MUSIC IN AMERICAN LIFE

Resources of American Music History

Volumes in the series Music in American Life
are listed at the end of this book.

RESOURCES OF AMERICAN MUSIC HISTORY

A Directory of Source Materials
from Colonial Times to World War II

D. W. KRUMMEL

JEAN GEIL

DORIS J. DYEN

DEANE L. ROOT

UNIVERSITY OF ILLINOIS PRESS

Urbana   Chicago   London

Preparation of this reference work has been made possible in part by a grant from the Research Tools and Reference Works Program of the National Endowment for the Humanities, an independent federal agency. Other assistance has been provided by the Graduate School of Library Science and the Research Board of the University of Illinois at Urbana-Champaign, and by the Martha Baird Rockefeller Fund for Music, Inc. The publishing expenses have also been supported by the National Endowment for the Humanities, through a grant from the Publication Program.

Library of Congress Cataloging in Publication Data
Main entry under title:

Resources of American music history.

(Music in American life)
  1. Music—United States—Bibliography—Union lists.
2. Music—United States—Directories. I. Krummel, Donald
William, 1929–   II. Title.
ML120.U5R47   016.78'0973   80-14873
ISBN 0-252-00828-6

∽◡ CONTENTS ◡∽

Introduction   1

Bibliography   11

Reference Works Cited in Short Form   13

Directory

   States: Alabama–Wyoming   17

   U.S. Territories   387

   Canada   388

   Other Countries   390

Index   395

INTRODUCTION

The scope of American music reaches in time from the days of the first settlers up to today; in space from the Atlantic to the Pacific; in situations from the campfire around which folksongs were sung to the steel and granite of the Metropolitan Opera. The musical activity itself extends from the casual circumstances of listening amusement to the demanding circumstances of a concert artist's career. Our national celebrities have ranged from William Billings to George Gershwin, from Stephen Foster to Charles Ives, from John Philip Sousa to Louis Armstrong. Beyond the limelights are those heroes who are unsung, as well as many who in their own days were not even singing: music teachers and critics, merchants and managers, patrons and listeners. America's musicians were not always able to read musical notation. But fortunately they lived in a literate society. Paper and ink—and later, sound recordings as well—were used to document their musical activities and their music. The present text is a survey of the evidence of this musical life, as recorded in documents located in 3000 repositories in the United States and abroad.

In 1975, a special committee of the Music Library Association began considering appropriate activities to commemorate the United States Bicentennial. One of the committee's suggestions was to compile a directory of musical resources throughout the country, and the Resources of American Music History project soon took shape. The American Musicological Society endorsed the proposal; the University of Illinois committed its resources; and the National Endowment for the Humanities provided the major funding. The first year of the project, from September 1976 to August 1977, was given over to planning, a thorough survey of the secondary literature, and extensive publicity. The second year was devoted largely to contacting potential respondents, in all somewhat over 20,000 of them. The staff spent the third year mostly in editorial work.[1]

As the work progressed, conspicuous gaps emerged, suggesting the need for a concerted effort in approaching organizations and canvassing our country's large urban musical centers. A supplementary matching grant was awarded in the fall of 1978 by the Martha Baird Rockefeller Fund for Music, Inc., and the National Endowment for the Humanities in order to secure better coverage in such areas. In approaching organizations, we have sought not only to describe their historic documents, but also to encourage them to consider a continuing archival program, as a step toward developing a systematic documentation of our country's continuing musical activity. This reference book is mostly concerned with the period up to World War II; but its momentum needs to be projected through subsequent generations, since present-day decisions affect the disposition of the source materials which scholars will need for the study of today's musical life.

Models for our reference book have been scarce, partly because the subject itself is rather new. The first general surveys of American library resources for particular subject areas,[2] from the turn of the century, make little mention of music. Several specific directories from the 1930s and earlier are concerned mostly either with treasures of European music or with the materials which were part of library service to the general public. Important as these materials may be (would that we had their circulating piano-roll collections today!), such directories suggest mostly the low awareness of American music itself. Our country had a musical present and Europe had a musical past: it was as simple as that. To be sure, a few notable music historians, such as Oscar Sonneck and Waldo Selden Pratt, were dealing with American materials.[3] Also active, fortunately, were our country's historical societies; the earliest private collectors of sheet music; musicians' descendants with plenty of room in the attic; organizations willing to trot out their charter and their

[1]For further information on the development and results of the project, see the brief article, "Little RAMH, Who Made Thee?," M.L.A. *Notes*, 37 (1980), 227–38.

[2]These are listed in the Bibliography, section A.

[3]Among the valuable reference books used in this project, Pratt's 1920 *American Supplement* to *Grove's Dictionary* deserves special praise.

Tschaikowsky letter for an annual exhibition; and a few retired music lovers who, wanting something interesting to do, cheerfully card-indexed anything musical they could lay their hands on. The situation was obviously ripe for the serious scholarly study, an endeavor which has gathered momentum since the 1950s.[4] It is time to survey the available resources. Some documents have already escaped into the bonfire; others will face the same fate unless we organize, develop, and promote our archival programs.

Part of the importance of this reference work should lie in its implied definition of a research field. Scholars have come to distinguish the study of "American music"—those works, idioms, and practices in which is variously manifest a distinctly American spirit—from the study of "music in America"—the more tangible but equally varied activities through which music functioned as part of the cultural life of the American populace.[5] Although the sources for the former will be covered in this book, our primary concern has been with that mixed assembly which comprises the latter. The wide range of musical activities has heretofore been mostly a noble vision of idealistic scholars, combining the wonder of William Blake, the detail of Pieter Breughel, and the democratic fervor of Joel Barlow. Now the panorama can be seen more clearly. Here is the evidence for identifying the spirit of pleasure experienced, both by the young lady who danced at the Mississippi soirée and by the Wyoming rancher who played the harmonica; the hard work and insecurity which were the lot both of the Hollywood studio musician and of the small-town Ohio music retailer; the striving for perfection, both by the symphony concertmaster and by the small-town Minnesota singing teacher; the idealism which characterized both the New England proponent of fuging tunes and the starving composers who aspired to be our very own Beethoven. For the retrospective vision of America's musical Jerusalem we thus have a few more of the footprints, some further suggestions of the varied countenances which have shone upon our musical nation.

Such a conception of scope must preclude value judgments; and it will make for curious juxtapositions as well. As a directory of resources, the entries have been compiled without the presumption of selectivity that a methodical dictionary would entail.

But what exactly is a "resource" of American music history? Specifically, what should one look for when approaching libraries and other repositories? Again with a view to the overall dimensions of music in America, our mailings to potential respondents mentioned ten general kinds of documents:

1. Sheet music: items singly or in bound volumes, vocal or instrumental, popular or classical
2. Songbooks: hymnals and tunebooks, school or community songbooks, either with music or with the words only
3. Other printed music: opera scores, cantatas and oratorios, band or orchestra music, solo or chamber music—particularly works by American composers
4. Manuscript music: parts copied out by hand for performance, for example, or personal music books found in family archives, as well as the holographs of composers
5. Programs: for concerts and operas, also playbills and music posters, which might be part of a theater collection, in scrapbooks, or part of a church, school, or civic group's archives
6. Catalogues: of music publishers, instrument or recording manufacturers, music shops, dealers, and suppliers
7. Organizational papers: archives, including records, publications, and memorabilia, of singing societies, local bands, orchestras, and other performing groups, music clubs, community concert series, opera houses and music auditoriums, local conservatories and music schools, and other commercial and non-commercial organizations
8. Personal papers: correspondence, scrapbooks, and diaries, for example, involving musicians or others concerned with music
9. Pictures: photographs, paintings, drawings, engravings, lithographs; singly or in albums and scrapbooks
10. Sound recordings: 78-rpm discs (singly or in albums), cylinders, and piano rolls, as well as oral-history tapes.

Each category has structural, geographical, and chronological limitations. Structurally, the documents are of two kinds: graphic evidence, on paper or on some other flat surface, and sound recordings of music or related in content to music. We have not sought systematically to collect in those interesting areas which generally fit under the rubric of "memorabilia": Theodore Thomas's

---

[4]Several of the most important of these, including in particular the writings of Allen P. Britton, H. Earle Johnson, and Irving Lowens, are included in the Bibliography, sections D and E.

[5]The most important exploration of this distinction, if not the earliest, is Irving Lowens, *Music in America and American Music: Two Views of the Scene*, I.S.A.M. Monographs, 8 (Brooklyn, 1978).

baton, locks of Gottschalk's hair, Grace Moore's Metropolitan Opera costumes, Jimmie Rodgers's guitars, and the like. We have excluded musical instruments, although piano rolls and other devices that provide the repertory for automatic musical instruments have been included as a kind of sound recording. The dividing lines admittedly are fine, and more than once even slightly mischievous: programs, posters, press clippings of reviews, even the torn ticket stubs for a performance of *Madama Butterfly* are in, but the fan used by Geraldine Farrar is out.

Geographically, our domain encompasses the territorial limits of the United States. Foreign works on American subjects—from J. C. F. Bach's lyric portrait *Die Amerikanerin* (Riga, 1776) to Debussy's "Gollywog's Cake-walk"—have not been included, even when their music was self-consciously written in an "American style." In borderline cases we erred on the side of inclusion, so as to include the careers of musicians from the United States working in Canada and elsewhere, or the activity of European musicians in the United States. To be sure, we have such delightfully perverse instances as the second *Kammersinfonie* of Arnold Schoenberg, conceived in Vienna in 1906, then set aside, and finally completed in Los Angeles in 1939. More bothersome has been the relatively sketchy documentation of the musical activity in such outlying areas as Puerto Rico, Hawaii, and Alaska.

Our terminal date of ca. 1941 is unfortunate but entirely necessary. Organizational files before World War II are generally archival, in function if not in designation and treatment. That is, they are likely to be inactive, whether or not they have been segregated and specially stored. The date has been loosely interpreted, insofar as we have not contacted organizations founded after 1940, yet have not attempted to exclude post-1940 archival materials that are part of the records of older organizations.

In the case of individuals—composers, performers, listeners, merchants, scholars, administrators—music manuscripts and personal papers are included for persons who were significantly active in the United States before 1941—generally those born before 1916 or who are now deceased. Descriptions of the materials emphasize the period before World War II, however.

There is still a problem of defining American musicians. It is impossible to distinguish composers on the basis of the American characteristics of their work, and nonsense even to think of such criteria for performers, musicologists, or music ad-

ministrators as groups. Our country's music was significantly enriched during the 1930s and 1940s by Jewish musicians and others fleeing Hitler; the close sense of community between so many of these musicians forbids us from stopping at the stroke of midnight on 31 December 1940, or the first bombs on 7 December 1941. Nor does it seem right to exclude performers who appeared frequently in America before 1941 but did not settle here until the war. There are other musicians who corresponded in Europe in the 1920s and 1930s, often about American matters, but did not settle in the United States until the 1940s. There are the European musicians who moved back to Europe after an American residence, under varying circumstances—from Henry Russell to Kirsten Flagstad, from Gustav Mahler to Bohuslav Martinů, from Frederick Delius to Paul Hindemith. There are also the Americans in Europe, from Lillian Nordica and Irving Schwerke (who returned) to Sir Francis J. Campbell and the younger George Templeton Strong (who stayed there). The expedient solution has been to single out when possible those materials which specifically concern musical activity in the United States before 1941.

For most kinds of commercial music, meanwhile, the meaningful dividing line is February 1942, the date of the so-called Petrillo ban. In soliciting information on and in reporting commercial sound recordings, the only conceivably effective dividing line was the decline of the 78-rpm phonodisc in favor of the 33⅓- and 45-rpm forms, which took place as late as the 1950s. Even harder to rationalize in any such plan are the oral-history tapes made in the 1970s which discuss music and musical activity before 1940.

As for music in oral tradition, as collected through transcripts and on field recordings by scholars and amateurs, it rarely accommodates any kind of chronological delimitation. Recorded or transcribed at a given date (most often after 1940), such documents reflect earlier repertories, practices, and attitudes; the extent to which they do so may be obvious (as, for instance, Child ballads recorded in Tennessee in 1948), but in some ways will always be unknown, if not even irrelevant for the purposes of this directory (as, for instance, on these same recordings, the question of whether certain practices of ornamentation derive from other local practices that may or may not pre-date 1940). Under such circumstances, our custom has been to recognize traditions of oral music rather than specific documents. Particular archival collections are included or excluded depending on whether the musical traditions they

3

cover date from before 1940. Black spirituals are in, for instance, but rock is out; hillbilly and country-and-western songs are in, but bebop improvisation is out. Obviously even this rule quickly becomes undermined by many specific instances—folk festivals, for example. Furthermore, this distinction was not settled on until fairly late in the project, leaving us without the time and publicity needed to conduct a thorough specialty survey. However ill-defined, our coverage we hope will result more in the discovery of useful surprises than in the embarrassment of shortcomings.

"There are two kinds of people," in the words of one of our respected gurus: "those who want to get their names in the paper, and those who want to keep theirs out." Accordingly, our strategies in contacting repositories have been varied. For both kinds of owners we have had to go to some pains simply to find respondents. Much of our early effort went into preparing mailing lists, for close to 12,000 libraries as listed by the R. R. Bowker Company; over 4000 historical societies and museums from the American Association for State and Local History; and a variety or organizations, orchestras, opera companies, scholars, collectors, dealers, agencies, unions, and commercial firms. Our pilot survey in autumn 1977 canvassed 1500 institutions in Illinois; its response told us what different kinds of results and problems to expect. In January 1978 our first nationwide mailings went out.

The initial response ran to about 12 percent for libraries and 30 percent for historical societies and museums. This was disappointing, although survey research advisors assured us that it was to be expected. The positive response did enable us to identify more exactly the groups to be selected for second mailings. Gradually our overall response has increased to about 25 percent. We have also made a special effort to contact organizations and individuals whose names were referred to us by our initial respondents. Our letters specifically asked that the postage-free reply cards be returned regardless of whether or not materials were reported. Even so, we believe that for the most part those who did not respond, if they had materials, were either unaware of them or too operationally disorganized to help; and, if they had no materials, were kindly saving us the postage. Thanks to our survey of secondary sources, we knew about many institutions that definitely had materials. These we pursued ruthlessly (but

also, we hope, politely); the resulting descriptions of only a few repositories are exclusively from other reference sources, and are so identified. In some instances the pressures of our deadline precluded the third and fourth follow-ups. Claims of completeness, of course, are another matter: if ever compilers needed to appeal for judgment on the basis of what they have done rather than what they have not done, this is the occasion.

To augment the impact of the mailings we tried other indirect approaches: besides reading papers and working the conferences, we placed notices (often several times) in leading music, library, archival, and other special-interest journals, and circulated a press release to newspapers.[6] An appeal appeared in the program of the homecoming football game (14 November 1977) between Illinois and Ohio State. (Illinois lost, RAMH won.) It is still likely that we have missed some important respondents.

A goodly number of owners were glad to share with us not only their materials, but often their exuberance as well. The gratuitous postscripts on the reply cards—"Good luck"; "A most worthwhile project"; "May we put a notice in our local newspapers?"—made many a day, and for the several dozen of these we are thankful indeed.

The wishes of some owners to remain anonymous also needed to be respected. Some musical organizations protested that they were simply too busy to be bothered. We could appreciate their feelings, considering that their primary objective is to make music itself: one wishes them well, so that eventually their history may demand to be preserved. We could understand the feelings of private collectors owning precious documents. For various reasons, some organizations declined to help us prepare a report, and occasionally collectors were unwilling to cooperate. The absence of their names may or may not be conspicuous. Usually we could do nothing but allow them to remain unidentified. In several instances, we were able to call on friends to intercede, and for all such help, we are most grateful. We also grumbled frequently at the bureaucratic vagaries which confronted us in even the most cooperative of re-

---

[6]Among the most important presentations were Jean Geil, "Resources of American Music History: A Progress Report," read at the national conference of the Organization of American Historians, New York, 15 April 1978; and Doris J. Dyen, "Ethnomusicological Study of Enclaves in America: Cross-Currents in the Mainstream," read at the annual conference of the Society for Ethnomusicology, 27 October 1978. Among the published presentations see particularly the short articles by Deane L. Root in the *Selmer Bandwagon*, 86 (May 1978), 19–20, and by D. W. Krummel in the *American Music Teacher*, 27/5 (1978), 8.

positories: materials scattered between the administrative units of even rather small institutions, some items in the music library, others in the music department, still others in the general collections or the rare-books department, occasionally in the audio-visual section, or the archives (not to be confused with manuscripts division), the museum, the Smith Memorial Room, or the Jones Collection of Local History, the office of vice-president, Professor Brown's study, the cataloguing arrearage of the technical department, also permutations of all of the above involving custody in one unit and expertise or even awareness elsewhere. Under such circumstances, the librarian's concept of materials being either "under" or "not under bibliographical control" seems meaningless.

There still remain the holdings we could not report because nobody told us about them. Though we apologize to our repositories for asking too many questions, such was the price of the classic response: "We didn't tell you because you didn't ask." There are still items—no doubt thousands of them—which we would gladly have cited had we known about them. While we must pass the buck to the owners, we pass it understandingly and sympathetically. Busy musicians, curators, and librarians cannot always bring to mind the odd lot of papers in the back basement or on the second shelf of the closet in the annex. The venerable walking encyclopedias too often seem to have ended their half-century incumbencies several days before our appeal arrived. Our directory, in sum, may be no better than our respondents; we still owe them the credit for its being as good as it is.

Our survey of the secondary literature turned up many useful leads. In all, upwards of 3000 different books, articles, and reference sources were examined. Many of them provided interesting anecdotes but, as seems endemic to musical legendry, no references to sources. Some of them mentioned documents in the casual way which could do no more than tantalize our staff. But, particularly in some of the most recent works, the documentation was effective enough to enable us to call materials to the attention of home institutions which were unaware of their existence. A wide range of doctoral dissertations[7] from the past two decades gave some of our most useful leads, as did many of the standard reference

works.[8] The help given by previous scholarship, even in a relatively new field like American music, cannot be underestimated.

The literature search was the key to a thorough, systematic canvass of musical materials. It was achieved at a significant cost. Except for repositories with minimal holdings (mostly as listed in the directory at the end of each state) we followed up nearly all written responses through phone calls, in which we could ask direct questions—questions which tested the credulity of the statements and often helped the respondent determine what exactly the institution had in its collections. Ultimately, we have had to rely almost exclusively on the word of our respondents. Our original plan included a rather Arcadian vision involving "traveling associates" working their way through an assigned area, from library to historical society to private attic, using a microbus equipped with dictaphone, microfilm camera, typewriter, card files, and cooking facilities, not inconceivably a diaper pail as well. However inspiring, the plan soon gave way as we came to realize how much material was likely to be involved; how cumbersome any such scheme would be to organize and to administer; and above all, how dependent we would be, even so, on the local staff for turning up the uncatalogued holdings.

In the end, then, our approach came to involve direct mailings, general publicity, and personal contacts based on leads provided by our literature survey and by other respondents. The personal approach was particularly needed in our dealings with musical institutions and private owners. When working with orchestras, opera companies, performing groups, and music organizations, a letter designed for libraries and historical societies would have been inappropriate. Direct questions were called for, referring to the specific kinds of documents likely to exist. Furthermore, the right persons needed to be approached. Often there were two persons, one in the front office with the power to make policy decisions but not likely to know much about the material itself; and one in the back room who had known the material in question for forty-five years but could not help where time, complex decisions, and access to potentially confidential material were involved. As for the private collectors, they ranged from a good many knowledgeable connoisseurs to a few uninterested investors, from the wealthy and

---

[7]Most of these are listed in Rita H. Mead, *Doctoral Dissertations in American Music*, I.S.A.M. Monographs, 3 (Brooklyn, 1974). We cite them with titles italicized rather than quoted, in view of their status of availability, which is now generally comparable to that of published rather than unpublished works.

[8]These are listed in the Bibliography, mostly in sections B, C, and E. Several works on this list, it should be mentioned—notably those by Fuld and Davidson and by Patterson—appeared too late to be used comprehensively in our survey.

usually stylish to the struggling and awkward, from the sociable (even the loquacious) to the suspicious (even the surly). Their specialties were almost always sound recordings, hymnals, or sheet music, seldom a mixture of them. Often the name of a respected associate was needed as our admission past the front door; once inside, our task was almost invariably pleasant, and almost invariably much too time-consuming. The extravagance of personal contact with most of our respondents, through the mail, over the phone, or in person, has been one of the pleasures of the project and is probably reflected in the quality and detail of the directory.

Much as we should have liked to check out all 4500 respondents to our mailings, we not only accepted an answer of "no" from about 1300 of them, but also regretfully consigned 1500 more to the supplementary lists at the end of each state in the directory. While our funds did not permit us to investigate the reports of limited holdings, particular users of this book may find further search there worth the effort. (The supplementary lists also include a very few responses that arrived too late to be incorporated as full entries in the directory.)

Our staff assumes responsibility for organizing the reports, also for the errors which inevitably have crept in. The most we can do is to identify those who answered our inquiries or otherwise supplied information; who often approved, corrected, or re-worked our early drafts; and who thus might serve the readers of this book as initial contacts in particular repositories. Unsigned reports are mostly by members of the project staff, as well as by the holders of private collections. A number of our 1689 detailed reports on specific repositories, especially the very large or very small ones, do less than justice to their collections. In a few instances nearby volunteers or project consultants were able to help us. Other institutions were anxious to publicize their holdings as part of their mandate for promoting scholarship. While the evidence of this should speak for itself, we must add a note of gratitude.

———————

In formulating practices for the descriptive citations which make up the directory, something of a departure from both library and archival practices has been appropriate, considering the material in question and the likely needs of our readers. Our practices stem from seven principles, of which the first six belong together, the second three being something of the inverse of the first three:[9]

1. A description has generally been contracted in deference to the quantity of material in question. A collection of 10,000 items will seldom need ten times as much description as one of 1000 items.

2. A description has generally been contracted in deference to the homogeneity of the forms or subjects of the material in question. A collection of 1000 pieces of sheet music usually needs less description than one the same size which includes programs, books, manuscripts, and pictures. Likewise, a collection of the papers of a single organization generally needs less description than one collection containing papers of several organizations.

3. A description has generally been contracted in deference to other descriptions of the material in question. If a full catalogue, check list, analysis of collection, or any other finding aid has been prepared—preferably in print, ideally available through a photocopy, but even in the form of a card index—a summary and a reference to the finding aid will usually suffice.

4. A description has generally been expanded in deference to the importance of the material in question, however that importance may be known or surmised.

5. A description has generally been expanded in deference to specific information regarding it. When a collection of music concerns several specific topics, we have tried to mention as many of those topics as would seem useful.

6. A description has generally been expanded for purposes of mentioning unexpected items or elements in it, when such are known. One does not expect to find, for example, information on Georgia music in Oregon, hymnals in a theater, or cowboy songs in Connecticut; when such surprises are discovered, they are mentioned.

Superseding these six is a seventh, much more pragmatic principle: the detail in a description must depend on the information supplied by the repository itself. We have taken the data that were given, and quite frankly have attempted to fit in as much as we could justify.

Two anomalies follow from these principles. First, printed editions are not cited specifically,

[9]These principles may be viewed as "degressive," in a sense not far removed from that introduced by early twentieth-century English bibliographers. The statements diminish from the ideal and fullest form along clearly indentified and rationalized lines (as in the first three principles), and at the same time incorporate relevant specifics (as in the second three).

except in very rare instances. The reasoning behind this decision may be convincing in its logic but the result is sometimes unfortunate. In theory, all printed materials should be covered in the bibliographical lists of printed sources.[10] Yet we know how small a fraction of America's music-publishing output is listed in these works. The *National Union Catalog* includes sheet music only when someone failed to follow instructions; most music directories are unlisted anywhere; the coverage of music periodicals in the Weichlein and Wunderlich lists suggests how incomplete the *Union List of Serials* really is; while many tunebooks and hymnals are recorded only in specialized short-title lists. In other words, deferring to other bibliographies will almost always mean deferring to sources that we know will let us down; and yet, with the output of our country's music press running into millions of items, there is no feasible alternative for this directory.

Second, we have not cited specifically the vast amount of material of musical interest buried in non-music sources, unless some obvious musical aspect can be brought out. References to concerts in newspapers, records of bands in military archives, vital biographical data about musicians in official records, addresses of firms in city directories, musical advertisements in general periodicals, interesting mention of personal impressions of concerts in the letters and diaries of music lovers: all this must regretfully lie beyond the scope of this directory for lack of any convenient way to conceive of it as a "resource," unless someone has already done this work for us in specific music-reference works we can quote or cite.

In the directory, the entries are arranged alphabetically by state, then by city, then by the name of the repository. The numerical sequence of entries in the directory is indicated by the number at the upper left corner of the entry. There is one number per entry; the index cites this number. (For the largest repositories, sections have been designated by letters, so as to facilitate the use of the index.) For entries other than private collections, the name in the heading is the primary organization, generally the largest administrative unit; beneath this are any subdivisions, indicating actual locations of the materials, and the mailing address. At the end of the line carrying an organization's name is the symbol assigned that repository by the *National Union Catalog*.[11]

The descriptive statement between the address and the main body of some entries describes special conditions of access or provenance, gives relevant bibliographic citations pertaining to the collection as a whole, or outlines the major sections of very long entries.

Each citation within the main body of an entry provides as much of the following basic descriptive information as was available: the category of materials (either the type of document or the name of the person or organization about which the materials center); quantity (in the most convenient terms, when these are known or meaningful at all, with sheet music figured at fifty items per inch, and with linear measure stated in metric units);[12] dates (usually approximations or inclusive dates); special finding aids, catalogues, inventories, or descriptions; further scope and description. Concluding each entry or section, as appropriate, is the name of the main respondent.

Arrangement of citations within each institution has called for special conventions, depending on the practices of the institution and the anticipated needs of our readers. A simple set of cataloguing main-entry rules, on which a simple plan for sequence might have been based, would have pleased our editorial staff no less than it would perhaps appeal to our readers, particularly those versed in library cataloguing or archival organizational practices. But our materials, ranging as they do from typical library and archival holdings to unsorted trunks, card indexes, and storage areas, will manifest a variety of relationships between source, form, and subject matter. (The archives of a hypothetical Monday Music Club, for instance, may consist of programs, mounted in scrapbooks, found in the personal papers of Mrs. John Doe.) Our ideal has been to bring out all these elements, insofar as this seemed meaningful and possible,

---

[10]The most important of these are listed in the Bibliography, section D.

[11]These are taken from the Library of Congress, *Symbols of American Libraries*, 11th ed. (Washington, 1976).

[12]A major difficulty in using metric forms involves the archival practice of using cubic rather than linear footage. Linear conversion is easy to comprehend, since 1 inch equals approximately 2.5 cm., and 1 foot equals approximately .3 meter. But 1 cubic foot equals .0283 cubic meter, 35.3 cubic feet making 1 cubic meter. Statements like .1416 cubic meter (5 cubic feet) may make sense some day, but not now. Under the circumstances, our practice of directly converting cubic feet to linear feet seemed best, all the more so since no great distortion was likely to be involved: most correspondence fits naturally into boxes of 1 cubic foot. As for materials of significantly different dimensions—sheet music, for instance, usually about 15 inches tall, or hymnals of various sizes—statement in cubic feet is odd to begin with. In many ways the philosophy of our project, as it has developed, has come to prefer archival practices to library practices; in this instance, a reconsideration seems appropriate, all the more so since most library and archival shelving runs 3 feet long, just under 1 linear meter: a collection running to 12 linear meters will fill approximately 12 standard-length shelves.

through specific statements that could be cited in our indexes.

The sequence of information has been determined individually for each repository. Ideally, general collections precede special collections, although highly miscellaneous collections usually fit best at the end. As a rule, like materials are kept together, and smaller or less important groups of materials are given last. Integrated groups of materials have often best been grouped by form rather than provenance. Manuscripts come before printed materials, music itself before writings about music, with sound recordings at the end—unless there are good reasons to do otherwise. Within each category, citations are arranged alphabetically (especially for very long entries in order to be more easily checked from the index), chronologically, or occasionally according to the importance of the material when the chronology is misleading or undetermined. An arrangement for each entry was chosen to bring out the specific character of each repository, with the assumption that the visual field on the page is small, and that our readers are accustomed and willing to scan. Sections with headings and subheadings occur mostly in the medium-size or larger entries, and introductory tables of contents in the very large ones.

Because of the diverse kinds and conditions of the materials reported, the varying musical and historical expertise of our respondents, and the limits of staff time, we have been unable and unwilling to impose rigid terminology. Most respondents did follow the basic categories of materials as described in our letter of inquiry. For purposes of clarity and as a general guide to our use of subject terms, the cross references and prefatory notes in the index should be particularly helpful.

Our information, like that in any directory, is surely out of date by the time it appears in print. In the course of our editorial work, we asked respondents to advise us of additions to their collections or of related collections of older materials omitted in earlier versions of the report, and quite often they have obliged. Very few of the repositories are closed collections; materials are constantly moving through their doors, in or out, so that the directory is something like a snapshot taken during the two years of its compilation.

Readers should be aware that an advance request for permission to see holdings of private collectors and of music organizations is appropriate. For the rarities owned by many public archives and libraries, permission is often specifically required. When we have known about them,

and unless there were misgivings on the part of the repository, materials on deposit are included, and not distinguished from materials formally owned by the host institution. Many materials are unaccessioned or in storage, and access to them may require advance preparation.

The physical locations of materials within repositories are dealt with in two ways in the directory. First, if there is a published inventory we have cited it, obviating much of the detail of the report. We have not mentioned general card catalogues, although we have included special card indexes which may be particularly useful in locating American materials within the holdings. Call numbers have generally been omitted, although reference or page numbers in many of the published guides to collections are included.

A date followed by a dash and no other number should indicate inclusion to the present (1880– , for instance, means from 1880 to the present), although in some cases, because of the intervention of our terminal date, this formulation may only indicate holdings that extend past 1940. Often there has been no practical way for us or our respondents to establish dates, however implicit they may be in the history of the subject being reported.

All graphic items are presumed to be printed, unless specified as manuscripts, papers, archives, etc. Furthermore, some manuscripts are in fact holographs; such a distinction has been made only when the information was confirmed by the respondent. The term "records" has been reserved for archival papers; sound discs, tapes, cylinders, and other forms are consistently called "recordings."

Many large collections of materials are unsorted, uninventoried, and uncounted. We have used numerical approximations throughout. The readers should assume that the following numbers, when used as quantities, are approximations: multiples of 10 from 30 to 200; multiples of 50 from 200 to 2000; and multiples of 100 above 2000. As approximations, we expect these numbers to be good within 20 percent either way; we hope they are good within 5 to 10 percent; but we cannot vouch for any better than 40 or 50 percent. This will be particularly true of numbers over 10,000.

Provenance has been particularly important in our citations, partly because benefactors deserve to be acknowledged, partly because the scope of a corpus of materials is often best explained in terms of its owner's career. Particularly rich and varied and troublesome to describe have been the "musical estates" (would that English had a counterpart to the German term "Nachlass"). We have also on occasion distinguished between "definitive" and "extensive" holdings. The former indicates the collection of working materials owned by a person at the time of his death—for instance, that of the Arnold Schoenberg Institute in Los Angeles—while the latter indicates a major repository, possibly as large and significant as the "definitive" collection, but acquired through other auspices—for instance, the Schoenberg Archives in the Library of Congress.

Biographical information has been held to a minimum, and while dates of lesser-known persons are not suppressed, dates of persons are generally omitted except when they clarify the scope of a collection.

The respondents to our inquiries are cited in the entries in the directory, while the staff members and consultants for the project are listed below.

Several other acknowledgments of a general nature are also appropriate. In the administration of our project at the University of Illinois, Ms. Donna Bigler and her staff were most supportive. We are pleased to have been able to work closely with the Music Library at the University of Illinois, out of our Pullman Nibelheim; and grateful for the services of the University Library in general, and for the comfortable and accommodating hospitality of the School of Music. Dr. Gerald P. Tyson was an admirably patient, sympathetic, and helpful liaison at the National Endowment for the Humanities. The special interest in American music at the University of Illinois Press, on the part of Richard Wentworth and Judith McCulloh in particular, has been the pleasant discovery and good fortune both of our project and of the users of our directory as well. In addition, we have received assistance, suggestions, advice, and encouragement from a multitude of other persons too numerous to list here but to whom our thanks are nonetheless profound.

Project Associates

D. W. Krummel, *Director*

Jean Geil, *Assistant Director*

Doris J. Dyen, *Field Supervisor*

Deane L. Root, *General Editor*

URBANA HEADQUARTERS STAFF: Aaron Appelstein, Dale Cockrell, Jeannette Cook, Peggy Daub, Alice Hanson, Thomasin LaMay, Carl Manns, Michelynn McKnight, Harriet Newman, Judy Rabin, Carolyn Rabson, Joan Schuitema, William Westcott, Vanessa Wilson, *and* Donna Zych

PLANNING ADVISORS: Otto E. Albrecht (*University of Pennsylvania*), Maynard Brichford (*University of Illinois*), Lenore Coral (*University of Wisconsin*), Richard Crawford (*University of Michigan*), Robert Bingham Downs (*University of Illinois*), Dena Epstein (*University of Chicago*), Lawrence Gushee (*University of Illinois*), H. Wiley Hitchcock (*Brooklyn College, Institute for Studies in American Music*), Richard Jackson (*New York*

Public Library), Anders Lönn (*Svenskt musikhistoriskt Arkiv, Stockholm*), Irving Lowens (*Peabody Conservatory of Music*), William McClellan (*University of Illinois*), Bruno Nettl (*University of Illinois*), Nicholas Temperley (*University of Illinois*), John Owen Ward (*Boosey & Hawkes*), *and* Thomas Willis (*Northwestern University*)

URBAN MUSIC AND OTHER SPECIAL CONSULTANTS: *Baltimore*: Edwin H. Quist, Jr.; *Boston*: H. Earle Johnson; *Cleveland*: Theodore J. Albrecht; *Detroit*: Mary D. Teal; *Kansas City*: Jack Ralston; *New Orleans*: John H. Baron; *New York*: Rita H. Mead, Amy Aaron, *and* Barton Cantrell; *Philadelphia*: Otto E. Albrecht; *Pittsburgh*: Irene Millen; *and Washington*: William Lichtenwanger

BIBLIOGRAPHY

In addition to the works cited in particular entries in the directory, the following works have been generally valuable:

A. Early Surveys of Music Library Resources (By Date)

Lane, William Coolidge, and Charles Knowles Benton. *Notes on Special Collections in American Libraries.* Library of Harvard University, Bibliographical Contributions, 45. Cambridge, 1892.

Johnston, W. Dawson, and Isadore G. Mudge. *Special Collections in Libraries in the United States.* U.S. Bureau of Education, Bulletin 23. Washington, 1912. (See esp. pp. 82–84.)

Music Teachers National Association. *Music Departments in Libraries.* U.S. Bureau of Education, Bulletin 33. Washington, 1922.

Richardson, Ernest Cushing. *An Index Directory to Special Collections in North American Libraries.* Yardley, Pa., 1927.

Pierre Key's International Music Year Book, 1928. New York, 1928 ("Music Collections in Libraries," pp. 292-98). *Pierre Key's International Music Year Book, 1929-30.* New York, 1929 ("Music Scores and Manuscripts in Libraries," pp. 314-23). *Pierre Key's Music Year Book . . . 1935 Edition.* New York, 1934 ("Library Music Reports," pp. 333-68). *Pierre Key's Music Year Book . . . 1938 Edition.* New York, 1938 ("Library Music Reports," pp. 462-76).

B. General Directories of Library Resources

American Association for State and Local History. *Directory of Historical Societies and Agencies.* Nashville, 1975.

American Library Directory: A Classified List of Libraries in the United States and Canada with Personnel and Statistical Data. 30th ed. New York and London, 1976.

American Literary Manuscripts: A Checklist of Holdings in Academic, Historical, and Public Libraries, Museums, and Authors' Homes in the United States. 2nd ed. Athens, Ga., 1977.

Americana in deutschen Sammlungen (ADS): Ein Verzeichnis von Materialen zur Geschichte der Vereinigten Staaten von Amerika in Archiven und Bibliothek der Bundesrepublik Deutschland und West-Berlins. Edited by Dietrich Gerhard, Egmont Zechlin, and Erich Angermann. N.p., 1967.

Ash, Lee. *Subject Collections: A Guide to Special Book Collections and Subject Emphases as Reported by University, College, Public and Special Libraries in the United States and Canada.* 5th ed. New York, 1978. (Cited as *Ash.*)

Downs, Robert Bingham. *American Library Resources: A Bibliographic Guide.* Urbana and Chicago, 1951. *First Supplement, 1950-61.* Chicago, 1961. *Second Supplement, 1961-70.* Chicago, 1971.

Greene, Evarts B., and Richard B. Morris. *A Guide to the Principal Sources for Early American History (1600-1800) in the City of New York.* 2nd ed. New York, 1953.

Hamer, Phillip. *A Guide to Archives and Manuscripts in the United States.* New Haven, 1961. (Cited as *Hamer.*)

Hines, Donald M. *An Index of Archival Resources for a Folklife and Cultural History of the Inland Pacific Northwest Frontier.* Ann Arbor, 1976.

Historical Records Survey. *Guide to Depositories of Manuscript Collections.* (Series for particular states, some with slightly different titles; vols. used as follows:) *California.* Sacramento, 1941. *Florida.* Jacksonville, 1940. *Illinois.* Preliminary ed. Chicago, 1940. *Iowa.* Preliminary ed. Des Moines, 1940. *Louisiana.* 2nd ed. University, La., 1941. *Massachusetts.* Preliminary ed. Boston, 1939. *Michigan.* Detroit, 1941. *Minnesota.* St. Paul, 1941. *Missouri.* St. Louis, 1940. *Nebraska.* Lincoln, 1940. *New Hampshire.* Preliminary ed. Manchester, 1940. *New Jersey.* Preliminary vol. Newark, 1941. *New York State (Exclusive of New York City).* Albany, 1941. *New York City.* New York, 1941. *North Carolina.* Raleigh, 1940. *Oregon–Washington.* Portland, 1940. *Pennsylvania.* Harrisburg, 1939. *Tennessee.* Nashville, 1941. *Wisconsin.* Preliminary ed. Madison, 1941. (All cited as *HRS.*)

Howell, John B. *Special Collections of the Southeast.* Jackson, Miss., 1978. (Cited as *Howell.*)

Jackson, William V. *Resources of Research Libraries: A Selected Bibliography.* Pittsburgh, 1969.

Meckler, Alan M., and Ruth McMillin. *Oral History Collections.* New York, 1975.

National Historical Projects and Records Commission. *Directory of Archives and Manuscript Repositories in the United States.* Washington, 1978. (Cited as *NHPRC.*)

National Union Catalog of Manuscript Collections. Ann Arbor and Washington, 1962– . (Cited as *NUCMC.*)

Spalek, John M. *Guide to the Archival Materials of the German-Speaking Emigration to the United States after 1933.* Charlottesville, 1978. (Cited as *Spalek.*)

Spiller, Robert E., et al. *Literary History of the United States.* Vol. 2, *Bibliography.* 4th ed. New York, 1974.

Subject Directory of Special Libraries and Information Centers. Vol. 4, *Social Sciences and Humanities Libraries.* Detroit, 1975.

Young, William C. *American Theatrical Arts: A Guide to Manuscripts and Special Collections in the United States and Canada.* Chicago, 1971.

C. Surveys of Music in Libraries

Albrecht, Otto E. "Collections, Private." *The New Grove Dictionary of Music and Musicians.* 6th ed. (London, 1980), vol. 4, pp. 536–58.

Association for Sound Recording Collections. *A Preliminary Directory of Sound Recordings Collections in the United States and Canada.* New York, 1967.

Benton, Rita. *Directory of Music Research Libraries, Part 1: Canada and the United States.* Iowa City, 1967.

Briegleb, Ann. *Directory of Ethnomusicological and Sound Recording Collections in the United States and Canada.* Ann Arbor, 1971. (Cited as *Briegleb.*)

Cipolla, Frank J. "An Annotated Guide for the Study and Performance of 19th-Century Band Music in the United States." *Journal of Band Research*, 14 (1978), 22–40.

Cook, Harold E. *Shaker Music: A Manifestation of American Folk Culture.* Lewisburg, Pa., 1973. (Cited as *Cook.*)

Crouch, Margaret Long, William J. Summers, and Karen Lueck. "An Annotated Bibliography and Commentary Concerning Mission Music of Alta California from 1769 to 1834." *Current Musicology*, 22 (1976), 88–99.

Dower, Catherine A. "Libraries with Music Collections in the Caribbean Islands." M.L.A. *Notes*, 34 (1977), 27–38.

Harris, Ernest E. *Music Education: A Guide to Information Sources.* Detroit, 1978.

Hickerson, Joseph C. "A List of Folklore and Folk Music Archives and Related Collections in the U.S. and Canada." Typescript. Washington: Library of Congress, Archive of Folk Song, 1979.

Johnson, H. Earle. "Notes on the Sources of Musical Americana." M.L.A. *Notes*, 5 (1948), 169–77.

Lichtenwanger, William, et al. *A Survey of Musical Instrument Collections in the United States and Canada.* Ann Arbor, 1974.

Lindsay, Bryan Eugene. *The English Glee in New England, 1815–1845.* Ph.D. diss. Nashville: George Peabody College for Teachers, 1966.

Messenger, Ruth, and Helen Pfatteicher. *A Short Bibliography for the Study of Hymns.* Hymn Society of America, Paper 25. New York, 1964.

Music Library Association, Southeast Chapter. *Directory of Music Collections in the Southeast.* Edited by Jerry Persons and Jeanette M. Drone. Campus Tower News, Special Issue 46. Memphis, 1979.

Patterson, Daniel W. *The Shaker Spiritual.* Princeton, 1979.

Seaton, Douglass. "Important Library Holdings at Forty-one North American Universities." *Current Musicology*, 17 (1974), 7–68.

D. Guides to United States Music Imprints

Britton, Allen P. *Theoretical Introductions in American Tune-Books to 1800.* Ph.D. diss. Ann Arbor: University of Michigan, 1949.

Britton, Allen P. and Irving Lowens. "Unlocated Titles in Early Sacred American Music." M.L.A. *Notes*, 11 (1953), 33–48.

Blanck, Jacob. *Bibliography of American Literature.* New Haven, 1955– .

Crandall, Marjorie Lyle. *Confederate Imprints: A Check List Based Principally on the Collection of the Boston Athenaeum.* Boston, 1955. (Cited as *Crandall.*)

Evans, Charles. *American Bibliography: A Chronological Dictionary of All Books, Pamphlets, and Periodical Publications Printed in the United States of America from the Genesis of Printing in 1639 down to and Including the Year (1800).* Chicago, 1903–34. Completed by Clifford K. Shipton. Worcester, 1955. Index by Roger P. Bristol. Worcester, 1959. See also Clifford K. Shipton

and James E. Mooney. *National Index of American Imprints through 1800: The Short-Title Evans.* Worcester and Barre, Mass., 1969; and Roger P. Bristol. *Supplement.* Charlottesville, 1970.

Fuld, James J. *American Popular Music (Reference Book), 1875–1950.* Philadelphia, 1955.

Fuld, James J., and Mary Wallace Davidson. *18th-Century American Secular Music Manuscripts: An Inventory.* M.L.A. Index & Bibliography Series, 20. Philadelphia, 1980.

Harwell, Richard B. *More Confederate Imprints.* Richmond, 1957. (Cited as *Harwell.*)

Heard, Priscilla S. *American Music, 1698–1800: An Annotated Bibliography.* Waco, Tex., 1975.

Hixon, Donald L. *Music in Early America: A Bibliography of Music in Evans.* Metuchen, N.J., 1970.

Janta, Alexander. "Early XIX Century American-Polish Music." *Polish Review*, 6 (1961), 73–105, and 10 (1965), 59–96.

Lowens, Irving. *A Bibliography of Songsters Printed in America before 1821.* Worcester, 1976. (Cited as *Lowens.*)

Metcalf, Frank J. *American Psalmody; or, Titles of Books Containing Tunes Printed in America from 1721 through 1820.* New York, 1917.

Rudolph, E. L. *Confederate Broadside Verse.* New Braunfels, Tex., 1950. (Cited as *Rudolph.*)

Shaw, Ralph R., and Richard H. Shoemaker. *American Bibliography: A Preliminary Checklist for 1801–1819.* New York and Metuchen, 1958–63. Continued by Richard H. Shoemaker, later Gayle Cooper, later Scott Bruntjen. *A Checklist of American Imprints for 1820– .* Metuchen, 1964– . See also D. W. Krummel. "American Music, 1801–1830, in Shaw–Shoemaker." *Yearbook for Inter-American Musical Research*, 11 (1975), 168–89.

Sonneck, Oscar. *A Bibliography of Early Secular American Music.* Revised and enlarged by William Treat Upton. Washington, 1945. (Cited as *Sonneck–Upton.*)

Springer, Nelson P., and A. J. Klassen. *Mennonite Bibliography, 1631–1961.* Kitchener, Ontario, 1977. See esp. vol. 2, pp. 285–97.

U.S. Board of Music Trade. *Complete Catalogue of Sheet Music and Musical Works.* New York, 1870. Reprint with new introduction by Dena J. Epstein. New York, 1973.

Weichlein, William J. *A Checklist of American Music Periodicals, 1850–1900.* Detroit Studies in Music Bibliography, 16. Detroit, 1970.

Wolf, Edward C. "Lutheran Hymnody and Music Published in America, 1700–1850: A Descriptive Bibliography." *Concordia Historical Institute Quarterly*, 50 (1977), 164–85.

Wolf, Edwin, II. *American Song Sheets, Slip Ballads, and Poetical Broadsides, 1850–1870.* Philadelphia, 1963.

Wolfe, Richard J. *Secular Music in America, 1801–1825.* New York, 1964. (Cited as *Wolfe.*)

Wunderlich, Charles Edward. *A History and Bibliography of Early American Music Periodicals, 1782–1852.* Ph.D. diss. Ann Arbor: University of Michigan, 1963.

E. Reference Guides to American Music and Culture

Baker's Biographical Dictionary of Musicians. 6th ed. Revised by Nicolas Slonimsky. New York, 1978.

Bio-Bibliographical Index of Musicians in the United States of America since Colonial Times. Edited by Keyes Porter and Leonard Ellinwood. Washington: Historical Records Survey, 1941.

Canon, Cornelius Baird. *The Federal Music Project of the Works Progress Administration: Music in a Democracy.* Ph.D. diss. Minneapolis: University of Minnesota, 1963.

Claghorn, Charles Eugene. *Biographical Dictionary of American Music.* West Nyack, N.Y. 1973.

Dichter, Harry, and Elliott Shapiro. *Early American Sheet Music, Its Lure and Its Lore, 1768–1889.* New York, 1941.

Epstein, Dena J. "Documenting the History of Black Folk Music in the United States: A Librarian's Odyssey." *Fontes artis musicae,* 23 (1976), 151–57.

———. *Sinful Tunes and Spirituals: Black Folk Music to the Civil War.* Urbana, 1977.

George, Zelma Watson. *A Guide to Negro Music: An Annotated Bibliography of Negro Folk Music, and Art Music by Negro Composers or Based on Negro Thematic Material.* Ed.D. diss. New York: New York University, 1953.

Harvard Guide to American History. Revised edition by Frank Friedel. Cambridge, 1974.

Haywood, Charles. *A Bibliography of North American Folklore and Folksong.* 2nd ed. New York, 1961.

Jackson, Richard. *United States Music: Sources of Bibliography and Collective Biography.* I.S.A.M. Monographs, 1. New York, 1973.

Johnson, H. Earle. "The Need for Research in the History of American Music." *Journal of Research in Music Education,* 6 (1958), 43–61.

Lawless, Ray M. *Folksingers and Folksongs in America: A Handbook of Biography, Bibliography, and Discography.* Rev. ed. New York, 1965.

Laws, G. Malcolm, Jr. *Native American Balladry: A Descriptive Study and a Bibliographical Syllabus.* Rev. ed. Philadelphia, 1964.

Marco, Guy A., Ann M. Garfield, and Sharon Paugh Ferris. *Information on Music: A Handbook of Reference Sources in European Languages.* Vol. 2, *The Americas.* Littleton, Colo., 1977.

Maultsby, Portia K., "Selective Bibliography: U.S. Black Music." *Ethnomusicology,* 19 (1975), 422–49.

Mead, Rita H. *Doctoral Dissertations in American Music: A Classified Bibliography.* I.S.A.M. Monographs, 3. New York, 1974.

Nettl, Bruno. *Folk Music in the United States: An Introduction.* 3rd ed., revised and expanded by Helen Myers. Detroit, 1976. See esp. the "Bibliographical Aids," pp. 170–77.

Pratt, Waldo Selden, and Charles N. Boyd. *Grove's Dictionary of Music and Musicians, American Supplement.* New York, 1920. Reissued with an "Appendix," pp. 413–38. New York, 1928.

Sonneck, Oscar. "The Bibliography of American Music." Bibliographical Society of America *Papers,* 1 (1906), 50–64.

Standifer, James A., and Barbara Reeder. *Source Book of African and Afro-American Materials for Music Educators.* Washington, 1972.

Tanselle, G. Thomas. *Guide to the Study of United States Imprints.* Cambridge, 1971. See also the music analysis and supplement by D. W. Krummel, *Yearbook for Inter-American Musical Research,* 8 (1972), 440–46.

Reference Works Cited in Short Form

Ash — Lee Ash. *Subject Collections* (Bibliography, B)

Briegleb — Ann Briegleb. *Directory of Ethnomusicological and Sound Recording Collections* (Bibliography, C)

Cook — Harold Cook. *Shaker Music* (Bibliography, C)

Crandall — Marjorie Crandall. *Confederate Imprints* (Bibliography, D)

Hamer — Phillip Hamer. *A Guide to Archives and Manuscripts* (Bibliography, B)

Harwell — Richard B. Harwell. *More Confederate Imprints.* (Bibliography, D)

Howell — John B. Howell. *Special Collections of the Southeast* (Bibliography, B)

HRS — U.S. Historical Records Survey. *Guide to Depositories of Manuscript Collections* series (Bibliography, B)

Lowens — Irving Lowens. *Bibliography of Songsters* (Bibliography, D)

NHPRC — U.S. National Historical Projects and Records Commission. *Directory of Archives and Manuscript Repositories* (Bibliography, B)

NUCMC — U.S. Library of Congress. *National Union Catalog of Manuscript Collections* (Bibliography, B)

Rudolph — E. L. Rudolph. *Confederate Broadside Verse* (Bibliography, D)

Sonneck–Upton — Oscar Sonneck. *Bibliography of Early American Secular Music.* Revised by William T. Upton (Bibliography, D)

Spalek — John M. Spalek. *Guide to the Archival Materials of the German-Speaking Emigration* (Bibliography, B)

Wolfe — Richard J. Wolfe. *Secular Music in America, 1800–1825* (Bibliography, D)

DIRECTORY

I labor on, hoping some day for success which will bring me reward for my labors—but if not—I will work in the mere hope of accomplishing something, of producing something truly great which may some day have some effect in raising the art which I so much love, tho it be after I myself have left this world.

—Frederic Grant Gleason

Alabama

1

AUBURN UNIVERSITY   AAP
Auburn, Alabama 36830

Ralph P. Draughon Library

Printed materials, including 50 sheet-music items in the Alabama and Auburn University collections; also 50 songbooks, and 25 New Orleans French opera libretti, 1869–90

—Mark Palkovic

University Archives

Vardaman–Gwin Collection, including 8 ms song lyrics by John Forsythe Vardaman, Coosa County, Ala., 1860–61

Auburn Knights Orchestra (University dance band, 1928–), papers, 1930–78, including sheet music, scrapbooks of press clippings, notebooks, correspondence, photographs, and recordings

—Bill Sumners

2

BIRMINGHAM PUBLIC LIBRARY   AB
2020 Park Place
Birmingham, Alabama 35203

Sheet music, 100 popular-music items, including some bound vols., 1846–

Other printed music, including several late 19th- and early 20th-century song collections and tune-books

Herbert Grieb, of Birmingham, 23 instrumental and sacred choral mss, ca. 1940–

Fred L. Grambs (Birmingham band leader), 12 scrapbooks of letters, programs, and press clippings, 1882–1938

Ruth Hannas, personal papers, 1922–75, including correspondence with Ernst Krenek and Ashley Pettis, in all 274 items

Collins Collection of the Dance, including books and articles on dance and ballet, music mss, programs, correspondence, photographs, and memorabilia, in all 1900 items

Birmingham Music Club, 24 scrapbooks, 1905– , including programs, 1923–76

Arion Club, Birmingham, minutes, 1915–20

Birmingham Civic Symphony Orchestra, 6 scrapbooks of clippings, programs, and memorabilia, 1930–42

—Robert G. Corley

3

SAMFORD UNIVERSITY   ABH
800 Lakeshore Drive
Birmingham, Alabama 35209

Included are holdings of the Birmingham–Jefferson Historical Society

School of Music Library

Edmund Simon Lorenz Collection of 3000 hymnals and songbooks, 1825– , published or collected by Lorenz and donated by his daughter, Ellen Jane Porter Lorenz

Elizabeth Jordan Brower (fl. 1930s, Metropolitan Opera singer), sheet music, programs, photographs, 6000 78-rpm operatic and classical discs, and musical memorabilia

Harwell Goodwin Davis Library

Sheet music, 4 bound vols., also separate items, printed in or relating to Alabama, 1840s–1900s

Hymnals, 200 19th-century vols.

—Annie Ford Wheeler, Margaret Sizemore

4

Margaret SIZEMORE
Samford University
800 Lakeshore Drive
Birmingham, Alabama 35209

Josef Casimir Hofmann (1876-1958), letters, notes, photographs, and 78-rpm discs, in all 1 linear meter; also records of the American Piano Society relating to Hofmann. See Margaret Sizemore, *The Amazing Marriage of Marie Eustis and Josef Hofmann* (Columbia, S.C., 1965)

5

EUFAULA HERITAGE ASSOCIATION
Box 486
Eufaula, Alabama 36027

Eufaula Music Club, papers, including minutes, 1912–36

Sheet music, 5 early 20th-century items; also several World War I songbooks; and 9 78-rpm disc recordings of popular music

—Hilda C. Sexton

6

W. C. HANDY HOME AND MUSEUM
620 West College Street
Florence, Alabama 35630

See the 4-page descriptive brochure

Sheet music of Handy and his associates, 1000 uncatalogued items

Holograph text of Handy's book, *Father of the Blues* (New York, 1941)

Pictures, including 5 oil portraits, paintings, and pencil sketches, and 5 albums of photographs of Handy and his friends

Recordings from Handy's personal collection, 5 78-rpm discs

—Mrs. W. Liner

7

Alvin DREGER
610 Holmes Avenue NE
Huntsville, Alabama 35801

Oscar Dreger (guitarist), ms music for guitar, and personal papers, pre-1898
Sheet music for cello, violin, and string ensemble
Other materials, including music catalogues, programs for local concerts, and photographs of local musicians

8

MOBILE HISTORIC PRESERVATION SOCIETY
1005 Government Street
Mobile, Alabama 36604

J. Clarendon McClure (organist, Government Street Temple and Christ Church, Mobile, 1825–52), scrapbook of press clippings of local musical events; photographs of local musicians; and a typescript account, "Mobile's Musical History," read before the Society, 1950s
Mobile Symphony Orchestra programs, 1909–12, in a scrapbook of Hugo Brown
Sheet music by local composers, among them Anne R. Boone, James G. Drake (1850), Anna Holberg (1896), John S. Holmes (1882), E. King, Kate Ayers Robert (1917–20), Mabel Schock, Glen Snelgrove (1921), and A. J. Staub; also a ms song by Hilton Jones and A. Browne
Miscellaneous 19th-century sheet music in 2 bound vols., also early programs and press clippings

—Sidney A. Smith

9

MUSEUMS OF THE CITY OF MOBILE
355 Government Street
Mobile, Alabama 36602

Sheet music, 3000 items, 1860s– , including 50 Civil War items, also minstrel music
Songbooks and hymnals, 25 items, ca. 1900
Manuscript music, 25 marches and keyboard works by Augustus J. Staub and Sigmund Schlesinger of Spring Hill College, late 19th century
Frohsinn Club (Mobile music group), papers, including published scores, press clippings, invitations, programs, and photographs, 1860s–1900s
Drago Band of Mobile, complete set of sheet music used 1883–1920s, also some photographs
Clara Schumann Club (founded 1894), papers
Recordings, including 197 cylinders and 125 78-rpm discs of popular and classical music

—Caldwell Delaney

10

SPRING HILL COLLEGE   AMobS
Thomas Byrne Memorial Library
4307 Old Shell Road
Mobile, Alabama 36608

Sigmund Schlesinger (faculty member, 1876–89), holograph score and ms piano score of his opera, *The Watchman*, 1884
Mrs. John J. Damrich (local music teacher), bound vol. of U.S. sheet music, 1850s–60s; also other sheet music and music editions including works by faculty members

—W. O. Livingston

11

STATE OF ALABAMA DEPARTMENT   A-Ar
OF ARCHIVES AND HISTORY
Montgomery, Alabama 36130

Alabama Federation of Music Clubs, proceedings, minutes, scrapbooks, and programs, 1927–42; also 5 boxes of papers, to 1977
Anne Eliza Coleman, typed class song written on her graduation from Mrs. Stafford's Finishing School for Young Ladies, Tuscaloosa, 1860
Program of commencement exercises at the Select School, Montgomery, ca. 1880, in the William B. Trimble papers
Programs of musical performances, ca. 1878 and 1895, in the Kate Duncan Smith papers
Kate Duncan Smith, ms song with violin obligato, composed for her graduation from Centenary Institute, Summerfield, 1860, in the Mrs. Samuel L. Earle papers
Lila Edwards Harper, of Montgomery, 3 scrapbooks of pictures, programs, notes on music history, and clippings, 1888–1908
Scrapbook of pictures and biographical sketches of opera performers, ca. 1896–
Herman Arnold, holograph band arrangement of Daniel Decatur Emmett's "Dixie's Land" (in the Museum—Music Room)
Songbooks, 30 items, 1829–1940
Sheet music, 300 songs and piano pieces, also 10 bound vols., 19th and early 20th centuries

—Milo B. Howard, Jr.

12

TALLADEGA COLLEGE   ATaT
Historical Collections
Talladega, Alabama 35160

Programs for College concerts, 300 items, 1877–
Oral-history tape recordings, 9 hours, including interviews with Teddy Wilson (b. 1912, jazz pianist and composer) and Frank Harrison (d. 1977, former faculty member), concerning the evolution of jazz, black jazz musicians, and the Harlem Renaissance

—Leon P. Spencer

13

TROY STATE UNIVERSITY   ATrT
Library
Troy, Alabama 36081

Paul V. Yoder, collection of 450 scores, printed and in ms, and 250 recordings of band music, mostly post-1940

14

TUSKEGEE INSTITUTE ATT

Hollis B. Frissell Library
Tuskegee Institute, Alabama 36088

Sheet music, 97 items relating to Afro-American music, 1915–38
Hymnals and school songbooks, 59 vols., 1899–1944
William Levi Dawson, 2 ms choral arrangements
Programs of Institute concerts, 432 items, also photographs of performing groups, 199 items, 1900–
Recordings, 214 78-rpm discs of choral music

—Daniel T. Williams

15

UNIVERSITY OF ALABAMA AU

Amelia Gayle Gorgas Library
University, Alabama 35486

All materials are in Special Collections, except as noted

T. P. Thompson Collection of 19th-century New Orleans imprints, including 50 items of sheet music, ca. 1856–97; 28 opera scores, 1843–99; and 30 programs of New Orleans operas and concerts before 1900. See Donald E. Thompson, *A Bibliography of Louisiana Books and Pamphlets in the T. P. Thompson Collection* (University, Ala., 1947)
Manuscript orchestral arrangement of A. P. Pfister's "Alabama University March," by Harkness, 1931
Peter Snow, ms songbook containing 42 popular songs, 1820
University of Alabama Glee Club, directed by Tom Garner, 16 scrapbooks containing clippings, programs, and photographs, ca. 1910–40
Sheet music, 120 pre-1930 American imprints in the Hill Ferguson collection, including works by Birmingham composer Daisy Woodruff Rowley; other items in the

papers of William Charles Cravner; and 250 items, 1900–1930
Programs, including 20 items of the Birmingham Music Club, early 20th century; 10 items of the Cadek Choral Society (Chattanooga, Tenn.), Birmingham Civic Opera Society, Birmingham Male Glee Club, and Apollo Boys Choir, all early 20th century; 25 items of Tuscaloosa musical organizations, ca. 1900–1925; and 12 items including 2 yearbooks of the Alabama Federation of Music Clubs, 1925–26
Recordings, including 150 78-rpm discs of early 20th-century American salon music, formerly in the collection of Margaret Christy of the University's Cadek Quartet; 2000 uncatalogued 78-rpm discs (in the Reserve Stacks); and 1000 field-recording discs of Alabama folksongs collected by Byron Arnold, ca. 1940–46

—Andrea Watson

In addition to the repositories listed above, the following have also reported holdings of the materials indicated:
Birmingham—Homewood Public Library: sheet music, songbooks
Birmingham—Southside Baptist Church: songbooks
Demopolis—Marengo County Historical Society: sheet music, songbooks
Florala—Florala Public Library: songbooks
Loachapoka—Lee County Historical Society: sheet music, songbooks
Mobile—Mobile Public Library: sheet music, songbooks, miscellaneous
Oneonta—Blount County Historical Society: sheet music, songbooks, programs, recordings
Scottsboro—Scottsboro Public Library: songbooks, recordings
Selma—Clifford P. Morrison: songbooks
Tuscaloosa—Tuscaloosa County Preservation Society: miscellaneous

Alaska

16

UNIVERSITY OF ALASKA AkU

Fairbanks, Alaska 99701

Elmer E. Rasmuson Library

Songbooks and hymnals, 350 items, mostly 20th century, including about 10 in Alaskan native languages, 5 of them hymnals
Printed scores, American materials in a general collection of 2550 items
Recordings, 50 78-rpm discs, including some of Alaskan native music or dance

University Archives

Programs and playbills of University or local theatrical and musical events, 15 items, ca. 1910–
Alaskan Native Literature Tapes, 450 reels of folklore

and folksong recordings collected 1972–74

—Sherry L. Abrahams, Paul McCarthy

17

SHELDON MUSEUM

Box 236
Haines, Alaska 99827

Published music for piano, violin, or orchestra, 40 items, ca. 1900–1940
Hymnals of various denominations, 20 items, ca. 1900–1930s
Popular and school songbooks, 70 linear cm., ca. 1900–1940
Sheet music, 5000 items, ca. 1890–1940, mostly popular songs; also 20 bound vols. of dance folios, ca. 1925–35
Recordings of popular and classical music, 150 78-rpm

discs, ca. 1900–1930s, and 12 Edison cylinders, ca. 1900–1920s

—Elisabeth S. Hakkinen

18

ALASKA HISTORICAL LIBRARY　　　**AkHi**
Pouch G
State Office Building
Juneau, Alaska 99811

Sheet music and songbooks relating to Alaska and the Yukon Territory, 36 items, of which 15 were published 1868–1907. See the Library's bibliographical list, *Musical Reflections of Alaska's History* (1974)

—Phyllis DeMuth

19

VALDEZ HISTORICAL SOCIETY
Box 6
Valdez, Alaska 99686

Hymnals, 6 items, ca. 1894–1917

School and popular songbooks and music pedagogy books, 30 items, ca. 1900–1932
Sheet music, ca. 1900, 12 items, including songs about Alaska and works by George V. Beck of Sitka
Programs of local musical events, including those of army bands and a dramatic club, 20 items, 1901–40; also 10 photographs, mostly of the local army band, ca. 1910
Recordings, 25 78-rpm discs, and 40 discs for a music box, ca. 1930

—Dorothy I. Clifton

In addition to the repositories listed above, the following have also reported holdings of the materials indicated:
Anchorage—Anchorage Historical and Fine Arts Museum: programs, pictures, recordings
Anchorage—University of Alaska: miscellaneous
Fort Yukon—Dinjii Zhuu Enjit Museum: recordings
Kodiak—Kodiak Public Library, A. Holmes Johnson Memorial: songbooks
Petersburg—Petersburg Public Library: songbooks

Arizona

20

CASA GRANDE VALLEY HISTORICAL SOCIETY
110 West Florence Boulevard
Casa Grande, Arizona 85222

Sheet music, 20 mostly popular items, ca. 1900–
Hymnals and piano-instruction books, ca. 1900–1940, 10 items
Papers of local music organizations, including the Matinee Musical Club, 1923–49
Photographs of local musicians and groups, 15 items, 1915–

—Kay Benedict

21

ARIZONA FRIENDS OF FOLKLORE　　**AzFU**
Box 5905
Northern Arizona University
Flagstaff, Arizona 86011

Folksongs and ballads of the Southwest, mostly Anglo-American, on tape recordings collected by Keith Cunningham and other University faculty and students, 1960s–70s

—Keith Cunningham

22

ARIZONA STATE PARKS BOARD
1688 West Adams
Phoenix, Arizona 85007

Materials are housed at various state historical sites

School, community, popular, and sacred songbooks, 120 items, ca. 1900–1950
Popular vocal sheet music, 500 items, ca. 1900–1950
Photographs of musicians and music groups in Arizona, 40 items, ca. 1890–1920

—Marcy-Jean Mattson

23

Temple BETH ISRAEL
Library
3310 North Tenth Avenue
Phoenix, Arizona 85013

Songbooks of Jewish folk and liturgical music, 50 items published ca. 1900–1940
Sheet music, mostly songs of Yiddish theater, 75 items, ca. 1920–40
Recordings of Jewish folk music, Israeli music, and liturgical music, 200 cassettes and 200 reels of tape, collected ca. 1972, mostly from the Phoenix area

—Lillian Tempkin

24

HEARD MUSEUM LIBRARY
22 East Monte Vista Road
Phoenix, Arizona 85004

Ethnomusicological archive, with 44 disc and tape recordings of music performed by American Indians at the Heard Museum Guild Indian Fair in Phoenix, ca.

1960–70; and photographs of American Indian musicians in a general photograph collection

—Mary Graham

25
PHOENIX HISTORICAL SOCIETY AND MUSEUM OF HISTORY

1242 North Central
Phoenix, Arizona 85004

Manuscript of the opera *Rosita*, written for the Amateur Theater in Chicago, 1939, with action set in Arizona's Superstition Mountains
Musicians' Club of Phoenix, 1.5 linear meters of materials, including scrapbooks, yearbooks, notebooks, programs, and printed music
Programs of musicians and groups in Phoenix, 15 linear cm., ca. 1890– ; also 40 photographs, ca. 1920–
Sheet music, 3 items, ca. 1900–1920; also recordings, including 3 linear meters of 78-rpm discs, mostly classical

—Richard Soine

26
Sharlot HALL HISTORICAL SOCIETY

415 West Gurley Street
Prescott, Arizona 86301

Manuscript compositions set to poetry of Sharlot Hall (1878–1943), 10 items, ca. 1900–1930
Songbooks for schools and organizations, and hymnals, in all 25 items, ca. 1900–1930
Popular or sacred sheet music including several works by Arizona composers, in all 120 items, ca. 1900–1930
Programs of local musical performances including events at Prescott opera houses and Fort Whipple military balls, 10 items, ca. 1860–1900
Photographs of local and military bands and other local music groups, 10 items, ca. 1880–1910, including some of Achille LaGuardia (father of the governor and bandmaster at Fort Whipple)
Recordings, including 15 cylinders, 12 tune sheets for music box, and 30 piano rolls

—Sue Chamberlain

27
Willard RHODES

13615 Redwood Drive
Sun City, Arizona 85351

Research notes on and field recordings of American Indian music, collected from tribes west of the Mississippi River, 1938–52 (materials deposited in the Archive of Folk Song, Library of Congress); white folk music from Ashland, Ky., recorded with Jean Thomas in 1940, and Sioux music recorded at Pine Ridge, S.D., in 1938–39 (materials deposited at the Archives of Traditional Music, Indiana University)

28
ARIZONA STATE UNIVERSITY   AzTeS

Tempe, Arizona 85281

Music Library

Wayne King Collection of orchestral and band materials, ca. 1930–65, 5600 popular items including ms arrangements, charts, and parts, some published music, a film of his television series, "The Wayne King Show" (1949–52), and 40 recordings
International Percussion Reference Library, 2400 items of published music for percussion solo or ensemble, ca. 1940–
Hymnals, 200 items, ca. 1836–
Popular sheet music, 2300 items, ca. 1836– , mostly 1920s–40s

—Arlys L. McDonald

Southwest Tape Archive, Department of Music

Tape recordings of music, mostly of the Southwest, especially from American Indian communities in Arizona, including Pima and Papago materials collected by Donald Bahr and J. Richard Haefer; also Spanish-American materials

—J. Richard Haefer

29
NAVAJO COMMUNITY COLLEGE

Naaltsoos Ba'Hooghan Library
Tsaile, Arizona 86556

Moses–Donner Collection on the Indians of North America, including recordings and other materials of American Indian music, as cited in *Ash*, p. 715

30
ARIZONA HISTORICAL SOCIETY   AzTP

949 East Second Street
Tucson, Arizona 85719

Herman Burr Leonard (1880–1935), programs and other materials relating to orchestra concerts and entertainment in Tucson, 70 linear cm., ca. 1915–38
Frederic Ronstadt (1880–1953), 30 linear cm. of papers including some relating to music in Tucson in the 1880s, with clippings on the musical career of his daughter, Luisa Ezpinal (Spanish concert singer), 1932–39
W. Arthur Sewell (1890–1968), 30 linear cm. of papers, including scrapbooks, letters, and programs, pertaining to his career as Tucson High School band director and supervisor of high school music
Papers and programs of local music groups, including the Phoenix Symphony Orchestra, Saturday Morning Music Club, and Temple of Music and Art, 2.5 linear meters, ca. 1890–
Published sheet music, 500 popular vocal items, ca. 1880–1920; also 10 items by Arizona composers or about Arizona, ca. 1890–1910
Henry and Albert Buehman Collection of photographs, with 250,000 glass plates and negatives, 1880s–1950s, including Arizona musicians, bands, and Indians
Pioneer Collection of photographs, including several photographs of bands, steamboat musicians, and other musicians or music groups

—Margaret S. Bret Harte

31

ARIZONA STATE MUSEUM
University of Arizona
Tucson, Arizona 85721

Collection of American Indian music recordings, with major holdings of Papago, Yaqui, Pueblo, Apache, and Tarahumara materials, some holdings of Seri, Chemehuevi, and Navajo, and a few holdings of non-Southwestern tribes

32

James GRIFFITH
Route 11, Box 624
Tucson, Arizona 85706

Field recordings of Anglo- and Mexican-American music, including cowboy songs and instrumental music; also southern Arizona vernacular music on commercial recordings, and photocopies of several ms songbooks

33

UNIVERSITY OF ARIZONA   AzU
Tucson, Arizona 85721

Music Collection, University Library

Sheet music, including 20,000 instrumental and vocal items, catalogued; the Historical American Collection, 9000 items, ca. 1850–1950, mostly 1920s–30s, arranged by title with card indexes by composer, title, and date; and the Grant L. Hill collection, 120,000 items, mostly 20th century, with a subject index on cards
Igor Gorin, personal music library, including 2000 printed editions of vocal music
Recordings, 13,000 early 78-rpm discs from the jazz collection of Louis Belden
National Flute Association collection, including 3000 editions of flute music, many U.S. imprints
National Opera Association collection, including printed editions, mss, and recordings of 20th-century operas, many of them American
National Trombone Association collection, including many U.S. editions of trombone music

—Elsie A. Phillips

Special Collections, University Library

Southwest Collection, 4 linear meters with published music and recordings, including music by Arizona composers or relating to Arizona or the Southwest, cowboy and folksongs, Mexican-American music, and American Indian music of the Southwest

—Elsie A. Phillips

Center for Creative Photography

Ernest Bloch (1880–1957), photographs made in Switzerland and in the U.S., as discussed by Eric Johnson, "A Composer's Vision, Photographs by Ernest Bloch," *Aperture*, 16/3 (1972); also his "Ernest Bloch," *Camera*, 55/2 (Feb., 1976), 6-17, 27, 37-38; and the exhibition catalogue, *Ernest Bloch, Photographer and Composer* (Tucson, 1979)

Southwestern Lore Center

1524 Gamma Apartments (Administrative Annex), Building 98

Collection of field recordings from Arizona, 1940s–60s, on tape and discs, mostly Anglo- and Mexican-American music, including folksongs, cowboy songs, *corridos*, and some fiddle music; also transcriptions. See the typescript report on the collection, 1966

—James Griffith

In addition to the repositories listed above, the following have also reported holdings of the materials indicated:

Gila Bend—Gila Bend Public Library: songbooks
Pearce—Arizona Sunsites Community Library: songbooks
Phoenix—Phoenix Public Library: sheet music
Phoenix—Southwestern College, Library: songbooks
Sierra Vista—Sierra Vista Municipal Library: recordings

Arkansas

34

ARKANSAS COLLEGE   ArBaA
Folklore Archive
Batesville, Arkansas 72501

Recordings of music collected in the Arkansas area, ca. 1976– , including English and American ballads, and square-dance and other music played on the fiddle or other string instruments; in all 60 tapes, also ms texts

—Diane Tebbetts

35

UNIVERSITY OF CENTRAL   ArCCA
ARKANSAS
Torreyson Library
Conway, Arkansas 72032

Manuscript music, mostly school songs by local composers, 10 items
Songbooks, 70 items containing mostly American folksongs, ca. 1930–40, including 10 locally published songbooks of Ozark folksongs, 1930s

Sheet music, mostly jazz and ragtime, 65 items, 1920s

—Patricia E. Lowrey

36

UNIVERSITY OF ARKANSAS ArU

Fayetteville, Arkansas 72701

See Samuel A. Sizer, *A Guide to Selected Manuscript Collections in the University of Arkansas Library* (Fayetteville, 1976; hereinafter cited as *Guide*)

David W. Mullins Library

Annie M. Caughey, 44 programs of operatic and concert performances in Little Rock, Dallas, Erie, Pa., and New York, 1928–48 (*Guide*, 42)

Theodore Thomas Frankenberg (1877–1958, Ohio newspaper critic), Theater Collection, 1872–1948, including published scores of Edgar Stillman Kelley's "Harrying Chorus" (autographed piano-vocal score) and "Alice in Wonderland" (piano arrangement), programs, photographs by Homer Alvan Rodeheaver, 1923–24, and correspondence with George H. Wilson (11 letters, 1904–6) and Eva Tanguay (1 letter, n. d.) (*Guide*, 80)

Scott Joplin, facsimile (1944) of the 1911 edition of his ragtime opera, *Treemonisha* (*Guide*, 112)

Mary Dengler Hudgins, 6 early published editions of the "Arkansas Traveller" tune, 1847–1905 (*Guide*, 104)

Vance Randolph (1892–1980), 4 vols. of ms and typescript Ozark folksongs, 1946–51, published folklore materials from Missouri and Arkansas, 1951–78, and tape recordings, 1978

Laurence Powell, 158 ms or published music scores, 1920–74

Arkansas and Ozark folklore collection, 442 tape recordings made by the University Folklore Research Project, 1949–65, directed by Mary Celestia Parler (Mrs. Randolph), including folksongs and instrumental music, 2.5 linear meters of typescript transcriptions, 9 linear meters of class reports (1958–74), and 1.2 linear meters of other typescript material. See "A Checklist of Arkansas Songs," *Arkansas Folklore*, 4 (1954), and occasional supplements

Mary Dengler Hudgins Collection, with 1 shelf box of Laurence Powell correspondence, writings, and compositions; 2 shelf boxes of published scores and writings about Scott Joplin's *Treemonisha*; 1 shelf box of gospel songbooks and writings; and 3 shelf boxes of mss, sheet music, scores, correspondence, and clippings on Arkansas composers or Arkansas musical subjects including Felix and Nola Locke Arndt, Samuel Bollinger, Imogen Carpenter, Butterfield Patricks, Lily Peter, Eddy Rogers, Harold L. Walters, Jule McIver Wood, the "Arkansas Traveler," William J. McDaniel, and William Merrell Paisley

William Grant Still (1895–1978), 88 ms scores and sketches of his compositions, with an 11-page typescript title index. The library is also to receive the composer's mss and papers

Florence Beatrice Smith Price (1888–1953, Arkansas-born composer), 64 items of papers, including 31 letters to or from John Alden Carpenter, Roland Hayes, Helen Armstrong Andrews, and others, 1933–50; 20 programs, mostly of Chicago organ or vocal recitals, 1906–75, including the dedication of the Florence B. Price School, Chicago, 1964; 2 folders of research

notes and photographs compiled by Mary Dengler Hudgins; 81 published scores and photocopies of ms music by Mrs. Price, 1928–53 and n.d.; and 30 other items, 1906–75, including clippings, photographs, an academic transcript, and biographical notes compiled by Florence Price Robinson

Music materials related to Arkansas, including 4 sacred or political songbooks, 1906–32; 4 items of sheet music, 1851–1927; and Arkansas State Music Teachers' Association publications, among them convention reports and bulletins, 1916– , and a music syllabus, 1929

Arkansas composers file, biographical materials in 1 file drawer, compiled in the preparation of James Pebworth's *A Directory of 132 Arkansas Composers* (Fayetteville, 1979)

—Barbara Garvey Jackson

Fine Arts Library

Published music for string instruments, a collection formerly belonging to Tosca Berger Kramer (string teacher in Tulsa, Okla.), 2000 items of American and European concert music, mostly for solo violin or viola, or chamber music, including autograph inscriptions of Henry Cowell and Alan Hovhaness

—Eloise McDonald

37

PHILLIPS COUNTY MUSEUM

623 Pecan Street
Helena, Arkansas 72342

Scrapbook with announcements, programs, and press clippings relating to the local opera house, mostly from 1920 until the burning of the house in 1926

Recordings, 35 wax cylinders, including items originally placed on permanent loan from the Edison Fund

—Dale P. Kirkman

38

ARKANSAS ARTS CENTER ArLA

MacArthur Park
Little Rock, Arkansas 72203

John D. Reid Collection of Early American Jazz, mostly of New Orleans performers ca. 1930–50, with correspondence, photographs, memorabilia, and several oral-history tapes; also 50 discographies and catalogues of recording companies or music publishers; and 4000 disc recordings, mostly 78-rpm discs, including some made by Reid. See Meredith McCoy and Barbara Parker, comp., *Catalog of the John D. Reid Collection of Early American Jazz* (Little Rock, 1975)

—Evelyn McCoy

39

ARKANSAS STATE LIBRARY Ar

One Capitol Mall
Little Rock, Arkansas 72201

Arkansas Authors and Composers Society, 50 linear cm. of papers, including 3 vols. of biographical material on Arkansas composers and writers, 1914–47; minutes, 1924–47; financial and presidents' reports; historian's record, 1935–44; and 11 scrapbooks, ca. 1918–47

—Dianne Williams

40

LITTLE ROCK PUBLIC LIBRARY   ArL
700 Louisiana Street
Little Rock, Arkansas 72201

Sheet music, 400 items, ca. 1900–1945, mostly popular, for voice or instruments, donated by the Little Rock Musical Coterie Society; indexed

—Bob Razer

41

DREW COUNTY HISTORICAL SOCIETY
Box 564
Monticello, Arkansas 71655

Hymnals, 3 items, ca. 1844–1900
Sheet music, mostly popular, 5 items and 1 bound vol.
Programs and photographs of bands from Monticello or from Midland, Tex., 5 items, 1893–1925
Popular recordings, including 26 78-rpm discs and 28 cylinders

—Margaret Rogers

42

OZARK FOLK CENTER
Library
Mountain View, Arkansas 72560

Published hymnals, ca. 1930–   , 100 items, mostly with hymns by Ozark composers
Popular and country-and-western sheet-music songs, 1000 items, ca. 1880–1940

Music catalogues of recording companies specializing in old-time and country-and-western music, 12 items, ca. 1910–30
Oral-history and music recordings, 1000 78-rpm discs or tapes concerning Ozark and Appalachian musicians, including several active ca. 1920–30, collected by W. K. McNeil

—W. K. McNeil

43

SOUTHWEST ARKANSAS REGIONAL ARCHIVES
Old Washington Historic State Park
Box 134
Washington, Arkansas 71862

Claud Garner (1890–1978), ms and published versions of 6 songs about Texas; also scrapbooks, clippings, correspondence, photographs, and 3 tape recordings of bands playing his music
Songbooks of popular and Civil War songs, 2 items, ca. 1890
Popular vocal sheet music including temperance songs, 500 items, ca. 1880–1925

—Mary Medearis

In addition to the repositories listed above, the following have also reported holdings of the materials indicated:

Fayetteville—Washington County Historical Society: songbooks, programs
Little Rock—Quapaq Quarter Association: sheet music
Searcy—Harding College, Beaumont Memorial Library: sheet music, songbooks, recordings
State University—Arkansas State University: sheet music, songbooks, other printed music, programs, miscellaneous

California

44

ARCADIA PUBLIC LIBRARY   CAr
20 West Duarte Road
Arcadia, California 91006

Anita Baldwin (1876–1939), 33 published songs in 2 bound vols. and 6 published orchestral works, ca. 1898–1932; also 1 linear cm. of biographical materials including clippings, reminiscences by Arcadia residents, a bibliography, and photographs

—Michelle A. Booth

45

S. E. BOYD SMITH
Azusa Pacific College
Highway 66 at Citrus Avenue
Azusa, California 91702

Camp-meeting songbooks, 1835–42, 3 items, 1 with words only
Popular sheet music in 12 bound vols., ca. 1840–80

46

**GRADUATE THEOLOGICAL   CBGTU
UNION LIBRARY**
2451 Ridge Road
Berkeley, California 94709

Hymnals, 200 items, mostly 20th-century U.S. imprints, and other materials relating to church music

47

INSTITUTE OF BUDDHIST STUDIES
2717 Haste Street
Berkeley, California 94704

Gagaku musical texts, imported for use in the U.S. in the 1930s

—Haruyoshi Kusada

48

Judah L. MAGNES MEMORIAL MUSEUM   CBM

Western Jewish History Center
2911 Russell Street
Berkeley, California 94705

Collection of Jewish music, emphasizing music of northern California and immigrants to the U.S., with 50 items of ms music, 200 songbooks, and 400 items of sheet music

—Harold M. Eiser

49

Chris STRACHWITZ

Arhoolie Records
Box 9195
Berkeley, California 94719

Recordings of blues, jazz, gospel, country, hillbilly, Texas-Mexican, and Cajun music, 10,000 78-rpm discs, 4500 other discs, and other materials

50

UNIVERSITY OF CALIFORNIA   CU

Berkeley, California 94720

Music Library

> See Audrey E. Phillips, *Guide to Special Collections, University of California, Berkeley, Library* (Metuchen, N.J., 1973); also Vincent Duckles, "The University of California, Berkeley, Music Library," *M.L.A. Notes*, 36 (1979), 7–22

Inez Fabbri-Mueller (1830–1909, San Francisco opera singer), personal papers, including scrapbooks, photographs, and memorabilia
Oscar Weil (1839–1921, San Francisco composer and music teacher), original compositions and teaching materials
Hugo Mansfeldt (1844–1931, San Francisco composer and music teacher), personal papers
Hermann Perlet (1863–1916, San Francisco impresario, composer, and author of musical comedies), ms scores, scrapbooks, and memorabilia
Alfred Hertz (1872–1942, conductor of the San Francisco Symphony Orchestra) and his wife, Lily (Dorn) Hertz (opera singer), personal papers, correspondence, photographs, and other memorabilia
Alfred Einstein (1880–1952), research papers and scrapbooks containing his music criticism
Ernest Bloch (1880–1959), music holographs, correspondence, and memorabilia. See Minnie Elmer, *Autograph Manuscripts of Ernest Bloch at the University of California* (Berkeley, 1962)
Albert I. Elkus (1884–1952, music professor, composer, and theorist), music compositions, correspondence, and scrapbooks

Sigurd Erhard Frederiksen (1884–1965, member of the Los Angeles Symphony Orchestra and the Hollywood Bowl Orchestra), music compositions
Charles Seeger (1886–1979), manuscripts and offprints of his writings
Sigmund Romberg (1887–1951), performance scores of his light operas, in 47 vols., also his personal collection of 4500 opera scores
Ivan Langstroth (1887–1971, pianist and composer), autograph music scores and correspondence
Manfred Bukofzer (1910–55), research materials, microfilms, and personal papers
Harris D. H. Connick (executive of Associated Music Publishers), collection of 4500 opera scores
Sheet music, 600 items, 1850s– , uncatalogued
Printed music in the general collections, including the collections of G. Camajani (San Francisco chorus director), 290 choral works in performance parts; Irving F. Morrow, 5500 items including 1500 opera scores; J. Louis and Fred Mundwyler, chamber music, 250 items; Henri E. Salz, 500 scores, mostly operas and piano works; and Ansley K. Salz, books on violins
Archives of the University Music Department, ca. 1940–
Scrapbooks and programs of Sacramento concerts and operas, particularly performances of the Saturday Club, 1893–1920
Pictures, including autographed photographs of musicians in the Koshland Photograph Collection and in the Wismer collection
Recordings, including 6000 early vocal discs in the Remo Bacigalupi collection, 450 jazz discs from the 1920s presented by A. Parker Stack, and 4000 discs, mostly vocal, presented by Prof. Paul Schaeffer

—Vincent Duckles

Bancroft Library

> See Dale L. Morgan and George P. Hammond, *Guide to the Manuscript Collections of the Bancroft Library* (Berkeley, 1963; hereinafter cited as *Guide*), also the *Catalog of Printed Books* (Boston, 1964; suppls., 1970 and 1975; hereinafter cited as *CPB*)

Sheet music, including a bound vol. with San Francisco imprints, 1867–77, owned by Zoe L. Green
Scrapbooks, including San Francisco concert and opera programs, 1 vol., 1882–88; Mary Randall and Marion Randall Parsons, 1 vol., 1890–1903; Charles Caldwell Dobie, 12 vols. including his newspaper criticism, 1890–1903; also Pomona College and Fresno theater and concert programs, 9 vols., 1921–48, collected by Anne Avakian
Programs of concerts and operas in San Francisco and other California cities, including the Arthur P. Agard collection, 1886–1957, in 20 vols.; Leonard W. Buck collection, 1915–53, in 7 vols.; and others as cited in *CPB*, vol. 5, pp. 475–76, also suppl. 1, pp. 129 and 292, and esp. the 120 entries in suppl. 2, pp. 191–97
Printed books, periodicals, directories, and organizational publications, including 91 San Francisco imprints, ca. 1873–1914, in the Music Pamphlet Collection; a 1912 *Constitution* and a 1914 *Price List* of the Musicians' Mutual Protective Union of San Francisco, in the Labor Union Constitutions and By-Laws collection; and various French materials, including a Lillian

Nordica autograph, from the Phoebe A. Hearst collection, in the Theater, Music, Dance and Art Miscellany. See *CPB*, vol. 14, pp. 453–64, also suppl. 1, pp. 291–93, and suppl. 2, pp. 566–68

Piper Opera House, Virginia City, Nev., business papers and correspondence of John and Edward Piper, 1877–1905, also contracts, printed circulars, and handbills (*Guide*, p. 142)

Miscellaneous ms documents, including Isaac Elder Blake (b. 1844), biographical materials, 1889–91, with musical references (*Guide*, p. 189); David Darling (1790–1867), hymns translated into Taheiti language, 1817 (*Guide*, p. 264); Father G. Gazzoli, prayers and hymns translated for Alphonse Pinart into the Skitswich language, 1876 (*Guide*, p. 157); Peter Hanson, journal, 1865–72, with Danish Mormon songs (*Guide*, p. 100); W. A. Houghton, letter to Rev. H. L. Foote, Carson City, Nev., and Stockton, Cal., 1876, concerning choral music (*Guide*, pp. 139–40); James Hampton Kuykendall (ca. 1820–82), biographical sketch, 1849, with song texts; William H. Nash, statement, 1886, discussing his musical interests (*Guide*, p. 224); and Alphonse Pinart (1852–1911, linguist and collector), Pima songs, some in a copy of an 1871 dictionary of Capt. F. E. Grossman, others obtained from John D. Walker, 1876 (*Guide*, p. 79)

—William M. Roberts

Lowie Museum of Anthropology

California Indian music and myths, of Yurok, Mohave, Yuki, Pomo, Modoc, Central Sierra Miwok, North Fork Mono, Yana, Eskimo, and other North American Indian tribes, including wire recordings, 3500 cylinders (also transcribed onto magnetic tape), and films, as cited in *Briegleb*, no. 5

Archive of California Folk Music

Field recordings of English- and Spanish-language folksongs collected by Sidney Robertson Cowell, early 1940s, including 15 paper tapes, also 7 cartons of related materials, with a card index

—John Emerson

University of California Folklore Archives

See Marsha Maguire's survey of University of California holdings, "Folklore and Folk Music Archives" (typescript, 1977)

Field-research collections, 15 filing cabinets of field reports by students in the U.S., ca. 1969– , alphabetized and indexed by genre, including Anglo-American, American Indian, Jewish, Chinese, German, Italian, and Russian materials

51

ACADEMY OF MOTION PICTURE ARTS AND SCIENCES CLAc

Margaret Herrick Library
8949 Wilshire Boulevard
Beverly Hills, California 90211

Sheet music, 1 box of background music for silent films,

ca. 1910–30, arranged by publisher

Conductor's scores for films, 50 published items, ca. 1941–50

Reference files, including 50,000 press clippings, photographs, and other documents, indexed by production titles; biographical subjects, including composers, arrangers, lyricists, and performers; and general topics, including a file on musicals

—Terry Roach, Stacy Endres

52

BEVERLY HILLS PUBLIC LIBRARY CBev

444 North Rexford Drive
Beverly Hills, California 90210

Dorothi Bock Pierre collection of 6000 photographs on dance, 1920s–60s, as cited by Sally Dumaux, *Sources for Photographs in the Los Angeles Metropolitan Area* (Los Angeles, 1977)

53

Q. David BOWERS

Beverly Hills, California

Bowers's mailing address is c/o Vestal Press, Box 97, Vestal, N.Y. 13850

Automatic musical instruments, music boxes, and related subjects, as treated in original literature, sales and trade catalogues, and printed ephemera, 1850–1930, and as shown on musical post cards, ca. 1900–1920. See Bowers's *Encyclopedia of Automatic Musical Instruments* (Vestal, N.Y., 1972) and *Guidebook to Automatic Musical Instruments* (Vestal, N.Y., 1967)

54

Walt DISNEY ARCHIVES

500 South Buena Vista Street
Burbank, California 91521

Walt Disney Music Co. correspondence, 7.5 linear meters, 1953– ; also 10 music catalogues, 1960–

Printed music, including 600 sheet-music items, ca. 1930– , with songs from Disney films and other songs owned by Walt Disney Music Co. and Wonderland Music Co.; also band and orchestral scores of Disney music, 1 linear meter, ca. 1955

Photographic negatives of Disney productions, 600,000 items, 1923– , including musical subjects such as the filming of *Fantasia*

Recordings released by Walt Disney Music Co. on the Disneyland and Vista labels, and Disney music on other labels, in all 12 linear meters of discs, 1933–

—David R. Smith

55

CLAREMONT COLLEGES CCC

Claremont, California 91711

Honnold Library

Robert G. McCutchan Collection of Hymns and Hymnology, including 650 18th- and 19th-century U.S.

tunebooks, books about hymnology, and other works, collected by McCutchan (1877–1958, who also wrote under the pseud. "John Porter") in his hymnological studies; also a biographical scrapbook on him by his wife, Helen McCutchan; and 3 loose-leaf binders containing his correspondence, published articles, and lecture notes. See Charles Edward Lindsley, "An Important Tunebook Collection in California," M.L.A. *Notes*, 29 (1973), 671–74; also A. Merril Smoak, Jr., "Hymnal Collections in the Greater Los Angeles Area," *The Hymn*, 30 (1979), 102–5

Joseph W. Clokey (1890–1960, professor of music and organist at Pomona College, 1926–39), personal papers, including 250 holograph compositions, both originals and in photocopy; 200 printed editions of his music; and 15 folders of correspondence

John Laurence Seymour Opera Collection, containing 600 vols. of books about opera, libretti, and scores, also several published editions of works by Seymour

Ernestine Schumann-Heink (1861–1936), 300 vocal scores used and annotated by her

—Ruth M. Hauser, Tania Rizzo

Claremont Graduate School

Lee Pattison (1890–1966, pianist and music educator), personal papers, 25 linear cm. with typescript inventory, including plans, notes, and minutes of the Liberal Arts Association of America, 1933–34; also materials of the WPA Federal Music Project in New York City, mostly 1936–37, including programs of the New York Festival Orchestra, Brooklyn Symphony, Knickerbocker Little Symphony, and New York Civic Orchestra, speeches and press releases by Pattison, programs and correspondence of the Music Education Division, and various WPA reports and correspondence

—Helen M. Smith

56
SCHOOL OF THEOLOGY   CCSC
AT CLAREMONT

Theology Library
1325 North College Avenue
Claremont, California 91711

Protestant hymnals, 30 linear meters, ca. 1750– , including some in German and Scandinavian, and some with words only

—James Overbeck

57
SCRIPPS COLLEGE   CCC

Ella Strong Denison Library
Claremont, California 91711

Fritz Bruch (German cellist, active in the U.S. after 1911, and a member of the Cincinnati Symphony Orchestra, 1940s), personal papers, including biographical press clippings and holograph performance materials for 21 music compositions

—Judy Harvey Sahak

58
George BRANDON

1010 East Eighth Street
Davis, California 95616

Hymnals and songbooks, 1790s– , mostly 1850s– , 200 items; also piano, organ, and choral music; programs of concerts and church services, 1930s– ; and 40 books on music and hymnology

59
UNIVERSITY OF CALIFORNIA   CU-A

Shields Library
Davis, California 95616

Woodland (Cal.) Opera House, 248 items of papers, 1896–1913, including programs, photographs, press clippings, ticket stubs, and other memorabilia; also a card index to performers and productions. See two papers written at the University, by John Eldridge and John Lamb, "The Woodland Opera House, 1896–1916," and by Janet Sullivan, "Woodland Theatre, 1892–1916"

Sheet music, 1208 items, 1900–1960, mostly popular and theater songs acquired for pictorial cover illustrations. A title index is maintained in the Special Collections Department

Programs, 15 file boxes of miscellaneous material, ca. 1869– , not indexed

—Marlene Wong

60
CALIFORNIA STATE UNIVERSITY—   CFS
FRESNO

Library
Department of Special Collections
Fresno, California 93740

Arthur C. Berdahl (former head of the Music Department), 17 scrapbooks of clippings concerning departmental activities, 1933–54

Mitchell P. Briggs (former dean of men at the University), scrapbook of clippings pertaining to local musical events, 1925–49

Pianoforte Club and Orchesis dance group, scrapbooks of clippings, programs, and photographs of local campus events, 1928–65, 1 linear meter

Programs of local musical events, including those of the Fresno Opera Association, Fresno Musical Club, and Fresno Theatre League, 60 linear cm., 1924–73

Programs of the University Music Department, 30 linear cm. of bound vols., 1947–72

Printed scores and parts for theater and silent-film orchestras, 14 linear meters, ca. 1860–1940

Engraved plates for 2 works by Gardner Eyre (pseud. of Agnes G. deJahn, local piano teacher), issued in 1926, 11 items

—Ronald J. Harlan

61
FRESNO CITY AND COUNTY HISTORICAL
SOCIETY

7160 West Kearney Boulevard
Fresno, California 93706

Bell T. Ritchie (local singer, teacher, and a founder of the Fresno Musical Club), programs of her recitals, reviews, articles, and 1 photograph

Programs of local musicians and groups, including the Fresno Male Chorus, Fresno Mandolin Club, Fresno Philharmonic Orchestra, Fresno Symphony, and Fresno Musical Club (established 1904; sponsored local performances by Feodor Chaliapin, Emmy Destinn, Mischa Elman, Ignace Jan Paderewski and other musicians), in all 100 items, ca. 1890–

Photographs of local music groups, mostly orchestras, ca. 1930s–40s

Sheet music, 43 items, ca. 1890–1930; also 3 popular songbooks, 1920s

Recordings, including 5 cylinders labeled in Chinese, and 80 78-rpm discs, ca. 1900–1930

—Dianne E. Seeger, Sharon Hiigel

62

Jack LONDON STATE HISTORIC PARK

Box 358
Glenn Ellen, California 95442

Materials of Charmian (Mrs. Jack) London (1871–1955, pianist), including 9 ms items for piano or voice written for her by acquaintances, 91 published piano works and 113 sheet-music items by American or European composers, and 37 78-rpm discs of classical music and sea chanteys

63

Ernest BLOCH SOCIETY ARCHIVES

Star Route 2
Gualala, California 95445

Ernest Bloch, 50 letters to his daughter, Lucienne Bloch Dimitroff, 1930–55; 100 letters to his mother, 1915–23, concerning his American experiences (photocopies; originals are in Switzerland); programs; 160 recordings of his music; 50 printed scores; published biographies and articles; drawings of him by Lucienne Bloch and others; 100 photographs, some by him; and memorabilia

—Lucienne Bloch Dimitroff

64

Louis A. GOTTSCHALK

Department of Psychiatry and Human Behavior
College of Medicine
University of California at Irvine
Irvine, California 92717

Max W. Gottschalk (1876–1961, St. Louis violinist, pianist, composer, and music critic), personal papers, including several published compositions

65

Corinne SWALL

36 Turnagain Road
Kentfield, California 94904

Collection of California music, 1848– , supporting re-

created performances of period productions, and emphasizing the 1850s; melodeon or saloon songs; parlor ballads; the repertory of early touring performers; and compositions by resident composers. Among the materials are sheet music (including numerous songs by George T. Evans and Stephen Massett, and the repertory of Lotta Crabtree, Jenny Lind, and E. Biscaccianti), songsters and songbooks, photographs and pictorial materials, biographical notes, early Spanish-Californian songs from the Jacob Leese family collection, and a library of books on theatrical and musical history

66

LIBRARY ASSOCIATION OF LA JOLLA   CLjL

Athenaeum Music and Arts Library
1008 Wall Street
La Jolla, California 92037

Musical Arts Society of La Jolla, scrapbook

Printed scores for operettas or instrumental music, 10 items

Sheet music, 3000 items, mostly popular songs, 1890–1950

Programs, 100 items, including those of the La Jolla Chamber Orchestra and the Musical Arts Society

Recordings, 1500 discs

—Carole Shipley

67

Merril SMOAK

823 Debra Street
Livermore, California 94550

Hymnals and tunebooks, 1744– , mostly 1800–1860, 200 items, including many shape-note vols., and pocket-size books with text only, especially editions of Isaac Watts

68

CALIFORNIA STATE UNIVERSITY   CLobS

Library
Long Beach, California 90840

Oral History of the Arts Archive

Begun in 1974, the Archive interviews and collects printed and ms documents concerning musicians active in southern California in the 1930s and 1940s

Richard Buhlig (1880–1952, pianist and teacher), biographical materials, letters, and programs and reviews of his concerts, mostly photocopies. See Nancy J. Wolbert, *Richard Buhlig, a Concert Pianist: His Career and Influence in the Twentieth Century* (Master's thesis, California State University, 1978)

Wesley Kuhnle (1898–1962, pianist and musicologist) Archive on Historic Tunings and Temperaments, with 56 tape recordings documenting his career and his work with keyboard performance practice, also 45 vols. of personal papers including notes, diagrams, correspondence, programs and reviews (1918–62), ms arrangements and compositions, photographs, biographical materials, and his personal library. See

C. G. Rayner, "The Wesley Kuhnle Repository," M.L.A. *Notes*, 33 (1976), 16–26

Dane Rudhyar, photocopies of many of his unpublished articles and books on music, also tapes of oral-history interviews and Rudhyar symposia. See Sheila Finch Rayner, ed., *An Oral History of Dane Rudhyar* (Long Beach, 1977)

Morris H. Ruger (1902–74, composer), ms autobiography, letters, clippings, reviews, a scrapbook, tapes of performances of his music and of interviews with friends and colleagues. See Leslie K. Greer, *Morris Hutchins Ruger: A Biography* (Master's thesis, California State University, 1977)

Gerald V. Strang, ms and published compositions, books, articles, and lectures, including the *New Music Quarterly* ed. by him; also biographical materials, student projects, materials from his oriental music studies, autographed scores by Arnold Schoenberg, Alban Berg, and Charles Ives, autographed writings by or about Schoenberg and Ernst Toch, articles collected by Strang, disc recordings of unpublished music, tape recordings of lectures and performances, and 15 hours of oral-history interviews. See Mitchel A. Berman, *Gerald Strang: Composer, Educator, Acoustician* (Master's thesis, California State University, 1977)

Southern California Chapter of the American Musicological Society Archive, materials from the Chapter's founding in 1939 to the present, with lists of officers and programs, a constitution, correspondence, and taped interviews with early participants including Ernst Krenek

Other oral-history recordings, 250 hours of interviews with 90 persons on such topics as pianists' careers in southern California, the rise of the university composer, new music in southern California, and chamber music and private performances. Persons interviewed include Gerhardt Albersheim, Pauline Alderman, William Audley Alexander, Victor Aller, Daniel Amtitheathof, Harry Anderson, Willi Apel, Milton Babbitt, Elmer Bernheimer, Vahdah Bickford, Emil Bisttram, Andrew Blakeney, Frank Bostwich, Teddy Buckner, Richard Bunger, Buddy Burns, Roxanne Byers, John Cage, Gaylord Carter, Winthrop B. Chandler, Abram Chasins, Marge Clauson, Joe Darensbourg, Hugo Davise, Mike Delay, Peter Dickinson, Akira Endo, Morton Feldman, Lukas Foss, Harold Gelman, Philip Glass, Felix Griessle, Dwane Gurnee, Roy Harris, Lou Harrison, Peter Hewitt, Joanna Hodges, Evelyn Hood, Leon Kirchner, Nicolai Kobzev, William Kraft, Ernst Krenek, Stanley Kurnik, Richard Lert, Helena Lewyn, Galen Lurwick, Leslie Maloche, Betty Olsson, George Orendorff, Harry Partch, Cesare Pascarella, Brent Pierce, Paul Pisk, Forest Powell, Edward Rebner, Roger Reynolds, Harry Rickel, Danny Robbins, Goldie Rodgers, Robert Ruger, Nicolas Slonimsky, Leonard Stein, Mrs. William Grant Still (Verna Arvey), Howard Swan, Edgar Thompson, George Tremblay, Floyd Turnham, Alfred Wallenstein, Garry White, Lucille Wilke, Peter Yates, and Florence Zook

—Clare G. Rayner

Other Collections

Metro–Goldwyn–Mayer Library of orchestral and piano-vocal scores for musical films, 170 printed items, 13

ms scores, and 5 ms vols., 1936–57

Songbooks, 7 items of war songs, school songs, and popular songs, 1813–87

Sheet music, 30 bound vols. of popular songs, 1847–1914

New Music Series and *New Music Orchestra* series, complete run, 1924–57

—Marilyn Moy

69

HISTORICAL SOCIETY OF LONG BEACH

4600 Virginia Road
Long Beach, California 90807

Musical Arts Club of Long Beach, 9 scrapbooks of press clippings, photographs of members, and programs, 35 linear cm., 1928–74

—Zona Gale Forbes

70

LONG BEACH PUBLIC LIBRARY　　　CLob

Literature and History Department
101 Pacific Avenue
Long Beach, California 90802

Programs, clippings, and photographs of local musical events, ca. 1920– , in a vertical file; scrapbooks of the Civic Concert Series, 1920s; a scrapbook of the Long Beach Symphony Orchestra, 1928–31; and a scrapbook of the Civic Light Opera

—Helene Silver

71

ARCHDIOCESE OF LOS ANGELES

Chancery Archives
1531 West Ninth Street
Los Angeles, California 90015

Manuscript music books, one of them copied by Arroyo de la Cuesta, 1834, and used in Mission San Miguel

—Francis Weber

72

CALIFORNIA STATE UNIVERSITY　　　CLS

John F. Kennedy Memorial Library
5151 State University Drive
Los Angeles, California 90032

Otto Klemperer (1885–1973, director of the Los Angeles Philharmonic Orchestra, 1933–39), library of musical scores, with personal annotations, 213 items

—Irving Cohen

73

Norm COHEN

Aerospace Corporation
Box 92957
Los Angeles, California 90009

Recordings of Anglo-American and Afro-American folk music, and commercial recordings of hillbilly, country and western, blues, Cajun, and other folk music, 30,000 78-rpm discs, 1000 other discs, and 250 tapes

74
John EDWARDS MEMORIAL FOUNDATION
Center for the Comparative Study of Folklore and
    Mythology
University of California
Los Angeles, California 90024

American folk music, hillbilly, country and western, blues, gospel, rhythm and blues, Cajun, and Hawaiian music on commercial recordings, 15,000 78-rpm discs, 12,000 other discs, 1500 tape recordings other than tape copies of discs, and 150 transcriptions. See the Foundation's *Newsletter* (1965–68) and its *Quarterly* journal (1969–); also Eugene W. Earle, "The John Edwards Memorial Foundation, Inc.," *Western Folklore*, 23 (1964), 111–13, and "The John Edwards Memorial Foundation," *Western Folklore*, 30 (1971), 177–81

—Norm Cohen

75
Joseph S. HALL
1455 Lemoyne Street
Los Angeles, California 90026

Music, folklore, and speech of the Great Smoky Mountains of Tennessee and North Carolina, including traditional ballads, fiddle tunes, square-dance music, commercial recordings, 20 aluminum discs, 50 acetate 78-rpm discs, 120 other 78-rpm discs, and tapes and films; also 30 ms ballads and folksongs, photographs of performers, and other papers

76
Herman LANGINGER
1349 North Highland Street
Los Angeles, California 90028

Correspondence and other transactions (bills, proof sheets, and music mss) of New Music Editions, Inc. (ca. 1932–59), involving composers, among them Carl Ruggles and Charles Ives; publishers, notably Henry Cowell, also Ray Green and Ingolf Dahl; and the publishers' main engraver, Herman Langinger (active at the Pacific Music Press in the late 1920s, and founder of the Golden West Music Press, ca. 1930ff). See Vivian Perlis, *Two Men for Modern Music*, ISAM Monographs, 9 (Brooklyn, 1978), esp. note 5 on p. 32

77
LOS ANGELES COUNTY   CLCM
MUSEUM OF NATURAL HISTORY
900 Exposition Boulevard
Los Angeles, California 90007

California mission music, 25 ms sheets, late 18th century

Sheet music, 1000 items, singly and in 3 bound vols., 1 of the latter stamped with the name of Mrs. Clara Patterson and including early Stephen Foster editions, another devoted to early keyboard music, mid-19th to early 20th centuries; also a Civil War songbook, 1863
Local theater and concert programs, late 19th and early 20th centuries, including many from the Belasco Theater
Cylinder and disc recordings, several items (in the Industrial Technology Section)

—Katharine Donahue, Sally Haimbridge

78
LOS ANGELES MUSIC CENTER ARCHIVES
135 North Grand Avenue
Los Angeles, California 90012

See Joel Pritkin, "The Music Center Archives," *Performing Arts*, 11 (1977), 61–62

Materials documenting the history of the Center and other performing-arts organizations in the Los Angeles area, including programs and photographs of the Los Angeles Philharmonic Orchestra, Hollywood Bowl, Los Angeles Civic Light Opera Association, Music Center Opera Association, and Los Angeles Master Chorale
Raymond F. Barnes Collection, with complete files on the early years of the Biltmore Theatre and Philharmonic Auditorium, including playbills, photographs, published books on theater, and a card index on Los Angeles theatrical productions, ca. 1850–1940, with some music materials
Kenn Randall Collection, including programs, promptbooks, press clippings, press books, and photographs pertaining to Los Angeles performing-arts events

—Joel Pritkin

79
LOS ANGELES PUBLIC LIBRARY   CL
630 West Fifth Street
Los Angeles, California 90017

Art and Music Department

Sheet music, 100,000 popular-music items, 1841–
Other printed music, 11,000 items, including operettas by John Philip Sousa and Victor Herbert, 19th-century popular songbooks, and 3000 items of the WPA
Music mss by California composers
Programs of local concerts, press clippings, and scrapbooks on music in Los Angeles, 1894–

Manuscripts and Special Collections

E. Lynden Behymer (20th-century impresario), 200 signed photographs of performers, also posters, programs, and memorabilia of theatrical events
Hal Weiner, photographs of musicians, 1920s–60s
Biographical collection of clippings, including concert reviews and professional and biographical information about musicians

—Katherine Grant

80

MOUNT SAINT MARY'S COLLEGE   CLMSM

Charles W. Coe Memorial Library
12001 Chalon Road
Los Angeles, California 90049

Popular sheet music, 13,000 items published ca. 1900–1950 by Mills Music, Inc., or by other firms acquired by Mills; in bound vols., donated by Irving Mills
Printed music for orchestra, chamber orchestra, and choir, 500 items, 1875–

—Mary L. Sedgwick

81

Arnold SCHOENBERG INSTITUTE

University of Southern California
Los Angeles, California 90007

For discussions involving the collection, see the Institute's *Journal* (1976–), particularly the continuing series "From the Archives," near the back of most issues, and esp. vol. 1, pp. 49–54

Musical mss of Arnold Schoenberg, as cited in Josef Rufer, *The Works of Arnold Schoenberg* (Glencoe, 1963). Original copies of mss are arranged in the order of this book, except for items noted in Rufer's first paragraph under each entry as being elsewhere; in all 3000 pages, catalogue in process
Literary manuscripts of Schoenberg, including textbooks, texts and libretti for vocal works, essays, poems, aphorisms, fragments, and sketches, 2000 pages, mostly as cited in Rufer, pp. 133–79
Published music, including all works by Schoenberg, many with his personal annotations; and 1500 works by other composers, many of which contain dedications to and/or annotations by Schoenberg
Other printed materials associated with Schoenberg, including libretti and periodicals, many of them annotated by Schoenberg
Schoenberg memorabilia, including biographical materials, birthday mementos, notebooks, calendars, indexes, pocket diaries, and teaching materials. See the *Journal*, 2 (1978), 143–60
Other materials, including photographs, posters, handbills, programs, press clippings, recordings, illustrative slides, and motion-picture films
Stiedry Collection of materials, assembled by Fritz Stiedry and Erika Stiedry-Wagner, with correspondence, programs, and other printed matter, mostly related to Schoenberg. See Jonathan M. Dunsby, "The Stiedry Collection," *Journal*, 1 (1977), 152–69
Steuermann Collection of printed music, other publications, typescripts, and other items from the library of Edward Steuermann. See Jonathan M. Dunsby, "The Steuermann Collection," *Journal*, 2 (1977), 63–71
Other "satellite collections," including materials presented by Mrs. Adolf Koldofsky, Lawrence Morton, Paul A. Pisk, Gerald Strang, Leonard Stein, and H. H. Stuckenschmidt

—Clara Steuermann

82

SOUTHWEST MUSEUM   CLSM

Box 128
Highland Park Station
Los Angeles, California 90042

Frances Densmore (folklorist), papers, ca. 1900–1957, including mss of books, also lectures, clippings, and correspondence
Eleanor Hague (folklorist), papers, ca. 1910–55, including the ms of her study, "Folk Music in the Southwest," photographs, Negro and Spanish-American folksongs, and miscellaneous correspondence
Charles Fletcher Lummis (folklorist), papers, 1898–1928, including correspondence with Los Angeles musicians, diaries and journals, photographs, ms and typescript writings, ms transcriptions of folksongs, and programs
Gamut Club, Los Angeles, 1 box of papers, 12 linear cm., ca. 1910–30
Recordings of southwestern U.S. folk music, 600 cylinders and 78-rpm discs, including Spanish and American Indian songs recorded 1904–7 by Charles Lummis, and partial collections of field recordings by Helen H. Roberts, Josephine P. Cook, and Frances Densmore
Sheet music, 600 items relating to American Indians of California, ca. 1910–30

—Glenna Schroeder

83

THEATRE AND FILM ARTS

c/o Carl Post
691 South Irolo Street
Los Angeles, California 90005

Manuscript materials, 200 items, including holograph music mss of Mario Castelnuovo-Tedesco, Henry Cowell, Charles Ives, Paul Amadeus Pisk, Cole Porter, Benjamin Lees, Roger Sessions, and Ernst Toch; also correspondence of Ernst Krenek, Darius Milhaud, and others
Published music, including editions of songs, orchestral works, and piano music by U.S. composers, 30 items; 50 sheet-music items, 1890–1914; 1 Harrigan and Hart songbook; and 50 published books on music, 1885–
Opera programs, 1500 items, including performances featuring Enrico Caruso, Geraldine Farrar, and Nellie Melba, productions by Oscar Hammerstein, and performances of the Metropolitan Opera (1910–20, including its Boston season, 1917), and of French opera and opéra comique
Theatrical and film collections with musical materials, 25,000 programs, photographs, window cards, and other materials, 1803–
Pictorial materials, including 100 posters and 100 photographs of opera performers

84

UNIVERSITY OF CALIFORNIA   CLU

Los Angeles, California 90024

This report has been assembled largely through the efforts of Stephen M. Fry

A. Music Library (1102 Schoenberg Hall)

Fannie Charles Dillon (1881–1947), personal papers, including 140 mss, published editions, and transparencies of her compositions; programs of the Dillon family, mostly in Los Angeles, 1912–39; programs and brochures for the MacDowell Colony (Peterborough, N.H.) and the MacDowell Colony League of Southern California, 1930s; personal correspondence involving Howard Hanson, Harry Woodhouse, and Willem Van Hoogstraten; photographs of and biographical material on Dillon; press clippings, mostly unorganized, and brochures on her life and works, mostly 1908–39; and press clippings, brochures, programs, and other materials, mostly on southern California music, mostly 1930s. See the inventory

Hal Levy Collection, including 120 tape recordings of lectures by popular-music composers and performers, used in Levy's course in lyric writing, as well as other materials in the Archive of Popular American Music (section B, below)

Earl Lowry collection, including 12 boxes of correspondence, documents, and drafts of his articles, also 35 mss and ozalid copies of mss by U.S. composers, ca. 1930–50

Edward B. Powell collection of film-music materials, including a piano-conductor score of Joseph Achron's music for *A Night with Pan,* 1935

Other collections of musicians' mss and personal papers, including Radie Britain, 7 holograph mss and editions of music; Hugo Davise, 125 mss and photocopies of his works; Rudolf Friml (1879–1972), 200 holograph mss, also 60 reproductions and recordings of his works, with an inventory; Colin McPhee (1900–1964), 40 mss, reproductions, published editions, and tapes of his works, with an inventory; P. A. Marquardt, book of 51 short scores of silent-film music for orchestra, and 2 cartons of ms orchestral music; Alfred Newman (1901–70), 29 recording albums and film scores, 1936–62; Alex North, mss of 39 film scores; Frances Marion Ralston (b. 1875), 10 mss and reproductions of her works; Joseph Rumshinsky, scores, parts, and libretti for his works, mostly for Yiddish theater, 115 items, with an inventory; Helen Louise Shaffer (ca. 1900–1950), 50 mss and published editions of her works; Edward Ward (1896–1971), 200 mss and reproductions of his film scores, 1935–40; Eugene Zador (1894–1977), 22 mss and reproductions of his works; also other extensive holdings of post-1940 film and television music

Archive Collections

Erich Wolfgang Korngold (1897–1957), archive in the process of being established

Clarence Mader (organist), holograph mss and sketches, correspondence, published books and music, some with annotations, and memorabilia

Mary Carr Moore (1873–1957), mss, reproductions, and published editions of her works, also correspondence, programs, and other materials

Ernst Toch (1877–1964), original mss, 40 items, as listed in Charles A. Johnson, *The Unpublished Works of Ernst Toch* (Ph.D. diss., UCLA, 1973), also 10 other holographs, most of them involving John Scott Trotter, presented by the Trotter family, and photocopies of Toch mss located in other collections; a complete file of Toch's published music, some copies with holo-

graph annotations; commercial and non-commercial recordings of music by Toch, 42 items; mss of Toch's literary works, including books, essays, and program notes; correspondence, 1906–72, 15,000 items, most of it arranged chronologically with indexes for correspondents, and described in Barbara Jane Davis, *The Organization of the Correspondence in the Ernst Toch Archive* (Master's thesis, UCLA, 1974); diaries, 1948–53 and 1956–64, 16 address books, and notebooks of personal financial accounts and first performances; sketches, cartoons, and drawings presented by Susi Loeb-Goehr; material about Toch, in reviews, programs, and articles, as described in Peter B. Brown, *A Guide to the Ephemera in the Ernst Toch Archive* (Master's thesis, UCLA, 1975); oral-history interviews of Toch, mostly by Robert Trotter, also a transcript of an interview with Toch's widow, Lilly, 2 vols., and written and oral-history material by other associates, among them Liesel Lehmann, Nikolai Lopatnikoff, Henry Temianka, John Scott Trotter, Herbert Zipper, and several family members; also 2 portrait sketches and 2 document boxes of photographs. See Lawrence Wechsler, *Ernst Toch, 1887–1964: A Biographical Essay* (booklet issued for the Ernst Toch Festival, Los Angeles, 1974–75); Barbara Barclay and Malcolm S. Cole, "The Toch and Zeisl Archives at UCLA," M.L.A. *Notes,* 35 (1979), esp. pp. 556–66; and *Placed as a Link in this Chain: A Medley of Observations by Ernst Toch* (Los Angeles, 1971)

John Vincent, holograph mss, sketches, printed editions, and recordings of his music, correspondence, press clippings, programs, photographs, memorabilia, and materials from his personal library. (Other materials, relating to his administrative work at UCLA and for the Huntington Hartford Foundation, are in the Department of Special Collections.)

Eric Zeisl (1905–59), music mss, 170 items, by copyists and in holograph, also 35 published editions and 15 recordings of his music; personal and professional correspondence, scrapbooks, literary writings by and about Zeisl, and other items relating to his career, mostly in film music. See Barbara Barclay and Malcolm S. Cole, "The Toch and Zeisl Archives at UCLA," M.L.A. *Notes,* 35 (1979), esp. pp. 566–77

B. Archive of Popular American Music (267 Kinsey Hall)

See the brochure on the collection; also Bob Thomas, "UCLA's Friend, the Music Man," *UCLA Alumni Magazine,* 39/3 (1965), 48–49. The sheet music from the various provenances below has been organized to form what is now designated as the Meredith Willson Library of Popular American Sheet Music. This is arranged by title within chronological groupings, i.e., 30,000 items, ca. 1830–90; 120,000 items, ca. 1890–1920; and 280,000 items, 1920–76. Also included are recordings, popular-song folios, and commercial band arrangements

Meredith Willson/Stanley Ring collection, containing 250,000 sheet-music items, ca. 1830–1960, also 250 cylinder recordings and 30,000 78-rpm discs, this material comprising the stock of the Stanley Ring music store, as acquired by Meredith Willson and presented to the University. See the descriptive report by Bob Thomas, 1976. The 100 bound vols. of music, 2500 music instruction books, 2000 books about music, and bound scores, libretti, and miniature scores which were also part of the collection are now mostly in the Music Library (section A, above)

Music Mart collection, 80,000 20th-century sheet-music items, 40,000 larger musical editions, and 20,000 commercial popular-music orchestrations, ca. 1920–60

Thomas Radcliff collection of popular 20th-century sheet music, ca. 1920–60

Hal Levy collection, including popular 20th-century sheet music, 5000 items; 600 song folios, 150 books on popular music, and 1500 issues of popular-music magazines (in addition to the lecture tapes in the Music Library, section A, above)

Harry Warren collection, 200 musical-comedy folios

C. Special Collections Department (A-1713 University Research Library)

George Pullen Jackson collection, 112 19th-century tunebooks and hymnals, also photocopies of Jackson's research notes (of originals in the Joint University Libraries, Nashville, Tenn., q.v.). See Paul J. Revitt, *The George Pullen Jackson Collection of Southern Hymnody: A Bibliography,* UCLA Library, Occasional Papers, 13 (Los Angeles, 1964)

Other U.S. hymnals and tunebooks, ca. 1840–80, 500 items, including materials from the Royal B. Stanton collection

Lionel Barrymore (1878–1954), mss of his musical compositions, in 13 boxes

Irving Bibo (songwriter and composer), personal papers, including sheet music and songbooks

Harry Kaufman (pianist and music teacher), personal papers, 17 boxes

Jeanette MacDonald, scrapbooks with press clippings, photographs, and programs, 1931–51

Ruth St. Denis, personal papers, 1886–1968, including music for her ballets

Joseph C. Stone (1758–1837, Boston poet and musician), 3 boxes of holograph music mss, as cited in William Salloch (antiquarian bookdealer), catalogue 237 (Oct. 1966), item 18

WPA Federal Theatre Project materials, including 3 vols. of folksongs and ballad transcriptions

Ephemeral materials relating to the theater, including press clippings, also 3 scrapbooks, ca. 1870–1900

D. Center for the Study of Comparative Folklore and Mythology Research Collection (1037 Graduate School of Management Building)

Research collections of commercial recordings, with particular strength in Anglo-American and Afro-American music, including 250 78-rpm discs and 6000 other discs

Western Kentucky Folklore Archive, including folksong and instrumental music, on 150 tape recordings, also incorporating the Josiah H. Combs collection of songs and rhymes, augmented by B. A. Botkin with materials collected in the 1920s, as indexed in D. K. Wilgus, *Folk-Songs of the Southern United States* (Austin, 1967). See also Wilgus, "The Western Kentucky Folklore Archive," *The Folklore and Folk Music Archivist,* 1/4 (1958), 3

Archive of California and Western Folklore, with international coverage but with particular strength in American folksong from California and Arkansas, in all 2000 tape recordings

E. Other Collections on the Main Campus

Ethnomusicology Archive (B-414 Schoenberg Hall), with recordings of folk, tribal, and traditional music of world cultures, including 1500 commercial 78-rpm discs, 6000 other commercial discs, and 6500 tape recordings. Special collections include the Colin McPhee library of 78-rpm discs, photographs, films, correspondence, and field notes; and field recordings of Cherokee Indian music by Charlotte Heth

—Ann Briegleb

Oral History Archives (136 Powell Library), with transcripts of interviews with Alice Ehlers (harpsichordist), Lawrence Morton, Jan Popper, Charles Seeger (1888–1979), Nicolas Slonimsky, Lilly Toch, Peter Yates, and Gertrud Zeisl; also other interviews in the various archive collections in the Music Library (section A, above)

Theater Arts Research Library (A-4509 University Research Library), including a collection of thematic cue sheets for use by motion picture companies

F. William Andrews Clark Memorial Library (2520 Cimarron Street, Los Angeles, 90018)

Letters of musicians, including those of David Bispham to Clarence Stedman, concerning the performance of Walter Damrosch's songs; Ernestine Schumann-Heink to William Andrews Clark, 1926; and Anton Seidl, 4 letters, to Gottfried Heinrich Federlein (New York organist), 1888, to Mrs. Abbe, 1895, to Engelbert Humperdinck, 1898, and to an unnamed correspondent, n.d., in praise of Sarah Bernhardt. See the *List of Letters and Manuscripts of Musicians* (Los Angeles, 1940)

William Andrews Clark, Jr. (1877–1934), papers relating to the founding and early history of the Los Angeles Philharmonic Orchestra, including a scrapbook of the first season, 1919–20; descriptive programs of the seasons 1919–34, in 15 vols.; letters exchanged 1923–34 with Caroline Estes Smith and George Leslie Smith, managers of the Orchestra; and 9 other documents

—Suellen Zecchini

85

UNIVERSITY OF SOUTHERN CALIFORNIA   CLSU

University Park
Los Angeles, California 90007

University Library

Mack David (1912–68, songwriter), collection mostly of ms sheet music, nearly all with lyrics or music by him, 579 items filed alphabetically by title and indexed chronologically, 1924–68, also including a few items of correspondence, scores, scripts, and other papers

Ernest Kanitz (1894–1978, professor of music), 23 boxes of ms and published music by himself and others, including sketches, performing parts, and scores for operas, orchestras, and chamber music, ca. 1920–78; also 17 items of personal papers, and 29 books on music. See *Spalek,* p. 457

Alfred Newman (1901–70, film composer), 97 film scores, bound and filed alphabetically by title; 16

bound vols. of film and thematic material, 1936–51; 4 boxes of unbound film music; and 11 boxes of miscellaneous books on music, published music scores, and film scripts

Harry Ruby (1895–1974, songwriter), 134 items of correspondence, filed alphabetically by author and listed chronologically, ca. 1920–59; also 5 ms songs by Ruby, 1928–

Dmitri Tiomkin, film scores (indexed), film scripts, and other music scores, in all 90 boxes, mid 1930s to late 1960s

Igor Stravinsky, holograph score of his opera, *The Rake's Progress*, 1948–51

Ingolf Dahl (1912–70), 92 cartons of papers, ca. 1935–70, including 250 envelopes of ms sketches and performance copies of his compositions; periodicals, lecture notes, scrapbooks, reviews, and programs; also his library of books on music and published scores of other composers, dispersed through the general collection

—Rodney D. Rolfs

School of Performing Arts

Inactive and archival files, including School of Music bulletins, 1934– , and faculty files, ca. 1940– (in the Office of the Director)

86
Leslie ZADOR
249 South Arden Boulevard
Los Angeles, California 90004

Eugene Zador (1894–1977), holograph music mss and sketches

87
MENLO PARK PUBLIC LIBRARY   CMen
Civic Center
Menlo Park, California 94025

Henry Cowell Music Center, a specially designated repository for published music editions and recordings of, and published writings about the music of Cowell

88
Ernst Werner KORNGOLD
9928 Toluca Lake Avenue
North Hollywood, California 91602

Erich Wolfgang Korngold (1897–1957), letters received from Hal Wallis and Jack Warner, and memorabilia, including a bronze bust of the composer by Alma Mahler. See *Spalek*, p. 492

Julius Korngold (1861–1945), personal papers, including correspondence and reviews from his American years. See *Spalek*, p. 501

89
George KORNGOLD
9936 Toluca Lake Avenue
North Hollywood, California 91602

Erich Wolfgang Korngold (1897–1957), personal papers, including correspondence, 48 holograph scores, autograph arrangements, scores for his operas, symphonic, chamber, and film music; reviews, articles, and programs; 350 scores of music by other composers; guest book, photographs, memorabilia; and other materials. See *Spalek*, pp. 492–96

Julius Korngold (1861–1945), personal papers, including correspondence and reviews from his American years, also memoirs, plays and photographs. See *Spalek*, p. 501

90
Robert JOHNSON
7961 Shay Drive
Oakland, California 94605

Collection of sheet music from films, emphasizing illustrated covers, 10,000 items; also complete scores for films

91
MILLS COLLEGE   CoMC [sic]
Oakland, California 94613

Darius Milhaud (1892–1974, faculty member) Collection, including 4 holograph scores; 200 letters; pictures and portraits; an extensive collection of published editions and ms copies of his music, with catalogues and a master file by opus number; and articles and other writings by or about him

Holograph scores of Ernest Bloch, Virgil Thomson, and Alexandre Tansman

—Eva Kreshka

92
OAKLAND MUSEUM
1000 Oak Street
Oakland, California 94607

Manuscript music, 10 items copied by various local persons, including Richard J. José, ca. 1880–1920

Richard J. José (silent-film and early recording performer), 2 linear meters of papers including photographs, sheet music, and other memorabilia, ca. 1875–1925

"Estrellita" (Stella Davenport Jones, ca. 1880–1969, singer and dancer), 10,000 items of papers, including music scores used by her, personal and business correspondence, photographs, costumes, and memorabilia

Music for piano or ukulele, 25 published items, ca. 1900–1925

Hymnals, 12 items, ca. 1880–1940

Popular and patriotic songbooks, 30 items, ca. 1880–1940

Popular vocal sheet music, ca. 1860–1950, 700 items including some by local composers or publishers

Programs, 1000 items, also 100 photographs, mostly of Oakland and San Francisco musical or theatrical events, organized by theater, ca. 1850–

Popular or classical recordings, 25 78-rpm discs

—J. Camille Showalter

93

OAKLAND PUBLIC LIBRARY   **CO**

125 Fourteenth Street
Oakland, California 94612

Hymnals of various denominations, 2 linear meters, ca. 1880–
Popular sheet music for voice or piano, 14 bound vols., ca. 1830–90, and 10,000 loose items arranged by date, 1890–
Programs from Oakland and Bay-area musical and theatrical events, including the Oakland and San Francisco symphony orchestras, 6 linear meters, ca. 1890–

—Richard Colvig

94

Morris J. SHENK

6159 Acacia Avenue
Oakland, California 94618

Collection of sheet music, with emphasis on 19th- and 20th-century political and presidential subjects, and including the *en bloc* contents of *Musical Americana, Catalog no. 10,* issued by the antiquarian sheet-music dealer Harry Dichter (Atlantic City, 1973)

95

ONTARIO CITY LIBRARY   **COn**

215 East C Street
Ontario, California 91764

Oral-history recordings of musicians, ca. 1970, including the pianists Clara Price (1889–1977) and Max Don

—Leonard Wheeler

96

Ernst KRENEK

623 Chino Canyon Drive
Palm Springs, California 92262

Ernst Krenek, personal papers from his years in America, 1938– , including correspondence, musical and literary mss, sketches, photographs, 37 folders of programs, memorabilia, and other materials. See *Spalek,* p. 504

97

Bruce E. DEAL

638 Towle Place
Palo Alto, California 94306

Hymnals, 350 items, 1800– , mostly Protestant with an emphasis on Methodist materials

98

Thomas E. WILSON

6686 Brook Way
Paradise, California 95969

Personal papers, 1939– , including correspondence and working files relating to his career as a band and orchestra conductor and educator in the Midwest and in California; files relating to organizations; 100 programs, loose and in scrapbooks, for concerts which he conducted, including performances of the Army–Air Force Symphony, Troop Carrier Command, 1940s; 50 photographs; 30 recordings; and memorabilia
Percy A. Grainger, 10 holograph music mss of large ensemble works, and 10 letters to Wilson, 1930s–40s; also 25 other autograph scores, as submitted to the National Oratorio Society
Published music, including 20 editions of music by Charles Ives sent by the composer to Wilson, 1920s; 150 orchestral scores used by the Boston Symphony Music Club, 1920s–30s; and 25 orchestral scores used by Thor Johnson with the Michigan Youth Symphony, 1930s
Sheet music, 1920s–30s, classical and popular, 1200 items; also hymnals and songbooks, mostly from the 1930s, 25 items

99

PASADENA HISTORICAL SOCIETY

470 Walnut Street
Pasadena, California 91103

Programs, clippings, and photographs pertaining to musical events in the Pasadena area, including the Pasadena Opera House, 25 items, ca. 1890–

—Sue Schechter

100

PASADENA PUBLIC LIBRARY   **CP**

Section of Fine Arts
Alice Coleman Batchelder Music Library
285 East Walnut Street
Pasadena, California 91101

Published music scores, 100 items; 150 songbooks and hymnals; and 640 items of sheet music, ca. 1858–1956
Programs, including local musical and theatrical performances, 250 items, and 500 related photographs; also 15 boxes of opera libretti
Music catalogues, 20 items
Recordings, 2000 items

—J. M. Pletscher

101

Barney CHILDS

School of Music
University of Redlands
Redlands, California 92373

Frederic Ayres (1876–1926), photocopies of his unpublished musical compositions, some of them ed. by Childs (originals are at the Library of Congress); also photocopies of other documents concerning Ayres
Barney Childs, personal papers, including ms sketches and compositions, correspondence, programs, and reviews

102

Barbara N. CRITCHLOW
854 Cedar Avenue
Redlands, California 92373

Collection of American folk and popular music with an emphasis on "heart songs" of the 19th and 20th centuries, in all 7 linear meters, comprising songsheets, sheet music, 200 songbooks and hymnals, Mrs. Critchlow's ms copies of songs with notes on history and provenance, and typed or ms interviews with family members concerning their folk music

103

A. K. SMILEY PUBLIC LIBRARY   CRedl
Box 751
Redlands, California 92373

> Musical materials from the local history collection are listed in *A Selective Bibliography of Books, Pamphlets, Letters, Documents and Other Materials in the Heritage Collection of the A. K. Smiley Public Library* (Redlands, 1975)

Papers of the Redlands Community Music Association, Redlands Clef Club, Friends of Music, Redlands Chorus, Redlands School of Music, Redlands Winter Concert at the University of Redlands, and Community Symphony Association, in all 200 items, ca. 1890–
Programs of the Calhoun Opera Company, Academy of Music, Wyatt Theater, Chautauqua, and other local and touring groups, in all 75 items, ca. 1890–1940 (in the Heritage Room)
Sheet music about Redlands or by local composers W. H. Pettibone, J. Hopkins Flinn, and Lucia W. Smith, 8 items (in the Heritage Room)

—Larry Burgess

104

UNIVERSITY OF CALIFORNIA   CU-Riv
Music Library
Riverside, California 92507

Oswald Jonas (1897–1978), research library devoted mostly to Heinrich Schenker and the Viennese classical composers, but also including a 7-page letter from Eduard Remenyi (1828–98, Hungarian violinist), addressed to Robert Underwood Johnson in New York, dated Waco, Tex., 1895, describing Texas and written in Remenyi's conception of a Texas dialect
Erich Wolfgang Korngold, correspondence with Raoul Auernheimer regarding an adaptation of Korngold's *Singspiel*, as cited in *Spalek*, p. 500
Phonograph recording catalogues, extensive but scattered holdings, chiefly for Columbia (1936–52), Decca (1942–48), and Victor (1921–51)
WPA Southern California Music Project, ms collection of orchestral performance parts and scores, 2000 titles

—John Tanno

105

**CALIFORNIA DEPARTMENT OF   CSPR
PARKS AND RECREATION**
Box 2390
Sacramento, California 95811

Materials are housed at various state historical sites

Published music, including 75 songbooks and 30 linear meters of sheet music, ca. 1880–1940
Programs of California musical and theatrical events, 35 linear meters, ca. 1900–
Photographs of California musicians, musical groups, and theatrical productions, 70 linear meters, ca. 1900–
Cylinder recordings, 25 items

—Elizabeth B. Smart

106

CALIFORNIA STATE LIBRARY   C
California Section
Library–Courts Building
Sacramento, California 95809

Published musical editions issued in or relating to California, 1250 sheet-music items, 60 songbooks, and numerous broadsides, ca. 1850s–1920s
Programs and musical announcements, 1 linear meter
Photographic materials, mostly portraits as part of a general collection, organized according to personal name
Newspaper and information files, containing 8000 references to music and musicians in California
Biographical files, containing information on 2000 musicians active in California, mostly pre-1930
Margaret (Blake) Alverson (1836–1923), personal papers, including correspondence, diaries, account books, programs, and clippings, in 10 archive boxes

—Kenneth I. Pettitt

107

CALIFORNIA STATE UNIVERSITY   CSS
Sacramento, California 95819

Archive of Folklore

Tape recordings and transcriptions of folk music, 10 items, including lullabies, cowboy songs, and southern blues, collected in the Sacramento area by University students, ca. 1968–   ; also published books on ballads

—Roland Dickison

Library

Songbooks, several items

—Donna Ridley Smith

108

SACRAMENTO MUSEUM AND HISTORY DEPARTMENT
1931 K Street
Sacramento, California 95814

KCRA radio station collection of recordings, 10,000 33⅓- , 45- , and 78-rpm discs, 1927–73 but mostly post-1940, including some non-union labels
Programs of musical events in the Sacramento area, 300 items, ca. 1895–1940

—Kathryn Gaeddert

109

Rev. Terry W. YORK

First Southern Baptist Church
4840 Fruitridge Road
Sacramento, California 95820

Hymnals and tunebooks, 250 items, 1744– , including pre-1860 books with words only and early 20th-century gospel songbooks

110

SILVERADO MUSEUM

Box 409
Saint Helena, California 94574

Musical settings of texts by Robert Louis Stevenson, including U.S. imprints of works by Robert Coningsby Clarke, Samuel Coleridge-Taylor, Ethel Crowninshield, David Elmore, Henry K. Hadley, and Graham Peel; also 6 ms songs by Dwight Fiske

—Ellen Shaffer

111

Richard SHEPHERD

191 Paradise Road
Salinas, California 93907

W. Franke Harling (1887–1958, composer), 9 linear meters of personal papers, including ms and published works, with 30 holograph songs, 75 holograph titles in complete orchestration with performance parts, and 200 published titles; 90 linear cm. of materials including photographs, correspondence, and mementos; recordings including 60 original wax discs of film soundtracks with his music for Paramount Pictures Corp., 1930s, and 100 78-rpm discs of light classical music; and a ms piano concerto by his teacher, Theo Ysaya

112

CALIFORNIA STATE COLLEGE AT   **CSbC**
SAN BERNARDINO

Library
5500 State College Parkway
San Bernardino, California 92407

Popular sheet music, 2500 items, ca. 1900–1940
Recordings, including 700 78-rpm discs

—Marty Bloomberg

113

POINT LOMA COLLEGE   **CSdP**

Ryan Library
3900 Lomaland Drive
San Diego, California 92106

Charles Brenton Widmeyer (1884–1974), 102 mss of hymns, gospel songs, and choral music, including "Come and Dine"; also, 6 gospel songbooks compiled and published by him, ca. 1900–1910; 2 linear meters of papers including typescript devotional talks, let-

ters, autobiographical sketches, and photographs; and *The Eureka Messenger* (Stigler, Okla.: Eureka Publishing Co., vols. 3–10, 1912–19, incomplete), of which he was associate editor
Hymnals and gospel songbooks, ca. 1880–1940, 150 items including many of the Church of the Nazarene, which were published by Nazarene Publishing Co. or Lillenas Publishing Co.
Sheet music, 5 gospel songs, 1930s
Children's sacred compositions, 2 items, 1921–36
Pasadena College (predecessor of Point Loma College), programs of cultural events, 5 linear cm., ca. 1910–

—Esther Schandorff

114

SAN DIEGO HISTORICAL SOCIETY   **CSdHi**

Library and Manuscripts Collection
Presidio Park
Box 81825
San Diego, California 92138

Nino Marcelli (composer and conductor), papers, 1920–43, including ms and published works mostly for school orchestra or band, 4 published music-education method books, 56 programs of San Diego music groups conducted by him, photographs, and correspondence
Alice Stevenson, ms compositions for voice, in notebooks, ca. 1909–31; also a photograph album, 1903–65, 3 scrapbooks, and correspondence
San Diego Symphony Orchestra, papers, 1928– , including articles of incorporation, 1928, correspondence, 50 programs, and a typed history
Amphion Club, papers, 1892–1948, with scrapbooks, photographs, clippings, 26 programs of concerts sponsored by the Club, and a ms history

—Sylvia Arden

115

SAN DIEGO PUBLIC LIBRARY   **CSd**

820 E Street
San Diego, California 92101

Art and Music Section

General collection of 9000 catalogued music items, ca. 1880– , including songbooks, operas, operettas, and choral, band, orchestral, and solo instrumental works
Hymnals, 75 items, ca. 1841–1940, some in Latin, French, or German
Popular sheet music in 109 bound vols., arranged chronologically ca. 1800– , of which 89 vols. are pre-1940
Recordings, 500 78-rpm discs

—Rhoda Kruse

California Room

Vashti Rogers Griffin Collection, including 90 ms songs, ca. 1920–50, and an envelope of clippings and programs
Programs, 1 linear meter, 1935– , mostly of local groups including the San Diego Ballet, Opera, Civic Orchestra, Old Globe Theatre, and La Jolla Playhouse
Constance Mills Herreshoff (local music critic and edi-

tor), 35 scrapbooks of clippings and programs, 1934–62

Songbooks of California, ca. 1850–1910, 7 items including *Putts Original California Songster* and *Putts Golden Songster*, ca. 1850, and a California mission hymnal

Sheet music of San Diego and California composers, ca. 1900–1935, 30 items including some by Charles Wakefield Cadman and Constance Mills Herreshoff

Index of newspaper reviews of local theatrical and musical activities from the *San Diego Union*, 1851–60, 1868–1903, and 1930–

—Don Silva

116
SAN DIEGO STATE UNIVERSITY   CSdS
Library
San Diego, California 92182

Special Collections

Sheet music, 2000 items, 1840– , including music of Stephen Collins Foster and other early minstrelsy, many from the 1890s. See the catalogue of 359 vocal-music titles, prepared by Dorothy Chiasera

Theater, concert, and film programs, 5000 items, 1830–

Jan Löwenbach (1880–1972, music critic, active in the U.S. after 1939), personal papers, including correspondence and research materials

—Jaroslav Mráček, Gordon Samples

American Studies Room

Scrapbook of press clippings of song texts, San Antonio, Tex., 1920s

Materials on folk humor, including poetry and song texts, 1 file drawer

Tape recordings of chants and religious music in the Diegueno language, 1/4 hour, and of early 20th-century local folksongs, 2 hours

—James N. Tidwell

117
BUREAU OF JEWISH EDUCATION
Jewish Community Library
601 Fourteenth Avenue
San Francisco, California 94118

Jewish liturgical songbooks, 75 linear cm., including items published in Israel; also published sheet music and choral music, mostly religious, 1 linear meter

Recordings of holiday songs, Yiddish and Hebrew folksongs, and liturgical music, 50 78-rpm discs

—Phyllis Blackman

118
CALIFORNIA HISTORICAL   CHi
SOCIETY LIBRARY
2099 Pacific Avenue
San Francisco, California 94109

Kirsten Flagstad Memorial Collection (MS 717), 3 linear meters, including her personal scores, ms tour sched-

ules, newspaper and magazine reviews and articles, programs and photographs from concerts and other performances, informal photographs, telegrams, personal and business correspondence, and recordings. See Bernice M. Nece, "The Kirsten Flagstad Memorial Collection," *American Archivist*, 30 (1967), 477–82

Sheet music, 10 boxes and 5 bound vols., 1895–1968, including songs by Californians or about California and the American West

—Karl Feichtmeir

119
Fitz Hugh LUDLOW MEMORIAL LIBRARY
Box 99346
San Francisco, California 94109

Materials relating to psychoactive drug-using musicians and their music, mostly post-1940s, including 200 vols. of published books, songbooks, discographies, and 600 disc recordings; also sheet music and photographs

120
NATIONAL MARITIME MUSEUM
Golden Gate National Recreation Area
Building 201
Fort Mason
San Francisco, California 94123

Sea chanteys, 15 published compilations, and textual materials pertaining to chanteys; 200 disc recordings of chanteys from the estate of Dr. John Lyman; and 6 oral-history tapes, ca. 1952–

Photographs of ships' bands and musicians at sea, in a general maritime photograph collection of 100,000 items, ca. 1850–1940

—David Hull

121
SAN FRANCISCO CONSERVATORY
OF MUSIC
1201 Ortega Street
San Francisco, California 94122

Ernest Bloch (1880–1959), personal papers and memorabilia, mostly relating to his tenure as director of the Conservatory, 1925–30, including holograph sketches; correspondence regarding the *Musical America* prize of 1930; autographed copies of his published music; 2 scrapbooks of press clippings, 1925–30; and photographs and memorabilia

—Viola Hagopian

122
SAN FRANCISCO PUBLIC LIBRARY   CSf
Civic Center
San Francisco, California 94102

Art and Music Department

Sheet music, 8500 songs in 250 bound vols., 1800–1950s, with title and first-line index; 979 songs, 1843–

58, given by Maurice Kursh, with title list; also 20 vols. of San Francisco imprints or songs about San Francisco or the West, mostly 19th century

Reference collection of California composers, 65 portfolios of ms scores and parts, copied for the WPA Federal Music Project

Alfred Hertz (1872–1942, San Francisco Symphony Orchestra conductor), letters and papers, 5 shelf boxes

Programs, including complete runs for the San Francisco Opera, 1923– , and San Francisco Symphony Orchestra, 1911– ; 5 scrapbooks of miscellaneous San Francisco programs; 1 scrapbook of programs and clippings of the San Francisco Public Library music department, 1917–50; San Francisco public-school music, 2 scrapbooks, 1881–1947; and 1 ring-binder on the musical events of the Panama–Pacific Exposition, San Francisco, 1915

Scrapbooks, 96 vols. of San Francisco–area music programs, clippings, flyers, and other items, 1850–1956

Letters of musicians, from 244 persons in Europe and the U.S., 1920–50

—Mary Ashe

San Francisco History Room

Sheet music on San Francisco and California subjects, 6000 19th- and 20th-century items, arranged by title

Programs and handbills of San Francisco–area musical and theatrical performances, ca. 1850s–1900

—Gladys Hansen

Archives of the Performing Arts

A major research collection concentrating in theatrical and other materials from San Francisco and the Bay area, 1840s– , and located at the Presidio Branch, 3150 Sacramento Street, San Francisco 94115

Chronological file of reviews, flyers, programs, advertisements, press clippings, and other materials, arranged chronologically by year, month, and day, with separate files for performers, theaters, and productions. The contents comprise 257 vols., 55 cartons, 64 legal-size file drawers, and 140 boxes

Photographic materials, including 3400 slides, 5000 negatives, 800 framed prints and photographs, 10,000 photographs of the San Francisco Ballet, 25,000 historical photographs, 10,000 film stills (many from the Sid Grauman collection), and 50,000 clipped pictures and reproductions

Theatrical prints, 12,000 items, including engravings, lithographs, and other forms

Sheet music, 10,000 items, with an emphasis on illustrated covers

Recordings, including 2500 acoustical 78-rpm discs of opera, black music, jazz, minstrel music, etc.; 1000 other discs; and 100 tapes of oral-history interviews

Scrapbooks, 100 items

Costumes and sets, including 200 original costume plates and set designs, and 50 costumes; also 500 other artifacts

Catalogues of Sherman and Clay (local music dealer), ca. 1930s

Books and periodicals, a reference library of 2100 vols., 8000 unbound periodicals, and 3600 miscellaneous periodicals with references to theater

Special subjects include the following: Vittorio Arimondi (operatic bass), scrapbook illustrated with his watercolors, programs, clippings, photographs, correspondence, sketch of him by Caruso, and a musical score notated by Arturo Toscanini; Marie (Alexandra) Baldini (ballerina with Diaghilev), letters; Harold, William and Lew Christensen (dancers), materials relating to their careers, the San Francisco Ballet, American Ballet, Ballet Caravan, and Ballet West; Isadora Duncan (dancer), materials on her family, particularly her father, Joseph Charles Duncan; Alexander Fried (music critic), clippings from the *San Francisco Examiner*, 1930s–78; Martha Graham (dancer), photographs, programs, and other materials on her San Francisco performances; Vaslav Nijinsky (dancer), photographs, programs, and clippings relating particularly to his 1917 performance in San Francisco, and photographs, programs, correspondence, and art work of his daughter, Kyra Nijinsky; Janet Reed (ballet dancer), materials on her early career in Portland, San Francisco, and the Ballet Theatre; and the San Francisco Opera Company

—Russell Hartley

123

SAN FRANCISCO STATE UNIVERSITY CSfSt

Frank V. de Bellis Collection
1630 Holloway Avenue
San Francisco, California 94132

Materials on the cultural and political history of Italy, including 600 editions of music by Italian composers published in the U.S., also archival cylinder and disc recordings of Italian music by American performers, among them Geraldine Farrar, Alma Gluck, Charles Hackett, Louise Homer, Alice Nielsen, Rosa Ponselle, Albert Spalding, and Reinald Werrenrath

—Serena de Bellis

124

SOCIETY OF CALIFORNIA PIONEERS CSfCP

456 McAllister Street
San Francisco, California 94102

Sherman Collection, ca. 1840–1940, 4 linear meters, including sheet music of early California publishers, programs of San Francisco concerts, extensive historical material collected by the publishing firm of Sherman and Clay (earlier Sherman and Hyde), a newsletter of the Sherman and Hyde firm, and biographical or historical material on early California performers and musical-instrument manufacturers

Manuscript and published biographies and biographical directories to California or western U.S. musicians, including ms memoirs and typed transcripts of letters, 50 linear cm., ca. 1900–

Popular songbooks, 20 items, ca. 1850–1915, mostly published in California; and other printed sheet music, ca. 1860–80

Programs, playbills, and posters of San Francisco–area theaters and musical productions including the San Francisco Opera, 1 linear meter, ca. 1860–1950

—Lucy Morey

125

SUTRO LIBRARY   C-S

2130 Fulton Street
San Francisco, California 94117

Laura Stephens (sister of Lincoln Stephens), music from
her library, including 19th-century opera libretti and
songbooks, mostly European, in all 5 linear meters
William Brown (British soldier of the Sixth Inniskilling
Dragoons), ms music book, 1770s–80s?, compiled in
Great Britain and probably partly in North America
Scrapbook devoted to late 19th-century drama and op-
era; also musical programs and other ephemera

—Geraldine Davis

126

SAN JOSE PUBLIC LIBRARY   CSj

180 West San Carlos
San Jose, California 95113

Sheet music and published scores for voice, orchestra,
piano, or choir, 25,000 items
David McDaniel Collection, including 800 vols. of
printed music, 10,000 disc recordings, and 300 cylinder recordings

127

Henry E. HUNTINGTON LIBRARY   CSmH

1151 Oxford Road
San Marino, California 91108

> See Edythe N. Backus, "The Music Resources of the
> Huntington Library," M.L.A. *Notes,* 14 (1942), 27–35;
> also her *Catalogue of Music in the Huntington Library
> Printed before 1801* (San Marino, 1949)

Catalogued music, 50 pre-1801 items, mostly tunebooks, including a special made-up copy of William
Billings's *Psalm-Singer's Amusement* (Backus *Catalogue,*
219); also *Das Gesäng der einsamen und verlassenen
Turtel-Taube* (Ephrata, 1747; Backus *Catalogue,* 733)
and Elias Mann, *The Northampton Collection* (Northampton, 1797; Backus *Catalogue,* 1201a), both with ms
music additions; and 500 tunebooks, hymnals, and
sheet-music items, 1801–75, including 35 Confederate sheet-music imprints
Uncatalogued sheet music, 1500 items, 1820–1940, described in a separate card index. Included are the collection of Robert Alonzo Brock; 106 items relating to
George Washington, in the collection of Walter Updike Lewisson (1855–1930); Lafayette, Civil War, and
other topical specialties, as cited in the 1942 Backus
article, p. 33; and 35 19th-century bound vols.
Music commonplace book, 18th century, in the papers
of Benjamin Trumbull
Songsters, mostly 1820–1900, some with musical notation, including many campaign songsters
Manuscript music, including fragments removed from
bound vols., of Virginia provenance, 1780–1860; and
Stephen Collins Foster, holograph ms of "Oh! boys,
carry me 'long"
Francis Hopkinson, 2 ms libretti of *The Temple of Minerva,* as discussed in Gillian B. Anderson, "'The Temple of Minerva' and Francis Hopkinson; a Reappraisal
of America's First Poet-Composer," American Philo-

sophical Society *Proceedings,* 120 (1976), 166–77, with
an inventory of the mss, pp. 174–77
Papers relating to music, including letters from composers and singers to William Raymond Sams (publisher), 1847–70; 2 letters from Stephen Collins Foster
to Edwin P. Christy, 1851; John Hill Hewitt (1801–90),
2 poems; James H. George, letters of a musician in
the Union army, 1862–65; Blinn Woodward to Samuel
Arnold Pearson, dated San Francisco, 1867; 15 letters,
1870–88, addressed to Charles L. Siegel (cobbler in
Richmond, Va., choirmaster, and secretary of the
Mozart Association); letter from Morrison Foster to
Robert Alonzo Brock, 1883; recollections of early San
Francisco theatrical productions, by John Quincy
Adams, 1890; May Irwin, questionnaire, ca. 1900,
filled in with information on local musical comedies;
Clarence Hungerford Mackay, letter concerning
American opera, 1911, to Augustus Thomas; Anita
M. Baldwin (1876–1939), personal papers, including 4
music copies, 1 music notebook, and 1 libretto; and
letters and mss of numerous authors concerning the
theater
Lynden Ellsworth Behymer (impresario and founder
and early manager of the Los Angeles Symphony
Orchestra), personal papers, 1881–1947, 3990 items,
including account books, contracts, and box-office
receipts

—Carey S. Bliss, Harriet McLoone

128

SAN MATEO COUNTY   CSmatHi
HISTORICAL ASSOCIATION

1700 West Hillsdale Boulevard
San Mateo, California 94402

Peninsula Philharmonic Orchestra, bound programs,
1926–33
Programs of 8 concerts sponsored by the Community
Concert Association of San Mateo County and
Friends of Music of San Mateo County, 1934–35; also
1 program of a local musical comedy performed by
the San Mateo Women's Club, 1922
Music Teachers' Association of California, 10 scrapbooks including photographs, programs, clippings,
and directories
Songbooks, including 7 hymnals, 1849–91, and 8 popular or school songbooks, 1 in Spanish, 1857–1923
Hymn sheet used in a local church on Easter Sunday,
1866, words only
Sheet music, 6 items, including M. A. Richter, "The
California Pioneers" (1852), the first sheet music published in California; also songs about the San Mateo
area by Lela France (photocopy), Roy A. Hohbargar,
and Otis M. Carrington
Recordings, 10 linear cm., also 2 albums of 78-rpm discs

—Marion C. Holmes

129

AMERICAN MUSIC RESEARCH   (CSrD)
CENTER

Dominican College
San Rafael, California 94901

Psalm books, 2 U.S. imprints, 1737 and 1818, and
others in photocopy

Tunebooks, 50 sacred items, 1726-1884, 41 secular items, 1798-1920, and 36 in facsimile editions, photocopies, or microfilms; also 1 ms book with syllabic notation, ca. 1726

Musical stage works, 15 piano-vocal scores and libretti of 18th-century works performed in America, 1735–1860; also 180 photocopies, mostly piano-vocal scores and libretti but also including full scores, instrumental parts, and vocal selections

Robert Louis Stevenson, photocopies of music composed by him, 2 linear cm.

Other published music, 18th to 20th centuries, some in photocopy, including chamber music, 90 linear cm.; orchestral scores, 60 linear cm.; choral music, operas, comic operas, and solo vocal music, 9 linear meters; piano music, 2.5 linear meters; and organ music, 30 linear cm.

California mission music collection, including a typescript copy of an 1842 inventory of musical items in the Mission San Antonio de Padua, near San Luis Obispo; microfilms, 500 photographs, and 160 slides of music mss and instruments of early padres and Indians; and typescripts of reminiscences of local life in the 1830s and 1840s, by Charles Lauff and Steven Richardson, 1916–18. Holdings include references to ms materials of other California missions; see also Margaret Long Crouch, "An Annotated Bibliography and Commentary Concerning Mission Music of Alta California from 1769 to 1834," *Current Musicology*, 22 (1976), 88–99

Slides, 2000 items, illustrating musical activities primarily in the U.S., 17th to 20th centuries, including psalmody, Moravian music, patriotic music, 18th-century comic opera and theater, California missions, black music, Louis Moreau Gottschalk, San Francisco, and St. Louis

Scrapbooks, 5 items containing theater programs and clippings from Boston, New York, and Chicago, 1880–91; photographs of opera and concert singers, 1900–1940; and concert and opera programs and clippings from New York, Chicago, San Francisco, and Los Angeles, 1885–1910

Photographs of concert and opera performers, 15 items, 1890–1940

Playbills of British performances of comic operas also performed in America, 4 items, 1786–99, and 2 early 19th century; also 85 miscellaneous concert and opera programs, 1862–1950

Recordings, 300 78-rpm discs of American music

Books on music, 600 vols., also a microfilm collection of early psalm books, tunebooks, late 18th-century concert music, California mission music, and Maryland playbills, 1782–83, as part of a reference collection supporting American musical studies

—Sister Mary Dominic Ray, O.P.

130

SANTA BARBARA MISSION ARCHIVE LIBRARY

Santa Barbara, California 93105

Music mss and ms fragments from California missions, 24 items; other musical items used in the missions, including 3 16th-century ms Spanish plainsong anti-phoners, 2 18th-century ms Mexican antiphoners, and 10 printed Spanish books, 1606–1848. See Margaret Long Crouch, "An Annotated Bibliography and Commentary Concerning Mission Music of Alta California from 1769 to 1834," *Current Musicology*, 22 (1976), 88–99

—William Summers

131

UNIVERSITY OF CALIFORNIA   CU-SB

Santa Barbara, California 93106

Lotte Lehmann collection, 3 linear meters of papers, including personal correspondence with Bruno Walter, Arturo Toscanini, and other musicians, also business papers, programs, clippings, photographs, and memorabilia of her life in Vienna, Salzburg, and Santa Barbara (in the Department of Special Collections, University Library)

Anthony Boucher Archival Record Collection, 10,000 78-rpm disc recordings of early opera, lieder, and instrumental music, 1904–68 (in the Arts Library)

—Martin Silver, Nancy Duby

132

WESTMONT COLLEGE   CStbW

Voskuyl Library
955 La Paz Road
Santa Barbara, California 93108

William Ripley Dorr (1891–1968, director of the St. Luke's Choristers, a boys' choir), 4.5 linear meters of papers, including his ms and published arrangements of sacred music; 15 scrapbooks of programs, clippings, and photographs; personal and business correspondence; and 11 78-rpm discs, 5 33⅓-rpm discs, and 60 tape recordings of his choir

—Marie Ensign

133

UNIVERSITY OF SANTA CLARA   CStclU

Santa Clara, California 95053

Michel Orradre Library, Special Collections

Lionel Newman, 121 film-music scores

Clay Meredith Greene, 1.5 linear meters of papers, 1875–1930, chiefly ms scripts of Victorian dramas, melodramas, and comedies produced in the San Francisco area and New York City, also letters and autobiographical material

—Mary Guedon

De Saisset Art Gallery and Museum

Music instruction book used by Franciscans to train Indians to sing Gregorian chant in the local mission church (on loan from the University Archives, below)

Printed sheet music, by G. Matter and Arnoldo Releider (Arnaldo Releida), in Italian

Edison cylinder recordings, 10 items, ca. 1900

—Georgianna M. Lagoria

University Archives

Liturgical music mss (in addition to the instruction book cited above), including 2 mass books, and a vol. called "Ybañez music manuscripts"

Programs of University musical and theatrical performances, 1855–

—Gerald McKevitt

134

Sara BOUTELLE

130 Getchell Street
Santa Cruz, California 95060

Charles Morrison (ca. 1840–1920, organist, educator, and composer), 1 trunk of materials including ms and published works, programs, 2 photographs, a portrait, and books from his personal library

135

FOREST HISTORY SOCIETY   **CStcrF**

109 Coral Street
Santa Cruz, California 95060

Rudolph Fromm, 52 ms sheets of loggers' songs and parodies, many of them used in U.S. Forest Service radio commercials, ca. 1940

Songbooks, 4 items of loggers' songs, ca. 1950

—Mary E. Johnson

136

MUSICIANS' PROTECTIVE UNION

Local 346, American Federation of Musicians
1383 Pacific Avenue
Santa Cruz, California 95060

Scores and parts used by the Hastings Band (established by George Hastings in 1873, active until 1907, and re-established in 1977), in all 12 linear meters, arranged by type of music; also photographs of the band

—Frances M. Doherty

137

SANTA CRUZ PUBLIC LIBRARY   **CStcrCL**

224 Church Street
Santa Cruz, California 95060

Edward Podesta Jazz Collection, 200 books, discographies, and journals, ca. 1920–60

Operas and musical comedies, 150 scores, 18th to 20th centuries

Songbooks, including 60 popular items, 12 school songbooks, and 30 hymnals, ca. 1880–1940

Sheet music, ca. 1850–1940, 7000 popular and classical items for voice or instruments, including some by Californians and some in Spanish

Photographs of local musicians and groups, 10 items, ca. 1870–1920

Recordings, 25 78-rpm discs, mostly classical or folk music

—Alma Westberg

138

SEASIDE COMPANY

400 Beach Street
Santa Cruz, California 95060

Archival records relating to George Hastings (1853–1923) and the Hastings Band, including photographs and press clippings, in the personal collection of Warren ("Skip") Littlefield

139

SANTA MONICA PUBLIC LIBRARY   **CStmo**

1343 Sixth Street
Box 1610
Santa Monica, California 90406

Geoffrey Francis Morgan, 16 published vocal scores of his operettas, 1927–34

Santa Monica Municipal Band, 10 linear cm. of concert programs, 1920–27

—Alice Fisher

140

SIMI VALLEY HISTORICAL SOCIETY

Box 351
Simi Valley, California 93065

Robert Perkins Strathearn (Simi Valley settler, ca. 1874), family papers, including 7 mss of church music, ca. 1900–1950; 29 hymnals and songbooks, some from Scotland; 20 programs of musical events at the local United Methodist Church, ca. 1900–1950; 40 published editions of choral music used by the family in the church choir; 200 items of popular sheet music, ca. 1900–1940; correspondence including letters mentioning music; and 1 photograph of the family singing

—Patricia Havens

141

TUOLUMNE COUNTY MUSEUM

Box 299
Sonora, California 95370

Programs of local musical performances by schools and other organizations, mostly 1880s–

Photographs of "mother lode" bands, 30 items; also several musical instruments used by local bands, late 1890s–1930

Sheet music, a general collection of popular items

Recordings, including cylinders, oral-history tapes, and 45 early discs

—Patricia H. Rhodes

142

STANFORD UNIVERSITY   **CSt**

Stanford, California 94305

Music Library (The Knoll)

Warren D. Allen (1885–1964, musicologist), personal papers, 60 linear cm.

—Jerry Persons

Archive of Recorded Sound

Recordings, including 869 cylinders and 130,000 78-rpm discs, the latter shelved by label and record number. Among the major gifts to the collection is that of W. R. Moran, including early operatic vocal recordings. Other gifts include early vocal recordings from Osborne Parker and Henry Taube, jazz from Arthur Schalow, and popular music from Dan Allen. See Edward E. Colby, "Recorded Sound Activities," Stanford University Library *Bulletin*, 23 (1971), 80–82

—Jerry Persons, Edward E. Colby

Department of Special Collections, Green Library

Music mss, printed music, and other documents of American composers, part of the collection presented by Mr. and Mrs. George Keating, as described in Nathan van Patten, *A Memorial Library of Music* (Stanford, 1950; entry numbers cited below in parentheses), including Samuel L. M. Barlow, inscribed 1st ed. of *Mon ami Pierrot*, 1924 (34); Irving Berlin, holograph fair copy of "White Christmas" (62); Ernest Bloch, inscribed 1st editions of *Macbeth*, 1910, and *Trois poems juifs*, 1918 (104–5); Samuel Coleridge-Taylor, inscribed 1st edition of *Scenes from the Song of Hiawatha*, op. 30, 1900 (229); Henry Cowell, holograph ms of the *Amerind Suite*, 1938, and *Ancient Desert Drone*, 1940 (231–32); Bainbridge Crist, holograph ms of *La nuit revécue*, ca. 1933 (234); Walter Damrosch, 1st edition of *Cyrano*, 1913, inscribed to the librettist, W. J. Henderson (239); Reginald De Koven, ms 1st draft and 1st edition of "Oh Promise Me," 1889 (248–49); George Gershwin, inscribed 1st editions of *Rhapsody in Blue*, 1924, and *Porgy and Bess*, 1935 (355–56); Ferde Grofé, inscribed 1st edition miniature score of *Grand Canyon Suite*, 1943 (435); W. C. Handy, 3 inscribed 1st editions, 1894–1949 (484–86); Victor Herbert, holograph ms of *The Debutante*, 1914, and 4 inscribed 1st editions, 1903–13 (501–5); J. Rosamond Johnson, 2 inscribed 1st editions, 1938–39 (549–50); Nelson Kneass, 1848 Louisville edition of "Ben Bolt" (557); Hermann Lohn, holograph of "Little Grey Home in the West" (617); Bohuslav Martinů, holograph sketches of the string sextet, dedicated to Mrs. Elizabeth Sprague Coolidge (647); Gian-Carlo Menotti, inscribed 1st editions of *The Medium* and *The Telephone*, 1947 (727–28); Louisa Morrison, inscribed 1st edition of "Sail on, My Boat, Sail on," 1887 (755); Frederick H. Opper, 1st editions of *Resurrection Morn* and its "Sanctus" section, Savannah, 1943 (797–98); Richard Rodgers and Oscar Hammerstein II, 2 inscribed 1st editions, 1943–45 (464–65, 880–81); John Philip Sousa, ms fragment of "Stars and Stripes Forever," dated 1901 (974); William Grant Still, inscribed 1st edition of *Six of the Twelve Negro Spirituals*, 1917 (996); Igor Stravinsky, holograph ms of *Danses concertantes*, 1941–42, also 16 inscribed 1st editions of his musical and literary works, 1910–47 (1028–44); Deems Taylor, inscribed 1st edition of *Peter Ibbetson*, 1930 (1066); and Virgil Thomson, holograph ms, 1942, and inscribed 1st edition of *The Seine at Night*, 1949 (1086–87); also 70 books about music, mostly U.S. imprints, 1890–1950, most of them inscribed by their authors (1157–1226)

Samuel Francis Smith, 100 items (30 linear cm.) of correspondence, photographs, and other documents relating to "My Country, 'Tis of Thee"

Jenny Lind and Otto Goldschmidt, personal papers, 500 items (60 linear cm.), including correspondence, a contract, a music ms, account book, pictures, press clippings, financial reports, and music editions, some of the latter with ms annotations by Jenny Lind

Juan B. Rael Collection, including 100 items (60 linear cm.) of religious songs (*alabados*) and folk plays from Colorado, New Mexico, and Latin America

Theatrical collections, with scattered materials on musical theater, including items in 5 scrapbooks from the Kate Felton Elkins collection; and acting scripts of *The Black Crook*, photographs, and other materials in the Samuel Stark collection, as cited in William C. Young, *American Theatrical Arts: A Guide to Manuscripts and Special Collections in the United States and Canada* (Chicago, 1971), no. 16

—J. Richard Phillips

Hoover Institution

Carol G. Wilson, personal papers relating to his books, including materials on Arthur Fiedler

Ignace Jan Paderewski, personal papers, including occasional music references

Song texts, as cited in Nina Almond and H. H. Fisher, *Special Collections in the Hoover Library on War, Revolution, and Peace* (Stanford, 1940), including World War I soldiers' songs, many with texts only (item 41), and other items in the Leipzig collection (item 93) and the Mönkemöller collection (item 95)

143
METHODIST HISTORICAL SOCIETY (CStoC)

Jab Fry Library
University of the Pacific
Stockton, California 95211

Hymnals of various denominations, ca. 1890–1920, 500 items including several in German, donated by Rev. Horace Hay

—Arthur W. Swann

144
PIONEER MUSEUM AND HAGGIN GALLERIES

Petzinger Library of Californiana
1201 North Pershing Avenue
Stockton, California 95203

Frank Thornton Smith (1912–50, local high-school choral director), scrapbook of programs, clippings, and photographs; also 2 diaries, 1915–17, recording his travels as a vocal entertainer through the Midwest (mostly Kansas, Missouri, and Nebraska), Canada, Montana, and Washington

Programs, 3.2 linear meters, devoted mostly to dramatic, operatic, and vaudeville productions in east- and west-coast theaters, collected by E. H. Charette and arranged in bound vols. by year, 1890–1934

Sheet music, 1200 items, 1880s-1920s, with a partial index to popular songs by title

Recordings, including 200 wax and hard-rubber cylinders

—Raymond W. Hillman

145

UNIVERSITY OF THE PACIFIC   CStoC
Stockton, California 95211

Holt–Atherton Pacific Center for Western Studies

Manuscript compositions of faculty members, alumni, and students, ca. 1900–1940, 12 items, in ms collections of individuals

Manuscript choir missal, on parchment, from an unidentified Spanish Southwest mission, ca. 1800

University of the Pacific Conservatory of Music papers, ca. 1880–1979, 1 linear meter including programs

Programs of regional musical events including minstrel shows, 25 items, ca. 1870–1940

Photographs of University and regional musical and theatrical events, 50 items, ca. 1890–1960

—R. H. Limbaugh

Irving Martin Library

Programs of the Conservatory of Music auditorium, ca. 1924–

—Sherman Spencer

146

PAJARO VALLEY HISTORICAL ASSOCIATION
261 East Beach Street
Watsonville, California 95076

Ladies' Hussar Band, 3 linear cm. of minutes, treasurers' records, and programs, ca. 1910–20

Band music, 2 linear cm. of published parts used by the Watsonville Band, ca. 1900

School songbooks, 6 items, ca. 1890–1900

Sheet music, ca. 1890–1940, 100 mostly popular-vocal items, including some about the Pajaro Valley

Programs of local school operettas and city bands, 12 items, ca. 1900–1940

Photographs of local musicians and groups, 50 items, ca. 1890–1950

—Alzora Snyder

147

MENDOCINO COUNTY MUSEUM
400 East Commercial Street
Willits, California 95490

Mabel Wymon Collection, ca. 1912–23, including 14 playbills from California cities and Honolulu

Other materials, including 46 items of sheet music used locally, ca. 1900, 6 of them published in California; a published compilation of piano music used locally, ca. 1900; 2 published songbooks; and a photograph of a band

—Kathleen Kane

148

WILLOWS PUBLIC LIBRARY   CWiW
201 North Lassen
Willows, California 95988

Hymnals of various denominations, 30 linear cm., ca. 1890–1940

Sheet music, including some about California, 2400 items, ca. 1900–1920

Recordings, 2 linear meters of 78-rpm discs

—Bonnie Arbogast

149

YOLO COUNTY HISTORICAL SOCIETY
Box 1447
Woodland, California 95695

Woodland Opera House, 25 programs, 1896–1916

—Nadine Salenites

In addition to the repositories listed above, the following have also reported holdings of the materials indicated:

Arcadia—Los Angeles County Department of Arboreta and Botanic Gardens: sheet music

Alameda—Alameda Free Library: sheet music, songbooks, recordings

Azusa—Azusa Pacific College, Marshburn Memorial Library: songbooks

Belmont—College of Notre Dame, Library: songbooks

Brawley—Brawley Public Library: sheet music, songbooks, recordings

Carmel—Mission San Carlos Borromeo: ms fragment of California mission music

Carpinteria—Carpinteria Valley Historical Society: sheet music, songbooks, pictures, recordings, miscellaneous

Chico—California State University, Library, Music Department: sheet music, songbooks, recordings, miscellaneous

Claremont—Disciples Seminary Foundation: songbooks

Coronado—Coronado Historical Association: sheet music, songbooks, programs

Covina—California Baptist Theological Seminary: songbooks, miscellaneous

Danville—San Ramon Valley Historical Society: recordings

Davis—Davis Community Church, Resource Center Library: songbooks

Desert Hot Springs—Desert Hot Springs Historical Society: sheet music, recordings, miscellaneous

Downey—Downey Historical Society, Museum: sheet music, songbooks, other printed music, programs, pictures, recordings, miscellaneous

Fall River Mills—Fort Crook Historical Society: songbooks, recordings

Fresno—Fresno County Free Library: sheet music, songbooks, other printed music

Fullerton—California State University, Library: songbooks, other printed music

Fullerton—Pacific Christian College, Hurst Memorial Library: songbooks, recordings

Glendale—Glendale Public Library: recordings

Hayward—California State University, Library: sheet music, songbooks, other printed music, catalogues, recordings

Hayward—Hayward Area Historical Society: sheet music, songbooks, other printed music

Independence—Eastern California Museum: sheet music, recordings

Irvine—Christ College, Library: songbooks

Jenner—Fort Ross State Historic Park: sheet music, songbooks

Lafayette—Lafayette Historical Society: songbooks, programs

La Jolla—University of California, Library: songbooks, other printed music

La Mirada—Biola College: songbooks, miscellaneous

Long Beach—Signal Hill Public Library: songbooks

Los Angeles—Occidental College, Mary Norton Clapp Library: sheet music, songbooks, recordings

Los Banos—Ralph L. Milliken Museum: sheet music, songbooks, programs, pictures, recordings, miscellaneous

Mission Hills—San Fernando Valley Historical Society: sheet music, songbooks, programs, recordings

Monterey—Monterey Public Library: songbooks, programs

Mountain View—St. Patricks College, Library: recordings

Napa—Napa County Historical Society: sheet music, songbooks, other printed music

National City—National City Public Library: songbooks

Newhall—Los Angeles Baptist College, Powell Memorial Library: songbooks

Northridge—California State University, Library: sheet music, recordings

Oroville—Butte County Historical Society: sheet music, songbooks, programs, miscellaneous

Oxnard—Oxnard Public Library: sheet music, songbooks, other printed music

Pacific Palisades—Yankee Doodle Society: miscellaneous

Pasadena—Ambassador College, Library: sheet music, recordings

Piedmont—Piedmont Historical Society: programs, pictures

Placerville—El Dorado County Historical Museum: sheet music

Pleasanton—Amador–Livermore Valley Historical Society: songbooks, programs, pictures

Quincy—Plumas County Historical Society: pictures

Red Bluff—Kelly–Griggs House Museum Association: pictures

Redding—Redding Museum and Art Center: sheet music, songbooks, programs

Redding—Shasta College Museum and Research Center: sheet music, songbooks, other printed music, programs, pictures, recordings

Redding—Shasta Historical Society: sheet music, songbooks, other printed music

Redondo Beach—Redondo Beach Public Library: sheet music

Rialto—Dorothy Galley: printed music

Rialto—Rialto Historical Society: sheet music, songbooks

Sacramento—Sacramento County Historical Society: printed music

San Andreas—Calaveras Heritage Council: recordings

San Clemente—San Clemente Historical Society: sheet music

San Diego—Diocese of San Diego, Chancery Office Archive: ms fragment of California mission music

San Diego—Miramar College, Library: songbooks

San Francisco—United Irish Cultural Center: catalogues

San Francisco—Wells Fargo Bank History: sheet music, songbooks, recordings, miscellaneous

San Jose—Santa Clara County Historical Heritage Commission: sheet music, songbooks, other printed music, recordings

San Juan Bautista—Mission San Juan Bautista: 2 Latin missals copied for use at the mission, ca. 1820

San Juan Bautista—San Juan Bautista Historical Society: photographs

San Leandro—San Leandro Community Library Center: songbooks, recordings

Santa Ana—Charles W. Bowers Memorial Museum: sheet music, songbooks, recordings

Santa Barbara—Santa Barbara Historical Society: programs

Santa Barbara—Trinity Church (Episcopal), Library: sheet music, songbooks, other printed music

Solvang—Mission Santa Inés: 6 ms fragments of California mission music

Sonoma—Sonoma State Historic Park: sheet music, songbooks

Sunnyvale—Sunnyvale Historical Society: sheet music, songbooks, programs

Truckee—Truckee–Donner Historical Society: miscellaneous

Valencia—California Institute of the Arts: songbooks, miscellaneous

Ventura—Ventura County Historical Society and Pioneer Museum: pictures

Visalia—Tulare County Historical Society Museum: sheet music, other printed music, recordings, miscellaneous

Walnut Creek—Walnut Creek Historical Society: sheet music, songbooks, pictures, recordings

Weaverville—Trinity County Historical Society: programs, pictures, miscellaneous

Whittier—Whittier College, Wardman Library: sheet music, songbooks, other printed music

Yreka—Siskiyou County Historical Society: sheet music, songbooks, pictures, recordings, miscellaneous

Colorado

150
UNIVERSITY OF COLORADO   CoU
Boulder, Colorado 80309

Music Library

Ben Gray Lumpkin Colorado Folklore Collection, containing 400 tape recordings of 700 songs in 2000 variants, collected 1949–69; also indexes for informants and tunes, biographies of informants, correspondence, and a collection of 250 books and articles that made use of the collection. See Gene Allen Culwell, *The English Language Songs in the Ben Gray Lumpkin Collection of Colorado Folklore* (Ph.D. diss., University of Colorado, 1976)

Joe Buzzard, Jr. (folklorist of Frederick, Md.), 48 reels of tape recordings, containing 800 hillbilly songs from his collection, assembled mostly 1940s–50s, with indexes by song title and reel. See William Kearns, "Hillbilly Music as a Tool in Music Education," *Colorado Journal of Research in Music Education,* 5 (1973), 1–13

Francis Wolle, programs, scores, and scripts of his musical comedies and operettas, 15 items

Published songbooks and instruction books, 150 19th-century U.S. imprints, as listed in a 1973 typescript inventory by William Kearns

—Arne Arneson

Western Historical Collections

See Ellen Arquimbau and John A. Brennan, *A Guide to Manuscript Collections* (Boulder, 1977)

Boulder Musical Society, 50 programs of the first 7 seasons, 1921–29

Frank W. Chace (ca. 1869–1947, director of the College of Music, University of Colorado), 1 box of papers concerning the organ in Mackey Auditorium, concerts at the University, and clippings, 1888–1926

George M. Bull (1873–1960, civil engineer), papers, including musical materials, 1862–1951

Programs of various Denver theaters, 50 items, 1887–1970s

Carl Conrad Eckhardt (ca. 1878–1946, historian), papers including musical materials, ca. 1926–46

John C. Kendel (d. 1970, Denver music educator), 3 notebooks and 1 tape recording, 1926–69, with typescripts of his writings and an interview

Marjorie Kimmerle (1906–63, folklorist), 27 boxes, 10 folders, and 2 card files of papers, 1942–62, including correspondence and other materials of the Colorado Folklore Society, and material on the folklore of Colorado and the western U.S.

Mrs. N. Koenig, 50 items of papers including recital programs, photographs, and clippings of musical activities in Golden and Denver, ca. 1900

Ben Gray Lumpkin, 50 items of pamphlets, magazines, and clippings about Colorado history and folklore, 1950s–60s

Sheet music, 1 suffrage song, words only, n.d.

Pamphlets describing local and regional music, performances, orchestras, festivals, and individuals, 50 items, 1860s–1970s

Photographs, several items depicting musical activities, in a general collection, filed by location

—John A. Brennan

University Memorial Center

Glenn Miller collection, assembled by Alan Cass, including memorabilia, photographs, Miller's holograph ms of the "Moonlight Serenade," his trombone, and pre-war Miller recordings

151
CANON CITY MUSIC CLUB

c/o Mrs. J. Vernon Wheeler
716 North Fifteenth Street
Canon City, Colorado 81212

Popular songbooks, sheet music, published orchestral arrangements, and Fox folios, 1 linear meter, ca. 1890–

—Virginia L. Blunt

152
COLORADO COLLEGE   CoCC

Colorado Springs, Colorado 80903

Southwest Studies Program

Southwest Folklore Collection, containing materials duplicated from the John D. Robb collection at the University of New Mexico, and materials collected by Ruben Cobos in southern Colorado and northern New Mexico, ca. 1940– , in all 100 hours of tape recordings including Hispanic music, mostly religious music or *alboradas*, with a partial index, annotated

—Rodolfo de la Garza

Music Department Library

Printed music, 2.5 linear meters, including several songbooks, and 2400 sheet-music items; also 1.5 linear meters of recordings

—Byron R. Levy

153
PIONEERS' MUSEUM

215 South Tejon Street
Colorado Springs, Colorado 80903

Nellie Cahn, 5 ms songs, ca. 1900–1910

Hymnals of various denominations, 12 items, ca. 1890–1920

Sheet music, ca. 1900–1930, 30 items, mostly popular songs including some about Colorado and Colorado Springs

Programs of the Colorado Springs Opera House, Temple Theater, City Auditorium, and Burns Theater, 20 items, ca. 1890–1930

Photographs, ca. 1890–1930, 15 items including some of local theaters, and some of the Midland Band, ca. 1900

Recordings, 337 78-rpm discs, mostly classical, and 181 metal discs for 120 music boxes

—Rosemary Hetzler

154
MOFFAT COUNTY MUSEUM

Court House
Craig, Colorado 81625

Piano music used by Edna French (local silent-film pianist), 112 sheet-music items and 9 printed editions, ca. 1890–1930

Hymnal, 1886

Piano method book, 1885

Programs of the Craig Orchestra and the Craig Brass

Band, 6 items, ca. 1898–1920; also 6 photographs of the Orchestra
Recordings, 14 78-rpm discs

—Louise Miller

155
CENTRAL CITY OPERA HOUSE ASSOCIATION

910 Sixteenth Street, Suite 636
Denver, Colorado 80202

Archives of the company, established in 1932, including official correspondence, reviews, and personal records, in 10 4-drawer file cabinets and miscellaneous portfolios; programs of all productions, 1932– ; pictures of the performers and other events; scores used in productions and miscellaneous other music; and memorabilia, including scenery, sketches and models, props, and costumes. Also some miscellaneous materials, 1878–1932

—Robert Edward Darling

156
COLORADO HISTORICAL SOCIETY   CoHi

Colorado Heritage Center
1300 Broadway
Denver, Colorado 80203

Mary Edna Guerber (1899–1956), 250 items of papers, including a diary (1912–56) and recital programs
Ella Bennett, 5 items of sheet music, ca. 1900, and photographs
Thomas F. Dawson, 80 bound vols. of scrapbooks, ca. 1880–1923, with references to music
Horace A. W. Tabor (1830–99) papers, 10,000 items including business records of the Tabor Grand Opera House, as used in E. S. Crowley, *History of the Tabor Grand Opera House* (M.A. thesis, University of Denver, 1940); see also the WPA, Colorado Writers' Program, *The Story of Denver's Theaters*, Life in Denver, 7 (Denver, 1942)
McClellan Opera House Collection of programs and advertisements, 75 items, 1898–1924
Programs of Colorado performing-arts organizations, 160 bound vols., ca. 1880–1920, organized by theater, including the Tabor Opera Theatre and Central City Opera Festival
Mountain and Plain Festival, Denver, 140 items, 1895–1940, including correspondence, minutes, program proposals, official programs and souvenir books, and press clippings
Sheet music, ca. 1858–1940, 3000 items, including works published in Colorado or pertaining to Colorado
Photographs, ca. 1858– , 300,000 items including some of Colorado musicians, bands, and theaters
Recordings of music of Colorado or Western Indians, 25 cylinders including those by Dr. James Walker on the Sun Dance, Pine Ridge Agency, ca. 1900, and 3 78-rpm discs (indexed)
Recordings of popular and classical works, 50 cylinders and 50 78-rpm discs
Al and Phoebe Birch, oral-history tape, 1964, on the

production of the *Denver Post* Summer Operas, 1934–72
Jean Chappell Cranmer, oral-history tape, 1959, "History of the Denver Symphony, Allied Arts, Friends of Chamber Music"

—Maxine Benson

157
DENVER PUBLIC LIBRARY   CoD

1357 Broadway
Denver, Colorado 80203

Western History Department

Organizational papers, including the Denver Männerchor, "Constitution und Neben-gesetze" (1875); Loretto Heights College, music scrapbook, 1864–1958; Colorado Federation of Music Clubs, 3 scrapbooks of which vol. 1 covers the period 1917–49; Western State College, Gunnison, scrapbook, 1919–58; Denver Symphony Orchestra, archives, 1930– , and scrapbooks, 1930–61; Allied Arts Foundation, scrapbook, 1933–35; and radio station KOA, music files, including Pro-Musica interviews with Denver cultural leaders, 1941
Other scrapbooks, including those of J. P. C. Poulton, containing lecture notes and musical criticism (written under the pseud. Fluke MacGilder) on operas in Denver and Colorado Springs, late 1870s; Alice Roeschlaub, programs and pictures in 1 vol., 1884–1950; Cuthbert Powell, scrapbook pertaining to the Denver Symphony Orchestra, 1945–64; and Saul Caston (1901–70, conductor of the Denver Symphony Orchestra, 1945–64), 33 vols., mostly post-1945
Miscellaneous music references, in the personal papers of Henry Faulkner (ms diary, 1859, including the song "Nancy Till"), Ruth Marie Colville, Jules Levy (1895), James G. Rogers, James Duncan (1910), W. C. Gerard (1890), Fred Haberl (6 letters, 1893–1900), Jacob Adriance, Addison Baker (23 diaries, 1859–83), George E. Turner (diary, 1881), May Arno, and Alice Lytle Weber. References are in various catalogues in the Department, also in Sanford A. Linscome *A History of Musical Development in Denver, Colorado, 1858–1908* (D.M.A. diss., University of Texas, 1970)
Music mss, including 10 scores by Denver composers in the J. Allen Grubb papers; holographs of May Arno and Milton Shrednick, in the Arno papers; and works by Max Zimmerman, in his personal papers
Sheet music, 500 items, arranged by composer, with composer and title indexes, emphasizing local imprints, composers, and subjects; also 2 items, 1907–15, in the papers of John Wallace Crawford
Musician's Directory for Denver, 1898–1932, 23 vols.
Accounts of musical life in the Denver area, including numerous theses and dissertations as cited in the published *Catalogue* of the collection (Boston, 1970; suppl., 1975), also Miriam S. Campbell, "Chamber Music in Denver, 1875–1959" (typescript, 7 pages); John C. Wilcox, 2 short papers with biographies of Colorado composers, ca. 1900; Colorado Federation of Music Clubs, 2 notebooks on Colorado composers, by Mrs. Garrett H. Sturr (1939) and Mrs. Luther Bolerjack (1946–47); Mrs. William E. Porter, "Music in Denver" (1936); Alice (Roeschlaub) Williams, "Early Music in Denver" (32 pages); and 13 boxes comprising the "Musician's Society of Denver's Centennial

Collection" (1958–59), assembled by Society members and including materials on local musicians (3 boxes), personalities (2 boxes), music schools, bands, concerts, organists, opera, orchestras and chamber music, Colorado towns, visiting musicians and artists, music mss, festivals, promotion groups, and radio stations

Photographic files, with a card index by towns, subjects, and topics such as music; and a clipping file, complemented by a general index to the contents of newspapers, journals, and books, with 500 entries under the heading "Music"

—Fred Yonce

Fine Arts and Recreation Department, Music Division

Folk-music collection, 2500 items, mostly published songbooks

Sheet music, 7300 items, mostly popular vocal, ca. 1850– ; and published scores, including those from the private collection of Charles Winfred Douglas (1867–1944)

—Marion Lonsberry

158
ILIFF SCHOOL OF THEOLOGY   CoDI

Ira J. Taylor Educational Resources Library
2233 South University Boulevard
Denver, Colorado 80210

Lindsay B. Longacre, 12 holograph mss and 19 published compositions, including piano solos and hymns, ca. 1912–50

Hymnals of various denominations, ca. 1800–1940, 800 items, including some without music and some in German

—Jerry Campbell

159
Austin C. LOVELACE

Wellshire Presbyterian Church
2999 South Colorado Boulevard
Denver, Colorado 80222

Hymnals and tunebooks, 1000 items, including many 19th-century imprints and shape-note vols.

Personal correspondence and research materials, including pamphlets and ephemera, used in the preparation of the *Companion to the Methodist Hymnal* (Nashville, 1966)

160
ROCKMONT COLLEGE

Library
8801 West Alameda Avenue
Denver, Colorado 80226

Hymnals of various denominations, 1808–1966, 250 items, some in German

—Jolene Mendrinos

161
UNIVERSITY OF DENVER   CoDU

Penrose Library, Special Collections
Denver, Colorado 80208

Levette Davidson, collection of folk materials including his mss and field notes on folk music, collected in Colorado and the western U.S.

—George Snyder

162
Ken PERIMAN

Fort Lewis College
Durango, Colorado 81301

Folklore tape recordings (some with transcriptions), including 20 hours of music, with the Ute Bear Dance, other Ute music, Pueblo and Navajo music, 16th- and 17th-century Spanish *alabados* (songs of praise) and secular songs, and cowboy songs, collected by Ken Periman and by students, ca. 1960–

163
FLORENCE PIONEER MUSEUM AND HISTORICAL SOCIETY

Pikes Peak and Front Streets
Florence, Colorado 81226

Margaret Ann Howell (ca. 1870–1960, local opera singer), personal papers including programs, autograph albums, scrapbooks, letters, and photographs of herself and other opera singers

Doris John Watkins (pianist), 2 78-rpm discs of popular and sacred music performed by her

Florence Lions' Club Hillbilly Band, papers, including 1 scrapbook of clippings prepared by the founder, programs, 10 photographs, and musical instruments and costumes of members, ca. 1935–55

Songbooks, 35 items, ca. 1900–1930, including popular songbooks and Protestant and Catholic hymnals

Sheet music, ca. 1900–1920, 25 items, including 1 by local composer Glenn Biglow

Programs of local performances, ca. 1885–1940, 30 items, including the visiting National Welsh Choir, ca. 1900, the Florence Opera House, and Chautauqua meetings

Photographs of local school and community groups, ca. 1890–1940, 100 items, including company bands of local mining towns financed by John D. Rockefeller; also uniforms and instruments of these bands

Recordings, including 75 Edison cylinders and 75 78-rpm discs

—Charles E. and Velma S. Price

164
FORT COLLINS MUSEUM

200 Mathews Street
Fort Collins, Colorado 80524

Sylvester H. Birdsall, portable instruction keyboard and instruction book, invented and patented by him, ca. 1870

Hymnals, 31 items, ca. 1840–1909
Songbooks, 14 items, ca. 1852–1913
Sheet music, 31 items, ca. 1850–1903, mostly for piano, including 1 song by D. S. McCosh (composer and publisher of Montelius and Denver)
Program of a local classical-music concert, ca. 1900
Recordings, including 4 cylinders, and 74 Edison or other 78-rpm discs

—Thomas Katsimpalis, Brian Moroney

165
FORT MORGAN HERITAGE FOUNDATION

Box 184
Fort Morgan, Colorado 80701

Songbooks, 12 items, 1902–6; also 5 hymnals, 1869–93, including 2 in German
Sheet music, 200 mostly popular items, ca. 1892–1952
Wiggins (Colo.) Beethoven Club, minutes of a 1922 meeting
Programs and clippings of concerts in Fort Morgan and the Denver area, 6 items, ca. 1922–33

—Sue Elliott

166
MUSEUM OF WESTERN COLORADO

Fourth and Ute Streets
Grand Junction, Colorado 81501

Songbooks, 1890–1912, 3 items, including sacred and school songs
Sheet music, 1900–1920, 127 items, some by local composers including Dr. E. F. Eldridge
Programs of local groups, 10 items, 1900–1930
Photographs of local music groups, 10 items

—Michael J. Menard

167
GREELEY MUNICIPAL MUSEUM

919 Seventh Street
Greeley, Colorado 80631

George Fisk (1838–1926, violin- and pattern-maker), 2 ms compositions for violin, music catalogues advertising his violins, 3 photographs of him, and other information including 1 oral-history tape collected ca. 1972 from a local acquaintance
Manuscript music by other local composers associated with the University of Northern Colorado, 5 items, ca. 1920–40
Opera House, 30 linear cm. of papers, ca. 1886–1961, including financial records
University of Northern Colorado (formerly Colorado Normal School), miscellaneous papers, including rosters of students, ca. 1890–1970
Programs of local events, including some at the Opera House, 150 items, ca. 1890–1940; also 10 related photographs
School songbooks and hymnals, 300 items, including hymnals in German and Swedish, ca. 1852–1960
Popular sheet music, 70 linear cm., ca. 1880–1940, including "Arabian Nights," an Oriental intermezzo played during Buffalo Bill's Show

Recordings, 30 piano rolls, 5 cylinders, 50 78-rpm discs; also 25 disc recordings made in Greeley, 1880–95, including "Just Break the News to Mother," 1880

—Sandra Cox

168
UNIVERSITY OF NORTHERN COLORADO   CoGrU

Music Library
Greeley, Colorado 80639

J. DeForest Cline (first dean of the School of Music), 75 ms items for orchestra, band, or voice, ca. 1920–50
Theater-orchestra music, published parts for 1000 items used in the Denver and Greeley area, ca. 1920–40, donated by Dr. Henry Ginsburg
Songbooks and hymnals, 350 items, ca. 1820–
Sheet music, 2000 mostly popular or semi-classical vocal items, ca. 1880–
Recordings, including 350 78-rpm discs, mostly classical

—Norman Savig

169
HEALY HOUSE AND DEXTER CABIN

Colorado Historical Society
912 Harrison Avenue
Leadville, Colorado 80461

Piano music and piano instruction books, 15 items, ca. 1880–1900
Hymnals, 5 items, and 5 school songbooks, ca. 1890–1920
Popular sheet music, 15 items, ca. 1880–1900
Recordings, including 40 78-rpm discs of popular music

—Edward Blair

170
LITTLETON HISTORICAL MUSEUM

6028 South Gallup Street
Littleton, Colorado 80120

Papers of the Women's Club of Littleton and other local organizations, including yearbooks, minutes, and programs, in all 45 linear cm., ca. 1880–1957
Published music, including 3 items for piano, 1878–1908; 30 popular, community, and school songbooks, ca. 1870–1925; 7 hymnals of various denominations, ca. 1880–1925; 300 sheet-music items, ca. 1850–1940; and 1 bound vol. of sheet music, mostly popular vocal music
Photographs of local musicians and groups, 5 items, ca. 1880–1940
Recordings, including 20 Amberol cylinders, ca. 1900–1915, 112 78-rpm discs, ca. 1905–15, and a Victor recording catalogue, 1923

—Lorena Orvañanos Donohue

171
LONGMONT PIONEER MUSEUM

375 Kimbark Street
Longmont, Colorado 80501

Hymnals of various denominations, 20 items, ca. 1880–1940, some of them in Swedish or German

School songbooks, ca. 1880–1940, 10 items including 1 with words only, and 1 used in Longmont schools, 1896

Sheet music, ca. 1860–1940, 450 items including music by local composers Edward Deville, Ferol Beckett, Noland Fry, Marian Kistler, and Seletha Brown

Programs of local or Denver school and community musicians, 25 items, ca. 1900–1940

Photographs of local school and community musicians and groups, 25 items, ca. 1890–1940

Recordings, including 140 cylinders, 185 78-rpm discs, and 67 piano rolls, mostly popular music

—Alberta Marlatt

172
SAN MIGUEL COUNTY HISTORICAL SOCIETY
Box 476
Telluride, Colorado 81435

Scrapbook of programs of musical events in Telluride, including some at the opera house, ca. 1900–1950

Published songbooks and sheet music, 6 linear meters, ca. 1890–1925

Recordings, 60 78-rpm discs

—Arlene Reed

In addition to the repositories listed above, the following have also reported holdings of the materials indicated:

Alamosa—Adams State College, Learning Resources Center: printed music, recordings

Aspen—Aspen Historical Society: sheet music, songbooks, programs

Aurora—Aurora Historical Society: sheet music

Bayfield—Gem Village Museum: recordings

Boulder—First Methodist Church, Library: songbooks

Brush—Brush Carnegie Library: songbooks, recordings

Canon City—Canon City Public Library: recordings, miscellaneous

Cascade—Ute Pass Historical Society: pictures, miscellaneous

Central City—Gilpin County Historical Society: sheet music, programs, pictures

Denver—Denver Art Museum: sheet music, other printed music

Denver—Loretto Heights College, May Bonfils-Stanton Library: songbooks, recordings

Denver—Regis College, Dayton Memorial Library: recordings

Denver—St. Thomas Seminary, Library: songbooks, recordings

Denver—Western Bible College: sheet music, songbooks, recordings, miscellaneous

Evergreen—Jefferson County Historical Society: sheet music, songbooks, other printed music

Evergreen—Jefferson County Public Library: songbooks, recordings

Frisco—Summit County Library: recordings

Georgetown—Georgetown Society: pictures

Golden—Colorado Railroad Historical Foundation: sheet music

Golden—Colorado School of Mines, Arthur Lakes Library: recordings

Golden—Buffalo Bill Memorial Museum: sheet music, songbooks, programs, pictures

Gunnison—Western State College, Savage Library: songbooks, other printed music, programs, pictures, recordings

Lafayette—Lafayette Public Library: songbooks

Longmont—Mrs. Donald J. Estes: sheet music

Montrose—Montrose County Regional Library: songbooks, other printed music, programs, catalogues, recordings

Pueblo—University of Southern Colorado, Library: Slovene sheet music and hymnals, and tamburitza programs and recordings

Strasburg—Comanche Crossing Historical Society: sheet music, songbooks, pictures, recordings, miscellaneous

Connecticut

173
BRIDGEPORT PUBLIC LIBRARY   CtB
Historical Collections
925 Broad Street
Bridgeport, Connecticut 06604

John Adam Hugo (1873–1945), 2.5 linear meters of mss, including his opera *The Temple Dancer*, orchestral music, and songs

Songbooks, 5 ms vols. of popular songs written in Connecticut, 1760s–1800

Published music, including 45 linear cm. of sheet music, 1920s, and 78 songbooks, 1780–1900

Music Research Club of Bridgeport, 75 linear cm. of papers, including minutes and scrapbooks, 1923–61

Wednesday Afternoon Musical Club, 60 linear cm. of papers, including minutes and yearbooks, 1898–1976

—David W. Palmquist

174
DANBURY SCOTT–FANTON MUSEUM AND HISTORICAL SOCIETY
43 Main Street
Danbury, Connecticut 06810

Charles Ives (1874–1954), family papers, wills, deeds, 50 family photographs, home furnishings, a death mask, and a bust

Sheet music, 50 items and 3 bound vols. of late l9th-century popular music owned by local residents
Hymnals, 25 19th-century items
Songbooks, 25 items, including early l9th-century tune-books and early 20th-century popular songbooks

—Dorothy T. Schling

175

DERBY PUBLIC LIBRARY CtDe
Elizabeth and Caroline Streets
Derby, Connecticut 06418

Sheet music, as cited in Charles E. Funk, Jr., *Directory of Subject Strengths in Connecticut Libraries* (Hartford, 1973)

176

EAST HADDAM HISTORICAL SOCIETY
Box 27
East Haddam, Connecticut 06423

Moodus Drum and Fife Corps, papers, 4 pictures, clippings, and memorabilia, 1887–92; also 2 fifes and a uniform, 1821–25
Maplewood Music Seminary, catalogue, 1874–75
Music ms of songs with words by local residents, ca. 1880–90
Sheet music, 10 items; also the *Soldiers Hymn Book* (1861)
Program of the Carvers Quarter Ball, n.d.

—Hazel J. Williams

177

GOODSPEED OPERA HOUSE
East Haddam, Connecticut 06423

Materials used at the theater, including 5000 items of sheet music, 200 vocal scores of musical shows, and 30 playbills
Musical Theatre Collection of Mr. and Mrs. Frank E. Tuit II, of Northampton, Mass., including 535 78-rpm disc recordings and a George Gershwin collection begun in 1925

—Prudence Hoffman

178

RATHBUN FREE MEMORIAL CtEhad
LIBRARY
East Haddam, Connecticut 06423

Moodus Drum and Fife Corps, 12 clippings, 1 ledger, and 3 photographs, ca. 1874
Songbooks, 3 items, 1771–1885

—Martha Monte

179

Marcella SEMBRICH MEMORIAL
ASSOCIATION
3236 Congress Street
Fairfield, Connecticut 06430

See also the Marcella Sembrich Memorial Studio, Lake George, N.Y.

Personal papers of Mme Sembrich (1858–1935), including correspondence, programs, contracts, and scrapbooks with concert and opera reviews, beginning in the U.S. at the Metropolitan Opera in 1883, and extending through her teaching career at the Juilliard School of Music and at the Curtis Institute with programs and reviews of U.S. tours; also reviews and programs of outstanding pupils
Autograph album, including testimonials from famous musicians and other associates (in special bank storage)

—Philip L. Miller

180

CONNECTICUT HISTORICAL CtHi
SOCIETY
Library
One Elizabeth Street
Hartford, Connecticut 06105

Joel Allen, ms draft of a music book, "Select Harmony," Southington, 1800
Eondias Bidwell, ms music book, 1772
Sidney Brooks, 4-page ms of music inserted in a printed book, *The Gamut* (1816)
Edwin R. Brown, 3 ms booklets of hymns and songs, in several hands, from Cheshire and Southington, 1815–30
Dudley Buck, autograph ms of a secular cantata
William Herbert Bush (1861–1952, organist), papers, 1885–1929, with a scrapbook of clippings and programs, a notebook with lists of pupils, and a calendar of services at the Second Congregational Church, New London, 1907–17
William Conner, papers relating to instruments, and an order for double-bass strings, Hartford, 1822–27
David Edgecombe, 15-page ms songbook, Groton, ca. 1827
Cushing Eells, ms music book, Norwich, 1789–91
Irving Emerson, of Hartford, account book of performance expenses and sales of music books, 1871–92, ledger with accounts of concert expenses, 1872–88, and a notebook with a record of ticket sales for *Iolanthe and Priscilla*, 1891–92
Charles Geer, ms music book, Groton, 1789–90
Ebenezer Geer, ms music book, Groton, 1799
Giles Gibbs, ms music book, "Giles Gibbs, His Book for the Fife," Ellington, 1777. See the modern edition prepared by Kate Van Winkle Keller (Hartford, 1975)
Alexander H. Griswold (d. 1881), papers with references to musical activities and singing schools in Granby, Simsbury, Windsor, and Middletown, 1813–21
Hartford Union Chorus, papers, 1883–84
James Bidwell Hosmer, 2 music mss, 1 for flute, n.d., the other 1798–99
Hosmer Hall Choral Union, Hartford, 1 folder of correspondence and records, 1886–89
John Ives, ms music, 1796
Andrew Law, *Rudiments of Music* (1792), with 1 page of ms music at the end
Maginnis and Morgan (New London flour merchants), account book, 1851–52 and 1856–58, including 12 pages concerning music lessons
Eneas Morgan, 2 vols. of ms music, Groton, 1790

Shubael Morgan, ms singing book

Solomon Porter, ms parts for anthems, ca. 1804

Ezekiel Spalding (b. 1782, of Killingly), ms music, 1802

Spencer Family Papers, 1742–1931, including some music mss, n.d.

Ishmael Spicer (of Chatham and Bozrah), ms songs, Chatham, 1797; ms music inserted after printed music in Samuel Green's *David's Harp*, 1816; and a ms music booklet, 1821

Sara Stevens (1833?–97, mandolin player, of Middletown and Hartford), scrapbook, graduation program, programs of concerts, and clippings, 1871–97

A. Storrs, ms songs, Mansfield, 1797

Timothy Swan, official ms copy of the copyright for his *New England Harmony* (1800), and 6 of his original compositions

Samuel Whitman, ms music book, 1768

Orramel Whittlesey (1801–76), 12-page music ms, 1850; 2 account books; 1 book of bills (1829–50) relating to transactions of the Music Vale Seminary and Normal Academy of Music of Salem; and a photocopy of a typescript commemorative vol. by Sara Augusta Shoner concerning Karolyn Bradford Whittlesey, containing material on the Music Vale Seminary

Miscellaneous materials, including 1 vol. of ms music with the bookplate of Benjamin Hastings, Suffield; and an arithmetic workbook of Sara M. Durand, Stamford Academy, 1853–55, with pages of ms music bound in, 1857

Songbooks, 300 items, including Connecticut sacred imprints. See Richard Crawford, "Connecticut Sacred Music Imprints, 1778–1810," M.L.A. *Notes*, 27 (1971), 445–52, 671–79

Broadsides, several hundred items including music-related materials, and 20 catalogued music broadsides, 1776–1814

Other materials, including programs for Hartford-area concerts (in the Prints Room), and early 19th-century American music periodicals

—Ruth Blair, Diana McCain

181
CONNECTICUT STATE LIBRARY   Ct

231 Capitol Avenue
Hartford, Connecticut 06115

History and Genealogy Department

Sheet music, 500 songs about Connecticut or published in Connecticut, 1890s–1935

Concert programs and catalogues of music schools, including the Julius Hartt School of Music, 1935–66, and the Hartt College of Music (see the University of Hartford), 60 linear cm.

Miscellaneous programs, pamphlets, and ephemera (scattered through the collections) of Hartford-area music groups including the Hartford Oratorio Society, 1923–49, and the Hartford Choral Club, 1903–65, in all 60 linear cm.; also 250 books including essays, reports, proceedings, histories, reference materials, instrumental instruction books, and biographies, among them Thomas Moore's *Melodies, Sacred Songs and National Airs* (Bridgeport, 1828), and early sacred-music imprints as cited in Richard Crawford, "Connecticut Sacred Music Imprints, 1778–1810," M.L.A. *Notes*, 27 (1971), 445–52, 671–79

—Julie Crawford

Connecticut State Archive

Priscilla Stoddard, ms book of hymns, 1816

Ralph Thompson, ms book of folk music, n.d.

Woodbury Harmonic Society, list of members and minutes, 1857, with court dockets of William Cothren (Society secretary)

Ralph Lyman Baldwin (director, Institute of Musical Pedagogy, Northampton, Mass., 1900–1929), 48 letters to Joseph H. Sofier, of West Hartford, 1935–43, concerning the Hartford School of Music; also Baldwin's 3-vol. scrapbook of programs and other materials concerning music in the Hartford area, 1898–1932

Logbooks, 18th and early 19th centuries, some containing song texts

Shaker hymnals, 2 vols., 1828 and 1852. See *Cook*, p. 290

—Eunice DiBella

182
HARTFORD PUBLIC LIBRARY   CtH

500 Main Street
Hartford, Connecticut 06103

Art and Music Department

Sheet music, including popular piano, vocal, and organ music, 1900–

Programs for opera and theater performances in Hartford, 1890s–

Clippings and photographs concerning local musicians, 1930s–

Historic Hartford Collection

Manuscript and published music of local composers including Dudley Buck (1839–1909) and John Spencer Camp (1858–1946), also WPA orchestral arrangements, 1930s

Scrapbooks of programs and memorabilia relating to music in Hartford

—Vernon Martin

183
HARTFORD SEMINARY   CtHC
FOUNDATION

Case Memorial Library
55 Elizabeth Street
Hartford, Connecticut 06105

Materials concerning the James Warrington, Silas K. Paine, and Waldo Selden Pratt collections of hymnals and tunebooks. The collections themselves, formerly in the Library, are now at the Pittsburgh Theological Seminary (Pittsburgh, Pa.) and Emory University (Atlanta, Ga.). Remaining materials include Warrington's diary, account book, clippings, notes, and an 18th-century music ms; Pratt's notebooks; and correspondence of all 3 collectors, and of Alfred Perry concerning the Hartford Seminary's acquisition of Warrington's collection

Frances Hall Johnson Program Collection, with programs of Hartford concerts, mid 19th and early 20th centuries

184

STOWE–DAY MEMORIAL LIBRARY   CtHSD
AND HISTORICAL FOUNDATION

77 Forest Street
Hartford, Connecticut 06105

Manuscript music relating to *Uncle Tom's Cabin*, including a music book with hymns by Asa Talcott (1778–1860), 1823, and a music book copied by Elisabeth Hooker Gillette (1813–93) at Farmington, ca. 1830
Sheet music, 109 items including dramatizations of *Uncle Tom's Cabin* and dances and songs about blacks, 1840–60
Congregational hymnals owned by the Lyman Beecher and Harriet Beecher Stowe families, 50 items, 1840–1900
Children's and school songbooks, 30 items, 1840–1900
Programs of European and American concerts, 1870–1910, 25 items formerly owned by John Calvin Day (1835–99) of Hartford, and his daughter, Katherine Seymour Day (1870–1964)

—Diana J. Royce

185

TRINITY COLLEGE   CtHT-W

Watkinson Library
Hartford, Connecticut 06106

See the exhibition catalogue, *Billings to Joplin: Popular Music in 19th Century America* (Hartford, 1980)

Music mss, including 25 18th- and 19th-century songbooks and copybooks; 33 19th-century organ and choir parts; 19 18th- and 19th-century printed songbooks and hymnals with ms additions; 2 boxes of compositions by Nathan Henry Allen and others, mostly for organ; and a book of patriotic song texts, dated 1783, owned by Joseph Kendal
Nathan Henry Allen (1848–1922, Hartford organist, and friend of Dudley Buck), personal papers, including 400 letters, 9 scrapbooks, photographs, and his ms study, "Music in a New England State, from Psalmody to Symphony in Connecticut" (1922)
Edward Abbe Niles (1894–1963) collection, including a ms music book, 1824, owned by Micah Hawkins, with commentary on dance in the 1830s added by Henry Mount and his brother, and a bound vol. of published sheet music owned by Hawkins, as cited in Oscar Wegelin, *Micah Hawkins and the Saw Mill* (New York, 1917), also in the *Magazine of History with Notes and Queries*, no. 127 (1927); also 200 letters of Irving Berlin, George Gershwin, W. C. Handy, Carl Sandburg, various publishers, and others; W. C. Handy memorabilia, a photograph album, and clippings; 900 miscellaneous sheet-music editions in 21 bound vols.; 225 sheet-music items, including minstrelsy, Stephen Foster, and early lithographed covers, from the collection of Bella C. Landauer; 102 items of sheet music in 3 bound vols., 1912–15; blues sheet–music editions, 81 items; and popular sheet music, 1900–1950, 1500 items arranged by composer
Songbooks, 2500 sacred and secular items, mostly 1780–1900, including minstrel and school books
Sheet music, 24,000 items, in 256 bound vols. and 130 boxes, 18th century to ca. 1940 (arranged mostly by composer)

Programs and playbills, 1870–1900, singly and in 20 scrapbooks, emphasizing items from Hartford, New York, and Boston, from the collection of Nathan Henry Allen
Printed music scores and 50 music-instruction books, 19th century
Music periodicals, 20 19th-century extended runs, also scattered issues of 10 other titles

—Margaret F. Sax

186

Mark TWAIN MEMORIAL   CtHMTH

351 Farmington Avenue
Hartford, Connecticut 06105

Sheet music, 30 items, including bound vols. of popular and classical music, 1889–1920s
Swiss music box owned by Mark Twain, built in 1865

—Margaret Cheney

187

Wallace CAMPBELL

Holly House
East Street
Litchfield, Connecticut 06759

Litchfield County Choral Union papers, including a complete run of concert programs, 1898– , and 2 scrapbooks of correspondence, records, and clippings

188

LITCHFIELD HISTORICAL SOCIETY   CtLHi

Box 385
Litchfield, Connecticut 06759

Sheet music, 35 19th-century items, including the "Litchfield Enquirer March"
Songbooks, 50 19th-century hymnals and secular songbooks, including 4 ms songbooks by Mary Sheldon, a local music student, ca. 1810–20
Manuscript music, 50 miscellaneous items, separate and in diaries in various collections
Adelaide Deming (New York City music teacher) Collection, 150 items of correspondence, 1880–1920, including papers of music groups of which she was a member, and 300 programs for concerts in New York City
Papers of local musicians and music groups, 50 items, 1831– , the subjects including bands and the purchase of a church organ
Programs of concerts in northwestern Connecticut, 1780–1920, 300 items
Photographs of local music groups, 25 items, 1860–
Musical instruments, 15 flutes and pitchpipes including some made at the Hopkins factory in the Fluteville section of Litchfield, 1800–1825

—Lockett Ford Ballard, Jr.

Mark SLOBIN

3 Brainerd Avenue
Middletown, Connecticut 06457

Jewish-American sheet music, 300 items, 1890s–1950s but mostly 1897–1930; also recordings of Yiddish music, 100 78-rpm discs, all copied on tapes, 1910s–50s

190

WESLEYAN UNIVERSITY CtW
Middletown, Connecticut 06457

Olin Library, Special Collections and Archives Department

Speirachordeon Band of Wesleyan University, ms book containing 8 compositions for wind instruments, dated 1838

Continental Vocalists (Connecticut ensemble that toured widely, 1854–85, co-founded and led by William D. Franklin), account book, 213 pages, covering the most active years, 1854–67, and including 6 pages of Franklin's personal accounts and 30 pages of Mrs. Franklin's millinery accounts; 2 scrapbooks, mostly of clippings, also programs, tickets, and 2 fan letters; 33 handbills, 28 of them for concert programs, 4 on temperance; lithograph portrait of Franklin, and 2 photographs of the quartet; ms music, songs, and arrangements by Franklin, in notebooks and portfolios, 8 linear cm.; sheet music, 170 items, including works by Franklin and from the Continental Vocalists' repertory, mostly with piano but some with guitar accompaniment; and 3 published vocal anthologies. (Franklin's velvet costume is in the Middlesex County Historical Society.) See Phyllis Bruce, "The Career of the Continental Vocalists and the Life of Its Co-Founder, William Dwight Franklin" (typescript, 1978)

Karl Pomeroy Harrington (1861–1953), ms and printed songs, 3 linear cm.; 3 printed music books by him; programs for his organ and choral concerts; and 3 unpublished papers on the history of local music. See his autobiography, *Karl Pomeroy Harrington: The Autobiography of a Versatile and Vigorous Professor*, ed. Mabel Harrington Potter (Boston, 1975)

William Butler Davis (1871–1936), original musical works, including ms piano-vocal scores and orchestral parts, and printed sheet music for 5 songs from *The Girl and the Graduate* (ca. 1908), his light opera with lyrics by K. M. Goode; also holograph mss of 8 songs

Carl Fowler Price (1881–1948), personal papers, including published vocal anthologies and writings on hymnology; a typescript bibliography of his writings and music compiled by Irene E. Snell (44 pages, 1942); 50 incoming letters, 1894–1929, also correspondence with Karl Pomeroy Harrington concerning editions of the *Wesleyan Song Book*, 1901–31; and 2 scrapbooks on hymnology, 1 owned by Charles Sumner Nutter

Emily S. Perkins, ms collection of 43 original hymn tunes, post-1921, entitled "Manuscripts and Printed Material Since Stonehurst Hymn-Tunes Publication"

Wesleyan University Musical Association, account book, 1908–30; and Music and Dramatics Board, papers for 1921–30, 2.5 linear cm.

Songs, 46 printed and ms items, many related to the University, including works by Adele M. Beattys, Calvin Sears Harrington, John Spencer Camp, Frederick L. Knowles, Henderson E. Van Surdam, Clifford L. Waite, Albert Sears Pruden, and Allie Wrubel

Hymnals, 1000 19th-century editions, some of them Methodist, including items acquired with the Carl F. Price collection, now dispersed but accessible through the subject heading "Hymns, English"

Wesleyan University music, including 7 editions of the *Wesleyan Song Book*, 1901–40, and 10 word books; also other items of individual fraternities

Programs of local performing groups, including the Glee Club and the Musical Association, 1869–1940, 20 linear cm.; of other Wesleyan events, including organ recitals, 1864–1940, 8 linear cm.; and of other Middletown musical events, ca. 1900

Photographs of Wesleyan University musical subjects, 1864–1940, 13 linear cm.

—Elizabeth A. Swaim

Department of Music, World Music Archives

Recordings of American Indian music, especially Navajo ceremonial music, formerly in the Laboratory of Ethnomusicology

—Mark Slobin

191

MOODUS DRUM AND FIFE CORPS
Falls Road
Moodus, Connecticut 06469

Archives and performance materials for the Corps, dating back to its founding in 1821 (available to members of the group)

—John Golet

192

NEW HAVEN COLONY CtNhHi
HISTORICAL SOCIETY
114 Whitney Avenue
New Haven, Connecticut 06510

Daniel Read (1757–1836), 57 linear cm. of papers, 1777–1853, deposited in 1855 by his son, George F. H. Read. See Irving Lowens, "Daniel Read's World: The Letters of an Early American Composer," *M.L.A. Notes*, 9 (1952), 233–48; also his *Music and Musicians in Early America* (New York, 1964), pp. 159–77. Materials include Read's ms journal, 2 ms letter books, 2 ms books of music, 1 folder of loose ms documents, and 14 published tunebooks or songbooks composed or used by Read; also 2 ms music books by Lucretia Champion of East Haddam, 1798 and 1799; ms music book for cornet by A. E. Lines, New Haven, n.d.; ms "Preceptor for Flute," possibly by Daniel Henry Huntington, ca. 1825, inscribed to Joseph Huntington; ms music book by J. Strong, Coventry, n.d.; ms music book possibly by Asahel Nettleton, ca. 1790, with related correspondence; and 1 unidentified ms music book for organ, choir, and piano, n.d.

New Haven Music Collection, 1798–1976, comprising 600 items published in New Haven or by local composers, 1798–1939, and including 18 songbooks, tunebooks, and hymnals, and 25 sheet-music items (mostly New Haven imprints, 1839–1932); 131 programs and 25 clippings of the New Haven Orchestral Club, 1885–95; 114 other programs for New Haven concerts, 1829–1975; Benjamin Jepson (1832–1914, New Haven music educator), song sheets, pamphlets, and music instruction books, including *The Elementary Music Reader* (1865) and *Selections for Devo-*

tional Exercises (n.d.); H. Earle Johnson, papers as music editor of the *New Haven Register*, including 4 folders and 2 scrapbooks of press clippings, 1933–42; Ethel Carmalt (former New Haven resident), folder and scrapbook of programs and clippings, 1881–1938; 2 issues of *The Green Room: A Record of Entertainments* (New Haven, 1867, 1872); and 2 issues of the *Shoninger Musical Monthly* (1888, 1890)

Sheet music, 25 19th-century items

Hymnals and school songbooks, 60 vols. used or published in New Haven, 19th century

Programs of concerts in New Haven, 20 pre-1895 items

Photographs of local musicians, 10 items, late 19th and early 20th centuries

Women's Choral Society of New Haven, 1708 items of papers including minutes, reports, and membership lists, 1927–59

New Haven Symphony Orchestra Collection, 1895– , 250 items including programs, press clippings in 5 scrapbooks (1939–49), and by-laws (1895)

—Irene K. Miller, Lysbeth Andrews-Zike

193
NEW HAVEN FREE PUBLIC LIBRARY
133 Elm Street
New Haven, Connecticut 06510

Sheet music, 68 items of popular music, 1920s

Songbooks, 58 secular items, and 18 early 20th-century hymnals

Programs of local concerts, 1930, 30 linear cm.

Pictures of musicians, instruments, and other musical subjects, in a general collection of 337,000 photographs, sketches, and reproductions (indexed)

—Helen Worobec

194
NEW HAVEN SECOND GOVERNOR'S FOOT GUARD BAND
Goffe Street Armory
45 Water Street
New Haven, Connecticut 06511

Band music, 5000 items, 1880– , including catalogues of earlier bands such as the Connecticut Second Regiment Band

195
YALE UNIVERSITY   CtY
New Haven, Connecticut 06520

A. John Herrick Jackson Music Library
B. Other of the Yale University Libraries
C. Other Music Collections

A. John Herrick Jackson Music Library (98 Wall Street)

The collection was established with the personal library of Lowell Mason, including materials he acquired on European trips, notably the collection of Johann Christian Heinrich Rinck of Darmstadt, Germany, purchased in 1852, donated to Yale after Mason's death in 1872,

and described then in a ms author-catalogue prepared by Joel Sumner Smith. (Some books from the collection are still located in the Divinity Library; see section B, below.) See Eva Judd O'Meara, "The Lowell Mason Library of Music," Yale University Library *Gazette,* 40 (1965), 57–74; also "The Lowell Mason Library," M.L.A. *Notes,* 28 (1971), 197–208

Marshall Bartholomew (1885–1978, conductor of the Yale Glee Club), personal papers, including music mss and documents relating to the Club and to the Whiffenpoofs, with a register

Hope Leroy Bartholomew (1891–1968), music holographs, also classroom materials and notes, in 4 boxes, with a register

Richard Donovan (1891–1970), holograph scores and sketches; correspondence, including materials relating to the Yaddo Festival and the American Composers' Alliance; programs for performances of his music, or which he conducted or attended; and classroom materials, including papers of his students; in all 30 boxes, with a register

Alonzo Elliot (1894–1964), music mss, 1.5 linear meters

Henry F. Gilbert (1868–1928), music mss, 4.5 linear meters, with a preliminary inventory; also correspondence, notebooks, sketches, pamphlets, programs, published books and music from his library, and printed and ms music by B. F. Gilbert and James L. Gilbert

Elliot Griffes (1893–1967), music holographs and other personal documents, 2 boxes, with a register

Paul Hindemith (1895–1963), personal papers and 9 holograph music mss, most of them from his years at Yale, 1940–53, including 100 letters and 300 photocopies; in all 5 linear meters, catalogued

Charles E. Ives (1874–1954), personal papers, including 8000 pages of music mss, also correspondence, diaries, photographs, scrapbooks, programs, press clippings, and memorabilia, with a register. See John Kirkpatrick, *A Temporary Mimeographed Catalogue of the Music Manuscripts and Related Materials of Charles Edward Ives* (New Haven, 1960)

J. Rosamond Johnson (1873–1954), personal papers, including music mss, correspondence, scrapbooks, and memorabilia, 3.5 linear meters

Ralph Kirkpatrick, personal papers, in all 27 boxes, with registers, comprising Series I: keyboard compositions, including holographs, photocopies, and published editions of contemporary American works; and Series II: materials relating to his research on Domenico Scarlatti

Armin Loos (1904–71), music mss, 1.8 linear meters, with an inventory

Love family papers, 1886–1960, including correspondence to Lucy Cleveland Prindle (Mrs. Edward Gurley) Love, and to her daughter, Helen Douglas (Love) Scranton (secretary to the Kneisel Quartet, and New York concert manager); also clippings, printed ephemera, and photographs; in all 11 boxes, with a register

Lowell Mason (1792–1872), personal papers, including correspondence, diaries, and literary mss; also materials of Henry Lowell Mason (1862–1957), including a ms biography of Lowell Mason; in all 3.5 linear meters, catalogued

Leo Ornstein, music mss, mostly in the hand of his wife, also photographs and tape recordings; in all 18 boxes, with a register

Horatio Parker (1863–1919), personal papers, including holograph music mss, correspondence, and other materials; in all 15 linear meters, catalogued

Quincy Porter (1897–1966), personal papers, including correspondence related to his activities with the American Composers' Alliance, the National Institute of Arts and Letters, the American Music Center, the Yaddo Festival, and Pierson College at Yale University; also a definitive collection of his music in holograph mss and printed editions; and music by other composers, mostly in photocopy; in all 66 boxes, with a register

Carl Ruggles (1876–1971), personal papers, a definitive collection, including holograph music mss, sketches, and correspondence, in all 9 linear meters

Schneeloch papers, 1886–93, including correspondence, diaries, photographs, and printed materials relating to the singers Emma Waleska Schneeloch Bacon (1862–1925) and Emelie A. ("Millie") Schneeloch (b. 1868) and their U.S. tours, 1891–92, with frequent mention of Patrick S. Gilmore; 2 boxes, with a register. (See also materials in the Sterling Memorial Library, Manuscripts and Archives Division, section B, below.)

Leo Schrade (1903–64), personal papers from both his European and American years, including classroom notes, copies of dissertations and other research projects prepared under his supervision, research notes and working photocopies, and portions of his personal library

David Stanley Smith (1877–1949), personal papers, including 350 music mss, and correspondence, in all 6 linear meters, catalogued

Thomas Max Smith (1874–1935), personal papers, 1879–1933, relating to his work as music editor and critic for the *New York Press* (1903–16) and the *New York American* (1916–19, 1923), in particular to his study of Arturo Toscanini and the New York Philharmonic Orchestra, 1926–30; in all 4 boxes, with a register

Gustave Jacob Stoeckel (1819–1907), music mss, 1 linear meter, catalogued

Virgil Thomson, personal papers, a definitive collection including holograph music mss and sketches, published literary and musical writings, correspondence, and memorabilia, in all 120 boxes, with registers

Wright papers, 1907–54, including clippings and photographs assembled by Helen Madeline Wright, also letters from her teachers, Teresa Carreño and Myra Hess; in 1 box, with a register

Single and smaller collections of music mss, including Samuel Holyoke (1762–1820), 3 ms books, the first containing sacred music, the second largely a copy of the first, the third called "Manuscript coll. anthems" and dated 1793; John F. Curtiss, "A most excellent and elegant collection of airs, marches, minuetts, duetts, &c. &c. set and adopted [sic] for two violins, and other instriments [sic]," dated Cheshire, Conn., ca. 1803, and including works attributed to Curtiss; Lowell Mason, original ms of the 1821 edition of the *Boston Handel & Haydn Society Collection*, dated Savannah, Ga., 1819–20; Isaac and Eliza Jane Waite, copyists' ms collection of vocal and piano music, dated New York, 1823 and 1825; Newton Ingram Alliger, "A collection of airs, preludes, marches, &c.," 4 vols., n.d., for piano and voice with German text; Charles Edward Horn (1786–1849), hymn, "Awake Thee, O Zion," holograph ms, dated 1847 and pre-

sented to Lowell Mason; 2 Shaker hymnals, post-1843, written by James Vail and by Henry Young, both of Enfield, Conn.; John Hill Hewitt (1801–90), holograph of *The Revellers*; George James Webb (1803–87), holograph of the song "My Little Wife and I"; Henry Stephen Cutler (1825–1902), fugue on "Jerusalem the Golden," with a letter to Lowell Mason, dated 1870; Robbins Battell (1819–95, of Norfolk, Conn.), 9 holograph music mss; I. J. Spiller, holograph mss of the "Waltz: Spring in Norfolk," n.d., dedicated to Carl Stoeckel, in both piano and orchestral arrangements; Julia Ludlow Rockwell, 2 boxes of original music mss, n.d.; Edward A. MacDowell, holographs of the "Étude, Wilde Jagd" (first 48 measures only) and "Polonaise," 1894, also copyists' mss for 2 songs, op. 34 [i.e., op. 33]; Leonard Woolsey Bacon (1865–1907), 2 boxes of music mss; A. Stevens Roe, "Voices from the Elms: Waltz," for piano, holograph ms, 1905; Samuel Coleridge-Taylor (1875–1912), "Keep Me from Sinkin' Down" (traditional Negro melody transcribed for violin and orchestra, first performed at the Norfolk Music Festival, 1912), holograph full score from the estate of Carl Stoeckel; Roger Sessions, Sonata for violin and piano (1916), the alternative violin part in the arrangement for violoncello, as copied by John Scudder Boyd, 1918; Henry Benjamin Jepson (1870–1952), holograph ms of his third Organ Sonata; the Frank Bozyan collection of 18 organ music holograph mss, including works by H. L. Baumgartner, H. F. Bozyan, Judd Cooke, J. J. Duffy, H. W. Kaufmann, Russell Keeney, Quincy Porter, Bruce Simonds, David Stanley Smith, and Dorothy Young; and silent-film music, 1910–28, 19 boxes of ms orchestral parts, along with dance music and synchronized scores for motion pictures

Literary mss relating to music, including Lowell Mason, 29 articles mounted in a scrapbook, of which 3 are in ms and 26 were published in the *New York Musical Review and Gazette*, some with ms marginalia, 1858–59; Albert A. Sprague (1835–1915), 1 folder of letters and other papers; Gustave Jacob Stoeckel (1819–1907), ms libretti for his dramatic works, *Harold der letzte Sachsenkönig, Miles Standish,* and *Münchhausen;.* Carl Stoeckel (1858–1925), typescript articles about Samuel Coleridge-Taylor and about Jean Sibelius's visit to the U.S., 1914; Olin Downes (1886–1955), typescript essay on Jean Sibelius; Gustave Holst, ms for his Howland Memorial Prize lecture, "The Teaching of Art," 1929; and John Carter Glenn, collection of musicians' autographs, mostly 19th-century European composers and performers, but including Eugène d'Albert, Rafael Joseffy, and Ignace Jan Paderewski

Organizational archives, including the New Haven Musical Association (1847–50?), prospectus and programs; Mendelssohn Society (1863–69), by-laws and programs; Apollo Club (1878–80?), programs, prospectuses, and membership announcements; Loomis Temple of Music (1878–1919), published music for piano, banjo, mandolin, violin, and voice; New Haven Concert Association (1884–88, founded by Theodore Thomas), programs and prospectuses; Church Choral Association (1886, founded by W. R. Hedden, Jr.), prospectuses and programs; Gounod Society (1888–1919), programs, membership lists, and other documents; Yale University School of Music, administrative correspondence of the School and relating to its students, 1897–1950; New Haven Oratorio Society (1903–13, conducted by Horatio Parker and David Stanley Smith), minutes and other official records; New Haven Music Club (1921–46), scrapbooks with programs and photographs; Society for the Publication of American Music (1924–74), archives, including correspondence and business records, in 4 boxes, with a register; and "Masters of Our Day Educational Series" (ed. by Lazare Saminsky and Isadore Freed, 1936–41), 69 editions of contemporary piano music for children

Sheet music and other published music, including 196 vocal and 67 instrumental pre-1830 imprints; 242 Confederate imprints; the Whitmark Library, 21 vols. of popular songs and condensed scores, 1910–40s; all of the above catalogued. In addition, U.S. imprints are scattered through the collections of songs (11,000 main entries), organ music (600 composer entries), and piano music (1900 composer entries). Of the uncatalogued collections, 1 linear meter of dance music and 4 linear meters of choral music are mostly American. There are also 1140 bound vols., uncatalogued, mostly with U.S. imprints

Tunebooks and other vocal anthologies, including 5 items before 1761, mostly psalm books and editions of Thomas Walter; 183 items before 1821 (class M 2116) and 188 later items (class M 2117), also 56 other items (classes M 2119–33), as well as 130 miscellaneous hymnals, school music books, juvenile psalm books, glee books, and other secular anthologies. Most of this material is from the collection of Lowell Mason

Music-instruction books, 60 items before 1850, as variously classified in the Library of Congress scheme as MT 165–950 and in the Yale scheme as Nd13–Np50

Music periodicals, an extensive collection, including 40 titles of journals begun before 1910, mostly complete runs

—Kathleen Moretto

B. Other of the Yale University Libraries

Historical Sound Recordings Collection

Sterling Memorial Library, Room 226. See Jerrold Moore, "The Historical Sound Recordings Program at Yale University," M.L.A. Notes, 19 (1962), 283–85; also his "The Purpose and Scope of the Historical Sound Recordings Program," Yale University Library Gazette, 38 (1964), 92–110; and Karol Berger, "The Yale Collection of Historical Sound Recordings," A.R.S.C. Journal, 6/1 (1974), 13–25

Recordings, 100,000 items, of which 40,000 are catalogued, the remainder arranged by label and performer, with an index by performer. Of the 300 linear meters devoted to discs, 260 are devoted to 78-rpm discs, and 5 more to instantaneous acetate discs. Also included are 25 linear meters of piano rolls and 100 linear meters of tapes. The original collection of 20,000 items from Laurence C. Witten II, specializing in early vocal recordings, included the collections of George T. Keating and Albert Wolf, and is still being expanded. Other personal collections now incorporated include those of H. William Fitelson (private recordings of Theatre Guild radio productions, mostly 1940s–50s), Warren Lowenhaupt (European recordings and radio broadcasts), S. J. Capes (piano record-

ings), C. O. Gray, Jr., Ralph Kirkpatrick, D. G. von Schrader, and materials from Joseph Strohl and H. D. Smith (early Victor Talking Machine Co. issues). Other specialties include composers' performances of their own works and the documentation of performance practice in general

Catalogues of recording companies, 15 linear meters, of which 8 meters are from U.S. companies, arranged alphabetically by company and partially catalogued

Programs, 1000 items, arranged by city and auditorium

Photographs, mostly of opera singers, 1890–1930, 12 file drawers, of which about one-third are from the U.S. or involve performers active in the U.S.

American Musical Theatre Collection

The collection is a separate entity, maintained by the staff of the Historical Sound Recordings Collection but located in the Beinecke Library, and serviced either by the Historical Sound Recordings Collection staff, or, for some materials, by the Beinecke Library on authorization of the Curator of Historical Sound Recordings. Recordings from or related to this collection have been incorporated into the Historical Sound Recordings Collection

Sheet music, 30,000 items, ca. 1890– , mostly but not exclusively for American musical-theater works, arranged by show title, uncatalogued but with an index by show title

E. Y. Harburg Archive, mostly his ms music but also letters and papers, in 41 boxes

Cole Porter (1891–1964), personal papers, mostly ms music for his shows, in 30 boxes, organized chronologically except for early material, which is by show title; also 32 scrapbooks, 28 of these for shows, containing correspondence, press clippings, and memorabilia, as organized by Mrs. Porter; and 4 personal scrapbooks, 12 photograph albums, also travel diaries and guidebooks. See Robert E. Kimball, "The Cole Porter Collection at Yale," Yale University Library Gazette, 44 (1969), 8–15

Programs for American musical-theater productions, 20 boxes, arranged alphabetically by title

Manuscripts and Archives Division, Sterling Memorial Library

Archives of music organizations of Yale University, including published catalogues and pamphlets, correspondence, minutes, programs, press clippings, and photographs relating to the School of Music; also materials on the Light Opera Guild of the School of Law, Yale Band, Yale Glee Club (ms records, 1879–84, also cash books and ledgers, 1903–5), Yale Glee and Banjo Club, Banjo Club, Beethoven Society, Yale Alumni Musical Association, Yale Guild of Harkness Bellringers, Yale University Jesters of Jonathan Edwards College, Yale Opera Association, Yale Russian Chorus, and Whiffenpoofs

Programs of University performances, singly, also in scrapbooks assembled by Joel Sumner Smith (1830–1903), 2 vols. for 1850–78; John Oxenbridge Heald (1850–1911), 2 vols., ca. 1872; Simon Metzger (1857–98), 1 vol., ca. 1880; and Thomas Griffin Shepard (b. 1848), 1 vol., ca. 1902; also programs of the New Haven Symphony Orchestra, 1895–

Songs associated with Yale University, including Joseph Washburn (1766–1805), ms book of vocal music, 1790, stamped "Social Hilarity and Musical Entertainment"; Simon Eben Baldwin (1840–1927), drafts of 2 songs and a resolution, 1858–61; Henry Strong Durand (1861–1929), holograph ms of his "Bright College Years," 1881; James Maurice Hubbard, 2 ms scores, 1887–88; George W. Chadwick, holograph ms of *Ecce jam noctes, Hymn by St. Gregory* (1897); Douglas Stuart Moore, holograph ms of "Good Night, Harvard"; and other items

Schneeloch family papers, including materials of Emma Waleska Schneeloch Bacon (1862–1925), Emelie A. ("Millie") Schneeloch (b. 1868), and Leonard Woolsey Bacon, Jr. (1865–1939), with a preliminary inventory by Vivian A. Perlis (other processed materials are in the Music Library, Section A, above)

Miscellaneous individual mss, including Aaron Thompson, fife music book used in the 3rd New Jersey Regiment, 1777–82; constitution, membership list, and minutes of the Hopkinton Musical Society, Hopkinton, N.H., 1828–37; 15 music mss and 1 printed edition, late 19th century, in the Daniel Collins papers; Frederick Acley Fowler, time book, 1880–81, and journal record, 1891, for music lessons given in New Haven; scattered references to Hawaiian music in the papers of Hiram Bingham; other references in the papers of Mabel Loomis Todd and of the Battell family

Charles A. Lindbergh, 50 musical pieces written in celebration of his trans-Atlantic flight, 1927, mostly in sheet-music editions but some in ms, including an inscribed copy of the 1930 edition of *Der Lindberghflug* by Kurt Weill and Bertold Brecht

Beinecke Rare Book and Manuscript Library

Early American imprints, including 5 Bay Psalm books, 1640–1758; 16 other 18th-century religious collections; and 19 19th-century vols.

Western Americana Collection holdings, with American Indian hymnals, including 10 manuals of hymns and chants for various tribes, printed in Kamloops, British Columbia, 1896–97; an Aleutian liturgy book for the Orthodox Eastern Church (New York, 1898), and 39 other hymnals in Amerindian languages; also 13 Mormon hymnals; and sheet music, including 100 items relating to the Mexican War and 35 items relating to California and the Gold Rush

James Weldon Johnson (1871–1938), personal papers, with extensive materials on black music, including 111 collections of black songs, 195 music editions with texts by blacks, 340 editions with music by blacks, and 52 editions on black subjects; 1200 recordings; and 62 autograph scores, including works by Chester Allen, Margaret Bonds, Henry Thacker Burleigh (4 items), Elliot Carpenter, Cecil Cohen, Samuel Coleridge-Taylor, William Levi Dawson (5 items), Daniel Decatur Emmett, George Gershwin (2 items), W. C. Handy (4 items), Hall Johnson (5 items), John Rosamond Johnson (5 items), Clarence Muse, Florence B. Price, William Grant Still (3 items), Roberta Summers Stone (5 items), Jean Stor, Maxine Sullivan, Howard Swanson (4 items), William H. Vodery (10 items), and Clarence Cameron White

Other Collections

J. R. Crawford Theatre Collection (409 Sterling Memorial Library), containing programs, photographs, press clippings, sketches, and engravings, many concerned with the musical theater, also with music halls, variety shows, circuses, and motion pictures. See Dorothy Crawford, "The Crawford Theatre Collection," Yale University Library *Gazette*, 41 (1967), 131–35

Reed Carol Collection (Sterling Memorial Library), 350 carol books, including 40 pre-1940 U.S. imprints

Hymnals without music from the Lowell Mason collection (Divinity School Library, 409 Prospect Street), including 200 catalogued and 150 uncatalogued U.S. and British imprints

C. Other Music Collections

Oral History, American Music
(School of Music, Stoeckel Hall)

Ives project, consisting of 60 tape recordings, including interviews with Eugene Becker, Mrs. John Becker, Mary Bell, Arthur Berger, Mrs. Samuel Berneri, Louis Bronson, Charles Buesing, Elliott Carter, Aaron Copland, Lehman Engel, Charles Farr, James Flexner, Peter Fraser, William Grey, Mina Hager, Arthur Hall, Harold A. Hatch, Bernard Herrmann, George Hofmann, Bigelow Ives, Brewster Ives, Chester Ives, Richard Ives, Charles H. Kauffman, John Kirkpatrick, Herman Langinger, A. J. La Pine, Monique Schmitz Leduc, Goddard Lieberson, Findlay Mackenzie, Debby Meeker, Jerome Moross, Julian S. Myrick, Mrs. Artur Nikoloric, Mary Howard Pickhardt, George Roberts, Mrs. George Roberts, Carl Ruggles, Mr. and Mrs. Will Ryder, Gertrude Sanford, Charles Seeger, Nicolas Slonimsky, Philip Sutherland, John S. Thompson, Mrs. Burton Twichell, Charles Ives Tyler, George Tyler, Louis Untermeyer, Mrs. Rodman S. Valentine, Amelia Van Wyck, Mrs. William Verplanck, William Verplanck, Jr., Lucille Fletcher Wallop, Watson Washburn, and Julia Zeigler, as reflected in Vivian Perlis, *Charles Ives Remembered* (New Haven, 1974)

Hindemith project, consisting of 75 interviews with Samuel Adler, Marshall Bartholomew, Mrs. Phyllis Bauer, Howard Boatwright, Sam diBonaventura, Martin Boykan, Mrs. Frank Bozyan, Rev. and Mrs. Calhoun, Beekman Cannon, John Colman, John Crosby, Donald Currier, Ward Davenny, Norman Dello Joio, Isabel De Witt, Leonard Doob, Antal Dorati, Leonard Feist, Lukas Foss, Richard French, Herbert Fromm, Thomas Frost, Margaret Grubb, Mr. and Mrs. Grumman, Mrs. Arthur Hague, Margaret Grady Hart, Fenno Heath, Louis Hemingway, Robert Hickok, Joseph Iadone, George Jacobson, Henry Kaufmann, Ulysses Kay, Ralph Kirkpatrick, David Kraehenbuehl, Mitch Leigh, Maurice Levine, Frank Lewin, Goddard Lieberson, Klaus Liepmann, Don Loach, George London, Mrs. John Lowe, Jean Mainous, Mason Martens, Paul Maynard, Arthur Mendel, Carl Miller, Jean Myer, Luther Noss, Osea Noss, Eva O'Meara, Aldo Parisot, Norman Pearson, Henri Peyre, Paul Pisk, Mel Powell, Mrs. Gustave Reese, Hermann Reutter, Eckhart Richter, Hugh Ross, Willie Ruff, Edmund Saranec, Karl Ulrich Schnabel, Ruth Seckel, Harold Shapero, Robert Shaw, Bruce and Rosalind Simonds, Kurt Stone, John Strauss, William Waite, Keith Wilson, Margaret Wimsatt, John Woldt, and Yehudi Wyner

Steinway & Sons project, including l00 interviews with family members, employees, piano technicians, dealers, and performers

Edward Kennedy ("Duke") Ellington project, including interviews with Aaron Bell, Eubie Blake, Dave Brubeck, Frank Driggs, Mercer Ellington, Ruth Ellington, Nat Hentoff, Russell Procope, and others

Major Figures in American Music project, including 66 interviews with Eubie Blake, Nadia Boulanger, John Cage, Carlos Chavez, Mr. and Mrs. Charles Clark (on Charles Martin Loeffler), Aaron Copland, Eleanor Cory, Burnett Cross (on Percy A. Grainger), Jacob Druckman, Valdo Freeman (on Harry Lawrence Freeman), Leopold Godowsky II, Ella (Mrs. Percy A.) Grainger, John Hammond, Lou Harrison, Mrs. Philip Gilbert Horton (on Henry F. B. Gilbert), Jean Eichelberger Ivey, Alan Jaffe (on Preservation Hall), Alexander Kipnis, Rudolf Kolisch, Olga Koussevitsky, Ernst Krenek, Herman Langinger, Minna Lederman, Noël Lee, Norman Lloyd, Josef Marx (on Stefan Wolpe), Darius Milhaud, Lawrence Morton, Nuria Schoenberg Nono, Eva J. O'Meara, Leo Ornstein, Harry Partch, Mrs. Quincy Porter, Claire Reis, Jim Robinson (on Preservation Hall), William Russell, Ronald Schoenberg, William Schuman, Charles Seeger, Victor Seroff, Roger Sessions, Alfred Simon, Bruce Simonds (on Quincy Porter), Noble Sissle, Carleton Sprague Smith, Leonard Stein (on Arnold Schoenberg), Leopold Stokowski, Gerald Strang, Oliver Strunk, Louis Sudler, Kay Swift, Virgil Thomson, Vladimir Ussachevsky, Vally Weigl, Keith Wilson (on Quincy Porter), and Stefan Wolpe

Materials from other formal and informal oral-history projects, including materials from radio stations WQXR in New York, WKPFK in Los Angeles, and WYBC in New Haven

—Vivian Perlis

Yale Band Library
(165 Elm Street)

Manuscript full scores and parts, including holograph music of Giuseppe Creatore, 6 items, early 1900s; and Carl Ruggles, ms scores prepared for the University of Miami Band, Coral Gables, Fla., 6 items, 1930s

Percy A. Grainger, band library, 7 linear meters, mostly published music, much of it with ms annotations of performance instructions by Grainger. Included are almost all the published editions of music by Grainger, including the "Chosen Gems for Winds" series

Other materials in photocopy from important early band collections, including the New Haven Second Company Governor's Foot Guard Band, and the Allentown (Pa.) Band

Programs of the Yale Band, extensive holdings, 1947– , and scattered holdings of earlier materials

Pictures, 1917– , in 2 vertical file drawers

Archival materials of the Yale Band, 1920s– , and of its forerunners, 1760s?–

—Keith Brion, Grant Cooper

196

CONNECTICUT COLLEGE   CtNlC

Greer Music Library
Mohegan Avenue
New London, Connecticut 06320

Sheet music, 17 bound vols., mostly American popular piano and piano-vocal music, 1830s–60s

Hymnals and sacred and secular songbooks, 100 items, 1783–1893

Louis Adolphe Coerne (1870–1922, first professor of music at the College), holograph 2-vol. orchestral and 3-vol. piano-vocal score of his opera *Nancy Thatcher, Woman of Marblehead*, 1895–98; ms copy of orchestral parts for his opera *Zenobia*, 1905; and a holograph vol. containing his String Quartet in C Minor op. 19 and Suite for String Quartet in D minor op. 10

Loraine Wyman (folksong collector), 21 linear meters of materials from her personal library, including composition books, sheet music, books on ballads, and research notes for her *Lonesome Tunes* (New York, 1916) and *Twenty Kentucky Mountain Songs* (Boston, 1920)

Programs of the Connecticut College Concert Series, 1918–40, 100 items

Correspondence, concert programs, financial records, and photographs of performing groups at the College, 10 folders (in the College Archives)

Recordings, including 30 linear meters of 78-rpm discs

—Philip Youngholm

197

NEW LONDON COUNTY   CtNlHi
HISTORICAL SOCIETY

11 Blinman Street
New London, Connecticut 06320

Music mss, 12 items, mostly single lines of notation, anonymous but including 1 by Joseph Willard, Jr., 1 by Sally Boynton, and 1 by H. L. G., late 18th or early 19th century

Sheet music, 26 items, mostly mid 19th century

Songbooks, 5 items, also 16 songsters, late 18th and mid 19th centuries

Other published music, 6 items, including piano albums, pedagogical books, and operas

Programs, 60 items, 1841–1907

Music periodicals, 2 published in New London, 1880–84

—Elizabeth B. Knox

198

NORFOLK HISTORICAL SOCIETY

Village Green
Norfolk, Connecticut 06058

Gustav Stoeckel (1819–1907, Norfolk resident, 1848–95, and professor of music at Yale University), 7 coon songs and sacred sheet-music editions, a portrait, and biographical materials

Hymnals, 7 items used locally, published 1784–1898

Litchfield County Choral Union, programs and clippings, 1899–1935 and 1958– , and 3 photographs, 1904–6; also programs of other local music groups, 1883–1941

—Mrs. William Walcott, Alice V. Waldecker

199

John Morgan BODMAN

Music Vale Farm
Route 3
Salem, Connecticut 06415

Materials relating to Bodman's great-great-grandfather, Orramel Whittlesey (1801–76, founder of the Salem Normal Academy of Music, which later became the Music Vale Seminary), including correspondence, photographs, published music, and biographical materials and histories of the Seminary, in all 1.2 linear meters. The correspondence includes materials from Orramel Whittlesey's daughter Eliza, who operated the Magennis Academy of Music, New London

200
SALEM HISTORICAL SOCIETY
Route 4
Salem, Connecticut 06415

Orramel Whittlesey (1801–76), biographical and other materials relating to the Music Vale Seminary (1835–76, originally the Salem Normal Academy of Music), which he founded, including administrative papers, 9 sheet-music items by him, 5 school songbooks, 8 issues of the school newspaper, *Gleaner of the Vale* (1859–74), miscellaneous concert programs, 11 diplomas, correspondence, photographs of students and buildings, and oil portraits of Whittlesey and his family; also a piano, built in 1829 by his brothers, Henry and John Whittlesey

—Louise S. Mutschler

201
TREE FARM ARCHIVES
272 Israel Hill Road
Shelton, Connecticut 06484

Sheet music, 600 popular-music items, 1830–1920, including some published locally for distribution by the Sterling Piano Co., Derby
Songbooks, 5 vols. of popular and religious music, 1850–1940

—Philip H. Jones

202
MANSFIELD HISTORICAL SOCIETY
Box 145
Storrs, Connecticut 06268

Luther Kingsley (local resident), 18th-century ms tunebook
Songbooks, 2 secular items, 1892 and 1893, and 3 sacred items, 1819–1912
Programs of local concerts, late 19th and early 20th centuries, 4 items
Playbill for *The Frogs of Windham*, 1889, an operetta by local composer Burton E. Leavitt
Meneely Bell Co., music catalogue, late 19th century

—Mrs. R. I. Munsell

203
UNIVERSITY OF CONNECTICUT   CtU
Storrs, Connecticut 06268

Special Collections Department

J. Louis von der Mehden, Jr. (1873–1954, cellist and conductor), ms and published music
Recordings, including 30 Edison cylinders, ca. 1903

Music Library

Published music, including 18 secular and sacred collections, 1883–1940, and 11.5 linear meters of theater music, ca. 1900, owned by Ernest E. Bullard of Norwich

—Dorothy Bognar

204
STRATFORD HISTORICAL SOCIETY
967 Academy Hill
Box 382
Stratford, Connecticut 06497

Manuscript vocal music, 2 items including "A Gamut of Music," 1805
Tunebooks, hymnals, and psalters, 50 items, 1801–97
Songbooks, 35 vols. of popular songs and choruses, 1830–91
Sheet music, 4 bound vols. and several separate popular and classical items, ca. 1830–1909
Method books for violin or keyboard, 4 items, 1850s

—Mrs. E. M. Larson

205
KENT MEMORIAL LIBRARY
Main Street
Suffield, Connecticut 06078

Timothy Swan (1758–1842, local composer), materials including a ms of "Denmark," 22 pages of ms drafts of vocal pieces, 3 pages of ms music lessons, published copies of *New England Harmony* (Northampton, Mass., 1801) and *The Songmaster's Assistant* (Suffield, ca. 1800), a brief ms biography by one of Swan's children, 1842, and a photograph of a portrait of Swan, ca. 1790 (original in the American Antiquarian Society, Worcester, Mass.)

—Anne W. Borg

206
UNIVERSITY OF HARTFORD   CtWeharU
200 Bloomfield Avenue
West Hartford, Connecticut 06117

Mildred P. Allen Memorial Library, Hartt College of Music

Arnold Franchetti (composer and faculty member), 40 holograph mss and 1 vol. of published piano works. See Watson Wilbur Morrison, *The Piano Sonatas of Arnold Franchetti* (D.M.A. diss., Boston University, 1971)
Sheet music, 50 items of 19th-century popular music
Hymnals, sacred and secular songbooks, and vocal method books, 100 19th-century vols.
Other printed music, 8 items, including works by Moshe Paranov (pianist) and Nathan H. Allen (1848–1925, organist)
Program for Virgil Thomson's opera *Four Saints in Three Acts*, Hartford, 1934

University Archives

Rosolino De Maria (1886–1970, cellist, conductor, and theorist), 150 mss of chamber, orchestral, and cello music
Julius Hartt, 60 letters to family members, early 20th century

Ernest Bloch, 53 letters to various musicians, 1918–20
Elizabeth (Mrs. George C.) Capen, scrapbook of operatic memorabilia, 1907–10
Harold Bauer (1873–1951, pianist), 1 unpublished photograph and 20 letters to Moshe Paranov, 1930–51
Waldo Selden Pratt, 1 photograph in his knickers, ca. 1910
Hartt College of Music, 1 linear meter of papers, 1920–

—Ethel Bacon

207

Ruth Steinkraus COHEN
28 Darbrook Road
Westport, Connecticut 06880

Vernon Duke, ms sketches from his Third Symphony, and a typescript paper on the history of American musical comedy
Keyboard music in early editions, 5000 items; also 10,000 books on keyboard music, published 18th to 20th centuries; and other published classical or popular music, mostly for keyboard instrument or voice
Recordings, including 500 78-rpm discs, mostly classical

208

WETHERSFIELD HISTORICAL SOCIETY
150 Main Street
Wethersfield, Connecticut 06109

Dudley Buck (1839–1909, local composer and organist), 12 items of sheet music, 12 music mss, and other materials
Songbooks, 25 items, late 18th and 19th centuries

—Doug Alves

209

WINDSOR HISTORICAL SOCIETY
96 Palisado Avenue
Windsor, Connecticut 06095

John Gaylord (1776–1856), ms vol. of dance tunes for violin
Samuel Clarke, ms book of song and dance tunes, n.d.; also an unidentified vol. of ms. music, without words
E-flat Cornet Windsor Band (1870–1926), ms vol. of music copied by E. L. Cobb, also a constitution, by-laws, membership list, and 4 photographs
Hymnals and songbooks, 4 19th-century items

—Edwinna C. Hillemeier

In addition to the repositories listed above, the following have also reported holdings of the materials indicated:

Bridgeport—Barnum Museum: programs, pictures, miscellaneous
Essex—Brenda Milkovsky: programs
Fairfield—Fairfield Historical Society: sheet music, songbooks
Guilford—Henry Whitfield State Historical Museum: songbooks, miscellaneous
Mystic—Mystic Seaport Association: recordings
New Fairfield—New Fairfield Free Library: songbooks
New Milford—New Milford Historical Society: songbooks, programs, pictures
Noank—Noank Historical Society: pictures
Norwalk—Norwalk Historical Commission: sheet music, miscellaneous
Norwalk—Henry Streb: sheet music, songbooks, pictures, miscellaneous
Old Lyme—Lyme Historical Society, Florence Griswold Association: sheet music
Preston—Preston Historical Society: songbooks, programs
Putnam—Putnam Public Library: miscellaneous
Rocky Hill—Rocky Hill Historical Society: songbooks, programs
Somers—Somers Historical Society: songbooks, programs
Stony Creek—Wallace Memorial Library: songbooks
Storrs—Congregational Church, Hale Donation Library: songbooks
Thomaston—Thomaston Historical Society: programs, pictures
Union—Union Historical Society: songbooks
Wallingford—Wallingford Historical Society: sheet music, songbooks, programs, pictures, recordings
Washington—American Indian Archaeological Institute: recordings
Washington—Gunn Memorial Library, Historical Museum: recordings
West Hartford—Emanuel Synagogue, Library: songbooks, recordings
West Hartford—Jewish Historical Society: programs, pictures, miscellaneous
West Willington—Willington Historical Society: songbooks, programs, pictures
Wethersfield—Webb–Deane–Stevens Museum: songbooks
Wilton—Wilton Library Association: songbooks, other printed music, programs, recordings
Windsor Locks—Connecticut Aeronautical Historical Association: sheet music

Delaware

210

DELAWARE DIVISION OF HISTORICAL AND CULTURAL AFFAIRS   De-Ar
Bureau of Archives and Records
Hall of Records
Dover, Delaware 19901

Eldridge Johnson (1867–1945, founder of the Victor Talking Machine Co.), personal papers, memorabilia, and photographs, in 1 file drawer; also 50 phonographs, 50 cylinders, and 12,000 78-rpm disc recordings

—Ann Baker

211
BRANDYWINE VALLEY FRIENDS OF OLD TIME MUSIC

Box 3504
Greenville, Delaware 19807

Materials concerning Appalachian, bluegrass, and other American folk music, including 3 linear meters of papers of the Friends, 1.8 linear meters of tape recordings of their performances, and their concert programs; also 60 linear cm. of photographs of musicians

—Carl Goldstein

212
ELEUTHERIAN MILLS–HAGLEY FOUNDATION   DeGE

Historical Library
Box 3630
Greenville, Delaware 19807

Sheet music, 2300 19th-century instrumental items, singly and in 42 bound vols.
Philadelphia Musical Saving and Loan Society, constitution and by-laws, 1857
Philadelphia Musical Fund Society, program of Haydn's *The Creation*, 1824
Music catalogues, 21 items from music and instrument dealers in Philadelphia and New York, 1880–1900

—Jon M. Williams

213
UNIVERSITY OF DELAWARE   DeU

Newark, Delaware 19711

Hugh M. Morris Library

Sheet music, 500 items; also 200 songsters and tunebooks, mostly pre-1860
Trade catalogues, ca. 1871–1924, 12 items, mostly for musical instruments and recordings

—Nathaniel H. Puffer

University of Delaware Folklore Archive

Folklore and Ethnic Art Center, 129 Memorial Hall

Materials documenting folk-music performers and musical traditions in Delaware and neighboring states, including 50 field collections, 100 audio- and video-tape recordings of concerts and festivals, and 300 slides, collected by students and campus folklorists. Subjects include black instrumental music and songs from Delaware and Maryland; local fiddle, banjo, and harmonica players and bluegrass groups; Maryland and Virginia ballad singing; Latin-American and other ethnic music in Wilmington; Nanticoke Indian music; and Eastern Shore commu-

nity minstrel shows. See the occasional publication *Delaware Folk Heritage* (Newark, 1978–   )

—Robert D. Bethke

214
FORT DELAWARE SOCIETY

Box 1251
Wilmington, Delaware 19899

Fort Delaware Cornet Band, sheet music of "Sounds from Fort Delaware," 1862; concert program from Salem, N.J., 1864; and 1 photograph, 1863
Ninth Delaware Regimental Band, 8 letters about band music, written by Sgt. Joseph Enos, 1864–65

—Gordon D. Patterson

215
HISTORICAL SOCIETY OF DELAWARE   DeHi

505 Market Street Mall
Wilmington, Delaware 19801

D. M. Grobe, ms music book with selections by I. A. and J. A. Grobe, n.d.; a music book with selections by Charles A. Grobe, ca. 1840; and 3 bound vols. of music owned by Nancy Elmer including some compositions by J. A. Grobe, 1840
Richard Hodgson's illuminated ms singing book, made by Capt. Richard Ellis, Maryland, 1787
Manuscript hymn tunes used at Old Swedes Church, 1828–45, in a notebook
William C. Lodge, ms music book for piano, including compositions by Isaac Solomons, n.d.
Philip P. Lyre, ms music book for tuba, Wilmington, 1879
Samuel Mansfield, ms tune book, Chestertown, Md., 1767
T. M. Todd, "Sounds from Fort Delaware," 1860s
Phoebe George Bradford, diaries, 1832–39, mentioning local musical entertainments
Felton Institute and Classical Seminary, 3 vols. of official records, 1869–1904
Masonic Hall (Wilmington opera house), documents relating to its construction, 1870s, and programs, 1879–80, in 12 folders
Millard Club (male chorus), ms book of minutes, and history of the Club, 1875–76
Musical Evening music club, minutes, 1891–96
National Association of Organists, Delaware Chapter, minutes, 1922–56
Orpheus Club papers, with programs, photographs, and records, 1917–68
Wilmington Music Commission, 2-vol. typescript (carbon copy) record of musical societies in Wilmington, 1800–1940, by T. Leslie Carpenter
Hymnals, ms and printed, of Alexander Armstrong (1833), Dr. John Brinckle (ca. 1839), John G. Robinson (1860), and Nathan Rumsey (ca. 1777)
Bound vols. of sheet music, 1830s

—Deborah J. Ancona

216

WILMINGTON INSTITUTE FREE   DeWI
LIBRARY AND NEW CASTLE COUNTY
FREE LIBRARY

Tenth and Market Streets
Wilmington, Delaware 19801

William M. S. Brown, "Heigho" for chamber orchestra, ms parts, ca. 1900; also published piano music and songs in 2 bound vols., ca. 1900–1910, and his "Our Delaware," 1907
David Kozinski, 2 ms items, n.d., and other choral music by him, in 1 bound vol.
Published sheet music and music for voice or piano, by composers from Wilmington or Delaware or of local interest, 150 items, ca. 1910–40
Hymnals, 5 items, ca. 1836– ; also Azariah Fobes, *Delaware Harmony* (1809)
Wilmington Choral Society, 1 bound vol. of programs, 1907–11
Recordings, including 25 78-rpm discs, ca. 1940

—Benedict Prestianni

217

Henry Francis du Pont   DeWint
WINTERTHUR MUSEUM

Winterthur, Delaware 19735

Joseph Downs Manuscript Collection, including 33 18th-century music mss, some of them Pennsylvania German and Ephrata items; 158 ms Shaker hymnals owned by Dr. Edward Deming Andrews, Pittsfield, Mass.; and 100 sheet-music items published before 1870, some with illustrated covers
Printed Books and Periodicals Collection, including 1 Germantown, Pa., hymnal, 1813; 12 bound vols. of 19th-century sheet music, indexed by engraver; and 35 late 18th- and early 19th-century popular songbooks, including John Aitken, *The Scots Musical Museum* (1790s)

—Eleanor McD. Thompson, Beatrice K. Taylor

In addition to the repositories listed above, the following have also reported holdings of the materials indicated:

Frederica—Commission on Archives and History, Barratt's Chapel Museum: songbooks
Milford—Milford Historical Society: pictures

District of Columbia

218

AMERICAN UNIVERSITY   DAU

Batelle–Tompkins Library
Massachusetts and Nebraska Avenues NW
Washington, D.C. 20016

Sheet music, 200 19th-century items owned by the Archibald Glover family of Washington, D.C.
Hymnals, 6 items, 1830–75
Esther Williamson Ballou (1915–73, composer and pianist), 750 items of personal papers including correspondence, music mss, notes, lectures, reviews of her performances, program notes, teaching materials, and 40 tape recordings of her performing and of first performances of her compositions

—James R. Heintze

219

Gillian B. ANDERSON

1320 North Carolina Avenue NE
Washington, D.C. 20002

Research materials concerning 18th- and 19th-century music in America, including photocopies of items documenting musical traditions in the colonies, and forming the basis of critical and performing editions by Anderson; photocopies, ms performing editions, and recordings of music from the colonies and early republic; lyrics of 1000 political and patriotic songs from colonial newspapers; notes on William Billings, Francis Hopkinson's *The Temple of Minerva*, and New England funeral practices; 10 early and mid 19th-

century tunebooks; and correspondence concerning American Bicentennial musical activities

220

ANDERSON HOUSE: MUSEUM OF THE SOCIETY OF THE CINCINNATI

2118 Massachusetts Avenue NW
Washington, D.C. 20008

Sheet music, 1 bound vol. containing 12 items of engraved dance music from Pennsylvania, dedicated to the Society of the Cincinnati, ca. 1790

—John D. Kilbourne

221

CATHOLIC UNIVERSITY OF AMERICA DCU

Music Library
Washington, D.C. 20064

Sheet music, 200 items, 1860–1940, including works by Amy Cheney (Mrs. H. H. A.) Beach and David Diamond, and Civil War songs
Songbooks, 8 vols. of popular music, late 19th century
Recordings, including 800 78-rpm discs and tapes of early classical-music releases

—Betty M. Libbey

222

COLUMBIA HISTORICAL SOCIETY   DCHi

1307 New Hampshire Avenue NW
Washington, D.C. 20036

Sheet music, 300 items from or about the District of Columbia, 19th and 20th centuries, including some by John Philip Sousa

Programs of local musical and theatrical events, mostly in scrapbooks; also papers of local theaters

—Perry Fisher

223
DISTRICT OF COLUMBIA PUBLIC LIBRARY   DWP

Martin Luther King Memorial Library
901 G Street NW
Washington, D.C. 20001

Washingtoniana Division

Hans Kindler (1892–1949, conductor of the National Symphony Orchestra), programs, 1931–49

Choral Society of Washington, minutes, 1892–1907, and bulletins, 1900–1905

National Symphony Orchestra, *Magazine*, 1930–70, and programs of the Watergate Concerts, 1935–50

National Theater of Washington, programs, 1876–1970

Files of clippings, leaflets, and pamphlets on Washington events, including music subjects, ca. 1930–

—Roxanna Deane

Music and Recreation Division

Hans Kindler Collection of orchestral parts, 600 sets; also 17 scrapbooks of press clippings about Kindler, including reviews

Sheet music, 6000 19th- and 20th-century items

Scores and other editions of all forms of music, 20,000 items, including American imprints and works by American composers

Vertical files of clippings and pamphlets, including 5 drawers of biographical materials, and 15 drawers of music and dance subjects of the U.S. and other countries

—Mary Lee Parker

224
FOLGER SHAKESPEARE LIBRARY   DFo

Washington, D.C. 20003

Charles B. Hanford (1859–1926), 10 boxes of ms part books for incidental orchestral music for Shakespearean plays, and 5 boxes of ms and published part books and musical scores for other plays and comic operas, ca. 1885–1915

Sheet music, 1 bound vol., mostly 19th-century English editions of works by Charles E. Horn

Playbills and programs, primarily 19th century, arranged by city, theater, and season. Items from opera houses and otherwise of musical interest are not separated or identified

—Sandra L. Powers

225
GEORGETOWN UNIVERSITY   DGU

Lauinger Memorial Library
Special Collections Department
Washington, D.C. 20057

Anton Gloetzner (faculty member, ca. 1875), 2 European music mss

John Gilmary Shea (1817–1891), personal papers, including 2 ms hymnals in Amerindian languages; also 14 late 19th- and early 20th-century published items

Sheet music, 300 popular-music items, late 19th and early 20th centuries

Programs of University concerts, 1820s–

Photographs of University concerts, 50 items, 1890s– , and 1 signed photograph of Oscar Hammerstein, Rudolph Friml, and Irving Berlin

Recordings of University music groups, 1930s–

—George M. Barringer

226
HOWARD UNIVERSITY   DHU

Washington, D.C. 20059

Moorland–Spingarn Research Center

Jesse E. Moorland Collection of Negro Life and History, including published materials described in the collection's *Dictionary Catalog* (Boston, 1970), vol. 6, pp. 190–270. Composers represented are Will Accooe (1 ms, ca. 1900), John S. Adams, Eubie Blake, James A. Bland, James T. Brymn, Henry T. Burleigh, Frank Albert Clark, Robert Cole (ms notebook), Samuel Coleridge-Taylor, Will Marion Cook, William Levi Dawson (3 mss), R. Nathaniel Dett, Carl Diton (1 ms), Edward Kennedy ("Duke") Ellington, Harry Lawrence Freeman, W. C. Handy, Donald Heywood, James Weldon Johnson, John Rosamond Johnson (1 ms), Edward Margetson, Lightfoot Solomon Michaux, Samuel Lucas Milady, Camille Nickerson, Maceo Pinkard, Florence B. Price (1 ms), Eli Shepperd, Christopher Smith, James M. Stewart, William Grant Still, Gerald Tyler, Joseph Josiah Walters, Clarence Cameron White (1 ms), Egbert Austin Williams, and John Wesley Work

Arthur B. Spingarn Collection of Negro Authors, including 2000 published sheet-music editions. The music holdings are described in the collection's *Dictionary Catalog* (Boston, 1970), vol. 2, pp. 657–784. Composers represented with extensive holdings include Amanda Ira Aldridge, J. Hubert Blake, James A. Bland, James T. Brymn, Henry T. Burleigh, Samuel Coleridge-Taylor, Will Marion Cook, Gussie Lord Davis, R. Nathaniel Dett, Edward Kennedy ("Duke") Ellington, Antonio Carlos Gomes, W. C. Handy, James B. Johnson, John Rosamond Johnson, John Turner Layton, Samuel Lucas Milady, Maceo Pinkard, Florence B. Price, Noble Sissle, Christopher Smith, William Grant Still, Thomas ("Fats") Waller, Clarence Augustus Williams, Egbert Austin Williams, and Spencer Williams

Marian Anderson Collection, chiefly microfilms of press clippings on the Daughters of the American Revolution controversy resulting from her being denied permission to perform at Constitution Hall in 1939, also papers of the Marian Anderson Citizens Committee, and the Marian Anderson Mural Fund Committee, including letters from Mary McLeod Bethune, Katharine Hepburn, Eleanor Roosevelt, and Leopold Stokowski, and programs and broadsides, 1939–45

Owen Vincent Dodson (b. 1914, playwright) Papers, ca. 1930–68, 1080 items, including ms plays and music, correspondence, photographs, clippings, programs, reviews, and other materials

Gregoria Fraser Goins (1883–1964, founder of the Gregorian Studio of Music and a women's string orchestra in Washington) Papers, 2.5 linear meters, including biographical materials, family correspondence, financial records, papers of the National Association of Negro Musicians, the Washington Music Teachers' Association, and the Treble Clef Club, also ms music, photographs, programs, clippings, diaries, notebooks, and memorabilia

Carl R. Gross Collection, with a press scrapbook of Sissieretta Jones (singer), 1891–93

Louis Vaughn Jones (1896–1965, violinist) Collection, with 4 scrapbooks of correspondence, programs, broadsides, photographs, financial papers, memorabilia, and biographical data

Andy Razaf (Paul Andreamentania Razafinlariefo, 1895–1973, songwriter), 30 linear cm. of papers, including correspondence, clippings, programs, photogrpahs, a scrapbook of published biographical information, 2 bound vols. of published songs, and memorabilia

Isabele Taliaferro Spiller (music teacher, a member of the "Musical Spillers" with her husband, William N. Spiller, 1912–26, and founder of the Spiller School of Music, 1926) Papers, 295 items, 1906–54, including photographs, correspondence, biographical materials, programs, clippings, and memorabilia; also programs of the Harlem Evening School, Wadleigh High School, and the WPA Federal Music Project in the New York City area

LeRoy Tibbs Collection, 3 scrapbooks documenting the New York nightclub and theater careers of Tibbs (a pianist) and his wife, Marie Young Tibbs (actress), including music scores, clippings, photographs, correspondence, and memorabilia, 1921–49

Washington Conservatory of Music Records, 5619 items, 1887–1966 but mostly 1905–41, including correspondence, organization and student records, financial papers, notebooks, programs, photographs, scrapbooks, sheet music, published musical scores, clippings, periodicals, and memorabilia; also biographical data, correspondence, and personal papers of the Conservatory's founder, Harriet Gibbs Marshall, and her husband, Napoleon Bonaparte Marshall, with drafts of her book, *Story of Haiti* (Boston, 1930)

—Thomas C. Battle, Esme E. Bhan

Fine Arts Library

Original mss and holograph scores by black composers, particularly Hall Johnson and James Rosamond Johnson, in all 300 items, mostly 1920s–40s

Published scores, American works scattered in a general collection of 5000 items, mostly classical

—Catherine Bounds

Channing Pollock Theatre Collection

500 Howard Place, Room 139. See the collection's descriptive brochure

William Warren II, 4 diaries, 2 dramatic scrapbooks, letters, and promptbooks concerning theater in the U.S., particularly the Boston Museum, 1847–88

Sheet music, 1500 items, 1880s– , mostly 1913–30s

Programs, contracts, photographs, and other musical-theater materials, scattered in various theatrical collections

—Marilyn Mahanand

227
LIBRARY OF CONGRESS　　　　DLC
Washington, D.C. 20540

Specific items as noted are mentioned in the *Annual Report of the Librarian of Congress*, 1909–39 (hereinafter cited as *AR*), and since 1941, usually in greater detail, in the *Library of Congress Quarterly Journal* (formerly the *Quarterly Journal of Current Acquisitions;* hereinafter cited as *QJ*). See also the Music Division's brochure, "Musical Americana on Microfilm" (1977; hereinafter cited as *MAM*)

Music Division

A. *Overview and Survey of the Americana Classes*
B. *Major Autonomous Americana Collections*
C. *Other Composers' Holograph Collections*
D. *Single Music Manuscripts*
E. *Personal Papers*
F. *Single Letters*
G. *Miscellaneous Manuscripts*
H. *Other Materials*

Other Units

J. *Copyright Records and Depository Copies*
K. *Archive of Folk Song*
L. *Motion Picture, Broadcasting, and Recorded Sound Division*
M. *Other Divisions*

A. Music Division: Overview and Survey of the Americana Classes

For general background see Harold Spivacke, "The Music Division of the Library of Congress," *Library Trends*, 8 (1960), 566–73; Carroll D. Wade, "The Music Division in the Library of Congress," *Fontes artis musicae*, 16 (1969), 109–12; and *The Music Division: A Guide to its Collections and Services* (Washington, 1972)

Materials in the collection will have received one of four forms of bibliographical organization, in matters of cataloguing, classification, and shelving identity. These forms are as follows:

First, cataloguing with classification. Most books about music (class ML), all libretti, many theoretical works (class MT), and a small but the most important part of the music (class M), have received descriptive cataloguing and classification within the general collections. Before 1939, this was done in the Music Division; thus this material is seldom found in the published Library of Congress catalogues, or in the *National Union Catalog,* except for most of the books about music. Important items which have been added to the collections or re-catalogued since 1939, on the other hand, have received their cataloguing in the library's Processing Department, or for a time through the Copyright Office

Second, classification only. A good deal of the published music, both in M and MT classes—copyright depository copies in particular—have been given a class number and a filing initial only. Since cataloguing is not involved, there is no record of the location. Users seeking music of a certain kind will find the item in its appropriate class, while the staff can usually find specific items on the basis of descriptive information

Third, special collections, mostly as listed in section B below, also often in sections C and E. The material is sometimes catalogued, in which case a special class number is assigned

Fourth, copyright depository materials arranged by copyright registration numbers, as discussed in section J below

Several classes in the music classification scheme are devoted entirely or mostly to U.S. music, as listed below. "Items" indicates the number of physical entities on the shelves. Of these, a high proportion may be duplicates, often as much as 30 percent in classes which contain mostly post-1900 copyright deposits. "Entries" includes the total number of cards in the Music Division's classed catalogues, or for ML and MT materials, in the official shelflist in the Processing Department. (The classed catalogue, it should be pointed out, often includes material relevant to the scope of the class, but which is classified elsewhere. Thus, for instance, there are 412 items in class M 2116, but 238 other pre-1820 hymnals elsewhere in the collections. Conversely, it will be seen that the vast majority of the songs in class M 1622 fall in the second category of treatment, i.e., classification only, with no cataloguing.)

Class	Items	Entries
American sheet music to 1860 (including the following:)		38,000
American sheet music to 1820		
M 1 .Al	5,000	
Copyright deposits		
M 1 .A12 I, V, Z	14,000	
Single sheets, 1820–60		
M 1 .A13	29,000	
Bound volumes (uncatalogued)		
M 1 .A15	10,000	
Civil War piano music		
M 20 .C58-61	944	75
American songsters		
M 1628	1122	1125
Popular songs		
M 1622	50,000	400
M 1630.2	97,000	64,000
(of the latter, 20% estimated pre-1941)		
Major patriotic songs		
M 1630.3	550	600
War songs, pre-Civil War		
M 1631.6	75	200
Civil War songs		
M 1637-42	1700	4850
Spanish-American War songs		
M 1643-44	700	625
World War I songs		
M 1646	2790	400

Class	Items	Entries
State and city songs		
M 1657-58.5	3500	3400
Songs in honor of particular persons		
M 1659	1125	1300
Songs for political parties		
M 1660-65	1320	375
Racial and emigré songs		
M 1668-71	3000	2850
Songs of patriotic societies		
M 1676-77	250	250
Songs of other societies		
M 1900-1921	700	600
College songs		
M 1945-60	1400	1100
Songs of trade, labor, professional, occupational, and other topical groups		
M 1977-78	1835	3750
Hymnals, pre-1820		
M 2116	412	650
Hymnals, post-1821		
M 2117-32	3650	3225
Temperance and gospel songbooks		
M 2198-99	11,500	9350
Journals and periodicals (titles, including post-1940 items)		
ML 1	4752	1500
Musical organizations		
ML 27	1050	400
Libretti, pre-1850		
ML 50.6	85	100
Books on U.S. music history		
ML 200	570	675
Books on U.S. folk music		
ML 3551-62	1344	1400
Publications of educational institutions		
MT 4	1000	500

Among the items included are many miscellaneous gifts, including Rev. Edwin H. Bookmyer, books and sheet music (AR, 1929, p. 163); Congressman Usher L. Burdick, sheet music (AR, 1937, p. 141); the Mendez Cohen estate, with much pre-1820 sheet music (AR, 1931, p. 200); Helen M. Craig (AR, 1931, p. 202); J. Francis Driscoll, sheet music (AR, 1928, p. 121, and 1929, p. 164), also materials from the library of Caroline Schetky Richardson (QJ, 16:12–13, 19–20); Charles J. Dyer (AR, 1925, p. 98); Hannah Fox, early U.S. sheet music (AR, 1928, p. 122); the Anna Maria Gansevoort Collection (AR, 1940, p. 144; complete list, pp. 476–85); Dr. Fielding H. Garrison (AR, 1915/16, p. 74); Edmond Charles Geñet (1763–1834), sheet music (AR, 1941, p. 122); Philip Hale, books about music, with his annotations (AR, 1939, p. 203); Miss J. L. Hart, sheet music (AR, 1921, p. 58); Micah Hawkins (1777–1825), sheet music; George S. Hodges (AR, 1919, p. 55); Dr. Clara S. Ludlow, music from 1830–50 (AR, 1919, p. 56); William Augustine Newland, music library (AR, 1930, pp. 198–208, with detailed lists); Thurlow W. Parker et al, sheet music, 1790–1830 (AR,

1915/16, p. 72); Mrs. E. R. Poole, sheet music, 1830–60 (*AR*, 1929, p. 168); Mrs. Harold Randolph, the collection assembled by Mrs. James A. Gary (*AR*, 1934, p. 118); Mrs. Francis Tazewell Redwood (*AR*, 1920, p. 69, and 1928, p. 123); Mrs. William Adams Slade (*AR*, 1939, p. 199, with a list); and Mrs. W. S. Telford, including flute music (*AR*, 1934, p. 118)

Other acquisitions, considered significant enough to be listed in the *AR* but without specific provenance, appear in 1903, p. 223 (psalmody); 1909, p. 37; 1913/14, p. 88 (editions of music by Edward A. MacDowell); 1915/16, p. 74; 1922, p. 73; 1925, p. 106 (sheet music, 1820–60); 1931, p. 231, (pre-1820 sheet music); 1934, p. 120; 1935, p. 136; 1940, p. 145 (pre-1820 imprints); 1940, p. 146 (tunebooks, including works by Lowell Mason); 1940, pp. 485–89; and 1943, p. 198 (pre-1820 imprints)

Class M 3.3 is devoted to first editions of music by major composers. Included here are published works of Stephen C. Foster and Edward A. MacDowell, as cited respectively in Oscar G. T. Sonneck and Walter Whittlesey, *Catalogue of the First Editions of Stephen Foster* (Washington, 1915), and Oscar G. T. Sonneck, *Catalogue of the First Editions of Edward MacDowell* (Washington, 1917)

In addition, other published music may be found in the various special collections listed below, e.g. the extensive collection of scores in the Tams–Witmark collection (section H below)

B. Music Division: Major Autonomous Americana Collections

Elizabeth Sprague Coolidge Foundation collection. The Foundation, established in 1925 by Mrs. Coolidge (1864–1953), is devoted to the commissioning of new chamber music, of which the holograph scores have come to be part of the Foundation's collection, as listed in *Autograph Musical Scores in the Coolidge Foundation Collection* (Washington, 1950). In addition, the collection includes 200 portrait photographs, many of them inscribed, also 16 linear meters of correspondence, including letters from Béla Bartók, Elliott Carter, Pablo Casals, Aaron Copland, Charles Ives, Serge Koussevitzky, Gustave Reese, and William Schuman

Damrosch family collection, comprising documents relating to the careers of Leopold Damrosch (1832–85), Frank Damrosch (1859–1937), and Walter Damrosch (1862–1950), and their various activities involving the Metropolitan Opera, the People's Choral Union, the Institute of Musical Art (precursor of the Juilliard School), and the NBC "Music Appreciation Hour." Included are music mss of Leopold and Walter Damrosch, biographical writings, programs, clippings, photographs, drawings, presentation copies of music editions, and scrapbooks, in all 16 linear meters. See the inventory, also *AR*, 1934, p. 118; and *QJ*, 20:33, 47; 21:44; 25:52–53; 28:46, 66–67; and 31:31–32

Geraldine Farrar (1882–1967), collection of scripts, contracts, programs, playbills, scrapbooks, and photographs, also 700 items of correspondence with Sarah Bernhardt, David Belasco, Lucrezia Bori, Georg Droescher, Emma Eames, Olive Fremstad, Amelita Galli-Curci, Giulio Gatti-Casazza, Lilli Lehmann, Lotte Lehmann, Lily Pons, Rosa Ponselle, and Kate Douglas Wiggin, in all 6 linear meters. See *The Autobiography of Geraldine Farrar: Such Sweet Compulsion*

(New York, 1938); also *QJ*, 12:48; 22:56; 25:75; and 28:56

George and Ira Gershwin Collection, including holograph scores and sketches, student notebooks, scrapbooks, financial statements, contracts, personal library vols., and film and stage production scripts of George Gershwin (1898–1937), as assembled by Ira Gershwin; also personal correspondence and drafts of lyrics by Ira Gershwin, including letters involving Merle Armitage and Kurt Weill, and photographs; in all 5.5 linear meters. See *AR*, 1939, p. 182; also *QJ*, 4:65; 11:127–39; 17:23; 18:23; 19:22; 21:23; 25:53, 75; 26:22; 27:68; 29:49; and 31:32; and Frank C. Campbell, "Some Manuscripts of George Gershwin," *Manuscripts*, 6 (1954), 66–75

Leopold Godowsky (1870–1938), 52 holograph mss of his virtuoso piano music, also business papers, clippings, printed music, photographs, notes for the biography of Godowsky by his nephew, Leonard Saxe, and records of legal disputes. See *AR*, 1938, p. 161; 1939, p. 187; and *QJ*, 17:24, 22:42; and 28:46–48

Koussevitzky Music Collection. The activity of the Koussevitzky Foundations (the one in Brookline, Mass. founded 1942, and the one in Washington, founded 1950) involves the commissioning of new music, for which the holographs mss are in the Library. In addition there are the correspondence, clippings, programs, photographs, business papers, and notebooks, mostly post-1920s, of Serge Koussevitzky (1874–1951), in all 11 linear meters. See *QJ*, 9:35–36, and 18:25. Also recently added to the collection are the correspondence and personal papers of Olga Koussevitzky

Charles Martin Loeffler (1861–1935), collection of holograph music, some of it provided by his publisher, G. Schirmer; literary mss, programs, and press clippings, 1882–1935; also correspondence with Pablo Casals, Elizabeth Sprague Coolidge, Isabella Stewart Gardner, Lawrence Gilman, Philip Hale, Edward Burlingame Hill, Amy Lowell, Pierre Monteux, John Singer Sargent, and Edgard Varèse, in all 2 linear meters. See *AR*, 1912, p. 74; 1935, p. 136; and 1937, p. 140; also *QJ*, 1:6–14; 6/1:31;`12:47; 14:15; 15:16, 33; and 23:32

Marian and Edward MacDowell Collection, including holographs of music by Edward A. MacDowell (1861–1908), some of them presented by George Templeton Strong; other letters, including 138 letters to his wife, Marian MacDowell (1857–1956); 300 photographs by or relating to MacDowell; his early self-portrait drawing; and letters to Mrs. MacDowell relating to the operation of the MacDowell Colony, Peterborough, N.H.; in all 3 linear meters. See *AR*, 1904, p. 318; 1905, p. 63; 1912, p. 74; 1930, pp. 189–90; 1940, p. 141; and 1942, p. 121; also *QJ*, 14:16; 15:26; 17:30; 30:39, 59; 26:23; 28:48; 30:310–11; and 31:32, 34, 41–42, 63–64

Leonora Jackson (Mrs. W. Duncan) McKim (1879–1969) Collection, including literary works and musical compositions, printed music, photographs, clippings, programs, and watercolors, in all 3.5 linear meters, as an adjunct to the McKim Fund, established 1970 for the support of chamber music for violin and piano. See *QJ*, 30:35

Dayton C. Miller Flute Collection, including books and music as well as the instruments assembled by Miller (1866–1941, professor of physics at the Case School of Applied Science, Cleveland). U.S. materials are included in the collections of 3000 books about music, 4000 published items, portraits and autographs of flautists and composers of flute music, programs, pamphlets, press clippings, patent specifications, prints and photographs, sales catalogues, correspondence with musicians, dealers, and instrument makers in 8 file drawers, and research notes. See *AR*, 1941, p. 121; *QJ*, 19:32 and 28:59; David Shorey, "Dayton C. Miller Collection," National Flute Association *Newsletter*, 2 (1977), 13; and Miller's *Catalogue of Books and Literary Material Relating to the Flute and Other Musical Instruments* (Cleveland, 1935)

Rachmaninoff Archive, including holograph mss, personal papers, and memorabilia of Sergei Rachmaninoff (1873–1943), 8 linear meters. Included is extensive correspondence with Feodor Chaliapin, Nina Koshets, Serge Koussevitzky, and Leopold Stokowski. See the detailed shelflist prepared by Sophie Satin, Rachmaninoff's sister-in-law; also *QJ*, 9:39–42; 14:19; 20:63–64; 28:46, 5l; and 29:54

Arthur C. Schmidt Collection, comprising 50 vols. of financial, organizational, and other archival records, including plate books; 100,000 items of correspondence in 114 boxes, of which 84 are devoted to work with composers; music mss, many of them holograph, used for published editions, including works of Gena Branscombe, Amy Cheney (Mrs. H. H. A.) Beach, George W. Chadwick (100 items), Henry Clough-Leighter, Charles Dennee, Arthur Foote (250 items), Leopold Godowsky, Henry K. Hadley, John Knowles Paine, and Margaret Ruthven Lang; signed photographs of musicians associated with the firm; and other documents

Arnold Schoenberg (1874–1951), collection of correspondence, mostly post-1933, including letters from Rudolf Kolisch, Ernst Krenek, Gustav Mahler, and Thomas Mann; drafts and carbon copies of business letters; programs; and press clippings; in all 1.5 linear meters. See *AR*, 1926, p. 135; 1928, p. 135; 1935, p. 135; 1939, p. 183; and 1940, p. 140; and *QJ*, 6/1:31, 7/1:36, 9/1:34, 36, 10:42–44, 11:20–22, 12:45, 14:20, 15:27, 16:16–17, 19:33, 20:47, 21:37, 22:32, 46, 23:34, 24:70, 25:78, 28:60, 29:54, and 31:43

C. Music Division: Other Composers' Holograph Collections

The following musicians are represented in the Library's holdings by definitive or extensive collections of music mss, also by other materials as noted: George Antheil, including letters to Mary Curtis Bok Zimbalist (*QJ*, 13:38, 20:31, 25:51, 26:21, 36, 30:48, 31:28, 59, and 34:2–22); Victor Babin (*QJ*, 11:25; 31:29); Samuel Barber (*QJ*, 1:87, 12:46, 13:26, 14:19, 15:15, 16:9, 17:19, 18:15, 19:17, 21:29, 23:20, 24:54, and 15:61); Amy Cheney (Mrs. H. H. A.) Beach (*AR*, 1924, p. 102; *QJ*, 5:46); Robert Russell Bennett (*QJ*, 25:59, 62); William Bergsma (*QJ*, 9/1:35, 16:8, 18:15, 19:19, 20:31, 21:29, 22:34, 23:20, 25:63); Leonard Bernstein, music mss (*QJ*, 13:23, 16:9, 17:20, 19:18, 21:29, 23:20, 24:56, 26:27), also 107 scrapbooks (*QJ*, 24:78, 31:56); Arthur Bird (*AR*, 1924, p. 103; *QJ*, 20:31); Ernest Bloch, music mss and sketches, scrapbooks, and family and personal papers (*AR*, 1929, p. 162; 1940, p. 450; 1925, p. 94; 1930, p. 188; and *QJ*, 27:51, 31:30, 12:50, 23:29, 24:27, 25:75, 26:36, 27:67); Dudley Buck, music mss and personal correspondence (*AR*, 1907, p. 47; 1912, p. 74; and *QJ*, 10/1:40); Charles Wakefield

Cadman, music mss and personal letters (*AR*, 1916, p. 74; *QJ*, 7/1:43, 22:35, 42); John Alden Carpenter, music mss, scrapbooks, and personal correspondence (*QJ*, 10/1:41, 11:20, 13:26, 18:17, 20:32, 60, 21:22, 36); Elliott Carter, music mss and personal correspondence (*QJ*, 17:48, 19:19, 20:32, 21:30, 22:35, 25:63, 26:27, 27:57, 31:35); Mario Castelnuovo-Tedesco, music mss and personal correspondence (see Nick Rossi, *Catalogue of Works by Mario Castelnuovo-Tedesco* [New York, 1977], pp. 142–47; also *QJ*, 25:63); George W. Chadwick (*AR*, 1910, p. 49; 1912, p. 74; and *QJ*, 9/1:38); Theodore Chanler, music mss and personal correspondence (*QJ*, 23:12); Aaron Copland, music mss and personal correspondence (*QJ*, 1/2:73, 5/1:43, 46, 9/1:35, 15:20, 16:9, 17:22, 18:21, 19:19, 20:32, 21:31, 22:36, 23:21, 24:56, 25:65, 26:28, 27:58, 28:52); Henry Cowell, music mss and personal correspondence (*QJ*, 5/1:46, 10/1:40, 13:20, 14:11, 15:17, 16:10, 17:23, 18:21, 19:21, 20:23, 21:31, 22:37, 23:21, 24:48, 25:52, 27:52, 30:49); Julian Edwards (*AR*, 1912, p. 74); Alvin Etler (*QJ*, 20:33, 21:31, 23:21, 25:66, 26:28, 27:59, 28:53); Irving Fine, music mss, scrapbooks, memorabilia, photographs, press clippings, and programs (*QJ*, 15:19, 21:31, 22:37, 24:50, 25:53, 26:22, 27:53, 82, 28:46, 29:49, 30:49, 31:32); Ross Lee Finney, music mss and personal papers (*QJ*, 7/1:35, 11:25, 15:23, 17:21, 18:22, 21:31, 22:38, 24:57, 25:66, 27:59, 27:35, 28:28); Arthur Foote, music mss and personal papers (*AR*, 1914, p. 88; 1936, p. 134; 1937, pp. 141–42; 1941, p. 125; and *QJ*, 16:15, 23:17); Eleanor Everest Freer (*AR*, 1919, p. 54; 1921, p. 57; 1925, p. 98; 1926, p. 126; 1928, p. 122; 1929, p. 164); Don Gillis (*QJ*, 23:21, 25:66, 26:29, 28:56); Anton Gloetzner; Percy Grainger, music mss and personal papers (*AR*, 1938, p. 161; *QJ*, 16:15, 20:35) on film, originals now at the Grainger Museum, University of Melbourne, Australia (q.v.); Roy Harris (*AR*, 1934, p. 118; 1935, p. 136; 1936, p. 133; 1940, p. 139; 1942, p. 123; and *QJ*, 5/1:46, 17:24, 18:23, 19:23, 21:32, 22:38, 25:66, 26:30, 28:53); Anthony Philip Heinrich, mss, published music, and memorabilia (*AR*, 1916/17, p. 61: *QJ*, 10/1:42); Victor Herbert, a "substantial portion of his musical estate" (*AR*, 1914, p. 88; 1925, p. 98; 1935, p. 134; 1936, p. 141; 1939, pp. 178, 182; and *QJ*, 1/3:87, 12:46, 13:22, 15:19, 17:25, 18:24, 19:31, 23:17, 24:50, 25:86, 26:22, 27:78); Alan Hovhaness (*QJ*, 13:38, 17:26, 18:24, 19:24, 21:32, 22:38, 23:22, 24:58, 25:67, 26:30, 27:60); Philip James (*QJ*, 17:35, 18:29, 25:67, 27:60, 68, 29:52); André Kostelanetz, ms copies of his music and personal papers; Fritz Kreisler, music mss, programs, clippings, photographs, and memorabilia (*AR*, 1939, p. 187; *QJ*, 13:23, 24:65, 29:50); Ernst Krenek, music mss and personal papers (*AR*, 1940, p. 140; *QJ*, 5/1:46, 15:19, 27:61); Ezra Laderman (*QJ*, 25:31); Hugo Leichtentritt, a few personal papers, mostly music compositions; Daniel Gregory Mason, music mss, correspondence, and personal papers (*AR*, 1921, p. 57; *QJ*, 6/1:32, 9/1:38); Arne Oldberg (*QJ*, 11:25, 29:54, 31:34, 64); George Perle, personal papers (*QJ*, 26:41); Walter Piston, music mss and personal papers (*AR*, 1937, p. 42; *QJ*, 5/1:46, 8/1:36, 10/1:40, 15:17, 20, 16:11, 17:30, 18:26, 19:27, 20:40, 21:34, 22:39, 23:25, 25:26, 72, 26:33); Cole Porter (*QJ*, 21:34, 22:40); David Raksin (*QJ*, 14:16, 26:33, 27:63, 28:55, and 35:142–72); Richard Rodgers (*QJ*, 13:24, 14:16, 15:22, 16:12, 17:31, 18:26, 19:28, 20:40, 21:34, 24:60, 26:34); Sigmund Romberg (*QJ*, 15:22, 16:12, 17:31, 18:26, 20:41, 21:26, 26:43–45);

William Schuman (*QJ*, 1/3:87, 5/1:43, 9/1:35, 12:49, 13:25, 14:17, 15:23, 16:13, 17:31, 19:29, 20:41, 25:72, 27:64, 28:55); Ruth Crawford Seeger (*AR*, 1938, p. 161; *QJ*, 13:25, 25:57); John Philip Sousa (*AR*, 1939, pp. 178, 184; *QJ*, 1/2:74, 5/1:45, 11:15, 12:47, 27:56); Leo Sowerby (*AR*, 1925, p. 96; *QJ*, 14:17, 17:32, 18:27, 19:30, 20:42, 21:35, 22:40, 23:26, 24:62, 25:73, 26:24); Eduard Steuermann; William Grant Still (*AR*, 1936, p. 133; *QJ*, 24:62); Igor Stravinsky (*AR*, 1929, p. 163; 1939, pp. 179, 184; 1942, p. 123; and *QJ*, 5/1:46, 7/1:34, 13:39, 20:42, 23:26, 24:62, 25:73, 26:35, 27:65, 28:55); George Templeton Strong (1856–1948), music mss and personal papers (*AR*, 1930, p. 189); Deems Taylor (*AR*, 1924, p. 103; 1940, p. 452; and *QJ*, 11:24, 17:34, 25:59); Virgil Thomson (*AR*, 1938, p. 162; *QJ*, 23:28); and Burnet C. Tuthill (*AR*, 1932, p. 154; *QJ*, 5/1:46, 7/1:40, 10/1:40, 11:25, 12:46, 14:18, 17:34, 19:30, 31:65)

D. Music Division: Single Music Manuscripts

The following composers are represented in the collection by one or more music mss: H. Aides (*AR*, 1919, p. 57), Percy Button Arant (*AR*, 1919, p. 57), Harry Armstrong (*AR*, 1938, p. 161), Percy Lee Atherton (*QJ*, 25:51), Frederic Ayres (*AR*, 1926, p. 125; 1927, p. 103), Milton Babbitt (*QJ*, 29:51), Parker Bailey (*AR*, 1942, p.22), John Epanimontas Balamos (*QJ*, 14:13), J. Murray Barbour (*QJ*, 25:62, 26:26), Edward Shippen Barnes (*QJ*, 17:23), Marion Bauer (*QJ*, 17:19), Daniel Melchior Beltzhoover (*AR*, 1925, p. 96), Paul Benoit (*QJ*, 15:18), Nicolai Berezowsky (*AR*, 1940, p. 450), Arthur Berger (*QJ*, 30:53), Irving Berlin (text of "God Bless America"), William Billings (*AR*, 1940, pp. 139, 450), Alberto Bimboni (*QJ*, 28:45), Seth Bingham (*QJ*, 5/1:46, 15:18), Eubie Blake ("Charleston Rag," 1917), Ralph Blane (*QJ*, 21:30), Marc Blitzstein (*QJ*, 9/1:36), Sol Bloom (*QJ*, 7/1:40), Edward W. Bok (*QJ*, 24:50), Samuel Bollinger, Eugene Bonner (*QJ*, 31:64), Joseph Bonnet (*QJ*, 14:13), Francis Boott (*AR*, 1938, p. 161), Felix Borowski (*QJ*, 10/1:40, 15:18), Paul Bowles (*QJ*, 26:27), George F. Boyle (*QJ*, 31:61), William B. Bradbury, Gena Branscombe, Henry Dreyfus Brant (*QJ*, 22:35, 28:52), George F. Bristow (*AR*, 1916, p. 73), Radie Britain (*QJ*, 28:52), Howard Brockway (*QJ*, 15:16), Charles Faulkner Bryan (*QJ*, 14:13, 15:18), Frederick Field Bullard (*AR*, 1928, p. 122; 1934, p. 117), Cecil Burleigh, Natalie Burlin, Frederick Russell Burton (*AR*, 1924, p. 102), Adolf Busch (*QJ*, 5/1:43), John Cage (*QJ*, 31:34), T. Frederick H. Candlyn (*QJ*, 29:49), Charles Frederick Carlson, Hoagy Carmichael, Benjamin Carr (2 vols.; *MAM*), Philip Greeley Clapp, Frederic Clay (*AR*, 1932, p. 154), Edward B. Claypoole, Grace Cotton Marshall Clough-Leighter, Henry Clough-Leighter (*AR*, 1912, p. 74), Louis Adolphe Coerne (*AR*, 1923, p. 74; 1924, p. 102; 1929, p. 163; 1932, p. 151), Rossetter Gleason Cole (5 mss), Ulric Cole (*AR*, 1932, p. 151), Zez (Edward Elezear) Confrey (*QJ*, 10/1:40), Frederick S. Converse (*AR*, 1912, p. 74; 1930, p. 188; 1941, p. 122; and *QJ*, 15:16), Carlton Cooley (*QJ*, 7/1:40), Helen C. Crane (*AR*, 1940, p. 450), Paul Creston (*QJ*, 15:17, 22:37, 23:21, 25:65, 26:28, 27:58, 28:52, 29:52), Ingolf Dahl (*QJ*, 15:19, 20:33), Carl Deis (*QJ*, 1/3:87), Reginald De Koven (*QJ*, 5/1:45), Eric De Lamarter (*QJ*, 19:21), Norman Dello Joio (*QJ*, 13:26, 15:23), William D. Denny (*QJ*, 13:21), David Diamond (*QJ*, 5/1:46, 9/1:36), Marcel Dick, Howard Dietz (*QJ*, 21:35), Fannie Charles Dillon (*AR*, 1938, p. 161), Laurence Dilsner (*QJ*, 17:23), William

H. Doane, W. O. Dolan (*AR*, 1919, p. 55), John Dressler (*QJ*, 15:18, 16:10), James Philip Dunn, Pierre Landrin Duport (dance and instrumental music, 1777-1834, in 3 vols., 1 prepared for his granddaughter, George Anne Reinagle; *MAM*), Garth Edmundson (*QJ*, 15:18, 16:10), Cecil Effinger (*QJ*, 5/1:46), Henry Eichheim, Georges Enesco (*QJ*, 10/1:40, 31:62), Carl Engel, Carl Eppert (*QJ*, 29:49), C. A. Erck (*AR*, 1920, p. 67), Blair Fairchild (*AR*, 1938, p. 182), Arthur Farwell (*QJ*, 15:18), Gottfried H. Federlein, Giuseppe Ferrata, John Alden Finckel (*QJ*, 13:21), Caryl Florio, Adolph Martin Foerster (*AR*, 1910, p. 49; 1924, p. 102), Cecil Forsyth, Fay Foster, Stephen Collins Foster, Arnold Franchetti (*QJ*, 20:34), Johan Franco (*QJ*, 13:26, 27:59), Marcel Gustave Frank (*QJ*, 14:13), Sigurd Frederiksen (*AR*, 1938, p. 161), James Friskin (*QJ*, 29:49), Genevieve Davisson Fritter (*AR*, 1941, p. 124), J. Frank Frysinger, Mrs. Lyman J. Gage, Rudolph Ganz (*QJ*, 14:13), Louis Gesensway, Robert Wilson Gibb (*QJ*, 17:23), Henry F. Gilbert (*AR*, 1914, p. 88; 1915, p. 93; 1928, p. 135), William Wallace Gilchrist (*AR*, 1933, p. 92), James Robert Gillette, Aurelio Giorni (*QJ*, 27:53), Edwin Franko Goldman, Wallace Goodrich (*AR*, 1942, p. 123), Eugene Goossens (*AR*, 1941, p. 122), Louis Moreau Gottschalk (*AR*, 1926, p. 132; 1928, p. 134), Morton Gould (*QJ*, 26:30, 28:53), Hans Gram, Marcel Grandjany (*AR*, 1940, p. 450), Charles Tomlinson Griffes (*AR*, 1923, p. 74; 1942, p. 123; and *QJ*, 21:24, 95), Elliot Griffis (*QJ*, 19:23), Carl Hugo Grimm (*QJ*, 15:18), Ferde Grofé (*QJ*, 13:26), Rudolph Gruen (*QJ*, 25:55), Louis Gruenberg (*AR*, 1938, p. 161), David W. Guion, Henry K. Hadley (*AR*, 1912, p. 74; 1931, p. 203; 1938, p. 161; and *QJ*, 13:27, 15:32), Alexei Haieff (*QJ*, 25:66, 26:30, 31:35), Edmund Haines (*QJ*, 27:59), W. C. Handy (*AR*, 1939, p. 182), Benjamin Hanna, Howard Hanson (*AR*, 1925, p. 96; *QJ*, 10/1:39, 15:24, 24:58, 25:66, 26:30, 27:60, 28:53), Erwin E. Harder (*AR*, 1919, p. 55), Lou Harrison (*QJ*, 13:21), Charles Haubiel (*QJ*, 29:52), Carl Hauser (*QJ*, 27:54), Roland Hayes (*QJ* 17:24), Bernhard Heiden (*QJ*, 15:19, 16:9), James G. Heller (*AR*, 1932, p. 152), Theodore Henckels (*AR*, 1919, p. 56), Francis Hendricks, Bernard Herrmann (*QJ*, 15:20), John Hill Hewitt (*AR*, 1929, p. 166), Edward Burlingame Hill (*AR*, 1938, p. 161; *QJ*, 15:32, 31:36, 63), M. Wood Hill, Paul Hindemith (*AR*, 1938, p. 161), Helen Hopekirk, Charles Jerome Hopkins (*AR*, 1931, p. 203), Francis Hopkinson (*AR*, 1920, p. 70), Edward Horsman (*AR*, 1929, p. 165), Elmer Arne Hovdesen (*QJ*, 15:18), Julia Ward Howe (*AR*, 1938, p. 162), Mary Howe (*AR*, 1940, pp. 139, 450; 1941, p. 125; and *QJ* 5/1:46, 7/1:40, 17:26), William Henry Humiston (*AR*, 1916, p. 74), Henry Holden Huss, Ernest Hutcheson (*AR*, 1930, p. 189), Charles Ives, Frederick Jacobi (*AR*, 1937, p. 142; 1938, p. 162; 1939, p. 182; and *QJ*, 27:54, 28:48), Werner Janssen (*AR*, 1931, p. 204), Clayton Johns, Francis Johnson "holograph ms" (*MAM*), J. Rosamond Johnson, Edgar Stillman Kelley (*AR*, 1914, p. 88; 1940, p. 451), Jerome Kern (*AR*, 1939, p. 182; *QJ*, 18:25), Harrison Kerr (*AR*, 1942, p. 123), George Kiallmark (*QJ*, 22:55), Ralph Kinder, Bruno Oscar Klein, Gustav Klemm (*QJ*, 6/1:30), Rudolf Kolisch (*AR*, 1940, p. 451), Boris Koutzen (*AR*, 1939, p. 183), A. Walter Kramer (*QJ*, 29:50), Ernest R. Kroeger (*QJ*, 24:51), Alexander Kyle (*AR*, 1923, p. 85), Charles Lagourgue (*AR*, 1941, p. 125), Burton Lane (*QJ*, 21:33, 24:59, 25:70), Henry Albert Lang (*AR*, 1941, p. 125;

QJ, 7/1:40), Margaret Ruthven Lang, Earl Roland Larson (QJ, 16:10), Wesley La Violette (AR, 1935, p. 136; 1936, p. 134; and QJ, 13:27, 18:25), Benjamin Lees (QJ, 31:35), Alois F. Lejeal, Leo Rich Lewis (AR, 1912, p. 73), Vachel Lindsay (AR, 1931, p. 203), Normand Lockwood (AR, 1942, p. 122; QJ, 16:11), Harvey Worthington Loomis (QJ, 9/1:38), Nikolai Lopatnikoff (QJ, 26:31, 27:61), Mary Lord (AR, 1921, p. 57), Louis Leslie Loth, Augusta Lowell, Robert Lowry, Frances McCollin (AR, 1940, p. 451), Alexander MacFadyen, Will C. Macfarlane, Francis Howard McKay (QJ, 29:52), George F. McKay (QJ, 14:13, 20:34, 24:59, 28:54), Colin McPhee (QJ, 13:23, 21:33), Hubert P. Main, Albert Hay Malotte (AR, 1938, p. 162), Simeon Buckley Marsh, Hugh Martin (QJ, 21:30), Eduardo Marzo, Lowell Mason, William Mason (AR, 1912, p. 74; 1930, p. 190), Alexander Matthews, Edward Gould Mead (QJ, 29:52), Gian Carlo Menotti (QJ, 13:38, 15:17, 16:8, 11), Jan Meyerowitz (QJ, 15:19), Paul Th. Miersch (AR, 1916, p. 74), Darius Milhaud (QJ, 27:62), Russell King Miller, Rodney Milns (QJ, 23:39), Douglas Stuart Moore (QJ, 5/1:46, 19:26, 20:40, 22:55, 26:32, 27:56, 29:51, 30:50), Mary Carr Moore, Haydn M. Morgan (QJ, 16:10), Harold Morris (AR, 1940, p. 451), Joseph Mosenthal (AR, 1935, p. 144), Thomas P. Murphy, Nicolas Nabokov (AR, 1942, p. 123; QJ, 5/1:46), W. H. Neidlinger (QJ, 7/1:40), Ethelbert Nevin (AR, 1909, p. 36; 1912, p. 74), George B. Nevin (AR, 1920, p.66), T. Tertius Noble (QJ, 10/1:40), John Jacob Niles, Geoffrey O'Hara, Leo Ornstein, Ignace Jan Paderewski (AR, 1940, p. 451), John Knowles Paine (AR, 1908, p. 39; 1941, p. 123), Mari Paldi, Robert Palmer (QJ, 9/1:35), Horatio Parker (AR, 1912, pp. 73–74), J. C. D. Parker (AR, 1920, p. 66), Harry Partch (QJ, 15:19), George Perle (QJ, 26:32, 27:63), Vincent Persichetti (QJ, 13:23, 15:24, 21:34, 22:39, 23:24, 24:60, 25:72, 26:33, 27:63, 28:55), George W. Persley, Burrill Phillips (QJ, 15:19, 24, 17:21, 23:24), Quincy Porter (QJ, 1/2:74, 5/1:43, 46, 7/1:40), Capt. A. Prevost (AR, 1929, p. 167), Francis Johnson Pyle (QJ, 15:24), Gardner Read (QJ, 26:33, 27:64), Robert B. Reed (QJ, 13:28, 20:34), Alexander Reinagle (AR, 1905, p. 63; MAM), Rudolf Réti (QJ, 30:50), Wallingford Riegger (QJ, 16:12, 19:28), Leroy Robertson (AR, 1937, p. 142; 1938, p. 162), Martin Röder, Clara Kathleen Rogers, Harold Rome (QJ, 21:34, 26:34), George F. Root, Edward Royce (QJ, 16:15), Beryl Rubinstein (AR, 1940, p. 451), Carl Ruggles, George Alexander Russell, Mary Turner (Mrs. Sumner) Salter, Carlos Salzedo (AR, 1924, p. 102; 1932, p. 153), Lazare Saminsky (AR, 1925, p. 98; 1937, p. 142; 1940, pp. 140, 451; and QJ, 7/1:40), Ira D. Sankey (AR, 1919, p. 55), Jacob Schaefer, Ernest Schelling (AR, 1912, p. 74; 1939, p. 183; 1941, p. 125), George J. Schetky (QJ, 16:12), Kurt Schindler, Charles Schirrmann (QJ, 17:23), Ludwig Schneider (AR, 1917, p. 57), Henry Schoenefeld, Alexander Schreiner (QJ, 15:18), Arthur Schwartz (QJ, 21:35), Roger Sessions (QJ, 9/1:36, 16:8, 18:26, 19:29, 20:42, 23:26), Abel Shattuck (AR, 1934, p. 119), Arthur Shepherd (AR, 1937, p. 142), Elie Siegmeister (QJ, 24:61, 29:53), Charles Sanford Skilton, David Stanley Smith (AR, 1940, p. 452; QJ, 10/1:40, 11:19), Oscar Sonneck, Charles Gilbert Spross, Patty Stair, Royal Stanton (QJ, 16:10), Constantin Sternberg (AR, 1926, p. 126), Augusta C. Stetson (AR, 1919, p. 55), Halsey Stevens (QJ, 15:19), Frederick A. Stock, Albert Stoessel (QJ, 17:33), Lily

Strickland, William Strickland (QJ, 24:63), Edwin John Stringham (QJ, 28:56), Gustav Strube (AR, 1940, p. 452), W. Oliver Strunk, Josef Suk (AR, 1933, p. 92), Alexandre Tansman (AR, 1942, p. 122), Albert Alfred Taylor (QJ, 14:13), Raynor Taylor (AR, 1936, p. 134), Arthur Wilder Thayer, Randall Thompson (AR, 1942, p. 122), Harry Tierney (QJ, 21:35, 26:25), Ernst Toch (AR, 1939, p. 184; QJ, 28:51), Arthur Tregina (AR, 1919, p. 56), Alfred Dudley Turner, Godfrey Turner (QJ, 5/1:46), Camil Van Hulse (QJ, 20:34), Carl Venth (AR, 1940, p. 452; 1941, p. 125), Robert E. Vick (AR, 1919, p. 56), Max Wilhelm Karl Vogrich (QJ, 30:53), Bernard Wagenaar (QJ, 5/1:46), Franz Wasner (QJ, 16:10), Joseph Watson (AR, 1935, p. 153), Franz Waxman (QJ, 14:18), Adolf Weidig (AR, 1914, p. 88), Hugo Weisgall (QJ, 18:28, 19:31, 20:43, 21:35, 27:65), Charles Wesley (AR, 1926, p. 132), D. Wescott (AR, 1919, p. 57), Willy White (AR, 1940, p. 452), Bessie M. Whiteley (AR, 1940, p. 452), Emerson Whithorne (AR, 1937, p. 141; QJ, 20:44), Arthur Whiting (AR, 1938, p. 162), Thomas Carl Whitmer (AR, 1917, p. 57; 1938, p. 162), John Wiegand, Christopher à Beckett Williams (QJ, 16:10), Owen Wister (QJ, 11:23, 13:157, 27:56, 26:246, 28:51), Stefan Wolpe (QJ 23:29), Louise Drake Wright, Robert Craig Wright (QJ, 28:56), Pietro Alessandro Yon, Vincent Youmans (QJ, 22:40, 24:54, 25:58), Eugene Ysaÿe, and Arnold Zemachson (QJ, 21:28)

E. Music Division: Personal Papers

Major collections of personal papers, including letters, correspondence, and other materials, from Hugh Aitken (QJ, 31:36), Harold Bauer (QJ, 16:14–15; 17:35; 19:18, 31), Paul Bekker (AR, 1940, p. 140), Carl Engel (AR, 1935, p. 135), Ossip and Clara (Clemens) Gabrilowitsch (QJ, 22:42), Richard Franko Goldman (QJ, 5/1:45), Glenn Dillard Gunn (QJ, 30:62), Oscar Hammerstein II (letters, scripts, notes, photographs, and other materials; QJ, 20:39), Richard S. Hill, Anne A. Hull, the Kneisel Quartet (QJ, 6/1:32), John McCormack (QJ, 28:59, 30:54), John Paul Morgan, Paul A. Pisk (QJ, 31:36, 65), Rudolf Réti (correspondence, printed and ms music, research materials, press clippings, and photographs), Francis Scala (correspondence, ms music, and other records of the U.S. Marine Band, 1855–74; QJ, 5/1:46; see also David M. Ingalls, *Francis Scala, Leader of the Marine Band from 1855 to 1871* [Master's thesis, Catholic University of America, 1957]), the Schirmer family (QJ, 6/1:33), Fabien Sevitzky, Nicolas Slonimsky, Oscar Sonneck (including materials from his personal library, programs, correspondence, research notes, music mss, and memorabilia, also materials involving Carl Engel and Nelson Eddy; AR, 1921, p. 57; 1926, p. 142; 1929, p. 168; 1930, p. 215; 1935, p. 135; 1942, p. 123; and QJ, 5/1:45, see also the reference by Allen P. Britton and Irving Lowens in M.L.A. *Notes*, 11 [1953], 34–35), Alexander Wheelock Thayer (AR, 1931, p. 204), Theodore Thomas (46 notebooks with ms programs of his concerts, also correspondence), Helen Traubel, William Treat Upton (research notes), Samuel Prowse Warren (correspondence and other personal documents, including 78 incoming letters, 19 of them from Dudley Buck; AR, 1939, pp. 187–88), Ethel Waters, Carl Wistach (sheet music and lecture notes), and Henry Clay Work (correspondence and other personal papers; *AR*, 1938, p. 167; 1939, p. 187; see also Richard S. Hill, "The Mysterious Chord of Henry Clay Work," M.L.A. *Notes*, 10 [1953], 211–25, 367–90)

F. Music Division: Single Letters

The various catalogued and uncatalogued collections also include one or several letters by Juliette (Mrs. Crosby) Adams, Clarence Adler, Richard Aldrich, Modest Altschuler (*QJ*, 17:14), Ugo Ara, Merle Armitage, Percy Lee Atherton, Frederic Ayres, Eben Howe Bailey, Theodore Baker, George Barati, Georges Barrère, Lionel Barrymore, Marion Bauer, John Parsons Beach, Wheeler Beckett, Nicolai Berezowsky, Arthur Berger, Charles-Wilfride de Beriot (*QJ*, 7/1:43), Irving Berlin, Adolfo Betti, Johanna M. Beyer, E. Power Biggs, Clarence C. Birchard, Arthur Bird, David S. Bispham, John Henry Blake (papers with material on "The Star-spangled Banner," *AR*, 1919, p. 55), Ralph Blane, Marc Blitzstein, Artur Bodanzky, Mary Louise Curtis Bok, Joseph Bonnet, Lucrezia Bori, Felix Borowski, Coenraad V. Bos, Catherine Drinker Bowen, Paul Bowles, William B. Bradbury, Marianne Brandt, Gena Branscombe, Carl Ernest Bricken (*QJ*, 31:36), Antonia Brico, George F. Bristow, Radie Britain, Horace Britt, Howard A. Brockway, Antonio Brosa, Mark Brunswick, Ole Bull, John N. Burk, Natalie Burlin, Adolph Busch, Carl Busch, W. Foley Bush, Irving Caesar, John Cage, Emma Calvé, Eddie Cantor, William Crane Carl, Julian Carrillo (*AR*, 1929, p. 163), Enrico Caruso, Minto Cato, Charles Chaplin, Mary Tibaldi Chiesa, Philip Greeley Clapp, Rebecca Clarke, Edward B. Claypoole, Charles V. Clifford (*NUCMC*, 72–1784), Chalmers Clifton, George M. Cohan, Rossetter Gleason Cole, C. C. Converse, Frederick S. Converse, Russell Ames Cook, James Francis Cooke, Richard Copley, Mildred Couper, Sidney Cowell, Paul Creston, Bainbridge Crist, Mrs. F. S. Crofts (*QJ*, 31:36), Ingolf Dahl, Walter Dahms, Hollis Ellsworth Dann, Mabel Wheeler Daniels, Archibald T. Davison, Mary Cardwell Dawson, Désiré Defauw, Carl Deis, Reginald De Koven, Eric De Lamarter, Norman Dello Joio, Frances Densmore, Joseph De Pasquale, Leonard De Paur, Elena De Sayn, Margarethe Dessoff, R. Nathaniel Dett, David Diamond, Clarence Dickinson, Howard Dietz, Angela Diller, Fannie Charles Dillon, Oliver Ditson, Mrs. Ernö Dohnányi, Richard F. Donovan, Antal Dorati, Tommy Dorsey, Celius Dougherty, Olin Downes, Jessica Dragonette, Ruth Draper, Paul Dresser, Henry S. Drinker, Arcady Dubensky, Vernon Duke, Paul Lawrence Dunbar, Katherine Dunham, John Sullivan Dwight, Peter Dykema, Emma Eames, Clarence Eddy (*QJ*, 6/1:35), Shepard N. Edmonds, Cecil Effinger, Henry Eichheim, Alfred Einstein (*AR*, 1941, p. 124), Leonard W. Ellinwood, Mischa Elman, Arthur Elson, Louis C. Elson, Herbert Elwell, Daniel Decatur Emmett, Lehman Engel, Carl Eppert, John Lawrence Erb, Heinrich Wilhelm Ernst (*QJ*, 7/1:43), John Erskine, Alvin Etler, Lillian Evanti, David Ewen, Blair Fairchild, W. Lynnwood Farnam, Geraldine Farrar, Arthur Farwell, Charles Norman Fay (*AR*, 1933, p. 92), Rodman Fay, Zoltan Fekete, Arthur Fickenscher, Arthur Fiedler, Henry T. Finck, Irving Fine, Ross Lee Finney, William Arms Fisher, Minnie Maddern Fiske, Jerzy Fitelberg, Harry Harkness Flagler, Harold Flammer, William Flanagan, Helen Harkness Flanders,

Carl Flesch, Alice C. Fletcher (*QJ*, 6/1:35), Charles Foley, Arthur Foote, Lukas Foss, Stephen Collins Foster (contract; *AR*, 1932, p. 153), Johan Franco, Alfred Frankenstein, Benjamin Franklin, Sam Franko, Isadore Freed, Harry Lawrence Freeman, Eleanor Everest Freer, Olive Fremstad, James Friskin, Anis Fuleihan, Clara Clemens Gabrilowitsch, Ossip Gabrilowitsch, Fortune Gallo, Rudolph Ganz (*QJ*, 14:19, 16:15), Mary Garden (*QJ*, 7/1:43), Giulio Gatti-Casazza, Harvey B. Gaul, Eva Gauthier, Karl Geiringer, George Gershwin, Ira Gershwin, Miriam Gideon, Henry F. Gilbert, Lawrence Gilman, Patrick S. Gilmore (*QJ*, 19:31), Harry Glantz, David Glazer, Anton Gloetzner, Leopold Godowsky, Percy Goetschius, Edwin Franko Goldman, Karl Goldmark (*QJ*, 20:46), Rubin Goldmark, Boris Goldovsky, Vladimir Golschmann, Otto Gombosi, Eugene Goossens, Jacques Gordon, Morton Gould, Martha Graham, Percy A. Grainger, Marcel Grandjany, Felix Greissle, Charles T. Griffes, Elliot Griffis, Sidney Griller, Ferde Grofé, Louis Gruenberg, Glenn Dillard Gunn, Henry K. Hadley (*QJ*, 14:19), B. H. Haggin, Philip Hale, Oscar Hammerstein, Oscar Hammerstein II, W. C. Handy, Howard Hanson, Otto Harbach, Edgar Y. Harburg, Ethel Ramos Harris, Roy Harris, Charles Haubiel, Roland Hayes, Jascha Heifetz, Hans Heinsheimer, W. J. Henderson, Victor Herbert, Bernard Herrmann, DuBose Heyward, Ethel Glenn Hier, Henry Lee Higginson, Edward Burlingame Hill, M. Wood Hill, Mildred J. Hill, Paul Hindemith, Theodor Hoch (*QJ*, 23:31), Josef Hofmann, Helen Hopekirk, Francis Hopkinson (letter from Benjamin Franklin; *QJ*, 20:46, 27:67), Vladimir Horowitz, Rosalie Housman, Alan Hovhaness, John Tasker Howard, Julia Ward Howe (*AR*, 1940, p. 141), Mary Howe, Anne Hull, Alfred Human, William Henry Humiston, James Gibbons Huneker, Sol Hurok, Zora Neale Hurston, Henry Holden Huss, Ernest Hutcheson, Ernest Hutchinson (*QJ* 7/1:43), Charles Ives, Mrs. Charles Ives (letters to Elliott Carter; *QJ*, 29:53), George Pullen Jackson (*QJ*, 19:32), Frederick Jacobi, Philip James, Werner Janssen, Alice C. Jennings (letter concerning Rev. Samuel F. Smith; *AR*, 1942, p. 120), Gunnar Johansen, Edward Johnson, James P. Johnson, James Weldon Johnson, Thor Johnson, Werner Josten, Arthur Judson, Otto Hermann Kahn (*QJ*, 7/1:43), Milton Katims, Edgar Stillman Kelley, Francis Scott Key, Pierre van Rensselaer Key, John Kiltz (letter to John Muir; *QJ*, 10/1:42), Hans Kindler, Omega King, Otto Kinkeldey, Hazel Gertrude Kinscella, John Kirkpatrick, Ralph Kirkpatrick, Lincoln Kirstein, Marc Klaw, Franz Kneisel, Erich Wolfgang Korngold, Hugo Kortschak, Serge Koussevitzky, A. Walter Kramer, Louis Krasner, Henry Edward Krehbiel, Fritz Kreisler, Boris Kroyt, Gail Kubik, Margaret Ruthven Lang, Paul Henry Lang, Nick La Rocca, Wesley La Violette, Lucile Lawrence, Warner Lawson, Filip Lazar, Minna Lederman, Ethel Leginska, Lille Lehmann, Hugo Leichtentritt, Erich Leinsdorf, Oscar Levant, Josef Lhévinne, Rosina Lhévinne, William Lichtenwanger, Goddard Lieberson, Jenny Lind (*AR*, 1919, p. 56; *QJ*, 21:36), Vachel Lindsay, Charles Martin Loeffler, Arthur Loesser, John Avery Lomax, Nikolai Lopatnikoff, Joseph Losey, Arthur Lourié, Amy Lowell, Otto Luening, Bascom Lamar Lunsford, Robert Guyn McBride, John McCormack, Harl McDonald, Edward A. MacDowell, Robert McFerrin, Robert MacGimsey,

George F. McKay, Colin McPhee, Joseph E. Maddy, Alma (Schindler) Mahler, Gustav Mahler, Edward M. Maisel, Joseph Malkin, Nicolai Malko, Thomas Mann, Clara Damrosch Mannes, David Mannes, Leopold Mannes, Robert W. Manton, Luther and Marian Marchant, Mathilde (Graumann) Marchesi, Harriet Gibbs Marshall, Bohuslav Martinů, Pietro Mascagni (*QJ*, 23:34), Daniel Gregory Mason, Henry Lowell Mason, Lowell Mason, William Mason, Elizabeth Mayer, Rosario and Mildred Mazzeo, Edward Gould Mead, Nellie Melba, Arthur Mendel, A. Tillman Merritt, Darius Milhaud, Dayton C. Miller, Renee Longy Miquelle, Howard Mitchell, Dimitri Mitropoulus, Richard Mohaupt, John Mokrejs, Hans Moldenhauer, Georges Moleux, Ferenc Molnar, Pierre Monteux, Douglas Stuart Moore, Earl V. Moore, Geraldine Morgan, J. P. Morgan, Mrs. John P. Morgan, Albert Morini, Jerome Moross, Lawrence Morton, Karl Muck, Nicolas Nabokov, Emma Nevada, Ethelbert Nevin (*AR*, 1940, p. 141), Camille Nickerson, Edouard Nies-Berger, Arthur Nikisch, John Jacob Niles, Christine Nilsson (*QJ*, 7/1:43), T. Tertius Noble, Lillian Nordica, Paul Nordoff, Charles O'Connell, Geoffrey O'Hara, Arne Oldberg (*QJ*, 29:54), Alphonse Onnou, Eugene Ormandy, Leo Ornstein, Vladimir de Pachmann, John Knowles Paine (*QJ*, 16:15), Henry Taylor Parker, Horatio Parker, Harry Partch, Radiana Pazmor, Arthur Penn (*QJ*, 16:15), Ashley Pettis, Carl Pfatteicher, Isidor Philipp (*QJ*, 14:19), Burrill Phillips, Michel Piastro, Gregor Piatigorsky, Jacques Pillois, Paul Amadeus Pisk, Walter Piston, Lily Pons, Cole Porter, Quincy Porter, Ezra Pound, John Powell, Maud Powell, Waldo Selden Pratt, Theodore Presser (*QJ*, 7/1:41), William Primrose, Sigurd Rascher, Gardner Read, Napoleon Reed, Gustave Reese, Fritz Reiner, Nathan Richardson, (*AR*, 1925, p. 97), Wallingford Riegger, Julie Rivé-King, Paul Robeson (form letter signed by stamp), Bill ("Bojangles") Robinson, Earl Robinson, Richard Rodgers, Artur Rodzinski, Bernard Rogers, Clara Kathleen Rogers, Mary R. Rogers, Ann Ronell, Julius Römtgen, George F. Root (*QJ*, 15:27), Paul Rosenfeld, Moriz Rosenthal, Hugh Ross, Anton Rubinstein (*QJ*, 22:46), Beryl Rubinstein, Olga Rudge, Dane Rudhyar, Carl Ruggles, César Saerchinger, Carlos Salzedo, Olga Samaroff, Lazare Saminsky, Pitts Sanborn, Eduardo Sanchez de Fuentes, Carl Sandburg, Jesús Mariá Sanromá, Winthrop Sargeant, Antonia Sawyer, Rosario Scalero, Ernest Schelling, Joseph Schillinger, Kurt Schindler (edited personal papers and mss; *AR*, 1936, p. 132; *QJ*, 31:64), Gustave Schirmer, Rudolph E. Schirmer, E. Robert Schmitz, Artur Schnabel, Georg Lennart Schnéevoigt, Alexander Schneider, Mischa Schneider, Arnold Schoenberg, William Schuman, Ernestine Schumann-Heink, Irving Schwerké, Carl Seashore, Charles Seeger, Ruth Crawford Seeger, Anton Seidl, Marcella Sembrich, Rudolf Serkin, Roger Sessions, Fabien Sevitzky, Harry Rowe Shelley, Arthur Shepherd, Elie Siegmeister, Ernest W. Simms, Noble Sissle, Charles Sanford Skilton, Lewis Slavit, Nicolas Slonimsky, Carleton Smith, Carleton Sprague Smith, David Stanley Smith, Melville M. Smith, Moses Smith, Samuel Francis Smith (*AR*, 1942, p. 120), Nikolai Sokoloff, Izler Solomon, Oscar Sonneck, John Philip Sousa, Leo Sowerby, Sigmund Spaeth, Albert Spalding, Walter Raymond Spalding, Timothy Mather Spelman, Harold Spivacke, William

Steinberg, Alexander Lang Steinert, Constantin Sternberg, Halsey Stevens, Fritz Stiedry, William Grant Still, Frederick A. Stock, Carl Stoeckel, Albert Stoessel, Sigismond Stojowski, Anson Phelps Stokes, Leopold Stokowski, Gerald Strang, Josef Stransky, Igor Stravinsky, William Strickland, George Templeton Strong, Gustav Strube, W. Oliver Strunk, Thomas Whitney Surette, Ottilie Sutro, Rose Laura Sutro, Alfred Swan, Donald M. Swarthout, Kay Swift, Raymond Gram Swing, George Szell, Joseph Szigeti, Alexandre Tansman, Davidson Taylor, Deems Taylor, Alexander Tcherepnin, Nicolas Tcherepnin, Henri Temianka, Leon Theremin, Theodore Thomas, Oscar Thompson, Randall Thompson, Virgil Thomson, Lawrence Tibbett, Glenn Tindall, Ernst Toch, Arturo Toscanini, Burnet C. Tuthill, William Treat Upton, Bruno David Ussher, David Van Vactor, Carl Van Vechten, Edgard Varèse, Isabelle Vengerova, John Verrall, John Vincent, Arnold Volpe, Bernard Wagenaar, Charles Ludwig Wagner, Joseph Frederick Wagner, Alfred Wallenstein, Bruno Walter, Samuel Prowse Warren, Edward N. Waters, Kurt Weill, Adolph Weiss, Roy Dickinson Welch, Clarence Cameron White, Paul Whiteman, Emerson Whithorne, Arthur Whiting, Gertrude Clarke Whittall, John Finlay Williamson, H. Wintter-Watts, Felix Wolfes, Mabel Wood-Hill, G. Wallace Woodworth, Henry Clay Work, Joseph Yasser, Eugen Zador, Fannie Bloomfield Zeisler, and Efrem Zimbalist

G. Music Division: Miscellaneous Manuscripts

Ephrata (Pa.) community, ms music books, including "Die bittre gute . . . Turtel-Taube," 1764; a copy of the *Paradisisches Wunder-Spiel*, 1751; and miscellaneous music books, ca. 1745–72, some from Henry D. Maxwell (*AR*, 1932, p. 157; 1928, p. 122; and *MAM*)

Music from the colonial and post-colonial periods, including William O. Adams, music book dated London, 1795, with American and English vocal and dance music (*MAM*); Wilkes Allen, "Apollo" collection, 1790 (*MAM*); Henry Beck, flute book with 180 tunes, dated 1786 (*MAM*); Bellamy Band, ms music book, 1799 (*MAM*); Israel L. Cohen, ms collections of marches, duets, songs, and dances, mostly "adopted to the violin"; D. Jesse Ewell, flute collection, 1826 (*MAM*); Eleanor Parke (Custis) Lewis (1779–1852), books of ms and printed music from the Washington family collection (*MAM*); Samuel Morse, marches and dances, dated Newburyport, Mass., 1811 (*MAM*); Edward Murphy, instrumental collection, 1790 (*MAM*); Abel Shattuck, instrumental collection, ca. 1801 (*MAM*); 3rd New Hampshire Volunteer Infantry, band music from Port Royal Island, S.C., ca. 1851 (*MAM*; other vols. are at the New Hampshire Antiquarian Society, Hopkinton, and the New Hampshire Historical Society, Concord); and Isaac Young, Shaker music treatise, New Lebanon, Ohio, 1833 (*Cook*, p. 286)

Biographical reports, including F. Nicholls Crouch, "holograph account" by Edward H. Droop (*AR*, 1932, p. 152); J. C. D. Parker, ms biographical sketch by Mary A. Thayer (*AR*, 1920, p. 70); and Henry M. Rogers, paper on John Barnett (*AR*, 1926, p. 127); also questionnaires from composers returned to Claire Reis in connection with her *Composers in America* (New York, 1930)

Miscellaneous composers' holographs presented by music publishers, among them John Church Co. (*AR*,

1915–16, p. 75), Oliver Ditson Co. (*AR*, 1930, p. 189; 1931, p. 202), J. Fischer & Bro. (*AR*, 1909, p. 36; 1921, p. 55), Hubert P. Main (*AR*, 1915–16, p. 75), Arthur P. Schmidt (*AR*, 1913–14, p. 89), C. F. Summy, and others (*AR*, 1917–18, p. 56)

Other collections of composers' holographs, including those of the National Federation of Music Clubs (*AR*, 1918, p. 57); Hugo Riesenfeld, collection of "classical jazz" (*AR*, 1924, p. 103); BMI traveling exhibition of serious and popular music (*QJ*, 14:10); sections of the autograph collection of Ernest Urchs (*AR*, 1931, p. 218); and miscellaneous items (*AR*, 1916–17, p. 58; 1923, p. 73; 1924, pp. 102, 105)

H. Music Division: Other Materials

Organizational archives, including the American Federation of Musicians, miscellaneous papers (*AR*, 1934, p. 117); California Federation of Music Clubs, records (*AR*, 1921, p. 57); *Modern Music* (formerly the League of Composers *Review*), business papers, including correspondence of its editor, Minna Lederman (Mrs. Mell Daniel), with letters from George Antheil, Theodore Chanler, Aaron Copland, Frederick Jacobi, Lincoln Kirstein, Lazare Saminski, and others, also typescripts of articles, including Bertold Brecht's unpublished "The Usage of Music in the Epic Theatre," photographs, 2 scrapbooks, and original drawings of composers, with a list of correspondents and introductory essay by Mrs. Daniel; Music Critics' Association; Music Educators' National Conference, archives and early materials on music education in the U.S. (*AR*, 1941, p. 123); Music Library Association; Music Teachers' National Association (*AR*, 1938, p. 159); National Federation of Music Clubs (*AR* 1940, p. 138), also an extensive card catalogue of contemporary American composers (*AR*, 1926, p. 127) and further material, including music mss (*AR*, 1941, p. 123; *QJ*, 1:88); National Music Council, collection of publications on patriotic themes (*AR*, 1942, p. 123); National Negro Opera Association; New York Philharmonic-Symphony Orchestra, microfilms of the archives, 1842–1956, known as the Bruno Walter Microfilm Collection (*QJ*, 17:47), also of the catalogue of works performed (*QJ*, 18:36) and of the Constitution of 1824 (*QJ*, 19:39); Society for the Foundation of a National Conservatory of Music, papers of Rose and Ottilie Sutro; Society for the Preservation of the American Musical Heritage, as directed by Karl Krueger (1894–1979); Society for the Publication of American Music (*AR*, 1920, p. 69); Society of Friends of Music in the Library of Congress (*AR*, 1921, p. 58); and WPA Federal Music Project, miscellaneous files, including a catalogue of the orchestral music in New York (United Service Organization, Raymond Kendall, coordinator) (*QJ*, 1:88) and a "Record of program operations and accomplishments," 1935–43, prepared by George Foster (*QJ*, 1:89). Material on music in the Federal Theatre Project is now located at George Mason University, Fairfax, Va. (q.v.)

Scrapbooks, of Mrs. Will C. Banks, with autographs of prominent midwestern musicians (*AR*, 1937, p. 141); John Alden Carpenter, 3 vols. (*QJ*, 20:60); E. E. Clarke, on Boston concert life, ca. 1870–83; Rebekah Crawford, various vols. devoted to autograph letters, musical post cards, press clippings, photographs, and other materials (*AR*, 1924, p. 101; 1925, p. 97; 1929, p. 164; 1930, p.

188; 1932, p. 202; 1933, p. 92; 1934, p. 116); Arthur Hauser, a vol. kept by his parents, 1882–83 (*QJ*, 12:50); Ada Joyce Jones, 17 vols. on concert life, ca. 1880–ca. 1916; Mrs. William Bruce King, scrapbook of writings by Henry E. Krehbiel in the *New York Tribune*, 1895; Elena de Sayn, 6 vols. concerned with the career of Amy Cheney (Mrs. H. H. A.) Beach (*QJ*, 17:35); Leo P. (Leonidas Polk) Wheat, autograph and photograph album (*AR*, 1932, p. 152); and Henry J. Winterton, 25 vols., also 5 additional linear meters of cartons of material on organists and organs. Other vols. are in the general collections and in the collections of special materials (see sections B and C above)

Programs (in addition to the general collection of bound vols. and other miscellaneous materials), including 5000 Baltimore items and related materials, 1915–55, in all 10 linear meters, from Broughton Tall (music critic); 200 Boston programs, tickets, and other materials, from the collection of William G. A. Turner (*AR*, 1926, p. 128); 38 Cornell University organ recitals, 1919–20, from James T. Quarles (*AR*, 1921, p. 59); New York opera and concert programs from Samuel Prowse Warren (*AR*, 1916–18, p. 61); New York programs of Ernest Schelling's children's and young people's concerts (*AR*, 1931, p. 204); San Francisco programs of the Bohemian Club, 10 items (*AR*, 1921, p. 58); Washington Choral Society, programs, 1884–1901, from H. M. Paul (*AR*, 1920, p. 69); programs sponsored by the National Broadcasting Company (*AR*, 1937, p. 146) and by the Columbia Broadcasting System (*AR*, 1921, p. 59); and miscellaneous foreign and U.S. programs, presented by Oscar Sonneck (*AR*, 1921, p. 59)

Pictorial materials, including 2 oil portraits of Arnold Schoenberg, 1 a self-portrait (*QJ*, 14:24) and the other by George Gershwin (*QJ* 16:17); miscellaneous portraits and photographs, including the collection of James T. Powers and Rachel Booth (*QJ*, 14:38), the collection of Mr. and Mrs. Patrick J. Hayes (*QJ*, 26:44), operetta composers of the 1920s (*QJ*, 7:36), and miscellaneous autographed collections (*QJ*, 20:59, 30:62); also a portrait index to the collection, on cards, compiled 1920s–30s?

Tams–Witmark Collection, 140 boxes of opera and operetta materials, including 650 complete and incomplete orchestral scores, 250 piano-vocal scores, 5 libretti, and sets of parts

Osbourne McConathy collection, 800 vols. on music instruction, mostly from Germany, acquired before 1891 by the family of Lowell Mason for use in their various educational activities

Material relating to "The Star-spangled Banner" (*AR*, 1941, p. 118); other materials presented by Joseph Muller (*AR*, 1935, p. 151) and in the papers of Richard S. Hill (section E, above). See also William Lichtenwanger, "The Music of 'The Star-spangled Banner'" (*QJ*, 34:136–70)

Publishing documents, including Simeon Wood (Boston music publisher), account book, 1818–21 (*QJ* 12:43); Lowell Mason, 322 proofsheets for a tunebook (*AR*, 1940, p. 145); and 94 phonograph-recording catalogues from Philip L. Miller (*AR*, 1942, p. 123)

Reference indexes, including the Music Division authority file, 16,000 cards, assembled 1902–43; an index of composers according to states, 2100 cards, assembled ca. 1925; and an index to theme-song titles from sound films, 7000 cards, assembled 1930s

—Barbara Henry, Gillian Anderson, Wayne Shirley

J. Copyright Records and Depository Copies

For the specific purpose of this report, the documentary evidence of music copyright in the U.S. is directed toward two topics: first, the copyright records and other copyright documents, in the Copyright Office of the Library of Congress and elsewhere, as a source of bibliographical information on U.S. published music; and second, the deployment of depository copies and other depository materials, especially those items—mostly sheet music—which are filed by copyright number, and hence accessible through copyright information. While many music copyright deposits have been added to the Library's classified collections, a large proportion of the material is still arranged by copyright number (cf. section A above). For general background, see G. Thomas Tanselle, "Copyright Records and the Bibliographer," *Studies in Bibliography*, 22 (1969), 77–124 (hereinafter cited as *Tanselle*); also William Lichtenwanger, "94–553 and All That; Ruminations on Copyright Today, Yesterday, and Tomorrow," M.L.A. *Notes*, 35 (1979), 803–18, and 36 (1980), 837–48

Copyright Records

U.S. District Court, copyright ledgers, 1790–1870, in the Rare Book and Special Collections Division, as summarized in *Tanselle*, pp. 122–23. Other ledgers, located in various regional repositories, are cited by *Tanselle*, pp. 83 and 123–24, along with various published transcripts of the records

Miscellaneous correspondence with claimants, duplicate ledgers, and other copyright documents of the U.S. District Courts, Department of the Interior, and Smithsonian Institution relating to their management of U.S. copyright activities before 1870, also in the Rare Book and Special Collections Division

Oscar Sonneck, ms transcript of the music copyright entries in the District Court record books, 1790–1825, in the Music Division

Letter-press copy of a "List of All Music Copyrighted in the United States," 1860–66, prepared 1911–12 for Leo Feist, Inc.

U.S. Copyright Office, official ledger books, 1870–1928, and bound copies of the certificates of copyright, 1928– , arranged by copyright number (i.e., chronologically). For the period 1870–99, all kinds of materials are arranged and numbered in one sequence. Beginning in 1900, materials were separated by form, with music in series E beginning in 1909; opera libretti in series D, as dramatic (i.e., musico-dramatic) works; and books about music in series A. Beginning in 1911, published and unpublished music has its separate record books even though they belong to the same numerical series. Beginning in 1928, separate numerical series were maintained for published and unpublished materials, in both the music and dramatic-works categories

The published *Catalogue of Copyright Entries* (Washington, 1891– ; from 1891 to 1906 known as the *Catalogue of Title-Entries*) transcribes information from the official records described above, generally reflecting the changing categories of classification by form. The *Catalogue* is of varying usefulness, depending mostly on the indexing, also on the changing practices of entry form and periodicity. (From 1939 to 1945, for instance, the index is solely by title, with no entries for composers or claimants.) In addition, musico-dramatic works are listed in the *Dramatic Compositions Copyrighted in the United States, 1870–1916* (Washington, 1916–18)

Miscellaneous Copyright Office correspondence with claimants, composers, and others, 1870– , in storage, arranged by period and names, and of occasional usefulness in determining names or information on name entries, or whether a work was made for hire or otherwise published

Card catalogues and indexes to copyright entries, in the Copyright Office, including (a) 1870–97 ("Old high"), with entries mostly for titles and claimants (rarely for composers), in one alphabet, with successive entries added to existing cards with the same first word or claimant name, and usually giving only the entry number; (b) 1898–1937, a separate music catalogue, with one entry to a card, arranged alphabetically by claimant, providing information on the entry number, date of registration, and composer, together with the claimant and names of author or arranger (if any); (c) also for 1898–1937, an alphabetical file of claimants' applications, occasionally with information not recorded elsewhere; (d) 1909–37, a separate catalogue for renewal entries, which in previous periods were recorded as new entries, alphabetized by title; and (e) 1938–45, one single card file for all forms of copyrighted material, music and musico-dramatic works included, with entries for each work under title, composer, author or arranger (if any), and claimant, for both new registrations and renewals

Depository Copies

Title pages and cover-title pages, as originally filed in the U.S. District Courts at the time of registration (and thus theoretically near the time of publication), and turned over to the Library of Congress in 1870. These sheets are particularly important for their handwritten notations by the clerks of the District Courts, which provide an exact date of registration. In the Music Division these fill 70 boxes (6.5 linear shelf meters) containing 25,000 items, in 5 chronological series (1841–50, 1851–60, 1861–70, 1871, and 1872), each arranged by composer; and in the Prints and Photographs Division, 25 boxes (3.2 linear meters) containing 5000 items, of special interest for their pictorial content, arranged chronologically; also other materials elsewhere, i.e., items from the District of Columbia in the National Archives, as noted in *Tanselle*, p. 123

Depository copies of pre-1860 published sheet music received in the District Courts, transferred variously by the Department of Interior, Department of State, and/or the Smithsonian Institution eventually to the Library of Congress, and now in bound vols. in class M 1. A12 in the Music Division, subdivided as Instrumental (M 1 .A12 I; 106 vols.), Vocal (M 1 .A12 V, 102 vols.), and Miscellaneous (M 1 .A12 Z, 102 vols., including instrumental and vocal editions intermixed). Included are 21,000 items in 310 vols., of which all but 31 vols. date from the period 1845–60. All of the items in question are accessible through the Music Division catalogues, notably through the classed catalogue for pre-1860 Americana (see section A of this entry, above)

Depository copies of other kinds of music (tunebooks, instruction books, books about music), ca. 1790–1870, dispersed through the Music Division collections and accessible through its various catalogues

Depository copies in other libraries, as summarized in *Tanselle*, pp. 83, 124, and 109–10; in addition, many items in the period 1910s–30s were returned to the claimants, as indicated on cards in the copyright catalogues (see above)

Civil War sheet music, 1861–65, dispersed through the Music Division collections, mostly in classes M 1631–36 and M 20 .C58–61, and mostly catalogued; also sheet music, 1865–70, classified under M numbers and thus dispersed through the Music Division collections, but mostly uncatalogued. The enforcement of copyright depository provisions may have been rather weak during and after the Civil War; in any event, there is no single collection of music arranged by copyright number for the decade 1861–70, comparable to M 1 .A12 above, or the "residual" collection below

Music copyright deposits, 1870–1928, the "residual" collection in the Music Division, consisting of materials originally not selected for addition to its collections, but transferred in 1939 from the Copyright Office. The collection comprises 1.2 million titles (600 linear meters) in 7285 boxes, and includes mostly sheet music, sets of parts for stock orchestrations or band arrangements (often represented only by a violin or cornet lead part), and choral octavos. Organization is by copyright number, i.e., for 1870–97, a distinctive numbering series for each year beginning with 1, and with a letter prefix for the year (A for 1870, C for 1871, etc.); 1898–99, distinctive numbering for each year, without prefixes; 1900, music numbered separately under class C; 1901–28, music numbered separately, 1–704999, with class C prefixes through June 1909, class E thereafter

Music Division "Reserve storage" collection, 1909–28, 800,000 items (400 linear meters) in 1683 boxes. The collection contains material originally selected by the Music Division to form an adjunct to its classified collections, but to be filed by copyright number as above. Included are sheet music, band and orchestra parts, and unpublished music mss; the collection is presumed to consist mostly of second copies, the first copy of which may be in either the classified collections or in the "residual" collection above

Music Division, 1943 "processing arrearage," of 330 linear meters, in cartons, in storage and not organized, presumed to consist mostly of second or additional copies of all kinds of music, including hymnals and opera vocal scores, almost all copyright deposits

Music Division, unfiled copyright deposits, 1938–40, 3 linear meters, consisting of items assigned classification numbers but without cataloguing, left unfiled because of World War II, and thus still accessible through the copyright number. Except for this material and the "processing arrearage" above, all published music copyright deposits after 1928 are in the classified collections of the Music Division, with or without cataloguing

Unpublished musico-dramatic works, 1870–1940, in the Music Division, with 6 linear meters for the period 1870–1928 and 14 meters for the period 1928–40. Included with these texts and libretti are many musical selections, ms or printed

Copyright Office, miscellaneous published and unpublished music and musico-dramatic works, 1901–35, filed by copyright number in the "unfinished business" and correspondence files

Unpublished music and musico-dramatic works ("E-unpub" and "D-unpub"), 1928– . Except for certain conspicuously important mss (i.e., works by recognized composers and in larger forms) which were transferred to the classified collections of the Music Division, this material has all been retained in the Copyright Office, where it is accessible through the copyright number

Film music, as variously submitted for copyright, in different forms (i.e., as full or condensed scores, published songs, dance band or simplified piano arrangements, or lead sheets), and in various published or unpublished copyright catagories. The location and organization of this material is now the subject of an extensive program

—William Lichtenwanger

K. Archive of Folk Song

The Archive is now a part of the American Folklife Center, and essentially a reference and research unit rather than a custodial division. Its extensive holdings of folk-music recordings are now under the custody of the Motion Picture, Broadcasting, and Recorded Sound Division (section L below), although the scholarly access to this material is through the Archive. From this collection, various important items have been made available for purchase through the Recording Laboratory, as listed in special catalogues distributed by the Archive. Reference lists on special topics are also available, as cited in Joseph C. Hickerson, "An Inventory of the Bibliographies and Other Reference and Finding Aids Prepared by the Archive of Folk Song," which itself is available from the Archive. For further information on the history and program of the Archive, see its special descriptive brochure. Among the special holdings of the Archive, the following are particularly important:

Reference information, in 94 vertical-file drawers (50 linear meters), for internal reference use. Among the major categories of material are bibliographies and finding aids, 5 drawers; catalogues of folk-music publishers and dealers, involving books, music, and recordings, 3 drawers; corporate subjects, 14 drawers; periodicals, 18 drawers; field notes, 5 drawers of the numerical file; projects, 6 drawers; and subjects, 15 drawers

Among the holdings are 225,000 pages of transcripts assembled by Robert W. Gordon, including T. B. Boyd (Alliance, N.C.), 125 songs, 1927–28; R. B. Davids, 33 songs, ca. 1924; Robert Frothingham, 127 letters received for his "Songs Old Men Have Sung" column in *Adventure* magazine, 1911–32, mostly 1923–29; James Holly Hanford, 8 songs from Iowa, transcribed 1930; Mellinger Edward Henry, 61 southern Appalachian ballads and songs, 1928–29; Guy B. Johnson, 15 ms texts by Walter Jordan, learned ca. 1910 in the South; Nettis F. McAdams, 140 black songs, presumably from *The Folksongs of the American Negro: A Collection of Unprinted Texts* (M.A. thesis, University of California, Berkeley, 1923); Joseph F. McGinnis, 130 sea chanteys and songs, 1928–29; E. A. McIlhenny, 325 pages and 125 texts and tunes of Louisiana black spirituals; Mary Newcomb (Louisville, Ky.), "Songs My Mother Sang," with 210 texts and 101 tunes, 1929–30, also 102 texts, 1930–31; Mabel Evangeline Neal, *Brown County Songs and Ballads* (M.A. thesis, Indiana University, 1926); Howard W. Odum, 83 texts obtained from J. D. Arthur in Tennessee, dated 1929; R. W. Phillips (Akeley, Minn.), 22 texts, 1924; Margaret Purcell (Greenwood, Va.), 108 song texts, ca. 1929; Betty Bush Winger, 125 black songs from the Missouri Ozarks, made in Point Pleasant, W.Va., 1931–32; also Gordon's own transcripts, including 400 California songs and texts from 1922–23, 374 from North Carolina in 1925, and 555 from Darien, Ga., 1926–28

Included in these files are 180,000 pages of folksong transcripts made by the WPA Federal Writers' Project in the late 1930s

Also included are transcripts and notes made in conjunction with early field recordings: while the recordings themselves are in the Motion Picture, Broadcasting, and Recorded Sound Division (section L below), the transcripts and notes are in the Archive. Among the collectors whose papers are in the Archive are James Madison Carpenter (papers and pictorial materials relating to British and American folk music, 1920s–30s), Woody Guthrie, and Vance Randolph (papers and photographs relating to Ozark folk music, 1930s–60s), also materials from the WPA Federal Music Project and Federal Theatre Project. In addition, notes and concordances on most of the Archive's recordings are maintained by the Archive

Reference books and periodicals relating to folk music, 3500 titles

—Joseph C. Hickerson

L. Motion Picture, Broadcasting, and Recorded Sound Division

Of the 1,000,000 recordings in the collection, 20,000 are cylinders, commercial and non-commercial; 200,000 are 78-rpm discs; and 200,000 are pre-1940 instantaneous lacquer recordings. Included in these totals are various special collections, some of the most important and frequently cited of which are given below. In addition to the various special finding aids mentioned below, there are 2 catalogues, one listing those items for which preservation copies have been made, with 75,000 entries, the other listing the pre–1942 radio transcriptions

Early discographic collections, including John Ross Frampton, 1879–1955, 747 discs of piano performances, 1912–30s (with a card index; *QJ*, 18:36–37), A. F. R. Lawrence (1922–72), 2320 test pressings and 745 instantaneous disc recordings, 1920s–30s, including serious and popular music mostly from CBS radio (with matrix lists and other research notes; *QJ*, 32:54–56, 69–73); John Secrist (1918–58), 1700 operatic and other vocal discs, with nearly comprehensive holdings of the recordings made by Enrico Caruso, Rosa Ponselle, and John MacCormack (with the personal catalogue of Secrist, also correspondence, research notes, catalogues, and photographs; *QJ*, 21:15–19, 30:80–81); and Benedict Stambler (d. 1967), 1400 commercial discs of Jewish music, including cantorial transcriptions and performances by Yiddish comedians and entertainers (with an inventory)

Recordings originally part of the collections of personal papers (see sections C, D, and E above), including George Antheil, 86 film-music "sequences" omitted from the soundtracks as finally released; Walter Damrosch, 254 instantaneous disc recordings for the "Music Appreciation Hour" on NBC radio, 1929–41; Geraldine Farrar, 50 discs of her radio broadcast transcriptions, and special pressings made by the Gramophone and Typewriter Co., Ltd., 1904–6; Irving Fine, 40 tapes of his works; George Gershwin, 250 commercial-recording discs made in London, 1926–28, also privately prepared transcriptions of broadcasts and rehearsals; Percy A. Grainger, field recordings of English and Danish folksongs, 1906–20s, wax cylinders copied on 93 discs; Sergei Rachmaninoff, 700 discs, mostly commercial recordings but also several unpublished items, including alternate "takes" for commercial releases,

several with Rachmaninoff's personal notations; Sigmund Romberg, 543 discs, many of them non-commercial recordings of his radio programs, also conversations with Jerome Kern, Deems Taylor, and Alexander Woollcott; and Arnold Schoenberg, drafts for letters, lectures, and a 1931 performance of the Variations for Orchestra op. 31

Jack Kapp (1901–49, president of Decca records), 65 original cartoon drawings relating to the history of the phonograph record and the recording industry, many of them concerning James C. Petrillo and the American Federation of Musicians

H. Rose Greenough, Jr. (acoustical consultant and owner of Technicord records), 1021 acetate discs and 793 tapes, also logbooks of performances of the Boston Symphony Orchestra, early Tanglewood Festivals, and local recitals, many by E. Power Biggs

Radio broadcast collections, including the "Major Bowes Amateur Hour," 1100 broadcast transcription discs, 1935–46, also films and applications; Jessica Dragonette, 369 discs of her performances on the NBC "Cities Service Concerts" series, 1929–37, and thereafter on the "Palmolive Beauty Box Theatre"; C. P. McGregor Co., 4200 discs and 1500 tape recordings from his sound-recording studio in San Francisco, 1929–36, thereafter in Los Angeles, featuring important jazz ensembles; NBC radio, 170,000 discs, 1933–70, including 300 Metropolitan Opera broadcasts, also most of those by the NBC Symphony Orchestra; and Wilfred Pelletier, 575 discs of Metropolitan Opera performances and auditions, 1938–49, of NBC Symphony Orchestra broadcasts, also other musical performances featuring Pelletier or Rose Bampton

—Gerald Gibson

Folk-Music Recordings

Materials mostly assembled by or in the Archive of Folk Song (see section K above), most with notes and concordances in the reference files of the Archive

Peabody Museum of Archaeology and Ethnology, Harvard University, early field recordings, comprising 264 wax cylinders, including Jesse Walter Fewkes, 50 cylinders of folksongs and tales of the Passamoquoddy Indians in Maine, 1890–91; Benjamin Ives Gilman, foreign folk music recorded at the World's Columbian Exposition, Chicago, 1893; Herbert J. Spinden, Nez Percé texts, 1907; Washington Matthews, Navajo music, 1900; and Roland Dixon, American Indian music from California, ca. 1910

Bureau of American Ethnology, Smithsonian Institution, 3591 wax cylinders of American Indian music, recorded by or under the supervision of Frances Densmore, 1907–40 (with a catalogue prepared by the National Archives)

Helen H. Roberts, field recordings and transcriptions of folk music of Jamaica, Hawaii, California, and the southwestern U.S., 1920s–40s, 250 cylinders and 363 discs, including also recordings by Walter McClintock of the Blackfoot Indians, 1898, and Charles Lummis in the southwestern U.S. See the bibliography of her writings in *Ethnomusicology*, 11 (1967), 118–33

Frank C. Brown (1870–1943), field recordings of North Carolina folk music, 1915–ca. 1940, transcribed from the original wax cylinders and instantaneous discs, now on transcription discs and ed. by Newman I. White in vols. 2–5 of *The Frank C. Brown Collection of North Carolina Folklore* (Durham, 1952–64)

Robert W. Gordon (1888–1960, first director of the Archive of Folk Song), 825 wax cylinder recordings of American folksongs, assembled 1918–26 through the University of California, Berkeley, and Harvard University, also 95 instantaneous disc recordings, 1928–30s (*AR*, 1928–32, passim; *QJ*, 35:218–33)

Other folksong collections commissioned by or complementary to the program of the Archive of Folk Song during the 1930s, including Laura Boulton, field recordings of traditional music on 1312 discs and 367 tapes, many of them devoted to American Indian and Eskimo groups; James Madison Carpenter, recordings of sea chanteys; Arthur Kyle Davis, Jr. (1897–1972), Appalachian Virginia folk music recorded in the 1930s–40s, including ballads, songs, fiddle tunes, and radio interviews, copied from originals of the Virginia Folklore Society; Woodrow Wilson ("Woody") Guthrie (1912–67), songs, also guitar and harmonica performances as part of his experience in Oklahoma, as recorded by Alan Lomax in 1940, on 17 discs; Joseph S. Hall, Great Smoky Mountain folklore, including folksongs, 1937–60s, on 161 discs; George Korson (1899–1967), Pennsylvania mining songs and music, collected 1924–60s; Bascom Lamar Lunsford, Appalachian music which he performed or collected, 1935–49, on 45 instantaneous disc recordings; Norman L. McNeil, Mexican border *corridas* (folk ballads), collected 1930s–40s (complemented by transcripts at Texas A & I University, Kingsville, q.v.); Ferdinand ("Jelly Roll") Morton (1885–1941), musical and narrative account of the development of jazz and of his role in that development, as recorded by Alan Lomax in 1938, on 45 discs, partially transcribed; Vance Randolph, Ozark field recordings, 1930s–60s, on 200 discs; Resettlement Administration Collection, field recordings of American folk music, 1936–37, made under the supervision of Charles Seeger, Sidney Robertson (later Mrs. Henry Cowell), Margaret Valiant, and others, also recorded American Indian, Finnish, Gaelic, Lithuanian, Serbian, and Swedish music in America, and Appalachian and Ozark songs and dance tunes, on 159 discs; Willard Rhodes, American Indian music field recordings on 270 discs and 50 tapes, 1940–52; Ruth Rubin, Yiddish folksongs and folklore, 139 tapes, collected in the U.S. and Canada (see *Briegleb*, no. 83); Charles Todd and Robert Sonkin, 119 disc recordings of music of California migratory labor camps, 1940–41, as discussed in their "Ballads of the Okies," *New York Times Magazine* (17 Nov. 1940), 6–7, 18; Frank M. and Anne Warner, field recordings on 105 discs and 19 tapes, collected mostly in North Carolina, New York, and New Hampshire, 1938–40s; University of Wisconsin field recordings of Wisconsin folk music, assembled 1940–46 under the supervision of Leland Coon, including Dutch, French-Canadian, German, Norwegian, and Swedish immigrant music, also occasional songs, 1940–46; and WPA materials, mostly from the Federal Writers' Project, 1936–39, and some from the Federal Music Project and the Federal Theatre Project, also discs produced in 1939 through the WPA Joint Committee on Folk Arts under the direction of Herbert Halpert, and including 419 discs of Southern transcriptions, and other materials from Florida, New York City, and California, the latter comprising 237 discs assembled through the work of

Sidney Robertson, this program as described in Herbert Halpert, "Federal Theatre and Folksong," *Southern Folklore Quarterly*, 2 (1938), 81–85, in Benjamin A. Botkin, "WPA and Folklore Research," *Southern Folkore Quarterly*, 3 (1939), 7–14, and in other writings cited in the Archive of Folk Song bibliography, "Folklore and the W.P.A."

M. Other Divisions

Manuscripts Division

Revolutionary War ms songs and references to music, including materials collected by Peter Force, notably the collection belonging to Joseph B. Walker of Concord, N.H., as transcribed in 1845 by Henry Stevens; a commonplace book written by American prisoners at Forton Prison, near Portsmouth, England, 1777–79, including 58 bawdy songs and ballads; 11 booklets copied by Christopher French (British officer), containing doggerel songs and verse villifying the American colonials; and Thomas Cole, orderly book, 1778, containing poems and songs. See Simon Vance Anderson, *American Music during the War for Independence* (Ph.D. diss., University of Michigan, 1965), and Gordon Eugene Beck, *British Military Theatricals in New York City during the Revolutionary War* (Ph.D. diss., University of Illinois, 1964); also *Manuscript Sources in the Library of Congress for Research on the American Revolution* (Washington, 1975), esp. entries 378, 397, and 873

Shaker music mss from Union Village, Ohio, mostly 1811–78, 50 items, as cited in *Cook*, pp. 286–90

Sir Francis J. Campbell (1832–1914, musician and teacher of the blind), correspondence sent and received, also biographical papers, photographs, and memorabilia, mostly from his years in Europe beginning 1869

Margaret Blaine (Mrs. Walter) Damrosch, diaries for 1878, 1880–82, and 1888; notebooks for 1875–76 and 1885; and an unpublished memoir fragment dated 1939, in the papers of her father, James G. Blaine

Marcia Davenport, notes, drafts, typescripts, and press clippings for her book, *Mozart* (New York, 1932)

Mary Elizabeth (Hallock) Greenewalt (pianist and manufacturer of light and color pianos), personal papers, 1918–42

John Hays Hammond, Jr. (1888–1965), papers and correspondence relating to the Hammond Organ Co. and to his mini-piano of 1937 (*QJ*, 24:178)

Harmon Foundation (established in 1922 by William Elmer Harmon, 1862–1928), archival records of philanthropic activities to blacks, 1913–67, mostly 1925–33, including records of its music awards, 1926–30

Francis Hopkinson, papers relating to music, and texts, including "The Temple of Minerva," as discussed in Gillian B. Anderson, "'The Temple of Minerva' and Francis Hopkinson: A Reappraisal of America's First Poet-Composer," American Philosophical Society *Proceedings*, 120 (1976), 166–77

Marian MacDowell (1857–1956), personal papers, 2000 items, mostly 1908–38, including correspondence, notably 100 letters to Nina Maud Richardson, messages of condolence on the death of Edward A. MacDowell in 1908, also letters from Aaron Copland, Roger Sessions, and others; papers related to the Edward MacDowell Association, Inc., and the MacDowell Colony, Peterborough, N.H.; and 20 music mss of Edward A. MacDowell, also 125 of his letters to Marian MacDowell, mostly 1880–1903

MacDowell Colony, Peterborough, N.H., archival records, 35,000 items, including personal correspondence of Marian MacDowell, administrators of the Colony, and others, 1895–1958; administrative papers, 1907–70; scrapbooks, 1869–1958, including press clippings, photographs, printed ephemera, and correspondence; and miscellaneous documents, 1884–1967

Margaret Webster (1905–72, actress and theatrical director), personal papers, including prompter's copies of opera libretti, music scores, and directorial materials

Owen Wister (1860–1938), personal papers, including materials on his operas *Dido and Aeneas, Kenilworth, Listen to Binks, Montezuma, Villon,* and *Watch your Thirst* (*QJ,* 10:155, 11:168–69, 16:243–46)

Prints and Photographs Division

Posters, including 2500 announcements of theatrical performances, mostly 1870s–ca. 1910, many for opera, minstrel, and other musical performances

Portraits of musicians, including engravings, lithographs, photographs, and documents in other media, accessible through personal name

Illustrated sheet music and sheet-music covers, including early lithographs, many of them copyright depository materials (see section J above)

Pictures of auditoriums, opera houses, and music halls, in the Pictorial Archives of Early American Architecture, the Carnegie Survey of the Architecture of the South, and the Historic American Buildings Survey, as mentioned in C. Ford Peatross, "Architectural Collections of the Library of Congress," *QJ,* 34:249–84 and 153–62

Rare Book and Special Collections Division

Abraham Lincoln sheet music and other musical materials, mostly cited in *A Catalog of the Alfred Whital Stern Collection of Lincolniana* (Washington, 1960), esp. pp. 449–56

Broadsides, mostly without music but many with indications of appropriate tunes, as cited in the *Catalog of Broadsides in the Rare Book Division* (Boston, 1972)

Joseph Meredith Toner (1825–96, American bibliophile), 40 mid 19th-century U.S. imprints of music and books related to music

District Court copyright record books, 1790–1870, as discussed in section J above

General Collections

U.S. songsters, including materials from the collection of Robert W. Gordon, classified as literature (see also *AR,* 1943, p. 201); hymnals without music and books on hymnology classified as religion; and libretti classified as dramatic texts

228
U.S. MARINE BAND

Marine Barracks
Eighth and Eye Streets SE
Washington, D.C. 20390

Papers of the Band, including official files and the leaders' logs, ca. 1900– , yearly and tour-program files, 1891– , ms and published materials concerning the Band and its leaders, and photographs and memorabilia of former bandsmen including Dr. Frank Simon

Music of the Band, ca. 1880– , 145 linear meters of items for band, symphonic band, and special groups; also 7.5 linear meters of piano music, 2000 standard marches, 6 linear meters of music for woodwind and brass ensembles, 3.6 linear meters of national anthems, and 5000 items for dance band or combo including state and college hymns and fanfares

Music of the former U.S. Marine Orchestra, 90 linear meters of items for orchestra and string ensemble

Reference library, 30 linear meters of books, hymnals, scores, catalogues, and piano-vocal collections

Library logs of the Band, 1919–

229
U.S. MARINE CORPS MUSEUM　　　DMam

Military Music Collection
Building 58, Washington Navy Yard
Washington, D.C. 20374

John Philip Sousa band library, 1110 printed band and orchestra arrangements, and 500 copyists' ms band and orchestra arrangements, formerly at Stetson University, De Land, Fla.; indexed

Other band arrangements, 3500 printed items, being indexed; 200 piano and piano-vocal sheet-music items, partially indexed; and the Leon Brusiloff collection of 14,000 dance-band arrangements, 1930s–50s, partially indexed

Other printed music, 50 songbooks and method books

Programs of musical organizations, 200 items

Sousa Band, archival records, 30 linear cm.; also artifacts of the Sousa Band, and microform copies of materials in other institutions relating to Sousa and to the U.S. Marine Band

John Philip Sousa, personal papers, 15 linear cm.

Photographs, 500 items, mostly of the U.S. Marine Band and John Philip Sousa

—J. E. Bennett

230
U.S. NATIONAL ARCHIVES　　　DNA

Washington, D.C. 20504

For general background see the brochure, *A Researcher's Guide to the National Archives* (Washington, 1977). The published *Guide to the National Archives of the United States* (Washington, 1974; hereinafter cited as *Guide*) and an updated loose-leaf copy (1977) may provide more specific information on particular holdings, although the more detailed finding aids, as prepared in various forms and variously located, are often a more valuable expedient when available

The materials are organized in terms of Record Groups according to their provenance, i.e., in terms of the governmental agency or program of origin. The materials in the collections which relate to music are thus widely scattered, and have never been systematically surveyed. The following items are among those known to be of importance:

Federal Music Project of the Works Progress Administration (Record Group 69), 10 linear meters of general holdings; 30 linear cm. of scrapbooks and other materials relating specifically to the Project; and 3 linear meters relating to the WPA administration and its various state agencies. See the *Guide,* pp. 693–99; the finding aid for the Federal Music Project records, prepared by Jim Glenn, 1971; Frances T. Bourne, *Preliminary Checklist of the Central Correspondence Files of the Works Projects Administration and Its Predecessors, 1933–1944* (Washington, 1946), esp. the general subject files in classes 211.1–211.13 and the state files in classes 651.311–651.3113; and William F. McDonald, *Federal Relief Administration and the Arts* (Columbus, 1969), passim

American Indian dances and ceremonies, pre–1920 motion pictures and photographs, from the Bureau of Indian Affairs, Record Group 75 (*Guide,* pp. 388–89)

Materials relating to military and other service bands, including documents in the War Department Collection of Revolutionary War Records (Record Group 93), also later material elsewhere (i.e., Record Groups 80, 111, 120, and 127)

Audiovisual Archives Division

Materials from various record groups, including items cited in Mayfield S. Bray and Leslie C. Waffen, *Sound Recordings in the Audiovisual Archives Division of the National Archives* (Washington, 1972; hereinafter cited as *SR*)

Recording entitled "U.S. Army and Navy Calls, Cavalry and Artillery," 1896, consisting of oral commands and the appropriate bugle call for each (*SR*, p. 8), in Record Group 94, Adjutant General's Office

Sound and linguistic material in Aleut, Mission, Chumash, Creek, Navajo, and other Amerindian languages, 1912–14 and 1930–41 (*SR*, p.8), in Record Group 106, Smithsonian Institution, Bureau of American Ethnology

Miscellaneous musical recordings, including Marian Anderson, also programs of religious and folk music (*SR*, pp. 4–5), in Record Group 48, Secretary of the Interior

Federal Music Project, 418 recordings, 1936–42, including folk singers, madrigal singers, a cappella choirs, Negro choruses, light- and grand-opera companies, symphony orchestras, concert bands, and other groups (*SR*, p. 8), in Record Group 69, Works Projects Administration

Miscellaneous recordings of speeches and discussions with prominent persons, among them musicians; an ASCAP concert, 1940; and *Wing of Expectation*, an opera by Kenneth Wright based on the life of Mary Todd Lincoln (*SR*, pp. 12–13), in Record Group 200, National Archives Gift Collection

German-American Band, recordings of German nationalist songs, symphonies, and operatic selections used at entertainments and rallies (*Guide*, p. 356; also *SR*, p. 9), in Record Group 131, Office of Alien Property

231
NAVAL HISTORICAL CENTER
Photographic Section
Washington Navy Yard
Washington, D.C. 20374

Photographs, 200 items principally concerning the U.S. Navy Band, with other subjects including miscellaneous groups, soloists, and sheet-music covers, 1860– , mostly 1900–1920

232
U.S. NAVY BAND
Washington Navy Yard
Washington, D.C. 20374

Music library of the Band, 11,600 items, including over 3000 published marches and many special ms arrangements, catalogued by title, composer, and format

U.S. Navy Orchestra library, scores and performance parts, to 1960

Programs of the Band, 1 file cabinet, 1925–

233
SCOTTISH RITE SUPREME COUNCIL   DSC
Library
1733 Sixteenth Street NW
Washington, D.C. 20009

Masonic music and hymnals, 25 items, 1850–1920
Manuscript copy of "Pleyel's Hymn," n.d.

—Inge Baum

234
SMITHSONIAN INSTITUTION   DSI
Washington, D.C. 20560

All units listed below are in the National Museum of History and Technology, unless otherwise noted. Specific items are cited in the *Guide to Manuscript Collections in the National Museum of History and Technology* (Washington, 1978; hereinafter cited as *Guide*)

Division of Community Life

Recordings, 1910s– , 1300 items, arranged by recording label

Hymnals, 20 items, including special-function materials

Swiss Singing Society of Boston, songbooks, photographs, and memorabilia, 1870s–90

Ken Sparnon (vaudeville-theater manager, 1930s), scrapbook, with autograph portraits of performers

Miscellaneous items, including a photograph of Arturo Toscanini; cigarette cards, including photographs of late 19th-century entertainers, in 1 cigar box; sheet music, 50 items, 1930s–50s; cabinet photographs of entertainers, ca. 1880–1910; circus programs; and playbills

Division of Electricity and Modern Physics

George H. Clark (1881–1956, radio engineer and Radio Corporation of America executive), personal papers, 70 linear meters, including correspondence, photographs, press clippings, technical materials, and other documents relating to the early history of radio, and his work relating to the manufacture of the theremin, 1922–34

William Joseph Hammer (1858–1934, inventor and associate of Thomas A. Edison), personal papers, ca. 1875–1934, 5 linear meters, including scientific notes, notebooks, articles and press clippings, and other technical materials

Division of Extractive Industries

Collection of Business Americana, begun ca. 1928 by Is-

adore Warshaw, 500 linear meters, of which 12 boxes
are related to music and 2 more boxes to musical instruments. Included are advertisements, catalogues,
price lists, bills, receipts, posters, magazines, and
other materials, among them Gilbert & Sullivan
memorabilia; sheet-music catalogues; business correspondence of G. Schirmer, Inc., Arthur W. Tams,
and other music publishers; shipping invoices for
musical instruments and accessories; programs for
the Cornell Banjo and Mandolin Club, Town Hall,
and others; and music posters

Division of Mechanisms

Papers concerning the early history of recordings, including archives of the American Graphophone Co.,
ca. 1888–90, 3 linear cm. (*Guide*, 76), and personal
papers of Charles Sumner Tainter, ca. 1878–80, 1915,
and 1919, 60 linear cm. (*Guide*, 79)
Early recordings, including tin-foil, cylinders, and experimental discs

Division of Musical Instruments

Photographs, slides, and other pictorial material on
musical instruments, 16 linear meters, devoted to (1)
photographs of instruments in the collections; (2)
2000 photographs showing details of keyboard construction and other subjects, assembled by Hugo
Worch (1855–1938, Washington, D.C., collector and
dealer), catalogued; and (3) musical instruments as
works of art, catalogued and cross-indexed by artist,
musical instrument, subject, place, and time
(*Guide*, 37)
Organ design, particularly in North America, correspondence, photographs, articles, and notes, 50
linear cm. (*Guide*, 38)
Musical programs, assembled by the Concert-Program
Exchange, 1916–17, from locations around the U.S.,
60 linear cm.
Copies of drawings of musical-instrument patents,
mostly U.S.
Published music, 2.5 linear meters, including 19th-
century sheet music, early 20th-century theater-music
parts, and 19th-century band-music copies
Musical-instrument trade catalogues, 2 linear meters;
catalogues of musical-instrument collections, 3 linear
meters; 40 periodical titles dealing with music and
musical instruments; and 1200 books about music
Piano rolls, 800 items

Division of Naval History

Albert F. Schroeck (member of the U.S. Marine Band
under John Philip Sousa), holograph music, ca. 1929–
39 and 1958, 3 linear cm. (*Guide*, 318)

Division of Political History

Helen May Butler (1866–1957, brass-band leader and
circus musician), personal papers, including scrapbooks, photographs, sheet music, and memorabilia
Adams Clement Collection of personal papers, including music books from the library of Mrs. John Quincy
Adams (1775–1852)
Sheet music, pamphlets, and songsters, 300 items relating to U.S. political campaigns, 1790–

Folklife Program (Office of American Studies)

Recordings of traditional music, 6000 reels of tape,
recorded in connection with the Festivals of American Folklife

Department of Anthropology (National Museum of Natural History; National Anthropology Archives)

Frances Densmore (1867–1957), personal papers, including portraits, diaries and extracts from diaries,
account book, scrapbook, correspondence, photographs, lectures, memoirs, and research notes concerning her field work with American Indian music,
in all 2 linear meters. See Helen Addison Howard, "A
Survey of the Densmore Collection of American Indian Music," *Journal of the West*, 13 (1974), 83–96
Alice Cunningham Fletcher (1845–1923), personal papers, including correspondence, research notes and
song transcriptions, diaries, and pictures, of which 40
linear cm. relate to her work with American Indian
music
John Harrington (1884–1961, ethnologist and student of
west-coast Amerindian languages), personal papers,
1907–19, including field recordings, 400 wax cylinders
and 1600 aluminum discs, with music
Division of Ethnology Manuscript and Pamphlet File, 15
boxes under the heading "Music," including obituaries of Frances Densmore, and correspondence of E.
H. Hawley (d. 1918, "preparator" in the Anthropology
Department) with letters involving Hugo Worch,
Frances Densmore, and others, also materials and research notes concerning his attempts to classify musical
instruments

—Caroline Baum, Cynthia Adams Hoover

Archives of American Art (National Collection of Fine Arts and National Portrait Gallery)

Carl Ruggles (1876–1971), 7 letters to Rockwell Kent, including ms musical passages
Walt Kuhn (1901–66), personal papers, including
designs and directions for musical productions, and
letters to his wife discussing music
Nina P. Collier (U.S. government official), materials relating to the WPA Federal Music Project, summer concerts of the National Symphony Orchestra, and planning of the 1939 World's Fair

—Garnett McCoy

National Air and Space Museum

Bella C. Landauer aeronautical sheet-music collection,
1500 items, as cited in *Ash*, p. 719. See also her *Some
Aeronautical Music* (Paris, 1933)

235
WASHINGTON CATHEDRAL LIBRARY DNC
Mount Saint Alban
Washington, D.C. 20016

Douglas Collection, 1000 items, mostly hymnals and
books about hymnology, as cited in the check list in
Leonard Ellinwod and Anne Woodward Douglas,
To Praise God: The Life and Work of Charles Winfred

Douglas, Hymn Society of America Papers, 23 (New York, 1958), pp. 38–72. The nucleus of the collection is the personal library of Canon Charles Winfred Douglas (1867–1944), which includes material acquired from Rev. Percival H. Hickman of Denver and from Rev. John Mott Williams, Bishop of Marquette

George C. Stebbins (1846–1945) Memorial Collection of gospel-song materials, containing 1200 hymnals and tunebooks, as organized by Rev. J. B. Clayton. The collection is strong in works of the Moody and Sankey movement, and includes complete files of music by P. P. Bliss and by Stebbins, as well as 100 working notebooks in which Stebbins pasted music taken from contemporary published books

Other smaller collections, including materials of Rev. John Sebastian Bach Hodges (1830–1915, composer, rector of St. Paul's Church, Baltimore, and active in the revision of the *Hymnal* of 1874 and 1892) and of Edgar Priest (1878–1935, first organist-choirmaster of the Cathedral)

—Leonard Ellinwood

236
Woodrow WILSON HOUSE
2340 S Street NW
Washington, D.C. 20008

Sheet music, 500 popular and theater songs, ca. 1890–1920, also several songbooks and editions of piano music

Recordings, 150 items, 1910s–20s, mostly the personal collection of President Wilson, but also including recordings of his voice

—Robert Mawson

In addition to the repositories listed above, the following have also reported holdings of the materials indicated:

Chevy Chase Presbyterian Church, Library: sheet music, songbooks

Frederick Douglass Museum of African Art: recordings

Washington Hebrew Congregation: sheet music, songbooks

Wesley Theological Seminary: songbooks

Florida

237
CAMERON–GRAHAM MEMORIAL BAND LIBRARY
Drawer 70
Altoona, Florida 32702

Sheet music, 2500 items, 1840s–1930s, being arranged by title; also music periodicals and books about music

Recordings, 25,000 items, including 20,000 78-rpm discs, 1887–1950s, 3000 16-inch radio-transcription discs, and 475 cylinder recordings, mostly of bands and band-instrument performances; arranged by performer, with a title index

Recording catalogues, including extensive runs of early serials, 1904–28, others to ca. 1950

Pictures, including 150 framed photographs of bands and bandsmen, also 150 post cards showing band gazebos, stands, and parks of the U.S.

—Oliver R. Graham

238
James A. LEWIS
213 Southeast Sixth Street, North
Belle Glade, Florida 33430

Hymnals, 150 items, mostly 20th century, also 100 books about music and hymnology

239
UNIVERSITY OF MIAMI   FMU
Box 248165
Coral Gables, Florida 33124

Music Library

Songbooks, 4 sacred collections bound in 1 vol., 1800–1802, given by Elmer Ziegler

Sheet music, 32 items published mid 19th century to 1890, donated by Malcolm Lovell; 15 bound vols., 19th century; and 1 box of miscellaneous novelty songs, early 20th century

Other published music, by University composers, editors, or arrangers, mostly recent editions, some autographed

Music mss, including Carl Ruggles, "Evocation No. 4" (Arlington, Vt., n.d.), photocopy with penciled corrections by Ruggles; and Jack Beeson, "Hello Out There," black-line print with corrections in pencil, 1953

Recordings, 33,000 items, including 17,000 78-rpm discs, arranged by manufacturer and number (in the Handleman Institute); recordings of American Indians, blacks, folk music, jazz, and American Yiddish songs; and field tapes of Yiddish songs, recorded in Miami Beach, 1976–

—Elsie Fardig

Band Department

Henry Fillmore (1881–1956, bandmaster, composer, and publisher), personal papers, including published compositions, ms scores, photographs, correspondence, business contracts, scrapbooks of clippings, programs, and memorabilia (in the Fillmore Museum)

Arthur Pryor (1870–1942, bandleader), 25 mss of original compositions, transcriptions, and arrangements (in the Band Library)

—William Russell

240

STETSON UNIVERSITY   FDS

Box 1418
De Land, Florida 32720

Sheet music, 600 popular 20th-century items; also 2 by
    Stephen Foster, 1849–51, and 1 bound vol. of songs,
    1850s–60s
Hymnals, 15 items of various denominations, 1844–1939
Other printed music, including 3 songbooks, 1882–1940
University concert programs, 1895– , and photographs
    of Music School groups

—Janice Jenkins

241

KORESHAN UNITY

Headquarter–Research Library
Estero, Florida 33928

Extensive music library assembled after the founding of
the community in 1893, including hymns with texts by
Koresh, also instrumental and vocal ensemble music
used in the annual Solar Festivals and other concerts.
The collection will be housed in the new Headquarter–
Research Library. See James A. McCoy, "The Musical
Life of the Koreshan Unity," *American Eagle,* 44/14
(1966), 2–4, and 44/15 (1966), 2–4

—Hedwig Michel

242

FORT LAUDERDALE HISTORICAL SOCIETY

219 Southwest Second Avenue
Fort Lauderdale, Florida 33301

Juliette Lange (d. 1977, New York opera singer, 1920s), 60
    linear cm. of papers, including 500 items of sheet music
    and music scores and 2 scrapbooks of clippings and
    programs
Songbooks, 2 vols., 1912
Programs of local choral groups, 1920s–40s; also photo-
    graphs of local bands

—Marjorie D. Patterson

243

INDIAN RIVER COMMUNITY COLLEGE   FFpI

3209 Virginia Avenue
Fort Pierce, Florida 33450

Vaughan Monroe (1912–73, singer), papers including ms
    arrangements, sheet music, and published scores with
    ms markings, in all 300 items

—Genevieve McMillan

244

UNIVERSITY OF FLORIDA LIBRARIES   FU

Gainesville, Florida 32611

Belknap Collection of the Performing Arts

    The collection includes non-book materials on theater,
    dance, music, and films, emphasizing U.S. and Canada

subjects from the mid 19th century to the present. See
Laraine Correll, "The Belknap Collection of Performing
Arts," *Performing Arts Resources,* 1 (1974), 56–65

Green Collection of American Sheet Music, including
    1000 illustrated items owned by a Florida family, 1830–
    1950, mostly popular burlesque and Broadway show
    tunes; 4 linear meters of Civil War songs, coon songs,
    and songs from musical theater, 1920s–40s; and 2
    bound vols., 1850s, also 53 songs published in news-
    papers, 1899–1920s
Songbooks, including 3 hymnals, 1918–53, and a comic
    songbook, 1890
Ringling Museum Theatre Collection of 19th- and early
    20th-century playbills and heralds (150,000 items),
    programs (2000 items), scripts, and scrapbooks from
    Dublin, London, and the U.S., mostly indexed
Programs, flyers, and clippings, 50,000 non-regional
    items arranged by medium (theater, dance, music,
    opera, and cinema); also programs of local concerts,
    1890s–1950s, in 12 scrapbooks; and program notes for
    U.S. orchestras, including some items in ephemera
    files
Production-information files, 4 linear meters of cata-
    logues and information sheets from performing-arts
    production companies, arranged by subject and
    alphabetically by company
Photographs, 10,000 items including opera and ballet
    subjects, arranged alphabetically by title of production,
    company, or person; also 1000 prints and engravings of
    famous theatrical personalities
Shakespearean collection, including programs of Shake-
    spearean companies and festivals, information on com-
    panies, 150 promptbooks, prints and engravings

—Marcia Brookbank

Music Library

Sheet music, 7 bound vols. and 45 separate items of
    popular music, 1890s–1940
Songbooks and hymnals, 172 early 20th-century items
Other printed music, including 27 solo-instrumental and
    ensemble scores, early 20th century
Programs of Metropolitan Opera performances, 23 early
    20th-century items
Lyon & Healy violin catalogue, Chicago, 1896
Recordings, including 21 linear meters of popular 78-rpm
    discs

—Robena Eng

Rare Books and Manuscripts Department

Zora Neale Hurston, 2 boxes of correspondence and 3
    boxes of mss, programs, and clippings, 1926–60,
    some concerning her activities with the Federal Ne-
    gro Theater Project and presentations of black folk-
    lore and folk music, 1930s
Florida Bandmasters' Association papers, 70 boxes of
    bulletins, programs, correspondence, and financial
    records, 1920s–

—Carmen Williams

University Archives

John W. DeBruyn, music mss, mid 1930s
Programs of University concerts and recitals, 1920s–30s,
    150 items

Photographs of University bands, glee clubs, and other groups, including pre-1940 items

—Maxine Hamilton

245
JACKSONVILLE PUBLIC LIBRARY   FJ

Haydn Burns Library
122 North Ocean Street
Jacksonville, Florida 32202

Art and Music Department

Frederick Delius, 70 published compositions including *Zum Carnival* (Jacksonville, 1892); also 1 linear meter of clippings, photographs, and memorabilia from his years in Florida
Music Teachers' Association of Jacksonville, annual programs and yearbooks, ca.1920–60

—Jeff Driggers

Florida Room

WPA Federal Writers' Project, original typescript of *The Negro Sings*, 1940, including work songs, blues, and rhythm-band arrangements of "God's Trombones" by James Weldon Johnson
James Weldon Johnson (1871–1938), published edition of the black national anthem, "Lift Every Voice and Sing"
Songbooks pertaining to Florida, including Alton C. Morris, *Folksongs of Florida* (Gainesville, 1950); also 2 sheet-music items pertaining to Jacksonville
Clipping file, with a section on Florida music and musicians, including programs of the Jacksonville Symphony Orchestra, the Friday Musicale (1897–), and local bands; also photographs of local private bands

—Carroll Harris

246
JACKSONVILLE UNIVERSITY   FJU

Swisher Library
Box 21
Jacksonville, Florida 32211·

Frederick Delius (1862–1934), music mss of "Koanga" and "Song of Summer," 40 published sheet-music items, and correspondence of his wife, Jelka Rosen
Hymnals and school songbooks, 60 late 19th-century items

—Thomas H. Gunn

247
BOK SINGING TOWER

Box 268
Lake Wales, Florida 33853

Research library including materials on carillons, and containing 6 linear meters of published and ms music for carillon, with works by Percival Price, Samuel Barber, Gian Carlo Menotti, and Anton Brees

—Milford Myhre

248
HISTORICAL ASSOCIATION OF   FMHiS
SOUTHERN FLORIDA

3280 South Miami Avenue
Miami, Florida 33129

Sheet music relating to Miami or Florida, including works by Florida composers, 1920s–30s
Miami Conservatory of Music, 1.2 linear meters of scrapbooks, including press clippings and curriculum materials, 1920s–
Photographs of musicians, in a general collection of 30,000 items, indexed
Recordings, including an oral-history tape concerning Mana-Zucca (pianist and composer)

—Becky Smith

249
MIAMI–DADE PUBLIC LIBRARY   FM

One Biscayne Boulevard
Miami, Florida 33132

Art and Music Division

Sheet music, 2000 popular-music items, 20th century
Other printed music, including 20th-century popular songbooks and operatic or piano scores

Florida Room

Sheet music relating to Miami or Florida, 43 items, 1920s–30s
Press clipping files, 1896– , indexed by subject
Romer collection of photographs, including 45 items relating to music or musicians in Florida, indexed

—Sam Boldrick

250
MANA-ZUCCA

4301 Adams Avenue
Miami Beach, Florida 33140

Mana-Zucca (Jesula Zuckerman, pseud. Augusta Zuckerman, pianist and composer), personal papers, including ms compositions, 1100 published compositions, 1000 programs and clippings, and memorabilia

251
ORANGE COUNTY HISTORICAL
COMMISSION

812 East Rollins Street
Orlando, Florida 32803

Sheet music, 200 popular-music items, 1920–35
Orlando Opera House, 3 programs and 1 photograph, 1890s
Mendelssohn Club, 2 photographs and 5 programs for Gilbert & Sullivan operettas, 1910–16
Photographs of local bandshells and band concerts, 1920s
Recordings, including 800 78-rpm discs and 50 cylinders of classical music

—Jean Yothers

252

ORLANDO PUBLIC LIBRARY   FO

10 Rosalind Avenue North
Orlando, Florida 32801

Sheet music, 2000 popular-music items, 1910–50
Songbooks, 525 vols. of popular music, ca. 1900
Music catalogues, 1 linear meter of late 19th-century
   items from Boston and New York City

—Paul Neal

253

PENSACOLA HISTORICAL SOCIETY

405 South Adams Street
Pensacola, Florida 32501

Research notes on musicians in Florida and on the activities of the Wyer family (Creole), 19th and 20th
   centuries, prepared by Karl Gert zur Heide (Achimer
   Str. 45, D–2800 Bremen 1, Germany/B.R.D.) for a
   monograph on Paul Wyer
Scrapbooks on music in Pensacola during the 1930s, 5
   vols., including 2 mss on music and the arts by Mary
   Lou Robson Flemina
Music Study Club of Pensacola, yearbook, 1930–31
Programs and advertisements for local concerts, including performances at the Pensacola Opera House, 300
   items, 1890–1917, and at the Saenger Theater, 30
   items, 1925–
Photographs of musicians, bands, and orchestras, 30
   items, 1890–1960
Sheet music, 12 items by Pensacola composers, 1898–
   1950
Recordings, including 2 tapes of songs about Pensacola
   or written or played by Pensacola musicians, 1907–
   50s, recorded in 1977

—Gordon N. Simons

254

Rev. Jacob BARKIN

535 Oak Drive
Pompano Beach, Florida 33060

Judeo-Hebraic music, including 10,000 items of sheet
   music, published music, and books about music; also
   original mss of his own and other composers' music
Personal papers relating to Barkin's career in the U.S.,
   1926– , including family correspondence, photographs, programs, and memorabilia

255

George W. CASE

2731 Northeast Fourteenth Street
Pompano Beach, Florida 33062

Henry Lincoln Case (d.1924), ms score to his opera
   Camaralzaman

256

POMPANO BEACH CITY LIBRARY

1213 East Atlantic Boulevard
Pompano Beach, Florida 33060

Davidson Collection of recordings, 1912–60s, comprising 5000 78-rpm discs, including many early vocal
   items and extensive holdings of Broadway show
   music

—Frank Trenery

257

SAINT PETERSBURG PUBLIC LIBRARY   FSp

3745 Ninth Avenue North
Saint Petersburg, Florida 33713

Sheet music, 3000 items, 1860s– ; 200 songbooks,
   1910–40; and 300 recordings

—Elizabeth R. Hartman

258

Sol KELLERMAN

810 Vista Del Lago
Stuart, Florida 33494

Sheet music, 5600 popular-music items, 1870–1965
Recordings, 500 78-rpm discs of jazz and popular music

259

FLORIDA AGRICULTURAL AND   FTaFA
MECHANICAL UNIVERSITY

Coleman Memorial Library
Tallahassee, Florida 32307

"Poetry of Sacred Song" collection of hymnals and gos-
   pel songbooks, including the personal collection of
   Robert Lowry (1826–99, hymn writer)
Louise Richardson, collection of settings of Clement C.
   Moore's "The Night before Christmas," including
   musical settings, as cited in *Howell*, p. 63

260

FLORIDA STATE UNIVERSITY   FTaSU

Tallahassee, Florida 32306

Warren D. Allen Music Library

Franciezek Zachara (1898–1966, pianist and professor of
   music at the University), 100 mss and 3 published
   compositions, ca. 1932–60; also 6 33⅓-rpm discs of
   him playing
Ella Scoble Opperman (dean of the School of Music,
   1911–44), personal papers, ca. 1901–44, including
   programs, clippings, correspondence, and printed
   scores
Florida Composers' League, 2 scrapbooks containing
   minutes, programs, and clippings, ca. 1945–65
Tunebooks, including some in shape notation, in all 200
   items, ca. 1840–1900
Popular vocal sheet music, ca. 1860–1940, 200 items,
   including several by composers from Florida or
   southern Georgia; also published scores, including

materials from the library of Olin Downes
Programs of the Boston Symphony Orchestra, 5 linear meters of bound vols.
Recordings, including the Carl Helwig collection of local-interest recordings, many of them of Hungarian and German ethnic background; 2500 78-rpm discs and 2500 tapes, collected by Helwig ca. 1948–62; also 1000 78-rpm discs, many of them of jazz

—Dale Hudson

Robert Manning Strozier Library, Special Collections Department

Olin Downes (1886–1955, music critic) Collection, including a Jean Sibelius ms of *Jedermann* op. 83
Programs of University musical and theatrical events, ca. 1927–

—Opal Free

261
UNIVERSITY OF SOUTH FLORIDA   FTS
Music Resources
4202 Fowler Avenue
Tampa, Florida 33520

Sheet music, 7000 popular- and classical-music items, ca. 1900
Other printed music, including 3 linear meters of band and theater items, 1900–1910
Recordings, including 7.6 linear meters of popular and classical 78-rpm discs

—Becky Miller

262
NORTH BREVARD PUBLIC LIBRARY   FTi
2121 South Hopkins Avenue
Titusville, Florida 32780

Jacob Hanneman (accompanist), 12 ms copies of concert music for piano, n.d.
Sheet music, 212 popular-music items, 1864–1940
Hymnals, 36 items of various denominations, 1881–1940
Songbooks, 32 vols. including popular, religious, and school songbooks, 1884–1940
Recordings, including 15 78-rpm discs, 1930s

—Verna Langlais

263
Stephen FOSTER CENTER AND FLORIDA FOLKLIFE ARCHIVE
Stephen Foster Memorial Park
White Springs, Florida 32096

Although the Florida Folk Festival dates from 1952, earlier materials are in the collections, including 20 sheet-music items, 30 *Sacred Harp* and other shape-note tunebooks and hymnals, archival materials from the Florida Federation of Music Clubs and the National Federation of Music Clubs, as well as 50 field recordings of Florida folk musicians

—James E. McDuffee

In addition to the repositories listed above, the following have also reported holdings of the materials indicated:
Belle Glade—Belle Glade Public Library: songbooks
Boynton Beach—Boynton Beach City Library: songbooks
Clearwater—Clearwater Christian College, Library: songbooks
De Land—De Land Free Public Library: songbooks
Largo—Pinnellas County History Museum: sheet music, songbooks, other printed music, pictures, recordings
Lehigh Acres—Lehigh Acres Public Library: sheet music, songbooks, recordings, miscellaneous
Opa Locka—Florida Memorial College, Jonathan Sewell Library: recordings
Palm Beach—Historical Society of Palm Beach County: sheet music, songbooks, programs, pictures
Riviera Beach—Riviera Beach Public Library: songbooks, recordings
St. Augustine—St. Augustine Historical Society: sheet music
St. Leo—St. Leo College, Library: songbooks, other printed music
St. Petersburg—Tampa College, Library: catalogues, recordings
Sanibel—Sanibel Public Library: songbooks
Stuart—Martin County Historical Society: sheet music, songbooks, programs, catalogues
Tavares—Lake County Historical Society: sheet music

Georgia

264
John GARST
123 Fortson Drive
Athens, Georgia 30606

Hymnals, 500 published vols., 1790–
Recordings, 500 78-rpm discs, including blues, hillbilly, and jazz

265
UNIVERSITY OF GEORGIA   GU
Athens, Georgia 30602

Guido Adler (1855–1941, Viennese music historian), personal library of 1200 books and periodicals (in the General Library) and music scores (in the Music Reference Library); also his personal papers (in Rare

Books and Manuscripts), 74 boxes, 1868–1935, with writings, correspondence, clippings, and personal records, including items on American subjects or from such colleagues as Alfred Einstein, Carl Engel, Arnold Schoenberg, and Oscar Sonneck. See Edward R. Reilly, "The Papers of Guido Adler at the University of Georgia: A Provisional Inventory" (typescript, 1975); also Mary Gail Means, *A Catalogue of Printed Books and Music in the Guido Adler Collection* (Master's thesis, University of Georgia, 1968)

Lucy Bates collection on dance, 892 items, including correspondence, diaries, photographs, post cards, and a scrapbook, 1711–1969

Arthur Mansfield Curry (1866–1953, composer), 50 music mss in 26 packets (in the Music Reference Library)

Katherine Cowen DeBaillou papers, including 34 items of correspondence with Paul Bowles (composer), 1930–47 (in Rare Books and Manuscripts)

Olin Downes (1886–1955, music critic), personal papers, including 50,000 letters, clippings, and personal artifacts (in Rare Books and Manuscripts), organized by subject (names and titles) and by persons, with a partial index. See Jean Réti-Forbes, "The Olin Downes Papers," *Georgia Review*, 21 (1967), 165–71

Georgia Folklore Society, copies of field recordings of sacred and secular folksongs including blues, shape-note singing, and black church music, collected from southern Georgia and the Sea Islands, 1960s–70s, 300 tapes (in the Electromedia Department)

Carol Robinson collection on 20th-century composers and performances, 419 items, including correspondence, concert programs (1919–68), photographs, libretti, clippings, contracts, and ms scores by George Antheil (*Fourth Sonata for Pianoforte)* and Bohuslav Martinu (*Par TSF),* donated in 1969 (in Rare Books and Manuscripts)

Archer Taylor (folklorist, Germanic scholar, and bibliographer), 10,000 vols. from his personal library (dispersed through the general stacks with 500 items in Rare Books and Manuscripts), also letters and 5 ms books (Rare Books and Manuscripts)

John B. Vaughan (hymn composer), papers, correspondence, ms music and verse, and printed materials, 252 items, 1884–1938 (in Rare Books and Manuscripts)

Musical comedies, 50 piano-vocal scores, 1891–1938, including 6 by May Hewes Dodge and John Wilson Dodge (in the Music Stacks)

Songbooks, including 25 shape-note hymnals published mostly in the southeastern U.S., and 30 other hymnals, all 20th century (in the Music Stacks and the Georgia Room); also 60 folksong collections (in the Music Stacks, Rare Books and Manuscripts, and the Georgia Room)

Sheet music, 10,000 items, mostly 1850–1920, indexed by title and date (in Rare Books and Manuscripts)

Programs of European and American concerts and stage productions, 9 linear meters, ca. 1890–1940, partly arranged by locality (in Rare Books and Manuscripts)

Periodicals, including 4 numbers of the *Southern Musical Journal,* 1874–81 (in the Music Stacks)

Recordings (in the Music Recordings Archive), 35 linear meters of 78-rpm discs, formerly used for instruction; also 8 linear meters of 78-rpm discs of jazz and dance

orchestras, formerly a radio-station collection, with a ms list

—Jerry Persons, J. Larry Gulley,
Harriet Newman, Béla Foltin

266
ATLANTA HISTORICAL SOCIETY   GAHi
Box 12423
Atlanta, Georgia 30305

Sheet music, 200 popular music items, 1860–

Hymnals and sacred songbooks, 62 vols., 19th and early 20th centuries

Helen Knox Spain, 45 linear cm. of programs of theatrical and musical events in New York and Atlanta, 1905–30

Bertha Harwood-Arrowood (president of the Atlanta Musical Association), papers, 1909–12, including accounts of the formation of public school bands and orchestras in Atlanta; an essay on blacks and black music; and a scrapbook of programs and clippings of the Atlanta Musical Association, clippings and correspondence with performers who came to Atlanta, and programs and clippings on Atlanta's opera season

Willie May (Mrs. James H.) Whitten (Atlanta singer), scrapbook, 1909–27, containing press clippings, programs of her performances, and photographs

Mary B. Griffith Dobbs (director of the Griffith School of Music, Atlanta), photographs, clippings, programs, and periodicals, 1915–40

Cornelia Jackson Moore family, 75 linear cm. of diaries and scrapbooks, 1865–1949, including press clippings and notes concerning the Atlanta Music Club and music in the U.S., 1920–40

Enrico Leide (composer, and conductor of the Atlanta Symphony Orchestra, 1920–39), personal papers, 1925–70, including 4 linear meters of music scores, recordings, programs, photographs, and 10 linear cm. of music mss, ca. 1926

Atlanta Music Club, papers, 1915–70, including 2 mss on the history of the organization, 1917 and 1940; a constitution and by-laws; minutes, 1919–70; programs; correspondence, 1917-50; 10 scrapbooks of clippings, programs, photographs, and calendars of monthly events, 1915–70; miscellaneous pamphlets; and constitutions for the National Federation of Musical Clubs, 1921, and for local clubs in Savannah, 1896, Macon, 1920, and Birmingham, Ala., 1920

Dorothy Haverty (Mrs. Lon) Grove (music patron), personal papers, 1938–55, including writings on music, and materials concerning the Atlanta Symphony Orchestra, Atlanta Symphony Guild, and Atlanta Music Club

—Mamie E. Locke

267
ATLANTA PUBLIC LIBRARY   GA
10 Pryor Street SW
Atlanta, Georgia 30303

Sheet music, 14 items, 1920s–30s

Hymnals and songbooks, 126 19th- and early 20th-century vols.

Other printed music, including 30 vols. of black spirituals, work songs, and blues, 1887–1940, in the Samuel Williams Collection of Afro-Americana

Georgia Federation of Music Clubs, minutes and reports, 5 vols., 1920–40, also 2 scrapbooks containing bulletins, concert programs, and membership lists, 1930s

Programs and clippings for local concerts, 1907–40

—Anthony G. Miller

268
ATLANTA UNIVERSITY   GAU
Trevor Arnett Library
273 Chestnut Street SW
Atlanta, Georgia 30314

See the *Guide to Manuscripts and Archives in the Negro Collection* (Atlanta, 1971)

Maud Cuney Hare (1874–1936, pianist), 83 items of papers, 1900–1936, with music mss, printed sheet music, photographs, programs, minstrel songs, and biographies of musicians including Henry T. Burleigh, B. Consuelo Cook, Will Marion Cook, Joseph S. Cotter, Sr., Gussie L. Davis, R. Nathaniel Dett, Carl R. Diton, Justin Elie, Taylor Gordon, E. Azalia Hackley, W. C. Handy, Justin Holland, Nora Douglas Holt, Laurence Hope, Henry Mather, Etta Moten, Noble Sissle, and others

Countee Cullen Memorial Collection, founded in 1942 by Harold Jackman (teacher, musician, and patron of the arts of New York City), 4800 items, including mss, broadsides, printers' proofs, photographs, periodicals, books, and theater programs dealing with contributions of the Negro to performing arts in the 20th century. The papers of Countee Cullen (1903–46) include typescripts of *Byword for Evil* (Cullen's *Medea* with music by Virgil Thomson) and *The Third Fourth of July*, a play with music; poems and songs by Cullen in sheet-music form; and photographs of Cullen. The collection also includes papers of W. C. Handy (1873–1958) concerning the Handy Brothers Music Co. and the W. C. Handy Foundation for the Blind, and Arna Bontemps's final draft of Handy's autobiography, *Father of the Blues*, 1941; Langston Hughes (1908–67), 3 cantatas set to music by Jan Meyerowitz; Eslanda Goode Robeson (1896–1965, anthropologist, and wife of Paul Robeson), letters from concert tours in England, Europe, and Russia, 1930s; Clarence Cameron White (1880-1960), papers concerning his fiftieth anniversary as a concert violinist, honors bestowed upon him in New Orleans, and advertisements for his opera *Ouanga*; also items by or about Marian Anderson, Henry T. Burleigh, Roland Hayes, Bill ("Bojangles") Robinson, Philippa D. Schuyler, Arthur B. Spingarn, and others

Henry P. Slaughter Collection, 1697–1946, 442 items including sheet music, clippings, pamphlets, books, portraits, and prints

George Alexander Towns Collection, including letters from James Weldon Johnson tracing his consular and literary careers, 1906-26, also letters of Percy Lee Atherton and Thomas W. Higginson

Southern Conference for Human Welfare Collection, 1938–67, including correspondence of Marian Anderson and others

—Gloria Mins

269
EMORY UNIVERSITY   GEU
University Libraries
Atlanta, Georgia 30322

All materials are in the Special Collections Department of the Woodruff Library, except as noted

Hartford collection of sacred music, 9000 hymnals, tunebooks, and sacred songsters, including materials formerly in the Warrington and Paine Collections at Hartford (Conn.) Theological Seminary, partly catalogued (in the Pitts Theology Library). See Irving Lowens, "The Warrington Collection, a Research Adventure at Case Memorial Library," *Hartford Seminary Foundation Bulletin*, 12 (1952), 29–38, also his *Music and Musicians in Early America* (New York, 1964), pp. 272–78

Wesleyana Collection, 2700 hymnals and books on hymnology and liturgy (in the Pitts Theology Library)

John Wesley (1703–91), papers including correspondence of Wesley and his family, mentioning music and musical activities

John Hill Hewitt (1801–90), 11 boxes of mss and published materials, including letters, plays, poems, songs and operettas, also scrapbooks of press clippings relating to his career as a playwright, songwriter, and journalist. See Richard B. Harwell, "John Hill Hewitt Collection," *South Atlantic Bulletin*, 13/4 (1948), 3–5

James Osgood Andrew Clark (1827–94), papers, including stories about and sheet music of black spirituals and hymns, collected by his wife, Ella Anderson Clark

Joel Chandler Harris (1848–1908, journalist and folklorist), personal papers, including letters, literary mss, Edward A. MacDowell's ms sketch for "Brer Rabbit" from *Fireside Tales* (1901), 1 other music ms, and 2 items of sheet music

Metropolitan Opera, materials relating to performances in Atlanta, including 5 shelf boxes of libretti, correspondence, clippings, and memorabilia in the papers of Charles Howard Candler (1878–1957), and other miscellaneous items, 1920s–, in various collections

Margaret Mitchell (1900–1949), personal papers, including 1 box of photographs, scripts, sheet music, and lyrics for Harold Rome's musical adaptation of *Gone with the Wind*

Gladys Hanson (early 20th-century Broadway actress), papers including 17 letters from Geraldine Farrar

Sheet music, including 150 Confederate imprints, and 150 other items mostly from the period of World War I. See Frank W. Hoogerwerf, "Confederate Sheet Music at the Robert W. Woodruff Library, Emory University," *M.L.A. Notes*, 34 (1977), 7–26

—Frank Hoogerwerf, Linda Matthews

270
GEORGIA DEPARTMENT OF   G-Ar
ARCHIVES AND HISTORY
330 Capitol Avenue SE
Atlanta, Georgia 30334

Published music, including 100 items of popular post-Civil War sheet music, also hymnals and other songbooks, scattered in various collections

Alfredo Barili (1854–1935, pianist and composer) and his wife, Emily Vezin Barili (1856–1940), 1.5 linear meters of personal papers, including biographical materials, correspondence, and photographs of Mr. Barili's aunt, Adelina Patti (1843–1919), and her family; also scrapbooks, sheet music, biographical and genealogical materials of the Barili and Vezin families, and materials concerning the Barili School of Music in Atlanta, founded 1899

Sarah Jane Thorne Brewton (1851–1929) and Margaret May Brewton Rabun (1882–1966, Georgia music teachers), personal papers, including sheet music, piano advertisements, ms copybook with accounts of music lessons, teaching materials, correspondence, and receipts for the rental of a piano in Hannibal, Mo.

Sacred Harp Convention, Georgia (Chattahoochee Musical Convention), membership lists, 1852–1922, minutes, 1865–1916, a constitution, and a list of annual sessions with an alphabetical list of members, 1852–1971

Music catalogues, 1879–84, 66 items, mostly from Ludden & Bates (Savannah music dealer), also from dealers in Boston and Worcester, Mass., New York City, and Brattleboro, Vt.

Programs of Atlanta operas and concerts, 100 items scattered in personal collections, 1840s–

—Peter E. Schinkel

271

GEORGIA STATE UNIVERSITY   GASU

104 Decatur Street SE
Atlanta, Georgia 30303

Georgia Folklore Archives, with recordings of white and black traditional singing and instrumental music from Georgia and the southern U.S., including black spirituals, gospel, blues, secular songs, white *Sacred Harp* singing, ballads, lyric songs, fiddle, banjo, dulcimer, mouth harp ("jew's harp"), mouth bow, accordion, pump organ, guitar, and mandolin; also some Ozark Mountain, Cajun, and southeastern American Indian music; in all 150 hours of tape recordings and 2 films, as cited in *Briegleb*, no. 24

William Russell Pullen Library, a collection of published music including sheet music and songbooks

272

William C. LORING

77 East Andrews Drive NW, Apt. 394
Atlanta, Georgia 30305

Music by American composers active in Europe, including scores by Arthur Bird and George Templeton Strong. Much of the collection has been donated to the Library of Congress, the New England Conservatory (Boston), and the Fleisher Collection of the Free Library of Philadelphia. See Loring's *The Music of Arthur Bird* (Atlanta, 1974)

273

Edmond D. KEITH

36 Kensington Road
Avondale Estates, Georgia 30002

Hymnals and tunebooks, 1000 items (in addition to the 5000 items in the Keith Collection at the New Orleans Baptist Theological Seminary, q.v.), mostly 20th-century imprints, and particularly strong in Baptist materials; also books on hymnology

274

SOUTHWEST GEORGIA REGIONAL LIBRARY

Shotwell and Monroe Streets
Bainbridge, Georgia 31717

Muscogee Indians of southern Georgia, tape recordings and video tapes of dances and dance music

275

WEST GEORGIA COLLEGE   GCarrWG

Library
Carrollton, Georgia 30118

Sacred Harp materials, 125 items, including photocopies of annual minutes of the Chattahoochee Valley Music Convention, 1852–1959, also hymnals and recordings, as cited in *Howell*, p. 90

276

COLUMBUS COLLEGE   GColuC

Archives
Columbus, Georgia 31907

Sheet music, 120 items, mostly early 20th century

Hymnals and school songbooks, 20 vols. used in the Columbus area, ca. 1890–1940

Chase Family (founders of the Chase Conservatory of Music, Columbus), papers, 1860s–1945, music mss, and programs of Conservatory recitals, 1894–1945

Other printed music, including 48 piano editions and a method book for reed organ, late 19th and early 20th centuries

Orpheus Club (Columbus music group), papers and yearbooks, 1890s

Programs of Springer Theatre Company (formerly Springer Opera House) concerts, 1871– , traveling shows, and other local concerts, late 19th and early 20th centuries

Papers and photographs of families musically active in Columbus before 1930, also music catalogues of 19th-century southern music dealers

—Katherine Mahan

277

Eugene WIGGINS

North Georgia College
Dahlonega, Georgia 30533

"Fiddlin' " John Carson materials, including 100 photographs, 20 hours of recorded interviews about him, and taped copies of 150 sides of 78-rpm discs, representing nearly all his recordings including unpublished items, 1923–34

Recordings, including 10 hours of non-commercial hillbilly recordings on tape, and taped copies of 30 hours of popular music on cylinders, ca. 1910–20

278
INSTITUTE FOR MUSIC IN GEORGIA (GDS)
Agnes Scott College
Decatur, Georgia 30030

Field recordings of Georgia music collected in the 1970s, including native blues, mostly urban (150 hours); country musicians, mostly rural, playing banjo or fiddle or in string bands (150 hours); radio broadcasts, predominantly evangelical services (100 hours); and interviews
Tunebooks, hymnals, songbooks, and books on music, 200 items, mid 19th century to the present
Memorabilia, local histories of church and music activities, photographs, scrapbooks, letters, and other materials, 100 items

—Ron Byrnside

279
METHODIST MUSEUM
South Georgia Conference
United Methodist Church
Box 407
Saint Simons Island, Georgia 31522

Methodist hymnals and revival-meeting songbooks, 40 vols., 1727– ; also Joseph Williams, *A Book of Psalmody* (1729), with ms markings

—Ethelene Sampley, Mary Fain

280
GEORGIA HISTORICAL SOCIETY   GHi
501 Whitaker Street
Savannah, Georgia 31401

Sheet music, 500 mid-19th-century and Civil War items, with title index

—Anthony R. Dees

281
Juliette Gordon LOW BIRTHPLACE
11 York Lane
Savannah, Georgia 31401

Sheet music, 5 bound vols., 1856–66, and 20 separate popular-music items, 1890–1910
Hymnals, 2 vols., 1838 and 1874
Ch. Davidoff, bass viol accompaniment to "Romance sans paroles" op. 23, n.d., owned by Eleanor Kinzie Gordon
Other printed music, including 3 vols. of vocal or religious music, ca. 1890
American music periodicals, including 1 issue of the *New York Music Echo* (May 1883)

—Charlotte P. Hallock

282
SAVANNAH PUBLIC AND   GS
CHATHAM–EFFINGHAM LIBERTY
REGIONAL LIBRARY
2002 Bull Street
Savannah, Georgia 31401

Sheet music, 1200 items of early 20th-century popular and religious music
Songbooks, 250 20th-century vols. of folksongs and slave songs
Programs of the Savannah Symphony Society, Inc. (formerly the Savannah Music Club), and the Savannah Community Chorale (formerly the Savannah Opera Association), 35 items, 1896–
Music catalogues, 25 items of early 20th-century music dealers

—Catherine A. Nathan

283
SAVANNAH STATE COLLEGE   GSSC
Asa H. Gordon Library
Savannah, Georgia 31404

James A. Bland (1854-1911), biographical materials, as reflected in Coleridge Alexander Braithwaite, "The Life and Creative Activities of James Allen Bland," Savannah State College *Faculty Research Edition*, 14/2 (1960), 15-20

284
Robert W. JOHN
105 Oakmont Court
Winterville, Georgia 30683

American church and school music, 400 vols., including 16th- to 18th-century English, German, and American psalm books; 18th- and 19th-century tunebooks; school music books, among them Pestalozzian materials, graded music readers, and songbooks, 1830s– , and revivalist songbooks of the late 19th and 20th centuries, mostly gospel songbooks and standard hymnals of Protestant denominations
Sheet music, popular songs and piano pieces, ca. 1790–1940s

In addition to the repositories listed above, the following have also reported holdings of the materials indicated:

Americus—Lake Blackshear Regional Library: sheet music, songbooks, other printed music, catalogues, recordings
Atlanta—Mercer University, Library: printed music, recordings
Atlanta—Oglethorpe University, Library: songbooks
Augusta—Augusta College, Reese Library: songbooks, other printed music, recordings

Augusta—Paine College, W. A. Candler Memorial Library: recordings

Dahlonega—North Georgia College, Stewart Memorial Library: songbooks, pictures, recordings

Dalton—Dalton Regional Library: sheet music

Decatur—Maud M. Burrus Library: songbooks, recordings

East Point—Atlanta Christian College, James A. Burns Memorial Library: songbooks

Jekyll Island—Jekyll Island State Park Authority: recordings

Marietta—Kennesaw Mountain Historical Society: songbooks

Oxford—Oxford Shrine Society: songbooks

Statesboro—Jack Broucek: sheet music, songbooks, other printed music

Statesboro—Georgia Southern College: sheet music, songbooks, other printed music

Tifton—Coastal Plain Regional Library: recordings

Tifton—Georgia Agrirama Development Authority: songbooks

Hawaii

285

Bernice P. BISHOP MUSEUM   HHB
1355 Kalihi Street
Box 6037
Honolulu, Hawaii 96818

Library

Liliuokalani collection, including 132 mss of music and lyrics, among them the first holograph ms of "Aloha Oe" and the published sheet music (1884), and ms booklets containing many of the Queen's lyrics

Manuscript notebooks of *mele* (words to chants), some copied by members of the royal family, in all 8 notebooks containing 150 items, ca. 1800–1915

Manuscript collections of ethnomusicologists, including Helen Roberts, ca. 1923–26, materials used in *Ancient Hawaiian Music* (Honolulu, 1926); Kenneth Pike Emory, 36 leaves of typescript notes and 5 pages of holograph notes pertaining to Hawaiian hulas, 1933; and Mary K. Pukui, ca. 1940–70, field notes

Jane Lathrop Winne (1885–1976), papers, including notes on Hawaiiana and Hawaiian music, and programs of musical events

Henri Berger, "Irwin March" (1897) and other items of his published music

Sheet music and published collections of Hawaiian music, 92 items, 1868–1940; also books about music, musical instruments, and dance of Hawaii and the Pacific islands

Programs of local musical events, including musicales, operettas, solo recitals, and band concerts, 100 items, ca. 1845–1950

Photographs of dancers, chanters, and musical instruments, 100 items, ca. 1923–70

—Cynthia Timberlake

Department of Anthropology, Audio-Recording Collection

Field recordings of music of the Pacific islands, especially of Hawaii and eastern Polynesia, ca. 1900–1960, 1500 items including wax cylinders, wire recordings, aluminum discs, other discs, and tapes (the latter ca. 1950–79)

Commercial recordings of Hawaiian or Pacific-island music, 2700 discs

Songbooks of Hawaiian music, 10 items, ca. 1880–1920; also 60 items of Hawaiian sheet music, ca. 1880–1960

Catalogues of Hawaiian music-recording companies, 15 items, ca. 1930–50

Photographs of Hawaiian chanters, 30 items, ca. 1923–70

Clippings on Hawaiian music, 150 items, ca. 1930–79

—Elizabeth Tatar

286

HAWAII STATE ARCHIVES   H-Ar
Iolani Palace Grounds
Honolulu, Hawaii 96813

Liliuokalani (1838–1917, Queen of the Hawaiian Islands), ms songbook, "He buke mele Hawaii" (Book of Hawaiian Songs), 1897, with songs by her and others; 12 other ms songs; and an oil portrait and photographs of her

Charles King (1874–1950), ms score of his opera *Prince of Hawaii*, 1925; 30 linear cm. of material about the opera, including a conductor's score, a typed précis of the action, and dialogue used in later productions; also 1 photograph of him

Henri Berger (1844–1929, leader of the Royal Hawaiian Band), 30 linear cm. of papers, including journals (1882–99), band accounts, mss of Hawaiian songs, ms band scores with marginal notes in English and Hawaiian for performers, and 6 photographs of Berger

—Agnes Conrad

287

HAWAIIAN HISTORICAL SOCIETY   HHi
560 Kawaiahao Street
Honolulu, Hawaii 96813

Honolulu Symphony Society, reports and programs, 1948–63, 20 linear cm.

Hymnals compiled by missionaries to Hawaii, 75 items published 1823–1900, mostly in Hawaiian; also 1 popular songbook in Hawaiian, 1898, and 1 bound vol. of popular sheet music, 1896

—Barbara Dunn

288

**HAWAIIAN MISSION CHILDRENS' HHMC
SOCIETY LIBRARY**
553 South King Street
Honolulu, Hawaii 96813

Hiram Bingham, folder with mss of traditional Protestant hymns, to which he added Hawaiian words, ca. 1820–90
Lorenzo Lyons, ms book of traditional hymns, with Hawaiian words, ca. 1820–90
Hymnals, 250 items, 1823–90s, mostly Protestant, including 160 in Hawaiian
Popular songbook, ca. 1870
Programs of local groups, 50 items, 1890s–1930s
Photographs of Hawaiian musicians, 20 items, 1890s
Folders with notes on songs and songwriters of Hawaii, and copies of music mss, in all 10 linear cm., 1890s–1970s

—Mary Jane Knight

289

UNIVERSITY OF HAWAII HU
Honolulu, Hawaii 96822

Sinclair Library, Special Collections
(2425 Campus Road)

Hawaiian music, including 40 songbooks, 30 sheet-music items, and 50 books, theses, and ms texts about Hawaiian music and musicians

—David Kittelson

Thomas Hale Hamilton Library (2550 The Mall)

Songbooks, 100 items; also 50 other published music editions

—Donald Matsumori

In addition to the repositories listed above, the following have also reported holdings of the materials indicated:
Honolulu—Christian Science Reading Room: songbooks, recordings
Honolulu—Hawaii Foundation for History and the Humanities: recordings
Laie—Church College of Hawaii, Ralph E. Woolley Library: songbooks, other printed music, programs, catalogues, pictures, recordings
Wailuku—Maui Historical Society: recordings

Idaho

290

IDAHO STATE HISTORICAL SOCIETY IdHi
610 North Julia Davis Drive
Boise, Idaho 83706

Programs, 25 local items, including Boise opera houses and Idaho dance halls, late 19th century, in various personal collections
Sheet music, 500 items, ca. 1860–1950, and 30 items relating to Idaho, ca. 1864–
Photographs of local musicians and music groups, 350 items
Recordings, including 50 Edison cylinders and 150 78-rpm discs; also 6 oral-history tapes concerning folk music, collected at the Sun Valley Folk Festival by the Idaho Oral History Center

—James H. Davis, Ken Swanson

291

COLLEGE OF IDAHO IdCaC
2112 Cleveland Boulevard
Caldwell, Idaho 83605

Terteling Library

Frederick Fleming Beale (fl. 1920s, local composer), 150 holograph music mss, mostly songs and operettas
—Richard G. Elliott

**College of Idaho Folklore Archive,
Department of English**

Field recordings collected by students of Louie Attebery, mostly of songs and fiddle music from the Snake River Basin, Idaho, Montana, Wyoming, eastern Oregon, and northern Utah, including music of American Indians, Mexican-Americans, and Anglo-Americans

292

LEWIS–CLARK STATE COLLEGE IdLN
Library
Lewiston, Idaho 83501

Sheet music and published compilations used by Gertrude Thompson (local silent-film organist), 2774 items including some cue music, ca. 1855–1930
Other published music, including 6 hymnals of various denominations, 1886–1906, and 1 cantata, 1877

—Lillian M. Martin

293

UNIVERSITY OF IDAHO IdU
Library
Moscow, Idaho 83843

Ballad texts, 15 linear cm. of typescripts; also 4 tape recordings of ballads (in the Folklore Archives)
Clarence Elzy Talbott, typed memoirs (1950) of the period ca. 1875–1900, including song texts
Musical compositions written by University students

in partial fulfillment of graduation requirements, 4 mss, 1940–

—Charles A. Webbert

294
IDAHO STATE UNIVERSITY   IdPl
Library
Pocatello, Idaho 83201

John Taylor (fl. ca. 1915–27, local silent-film organist), 2500 sheet-music items, some with ms notations
Recordings, including 60 linear cm. of 78-rpm discs

—Douglas Birdsall

295
Ruth H. BARRUS
Program Director
Musical Heritage Studies
Ricks College
Rexburg, Idaho 83440

Scrapbooks, 10 vols., containing pictures, programs, and press clippings, documenting the musical activity of Ricks College and the Rexburg community, 1935–

Material collected in connection with a project entitled "The Musical Heritage of the Upper Snake River Valley," supported by the Association for the Humanities in Idaho, 1976–79, including documentation of the work of private music teachers, civic music groups, and public schools, and musical histories of Idaho State University, Ricks College, and 33 southeastern Idaho communities

296
BONNER COUNTY HISTORICAL SOCIETY
Box 1063
Sandpoint, Idaho 83864

Sheet music, ca. 1900–1945, 1000 items, mostly songs of World Wars I and II, including some by local composers Mira H. Persons, Robert E. McFarland, and Agnes Schaffenberg
Recordings, including 1 linear meter of 78-rpm discs

—Betty Dunlap

In addition to the repositories listed above, the following have also reported holdings of the materials indicated:
Boise—Boise Public Library: songbooks
Boise—Garden City Community Library: sheet music, songbooks
Cambridge—Cambridge Community Library: songbooks
Coeur D'Alene—Museum of North Idaho: sheet music, songbooks, pictures, recordings
Gooding—Gooding Public Library: songbooks, other printed music
Hansen—Hansen Public Library: songbooks
Horseshoe Bend—Community Library: recordings
Middleton—Cowden Memorial Library: songbooks
Moscow—Latah County Historical Society: sheet music, pictures, recordings
Mountain Home—Mountain Home Public Library: songbooks, miscellaneous

Illinois

297
AURORA COLLEGE   IAurC
Library
347 South Gladstone
Aurora, Illinois 60507

Hymnals and sacred songbooks of the Adventist and Millerite movements, 75 items, 1840– , and printed hymns and sacred songs of Millerite and Adventist hymn writers, on 26 printed leaflets, 1840– (largely in the Jenks Memorial Collection of Adventual Materials)
Singing-school and popular songbooks, 20 secular or sacred items, ca. 1800–1900
Recordings of sacred music, including 3 78-rpm discs and 1 radio-transcription disc, ca. 1930–50

—Doris Colby

298
AURORA HISTORICAL MUSEUM
304 Oak Avenue
Box 905
Aurora, Illinois 60507

Charles E. Gridley (1875–1965, violinist and theater musician), 2 scrapbooks containing press clippings of minstrel-show tours and vaudeville productions, also programs, mostly local
Emma Maybelle Baker Broderick (opera singer), 1 scrapbook, n.d.
St. Cecilia Musical Club, 70 linear cm. of minutes, programs, and clippings, ca. 1880–1976
School songbooks, 10 items, ca. 1920–40
Sheet music, 50 mostly popular items, ca. 1910–40
Programs of local musical events, 500 items, some of them in scrapbooks, ca. 1870–1940
Photographs and drawings of local musicians and groups, 25 items, ca. 1866–

—Robert W. Barclay

299
BARRINGTON HISTORICAL SOCIETY
111 West Station Street
Barrington, Illinois 60010

Sears School of Music, Barrington, programs of concerts and 6 catalogues, ca. 1902–30

Sheet music and songbooks, 60 linear cm., ca. 1900–1940

Recordings, including 50 Edison amberol cylinders, and 30 78-rpm discs

—Donna Hellman

300

CENTRAL ILLINOIS CONFERENCE— THE UNITED METHODIST CHURCH

Commission on Archives and History
Box 2050
Bloomington, Illinois 61701

Hymnals of the Methodist, Evangelical, and United Brethren churches, 86 items, 1817–1976

Programs and photographs of musical events in churches, included in a collection of historical materials on 600 local churches, 1820–

—Lynn W. Turner

301

ILLINOIS WESLEYAN UNIVERSITY   IBloW

Bloomington, Illinois 61701

Archives of the School of Music and its precursor, the Bloomington College of Music, 1887– , including catalogues, programs, curriculum materials, and correspondence

Scrapbooks of press clippings and programs related to the School of Music, its faculty and students, also to other Bloomington–Normal musical events, 5 vols., 1924–60 (in the University Archives)

—Glenn Patton

302

McLEAN COUNTY HISTORICAL SOCIETY LIBRARY

201 East Grove
Bloomington, Illinois 61701

Personal papers of musicians, including an anonymous ms biography of Charles E. Ballard (composer), 1867–91, also a typescript copy; William Brigham, early 20th century; Emma Wissmiller; C.H. Chamberlain; Eileen Foley; Sarah Raymond Fitzwilliam; Hutton family (publishers), including notebooks, scrapbooks, bills, and correspondence; Charles Morgan, 18 diaries, 1896–1925; G. H. Sitherwood; and Minnie Saltzman Stevens, ms memoirs

Music exercise and theory books, 5 items printed in Bloomington by local music schools, ca. 1910

Hymnals with words only, 15 items, 1790–1900

Songbooks used in local schools, 5 items, ca. 1855–70

Sheet music by local composers, 10 items, ca. 1890–1917, including works by Fred T. Ashton, also a photograph of him

Civil War broadsides, 2 items

Programs of local organizations, 80 items, 1888–1935, including the Amateur Musical Club, Bloomington Band, Bloomington Conservatory of Music, Chatterton Opera House, Coliseum, Curley Theatre, Grand Opera House, Illini Theatre, Mardi-Carnival Association, and Skinner School

Bloomington School of Music, 1921 catalogue

—Greg Koos, Barbara Dunbar

303

CAIRO PUBLIC LIBRARY   ICa

1609 Washington Avenue
Cairo, Illinois 62914

Malvin Franklin (local composer), personal papers, including photographs and a holograph ms of his song "Cairo, Illinois"

Sheet music, several songs, relating to Cairo, 1920–

French's *New Sensation* (river showboat), 3 cashbooks, 1882–1922

304

FULTON COUNTY HISTORICAL SOCIETY

45 North Park Drive
Canton, Illinois 61520

Sheet music, 2000 popular items, including 3 by local composer Bert Morgan, ca. 1900

Band and orchestra scores and parts, 10 items used by local groups, ca. 1930–40

School songbooks and hymnals, 25 items used locally, ca. 1880–1920

Programs of local musical events, 10 items, ca. 1880–1920, including 1 from the Canton Opera House

Parlin and Orendorff (farm-implement manufacturers) Band, clippings in scrapbooks of various individuals, also 25 photographs and a uniform, ca. 1850–1940

—Mrs. Lawrence I. Bordner

305

SOUTHERN ILLINOIS UNIVERSITY   ICarbS

Carbondale, Illinois 62901

Morris Library

Vocal sheet music, secular and sacred, 2500 items, 1860– , mostly 1890–1940, including personal copies owned by Marjorie Lawrence (1907–79); arranged by composer, with partial index by titles and composers

Pearl White Walker (singer and professor of music at Lindenwood College, St. Charles, Mo.), personal library of music scores, and several hundred books on music

Marjorie Lawrence (1907–79), personal papers, 1926–77, 10 linear meters of correspondence, libretti, pictures, and programs, also 289 bound vols.

Katherine Mary Dunham, personal papers, 1919–68, relating to her career in dance, including 28 boxes of ms orchestral arrangements for her dance troupe

Belleville (Ill.) Band, bound vol. of official records, 1842–48, including membership lists, constitution, and reports

—Theophil M. Otto

Project in Ethnomusicology, Department of Anthropology

World-music collection of 245 tape recordings, 140 LP disc recordings, and 100 musical instruments, with an emphasis on Indochinese and Vietnamese music; also 40 tape copies of folk music of Kentucky, Missouri, and southern Illinois, recorded by David MacIntosh; and recordings of Afro-American music, tape copies of commercial ethnic recordings, and publicity and other materials about folk festivals

—Joel Maring

Department of Music

Printed music, including 200 sheet-music items, 6 song-books, and 30 other items, some of them from the library of the American Kantorei

—Robert R. Bergt

306
HOPE PUBLISHING COMPANY
380 South Main Place
Carol Stream, Illinois 60187

Fanny Crosby, 1000 mss of hymn texts, ca. 1870–1902 (in storage at the Billy Graham School of Evangelism, Wheaton, Ill.)
Notebooks pertaining to the history of the Company, 3 items compiled by George H. Shorney, including catalogues, prefaces, and hymns; a Lowell Mason ms; letters of Dwight L. Moody, Ira D. Sankey, and James McGranahan, also programs, ca. 1878–1975; and Fanny Crosby hymns, photographs, articles, and memorabilia
Hymnals, 2000 items, mostly Baptist and Methodist, 1832–1900

—George H. Shorney

307
Pauline LANGER
West Maple Avenue
Carrollton, Illinois 62016

J. A. Carson (1862–1944, music publisher and teacher), 12 ms organ and piano duets for use in his church, ca. 1942–44; 5 published compositions; programs for 10 recitals of his and his wife's students, ca. 1900–1950; and 10 published orchestral works used by him
Nita Ford (ca. 1900–1975, local piano teacher), 50 programs, ca. 1930–75
Hymnals of various denominations, 40 items, ca. 1880–1930
Popular vocal sheet music, 1400 items, ca. 1900–1930

308
Doris J. DYEN and Deane L. ROOT
1416 South Mattis Avenue
Champaign, Illinois 61820

Materials concerning the music of ethnic groups in the U.S., as partly reflected in Dyen's *The Role of Shape-Note Singing in the Musical Culture of Black Communities in Southeast Alabama* (Ph.D. diss., University of Illinois, 1977), including field recordings, interviews, photographs, minutes of singing conventions, singing-school materials, songbooks, and gospel songbooks; research files concerning theater music, as reflected in Root's *American Popular Stage Music, 1860–80* (Ph.D. diss., University of Illinois, 1977); and oral-history and field recordings of German-American music in central Illinois
Published music, including 2000 popular sheet-music items, also vocal anthologies, organ instruction books, hymnals and tunebooks, and books on music, mid 19th and 20th centuries
Recordings, including 100 78-rpm discs of classical and popular music

309
AMERICAN CONSERVATORY OF MUSIC
116 South Michigan Avenue
Chicago, Illinois 60603

Edward Collins (1889–1951, composer, conductor, and teacher), holograph music mss, comprising 19 orchestral works (scores and some parts), 4 chamber works, 21 piano works, and 16 art songs, also sketchbooks (located in the dean's office; inventory list)
Gibson Walters, personal music library, mostly published string music, 3 linear meters (being integrated into the Music Library collections)

310
Carl E. ANDERSON
1941 Farragut Avenue
Chicago, Illinois 60640

American Union of Swedish Singers, archives, 1892– , including 3000 musical works, in ms and printed editions, the latter mostly from Sweden, as used by the Union and its 30 component groups; songbooks used at the quadrennial conventions; archival records of affiliated groups, including ledgers, minutes, programs, and photographs; and copies of the Union's journal, *Musiktidning*. The archives are being organized and transferred to the Rockford (Ill.) Museum Center

311
Elisabeth H. BUCHHALTER
77 West Washington Street
Chicago, Illinois 60602

Simon Bucharoff (1881–1955), ms compositions and papers

312
CENTER FOR RESEARCH LIBRARIES   ICRL
5721 South Cottage Grove Avenue
Chicago, Illinois 60637

School music textbooks, 10,000 titles (30 linear meters), mostly 19th and 20th centuries, shelved by size, alphabetized by author, uncatalogued

313
CHICAGO ARCHITECTURE FOUNDATION
Glessner House
1800 Prairie Avenue
Chicago, Illinois 60616

Materials collected by Mr. and Mrs. John Jacob Glessner and family as patrons of music in Chicago, including a library of 100 books on music, ca. 1880–1920, and 80 music scores; programs of 80 opera and musical-theater productions, 1885–93, assembled in a scrapbook by Frances Glessner (b. 1878, the Glessners' daughter); and pictures, among them a self-portrait in ink by Enrico Caruso, sketches of Theodore Thomas, 2 portraits of Ignace Jan Paderewski, and 20 photographs of musicians (ca. 1900) donated by Mrs. Charles F. Batchelder (Frances Glessner's daughter)

—Jethro Hurt

314

CHICAGO HISTORICAL SOCIETY   ICHi

North Avenue and Clark Street
Chicago, Illinois 60614

Sheet music, in 4 groups: Chicago pictorial imprints, 1846– , 800 items; Chicago non-pictorial imprints, 1846– , 1200 items; music by George F. Root, 1845–93, 250 items; and other materials, ca. 1807– , 5000 items. Each group is arranged chronologically, and there is a general typescript index by title and by subject. See "Chicago: A Musical Accomplishment," *Chicago History*, 8 (1969), 353–74

Songbooks, secular and sacred, 200 items in the classes for Chicago imprints and general materials, catalogued

Programs of concerts, operas, and other musical performances, 13 linear meters, in bound vols., scrapbooks, and singly. The arrangement is by sponsoring organization or, lacking this, by concert hall, subdivided by date. Some of this material is included in the organizational archives (see below). Also broadside announcements of musical events, 45 items, 1840– , mostly 19th century

Broadside literary texts with musical association, 29 general items, 1834– ; 4 American Revolution items, 1775–1860s; 6 slavery items, ca. 1855–89?; 4 John Brown items, 1860–95; 18 Abraham Lincoln items, 1860–1911; 43 Confederate items, 1860s; 4 other Civil War items, 1860–89; and 8 political-campaign items, 1856–1936

Manuscripts of music and musical texts, including an Ephrata Cloister hymnal, ca. 1740, 200 pages in 2 vols.; 1 vol. of secular music, with colophon "Copy'd October 12th 1826 Thursday by Esther Maria Coxe," said to have been in the possession of the Custis family; James G. Drake, words to the song beginning "Sleep my love and sweetly sleep," dated Louisville, 1839; Joseph M. Dunavan, music for "Twas a Pleasant Home of Ours, Sister," with hand-drawn cover in the style of an illustrated sheet-music cover ("Composed and arranged in Camp Douglas by a Prisoner of War"); E. N., "Gov. Bross' March," dated Christmas, 1889, written for Gov. William Bross; Virginia Buckley Wallace (composer) and Martin E. Buckley (poet), song about Mrs. O'Leary's cow, 1895; M. Stead, music to Eugene Field's poem, "Little Boy Blue," 1896; Willetta Parker (composer) and Mary Mapes Dodge (poet), song "Coming," 1889, written for the mother of William Bross Lloyd; Edith Ogden (Mrs. Carter II) Harrison and L. Frank Baum, typescript text of "Prince Silverwings, a 3-Act Musical Fairy-Tail [sic]," 1902; Caspar J. Goudy, song "So Long Bill," written for Chicago mayor William Hale Thompson, 1931?; and William Mathieu, score of the musical play *Big Deal*, n.d.

Holograph fair copies of famous songs, including Daniel Decatur Emmett, "I Wish I Was in Dixie's Land," ca. 1900; Joseph Hopkinson, "Hail Columbia!", dated 1838; Walter Kittredge, "Tenting on the Old Camp Ground," dated 1900; James R. Randall, "Maryland, My Maryland," n.d.; George F. Root, "The Battle Cry of Freedom," dated 1885; Samuel F. Smith, "America," dated 1892; William Ross Wallace, "Keep Step with the Music of the Union" and "The Fall of Richmond," dated 1865; J. P. Webster, "Softly, Lightly," n.d.; and Henry Clay Work, text only and text with music for "My Grandfather's Clock," dated 1878, and chorus of "Marching through Georgia," n.d.

Transcripts of source materials on Chicago music, including George P. Upton, 6 vols. of notes and clippings, 1847–81; and Richard Longley Kilmer (1921–65), 3 boxes of materials toward a history of opera in Chicago, 1883–1962

Musical organizations' publications, programs, histories, scrapbooks, and archives, 200 files (as entered in the shelflist for class F38RL), also 25 files for operatic groups (class F38RM), including Ballman's Orchestra and Symphonic Band, scrapbooks, 1917–18; Bush Temple of Music and Conservatory, 1901–28; Chicago Band Association, 1901–24; Chicago Business Men's Orchestra, programs and clippings, 1932–35; Columbian Exposition, 1893, 2 vols. of official programs of the Bureau of Music; Fine Art Club, minutes, programs, and other archives, 1938–60; Germania Club, 27 vols. of verses and songs in German, many translated from English, 1869?–87, and 4 vols. of annual ledgers, 1939–48; Great Lakes Dredge and Philharmonic Society, archives, 1934– ; Illinois National Guard, 2nd Regiment, Field Music Association, record book, 1890–93; Jewish Community Centers of Chicago, extensive archives, 1904–54, with important music references; Klio Association (formerly the Emerson Gounod Club), 3 vols. of official archives, 1887–1901; Chicago Mendelssohn Club, extensive program books and official files, mostly of Charles Heber Strawbridge, 1894–1943; Musicians Club of Women (formerly Amateur Musical Club), extensive files of programs and archives, also an important history of the club by Ruth Klauber Friedman, 1967; National Convention of Women's Amateur Music Clubs, records, 1893; Nordamerikanischer Sängerbund; Philharmonic Society of Chicago, ms constitution, 1860, and programs, 1860–82; and the Teutonia Männerchor, pamphlets and songbooks

Henry E. Voegeli (1876–1943, manager of the Chicago Symphony Orchestra, 1927–43, and active at Orchestra Hall as of 1909), personal papers, 200 items, 1909–53, including extensive correspondence from Frederick Stock, 1931–40; letters from other colleagues, including Sol Bloom, Ossip Gabrilowitsch, Serge Prokofiev, Eugene Ormandy, and Percy Grainger; memorial vol. with tributes on his death; and miscellaneous items, mostly related to Jenny Lind

Miscellaneous references to Chicago musical activity, including Orlando Blackman (1835–99, public-school music administrator), biographical scrapbook; Charles Page Bryan, letter describing the conflict over alleged immorality in the performance of the American Opera Company ballet, 1886; James B. Campbell, inquiry about the sale of Dr. Kimberly's piano, 1836; George Benedict Carpenter, letter describing insolence of ushers at Central Music Hall, 1880; Herma Naomi Clark, songs supplied by readers for her *Chicago Tribune* column, "When Chicago Was Young," 1931–56; Giovanni Batista Contin, letter on his concert and other musical affairs, 1892; William James

Davis (1884–1919, Chicago theater manager), personal papers, including those of his wife, Jessie Bartlett Davis (professional singer), also incoming letters and letterpress copies of outgoing correspondence of the Carleton English Opera Company tour, 1883–85, and the 1883 tour of the Southwest by the Chicago Ideal Company, a ms music book copied by John E. McWade, including some of McWade's own songs, and miscellaneous theatrical correspondence, 10 bound vols. and 340 letters; Zdenka Cerny De Lacey, "Memories of a Musical Girlhood in Chicago," as told to Katherine Wagner Seineke; Julia Gerstenberg, letters and clippings on Chicago cultural affairs, notably on the Arts Club of Chicago and on Chicago opera, 1872–1942; Frances Macbeth (Mrs. John J.) Glessner, journals, 1879–1921, in 53 vols., including many references to Theodore Thomas and other musical subjects; Charles F. Gunther, 25 scrapbooks of Theodore Thomas concert programs; John Maynard Hubbard, letter to Philo A. Otis, 1912, recalling Jules Lumbard and the first singing of "Tramp, Tramp, Tramp"; John Sturge Johnston, diary with references to the opening of Crosby's Opera House, 1865; Archie H. Jones, notes for radio programs on the history of Chicago opera houses; Emil Liebling, programs of his piano students' recitals, 1879–94; Horace Jay Mellum, memoirs with references to the Central Music Hall; John Munn, journal, with references to concerts of Jenny Lind, Ole Bull, and Louis Jullien, 1851–53; J. A. J. Reading, report to the *Ashland Times* describing German opera in Chicago, 1895; John Blake Rice, account book, 1851–57, and day book, 1858–72, for Rice's Theatre; Edward L. Ryerson, stock certificate for the Chicago Grand Opera Company, 1910; William David Saltiel, archival records for his activity as an officer of the Chicago City Opera Company, 1929–53, and scrapbooks of clippings, 1921–61; and James Whittaker, transcripts of his letters describing theatrical and musical performances, 1885–87

Miscellaneous references to musical activities elsewhere, including John Hiwill, inspection return of the music in Gen. Washington's army, dated West Point, 1782; 5 vols. of early 19th-century European and American published music, formerly in the possession of the Custis family; Henry Warren, 100 letters received regarding bookings for theatrical and musical performances in Buffalo, 1846–58; C. M. Bochsa, letter dated Louisville, 1848, to Messrs. Peters and Field in Cincinnati, engaging rooms for a concert by Mme Anna Bishop; Sara Blakely, diary, involving her tour with a midwestern concert troupe, 1852–54; Henry H. Miller, letters written in 1914 concerning soldiers' performances of songs during the Civil War, with a copy of "A Soldier's Letter"; W. H. Engle, 2 letters dated Columbia, Tenn., 1882, concerning his song "Soldiers Are Wanted"; and Zerlina (Muhlmann) Metzger, autobiographical data, and biographical data on her father, Adolf Mühlmann (Metropolitan Opera baritone), 1889–1910

Autograph albums with musicians' signatures, owned by Walter H. Parcells, 1883–84, Carrie M. Watkins, 1892–95, and Aline Sue DeVany, 1911–12

Pictorial materials, extensive files of photographs and lithographs, with music content indexed through personal names only

Music-box discs, 1890s, 50 items

—Grant Talbot Dean

315

CHICAGO PUBLIC LIBRARY   IC

78 East Washington Street
Chicago, Illinois 60602

See *Treasures of the Chicago Public Library* (Chicago, 1977) and *One Hundred Important Additions to the Civil War and American History Research Collection: An Exhibition of Acquisitions, 1974–78* (Chicago, 1978), both prepared by the Special Collections Division

Special Collections Division

Grand Army Hall and Memorial Association Collection, with the broadside "Song on the Death of Col. Ellsworth," 1861; autograph ms text of George F. Root, "On, On, On, the Boys Came Marching," ca. 1865; 28 published music items, 1845–96, including songs about slavery, the Civil War, Col. Ellsworth, Abraham Lincoln, and political campaigns, also patriotic songbooks; diaries of William T. Humphrey and LeRoy Van Horn (Civil War military musicians); 4 photographs of Civil War musicians and bands, including 1 of Van Horn; and a picture of George F. Root

Broadcast Music Incorporated (BMI) collection, 30 vocal or piano sheet-music items, 1863–1969, all published in Chicago, including several by Henry Clay Work, Fred W. Root, and George F. Root, including his "Tramp, Tramp, Tramp! The Prisoners Hope," 1864

James G. Roy, Jr., Collection, with 5 linear cm. of piano or vocal sheet music, ca. 1840–1915; 5 tunebooks, 1835–56; 2 bound vols. of sheet music, ca. 1850–70; and a piano instruction book by Bertini, ca. 1860

Plitt Theatre Collection of materials from Chicago theaters, 1920–50, 250 linear meters, including ms and published compositions and arrangements of popular and classical music for band or orchestra (indexed), fashion-show music, piano and choral parts, sheet music, opera and operetta libretti, scripts, programs, correspondence, financial records, music-publishers' catalogues, and photographs; also Ettore Panizza (1875–1967, conductor of the Chicago Civic Opera Co., 1922), letters, documents, and a ms of his opera *Il fidanzato del mare*, 1897

Chicago theater programs and clippings, a general collection of 1.7 linear meters, singly or in scrapbooks, ca. 1860–1940 but mostly after the 1871 Chicago fire, including programs and clippings of the Grand Opera House, Washington Park concerts, Academy of Music, New Academy of Music, Chicago Orchestra, and WPA concerts; scrapbooks of Claudia Cassidy; 9 vols. of Chicago theater-history notebooks, 1847–1928, compiled by Rosalie Lang; the Lawrence Dicke Collection, including 30 pre-fire Chicago theater broadsides, ca. 1840–70; Crosby's Opera House Collection, with a broadside for a ballet and 2 opera programs, 1867–70; and a broadside of a concert by Miss Fred'rica Magnuson, 1864

World's Columbian Exposition Collection, including an official scrapbook, report of the Music Division, 1 bound vol. of all the musical events' programs, and a book on musical instruments at the Exposition, 1893

—Thomas A. Orlando,
Susan Prendergast Schoelwer

Fine Arts Division, Music Section

Published piano-vocal scores of operas and operettas, 74 items, 1881–1940

Hymnals, 25 items, ca. 1860–1940

Songbooks, 40 mostly popular items, ca. 1865–1940

Sheet music, 2000 popular items arranged by title, ca. 1830–1940, some of them by Chicago composers and publishers

Programs, program notes, and handbills of major U.S. performing organizations, 20 linear meters of bound and separate items, 1873–1940, including the Chicago Symphony Orchestra (complete from 1897, indexed), Grant Park Symphony Orchestra, Chicago Grand Opera, Chicago Civic Opera, Chicago Lyric Opera, and the Apollo Musical Club Directory plus 7 vols. of the Club's programs

Musical Leader (music journal, 1900–1967), extensive run, for which an index is being prepared

Recordings, including 16 78-rpm discs

Vertical files, including materials on "Chicago—Music," "Lincoln, Abraham—Music," and "Songs—U.S."; also card files with information about Chicago musical premières, ca. 1933– , and bio-bibliographical information on Illinois composers

—Marjorie Adkins, Rosalinda Hack

Woodson Regional Library, Vivian G. Harsh Collection of Afro-American History and Literature

9525 South Halstead Street
Chicago 60628

WPA project typescript, "The Negro in Illinois—Music and Musicians in Illinois, to 1939," discussing Chicago jazz and gospel music, and including a complete run of the *Negro Music Journal* (1902–3), in all 6 linear meters

Published songbooks and sheet music of jazz and spirituals, 50 items, ca. 1900–1940

Recordings of Afro-American music, including many re-recordings, 2000 items

—Donald F. Joyce

316
CHICAGO SWEDISH GLEE CLUB

Swedish Club Foundation
1258 North LaSalle Street
Chicago, Illinois 60610

Glee Club materials, including a charter issued in 1874 under an earlier name, Freja Singing Society (founded 1864); 80 programs of annual concerts, 1893– ; 12 photographs of concerts and tours, ca. 1900– ; 3 disc recordings, 1953–75; and 400 published sheet-music items or songbooks, ca. 1900– , with songs in Swedish, Norwegian, Danish, German, Latin, Russian, and Italian

—Carl E. Rosén

317
CHICAGO SYMPHONY ORCHESTRA

Orchestra Hall
220 South Michigan Avenue
Chicago, Illinois 60604

Administrative Offices

Correspondence, official records, scrapbooks, and other memorabilia relating to the Orchestra and to Orchestra Hall, not organized archivally but rather as part of the working files. See the commemorative book, *Chicago Symphony Orchestra, 75th Anniversary, Diamond Jubilee* (Chicago, 1966). Other materials, including correspondence and scrapbooks of press clippings, are at the Newberry Library (q.v.)

—Evelyn Meine

Music Library

Scores and parts for the use of the Orchestra, including holograph materials of Felix Borowski, others possibly holograph of Thorvald Otterström and John Knowles Paine, as well as arrangements and markings in the hands of Theodore Thomas and Frederick Stock. Also ms and printed performance scores and parts for works by Ernest Bloch, Dudley Buck, Charles Wakefield Cadman, John Alden Carpenter, George W. Chadwick, Eric DeLamarter, Arthur Foote, Eugene Goossens, Percy A. Grainger, Howard Hanson, Roy Harris, Victor Herbert, Edward A. MacDowell, Daniel Gregory Mason, George B. Nevin, Arne Oldberg, Ignace Jan Paderewski, and Adolph Weidig; and printed materials of U.S. composers, among them Edward Ballantine, Amy Cheney (Mrs. H. H. A.) Beach, Howard Brockway, Carl Busch, Rossetter G. Cole, C. C. Converse, Henry Eichheim, Adolph M. Foerster, Rudolph Ganz, Charles Tomlinson Griffes, Henry K. Hadley, Edward Burlingame Hill, Werner Janssen, Hugo Kaun, Edgar Stillman Kelly, Emil Moor, Ernest Schelling, W. C. E. Seeboeck, Charles Sanford Skilton, Bernard Wagenaar, and Jaromir Weinberger. For further identification of specific works, see the cumulative repertory indexes at the end of the annual vols. of the Orchestra's program notes. In addition, the library includes holdings of ms and printed scores and parts for works not listed in this index, including works by F. A. Bridgman, Charles G. Dawes, John Hopkins Densmore (1880–1943; *The Flowers' Revenge, Overture*), Julian Edwards (1855–1910; *My Own United States*), Charles Elliott Fouser (2nd movement of the *Prairie Symphony*), Thomas William Lester (b. 1889; *Manabozo, Suite*), and John Philip Sousa

—Lionel Sayers

318
CONGREGATION RODFEI ZEDEK

J. S. Hoffman Memorial Library
5200 Hyde Park Boulevard
Chicago, Illinois 60615

Jewish music collection, including 30 liturgical songbooks, programs of musical events, ca. 1890– , organizational papers, and 78-rpm disc recordings of sacred or classical music

—Henrietta Schulz

319

Herbert CURTIS

Mathematics Department
University of Illinois
Chicago Circle Campus
Chicago, Illinois 60680

Programs of ballet and opera in Chicago, 1934– , 1600 items, including local and touring companies, with an index by title of work

Civil War fife book with marching tunes, including some in ms

Sheet music, 1 bound vol. containing 22 piano-music items, mid to late 19th century

320

Harlan DANIEL

Box A-3250
Chicago, Illinois 60690

Songbooks, 1802– , 3000 items, including tunebooks and hymnals, some shape-note and gospel songbooks among them; Christy Minstrel songsters, 1840s–70s, 8 items, 4 of them genuine; 20 pre-1850 Scottish songbooks; and songbooks on various topics such as abolition, temperance, the Civil War, and elections

Sheet music, 2500 items, ca. 1830– , mostly topical songs, some relating to historical events; also 100 19th-century broadsides

Music periodicals, 1914–65, including 250 issues of little-known and ephemeral publications

Recordings of country, folk, gospel, and singing-convention music, 1903– , including 20 cylinders and 6000 78-rpm discs

321

J. C. DEAGAN COMPANY

Division of Slingerland Drum Company
1770 West Bertreau Avenue
Chicago, Illinois 60613

Company records, including ledger books, advertising, and product descriptions, dating from the founding in 1880 to the present

Photographs of jazz musicians, including Lionel Hampton and Red Norvo, 1930s, and of other mallet instruments and performers, 1920s–

Catalogues of mallet-percussion instruments, 30 items, 1890s–

—Hal Trommer

322

DELMARK RECORDS

4243 North Lincoln Avenue
Chicago, Illinois 60618

Programs, advertising brochures, recording catalogues (of Paramount, Columbia, and other companies), photographs, and periodicals, all pertaining to jazz and blues, 45 linear meters

Jazz recordings, a small collection of 78-rpm discs (at the company's retail outlet, 7 West Grand Avenue, Chicago 60610)

—Steve Tomashefsky

323

DE PAUL UNIVERSITY ICD

Lincoln Park Campus
2323 North Seminary
Chicago, Illinois 60614

WPA Music Periodicals Index, 400,000 cards indexing articles in 111 European and American periodicals (61 of them completely indexed), late 1700s–1935 (at the Frank J. Lewis Center Library). See Judith Labash, "The Condition of the Federal Works Agency Work Projects Administration Music Index Project" (typescript, 1976), on file with the Index

Leon Stein (professor of music), published chamber music and music textbooks, 1920s–30s

Alexander Tcherepnin (professor of music, 1949–64), 50 published music scores, 1920s–50s

Wesley La Violette (chairman of the music theory department, 1938–40), 10 published music scores, 1930s

Sheet music, 2 shelf boxes of piano and vocal items, catalogued by composer

—Robert Acker

324

EPISCOPAL DIOCESE OF CHICAGO

65 East Huron Street
Chicago, Illinois 60611

John Leo Lewis (organist and choirmaster at St. James Cathedral, Chicago), personal papers, including ms works and his complete published works for organ or choir, scrapbooks, correspondence, and photographs

Leo Sowerby (1895–1968, organist at St. James Cathedral, 1927–62), personal papers, including music mss and photographs

Liturgical Commission, Music Commission, and St. James Cathedral Choir, 1.5 linear meters of papers including minutes and correspondence

Diocese materials, including 2 linear meters of programs, 1847– , among them pontifical events and bulletins from St. James Cathedral and local parishes; photographs of musicians and music groups; and ms music commissioned for Episcopal Church events

Published choral or instrumental music, 15 linear meters in a general collection, including American imprints, 1860– ; also 1.2 linear meters of hymnals and chant books, mostly Anglican, ca. 1850–

—Chester LaRue

325

EVANGELICAL COVENANT (ICNPT)
CHURCH OF AMERICA

Archives and Historical Library
North Park College
5125 North Spaulding Avenue
Chicago, Illinois 60625

Swedish-language songbooks, including 82 hymnals, 12 books of gospel songs, and 14 secular songbooks used in the U.S., chiefly 1880s–1920s

English-language hymnals, 70 items

Music for choirs, male choruses, and quartets, 45 Swedish-language and 6 English-language vols.; also a complete run of *Gittit* (1892–1908), a monthly sacred-music journal usually containing original anthems and choral music, ed. by A. L. Skoog

Biographical materials on Swedish hymn writers, including Lina Sandell Berg, A. L. Skoog, Nils Frykman, and J. A. Hultman, consisting chiefly of published books and articles but also including correspondence, diaries, personal papers, and music

Photographs of singing groups and church choirs, 25 items, ca. 1900–1920

—Sigurd F. Westberg

326
H. T. FITZSIMONS COMPANY

615 North LaSalle Street
Chicago, Illinois 60610

Operettas, sacred and secular choral music, organ music, and piano-vocal sheet music, published by the Company from its founding in 1923 to the present, in its FitzSimons Band Library series, Aeolian Choral Series, Aeolian Band & Orchestra Library, Aeolian Organ Series, and Canterbury Choral Series; also catalogues of the Company's publications

Rossetter Gleason Cole (1866–1952), several boxes of papers, including music mss and photographs, given to his pupil, H. T. FitzSimons

—Ruth FitzSimons

327
Michael GILLIGAN

10809 South State Street
Chicago, Illinois 60628

Hymnals, 1847– , 200 items, mostly Roman Catholic works issued in North America

328
GRANT PARK SYMPHONY ORCHESTRA

425 East McFetridge Drive
Chicago, Illinois 60605

Papers of the Orchestra, 1934– , including business records, a complete file of progams, photographs in scrapbooks and singly, press clippings, and lists of personnel with some biographical material

—Robert Wilkins

329
Edward LOWINSKY

7440 South Constance Avenue
Chicago, Illinois 60649

Edward Lowinsky, personal papers, including correspondence, literary mss and offprints, personal library, teaching and research materials, scrapbook, photographs, and memorabilia. See *Spalek*, pp. 556–57

330
LUTHERAN SCHOOL OF THEOLOGY   ICLT

1100 East Fifty-fifth Street
Chicago, Illinois 60615

See Joel W. Lundeen, *Preserving Yesterday for Tomorrow: A Guide to the Archives of the Lutheran Church in America* (Chicago, 1977)

Lutheran Church in America Archives, with papers of the hymnal, worship, and other committees of the former Danish, Augustana, and United Lutheran Church in America, 1892– , including minutes, correspondence, and ms reports, also 15 ms hymnals with words only, late 18th century, and ms versions of the Augustana and United Lutheran Church hymnals

Lutheran hymnals and liturgies, a nearly complete collection of all such books published or used by Lutheran Church groups in America; also published anthems, especially by composers active in the LCA and its predecessors, with a large proportion of materials from the Swedish and American traditions of the Augustana Church

—Joel W. Lundeen

331
MEADVILLE / LOMBARD   ICMe
THEOLOGICAL SCHOOL

5701 South Woodlawn Avenue
Chicago, Illinois 60637

Hymnals, 200 items, including many of the Unitarian-Universalist denomination, ca. 1750–1940

—Neil Gerdes

332
Elizabeth Blackman MOFFATT

880 Lake Shore Drive
Chicago, Illinois 60611

Orlando Blackman, letters and memorabilia, as reproduced and discussed in Royce Devon Devick, *Orlando Blackman: A Study of His Contribution to Music Education in the Chicago Public Schools, 1863–1899* (Ph.D. diss., University of Iowa, 1972)

333
MOODY BIBLE INSTITUTE   ICMB

Library
820 North LaSalle Street
Chicago, Illinois 60610

Songbooks, 2000 items, mostly gospel songs and revival hymnody but also including many shape-note tunebooks, Protestant hymnals, and some songsters, ca. 1825–

Sheet music and songbooks, 34 file drawers, mostly 20th-century classical music (in the Music Library, Doan Memorial)

Biographical files on 12 hymn writers, performers, and other subjects, with clippings, pamphlets, and correspondence, including major files on P. P. Bliss, Ira Sankey, D. L. Moody, George C. Stebbins, Maj. D. W. Whittle, James McGranahan, and Daniel B. Towner

Pictures, 10 file folders of photographs of musicians and gospel singers, some of them associated with the Institute

Recordings, including 3 78-rpm discs of gospel music played by radio station WMBI, 1930s

—Walter Osborn

334
NEWBERRY LIBRARY   ICN
60 West Walton Street
Chicago, Illinois 60610

See the *Proceedings* of the Library's Trustees, 1887–1941 (hereinafter cited as *Proc.*); the Newberry Library *Bulletin*, 1944– (hereinafter cited as *NLB*); and the *Bibliographical Inventory to the Early Music in the Newberry Library* (Boston, 1977), esp. the U.S. sections, classes I.D. (pp. 19–21) and IX. (pp. 452–525; hereinafter cited as *BI*, followed by entry numbers)

Personal Papers

Theodore Thomas (1835–1905), personal papers, including 400 vols. from his personal music library, mostly conducting scores with extensive markings and re-orchestrations in his own hand, also books from his personal library, photographs, and 50 scrapbooks of programs for his concerts, 1864–1903. See the *Catalogue of the Musical Library of Theodore Thomas* (Chicago, 1904). Also 6 boxes of correspondence; and the autograph album of his wife, Rose Fay Thomas, with signatures of musicians and other guests, 1879–1927

Frederic Grant Gleason (1849–1903), personal papers, with 38 scrapbooks of Chicago concerts and musical life, 1872–1903, including 8 vols. devoted to the Hershey School of Musical Art, 1876–84, 3 vols. on the Chicago Auditorium Conservatory, 1900–1902, and 1 vol. on the American Music Society, 1892–93; music mss, including 36 holograph scores of his works, and performance parts in 19 boxes; and diaries, notebooks, photographs, and correspondence, in the form of incoming original letters and 5 vols. of letterpress books, including materials relating to the Manuscript Society and the music program at the 1893 World's Columbian Exposition. See the notice by Thomas Willis in the *Chicago Tribune* (8 Sept. 1963), sec. 5, p. 10; also Aileen M. Peters, *Analysis of the Frederic Grant Gleason Collection* (Thesis, Chicago Teachers College South, 1964)

Frederick Stock (1872–1942), personal papers, including 1 box of correspondence, photographs, and 5 boxes of music holographs, 1886–1930s, notably the *Rhapsody for Orchestra* (1925) (*Proc.* 1937, p. 10)

Rudolph Ganz (1877–1972), personal papers, including correspondence, programs for his performances or concerts of his music, scrapbooks, photographs, loose clippings, speeches, lectures, and published and ms scores from his personal library

Personal papers of musicians, including Eric DeLamarter (1880–1953), 151 items, 1904–71; Henry Royal Hoaré (1882–1959), 28 printed and ms music works and other personal papers; Heniot Levy (1879–1946), 34 music mss and other personal papers; Thorvald Otterström (1868–1942), 89 printed and ms music works, and other personal papers; and Bernhard Ziehn (1845–1912), 116 items of music, published writings, press clippings, photographs, and correspondence between his pupils Julius Gold and Mrs. Albert Heller relating to him. See the facsimile ed. of Ziehn's *Doric Hymns of Mesomedes* (Chicago, 1979)

Horace Oakley (1861–1929, music patron), personal papers, including 1 box devoted to his activities with the Chicago Symphony Orchestra, mostly 1919–29

Music Manuscripts

Pre-1861 items as listed in *BI*, 323–50, including books of Stephen Jenks (*BI*, 326); Francesco Masi (*BI*, 214); Benjamin Carr, including "The Clouds Were Dispers'd," extracts from his ms organ book, a copy of his *Te Deum* dated Philadelphia, 1868, and his harmonization of "I'll Ask the Sylph," by E. Hudson; a book of 2- to 4-voice unaccompanied hymns and other sacred music, ca. 1810; and 4 vols. owned by Samuel Willard of Upper Alton and Jacksonville, Ill., devoted to marches, part songs, hymns, and dance music (*BI*, 329, 332, 337, and 343)

J. G. C. Schetky (1740–1824), 5 mss, ca. 1800, several of Edinburgh provenance, from the collection of Caroline Schetky Richardson of Philadelphia

Gaetano Capocci (1811–98), book on introits from Christmas to Corpus Christi Sunday, inscribed by Rev. Sherwood Healy, Boston Cathedral, 1874; a copyist's score of the "Christus and Miserere," dated Boston, 1872, by copyist John P. Endress; 2 other sacred-music ms vols.; and a copy of Thomas Bissell, "Trust in the Lord"

Chicago composers' holographs, including Felix Borowski, A-Minor Organ Sonata (1930s); Rossetter G. Cole, *The Rock of Liberty* op. 36 (1919/20); John Alden Carpenter, *The Debutante* (1908), *Krazy Kat* (1921), and *Lullaby* (1910s?), the latter probably in the hand of Janet Ayer Fairbank; Henry Eichheim, 35 items, from the collections of Dr. Ethel J. Lindgren and others; Hamilton Forrest, full score of his opera *Camille* (1930), written for Mary Garden; Robert H. Just (b.1875), 23 scores in ms, photocopy, and printed editions; Buren Roscoe Schryock (1881–1974), overture to *Flavia* (ca. 1940), *Mary and John* (1948), and *Grndp' Sgtlsg* (1960); William C. E. Seeboeck (1860–1907), unidentified piano work in A major; Leo Sowerby (1895–1968), *Songs* for soprano and organ (1933), and 11 other items; Alexander Tcherepnin (1899–1977), various materials from op. 67–93 passim; Adolph Weidig (1867–1931), 6 boxes of holograph materials; and 63 items of harp music in various hands, copied ca. 1900 in Chicago

Other U.S. holograph materials, including George Bristow (1825–98), *The Great Republic* (ca. 1880); Edward A. MacDowell (1861–1908), 1st Piano Concerto (*Proc.*, 1915, p. 16), and a "Pizzicatti" for piano solo, attributed to Victor Herbert (1859–1924); also Richard Wagner, *Grosses Festmarsch*, written for the Philadelphia Exhibition of 1876, from the collection of Theodore Thomas

Published Music

Sheet music, 100,000 items, 240 of them before 1801, and 2500 more from the period 1801–25. All pre-1825 items as well as imprints of selected publishers, 1826–50, are catalogued. The total comprises three groups: (1) 15,000 miscellaneous unbound items, including duplicates from the Grosvenor Library (Buffalo and Erie County Public Library, N.Y.), also gifts of Helen Rand Clarke (*Proc.*, 1935, p. 9) and Mrs. Henry V. Friedman (*NLB*, 1:19), separated into pre- and post-1870 groups under the class usVM, and not represented in the library's catalogues; (2) miscellaneous bound vols. in the classified collections (i.e., *BI*, 8919–49, 9822–23), mostly not analyzed; and (3) the collection of J. Francis Driscoll (1875–1959, of Brookline, Mass.), 83,000 items, strong in materials from and relating to Boston (including 825 Graupner imprints, 600 Bradlee imprints, and 7100 other editions on Massachusetts topics), Stephen C. Foster (700 items; others now in Foster Hall, University of Pittsburgh, Pa.); and minstrel and blackface music (3400 items). See Richard L. Castner's "Introduction" to the collection (Boston, ca. 1960); Samuel A. Floyd, Jr., "Black Music in the Driscoll Collection," *Black Perspectives in Music*, 2 (1974), 158–71, with supplemental information available at the Library; and the 34-page "Introduction" at the Library, which follows Driscoll's organization of his collection and thus serves as a temporary finding aid for uncatalogued items

Tunebooks and hymnals, 3500 items, 1600 of them accessible through the shelflist for class VM 2116, in all 825 items before 1860 as listed in *BI*, 8950–9774, 9817–21. A copy of Samuel Holyoke, *Harmonia Americana* (1791), has important psalms, hymns, and anthems added in ms. Most of the collection is that of Hubert P. Main (1839–1925), purchased in 1891 (*Proc.*, 1909, p. 16); recent acquisitions come from Don Bloch, Denver, Colo., 1966, and through the Driscoll collection

Printed music, scattered through the collection. For selected pre-1861 items, see *BI*, 8736–8919. Included are the music libraries of the Beethoven Society of Chicago, rich in vocal music, acquired in 1890; Dr. Julius Fuchs, including orchestral scores, also acquired in 1890; Mrs. T. R. Charpentier-Morphy of New Orleans (*Proc.*, 1911, p. 8); Fannie Bloomfield Zeisler, mostly the repertory of her concert career (*Proc.*, 1927, p. 14); Prof. Heman Allen (1836–93), the gift of William Stetson Merrill (*Proc.*, 1928, p. 20); Adolf Weidig (*Proc.*, 1936, p. 10) and Mrs. Thomas Marsten (*Proc.*, 1938, p. 9), both rich in chamber music; and Janet Fairbank (1903–47), including 1500 art songs, published and in ms photocopy, mostly by American composers, comprising her concert repertory (*NLB*, 2/1:25–26, 1948; see also Edith Borroff, "The Fairbank Collection," *College Music Symposium*, 16 [1976], 105–22)

Scrapbooks (in addition to the Thomas, Ganz, and Gleason materials cited above), of George P. Upton, 3 vols. on Chicago music, 1860–76, presented by Mrs. Karleton Hackett; 1 vol. on Chicago music and theater of the late 1860s; 5 vols. on Chicago music, 1865–72; W. S. B. Matthews, 4 vols. covering 1872–1908; 1 vol. of Boston programs, 1873–84; Mrs. John A. Holabird, 7 vols. and 1 box on Chicago music, 1886–1930; Rossetter G. Cole, 1 vol. with programs for concerts in which his works were first performed, 1888–1941; 1 vol. on miscellaneous events, 1892–98; Mary Slaughter Field, 34 vols. on Chicago symphony and opera, 1893–1950; and Janet Fairbank, 1 vol. documenting her vocal career, 1931–47. Also on deposit are the press books of the Chicago Symphony Orchestra, 1894–   , 50 vols. through 1940, and 4 vols. of official documents and clippings relating to the music of the 1893 Columbian Exposition

Collections of loose programs of Chicago musical events, as presented by Mrs. W. C. Wright, covering 1843–76 (*Proc.*, 1911, p. 20); by Philo A. Otis, 579

items, 1860–1920s (*Proc.*, 1936, p. 8); by Bertha Rudolph, 1880–1910 (*NLB*, 2/1, 26:1948); and by Mrs. Charles C. Willson, on Chicago opera, 1911–36 (*Proc.*, 1936, p. 10)

Photographs, including files assembled by Mae Valentine, active in Chicago opera, ca. 1920–65, 70 items; Nathaniel Gates Chapin (1817–93), 136 items relating to Boston music (*Proc.*, 1930, p. 17); and 130 inscribed photographs in 12 vols., assembled by Milward Adams, manager of the Auditorium Theatre (*Proc.*, 1910, p. 11)

Books about music, libretti, and songsters, scattered through the collection, including 365 items before 1861 (*BI*, 8421–785), and incorporating the working music libraries of George P. Upton (*Proc.*, 1920, p. 19), George F. Root (*Proc.*, 1934, p. 9), and some items from the library of Frédéric Louis Ritter

Amerindian hymnals, in the Edward E. Ayer Collection, as described in the *Dictionary Catalog* of the Collection (Boston, 1961), vol. 7, p. 3256

—Diana Haskell, Bernard E. Wilson

335

NORTH PARK COLLEGE   ICNPT

Wallgren Library
5125 North Spaulding Avenue
Chicago, Illinois 60625

Jenny Lind Collection, including 35 linear cm. of her correspondence with Otto Goldschmidt, P. T. Barnum, and others (with an inventory); press clippings, books, memorabilia, and 6 scrapbooks documenting her American career; 70 pictures, mostly reproductions of her portraits; and 650 19th-century sheet-music items, many with U.S. imprints, mostly with cover portraits of her

—Kay King

336

POLISH MUSEUM OF AMERICA

984 Milwaukee Avenue
Chicago, Illinois 60622

Ignace Jan Paderewski, materials including his ms military marching song "Hey White Eagle," 1917; 4 vols. and other items of classical piano music with his ms notes; letters from his diplomatic career; biographical notes by Rudolf Ganz made in dedicating the Paderewski Biographical Room, 1941; programs of Paderewski performances in the U.S., Latin America, and Europe, 20 items, 1893–1930s; and other papers

Sheet music, 30 boxes and cartons, mostly 19th-century vocal works by Polish composers, including some by Jerzy Bojanowsky (Polish-American conductor and composer) and by an organist at St. Peters Church, Stevens Point, Wis.

Books with or about music, 600 items, including songbooks and hymnals, some in Polish, used by Polish school children in the U.S.

Sajewski Music Store, Chicago, catalogues and brochures

Programs of local dramatic groups and of the Chopin Singers

Mazowsze Troupe (dance group), costumes used on their U.S. tour

—Rev. Donald Bilinski

337

RAVINIA FESTIVAL ASSOCIATION

22 West Monroe Street
Chicago, Illinois 60603

Archival files relating to the Festivals (1936– , previously the Opera Festivals, 1911– , and earlier the amusement park), including programs, photographs, and other memorabilia

338

ROOSEVELT UNIVERSITY   ICRC

Chicago Musical College
430 South Michigan Avenue
Chicago, Illinois 60605

Music Library

Rudolph Ganz (1877–1972), holograph mss of "And So We Marched" (1972), *Strings in Variations* op. 33 no. 2, and *Woody Scherzo* op. 33 no. 3; copies of his published books on music and 30 published editions of his music, also 200 piano-music editions from his library; and 8 broadcast tapes on the centenary of his birth, 1977, from radio station WFMT, Chicago

Karel Bohuslav Jirák (1891–1972), 5 holograph mss, in original or photocopy, and 25 published editions of his music, ca. 1921–69

Gena Branscombe (1881–1977), holograph mss of 3 choral compositions, ca. 1911–67, and published editions of 47 vocal or choral works and arrangements, ca. 1911–58

—Donald Draganski

University Archives

Archives of the Chicago Musical College and its precursors, as begun by Florenz Ziegfeld, 1867, including financial records (ca. 1904–52), programs, publications, photographs, and memorabilia, also incomplete records of the Metropolitan School of Music (absorbed by the College, 1949–50), as reflected in Felix Ganz, "Chicago Musical College, 1867–1967, an Historical Sketch" (typescript, 1967)

Tibor Heisler Collection of 85 autographs, assembled in Budapest but including signatures of musicians later active in the U.S.

—Frankie Kozuch

339

SWEDISH PIONEER   (ICNPT)
HISTORICAL SOCIETY

Archives
5125 North Spaulding Avenue
Chicago, Illinois 60625

Songbooks, including 2000 copies of *Dalkullans Sångbok* with Swedish folksong texts, some with music (Chicago, 1930–33), and 126 miscellaneous songbooks, mostly sacred, mid 19th and 20th centuries

Sheet music, 500 folders, mostly popular vocal ca. 1900–1933, formerly in the stock of the Dalkullan shop in Chicago

Music published for Swedish orchestras, several items

—Selma Jacobson

340

UNIVERSITY OF CHICAGO   ICU

Joseph Regenstein Library
1100 East Fifty-seventh Street
Chicago, Illinois 60637

All items are in the Special Collections Department, except as noted

University of Chicago materials, including 1 box of ms music for the University of Chicago Band, 1890–1940s, and holograph mss of music by University faculty and students, 1950s– ; Blackfriars (organization for student productions), 6 boxes of music scores, programs, and libretti, 1892– (in the Archives); Rockefeller Chapel correspondence files, 1950– , with letters from musicians including Virgil Thomson and E. Power Biggs; and Music Department working files, 1950– (in the Music Department offices)

Otto Gombosi, personal papers relating to his musicological work at the University, 1940s, 1 box

John U. and Elinor Castle Nef, personal papers involving their activities as founders of the Committee on Social Thought, including 27 letters from Ernst Krenek, 1943–62, 10 letters from Arnold Schoenberg, 1946–47, 115 letters from Artur Schnabel, 1939–51, including his 51-page typescript "Recollections of Our Time," and 1 letter from Bruno Walter, 1946

Music mss, in a "Collection of Songs, 1800–1830" (Aldine Collection, Ms. 735)

Sheet music, including 7 bound vols. of 19th-century piano or vocal music; the William E. Barton Collection of Lincolniana, containing 35 Lincoln items, 24 Civil War imprints, 40 other 19th-century American items, and 33 folders of broadsides and song sheets; the Lt. Joseph Benedict Starshak Collection of 300 items, late 19th and early 20th centuries; and 2 vols. in the Rare Book Collection (M20.M9), acquired in 1913 as part of the Reuben T. Durrett Collection of materials concerning Ohio Valley history, vol. 1 containing 31 vocal and 8 instrumental items, mostly published in Philadelphia, ca. 1800, and vol. 2 containing piano scores of five operas, ca. 1800–1823

Tunebooks and hymnals, 250 items, 1772–1940, some with words only (partly in General Collections)

Songbooks, 16 items in the Lincoln Collection, 4 of them early black-spiritual collections, and 7 other items in the Rare Book Collection; also books on music, 1808– , and other printed music, 1827–

Fred W. Atkinson Collection of American Drama, including 44 opera libretti, 54 light-opera libretti, and miscellaneous musical-play texts, 18th century to the present, mostly 19th century

Allied Artists (Harry Zelzer Concert Management), programs, 1937–77, in 40 bound vols. (in the Music Collection)

—Dena J. Epstein

341

UNIVERSITY OF ILLINOIS AT   ICIU
CHICAGO CIRCLE

Chicago, Illinois 60680

Department of Special Collections (Box 8198)

See the *Guide to the Manuscript Collections in the Department of Special Collections, The Library* (Chicago, 1969)

Franklin J. Meine (1898–1968, collector of folk humor), 3.6 linear meters of papers, including sheet music, broadsides, clippings, and scrapbooks

Eric Hjorth (member of the Hull House Players), papers, 1879–1940, including clippings, notes, and programs, 1.5 linear meters

William Fee McDermott (1894–1966, minister), papers relating to music in Winfield, Kan.

Lenox Riley Lohr (1891–1968, president of the National Broadcasting Corp., 1936–40, and nephew of John Philip Sousa), 30 linear meters of papers, including memorabilia of Sousa and of NBC

Inidana Society of Chicago (men's social club), 1.4 linear meters of papers, 1905–73, including correspondence, minutes, programs, scrapbooks, songbooks, and recordings

Eleanor Hammer, 40 linear cm. of papers relating to the Hull House Music School

—Robert Adlesberger

Jane Addams' Hull House (Box 4348)

Manuscript music, 50 items, mostly by Eleanor Smith (composer at Hull House), including children's music, concert songs performed by Hull House Music School students, and a cantata, *The Golden Asp*; also 4 78-rpm recordings of Eleanor Smith's students

Hull House Association Collection, 9 linear meters of materials, 1889– , containing financial records, correspondence, and yearly reports of musical activities of the Music School, Hull House Theater, dance groups, and a women's orchestra

Alma Birmingham (pianist and teacher at the Music School), personal papers, ca. 1907–50, 1.2 linear meters, including a complete listing of Music School recitals, and a 78-rpm recording of her students

Shipps–Smith Collection of clippings, programs, and correspondence of Eleanor Smith and her niece, Barbara Shipps, ca. 1890–1940

Songbooks, of children's and social-protest songs, 10 items, 1898–1934, including 1 vol. of songs by Hull House residents and neighbors

Pictures of Hull House students, teachers, performances, and buildings, 50 items, ca. 1920–60

—Mary Lynn McCree

342

VANDERCOOK COLLEGE OF MUSIC

Harry Ruppel Memorial Library
3209 South Michigan Avenue
Chicago, Illinois 60616

Published band scores and parts, 5000 pre-1940 titles
Community songbooks, 25 items, ca. 1920

—John E. Sayers

343

J. Sterling MORTON HIGH SCHOOL

2423 South Austin Boulevard
Cicero, Illinois 60650

John Philip Sousa (1854–1932), 13 mss or ms arrangements for band, as cited by Paul Bierley, *John Philip Sousa: A Descriptive Catalog of His Works* (Urbana, 1973)

—Joseph Ondrus

344

ELLWOOD HOUSE MUSEUM

509 North First Street
DeKalb, Illinois 60115

Music used by the Ellwood family, ca. 1890–1940, with 7 hymnals, including 1 of the Christian Scientist Church, 1150 items of popular sheet music, and 200 songbooks; also 100 photographs of the family and home, and 21 photograph albums

Published school songbooks by Alice Barber Whitmore, 2 items, and 2 ms songs by her for her children, ca. 1910–15; also 1 ms song each by Jessie L. Bodueau and Angeline Maccaroni

Programs of 18 local concerts

Recordings, including 20 cylinders, and 2 punched-paper cylinders for a music box

—Laurel L. Fant

345

NORTHERN ILLINOIS UNIVERSITY   IDeKN

DeKalb, Illinois 60115

Charles Elliott Fouser (1889–1946), mss, photocopies of mss, and published scores of symphonies, a violin concerto, and sacred choral compositions (in the Archives)

Songbooks, 5 items, 18th and 19th centuries (in Special Collections)

Recordings, mostly of jazz and musical theater, 1500 78-rpm discs, formerly in the American Music Collection (in the Audio-Score Library)

—Gordon Rowley, J. Joe Bauxar

346

The DIAPASON

380 Northwest Highway
Des Plaines, Illinois 60016

Archival file copies of *The Diapason*, 1909–

—Arthur Lawrence

347

SUBURBAN LIBRARY SYSTEM

Downers Grove Public Library
1050 Curtiss Street
Downers Grove, Illinois 60515

Popular sheet-music songs and piano-vocal scores of musical productions, 1700 items, ca. 1920–

—Joanne Klene

348

MADISON COUNTY HISTORICAL SOCIETY

715 North Main Street
Edwardsville, Illinois 62025

Annie C. W. Burton, 2 ms songs, ca. 1918, and a printing plate for a song

William D. Armstrong (1868–1936, pianist, organist, and composer), 14 scrapbooks with programs, clippings, correspondence, and financial material; also 1 published composition by him, 1928

Songbooks used by singing societies, 13 items, 1849–1905

Sheet music, 75 vocal and 25 instrumental items, late 19th and mid 20th centuries

Posters for local musical events, 20 items, late 19th and early 20th centuries

Photographs of local music groups, 5 items, late 19th century

—Katharine Moorhead

349

SOUTHERN ILLINOIS UNIVERSITY   IEdS

Lovejoy Library
Edwardsville, Illinois 62025

Music materials were assembled mostly in the 1960s, including 4000 items from the estate of Carl Tollefsen (1882–1963, violinist, collector, and founder of the Brooklyn Chamber Music Society, N.Y.), and many items formerly in the collections of the Essex Institute, Salem, Mass. For information on the Tollefsen collection, see "The Ink Path of the Great: Some Thoughts of an Autograph Collector," *Musical Courier*, 109 (3 Nov. 1934), p. 6. The University's special holdings are summarized in Linda McKee, *Guide to Research Collections* (Edwardsville, 1971). Most of the individual collections cited below are kept separately, and have their own accessions lists or card indexes

Sheet music, 55,000 items, ca. 1840– , particularly strong in ragtime and St. Louis imprints, and including 150 bound vols.; 30,000 items from the library of radio station KMOX, St. Louis; 10,000 items from the Essex Institute, particularly strong in 1830s–40s imprints; the collection of Gordon Wright Colket, 120 editions, mostly 1840s–50s; and those of the Hewitt family and of Laura Baker

Tunebooks and songbooks, 700 items, 1810s– , including 52 songbooks, 1838–74

Other printed music, 36,000 items, including light opera and chamber music from the collection of Max Autenrieb, European editions used in the Edwardsville area, 1923–60s, 2 linear meters; Elmer Booker, 1657 orchestral parts for silent films; Warren Brown, 325 stock band charts for high school bands; Walter Deller, 10,000 vocal- and violin-music editions used in his work as a violinist and vocal-ensemble coach in Chicago, 1930s–50s; Eugene Eichar, 2955 vocal octavos and orchestral parts for silent films; Henry M. Johnson, 914 scores and parts for band music used in the Spanish-American War and in his later community music work in the Midwest; A. Kennedy, 150 miscellaneous items for silent films; John Kiburz, Sr. and Jr. (flautists with the St. Louis Symphony Orchestra), 1500 solo and ensemble flute editions, also a scrapbook of memorabilia; David Mohler, 575 miscellaneous items; Ben Rader and Russ David, 15,000 stock band charts used by their

dance and theater orchestra in St. Louis, 1920s–50s; and John Schnabel, 293 editions of high school band parts

KMOX (St. Louis radio station), music library, 15,195 original and stock arrangements, 1930s–40s; and Carl Hohengarten, 1714 ms scores, arrangements, and other music used at KMOX, also from CBS network programs from Chicago and New York

Earl Robinson, personal papers, 42 linear meters of correspondence, music mss, and books

Music periodicals, 139 items, 1880–1912, from the collection of Gerald A. Reiss (St. Louis music publisher)

Photographs, including 600 items relating to Walter Damrosch and his family; also 3 large cartons of autographed portraits from the Carl Tollefsen collection

Recordings, including 8000 78-rpm discs of jazz, mostly pre-1945; other classical and popular 78-rpm discs, 30 linear meters; and 258 piano rolls, including items from the collections of Christ Pashkoff, others from Russell and Ruby Ames

Slavic-American music in general, including 300 music editions scattered through the collections, and 70 ' 78-rpm discs

—Marianne Kozlowski

350

CHURCH OF THE BRETHREN
GENERAL BOARD

Staff Library and Historical Library
1451 Dundee Avenue
Elgin, Illinois 60120

Hymnals, 18th and 19th centuries, including some published by the Ephrata Cloister; also 1 ms 18th-century choral book of the Snow Hill Cloister of the Ephrata group

—Gwendolyn Bobb

351

JUDSON COLLEGE

Benjamin P. Browne Library
1151 North State Street
Elgin, Illinois 60120

Robert Schofield (local organist), collection of sheet music and published instrumental music, including some for organ or piano, with autographed works of Charles W. Cadman; also other published sheet music, instrumental music, and dance folios; in all 200 items, ca. 1890–1940

Hymnals of various denominations, 40 items, ca. 1860–1940

Programs of local and Chicago concerts, donated by Robert Schofield, including some of the Chicago Opera, ca. 1910, and some of Schofield's performances

—Elsie Smith

352

ELMHURST COLLEGE   IElmC

A. C. Buehler Library
Elmhurst, Illinois 60126

Armin Haeussler (1891–1967), research notes for his book *The Story of Our Hymns* (St. Louis, 1952), 1.5 linear meters

Hymnals and other vocal anthologies, including 60 19th-century German items

—Mel Klatt

353

ELMHURST HISTORICAL MUSEUM

Glos Mansion
120 East Park Avenue
Elmhurst, Illinois 60126

Hymnals, 10 items, 1920s, donated by local Lutheran churches

Sheet music, 50 items published before World War I, and several from World War I with illustrations of military uniforms

Programs of 40 local piano recitals and annual park-district choral concerts, 1930s

Pictures, 5 items, including a boy-scout band, n.d.

Recordings, including 20 cylinders and 80 78-rpm discs, mostly classical

—Mrs. Wayne Harlan

354

EVANSTON PUBLIC LIBRARY   IE

1703 Orrington Avenue
Evanston, Illinois 60201

Sadie Knowland Coe Collection, established in 1907 by her busband, Prof. George Albert Coe, based on her library and enriched by gifts, particularly from Mrs. Hannah B. Knowland of Alameda, Cal. According to Gertrude L. Brown's *Catalogue of the Coe Music Collection and Other Musical Literature* (Evanston, 1916), the collection then included 1600 scores and books about music, and 400 items of sheet music. The collection has been integrated into the main library music holdings, mostly in class 780. The 572 pianola rolls and a player piano, part of the collection in 1916, are no longer there

Published sheet music, 1000 items for piano or voice and piano, including works by Evanston composers L. J. Downing (7 songs), Mrs. Louise Ayers Garnett (14 songs), G. A. Grant-Schaefer (62 items), Peter C. Lutkin (3 items), Arne Oldberg (17 items), and Gardner Read (15 items)

Music folders in the pamphlet collection, including materials on American music (50 clippings and 5 pamphlets, 1925–), bands (6 miscellaneous items, 1918–), Evanston–Coe Collection (clippings, photographs, a catalogue, and descriptive pamphlets, 1916–), the MacDowell Colony (clippings, booklets, and photographs, 1922–), and music in the war (songs and clippings, 1919–43)

Printed music, 2000 items, mostly 20th century, including scores for operas and musical shows, piano and vocal anthologies, and school and camp songbooks

Libretti, 400 items, mostly for Chicago productions, ca. 1880– , arranged alphabetically by composer

Evanstoniana Collection of unprocessed materials relating to the cultural life of Evanston, including programs of the North Shore Music Festival, 1909–39,

and the Evanston Music Festival, mid 1930s; local guide books, histories, and annual business directories, 1882– , including addresses for musical-instrument manufacturers; handbooks, programs, and yearbooks of the Music Study Club of Evanston, 1915–40s; and bulletins and yearbooks of the Woman's Club of Evanston, listing musical events, 1889–1940s

Chamber- and orchestral-music scores and parts, mostly 19th-century European works, prepared by the WPA Illinois Music Project in the 1930s and donated by the Newberry Library, with a partial inventory (non-circulating)

—Linda Seckelson-Simpson

355

GARRETT–EVANGELICAL   IEG
THEOLOGICAL SEMINARY

Library
2121 Sheridan Road
Evanston, Illinois 60201

Hymnals, 700 items, ca. 1850–1940, including those of the Methodist and Evangelical United Brethren churches and some in Choctaw, Chippewa, and Mohawk

Songbooks of black spirituals, 22 items, 19th and 20th centuries

—Leo M. Constantino

356

NATIONAL WOMEN'S CHRISTIAN   IEWT
TEMPERANCE UNION

1730 Chicago Avenue
Evanston, Illinois 60201

Frances E. Willard Memorial Library

Temperance cantata by E. C. Knapp, *The Liquor Traffic Must Go*, ca. 1920

Sheet music, 7 temperance songs and one 4-part chorus by F. M. Lehman, I. Van Etten, and Stephen Glover 1877–1920

Songbooks with temperance and gospel songs for use by temperance organizations, 72 items published 1847– , but mostly 1870–1910, including 2 hymnals, 2 books of children's songs, 1 book of songs in Hawaiian, and 4 collections of songs of the Silver Lake Quartette (upstate New York temperance singers)

Songsters containing temperance texts, 5 items, 1880s–1920s

Photocopied and mimeographed songs, 4 items, ca. 1920, 2 of them by J. G. Dailey

Biography of Anna Adams Gordon, by Julia Freeman Deane (Evanston, n.d.)

Museum

Scrapbooks, 2 items relating to temperance work of Frances E. Willard (first president of the WCTU) and her secretary, Anna Adams Gordon (organist)

Photographs, 100 items documenting the careers of Willard and Gordon, late 19th and early 20th centuries

Musical instruments, including organs used by Gordon and Willard

—Grace Storer, Juanita Whisler

357
NORTHWESTERN UNIVERSITY   IEN
Evanston, Illinois 60201

Music Library

Holograph music mss of composers associated with the University or from the Chicago–Evanston area, including Anthony Donato, 50 items; Karel Jirak, definitive holdings as cited in Alice Tischler, *Karel Bohuslav Jirak: A Catalog of his Works*, Detroit Studies in Music Bibliography, 32 (Detroit, 1975); and Albert Noelte, 10 items; also holograph mss of George Heussenstamm, 30 items, and Sigmund Landsberg, 50 items

Camille Saint-Saens, correspondence, 500 items, including many letters written in the course of his American tours

Eric Oldberg (president of the Chicago Symphony Orchestra Association), 310 letters received, mostly personal letters to him and his wife, from Fritz Reiner (10 items) and Carlotta Reiner (26 items), George Szell (36 items) and Helene Szell (4 items), Bruno Walter (102 items) and Lotte Walter (5 items), and Artur Schnabel (29 items) and Therese Schnabel (95 items); also mss, photocopies, and published editions of music by his father, Arne Oldberg (1874–1962)

John Cage Collection, comprising the original mss of the works reproduced in his book *Notations* (New York, 1969), with several additional items

Published music editions and recordings of the music of Henry Cowell, also published writings about Cowell. The Library is a specially designated repository for Cowell materials

Some materials from the Moldenhauer Archive, of Spokane, Wash. (q.v.)

Summy–Birchard Co., microfilm archive of the published music issued by the firm, also by the Clayton F. Summy Co., C. C. Birchard & Co., McLaughlin & Reilly, Chart Music Publishing House, and Arthur P. Schmidt Co.

Published music editions and books about music, including 20,000 U.S. and foreign sheet-music editions in 100 file drawers; also pamphlets, catalogues, brochures, and press clippings, in 25 drawers

Recordings, including 25,000 78-rpm discs

—Don L. Roberts

Special Collections Department

Charles G. Dawes (1865–1931, U.S. vice president), several holograph music mss

Abraham D. Graves (farmer of DeKalb County, Ill.), 55 diary notebooks, 1847–1907, describing rural Illinois social events, including singing schools

Africana Collection

Melville Herskovitz (1895–1963), personal papers, including ethnomusicological field notes and research correspondence

University Archives

Peter Christian Lutkin (1858–1931), personal papers, including correspondence, 1889–1928, mostly related to his work with the University's School of Music; press clippings and other biographical materials; lectures and addresses, ca. 1891–1928; his Christmas cards, with original music; and other memorabilia

John Walter Beattie (1885–1962), personal papers, including correspondence, press clippings, notes relating to his published music-education works and songbooks, published writings, and memorabilia. See Larry Wayne Edwards, *John Walter Beattie, 1885–1962, Pragmatic Music Educator* (Ph.D. diss., University of Michigan, 1971)

School of Music files, including 3 boxes of alumni biographical records, 1873–1925; 12 vols. of catalogues, 1892– ; concert and recital programs; and 40 vols. and 17 boxes of student grade reports, 1892–1959; also correspondence relating to School of Music matters in the papers of the University presidents, including Walter Dill Scott, Franklyn Bliss Snyder, and J. Roscoe Miller

—Patrick M. Quinn

358
SEABURY–WESTERN THEOLOGICAL   (IEG)
SEMINARY
Library
2122 Sheridan Road
Evanston, Illinois 60201

Hymnals and psalm books, 11 19th-century and 4 20th-century items

Hymnals of the Episcopal Church, 40 linear cm., 19th and 20th centuries

—Newland Smith

359
HISTORICAL SOCIETY OF FOREST PARK
7555 Jackson Boulevard
Forest Park, Illinois 60130

Harlem Männerchor (founded 1890), materials including vocal music of German origin, 6 folders, 25 photographs of the Männerchor and affiliated Damenchor, 1890–1970s, and 3 anniversary programs, 1915, 1940, and 1965

—Josephine Austin

360
KNOX COLLEGE   IGK
Seymour Library, Archives
Galesburg, Illinois 61401

Otto A. Harbach (Hauerbach, 1873–1963, librettist), personal papers, 1907–63, 40 linear cm. and 44 separate items, including documents relating to his student days at Knox College and to the founding of ASCAP; 39 libretti, in transcript, original, carbon copy, and photocopy, also other sketches, ms leaves, and notes; holograph ms of Carl Sandburg, "Peg," written for Harbach; materials relating to "Smoke Gets in Your

Eyes"; and tapes, films, and recordings relating to Harbach's career; inventoried

Musicians' Club of Galesburg, archives, including minutes, 1917– , account book, 1938–59, membership lists, 1925– , concert programs, 1924–73, and letters; in all 40 linear cm.

George F. Root, autograph album leaf dated 1890, in the Donna Workman collection

Sheet-music editions and music mss by former College faculty members and students; also 22 songs by Noel Hudson Stearn

Programs of musical events in Galesburg and the local area, 1874–

Monthly Musical Review (Galesburg, 1881–84)

—Lynn Metz

361
GOLCONDA PUBLIC LIBRARY
Box 424
Main Street
Golconda, Illinois 62938

Blaine Boicourt (fl. 1920s–50s, local music teacher), music library, mostly books about music and some songbooks, 100 vols.

362
Lyle and Doris MAYFIELD
820 Trindle
Greenville, Illinois 62246

Illinois folk-music collection, including 400 hours of field recordings on tape, indexed by performer; 30 biographical sketches of performers; and 18 hours of tapes of the annual FolKonvention of southwestern Illinois traditional music at Greenville, 1969–75

363
HIGHLAND PARK HISTORICAL SOCIETY
326 Central Avenue
Highland Park, Illinois 60035

"Ravinia Festival Mini-Museum," including programs, photographs, and other documents of the Ravinia festivals, ca. 1904–

364
MacMURRAY COLLEGE   IJMac
Henry Pfeiffer Library
Beecher and Clay Avenues
Jacksonville, Illinois 62650

Thomas Austin-Ball (1872–ca. 1944, professor of voice at Eastman School of Music), typescript of his "Vocal Pedagogy" (Rochester, ca. 1936), and his personal library of 150 books on music and 250 vocal or choral scores

Virginia (Vasey) Fulkerson (b. ca. 1870, piano teacher in Jerseyville and Jacksonville, and leader of the Chaminade Club), personal music library, comprising 700 items of catalogued sheet music including 2 bound vols. formerly owned by Sarah Cory, ca. 1860, also

tunebooks, hymnals, choral and instrumental music, and books and journals on music; in all 1.5 linear meters

Theater-orchestra music, 50 linear cm. of scores and parts, ca. 1900–1930, from the collection of Hazel (Claus) Wilson (local music teacher)

MacMurray College materials, including 1 linear meter of programs for musical events, ca. 1852– ; also 5 pre-1930 student scrapbooks including programs, and 4 file drawers of photographs, including musical subjects

—Victoria E. Hargrave

365
SCHOOL MUSICIAN, DIRECTOR, AND TEACHER
4 East Clinton Street
Joliet, Illinois 60431

Photographic archives, 1929–40s, partly reproduced in the "Golden Anniversary" issue of *The School Musician, Director, and Teacher*, 50/2 (1978), 87–97

—George Littlefield

366
LAKE FOREST COLLEGE   ILfC
Donnelley Library
Sheridan and College Roads
Lake Forest, Illinois 60045

Songbooks, 100 items, 1920s–30s, including hymnals (1 of them Scottish) and American ballad collections

Programs, including 4 bound vols. of Paterson's Orchestral Concerts, 1920s–30s

Libretti of Chicago productions of the 1920s, some donated by Edwin N. Asmann of Chicago, in all 1 linear meter

Recordings, including 30 78-rpm discs (in the Audio-Visual Center), and 1 78-rpm disc and a booklet of college songs, 1930s (in the Archives)

—Joel M. Lee

367
McKENDREE COLLEGE   ILebM
Holman Library
Lebanon, Illinois 62254

The collection of rare works and hymns, reportedly part of the former Benson Wood Library (see, for instance, *Ash*, 4th ed., p. 513), cannot now be located

Hymnals, 15 items

—Helen E. Gilbert

368
LINCOLN CHRISTIAN COLLEGE
Jessie C. Eury Library
Limit Street and Route 10
Box 178
Lincoln, Illinois 62656

Hymnals, 2800 items, including 800 of the Christian

Church, ca. 1804–1940
Published choral and organ music, 150 items

—Jessie Eury

369

WESTERN ILLINOIS UNIVERSITY   IMacoW

Macomb, Illinois 61455

Music Library

Sheet music for violin, voice, or piano, 5 bound vols., mid 19th century

Archives

Music programs, brochures, catalogues, and posters of the University Music Department, 1906–
Theater training-school programs, 1906–
Sacred and popular songbooks, 4 items, ca. 1855–1900; a book of violin music, 1895; and 4 sheet-music items by Henry Clay Work, 1862–63

—Allie Wise

370

John HANSEN

Malta High School
Malta, Illinois 60150

School songbooks, 5 items, ca. 1880–1900
Band scores and parts, 60 published items, ca. 1900–
Programs, 50 items, ca. 1930– , mostly of local or Chicago school events including some in which Hansen participated as a band member or director
Recordings, 200 78-rpm discs, including Edison discs, some by the Sousa Band

371

John CONNELLY

Box 64
Matteson, Illinois 60443

Collection of 19th- and 20th-century pianos, player pianos, and other musical instruments, including 65- and 88-note piano rolls
Other recordings, including London 78-rpm discs; also Vitaphone 16-inch transcription discs for films, 1927–33, and radio transcription discs

372

Gerald and Delight BELT

429 West Avenue
Morris, Illinois 60450

Published choral music used locally, ca. 1900, 70 linear cm.
Hymnals and popular songbooks, 70 linear cm., ca. 1900
Popular vocal sheet music, 1400 items, ca. 1900
Music publishers' catalogues, 1 linear meter, ca. 1900

373

ILLINOIS VALLEY HISTORICAL SOCIETY

385 East Southmor Road
Morris, Illinois 60450

School songbooks, 8 items, ca. 1930–50
Hymnals, mostly Methodist, 30 items, ca. 1870–1940
Popular vocal sheet music, 1200 items, ca. 1860–1930

—Helen Ullrich

374

MOUNT PROSPECT HISTORICAL SOCIETY

1100 South Linneman Road
Box 81
Mount Prospect, Illinois 60056

Printed music, including 2 German-language hymnals published in the U.S., ca. 1903, donated by local residents, and 40 popular sheet-music items, ca. 1920–
Mount Prospect Citizen's Band, picture, 1920
Recordings, including 100 78-rpm discs of popular music including German waltzes and operettas, recorded in the U.S.; and 3 oral-history tapes in English (recorded in 1968–70), of descendants of German settlers in Mount Prospect, ca. 1848

—Gertrude M. Francek

375

SAINT MARY OF THE LAKE   IMunS
SEMINARY

Feehan Memorial Library
Mundelein, Illinois 60060

Catholic hymnals, 150 late 19th-century items, some with words only, and some in Latin
Hymns and organ compositions by Johann Baptist Singenberger (1884–1924) and his son, John Singenberger, 15 items published mostly in Chicago and Milwaukee, ca. 1900–1930

—Gloria Sieben

376

Caroline MARTIN-MITCHELL MUSEUM

201 West Porter
Naperville, Illinois 60540

Hannah Ditzler Alspaugh (1848–1938), 6 diaries with references to local music and lyrics for children's songs, 1848–73
Piano or organ instruction and repertory books, 4 items, 1842–71
Hymnals and Sunday-school songbooks, 17 items, 1854–1918; also 5 popular songbooks, ca. 1847–91
Sheet music, 21 popular or classical items, 1852–1920
Programs of local church or school musical events, 6 items, ca. 1870–1910; also clippings on local or Chicago-area theater
Recordings, 11 78-rpm discs, including 1 of Boy Scout songs, ca. 1920, and others of orchestral instruments by the Society of Visual Education

—Helen Fraser

377

NAPERVILLE MUNICIPAL BAND

c/o Ronald Keller
24W623 Burlington Avenue
Naperville, Illinois 60540

Materials of the Band, including a 1928 charter, 5 scrapbooks of clippings and photographs, ca. 1930– , and 2.5 linear meters of published scores and parts, ca. 1890–1940

378
NORTH CENTRAL COLLEGE   (INapC)
Library
320 East School Avenue
Naperville, Illinois 60540

Philip D. Sang Jazz Collection, including 200 original editions of books on jazz, and articles on American jazz

379
ILLINOIS STATE UNIVERSITY   INS
Normal, Illinois 61761

Milner Library

George K. Jackson (1745–1822, Boston composer, teacher, and performer), 12 vols. containing 300 items from his music library; 6 ms vols., mostly in Jackson's hand, including his theory method book and music compositions; 5 vols. containing 77 items of published music, 2 of the vols. containing editions issued by Jackson, others containing London editions; and 1 vol. of ms and printed viola parts. See William Salloch (antiquarian book dealer, Ossining, N.Y.), *Catalogue 301* (1973), pp. 16–22, item 37

Circus and Related Arts Collection, including materials acquired from Walter Scholl, Sverre O. Braathen, and Jo van Doveren, also the Charles H. Tinney Collection of Circus Band Scores, 121 items, 1882–1916. Holdings include band scores from the Braathen collection, 60 linear cm.; several essays by Braathen on the historical development of the circus band, ca. 1940; 14 circus songsters, mostly 1880s–90s; 59 songbooks on circus and related topics from the Scholl collection; 25 catalogues of band music and musical instruments from the Braathen collection; and other musical items scattered through 70 scrapbooks, 1890s–1970s, 50,000 pictures, several hundred programs, and extensive personal papers. See Robert Sokan, *A Descriptive and Bibliographic Catalog of the Circus and Related Arts Collection*, (Bloomington, 1976)

Minnie Saltzmann-Stevens (1874–1950, Wagnerian soprano), personal papers, including her diary, 1904–6, photographs, clippings in 4 scrapbooks, and correspondence

Correspondence of Julia Ward Howe, 2 items, and of Lowell Mason, 1 letter dated 1867

Oratorical Association, documents of musical and literary contests between the oratorical societies of Bloomington and Carbondale, 1878–81, and 1 ledger, 1899

Sheet music, 1200 items, 1820s–1940, 600 separate items and 15 bound vols., all uncatalogued except for a contents list of 400 unbound items

Hymnals, tunebooks, and school songbooks, 52 items, 1794–1900, including 15 by Lowell Mason

—Mary Jo Brown, Robert Sokan

University Museums

Oblong music copybook with ms marches, waltzes, and instrumental works, by Job Farly of Monkton, Vt., 1851

Book of music for parlor organ, 1892

Hymnal and popular songbooks, 6 items, ca. 1886–1923

Vocal sheet music, 4 items, 1844–1917; also 2 sheet-music items clipped from a local newspaper, ca. 1900

Programs of musical events in Normal and in St. Louis, Mo., 21 items, ca. 1890–1940

Minnie Saltzman-Stevens, 2 opera costumes

Marie Litta (1856–83, opera singer), 1 photograph

Cylinder recordings, 7 items

—Virgina M. Wright

380
BETHANY AND NORTHERN BAPTIST   IObT
THEOLOGICAL SEMINARIES
Library
Butterfield and Meyers Roads
Oak Brook, Illinois 60521

Cassell Collection, containing the *Zionitischer Weyrauchs Hügel* (Germantown, Pa., 1739) and *Das kleine Davidische Psalterspiel*, 2nd ed. (Germantown, Pa., 1760), of the Ephrata community, and 450 other tunebooks or hymnals published or used in the U.S., many in German, ca. 1730–1920

—Hedda Durnbaugh

381
PEORIA PUBLIC LIBRARY   IP
107 Northeast Monroe Street
Peoria, Illinois 61602

Art and Music Department

Piano-vocal scores for 25 musical comedies, ca. 1905–40

Hymnals and popular songbooks, 2 linear meters, ca. 1836–1940

Vocal sheet music, 2000 mostly popular items, ca. 1838–1940

—Velma Gorsage

Reference Department

Programs from Peoria-area musical events, 1890– , in 7 envelopes, including the Amateur Musical Club, Bradley University School of Music, Peoria Civic Opera, and Peoria Symphony Orchestra; also clippings and photographs of Peoria-area musical events, ca. 1900– , in 11 envelopes

—Joyce Johnson

382
HISTORICAL SOCIETY OF QUINCY AND
ADAMS COUNTY
425 South Twelfth Street
Quincy, Illinois 62301

Popular sheet music and songbooks of the Civil War, 2 linear meters

Programs of the Quincy Opera House and Theatre, 30 items, ca. 1865–89

—Julia Scofield

383

George M. IRWIN
428 Main Street
Quincy, Illinois 62301

Leonard ("Ned") Picerno (1889–1947), 3 linear meters of performance materials used by him in vaudeville, silent films, and other theater pit orchestras in the Quincy area, mostly 1910s–30s

384

QUINCY PUBLIC LIBRARY   **IQ**
526 Jersey Street
Quincy, Illinois 62301

William Spencer Johnson (1883–1967), 250 items of papers, including ms and published compositions, correspondence with Bliss Carman (poet) and with publishers, programs of performances of his works, clippings, and photographs

—Bonnie Robinson

385

CONCORDIA TEACHERS COLLEGE   **IRivfT**
Klinck Memorial Library
7400 Augusta Street
River Forest, Illinois 60305

Hymnals and tunebooks, 300 items, mostly from Lutheran churches in the U.S., 1770–1940; also 16 chorale books, 1847–1906, and 13 singing-school songbooks, 1839–84. See the catalogue by Carl Schalk, *Hymnals and Chorale Books of the Klinck Memorial Library* (River Forest, 1975)

—Carl Schalk

386

AUGUSTANA COLLEGE   **IRA**
Denkmann Memorial Library
Rock Island, Illinois 61201

Hymnals in Swedish and English, mostly Lutheran, 1853–1940, 112 items, including many without music, and 8 in "Dutch door" format
Sheet music, 422 items, mostly 1910s–20s, including World War I songs and music written for performance in Swedish-American Lutheran Churches
Oliver A. Linder, press clippings relating to Swedish theater in Chicago, 1869–1950, with references to musical productions, accessible through a personal-name index

—John Caldwell

387

ROCKFORD COLLEGE   **IRoC**
Howard Colman Library
5050 East State Street
Rockford, Illinois 61101

Clarence Joseph Bulliet (1883–1952, music critic for the *Indianapolis Star*, 1906–12, *Louisville Herald*, 1922–23, *Chicago Evening Post*, 1924–32, and *Chicago Daily News*, 1932–48), personal papers, in 5 vertical-file cabinets, including research materials, drafts of his writings, and extensive photographic files of theatrical and musical celebrities

—Joan B. Surrey

388

ROCKFORD MUSEUM CENTER
6799 Guilford Road
Rockford, Illinois 61107

American Union of Swedish Singers, archives, 1892– , materials being transferred from the custody of Carl E. Anderson, Chicago, q.v.

389

David D. BENNETT
4N 970 Highway 25
Saint Charles, Illinois 60174

David D. Bennett, complete published compositions and arrangements, 150 items, including "Bye, Bye Blues," also some ms items, ca. 1920– ; ms memoirs written 1976–79; royalty contracts from U.S. publishers; publishers' catalogues; photographs of Bennett and of groups directed by him; tape recordings of his compositions and arrangements, played by various bands including the U.S. Marine Band; and programs and clippings
Radio-orchestra scores and parts, 1 linear meter, used by the WJJD Studio Orchestra, Chicago, ca. 1930–50
Popular sheet music, 1500 items, ca. 1900–1940

390

ILLINOIS STATE ARCHIVES
Archives Building
Springfield, Illinois 62756

See the *Descriptive Inventory of the Archives of the State of Illinois* (Springfield, 1978)

Muster rolls of musicians from Illinois serving in the Civil War, 1861–65, 7 folders
Tax assessments of musical instruments (i.e., organs, pianos, and melodeons), 1867–1903

—Patricia Brennan

391

ILLINOIS STATE HISTORICAL LIBRARY **IHi**
Old State Capitol Building
Springfield, Illinois 62706

General collections

William Black (1796–1884), ms music book with 3-voice hymns, begun in Georgia in 1818, and continued in Tennessee and at Walnut Grove farm, Ill.
Riley Root (1795–1870), papers and patents, 1855–66, in-

cluding materials relating to his "new musical transposition keyboard"

Civil War song texts, diaries, letters, and papers mentioning music, including a diary of Francis Marion Johnson (principal musician, 32nd regiment, Illinois Infantry), 1862–63

Benjamin Grierson (1826–1911, Union officer, later band and orchestra director and music teacher in Pittsburgh and in Jacksonville, Ill.), ms band and orchestra parts, also correspondence mentioning his musical activity

Alfredo Jannotta (composer and teacher), holograph and published music, 1860s–70s, letters in Italian, and brochures describing his music classes and his vocal school in Chicago and Los Angeles, 1881–97

Carrie Jacobs Bond, press clipping on her Chicago Boarding house, ms note, and a typed letter

Monticello (Ill.) College (formerly Monticello Female Seminary), archives, including photographs; press clippings; scrapbooks; 8 boxes of programs, including recitals, 1869– , and anniversary and commencement programs, 1847– ; also other programs, published poems and songs, 1879–1939, and other college hymns and songs; and Philena Fobes's copy of the *Music Vale Academy Catalogue*, 1860–61

Parmelia Elizabeth (Cox) Goodwin, "Folk Songs of Crawford County, Ill., c. 1870–1890," with texts for 32 songs

Sheet music, 800 items, ca. 1830– , mostly 1850–1900, in 6 bound vols. and singly (the latter arranged by title), mostly songs and solo keyboard music, with special emphasis on Abraham Lincoln (200 items), the Civil War, and Illinois subjects

Printed music, including 35 vocal anthologies, 1844–1924; 50 songsters, 1860–1908; 250 broadsides, ca. 1850–76; 40 tunebooks and hymnals, 1835–70; and other books and periodicals about music. Many of these items date from or concern the Civil War

Programs, including a Jenny Lind concert, ca. 1850; 36 Chautauqua programs, 1898–1923, 14 of them from Galesburg; and miscellaneous other items, 1882–1914

Scrapbook on "Music and Churches in Springfield," ca. 1936

Printed reports, including brochures of Chicago musical societies, 1874, 1921, and 1955; Springfield Conservatory of Music, *Annual Catalogue*, 1910–12; and music publishers' catalogues

Archives of the Illinois Writers' Project

Files assembled in connection with the WPA project in its Chicago office, 1930s–40s, in 307 boxes with a typescript inventory

Material from Illinois cities other than Chicago, in 51 boxes, some with musical subject matter; also short essays, including L. Gregory on early rural music in Illinois, a survey of "Galesburg as a Music Center," Grace Armstrong on music in Springfield, and on Illinois music schools, high-school band contests, and a biography of Dr. William F. Bentley

Chicago materials, in 51 boxes as well as in other parts of the collection, some with musical subject matter, including sections on (1) buildings, with folders on Orchestra Hall and the Civic Opera Building; (2) organizations, including short essays by Eric Stigler on the "Little Theater at the Jewish People's Insti-

tute," Mabel Locke on "'Song Sharks' and the Amateur Songwriters' Protective Societies," Harold Rogers on "The Negro Light Opera Company and the Center of Negro Art," and Theodora Picard on "The Chicago Classical Guitar Society"; (3) industry, including essays on Chicago music manufacturers, retailers, and publishers, notably Elizabeth Drury, "Early History and Development of Musical Instrument Making in Chicago," (1850s–ca. 1914), 75 pages, and Carroll Whaley's memoirs, "An Organ Builder's Soliloquy," ca. 1919–30; (4) a chronological history of opera in Chicago, with details on the seasons, 1850–1937; (5) Charles Ellis's "History of the Chicago Theatres, 1837–1937," 634 pages, and other essays on Chicago theater; (6) Laura Antoinette Large, "Musical Chicago: A History of Music in Chicago," 146 pages; (7) and other miscellaneous surveys of music organizations, festivals, schools, patronage, and collections

Detailed annals of the theater in Chicago and other cities, 1813–1910, in 4 boxes

Ethnic music in Illinois, including 6 boxes containing transcriptions of texts and essays, many of these by Mary Mears and Grace Levy, on European-immigrant, American Indian, Negro, and Afro-American traditions, also comic songs, vaudeville, camp meetings, party and chidrens' games, and labor and protest songs, with special concern for George Evans and the Honey Boy Minstrels, John Skelton, Luke Slick, the Holiness Church in Chicago, the National Folk Festivals of 1934–37, and Slovenian, Lithuanian, Italian, and Polish traditional music; also a bibliography of American Indian music, a description of ethnic festivals in the Chicago area, 1930s, and essays on black theater including Kitty Chapelle, "Development of Negro Culture in Chicago," 690 pages

Federal Music Project in Illinois, archives, 1935–43, in 36 boxes, including administrative records, publicity announcements, press clippings, ms and published performance parts and catalogues to this and other of the Illinois Project's music libraries, concert materials, mailing lists, photographs of 200 musicians and musical groups, and audition records

392
LINCOLN LIBRARY   ISL
Sangamon Valley Collection
326 South Seventh Street
Springfield, Illinois 62701

Illinois Federation of Music Clubs, 10 scrapbooks, 1918–44

Springfield chapter of the Illinois Federation of Music Clubs, 40 scrapbooks, 20 of them pre-1940

—Edward J. Russo

393
James A. ROGERS
First United Methodist Church
501 East Capitol Avenue
Springfield, Illinois 62702

Materials on hymnology, including 2000 hymnals, mostly published in the U.S., 1790– , and 500 books on hymnology and church music

394

Chaw MANK

Box 30
Staunton, Illinois 62088

Manuscript and published compositions by Chaw Mank, 400 items, ca. 1935– ; 15 scrapbooks with programs including performances of his compositions; and recordings produced by his Blue Ribbon Record Co., 50 78-rpm discs, ca. 1935–40
Photographs of musical, theatrical, and Hollywood personalities, 25,000 items, ca. 1914–

395

SEVEN ACRES MUSEUM

Union, Illinois 60180

Materials were purchased mostly in the early 1970s from Clarence Ferguson, a former employee of Thomas A. Edison

Recordings, 15,000 cylinders and 10,000 80-rpm discs of popular and classical music and the spoken word, recorded by Leo Slezak, Sarah Bernhardt, and others
Catalogues of music dealers and publishers in West Orange, N.J., and in New York, 200 items, ca. 1895–
Musicians' portraits, 100 items
Phonographs, 600 items manufactured 1870s–1920
Books on sound reproduction, with 19th-century imprints

—Larry Donley

396

Philip V. BOHLMAN

509 West Green Street
Urbana, Illinois 61801

Wallee Brown (1888–1956) and Mayme Brown (b. 1889, composers and music publishers in Chicago and in Boscobel, Wis.), original compositions including religious and popular music and selections from stage musicals; also clippings and printers' paste-ups
William Kinder (1864–1947, composer and publisher in Blue River, Wis.), materials on his career, ca. 1900–1930, including 2 interviews with his daughter, Mrs. Bessie Barta, 1978
Printed music of German-American publishers in Wisconsin, Missouri, Illinois, and Ohio, ca. 1890–1920, including 3 songbooks, 4 hymnals (3 with words only), 3 chorale books for organ, 8 sheet-music items, pedagogical publications, and a church band book; also a Danish hymnal (Askov, Minn., 1920) with words only

397

D. W. KRUMMEL

702 West Delaware Avenue
Urbana, Illinois 61801

Research notes, including transcripts of music notices in Philadelphia newspapers, 1800–1820, with card indexes; also files relating to American music printing and publishing, including card indexes of publishers'

plate numbers, maintained in connection with the International Association of Music Libraries, Commission for Bibliographic Research
Sheet music, 1800–1940, 5000 miscellaneous items, mostly in bound vols.

398

UNIVERSITY OF ILLINOIS   IU

Urbana, Illinois 61801

See Jean A. Major, *Collections Acquired by the University of Illinois Library at Urbana–Champaign, 1897–1974* (Urbana, 1974)

Music Library

Sheet music, 1790s– , 30,000 items in 40 bound vols. and singly, the latter divided into vocal and piano sections, each subdivided by year of imprint and arranged by title. Included are items from the collections of Bly Corning, Harry Dichter (3021 items), Millie Emory (450 Von Tilzer Music Publishing Co. imprints), Richard B. Harwell (445 topical southern U.S. items), Lester S. Levy, Thomas A. Radcliffe, and the American Antiquarian Society
Tunebooks and hymnals, 350 items, mostly with music, 1771–ca. 1900, mostly post-1830; also 291 broadsides, mostly 1850s–60s
Other printed and ms music, including items from the libraries of Rafael Joseffy (1852–1915), 2000 items as cited in the sale catalogue, *Musical Library Owned by Rafael Joseffy* (New York, 1930s); Lloyd Morey (1886–1965, organist and University president), organ and vocal music; Heinrich A. Rattermann (1832–1923), German choral music from Cincinnati; Soulima Stravinsky, 200 piano editions; Joseph Szigeti (1892–1973), 850 violin editions; and Ludwig Zirner (1917–71), 450 opera scores, many with ms translations, also piano editions and other music
Hunleth Music Store, of St. Louis, Mo., dispersal stock of 500,000 items, including a separate collection of 20,000 dance-band items; 14,000 items of orchestral music for silent films from the Fox Theatre, St. Louis; 37,000 items of other theater-orchestra parts; and other items, partly integrated into the Library's music collections
Radio station WGN, Chicago, music library, 1930s–50s, containing 2900 vocal scores and sets of orchestral parts; also programs, scripts, and other documents of music broadcasts, 1935–
Rafael Joseffy, 200 mss and ms sketches for his piano compositions and exercises; also 270 ms sheets and fragments for his *First Studies for the Piano*; 40 programs, letters, press clippings, and other documents relating to his career; and ms music documents from his associates, many with inscriptions to him
Philander Seward (grandfather of William H. Seward), musical commonplace book, New England, ca. 1808
Frank Skinner (1897–1968), 80 film scores, 1941–66
Harry Partch (1901–74), black-line prints of his mss, 36 items, 1930s–60s; also miscellaneous personal papers
Joseph Szigeti, 51 mss and black-line prints of mss by his associates, mostly European but including works by Charles Wakefield Cadman, Henry Cowell, and S. Stillman (probably Mitya Stillman, 1893–1936)
Miscellaneous ms materials, including Edward Bailey Birge, "Concord Hymn," n.d.; documents relating to

J. W. ("Captain Jack") Crawford, ca. 1907; Alvin Etler, score and parts for his arrangement of J. S. Bach's *Wenn wir in höchsten Nöten sein;* Lloyd Morey, 12 orchestral and chamber works, 1910–36; Nicholas Van Slyck, 8 items, mostly 1940s; and W. E. Watt, 20 mss

Programs of performances of music by American composers, including items relating to Henry K. Hadley, Henry Holden Huss, William J. McCoy (1848–1926), and others, acquired from the collection of Barton Cantrell

Scrapbooks and other collections of miscellaneous documents, including materials relating to the career of Maud Powell (1868–1920, violinist); 15 scrapbooks assembled by William Allen Shirk, relating to operatic and other singers; and documents on local musical activities assembled by Edna Morey, Charlotte B. Ward (1914–21), and Ludwig Zirner

Catalogues of music publishers and dealers, 150 items, ca. 1915–40

Photographs and pictorial materials relating to materials in collections described above

Recordings, 35,000 78-rpm discs, including 1200 Edison discs, and materials from the collections of John Kirker Quinn (4022 items, including important early jazz), Edward Vollintine (1397 items), William A. Shirk (1165 discs, including early vocal items), Frank Skinner (400 items, commercial and noncommercial, mostly film music), Joseph Szigeti (155 items, mostly non-commercial), and Sterling Hackman (4650 items); also 85 early piano rolls

Rare Book Room, University Library

Sheet music, including 830 pre-fire Chicago imprints, as cited in Dena J. Epstein, *Music Publishing in Chicago before 1871: The Firm of Root & Cady*, Detroit Studies in Music Bibliography, 14 (Detroit, 1969); and 215 Confederate imprints, arranged by and accessible through marked copies of *Crandall* and *Harwell*

Franklin Meine Collection of American humor, 15 music items, including songbooks, songsters, and minstrel-show materials, also an extra-illustrated copy of *Jubilee Days* (Boston, 1872), containing pamphlets, pictures, press clippings, and other materials on the World's Peace Jubilee

Carl Sandburg, published editions and materials used in the preparation of the *American Song Bag* (New York, 1927); also photographs and other materials

Frederick B. Stiven, holograph ms of his "Hymn for Mother's Day"

Printed music and music books, including 30 tunebooks and hymnals, 1772–1845, in English and German; 3 libretti, 1805–27; 2 political songsters, 1863–68; and 6 19th-century published music editions

University Archives

> See Maynard J. Brichford, *Guide to the Manuscript Collection at the University of Illinois* (Urbana, 1976)

Personal papers of University faculty, alumni, and administrators, including Samuel Abrams, scrapbook, 1902–6, relating to his violin school in Chicago; Arthur E. Bestor, Sr., papers relating to his work as a director and president of the Chautauqua Institution; Marcus Selden Goldman (English professor), notes on his student years in Paris, including references to James Joyce as music and literary critic for the Euro-

pean edition of the *New York Herald;* Mark Hindsley, papers and an interview relating to early University bands, former director Austin A. Harding, John Philip Sousa, and college songs; Stewart S. Howe, fraternity songbooks, 1871–1961, 1 linear meter; Herman G. James, student notes for music courses, 1907–9; Everett D. Kisinger, correspondence, charts, announcements, music, programs, and other materials relating to bands at the University of Illinois and the University of Michigan; Albert Lee, papers relating to the music program of the Bethel A.M.E. Church, Champaign, 1912–28; Jennette E. C. Lincoln (University director of physical education for women), papers, sheet music, and photographs, 1892–1916, including material on May Day fetes; Russell H. Miles, personal papers, 1928–72, including 3 published editions of his music; Lloyd Morey, programs of University musical events and of the Trinity Methodist Church, Urbana, also his music scrapbook, 1908–53; J. Kerker Quinn (English professor), personal papers, including sheet music; Samson Raphaelson, materials on his short story (and its later stage and film versions), "The Jazz Singer," as discussed in Robert L. Carringer, *The Jazz Singer* (Madison, 1979); Ernest A. Scott (director of the Natural History Survey), personal papers, including programs, orders for sheet music, and press clippings concerning his work as choir director of the Bethel A.M.E. Church, Champaign; Frederic B. Stiven (1882–1947, director of the School of Music), papers, including correspondence, programs, notes, a journal from 1910, and photographs

Songs and music of the University, collected as a group and in the papers of individuals; also a scrapbook of Thacher Howland Guild (composer of the "Illinois Loyalty" song)

Scrapbooks, programs, press clippings, and memorabilia relating to music at the University, as a group and in various other files; also photographs of University performing groups and relating to University musical events

Radio station WILL, administrative records, 1933– , including program notes, schedules, scripts, documents, commentary, reports, audience surveys, and recordings, also materials concerning the gift of the John Philip Sousa collection (see under Band Department Collections, below)

Printed programs for the Illinois Rural Music and Drama Festivals, 1931–52, sponsored annually by the Agriculture Extension Service

Administrative files, course announcements, and miscellaneous materials pertaining to the School of Music, and to the University's earlier academic programs in music

Administrative files pertaining to student musical programs and services, also records of student music organizations, and miscellaneous information on recreational musical activities for students

Illinois Historical Survey

Heinrich A. Rattermann (1832–1923, Cincinnati publisher and German-cultural leader), personal papers, including 6 account books and songbooks of the Cincinnati Liedertafel, 1851–57; letter book and minute book of the Erster deutscher Sängerbund von Nordamerika, 1859–68; German folksongs; leases from German music societies for the use of concert halls; 20 ms libretti, mostly in Rattermann's hand, also 26 other ms and 2 published music texts; and correspondence relating to music organizations including the Cincinnati Männerchor and the Cincinnati Orpheus, and musicians, among them Hans Balatka, Otto Dresel, and George S. Schuhmann in Louisville. See Dennis E. Walle and Donna Sell, *Guide to the Heinrich A. Rattermann Collection* (Urbana, 1979), esp. pp. 93–96 and 202–3

Songbooks, pamphlets, programs, and printed announcements, 10 items, relating to Alfredo Janotta's music studio, 1880s; the Chicago Mendelssohn Club, 1908; and the Litta Conservatory of Music, Bloomington, Ill., 1903–4

Band Department Collections

Albert A. Harding (1880–1958), personal papers. Music scores include marching- and concert-band scores and parts, many in ms copied by Harding and others, 500 sets; orchestral scores and parts, 125 items; and miscellaneous music mss, including 2 portfolios of music by Herman Bellstedt (1858–1926), largely band music, Victor Herbert's "Encore for 3 Cornets," ca. 1895, Percy Grainger's "Molly on the Shore" (inscribed to John Philip Sousa), mss of Illinois college songs by R. S. Howland, H. L. Alford, and others, "Hail to the Orange" arranged for performance by Tito Schipa at a football game in 1927, and mss in the hands of John Philip Sousa, Carl Busch, Arthur Seidel, Vincent Ragone, and others. Among the programs and other documents, which are bound, in scrapbooks, or separate, are materials relating to University band groups and band clinics, 1906–48, also programs of the Colorado Midland Band, the Goldman Band, and other groups, and an extensive collection of photographs. Organizational files relate to the American School Band Directors' Association, National Music Camp, American Bandmasters' Association, and the Tri-State Band Festival of Enid, Okla. Harding's personal library contains 100 books, 250 vols., and 4 linear meters of printed music, also periodicals, 100 pamphlets, and 200 78-rpm discs. Administrative files include correspondence, notably 16 letters from Percy Grainger, 4 from Leo Sowerby, and others; also extensive correspondence with the Victor Talking Machine Co., honors and citations, posters, repertory lists, and extensive card indexes

Herbert L. Clarke (1867–1945), personal papers, including 625 sets of band-music parts, published and ms, used mostly by the Long Beach (Cal.) Municipal Band, 1923–43, of which 50 works are by Clarke; 30 published and ms sets of orchestral parts; published music, including songs, instrumental works, and method books, 1.2 linear meters; 30 mss of works by Clarke, including the "Toronto Yacht Club Polka"; and other mss of Charles W. Storm, Sallie J. Shull, A. H. Knoll, O. H. Schemmer, and J. Salcedo. Other materials include ms texts of articles, press clippings, 1931–47, and contest materials; 100 photographs, mostly related to bands; 100 78-rpm discs of privately and commercially recorded band music; 65 books and pamphlets; and memorabilia, including a "Book of Friendship" prepared by the Women's Symphony Orchestra of Long Beach, Cal., 1937

John Philip Sousa Museum, including the Sousa Band Library of 3000 sets of scores and parts, published

and in ms; 1 linear meter of books and music from Sousa's personal library; 25 mss of works by Sousa, as cited in Paul E. Bierley, *John Philip Sousa: A Descriptive Catalogue of His Works* (Urbana, 1973); 35 mss of works by other composers, among them Henri S. Brandt, Mabel W. Daniels, John Gready, C. M. Long, Morton F. Mason, Byron Tapley, and N. van Westerhout, also other mss bearing the stamp "Property of Victor Herbert"; 100 programs, mostly of Sousa Band performances, 1882–1920s; personal papers, including 2 letters, press clippings, and radio scripts; 70 photographs of Sousa and his associates, 1893–1932, and an oil portrait; and memorabilia

Carl Busch (1862–1943) Collection of Musical Instruments, including press clippings and other writings by Busch; a photograph album, 1924, with a Sousa letter; ms band books used in Humboldt, Kan., ca. 1864; 6 published and 5 ms works by Busch; 35 photographs of Busch and his associates; books on music; and memorabilia

Band Department Museum, including zither music of C. J. F. Umlauf from the library of J. W. Woodrow, and other items sold by Franz Schwarzer (zither dealer, of Washington, Mo.); photographs relating to local and University bands, 1893–1936; and posters, programs, and memorabilia

Ethnomusicology Archive

A research collection established and maintained by the School of Music, containing tape recordings and related documents and including 52 American collections

American Indian music, 36 collections on 100 tapes, many of Blackfoot music as collected by Bruno Nettl or Robert Witmer, 1950s–60s; also of 20 other tribes from various collectors, 1930s–70s; and copies of early recordings, 1890s–1930s

Other American materials, collected mostly 1960s–70s, including Anglo-American fiddle tunes in Arkansas, black revival church music in Virginia, black "Sacred Harp" singing in Alabama, Amish music in Indiana and Illinois, German (East Frisian) songs and hymns in Illinois, Czech and other folksongs in Wisconsin, music of Pakistani-Americans, folksongs of southern Illinois, and sacred music from commercial recordings

Other Collections

Abraham Lincoln collection, including Benjamin Henry Grierson (1826–1911), holograph ms text of the words of his "Song of Jubilee," celebrating the Republican party victory of 1860; an 1864 campaign songster; 2 sheet-music items of 1865; and a printed text for Dan B. Brunnitt's *Let My People Go! A Service for the 44th Anniversary of the Freedmen's Aid Society* (Cincinnati, n.d.)

Theodore Leavitt Theatrical Print Collection, 5000 items, mostly British but partly American, including illustrations of composers, dancers, singers, and instrumental performers, with card indexes by personal names as well as for scenes, theaters, and roles

Theatre Reference Room collections, including a score of Hall Macklin's *Nada* (Champaign, 1928), and 13 programs of University dramatic musical productions, 1930s

Theater program collections, including 2500 items, many for Chicago productions, assembled by Mrs. E.

G. Stetson and her father, D. C. Burdick, and presented by Alyene Westall Prehn; 91 items assembled by Hattie F. Kaufman, many for early events in Chicago, Champaign, and Urbana; T. E. Ratcliffe, 1 linear meter of music and drama programs, 1930s–50s; and 40 linear cm. of programs of local and University events, 1911–49

General library holdings, including 35 vocal part books, 15 hymnals with words only, and 65 programs in German, mostly relating to Cincinnati, acquired from Heinrich Rattermann and Julius Doerner; 100 other hymnals with words only, 1825–1940; 200 hymnals with music, including gospel songbooks; 16 catalogues of Victor recordings, 1915-40s; and 15 runs of pre-1915 music periodicals

Archival records of the Resources of American Music History project, including 3 linear meters of reports from the repositories covered in the published directory, also staff notes and draft entries; 1 linear meter of administrative records and other correspondence; and 8 linear meters of card indexes, including biographical files (3000 entries), bibliographical files (2500 entries), reply-card files (4000 entries), and control files for respondents approached (20,000 entries)

399
IROQUOIS COUNTY HISTORICAL SOCIETY
Old Court House
Watseka, Illinois 60970

Sheet music, 600 items, 1870s–1920s
Hymnals, 50 items, 1856–1917, half of them pre-1900
Secular songbooks and instrumental-music collections, 22 items, 1867–1930; also 1 music periodical vol., 1863–64
Recordings, 1 linear meter of popular 78-rpm discs, 1908–20s

—Lorraine Schriefer

400
LAKE COUNTY MUSEUM
Lakewood Forest Preserve
Wauconda, Illinois 60084

Sheet music, 4 bound vols. and 5 separate items, ca. 1867–1917
Songbooks, 15 sacred and secular items, 19th century, including A. S. Hayden, *Introduction to Sacred Music* (Pittsburgh, 1838)
Instrumental method books, 4 items, ca. 1900
Programs for opera houses and other theaters in Chicago and Waukegan, ca. 75 items, late 19th century
Photograph of the Apollo Quartette, Waukegan, 1890s

—Andrea Zolle

401
WAUKEGAN HISTORICAL SOCIETY
1917 North Sheridan Road
Waukegan, Illinois 60085

Music by local composers, including John D. Thomas, ms "Centenial [sic] Ode," 1935, and Otto Graham, ms conductor's score of a march for band

Waukegan Philharmonic Chorus, membership lists and programs of operettas
Popular, campaign, and school songbooks, also hymnals, in all 10 items, ca. 1887–1934; and chorus books for men's or mixed choruses, 7 items used locally
Cylinder recordings, 6 items

—Phyllis E. Ball

402
WAUKEGAN SWEDISH GLEE CLUB
c/o Gerald Johnson, Secretary
621 Belvidere Street
Waukegan, Illinois 60085

Archival records of the Club, 1913– , including official minutes, press clippings, 500 photographs, 300 programs, 50 items of personal papers, 500 sheet-music items, 50 songbooks, and 20 music mss

—Fred Fortney

403
WEST CHICAGO HISTORICAL MUSEUM
132 Main Street
West Chicago, Illinois 60185

Materials relating to John West (local composer)

—Jerry Musich

404
WHEATON COLLEGE   IWW
Wheaton, Illinois 60187

Wheaton College Library

Hymnals and Sunday-school songbooks, 300 vols., ca. 1870– , including items in Spanish, French, German, and Scottish (10 of them in Special Collections); also 47 community songbooks including 2 in French and 4 in Spanish, and 11 school songbooks including 1 in German, ca. 1870–

—Virginia L. Powell

Billy Graham Center Library

Gospel hymnals, and mission and Sunday-school songbooks, 19th and 20th centuries

—Fern Weimer

Billy Graham Center Archives

Fanny Crosby, 1000 ms lyrics, as copied by her husband, ca. 1865–1915
Sheet music and songbooks in collections of evangelists, radio preachers, and missionaries, including Paul Rader, Billy Sunday, and Amie Semple McPherson

—Robert Schuster

In addition to the repositories listed above, the following have also reported holdings of the materials indicated:

Andover—Andover Historical Society: songbooks, programs, miscellaneous

Anna—Stinson Memorial Library: songbooks

Arlington Heights—Historical Society and Museum of Arlington Heights: songbooks, pictures, recordings, miscellaneous

Barrington—Barrington Area Library: songbooks, other printed music

Berwyn—Stickney–Forest View Library District: songbooks, recordings

Blue Island—Blue Island Historical Society: sheet music, songbooks, miscellaneous

Blue Island—Blue Island Public Library: sheet music, songbooks

Breese—Breese Public Library: songbooks

Brookfield—Brookfield Free Public Library: recordings

Calumet Park—Calumet Park Public Library: songbooks

Camp Point—Camp Point Free Public Library: songbooks, other printed music, pictures, recordings

Carbondale—Carbondale Public Library: songbooks

Carrollton—Greene County Historical Society and Museum: programs, pictures

Catlin—Catlin Public Library District: songbooks

Centralia—Kaskaskia College, Kaskaskia Theatre Association: programs, recordings

Champaign—John and Jean Boyer: sheet music, songbooks

Champaign — Byerly Music: sheet music, songbooks, other printed music

Champaign—Champaign County Historical Museum: songbooks, programs, recordings

Charleston—Carnegie Public Library: songbooks, programs, recordings, miscellaneous

Charleston—Eastern Illinois University: sheet music, songbooks, recordings

Chicago—Chicago Artists Orchestra: sheet music, songbooks

Chicago—Chicago Board of Education Library: songbooks, miscellaneous

Chicago—Elmwood Park Public Library: songbooks

Chicago—Forest Fund: recordings

Chicago—Historic Pullman Foundation: programs, pictures

Chicago—Malcolm X College, City College of Chicago: songbooks, recordings

Chicago—National College of Education, Herman H. Hegner Library: songbooks

Chicago—North Park Theological Seminary, Mellander Library: songbooks

Chicago—Ridge Historical Society Library: sheet music, songbooks

Chicago Ridge—Chicago Ridge Public Library: songbooks

Clinton—Fine Arts Center of Clinton: sheet music, songbooks, other printed music

Creve Coeur—Creve Coeur Public Library: sheet music, songbooks

Danville—Danville Public Library: sheet music, recordings

Deerfield—Deerfield Public Library: songbooks

Deerfield—Trinity College Library: songbooks

Deerfield—Village School of Folk Music: songbooks

DePue—DePue Public Library: songbooks

Des Plaines—Des Plaines Historical Society, Library: sheet music, songbooks, programs, pictures, recordings

Dundee—Dundee Township Historical Society: sheet music, songbooks

Dunlap—Dunlap Public Library District: songbooks

Earlville—Earl Township Public Library: songbooks

Elgin—Gail Borden Public Library District: songbooks, recordings

Elgin—Robert Harris: sheet music, songbooks, recordings

Elsah—Principia College, School of Nations Museum: recordings

Evansville—Evansville Public Library: songbooks, programs, catalogues, recordings, miscellaneous

Fort Sheridan—United States Army Post, Library: songbooks

Fox River Grove—Fox River Grove Public Library District: songbooks

Frankfort—Frankfort Area Historical Society of Will County: sheet music, songbooks, programs, recordings

Frankfort—Marian R. Nordsell: sheet music, songbooks, recordings

Freeport—Freeport Mennonite Church, Library: sheet music, songbooks

Freeport—Stephenson County Historical Society: songbooks, programs, miscellaneous

Galesburg—Knox–Galesburg Symphony, Knox College: printed music, programs

Geneva—Geneva Historical Society: sheet music, songbooks, programs, pictures

Genoa—Genoa Public Library: songbooks, pictures, recordings

Glen Ellyn—College of DuPage, Learning Resources Center: recordings

Glenview—Glenview Public Library: songbooks

Greenup—Greenup Township Carnegie Library: songbooks, recordings

Greenville—Greenville College: songbooks, miscellaneous

Harrisburg—Curt Burklow: sheet music

Hillsboro—Historical Society of Montgomery County: songbooks, programs, pictures, recordings

Hillside—Hillside Public Library: songbooks, recordings

Jacksonville—Philip Bradish: pictures

Jacksonville—Jacksonville Symphony Orchestra: printed music

Kankakee—Kankakee County Historical Society Library and Museum: sheet music, songbooks, programs, miscellaneous

Kankakee—Kankakee Public Library: recordings

Kewanee—Kewanee Historical Society: sheet music, songbooks

Kewanee—Kewanee Public Library: songbooks

LaGrange—LaGrange Public Library: songbooks

Lake Forest—Barat College, Library: songbooks, other printed music, recordings

Lake Forest—Lake Forest Library: songbooks

Lebanon—Lebanon Public Library: songbooks

Libertyville—Cook Memorial Public Library District: sheet music, programs

Lombard—Lombard Historical Society: sheet music

Lombard—Lombard Public Library: sheet music, songbooks

Macomb—Macomb City Public Library: sheet music, songbooks

Manhattan—Manhattan Township Free Public Library: songbooks, recordings

Marion—Marion Carnegie Public Library: songbooks, programs

Maywood—Maywood Public Library: programs, pictures

Mendota—Time Was Village Museum: sheet music, songbooks, programs

Moline—Black Hawk College, Learning Resource Center: recordings

Moline—Rock Island County Historical Society: sheet music, songbooks, other printed music

Morrison—Odell Public Library: songbooks, other printed music, programs, recordings

Morton Grove—Morton Grove Public Library: songbooks

Mount Carmel—Mount Carmel Public Library: songbooks, programs, pictures, miscellaneous

Mount Carroll—Mount Carroll Township Public Library: printed music

Mount Prospect—Mr. and Mrs. Hansen: sheet music, recordings

Mount Prospect—Carol Stein: sheet music, songbooks, other printed music

Murphysboro—Vivian M. Parrish: sheet music, other printed music, miscellaneous

Naperville—Naperville Heritage Society: sheet music, pictures

Naperville—Nichols Library: songbooks, other printed music

Oak Forest—Acorn Public Library District: songbooks, recordings

Oak Lawn—Oak Lawn Historical Society: recordings

Oak Park—American Catholic Press: songbooks

Oak Park—Scoville Institute, Oak Park Public Library: songbooks

Oakland—Rutherford Home: sheet music, songbooks

O'Fallon—O'Fallon Public Library: songbooks, recordings

Olney—Olney Central College, Anderson Library: songbooks

Ottawa—LaSalle County Historical Society: sheet music, pictures

Park Ridge—Park Ridge Public Library: songbooks

Paxton—Ford County Historical Society: songbooks, programs, pictures

Paxton—Paxton Carnegie Library: songbooks

Pekin—Pekin Public Library: songbooks

Peoria—Bradley University, Cullom–Davis Library: sheet music, songbooks

Peoria—Peoria Historical Society, H. L. Spencer Memorial Library: sheet music, recordings

Polo—Mrs. Craig McGuire: sheet music, catalogues

Prairie View—Vernon Area Public Library: sheet music, songbooks, catalogues, pictures

Princeton—Bureau County Historical Society Museum and Library: sheet music, songbooks, pictures

Quincy—Musicians' Protective Association: sheet music, other printed music, catalogues, pictures

Quincy—Quincy College, Library and Music Department: sheet music, song books, other printed music, recordings

Quincy—Lavern Wagner: sheet music

Quincy—Quincy Society of Fine Arts: miscellaneous

Richmond—Nippersink District Library: songbooks, recordings

Riverdale—Riverdale Public Library: songbooks

Riverside—Riverside–Brookfield High School: miscellaneous

Roselle—Roselle Public Library District: songbooks

Rock Island—Rock Island Public Library: songbooks

Rockford—Rock Valley College Educational Resources Center: songbooks, recordings

Rolling Meadows—Helen Heeter: sheet music, programs, recordings, miscellaneous

Roseville—Warren County Historical Society: sheet music, songbooks

Saint Charles—Bethlehem Evangelical Lutheran Church Library: songbooks

Saint Charles—Saint Charles Public Library: songbooks, miscellaneous

Sandwich—Sandwich Township Public Library: sheet music

Seneca—Seneca Public Library: songbooks

Skokie—Chordcraft Music Publishing Company: sheet music, songbooks, miscellaneous

Springfield—Vachel Lindsay Association: pictures, recordings, miscellaneous

Staunton—Macoupin County Historical Society: sheet music, songbooks

Stillman Valley—Armour Van Briesen: sheet music

Sullivan—Moultrie County Historical and Genealogical Society: sheet music, songbooks, programs, pictures, recordings

Union—McHenry County Historical Society: sheet music, songbooks, recordings, miscellaneous

Urbana—Urbana Free Library: programs, pictures

Vandalia—Evans Public Library: sheet music

Vandalia—Vandalia Historical Society: sheet music, songbooks, other printed music, programs

Vergennes—Naomi Williams: sheet music, miscellaneous

Warsaw—Warsaw Free Public Library: songbooks, pictures, miscellaneous

Wauconda—Lake County Museum, Lakewood Forest Preserve: songbooks

Waukegan—Waukegan Public Library: songbooks, other printed music, pictures

Western Springs—Western Springs Historical Society: sheet music, songbooks, programs, recordings

Wilmette—Malinckrodt College, Library: sheet music, songbooks, other printed music, recordings

Wilmette—Wilmette Historical Museum: songbooks, programs

Wilmette—Wilmette Public Library District: songbooks, pictures, recordings

Winfield—Winfield Public Library: recordings

Winnetka—Winnetka Congregational Church: sheet music, songbooks, programs, catalogues, pictures, miscellaneous

Witt—Witt Memorial Public Library: songbooks

Wood Dale—Wood Dale Library: songbooks

Woodridge—Woodridge Public Library: sheet music, songbooks

Woodstock—Woodstock Public Library: songbooks

Yates City—Salem Township Free Public Library, Jaquith–Corbin Memorial Library: songbooks, recordings

Yorkville—Yorkville Public Library: sheet music, other printed music

Indiana

405

ANDERSON SCHOOL   InAndC
OF THEOLOGY

Library
Anderson College
Anderson, Indiana 46011

Barney Warren, ms hymns, ca. 1867–1951
A. L. Byers (1869–1952, hymn writer), personal papers, including a list of his hymns
Church of God hymnals, a comp'ete set, ca. 1885–1940

—Delena Goodman

406

INDIANA UNIVERSITY   InU

Bloomington, Indiana 47401

Music Library

Black Music Collection, including books, printed music, and other writings by and about black American composers, with some holdings before 1940. See Michael Williams, "Indiana University Black Music Project," *Current Musicology*, 10 (1970), 8–10; also "Black Music Center," *Music Educators Journal*, 57 (1970), 81

Harold Wansborough (1893–1954, composer and educator), personal papers, including ms scores, correspondence, and memorabilia, in 3 boxes

Robert L. Sanders (1906–74, composer and educator), personal papers, including his own compositions, many in holograph, and his music library

Ferdinand Schaefer (1861–1953, founder of the Indianapolis Symphony Orchestra), scrapbook of memorabilia

Paul Nettl (1889–1972, musicologist), lecture and research notes, and memorabilia, 2.5 linear meters

Charles Diven Campbell, ms scores and parts for his *Pageant of Indiana* (1916) and *Indiana University Foundation Day Ceremonial* (n.d.)

Miscellaneous materials donated by former faculty members and now incorporated into the general music collections, including 2500 opera scores from Tibor Kozma (1909–76) and other music, mostly opera scores, from Wilfred Bain

Programs, of the Indianapolis Männerchor, 1930–34; Indianapolis Symphony Orchestra, 1937– ; Indiana University School of Music, annual recitals of the composition class, 1924–36, and other programs, 1936–

Scrapbooks, 2 vols. of programs and reviews from the Metropolitan Opera, New York, 1912–16 and 1937–39

Hoagy Carmichael Collection, 60 reels of tape recordings copied from his collection of 78-rpm discs, including works by Louis Armstrong, Bob Crosby, Duke Ellington, and others; also 2 letters by Carmichael, and a holograph ms of a choral pastiche of his works

Fritz Busch (1890–1951), 91 reels of tape recordings of rehearsals, performances, and other events in his career

Leopold Stokowski, 63 reels of tape recordings of his rehearsals

—Michael Fling

Lilly Library

Rappite and Harmony Society ms music books, including a hymnal inscribed Fridrika Welhafin, 1817; an 1822 book, using both roman and gothic scripts, with added drawings and water-color illustrations; a book inscribed "Secondo flouto. W. Weingartner," n.d.; a book inscribed "Jacob Wagner," elsewhere "Wolf," n.d.; and a *Grammar of Music*, referring to Thomas Busby

Paul Dresser (1857–1906), personal papers, 17 items, 1897–1904, including his letters to Mary Ellis South, press clippings, photographs, and a ms copy of Louise Dresser's reminiscences, also photographs in the family correspondence between the Flanagan and Dreiser families

Barclay Walker (1859–1927), 23 music mss, also a folder of printed music, including materials for *The Girl of Yesterday*, *Griggsby's Station*, *Kettledrum*, *Life de luxe*, and *Marigold*

Paul Nettl (1880–1972), correspondence received from colleagues, 1927–67, 54 items, as cited in *Spalek*

Hoagy Carmichael, personal papers, 56 items, presented by the composer and by Judge Ora L. Wildermuth (of Gary, Ind.), including correspondence, programs, articles, press clippings, and holograph music mss, as referred to in the catalogue of *An Exhibition Honoring the Seventy-fifth Birthday of Hoagland Howard Carmichael* (Bloomington, 1974)

Sidney C. Woodward, collection of autographs of theatrical celebrities, mostly British and U.S., 1235 items, including letters and photographs from American composers and singers, as listed in the catalogue on 80 cards

Miscellaneous mss from the collection of Dr. Saul Starr (1907–64, sheet-music collector of Eastchester, N.Y.; see below), including 11 bound vols., several of them ca. 1800, among them books inscribed by B. E. Ratliff, and George W. B. Felten, also an exercise book of Alice E. Downs, Oberlin, Ohio; and separate sheets, with references to W. Naze, A. Vulliet, the Orphéon Française de la Nouvelle Orléans Bibliothèque, Miss A. Fenner (of Portsmouth, Ohio, 1867), Anna Edna VanderKiste, Mary B. (Marie) Woodruff (New York, 1859), Mary Hills Catskill, Benjamin K. Browne (inscription to Augusta H. Farrar), Henri Mérou (French consul in New Orleans) and Antoinie Mérou-Grevemeyer, H. Piano (dedication to Ann Agusta Chattle, of Middletown, Orange County, N.Y.), J. J. Kimball (1892), Virgil Corydon Taylor, Anton Wallerstein (1813–92), and Joseph Snively (copy of Jezaniah Sumner's "Ode to Science," dated 1820), some of the materials from the collections of Fannie C. Johnson and James H. Snakenberg (of Baton Rouge, La.)

—Saundra Taylor

Starr sheet music collection, 100,000 items assembled by Dr. Starr (see above), as described in "A Guide to the

Starr Sheet Music Collection" (4 pages). The collection is arranged in 3 sections: (1) by personal names of composers, lyricists, performers, and literary figures, as listed in the 14-page index (which includes cross-references to subject entries, and contains 600 names in all); (2) by subjects and types of music, as listed in the 19-page index (also with cross-references; 800 terms in all); and (3) chronologically, as anthologies and undated miscellaneous, pre-1825, 1825–79 (illustrated materials separate), and by decade beginning 1880. Among the materials of particular importance are the early patriotic imprints, as described in the exhibition catalogue, *American Patriotic Songs, Yankee Doodle to The Conquered Banner, with Emphasis on The Star-spangled Banner* (Bloomington, 1968). See also Joan Falconer, "Music in the Lilly Library," M.L.A. *Notes*, 29 (1972), 5–9

Gilbert & Sullivan materials, 1200 items, in 5 boxes and 251 folders, containing mostly programs, but also posters, press clippings, playbills, articles, and photographs, mostly 1870–1908, with both U.S. and English items, many from the collection of Carroll Wilson. See the 10-page inventory

—Susan Glover Godlewski

University Archives (201 Bryan Hall)

Archives of the School of Music, 1893– (i.e., relating to private classes, 1893–1903, the Department of Music, 1904–21, and the School of Music, 1921–   ), including central University administative records relating to the deans, faculty, and alumni, also including programs, brochures, and other printed materials

—Dolores M. Lahrman

Afro-American Arts Institute

Materials from the Black Music Center, including research notes, mss, and oral-history recordings of interviews with black composers

—Leslie Simpson

Archives of Traditional Music (057 Maxwell Hall)

A part of the Folklore Institute. See the *Catalog of Phonorecordings of Music and Oral Data Held by the Archives of Traditional Music* (Boston, 1975); also "Archives of Traditional Music," *Library News Letter*, 5 (Bloomington, Feb. 1970), 13–14, reprinted in the Society for Ethnomusicology *Newsletter*, 4 (1973), 203–5

Recordings documenting oral tradition throughout the world, including folk music, music of non-literate societies, non-European classical or art music, and popular music. The holdings of commercial and field recordings include 125 wire recordings, 6300 cylinders, 3500 discs, and 18,000 tapes; the geographical strengths include North America (notably Indiana), Latin America, and Africa; subject areas and forms include Afro-American and Anglo-American ballads, ragtime, jazz, blues, country music, and commercial styles; American Indian materials include 5000 items from 205 culture groups, 1893– . See Dorothy Sara Lee, *Native North American Music and Oral Data: A Catalogue of Sound Recordings, 1893–1976* (Bloomington, 1979)

Reference collection of books, periodicals, microfilms, and memorabilia relating to traditional music

Folklore Archives

Also a part of the Folklore Institute, located at 506 North Fess Street

Folklore materials collected by students, 1950– , in 10 filing cabinets, organized by ethnic or religious group, predominantly written transcriptions of Anglo-American song texts and contextual data, including ballads, dance music, college songs, drinking songs, game songs, and occupational songs; also tape recordings of lectures and oral-history interviews

Richard Dorson Collection of World War II soldiers' songs, transcribed from interviews collected at Michigan State University

—Harry Gammerdinger

407
INSTITUTE FOR SEX RESEARCH   InU-ISR
416 Morrison Hall
Indiana University
Bloomington, Indiana 47405

Folksongs and party songs, 130 disc and tape recordings, also transcriptions of song lyrics, ca. 1930–

408
Hans TISCHLER
711 East First Street
Bloomington, Indiana 47401

Hans Tischler, personal papers, including correspondence, lecture and research notes, personal library, photographs, programs, and memorabilia. See *Spalek*, p. 883

409
BARTHOLOMEW COUNTY
HISTORICAL SOCIETY
524 Third Street
Columbus, Indiana 47201

Manuscript hymns, 10 items, late 19th century

Bates Conservatory of Music papers, 10 items including clippings, programs, and photographs, 1880s

Hymnals, 35 items including some with words only and some in German, 1830–1900

Sheet music, 400 items for clarinet or voice, ca. 1900–1935

Programs from Columbus, Indianapolis, Indiana University, and other area events, 35 items, ca. 1900–1930

Catalogues of sheet-music publishers and recording companies, 10 items, early 20th century

Photographs of local musicians and groups, 20 items, ca. 1880–1940, and a tintype of the Hartsville (Ind.) Serenaders, 1859

Recordings, including 60 Edison discs or cylinders

—Gary Schalliol

410
ALLEN COUNTY–FORT WAYNE
HISTORICAL SOCIETY
1424 West Jefferson Street
Fort Wayne, Indiana 46804

Manuscript scores by local composers, 3 items by Marshall Turkin ("Homage at Three Rivers," 1857), Nano H. Coffman and Fred Busch, and Grace C. Philley
Published sheet music, 10 items with Fort Wayne imprints or of local interest, and 100 non-local items, mostly popular, ca. 1869–1940

—Doris Perry

411
Sam DEVINCENT
3424 Contessa Drive
Fort Wayne, Indiana 46816

Sheet music, 100,000 items, ca. 1790–1960s, particularly strong in instrumental ragtime (1000 items, ca. 1887–1918), automobile subjects (600 items, ca. 1897–), aviation/balloon subjects (400 items, ca. 1855–), and Indiana composers
Song folios, several hundred items of many styles of music
Dance folios, 1900–1930s, several hundred items including country and western and other popular music

412
PUBLIC LIBRARY OF FORT WAYNE   InFw
AND ALLEN COUNTY
900 Webster Street
Fort Wayne, Indiana 46802

Published sheet music, songbooks, and books of music for voice, piano, or guitar, 7500 20th-century items
Recordings, 16,195 78-rpm discs

—Helen Colchin

413
Louis A. WARREN LINCOLN   InFwL
LIBRARY AND MUSEUM
Lincoln National Life Foundation
1300 South Clinton Street
Box 1110
Fort Wayne, Indiana 46801

Materials concerning Abraham Lincoln, including 250 items of published sheet music, ca. 1860– , ms music compositions, and 78-rpm disc recordings. See the *Lincoln Sheet Music Check List* (Fort Wayne, 1940)

—Mark E. Neely, Jr.

414
GARY PUBLIC LIBRARY   InG
220 West Fifth Avenue
Gary, Indiana 46402

Scrapbooks concerning 500 black performers, with biographical material and photographs, 40 vols. comp. 1970–
Hymnals and community songbooks, 30 items, and 60 items of popular vocal sheet music, 19th and 20th centuries

—Jean M. Isaacs

415
ARCHIVES OF THE   (InGo)
MENNONITE CHURCH
Goshen College
Goshen, Indiana 46526

The Archives are administered by the Historical Committee of the Mennonite Church, formerly the Mennonite Historical and Research Committee

John David Brunk (1872–1926, musician and college professor), drafts of hymns for which he composed the music, 23 linear cm.
S. F. Coffman (1872–1954, editor), 23 linear cm. of ms hymns
Walter E. Yoder (1889–1964, musician and college professor), 38 linear cm. of ms hymns
A. J. F. Zieglschmid (college professor), 16th-century Hutterian (Anabaptist) hymns and songs in German, a ms of 4000 pages
Mennonite Church Music Committee, ms hymns used in preparing 20th-century Mennonite hymnals, 2.5 linear meters

—Leonard Gross

416
GOSHEN COLLEGE   InGo
Harold & Wilma Good Library
Goshen, Indiana 46526

Hartzler Collection of 2750 American imprints formerly in the private library of Rev. J. D. Hartzler, Wellman, Iowa, including early Protestant hymnals, tunebooks, psalm books, sacred song collections, and gospel songbooks, mostly 19th century but including 24 late 18th-century items, also late 19th-century histories of church music. See Gordon E. Fouts, *Music Instruction in America to around 1830 Suggested by the Hartzler Collection of Early Protestant American Tune Books* (Ph.D. diss., University of Iowa, 1968)

—James Clemens

417
MENNONITE HISTORICAL LIBRARY   InGoM
Goshen College
Goshen, Indiana 46526

Materials relating to the Mennonite church, including 15 ms singing-school books, early 18th century, and 500 published Mennonite hymnals, as listed in Nelson P. Springer and A. J. Klassen, *Mennonite Bibliography, 1631–1961* (Scottsdale, Pa., 1977), vol. 2, pp. 285–97

—Nelson P. Springer

418
DE PAUW UNIVERSITY   InGrD
Greencastle, Indiana 46135

Marjorie Gaston (1906–74, De Pauw graduate, and music teacher), 500 items of personal papers concerning music education in Indianapolis, 1930–70 (in the Archives)

Methodist hymnals, 100 published vols., 1812–1970 (in the Archives)

Programs of concerts at the University, 1876– , a complete set (in the Archives)

Official records, correspondence, reports, scrapbooks and programs of the Music School, 5 linear meters, 1884– (in the Music School)

Sheet music, 700 items for piano or voice, 1920–70 (in the Music Library)

—David E. Horn

419
HOBART HISTORICAL SOCIETY

Box 24
Hobart, Indiana 46342

Singing Society, 15 linear cm. of minutes, ca. 1870–1900

Programs, clippings, and photographs of local musicians and groups, including the Hobart High School Band, 10 linear cm., ca. 1890–

Hymnals and school songbooks used locally, 25 items including 2 hymnals in Swedish, ca. 1880–1930

Sheet music, 100 items, mostly popular music for voice, ca. 1890–1910, including several local items

—Elin Christianson

420
Jussi BJOERLING MEMORIAL ARCHIVE

Box 2638
Indianapolis, Indiana 46206

Collection pertaining to Jussi Bjoerling (1920–75, Swedish tenor), with 2500 disc or tape recordings, and 9 linear meters of other materials including programs, clippings, photographs, magazines, and books

—Jack W. Porter

421
BUTLER UNIVERSITY InIB

Jordan College of Music Library
4600 Sunset Avenue
Indianapolis, Indiana 46208

Eddy Brown (1895–1974, violinist), scrapbook of programs and clippings

Indianapolis Symphony Orchestra programs, 10 bound vols., ca. 1934–

Published community songbooks, 5 items, ca. 1872–1920

Sheet music, 1500 mostly popular-vocal items including some published locally, ca. 1890–1940

—Phyllis J. Schoonover

422
CHRISTIAN CHURCH (DISCIPLES OF CHRIST)

National Headquarters Library
Box 1986
222 South Downey Avenue
Indianapolis, Indiana 46206

Hymnals of various denominations, 150 items, ca. 1860– , some with words only

—Doris Autrey Kennedy

423
CHRISTIAN THEOLOGICAL InIT
SEMINARY

Library
Box 88267
Indianapolis, Indiana 46208

Hymnals, mostly pertaining to the Disciples of Christ, including some used by circuit riders in the Midwest, ca. 1820–

—Leslie R. Galbraith

424
President Benjamin HARRISON FOUNDATION

1230 North Delaware Street
Indianapolis, Indiana 46202

Materials owned by the Harrison family during their years in the White House, 1889–93, including 90 items of sheet music, some inscribed to Mrs. Harrison; 21 hymnals and songbooks; songsters of the 1888 campaign; 9 ms songs given to Mrs. Harrison; and 5 programs for concerts attended by the Harrisons

Recordings, including 35 copper or steel discs for an 1893 Reginaphone, and 4 piano rolls

—Katherine Svarczkopf

425
INDIANA HISTORICAL SOCIETY InHi

315 West Ohio Street
Indianapolis, Indiana 46202

Sheet music, 90 items, mostly 19th century, including 20 campaign songs for William Henry Harrison, 1848

Songbooks and hymnals, 40 19th-century vols.

Jacob Zimmerman, ms copy of a liturgy and hymnal, 1822, used by the Rappites in New Harmony, Ind., 1814–24

William Owen, music book prepared in England, 1820, used in New Harmony after 1825

Robert Dale Owen, 6 ms music books used in New Harmony after 1825

Jane Short, 2 ms music books, Lexington, Ky., 1815–18

Eliza Sprole (Mrs. James) Blake, 1 vol. of published music including ms copies, 1821

John M. Fisher, 1 ms vol. of clarinet music, from Crawfordsville, Ind., 1830

Manuscript songs for guitar, 8 items, 1880s, in the Hutchings–Koehlar papers

Civil War song texts, 26 items

Photographs of bands in Indiana, 1871–1910, 5 items

—Leona T. Alig

426
INDIANA STATE LIBRARY In

Indiana Division
140 North Senate Avenue
Indianapolis, Indiana 46204

Indianapolis Matinee Musicale, 3 linear meters of papers, including programs, scrapbooks, yearbooks, and minutes, 1877–

Songbooks, 60 items, ca. 1870–1930, including popular, school, and sacred anthologies, mostly relating to Indiana; also 1800 sheet-music items, ca. 1880–1940, by Indiana composers and lyricists or pertaining to Indiana

Programs of Indiana musical events, ca. 1870– ; also several photographs of musical subjects, in a general photograph collection

—Jean Singleton

427
INDIANAPOLIS–MARION COUNTY   InI
PUBLIC LIBRARY
40 East Saint Clair Street
Indianapolis, Indiana 46204

Ferdinand Schaefer (1861–1953, first conductor of the Indianapolis Symphony Orchestra), ms scores and parts for "Scherzo" for string quintet and "Forest scene," orchestral sketch, n.d.

Indianapolis Symphony Orchestra, 3 linear meters of transcriptions of live radio broadcasts from the Murat Theatre, Indianapolis, to Europe, South America, and the U.S., 1939–45, and scrapbooks of programs and press reviews, 1896–1955

Programs and press clippings of local musical events, 1898– , 3 linear meters, including the Ona B. Talbott Concert Series, Martens Concerts, English's Theatre and Opera House, and the Indianapolis Männerchor

Popular sheet music, 60,000 items, ca. 1880–1940

Printed scores and parts, including the Ernestinoff collection of 200 scores and parts by U.S. and European composers of the 19th and early 20th centuries, presented to the Library ca. 1924 in honor of Alexander Ernestinoff (conductor of the Indianapolis Orchestra, ca. 1910–17)

Matinee Musicale—Indianapolis, 3 vols. of programs, 1882–1912

Artists' and musicians' miscellanea, 87 items, 1800–1950, including musicians' autograph letters, papers, and music scores

—Nancy N. Gootee

428
SAINT MAUR MONASTERY LIBRARY
4545 Northwestern Avenue
Indianapolis, Indiana 46208

Liturgical books of the Roman Catholic Church, 150 items published in the U.S.

Recordings of sacred music, 200 78-rpm discs

—Rev. Joseph C. Bell III

429
PHILHARMONIC MUSIC CLUB
c/o Sarah Krodel, Librarian
715 Clay Street
Jasper, Indiana 47546

Papers of the Club, including programs, 1922– , also sheet music and vocal anthologies

430
Carroll H. COPELAND
814 Shawnee Avenue
Lafayette, Indiana 47905

Materials relating to the band-conducting career of Carroll H. Copeland, 1938–75, including 100 programs of Indiana high-school concerts, attendance records, magazine articles on band music, annual scrapbooks of programs, photographs, and clippings, 200 photographs of bands, and 90 disc or tape recordings of his bands

Sheet music, 300 mostly popular items, ca. 1920–55

431
MICHIGAN CITY HISTORICAL SOCIETY
Box 512
Michigan City, Indiana 46360

Histories of the Monday Musicale, 1909–71, and the Michigan City Municipal Band, 1869–1969, 2 items

Photographs of local musical events, including the Michigan City Municipal Band, the Michigan City Symphony Orchestra, and various school symphony orchestras, 25 items, ca. 1890–1940

Hymnals and popular songbooks, 5 items, ca. 1890–1922

Sheet music, ca. 1890–1920, 100 items, including several with references to local events and places

—Mrs. William H. Harris

432
Carolyn Campbell ESTES
Route 1, Box 26-B
Mulberry, Indiana 46058

James Emmett Campbell (1892–1972) and Elsie Benjamin Campbell (song evangelists and members of the Westminster Choir of Dayton, Ohio), 300 gospel songbooks, 1 78-rpm disc of James Emmett Campbell accompanied by the Tovian Trio, 1920, and published songs written for him by Rev. Edward Cornelius

433
BALL STATE UNIVERSITY   InMuB
Department of Library Science
Muncie, Indiana 47306

C. G. Conn Instrument Manufacturing Co., Elkhart, archival materials, 1.2 linear meters

Buescher Saxophone Co., Elkhart, archival materials

Vocal music, comprising the personal art-song libraries of Earl Cartwright (1879–1931) and Carl Sobeski, mostly standard repertory works but with many promotional copies from U.S. publishers, ca. 1900–1920, in all 1500 items

Cecil Leeson (concert saxophonist), personal papers, including correspondence, scrapbooks, diaries, and mss, both of his own compositions and works commissioned from other composers; also archival material

Max Pottag (1875–1970, horn player with the Chicago Symphony Orchestra), music for the horn and books relating to horn playing, 300 items, also such memorabilia as mouthpieces

John J. Graas (1917–64?, Hollywood studio-orchestra horn player), collection of big-band and studio-orchestra jazz music, mostly parts, including 16 jazz-band arrangements, 50 original jazz compositions, 12 original works for horn, a jazz symphony, and miscellaneous sketches, in all 8 linear cm.

—Nyal Williams

434

BROWN COUNTY HISTORICAL MUSEUM

Route 4, Box 65
Nashville, Indiana 47448

Oral-history tapes of Brown County natives, among them Samuel Allison Rednour, reminiscences of musical activity in Nashville, 1899–1907, concerning his work in the Sheepskin Band, Needmore Band, Mark Hoffer's orchestra, and the Knights of Pythias Band; and in Columbus, 1917–74, including work in Jo Sheets' band, Raleigh Vandergriff's band, the United Brethren band, the Christian Church band, and the American Theatre band

Photographs of local bands, ca. 1900

—Dorothy Bailey

435

Earl G. HEDDEN and Will J. HEDDEN

801 Vincennes Street
New Albany, Indiana 47150

Hedden family papers, documenting musical life in New Albany, 1863– . Materials include programs, recordings, correspondence, and published music, also materials of the Jennie Gebhart Hedden Music Study Club, and a ms history of music in Louisville and New Albany, 1880–1920

436

INDIANA UNIVERSITY SOUTHEAST   InU-Se

Library
4201 Grant Line Road
Box 679
New Albany, Indiana 47150

Musical materials from the collection of Earl G. Hedden and the Hedden family of New Albany

437

NEW ALBANY–FLOYD COUNTY   InNea
PUBLIC LIBRARY

180 West Spring Street
New Albany, Indiana 47150

Programs, papers, and photographs of 25 local music organizations, including the Handel and Haydn Society (constitution and by-laws, 1854), Haydn Male Chorus (1907–), Jenny Gebhart Hedden Music Study Club (1929–), New Albany Civic Orchestra (programs, minutes, and press clippings, ca. 1932–), New Albany Musical Society (1859–), and

the Treble Clef Club (1890–), in all 2 linear meters, ca. 1850–

School songbooks, 2 items, ca. 1881–87

Published sheet music by local composers, 17 items, mostly popular piano or vocal music, 1890–1918; also 20 file drawers of other published music

Clippings on 25 local musicians and on local school-music activities, 300 items, ca. 1920–40

Index to local newspapers, 1838–1930, including musical subjects (in process)

—Ruth Ann Kramer

438

NEW HARMONY WORKINGMEN'S   InNhW
INSTITUTE LIBRARY

Box 368
New Harmony, Indiana 47631

Manuscript music, including a book of music and dance instructions written in New Harmony, ca. 1826

Personal papers of local musicians

Programs of local musical and theatrical performances, including some at the Opera House, ca. 1850– , and related photographs in a collection of 2500 items, ca. 1870–

Hymnals, songbooks, and sheet music of 19th-century New Harmony residents

—Mary A. Cook

439

MANCHESTER COLLEGE   InNomanC

Funderburg Library
North Manchester, Indiana 46962

Gottfried Lehman, ms notebook of hymn tunes, early 18th century

Howerton–Holsinger Collection of choral octavos, 15 linear meters of U.S. and European compositions, from the collections of George Howerton and Clyde Holsinger

Psalm books in German, 8 published items, late 18th and early 19th centuries, mostly of the Church of the Brethren; also 120 hymnals including some in German, ca. 1840–1940

Published sheet music for voice, ca. 1915–1930

Programs of the Manchester Civic Symphony, a complete run, 1939–

Recordings, including 200 78-rpm discs, mostly classical

—J. Allen Willmert

440

UNIVERSITY OF NOTRE DAME   InNd

Notre Dame, Indiana 46556

Memorial Library

William Bacon Stevens (1815–87), 30,000 religious books from his library, mostly liturgical vols., formerly maintained as the William Bacon Stevens Library by the Protestant Episcopal Church in Philadelphia (Pa.) Divinity School

University Archives

Rev. Michael Mathis, 60 linear meters of personal papers, mostly ca. 1940–70, including programs, correspondence with publishers and composers of liturgical music, and ms and published settings of the Mass

Sheet music editions of Notre Dame songs, 1898–

Programs of University music performances, 1 linear meter, ca. 1910– , and related photographs and rosters

Liturgical Arts Society, archival papers, 1928–72, 20 linear meters, including minutes, business correspondence, financial reports, slides, and films

—Peter J. Lombardo

441

Mr. and Mrs. Owen STOUT

"Valhalla," Route 3
Paoli, Indiana 47454

Sheet music, 1600 items, and 500 hymnals, mostly 20th century; 500 orchestrations, mostly for theater orchestra but a few for dance band; and 50 pre-1940 recordings

442

MIAMI COUNTY HISTORICAL MUSEUM AND PUTERBAUGH MUSEUM

Court House
Peru, Indiana 46970

Papers of musicians and organizations, including 1 letter of John Philip Sousa, 1926; 1 letter from Cole Porter to Grant S. Ray, 1954; a scrapbook compiled by John Charters of Peru, Ind.; the original charter of the Third Regiment Band, 1902; and a printed advertisement for Gordon Balch Nevin (1892–1943, organist)

Songbooks, 90 items, ca. 1825– , mostly mid 19th century and largely Methodist Episcopal hymnals; also including popular songbooks, political and war songbooks, and gospel hymnals, among them 1 autographed by Homer Rodeheaver

Other published music, including 9 partbooks for circus band, 1920s–30s

Pictures, 60 items, including autographed photographs of such composers as B. D. Ackley, Carrie Jacobs Bond, George Balch Nevin, Gordon Balch Nevin, Cole Porter, and Homer Rodeheaver; 42 photographs of local bands and orchestras, 1880s–1950s, along with 5 items of band uniforms; and 2 photographs of Ernst Rufser's Zither Club, 1888

Programs of local opera performances, 4 items, 1891–1910

—Mrs. Horace D. Cook

443

MARSHALL COUNTY HISTORICAL SOCIETY

317 West Monroe Street
Plymouth, Indiana 46563

George Ade (1866–1944), brochures and materials related to the Indiana Society of Chicago, 1925, 1 folder

Jean Goldkette (1899–1962, musician and dance-band promoter), 18 78-rpm Victor disc recordings; also biographical materials including clippings and photographs

Elizabeth Hubbell (1880–1965, pianist and music educator), 1 folder of clippings

Joshua Logan (student of Elizabeth Hubbell), correspondence with Elizabeth Hubbell, much of it pertaining to musical comedy, and clippings, portraits, and photographs, 9 items, ca. 1920–50

Dan McDonald (1833–1916, newspaper editor), clippings of his articles concerning local musical events, and his personal notebook, 1855–1916

Edward Payson (1902–77, educator, cellist, and composer), 4 folders of programs, clippings, and photographs, some of them pertaining to the founding of the South Bend Symphony Orchestra and the development of music at Culver Military Academy, also photocopies of 2 of his ms music compositions

Ernestine Schumann-Heink, 1 folder of materials pertaining to her visits when her son was a student at the Culver Military Academy in Plymouth, with clippings and oral-history transcripts from other persons in Plymouth

Hazel Dell Neff Smelzer (1886–1942, vocalist and educator), 1 folder of programs, clippings, and photographs, plus a personal scrapbook, ca. 1905–38

Wilbur Wright Swihart ("Bugler Bill" from the Virginia Military Institute), 1 folder of clippings and photographs

David Van Vactor, photocopy of the ms of his Fifth Symphony, 1975; also photographs, clippings, and programs, in 1 folder, ca. 1917–76

Hymnals, 25 items including 1 in German, 1837–1916

Sheet music, 350 items, ca. 1870–1940

—Frances Hewitt

444

EARLHAM COLLEGE   InRE

Lilly Library Archives
Richmond, Indiana 47374

Esther Griffin White (1869–1954, journalist), papers, including 12 items of musical criticism written for the *Richmond Palladium and Sun-Telegram*, 1912, and an unpublished essay on the future of American music

—Philip Shore

445

MORRISSON–REEVES LIBRARY   InRM

48 North Sixth Street
Richmond, Indiana 47374

"Singin' Sam Collection," 4300 sheet-music items, mostly popular, ca. 1895–1940, from the personal collection of Harry A. Frankel ("Singin' Sam")

—Harriet E. Bard

446

FULTON COUNTY HISTORICAL SOCIETY

Civic Center
Seventh and Pontiac Streets
Rochester, Indiana 46975

Hymnals and school songbooks, ca. 1870–1930, 50 items including 2 hymnals in German

Popular vocal sheet music, 50 items, ca. 1900–1930

Programs of local musical events, including opera houses and town bands in the county, ca. 1890–1940, 20 items; also 50 photographs of musical events

Recordings, 77 78-rpm discs including Paul Spotts Emrick directing the Purdue University Marching Band, and 31 piano rolls

Oral-history interviews with members and friends of the Rochester Band, ca. 1855–1935, 20 pages of typed transcripts, collected 1977–79

—Shirley Willard

447

SAINT MEINRAD COLLEGE &   InStme SCHOOL OF THEOLOGY

Archabbey Library
Saint Meinrad, Indiana 47577

Manuscript music, 1 box, including some 19th-century American sacred music

Papers of persons and organizations, 3 boxes, with some musical materials; also 1 scrapbook of pictures, and 4 notebooks of programs

Published sheet music, 1 box; also 10 songbooks

Recordings, 4 items

—Samuel Weber

448

INDIANA UNIVERSITY AT   InU-Sb SOUTH BEND

University Library
1700 Mishawaka Avenue
South Bend, Indiana 46615

James Lewis Casaday collection, 4.5 linear meters of printed scores and parts for theatrical productions at the University or in the community, ca. 1930–70; also 10 linear meters of 78-rpm discs

—James L. Mullins

449

NORTHERN INDIANA   InSNHi HISTORICAL SOCIETY

112 South Lafayette Boulevard
South Bend, Indiana 46601

Sheet music, 1852–1940, also 16 bound vols. of editions dated 1840–75

—Nathalie D. Perkins

450

VIGO COUNTY PUBLIC LIBRARY   InTV

222 North Seventh Street
Terre Haute, Indiana 47801

Press clippings relating to music in Terre Haute, 6 folders in the Community Affairs files, including information on local institutions such as the Terre Haute Opera House, and musicians, among them

Paul Dresser. Also 2 microfilms of 19th-century theater and opera press clippings; and other press clippings on local music and musicians in the genealogy collection

Scrapbooks and indexes of local music references in the newspapers and journals in the Library, also in the genealogy collection

—Lois Harris

451

TAYLOR UNIVERSITY   InUpT

Upland, Indiana 56989

Hymnals, ca. 1860–1940, 200 items including Methodist and interdenominational hymnals, in the Ayres–Alumni Memorial Library

Conservatory of Music and Taylor University Music Department papers, including programs, in the University Archives

—David Dickey

452

GRACE COLLEGE   InWinG

Winona Lake, Indiana 46590

Hymnals and gospel songbooks from the library of the Rodeheaver Music Publishing Co., 200 19th- and 20th-century items; also memorabilia of evangelist Billy Sunday

Other published music, including choral scores and 100 items of popular sheet music

—Don Ogden

In addition to the repositories listed above, the following have also reported holdings of the materials indicated:

Anderson—Anderson College, Charles E. Wilson Library: sheet music, songbooks

Auburn—Auburn Automotive Heritage: recordings

Bloomfield—Bloomfield Public Library: songbooks, recordings

Bristol—Elkhart County Historical Society: sheet music, songbooks, programs, pictures, recordings, miscellaneous

Connersville—Historic Connersville, Canal House: sheet music, songbooks, miscellaneous

English—Crawford County Public Library: sheet music, songbooks, other printed music, programs, recordings, miscellaneous

Evansville—Evansville Public and Vanderburgh County Library: catalogues, recordings

Evansville—St. Paul Church, Educational Resources Center: songbooks, other printed music

Ferdinand—Convent of the Immaculate Conception: sheet music, songbooks, other printed music, pictures, miscellaneous

Greensburg—Greensburg Public Library: sheet music, recordings

Hanover—Hanover College, Duggan Library: programs, pictures

Indianapolis—Childrens Museum of Indianapolis: sheet music, songbooks, programs, catalogues

Indianapolis—Indiana Central University, Library: songbooks, programs, recordings

Jasper—Jasper Public Library: sheet music, songbooks, other printed music, recordings, miscellaneous

Kingman—Fountain County Historical Society: pictures, miscellaneous

Knightstown—Knightstown Public Library: sheet music, songbooks

Kokomo—Howard County Historical Museum: miscellaneous

Ladoga—Ladoga–Clark Township Public Library: songbooks

Lafayette—Tippecanoe County Historical Association: sheet music, songbooks, other printed music, programs, recordings, miscellaneous

LaGrange—LaGrange County Historical Society: sheet music, songbooks, catalogues, recordings

Logansport—Cass County Historical Society Museum: sheet music, songbooks, programs, catalogues, pictures, recordings

Marion—Marion College, Library: songbooks

Mentone—Bell Memorial Library: songbooks, recordings

Michigan City—Michigan City Municipal Band: printed music

Mooresville—Mooresville Public Library: sheet music, songbooks, programs, recordings

New Albany—Mrs. Ferd Wrege: sheet music, programs

New Carlisle—New Carlisle–Olive Township Public Library: songbooks, pictures

New Castle—Henry County Historical Society: recordings

North Manchester—North Manchester Public Library: sheet music, songbooks

North Vernon—Jennings County Public Library: sheet music, songbooks, other printed music, programs, recordings, miscellaneous

Notre Dame—Alumnae Centennial Library: sheet music, songbooks, other printed music, recordings

Oxford—Irvin K. Williams: miscellaneous

Paoli—Paoli Public Library: songbooks

Remington—Remington–Carpenter Township Public Library: songbooks, recordings

Richmond—Wayne County, Indiana, Historical Society: sheet music, songbooks, pictures, recordings, miscellaneous

Salem—Washington County Historical Society: sheet music, songbooks

South Bend—South Bend Public Library, Art and Music Department: sheet music, songbooks, programs, recordings

Tell City—Tell City Historical Society: pictures

Terre Haute—Eugene V. Debs Foundation: sheet music

Terre Haute—Malcolm C. Scott: sheet music, songbooks, programs, pictures, miscellaneous

Terre Haute—Vigo County Historical Society: sheet music, songbooks, programs

Tipton—Tipton County Public Library: sheet music songbooks, other printed music, programs, miscellaneous

West Lafayette—Mrs. M. E. Shanks: recordings, miscellaneous

West Lafayette—West Lafayette Public Library: sheet music, songbooks, recordings

Wolcott—Wolcott Community Library: songbooks, recordings

Iowa

453
AMANA HERITAGE SOCIETY
Amana, Iowa 52203

William Graichen, 2 ms songbooks, and Jacob Graichen, 1 ms songbook, ca. 1917, used by local male choruses

German-language hymnals, 3 items, including *Davidisches Psalter-Spiel* (Ebenezer, N.Y., 1854); also English translations of hymns from the *Psalter-Spiel* printed on loose-leaf sheets and used locally

School songbooks used locally, 2 items in German, 1905–6, including 1 published in Amana

—Henrietta M. Ruff

454
BURLINGTON PUBLIC LIBRARY IaB
501 North Fourth Street
Burlington, Iowa 52601

William Leander Sheetz, 16 sheet-music items published by the White–Sheetz Publishing Co. of Burlington, 1889–1922

Programs of events at the Grand Opera House in Burlington, 1905–18

—J. Guest

455
DES MOINES COUNTY HISTORICAL SOCIETY
1616 Dill Street
Burlington, Iowa 52601

William Leander Sheetz (music teacher and publisher with the White–Sheetz Publishing Co., Burlington), 100 popular sheet-music items including 26 mss, 1892–1921, for piano, chamber ensemble, voice, or choir, also including state and national songs; his "Method of Teaching" (15-page typescript, ca. 1912); and 1 photograph of him, ca. 1916

Sheet music, 30 items, 1894–1952, including 6 by local composers other than Sheetz

Hymnals, 40 items, 1886–1915, including 4 in German

School songbooks, 9 items, 1882–1917

Programs of local musicians and groups, 108 items, 1882–1924; also a scrapbook mostly of local concert programs, 1876–94

Photographs, 12 items, 1895–1915, including 1 of Martin Bruhl (Burlington musician, member of the New York Philharmonic), ca. 1915

—Helen Parsons

456

UNIVERSITY OF NORTHERN IOWA   IaCfT
Library
Cedar Falls, Iowa 50613

Audio Collection of recordings, including 100 ethnic items, among them folk music, jazz, and other music of Canada, Mexico, and the U.S., as cited in *Briegleb*, no. 32

457

COE COLLEGE   IaCrC
Music Library
Cedar Rapids, Iowa 52402

R. L. Moehlmann, 10 original compositions and 70 arrangements for band, including published and ms copies, ca. 1929–72
John Mokrejs (1875–1968), 20 piano compositions published ca. 1902–68, including some published in Iowa
Vaudeville collection, used at the Iowa Theater in Cedar Rapids, ca. 1915–35, donated by the conductor George Cervenka, including published theater-orchestra scores and parts for 500 titles, 100 sheet-music items, and 100 photographs of performers, some autographed
BMI radio-orchestra collection used at station WMT in Cedar Rapids, ca. 1935–40, including published piano-conductor scores and parts for 1000 titles
Published dance-orchestra music donated by Charles Havlena, with conductor's scores and parts for 500 titles, ca. 1920–50
Songbooks and hymnals, 5 items, ca. 1910–40
Sheet music, 300 vocal items, ca. 1910–50
Coe College Music Department, minutes of faculty meetings, ca. 1900– , 100 pages
Programs of musical and theatrical events at the College, ca. 1900– , 1000 items, mostly in scrapbooks
Recordings, including 3000 78-rpm discs, mostly classical

—Richard Adkins, Bernice Bergup

458

IOWA MASONIC LIBRARY   IaCrM
813 First Avenue SE
Box 279
Cedar Rapids, Iowa 52406

Jean Sibelius, ms *Masonic Ritual Music* op. 113, for piano (with "Finlandia" included), for the Grand Lodge of Iowa, Ancient Free and Accepted Masons, 1927, autographed by the composer, in 1 bound vol.
Songbooks of Masonic songs, 60 items, 1795–
Hymnals of various denominations, 75 items, ca. 1850–
Sheet music, 150 items, ca. 1900–1940, including Masonic songs and popular music
Programs of Greene's Opera House, Cedar Rapids, 1880–1926, collected by Charles Laurance in 31 bound vols.

—Keith Arrington

459

SANFORD MUSEUM AND PLANETARIUM
117 East Willow Street
Cherokee, Iowa 51012

Tone Circle (local music group), 39 yearbooks, 1908–11 and 1915–62, also 19 programs, 1895–1961
Published music, including 6 sheet-music items, 1881– , and 1 songbook, 1893

—Linda Burkhart

460

MONTAUK, DIVISION OF HISTORIC PRESERVATION, IOWA DEPARTMENT OF HISTORY
Box 372
Clermont, Iowa 52135

William Larrabee (governor of Iowa, 1886–90), personal papers, including a diary with passages relating to music, 1900; 100 items of letters, receipts, and contracts concerning 3 pipe organs purchased by him; 10 letters and bills concerning the sale of a Victrola and recordings, ca. 1910; a certificate for a grand piano, 1914; 10 letters received by him concerning music and musicians in Iowa, 1901–4; and an essay by Mrs. Larrabee on "Music," pencil ms, ca. 1900–1910
Printed music, including method books for voice, piano, violin, harp, and brass instruments, 45 linear cm. of bound vols., 1882–1913
School and community songbooks, 70 items, 1888–1917
Hymnals, 20 items, 1875–1928
Sheet music, 200 items of classical and popular music for piano, voice, or violin, 1890s–1940s
Programs, 25 items, including musical organizations in Iowa, the 1904 St. Louis World's Fair, and other events attended by Governor Larrabee, 1888–1910
Recordings, 255 78-rpm discs of classical and popular music, ca. 1910

—Arlinda Abbott, Tom McKay

461

LUTHER COLLEGE   IaDL
Preus Library
Decorah, Iowa 52101

Loren Singers, 1895– , 60 linear cm. of correspondence and 100 photographs
Norwegian-American hymnals, ca. 1870–1913, 500 items, including some published by the Lutheran Publishing Co., Decorah
World War I songs, 36 sheet-music items
Programs of Luther College and local civic organizations, 400 items, ca. 1863–
Recordings, 65 piano rolls and 241 78-rpm discs

—Leigh D. Jordahl

462

**VESTERHEIM NORWEGIAN-   IaDN
AMERICAN MUSEUM**
502 West Water Street
Decorah, Iowa 52101

Songbooks of Norwegian-American music, 40 items, mostly sacred choral, 1875–1925

Recording of M. A. Gauper playing 49 Hardanger-fiddle tunes from the region of Gudbrandsdalen, Norway, learned from his father, 1928

Photographs, 100 items of Norwegian-American bands, choruses, and other musical groups, 1875–1940

Norwegian traditional instruments used in the U.S., 30 items, 18th and 19th centuries

—Marion Nelson

463

DES MOINES PUBLIC LIBRARY   IaDm

100 Locust Street
Des Moines, Iowa 50309

Karl King (1891–1971), holograph band ms of *A Hometown Boy*

Sheet music, 2500 items, ca. 1900–1940s, mostly by Iowa composers, including Meredith Willson, Alice Jordan, Bix Beiderbecke, Sven Lekberg, Mildred Souers, Karl King, and Frederick Knight

Programs of the Des Moines Symphony Orchestra, 1938– , complete, and reviews, in scrapbooks

—Marjorie Benton

464

GRAND VIEW COLLEGE   IaDmG

Archives
1200 Grandview Avenue
Des Moines, Iowa 50316

Danish-American materials, including 6 published piano-music items, ca. 1900–1940; 30 school songbooks of folk music and 25 hymnals in Danish, ca. 1875–1938; 12 hymnals and school songbooks of folk music in English, ca. 1925–60; and 4 sheet-music items, ca. 1904–40

Programs of musical events at the College, ca. 1896–1940, 6 items

—Thorvald Hansen

465

IOWA STATE HISTORICAL   Ia-HA
DEPARTMENT

Division of Historical Museum and Archives
East Twelfth and Grand Avenue
Des Moines, Iowa 50319

Army band books, 3 boxes of ms vols. used during the Civil War; later used by the West Liberty (Iowa) Band, ca. 1885–90, as directed by W. H. Shipman; and presented by his son, C. E. Shipman

Conrad Beck, 2 ms music books copied by him at Heidelberg University, and brought to the U.S. in 1854

Meredith Willson, "Iowa, It's a Beautiful Name," autographed by him and by Bing Crosby; also miscellaneous biographical materials concerning Willson and Crosby

Manuscript music, including a copy of "Hail Columbia"; Tacitus Hussey, *New Praises of Jesus*, song-book, 1869; and "Blue-eyed Mary" and other items donated by Laura Miller

Published music by Iowa composers, including S. H. M. Byers, "Song of Iowa," and William Lehman, "Des Moines City Waltz" (1864)

Agnes V. Flannery (b. 1879, author), papers, including programs of the Iowa Federation of Music Clubs, and clippings on Iowa musicians; also her compilation, "Musical Iowana, 1838–1938" (4-page typescript, n.d.), listing Iowa artists and musicians

Iowa Society of Music Teachers, program of the annual meeting, 1903

Autographs of musicians, including composer Arthur Nevin, in a collection donated by Arthur Hartman

Photographs and clippings of performers, mostly ca. 1920–40, including Joy Hodges (actress and singer, ca. 1930s–40s)

Published music for guitar, piano, or choir, 10 items, ca. 1842–1900

Music theory and method books used in schools, 10 items, ca. 1854–1910

Hymnals and tunebooks, including vols. for youth and Sunday school, ca. 1850–1920, 30 items, some with Iowa imprints

Songbooks of popular, folk, patriotic, and Civil War music, ca. 1814–1940, 60 items, including some Iowa-related items and the *Missouri Harmony* (1848)

Russ Levine Collection of Sheet Music, 150 items, including musical-theater selections; also 125 other items of sheet music, including Iowa-related items, ca. 1825–1930

Programs, mostly of musical events, in Iowa, including Greene's Opera House, Cedar Rapids; Conservatory of Music of Callanan College (1885); Hildreth Opera House, Charles City; Ames Glee Club (1913); and the Des Moines Philharmonic Society (1886)

Presto, the Northwestern Journal of Music, 1 issue, published in Des Moines, 1886

Biographical files on Iowa musicians, containing press clippings, letters, and responses to a questionnaire circulated ca. 1920 by Edgar R. Harlan, curator of the Historical Department of Iowa. Among the musicians included are Fanny Kellogg Backert, George S. Bassett (sheriff of Webster County), Cora Beck, Maro Loomis Bartlett, Mrs. Ida Work Bartlett, M. L. Bartlett, C. L. Barnhouse, Isabella Beaton, Loretta M. Hubbard (Mrs. William) Beaton, Opal Bullard, Mrs. Kate Holmes Cooper, Grace Clark DeGraff, Catherine McFarland (Mrs. George M.) Dwight, Dudley Warner Fitch, John S. Fearis, Charles Hutchinson Gabriel, J. F. Galuska, Guy Greason, Emma McHenry Glenn, Alberta Powell Heald (Mrs. H. Austin) Graham, Mabelle Graham, Elliot Griffis, George E. Hamilton, Philip Cady Hayden, S. M. Helmick, W. C. Hoff, Louis J. Kelsey, Maj. George W. Landers, Will Lehman, Ernest Leo, Thurlowe Lieurance, Amelia Timm (Mrs. F. H.) Little, Frederick Knight Logan, Emma Mershon Konschine, Hans Mettke, Horace Alden Miller, John Mokrejs, Robert B. McGregor, Hugh R. Newsom, O. M. Oleson, Webb M. Oungst, Mildred Souers, Carlo A. Sperati, Erwin Swindell, Virgil Corydon Taylor, Althea Snider Turner, Gilbert Wells, Ira B. Wilson, Harriet Vivian Woodland, and George A. Wrightman

—Phyllis E. McLaughlin

466

AMERICAN LUTHERAN CHURCH ARCHIVES

(IaDuW)

Wartburg Theological Seminary
Dubuque, Iowa 52001

Hymnal Committee of the American Lutheran Church, minutes
Lutheran hymnals, 1750– , 25 English-language items and others in German; also printed organ music

—Robert Wiederanders

467

DUBUQUE COUNTY HISTORICAL SOCIETY

Box 305
Dubuque, Iowa 52001

Printed music, for piano and organ, 3 items, 1860–1910
Songbook of sacred and secular music, 1881
Sheet music, 400 items, 1870s–1940, including popular, children's, and wartime music; also 1 bound vol. containing 40 vocal works, 1877–1910
Lee and Walker, *Catalogue of Books and Exercises* (Philadelphia, 1890)
Recordings, including 4 albums and 10 separate 78-rpm discs of popular music, ca. 1910–30

—Debora Griesinger

468

SCHOOLS OF THEOLOGY IN DUBUQUE

Library
333 Wartburg Place
Dubuque, Iowa 52001

Hymnals, mostly of Lutheran denominations in the U.S., 56 items, ca. 1850– , 15 of them in German

—Duncan Brockway

469

WRIGHT COUNTY HISTORICAL SOCIETY

Eagle Grove Chapter, Museum
401 Broadway
Eagle Grove, Iowa 50533

Cecilian Music Club materials, including 25 printed songbooks, cantatas, and choral-music items for 3 female voices, ca. 1925–40; a complete run of programs, 1920s–60s; and 3 scrapbooks, 1913– , with yearbooks, press clippings, and photographs

—Mrs. John Henneberry, Mrs. Forrest Fromm

470

FORT MUSEUM

Museum Road
Fort Dodge, Iowa 50501

Karl L. King (1891–1971, composer and bandmaster), photographs, awards, his gold cornet, and his desk
Other materials relating to the musical history of Fort Dodge

—Betty Smith

471

NORTH LEE COUNTY HISTORICAL SOCIETY

Box 385
Fort Madison, Iowa 52627

Prof. Alfred Sommers (local cello instructor), programs of a farewell concert, and 1 photograph, 1898
Recordings of popular and classical music, including 24 Edison cylinders, 1900–1919, and 107 78-rpm discs, 1910–25, with Edison, Columbia, Aeolian Vocalian, Brunswick, Victrola, Emerson, Gennett, and New Moon labels

—Mrs. William R. Sopher

472

GARNAVILLO HISTORICAL SOCIETY

Garnavillo, Iowa 52049

Lucille Roggman (fl. 1905, music teacher), papers
Hymnals and songbooks, 1835–76
Other materials, including programs of local recitals, late 19th and early 20th centuries; photographs of local 19th-century bands, including the Garnavillo Brass Band and the Elkader Band; and cylinder recordings

—Arnold Roggman

473

GRINNELL COLLEGE

IaGG

Burling Library—Archives
Grinnell, Iowa 50112

Manuscript music by faculty members, 70 items, ca. 1915–30
Music Department faculty papers, 10 items, including correspondence, lists of faculty, a tour diary, and a history of the Department, ca. 1909–63
Songbooks of Grinnell College and of social organizations, 7 items, ca. 1900–1920; also sheet music of College songs, 10 items, ca. 1897–1942; programs of the College, 100 items, ca. 1879–1940; and photographs of College music groups, 25 items, ca. 1900–

—Anne G. Kintner

474

Frederick CRANE

930 Talwrn Court
Iowa City, Iowa 52240

Research materials relating to music in Iowa, 60 linear cm., including press clippings and programs, 80 sheet-music imprints, ca. 1890– , and research notes and bibliographical references
Research notes on Chautauqua music, also 200 advertising flyers
Pictorial materials, including post cards, relating to music in the U.S.

475

STATE HISTORICAL SOCIETY OF IOWA

IaHi

402 Iowa Avenue
Iowa City, Iowa 52240

Music Study Club, Iowa City, 1916– , 30 cm. of papers including minutes and program books

Papers of 10 other Iowa music organizations, ca. 1900– , 1 linear meter

Wallace E. Atkinson (trombonist) and his wife, Buena Vista Atkinson (vaudeville pianist and singer), 30 linear cm. of papers, 1899–1925, including letters, diaries, scrapbooks, account books, and photographs

Henry Givin Cox (violinist and music teacher at the University of Iowa; Central College, Pella; and Omaha, Neb.), 15 cm. of papers, 1897–1964, including contracts, writings on music, autobiographical materials, and curricular information

George W. Landers (bandleader and music dealer, "Father of the Iowa Band Law"), 50 cm. of materials, 1898–1955, related to the Iowa Band Law, the Spanish-American War, and state and national band associations

William Oscar Perkins and Henry Southwick Perkins, ms music book, as cited in Raymond Comstock, *Contributions of the Orson Perkins Family to Nineteenth Century American Music Education* (Ph.D. diss., University of Iowa, 1970)

Helen Katz Robeson (violinist and teacher at Yankton, S.D., and the University of Iowa until 1919), 10 cm. of papers, 1903–60, with diplomas, programs, photographs, letters, certificates, and a diary written during the 1916 Chautauqua tour

Streed Family Orchestra, papers, including 1 scrapbook, 1911–14, with correspondence, clippings and photographs relating to their vaudeville performances, mostly for Chautauqua events in Iowa

Manuscript music, 50 items, late 19th century, in collections of personal papers

Hymnals, 100 items, including some in German or Norwegian

Songbooks, 20 items used in schools, 1880s–1940; also 10 World War I songbooks for the armed forces

Sheet music, 1300 items, ca. 1900–1940s, including 200 by Iowa composers; also 300 items bound in 6 vols., 1860s–70s

Programs of the Burlington (Iowa) Opera House, 1892–1904, 15 linear cm.; also recital programs of E. D. Keck (vocal music teacher) in 1 unbound scrapbook, 1889–1902, and of A. Bullock (singer and teacher), 25 items, 1893–1913

Photographs of Iowa music groups and musicians, 200 items, 1880s–1940s, arranged by subject, including William Leander Sheetz and Karl King

Oral-history tape recordings, 10 of them with transcriptions relating to the 1915–1940 period

—Joyce Giaquinta

476

UNIVERSITY OF IOWA   **IaU**

Iowa City, Iowa 55242

See Boyd Keith Swigger, *A Guide to Resources for the Study of Recent History of the United States in the Libraries of the University of Iowa [and Others]* (Iowa City, 1973), esp. pp. 131–37; also Dennis R. Martin, "Musical Items with pre-1875 American Imprints in the University of Iowa Libraries" (typescript, 1975)

Music Library

Sheet music, 300 pre-1860 items

A. Louis Scarmolin, 200 editions of his music in various forms, as cited in M.L.A. *Notes*, 30 (1973), 163

Published music books, 1791–1863, as cited in Frederick K. Gable, *An Annotated Catalog of Rare Musical Items in the Libraries of the University of Iowa* (Iowa City, 1963), and in Gordon Rowley, *An Annotated Catalog . . . , Additions, 1963–1972* (Iowa City, 1973)

Clifford Hesser, 78-rpm recordings, mostly early vocal

—Rita Benton

Main Library, Special Collections Department

Early U.S. imprints, including 3 libretti, 1806–11, as cited in Gable (see above)

Chautauqua collection, 1902–36, 270 linear meters, including archives of the Redpath–Vawter Bureau of Cedar Rapids, the Redpath Bureau of Chicago, and the Redpath Bureau of Kansas City. See Robert A. McCown, "Records of the Redpath Chautauqua," *Books at Iowa*, 19 (1973), 8–23

Keith/Albee vaudeville circuit, 200 scrapbooks, 1895–1945, from vaudeville, burlesque, and movie theaters, mostly in New England; also business records of the Albee Theater, Providence, R.I., mostly 1940s

Cedar Rapids Symphony Orchestra, archives, 1923–57, including attendance registers, programs and financial accounts

Archival records of the School of Music, including programs, 1909– , photographs, official records, and related inter-university correspondence, all as part of the University Archives. Also papers of faculty members, including Philip Greeley Clapp (1888–1954), music mss and correspondence, 40 linear cm., as discussed in Dorothy R. Holcomb, "Philip Greeley Clapp," *Books at Iowa*, 17 (1972), 3–14; and Philip Bezanson (1916–75), 10 editions of his music

Dessa Manion, music collection, 3.6 linear meters, 1900–1960, including transcriptions of popular and folk songs, sheet music, and a card index

Elmer Joseph Miller, collection of concert and theater programs, 1872–1975, 1.5 linear meters

Edwin Ford Piper (1871–1939), folklore collection, 60 linear cm., including western ballads, with notes on some items. See Harold D. Peterson, *Syllabus of the Ballad Collection of Edwin Ford Piper* (M.A. thesis, University of Iowa, 1934); also Harry Oster, "The Edwin Ford Piper Collection of Folksongs," *Books at Iowa*, 1 (1964), 28–33

Carl E. Seashore (1866–1949, psychologist of music), published writings, including memoirs

—Robert A. McCown, Earl M. Rogers

University Bands

Goldman Band, performance materials formerly used by the Band, 2204 scores and parts, mostly published but some in ms, as cited in the catalogue, "Goldman Band Library" (typescript)

—Frank A. Piersol

477

GRACELAND COLLEGE   **IaLG**

Restoration History Manuscript Collection
Frederick Madison Smith Library
Lamoni, Iowa 50140

Virgil Thomson, ms score and parts for *Songs of the Restoration*, for chorus and orchestra, 1918, in the Alice M. Edwards Collection

William Gould, 8 ms items for orchestra or piano, ca. 1935–45

Manuscript and published music by College faculty and local composers, 4 items, by J. H. Anthony, Myron McTavish, and Frederick M. Smith

Hymnals, ca. 1833–1975, 150 items including many of the Reorganized Latter-day Saints Church and the Latter-day Saints Church, among them *The Saints Harmony* (1842) and *The Saints Harp* (1889)

Graceland Singers, 2 linear meters of papers, ca. 1895– , including correspondence relating to the founding of the group, programs, clippings, and 200 photographs (in the Rare Book Room)

—Paul M. Edwards

478
Helen DUCOMMUN
122 West Main Street
Laurens, Iowa 50554

Hymnals, 100 items of various denominations, 1890–1940, including several in Swedish or German

Sheet music, 1000 items, ca. 1890–1940, mostly popular songs arranged for piano, organized by copyright date; popular songs arranged in dance folios, 20 items, 1920s; and printed music for mandolin, guitar, piano, or reed organ

Programs of school and community concerts in Laurens, 12 items, ca. 1896–1930

Photographs of town bands in Laurens and Lamoni, 2 items, ca. 1920

Edison discs of popular and classical music, 20 items, 1915–30

479
IOWA WESLEYAN COLLEGE   IaMpI
College Archives
J. Raymond Chadwick Library
Mount Pleasant, Iowa 52641

Alexander Rommel (1843–1934), personal papers, 40 linear cm., including 4 holograph compositions; and materials of his Academy of Music (affiliated with the College, 1877–1918), with programs of Rommel and his students, a scrapbook of clippings, programs, correspondence, and photographs, and program booklets of the Rommel Music Club

Materials pertaining to College musicians and musical activities, including programs of the Music Department, ca. 1860–1940

Methodist hymnals, 40 items, ca. 1870–1940

—Carl Moehlman, Patricia Newcomer

480
MUSEUM OF REPERTOIRE AMERICANA
Mid-West Old Settlers
Route 1
Mount Pleasant, Iowa 52641

Materials related to theatrical music, mostly of traveling troupes in the Midwest, ca. 1920–50, including 2

cubic meters of orchestral parts with mss and lead sheets, 10,000 programs, 2000 photographs of productions, orchestras, bands, and individuals, 20 diaries, and 50 scrapbooks of clippings

—Michael Kramme

481
CORNELL COLLEGE   IaMvC
Russell D. Cole Library
Mount Vernon, Iowa 52314

Manuscript music by College faculty members Jacques Jolas (1895–1957), 2 compositions for choir, and Horace Alden Miller (b. 1872), 3 compositions for orchestra, choir, or organ

Cornell College May Festival, 30 linear cm. of programs, clippings, press releases, and memorabilia, 1899–

Cornell College songbooks, 8 published items, ca. 1908–

—Karen Houkom

482
D. D. HUNDLING
1020 South Eighth Avenue West
Newton, Iowa 50208

Theater orchestrations for silent films, 2000 printed arrangements of popular, classical, and semi-classical works, 1921–28, used by the Hundling family at the Capitol Theatre, Newton, 1920s, with a ms index of composers, titles, and publication dates

Recordings, 100 78-rpm discs, some used during silent films at the Capitol Theatre, 1920s, and some from the Big Band Era

483
Ruth JACKSON
Route 2
Newton, Iowa 50208

Sheet music, 300 items of piano and vocal popular music, ca. 1860–1945

Hymnals, 40 vols., late 19th and early 20th centuries

484
William PENN COLLEGE   IaOskW
Wilcox Library
Trueblood Avenue
Oskaloosa, Iowa 52577

Manuscript songs for the College, 4 items, 1905–42, in the Quaker Collection

Hymnals of various denominations, 300 items, 1910s–30s, mostly from the collections of Clarence E. Pickett and Charles L. Griffith

—Marion E. Rains

485
ROCK RAPIDS PUBLIC LIBRARY
102 South Green Street
Rock Rapids, Iowa 51246

Sheet music, 3000 popular and classical items, mostly vocal, ca. 1900–1940

Hymnals, 1.5 linear meters, early 20th century, some in German

—Linda Haegele

486
CALHOUN COUNTY HISTORICAL SOCIETY
Rockwell City, Iowa 50579

George A. Craft collection, including 150 ms and printed band and choral works composed or arranged by him, financial records, programs of his band concerts, and his trumpet

Sheet music, 800 popular-music items for piano or organ, 1920s–40s

Hymnals, 30 items, 1860–1940, including 5 with words only

Programs of concerts in Rockwell City schools, 15 items, 1930s

Recordings, including 60 78-rpm discs

—Judy Webb

487
Lois (Mrs. Neil) DAWSON
138 Lake Street
Rockwell City, Iowa 50579

George A. Craft (Mrs. Dawson's grandfather), personal papers, including holograph music mss, ca. 1900–1940s, 75 original compositions and arrangements for band, and 100 sacred or secular vocal and choral works; 100 items of printed music, comprising his complete published works; a scrapbook of press clippings, correspondence, pictures, and programs (including a 1943 Rockwell City concert in his honor), ca. 1910–45; 20 photographs of him, 1930s–40s; 15 linear cm. of wax-disc recordings made by Craft and his son, including music performed at family gatherings and a concert of his music; and a valve herald trumpet and violin

488
MORNINGSIDE COLLEGE   IaScM
Sioux City, Iowa 51106

Archival records of music at Morningside College, including subject files on the Conservatory of Music, Madrigal Club, Master Melodiers, and other activities, also programs for music festivals, recitals, and other concerts

—Orpha M. Jarman

489
TAMA COUNTY HISTORICAL SOCIETY
State and Broadway
Box 64
Toledo, Iowa 52342

David F. Bruner, "Parting Song," in holograph ms, 1848, and published version, 1852

William H. Malin, ms hymns, ca. 1930

Popular vocal sheet music, 112 items, ca. 1900–1940

Other published music, including 20 hymnals, 20 popular songbooks, and 25 choral scores, ca. 1900–1930

—Marie K. Vileta

490
Herbert HOOVER PRESIDENTIAL LIBRARY
Box 488
West Branch, Iowa 52358

Manuscript music, 5 unsolicited works from the 1928 campaign, including William Balzer, "Presidential March" for piano, also Mary A. Bremond, "Hoover Is the Man for Me," Harriet Thorne Rhoads, "Hoover's March of Progress" and "Climbing the White House Stairs," and Mrs. E. Rogers and George Careless, "Hoover for President," all vocal

Sheet music, 24 songs and marches, 1921–33, for voice, chorus, piano, band, or orchestra

Correspondence concerning such subjects as Department of Commerce business, performers wishing to appear at the White House, and National Music Week, 15 linear cm., 1921–33

Programs, 20 items, 1929–33, from receptions and dinners, including White House events

Recordings, 7 78-rpm discs of popular, political, and classical music, 1920s–30s

—Nancy DeHamer

In addition to the repositories listed above, the following have also reported holdings of the materials indicated:

Albert City—Albert City Historical Association: recordings

Allison—Butler County Historical Society: sheet music, songbooks, other printed music

Audubon—Audubon Public Library: sheet music

Bettendorf—Bettendorf Museum, Bettendorf High School Library: recordings

Burr Oak—Laura Ingalls Wilder Park and Museum: songbooks

Cedar Falls—Cedar Falls Historical Society: sheet music, songbooks, programs, pictures

Charles City—Charles City Public Library: sheet music, recordings

Cherokee—Cherokee Public Library: songbooks, recordings

Cresco—Howard County Historical Society: sheet music, songbooks

Davenport—St. Ambrose College: songbooks, recordings

Davenport—Marycrest College, Cone Library: recordings

Des Moines—Drake University, Cowles Library: songbooks, pictures, miscellaneous

Des Moines—Living History Farms: sheet music, songbooks

Dyersville—Dyersville Historical Society: pictures

Earlham—Earlham Public Library: songbooks, recordings

Eldora—Hardin County Historical Society: sheet music, songbooks, programs, pictures, recordings, miscellaneous

Elliott—Elliott Public Library: songbooks
Farmersburg—Farmersburg Public Library: printed music
Fort Dodge—Fort Dodge Historical Foundation: songbooks, other printed music, pictures, miscellaneous materials of Karl King
Grundy Center—Jean Evans: sheet music, songbooks
Hampton—Franklin County Historical Society: sheet music, songbooks, pictures
Hampton—Hampton Public Library: sheet music, songbooks, pictures, miscellaneous
Harlan—Shelby County Historical Society: sheet music, songbooks, other printed music
Ida Grove—Ida County Historical Society: recordings
Jefferson—Greene County Historical Society: pictures
Keokuk—Lee County Historical Society: sheet music
Keosauqua—Van Buren County Historical Society: songbooks, miscellaneous
Knoxville—Knoxville Public Library: songbooks, recordings
Logan—Harrison County Historical Society: sheet music, songbooks, other printed music, recordings
Lovilia—Monroe County Genealogical Society: sheet music, songbooks, programs, recordings
Malvern—Malvern Public Library: songbooks
Maquoketa—Maquoketa Public Library: songbooks, recordings
Marshalltown—Historical Society of Marshall County: sheet music, songbooks, other printed music, programs, miscellaneous
Martelle—Martelle Public Library: songbooks
Mediapolis—Rhonda Winegard: sheet music, songbooks, miscellaneous
Monona—Monona Historical Society: sheet music, songbooks, other printed music, recordings
Monticello—Jones County Iowa Historical Society: sheet music, songbooks, pictures
Mt. Ayr—Ringgold County Historical Society: pictures, miscellaneous

Mt. Pleasant—Mt. Pleasant Public Library: songbooks, recordings
Nashua—Chickasaw County Historical County Museum: sheet music, songbooks, miscellaneous
New London—New London Public Library: songbooks
New Virginia—New Virginia Public Library: songbooks
Oakland—Oakland Historical Society: sheet music, songbooks, other printed music, programs, miscellaneous
Oelwein—Oelwein Public Library: songbooks
Onawa—Onawa Public Library: sheet music, songbooks, other printed music, programs
Osage—Mitchell County Historical Society: sheet music, songbooks, recordings
Osage—Osage Public Library: songbooks
Oskaloosa—Oskaloosa Public Library: catalogues
Rock Valley—Gary Ritsemer: sheet music, songbooks
Rock Valley—Rock Valley Public Library: songbooks, pictures, recordings
Sac City—Sac County Historical Society: songbooks
Terril—Terril Community Library: songbooks
Vinton—Vinton Free Public Library: songbooks, other printed music
Wadena—Wadena Public Library: songbooks
Waterloo—Grout Museum of History and Science: sheet music, songbooks, recordings
Waverly—Waverly Public Library: songbooks, recordings
Wellsburg—Burdette Walters: sheet music, songbooks, recordings, miscellaneous
West Point—West Point Public Library: songbooks
West Union—Fayette County Helpers Club and Historical Society: songbooks, other printed music, pictures
Woodward—Mrs. Kenneth Beck: sheet music, songbooks, recordings
Woodward—Irene Hartman: sheet music
Woodward—Dick and Betty Krasche: recordings
Woodward—Alvera Maas: sheet music

Kansas

491

DICKINSON COUNTY HISTORICAL SOCIETY

Box 506
412 South Campbell Street
Abilene, Kansas 67410

Manuscript music for calliope, 5 anonymous items, ca. 1905–20, donated by the family of C. W. Parker (local amusement-device manufacturer)
Song sheets of popular and Civil War songs, 200 items with words only, mostly printed, ca. 1890–1910
Popular recordings, including 40 Edison cylinders, ca. 1890–1910, and 40 78-rpm discs, ca. 1910–30

—Susan Traub

492

MUSEUM OF INDEPENDENT TELEPHONY

412 South Campbell Street
Abilene, Kansas 67410

Sheet music on the subject of the telephone, 50 items, ca. 1900–1970
"My Lady of the Telephone," the first recorded song about the telephone, 3 tape copies of the 1905 recording

—Susan Traub

493

CLARK COUNTY HISTORICAL SOCIETY

Pioneer Museum
Box 613
Ashland, Kansas 67831

Hymnals of various denominations, 40 items, ca. 1880–1940
Popular sheet music for voice, 15 items, 1920s
Recordings, including 100 Edison cylinders, ca. 1890–1910, 150 78-rpm discs, ca. 1890–1920, and 31 Ehrlich slotted discs, ca. 1900

—Florence E. Hurd

494
ATCHISON LIBRARY
401 Kansas Avenue
Atchison, Kansas 66002

Sheet music and other printed music, ca. 1900–1955, 2300 mostly vocal items, donated by a local music teacher

Popular and community songbooks, 350 items, ca. 1935–55

—Mrs. Freund

495
Robert A. ROBISON
Route 1, Box 87AB
Chetopa, Kansas 67336

Carson J. Robison (country-and-western and novelty-music composer), 3 compilations and 10 items of sheet music, ca. 1920–57; 6 photographs, ca. 1940–57; and 3600 linear meters of tape recordings of Robison, Frank Luther, and Vernon Dalhart, copied from 78-rpm discs, ca. 1920–55

496
Kay H. BEACH
Box 13246
Edwardsville, Kansas 66113

Hymnals, 100 items, 1850– , mostly Methodist; also sheet music, printed music in vocal and piano collections, books on hymnology, programs, and pictures

497
BUTLER COUNTY HISTORICAL SOCIETY MUSEUM
381 East Central Avenue
Box 696
El Dorado, Kansas 67042

Robert Graham (b. 1912), 300 ms and 500 published compositions, including piano instruction works, sacred cantatas and anthems, oratorios, vocal solos, and organ and orchestral works, ca. 1933– , partially indexed; also a 4-vol. scrapbook documenting his life and career

—Anna Louise Borger

498
LYON COUNTY HISTORICAL SOCIETY
Box 1224
Emporia, Kansas 66801

Hymnals of various denominations, ca. 1890–1930, 20 items including 5 in Welsh

Popular sheet music for voice or piano, 200 items, ca. 1890–1930, including 2 by Kansas composers Irma Doster and Rebecca Welty Dunn, and lyricists Esther Clark Hill and Edna Becker

Programs of local schools, churches, and theaters, 200

items, ca. 1880– , including Emporia State University, the College of Emporia, and Whitley Opera House

Recordings, 30 cylinders and 100 78-rpm discs

—Gayle Graham

499
FORT HAYS KANSAS STATE COLLEGE   KHayF
Forsyth Library
Hays, Kansas 67601

Folklore collection, including 50 tape recordings of music and songs, mostly of western Kansas, collected by the College's English Department, 1960s

—Rachel Christopher

500
KINGMAN HISTORICAL MUSEUM
242 Avenue A West
Kingman, Kansas 67068

Oscar Capp's Kid Band, printed marches used by the Band ca. 1910–50, 4 linear meters, and 1 photograph, ca. 1915

Hymnals, ca. 1870–1930, including 2 items with words only; also school songbooks, ca. 1900–1920

Sheet music, 10 items, ca. 1920–30, mostly popular vocal

Programs of local high-school music performances, 10 items, ca. 1900–1920

Photograph of Kingman Band members with their Kansas regiment during the Spanish-American War

—Sadie F. Jurney

501
KINSLEY LIBRARY
208 East Eighth Street
Kinsley, Kansas 67547

Kinsley Music Club, minutes, 15 linear cm., ca. 1920–50

Hymnals, 2 items published by the Rodeheaver Co., 1927 and 1929

Sheet music and printed choral music, 75 items, ca. 1930–

—Beverly J. Craft

502
UNIVERSITY OF KANSAS   KU
Lawrence, Kansas 66045

Thomas Gorton Music Library

Sheet music, 500 items in 6 boxes, unsorted, and 17 bound vols., one of the latter stamped "Czarina Macomb," with 50 imprints of the 1810s–20s, including early lithographs by Henry Stone, another vol. stamped "Miss M. E. Rice," with imprints of the 1850s, including early St. Louis imprints

Music editions and books about music from the libraries of Carl E. Preyer (1863–1947, composer and University piano professor) and Charles Sanford Skilton (1868–1941, American Indianist composer and University professor)

James E. Seaver, 17,400 recordings, 1896– , including 440 cylinders, 12,000 78-rpm discs, and 440 albums, with special emphasis on operatic recordings

—Ellen Johnson, J. Bunker Clark

Kenneth Spencer Research Library, Department of Special Collections

"Miss Berkley's commonplace book," 1803, including a chronicle of performances at the Theatre Royal in New York, 1778

John Beach, ms music book, pre-1817, derived in part from Samuel Holyoke's *Instrumental Assistant* (1800), and including airs, marches, and instructional text for various instruments. See Raoul Camus, "Some Thoughts on Early American Band Music" (typescript, Lawrence, 1978)

Elizabeth Smith, bound vol. containing sheet music with U.S. imprints, 1830s, also 10 pages of ms piano music and songs

Lowell Mason, letter, 1842, to A. M. Merrill of Hamstead, N.Y., concerning musical matters

Roger Imhof (1875–1958, vaudeville and burlesque actor), 12 boxes of personal papers, including scrapbooks, correspondence, songs and lyrics by him, and scripts

Henry M. Katzman, collection of materials used in radio programs featuring George Gershwin, 1933–34, including 42 performance parts, 22 of these for Gershwin compositions, and consisting of ms materials in various hands, including Katzman's, with passages from printed sheet-music editions pasted on; 102 sheet-music items, many with annotations in pencil, including 25 early Gershwin editions; and a commentary by Katzman describing his work with Gershwin. See the typescript inventory by Donald Frueh, 1972

Tunebooks and other vocal anthologies, 10 items, 1788–1937

James Joyce, 8 of his poems set to music, issued under U.S. imprints, 1930s–40s

—Alexandra Mason, J. Bunker Clark

University Archives

Charles Sanford Skilton, personal papers, 1917–38, including music in holograph mss and printed editions

Carl Preyer, personal papers, 1920–45, including holograph music mss, correspondence, and scrapbooks, in all 30 linear cm.

School of Fine Arts, scrapbooks containing programs, photographs, press clippings, and other materials, 1919– , 28 vols.

—John Nugent

503
Elizabeth M. WATKINS COMMUNITY MUSEUM

Douglas County Historical Society
1047 Massachusetts
Lawrence, Kansas 66044

Hymnals of various denominations, 10 items, 1868–1915, including 1 in German

Songbooks for schools and singing societies, 5 items, 1861–97

Sheet music, 170 items, 1868–1940, in 1 bound vol. and singly

Sheet-music catalogue of the Century Music Publishing Co., n.d.

Programs, 6 items, 1886–1948, including 1 of Sousa's Band in Lawrence

Photographs of local music organizations, 10 items, ca. 1890–1920

—Ann Clausen

504
SAINT MARY COLLEGE   KLeS

Leavenworth, Kansas 66048

Nazarene De Rubertis (ca. 1880–1956, Kansas City composer and conductor), autograph holograph orchestral and band scores, 100 items, catalogued

Virgil Thomson, ms of "Two Sentimental Tangos"

—Sister Anne Callahan

505
BETHANY COLLEGE   KLindB

Wallerstedt Learning Center
Lindsborg, Kansas 67456

Messiah Festival of the Bethany Oratorical Society, press clippings, 80 programs, 2 posters, and 8 photographs, 1882–

—Dixie Lanning

506
McPHERSON COLLEGE   KMcpC

Miller Library
1600 East Euclid Street
McPherson, Kansas 67460

McPherson College music groups, 1 folder of programs and 1 photograph, ca. 1900–

Church of the Brethren hymnals, 50 items, ca. 1875–1940

—Rowena Olsen, Joan Johnson

507
RILEY COUNTY HISTORICAL MUSEUM

2309 Claflin Road
Manhattan, Kansas 66502

Hymnals of various denominations, 50 items, ca. 1840–1940, some of them with words only, and some in Swedish or German

Popular songbooks, 4 items, ca. 1910–30

Laura E. Newell (local composer), 20 sheet-music items for piano and voice, ca. 1890–1920, donated by her granddaughter, Esther Toothaker

Popular sheet music for voice, 200 items, ca. 1900–1940

Programs of Kansas State University musicians and groups, 50 items, ca. 1880–1940

Photographs of local music groups, 25 items, ca. 1890–1950

Recordings, including 200 78-rpm discs, ca. 1900–1940

—Jean Dallas

508

Jean SLOOP

Music Department
Kansas State University
Manhattan, Kansas 66502

American art songs, ca. 1750–1960, photocopies of 250 out-of-print items located primarily at the Library of Congress, indexed

509

**MENNONITE LIBRARY AND   KNM
ARCHIVES**

Bethel College Library
North Newton, Kansas 67117

Walter H. Hohmann (1892–1971, music educator and editor of Mennonite hymnals), 35 linear cm. of papers, including ms compositions for the A Capella Choir at Bethel College, correspondence concerning the hymnals, and a typescript history of German evangelical hymnody

Mennonite Song Festival Society, complete papers including correspondence, programs, and minutes, 1930–

Hymnals, mostly Mennonite, 100 items published in the U.S., 1742–1978, and 600 published in Europe but used in the U.S.

Recordings of Amish singers and various Mennonite groups, 1 hour of tapes recorded ca. 1945–50

Sheet music, 20 sacred items for mixed chorus, 1922–48

—John F. Schmidt, Rita Romeijn

510

Walter BUTLER

322 South Main
Ottawa, Kansas 66067

Music for ukelin, pianolin, or piano-harp, 100 items, ca. 1900–1920; also published music for zither, mandolin, or banjo, ca. 1875

Popular, folk, and school songbooks, 50 items including some with shape notes, ca. 1840–1940; also a published method book for parlor organ, 1900

Recordings, 1000 78-rpm discs, including many of operas and musical comedies, ca. 1890–1940

511

PITTSBURG STATE UNIVERSITY   KPT

Porter Library
Pittsburg, Kansas 66762

Eva Jessye papers, including a ms oratorio "Paradise Lost and Regained," 1937; published works, ca. 1920–50, 20 items, mostly for choir; personal papers, including scrapbooks, diaries, correspondence, and programs, 1 linear meter, ca. 1900–1978; photographs of her, 40 items, ca. 1899–1978; and photographs of the 1934 production of Virgil Thomson's opera, *Four Saints in Three Acts*, for which she was choral director

Manuscript works by Kansas composers, 20 items, ca. 1900–1930

Sigma Alpha Iota, Alpha Kappa Chapter, 1 linear meter of papers, ca. 1920–40, including scrapbooks, membership lists, minutes, and books of photographs of members

J. J. Richards, printed band music and ms conductor's score

Published music, including hymnals of various denominations, 1796–1926; 600 items of sheet music, ca. 1860–1945, mostly popular, including some by Kansas composers; 8 fake books, ca. 1930–50; and band music

Programs of University musical productions, 1 linear meter, 1903– ; bound programs of area performances, 70 linear cm., ca. 1890–1940, in the collection of Walter McRay; and 50 Chautauqua programs, 1920s, in the Rodley Collection

Photographs of University music organizations and productions, 200 items

—Gene DeGruson

512

Gayle GRAHAM

Route 2, Box 42
Reading, Kansas 66868

Popular sheet music, 300 items, ca. 1890– , including songs about prohibition and about blacks

513

Ida Long GOODMAN MEMORIAL LIBRARY

Box 277
406 North Monroe Street
Saint John, Kansas 67576

Hymnals, 50 items of various denominations, also 50 popular songbooks, 19th and 20th centuries

Sheet music, 780 items, ca. 1880–1940

Recordings, including 1000 78-rpm discs

—Verl L. Manwarren

514

KANSAS STATE HISTORICAL SOCIETY   KHi

Memorial Building
120 West Tenth Street
Topeka, Kansas 66612

Manuscript Department

Music mss, including Jacob Spengler, music "notebook," 1784, with instrumental music and English and German songs

Personal papers, of Annie Marie Pest (d. 1837); Lillian Forrest, including 5 songs; Winfield Miller; Henry Clay Corbett (1886–1972); Mrs. A. H. Lehman; Esther Munson (Topeka piano teacher); and Harvey Worrall (1860–1936)

Organizational archives, including minutes of the Handel & Haydn Society, Lawrence, 1885–86; constitution of the Lawrence Musical Association; and papers of the bands in Clay Center (1938), Concordia (1938), Hope, and Olathe (1888)

Mrs. Frank C. Montgomery, ms notes and press clippings on early Kansas music

Library

Sheet music, including 300 "Kansas Songs" and 900 other items, catalogued by composer and title
Singing-school books, 1850– , 30 items
Kansas folk songs, mostly photocopies from periodicals
Press clippings relating to bands and choral groups in Kansas
Programs of Kansas musical events, including 200 instrumental and 300 vocal performances
Pamphlets on Kansas band and choral music, 50 items

515
SHAWNEE COUNTY HISTORICAL SOCIETY
Box 56
Topeka, Kansas 66601

Sheet music, photographs, press clippings, and memorabilia related to music in Topeka, 1860s–1950s, as reflected in John W. Ripley and Robert W. Richmond, *A Century of Music*, Shawnee County Historical Society Bulletin 54 (1977), relating to local performers, ensembles, teachers, merchants, publishers, and music clubs, with a list (pp. 123–27) of 145 sheet-music titles composed or published in Shawnee County, 1878–1954; also glass lantern slides to illustrate theatrical performances of popular songs, 1895–1914, with a catalogue

—John W. Ripley

516
TOPEKA PUBLIC LIBRARY   KT
1515 West Tenth Street
Topeka, Kansas 66604

Sheet music, including 30 items by Topeka composers or relating to Topeka, in the Special Collections Department; and 1200 popular-music items, including ragtime editions, ca. 1900, in the Fine Arts Department

517
WASHBURN UNIVERSITY   KTW
Topeka, Kansas 66621

Published scores for orchestra, piano, or voice, ca. 1900–1940, 200 items including some by Kansas composer Sam Bradshaw (in the Orchestra Library)
Other published music, including popular songbooks, 10 hymnals, and 20 file drawers of sheet music for voice, piano, or other instruments

—John Iltis

518
CHISHOLM TRAIL MUSEUM
502 North Washington Street
Wellington, Kansas 67152

Joseph E. Maddy (1891–1966), personal papers, 50 linear meters, ca. 1891–1970, including correspondence, 2 published biographies, photographs of his family and of Interlochen, Mich., and programs

Popular songbooks, 15 items, ca. 1880–1930, some of them brought to Wellington by pioneers
Hymnals of various denominations, 20 items, ca. 1880–1930, including 2 in German
Popular sheet music for voice or piano, 125 items, ca. 1860–1940, including works by Bill Post and other local composers
Photographs of local musicians, ca. 1880– , 50 items, some of them with biographical sketches
Band memorabilia of Olaf Theodore Nielsen Huuse, ca. 1855–1940

—Dorothea W. Miller

519
WICHITA PUBLIC LIBRARY   KWi
223 South Main Street
Wichita, Kansas 67202

Popular songbooks, 400 items, ca. 1900–
Hymnals of various denominations, 25 items, ca. 1900–
Popular sheet music, 200 items, ca. 1900–1950
Clippings on Wichita music, ca. 1920– , mounted on 500 pages
Tape recordings of Kansas and midwestern folksongs, collected by Wichita State University students, 1950s–60s

—Arlene V. Root, Shirley Holmes

520
COWLEY COUNTY HISTORICAL SOCIETY
1011 Mansfield Street
Winfield, Kansas 67156

Papers of the Winfield Music Club and the Apollo Club, ca. 1920–60
Hymnals of various denominations, 32 items, ca. 1900, including 1 with words only
Sheet music, 67 items, ca. 1920, and 100 items in 1 bound vol., ca. 1850–1910
Programs, 25 items, ca. 1885–1940, of Chautauqua events, local high schools, St. John's College, Southwestern College, and local organizations
Popular recordings, including 30 Edison cylinders, ca. 1890–1910, and 100 78-rpm discs, ca. 1900–1940

—Mrs. Frankie S. Cullison

In addition to the repositories listed above, the following have also reported holdings of the materials indicated:

Baldwin—Baker University, Old Castle Museum, and United Methodist Historical Library: sheet music, songbooks, programs, pictures, recordings
Bonner Springs—Wyandotte County Historical Society: sheet music, songbooks, recordings
Colby—Thomas County Historical Society: sheet music
Concordia—Cloud County Historical Society: sheet music, songbooks, pictures, recordings, miscellaneous
Dodge City—Southwest Kansas Library System: songbooks
Douglass—Douglass Historical Society: sheet music, songbooks
Emporia—Emporia Kansas State College, William A.

White Library: songbooks, other printed music, programs, pictures

Eureka—Eureka Carnegie Library: songbooks, recordings

Ft. Leavenworth—Historical Society of Ft. Leavenworth: sheet music, songbooks, recordings

Hesston—Hesston College, Mary Miller Library: songbooks, other printed music, pictures, recordings

Jetmore—Haun Museum: songbooks

Kingman—Kingman County Historical Society: sheet music, songbooks, printed music for the city band up to the 1920s

Larned—Santa Fe Trail Center: sheet music, songbooks, recordings

Lawrence—Kansas School of Religion Library: songbooks

McPherson—Central College, Library: songbooks

McPherson—Kay Kline: sheet music, songbooks, other printed music, programs, recordings, miscellaneous

McPherson—McPherson County Historical Museum: sheet music, songbooks, miscellaneous

Manhattan—Kansas State University, Farrell Library: sheet music, songbooks, other printed music, recordings

Medicine Lodge—Lincoln Library: songbooks

Mound Valley—Mound Valley Public Library: songbooks, other printed music, programs, recordings, miscellaneous

North Newton—Bethel College, Music Library: songbooks, programs, recordings

Ottawa—Franklin County Historical Society: sheet music, songbooks, other printed music

Parsons—Parsons Public Library: songbooks, recordings

Troy—Library District One: songbooks, recordings

Wetmore—Wetmore Library: songbooks, other printed music, pictures

Wichita—Friends University, Edmund Stanley Library: sheet music, songbooks, recordings

Wichita—Historic Wichita: sheet music, songbooks, recordings

Wichita—Wichita State University, Thurlow Lieurance Memorial Music Library: sheet music, songbooks, other printed music

Kentucky

521

NELSON COUNTY PUBLIC LIBRARY

90 Court Square
Bardstown, Kentucky 40004

Miscellaneous secondary material relating to Stephen Collins Foster and the original site of My Old Kentucky Home

522

BEREA COLLEGE   KyBB

Berea, Kentucky 40403

Appalachian Center

Bascom Lamar Lunsford (1882–1973, singer and banjoist), personal papers, interviews, correspondence concerning him, and taped copies of recordings

Bradley Kincaid (b. 1895, singer), songbooks and sheet music from his personal collection, correspondence with or about him, photographs, interviews, a copy of his repertory wordbook, a book of his poems, and tape recordings of his performances

Buell Kazee (b. 1900, singer and banjoist), correspondence, interviews, and tape recordings of him performing and of his sermons

Asa Martin, interviews, and tapes and 78-rpm recordings of him performing

General collection on Appalachian culture, including field recordings, oral-history recordings, video tapes of musicians, photographs, correpondence, songbooks and writings, some of them from the annual symposium on Appalachian culture, the annual Berea Festival, and the annual summer workshop on Appalachian studies

—Loyal Jones

Weatherford–Hammond Appalachian Collection

Books, articles, typescript and ms papers, clippings, photographs, ballad transcriptions, and tape recordings, all concerning Appalachian studies, including some relating to music. Materials in the Archives of Traditional Music, on tape, are shared with the Appalachian Center (see above)

—Alfred H. Perrin

Hutchins Library

Hymnals, 300 vols., 1805– , including early Baptist and Primitive Baptist items

Appalachian Ballad Collection, a research library of 340 books on British and American ballads and folksongs

Katharine Jackson French, 28 pages of ms Appalachian ballad texts collected ca. 1909

Gladys Jameson, 25 pages of ms choral arrangements of Appalachian ballads, hymn tunes, and other melodies collected ca. 1930

John F. Smith, 450 ms ballad and hymn texts documenting family singing by his students at the Foundation School, Berea, ca. 1910–30

James Watt Raine, collection of mountain speech patterns and song texts, 1906–35

—Alfred H. Perrin

523

WESTERN KENTUCKY UNIVERSITY   KyBgW

Bowling Green, Kentucky 42101

Kentucky Library

Songbooks, including hymnals of Baptists, Methodists, and other denominations, also tunebooks, folksongs, and Civil War songs, some published in Kentucky, in all 200 items, 1810s–

Sheet music, 1650 items and 47 bound vols., 19th and 20th centuries

Programs of local musical events, 7 linear cm., 1910s–30s; also 1 scrapbook of programs of Kentucky music clubs

Recordings, including 181 78-rpm discs, mostly popular music

St. Joseph Catholic Church, Bowling Green, 1 linear meter of music used in the Church

Franz Joseph Strahm (1867–1941, professor of music), ms music, including marches and school songs, 22 linear cm.; also published music and 6 letters, 1934–37

—Jeanette Farley

Kentucky Library—Manuscript Division

Music mss, including 21 19th-century Shaker hymnals from South Union, Ky., 8 of them in the Coke Collection; 3 anonymous music books from the Bluegrass area, ca. 1805–30; and a booklet of lyrics to published songs, compiled by Henry Kerr McGoodwin, with comments on their emotional effects, 1894

Will S. Hays (1837–1907, composer and author), 1045 items of personal papers, including lyrics, 175 sheet-music items, photographs, and a diary

David Morton (1886–1957, educator), ms diary "The Amateur Listener," with comments on music and musicians, 1952–55

Henry Clay Northcott (1851–1918, Methodist preacher), 1.9 linear meters of papers, including correspondence about opera in Boston, Cincinnati, and northern Kentucky, 1873–81

Cale Young Rice (1872–1943, poet), 80 items of papers, including correspondence, clippings, and music programs, 1916–35, also his typescript play *Yolanda of Cyprus*, performed as an opera, 1929

James Proctor Knott (1830–1911) collection, including 1 letter concerning a music festival in Bowling Green, 1912

Martha Allen Woods Potter (1868–1963, church organist), letters with references to musical activity in Bowling Green

Courtney M. Ellis (1888–1964), collection of materials concerning steamboats, with 1 tape recording of songs and *Delta Queen* (riverboat) calliope tunes, 1960s

—Pat Hodges

Folklore, Folklife, and Oral History Archives—Helms–Cravens Library

See the *Research Guide to Western Kentucky University Folk-lore and Folk-life Archive*, Academic Services Library Bulletin, 8 (Bowling Green, 1974)

Recordings of traditional music of Kentucky, including local performers of bluegrass, country music, and folksongs, oral-history interviews and transcriptions, and tapes of commercial disc recordings, among them the collection of Freeman Kitchens, in all 1600 tapes, indexed by performer, song title, geographical area, and subject, with a separate index of fiddle tunes

Field projects by University students and faculty, typescripts and ms notes of studies on local musical activ-

ities, instrument making, and folksong collecting, ca. 1960–

Folksong lyrics collection, including traditional ballads and songs of western Kentucky, collected by D. K. Wilgus, L. Montell, H. Halpert, and G. Boswell; indexed

—Robert Turek

524
HENDERSON SETTLEMENT SCHOOL
Frakes, Kentucky 40940

Materials concerning the musical history of the School, as cited by Virginia Anne Chambers, *Music in Four Kentucky Mountain Settlement Schools* (Ph.D. diss., University of Michigan, 1970)

525
KENTUCKY HISTORICAL SOCIETY   KyHi
200 Broadway
Frankfort, Kentucky 40601

Sheet music, 2400 items, including some Kentucky imprints, 1800s– , also hymnals from South Union, Ky.

—Ann McDonnell

526
SHAKERTOWN AT PLEASANT HILL, KENTUCKY
Route 4
Harrodsburg, Kentucky 40330

Manuscript music in Shaker letter notation, 1 sheet, early 19th century

—Ed Nichols

527
HOPKINSVILLE COMMUNITY COLLEGE
Library
North Drive
Hopkinsville, Kentucky 42240

Collection of popular music, 100 vols., ca. 1925– , including published piano-vocal and conductor's scores of Broadway musicals, collected editions of songs by Irving Berlin, George Gershwin, Jerome Kern, Cole Porter, and others, editions of traditional and folk music, and recordings of musicals on 3000 33⅓- rpm discs, many of them re-recordings

—Marjanna J. Frising

528
TRANSYLVANIA UNIVERSITY   KyLxT
Lexington, Kentucky 40508

Sheet music, 700 items, mostly 1860–1900, including works by Stephen Foster, 38 items autographed by Carrie Jacobs Bond, and several items from the 1820s

Songbooks, 2 vols. of popular songs, 1923 and 1928

Constantine S. Rafinesque, 1 ms sheet of music, ca. 1825

Mary Austin Holley (wife of the University president), letters on music in New Orleans and Texas, pre-1846; autograph copy of Wilhelm Iucho, "The Brazos Boat Glee," 1838; and a picture of Ole Bull presented to Mrs. Holley in 1845

Lexington Opera House programs, late 19th and early 20th centuries

Programs and archival records of University music groups, 1898–

—Hogan Trammell

529
UNIVERSITY OF KENTUCKY   KyU

M. I. King Library
Lexington, Kentucky 40506

Shaker ms songbooks and correspondence from Pleasant Hill, Ky., 19th century, on deposit

American Federation of Musicians, Local 11, Louisville, 35 vols. of papers, 1890–1960, also a list of officers, 1871–1960

Kentucky Music Educators' Association Collection, 5 boxes, including school programs, textbooks (1910s–40s), periodicals, and other materials relating to the history of music education in Kentucky, also with KMEA convention programs, All-State band, orchestra, and chorus programs, photographs, and workshop notebooks

University of Kentucky College of Arts and Sciences Collection, with 2 boxes of Department of Music materials, including concert notices and programs, 1930s–60s, brochures of the Department, 1919–59, and clippings and papers concerning high-school music festivals, 1926–48

University of Kentucky Sunday afternoon musicales, 4 vols. of programs, 1938–42

Handbill advertising music for sale by H. P. Hitchcock in Lexington, ca. 1840s, entitled "Select Catalogue of New Music"; also a broadside advertising Al G. Field & Co.'s Operatic Ministrels, n.d.

Sheet music, 7000 items, catalogued

Tunebooks and hymnals, 64 items, 1760s– , some of them published in Indiana, Kentucky, and Cincinnati, also reprint editions

—Adelle Dailey, Claire McCann

530
S. A. CISLER

Orbit Radio
Box 1644
Louisville, Kentucky 40201

Recordings of early radio programs and folksongs of the southern U.S., including 150 cylinders, 5000 78-rpm discs, 2000 16-inch transcription discs, 12,000 other discs, and 2000 tapes

531
FILSON CLUB   KyLoF

118 West Breckinridge Street
Louisville, Kentucky 40203

Mildred Hill (1859–1916), *Mermaid's Dance*, autograph ms orchestration and piano arrangement

Mary Newcomb, "Songs My Mother Sang," typescript with ms music and drawings, containing 210 Kentucky folksong and ballad texts and 101 transcribed tunes, collected 1926–29

Joseph Brown Smith (1823–59, first blind student to receive a degree from Harvard University, and later professor of music at the Kentucky School for the Blind, Louisville), materials including John H. Heywood, *Discourse on the Life and Character of Joseph Brown Smith* (Louisville, 1859), and correspondence of Mrs. Melville O. Briney, 1958

Programs of 8 concerts in Cincinnati and central Kentucky, 1866–87, in the Levassor Family papers

Young Ewing Allison (1878–1943, journalist and songwriter), personal papers, including extensive correspondence with James Whitcomb Riley, 2 items of correspondence with Albert Matthews concerning "Dixie," 1915, research notes and a ms of his study "Stephen Collins Foster and American Songs," 4 items of his published sheet music, a published score of Henry Waller's opera *The Mouse and the Garter* with words by Allison (1897), and a bibliography of his writings

William Frederick Norton (pseud. Daniel Quilp, owner and manager of the Amphitheatre Auditorium), autograph album, 1889–96, with autographs of musicians and actors who performed at his Auditorium

Champion Ingraham Hitchcock papers, including 6 items of correspondence, 1915–18, concerning Young Ewing Allison's poem "Fifteen Men on the Dead Man's Chest"

Kentucky Federation of Music Clubs archives, 1921–

"Classical Music in Early Kentucky under Louis H. Hast," a ms history of the period 1850–89, compiled in 1947 by Hast's daughter, Lisette Hast, and issued in an offset printing; also a notebook containing letters, clippings, and notes for the study

Songbooks, 10 19th-century items, including kindergarten and Sunday-school songbooks, war songs, and tunebooks; also 12 hymnals, 1821–96

Sheet music, 4000 items of 19th-century popular piano and vocal music

Programs of Louisville theaters and concert halls, 100 items, 1850–1970

—James R. Bentley, Martin F. Schmidt

532
LOUISVILLE ACADEMY OF MUSIC

Library
2740 Frankfort Avenue
Louisville, Kentucky 40206

Roy Harris, personal papers, including a ms of his Seventh Symphony in several versions; other ms and published music; a ms biography by Nicolas Slonimsky; and programs, brochures, letters, photographs, clippings, and disc and tape recordings of his works

Hattie Bishop Speed (Louisville pianist), personal papers, including programs of her local performances, ca. 1870–1930, and other Louisville programs, 1870–1942

Clippings and other miscellanea pertaining to 700 Louisville musicians, ca. 1850–

—Robert B. French

533

LOUISVILLE FREE PUBLIC LIBRARY   KyLo

Fourth and York Streets
Louisville, Kentucky 40203

Fine Arts Division

Hymnals, 40 items, ca. 1890–1940
Sheet music, 2100 mostly popular items, ca. 1890–1940; also 30 linear meters of printed scores and parts, mostly for piano, voice, chorus, or orchestra

—Tim Hellner

Audio-Visual Department

Phonograph and tape archives, containing 30,000 discs of music and 300,000 tapes including some of music, used on the Library's radio station, WFPK-FM

Kentucky Division

Scrapbooks of programs and clippings relating to music and theater in Louisville and in Kentucky, ca. 1873– , 8 linear meters, mostly compiled by the Library

—Mark Harris

534

SOUTHERN BAPTIST   KyLoS
THEOLOGICAL SEMINARY

Music Library
2825 Lexington Road
Louisville, Kentucky 40206

Hymnals, tunebooks, and gospel songbooks, 1450 items, ca. 1770–1940, including the Converse Hymnal Collection, also including Baptist publications, and 160 published books on hymnology
Scores and anthems, largely of sacred music, 30,000 items published ca. 1880– , including the Janet T. Ingersoll Gospel Music Collection
Recordings, 6800 discs and 3100 tapes

—Martha Powell

535

UNIVERSITY OF LOUISVILLE   KyLoU

Louisville, Kentucky 40208

Dwight Anderson Memorial Music Library
(2301 South Third Street)

Isidor Philipp (1863–1958, piano pedagogue) Archive and Memorial Library, established under the aegis of the American Liszt Society, with 100 catalogued items, 1880s–1950s, including pedagogical materials, original compositions, and editions by Philipp; also a collection of letters
Jean Thomas (the "Traipsin' Woman"), collection of eastern-Kentucky mountain folklore and Americana, 1898–1969, including 46 sound tapes and films, 25 folders of

correspondence, clippings, and other materials, and 29 items of memorabilia
Kentucky Composers collection, 6 shelf boxes of ms and published sheet music, some autographed, 1840– , including works by Claude Marion Almand (1915–57), Mildred J. Hill (1859–1916), Josephine McGill, Buddy Pepper, Zudie Harris Reinecke (d. 1924), Clifford Shaw, and Alicia Van Buren
Sheet music, 275 items of vocal or piano music published in Louisville by W. C. Peters, David P. Faulds, G. W. Brainard, and others, mostly 1840–1900; also 325 separate items and 184 bound vols. of early American piano or vocal music, the bound vols. also containing many Louisville imprints
Songbooks, mostly tunebooks, 72 items, 1830–1900
Dwight Anderson (music critic and dean of the School of Music), 7 scrapbooks of reviews for the Courier-Journal, 1945–62; also 6 vols. of Louisville and other U.S. programs, 1919–56, including 1 vol. of his piano programs with reviews
Letters of musicians, 1885– , in 2 albums
Louisville Orchestra archives, 1866– , including papers, scores, and recordings from the commissioning project
Hattie Bishop Speed collection, 21 vols. of programs for concerts at the Speed Music Room, Louisville, 1914–52; also 17 vols. of American and European concert programs, 1877–1926
Davison–Belknap collection of American and European concert programs, 16 vols., 1867–1926
University of Louisville Chamber Music Society, programs, 1938–
Photographs of local and international musicians, 3 albums, 1900–
Recordings, including 80 piano rolls

—Marion Korda

University Archives and Records Center
(Belknap Campus)

University of Louisville School of Music (1932–), papers, including 30 linear cm. of president's office records on the closing of the Louisville Conservatory of Music, the University's relationship with the Juilliard School of Music, the Recital Hall fund, résumés and appointment information, memorandums, and a history of the School of Music at the Gardencourt Campus, 1931–67; records of the dean of the School of Music, including 1.8 linear meters of personnel and biographical data, notices of appointment, correspondence, reports, programs, and publicity material, 1932–72; School of Music catalogues, 1932– ; School of Music faculty minutes, 1936–66, 1976– ; miscellaneous programs, journals, and publicity materials, 1950s–70s; and general files of clippings, photographs, faculty biographies, and faculty publications. See the WPA Kentucky Writer's Project, A Centennial History of the University of Louisville, American Guide Series (Louisville, 1939), and Mary Grace Money, A History of the Louisville Conservatory of Music and Music at the University of Louisville, 1907–1935 (Master's thesis, University of Louisville, 1976)
Louisville Orchestra (founded 1937), papers, 38 linear meters, 1934–71, including records of its predecessors, the Louisville Civic Arts Association and the Louisville Philharmonic Society, consisting of by-laws and articles of incorporation, correspondence 1935–

69, Board of Directors minutes, 1941–62, files on concert series, tours, and programs, 1937–75, financial records, 1934–71, and publicity releases and scrapbooks; also records of the commissioning and recording projects, including 124 commissioned scores by George Antheil, Elliot Carter, Aaron Copland, Lou Harrison, Alan Hovhaness, Ernst Krenek, Benjamin Lees, Walter Piston, Wallingford Riegger, Ned Rorem, William Schuman, Roger Sessions, Halsey Stevens, Ernst Toch, Chou Wen-Chung, and others

Louisville Conservatory of Music (fl. 1913–32), yearbooks for 1926–27

Oral-history interviews, 20 tape recordings of local musicians and patrons of the performing arts, documenting music history in Louisville; also 10 interviews by Robert S. Whitney with composers and performers, for a 1977 radio program on the history of the Louisville Orchestra

Programs of musical performances in Louisville, 1932–38, 21 items

—Sherrill McConnell

536
Glenn WILCOX
Box 649
Murray, Kentucky 42071

Collection of American tunebooks, hymnals, psalm books, and other printed books of music, 5000 items

Recordings, 2000 items, including 78-rpm discs

537
Leonard ROBERTS
Appalachian Studies Center
Pikeville College
Pikeville, Kentucky 41501

Folksong materials of the Kentucky Appalachian area, collected mostly 1950s by Roberts and his students at Pikeville College, including 100 tape recordings, transcripts of music and words, and related published materials

538
PINE MOUNTAIN SETTLEMENT SCHOOL
Pine Mountain, Kentucky 40810

Letters, notes, and other papers concerning folklore and folk music of the Pine Mountain area, 1910s– , including materials by or about folklorists and ballad collectors such as Richard Chase, Jean and Edna Ritchie, Cecil Sharp, and Evelyn Wells; also songs and songbooks used at the School

—Alvin Boggs

539
Alice LLOYD COLLEGE
Pippa Passes, Kentucky 41844

Field recordings of interviews with musicians and instrument makers, 1900– , taped during the 1970s (in the Appalachian Oral History Program)

Alice Lloyd (founder of the College), scrapbooks of materials relating to music in Kentucky-mountain settlement schools, 1902–10 (in the Archives)

—Ron Daley

540
EASTERN KENTUCKY UNIVERSITY   KyRE
Jonathan Truman Dorris Museum
Richmond, Kentucky 40475

Sheet music, in 1 bound vol., ca. 1845, and 4 early vocal anthologies

—Jane Munson

541
WASHINGTON COUNTY HISTORICAL SOCIETY
Simmstown
Springfield, Kentucky 40069

Sheet music, 2 bound vols. of popular music, 1860–1916

Frances R. Schultz (d. 1975, music teacher), papers and programs, also music mss copied by her mother

—Mrs. E. O. Kelly, Jr.

In addition to the repositories listed above, the following have also reported holdings of the materials indicated:

Edmonton—Metcalfe County Public Library: songbooks

Harrodsburg—Harrodsburg Historical Society: songbooks, miscellaneous

Henderson—Henderson Public Library: sheet music, songbooks

Lexington—Lexington Theological Seminary, Bosworth Memorial Library: songbooks

Lexington—Waveland State Shrine: sheet music, songbooks

Louisa—Lawrence County Library: songbooks, programs

Louisville—Bellarmine College, Library: sheet music, songbooks

Louisville—Locust Grove Historic Home Museum: sheet music, pictures, miscellaneous

Louisville—Museum of Natural History and Science: recordings

Manchester—Clay County Public Library: songbooks

Morehead—Morehead State University, Johnson Camden Library: songbooks, other printed music

Owensboro—Brescia College, Library: sheet music, songbooks, programs, pictures, miscellaneous

Owensboro—Kentucky Wesleyan College Library: songbooks, other printed music

Wilmore—Asbury College, Morrison–Kenyon Library: songbooks, other printed music, recordings

Wilmore—Asbury Theological Seminary, B. L. Fisher Library: songbooks

Louisiana

542

Catherine B. BLANCHET

Route 4, Box 397
Abbeville, Louisiana 70510

Field recordings of 300 Louisiana French songs sung by children, 1946–54, with 60 ms transcriptions, which were the basis for Blanchet's *Louisiana French Folksongs among Children in Vermillion Parish, 1942–1954* (Master's thesis, University of Southwestern Louisiana, 1970)

Sheet music, 300 popular items, 1905–39

543

LOUISIANA STATE LIBRARY   L

Box 131
Baton Rouge, Louisiana 70821

Popular, folk, and religious songbooks, 260 items, ca. 1900–1940, 10 of them from Louisiana

Sheet music, ca. 1920–50, 1500 mostly popular items, including 50 by Louisiana composers

—Blanche M. Cretini

544

LOUISIANA STATE UNIVERSITY   LU

Baton Rouge, Louisiana 70803

University Library

Sheet music, 1500 items, ca. 1800–1940, including bound vols. and special groups as follows: New Orleans imprints, 350 items in 7 boxes, mostly 1830s–40s; 3 vols. with mostly early New Orleans imprints, also "Mexican music" published by Junius Hart, 1890–91; the Himel family music collection, 458 items, ca. 1800–1931, in folders; piano music by L. M. Gottschalk, 1853–93, 20 items in 1 box, and 8 items in 1 vol.; works by Henri Fourrier, 1855–88, 19 items in 1 vol., also 5 vols. of religious music and 1 vol. of music by Benjamin Carr from Fourrier's library; Stephen Foster songs, 1851–56, 5 items in 1 vol.; minstrel songs, 1848–53, 61 items in 1 vol.; Civil War songs and marches, mostly published in Georgia, 1860–1901, 15 items in 1 vol.; ragtime, jazz, cakewalk, and two-step, 1877–1916, 13 items in 1 vol.; John Philip Sousa marches, 1889–99, 8 items in 1 vol.; Bromo-Seltzer songs, 1890s, 75 items in 1 vol.; military and patriotic songs, 1840–1931, 20 items in 1 vol.; piano and vocal music, 1842–59, 35 items in 1 vol.; piano music, 1846–1906, 48 items in 1 vol.; 126 miscellaneous items in 3 vols., 1884–1936; piano music, ca. 1870, 50 items in 2 vols. owned by Bessie Lamon; 75 19th-century items in 2 vols., owned by Kaite A. Porter; and miscellaneous 19th-century items in 4 vols.

Songbooks, 300 items, ca. 1831–1920, including hymnals and community and school songbooks

Published art music, 150 items, ca. 1880s–1920s, mostly vocal, with an emphasis on children's music of the 1920s

St. Louis Philharmonic Society, music library for the period 1832 (or earlier) to 1838, including opera scores and performance parts and 3 published instrumental works. Acquired in 1939 from the Hunleth Music Store of St. Louis, through the efforts of Henri Wehrmann (former violinist with the French Opera Company of New Orleans) and H. W. Stopher (former dean of the School of Music), the collection was previously stored by the Balmer & Weber music shop in St. Louis

LSU School of Music programs, 28 vols., 1915– , complete and bound, the early vols. including ms logs of faculty and student performances on and off campus; also other recital and concert programs

Scrapbooks of University opera productions, mid 1930s, sponsored by the Baton Rouge Grand Opera Committee, 3 items; also other archival scrapbooks, and School of Music scrapbooks

Catalogues of New Orleans music publishers, 1888– , and of player-piano music and violins, 7 items

Music periodicals, scattered issues of 4 titles, 1876–86

Instructional materials, including instrumental and vocal method books and music-theory texts, 100 items, 1860–1940

Libretti, 30 items, mostly published in Napoléonville and New Orleans, 1850s–60s

Vertical files on local music subjects, including clippings, reports, photographs, programs, and biographical files on musicians

Department of Archives and Manuscripts

Personal Papers of Musicians

Henri Fourrier (emigré French composer) and Joseph Amedee Fourrier (1853–1939, his son, born in Plaquemine, Iberville Parish, organist at St. Joseph Catholic Church, and director of the Fourrier Concert Band in Baton Rouge), papers, 1838–1915, 240 items and 2 ms. vols. of original compositions, arrangements, and copies. Included is a 1915 report on choir members. Index cards and a list of titles of the music, ca. 1967, are to be found in the personal papers of Prof. John G. Cale

Emmanuel Chol (French musician in Thibodaux, La.), 1231 items and 6 ms vols. of papers, 1845–1921, including ms and printed sheet music, pamphlets, publishers' and dealers' catalogues, broadside advertisements, correspondence, bills, and receipts, with an itemized list

Caralie Leblond (New Orleans pianist and composer), 3 ms vols., 1850s–60s, including original compositions, and works by other local composers

Joseph Ward (teacher in Baton Rouge), ms record book, 1894, with music and texts

John L. Peytavin (1859–1937, attorney, planter, and composer, of St. James Parish), papers, ca. 1900, including 30 programs, 2 bound vols. of sheet music, 10 original compositions, and musical references in correspondence

Lillie Trust Gray (music teacher at the Convent of the Sacred Heart, St. James Parish), papers, 1860–1920,

178 items and 8 vols., including bills for music purchased from the Philip Werlein Co. in New Orleans, receipt books, 1874–1902, and her diary, 1900–1905, with comments on Catholic liturgical and choral music

Kate Lee Ferguson (Mississippi novelist, poet, and composer), papers, 1857–1911, 38 items and 7 vols., with published and ms music including the operetta *A Tempest in a Tea Pot*

Louis Hasselmans (conductor at the Metropolitan Opera, New York, and the Opéra Comique, Paris, and professor of music at the University) Collection, 116 items and 4 printed vols., including photographs, programs, clippings, and personal papers from his career and that of his grandfather, Joseph Hasselmans (1814–1902, French theater-orchestra conductor)

Frank Crawford Page (professor of music and organist at the University), papers, 1923–72, 360 items and 10 ms vols., including correspondence, printed items, and lecture and research notes

Lloyd V. Funchess, oral-history interview, 1976, concerning music education in Louisiana in the 1930s, and his composition of the University "Alma Mater" song, ca. 1922

Other Personal Papers

Thomas Butler and Family Papers, mid 19th century, including ms and published music and music notebooks of John Thuer, music notebooks of family members, and 2 published sheet-music items

Charles Cior (b. Paris, 1814, New Orleans music teacher), ms theory method book in 2 vols., 1885

Nathaniel Evans Family Papers, including 2 bound vols. of sheet music, and 1 letter describing a band concert, 1892

Robert de Lapouyade (theatrical scenic artist) Collection, 1848–1936, 204 items and 11 vols., including correspondence and a scrapbook of press clippings, 1905–11, also theatrical photographs, programs, and scores

Henry D. Mandeville Family Papers, including letters with references to music performed at resorts in Arkansas and Virginia, 1840s–50s, performances in Natchez, Miss., and New Orleans, 1850s–60s, and in Chicago, 1870s–80s, and performances by Christy's Minstrels, 1850, and L. M. Gottschalk, 1853; also a diary with references to music education for children, 1848

Lemuel Parker Conner Family Papers, including 256 sheet-music items, 1824–83, a minstrel program, 1879, and other programs of Natchez concerts and recitals

Anton Reiff (musician with the Pyne and Harrison Opera Company), journal of a southeastern U.S. tour, 1856–57, with comments on theater facilities, concerts, and church music

John E. Uhler, Sr. (1891–1962, professor of English at the University), papers, 4848 items with 8 ms vols. and 394 printed vols., including materials for his research on Thomas Morley, also research materials and an unpublished ms biography of Pasquale Amato and correspondence with prominent musicians at the Metropolitan Opera

Edward Clifton Wharton Family Papers, including 8

music mss by family members and a program for a performance by Gottschalk, 1852

Michael D. Wynne Collection, including a minute and record book, bills, and receipts of the Mayer Brass Band of Opelousas, 1892–1909; 31 Civil War sheet-music items, published and in ms copy from published editions; and 5 published World War I sheet-music editions

Major Correspondence Files

August Girault (French emigré music professor in New Orleans), papers, 1808–45, 12 items of official documents and correspondence

Luther Field Tower (cotton broker), diary, 1845–46, with references to operatic and other musical performances in New Orleans

Louis Placide Canonge (poet and lyricist), 87 letters in the Leona Queyrouze Papers, and 75 letters, 1865–92, in the Henry Vignaud Papers

Adelina Patti, 15 letters, 1889–91, discussing her personal plans

J. G. Kilbourne family papers, including letters concerning piano repair, music teaching, and performances of a black band, 1890–92

Grace King, papers, including letters mentioning performances in New Orleans, New York, and Europe, ca. 1900

Henry Wallace Stopher (University music administrator), papers, 1882–1944, 313 items and 11 ms vols., also a notebook containing a list of Louisiana composers and their published works

Other Letters

Frederick F. Miller, letter, ca. 1840, concerning New Orleans music and his conducting activity

Materials concerning Jenny Lind concerts, 1851, including reactions in an anonymous letter from Alexandria, Rapides Parish; in a letter in the John A. Quitman and Family Papers; and in a letter in the Benjamin Tureaud Papers

Elijah Dunbar (Massachusetts native, employee of a New Orleans music dealer), 3 letters, 1851, commenting on church music, concerts, and Jenny Lind

Lizzie Randall, 1851 letter concerning her visit to New Orleans, with comments on Jenny Lind, Rosa Devries, and the French Opera

Materials concerning Thomas B. ("Blind Tom") Bethune concerts, including comments in an anonymous letter from Trenton, N.J., 1867, and in a letter in the papers of Sen. Donelson Caffery, 1883

Alfred Mapleson, 3 letters, 1891, concerning Giulia Valda Cameron ("Madame Valda")

Edwin L. Stephens, 6 letters, 1902–3, concerning a concert by William Hayden (blind musician)

Receipts for purchases of musical instruments, and 1 letter concerning the circus, 1821, in the David Weeks and Family Papers

Organizational Materials

Philharmonic Society of Thibodaux, constitution and minute book, 1861, in the H. Dansereau collection

Philharmonic Society of Vicksburg, Miss., programs and letters, 1869, in the Eggelston–Roach papers

New Orleans Conservatory of Music, prospectus, n.d., in the Robert Ormond Butler Papers

French Opera Association, Ltd., certificate for 1 share of capital stock, 1910

University Music School class registers, 1917–30, 96 vols.

New Orleans Grand Opera Company, checkbook, 1919–20, 1 ms vol.

WPA Federal Music Project, Louisiana State-Wide Music Project, 1940 annual report

Manuscript Music

Eddie Moore (New Orleans mulatto, a music student in Stuttgart), microfilm of his ms "Mazurka d'Encore," 1893

Edward Gabrielli, ms "Washington Artillery Triumphal March," n.d., in the William Miller and Allison Owen Papers

Margaret G. Kilbourne Breedlove, ms music, n.d., in the J. G. Kilbourne family papers

Sheet Music

General collection, 53 items and 2 vols. composed or sold in Baton Rouge and New Orleans, 1826–1912, including European and American vocal or piano music

Bartholomew Barrow (sugar planter and politician of Pointe Coupée Parish), collection, 1848–1901, 4 separate items and 3 bound vols. containing ca. 120 vocal and piano items, including Confederate and New Orleans imprints

Ellen M. Cox, 1 bound vol., 1850s, the items published mostly in Paris and purchased from New Orleans dealers

Himel family sheet music, 1870–1913, 48 items, some in hand-sewn vols.

Leona Queyrouze, papers, including 11 bound vols., 1885–98

William T. Johnson and Family Memorial Collection, including 5 bound vols. and single sheets

Miscellaneous single items or small groups, including 1 item, 1845, in the Eleanor Percy and Catherine Ann Ware papers; 1 item, 1854, in the New Orleans Municipal Records—Fire Protection; 1 item, of P. G. T. Beauregard, 1861; "Kingdom Coming," songsheet, ca. 1862; 1 item of Edward O. Eaton–Charles Lever, 1864; 9 items, including songs by Regina Morphy Voitier, in the Percy Ferguson papers; 7 items, late 19th century, in the Baughman family collection; 4 presidential campaign songs, 1876–84; 1 E. T. Paull item, 1898; 1 Alice Webb item, 1904; 1 University item, 1910; 2 items, 1910–18, in the William W. Garig papers; 1 item, 1918, in the Historical Society of East and West Baton Rouge collection; 1 item, 1935, in the Huey P. Long papers; and 1 item, n.d., in the Donelson Caffery papers

Scrapbooks

Anonymous poetry scrapbooks, 1833–83, 2 vols., including election-campaign and Confederate song texts

Hubert Rolling (1823–98, New Orleans pianist, composer, and teacher), 1 scrapbook and 14 separate items, including programs, clippings, and Gottschalk letters

Edward Everett, scrapbook, 1893–1916, with programs and announcements from northern and eastern U.S. cities

New Orleans opera-theater scrapbook, 1899–1937, 8 items and 1 vol. with programs

Estelle Hayden theater scrapbooks, 1899–1949, 12 vols. of New York programs and pictures

Mildred Orkney Wurtele, scrapbook, 1910–12, with programs, clippings, and pictures from Chicago and New Orleans, and ms commentary

Pasquale Amato (operatic baritone), scrapbook, 1913–29, 26 items and 1 vol., with pictures, clippings, and other items

Programs

Baton Rouge Sacred Music Society, program of the first concert, 1845

Programs of New Orleans musical and theatrical performances, 1875–1924, in the William W. King family papers

Adelina Patti, concert program, Los Angeles, 1887, in the George Lanaux family papers

New Orleans Grand Opera House, 2 programs, 1901–2, in the W. Frank Witherell papers

New York theater programs, 161 items and 1 vol., 1916–25, including opera and nightclub programs and handbills

Program for a production of *The James Boys in Missouri*, Thibodaux, n.d., in the Joseph P. Horner Collection

Miscellaneous musical programs in the papers of Norbert Badin (free black planter of Melrose, Natchitoches Parish), n.d. (ca. 1900?)

Playbill for Callender's Georgia Minstrels, n.d.

WPA programs, 1938

Miscellaneous Items

Revolutionary War broadsides, 5 items, in the Richard T. Ely Memorial Collection

Civil War and mid-19th-century broadsides, 8 items, in the Lyrics Collection

"We Are for the Union," Civil War broadside

"Skidmore Guard" (Ed Harrigan?), broadside of a New York black military unit, ca. 1863

Music journal collection, 1876–99, 34 items, including issues of *The Music Record* (Boston), *The Song Journal* (Detroit, 1876–77), and *The Musical Visitor* (Cincinnati, 1883)

Thomas ("Blind Tom") Bethune, 1903 clipping, in the Sylvester L. Cary scrapbook

New Orleans Opera Company, 5 subscription tickets for the 1919–20 season

—Barbara Jean Meades, Margaret Dalrymple

545

CENTER FOR ACADIAN AND CREOLE FOLKLORE   (LLafS)

University of Southwestern Louisiana
Lafayette, Louisiana 70504

Joseph Carriere collection of ballads, folksongs, and instrumental music of French-speaking Louisiana, collected on 100 wax cylinders, 1930s

Field recordings of songs (many transcribed), instrumental music, and interviews (transcribed) with fiddle and accordion players, ballad singers, and other musicians, in all 300 hours of tape, collected mostly 1974– , but also including collections by Corinne Saucier, 1930s, Harry Oster, 1950s, and Ralph Rinzler, 1960s

Recordings on LP and 78-rpm discs, also tape copies of
78-rpm discs, including nearly the entire RCA Bluebird
label series of Louisiana French music
Discography of all recorded Acadian and Creole music
from Louisiana
Other materials, including slides and photographs of
musicians, clippings, and biographical information
—Barry Ancelet

546
Ernest FERRATA
123 Sierra Place
Metairie, Louisiana 70001

Giuseppe Ferrata (1865–1928, composer and pianist),
published and ms compositions including 3 ms
operas, also letters and other papers

547
Walter S. JENKINS
400 Dorrington Boulevard
Metairie, Louisiana 70005

Amy Cheney (Mrs. H. H. A.) Beach, personal papers,
including diaries, mss, press clippings, incoming correspondence, programs, and photographs

548
MUSEUM CONTENTS, Inc.
Box 37
Natchitoches, Louisiana 71457

Manuscript flute music, composed or copied by a local
musician, identified as "Breda," 1 bound vol., ca. 1830
Sheet music, ca. 1820–70, 500 items and 8 bound vols.,
including several works written locally, ca. 1850
—Robert B. DeBlieux

549
John H. BARON
4527 South Tonti Street
New Orleans, Louisiana 70125

Julius Singer (1878–1934, grandfather of Baron, and
violinist with the Cincinnati and Buffalo symphony
orchestras, 1906–34), personal papers, including correspondence, documents, diary, programs, photographs, and scrapbooks
Joshua Heschel Singer (1848–1925, father of Julius Singer, and cantor of the Pine Street Synagogue, Buffalo,
N.Y., 1888–1925), books, photographs, and other
documents
Other family correspondence, 1910– , including numerous letters to and from the Menuhin family in San
Francisco
Sheet music, 1 bound vol. with 19th-century American
piano music, including New Orleans imprints
John Alden Carpenter, letter to Mrs. Alfonso Del Marmol, dated 1923, concerning his songs
Ursuline Convent, New Orleans, de-accessioned music
books, 2 items, including a *Vesperal Romain* (Quebec,
1886)

550
Raymond BARROIS
2711 Ursulines Avenue
New Orleans, Louisiana 70119

Jazz recordings, 1920–40s

551
Jack BELSOM
721 Barracks Street
New Orleans, Louisiana 70116

Materials relating to New Orleans, from the 19th century to the present (Belsom is archivist of the New
Orleans Opera Association), including programs and
playbills, particularly of opera but also of concerts
and recitals

552
CHRIST CHURCH CATHEDRAL
2919 Saint Charles Avenue
New Orleans, Louisiana 70115

Florian Schaffter (1850–1921, organist of Christ Church
at various times, 1872–1919), original church music
Ferdinand Dunkley (1869–1926, sometime organist at
Christ Church), original church music

553
Mrs. Pierre CLEMENCEAU
465 Lowerline Street
New Orleans, Louisiana 70118

Scrapbook compiled by Mrs. Clemenceau's father,
Benedict Grunewald, and her grandfather, Louis
Grunewald, with clippings concerning the history of
the Grunewald music-publishing and retailing firm in
New Orleans, 1880s–1940s, also including information on Louis Eckert and other employees, and on
concerts sponsored by the Grunewalds, ca. 1900–
1920s
Family photograph albums, including pictures of
famous musicians shown with members of the
Grunewald family

554
Vaughn L. GLASGOW
Louisiana State Museum
751 Chartres Street
New Orleans, Louisiana 70116

Sheet-music collection, including 60 Louisiana imprints,
1845–1920; 700 European illustrated covers, many
with U.S. dealers' stamps; and 200 U.S. illustrated
covers, 1845–1930s

555
HISTORIC NEW ORLEANS COLLECTION
533 Royal Street
New Orleans, Louisiana 70130

Louis Moreau Gottschalk Collection, 358 items, including 2 Gottschalk letters, 1842, 1869; correspondence between William L. Hawes and Clara Gottschalk Peterson concerning Gottschalk editions and memorabilia, and to Hawes from Philip Hale, William A. Pond & Co., Louis G. Gottschalk, Biglow & Main Co., and others, 1895–1909; 4 music mss, including *Manchega* and *Scherzo Romantique* autographs and Mrs. Peterson's *Ou Som Souroucou*; published sheet music by Gottschalk (87 items), Mrs. Peterson (6 items), and W. J. Francis (1 item); and Gottschalk memorabilia

Euphemie Aimée Lambert, 2 bound vols. of unattributed ms music for piano, copied in Louisiana, 1850s

Piano-music album, *La Louisianaise* (Paris: F. Pleyel; New Orleans: Emile Johns, 1837), with the imprint of Johns, the first music publisher in New Orleans

William Couret music collection, 89 published or ms items of piano or vocal sheet music, 1880–1914

Sheet music with New Orleans imprints, 1838– , 524 items, composed by Theodore von La Hache, Basile Bares, Brinley Richards, Auguste Davis, Harry McCarthy, J. C. Viereck, Gottschalk, and others, and published by Charles Horst, Philip Werlein, A. E. Blackmar, S. Chassaignac, A. Elie, Louis Grunewald, Junius Hart, William T. Mayo, Henri Wehrmann, and others; indexed by title, composer, and publisher

Confederate sheet music, 31 items, mostly published by A. E. Blackmar in New Orleans before the occupation in 1862

Sheet music published in the South, including occupied New Orleans, 1860–65, 76 items

Libretti of operas, mostly performed at the French Opera House in New Orleans, as published in Napoléonville; also programs of the French Opera House, 1888–1920

Programs, 350 items of theater, opera, and concert performances at the Grand Opera House, 1889–1900; complete seasons of Le Petite Théâtre du Vieux Carré, 1920– ; and other 20th-century performances

—Susan Cole

556

LOUISIANA STATE MUSEUM   L-M

751 Chartres Street
New Orleans, Louisiana 70116

Louisiana Historical Center

Sheet music, 5000 items being arranged, with composer, title, and publisher indexes, particularly strong in imprints of Willig and Fiot in Philadelphia, and Blackmar, Grunewald, Mayo, and Wehrmann in New Orleans

Concert and opera programs, mostly for New Orleans performances, 1 linear meter

Music ms copy books, including pre-Civil War vols. prepared by students at the Ursuline Convent

Painting and Graphic Arts Collection

Photographs, 60,000 items, including a few of musical interest, notably a daguerreotype of a young black musician, ca. 1850, and a picture of Louis Armstrong on a steamboat, ca. 1916

New Orleans Jazz Club Collection

Photographs, 10,000 items relating to jazz, arranged alphabetically by musician, subdivided chronologically

Sheet music, 1000 items, 1850s–1950s

Recordings, including 2 cylinders, 7000 78-rpm discs, 1917– , and 20 piano rolls

Miscellaneous letters, post cards, printed ephemera, and other documents, 500 items

—Vaughn L. Glasgow

557

Bill C. MALONE

History Department
Tulane University
New Orleans, Louisiana 70118

Research collection supporting writings and publications on country music, gospel music, and southern and rural hymnody. Materials include taped and transcribed interviews, correspondence, songbooks, sheet music, hymnals, song folios, and periodicals

Henry Kmen, research notes on music in New Orleans, drawn from newspapers, travel accounts, and other sources, in 15 file boxes; also published materials

558

MUSICIANS' MUTUAL PROTECTIVE UNION, LOCAL 174–496

2401 Esplanade Avenue
New Orleans, Louisiana 70119

Although the files for Local 496 (black) do not predate the merger in 1969, the minutes and records for Local 174 (white) are preserved back to the 1920s, and are accessible for special consultation through the offices of Bernie Winstein or John Scheuermann at the above address

559

NEW ORLEANS BAPTIST   LNB
THEOLOGICAL SEMINARY

Martin Music Library
3939 Gentilly Boulevard
New Orleans, Louisiana 70126

Edmond D. Keith Collection, 3000 published hymnals and psalm books, particularly rich in Baptist and gospel hymnody, also including 50 early 19th-century tunebooks

Anthems, 3500 published items

Music scores, hymnals, and psalm books, 7200 items. See Ann Hayes Daniel, *The Sellers–Martin Hymnal Collection: A Source for the History of Gospel Hymnody* (Master's thesis, 1970)

Ernest O. Sellers (Seminary faculty member), ms hymn texts, early 20th century

Recordings, including 10 78-rpm discs

—Harry Eskew, Paul Gericke

560

NEW ORLEANS PHILHARMONIC SYMPHONY ORCHESTRA

Maritime Building
203 Carondelet Street
New Orleans, Louisiana 70130

Programs for non-subscription concerts, 3000 items. (The subscription-concert programs are in the New Orleans Public Library.)

Mike Caplan (last surviving member of the French Opera Orchestra, before 1919, and trumpet player in the Philharmonic from its founding in 1936 to ca. 1970), personal papers, including correspondence, programs, and press clippings

Archival records of the Orchestra, including correspondence, minutes of board meetings, office memoranda, and photographs, in storage. For general background see Cintra Shober Austin, *The History of the New Orleans Philharmonic Symphony to 1942* (M.A. thesis, University of New Orleans, 1972), and Elizabeth Jane Vallas, *The Philharmonic Society of New Orleans, 1906–1947* (M.A. thesis, Tulane University, 1948), the latter with extensive bibliography, pp. 163–86, relating to this women's concert-sponsorship group

561

NEW ORLEANS PUBLIC LIBRARY   LN

219 Loyola Avenue
New Orleans, Louisiana 70140

All items are in the Art, Music, and Recreation Division, unless otherwise noted

Theodor Von La Hache (1823–67), ms "Grand Etude de Salon" for piano

Historical Sheet Music Collection, ca. 1865–1900, 453 separate items and 160 bound vols., including works of Von La Hache and other New Orleans and southern composers or publishers

Concert programs of New Orleans, 1839–1923, 5 vols. collected by the WPA (in the Louisiana Division)

New Orleans Municipal Auditorium, scrapbook and rental fee book, ca. 1925–65 (in the Louisiana Division)

Libretti for operas performed in New Orleans theaters during the 19th century

Published music, including hymnals, songbooks, and scores, 19th and 20th centuries

Photographs of singers, pianists, jazz musicians, and Mardi Gras events

Fischer Collection of Early Vocal Recordings, 2500 78-rpm discs

"Louisiana News Index" of early New Orleans newspapers, including music subjects (in the Louisiana Division)

—Marilyn Wilkins

562

Louis PANZERI

1030 Saint Philip Street
New Orleans, Louisiana 70116

Other items in the Panzeri collection have been donated to the University of New Orleans Library, q.v.

Opera scores, including some used in New Orleans productions, and sheet music, 50 items, ca. 1860–

563

George REINECKE

1548 Leda Court
New Orleans, Louisiana 70119

Recordings of French music of Louisiana, 250 78-rpm discs or tapes, with New Orleans-area colonial French folksongs, Acadian folksongs, and Creole folksongs, collected by Corinne Saucier, Louise Olivier, and George Reinecke, 1948–70; also ms transcriptions of folksongs and piano arrangements

564

Al ROSE

3135 Bell Street
New Orleans, Louisiana 70119

Sheet music, including 1200 ragtime editions, 750 New Orleans imprints, and 500 miscellaneous items, arranged by year

Photographs of jazz musicians and subjects, 2000 items, in addition to materials in the Hogan Jazz Archive, Tulane University (q.v.), used in *New Orleans Jazz: A Family Album* (Baton Rouge, 1967)

Original documents relating to the jazz concert at Mercantile Hall, Philadelphia, sponsored by the American Newspaper Guild, 1936

Correspondence with jazz and popular musicians, 1930s, among them Eubie Blake, Perry Bradford, and W. C. Handy

565

Diana ROSE

3135 Bell Street
New Orleans, Louisiana 70119

Sheet music, 1000 items, ca. 1860– , specializing in Civil War music and illustrated covers, the latter emphasizing E. T. Paull illustrations and pictures of bluebirds and of roses; also several published silent-film folios

566

TEMPLE SINAI

6222 Saint Charles Avenue
New Orleans, Louisiana 70118

Henry Jacobs (1907–64, organist and choir director at Temple Sinai, 1939–64), original works in holograph, and 70 linear cm. of printed editions for use in services

567

TRINITY EPISCOPAL CHURCH

1329 Jackson Avenue
New Orleans, Louisiana 70130

Ferdinand Schaffter, mss, probably holograph, of 2 settings of the *Te Deum*
Music used by the church choir, ca. 1900, 60 items
—Thomas Rushing

568
TULANE UNIVERSITY   LNT
New Orleans, Louisiana 70118

A. *Maxwell Music Library*
B. *William Ransom Hogan Jazz Archive (in the Howard–Tilton Memorial Library)*
C. *Other Materials in the Special Collections Division, Howard–Tilton Memorial Library*

A. Maxwell Music Library

Includes materials presented and collected by the founder, Leon R. Maxwell (1882–1956, chairman of the University Music Department)

Sheet music, 14,000 items, including 19 miscellaneous bound vols.; 300 items, ca. 1860–1930, mostly the gift of Anna Ludwig Drysdale (New Orleans singer); 2500 items, mostly U.S. imprints, from the Maxwell collection; and other materials, 8000 unbound items and 62 bound vols., estimated to contain one-third each from the periods 1830–1900, 1901–20, and 1921–40, and one-fourth with New Orleans imprints or otherwise associated with New Orleans
Music editions, including materials from the collections of Prof. Maxwell; Giuseppe Ferrata (1865–1928, professor of music at the University), including 43 editions of his own music; Violet Hart (local singer and benefactor), mostly vocal music; and Henry Wehrmann (1870–1956, violinist in the French Opera House to 1919, and son of Henri Wehrmann, local music printer), 300 chamber-music and string editions from the standard repertory
Tunebooks, 23 items, including 8 pre-1801 editions and 5 Joseph Funk collections
Opera libretti, 10 boxes, mostly pre-1919, from the French Opera House, arranged by title
Programs, 50 items, mostly local, not arranged
Anni Frind-Sperling, 2 scrapbooks of pictures, press clippings, and a list of roles relating to her singing career in Europe, pre-1940, and her later teaching career in New Orleans
Leon R. Maxwell, personal workbooks, with teaching notes, bibliographical lists, and scholarly translations
—Liselotte Andersson

B. William Ransom Hogan Jazz Archive (in the Howard–Tilton Memorial Library)

Founded in 1958 in honor of Hogan (1908–71, professor of history, with William Russell as first curator, the Archive is housed in the Howard–Tilton Memorial Library. See the Archive's brochure, 8 pages, also Richard B. Allen, "The Archive of New Orleans Jazz," *Yearbook for Inter-American Musical Research*, 3 (1967), 141–47; "New Orleans Jazz Archive at Tulane," *Wilson Library Bulletin*, 40 (1966), 619–23; and discussions of the Archive in such books as Whitney Balliet, *Such Sweet Thunder* (Indianapolis, 1966); William J. Schaefer, *Brass Bands and New Orleans Jazz* (Baton Rouge, 1977); and Donald M. Marquis, *The Buddy Bolden Story* (Baton Rouge, 1978)

Recordings, 23,000 items, including 21,000 78-rpm discs, 24 cylinders, and 59 piano rolls; also tape recordings, including 1466 reels of interviews and 783 reels of music, many of the latter acquired with the assistance of the American Federation of Musicians, 20 from Herbert O. Otto
Motion pictures, 32 reels of film, and 3 video tapes
Sheet music, 13,000 items, including the collection of John Robichaux comprising the music later arranged for his society jazz band
Archival materials, 27,000 items, including the collections of Dominic James ("Nick") LaRocca (1889–1961, member of the Original Dixieland Jazz Band), 2644 items, among them scrapbooks, clippings, correspondence, sheet music, and advertisements; Robert Greenwood, 240 items, also 105 photographs; and Al Rose, 2083 items, also 522 photographs. In all there are 6000 photographs (including items mentioned above) and 18,000 other miscellaneous notes, clippings, and posters
Reference materials, 12,000 items, including 1300 books, 10,500 issues of serials, and 284 recording-company catalogues
—Richard B. Allen

C. Other Materials in the Special Collections Division, Howard–Tilton Memorial Library

Harry Brunswick Loeb (1884–1957), personal papers, 1911–56, 176 items, including correspondence with Leopold Godowsky, Joseph Hofmann, Mischa Elman, Harold Bauer, and others; photographs of famous musical friends; original song texts and prose works, many of the latter relating to opera, also a history of the opera in New Orleans; concert programs; and sheet music of his songs
Leon R. Maxwell, personal papers, 1181 items, including letters, papers, programs, scrapbooks, and journals of Maxwell and his wife, Ruth Nottage Maxwell, relating mostly to music in New Orleans and at Tulane University, also to the Music Teachers' National Association
Music mss, including George Washington Cable, 47 holographs, mostly 1920s?, in 1 bound vol.; Eugene Chassaignac, 80 holographs, ca. 1867–73; and Philip P. Werlein, "Life's Best Dream; or, Woodville Galopade," 1843
Correspondence, including Henry Edward Krehbiel, 2 letters to Lafcadio Hearn, dated Cincinnati, 1878, as cited in Ann S. Gwyn, *Lafcadio Hearn, a Catalogue of the Collection . . . at Tulane University* (New Orleans, 1977), p. 54; Willie Pape (Mobile, Ala., performer), letters to Master Freddy Hartel of Grunewald's Music Store, dated London, 1863–68; and Samuel Snaer (Louisiana music publisher), letter to M. Mazet, ca. 1880
Theses and studies on New Orleans music, including Gaston Rondeau, ledger listing the members of the French Opera company, 1859–1900, and related memorabilia; and Virginia Westbrooke, "Old New Orleans and the Opera" (typescript history)
Armand Edward Blackmar, typescript memoir by his granddaughter, Dorothy Blackmar, 1972
New Orleans Sheet Music Collection, 3350 items, 1830s–ca. 1910, mostly piano music by Louisiana composers, from the Howard Library collection, with a card catalogue for composers and titles

Louisiana Historical Association, sheet music, 205 items, 1838–1933, including 126 Confederate imprints, 17 of them not cited in *Crandall;* 9 Union items; and other sheet music mostly on local topics, 42 items dated 1865–1930, mostly pre-1900

Additional sheet music, including 7 bound vols. of Civil War publications, mostly New Orleans imprints; August Davis, 1 bound vol. with music, 1851–76, including Davis's compositions and other New Orleans publications; Sarah E. Archer, 1 bound vol. with music, 1854–90, mostly New Orleans imprints; and Eleanor P. Thompson, 8 sheet-music items, late 19th century (?)

Rosamonde E. and Emile Kuntz, New Orleans history collection, including Louis Moreau Gottschalk memorabilia, 1853–65, 6 items; 50 opera programs, 1866–1924, and bound vols. of programs of the French Opera House, 1905–8; and 5 libretti published in Napoléonville, 1858–61, also others published in New Orleans. See Guillermo Nuñez Falcon, *The Kuntz Collection: A Catalogue* (New Orleans, 1979)

Other programs of New Orleans musical events, 9 items, 1876–1917, in the Eleanor P. Thompson collection and elsewhere

—Daniel R. Todd

569
UNIVERSITY OF NEW ORLEANS   LNU
Earl K. Long Library
Lake Front
New Orleans, Louisiana 70122

Sheet music for solo piano or piano ensemble, organ, solo voice, or choir, 5 linear meters, ca. 1860–1900, also 30 piano-vocal scores used at the French Opera House in New Orleans, ca. 1830–1920, donated by Louis Panzeri

—Beth Barrett

570
Nancy C. VAN DEN AKKER
6230 Saint Anthony Avenue
New Orleans, Louisiana 70122

Hymnals and songbooks, 175 items, 1880– , mostly 1900–1930s, largely Roman Catholic and gospel vols.

571
WERLEIN'S FOR MUSIC
605 Canal Street
New Orleans, Louisiana 70112

Scrapbooks, 8 vols., including clippings, advertisements, and programs for musical events and concerts underwritten by the Werlein firm, ca. 1890–

Printed music, mostly file copies of editions published by Werlein, including the first edition of "Dixie"

572
XAVIER UNIVERSITY OF LOUISIANA   LNX
7325 Palmetto Street
New Orleans, Louisiana 70125

Daybooks, 1829 and 1872, containing songs and other ms music, as cited in *HRS*

573
LOUISIANA COLLEGE   LPiL
Richard W. Norton Memorial Library
Pineville, Louisiana 71360

Robert Hunter MacGimsey (1898–1979, composer, Louisiana folksong collector, and professional whistler), personal papers, including field recordings and transcripts of black spirituals, other research and personal papers, and scrapbooks, mostly 1930s–40s, acquired through the auspices of the Historical Association of Central Louisiana, Alexandria

—Landrum Salley

574
Norman Z. FISHER
First Presbyterian Church
900 Jordan Street
Shreveport, Louisiana 71101

Hymnals, 125 items, 1800– , including materials in German, Welsh, and Japanese; organ and piano music, 1875– ; and Eugene Mayer, *The Organist's Journal and Review*, 1874–77

575
NICHOLLS STATE UNIVERSITY   LTF
Leonidas Polk Library
Division of Archives
Thibodaux, Louisiana 70301

Manuscript materials relating to south-central Louisiana, as cited in *NHPRC*, p. 233, are partly in the Maude Billin Collection, including 25 published items, 1860s–1930s

—Philip D. Uzee

In addition to the repositories listed above, the following have also reported holdings of the materials indicated:

Lake Charles—Imperial Calcasieu Museum: sheet music, songbooks, other printed music

Metairie—Jefferson Parish Library: songbooks

Natchitoches—Northwestern State University, Watson Library: sheet music, songbooks, miscellaneous

New Orleans—Gallier House: sheet music

New Orleans—Preservation Hall: sheet music, songbooks, other printed music, programs, catalogues, pictures, recordings, miscellaneous

Ruston—Louisiana Technological University, Prescott Memorial Library: sheet music, songbooks, programs, miscellaneous

Thibodaux—La Fourche Parish Library: songbooks, pictures

Maine

576
MAINE STATE LIBRARY — Me
Cultural Building
Augusta, Maine 04330

Robert Browne Hall (1858–1907), ms music, correspondence, pictures of his band, programs, a biography, and other items in 10 folders, compiled by Ralph T. Gould for his article, "R. B. Hall: Maine Music Man," *Down East* (Oct. 1967)
Samuel Thurston, "Musical Reminiscences of Seventy-five Years" (typescript, 1911)
Kotzschmar Club, Portland, papers, 1920–58, 1 vol.
Sheet music of Maine composers, 125 linear cm. comprising 1000 works, some in ms
Programs, including items of the Augusta Opera House, 1905–11; various music clubs in Maine, 1920–63; Eastern Music Camp, Sidney, 1931–32; New England Music Camp, 1938–50; and souvenir programs of the Maine Music Festival, 1897–1926, indexed, with a list of Maine music performed at the Festivals, 1897–1920, in 3 notebooks
Libretto for the opera *Pepita* (Augusta, 1883)
Hymnals, 2 items published in Maine, 1807 and 1817
Books on music in Maine and on music pedagogy, 1854– , 20 items

—Shirley M. Thayer

577
MAINE STATE MUSEUM — MeAMM
State House Complex
Augusta, Maine 04330

Sheet music, 200 items, including popular dances, ca. 1845–55, and popular songs, 1900–1930
Songbooks, including 4 temperance items published by the National Temperance Society, New York, ca. 1850–88; 4 hymnals, ca. 1796–1855; and 2 seminary songbooks published in Boston, 1854–55
Programs of the Maine Music Festival, 1912
Dyer and Hughes Co. (organ dealer in Dover-Foxcroft), 3 music catalogues, also trade cards, mid 19th century
Photographs, including the Cherryfield Marching Band, ca. 1870; a family of musicians, ca. 1890; the Gardiner Drum Corps, 19th century; and the Dyer and Hughes factory and products, 11 items, n.d.

—Susan Ostroff

578
BANGOR HISTORICAL SOCIETY — MeBaHi
159 Union Street
Bangor, Maine 04401

Music relating to early local and regional events, as cited in *NHPRC*, p. 235

579
BAR HARBOR HISTORICAL SOCIETY
34 Mount Desert Street
Bar Harbor, Maine 04069

David L. Carver, 1 sheet-music item composed for the opening of the Kebo Valley Golf Club, 1896
Bar Harbor Choral Society, constitution, 1903; Building of Arts Association (local choral society), ledger, and 1 scrapbook of papers, press releases, and programs, 1907–36; and programs of the Bar Harbor Choral Society and the Building of Arts Association, 50 items, 1902–39
Photographs of local bands, choral groups, and musicians, 19 items, 1883–1940

—Gladys O'Neil

580
BELFAST MUSEUM
66 Church Street
Belfast, Maine 04915

Gladys Pitcher (composer), scrapbooks of musical memorabilia, including business cards from her father's piano business, n.d.
Maine Music Festival programs, 1897–1900; also posters for organ concerts
Photographs of local musicians, late 19th and early 20th centuries

—Andrew Kuby

581
BETHEL HISTORICAL SOCIETY
Box 12
Bethel, Maine 04217

William Rogers Chapman (1855–1935, conductor), materials including 30 vols. of popular sheet music and 6 popular songbooks, ca. 1900; 25 photographs of him and his performance groups; and papers of the Rubinstein Club (choral group formed by Chapman in New York City), 9 linear cm., ca. 1911
Programs of concerts in New England, 30 items, 1897–1901

—Stanley R. Howe

582
Jon F. HALL
Box 26
Bingham, Maine 04920

Manuscript tunebook, 66 pages, mostly of country fiddle music, including waltzes, polkas, hornpipes, cotillions, and other dances, compiled in Maine, ca. 1870–90

583

KNEISEL HALL

Blue Hill, Maine 04614

Franz Kneisel (1865–1926, violinist), materials including published chamber music of Johannes Brahms with the composer's markings, and an autographed picture of Brahms; leather-bound chamber music owned by Gustav Schirmer; programs, photographs, and scrapbooks of reviews (1885–1917) of the Kneisel Quartet; and correspondence and memorabilia of Kneisel

—Ruth B. Kneisel

584

Miriam BARNDT-WEBB

153-A Park Row
Brunswick, Maine 04011

Secular and sacred tunebooks, 30 19th-century editions; also 300 sheet-music items, 1820s–60s

585

BOWDOIN COLLEGE　　　　　　　　**MeB**

Brunswick, Maine 04011

Hawthorne–Longfellow Library

Sheet music, 665 items, consisting of settings of poems by Henry Wadsworth Longfellow
Programs of College concerts and student recitals, 1808–
Early American Imprints Collection, containing American imprints to 1820 and Maine imprints to 1835, including 50 tunebooks

—Mary Hughes

Music Library, Gibson Hall

U.S. music imprints, acquired from Bates College, in 25 cartons, unsorted, and including 18th-century printed tunebooks and extensive holdings of 19th-century sheet music

—Miriam Barndt-Webb

586

PEJEPSCOT HISTORICAL SOCIETY

11 Lincoln Street
Brunswick, Maine 04011

Joseph Merrill, ms music book dated Topsham, Me., 1795, entitled "New Country Dances" and containing directions for 25 dances
Archival files of local music organizations, mostly programs and photographs, including materials of the Brunswick and Topsham Choral Society, 1897–1919; Brunswick Juvenile Band; Brunswick Musical Education Society, 1856–59; Haydn Society; Orpheus Music Club; and Saturday Club of Brunswick, 1895–

—Eileen Banashek, Pamela Rogers

587

CASTINE SCIENTIFIC SOCIETY

Wilson Museum
Castine, Maine 04421

Advertisements for local musical activities, 1846 and 1873
Published music, including a sacred songbook, 1833; V. Nicolai's Sonatas for violin and piano (Boston, Graupner), inscribed "Dorothy & Phebe W. Little, Castine, 1820"; and other 19th-century songbooks and hymnals
Hosea Wardwell, typed copy of a late 19th-century diary, with a photograph and references to musical activities in Penobscot; also various other ms and published materials, 1814–1940, mentioning local musical activities, including dances, bands, and glee clubs
Subscription lists for sponsors of local bands, early 19th century
Programs of glee clubs and local concerts, ca. 1870–1940, and of local dances, 1880s–90s

—E. W. Doudiet

588

Jane Plonski FORD

Box 6
East Stoneham, Maine 04231

Materials purchased from the Jones family, of Jones Beach, Long Island, N.Y., including 7 bound vols. of sheet music, 1840–90, 10 songbooks and hymnals, 10 vols. of other printed music, 10 libretti, 2 programs, and 2 music mss

589

WINTHROP HISTORICAL SOCIETY

Box 111
East Winthrop, Maine 04343

The materials are owned by individual members of the Society, and are not part of the Society's own holdings

Winthrop Military Band (fl. 1860s–1920s), photographs, personal papers, and sheet music, in all 15 linear cm.
George Henry Kilbreth (singing-school master), personal papers, music books, and late 19th-century sheet music, in all 1200 items, ca. 1900

—Ronald J. Kley

590

NORDICA HOMESTEAD MUSEUM

Holley Road, Route 3
Farmington, Maine 01938

Lillian Nordica (1857–1914), 100 letters from her and from her mother, Mrs. Amanda Allen Norton, many of them quoted in Ira Glackens, *Yankee Diva: Lillian Nordica and the Golden Days of Opera* (New York, 1963); also her personal music library (with inventory), including 700 editions of songs, and opera scores with markings (all materials are in storage)

Edward A. MacDowell, leather-bound vol. of published songs, with autograph dedications to Mme Nordica
Charles Wakefield Cadman, letters to Ben Stinchfield, 1940s, recognizing the contribution of Mme Nordica to his reputation as a composer

—Ben Stinchfield

591
UNION EVANGELICAL CHURCH

Box 448
Greenville, Maine 04441

Sheet music, 600 popular songs, 1930s
Evangelistic hymnals, 25 items, ca. 1900
Sunday-school and community songbooks, 10 items, ca. 1900

—Rev. Robert E. Simon

592
UNIVERSITY OF MAINE   MeU

Orono, Maine 04473

Raymond H. Fogler Library

Fannie (Hardy) Eckstorm (1865–1946, folklorist), 1.2 linear meters of papers, including notes on ballads, transcriptions of lumbering songs and songs of Maine and New Brunswick, and programs. See the unpublished guide, on file with the collection; also Jeane Patten Whitten, *Fannie Hardy Eckstorm: A Descriptive Bibliography of Her Writings Published and Unpublished* (Master's thesis, University of Maine, 1975), also issued as vol. 16 (1975) of *Northeast Folklore*

—Eric Flower

Northeast Archives of Folklore and Oral History

See Florence Ireland, "The Northeast Archives of Folklore and Oral History: A Brief Description and a Catalog of Its Holdings, 1958–1972," *Northeast Folklore*, 13 (1972)

Field recordings of turn-of-the-century lumber-camp songs from Maine, New Brunswick, and Prince Edward Island, ca. 350 hours, recorded 1956–70
Oral-history interviews with early country-and-western performers in Maine, ca. 40 hours, recorded 1975–77

—Edward D. Ives

593
UNITED SOCIETY OF SHAKERS LIBRARY

Route 1, Sabbathday Lake
Poland Springs, Maine 04274

Shaker music materials, including 200 sheet-music items and 40 miscellaneous published songs, 100 ms hymnals, 340 ms songs, 88 Maine and New Hampshire concert programs, 1810–1920, and 30 archival recordings of earlier music, produced 1940s–70s
Music catalogues, 5 items used by Shakers

—Theodore E. Johnson

594
Clinton GRAFFAM

18 Lawn Avenue
Portland, Maine 04103

Portland Symphony Orchestra, scrapbooks of programs and clippings, 1927–

595
MAINE HISTORICAL SOCIETY   MeHi

485 Congress Street
Portland, Maine 04101

Sheet music, 20 items, 1870s–
Hymnals, 22 items, 1803–1945
Oliver Bray, published oration on music, 1807
Papers of Maine musical organizations, including scrapbooks and newspaper clippings, records of early Portland churches, and scrapbooks of the Rossini Club, Portland
Programs of local concerts and theaters, 200 items, 1868–1971

—Rae R. Brown

596
PORTLAND PUBLIC LIBRARY   MeP

619 Congress Street
Portland, Maine 04101

Sheet music, 1.2 linear meters of popular and classical 19th-century music, and 3 file drawers of music by Maine composers, some in ms
Other printed music, including 2 songbooks and 2 file drawers of choral music used by a local music club
Organizations' papers, including the Kotzschmar Club of Portland, 1 scrapbook with ms materials; Portland Haydn Club, papers and memorabilia; and a few items each of the Portland Womens' Chorus, Portland Music Commission, and Portland Rossini Club
Photographs of Maine composers

—Judith Wentzell

597
ROSSINI CLUB

c/o Marjorie Anderson
96 Park Street
Portland, Maine 04101

Rossini Club (founded 1869, oldest women's music club in the U.S.), scrapbooks, including programs, press clippings, and other historical information

598
SCARBOROUGH PUBLIC LIBRARY

165 Black Point Road
Scarborough, Maine 04074

Congregational hymnal, 1881
Annie Louise Cary Raymond (1841–1921, opera singer), scrapbook with clippings, correspondence dated 1916–17, and an 1876 concert program from Unity Church, Chicago, autographed by her

—Nancy E. Crowell

599

WATERVILLE HISTORICAL SOCIETY
64 Silver Street
Waterville, Maine 04901

Sheet music by local women composers including Harriet Reddington, 5 items, ca. 1865
Tunebooks, 20 items, mid 19th century
Programs of local concerts, ca. 1853
Robert Browne Hall (1857–1908), concert program from Waterville, late 1890s, and memorabilia

—Jon F. Hall, Agatha Fullam

600

MUSICAL WONDER HOUSE AND MUSIC MUSEUM
18 High Street
Box 274
Wiscasset, Maine 04578

Mechanical musical instruments, including 400 music boxes, ca. 1750–1930; discs and cylinders for music boxes; 10,000 rolls for piano or organ, including many made locally; 10,000 disc recordings, ca. 1890–1940; and 5000 cylinder recordings, ca. 1895–1930

—Douglas Henderson

601

OLD GAOL MUSEUM
Box 188
York, Maine 03909

Rufus Bragdon, book of ms song texts, 1798
John W. Stiles, *Music Book*, with 30 ms marches, 1807

Songbooks, 12 items, 1736–1940; also Thomas Walter, *Grounds and Rules of Musick* (1764)

—Eldridge H. Pendleton

In addition to the repositories listed above, the following have also reported holdings of the materials indicated:

Bangor—Bangor Theological Seminary, Moulton Library: songbooks
Belfast—Belfast Free Library: programs
Bucksport—Bucksport Historical Society: sheet music, songbooks, other printed music, recordings, miscellaneous
Camden—Camden Public Library: recordings
Dexter—Dexter Historical Society: sheet music, songbooks, programs, pictures
Dixfield—Ludden Memorial Library: songbooks, recordings
Dresden—Dresden Historical Society: programs, pictures
Gorham—University of Southern Maine, Gorham Campus, Library: sheet music, songbooks, other printed music
Greenville—Moosehead Historical Society: songbooks
Millinocket—Millinocket Memorial Library: sheet music, songbooks
Orland—Orland Historical Society: songbooks, recordings
Owl's Head—Owl's Head Village Library: songbooks
Portland—State Street Church, Music Department: songbooks, other printed music
Rockland—William A. Farnsworth Library and Art Museum: songbooks
Thomaston—Knox Memorial Association: songbooks
Waterville—Colby College, Miller Library: songbooks, other printed music
Wilton—Wilton Historical Society: sheet music, songbooks, programs, pictures

Maryland

602

U.S. NAVAL ACADEMY   MdAN
Museum
Annapolis, Maryland 21402

Charles A. Zimmermann (1862–1916, bandmaster and composer at the United States Naval Academy Museum), scrapbook of clippings, 1887–1916
Navy songs, including 9 songbooks, 1813–1938, and 6 sheet-music items, 1906–62; also other songbooks (in the Nimitz Library)

—James W. Cheevers

603

AMERICAN GUILD OF ORGANISTS
Chesapeake (formerly Baltimore) Chapter
John Heizer, Dean
Zion Lutheran Church
City Hall Plaza
Baltimore, Maryland 21202

Archives of the Chapter, 1921– , including correspondence of W. Henry Baker, 1922–35, and others; also programs, minutes, press clippings, and photographs

604

BALTIMORE MUSIC CLUB
19 East Mount Vernon Place
Baltimore, Maryland 21202

Archives of the Club, 15 linear meters, 1923– , including scrapbooks, programs, information on contests, and membership files

605

BALTIMORE SYMPHONY ORCHESTRA ASSOCIATION
5204 Roland Avenue
Baltimore, Maryland 21210

See the anniversary booklet, *The Baltimore Symphony Orchestra, 1916–76: A Memento*, which includes John Brain, "A History of the Baltimore Symphony Orchestra"

Archives of the Orchestra, 1916– , mostly post-1942, with a card index for composers and guest performers, 1942–
Programs, 1916–42, in 1 box
Orchestral Library (at the Lyric Theatre, 120 West Mount Royal Avenue), including ms scores and parts for works and arrangements by Gustav Strube (1876–1953), the Orchestra's first conductor

606

EVERGREEN HOUSE   MdBJ-G

John Work Garrett Library
4545 North Charles Street
Baltimore, Maryland 21210

The Evergreen House and the Library are part of Johns Hopkins University

Tuesday Club of Annapolis, book of archival documents, 1740s–60s, including early minutes, with references to Alexander Malcolm; 58 leaves of ms music, with suggestions of instrumentation, this presumably being the earliest extent ms devoted to secular music composed in the American colonies; and later descriptive historical information on the Club
Sidney Lanier, personal papers, including 50 music mss and 3600 letters and personal papers, many with musical references, as discussed in Richard Higgins, *Sidney Lanier, Musician* (D.M.A. diss., Peabody Conservatory of Music, 1969)
Hugo Weisgall, 4 holograph music mss (sketches and complete copies) along with their printed editions, 1937–41
Sheet music, including the "Peabody Collection" of 4000 items, mostly vocal music, ca. 1830–80, transferred from the Peabody Institute, 1938–40, and arranged alphabetically by composer; also the "miscellaneous" collection, mostly U.S. imprints, 1830s–1920s, arranged alphabetically by composer, and including materials from the collections of Clifton Andrews, Charles H. Carey, B. M. Hopkinson, Emilie Shartkloff, Hinkley and Singley, May Smith, and Grace Turnbull; and 250 items from the collection of Henry Phillips, Jr., including piano music printed in Philadelphia, ca. 1870–90, some of it by Phillips, privately printed for him, 1877
Edwin Litchfield Turnbull (1872–1928), music library, 1.8 linear meters in 16 boxes, including 2 boxes of ms music by Turnbull, 4 boxes of his ms arrangements of music by other composers, and 10 boxes of instrumental performance parts and piano scores, mostly in European editions but including music by Dudley Buck, Edwin Grasse, and Victor Herbert, mss of 4 songs by John Hullah, and the ms parts to Grasse's Second Violin Concerto, op. 43
Gottlieb Musical Collection, 8 linear meters of chamber and orchestral music, mostly European imprints, but including printed editions of Edward A. MacDowell and Amy Cheney (Mrs. H. H. A.) Beach; also John Itzel's arrangements of MacDowell's "Woodland Sketches" in ms scores and parts, 3 printed songs,

and the ms Sonata for Flute by W. G. Owst (Baltimore composer)
Edgar Allan Poe, songs and choral works based on his texts, in ms, printed editions, and photocopies, 80 linear cm., purportedly assembled in connection with May Garrettson Evans' book *Music and Edgar Allan Poe* (Baltimore, 1939)

—Ben C. Bowman

607

FORT McHENRY NATIONAL MONUMENT AND HISTORIC SHRINE

Baltimore, Maryland 21230

Mrs. Reuben Ross Holloway, 50 items of papers, 1917–31, concerning the movement to adopt the "Star-spangled Banner" as the national anthem

—Paul Plamann

608

GERHARDT MARIMBA AND   (MdBT)
XYLOPHONE COLLECTION

Fine Arts Building, Room 457
Towson State University
Baltimore, Maryland 21204

Materials relating to the marimba and xylophone, including Edison cylinders, 78-rpm discs, music catalogues, and an Edison phonograph, 1905; correspondence and personal memorabilia of Edwin L. Gerhardt; method books; and photographs of musicians and instruments

609

HANDEL CHOIR OF BALTIMORE

c/o Gilbert French, President
2923 Gilford Avenue
Baltimore, Maryland 21218

Scrapbooks, lists of members, and scattered runs of programs, 1939–

610

Johns HOPKINS UNIVERSITY   MdBJ

Milton S. Eisenhower Library
Baltimore, Maryland 21218

Lester S. Levy, sections of his sheet-music collection, including 1000 presidential items and 1000 political items, 1795–
Andrew Salmieri jazz collection, including 6 linear meters of 78-rpm discs, mostly 1940s–50s with a few earlier items, indexed by performers, among them Big Bill Broonzy, Bing Crosby, Tommy Dorsey, Bessie Smith, and Teddy Wilson

611

Irving and Margery LOWENS

5511 North Charles Street
Baltimore, Maryland 21210

Edward A. MacDowell, 50 letters; holograph ms sketches and complete works; 500 published editions, including early German editions of his music; and miscellaneous early recordings of his music

W. L. Hubbard (1867–1951, editor and Chicago music critic), personal papers, 10,000 items, including letters to his family, 1880s–1951; letters to Hubbard, including 60 items from Frederick Stock, 35 from Riccardo Martin, and 200 from other Chicago musicians; and 200 photographs, 1880s–1920

Music mss of U.S. composers, 100 items, including unpublished songs by Jerome Kern; also 2000 letters of American composers, performers, and critics, 1850–

Commonplace books with ms musical notation, 1750s–ca. 1850, 150 items, mostly sacred, including many Pennsylvania German items, and many with macaronic and bilingual texts

American music publications, 300 pre-1861 items, including 50 singing-school lectures, 100 songsters, and 50 tunebooks (in addition to the collection in the Moravian Music Foundation, Winston-Salem, N.C., q.v.), also 35 bound vols. of American music periodicals, 1840s–80s

Printed musical ephemera, 7500 items, including trade cards, post cards, postage stamps, and programs

612

MARYLAND HISTORICAL SOCIETY   MdHi

201 West Monument Street
Baltimore, Maryland 21201

> See P. William Filby, "Music in the Maryland Historical Society," *M.L.A. Notes*, 32 (1976), 503–17; also Avril J. M. Pedley, *The Manuscript Collections of the Maryland Historical Society* (Baltimore, 1968; hereinafter cited as *Pedley*), and the suppl. (to be issued 1980; hereinafter cited as *Ms*, which entry numbers identify the call numbers as well)

Francis Scott Key, original holograph of the text of "The Star-spangled Banner." See P. W. Filby and Edward G. Howard, *Star-spangled Books* (Baltimore, 1972), pp. 152 and 154–57; also *Pedley*, 819 no. 3, 861, and 910 for related materials

Musical mss, including a book of German religious songs, later used as a receipt book, belonging to Thomas Cronmiller, Baltimore, 1790 (*Pedley*, 412); ms music book copied by Mary Ann Johnson, ca. 1830 (*Pedley*, 871); Marion Dodson (1812–96, surgeon), ms of "Tunes Used Aboard the *U.S. Pocahontas*, 1864" (*Pedley*, 477); Horatio D. Hewitt, full score and parts for the comic opera *Pearl of Granada* (1878); and Franz Bornschein (1879–1948), music holographs along with printed editions of his works, including 30 works in 47 boxes, with a register (*Ms*, 2254)

Personal papers related to music or of musicians, including John Coleman, hymn texts, in his personal papers, 1775–1815 (*Pedley*, 442); Willard G. Day (1856–1913, inventor), scrapbooks on Baltimore music, also musical instrument patents (*Pedley*, 442); John Hill Hewitt, scrapbook, 1884–87 (*Pedley*, 762), and his history of the Marion Rifle Corps, 1888 (*Pedley*, 1041); Francis Hopkinson, transcripts of letters in other repositories (*Pedley*, 1283); Leonora Jackson (McKim) (1852–1931, violinist), diaries, programs, press clip-

pings, and correspondence, 1890–1931 (*Ms*, 1780); Benjamin Henry Latrobe (1764–1820), personal papers, with references to music (*Pedley*, 942); W. G. Owst, music criticism, 1899–1927, 5 vols. (*Pedley*, 1151); James R. Randall (1839–1905, author of "Maryland My Maryland"), personal papers, 1861–1905, 15 items (*Pedley*, 1270); Andrew Schad (musician of Georgetown, D.C.), personal papers, 9 items, 1850–65 (*Pedley*, 1368); Rose and Ottilie Sutro (duo-pianists), correspondence, recital programs, press clippings, and scrapbooks, also other materials relating to the Society for the Foundation of a National Conservatory of Music, 1890–1930 (*Ms*, 1867); and Frank Rush Webb (1851–1934, composer), diaries and logs, 46 vols., 1868–1932, kept in Staunton, Va., Covington, Ill., and Baltimore (*Pedley*, 1626)

Organizational archives, including the Baltimore Harmonic Society, record book, 1809, with a newspaper account of the history of the Society by Leo McCardell, n.d. (*Pedley*, 112); Anacreontic Society, official record book, with repertory lists, 1820–26 (*Ms*, 1793); Baltimore Musical Association, minutes, 1835–38 (*Pedley*, 124); Otto Sutro Wednesday Club, official records and programs, 1869–1903, 4 vols. (*Pedley*, 1629–30, 473); Ford's Theatre, 35 vols. of records, 1875–1919, including accounts, programs, and a libretto for the comic opera *Billie Taylor* (*Pedley*, 579; cf. 1088); Charles M. Stieff Piano Co., archives, 1873–1909, including posters, shipping records, and music photographs, 7 vols. and 75 items (*Pedley*, 1477); Baltimore Oratorio Society, scrapbook, 1880–1926, and minute book, 1897–1914 (*Pedley*, 127–28); Paint and Powder Club, official records, programs, press clippings, and music scores, 1894– (*Pedley*, 1200); Academy of Music, 37 scrapbooks, 1896–1930 (*Pedley*, 4); and Johns Hopkins Orchestra and Musical Association, records, 1930–42, as collected by Dr. W. R. Dunton, Jr. (*Pedley*, 803)

Song texts, including 18th-century ms songs and ballads in the Watkinson record book (*Pedley*, 1623); "Hail Columbia!", printed text in German, 1810s?, in the Henry Schroeder papers (*Pedley*, 1374; *Ms*, 1417); and the Birckhead Civil War scrapbook, 1861–62, including war songs (*Pedley*, 179)

Sheet music, 8000 Baltimore imprints, mostly 19th century, and highlighted by the first and most other early editions of "The Star-spangled Banner." Among the Baltimore music publishers represented are Carr, 403 items, 1794–1823; Cole, 900 items, 1799–1855; Willig, 1400 items, 1822–1910; Benteen, 1500 items, 1838–53; Miller & Beacham, 1000 items, 1838–72; and McCaffrey, 500 items, 1853–95. See William Treat Upton, "Eighteenth-Century American Imprints in the Society's Dielman Collection of Music," *Maryland Historical Magazine*, 35 (1940), 374–81

Songbooks, 120 items, many with "Star-spangled Banner" association; music broadsides, 1200 items, mostly related to the Civil War; and music programs, arranged by theater, with musical items not separated or identified, mostly 1880s–1920s

Hymnals, mostly early and mid-19th-century Baltimore imprints, including 20 tunebooks, several of them compilations by John Cole and Samuel Dyer, and 20 books with texts only

Maryland Diocesan Archives, with specific items on Protestant Episcopal church music as cited under the heading "Music—church," including 14 letters from

Rev. Thomas Bacon, John Glassell, and others, to Henry and Francis Callister, 1746–59?; Rev. Thomas John Claggett, 5 items, 1792–1815; Rev. James Kemp, 12 letters and documents, 1802–27, including documents relating to the slanderous allegations that Rev. J. G. J. Bend sang the obscene song "The Done Over Tailor" at a wedding in 1802; Rev. William R. Whittingham, 50 letters, programs, and other documents, 1830–83, regarding his personal interests in art music, church-music practice and development, objections to opera singers in church choirs, and excommunicating those who attend opera; Rev. William A. Muhlenberg, 2 items, 1856–62; Leah H. Reese, "A History of Messiah" (i.e., Church of the Messiah, Baltimore), with music references; and other miscellaneous items, 1770–1903

—P. William Filby, Larry Sullivan

613

PEABODY INSTITUTE OF THE JOHNS HOPKINS UNIVERSITY LIBRARY
(Peabody Conservatory of Music)
17 East Mount Vernon Place
Baltimore, Maryland 21202

The music collection was formerly part of the Peabody Institute Library. For other materials relating to the Institute, see the Enoch Pratt Free Library, George Peabody Department

Sheet music, 1810s–80s, in 20 bound vols., uncatalogued

Songbooks, 200 items, including several pre-1850 but mostly post-1850 imprints; also books about music, including 5 pre-1860 periodical sets

Programs of Baltimore performances, including Theodore Thomas Orchestra visits from Chicago, 1887–88; Boston Symphony Orchestra visits, 1892–93; Baltimore Musical Thieves, 1894–97; Germania Männerchor, 1904–16; miscellaneous operas, ca. 1873–1917; and Baltimore Symphony Orchestra concerts

Hugh Newsom (1891–1978), personal papers, including holograph mss, ozalid scores, and printed editions of his music

Otto Ortmann (physicist), books from his library pertaining to the physics of music

614

Enoch PRATT FREE LIBRARY   MdBE
400 Cathedral Street
Baltimore, Maryland 21201

Fine Arts Department

William Wallace Furst (1852–1917), ms opera *Theodora*
Sheet music, 4200 items, 1865– ; also 320 popular and classical songbooks, early 20th century

—Ruth Sundermeyer

Maryland Department

Programs and press clippings of Baltimore operas, 1856–1955, and concerts, 1839–1951; 30 photographs relating to music and musicians in Baltimore; pamphlets and press clippings on "The Star-spangled Banner," 15 linear cm.; and 78 Confederate broadside ballads, as cited in *Rudolph*

George Peabody Department

Materials from the Peabody Institute Library, excluding musical materials at the Peabody Conservatory (q.v.). Also present are materials on the Peabody Institute itself (i.e., the general organization which formerly comprised the Peabody Library, the Peabody Conservatory, and the Peabody Art Collection), which materials are now under the joint custody of the Pratt Library and the Peabody Conservatory

Archives of the Peabody Institute, including miscellaneous correspondence, 1830–75, and the *Annual Reports*, 1868–1916, both of which discuss musical matters

Archives of the Peabody Conservatory, including account books and recital programs, 1 linear meter; correspondence and scrapbooks, 70 linear cm.; concert programs, 1866– , in 87 bound vols.; catalogues and yearbooks, 1868– , in 87 bound vols.; dissertations, 58 vols.; scrapbooks, music-acquisitions lists, and alumni files, 26 bound vols.; public-relations scrapbooks, 1900– , 55 vols.; records of the Business Office and preparatory program, 15 linear meters; and 600 photographs, 1860– . Among the scrapbooks are vols. assembled by Clara Ascherfeld

Music mss of Peabody Conservatory faculty members, including O. B. Boise, Franz Bornschein (also his published editions, with a finding list), George F. Boyle, Louis Cheslock, Asger Hamerik, Theodore Hemberger, John Itzel, Katherine Lucke, Robert L. Paul, Gustav Strube, Howard Thatcher, and Leon L. Werner

John Charles Thomas, personal papers, including programs, photographs; also materials relating to Albert Hay Malotte

Enrico Caruso, 14 scrapbooks, with clippings, programs, and caricatures, also 4 vocal scores, and 3 boxes of photographs and other memorabilia, presumably presented by Mrs. Caruso

Metropolitan Opera and Manhattan Opera House, 6 vols. of scrapbooks, 1906–10

615

SAINT MARY'S SEMINARY   MdBS
AND UNIVERSITY
5400 Roland Avenue
Baltimore, Maryland 21210

Sheet music, 30 bound vols., 1889–1937, mostly sacred items

Songbooks, hymnals, and liturgical music, 13 linear meters of European and American publications, 1660–

—Norman Desmarais

616

STAR-SPANGLED BANNER FLAG HOUSE
844 East Pratt Street
Baltimore, Maryland 21202

Materials relating to the U.S. national anthem, including 19 items collected by the former curator, Arthur Sewell, with the help of Sen. Millard Tydings; 5 early editions and 2 bound vols. of sheet music, including "The Star-spangled Banner"

Other printed music, including 2 folders of assorted 20th-century sheet music

617

Jean E. GARRIOTT
8808 Kensington Parkway
Chevy Chase, Maryland 20015

Hymnals of various denominations, including gospel songbooks, 86 vols., 1700s–

618

UNIVERSITY OF MARYLAND   MdU
College Park, Maryland 20742

Special Collections in Music

Maintained within the McKeldin Library, as a part of the collections of the Music Library

American Bandmasters' Association Research Center

American Bandmasters' Association, archives, 1929–

Banda Mexicana (75-piece early 20th-century touring band), music library, consisting of conductors' scores and parts for 200 arrangements and original works marked for performance by the band, and including many Patrick S. Gilmore Co. imprints

J. Frank Elsass collection, the library of the "Symphony in Gold for Brass and Percussion," with 4 file drawers of ms music, including arrangements by M. S. Lake

Edwin Franko Goldman collection, comprising 22 scrapbooks of clippings, programs, and other materials relating to Goldman and the Goldman Band, 1893–1955, as discussed in Kirby Reed Jolly, *Edwin Franko Goldman and the Goldman Band* (Ph.D. diss., New York University, 1971); also recordings, letters, scores, photographs, and other materials, mostly presented by Richard Franko Goldman

Col. George S. Howard, personal papers documenting his career with the Patrick Conway Band and with the Ernst Williams School of Music (Boston), also the founding and early years of the U.S. Army–Air Force Band

Karl L. King collection, 243 published scores for band, donated by Samuel Kurtz

Star Music Co. (Elred, Pa.) collection, comprising 50 published works for band and small orchestra by R. B. Hall, F. H. Losey, and others, donated by Loren Geiger

Miscellaneous correspondence, clippings, programs, and photographs of Herbert L. Clarke, Patrick Conway, Patrick S. Gilmore, Arthur Pryor, John Philip Sousa, John W. ("Jack") Wainwright, and others

Recordings, mostly from the David Burchuk and Kenneth Slater collections, including discs, cylinders, and tapes of early 20th-century bands, among them Vessella's Italian Band, Creatore's Band, and the bands of Clarke, Conway, Pryor, Sousa, and others

Books pertaining to band history and instruction

Music Educators' National Conference Historical Center

Music Educators' National Conference, records, 1907– , including minutes, proceedings, reports, memorandums, correspondence, programs, membership records, photographs, scrapbooks, special-project files, biographical files, and subject files

Clifford V. Buttelman (1886–1970), personal papers, containing working papers for a history of the Music Educators' National Conference, in progress at the time of his death; biographical data on 20th-century music educators; and correspondence relating to the Music Educators' National Conference before 1956

Frances Elliott Clark (1860–1958) collection, including 500 books and pamphlets, 100 recordings, memorabilia, addresses and lectures, articles, correspondence (relating to the Music Educators' National Conference and its predecessor, the Music Supervisors' National Conference; the educational department of the Victor Talking Machine Co.; the National Federation of Music Clubs; Lowell Mason; Stephen Foster; and the Philadelphia Mayor's Committee), programs of the National Summer School of Music before 1919, and notes on her trip to Europe (1928, including meetings with Percy A. Scholes in order to establish the Anglo-American Music Conference)

Ginn & Co., music library, 100 cartons of editorial materials, including books, *Ginn Music News*, advertising circulars, source notebooks, historical files, records of the National Summer School of Music from 1886 to 1919, and catalogue information. See the notice in M.L.A. *Notes*, 31 (1975), 768

Lowell Mason collection, 100 items, mostly published tunebooks, textbooks, and hymnals by Mason and various collaborators, also including periodicals, a scrapbook of press clippings, printed addresses, programs, and several Mason holograph mss, as collected by his grandson, Henry Lowell Mason

Luther Whiting Mason (1818–96) collection, 250 items, including Japanese musical instruments, art, and artifacts presented to Mason while he was in Japan, 1880–82, as well as books, papers, and photographs (materials on deposit)

Pillsbury Foundation School (experimental music nursery school), daily observation notes and other analytical records of students, correspondence, reports and writings, 600 disc recordings of spontaneous musical creations, press clippings, photographs, and oral-history materials

Charles M. Tremaine, personal papers, including correspondence and other documents relating to the National Bureau for the Advancement of Music, and its work in support of National Music Week, the Music Memory Contest, class piano instruction, and community music programs, in all 50 linear cm. See Franklin W. Koch, *The History and Promotional Activities of the National Bureau for the Advancement of Music* (Ph.D. diss., University of Michigan, 1973)

Personal papers of Will Earhart, Russell and Hazel Morgan, Gladys Pitcher, and Lilla Belle Pitts

Organizational papers of the American Institute of Normal Methods; Chicago In-and-About Music Educators Club; College Band Directors' National Association; Music Industries Council; National School Band, Orchestra, and Vocal Association; and others

Books and periodicals, a collection strong in graded

series, music appreciation, song collections, and methodology and philosophy of music education

Oral history of the Music Educators' National Conference, including interviews with former presidents

Other Major Collections

International Clarinet Society Research Center, including the Burnet C. Tuthill Library of 2000 ms and printed editions of music for clarinet solo and ensemble as well as books about the clarinet; and the Joseph Ierardi Collection of articles, periodicals, pamphlets, scores, programs, and memorabilia pertaining to clarinet instruction and performance

National Association of College Wind and Percussion Instructors Research Center, mostly post-1940 scores and archival materials

—Bruce Wilson, Fred Heutte

Other McKeldin Library Collections

Alfred Wallenstein Collection, consisting of the working library of radio station WOR in New York, 1920s–50s, containing 28,000 titles in 110 file cabinets, including sheet music and scores and parts for operas and orchestral works (in the Music Library)

—Fred Heutte

Maryland sheet music, including Bromo-Seltzer editions, Maryland imprints, and music by Maryland composers, 1044 items (in the Archives and Manuscripts Department)

—Mary Boccaccio

Other Collections

Andre Kostelanetz collection, including 300 original compositions and arrangements by Kostelanetz, also other works performed by his orchestra, 1930s–70s (in the Department of Music)

Maryland Folklore Archive, including 10 hours of tape recordings of Maryland college songs, folksongs, Afro-American folk music, and traditional instrumental music, as cited in *Briegleb*, no. 43 (in the Department of English)

619
ALLEGANY COUNTY HISTORICAL SOCIETY
218 Washington Street
Cumberland, Maryland 21502

Manuscript music, 3 sacred items copied locally, late 19th century

Printed music, including 123 popular and religious sheet-music items, ca. 1880–1900; 6 late 19th-century hymnals; and 9 19th- and 20th-century school songbooks

Programs of late 19th-century local concerts, 10 items

Photographs of local orchestras, bands, and choral groups, 6 items, late 19th century

Recordings, including 7 cylinders; also 1 Edison phonograph

—Joan Baldwin, Rita Knox

620
FREDERICK COUNTY HISTORICAL SOCIETY
24 East Church Street
Frederick, Maryland 21701

Johannes Schley (1712–89, German schoolmaster and musician in the Frederick area, ca. 1750), ms songbook in German; also 8 bound vols. of printed sheet music, 1826–76, including 1 in French, owned by other members of his family

Recordings, including 20 78-rpm discs and 12 wax cylinders

—Mary Winslow

621
FREDERICK COUNTY PUBLIC LIBRARY
116 Record Street
Frederick, Maryland 21701

Jacob Engelbrecht, ms diary with information on church and band music in Frederick, ca. 1820–77. See William R. Quynn, ed., *The Diary of Jacob Engelbrecht, 1818–1878* (Frederick, 1976)

—Jean Davis

622
Wayne WOLD
Saint John's Lutheran Church
141 South Potomac Street
Hagerstown, Maryland 21740

Hymnals and books on hymnology, 350 items, ca. 1772– , mostly 1850–1900, including Sunday-school books, Lutheran hymnals, and Isaac Watts editions

623
Mark ELROD
1301 Potomac Heights Drive
Oxon Hill, Maryland 20022

Research materials concerning military brass bands, 1815–90, centering on the Civil War era, and including original editions and copies of band music, transcriptions of parts into full conductor's scores, 40 photographs, 100 sheet-music items for piano, research notes, and reference works

624
Lester S. LEVY
2 Slade Avenue
Pikesville, Maryland 21208

Sheet music, 30,000 items, mostly arranged in categories by subject or composer, and including 600 *Sonneck–Upton* and 1800 *Wolfe* titles. Among the important subjects are blackface minstrelsy, 1000 items, 1820s–80s; war and military music, 2000 items, including 900 Union and 300 Confederate Civil War items and 500 items from World War I; railroads, 500 items, 1828–1928, and other forms of transportation, 300 items, 1850s–1920s; dance music, 400 items, mostly

1830s–60s; comic songs, 1000 items, ca. 1800–90; fires, 75 items, 1814–90; illustrations, 80 Currier & Ives items and 10 Winslow Homer items, also 75 views of music stores, 1820s–70s, and 900 portraits of actors and screen stars, 1905–50; 600 songs with texts by famous poets; 500 sports items; 400 maritime items; and others. (The collections of patriotic and presidential items are now at the Eisenhower Library, Johns Hopkins University, Baltimore, q.v.) Among the composer collections are 650 items by Irving Berlin, 125 by George M. Cohan, 250 by Stephen Collins Foster, 200 by George Gershwin, 100 of Harrigan and Hart, 400 by Victor Herbert, 550 by Jerome Kern, 250 by Cole Porter, 250 by Richard Rodgers, and 110 by John Philip Sousa. See the books based on the collection, *Grace Notes in American History* (Norman, Okla., 1967), *Flashes of Merriment* (Norman, 1971), *Give Me Yesterday* (Norman, 1976), and *Picture the Songs* (Baltimore, 1977)

Songsters, 150 U.S. imprints, ca. 1790–1880s, mostly 1820s–60s

Broadsides, 300 items, mostly Civil War editions

625
MONTGOMERY COUNTY HISTORICAL SOCIETY
103 West Montgomery Avenue
Rockville, Maryland 20850

Sheet music, 550 popular-music items, mostly 1840–80

School songbooks, 2 items used ca. 1900 at the National Park Seminary, Forest Glen, Md., and 1 vol. published and arranged by Harvard University students, 1880

Manuscript music, 1 vol. of patriotic ballads, ca. 1790–1800, formerly owned by the Clopper family, Cloppers, Md.

Programs of local concerts, 4 items, ca. 1895

Papers and photographs of the Browningsville Coronet Band, founded 1844, and the Clarksburg Band, founded 1845, in all 8 items; also 1 etching of Prof. George Wesley Walker (1837–1913, first music teacher in Montgomery County)

—Mark Walston

626
Richard K. SPOTTSWOOD
711 Boundary Avenue
Silver Spring, Maryland 20910

Materials on American vernacular music in all forms except pop, and emphasizing non-English-speaking ethnic groups such as Slavic, Middle Eastern, Mediterranean, and Irish. Included are 8000 disc recordings, mostly 78-rpm; research notes on recording companies; and other research materials

———————

In addition to the repositories listed above, the following have also reported holdings of the materials indicated:

Baltimore—Flickinger Foundation for American Studies: printed music

Baltimore—Morgan State University: sheet music

Baltimore—United Methodist Historical Society, Baltimore Annual Conference: songbooks

Baltimore— University of Maryland, Baltimore County, Library: sheet music, songbooks

Cambridge—Dorchester County Historical Society: sheet music, songbooks, other printed music

Chestertown—Washington College: sheet music, songbooks, recordings

Ft. Meade—Ft. Meade Museum: sheet music, songbooks, programs, pictures

Preston—Caroline County Historical Society: sheet music, songbooks, programs, catalogues

Sharpsburg—Chesapeake and Ohio Canal National Historical Park: pictures

Snow Hill—Worcester City Historical Society: sheet music, songbooks, programs

Takoma Park—Columbia Union College, Weis Library: songbooks, recordings

Westminster—Historical Society of Carrol County: sheet music

Massachusetts

627
UNIVERSITY OF MASSACHUSETTS   MU
Music Library
Amherst, Massachusetts 01002

Howard M. Lebow (d. 1968, faculty member), piano, instrumental, and vocal scores, also books on music from his personal library

—Catherine D. Collins

628
ANDOVER HISTORICAL SOCIETY   MAnHi
Amos Blanchard House
97 Main Street
Andover, Massachusetts 01810

Manuscript entitled "Original Jim Crow," with name of Joseph Farnham, Andover, and reference note to Thomas D. Rice, 1835

Manuscript hymns by local composers Henry J. Stevenson and Jonathan French, 2 items, 1762 and ca. 1890

Printed songbooks and hymnals, 40 items, 1721–1900, including *The Essex Harmony* (1770) and Thomas Walter, *The Grounds and Rules of Musick* (1721); also 5 printed sheet-music items, including hymns and a march

Programs of local school and community musical events, 10 items, ca. 1840–90

—Kathleen E. Greer

629

PHILLIPS ACADEMY MAnP

Archives
Andover, Massachusetts 01810

Oliver Holden, 12 letters, 1798–1804, written from Charlestown, Mass.

—Ruth Quattlebaum

630

Howard T. GLASSER

28 Forge Road
Assonet, Massachusetts 02702

Field recordings, 400 hours of tapes recorded in Scotland and West Virginia, including songs and ballads, stories, and fiddle and banjo players
Commercial recordings, 2 linear meters of 78-rpm discs of folk and folk-revival recordings, and 12 linear meters of LP discs of European and American folk music

631

Janet White FRAZIER

32 Clifton Street
Attleboro, Massachusetts 02703

Sheet music, 2000 popular and classical items, 18th to 20th centuries; also "Melodies pour Chant et Piano par C. Chaminade" (Paris, 1912) presented to the local Chaminade Club
Dance programs, 5 items, including performances by Pavlova and the Ballet Russe, 1918 and 1930s
Dance notations, 6 items, 1874–1900
Recordings, 35 78-rpm discs of semi-classical and popular music and jazz

632

F. B. BELCOUR

121 Day Street
Auburndale, Massachusetts 02166

Recordings, 4.3 linear meters of 78-rpm discs, mostly jazz, 1920s–30s, also music broadcast over radio

633

BEDFORD HISTORICAL SOCIETY

15 Great Road
Bedford, Massachusetts 01730

Hymnals, 10 printed items, 1819–1914; also 7 ms hymns, 19th century
Tunebooks, 2 printed items, 1787 and 1796, the latter with extensive ms sacred music, inscribed by Asa Webber, 1799, and Buhamah Webber, of Mount Vernon, N.H.
Republican campaign songster, 1884
Bedford Band, papers, including a notebook with history and records of the organization, 1843–46; 4 vols. of ms bass-drum music, ca. 1840; and 2 photographs, 1878 and early 20th century
Programs of local singing groups and bands, 10 items, 1840s–1900s

—Mary S. Hafer, Mary Wallace Davidson

634

AMERICAN CONGREGATIONAL MBC
ASSOCIATION

Congregational Library
14 Beacon Street
Boston, Massachusetts 02108

Hymnals of various denominations, some with words only, 18th and 19th centuries, 60 linear meters
Sheet music, 600 items of late 19th-century popular, classical, and religious music, published locally
Tunebooks, 59 Lowell Mason items, 1835–45

—Harold F. Worthley

635

BOSTON ATHENAEUM MBAt

10½ Beacon Street
Boston, Massachusetts 02108

Confederate imprints, including 400 sheet-music items, 15 songsters, 10 hymnals, and other music items, mostly as described in *Crandall*, esp. vol. 2, pp. 553–56, 561–669, and 719–21; also in *Harwell*
Other sheet music, including 300 miscellaneous items, mostly Boston imprints; Louisa Brown, 1 bound vol. containing 43 songs, early 19th century; and 373 items with illustrated covers, maintained as part of the print collection
Arthur Howard Nichols and Margaret Homer Nichols Shurcliff, materials relating to bells, bell ringing, and the Bell-Ringers Guild of Boston, 1854–1952, in 10 boxes and 1 vol.

—Cynthia English

636

BOSTON PUBLIC LIBRARY MB

Copley Square
Boston, Massachusetts 02117

See the *Dictionary Catalogue of the Music Collection* (Boston, 1972; suppl., 1976; hereinafter cited as *DC*), which includes not only materials in the Music Department, but also a number of items now in the custody of the Rare Books and Manuscripts Department; also the reading list, *Landmarks in Music, Boston, 1630–1924* (Boston, 1924)

Music Department

The collection dates from the first attempt in the U.S. to develop specialized music holdings in an American institutional library: in 1858, Joshua Bates (1788–1864, Massachusetts-born financier working in London) commissioned Alexander Wheelock Thayer, then in Europe, to acquire music for the newly founded Library's collections. Among Thayer's acquisitions were the collection of rare European music books assembled by Josef Koudelka (1773–1850, Viennese army officer), and 100 vols. from Thayer's own personal library. The noted music collection of Allen A. Brown (1835–1916) was presented in 1894; its 7000 vols., devoted mostly to European music, are described by Barbara Duncan, *Catalogue of the Allen A. Brown Collection*, 4 vols. (Boston, 1910–16).

Sheet music, scattered through the collection. The catalogued items are accessible in *DC* through composer entries, also through form and subject headings, particularly "Songs. With Music" (6000 entries, mostly pre-1940 U.S.), as well as such specific headings as "European War," "U.S. History, 19th Century," "Civil War," and "Campaign Songs." In addition, there are bound vols. cited throughout the Duncan *Catalogue of the Allen A. Brown Collection*, but mostly not analyzed; also in class "SP," some pre-1865 items, numbered but not catalogued, most of them accessible through the "Song Index" maintained in the Music Department

Songbooks, catalogued and cited in *DC*. Religious works are mostly collected under the heading "Church Music. Psalmody," which includes 500 items, mostly pre-1940 U.S., arranged in several alphabets. See also the 300 entries under "Singing. Instruction Books." Of the 3000 secular songbooks listed under "Songs with Music. Collections," many are pre-1940 U.S. imprints

Scrapbooks, as cited in *DC*, vol. 16, pp. 683–95, and the suppl., vol. 4, p. 166. Most of the vols. were assembled by the Library staff, working with materials from the vertical files; many were compiled by Allen A. Brown, including vols. on Boston musical events and on special subjects, such as child prodigies, necrology (1884–1907, 7 vols.), the first U.S. performance of Richard Strauss's *Salome* in 1910, and music departments in U.S. public libraries. Other collectors and compilers of scrapbooks include Adelina Marie Armistead, Giuseppe de Begnis, Arthur King Brown, William Taylor Campbell, Rebekah Crawford, John W. Cummin, Abram Edmands Cutter (Jenny Lind concerts in Boston), Charlotte Jones Davis, Julius Eichberg (3 vols., 1843–94), Mary Hallock Greenewalt (on color music), Arthur Foote, Franklin Hunt, Mrs. John Henry Long, Mrs. N. Manley, Charles C. Moreau, Alfred Edgar Mullet, Henry F. Oates, Mrs. James S. Pray (on hymnal references in the *Christian Science Monitor*, 1932–33), Mary G. Reed, Gustav Schirmer (on the Boston Orchestra, 1885–86), Nicolas Slonimsky, Lucien H. Southard, Warren Storey Smith, Rose Stewart, Pearl Strachan, Everett E. Truette (12 vols. on organs and organ music), William E. Walter, Mary Elizabeth Walton, Frederic Wilder Wheildon (Civil War songs, comp. 1861), Isabel Wesson, Suza Doane White, J. Angus Winter, and Henry Woelber (on famous bandmasters, 1934). Among the topics covered by special scrapbooks are The American Opera Co., New York, 1927–30; ASCAP, 1939–45; the Apollo Society, concerts, 1824–26; La Argentina, 1928–35; band music in Boston, 1902–47; the Beethoven centenary of 1927; bells and carillons; Thomas B. ("Blind Tom") Bethune, comp. 1918; Anna Bishop, including visiting cards received, and programs of her concerts, 1856–73; the Boston Chamber Music Society, 1886–87; Boston Conservatory of Music, 1870–80; Boston Music Hall, 1859–79; Boston Music Week, 1924–25; Boston Opera Co., 1913–14; Boston Orchestral Club, 1885–91 and 1903–11; Boston Philharmonic Orchestra, 1890–92; Boston Singing Club, 1902–11; Boston Woman's Symphony Orchestra, 1927–30; Nadia Boulanger, visit to Boston, 1838–39; "Canned Music" symposium, 1931; the carillon of St. Stephen's Church, Cohasset, Mass., 1924–25; Feodor Chaliapin, 1921–38; Composer's Forum-Laboratory (WPA Federal Music Project, 1936–37); Archibald T. Davison, lectures at the Lowell Institute, 1924–25; Electrical musical instruments, 1909–35;

Euterpe concerts, Boston, 1879–89; Faelten Pianoforte School programs, 1897–1913; Lynnwood Farnam, 1931; Arthur Foote, 1942; Flonzaley Quartet, 1908–15; Clara and Ossip Gabrilowitsch, 1901–37; Mary Garden, 1907–26; George Gershwin, 1931–38; Philip Hale, scrapbook of writings on his music library, 1942; Helsinki University (Finland) Chorus (Ylioppilaskunnan Laulajat), U.S. tour, 1937–38; jazz, 1922–29; Maxim Karolik, 1930–33; Serge Koussevitzky, 1924–39; B. J. Lang, Boston concert programs, 1861–1906; Jenny Lind, 1890s; Longy Club, Boston, 1901–15 and 1932–65; Lowell Institute lectures, 1900– ; MacDowell Club, 1904–37; the Manhattan Opera Co., 1906–10; Mariarden (events at Peterborough, N.H.), 1925–26; Redfern Mason, *Boston Transcript* writings, 1927–37; the Massachusetts Federation of Music Clubs, 1902–51; the Mendelssohn Quintette Club, 1852–55; Frank Metcalf, articles on hymnology, 1914–22; Hiram Motherwell, Harvard lectures, 1912; National Music Week, 1926–41; Old South Church, special musical services, 1886–1904; Orpheus Musical Society, Boston, 1853–1909; Vladimir de Pachmann, 1890–1911; Ignace Jan Paderewski, 1909–41; George W. Palmer, singing school, 1830s; Henry Taylor Parker, 1928–31; Adelina Patti, 1881–1903; People's Choral Union, 1898–1914; Johann Ernst Perabo concerts, 1866–1909; Roman Polyphonic Singers, 1927–28 tour; Russian Symphonic Choir, 1925–37; Saturday Morning Junior Concerts, 1935–37; Ernestine Schumann-Heink, 1889–1936; William H. Sherwood, 1876–97; Uday Shan-Kar, 1936; Leon Vartanian (d. 1931); Winchester Orchestral Society, 1909–15; and the Women's Symphony Society of Boston, 1939–42

Concert and opera programs, as cited in *DC*, vol. 5, pp. 1–19 and suppl., vol. 1, p. 576, including early events sponsored by the Boston Academy of Music, 1833–47; the Musical Education Society, 1846–56; and the Handel and Haydn Society, 1815–1905 (nos. 1–748)

Serge Koussevitzky, holographs of his works for double bass, autograph copies of music dedicated to him, personal library of scores with his performance markings, and memorabilia, as maintained in the Koussevitzky Room. See the typescript inventory, also *DC*, suppl. 1, vol. 2, pp. 592–98

Special Music Collections in the Rare Books and Manuscripts Department

Handel and Haydn Society, music library, including scores with markings for use in the Society's performances, 1815– . See the typescript inventory by Joel Sheveloff, *Rare Old Music and Books on Music in Boston* (Boston, 1972)

Walter Piston, 14 holograph music mss, 1933–70s

Victor Young (1900–56), mss and printed editions of his original music and arrangements

Holograph music mss, including Dudley Buck, Psalm 46 ("God Is Our Refuge," 1872), and the operas *Don Munio* (1873) and *Serapis*; George W. Chadwick, small works; Philip Greeley Clapp, "O Gladsome Light" (1908); Louis A. Coerne, extensive holdings; Frederick S. Converse, *The Sacrifice* op. 27 (1910); Mabel Daniels, autograph scores and corrected proofs for 12 major works, 1917–40, with other personal papers; Julius Eichberg, *The Doctor of Alcantara* (1862) and other operas; Arthur Foote, String Quartet op. 4 (1890), and other mss; Henry F. B. Gilbert, *Negro*

Rhapsody for Orchestra (1913); Edward Burlingame Hill, *Stevensonia* (1924); Edward A. MacDowell, first sketch of the "Dirge" from the *Indian Suite* (1891?); Maria Malibran, song, "Le retour de la Tyrolienne"; Edward Maryon (1867–1954), many unpublished works, mostly operas; Daniel Gregory Mason, *Three Pieces* op. 13; William Mason, piano works, "Valse" and "A Pastorale Novelette"; John Knowles Paine, opera *Azara* (1890s?), "Centennial Hymn" (1876), and other works; Horatio Parker, Concerto for Organ and Orchestra op. 55 (1902?); C. C. Perkins (1823–86), several small works written for his sister; Gardner Read, Symphony no. 2; Clara K. (Barnett) Rogers, 2 small ms works for piano, also extensive holograph mss of her father, John Barnett (1802–90, English composer), and personal correspondence; Robert Stoepel, *Hiawatha, an Indian Symphony* (1863); Nicolas Slonimsky, several small pieces with Slonimskonian titles; Lucien Southard (1827–81), full score of the opera *Oomano*, and a scene from *The Scarlet Letter* (both 1850s?); Samuel Coleridge Taylor, *Hiawatha*, acquired with the Beerbohm Tree collection on British theater; George J. Webb, "Great Is the Lord: Anthem for Thanksgiving Day" (1830); George Whiting (1840–1923), numerous unpublished works, also correspondence; and Carl Wilmore, 33 mss, also letters

Other Music Materials in the Rare Books and Manuscripts Department

John S. Dwight (1832–92), personal papers, 329 items, relating to his activity at Brook Farm, as editor of *Dwight's Journal of Music*, and elsewhere, including 94 personal documents, also 233 incoming letters, many from musical associates, among them Otto Dresel (18 letters), Frédéric Louis Ritter, Thomas Ryan, Wilhelm Scharffenberg (9 letters, mostly concerning funds to support the study of Johann Ernst Perabo in Europe), and Alexander Wheelock Thayer (17 letters, also his essay "The Musical Culture and Advantages of Boston," signed jointly by Thayer and C. C. Perkins). See Honor McCusker, "Fifty Years of Music in Boston," *More Books*, 12 (1937), 341–59, 397–408, and 451–62

Richard Appel, letters, mostly in connection with his studies of the *Bay Psalm Book* and his duties at the Library

H. Earle Johnson, correspondence, mostly post-1940, relating to research in early American music

John Cotton (also attributed to Richard Mather), draft of the preface to the *Bay Psalm Book*, 1640, in the Thomas Prince mss, as discussed in Zoltán Haraszti, *The Enigma of the Bay Psalm Book* (Chicago, 1956), 18–27, the text reprinted on pp. 107–15

George Hood (1807–82), ms letters received, 1842–64, relating to Oliver Holden, Andrew Law, Elias Mann, Lowell Mason, Daniel Read, and Timothy Swan

Harriet C. Bond Long (1830–98), diaries, 1854–69, describing Boston concert life; also a partial transcript of these by H. Earle Johnson, 1947

Lang family papers, including B. J. Lang, lectures and career letters, 1876–1909; Francis (Mrs. B. J.) Lang, diaries, 1876–1920; Malcolm Lang, European and American diaries, 1876–1920; and Margaret Ruthven Lang, 3 vols. of scrapbooks, 1887–1967. (She is said to have destroyed her scores.)

Miscellaneous letters, of William Foster Apthorp; Amelita Galli Curci (1882–1963), letter discussing her vocal techniques, 1920; Henry Lee Higginson, letters as described in the *Catalogue of Old Boston Dining Club Papers*, mostly non-musical but with several musical discussions; Mrs. Marian MacDowell, 3 letters to Mrs. Mary H. MacNaught; and Johann Ernst Perabo, 20 items; also other items mentioned with the holograph materials above

Everette Truette, 2 vols. of travel diaries, 1883–84; also autograph albums, church music, and lectures

Other miscellaneous ms materials, including Quaintance Eaton, draft of her book *The Boston Opera Company* (New York, 1965), with typescript lists of casts, 1909–17; and Lucile Wilkin, notebook bibliography of pre-1851 U.S. songsters (1953)

Organizational archives, of the Boylston Club, 1873– , including papers of B. J. Lang; Boston Academy of Music, treasurer's reports, 1833–39, and lists of subscribers; Federal Street Theatre, Boston, 2 vols. of records, 1790s, including a contract with P. Landrin Duport; and ms record book of the Tremont Theatre

637
BOSTON UNIVERSITY   MBU
Mugar Memorial Library
Boston, Massachusetts 02215

Special Collections Department

Holdings are personal papers of musicians, and other papers with significant musical content

Rudolf Bing, correspondence and other mss, printed materials, photographs, and memorabilia, 40 linear cm.

Alexander Brailowsky (1896–1976), correspondence, programs, publicity materials, financial records, scrapbooks, and photographs, 2.5 linear meters

Cab Calloway, autobiographical materials, scrapbook, music, and photographs, 4 linear meters

Samuel Chotzinoff, correspondence and other ms materials, and printed matter, 90 linear cm.

Sylvia Dee (Josephine M. Profitt), ms materials, scrapbooks, printed materials, recordings, and memorabilia, 2 linear meters

Mischa Elman (1891–1967), correspondence and other ms materials, scrapbooks, programs, photographs, and publicity materials, 2.5 linear meters

Ella Fitzgerald, musical materials with ms annotations for her use, many by her arranger, also photographs, 65 linear cm.

Tamara Geva, ms autobiography

Martyn Green, correspondence, scrapbooks, scripts, playbills, photographs, posters, and memorabilia, 3.6 linear meters

Ervin Henning, printed and ms music, correspondence, and recordings, 60 linear cm.

Nora Kaye, material relating to her career, including correspondence, printed materials, programs, and photographs, 30 linear cm.

Marks Levine, correspondence, other ms and printed materials, and publicity, 15 linear cm.

Norman Lloyd, correspondence and other ms materials, 1.5 linear meters

George Marek, research correspondence and other ms materials, 1.2 linear meters

Vaughan Monroe, correspondence, scrapbook, recordings, photographs, and memorabilia, 90 linear cm.

Anthony Newley, correspondence and other ms material, music scores, scrapbooks, financial records, posters, and extensive memorabilia, 7 linear meters

Henry Pleasants, correspondence and scrapbooks, 1.2 linear meters

Harry Richman, correspondence and other mss, including an autobiography, scrapbooks, recordings, photographs, and memorabilia, 4.5 linear meters

Winthrop Sargeant, research notes, diaries, autobiographical materials, music scores, contracts, photographs, and memorabilia, 1.2 linear meters

Harold Schonberg, correspondence and other ms materials, programs, and other printed matter, 18 linear meters

Artie Shaw, scrapbooks, musical materials, and publicity, 6 linear meters

Albert Spalding (1888–1953), correspondence and other ms materials, scrapbooks, photographs, and printed music, 6 linear meters

Risë Stevens, scrapbooks, press clippings, programs, music with annotations, and memorabilia, 3.6 linear meters

Joseph Szigeti (1892–1973), correspondence, photographs, and other ms and printed items, 35 linear cm.

Rosalyn Tureck, correspondence, archives of the International Bach Society, financial records, ms research materials, interview transcripts, photographs, and other publicity materials, 10 linear meters

Boston Symphony Orchestra, archives, including all programs, 1881– ; holograph mss music commissioned by the Orchestra, including works by Igor Stravinsky, Paul Hindemith, Walter Piston, and Randall Thompson; and a miscellaneous collection of 18th- and 19th-century Italian opera music in ms

Veteran Association of the First Corps of Cadets (of 227 Commonwealth Avenue, Boston), and the Military Historical Society of Massachusetts, archives, including organizational records, sheet music and other printed music, programs, pictures, and recordings

School of Theology Library

Hymnology collection, 5000 items, including many U.S. imprints, mostly early Methodist and other Protestant, including materials from the collections of Frank E. Metcalf and Charles S. Nutter

—Francis Gramenz

638
BOSTONIAN SOCIETY   MBBS
Washington Street
Boston, Massachusetts 02109

Manuscript music, 12 items, including 19th-century songs about Boston by local composers

Materials relating to Oliver Holden, including 4 mss, 3 tunebooks, and an organ owned by him

Abel Bowen (early 19th-century music engraver), scrapbook containing proofs of music engravings and woodcut illustrations

Hymnals, 6 items, also 6 songbooks, late 18th and mid 19th centuries

Sheet music, 250 19th-century Boston imprints

Programs of local operas and concerts, mid to late 19th century, 60 linear cm.

Papers relating to 19th-century musical theater in Boston, 60 linear cm.

—Mary Leen

639
Isabella Stewart GARDNER   MBG
MUSEUM
2 Palace Road
Boston, Massachusetts 02115

Letters, ms scores, and memorabilia of musicians, located mainly in two showcases in the Yellow Room, including single letters or music mss of famous European musicians from the past or of contemporaries whom Mrs. Gardner did not know. Contemporary composers, performers, critics, and musicians whom she knew or helped support are represented more extensively, through letters, signed photographs, signed musical quotations, and scores; these include William F. Apthorp, Ferruccio Busoni, Gabriel Fauré, Heinrich Gebhard, Wilhelm Gericke, George Henschel, Vincent d'Indy, Henry Lee Higginson, Clayton Johns, Theodor Leschetizky, Charles Martin Loeffler (116 letters to Mrs. Gardner, and 2 music mss), Edward A. and Marian MacDowell, Nellie Melba, Karl Muck, Ethelbert Nevin, Ignace Jan Paderewski, Gustav Schirmer, Dame Ethel Smyth, Johann Strauss, Jr., Theodore Thomas, Pietro Adolfo Tirindelli (mss of 20 works, mostly songs), Francesco Paolo Tosti, and Amherst Webber. The Collection also includes concert programs, musical instruments, a John Singer Sargent painting of Loeffler, and a drawing of Fauré. See the typescript catalogue by Ralph P. Locke, also Locke's articles on Loeffler and Wagner items in the Museum's annual *Fenway Court: Isabella Stewart Gardner Museum* (1974, 1975)

—Ralph P. Locke

640
GIBSON SOCIETY
137 Beacon Street
Boston, Massachusetts 02116

Sheet music and songbooks, 2 linear meters; also press clippings on music, and recordings, including 25 78-rpm discs

—David Sweeney

641
GRAND LODGE OF MASONS IN
MASSACHUSETTS
Library
Masonic Temple
186 Tremont Street
Boston, Massachusetts 02111

Masonic songbooks, 2 linear meters, published ca. 1820– ; and Masonic sheet music, 150 items, 1826–1900s

—John Sherman

642

HARVARD MUSICAL ASSOCIATION   MBHM

57-A Chestnut Street
Boston, Massachusetts 02108

> See the issues of the *Bulletin* (later *Report*) of the Harvard Musical Association, 1934–59; also Charles Read Nutter, *History of the Harvard Musical Association* (Boston, 1968)

Charles E. Horn, holograph of "A Charter Glee for the Tremont Beef Steak Club," 1832

Arthur Foote, holograph ms of the Sonata for violoncello and piano op. 78, in a collection of 8 vols. of his music, both ms and published, presented in 1945

Frederick S. Converse, holograph ms of "Silent Noon," reverie for violoncello and piano

Sheet music and other published music from the library of Theodore Chase, originally 816 bound vols., including 409 operas, 118 chamber music works, and 185 miscellaneous vols., mostly collected in the 1860s; 120 vols., mostly piano music, from William Dietrich Strong; other vols. from the estates of Wulf Fries, Charles Peabody, and Mrs. Frances G. Lee; and many vols. from the library of Arthur Foote

George K. Jackson, personal copy of a bound vol. containing his own published music, some of it issued in England

Tunebooks, 40 items, 1752–1857, mostly ca. 1800

Periodicals, 47 pre-1914 titles, including a complete run of *Dwight's Journal of Music*

Programs of all concerts presented by the Association, 1865–   , and 35 other miscellaneous collections of programs

Photographs, formal and informal, including 15 items on display and 1 box in storage, also oil portraits of important leaders and associates of the Association, including John S. Dwight, Henry Gassett, Jr., Julia Marsh (also Charles Marsh, and Charles and Abby B. Barrett), and Courtney Guild

Archival documents relating to the Ariontic Sodality (1813–31?) and the Pieran Sodality (1837–40), precursors of the Harvard Musical Association, as discussed in the *Bulletin*, 20 (1952) and 23 (1955)

John S. Dwight, correspondence offering Hans von Bülow the position of conductor of the Harvard Orchestra, as discussed in the *Bulletin*, 7 (1938) and 12 (1942)

Dr. Newell S. Jenkins, letters concerning his friendship with Richard Wagner, 1875–83, and his invitation to Wagner to settle in the U.S., as reproduced in the *Bulletin*, 21 (1953)

—Barbara Winchester

643

MASSACHUSETTS HISTORICAL   MHi
SOCIETY

1154 Boylston Street
Boston, Massachusetts 02215

Sheet music, mostly 1830s–80s, 1000 items, arranged by composer (anonymous works by publisher), with a partial catalogue, and including 2 songs by Martha Harris Hastings

Printed flute music belonging to John Quincy Adams,

several items with a conjectural date of 1786, in the Cranch family papers

Tunebooks and hymnals, several 18th-century items and 3.5 linear meters of 19th-century items

Music mss, including Rev. Ebenezer Parkman, singing book, dated Westborough, Mass., 1721; Shepard Fish, ms music, dated 1730 and 1790; march music for drum, ca. 1776; 2 sheets of secular music with 17 tunes for flute, 1 page with "John Quincy Adams" written on it; and John Maxim, sacred-music ms, n.d.

Thomas Jefferson, ms lists of publications, including 80 music titles as cited in H. Earle Johnson, "Musical Interest of Certain American Literary and Political Figures," *Journal of Research in Music Education*, 19 (1971), 272–94

Shaker music, 5 printed editions, in the Knight–Shaker Collection

Miscellaneous musical correspondence, including letters of Oliver Holden, 1806–11; George Homer, letter concerning a singing school, 1806; and Robert Treat Paine, diary entries, 1749

—John D. Cushing

644

Thomas MURRAY

Saint Paul's Cathedral
138 Tremont Street
Boston, Massachusetts 02111

Sheet music and other published music, 300 mid-19th-century sacred choral editions

645

MUSEUM OF FINE ARTS   MBMu

465 Huntington Avenue
Boston, Massachusetts 02115

Manuscript book of flute music, ca. 1820, owned by George Briard, Portsmouth, N.H.

—Barbara Lambert

646

NEW ENGLAND CONSERVATORY   MBCM
OF MUSIC

Harriet M. Spaulding Library
33 Gainsborough Street; *and*
Idabelle Firestone Audio Library
290 Huntington Avenue
Boston, Massachusetts 02115

Papers of Musicians and Groups

Maud D. Brooks, 9 letters to Virginia Richmond, written while she was a student at the Conservatory, 1888–90

Chromatic Club, Boston, programs of 32nd to 60th seasons, 1918–47

Silvio Coscia (1899–1977, horn player), papers, including correspondence, ca. 1927–72, publicity, and clippings; also photographs, ca. 1916–66, mostly signed portraits of conductors and singers, many of the latter attached to typed transcriptions of responses to questions from Coscia about voice production

Arthur Foote (1853–1937), 180 items of correspondence, 1883–1922, mostly from European and American musicians, some also to Mrs. Foote

Wallace Goodrich (1871–1952, organist and conductor), 179 items of correspondence, 1895–1953, from American and European musicians, some also to Mrs. Goodrich

Ernest H. Jackson annotated programs, souvenir items, and press clippings, 1922–43; also memorabilia of the World's Peace Jubilee, Boston, 1872

Isabelle Tompson Moore, personal papers, 70 items, including correspondence, clippings, and programs, 1890–ca. 1955, with letters from Ethelbert Nevin, Anne Paul Nevin, Edward A. MacDowell, Marian MacDowell, and Johann Ernst Perabo, also with assignments of piano pieces by MacDowell (her teacher), and her music notebook of finger exercises, partly in the ms hands of Nevin and MacDowell

National Peace Jubilee, Boston, 1869, programs and memorabilia, ca. 1869, and selected serial publications

Gertrude Norman, 51 items of correspondence, 1938–51, mostly relating to the Marcia Van Dresser Memorial Room at the Conservatory; also 6 scrapbooks of photographs, clippings, programs, and other materials relating to Marcia Van Dresser, with commentary by Norman

John A. Preston Collection of autograph letters of celebrated European musicians, 55 items, 1807–88

Gunther Schuller, collection of 19 documents and letters concerning Carl Baermann (1839–1913) and the Baermann Society, 1909–68, including letters from Baermann to Lee Marian Pattison

Walter F. Starbuck, album of 53 autographs, autograph letters, and programs, mostly of American and European musicians, ca. 1894–1940

Helen Ingersoll Tetlow, 58 portraits and letters of musicians, 1878–1945, mostly involving Helen Hopekirk

Eben Tourjée (1834–91, educator), 30 items of letters, documents, and clippings, 1850s–ca. 1934

"Voice of Firestone" (radio and television broadcasts sponsored by the Firestone Tire and Rubber Co., ca. 1928–58), 1 box of correspondence, documents, and memorabilia

William W. Wheildon, scrapbook of press clippings, memorabilia, and programs of the National Peace Jubilee, Boston, 1869, and scrapbook of press clippings, programs, journals, and memorabilia of the World's Peace Jubilee, Boston, 1872

Programs of various Boston concert series, ca. 1865–ca. 1932

Manuscript and Published Music

Edward Ballantine, 135 mss including 67 songs, 38 piano works, and 26 chamber, choral, and orchestral works, ca. 1904–54; also printed music

Amy Cheney (Mrs. H. H. A.) Beach, 19 holograph mss including "The Canticle of the Sun," "Festival Jubilate," "The Rose of Avontown," "The Sea-Fairies," and other works, 1880–ca. 1929; also printed music

John Parsons Beach, 2 music mss

John Alden Carpenter, 3 music mss, ca. 1934–47

George W. Chadwick, 55 mss including holographs, photostats of holographs, and copyists' mss, ca. 1878–ca. 1928; also 100 first editions of printed music

Frederick S. Converse, 120 mss, mostly holographs, ca. 1890–ca. 1940; also printed music

Silvio Coscia, 260 music mss, mostly holographs, 1916–71

Mabel Wheeler Daniels, 3 music mss, 1913–29

John Lodge Ellerton, 2 holograph music mss, ca. 1857

Arthur Elson, 14 music mss

Louis Charles Elson, 25 music mss, some in holograph; also printed music

Norma Farber, 100 songs, mostly by 20th-century American composers, with holographs, reproductions from holographs, and copyists' mss, including works by Theodore Chanler (19 items), David Diamond (11 items), Normand Lockwood (8 items), Daniel Pinkham (11 items), and Arthur Shepherd (9 items)

Arthur Foote, 32 music mss, 1906–23, including 1 vol. containing 14 holographs

George Luther Foote, 120 music mss, ca. 1900–1954, mostly holographs, including 5 vols. of sketches

Wallace Goodrich, 27 holograph mss of 16 original works and 11 arrangements

Elise Coolidge (Mrs. Richard J.) Hall, 19 mss of works she commissioned featuring the saxophone, 1901–15, with copyists' mss and holograph scores, the latter including works by Charles Martin Loeffler, André Caplet, Debussy, Jean Huré, and Henry Woollett; also 19 printed orchestral works and selections from operas, principally by French composers

Henry K. Hadley, 4 holograph music mss, ca. 1891–1918

Edward Burlingame Hill, 13 music mss, mostly in holograph, 1898–1943

Napier Lothian Theater Orchestra Collection, partly consisting of orchestrations of works by Johann Strauss, Jr. (50 items), Josef Strauss (25 items), and Eduard Strauss (26 items), some of them published in Boston and New York

Horatio Parker, 7 music mss, principally in holograph, 1890–1914, including "Cahál Mór," "Collegiate Overture," "Fairyland," and "A Northern Ballad"

J. C. D. Parker, 3 holograph music mss, 1854–90, including "The Life of Man"

Adelaide and Mathilde Phillipps Memorial Collection, principally orchestrations for vocal selections; also selections from vocal works by various composers, copied by Adelaide Phillipps (d. 1880), some with her annotations for study. Their opera scores, songs, and books on music are in the Boston Public Library, q.v.

Thomas Ryan, 32 holograph music mss, 1850–1902, including 29 original works and 3 arrangements, some written for the Mendelssohn Quintet Club of Boston

George Siemonn, 4 holograph music mss, ca. 1916–20

Marcia Van Dresser (1880–1937, soprano), 15 ms and printed songs, some of them in holograph, including works by Lyell Barbour, Gordon Bryan, Tom Dobson, Sinclair Logan, Roger Quilter, and Leila Von Meister

"Voice of Firestone," 1639 ms instrumental and vocal arrangements used for broadcasts; also 485 kinescopes of the television program, and 42 master tapes of radio broadcasts

Thomas Carl Whitmer, 2 holograph music mss, ca. 1942

Other holograph music mss, 1 item each by Percy Lee Atherton, Rossitter Gleason Cole, Charles Frederick Dennée, Carl Engel, James Remington Fairlamb, Arthur Farwell, Heinrich Gebhard, Richard Hageman, Rheinhold Ludwig Herman, Frederick Jacobi, Stuart Mason, and Whitney Eugene Thayer

—Geraldine Ostrove

647

NORTHEASTERN UNIVERSITY   MBNU

Robert G. Dodge Library
360 Huntington Avenue
Boston, Massachusetts 02115

Materials from the cornerstone of the Boston Opera House, including 6 music-periodical issues, 1908, 10 music scores, 1885–1907, and 11 programs, 1907–8
Songbooks, 40 items, 1776–1940
Recordings, including 700 78-rpm discs
          —Vivian A. Rosenberg

648

SAINT PAUL'S CATHEDRAL

138 Tremont Street
Boston, Massachusetts 02111

Personal correspondence of Samuel Parkman Tuckerman (1819–90), John Paddon, and other Boston musicians, ca. 1850, relating to music at the Cathedral, including financial documents of George K. Jackson (1745–1822) and Thomas Ball (fl. 1848, sculptor and musician)
          —Thomas Murray

649

SOCIETY FOR THE   MBSpnea
PRESERVATION OF NEW ENGLAND
ANTIQUITIES

Harrison Gray Otis House
141 Cambridge Street
Boston, Massachusetts 02114

The collection of miscellaneous late 18th- and 19th-century materials, including 2 drawers of sheet music, various printed editions of music, mss, and programs, is now dispersed

650

UNIVERSITY OF MASSACHUSETTS   MBMU

Harbor Campus
Fine Arts Library
Boston, Massachusetts 02125

Sheet music, 10,000 popular songs, mostly 1900–1950; also 1200 photocopies of 19th-century parlor music
          —Andrew Castiglione

651

Dorothy WATERHOUSE

313 Commonwealth Avenue
Boston, Massachusetts 02115

Susanna ("Sukey") Heath (1758–87), ms music book, copied 1780–81 and dated 1782, entitled "Collection from Sundry Authors," and including sacred and secular vocal music, with important texts of works by William Billings. See Richard Crawford and David P. McKay, "Music in Manuscript: A Massachusetts Tune-Book of 1782," *American Antiquarian Society Proceedings*, 84 (1974), 43–64

652

PUBLIC LIBRARY OF BROOKLINE   MBr

361 Washington Street
Brookline, Massachusetts 02146

Sheet music, 315 items, 1880–1940, including popular and World War I songs
Protestant hymnals, 70 items
Piano and piano-vocal music, 1883–1943, 45 items
          —Judith Jackson Long

653

EPISCOPAL DIVINITY SCHOOL   MCE

Sherrill Memorial Library
99 Brattle Street
Cambridge, Massachusetts 02138

William Bacon Stevens (1815–87), 30,000 vols. from his library, formerly maintained by the Protestant Episcopal Church in Philadelphia Divinity School. (Other parts of the collection are at the University of Notre Dame, Ind., and the University of Pennsylvania, Philadelphia, q.v.) Among the Cambridge holdings are hymnals and hymnology books, including the collection assembled by Rev. Charles L. Hutchins (1838–1919, hymnologist)
Additional hymnals, 6 linear meters, and liturgical music, 12 linear meters
          —John E. Lamb, Sandra Boyd

654

HARVARD UNIVERSITY   MH, MCR

Cambridge, Massachusetts 02138

This report on the various collections of Harvard University and Radcliffe College has been coordinated by Michael Ochs; unless otherwise noted, the reports have been prepared by Honey Meconi. For a list of pre-1801 materials, including some U.S. items, see David A. Wood, *Music in Harvard Libraries* (Cambridge, 1980)

Eda Kuhn Loeb Music Library

See Nino Pirrotta, "The Eda Kuhn Loeb Music Library," *Harvard Library Bulletin*, 12 (1958), 410–17

Richard Aldrich, selected materials from his collection, as cited in his *Catalogue of Books Relating to Music* (New York, 1931). Other materials listed in this catalogue have been assigned to other Harvard Libraries
Vocal anthologies, including 140 school songbooks, 75 hymnals and other sacred collections, and 50 glee and other secular songbooks, mostly Boston imprints, mid 19th century
Sheet music, in several bound vols., including a collection of glees, rounds, and madrigals assembled in New York by M. Johnson, Jr., after 1832
          —Florence Lynch

Houghton Library

Music mss, including Louis Adolphe Coerne (1870–1922), *Excalibur*, 1921, and *Two Studies in Mood*, 1914; Frederick Shepherd Converse (1871–1940), 9 mss, including the *Fantasy for Piano and Orchestra*, 1922, Serenade, 1907, Symphony in A Minor, 1898, and

Laudate Dominum, 1936, also a copyist's ms of his arrangement of Brahms's Haydn variations; Archibald T. Davison (1883–1961), conductor's score of "O Gladsome Light"; Edward Burlingame Hill (1872–1960), *Lilacs* op. 33, 1926; Charles Jerome Hopkins (1836–1898), 12 boxes of music mss on deposit, including the Symphony in A, Piano Concerto no. 1, *Paraphrase of Cherubini's Fugue in D, Sepoy March, Nuptial March, Child's Symphony for Strings, Manhood Overture, Victory Te Deum,* Trio Concerto, Serenade, and *Dramatic Caprice for 5 Pianos;* Darius Milhaud (1892–1974), *Psaume 121,* 1921; John Knowles Paine (1839–1906), 77 items, as cited in John Calvitt Huxford, *John Knowles Paine, His Life and Works* (Ph.D. diss., Florida State University, 1968), also copies of some of his students' music; and Randall Thompson, 152 holograph scores and sketches on deposit including most of his works

Letters of musicians, including Frederick Shepherd Converse, 5 items, 1919–39; George Gershwin, 35 letters to Isaac Goldberg, 1929–37; Edward Burlingame Hill, 10 cartons of personal papers containing 12 letters to and 8 letters from Amy Lowell, 1918–25, and 12 letters to and 13 letters from Houghton, Mifflin, & Co., 1924; Louis Krasner, 70 letters from various correspondents, including Alban Berg, Helene Berg, Serge Koussevitzky, Alma Mahler, Nathan Milstein, Arnold Schoenberg, Roger Sessions, Harold Spivacke, Leopold Stokowski, and Anton Webern, also other materials, on deposit; Jenny Lind, 32 letters, 1851–78, including 2 to Henry Wadsworth Longfellow, 1851, and 28 to Anna Hazard Barker Ward, 1852–78, also other materials; correspondence of the members of the McKim and Garrison families, 1866–90; John Knowles Paine, 7 letters to various correspondents, 1874–1902, also an 87-page ms about Paine by Mark Antony DeWolfe Howe; Walter Piston, 3 letters to Howe, 1936–37; Randall Thompson, 8 letters to Howe, 1935–55; and Oswald Garrison Villard (1872–1949), papers relating to his work with the New York Philharmonic–Symphony Orchestra

Other music mss, including the archives of the Cambridge Music Club, 1916–56; a ms glee book of Augustus Peabody, ca. 1820, and a glee book stamped, "Harvard Glee Club, vol. 3," 1836–37, as described in Bryan Eugene Lindsay, *The English Glee in New England, 1815–1845* (Ph.D. diss., George Peabody College for Teachers, 1966); miscellaneous vols., including John Bryden, psalm tunes and church music, dated Cumberland (Md.?), 1838; John Fowle, collection of musical airs, instrumental and vocal, early 19th century?; Abiel How, collection of hymn tunes, compiled in Methuen, Mass., 1791–1801; Samuel Mowrer, collection of musical airs, written in Boston and at Union College, Schenectady, N.Y., 1828–30; Emily Rand, holograph ms "Musick Book," Boston?, 1830–37; John Wright Taylor, "Method of Writing Music," typescript with ms music, Worcester, 1921; an anonymous "Collection of Musical Airs," early 19th century?; a "Collection of Dance Tunes and Marches," late 18th century?, possibly in the hand of Elisha Belknap; and Hugh Stalker, collection of musicians' autographs

Francis James Child (1825–96), personal papers, including research materials on the history of British ballads

Henry Lee Higginson, personal correspondence, including 118 outgoing letters, 1875–1917, and 28 incoming letters, 1863–1917

Sheet music, 225,000 items (estimate based on an average of 200 items per box), including the collection of Raymond Sanger Wilkins (1891–1971, chief justice of Massachusetts Commonwealth), in 409 boxes, of which 121 are arranged by title, 162 by composer, and 124 by composer for Tin Pan Alley and Broadway music; the general collection, in 658 boxes, incorporating the collections of Clara de Windt and of Evert J. Wendell, arranged by title; 43 boxes arranged by literary association, 13 boxes of ragtime, and 13 boxes of music by popular composers; and 400 bound vols. of sheet music

Songsters, 1500 items, including 78 pre-1921 imprints

Theatre Collection

A Department of the Houghton Library; materials are housed in the Pusey Library. See William Van Lennep, "The Harvard Theatre Collection," Harvard Library *Bulletin,* 6 (1952), 281–301

Dramatic ms materials of musical significance, including William Dunlap, promptbook for *The Virgin of the Sun,* and Charles M. Barras, ms for *The Black Crook*

Dramatic portraits, in 88 boxes and including many American and many musical portraits, as indexed in Lillian A. Hall, *Catalogue of Dramatic Portraits,* 4 vols. (Cambridge, 1930–34); also 9 boxes of pictorial material on minstrelsy, arranged by performer or troupe

Edwin Vose, sheet music, 12,000 items, mostly from American musical comedies, 1920s–50s, arranged by show; and recordings, including 2800 10-inch 17-rpm Victor discs, mostly popular, 1911–50s, indexed but not presently available for consultation

Playbill collection, including many programs of operatic and other musical events, many of them local or from New Orleans

Theatrical press clippings, including musical events

Opera libretti, arranged by title

Andover–Harvard Theological Library, Harvard Divinity School

Hymnals and tunebooks, 85 linear meters of catalogued books, and 75 linear meters of uncatalogued books, 1713– , mostly 19th-century U.S. imprints, with and without music; also 16 linear meters of books on hymnology, catalogued. Included are 175 vols. from the Universalist Historical Society

Archival records of the Universalist Historical Society and of the Singing Committee of the Hollis Street Church, Boston, the latter including an inventory of music books, 1800s

Henry Wilder Foote (1875–1964), personal papers, uncatalogued

Monroe C. Gutman Library, Graduate School of Education

Music textbooks, including 175 vols. published 1870–99, and 200 vols. published 1900–1936, arranged chronologically

—Marcia J. Kindzerske, Honey Meconi

Baker Library, Graduate School of Business Administration

Henry Lee Higginson, personal papers, 1870–1919, 11 linear meters, including extensive documents relating to the founding and management of the Boston Symphony Orchestra

Brighton Beach Music Hall, Brooklyn, N.Y., archives, including contracts with performers, account books, and programs, 1908–14; also related account books and other archival records of the firm of Ward and Gow, New York, involving advertising on behalf of the Hall and related matters, 1895–1919

—Honey Meconi, Florence Lynch

Arthur and Elizabeth Schlesinger Library on the History of Women in America

A research collection maintained as a part of Radcliffe College. See the catalogue of the collection (Boston, 1973)

Mabel Wheeler Daniels (1884–1971), personal papers, including extensive correspondence with musicians, notably with Marian MacDowell; holograph music mss, in 15 folders, with a list; biographical material, including an extensive collection of photographs; 7 scrapbooks, 1884–1935, and several folders of materials removed from scrapbooks; and programs, press clippings, and other materials, some of it relating to the MacDowell Colony. See the detailed inventory

Vera Curtis (1879–1962), personal papers, 1907–43, 1962, including correspondence, photographs, programs, press clippings, and writings and lecture notes relating to her singing career at the Metropolitan Opera and elsewhere; also her scrapbook of programs, announcements, and press clippings, 1915–26

Emma Eames (1865–1952), 76 letters to Francis Wilson Lee, regarding funds raised to finance her studies abroad, 1886–91

Marie Reuter Gallison (b. 1861, singer, teacher at Radcliffe College, and founder of the Choral Society), typescript autobiography, *My Life in Two Continents,* Kaiserswerth, Germany, 1949

Josephine Sherwood Hull, personal papers, including 13 college songbooks containing her musical works

—Elizabeth Shenton, Madeleine Bagwell Perez

Peabody Museum of Archaeology and Ethnology

Musical materials and artifacts of American Indians, including musical instruments of Plains and northwest-coast tribes, also materials collected by Alice Fletcher

Milman Parry Collection, Widener Library

Recordings of folklore materials, mostly non-American, but with musical materials including several field recordings of Hungarian immigrants in Pittsburgh; oral-history common-meter monologues recorded in Newton, Mass.; 6 tapes of Afro-American preaching collected by Jeff Titon; and 12 hours of copies of early blues recordings, 1920s. See David Bynum, "Child's Legacy Enlarged," Harvard Library *Bulletin,* 22/3 (1974), 237–67

—David Bynum

Harvard University Archives

University records, including archives of the Music Department, with minutes, correspondence, records of concerts, student folders, and other documents, 1904–59, in 42 vols.; the Faculty Committee of Dramatic and Musical Entertainments, rules and forms, 1899–1901; the Board of Overseers, Reports of the Committee to Visit the Department of Music, 1890–1953, 1 folder; and theses, as cited in Alan C. Buechner, *Yankee Singing Schools and the Golden Age of Choral Music in New England* (Ed.D. diss., Harvard University, 1960), Appendix A

Student/alumni organization records, including musical works written by students and relating to Harvard; Alumni Chorus, 1 folder, 1910– ; Harvard University Band, 4 vols. of publications and reference material, a scrapbook, recording, and correspondence relating to the tercentenary celebration, 1938, also photographs and music arranged by Leroy Anderson and G. W. Griggs, 1922–51, in 3 vols.; University Choir, 2 vols. of official records, 1834–48; Freshman Glee Club, programs, general folder, and account book, 1870– , in 4 vols.; Glee Club, 52 vols. of publications and reference material, and 165 vols. of correspondence and minutes of the Executive Committee, including printed notices and operational manuals and documents, recordings, contracts, scrapbooks of press clippings, songbooks, and other materials, 1860–ca. 1969, also 2 vols. of publications and reference materials on earlier glee clubs, 1835? and ca. 1850?; Handel Sodality, constitution, list of members, and minutes, 1807, in 1 vol.; instrumental clubs, 2 vols. of publications and reference material, 14 vols. of correspondence, minutes, scrapbooks, and other documents, and 18 vols. of similar material relating to tours, 1911– ; Pierian Sodality, publications and reference materials in 16 vols., minutes, correspondence, music, recordings, and other papers, 1808–ca. 1968, in 57 vols., and correspondence and other records of the Pierian Sodality Alumni, 1929–30; Harvard Singing Society, 1840– , constitution and minutes, in 1 vol.; also general folders on the Alumni Chorus, 1910– , Harvard Banjo Club, 1886– , Harvard Brass Band, 1883– , Collegium musicum of the Division of Music, ca. 1938, Friends of Art, Archaeology, and Music at Harvard, 1939– , Guitar and Mandolin Club, 1887– , Mandolin Club, 1887– , Opera Association, 1912– , Summer School Chorus, ca. 1931?, and 57 vols. of college music other than religious and dramatic, including clippings and reprints, sheet music, songbooks, and songs in ms

Personal papers, including John Knowles Paine (1839–1906), 3 folders of correspondence, ms music fragments, and other documents, also 1 vol. of his autograph collection; George Lyman Kittredge (1860–1941); Walter R. Spaulding (1865–1962), 1 vol. of publications and reference material, and 1 ms music arrangement; and G. Wallace Woodworth (1902–69), 2 vols. of publications and reference materials, and 13 vols. of correspondence and papers relating to Harvard musical activities

—Jennifer Zukowski

Radcliffe College Archives

Archives of music organizations, including the Radcliffe Choral Society, Glee Club, Operetta Society, and Mandolin Club, 1 linear meter; Harvard Radcliffe Orchestra, 15 linear cm.; and Radcliffe Musical Association (alumnae organization), 30 linear cm.

College songbooks, 5 items, 1909–43

Sheet music, published and in ms, 15 linear cm.

Music, programs, and memorabilia of Mabel Daniels and Rhoda Crowell, 30 linear cm.

Programs and records of concerts, 30 linear cm.

Photographs of musicians and musical activities, 30 linear cm.

—Jane S. Knowles

655

MASSACHUSETTS INSTITUTE OF   MCM TECHNOLOGY

Institute Archives and Special Collections
MIT Libraries, Room 14N-118
Cambridge, Massachusetts 02139

Tech Show (annual student revue or vaudeville comedy), archives, 1899–1968, 3 linear meters, comprising posters, programs, scripts, orchestral parts, published scores, photographs, and recordings

—Karen Temple Lynch

656

Joseph A. BASSETT

First Church
26 Suffolk Road
Chestnut Hill, Massachusetts 02167

Howard E. Pomeroy (1900–1975, pastor of the Boylston Congregational Church, Jamaica Plain, Mass.), correspondence with American hymn writers describing the circumstances in which hymns were written, 80 letters, 1930–40

657

Louisa May ALCOTT MEMORIAL ASSOCIATION

Box 343
Concord, Massachusetts 01742

Manuscript music for flute, 2 bound vols. owned by Frederick Alcott Pratt (b. 1863)

Hymnal, prepared by Rev. David Palmer, Middlesex Musical Society, 1807, and owned by Joseph May (father of Louisa May Alcott)

Songbook containing Irish melodies and sacred, moral, and sentimental songs, ca. 1825, owned by Louisa May Alcott (1840–79)

—Jayne Gordon

658

CONCORD ANTIQUARIAN SOCIETY

Box 146
Concord, Massachusetts 01742

Songbooks, 2 items in the Thoreau Collection, one of them a copy of Oliver Holden's *Rudiments of Music*, signed by Samuel Blake, 1801, the other a vol. of antislavery songs published by Jairus Lincoln (Boston, 1853); also Isaac Watts, *The Union Harmony* (n.d.)

—Barbara Oster

659

CONCORD FREE PUBLIC LIBRARY   MCo

129 Main Street
Concord, Massachusetts 01742

Thomas Whitney Surette (1861–1941), 1 linear meter of papers relating to the Surette School of Music and the Concord Academy, including scrapbooks, programs, letters, press clippings, and photographs; also published songbooks including his *Concord Series*, ca. 1925

Kay Davis (b. 1892, composer and teacher), published music, and letters to Surette

Sophia Thoreau, 5 mss of popular songs, and published sheet music owned by her family. See "Some Observations on the Thoreau Family's Sheet Music," Thoreau Society *Bulletin*, 142 (Winter, 1977)

Ellen Emerson (1839–1909, dance teacher, daughter of Ralph Waldo Emerson), published dance music used by her, with ms notes

Sheet music, 15 vols. of popular music, ca. 1900

Concord Choral Club, programs, 1887–92

Programs for local concerts, 1800s–1930

—Marcia E. Moss

660

DEDHAM HISTORICAL SOCIETY   MDedHi

Box 215
Dedham, Massachusetts 02026

Hymnals, 2 18th-century ms vols.

Sacred songbooks, 10 items, 1812–60, mostly Boston imprints

Supply Belcher, *Harmony of Maine* (Farmington, Me., 1794)

—Muriel N. Peters

661

Henry Leland CLARKE

1 Watting Road
Deerfield, Massachusetts 01342

Personal papers, including sketches of Clarke's musical compositions; correspondence with composers, musicologists, and other musicians, among them Otto Luening and G. Wallace Woodworth; and research notes for his studies, mostly in early English and American music

662

HISTORIC DEERFIELD   MDeeH

Box 231
Deerfield, Massachusetts 01342

Manuscript music by local amateur composers and students, including singing-school items, scattered among 500 boxes

Protestant hymnals, 100 items published ca. 1770–1890, some with words only

Tunebooks, 50 items published ca. 1780–1890, the earliest of them in shape notation

Justin Hitchcock (1752–1822, fifer who moved to Deerfield in 1774, and marched at Lexington), diary

Sheet music, 25 items of 19th-century popular piano music, some bound; also 5 items by Matilde Hyde (local composer), 1920s–30s

William Bull (1762–1842, Deerfield composer), a copy of his instruction book and hymnal, *Music, Adapted to Language* (Greenfield, Mass., 1819)

Programs of mid-19th-century local concerts, 75 items, scattered among personal collections

—David R. Proper

663
DUKES COUNTY HISTORICAL SOCIETY
Box 827
Edgartown, Massachusetts 02539

John Pease, Jr., ms music book, ca. 1795

William Litten, ms fiddle music, 2 bound vols., ca. 1790

Joseph Thaxter, (chaplain at the Battle of Bunker Hill), ms copies of church music, 50 items

Manuscript music for clarinet, 30 items, ca. 1830

Will Hardy (local composer), 6 sheet-music items, mostly 1880s

—Thomas E. Norton

664
FALL RIVER HISTORICAL SOCIETY
451 Rock Street
Fall River, Massachusetts 02720

Sheet music, 75 items, some by local composers including George H. Foley, J. C. Hurley, and Annie Burgess Buffinton, published locally, ca. 1911

Songbooks, 20 items, used locally in Methodist Sunday schools, 1890–1900

Programs, 6 items, of local music groups and of concerts given locally by Eben Tourjée, 1880–90

Scrapbooks, 50 items containing local concert programs and press clippings, 1900–1910

—Florence C. Brigham

665
FITCHBURG HISTORICAL SOCIETY
Box 953
Fitchburg, Massachusetts 01420

Hymnals, 15 early 19th-century items, some with words only, used in the local Congregational church

Songbooks, 15 items, early 19th to early 20th century, used by local bands

Sheet music, 20 popular vocal and piano-vocal items, some of them composed and published locally, late 19th century

Fitchburg Cornet Band, 2 notebooks of papers, 19th century

Programs of local music groups, 1 linear meter, mid 19th and early 20th centuries

Pictures of local music groups and musicians including Gustav Patz and Andrew Whitney, 25 items, 1870s to early 20th century

Melodeons, 2 instruments built in Fitchburg, and formerly owned by Andrew Whitney

—Eleanora F. West

666
FITCHBURG PUBLIC LIBRARY   MFi
610 Main Street
Fitchburg, Massachusetts 01420

Music scores from the Francis H. Jenks Collection, donated in 1906. The majority of the collection is housed in the Fitchburg State College Library (q.v.)

667
FITCHBURG STATE COLLEGE   MFiT
Library
Pearl Street
Fitchburg, Massachusetts 01420

Francis H. Jenks (1838–94) Collection of 19th-century music scores, 1000 printed and ms items, formerly at the Fitchburg Public Library. Materials include reviews, programs, publicity, illustrations, correspondence, and Jenks's notations of dates and personnel of American performances. Scores are mostly of European compositions, but the numerous American items include hymns and anthems, songs, choral music, keyboard and chamber music, and orchestral scores

Belding collection of 19th-century music for piano four-hand, 600 items, mostly arrangements of symphonic and chamber music

668
FOXBOROUGH HISTORICAL COMMISSION
Memorial Hall
Foxborough, Massachusetts 02035

Foxboro Brass Band, instruments and descriptive materials

Sheet music, 10 items, also 10 songbooks, 1 music ms, 30 programs, and 20 photographs concerning local musical activities

—Ed Heinricher

669
FRAMINGHAM HISTORICAL SOCIETY
Box 2032
Framingham, Massachusetts 01701

Framingham Musical Association, papers, ca. 1870–1910

Songbooks, including 50 early 19th-century hymnals and 10 late 19th-century popular songbooks

Sheet music, 100 items, late 19th century

Programs of 50 late 19th-century local musical events, involving the Elmwood Opera House, charitable organizations, and community and military groups

—Stephen W. Herring

670

FRUITLANDS MUSEUMS
Prospect Hill
Harvard, Massachusetts 01451

Shaker hymnals in letter notation, 20 items, 1840s, and
an 1843 book concerning letter notation
—William Harrison

671

HAVERHILL PUBLIC LIBRARY   MHa
99 Main Street
Haverhill, Massachusetts 01830

Sheet music, 750 bound vols. for piano, early 20th
century
Photographs, including Rufus Williams (local music
publisher) and his daughter, Annie Williams Chick
(violinist), late 19th century; John Nichols (local
violin-maker and conductor of the Pentucket Orchestra), ca. 1910; and Julia Houston West (local singer),
1869
Haverhill Academy of Music, 30 linear cm. of papers
concerning James West (director of the Academy),
1880s; also programs, 1884–89
Frank G. Holt (drummer with John Philip Sousa's
band), papers, 1860–1910
Grace Spofford (Haverhill resident and director of the
Curtis Institute of Music, 1930s), 5 clippings
—Greg Laing

672

MEANS LIBRARY
5 Vautrinot Avenue
Hull, Massachusetts 02045

Bernice De Pasquali (Metropolitan Opera coloratura
soprano, 1907–13) and her husband, Salvatore De
Pasquali (opera manager), materials including 3 letters from Pietro Mascagni, 30 linear cm. of papers,
diaries of Bernice's mother at the start of the singer's
career, 15 linear cm. of programs, 20 linear cm. of
pictures, and 8 recordings, ca. 1910
Photographs of local bands, 6 items, 1890s
—Dennis Means

673

TALES OF CAPE COD
47 Cherry Street
Hyannis, Massachusetts 02601

Hymnals, 50 items used by the local Third Baptist
Church, ca. 1900
Photographs of local bands, 6 items, 1880s
Oral-history materials, 200 tape recordings about the
history of Cape Cod since the 1880s, cross-referenced
and briefly summarized
—Louis Cataldo

674

LANCASTER TOWN LIBRARY   MLanc
Main Street
Lancaster, Massachusetts 01523

Sheet music, 20,000 items in 455 bound vols., which also
include instruction books and other published editions, some European
Music periodicals, 1839–48, 6 vols.

675

BERKSHIRE CHRISTIAN COLLEGE   MLenB
Library
200 Stockbridge Road
Lenox, Massachusetts 01240

Hymnals, 788 items of various Protestant denominations,
ca. 1800–   , some with words only
—Lois Jones

676

UNIVERSITY OF LOWELL   MLowTC
Lydon Library
Lowell, Massachusetts 01854

Sheet music, 50 items, mostly French-Canadian, published locally by the Champagne brothers, 1909–28
Solon Stevens (editor of the *Vox Populi*, a Lowell newspaper, 1836–1919), papers, 60 linear cm.
Lowell Historical Society Book, Manuscript and Photograph Collection, including papers of local music
groups, 1850–80, 1 linear meter; a complete run of the
Lowell Offering (local women's journal with music,
1840–45) and other journals with music, including *The
Album* (1932–33), *The Ladies' Pearl* (1840–43), and the
Middlesex Hearthstone (1895–96); 500 programs of local
concerts and musical events, 1850–1900, arranged
alphabetically by concert hall; and photographs of local
19th-century musicians and music buildings in a general collection of 5000 photographs of local subjects
—Martha Mayo

677

LYNN HISTORICAL SOCIETY
125 Green Street
Lynn, Massachusetts 01902

Materials used by the Hutchinson Family Singers,
donated by John W. Hutchinson shortly after 1900,
including 10 popular sheet-music songs; 4 songbooks,
some with religious songs; programs of Hutchinson
Family concerts; a scrapbook of John W. Hutchinson,
including programs, tickets, and photographs of the
Hutchinson family; and 5 photographs of the Hutchinson Family Singers
—Susan Eastwood

678

MARSHFIELD HISTORICAL SOCIETY
Box 1244
Marshfield, Massachusetts 02050

Adelaide Phillipps (1833–82, local singer), sheet music, programs, photographs, and a biography
Songbooks, several items from schools and churches

—Janet E. Peterson

679

TUFTS UNIVERSITY   MMeT

Medford, Massachusetts 02155

Nils Yngve Wessell Library

Frédéric Louis Ritter (1834–91, historian and professor of music at Vassar College), music library, as described in the *Catalogue of the Music Library of the Late Frédéric Louis Ritter* (n.p., 189–?)
Asa Alford Tufts (1798–1884), family music library, including songbooks, sheet music, and other materials, mostly 19th-century Boston imprints
Leo Rich Lewis (1865–1945, professor of music at Tufts College, 1895–1945), personal papers, including 100 letters and 2 scrapbooks
Programs and playbills, 3 linear meters
Popular sheet music, 1900–1930, 150 items

—Brenda Chasen Goldman

Tufts University Collection of Oral Literature
(Reference Division, University Library)

Vertical file containing 4 folders of printed materials and transcriptions pertaining to work-play songs, jump-rope songs, slang folksongs, and folktales from Massachusetts and from Beaver Falls, Pa.; also an index to folksongs and camp songs; and discussions with guitarists, collected by University students, 1970s

—Ray Gerke

680

Michael CUMMINGS

16 Cedar Terrace
Milton, Massachusetts 02186

Patrick S. Gilmore (1829–92), songs and band music by him, also letters, clippings, programs, photographs, and memorabilia

681

NEEDHAM HISTORICAL SOCIETY

53 Glendoon Road
Needham, Massachusetts 02192

Sheet music, "The Lancers' Quick Step," performed by Bartlett's Brass Band, 1837
Hymnals and sacred songbooks, 4 items, 1805–83, also a Grover Cleveland campaign songster, 1884
Other printed music, 2 vols. for the Boston Peace Jubilees of 1869 and 1872
Programs for local concerts and photographs of local 19th-century cornet bands

—Leslie G. Crumbaker

682

Harrie W. JOHNSTON

144 Campbell Street
New Bedford, Massachusetts 02740

Songs written and published by New Bedford residents, including Len Gray, George Ramsden, and Edgar Barrell, 150 items, ca. 1897–
Orchestral arrangements, 400 published items, including Theodore Thomas arrangements, and folios published by Carl Fisher, New York
Chamber music, 500 items, late 19th and 20th centuries
Scrapbooks, 10 vols. containing programs and photographs of local instrumental and vocal groups, ca. 1916–   , including Le Cercle Gounod and the New Bedford Chamber Music Society
Autographs of musicians, 100 items, 1814–   , including all conductors of the Boston Symphony Orchestra, and members of string ensembles, notably the Kneisel Quartet and the Mendelssohn Quintet Club

683

NEW BEDFORD FREE PUBLIC   MNBedf
LIBRARY

Box C-902
New Bedford, Massachusetts 02741

Manuscript sea chanteys, 1 bound vol., ca. 1850, attributed to William Histed
Programs, 1100 playbills from traveling shows at Liberty Hall, New Bedford, 1865–79

—Bruce Barnes

684

NEWBURYPORT PUBLIC LIBRARY   MNe

94 State Street
Newburyport, Massachusetts 01950

The music collection (as cited, for instance, in Louis Pichierri, *Music in New Hampshire* [New York, 1966], p. xv) was extensively damaged by fire on 2 June 1977. The Scott Richard and Kevin MacDonald Music Room was involved, and 80 percent of the sheet music was destroyed. A detailed report on specific holdings is thus impossible at this time

685

ANDOVER NEWTON   MNtcA
THEOLOGICAL SCHOOL

Library
169 Herrick Road
Newton Center, Massachusetts 02159

Protestant hymnals, 500 vols., 18th to 20th centuries
Lockhart Society (19th-century student group at Andover Theological Seminary, devoted to worship through music), papers, 10 linear cm.
Samuel Francis Smith (1808–93, author of the text to "America"), 15 linear cm. of photographs and memorabilia

—Diana Yount

686

NORTH ANDOVER HISTORICAL SOCIETY

153 Academy Road
North Andover, Massachusetts 01845

Manuscript music for clarinet, 2 items, early 19th century
Protestant hymnals, 13 early 19th-century Boston imprints
Community songbook and school songbook, used locally, early 19th century

—Martha Larson

687

Florence E. BRUNNINGS

231 Bridge Street
North Weymouth, Massachusetts 02191

Folk-music archive, comprising a 50,000-card index of ballads, folksongs, sea chanteys, and lumbering, cowboy, humorous, children's seasonal, and other favorite songs and hymns, derived from 1000 books and 700 recordings

688

FORBES LIBRARY   MNF

Art and Music Department
Northampton, Massachusetts 01060

Sheet music, 3000 items, including 27 bound vols. of 18th- and 19th-century British and U.S. vocal music, with a composer index; 900 popular song sheets, with composer and title index; and 900 classical songs, ca. 1850–ca. 1920, with composer and title index
Tunebooks, hymnals, and songbooks, 162 items, 18th and 19th centuries, mostly in the Elbridge Kingsley collection
Other U.S. music imprints, scattered through the collection of 21,000 bound music scores
Jenny Lind, a special collection of miscellaneous materials following her Northampton residency, 1852, including programs, scrapbooks of clippings, and promotional publications
Programs, 1.2 linear meters, mostly in the Kingsley collection, including bound vols. listing bookings at the Northampton Academy of Music, 1891–1913, also programs, 1911–38, programs for the Northampton Vocal Club, 1897–1905, and programs for the Northampton Clef Club, 1908–30
Pictorial materials, including 12 photographs of the Academy of Music (in the Northampton Collection of Photographs), and 2½ file drawers of pictures of composers and instruments, clipped from early 20th-century periodicals

—Daniel J. Lombardo

689

NORTHAMPTON HISTORICAL SOCIETY

58 Bridge Street
Northampton, Massachusetts 01060

Hymnals (some with words only), Sunday-school and prayer-meeting books, glee books, and tunebooks,

100 19th-century items, donated by local churches and residents
Sheet music, including 12 Civil War songs; 6 Jenny Lind lithographs, ca. 1860; and 36 bound vols. of 19th-century instrumental and vocal music, including works by local composers Dana Henshaw and George Kingsley
Clef Club (local music group), papers, 1913–39, 45 linear cm.
Programs of Smith College concerts, ca. 1900– , and of the Academy of Music (city-owned theater), early 20th century
Pictures, 24 items, late 19th and early 20th centuries, including an oil painting of Jenny Lind, ca. 1890, and 1 of George Kingsley playing the piano, also photographs of local bands, musicals at the Academy of Music, and of Myron Kidder (local violin-maker)
Pianola rolls of operatic and classical music, 64 items
Music boxes, 3 items, 19th century

—Ruth F. Wilbur

690

Yella PESSL-SOBOTKA

54 Allison Street
Northampton, Massachusetts 01060

Yella Pessl-Sobotka, personal papers, including correspondence, notebooks, personal library, music mss, programs, and press clippings. See *Spalek*, p. 697

691

SMITH COLLEGE   MNS

Center for the Performing Arts
Werner Josten Library
Northampton, Massachusetts 01060

Sheet music, pre-Civil War to late 19th century, including 17 bound vols. indexed by composer and title, and 3 boxes of items partly catalogued
Werner Josten (1885–1963), personal papers, including correspondence and music mss.
Additional ms music, including works by John Woods Duke (in the Archives); Ross Lee Finney, holograph of the Sinfonietta for small orchestra, and blueprint reproductions of other early works; and Roger Sessions, 2 holographs of the Sonata for piano
Cinema and theater ephemera, including 38 looseleaf notebooks of playbills and theatrical clippings, 1863–1934, and clippings about films, including musicals, 1915–34, indexed by donor; also 8 cartons of playbills, probably including musical-theater productions
Alfred Einstein (1880–1952), research materials, including 16th- to 18th-century European vocal and instrumental music copied in score by him from part-books in European libraries, for his musicological research
Philip Hale (1854–1934), personal collection of early music treatises

—Mary M. Ankudowich

692

Sophia SMITH COLLECTION   MNS-S

Women's History Archive
Smith College
Northampton, Massachusetts 01060

Women's history materials, including published biographies of women musicians, and papers of Sophie Drinker (musicologist), 16 vols., 1933–48; Geraldine Farrar (soprano), correspondence, after 1925; and the Garrison Family, with correspondence and memorabilia of Ellen Wright (Mrs. William Lloyd Garrison II, sister-in-law of Lucy McKim Garrison). See the *Catalogs of the Sophia Smith Collection*, vol. 4 (Boston, 1975), pp. 565–74

—Mary-Elizabeth Murdock

693
NORTHBOROUGH HISTORICAL SOCIETY
52 Main Street
Northborough, Massachusetts 01532

Papers of the Northboro Choral Union and other local societies, 1800–1946
Published music, including 1 box each of sheet music, songbooks, and other printed music; also 5 music mss
Programs, 1 box, and several photographs
Edison cylinder recordings, with 1 phonograph
Musical instruments and accessories manufactured in Northborough

—Louise H. Benton

694
WHEATON COLLEGE   MNoW
Norton, Massachusetts 02766

Lucy Larcom (poet, and faculty member, 1855–63 and 1865–67), papers, including poems that were set to music, some in ms; also a music edition of her "Kansas Prize Song"
Wheaton Female Seminary (renamed Wheaton College in 1912), hymnals and seminary workbooks containing music
Songbooks of College songs, 1918–

—Ruth Fletcher, Kersti Tannberg

695
PETERSHAM HISTORICAL SOCIETY
North Main Street
Petersham, Massachusetts 01366

Protestant hymnals, 12 items, some with words only, 1794–1850
Hymnal by Rev. Samuel Willard (blind preacher of Deerfield, Mass.), published in Greenfield, Mass., 1824
Henry R. Wheeler (local church organist), scrapbook containing local concert programs, with ms notes, 1910–45

—Delight Haines

696
BERKSHIRE ATHENAEUM   MPB
1 Wendell Avenue
Pittsfield, Massachusetts 01201

Edward Boltwood (composer), 3 linear meters of ms operettas and show music, 1850–1920
Shaker hymnals and mss, 20 items, 18th and 19th centuries. See *Cook*, pp. 285–86
Tunebooks, 20 19th-century items bound in leather, used in Massachusetts or Connecticut

—Denis J. Lesieur

697
SHAKER COMMUNITY
Box 898
Pittsfield, Massachusetts 01201

Manuscript music, 6 vols. in Shaker letter notation, from Hancock, Mass., and New Lebanon, N.Y., 3 of them from the collection of Harold Cook. See *Cook*, p. 291
Shaker hymnals, 25 items, published ca. 1884; also Isaac N. Young, *A Short Abridgement of the Rules of Music* (1846)
Harold Cook (1904–68, musicologist), 4 items of correspondence
Photographs of Shaker singers and composers, 1870–90, 6 items

—June Sprigg

698
PILGRIM SOCIETY   MPlPS
75 Court Street
Plymouth, Massachusetts 02360

Materials relating to Pilgrim history, including 55 published sacred and secular song collections, 1807–76, mostly pre-1860
Briggs Family Collection, with 1 ms hymn, "Kendall Hall," 1889; also a ms score, scripts, photographs, playbills, and clippings of *The Mirror of the Fairest*, operetta first performed in Plymouth, 1879
Manuscript songs, including William Thomas Davis, "On Shiloh's Plain," 1889; Birge Harrison, "The Ballad of the Mayflower," n.d.; and Felicia Hemans, "The Pilgrim Fathers," n.d.
Manuscript music notebooks, 1 by Stephen Parker, 1775, and 1 anonymous vol., n.d.
Other printed music, including Felicia Hemans, "The Landing of the Pilgrims in New England," 1825, and 1 published hymn, 1888, in the Ralph Waldo Emerson Collection

—Jeanne M. Mills

699
READING ANTIQUARIAN SOCIETY
26 Vine Street
Reading, Massachusetts 01867

Songbooks, 4 items used by Father Kemp's Old Folks, 1850s–60s; also 1 photograph of the group, 1860s?
Music mss, 16 pages of country-dance tunes, signed by Abel Farnsworth Knight, South Reading, 1821, and by Robert Stimpson (1800–1887)
Programs of local concerts, 16 items, 1840–80, and of the Tourjee Club, 1898–1916

—Miriam Barclay

700

Barbara OWEN

46-A Curtis Street
Rockport, Massachusetts 01966

Materials relating to the history of organs and organ music in the U.S., mostly from the 19th and early 20th centuries, including 50 organ-builders' catalogues; 50 programs, mostly for organ dedications; 40 published editions of early American organ music; issues of periodicals; fragments of early mss of organ music; and clippings and other ephemera, now in 8 scrapbooks

Personal papers of organ historians John Van Varick Elsworth (mostly concerning the history of the Johnson Organ Co., ca. 1940–70) and William King Covell (including notes on the Aeolian Skinner Co., ca. 1930–70)

Tunebooks and hymnals, mostly mid 19th-century New England imprints, 100 items

701

ESSEX INSTITUTE   **MSaE**

132 Essex Street
Salem, Massachusetts 01970

Sheet music, 500 items, mostly relating to Salem and Essex County, including works by local composers Thomas Bricher, Luther O. Emerson, Arthur Foote, Patrick S. Gilmore, Jean M. Massud, John P. Ordway, Henry S. Thompson, Edward L. White, and Isaac B. Woodbury, and songs with texts by local authors Hanna Flagg Gould, Lucy Larcom, and John Greenleaf Whittier; also 68 items used by the Hutchinson Family. (Other sheet music formerly in the Essex Institute collection is now at Southern Illinois University, Edwardsville, Ill., q.v.)

Tunebooks and hymnals, 200 items, mostly pre-1860, including 30 18th-century imprints

Broadside texts of songs, 300 items, 1750s–1860s

Programs of Essex County musical events, 3000 items, pre-1920, particularly 1860–70s

Manuscript music, 1785–1860, as listed in an inventory with an analytical index of texts, and including 2 books for William A. Brown (of Hamilton, Mass.), the first dated 1847 for flute or clarinet, the second an undated clarinet instruction text; Jacob Cabot, "New Instructions for the German Flute," n.d.; Cabot, Nathaniel Lee, and Wendall, flute music book, n.d.; Harriet Orne Clarke, song and piano book, 1810; William Cleveland, book dated 1797, possibly for clarinet; Driver, untitled music, dated 1860; David Jewett, holograph of "Princess Helena's Grand March," arranged for pianoforte; Benjamin Lynde Oliver, keyboard music, mostly original but also including works by Raynor Taylor, Peter von Hagen, Jr., and other American composers; Sally Pickman and Rebecca Taylor Pickman, book of songs and instrumental music, ca. 1785–95; Anna Richardson (of Moultonborough, N.H.), choir singer's book, dated 1793; Harriet Rose, book of songs and piano music, dated 1814; L. L. A. Very, exercise book, dated 1846; fife book with names of Matthew Vincent, Benjamin Gardner (1788), and Benjamin Dowling (1794); Stephen Wheatland (of Cambridge and Salem), un-

dated book; 2 catalogued books, 1 of them for flute, and miscellaneous pieces, catalogued; and 24 uncatalogued books, along with uncatalogued loose papers

Dance mss, including 1 page of "Figures of the Polka," n.d., and a book of "Contra Dance Steps," ca. 1830

Jean Missud (1852–1941, leader of the Salem Cadet Band), personal papers, including appointment books, 1879–1941; 3 boxes of band-music sets of parts, including 66 titles; miscellaneous photographs, printed ephemera, correspondence, programs, and press clippings, singly and in scrapbooks; and records of the Committee of the Salem Cadet Band, 1879–85; with a detailed inventory

Frederick E. Bigelow (1873–1929), personal papers, including 18 folders of ms music, mostly songs and instrumental parts; also folders of biographical materials; with an inventory

Musical materials in various family papers, including Manuel Emilio, holograph ms "Nocturno de Concerto" for piano, dedicated to Mary Silsbee; Arthur Foote, 24 letters sent and received, and 5 other documents, 1874–1936; Ephraim Foster (b. 1832?, of Ipswich, Mass.), 3 mss including "The Universe" and "Quick Step," both dated 1849; Benjamin Holt, ms book of psalms and hymns, ca. 1776; J. Maurice Hubbard, ms "Shepherd with Thy Tenderest Care," inscribed to Prof. Edward Morse; Caleb Jackson, Jr. (of Boxford, Mass.), 2 musical works, along with his commonplace book and daily journal, 1799–1805; Jacob Kimball, personal papers, including ms music, as discussed and partly reproduced in Glenn C. Wilcox, *Jacob Kimball, Jr. (1761–1826), His Life and Works* (Ph.D. diss. University of Southern California, 1957); Lowell Mason, 3 holograph music mss, including "Good Advice" and "Birmey, L. M."; Henry K. Oliver (1800–1885), 5 boxes of choral music, mostly English anthems, also a book of "Hymn Tunes and Chants," dated 1832–63, 1 leaf of ms copies of songs, dated 1880–83, and a ms fair copy of "Federal Street," dated 1884; James Upton, ms hymn book entitled "Musical Miscellany"; and W. Wood, ms book of voluntaries, sacred music and organ works, dated 1812, for use in the Church in Pleasant Street, Newburyport, Mass. Also other materials scattered through the various collections, as cited, for instance, in Bryan Eugene Lindsay, *The English Glee in New England, 1815–1845* (Ph.D. diss., George Peabody College for Teachers, 1966), esp. pp. 332–45

Salem Academy of Music, 6 vols. and items of archival records, including an account book, 1846–57; bills, 1854–56; letters and reports, 1848–55; and record books, 1846–57, with a constitution

Salem Oratorio Society, 31 vols. and items of archival records, including an account book, 1886–1916; by-laws and incorporation, 1873–1909; checkbook stubs, 1913–17; "History: Salem Oratorio Society, 1868–1891"; lists of performers for special concerts, 1889; lists of members, 1868–1909, in 20 vols.; recital programs, 1889–1907; record books, 1870–1909; scrapbook of press clippings, programs, and announcements, 1868–93; subscription list for testimonials to Carl Zerrahn, 1892–93; and other items

Archives of other local music groups, including the Madrigal Club, miscellaneous papers, 1892–93; Mendelssohn Choral Society, notebook of educational material, n.d., also 1 sheet-music item; Mozart Association, record book, 1825–29; National Peace Jubilee, official program, 1869; Salem Choral Society, constitution and by-laws, n.d.; Salem Concert Hall, account book, 1782–86; Salem Glee Club, record book, 1832–45; Salem Schubert Club, by-laws, 1880, miscellaneous papers dated 1878–87, and record book, 1878–79; and Salem Social Singing Society, record book, 1830–46

Singing-school materials, including a list of the 26 students in Samuel Holyoke's school, Danvers, Mass., 1804, with amounts of tuition received from each; also a school's maintenance records, 1808–15

Archives of musical organizations outside Salem, including the Georgetown Musical Union, 1 vol. of account books, 1869–77; and the Groveland Organ Association, record book, 1865–71

Essex Institute Musical library, archival records, including a list of members, dated 1869, and a catalogue of the Salem Musical Library

—Robinson Murray III

702
PEABODY MUSEUM OF SALEM MSaP
East India Square
Salem, Massachusetts 01970

Sheet music, 2000 items concerning the sea, mostly published in Boston, 1850–1900

Collection of 60 ship's logs, 1795–1860, some of which include texts of poems, songs, and song fragments

—Barbara Edkins

703
SANDWICH HISTORICAL SOCIETY
Glass Museum
Box 103
Sandwich, Massachusetts 02563

Tunebooks and hymnals, 16 items, 1821–74; also local materials, including an 1863 poster for the Peak Family Bell Ringers, an 1880 band picture, and descriptive material on the town's Tricentennial Ball, 1889

—Russell A. Lovell, Jr.

704
CONNECTICUT VALLEY MSCV
HISTORICAL MUSEUM
194 State Street
Springfield, Massachusetts 01103

Bathshua Pynchon, ms music book of popular songs and dances, compiled 1797–1805

—Gregory Farmer

705
SPRINGFIELD CITY LIBRARY MS
220 State Street
Springfield, Massachusetts 01103

Sheet music, 2000 popular-music items, 1854–1940
Hymnals, songbooks, and tunebooks, late 18th and 19th centuries

Other printed music, including 100 choral-music vols.

George W. Chadwick, ms score, *Phoenix Expirans,* 1892

Programs and 10 scrapbooks with pictures, clippings, and tickets for the Hampden County Musical Association, 1807–1904, Junior League Concert Series, 1930– , Musical Art Society, 1906–12, Orpheus Club (also with secretary's reports), n.d., Springfield Music Festival Association, 1903–31, Springfield Oratorio Society, 1901–2, and Springfield Symphony Orchestra, 1922–33

—Sylvia A. St. Amand

706
STOUGHTON HISTORICAL SOCIETY
Box 542
Stoughton, Massachusetts 02072

> Materials are owned by the Old Stoughton Musical Society and the Musical Society in Stoughton

Archives of the Old Stoughton Musical Society, 1786– , and of the Musical Society in Stoughton, 1802– , 3 file drawers, including 200 concert programs, 125 photographs, letters and diaries of members, and complete runs of their respective journals

William Capen (1871–1939, member of both Musical Societies), personal papers, 1 file drawer

Edwin Arthur Jones (1853–1911), 12 ms music books, containing oratorios and chamber music

Tunebooks, 75 18th- and 19th-century items used in New England, including 2 compiled by the Old Stoughton Musical Society

Other printed music, 100 items, mostly oratorios and anthems, including Boston imprints, 1820s–70s

—Roger Hall

707
OLD STURBRIDGE VILLAGE MStuO
Research Library
Sturbridge, Massachusetts 01566

Music books, 19 ms items, 1776–ca. 1850, comprising Joseph Akerman, singing instructions, flute fingering chart, and vocal music, Portsmouth, N.H., 1795; Thomas Bigelow, mostly hymns, Sherburne, Mass., 1809–ca. 1842; David McLaughlin Brown, fife book, songs and marches, Corinth, Vt., n.d.; Jonathan Shipley Copp, secular and sacred music, 1 vol. without words and a 2nd vol. with words, also moral and musical observations, 1799; Eldredge family (?), 5 items, Willington and Tolland, Conn., ca. 1850, 1 vol. inscribed by Simon Chapman, Tolland and East Windsor, 1822, 1833; Moses F. Geer, hymns at the end of a *A Gamut, or Scale of Music* (1814), inscribed Griswold, Conn., 1824; Anna Grant, also Lora Ann, Juliett, and Anna Root, church music, 1803–26; Hez Goddard, hymns, 1801; Abel Joslen, flute or fife exercises, Thompson, Conn. (?), n.d.; S. Knaebel, first-trumpet part for 26 band pieces, n.d.; Jacob Leonard, hymns and secular songs, 1790; E. W. Spalding, hymns, Foxborough, Mass. (?), early 19th century; Elijah Stone, 2 pieces, Whittingham, Vt. (?), mid 19th century; P. Van Schaack, Jr., songs, dances, and marches, Kinderhook, N.Y., 1820. Also 5 anonymous vols., including singing instructions, with "The British Hero," Northfield, Mass., ca. 1776; "A Collection of Songs" (known as the "Thompson ms. songster"), ca. 1800; 12 pages of hymn tunes without words, ca. 1800; words and music of sacred songs, ca. 1810; and hymns and patriotic songs, 1819–33

Single sheets of ms music, 6 items, including "Elegy on Sophronia," Durham, 1800; Newton S. Hatch, 3 pages of music in his farm account book, Tamworth, N.H., 1827–66; "La pipe de tabac," ca. 1830; "Nestor, C.M.," n.d.; "Sorrow's Tear," n.d.; and "Children of the Heavenly King" with "Robert Girling's Tune", n.d.

Song texts in ms, 3 items, including "Ship in Distress" and "A Song to the Tune of Old Man," at the back of a copy of the 1755 *Acts and Laws of the Colony of Connecticut*; 4 texts in the daybook of Jonathan Reynolds, Jr., South Kingston, R.I., 1796–1809; and "The Doctor and Squire," in the account book of Thaddeus Fish, Kingston, Mass., 1767–80

Military music documents, 3 items, including Ephraim B. Hardy, appointment to the band, 2nd Brigade, 7th Division of the Militia of Massachusetts, Boston, 1807; 2nd Regiment, 2nd Brigade, 1st Division of the State Militia of Vermont (also known as the Springfield Military Band of Music), by-laws, minutes of monthly meetings, and attendance records, 1815–30; and Light Infantry Company of Otisfield, Harrison, and Raymond, Me., military record book, 1821–41, also a letter dated 1886 describing the musicians of the company in 1823

Letters relating to music, including the Isaac Hayden family papers, with a receipt from Joseph B. Wadsworth for keeping a singing school, 1770, and a subscription payment for sacred-music instruction, 1780; Hannah Lewis, letter book, Dorchester and Boston, Mass., and Augusta, Me., 1807–16, with references to music in Augusta, the *Suffolk Collection*, singers, and other musical matters; Edmund Firmin, letter mentioning a local music school, Monson, Mass., 1835; and Anna Louisa Tufts (Mrs. Theodore) Atkinson, letter dated Boston, 1849, with references to singing

Programs, including the Washington Benevolent Society of Massachusetts, 4th annual celebration in the Old South Church, 1815; Select Oratorio, directed by Capt. B. Salisbury, Brimfield, Mass., 1825; 50th anniversary of U.S. independence, n.p., 1826; Mr. Friend, vocal concert, followed by contra-dancing, Milltown (Me.?), ca. 1840?; Ole Bull, concert in Worcester, 1844; choral concert directed by F. A. Noble, Globe Village, Southbridge, Mass., 1856; and Shelburne Falls (Mass.) Academy, exhibition, 1857

Printed ephemera concerning music, 4 items, including 1 broadside ballad, Boston, 1821?; announcement of the Lunenburg (Mass.) Academy, 1843, specifying musical instruction; T. Gilbert, trade card for his Piano Forte Manufactory, Boston, ca. 1850, with an engraving of his building; and J. F. Browne & Co. of London and New York, harp makers, circular, ca. 1845

Pictorial materials, including lithograph portraits, also musical illustrations and designs on decorative-arts objects in the Museum's general Curatorial Collections, with musical content not separately identified

Sheet music, 600 items, singly and in 12 bound vols., mostly published or used in New England before 1850. The unbound items are uncatalogued, but the bound vols. have contents lists as well as a card index of titles and first lines

Hymnals and tunebooks, 340 items, also 140 music editions and instruction books, mostly from New England, pre-1850, catalogued

—Etta Falkner

708

OLD COLONY HISTORICAL SOCIETY   MTaHi
66 Church Green
Taunton, Massachusetts 02780

Sheet music, 800 items in 20 bound vols., ca. 1820–1910s, with a title index, including Hutchinson Family materials

Jacob Orth (1822–77, local music teacher and organist, a pupil of Franz Liszt), holograph ms music, including 1 vol. of his preludes and fugues, also copies of works by Mozart and Rinck; a copy of Jezaniah Sumner, "Ode on Science," written ca. 1820 for the Bristol Academy and later published by Father Kemp; and scores and parts for 25 band and orchestra works, some by Orth

Tunebooks and hymnals, 40 items, 1770s?–1860s; also 20 19th-century secular and sacred song anthologies, and 5 literary works about music

—Richard Hill

709

Stewart ALLEN
Tashmoo Avenue
Box 286
Vineyard Haven, Massachusetts 02568

Recordings, including 10,000 78-rpm discs, and tape copies of all commercial and unpublished recordings of Lillian Nordica

Photographs of Mme Nordica, 4 items

Episcopal hymnals, 3 items, ca. 1898

710

VINEYARD PUBLIC LIBRARY
Main Street
Vineyard Haven, Massachusetts 02568

Will Hardy, 2 sheet-music items, 1913

Lillian Nordica (1857–1914), tape recording entitled "Yankee Diva," of performances at the Metropolitan Opera House, New York, 1903–11

—Jean Gross

711

AMERICAN JEWISH HISTORICAL SOCIETY   MWalA
2 Thornton Road
Waltham, Massachusetts 02154

Sheet music, 3500 items from American Yiddish theater, 1890–1950

Molly Picon (1876–1967, actress), papers, 3000 items, including theater-song lyrics, Yiddish songbooks, and sheet music

Abraham Ellstein (1907–63, composer), papers, 325 items, including Hebrew and Yiddish sheet music, material for his opera *The Gholem,* and items from Yiddish musicals

Israel Goldberg (1887-1964, author and historian), personal papers, including 14 ms songs

Edward Bernard, ms choral exercises and compositions

Programs of Jewish composers or performers, ca. 1865– , 35 linear cm.

Photographs of Jewish performers and theatrical scenes, 100 items, ca. 1900

Posters of Yiddish theater, 500 items, ca. 1900

—Nathan M. Kaganoff

712

BRANDEIS UNIVERSITY   MWalB
Goldfarb Library
Creative Arts Division
Waltham, Massachusetts 02254

Reginal De Koven, holograph mss of 30 operas and 70 songs, and 400 printed editions of his music

Eleanora Mendelssohn, 2 scrapbooks containing photographs, sketches of Arturo Toscanini, and correspondence

Sheet music, 9000 19th-century items, many of them from the collection of Daniel and Ruth Siegel; also 800 items, ca. 1850–1900, presented by James J. Fuld; 2500 early 20th-century items; 300 20th-century sacred items presented by Ed Levy; 150 19th-century items on black subjects, maintained as a separate collection; and 1 bound vol. of U.S. imprints, ca. 1800

Piano music in ms fragments, mid 19th century, 2.5 linear meters

Published editions of music by American composers, mostly Boston imprints, 1870s–1920s, including 35 oratorios and 30 vocal anthologies; also a collection of U.S. libretti from this period

Programs, including 10 linear cm. of Boston and Metropolitan Opera programs, pre-1917; also a scrapbook of opera, concert, and theater programs, 1882–1908, compiled by John C. Abbott

—Robert L. Evensen

713

Angelica B. LEE
353 School Street
Watertown, Massachusetts 02172

Erwin Bodky (1896–1958, harpsichordist), personal papers, including 2 boxes of correspondence received, 13 musical mss, and photographs, many relating to his studies in the interpretation of early music. See *Spalek,* p. 108

714

PERKINS SCHOOL FOR THE BLIND   MWatP
Samuel P. Hayes Research Library and Music Library
175 North Beacon Street
Watertown, Massachusetts 02172

Historical information on the production of braille music and the education of children through braille music, as introduced in the U.S. ca. 1850, in all 1.5 linear meters of archival materials

Braille music, 3000 items, including some items produced in the U.S. before 1940

Books of blind musicians, and biographical files of articles and press clippings on blind musicians, among them persons from or active in the U.S. before 1940, and including Thomas B. ("Blind Tom") Bethune, George Shearing, and Alec Templeton

—Kenneth Stuckey

715

WAYLAND FREE PUBLIC LIBRARY
5 Concord Road
Wayland, Massachusetts 01778

Theater and concert programs, 1840–1900, in 4 scrapbooks, collected by Beatrice Hereford Haywood (local monologist)

—Phoebe Homans

716

WELLESLEY COLLEGE   MWelC
Wellesley, Massachusetts 02181

Margaret Clapp Library, Special Collections

Hamilton C. Macdougall (1858–1945), holograph ms, "Teach Me, O Lord," n.d.

Wellesley College Archives

Hamilton C. Macdougall, 12 letters concerning the founding of the Wellesley College Choir

Katherine Kennicott Davis, personal papers, including 3 notebooks of correspondence with Thomas Whitney Surette (1862–1941) during the period of his greatest influence in the music appreciation movement, also correspondence with Hamilton C. Macdougall

—Mary Wallace Davidson

717

GORDON COLLEGE   MWenhG
Winn Library
255 Grapevine Road
Wenham, Massachusetts 01984

A. J. Gordon (1836–95), personal papers, including materials relating to the publication of the *Coronation Hymnal* (1895)

—John Beauregard

718

Kenneth ROBERTS
Williams College
Williamstown, Massachusetts 02167

John Knowles Paine, personal papers, including holograph mss, 100 pages, 1870–95, mostly variant texts for published works; also the Paine family scrapbook, including photographs of Paine with such associates as John Fiske and Owen Wister, also letters from Paine to his nephew, William Roger Greeley, and press clippings regarding first performances of his music

719
WILLIAMS COLLEGE   MWiW
Williamstown, Massachusetts 02167

Sawyer Library

Shaker music, 50 printed and ms vols., some with words only, 1836–64, as cited in *Cook*, pp. 292–93; see also Mary L. Richmond, *Shaker Literature* (Hanover, N.H, 1977), vol. 1, pp. 152–55
Sumner Salter (1856–1944), 5 mss of organ music and songs written at Williams College
Williamsiana Collection, including 4 college songbooks, 1904–33, and 5 sheet-music items, mid 19th century; also programs for 239 organ recitals by Sumner Salter, 1905–33, in Thompson Memorial Chapel and Grace (now Chapin) Hall
Scrapbooks kept by individual students, mostly 19th century, 100 vols., many of them including concert tickets, pictures, and programs
Programs of regional music clubs, 1862–1944
Scrapbook containing annual programs of the Flonzaley Quartet, 1912–28

—Lawrence E. Wikander

Chapin Library

For the music holdings of this important rare-book collection, see the 1950 exhibition catalogue, *Four Hundred Years of Music*, prepared by Joaquin Nin-Culmell and Mary L. Richmond. Other early American music is entered in a special card file maintained by the Library

—Robert L. Volz

Whiteman Collection

Paul Whiteman (1890–1967), materials including orchestrations used by his band for concerts, recording sessions, radio broadcasts, and ballroom performances, 4000 scores and parts, catalogued by title, composer, and arranger; sheet music, 2000 items, 1885–1940s, including the collections of George Eberle, George Royal, and Stanley W. Stearns, now integrated and catalogued by title, composer, and lyricist; 20 scrapbooks of press clippings relating to Whiteman's career, also photographs, other press clippings, concert programs, route sheets, and a personnel roster with salaries; 2000 recordings, including 600 78-rpm discs by Whiteman and 200 hours of his radio broadcasts, transcribed on tape; and films, including *King of Jazz* (1930) and *Rhapsody in Blue* (1945), featuring Paul Whiteman and His Orchestra, and 30 Whiteman television shows. Some of these materials were presented by H. Richard Archer, the Cole Porter Estate, and various Williams College alumni. For further information see Carl Johnson, *Paul Whiteman: A Chronology* (Williamstown, 1976)

Other materials, including books and periodicals concerned with American popular music; and 3 letters from Bix Beiderbecke to his parents, 1931, as published in the campus literary magazine, *Pique* (Feb. 1978), p. 31

—Carl Johnson

Music Department
Archives of the Music Department of Williams College, 1923– , including correspondence and concert programs

720
WINCHENDON HISTORICAL SOCIETY
Beals Memorial Library
Pleasant Street
Winchendon, Massachusetts 01475

Hymnals of various Protestant denominations, 20 items, 1840–1926
Songbooks and instrumental method books, 10 mid-19th-century items
Programs of local concerts, mid 19th century, 30 linear cm.
Pictures, 25 items, including mid-19th-century photographs of local bands

—Lois Greenwood

721
AMERICAN ANTIQUARIAN SOCIETY   MWA
185 Salisbury Street
Worcester, Massachusetts 01609

A research collection which has grown out of the personal library of Isaiah Thomas (1749–1831), concentrating in Americana before 1876, with special emphasis on printed materials before 1821. The Society's *Dictionary Catalog of American Books Pertaining to the 17th through 19th Centuries* (Westport, Conn., 1971; hereinafter cited as *DC*) covers monographic materials printed before 1821, with several kinds of material excepted, sheet music among them. None of the holdings printed between 1821 and 1876 are cited in the *DC* , except for genealogy books and works by writers included in P. K. Foley's *American Authors, 1795–1895* (New York, 1897). In the *DC*, subject headings appear for only the earliest edition to be catalogued; the main entry should be consulted for other editions

Printed Materials

Sheet music, 60,000 items, arranged by composer, with partial indexes for titles and illustrated covers. Included are 555 titles before 1801, and 3500 titles, 1801–25. The collection of Boston imprints is particularly strong. Several "Songs" are cited in *DC*, vol. 14, p. 400
Songsters, 1000 items printed before 1877. Pre-1821 imprints are cited in *DC*, vol. 16, pp. 407–17, also in Irving Lowens, *Bibliography of Songsters Printed in America before 1821* (Worcester, 1976). In addition to the 240 items before 1821, there are 270 items dated 1821–50. The post-1820 songsters are not catalogued, but are shelved separately and divided into two chronological periods, each arranged by title. There is

a ms checklist by Lucile K. Wilkin of the pre-1851 songsters in the Society and at Brown University, also other ms checklists that describe the holdings of the New York Public Library, New-York Historical Society, Harvard University, Boston Public Library, and Massachusetts Historical Society. Many of the songsters come from the collection of H. Douglass Dana

Tunebooks and hymnals, including 1600 pre-1821 items, as cited in *DC*, vol. 9, pp. 132–93, especially pp. 175–93 ("Hymns with Music"), and in Richard Crawford, *Bibliography of American Sacred Music through 1810* (Worcester, forthcoming). The collection of later hymnals, uncatalogued, includes 3900 items. Included are 4400 items from the collection of Bishop Robert W. Peach (d. 1936), and 800 items from the collection of Frank J. Metcalf. Also located in the Society is the catalogue of Valmore X. Gaucher, who was engaged to catalogue the holdings of the Society and to prepare a bibliography of U.S. hymnals to 1880

Music instruction books, 1300 items, including pre-1821 items as cited in *DC*, vol. 12, pp. 281–95, and post-1820 items, uncatalogued but shelved by composer or compiler in the collection of secular songbooks

Broadside ballads, 3000 items, 1780s–1880, partly interfiled in the broadside collection in the Graphic Arts Department, partly filed by title. Pre-1831 items are being catalogued. The Isaiah Thomas Collection of Ballads contains 302 items, including popular songs of the War of 1812, which Thomas purchased from a ballad printer in 1814. See Worthington C. Ford, "The Isaiah Thomas Collection of Ballads", American Antiquarian Society *Proceedings*, 33 (1924), 34–112

Secular songbooks, other printed music, and books about music, as cited in *DC*, vol. 16, pp. 401–2, also in vol. 12, pp. 279–301, and under other subject headings mentioned on p. 279. Post-1820 imprints include 400 items collected under the subject heading "Music"

Music catalogues, beginning with a list from John Rowe Parker (Boston, 1820), and including lists for E. S. Mesier, J. E. Gould, Joseph F. Atwill, Oliver Ditson, S. Brainard, and Beck & Lawton, also other uncatalogued items in the broadside collection

Programs of musical events (in the Graphic Arts department, uncatalogued), the pre-1821 items interfiled with the broadsides, the post-1820 items shelved separately and consisting of 62 items, 1820–49; 151 items, 1850–59; 234 items, 1860–76; 79 undated items and 29 minstrel-show items. Worcester community materials include 94 items, 1822–50; 247 items, 1851–61; 247 items, 1862–72; 162 items, 1873–76; and 207 undated items; also 58 Worcester County Music Association programs, 1859–75; 54 Worcester Opera programs, 1851–76; 78 programs of the Worcester Mozart Society and the Germania Musical Society of Worcester; and Worcester minstrel programs, 38 items, 1846–61, 30 items, 1862–69, and 10 items, 1870–76

American music periodicals, extensive holdings, particularly of pre-1853 titles

Pictorial materials, including 60 19th-century lithographed portraits of musicians, and others in the uncatalogued portrait file; an oil portrait of Timothy Swan, late 18th century; and 25 engraved or printed trade cards and lithographed advertisements for music publishers and stores

Manuscripts

Maj. Henry Blake (1755–1833, Revolutionary War soldier), diary for 1776, including tunes with music

Thomas Fanning (1755–1828, Revolutionary War Soldier and Connecticut artisan), notebooks, 1779–80 and 1814, including song texts

Timothy Swan (1758–1842, composer and music teacher), personal papers, 1783–1844, including ms music and correspondence concerning his music-publishing activities

Susannah Perkins, songbook, 1786–1804, with 61 tunes

Ebenezer Martin (minister and cooper), diary for 1796, written near Binghamton, N.Y., with song texts

Timothy Minot Baker, songbook, 1809, with tunes and texts, some with authorship attributions

Isaiah Thomas, invoice relating to the purchase of music type from Edmund Fry & Co., 13 July 1790, and other letters relating to Thomas's activity as a music printer, as cited in Karl Kroeger, "Isaiah Thomas as a Music Publisher," American Antiquarian Society *Proceedings*, 86/2 (1976), 321–41

Edward Shepard Nason (Worcester music teacher), correspondence with Elias Nason, 1831–84, with frequent mention of musical topics

Joseph Funk and his sons (Mennonite music teachers and publishers in Virginia and areas westward), family correspondence, 1833–54 and ca. 1860; also Joseph Funk's letter book, 1856–59, with personal and business correspondence (an item formerly attributed to John B. Engelman); and an unpublished text by Joseph Funk in answer to his criticism of a religious piece, entitled "John Kline's Strictures and Reply"

Samuel Elias Staples (Worcester composer and administrator of the Worcester Music Festival), correspondence, 1840–1900, relating to Festival performances, also books from his music library

Worcester Choral Union, archives, 1850–1930, in 14 vols. and 1 box, including officers' reports, minutes, membership lists, constitution and by-laws, programs, press clippings, financial records, and business correspondence, also an official history of the group, issued 1875

Don Avery Winslow (farmer and musician of St. Albans and Westfield, Vt.), diaries, 1857–65, mentioning his work as a composer, performer, and teacher, also financial records of his piano lessons and the sale of music to his pupils

Twenty-fifth Regiment, Massachusetts Volunteer Infantry, 18 band books, 1861–65, each with about 70 items of music, including waltzes, marches, polkas, and patriotic songs

Alexander Cole Munroe (1831–1911, Worcester businessman), business papers, 1868–97, including accounts, correspondence, and other documents relating to the funding and the programs of the Worcester Music Festival

Worcester Opera Company, business records, 1876–77, including by-laws, lists of shareholders, minutes of shareholders' meetings, and a certificate of payment of capital

Frank J. Metcalf (1865–1945, Washington, D.C., hymnologist), personal papers, ca. 1917–45, in 2 boxes, including biographical sketches, lists of sacred music published in America, 1720–1880, an alphabetical list of tunes, and a list of American music printers

Anthony Haswell (1756–1816, printer and ballad writer) and his son, Nathan Baldwin Haswell (b. 1786, member of the Vermont House of Representatives), family papers, including song texts

Miscellaneous music mss, 3 folders, including 9 bound blank books, early and mid 19th century, shelved with the sheet-music collection

—Georgia B. Bumgardner

722
Ronald STALFORD
136 Coolidge Road
Worcester, Massachusetts 01602

Leo Sowerby (1895–1968), personal papers, including holograph mss of unpublished music (125 songs, 5 symphonies, concertos, and many works in other forms; holograph mss of the published music are at the Library of Congress, q.v.); also 10 personal scrapbooks and photograph albums, including programs, press clippings, and other memorabilia, mostly dating from his activity at the Cathedral of St. James, Chicago

723
WORCESTER COUNTY MUSIC ASSOCIATION
Highland Street
Worcester, Massachusetts 01608

Archives of the Association, including 10 ledgers and 1 account book, indexes of works performed, and lists of performers, and catalogues of the music collection

Printed music performed by the Association, including 300 choral and 250 orchestral works

Photographs, press clippings, and other memorabilia relating to the Association, 1858– , in 4 boxes

—Jeanne Berggren

724
WORCESTER HISTORICAL   MWHi
MUSEUM
39 Salisbury Street
Worcester, Massachusetts 01608

Music mss, several items by A. Soderman and other local composers, n.d.

Carl (Charles) F. Hanson, 6 operettas in multiple copies, some with performance parts, composed arranged, or sold by him, ca. 1890–1910; also 10 catalogues of his publishing business, ca. 1880–1910

Sheet music, 60 items and 2 bound vols., ca. 1840–1920

Songbooks, 25 items, mostly 19th century

Programs, 300 local items, ca. 1850– , including many from Mechanics' Hall

Portrait file, with photographs, engravings, and clippings of pictures, mostly of local subjects including musicians, ca. 1860–1920

Clippings file, with materials on local musicians and music organizations, 1870s–

Recordings, including 25 78-rpm discs and 70 Simplex player-piano rolls

—Jessica S. Goss

In addition to the repositories listed above, the following have also reported holdings of the materials indicated:

Acton—Acton Memorial Library: songbooks, programs

Amherst—Amherst Historical Society: songbooks

Ashburnham—Ashburnham Historical Society: songbooks, recordings, miscellaneous

Ashland—Ashland Historical Society: sheet music, songbooks, pictures, miscellaneous

Attleboro—Elizabeth H. Phillips: songbooks

Barre—Barre Historical Society: sheet music, songbooks

Belchertown—Belchertown Historical Association: sheet music, songbooks, programs, miscellaneous

Boston—Boston College, Bapst Library: miscellaneous

Boston—Episcopal Diocese of Massachusetts, Library: songbooks

Boston—General Theological Library: songbooks, miscellaneous

Boston—Simmons College, Beatley Library: songbooks

Boston—USS Constitution Museum Foundation: sheet music

Brookline—Longyear Historical Society: songbooks, recordings

Chesterfield—Chesterfield Historical Society: sheet music, songbooks

Concord—Minute Man National Historical Park: songbooks

Dighton—Dighton Historical Society: sheet music, songbooks

Dorchester—Dorchester Historical Society: songbooks

East Douglas—Simon Fairfield Public Library: songbooks, other printed music, recordings

Framingham—Framingham State College, Whittemore Library: programs

Halifax — Halifax Historical Society: songbooks, recordings

Hanover—Esther T. Josselyn: sheet music, songbooks, programs

Hingham—Hingham Historical Society: songbooks, miscellaneous

Ipswich—Ipswich Historical Society: sheet music, songbooks

Leominster—Leominster Historical Society: songbooks

Lexington—Lexington Historical Society: songbooks

Lowell—Lowell City Library: songbooks

Manchester—Manchester Historical Society: sheet music, songbooks, programs

New Bedford—Old Dartmouth Historical Society: sheet music, songbooks, programs, miscellaneous

New Salem—Swift River Valley Historical Society: songbooks

Newton—Jackson Homestead: sheet music, songbooks, programs, pictures

North Adams—North Adams Public Library: songbooks

North Andover—Merrimack Valley Textile Museum: sheet music

North Reading—Flint Memorial Library: sheet music, other printed music

Petersham—Ruth B. Robinson: sheet music, songbooks, other printed music

Plymouth—Plymouth Antiquarian Society: sheet music, songbooks, programs

Quincy—Quincy Historical Society: sheet music

Rowley—Free Public Library: songbooks

Scituate—Scituate Historical Society: sheet music, song-books, pictures

Shirley—Shirley Historical Society: sheet music, song-books, other printed music, programs, catalogues, miscellaneous

South Egremont—Egremont Free Library: sheet music

South Lancaster—Atlantic Union College: sheet music, songbooks, other printed music, catalogues, recordings

Topsfield—Topsfield Town Library: songbooks

Waltham—Gore Place Society: sheet music, songbooks

Ware—Young Men's Library Association: sheet music, songbooks

Wenham—Wenham Historical Association and Muse-um: songbooks

Worcester—Assumption College, Library: songbooks, recordings

Michigan

725

ALBION COLLEGE   MiAlbC

Library

Albion, Michigan 49224

F. Dudleigh Vernor (college organist), "Sweetheart of Sigma Chi," 20 ms or published items, some auto-graphed, ca. 1912

Music Department materials, 36 items, including pro-grams, minutes, and photographs of musicians, ca. 1920– ; printed college or fraternity songs; and papers of music-faculty members, 8 items, includ-ing personal correspondence, clippings, and college publications

Published music, including 100 hymnals, mostly Methodist, also college songs, ca. 1900–

Recordings, including 50 78-rpm discs

—William Miller

726

Richard CRAWFORD

1158 Baldwin Avenue

Ann Arbor, Michigan 48104

Thematic index to musical works in sacred music vols. published in the U.S. to 1810, 7500 entries

727

Glenn HENDRIX

1139 Vesper

Ann Arbor, Michigan 48103

Folksongs of Beaver Island, Mich., 31 ms texts or frag-ments and 9 music mss including material copied from items in the Ivan Walton Collection, Bentley Historical Library, University of Michigan (q.v.); also tapes of folk music, copied from recordings in the Walton Collection, 32 items mostly concerning Beaver Island folk music

Tape recording of Pat Bonner (Beaver Island fiddler), 1971

728

David Warren and Suzanne Flandreau STEEL

511 West Summit Street

Ann Arbor, Michigan 48103

Tunebooks, 24 items, 1823–96; psalm books and hym-nals, 12 items, 1794–1853; sheet music, 70 items in 2 bound vols., 1830–70; and miscellaneous music books, 6 items, ca. 1820–80

Music mss of violin quadrilles, 4 late 19th-century items

729

UNIVERSITY OF MICHIGAN   MiU

Ann Arbor, Michigan 48109

A. *William L. Clements Library*

B. *Bentley Historical Library/Michigan Historical Collections*

C. *School of Music Collections (Frederick H. Stearns Building)*

D. *University Libraries: School of Music Library (Earl V. Moore Building)*

E. *University Libraries: Rare Book Room (Harlan Hatcher Research Library)*

A. William L. Clements Library

Andrew Law (1749–1821), personal papers, 1775–1821, including 500 items of family, business, and personal correspondence, 700 business papers, 350 pages of memorandums, 35 lists of students in his singing schools, and 188 leaves of ms music. See Richard Crawford and H. Wiley Hitchcock, *The Papers of Andrew Law* (Ann Arbor, 1961), also Richard Craw-ford, *Andrew Law, American Psalmodist* (Evanston, 1968), pp. 388–99

George Philip Hooke (British army officer during the Revolution), ms journal, 1779–80, including 25 leaves of secular music, mostly catches

Sacred ms tunebooks, 6 items, including 2 signed by Ishmael Spicer of Bozrah, Conn., ca. 1804–24, and 1 shape-note vol. by Catherine Alderdice, Emmitsburg, Md., ca. 1830; also Eleazar Everett, ms orderly book, dated West Point, 1780, with 25 leaves of sacred music, mostly by native composers

Secular music ms, undated, 80 pages with 45 titles dat-ing 1800–1825

Cantelo, *Twenty-four American Country Dances* (London, 1785; RISM C-880)

Published and ms music in honor of the return visit of Gen. LaFayette, as discussed in J. Bunker Clark, "American Musical Tributes of 1824–25 to LaFayette; a Report and Inventory," *Fontes artis musicae*, 26 (1979), 17–35

Corning Sheet Music Collection, 30,000 items from the collection of Bly Corning, of Flint, Mich., and other sources. Included are 135 *Sonneck–Upton* titles, 1800 *Wolfe* titles; 600 Civil War items, 300 blackface-minstrelsy items, and 1100 Negro items; and many works by Benjamin Carr, Daniel Decatur Emmett, Stephen C. Foster, Patrick S. Gilmore, Louis M. Gottschalk, James Hewitt, John Hill Hewitt, Lowell Mason, Harrison Millard, George F. Root, Henry Russell, John Philip Sousa, and Septimus Winner. Items are arranged by year, subdivided by composer. Music with illustrated covers, including 2500 items pre-1871, other items to 1899, is kept separately; see Nancy Davison, *American Sheet Music Illustration: Reflections on the Nineteenth Century* (Ann Arbor, 1973). Cataloguing of the entire collection, with detailed subject indexing, is in progress

Tunebooks, 217 items, including 5 items, 1700–1760; 75 items, 1761–1800; 85 items, 1801–20; 34 items, 1821–40; 17 items, 1841–60; and 12 items, 1861–1900. Included are 26 Andrew Law editions, 10 editions of the Little and Smith *Easy Instructor*, and a copy of William Billings's *Singing Master's Assistant* (Boston, 1778) with ms additions, including Billings music not otherwise extant; also 72 hymnals pre-1861, mostly without music, 29 of them pre-1801, 26 of them 1801–20, and others after 1820; and 26 German-language hymnals published in the U.S., 11 of them pre-1801, 10 of them 1801–20, and others after 1820

Songsters, 74 items, 24 of them pre-1821

Music books, including 34 items pre-1821, particularly strong in singing-school and other music-instruction materials. See Beula Blanche Eisenstadt Blum, *Solmization in Nineteenth-Century American Sight-Singing Instruction* (Ph.D. diss., Univ. of Michigan, 1968), pp. 238–67

—Richard Crawford

B. Bentley Historical Library/Michigan Historical Collections

Personal papers of Michigan musicians and concerning musical activity in Michigan, including David F. Allmendinger, family papers, 1890–1974, with 2 folders of music by Helene Allmendinger, 3 folders of records of the Ann Arbor Organ Co., scrapbooks, photographs, and memorabilia of the family and of the organ firm, and drawings for Allmendinger organs; George Bennard (clergyman, Albion, Mich.), 26 letters, programs, clippings, and invitations, 1938–39, relating to his authorship of "The Old Rugged Cross" and other hymns; Roy D. Chapin (1880–1936, industrialist), papers relating to his activity in the Detroit Symphony Society, 1917–18; D. Palmer Christian (1885–1947, organ professor), personal papers, 30 linear cm., including correspondence, programs, clippings, and notes, 4 boxes; Henry Simmons Frieze (1817–89, president of the University), personal papers, 30 linear cm., including minutes of the Philharmonic Society of Providence, R.I., 1834–35, also diaries during his sabbatical in Germany, 1855–56, with musical references and mention of Alexander Wheelock Thayer; Carl E. Gehring (Ann Arbor composer and critic), personal papers, 3.2 linear meters, including scrapbooks, music mss, tapes, and microfilms, 1925–65; Mabelle Gilbert (West Bay City music teacher), diaries, school grade books, account books, and a scrapbook from her Ann Arbor student days, 1889–1914; Edgar A. Guest (1881–1959), 28 ms

and published settings of his poems by various composers, ca. 1900–1931; Francis W. Kelsey (1858–1927, classical archaeologist), papers relating to Ann Arbor musical activity, particularly to the Frieze Memorial Organ and its acquisition from the World's Columbian Exposition, Chicago, 1893; Edward G. Kemp (1887–1962, Detroit attorney, diplomat, and music patron), correspondence and papers, 1920–61; Ring Lardner (1885–1933), lyrics for a song and text for a musical show; David E. Mattern (1890–1959, music educator), correspondence, 60 linear cm., 1930–57, including documents on the Summer Conference on Music Education; George S. Morris (1857–1935, philology professor), personal papers, including a hymn-tune text and music lecture notes, 1887; Rudolf Muenzinger (Lutheran pastor at Metz and Lupton, Mich., and Toledo, Ohio), papers, 1859–1936, including sacred music mss, 100 items and 2 vols.; Otto family of Ann Arbor, clippings, photographs, and other materials on the Otto family band, 25 items, ca. 1875–1927; Minnie Root (Ann Arbor publisher of college and patriotic songs), 11 items of correspondence and papers, 1928–42; Gilbert Ross (violin professor), 2 linear meters of scrapbooks, programs, and correspondence, 1911–70; Charles A. Sink (1879–1972, president of the University Musical Society), personal papers, 1907–57, 5.5 linear meters; Victor C. Squier (1866–1949, Battle Creek music manufacturer, especially of violin strings), correspondence, papers, and clippings, 1926–63; Albert A. Stanley (1851–1932, music professor), correspondence and administrative records, teaching and lecture materials, and autobiography, 1907–32, 1 linear meter, also other of his letters in the papers of Warren Lombard, as discussed in Kenneth Roberts, "Music in America: A Proper View before Howard," *Music Review*, 32 (1971), 254–64; John D. Towne (1842–1910, Grand Rapids musician), 6 items of correspondence and a biographical sketch, 1862–1910; Charles M. Tremaine (1870–1963, music executive), correspondence and reports relating to his work as trustee and financial officer of the National Music Camp, Interlochen, 30 linear cm.; Ivan Walton (1893–1968, English professor), correspondence, research notes, and recordings relating to his studies of Michigan folksongs, 6 linear meters; Mattie Azalia Willis (1912–70, Battle Creek singer and music teacher), diaries, correspondence, clippings, and papers, including materials on the Battle Creek Chapter of the National Association for the Advancement of Colored People, 60 linear cm.; and Alexander Winchell (1824–91, scientist), papers relating to the University Musical Society, 1880–83

Civil War music references, accessible through a card index of subjects referring to entries cited in Ida C. Brown, *Michigan Men in the Civil War* (Ann Arbor, 1977), including 50 entries under the heading "Bands"

Organizational archives, of the University Musical Society, Ann Arbor, 1879–1943, including files of Albert A. Stanley and Charles A. Sink, with correspondence, ledgers, and account books concerning concerts, the activities of the Choral Union, the early operation of the School of Music, and the Henry S. Frieze Memorial Organ Fund; the University of Michigan School of Music, 1880 and 1924–62, including minutes of the faculty and executive committee meetings, clippings, correspondence of William D.

Revelli and others, and files relating to performances (see Richard Crawford, "Music at Michigan: A Historical Perspective," in *One Hundred Years of Music at Michigan, 1880–1980* [Ann Arbor, 1979], pp. 9-37); the Frederick H. Stearns Collection of Musical Instruments, correspondence and papers relating to the development of the collection, 1897–1907; the University of Michigan Band, 1931– , 1 box, and its predecessor, the Student Volunteer Band, 1914–15, minutes, 1 vol.; the National Music Camp, Interlochen, 1925–62, 12 linear meters and 29 bound vols., including correspondence and files of Joseph E. Maddy, also scrapbooks and papers relating to his dispute with James C. Petrillo, the latter presented by the American Federation of Musicians, as discussed in Neil A. Miller, *A History of the National Music Camp* (thesis, Univ. of Michigan, 1965); the Chamber Music Society of Ann Arbor, 1920–56, and its predecessor, the Ann Arbor Matinee Musicale, minutes, financial records, and membership material, also a history of this group and its companion, the Ann Arbor Wednesday Music Club, prepared by Emil Lorch; and the Ann Arbor Symphony, formerly the Ann Arbor Civic Orchestra, and its Women's Association, 1931–67, scrapbooks, clippings, programs, and reports, 1 linear meter

James E. Harkins, scrapbook with playbills, posters, and clippings, documenting his activity as a minstrel-show entertainer, 1873–1901

John Robert Crouse collection of mss, including autographed documents of George Cooper (1912), Reginald De Koven, Victor Herbert, Josef Hofmann (1926), Ignace Jan Paderewski, John Philip Sousa (1931), and Arturo Toscanini (1934)

University of Michigan scrapbooks, vocal scores for Michigan Union Operas and other campus dramatic productions, and sheet music, 1875– , in all 40 items

Sheet music published in or relating to Michigan, 1852– , 150 items and 3 bound vols., 1 owned by E. M. Orrell, another by John W. Williams

German singing societies in Detroit, programs and historical studies, 1909–46, 7 items

Songbooks and songsters, including 1 abolitionist book, 1846; 10 temperance books, 1876–1928, including materials from the Women's Christian Temperance Union, Battle Creek, Mich., and the Partisan Prohibition Historical Society, Lee, Me.; and 3 religious vols. published in Michigan, 1880s

Programs for concerts of the University of Michigan School of Music, 1927– , and of the National Music Camp, 1920s–

Photographs, of the Victor C. Squier shop, ca. 1910–72; of Rev. E. H. Lindsay, 9 items, ca. 1900, relating to his musical work among the Indians for the Christian Crusaders of Wisconsin; and of local music organizations, as part of the Sam Sturgis collection

Transcripts of music references in Ann Arbor newspapers, 1829–44, prepared by Lloyd E. Biggle, 1949

—Martha D. Burns, Mary Jo Pugh

C. School of Music Collections

Eva Jessye Afro-American Music Collection, including 100 books about music, texts of films and musicals, and periodical issues; 150 editions of music; 3 file drawers of programs, pamphlets, and clippings referring to black performers, writers, and subjects; photographs of 400 subjects, also 22 portrait sketches by Bill Strong, 20 Hirschfield caricatures, and 17 miscellaneous paintings and sketches; and ms materials of Eubie Blake, Arthur Cunningham, William Dawson, Eva Jessye, and William Grant Still. See Mary Catherine Blanding, *A Catalogue of the Eva Jessye Afro-American Music Collection* (thesis, University of Michigan, 1974)

Albert A. Stanley, 34 letters received, 1909-11, including 15 letters and 3 documents from Oscar Sonneck, relating to the formation of a North American Section of the International Music Society

David E. Mattern Collection, 40 linear meters of music-education and related materials, including books, theses, journals, and performing editions, with a separate catalogue (housed in the Music Library)

D. University Libraries: School of Music Library

Sheet music, ca. 1840–70, 1500 items in 34 bound vols., not separately catalogued

General music collections, including extensive holdings of organ music from the estate of Palmer Christian, and violin music from the estate of Joseph Knitzer

Jacob Maurice Coopersmith (1903–68), research notes and materials, comprising the Coopersmith Handel Collection

Glenn Osser, ms arrangements used by his dance orchestra, 1930s–50s, 10 linear meters with 600 arrangements, with a card index by title

E. University Libraries: Rare Book Room

Lorenzo da Ponte, *Versi* (New York, 1832), with his ms additions and corrections

Shaker music books, including 3 vols. of texts and history, 1813–50, and 6 ms vols. with music, 1840–80, among them books signed by Levi Shaw, John M. Brown, Maria Blow, and Martha J. Anderson. See *Cook*, p. 291

Albert A. Stanley, music mss, including 26 choral, 19 vocal, and 9 instrumental works in score; also 6 scores of his modern settings of ancient Greek music, 8 letters, and 14 mss of his lectures on music history ca. 1900–1921

Albert Lockwood (1871–1933), 15 ms transcripts of chamber-music arrangements

Frederick Stock (1872–1942), personal papers, 77 items, including letters from Arthur Bodanzky, Nadia Boulanger, Ferruccio Busoni, John Alden Carpenter, Pablo Casals, Walter Damrosch, Ernö Dohnányi, Clara Clemens Gabrilowitsch, Mary Garden, Rubin Goldmark, Percy Grainger, Victor Herbert, Charles Martin Loeffler, Pierre Monteux, Isidor Philipp, Edward C. Potter, Serge Prokofiev, Sergei Rachmaninoff, Olga Samaroff, Ernestine Schumann-Heink, Leopold Stokowski, Rose Fay (Mrs. Theodore) Thomas, Frank Van der Stucken, Eugene Ysaÿe, and Bernhard Ziehn

Arnold Schoenberg, correspondence, 1901–50, 182 items, mostly addressed to him in the U.S., including 89 letters from Heinrich Jalowitz, 76 from René Leibowitz, others from Wilhelm Furtwängler, Klaus and Monika Mann, Artur Schnabel, and Alfred Wallenstein

Gustav Holst (1874–1934, English composer), holograph ms of *A Fugal Concerto for Flute and Oboe* op. 40 no. 2, 1923, with the note "This score was written in the Library of the University of Michigan"

Labadie collection relating to anarchism, socialism, communism, and other protest movements, including workers' songbooks with U.S. imprints, mostly with texts only, and a few with music, 1900–1910 and 1930s

Theater promptbooks in the VanVolkenburg–Browne Collection, several with ms music used in performances of the Chicago Little Theatre, 1910s

Miscellaneous songbooks, 34 items, including hymnals, with and without music, and tunebooks in English, 1758–1848; German hymnals, 1760–1834; children's music books; and other items

—Harriet C. Jameson, Margaret E. Berg

730

KIMBALL HOUSE HISTORICAL SOCIETY

196 Capital Avenue NE
Battle Creek, Michigan 49017

Sheet music, 600 items, including local imprints

Other printed music, including 2 boxes of hymnals; also parts for music performed by the Germania Band of Battle Creek, 1870s–99, 36 titles

Programs, including concerts performed by John B. Martin; (1866–1940) in Battle Creek, also at Albion College and Olivet College; Battle Creek Symphony Orchestra, 1899– , including performances conducted by John B. Martin; vaudeville, concerts, and other events at the Post Theatre, 1903–30s, 18 linear cm.; recitals by Bendetson Netsorg (pianist), ca. 1900–1910; and other local performances of Community Concerts, the Community Chorus, the Amateur Musical Club of Battle Creek, the Civic Music Association, the Pedro Paz Orchestra, and church and public-school events, in all 15 linear cm.

Organizational archives, of the Amateur Musical Club of Battle Creek, 3 vols. of minutes, 1896–1905, also programs; Treble Clef Musical Club, 1 vol. of papers and minutes, 1891–1905; and the John B. Martin and Sherwood School of Music of Battle Creek, press clippings, 1880s–1920s

Materials on the history of music in Battle Creek, including Lela M. Hart, "Comprehensive Musical History of Battle Creek, 1842–1904"; Lenora M. McBain (music teacher and principal in the Battle Creek public schools), scrapbook, 1901–34, with photographs, letters, and press clippings; William F. Neale, historical studies, including "Music in Common Life" (1898, relating to Battle Creek music) and "A Story of Music in Battle Creek" (1911); Maurice H. Neale, "A Story of Two Cremona Violins," ed. W. F. Neale (ca. 1900); and Julia A. Walton, "The First 75 Years: Battle Creek Symphony Orchestra" (honors term paper, Western Michigan University, 1974). Also folders on local-history topics, among them the Battle Creek Conservatory of Music, Edwin Barnes, the Morning Musical Club, industrial, military, and dance bands, and talent shows

Photographs of the Germania Band, Battle Creek Symphony Orchestra, John B. Martin, and Raymond Gould

Press clippings of reviews of the Battle Creek Symphony Orchestra, John B. Martin, Raymond Gould, Olive Gould Parkes, and Roger Parkes, 1 box, 1880s–1950s

Recordings, including 200 Edison cylinders, 1892–1905, and 60 linear cm. of 78-rpm discs

—Arlene Lavigna

731

BAY CITY BRANCH LIBRARY   **MiBay**

Bay County Library System
708 Center Avenue
Bay City, Michigan 48706

Sheet music, 500 items, mostly early 20th-century American imprints for keyboard

Songbooks of various kinds, 200 items

—Barbara Fisher Miles

732

ANDREWS UNIVERSITY   **MiBsA**

James White Library, Heritage Room
University Station
Berrien Springs, Michigan 49104

Seventh-Day Adventist hymnals, 64 items, ca. 1849–1940

—Elaine L. Waller

733

John MORRIS

6241 Three Lakes Drive
Brighton, Michigan 48116

Recordings of American folk and hillbilly music, 1920s–50s, 50 cylinders, 15,000 78-rpm discs, 3000 other discs, and 500 tapes; also materials concerning bluegrass and old-time music, used for reissued recordings by the Old Homestead Records Company

734

IRON COUNTY HISTORICAL AND MUSEUM SOCIETY

Route 424, Museum Street
Caspian, Michigan 49915

Carrie Jacobs Bond, 3 published compositions, words to 20 compositions, 40 letters, 10 photographs, and 2 programs (from Caspian and Chicago)

Other published sheet music, including piano music, ca. 1920–30

—Harold Bernhardt, Marcia A. Bernhardt

735

DEARBORN HISTORICAL   **MiDbHi**
MUSEUM

915 Brady Street
Dearborn, Michigan 48124

Hymnals and popular songbooks, 100 items, 1850s–1940

Sheet music, 200 mostly popular items, ca. 1890–1940, including 1 song referring to Dearborn

Photographs of local musicians and music groups, and of the Henry Ford early American dances, 15 items, ca. 1900–1940

Recordings, including piano rolls and 5 linear meters of 78-rpm discs and cylinders

—Donald V. Baut

736

GREENFIELD VILLAGE AND HENRY FORD MUSEUM (Edison Institute)

MiDbEI

Oakwood Boulevard
Dearborn, Michigan 48121

Robert H. Tannahill Research Library

Stephen Collins Foster, holograph mss of songs, including "Come Where My Love Lies Dreaming," "Open Thy Lattice, Love," and a fragment of "Nelly Bly"; also a nearly complete set of first editions of his published music

Orchestral arrangements of Henry Ford's favorite tunes, played by dance bands, 1920s; also a ms field transcription of fiddle tunes and dance music

Public relations files on Edison recording artists, including photographs and biographical information

Musical-instrument trade catalogues, late 19th and early 20th centuries, 12 items

Hymnals, 15 pre-1850 vols., other later items

—Joan Gartland

Henry Ford Museum

Recordings, including 5000 cylinders and 10,000 discs, early 20th century, in various musical and spoken forms; also 10,000 master metal moulds for all Edison Co. discs, 1912–29

Materials on the history of American musical instruments, including catalogues, method books, printed ephemera, and facsimiles

—Robert E. Eliason

Ford Archives

"Ford Sunday Evening Hour" and other radio-broadcast music programs, 1934–47, archival materials in the following files: Acc. 44, Boxes 15–16; Acc. 149, Boxes 10–40, 91–147; Acc. 454, Box 1; and Acc. 572, Box 10. See David L. Lewis, *The Public Image of Henry Ford* (Detroit, 1976), pp. 315–29 and 453–58, also the footnotes on pp. 533–35, 555–56

Oral-history interviews used for Allan Nevins and Frank Ernest Hill, *Ford* (New York, 1954–63), with some musical materials accessible through a partial card index

Scrapbooks of press clippings, 1912– , in 200 vols., with occasional musical references

Sheet music, 10 songs relating to the Model-T Ford. See Faye Witt Moreland, *Greenfield and Fairer Lanes: Music in the Life of Henry Ford* (Tupelo, Miss., 1969)

—Winthrop Sears

737

DETROIT FEDERATION OF MUSICIANS

1916 Schaefer Highway
Detroit, Michigan 48235

Archives of the Federation, established 1897, including 30 books of minutes, 1897– ; various financial and official records, including 25 account books; personnel records, consisting of applications, accounts, necrology materials, and miscellanea; scrapbooks, including 12 vols. of general press clippings, programs, and announcements, 1919– , also vols. on the Graystone Ballroom; files of the *Keynote,* and of the official bulletin which preceded it; photographs; and miscellaneous other papers. Apart from the bound vols., the archives fill 34 4-drawer files. Included are important data on William Finzel, Jean Goldkette, Hugo Kalsow, and Hermann Schmeman, also on the Detroit Symphony Orchestra, the J. L. Hudson Company Band and Orchestra, the Ford Motor Company Band, and other theater orchestras and dance bands

738

DETROIT INSTITUTE OF ARTS

MiDA

5200 Woodward Avenue
Detroit, Michigan 48202

Archives of the Institute, including issues of the Institute's *Bulletin* with information on concerts; minutes of the City of Detroit Arts Commission, and correspondence of Clyde Burrows (secretary of the Commission); programs, including events at the Bonstelle Theatre; and information on the Pro Musica concert series

739

DETROIT PUBLIC LIBRARY

MiD

5201 Woodward Avenue
Detroit, Michigan 48202

Music and Performing Arts Department

E. Azalia Hackley Memorial Collection of Negro Music, Dance, and Drama, established 1943 by the Detroit Musicians' Association (local chapter of the National Association of Negro Musicians), in honor of Mme Hackley (1867–1922, singer and music teacher), including 900 books about black music and musicians; music by black composers, 1200 items; 1600 recordings; and programs, playbills, scrapbooks, press clippings, letters, and ephemera. The sheet-music collection includes 19th-century songs and descriptive pieces on Negro themes, 95 items; songs and descriptive music by non-Negro composers on Negro themes, 384 items; songs and pieces by Negro composers and lyricists, 900 items; and popular songs written by or featuring Bert Williams, 68 items. Among the important holdings are a ms copy of Samuel Coleridge-Taylor's Violin Concerto, formerly owned by Maud Powell; 3 scrapbooks of concert tours by the Fisk Jubilee Singers, 1875–98, and an early photograph of the group; a working script for *Haiti,* as produced by the Federal Theatre Project, 1938; 2000 photographs of black singers and actors, including some from Carl Van Vechten, 1920s–30s;

and autograph copies of songs by Lillian Evanti, W. C. Handy, and Langston Hughes. See the published catalogue (Boston, 1979)

Michigan Collection, containing books, music, and recordings by authors, composers, and performers who were either born or resident in Michigan, 400 items, published or in ms photocopy. Among the composers are Roberta Bitgood, 63 works; Julius Chajes, 60 works; Charles N. Daniels (1878–1943), 126 works; Clark Eastham, 26 works; Arthur Farwell, 23 works; Ross Lee Finney, 46 works; Ossip Gabrilowitsch (1878–1936), 9 works; Leo Sowerby (1895–1968), 62 works; and Harry von Tilzer (1872–1946), 155 works. Other items include 250 books, 150 recordings, and 10 file drawers of materials. Related to this collection is the 30-drawer card file assembled by Lawrence W. Brown, documenting all aspects of musical life in the state. See his article "An Awful Lot of Music in Detroit," *Among Friends*, 13 (1958–59), 58–59

Historical Sheet Music Collection, 17,000 items, of which 12,000 are pre-1940; arranged by title, with a chronological index on 15,000 cards

Scrapbooks, of the Tuesday Musicale, 1908– , in 21 vols.; Detroit Symphony Season, 1914–62, in 9 vols.; Madrigal Club of Detroit, 1915– , in 8 vols.; Detroit Season, 1923–62, in 30 vols.; and Pro Musica, 1927– , in 3 vols.; also 2 linear meters of programs, press clippings and ephemera on Detroit musical activities, arranged chronologically

Hymnals and tunebooks, 450 items, most of them pre-1940

Kling's orchestral music library, performance materials for 500 works, mostly in European editions, ca. 1900

Alma Josenhans, research notes on Detroit theater history, 1811–1908, mostly transcripts of newspaper notices, covering concerts and operas; in 33 notebooks, 1.4 linear meters

Song index, 60,000 cards, including the titles in the Historical Sheet Music Collection, also the contents of the Library's collection of song anthologies

—Agatha Pfeiffer Kalkanis

Burton Historical Collection

Personal papers, of Rossetter G. Cole (1866–1952), correspondence, programs, and genealogy, including information on his activities at Ripon College, Grinnell College, and the University of Wisconsin, 15 linear cm.; Marian Coryell, holograph music mss, 15 linear cm.; Ossip Gabrilowitsch, correspondence, 1920–37, 5.5 linear meters; Thomas Hastings, letters to his brother, E. P. Hastings, 1817–52, as discussed in Mary Teal, "Letters of Thomas Hastings, M.L.A. Notes, 3 (1978), 303–18; Ralph F. Holmes, correspondence, plays, reviews, and scrapbooks for his work as music critic of the *Detroit Times*, 1908–39, 1.3 linear meters; the Humphries family papers, including diaries and papers of Martha Humphrey, 1864–77, and working files of Mary Humphrey in connection with her columns in the *Detroit News*, 1938–57, with scattered music references; Fritz Kalsow, subscription books for the Detroit Symphony Orchestra and records of his music students, 1891–99, 30 linear cm.; Charles Julius Simon (1815–89), personal correspondence, 4.5 linear meters; and scrapbook concerning Thaddeus Wronski (director of the Detroit Opera Company, 1920s–30s)

Organizational archives, of Cass Technical High School, papers regarding its music program, 1919–72, including correspondence of Clarence Burn (founder of the program) and of Gordon Allen (later his assistant), scrapbooks, programs, school papers, photographs, and band journals, among them *Jacobs Band and Orchestra Monthly*; Detroit Conservatory of Music, 1886–1915, 75 linear cm.; Detroit Symphony Society, correspondence and official records, 1915–45, 75 linear cm.; Women's Association for the Detroit Symphony Orchestra, official records, correspondence, programs, and scrapbooks, 1933– , 1.8 linear meters, also the Junior Woman's Association, similar materials, 1939– , 2.5 linear meters; and Harmonie Society of Detroit, official and financial records, correspondence, programs, and photographs, 1881– , 5 linear meters

Sheet music published in Detroit and elsewhere in Michigan, 1851–1961, 9000 items

—Alice C. Dalligan, Joseph F. Oldenburg

National Automotive History Collection

Sheet music relating to automobiles, 127 items

740
DETROIT SYMPHONY ORCHESTRA
Ford Auditorium
Detroit, Michigan 48226

Program books for the Orchestra and its two predecessors (1914–42, 1943–49, 1951–), in bound vols.

Card indexes covering repertory, conductors and soloists, members of the orchestra, and performances outside Detroit, being assembled

—Bruce Carr

741
Arthur R. LaBREW
13560 Goddard Street
Detroit, Michigan 48212

Research materials used in his publications, which include *Black Musicians of the Colonial Period, 1700–1800: A Preliminary Index of Names* (Detroit, 1977), *Black Music of the 19th Century: The Exodus to Europe* (Detroit, 1974), *Elizabeth T. Greenfield, the Black Swan* (Detroit, 1969–79), *Free at Last: Legal Aspects of Blind Tom Bethune's Career* (Detroit, 1976), *Selected Works of Francis Johnson* (Detroit, 1979), and *Studies in 19th-Century Afro-American Music* (Detroit, 1979). Specific holdings include Melville Charlton (organist), letters and correspondence; Edgar Rogie Clark (1913–78, folklorist), letters, musical and poetical works, papers, and pictures; Carl Diton (1860–1970, Philadelphia concert pianist and founder and president of the National Association of Negro Musicians), correspondence; John Eccles (singer), memorabilia of his career and notices of black performers in New York, 1920–70; Helen Jones (choral director and accompanist to Abbie Mitchell), scrapbooks; Cora Smith, 19th-century documents, and a score for the first performance of Scott Joplin's *Treemonisha*, in which she performed; documents relating to the National Association of

Negro Musicians; published music by 19th-century black musicians, including black minstrelsy, 1865–1900; materials on black music in Detroit, 1881–1940; and other memorabilia relating to black music and musicians

742
WAYNE STATE UNIVERSITY   MiDW
Walter P. Reuther Library
Detroit, Michigan 48202

Archives of Labor History and Urban Affairs

See Warner W. Pflug, ed., *A Guide to the Archives of Labor History and Urban Affairs, Wayne State University* (Detroit, 1974)

People's Song Library, papers including songs and song texts on civil rights, elections, hootenannies, and the folk revival, also songs of the Almanac Singers, 1937–70

Humphrey family papers, including diaries and letters mentioning opera in Detroit

John Oneka (1937–64, union official), songs and press clippings relating to the National War Labor Board

Industrial Workers of the World (IWW), poems, cartoons, pictures, songs, and lyrics relating to labor movements of the early 20th century

American Federation of State, County, and Municipal Employees (AFSCME), papers, including songs and lyrics emphasizing labor struggles, 1900–1950

Audio Collection of tape and disc recordings, including the United Auto Workers labor-song collection, and the Joe Glazer collection of songs of coal miners, textile workers, garbage collectors, and steel workers

Folklore Archive

Folk music relating to urban America, particularly of ethnic groups and culture groups of Detroit, as cited in *Briegleb*, no. 53

Elinor Aumann (student), 7-page ms of folksongs, written for a folklore class at the University, 1939

—Carrolyn A. Davis, Janet Langlois

743
MICHIGAN STATE UNIVERSITY   MiEM
East Lansing, Michigan 48824

Special Collections Department, University Library

Popular Culture Collection, including popular and sacred songbooks, ca. 1890–1920

American Radicalism Collection, containing IWW songs

Sheet music, 30 linear cm., including 3 Ku Klux Klan songs, ca. 1900–1920

Popular Theater Collection, including programs of local musical events at the Lansing Opera House and elsewhere, ca. 1900

—Jeannette Fiore

Museum

Programs, publicity materials, and tickets, mostly of local musical events and dances, 209 items, ca. 1849–1957

Photograph of a boys' band from Three Oaks, Mich., 1896

Songbooks, 100 popular, school, and sacred items, ca. 1880–1930

Sheet music, 1200 items, ca. 1860–1940

Advertising cards for organs, pianos, and musical-instrument dealers, 27 items, ca. 1850–1920

Recordings, including 175 78-rpm discs, 178 cylinders, and 103 piano rolls

—Val Roy Berryman

University Archives and Historical Collections

University Department of Music papers, 30 linear cm., 1910–73, including descriptions and diagrams of marching-band formations, programs, reports, and a statement of requirements for the Ph.D. in music

University Cooperative Extension Service, Music Extension Program, 30 linear cm. of papers, ca. 1929–64, including annual reports and song lists for Michigan counties

R. Nathanial Dett, 70 linear cm. of papers, 1913–43, including 33 sacred compositions by him

Photographs of musicians and music groups at the University, 200 photographs, ca. 1884–1959

—Frederick L. Honhart

744
Bly CORNING
1902 Hampden Road
Flint, Michigan 48500

Materials assembled for the use of Thomas A. Edison in connection with his program for issuing recordings, as collected by Messrs. Hayes and Welch, ca. 1900–1922 on a worldwide basis for all kinds of music; also archival records from the Edison Co. Portions of the collection are at the University of Michigan, Ann Arbor, and at Central Michigan University, Mount Pleasant, q.v.

Sheet music, 300,000 items, all pre-1921 and mostly U.S. imprints, including 800 *Sonneck–Upton* titles; 3000 *Wolfe* titles; 3000 Civil War editions, including 500 Confederate imprints; and 3000 presidential and campaign editions. The collection is arranged mostly by subject and name categories, i.e., presidential materials, patriotic songs, the U.S. flag, transportation, sport, Stephen Collins Foster, and Louis Moreau Gottschalk

Miscellaneous music mss, 1.2 linear meters, including 4 fair copies of marches by John Philip Sousa, inscribed to Edison

Papers of the Edison Co., including the 3000 questionnaires returned for a 1924–25 survey of the musical repertory, directed through phonograph dealers; also 150 letters to Edison from composers, 1900–1925; and copies of Edison house publications, including the *Talking Machine World*; in all 1.2 linear meters

Recordings, including 700 cylinders

745
FLINT PUBLIC LIBRARY   MiFli
Art, Music, and Drama Department
1026 East Kearsley Street
Flint, Michigan 48502

Popular sheet music, 2500 items, ca. 1880–1940

Hymnals of various denominations, 30 items, ca. 1883–1940

Clippings, programs, and photographs of local musicians and music groups in a vertical file, ca. 1890– , including minute books and scrapbooks of the St. Cecilia Society, 1890– , and scrapbooks of the MacDowell Club, 1935–

—Forrest Alter

746

FRANKENMUTH HISTORICAL MUSEUM

613 South Main Street
Frankenmuth, Michigan 48734

Laura Bernthal Nuechterlein (b. ca. 1885, of Frankenmuth), music copybook containing ms music for a brass band, ca. 1900

Photographs of a local band, ca. 1900, the Concordia Male Choir, ca. 1900–1940, and the Frankenmuth Band, ca. 1890–1903, in all 23 items

Hymnals and school songbooks, 12 items, ca. 1880–1920, including German-language items published in the U.S. or in Germany and used in the U.S.

Popular vocal sheet music, 10 items, ca. 1880–1920

Marching-band scores and sacred arrangements, 2 published items, 1875–1900

—Carl R. Hansen

747

ARNOLD'S ARCHIVES

c/o Arnold Jacobsen
1106 Eastwood SE
Grand Rapids, Michigan 49506

Recordings of 200,000 songs on discs and tapes, accessible through subject classification, mostly in the form of special subject lists prepared for circulation. Among the subjects of the discographies are dance bands, jazz bands, blues, and country-and-western music, also composers including Ernest R. Ball, Irving Berlin, Gus Edwards, Jerome Kern, Victor Herbert, and Sigmund Romberg

748

GRAND RAPIDS PUBLIC LIBRARY   MiGr

Library Plaza
Grand Rapids, Michigan 49502

Music and Art Department

Popular and classical sheet music, mostly for voice, 2000 items, including works pertaining to Grand Rapids, ca. 1870–1930

Hymnals, 12 items, ca. 1870–1940, including 1 in Dutch

Popular and community songbooks, 12 items, ca. 1870–1940

Recordings, including 900 78-rpm discs or albums

—Helen Vanden Engel

Michigan History Collection

School and university songbooks, 7 items, ca. 1885–1953

Programs and papers of local musical events, 1857– , including those of the Bach Festival, Grand Rapids Conservatory of Music, Grand Rapids Symphony Orchestra, Luce's Hall, National Federation of Music Clubs Sixth Biennial Festival and Convention, National Music Camp (Interlochen), Powers Opera House, Redmond's Opera House, St. Cecilia Society, Schubert Club, Squier's Opera House, and University of Michigan; also related photographs, 25 items, including the Newsboys' Band

Friedrich Brothers Musical Journal, published by a local music dealer, 2 issues, 1882–83

Sheet music published in Grand Rapids, 3 items, 1851–1901; also F. L. Grundtvig, *Sangbog for det Danske folk in Amerika* (Manistee, Mich., n.d.)

—Celene E. Idema

749

GRAND RAPIDS PUBLIC MUSEUM

54 Jefferson Avenue SE
Grand Rapids, Michigan 49503

Hymnals, 14 items, ca. 1850–1915; also several 20th-century popular and school songbooks

Popular vocal sheet music and published classical-music scores for piano or orchestra, 3000 items, ca. 1870–1930

Programs of local musical events, including those of bands and at the Powers Theater, 20 linear cm., ca. 1887– ; also photographs, 120 items, ca. 1890–1950

Recordings, including 1065 78-rpm discs, 300 cylinders, 194 piano rolls, and 30 wire or tape recordings

750

John H. PERSCHBACHER

58 Baynton NE
Grand Rapids, Michigan 49503

Early recordings, including 1000 cylinders of bands, orchestras, vaudeville, and political and other spoken material, 1890–1929; 200 78-rpm discs of speeches, sketches, songs, and bands, 1895–1940; several hundred 88-note music rolls of rags, dance music, blues, and classical music, mostly for coin-operated pianos; and piano rolls made by composers, among them 85 Violano rolls, 1912–32, 90 Wurlitzer 65-note rolls, 1905–30, 30 A rolls, 1907–37, 20 G rolls, 1910–30, and 25 Pianolin 49-note rolls, 1910–28

Songbooks, several early 19th-century items

751

BOHEMIAN MUSICIANS' CLUB OF DETROIT

c/o Edward P. Frohlich
30 Preston Place
Grosse Pointe Farms, Michigan 48236

Archives of the Club, 1930s–70s, 70 linear cm., including correspondence, scrapbooks, minute books, programs, bulletins, and miscellanea

752

GUILD OF CARILLONNEURS IN NORTH AMERICA

c/o Grosse Pointe Memorial Church
16 Lakeshore Drive
Grosse Pointe Farms, Michigan 48236

Archives of the Guild, 1920s– , including 75 ms and 100 published scores, and papers of such carillonneurs as Anton Brees, Percival Price, and Kamiel Lefevere; also numerous programs, press clippings, photographs, and catalogues of carillon music

—William De Turk

753

SUOMI COLLEGE   MiHanS

Finnish-American Historical Archives
Hancock, Michigan 49930

Materials relating to the life and work of Finnish-Americans, including 5 boxes of ms music and 15 cm. of sheet music, also songbooks, programs, organizational papers, and 12 photographs, 1890s–
Martti Nisonen (faculty member, 1922–46), music mss, 4 boxes

—Ellen M. Ryynanen

754

CROMAINE LIBRARY

3688 North Hartland Road
Hartland, Michigan 48029

Programs of local musical events, including those at Hartland Music Hall

—Sandra Scherba

755

HARTLAND MUSIC HALL

Hartland, Michigan 48029

Sheet music, popular and sacred items, also topical items relating to Hartland, 1930s–40s

—Sandra Scherba

756

Joseph F. KAWECKI

10 Louise Street, Apt. 315
Highland Park, Michigan 48203

Hymnals, 1880– , 100 items, mostly Roman Catholic and in Polish

757

HOPE COLLEGE   MiHolH

Holland, Michigan 49423

Helene P. Karsten (piano teacher), papers, 1929–72, including a ms score, "Cosmopolitan Fraternity," and clippings, programs, and course notes

Willard C. Snow (music administrator), papers, 1929–36, including correspondence, programs, and minutes of the Holland Civic Chorus

758

NETHERLANDS MUSEUM

8 East Twelfth Street
Holland, Michigan 49423

Holland Musicians' Club, archives, 1928–33

—Barbara Lampen

759

WESTERN THEOLOGICAL   MiHolW SEMINARY OF THE REFORMED CHURCH OF AMERICA

Beardslee Library
86 East Twelfth Street
Holland, Michigan 49423

Hymnals of the Reformed Church and other denominations, ca. 1800–1950, 140 items, including some in Dutch and other non-English languages

—Norman J. Kansfield

760

BARTLETT MEMORIAL LIBRARY OF EXPLORATION

American Institute for Exploration
1809 Nichols Road
Kalamazoo, Michigan 49007

Recordings of Aleut-Eskimo religious (Russian Orthodox) chants, 10 7-inch reels of tape

—Ted P. Bank II

761

WESTERN MICHIGAN UNIVERSITY   MiKW

Kalamazoo, Michigan 49008

Music Library

Hymnals, ca. 1825–1940, 25 items, including 1 in German
Sheet music, 8000 mostly popular-vocal items, ca. 1890–1930, indexed by title

—Evan Bonds

University Archives and Regional History Collections

Milton Sawyer (Civil War musician), diary, 1863
Robert A. Simonds (Army bandleader with the American Expeditionary Force in Russia, 1918–19), papers, including 43 letters
Florence T. Dewing collection, 1862–1938, with programs of the Kalamazoo Symphony Orchestra, 1922, and copies of *The Sounding Board*, issued by Mandolin/Guitar Co.,1916–19
Robert Somers collection, 1876–1907, including the ms song "The Happiest Boys That's Out," dated West Lake, 1877

Mrs. Lynn Stoddar collection, including printed song sheets for 3 popular or campaign songs, 1926–40

Printed music, including the *Seventh Day Adventist Hymn and Tune Book* (Battle Creek, 1887), in the Orrin Lathrop Collection; a popular song, 1910, in the Mutual Improvement Club of Galesburg Collection; and the *Michigan State Grange Song Collection* (1929); also *The American College Songster* (1876) and *Whitney Family's Merry Moments Songster* (1884), in the McReakin and Somers collections

Broadsides and handbills, 4 items, 1866–1917, for the Galesburg Musical Society, Galesburg Musical Union, Kalamazoo Choral Union, and Orpheum Theater (Kalamazoo), in the Fink, Fisher, and Hirschy collections

Programs, 120 items from Decatur (N.D.), Battle Creek, Dowagiac, and Kalamazoo, including those of the Academy of Music, Kalamazoo Choral Union, Kalamazoo Musical Society, Kalamazoo Symphony Orchestra, Fritz Kreisler, and the Sousa Band, 1889–1958, in the Beeby, Cousins, Krause, Ihling, Rogers, Shutes, Starring, Stevens, Suck, Van Allen, and Wilhelm collections

Eckford Cornet Band, rules and by-laws (photocopy), ca. 1880, in the Youngs collection

Schoolcraft Musical Association, minute book and calls for dance steps, 1869, in the Stanley B. Smith family papers

Histories of the Battle Creek Symphony Orchestra, by Julie A. Walton, 1974; music in Kalamazoo, by Philip Proud, n.d.; and theaters in Kalamazoo, by Viola Ross, 1946

— Phyllis Burnham

762
KALKASKA COUNTY HISTORICAL SOCIETY
Kalkaska, Michigan 49646

Chauncey C. Jencks (1853–1932), 1 published popular sheet-music item for voice, ca. 1900, and 1 photograph

Grange songbooks, 3 items, 1900–1940; also a Methodist hymnal, 1894

Programs of local musicians or groups, 50 items, including those of the Opera House, 1880–1908, and the Kalkaska County Ladies' Concert Band, 1906–12; also photographs, press clippings, and memorabilia of the Ladies' Band

—Neva Wolfe

763
MICHIGAN HISTORY DIVISION,   Mi-HC
DEPARTMENT OF STATE
208 North Capitol Avenue
Lansing, Michigan 48918

Hugo Richter, Jr., song "Dreams of Nature," n.d.

Michigan Federation of Music Clubs, minutes, reports, scrapbooks, and publications, 1916–78

Saginaw Academy of Music, 2 programs, ca. 1910

Photographs, 10 items, including Michigan orchestras and bands, and the Michigan Music Club

—LeRoy Barnett, Ruby Rogers

764
MANISTEE COUNTY HISTORICAL MUSEUM
425 River Street
Manistee, Michigan 49660

Tuesday Music Club, 60 linear cm. of papers, including programs, clippings, and printed music, ca. 1925–75

Hymnals, 50 items, including books in German and Polish, ca. 1875–1925

Sheet music, 3000 items, ca. 1875–1925

Photographs of local musical events, 50 items, ca. 1880–1910

Recordings, including 75 cylinders and 75 78-rpm discs

—Steve Harold

765
MENOMINEE COUNTY HISTORICAL SOCIETY
Box 151
Menominee, Michigan 49858

Menominee Opera House, official record books, 2 vols., 1902–6 and 1915–19, with information on financial matters (payroll, tickets sold, etc.), weather, and competing events

—D. M. Swanson

766
CENTRAL MICHIGAN UNIVERSITY   MiMtpT
Clarke Historical Library
Mount Pleasant, Michigan 48859

Marie Curtis (music director of Detroit high schools), 2 scrapbooks of business correspondence, programs, clippings, and photographs, 1932–54

Michigan Music Teachers' Association archives, consisting of 1660 items and 14 bound vols., 1867– , including minutes, programs, and correspondence

Published sheet music, 3350 items and 8 bound vols., ca. 1800–1940, including coon songs, mostly from the Thomas A. Edison collection, later acquired by Bly Corning, of Flint, Mich. (q.v.)

Patriotic, popular, and school songbooks, 90 items, ca. 1850–1920, including a few local items, and several editions of *School Song Knapsack*; also 23 other items of published music, some for piano

Programs of Michigan cities and of the University, ca. 1850–1940, in local collections

Catalogues of Michigan music dealers and instrument manufacturers, 15 items, 1880s

Photographs, 3000 19th-century cabinet photographs, including many of such musicians as Ole Bull and Jenny Lind

Recordings, including 2 tapes of Chippewa Indian hymns collected in 1965 by John Cumming, and 2 78-rpm discs of lumbermen's ballads collected 1930s–40s by Earl C. Beck

—John Cumming, William Miles

767
OLIVET COLLEGE   MiOC
Library
333 South Main Street
Olivet, Michigan 49076

Autograph ms music in 3 notebooks, by faculty members of the College's Conservatory of Music, including Olivet College songs

Programs and papers of community or College musical events, including correspondence, minutes, scrapbooks, photographs, and 100 programs

Printed music for piano, voice, or orchestra, 200 items, ca. 1870–1900

Songbooks of community or College music societies, 8 printed items, ca. 1860–1940

—John P. Kondelik

768

BEAVER ISLAND HISTORICAL SOCIETY

Main and Forest
Saint James, Michigan 49782

Local musical materials, including a photocopy of the ms song by Isaac Wright, "Beaver Island Girls," 1874; tape recordings of local fiddlers, collected ca. 1970; and 5 photographs of local bands, ca. 1880–1930

769

CONGREGATION B'NAI DAVID

Isadore Gruskin Library
24350 Southfield Road
Southfield, Michigan 48075

Liturgical music, including ms and published Jewish liturgical books and sheet music, and recordings of sacred music

Published secular music, including Hebrew songs, Jewish folksongs, and Israeli, Hasidic, and Sephardic festival music

Programs of concerts at the synagogue

—Hyman J. Adler

770

DUNS SCOTUS COLLEGE LIBRARY   MiDDS

Nine Mile Road and Evergreen Street
Southfield, Michigan 48076

Hymnals, 75 items, ca. 1855– , mostly Roman Catholic
Sheet music, including 100 items in 2 bound vols., ca. 1855–69; also 250 songs, mostly 20th century

—Brother Gabriel Balassone

771

Michael MONTGOMERY

17601 Cornell Street
Southfield, Michigan 48075

Collection of 2000 U.S. piano rolls, mostly hand-played, 1900–1940, primarily jazz, ragtime, and blues, and a related library of piano-roll catalogues and rollographical data

Sheet-music collection, emphasizing black composers and publishers, 1890–1940, primarily jazz, ragtime, and blues

772

STURGIS PUBLIC LIBRARY

North Nottawa at West Street
Sturgis, Michigan 49091

Sturgis Music Club, archives, 1924–28, including a secretary's book, a treasurer's book, and programs

—Betty Freeland

773

WAYNE HISTORICAL COMMISSION

1 Town Square
Wayne, Michigan 48184

Oddfellows Band, 1 bound vol. of minutes, 1920–21
Sheet music, including 69 vocal items, 1899–1945, and 65 piano items, 1892–1922; also 5 instruction books for piano, 1892–1942

Hymnals, 32 items, and 12 popular or school songbooks, ca. 1874–1930

Recordings, including 33 cylinders and 65 78-rpm discs

—Mildred Hanchett

774

WYANDOTTE HISTORICAL SOCIETY

2610 Biddle Avenue
Wyandotte, Michigan 48192

Local music materials, including 3 linear cm. of programs; papers of a local music organization, and 3 linear cm. of photographs

Songbooks, 3 linear cm. of sacred, popular, school, and community items, ca. 1930–60

Popular or sacred sheet music for voice or piano, 240 items, ca. 1890–1915

Recordings, including 5 linear cm. of 78-rpm discs, and 10 cylinders and piano rolls

—Timothy Caldwell

775

Nym COOKE

4847 Merritt Road
Ypsilanti, Michigan 48197

Tunebooks, 20 items published 1782–1878, including a copy of Andrew Law's *Select Harmony* (1782) with 46 pages of ms music at the end; also 10 19th-century gospel and popular songbooks

---

In addition to the repositories listed above, the following have also reported holdings of the materials indicated:

Adrian—Adrian College, Shipman Library: sheet music, songbooks, other printed music, programs, catalogues

Adrian—Lenawee County Historical Museum: sheet music, songbooks, programs, catalogues, pictures, recordings

Albion—Albion Historical Society: sheet music, songbooks, pictures, recordings

Alma—Alma Public Library: songbooks, miscellaneous

Alpena—Jesse Besser Museum: sheet music, songbooks, recordings

Au Gres—Arneac County Historical Society: sheet music, songbooks, programs, recordings

Battle Creek—Kingman Museum of Natural History: sheet music, programs, recordings

Bay City—Bay County Historical Society and Museum: sheet music, songbooks, programs, pictures, recordings

Bellevue—Bellevue Historical Society: songbooks

Caro—Indianfields Public Library: recordings

Caro—Watrousville–Caro Area Historical Society: songbooks

Clawson—Clawson Historical Society: sheet music, songbooks

Corunna—Corunna Public Library: songbooks

Dearborn—Dearborn Department of Libraries: songbooks

Detroit—University of Detroit, Library: sheet music, songbooks, other printed music

Durand—Shiawassee County Historical Society: songbooks

Farmington Hills—Detroit Bible College, Library: songbooks

Grand Haven—Tri-Cities Historical Society: sheet music, songbooks, other printed music, programs, recordings, miscellaneous

Grand Ledge—Grand Ledge Area Historical Society: programs

Grand Rapids—Congregational Church, Library: sheet music, songbooks, programs

Grand Rapids— St. Cecilia Music Society: sheet music, songbooks, pictures, recordings

Greenville—Flat River Historical Society: sheet music, songbooks, pictures

Grosse Ile—Grosse Ile Historical Society: sheet music, songbooks, programs

Hamburg—Hamburg Township Library: songbooks, recordings

Hancock—Hancock School Public Library: songbooks

Harbor Beach—Huron County Historical Society: sheet music, songbooks

Huntington Woods—Huntington Woods Public Library: songbooks, pictures

Ironwood—Ironwood Area Historical Society: sheet music, songbooks, pictures, recordings, miscellaneous

Lansing—Department of Education, State Library Services: sheet music (Michigan imprints)

Lansing—Great Lakes Bible College, Louis M. Detro Memorial Library: songbooks, other printed music

Lansing—Lansing Public Library: sheet music, songbooks, programs, pictures, recordings

Marquette—Marquette County Historical Society: sheet music, songbooks

Marquette—Northern Michigan University, Olson Library: songbooks

Mayville—Mayville Historical Museum: sheet music, songbooks, other printed music, programs, recordings

Montague—Montague Museum and Historical Society: sheet music, songbooks, other printed music, pictures, recordings, miscellaneous

Muskegon—Hackley Public Library: songbooks, programs

New Haven—Jean Waterloo: sheet music

Ontonagon—Ontonagon County Historical Society: sheet music, songbooks, other printed music, programs, catalogues, pictures, recordings, miscellaneous

Plymouth—St. John's Provincial Seminary, Library: songbooks, miscellaneous

Pontiac—Oakland County Pioneer Historical Society: sheet music, songbooks, programs, pictures

Port Huron—Museum of Arts and History: programs, pictures, recordings

Saginaw—Saginaw Historical Society Museum: sheet music, songbooks, pictures, recordings

Sault Ste. Marie—Bayliss Public Library: songbooks, programs

Sault Ste. Marie—Lake Superior State College, Library: miscellaneous

Spring Arbor—Spring Arbor College, Hugh A. White Library: sheet music, songbooks, other printed music, recordings

Stevensville—Lincoln Township Library: sheet music, recordings

Troy—Troy Public Library: songbooks, catalogues, pictures, recordings

Vermontville—Kalamo Township Historical Society: programs

Wixom—Wixom Public Library: songbooks

Ypsilanti—Ypsilanti Historical Society: sheet music, songbooks, programs

Minasota

776

CROW WING COUNTY HISTORICAL SOCIETY

Court House
Box 722
Brainerd, Minnesota 56401

Sheet music for piano, 1200 items, ca. 1880–1920, including 20 ms copies, and printed works by local composers William Bartsch, Jennie Johnson, and A. J. Crone

Other printed music, including 4 hymnals, 1849–1914, 1 of them in Swedish; 6 popular songbooks, 1881–1906; and 5 items of instrumental music, 1875–1910

Brainerd Ladies Musical, 60 linear cm. of minutes and account books, 1903–21

Programs of 10 local groups, 1892–1907, 50 linear cm.; also several photographs of local bands and music groups, ca. 1880–1920

Recordings, 1 linear meter, 1930–40

—Catherine M. Ebert

777

WRIGHT COUNTY HISTORICAL SOCIETY

101 Lake Boulevard NW
Buffalo, Minnesota 55313

Albert Nelson, typescript biography, 1916–50, with photographs of his Nelsonian one-man-band of 32 instruments, assembled in Buffalo and displayed at the 1933 World's Fair; also the one-man-band, with silent films and a 3-minute tape recording of Nelson performing

Hymnals, 75 items, 1900– , mostly Lutheran, including some in Swedish

School songbooks, 20 of them in English, 1860–1945, and 5 local items in Norwegian, Swedish, and Finnish, 1860s–70s

Sheet music, 40 popular items, 1910–30

Programs, 25 items, 1880s, including school events in Monticello, Minn. and patriotic festivals in Montrose, Minn.

Photographs of local musicians and town bands, 20 items, 1880s–1920s

Recordings, including 35 78-rpm discs, 1920s–40s

—Marion Jameson

778

CHATFIELD BRASS BAND
FREE MUSIC LENDING LIBRARY

Thurber Community Building
Chatfield, Minnesota 55923

> Since its founding in 1969, the Library has accumulated, indexed, and made available on free loan over 25,000 items of music as well as biographical essays pertaining to bands in America. See the typescript "History and Purpose," and various catalogues

Band music in printed scores and parts, 20,000 items as separate pieces and sets, ca. 1880– , with composer, title, and classification indexes. Classes include popular music for band, 2600 items, 1896– ; marches for band, 5400 items, 1880– ; music for string orchestra, 1300 classical or popular items, 1884– ; and music for big bands with strings, 1000 items, 1911–

Songbooks, 80 items, 1880– , including hymnals and military and popular songbooks

Vocal sheet music, 1700 items, 1846–

Manuscript arrangements, scores, and parts used by the University of Minnesota Marching Band, 1941– , 37 linear meters

Recordings, 500 items, mostly 78-rpm discs of band, orchestra, and piano music

—James A. Perkins

779

COKATO HISTORICAL SOCIETY

95 West Fourth Street
Cokato, Minnesota 55321

Emma and Lena Seidel (piano teachers in Cokato, 1880s–1920s), 100 pages of ms papers, including letters and account books; also photographs of their piano classes

Town bands of Cokato and neighboring towns, 1880s–1950s, membership lists, uniforms, instruments and oral-history tapes by former members

Hymnals in Finnish, Swedish, or Norwegian, 10 items, 1864–1911

Piano music, 4 collections published 1880–1910; also 2 pump-organ method books, 1884–90, and 25 sheet-music items for piano or organ, ca. 1900–1910

Photographs of local musicians and town bands, 50 items, 1895–1940

Tape recordings of Cokato musicians, including Clarence Anderson, playing the musical saw; May Redman, playing piano music for silent films; Mrs. Bailey Gobel (piano teacher), discussing the teaching of music in Cokato, 1920s–60s; and Carlton Lee, discussing and performing music from his career as a jazz-band pianist, 1920s

—Patricia Haloven

780

SAINT LOUIS COUNTY
HISTORICAL SOCIETY

Duluth, Minnesota 55812

> All materials are on deposit in the Northeast Minnesota Historical Center, University of Minnesota at Duluth, Duluth, Minnesota 55812

Matinee Musicale, papers, 1900–1976, 4 linear meters, including minutes, scrapbooks, annual reports, photographs, and other materials

—David Gaynon

781

John W. BERQUIST

Route 1, Box 478
Eveleth, Minnesota 55734

Folk music from the Iron Range, including papers and tape recordings of Scandinavian, Italian, southern Slavic, and Finnish musicians

782

IRON RANGE HISTORICAL SOCIETY

Gilbert, Minnesota 55741

Field recordings of ethnic music on the Iron Range, including tapes of southern Slavic and Finnish folk music, collected in 1978 by the Iron Range Folklife Project, and indexed; also recordings of Ethnic Heritage on Iron Range Music Festivals, including southern Slavs, Swedes, Norwegians, Finns, Italians, and French, 1978, and field recordings of Finnish Laskiainen, Palo, Minn., 1979, in all 30 hours

—Jean Stimac, Larry Danielson

783

ITASCA COUNTY HISTORICAL SOCIETY

Box 664
Grand Rapids, Minnesota 55744

Judy Garland, 15 photographs of her and of her parents, ca. 1915–42
Songbooks, 1 sacred and 2 school items, ca. 1900
Sheet music, 14 items, ca. 1920–35

—Agnes Rajala

784
HIBBING HISTORICAL SOCIETY
Twenty-first Street and Fourth Avenue East
Hibbing, Minnesota 55746

Hibbing Concert Band, record book, 1912–16, including minutes, clippings, correspondence, and rosters of members
Lions' Club songbook, ca. 1929
Sheet music, 20 mostly popular items, 1924–34
Photographs of local musicians and groups, 23 items, ca. 1900–1920
Recordings, 36 78-rpm discs, mostly popular

—Patricia Mestek

785
McLEOD COUNTY HISTORICAL SOCIETY
209 Hassam Street
Hutchinson, Minnesota 55350

Asa B. Hutchinson (1823–84), personal diary, January 1875–June 1876
Other materials of the Hutchinson family, including 20 sheet-music editions used in their concerts, and a large furniture cabinet containing family papers, scrapbooks, prayer books, pictures, maps, and memorabilia. See the notice by Bertha L. Heilbron, in *Minnesota History*, 30 (1939), 347

—Mrs. Henry Steinke

786
Olive WAGNESS
Island View Route
International Falls, Minnesota 56649

Scrapbooks, 2 vols. compiled by Olive Wagness, containing programs and clippings on music history, and on musical events at Northland College, Ashland, Wis., ca. 1929–35
Tuesday Musicale, minutes and programs, n.d.
Hymnals, 10 items, mostly Methodist and Congregational, ca. 1900–
Published music, including sheet music for voice, organ, or piano, 1.5 linear meters, ca. 1910–40
Recordings, 2 albums and 10 single 78-rpm discs; also 30 Victor recording catalogues, ca. 1910

787
MORRISON COUNTY HISTORICAL SOCIETY
Box 239
Little Falls, Minnesota 56345

August Wroblewski (August Roble, of Morrison County), ms song in Polish, 1864
Cantatas and operettas, 3 items published 1904–17

Method books for violin, autoharp, or on general musicianship, 4 items, 1883–1914
Hymnbooks and sacred songbooks, 1864–1924, 8 items, including 1 in German; also 6 popular songbooks, 1874–1919, and 1 German songbook, *Der Kinder Luft* (St. Louis, 1893)
Sheet music, 1905–15, 3 items including "Lake of the Woods," n.d., by Dr. Laurence Parker of Warroad, Minn.
Programs of 8 local high-school and community performances, 1901–37, including those of the Musical Arts Club
Photographs of a Little Falls band, 3 items, 1890
Recordings on tape, including Clara Wright Temple, 1 hour of ragtime piano-playing, also a photograph; Irene Rudie and Olga Holmen, 1 hour of songs of childhood; Charles Martin, 1 hour of Irish songs and ballads; Franciscan Sisters of Little Falls, 30 minutes of Polish songs; and songs of various ethnic groups, 3 hours

—Jan Warner, Nancy Zarns

788
WESTERN HENNEPIN COUNTY PIONEERS ASSOCIATION
Highway 12
Long Lake, Minnesota 55356

Printed operettas, 5 items used by a local high school, ca. 1928–32; also 10 school songbooks, ca. 1880–1925; 25 hymnals, ca. 1880–1940; and 100 sheet-music items, ca. 1915–40
Recordings, including 10 cylinders and 75 78-rpm discs

—Delphine W. Sprague

789
WATONWAN COUNTY HISTORICAL SOCIETY
Box 126
Madelia, Minnesota 56062

Frank Morris (local ballad collector), 1 bound vol. of carbon copies of ballad texts, collected ca. 1900
Songbooks, 25 mostly sacred items, ca. 1890–1910
Sheet music, 6 items, ca. 1890–1910, including the "Watonwan Waltz"

—Mrs. Alton Anderson

790
BETHANY LUTHERAN COLLEGE   MnManBC
Memorial Library
734 Marsh Street
Mankato, Minnesota 56001

Walter Buszin, personal papers, including published books on Lutheran church music and published articles or reprints

—Mary Birmingham

791

BETHANY LUTHERAN THEOLOGICAL SEMINARY   MnManBS

Library
Mankato, Minnesota 56001

Hymnals, ca. 1836–1940, 300 items, including 100 in Norwegian, 60 in German, 10 in Swedish, 3 in French, 1 in Danish, and 1 in Latin

—Mary Birmingham

792

BLUE EARTH COUNTY HISTORICAL SOCIETY

606 South Broad Street
Mankato, Minnesota 56001

Minnie Shoyen Hubbard (1883–1960, violinist), personal papers, including scrapbooks of programs and reviews of her concerts, personal and business correspondence, clippings, and photographs; also 7 78-rpm discs, 1927
Mankato Musical Association, papers, 1872–73, including a constitution and by-laws, minutes, list of members, annual report, and programs of 4 concerts
Songbooks and hymnals, 12 items, 1868–1920
Sheet music, 240 items, 1887–1920, including some by Minnesota composers
Programs of local concerts and theatrical performances, 15 linear cm.
Photographs of local musicians and groups, 40 items, ca. 1880–1950
Recordings, including 80 78-rpm discs, 60 cylinders, and 25 piano rolls
Files of press clippings concerning Mankato State University and other local musicians, 2 linear cm., 1880–

—Jeanne D. Kress

793

SOUTHWEST STATE UNIVERSITY   MnMarS

Library
Marshall, Minnesota 56258

Sheet music, 500 dance-orchestra arrangements of popular works, published 1930s–40s
Recordings, including 50 78-rpm albums of opera and other classical works, 1915–25

—John Robson

794

AMERICAN SWEDISH INSTITUTE

2600 Park Avenue South
Minneapolis, Minnesota 55407

Margareta Liljenstope Astroth (piano teacher), ledgers, diaries, clippings, and photographs, n.d.
Odin Male Chorus, 3 cartons of choral music in Swedish, Norwegian, German, and English, 1890s–1940s, and 1 photograph, 1926
American Swedish Institute Male Chorus, 25 photographs, some on engraved plates, n.d. and 1954
Turnblad Society, 1 carton and 300 items of sheet music for male or mixed chorus, solo voice with piano

accompaniment, orchestra, or string quartet, the vocal works mostly in Swedish, some published in Minneapolis, 1880s–1940s
Wennerburg Choral Society, 9 file drawers and other cartons of male-chorus and mixed-chorus music published in Sweden and the U.S., late 19th and mid 20th centuries, including sheet music, songbooks, and anthologies; also 2 scrapbooks of correspondence, programs, clippings, and posters, 1937–50
Other published music, including choral sheet music, mostly for 4-part male chorus, 350 items, mostly American imprints, 1880s to mid 20th century; songbooks, among them 30 linear cm. of sacred items, 90 popular items mostly for men's chorus, and some folksong items; vocal anthologies, mostly published in the U.S., late 19th century, 15 linear cm.; and 50 items of salon-orchestra music, published in Sweden and performed in Minneapolis, 1930s
Manuscript music, including 23 dances for piano, 18 songs, and a cantata, by various composers, n.d., partly from the collection of L. P. Bergstrom of Winthrop, Minn.

795

AUGSBURG COLLEGE   MnMA

George Sverdrup Library
731 Twenty-first Avenue South
Minneapolis, Minnesota 55404

Manuscript Finnish-American *valssi* (folk dances) used in Minnesota communities in the 1930s, 218 items in 1 loose-leaf vol., compiled by Lionel B. Davis
Augsburg College Band and Choir, papers, 70 linear cm., 1922–42 and 1959–60, including scrapbooks of programs, photographs, financial records, correspondence, and 10 recordings

—Irene Schilling

796

Kenneth CARLEY

3442 Ulysses Street
Minneapolis, Minnesota 55418

Sheet-music collection of 30,000 items, including 13,000 stage-music items, 1870– ; 3500 film-music items, ca. 1910– ; and 13,500 non-show items on such subjects as transportation, sports, and communication media

797

Norman HEITZ

Augsburg Publishing House
426 South Fifth Street
Minneapolis, Minnesota 55408

Hymnals, 125 19th- and 20th-century items, mostly Lutheran

798

MINNEAPOLIS PUBLIC LIBRARY   MnM

300 Nicollet Mall
Minneapolis, Minnesota 55401

Art and Music Department

Manuscript music, 200 items by local composers, including 3 scores by Stanley R. Avery (1879–1967), 21 by Emil Oberhoffer (1867–1933), and 80 by Willard Patton (1853–1924)

Paul McDonald, 2 file drawers of personal papers and ms compositions

John C. Hinderer (1885–1963), personal papers, including 15 drawers of scrapbooks, teaching materials, photographs, and paintings

Emil Oberhoffer, 40 pages of notes for remarks presented during Minneapolis Symphony Orchestra children's concerts

Programs, mostly of local performances, 1875–1930, in 1½ file drawers, with a card index of organizations

Elmer Brooks collection of pictures and photographs of musicians who performed with the Minneapolis Symphony Orchestra, 600 items

Songbooks, 19th and 20th centuries, including 400 school songbooks, 1000 hymnals, tunebooks, and books on hymnody, and 1000 popular songbooks

Sheet music, 200 shelf boxes of 19th- and 20th-century popular songs, indexed by title

Printed music for band, 400 catalogued and 1000 uncatalogued parts; for orchestra, 3000 items, of which half are catalogued; for chorus, 10,000 items, of which 2000 are catalogued; for solo voice, 5500 uncatalogued items published before 1900; and for solo piano, 3500 uncatalogued items published before 1900

Athenaeum and Rare Book Room

Manuscript music by Stanley Avery, "Ichabod Crane"; and by Willard Patton, "Spirit of '61" and "USONA, a Paean of Freedom"

Dodge Autograph Collection, with letters and autographs of musicians (in vol. 7) and of hymn writers (in vol. 9)

North Regional Library

Rev. Samuel Francis Smith (1808–93), 12 letters, dated 1883–94

—Marlea R. Warren

Minneapolis History Collection

Louise Chapman, correspondence, 1954, and ms of her study, *First Fifty Years of Music in Minneapolis, 1850–1900*, 1944

Apollo Club, 5 linear cm. of clippings and programs

Thursday Musical Club, 3 cartons of papers, including minutes, 1892– , and vols. 1–9 of the *Thursday Musical Clarion* (1909–18)

Minneapolis Symphony Orchestra (now the Minnesota Orchestra), 4 file drawers of clippings, 1912–

Scrapbook of clippings from the *Musical Courier*, 1892–1900, concerning music in Minneapolis

Programs of local performances, in 2 scrapbooks compiled by A. M. Shuey, 1868–81 and 1891–97; in 2 boxes of church programs, mostly after 1900; and of the University Artist Course, 1920–74

Published sheet music by Minneapolis composers, 10 items

Arthur Mellon collection of 100 photographs of dance-band leaders, 1920–30

Photographs of members of the Minneapolis Symphony Orchestra, 200 items, 1905– , in various collections; and 20 oral-history interviews of Orchestra members

Clippings on music and musicians in Minneapolis and Minnesota, 6 linear meters of vertical-file material, ca. 1897–

—Dorothy M. Burke

799

UNITED METHODIST CHURCH, MINNESOTA ANNUAL CONFERENCE

Commission on Archives and History
122 West Franklin Avenue
Suite 400
Minneapolis, Minnesota 55404

Hymnals, mostly of the United Methodist Church and its antecedents, 100 items, 1819– , including some in Norwegian

—Thelma Boeder

800

UNIVERSITY OF MINNESOTA   MnU
LIBRARIES

Twin Cities Campus
Minneapolis, Minnesota 55455

Music Library

Sheet music, 2980 separate items and 16 bound vols., 1848–1940, including lithographed covers from the collection of Edward Miller

Tunebooks, 107 items, 1794–1859; hymnals, 386 items, 1880–1920, including 200 "pioneer" hymnals in European languages but published in the midwestern U.S.; and 60 secular songbooks, 1850–1920

Music scores by U.S. composers, 700 vols., 1864–1940, including collections and method books; books about American music or composers, 95 items, 1880–1914; and periodicals published in the U.S., 27 titles in 145 vols., 1834–1914. Some of these items are from the Kenneth Berger Band Collection, among them band scores (in the University Band Library), and books and journals on wind instruments, 1890–1920s

Latin American music scores, 500 vols., 19th and 20th centuries

Recordings, including 500 78-rpm discs of opera, classical and popular music, and jazz, also 100 Edison discs

Stanley R. Avery (1879–1967, Minneapolis teacher, organist, and composer), 2 boxes of ms scores

Donald N. Ferguson (b. 1882), 12 ms compositions, 1927–29, and typescripts of 2 books

Thorvald Otterström (1868–1942), 2 ms compositions, 1930s, 6 transcriptions for violin or cello, and 1 composition/harmony exercise

Children's Literature Research Collections

Children's songbooks, 21 vols., 1840–1937

Performing Arts Archive

Malcolm Dana McMillan (St. Paul composer and director of the Orpheus Club), 30 linear cm. of papers,

1809–1936, including clippings, programs, correspondence, music compositions, scrapbooks, financial records, and photographs

Louis N. Scott (manager of the Metropolitan Opera House, St. Paul), 30 scrapbooks, 1890–1930

John K. Sherman (1898–1968, critic for the *Minneapolis Star Journal* and *Star*), 2 linear meters of papers, 1916–68, mostly clippings with some correspondence

Minnesota Orchestra (formerly the Minneapolis Symphony Orchestra), papers, 1909–78, including scrapbooks, programs, photographs, clippings, financial records, correspondence, and files on guest performers

St. Paul Opera Company, papers, 1933–75, including personnel reports, reviews, press releases, programs, financial records, minutes, clippings, and photographs

Immigrant History Research Center

See the Center's *Guide to Manuscript Holdings* (Minneapolis, 1976)

John Berlisg (1882–1945, Slovenian-American leader of the Svoboda singing society, Detroit), 60 linear cm. of papers, 1920–45

Peter Czopiwsky, papers, 36 linear cm., ca. 1925–65, including correspondence and ms and published scores of operas and operettas by M. Arkas and others

Fortune Gallo, 30 linear cm. of papers, ca. 1930–60, including personal library materials, and programs and clippings of his San Carlo Opera Company

Zlatko I. Kerhin (1881–1968, president of the Croatian American Singers), 75 linear cm. of papers, ca. 1918–71, with programs and other materials concerning Croatian singing societies in Chicago, Pittsburgh, Pueblo, Colo., and Gary, Ind.

Edith Koivisto (b. 1889, Finnish-American playwright, director, and singer active in Duluth), 2 linear meters of papers, ca. 1910–77, including diaries, photographs, scrapbooks, ms and published writings, sheet music, correspondence, and minutes

Stephen Kuropas, 3 linear meters of papers, ca. 1940– , including correspondence and programs of Ukrainian cultural events in the U.S.

Eduardo Migliaccio (1882–1946), 3 linear meters of papers, ca. 1909–58, including ms and published sheet music, photographs, contracts, playbills, correspondence, and scrapbooks

John Panchuk, 1.6 linear meters of papers, ca. 1932– , including materials concerning the Bandurist Chorus and Ukrainian cultural events in Detroit

John K. Sherman, scrapbooks concerning 19th-century choral music in Minneapolis and St. Paul

Vera Stetkevicz Stangl, 45 linear cm. of papers, ca. 1910–72, including 2 hymns by Liudkevych dedicated to Ukrainian-Americans, 1913

University Archives

Walter Castella Coffey (1876–1956, president of the University), 4 folders of correspondence, 1927–32, concerning his sponsorship of Inga Hill for vocal study with Anna Shoen-René in New York

Donald N. Ferguson, 2 boxes of papers, including clippings, photographs, opera-broadcast typescripts, and a taped interview, 1968

Isabel Gale, 6 linear cm. of papers, 1878–84, including 1 scrapbook on theatrical and musical events in Minneapolis

Truman Rickard (1882–1948, composer of college songs), 6 folders and 11 vols. of papers, 1904–72, including 2 scrapbooks, and mss and copies of songs

Carlyle McRoberts Scott (1873–1945, chairman of the University's Music Department), 3 boxes of papers, 1917–31, including correspondence, financial records, programs, announcements, and photographs

Verna Golden (Mrs. C. M.) Scott (1876–1964, founder of the University Artists Course and manager of the Minneapolis Symphony Orchestra), papers, 1919–30, including correspondence, financial records, programs, announcements, and photographs

University of Minnesota materials, including Concerts and Lectures papers, 1934–68, with biennial reports, programs, photographs, and correspondence; Music Department papers, 51 folders and 1 vol., 1922–42, with correspondence, programs, and clippings; and student organizations' activities papers, 1940s–

—Katharine Holum

Collection of Minnesota Ethnic Music, Music Department

Field recordings, 250 items totaling 400 hours, collected 1950s– , major subjects comprising Norwegian or Norwegian-Minnesotan fiddlers including Hardanger fiddlers, collected by Daniel Aakhus; miscellaneous fiddle traditions of Wisconsin, Minnesota, Iowa, and the Dakotas, collected by Otto Rindlichbaker; U.S. Finnish songs; and Estonian songs of Minnesota

Manuscripts of 150 fiddle tunes, written by the fiddlers, along with photographs of the fiddlers, 1930s–40s

Transcriptions of fiddle tunes from field recordings, also field notes

Published sheet music for accordion, 300 items in 5 bound vols., representing Italian-American publishers in Ohio and New York, 1920s

—Alan Kagan

Social Welfare History Archives Center

See the *Descriptive Inventories of Collections in the Social Welfare History Archives Center* (Westport, Conn., 1970)

National Federation of Settlements and Neighborhood Centers, records, 1891–1965, including Music Division papers, 30 linear cm., mostly 1920–40, with minutes, financial records, correspondence, press clippings, photographs, songbooks, and other papers, concerning music education of children in cities, music appreciation, and musical recreation, and involving Martha Cruikshank, Johann Grolle (chairman of the Division), Frances M. McFarland (1931–40, including her report on the Anglo-American Music Conference, Lausanne, 1931), and Janet D. Schenck, as well as the International Toy Festival, Elizabeth Peabody House in Boston (1936–50), Hull House in Chicago, Cleveland Music School Settlement (reports and correspondence, 1931–54), New York City Welfare Council (1912–43), New York Association of Music Schools (minutes and reports, 1924–33), Greenwich House in New York (1921–54), Henry Street Settlement in New York (1903–58), Lenox Hill Neighborhood Association in New York (1928–47), University Settlement in New York, San Francisco Community Music School (correspondence and reports, 1929–42), and Community Music Schools Foundation in St. Louis (correspondence and annual reports, 1930–50)

United Neighborhood Houses of New York City, records, 1891–1961, including 1 folder of music-committee papers concerning settlement-school music, the WPA Federal Music Project, World War II patriotic songs, and programs of folk-dance and music festivals, mostly 1930–50

Henry Street Settlement Music School, 6 linear meters of records, 1927–69, including scrapbooks, programs, photographs, clippings, annual reports, minutes, correspondence, financial records, and other papers, concerning the 1937 première of Aaron Copland's opera *The Second Hurricane*, advisory committee members Copland, George Gershwin, and Jascha Heifetz, and School directors Hedi Katz, Grace Spofford, and Robert Egan

Association of Junior Leagues of America, records, 1921–64 but largely 1940s, partly concerning community music activities in the U.S. and Canada, including children's concerts, local symphony orchestras, and choral ensembles, and radio music programs

National Recreation and Park Association (formerly the Playground Association of America), records, 1907–65, including 15 linear cm. of bulletins, 1918–45, promoting community singing to raise morale near military bases during World War I, also concerning music for camps, playgrounds, recreation centers, patriotic festivals, and children's songs

National Guild of Community Music Schools (founded 1937), 1 linear meter of records, 1948–65

—David Klaassen

801

BROWN COUNTY HISTORICAL SOCIETY

27 North Broadway
New Ulm, Minnesota 56073

Vogelpohl and Spaeth (organ builders, later Vogelpohl and Sons, Organ Co.), papers, including published books about the organ, and contracts, ca. 1890–

Popular songbooks and hymnals, 50 items, ca. 1890–1940, including some in German, Norwegian, and Danish

Popular sheet music for voice or piano, 50 items, ca. 1920–40

Programs of local and touring musicians and groups, mostly at Turner Hall, 125 items, ca. 1860–1940

Photographs of local musicians and groups, 200 items, ca. 1880–1940

Recordings, including 75 78-rpm discs and 15 cylinders

—Paul Klammer

802

NORWEGIAN-AMERICAN   MnNHi HISTORICAL ASSOCIATION

Saint Olaf College
Northfield, Minnesota 55057

F. Melius Christiansen, 17 published choral-music items, ca. 1896–1920, also clippings, 1897–1955

Knud Henderson (1835–1930), 30 linear cm. of papers relating to his musical and artistic activities in Chicago and in Cambridge, Wis.

J. Jørgen Thompson (1896–1963, St. Olaf educator), 70 linear cm. of papers, including materials pertaining to Norwegian-American culture, and notes about the St. Olaf College band and choir tours

Olav Lee (1880–1938, minister and professor), 30 linear cm. of papers, including hymns, also songs by F. M. Christiansen and Bernt Muus

Norwegian American Music Collection, ca. 1882–1966, 1.5 linear meters, including biographical material on Lorentz S. Skougaard, and clippings concerning Ole Bull

Church convention materials pertaining to music in the Lutheran church, 14 items, ca. 1890–1950

Printed vocal and choral music, mostly sacred, ca. 1890–1950, 480 items, mostly by Norwegian and Norwegian-American composers, including some published by the Northern Book & Music Co.

Hymnals, ca. 1890–1950, 60 items, mostly Lutheran, including 10 of the Norwegian Synod

Songbooks, mostly of Norwegian folksongs or temperance songs, 75 items, including some published by E. Jensen, Northern Book & Music Co., and Samhold Sanger-Forbund

Christmas programs of Lutheran churches and Sunday schools, 75 items

Music periodicals edited and published by John Dahle, including *Jubilate,* vols. 1–16 (1901–5), and *Norsk Amerikansk Musiktidende,* vols. 1–11 (1890–95)

—Charlotte Jacobson

803

SAINT OLAF COLLEGE   MnNS

Northfield, Minnesota 55057

Music Library

F. Melius Christiansen, ed., *St. Olaf Choir Series,* 128 works (Minneapolis, 1919–32)

John Dahle (1876–1931), 25 works published 1900–1910, mostly sacred or secular songbooks for men's or mixed choir

Ella Hjertaas-Roe (former St. Olaf faculty member), scrapbook with 140 programs, mostly of vocal concerts in Carnegie Hall and Aeolian Hall, New York, ca. 1920–25

Hymnals, 100 items, ca. 1860–1910, including 50 in Norwegian

Archives

F. Melius Christiansen, complete mss of his published works; also 1 box of papers, ca. 1890–1951, donated by his son, Olaf Christiansen, 1969, including a scrapbook of programs and clippings, 1890s, other clippings and programs, lectures on church music (in Norwegian), pamphlets, lists of materials given to the St. Olaf College Library, and 200 photographs of the Christiansen family and of St. Olaf College music groups; 1 box of notebooks and non-music materials from his teaching career; and 1 file folder of clippings and programs of his eightieth-birthday celebration at St. Olaf, 1951. See the 12-page inventory, 1980

St. Olaf Choir Collection, 1891–1960, 6 linear meters of materials of the Choir and Band, including tour contracts, budgets, itineraries, posters, programs, personal diaries, scrapbooks, tape and disc recordings, videotapes, and photographs

Ella Hjertaas-Roe, papers, 1919–57, including 2 scrapbooks, 1 of the St. Olaf Choir tour of Europe, 1930; clippings and programs, including some of her performances; personal and business correspondence; and photographs of St. Olaf musicians and groups

—Beth Christensen

804
GOODHUE COUNTY HISTORICAL SOCIETY
Red Wing, Minnesota 55066

Frances Densmore (1867–1957), published articles, monographs, and recordings, 1904–45, including miscellaneous pre-1910 writings on subjects other than music

—Orville Olson

805
RED WING PUBLIC LIBRARY   MnRw
225 Broadway
Red Wing, Minnesota 55066

Frances Densmore, Smithsonian publications on American Indian music, 20 items

—Nancy Thorson

806
CENTRAL MINNESOTA HISTORICAL CENTER
Saint Cloud State University
Saint Cloud, Minnesota 56301

St. Cloud Musicians' Association, AFM Local 536, photocopy of the printed union membership book, 1921–22, owned by James McNeal, listing officers, board of directors, members, and wage rates

—Calvin W. Gower, John LeDoux

807
STEARNS COUNTY HISTORICAL SOCIETY
Court House, Third Floor
Box 702
Saint Cloud, Minnesota 56301

School and popular songbooks, 20 items, 1880s–1940s
Posters of local high-school, polka-band, and big band performances, 4 items, 1890s–1960s
Photographs of local musicians and groups and of visiting Metropolitan Opera performers, 45 items, 1890s–1960s
Recordings, including 80 oral-history tapes of musicians, recorded 1977–78

—John Decker

808
ARCHIVES OF THE AMERICAN LUTHERAN CHURCH
2375 Como Avenue West
Saint Paul, Minnesota 55108

John Dahle (1853–1931, professor and compiler of sacred music, active in the U.S. after 1889), personal papers, including holograph music mss, published editions of music by Dahle and by F. Melius Christiansen, and other materials

—Della Olson

809
BETHEL THEOLOGICAL SEMINARY   (MnSB)
Seminary Library
3949 Bethel Drive
Saint Paul, Minnesota 55112

Hymnals of various denominations, 500 items, 1628–1940, including some with words only; also 200 in Swedish, several of them compiled and published in the U.S.

—Betty Kleinschmidt, David Guston

810
COLLEGE OF SAINT CATHERINE   MnSSC
Performing Arts Library
2004 Randolph Avenue
Saint Paul, Minnesota 55105

Leopold Bruenner, holograph mss of 7 sacred works, including a mass, 1924
Other music ms materials by Glenn L. Glasaw, Sister Lucia Graham, and Johann A. Hein
Published opera and oratorio scores, 200 items, mostly late 19th-century English and American works, as used extensively in Maurice Jones, *American Theatre Cantatas, 1852–1907* (D.M.A. diss., University of Illinois, 1975)

—Sister Anne Godine

811
CONCORDIA COLLEGE   MnSCC
Buenger Memorial Library
275 North Syndicate Street
Saint Paul, Minnesota 55104

Hymnals, 16th to 20th centuries, 230 items, including some published in Europe and used in the U.S., emphasizing materials of the Lutheran Church—Missouri Synod; also several sheet-music items and recordings

—Glenn W. Offermann, Margaret Horn

812
Mrs. Michael F. ETTEL
465 West Wheelock Parkway
Saint Paul, Minnesota 55117

Collection of bound and separate items of 19th-century popular sheet music, 1200 lithographed covers, late 1820s–60s, with a checklist of the lithographic covers, and an index to the music, in process

813

LUTHER THEOLOGICAL SEMINARY   MnSL

Library
12375 Como Avenue West
Saint Paul, Minnesota 55108

Carl Døving (1867–1937, Norwegian Lutheran hymnologist active in the U.S. after 1890), hymnology collection, 800 late 19th- and early 20th-century items, 200 of them in English and 100 with U.S. imprints

—Della Olson

814

MACALESTER COLLEGE   MnSM

Weyerhauser Library
Grand and Macalester Streets
Saint Paul, Minnesota 55105

Arthur Billings Hunt Hymnology Collection, 700 vols. pre-1940

—Jean K. Archibald

815

MINNESOTA HISTORICAL SOCIETY   MnHi

690 Cedar Street
Saint Paul, Minnesota 55101

Archives and Manuscripts (1500 Mississippi Street)

Papers of Organizations

American Guild of Music Teachers, St. Paul and Minneapolis, papers, 9 vols., including minutes, clippings, programs, bulletins, financial statements, and biographical materials, 1926–58

Andrews Opera Company, ms history by Harry Sweet, "Farmhouse to Footlights," n.d., in the Albert Burbank Sweet papers

Arlington Hills Mother's Club, 1 vol., including music programs, 1897–99

Baldishol Committee, Minneapolis, papers, including ms "March of the Vikings" by Anna Farcloh, 1925

Chicago Symphony Orchestra, list of subscribers to 2 concerts in St. Paul, 1895

Club Montparnasse, St. Paul, 1 vol. of clippings concerning efforts to stimulate performances of music and dramatic arts, 1930–50

Maude S. Cooper, "History of the Minneapolis Symphony and Associated Organizations," 30-page typescript, 1956–58

L. S. Donaldson Co., Minneapolis, papers, including ms "Golden Jubilee March," n.d.

Folk Arts Foundation of America, St. Paul, papers, 1943–65, 1 box containing correspondence, minutes, programs, and writings, including reports on the musical studies of Frances Densmore and Marjorie Edgar, and projects to preserve folk dancing

Fort Snelling, program of a concert by the Twenty-first Infantry Band, n.d.

Hotel Ryan, St. Paul, program of chamber concerts, 1885

Minnesota Music Teachers' Association, papers, 5 vols., including correspondence, minutes, convention proceedings, and clippings, 1913–60

Zylpha S. Morton, "A Brief History of the Schubert Club, 1882–1962," 49-page typescript, 1964

Mount Zion Hebrew Congregation, St. Paul, contracts for choir singers, 1910–20s

Musical Society of Newark, N.J., scrapbook in German, 1880s, in the Charles William Bachmann papers

Nordic Choral Ensemble Association, Duluth, scrapbook containing photographs, programs, clippings, circulars, and other materials, 1939–50

Normändenes Sangforening, Minneapolis, papers, 4 vols., 1886–1903, including a constitution, list of societies in the Scandinavian Singers' Union of America, membership rolls, lists of engagements, minutes, and a program of the Northwestern Singers' Association, 1894

St. Paul and Ramsey County War History Committee, papers, including an interview with Frances Boardman concerning the history of music and fine arts in Minnesota, 1944

St. Paul Choral Club, scrapbook with programs, clippings, correspondence, financial records, and tickets, 1898–1907

St. Paul Municipal Chorus, 1 box and 1 vol. of papers, 1920–34, including minutes, records of rehearsals, programs, clippings, and correspondence

St. Paul Musical Society, scrapbook, 1863–79

Schubert Club (formerly Ladies' Musical), St. Paul, 2 boxes and 56 vols. of papers, 1885–1968, including minutes, annual reports, financial records, scrapbooks, programs, clippings, and correspondence

Swedish Historical Society of America, papers, 10 boxes and 20 vols., 1905–32, including a constitution, a program of Jenny Lind's concert at Hartford, Conn., correspondence, business papers, minutes, membership lists, and other mss, also papers of A. A. Magnusson concerning the Augustana Synod and music, and materials of the Swedish Festival Chorus

U.S. Infantry, 5th Regiment, 73-page letterbook, 1819–28, with information on the post band and musicians in Minnesota

Albert Woolson, reminiscences of the Signora Ethiopian Minstrel Burlesque Troop, 1868 ms and 1949 typed copy

WPA papers, including 3 boxes of newspaper transcripts concerning musical societies and concerts in Minnesota during the period 1850–1941

Papers of Musicians

Richard J. Barton (1860–1939, Minneapolis orchestra leader whose orchestra also performed in Arkansas and Ohio), 24 items of papers, 1894–1942, including clippings and biographical materials

Irja Wilhelmina Laaksonen Beckman, 156-page typescript reminiscences, ca. 1903, including information about early amateur theatricals and musical instruments in Minnesota

Beatrice Gjertsen Bessesen (1886–1935, singer) scrapbook, 1904–34, concerning her career, and her organization of conservatories of music in Albert Lea and Minneapolis

Evelyn Graber Cosandy, transcript of her radio address concerning the Range Symphony Orchestra, 1931, in the Albert Graber and family papers

George Crosby (music publisher and organizer of bands in Hudson, Wis.), 2 boxes of papers, 1866–1930

William Fuson Davidson, papers, 172 boxes, 1817–1919,

documenting his participation in civic and commercial organizations in St. Paul, including opera houses and the engaging of performers

Frances Densmore (1867–1957), 13 linear cm. of papers, 1927–39, comprising writings and photographs on folklore and music of the Dakota, Ojibway, and other Minnesota Indians; also materials concerning the presentation of her papers, in the Benjamin Densmore papers

Iva Andrus Dingwall, 3 typescript reminiscences of old-time Minnesota country-dance steps and verses, 1954

Bessie P. Douglas, "A Patti Concert," ms description of an Adelina Patti concert in Minneapolis, 1887, in the Bessie P. and George Perkins Douglas papers

Marjorie Edgar, 1 vol. of ms notes including words and music to Finnish songs in Minnesota, 1928–32, in the William Crowell Edgar and family papers

George Herbert Fairclough, 3 music mss, including organ and choral music, 1869–1954

William Foulke papers, including a music- and lecture-program pamphlet, St. Paul, 1898–99

Hiram Davis Frankel papers, 1873–1930, 6.4 linear meters, including materials from committees for seasons of grand opera in St. Paul

Agnes Moore Fryberger (1868–1939, teacher of music appreciation at the University of Louisville), 6 items of papers, 1931–38, including 4 published articles concerning her career

William Dinsmore Hale and family papers, 21 boxes, 45 vols., and 1 microfilm reel, including correspondence concerning the Allegany Academy of Music in New York, and between Lucie Hale (music teacher at the St. Croix Valley Academy, Afon, Minn.) and O. D. Adams (proprietor of the Academy of Music and a music dealer, Winona, Minn.)

Oscar Hallam, 350-page typescript reminiscences of life in rural Wisconsin, 1870s, mentioning music

Frank Hasty, typescript song, "Pokegama Bear," n.d.

Theodore L. Hays (d. 1941, owner of the Bijou Opera House, Minneapolis; manager of the Grand Opera House, St. Paul, and People's Theatre and Metropolitan Theatre, Minneapolis; and general manager of Finkelstein and Ruben Co., reorganized in 1928 as the Minnesota Amusements Co.), papers, 1887–1921, including correspondence, minutes, account books, and scrapbooks on his career

Julius Heilbron, papers, including a ms diary mentioning band concerts in the St. Paul area, 1884–91

Samuel Hill, papers, 1895–1902, 1 box, including programs and notices of concerts of the Apollo Club (Minneapolis men's choral society)

Johan A. Holvik, papers on music presented at Concordia College, Moorhead, Minn., 1920s

Gordon How (member of the regimental band of the 216th Coast Artillery, at Camp Haan, Riverside, Cal., and at San Francisco), 20 letters, 1933–42

Hutchinson family, microfilm of diaries and scrapbooks, also concert tour materials, programs, and words and music, 1844–99

Dorothy Hatch Langlie (b. 1902, Minneapolis violinist), 69-page typescript reminiscences, 1963

Louis E. Larson, papers, including 500 programs of the Winona Opera House, 1857–1916

J. M. Leland, 1 ms vol. of piano music, n.d., in the Charles Roos and family papers

Emil Oberhoffer (1867–1933, conductor of the Minneapolis Symphony Orchestra), 53 letters, 1895–1922,

from Henry A. Bellows, Mrs. Elbert L. Carpenter, Louis Eckstein, Percy Grainger, George Klass, Marian MacDowell, Frederick A. Stock, John R. Van Derlip, and others

Charles Astor Parker (owner of the Grand Opera House, Minneapolis, 1880s–90s), oral-history interviews on tape

Andrew Peterson, papers, including 1 ms vol. of bugle calls kept by him during his service in the Civil War

Arvid Reuterdahl, papers, including correspondence and clippings

Charles E. Roussain, 1 ms vol. of music for old Scottish reels, 1864

Charlotte Mead Sanford (b. 1871, singer and patron), 5 boxes of materials concerning concerts, opera, and performances by musicians in America and Europe, n.d. and 1836–1954, in the Edward Rollin Sanford and family papers

Gertrude Sans Souci (Mrs. William C. Toomey, 1873–1913), papers containing 30 ms songs and works for piano, a printed brochure on her, 1904, an invoice of royalties paid her by Paul A. Schmitt Music Co., Minneapolis, and an obituary

Frances Mae Howe Satterlee (church-choir director, teacher, and booking-agency manager), 10 vols. of papers, 1892–1948, including her diploma from Parker College of Music, Winnebago (1908), also concerning her career in southern Minnesota, at the St. Paul College of Music, the Thurston School of Music in St. Paul and Minneapolis, and the Music and Applied Arts Bureau agency, Minneapolis

Ferdinand Peter Schultz, 39-page typescript, "The Andrews Family: Up from the Frontier in Music and Opera," n.d.

Verna Golden Scott, 12 items of papers, 1940–54, including clippings and biographical materials concerning her early musical career and that of her husband, Carlyle M. Scott (founder of the University of Minnesota Music Department)

Elsie M. Shawe (supervisor of music in St. Paul schools), 7 items of papers, 1907

Bessie Mae Stanchfield, 2 boxes of papers, 1935–47, including 4 published articles by her concerning early music and folk music in Minnesota, also correspondence, clippings, and ms words and music of Minnesota folk and lumberjack songs

Olin Dunbar Wheeler, papers, 1 box and 1 vol., including clippings of concerts in St. Paul and Washington, D.C., 1875–91

Gilbert Livingstone Wilson, papers, with Dakota (Sioux) songs and materials on the grass dance and Indian ceremonies

Newton H. Winchell and family papers, 17 boxes and 108 vols., 1814–1958, including letters from Mrs. Horace V. Winchell concerning concerts in Philadelphia, 1889–99, and programs of concerts at which she performed in Minneapolis and elsewhere; also letters of Alexander Winchell and his daughter who studied music at Lynn, Mass., 1871–72

Other Published Materials

Broadside Collection, including a Sunday-school hymnal, 1842; 11 local programs, 1865–87; 2 issues of the *Journal of Music and Dramatics* (St. Paul, 1885), published by George Seibert with advertisements and programs of his orchestra; and 1 issue of *The Opera*

Companion, 4 pages describing operas presented in St. Paul, n.d.

Sheet music, including 50 items from World War I, in the War History Committee papers; John Philip Sousa's march for the dedication of Foshay Tower, Minneapolis, 1929, in the Frazer Arnold papers; R. D. Vann, "Itasca Maid," 1932, in the papers of the lyricist, Flora Ann Dean; Frank J. Black's Minnesota field song, "We're on Our Way," 1937, photocopy; Agnes Helenius Luoma, "Minnesota, Land of Charm," n.d.; and "Liberty Chorus" of the Northern Pacific singers, n.d., in the Northern Pacific Railway Records

William W. Woodbury, book of music for snare drum, also snare-drum parts for band music of Ft. Snelling, 1860s

Pamphlet of popular reform songs, published by C. St. John Cole (Minneapolis, 1895), in the Gustavus A. Westphal papers

—Ruth Ellen Bauer

Special Libraries

Photographs of Minnesota bands, orchestras, and instrumentalists, 575 items, and 100 items of singers and choral groups

Oral-history tapes, mostly concerning music in Minnesota, including interviews with Jan (John F.) Bílý (b. ca. 1881, violinist) concerning Antonín Dvořák, 1968; Mary Ann Feldman on "Music in St. Paul and Minneapolis, 1850–1900," 1974; Johannes Riedel on Minnesota music, 1920–40, 1976; and concerning Scandinavian-American choral music, 1972

Recordings, including 200 cylinders and 200 78-rpm discs (in the Museum Collections)

—Bonnie Wilson

Reference Library

Songbooks, 100 items, 1834– , mostly 20th century, including popular songbooks, also Amerindian, French Canadian, Scandinavian, and English-language hymnals, some with words only

Sheet music, 500 items, ca. 1855– , on Minnesota subjects, by Minnesota composers, or published in Minnesota, catalogued by title. See James Taylor Dunn, "A Century of Song: Popular Music in Minnesota," *Minnesota History*, 44 (1974), 122–41

—Patricia Harpole

Minnesota Folklife Center

Founded in 1976, the Center is developing an archive of Minnesota folksong tapes, transcriptions, and writings, covering such subjects as polkas, German-American music, lumbering songs, Serbian-American music, and urban folksong

—Ellen Stekert

816

SAINT PAUL PUBLIC LIBRARY   **MnS**
90 West Fourth Street
Saint Paul, Minnesota 55102

Harold Field, sheet music collection, 9000 items, 1865–1950, including 1500 pre-1914 items; title index with thematic incipits

Miller Index of Songs, a title index to 45,000 works in the collection of hymnals and songbooks

—Carole King

817

SAINT PAUL PUBLIC LIBRARY,   **(MnS)**
HIGHLAND PARK BRANCH
Perrie Jones Rare Book Room
1974 Ford Parkway
Saint Paul, Minnesota 55116

Robert Robitschek (1874–1967, Czech–American composer), personal correspondence with musicians, mostly from Europe but including letters from Wilhelm Berger, Arthur Bodanzky, and Edgar Stillman Kelley

Published music books, several items, 1816–64, from the Johnston Collection

—Elizabeth McMonigal

818

SAINT PAUL SEMINARY   **MnSS**
2260 Summit Avenue
Saint Paul, Minnesota 55105

Francis Missia (choral director at the Seminary, ca. 1930–55), 1.8 linear meters of papers, ca. 1930–55, including recordings of his music groups at the Seminary

—Leo J. Tibesar

819

GUSTAVUS ADOLPHUS COLLEGE   **MnStpeG**
Folke Bernadotte Memorial Library
Saint Peter, Minnesota 56082

Jerome Mettetal (Presbyterian minister, 1925–77), collection mostly of opera materials, including correspondence with or about Dorothy Duckwitz (1931–67), Jussi Björling (1950–76), Guiomar Novaes (1960s), and Frederick Schauwecker (1972); scores and books, 11 linear meters, 1883–1977; photographs, clippings, and autographed programs, 30 linear cm., 1890–1977; and 2000 disc and 257 tape recordings of the New York Metropolitan Opera, Jussi Björling, Toscanini, and others

J. Victor Bergquist (1877–1935), papers, including his ms oratorio *Davids II. Psalm*, 1899, 8 ms copy books, ca. 1900, correspondence, and 2 pages of press clippings, 1905–7

Reinhold Lagerstroms, ms score and parts for *Tonbilder ur Jesur lif*, 1899, and other compositions; also 5 printed works, 1898–1927, and letters, clippings, and photographs, 1896–1937

Hymnals, primarily Swedish–Lutheran, 1859–1958, 184 items, including 52 without music

Songbooks, mostly for community use, 32 items, 1872–1938, in Swedish, English, Norwegian, or Italian, including 5 compiled in Minnesota, 1889–1929, and 4 with words only

Sheet music, 2000 items bound in 64 vols., 1859–1905; also 700 separate items, 1883–1950, for organ, piano, band, orchestra, or voice (in the Archives)

Programs, 5 linear cm., 1877–1971, including events at the College and at Björling Concert Hall

Lorenz Publishing Co., catalogue of organ music for church use, ca. 1926

Pictures, 20 linear cm., 1890–1978, including photographs of Jussi Björling, Guiomar Novaes, Dorothy Duckwitz, and L. Philip; also press clippings with pictures

Recordings, 100 78-rpm discs and 240 tapes, ca. 1940–70, including private recordings of performances at the New York Metropolitan Opera and the San Francisco Opera House, 1939–65

—Edith J. Tibbits

820
LAKE COUNTY HISTORICAL SOCIETY

Railroad and Historical Museum
Two Harbors, Minnesota 55616

Hymnals, ca. 1900–1930, 35 items, mostly Presbyterian, also 1 sacred cantata used locally, ca. 1900–1960, donated by Madeline (Mrs. James) Fillenger

Sheet music, 200 classical vocal items, ca. 1900–1950, and 240 piano-music items

Programs of local musicales, 5 items, ca. 1915–30

Photographs of local groups and musicians including Mrs. Fillenger, 8 items, ca. 1920–35

Edison cylinder recordings, 50 items, mostly of Enrico Caruso

—Elfa M. Setterlund

821
CARVER COUNTY HISTORICAL SOCIETY

119 Cherry Street
Waconia, Minnesota 55387

Pioneer Mennenchor Association, Young America, Minnesota (1861–1900), 1 linear meter of materials, including printed music and minute books

Hymnals used locally by German and Swedish immigrants and their descendants, 100 items, including some published in the U.S., ca. 1860–1940, and some with words only; also published band and orchestra music used locally

Photographs of local bands, 20 items, ca. 1890–1940

Recordings, including 100 Edison cylinders, 4 78-rpm discs, and 15 discs for music boxes

—Estelle W. Mueller

822
SOUTHEAST MINNESOTA   (MnWinoS)
HISTORICAL CENTER

122 Maxwell Library
Winona State University
Winona, Minnesota 55987

Faculty papers and student diaries, ca. 1860–1920, including scattered references to music

Papers of local music clubs, 8 linear cm., ca. 1860–1920, including minutes and constitutions

Hymnals, 2 items, 1880s, used in Normal School and College chapel meetings

Programs of University musical and theatrical events, 40 items, ca. 1860–1920

Photographs of musical performances by students at the Normal School and College, and by grade-school students in the Model School, 15 linear cm., ca. 1900–1940s

—George E. Bates, Jr.

823
WINONA COUNTY HISTORICAL SOCIETY

160 Johnson Street
Winona, Minnesota 55987

Carl Ruggles, 1 ms page from *Men and Mountains,* and 1 linear cm. of correspondence, ca. 1907–17

Manuscript music by Horace Seaton, 1907, and Bert Beyerstedt, 1925

Beyerstedt Theater Orchestra, parts and scores, 15 linear cm., ca. 1920–30

Songbooks, 70 linear cm. of sacred, popular, and school songbooks, ca. 1890–1940, including some in German and Polish

Popular sheet music, 1.4 linear meters, ca. 1900–1930

Programs of local events, including those of the Winona Opera House, 30 linear cm., 1892–1940

Photographs of local groups, including bands and orchestras, 15 linear cm., ca. 1910–40

Recordings, including 6 cylinders and 15 78-rpm discs

—C. J. Vincent

824
NOBLES COUNTY HISTORICAL SOCIETY

Box 213
Worthington, Minnesota 56187

Noblemen's Chorus (ca. 1938–60), papers in 1 envelope, including minutes, printed programs, and photographs

Published hymnals, including some in German, also school songbooks and songbooks advertising products of the issuing company, 20 items, ca. 1880–1910; and other printed music for piano or voice

Popular sheet music, 1000 items, ca. 1880–1930

Photographs of local musicians and music groups, 1 envelope

Recordings, including 50 linear cm. of 78-rpm discs and cylinders

—Helen Towne

In addition to the repositories listed above, the following also reported holdings of the materials indicated:

Ada—Norman County Historical Society: sheet music, songbooks, other printed music, programs, pictures, recordings, miscellaneous

Albert Lea—Albert Lea Public Library: songbooks

Albert Lea—Freeborn County Historical Society: sheet music, songbooks, pictures

Anoka—Anoka County Historical Society: songbooks, programs, recordings

Austin—Mower County Historical Society: sheet music

Bemidji—Bemidji State University, A. C. Clark Library: songbooks, other printed music, catalogues, recordings

Bemidji—Oak Hills Bible Institute, Library: songbooks

Bertha—Bertha Historical Society: songbooks, recordings

Blue Earth—Faribault County Historical Society: sheet music, songbooks, other printed music

Carlton—Carlton County Historical Society: songbooks, other printed music, recordings

Collegeville—St. John's University, Alcuin Library: sheet music, songbooks

Edina—Edina Historical Society: sheet music, songbooks

Elbow Lake—Grant County Historical Society: printed music

Elysian—Le Sueur County Historical Society: songbooks, programs, catalogues, miscellaneous

Fairmont—Martin County Historical Society: sheet music, songbooks

Grand Rapids—Grand Rapids Public Library: songbooks

Granite Falls—Granite Falls Public Library: printed music

Hallock—Hallock Public Library: songbooks

International Falls—Koochiching County Historical Society: sheet music, pictures, recordings

Lakefield—Jackson County Historical Society: sheet music, songbooks, pictures, recordings

Litchfield—Baker County Historical Society: pictures, recordings

Little Falls—Little Falls Public Library: printed music

Mankato—Mankato State University, Music Department: sheet music, songbooks

Mantorville—Dodge County Historical Society: songbooks

Minneapolis—Caroline Bliss: songbooks

Minneapolis—Billy Graham Evangelistic Association, Library: songbooks

Mora—Kanabec County Historical Society: songbooks, programs, pictures

Moorhead—Comstock Historic House Society: sheet music, songbooks

Morris—University of Minnesota, West Central Minnesota Historical Research Center: sheet music, programs, pictures, recordings, miscellaneous

New Brighton—United Theological Seminary of the Twin Cities, Library: songbooks

New London—Monongalia Historical Society: songbooks

Paynesville—Paynesville Historical Society: songbooks, recordings

Rochester—Minnesota Bible College, Library: songbooks

Roseau—Roseau County Historical Society: songbooks, pictures

Royalton—Royalton Historical Society: songbooks, other printed music

St. Joseph—College of St. Benedict, Library: sheet music, songbooks, other printed music, recordings

St. Paul Bethel College, Learning Resources Center: songbooks, other printed music, recordings, miscellaneous

St. Paul—Hamline University, Bush Memorial Library: sheet music

St. Paul—Ramsey County Historical Society: sheet music, songbooks

St. Paul—Rev. Leo J. Tibesar: recordings

Spring Valley—Spring Valley Community Historical Society: sheet music, songbooks

Warren—Marshall County Historical Society: songbooks, recordings

Williams—Lake of the Woods County Historical Society: programs, pictures, recordings

Winona—St. Mary's College, Fitzgerald Library: programs, recordings

Winona—Winona State College, Maxwell Library: sheet music, other printed music

Mississippi

825

William CAREY COLLEGE   MsHaW
I. E. Rouse Library
Hattiesburg, Mississippi 39401

Clarence Dickinson (1873–1969) Collection, including his ms and published anthems; 100 hymnals; printed Christmas carols, some with words only; opera libretti; papers related to the compiling of the 1937 *Presbyterian Hymnal;* papers from his term as professor and director of sacred music at Union Theological Seminary, New York, 1912–45; annotated programs of Friday-afternoon recitals at Brick Presbyterian Church, New York, with tape recordings of the performances; his complete publications on organ and sacred music; a folk-music collection compiled by him and his wife, Helen, mostly concerning Slovakian folk music, with her typescript translations and his ms music, also related publications; and personal correspondence, scrapbooks, and printed memoirs

—Marilyn M. Pound

826

MARSHALL COUNTY HISTORICAL SOCIETY
Box 806
Holly Springs, Mississippi 38635

Kate Freeman Clark (1875–1957, artist) Manuscript Collection, 3.6 linear meters of materials from her estate, 1840–1957, including correspondence, diaries, journals, photographs, clippings, biographical information, and other papers, among them an 1840 receipt for piano tuning, 286 items of popular sheet music, 1834–1917, and 7 ms songs by her and her mother and grandmother, ca. 1870–1920; also 1500 books, including 10 hymnals, 1850–94, and 16 songbooks, 1817–93

Philharmonic Society of Holly Springs, minute book, 1868–71

Programs for commencement recitals in Holly Springs, 6 items

Sheet music, several items, 1930–50

—Mrs. R. L. Wyatt

827
JACKSON STATE UNIVERSITY   MsJS
Henry T. Sampson Library
1400 John R. Lynch Street
Jackson, Mississippi 39217

William Grant Still, ms and published compositions, including a ms opera; also programs and clippings relating to his career, and a tape recording of the opera *Bayou Legend*

Music Department and University papers pertaining to music, including programs of musical events, especially involving black performers

Sheet music, 3 items, including a first edition of a Scott Joplin composition, ca. 1900

—Berniece Bell

828
MILLSAPS COLLEGE   MsJMC
Millsaps–Wilson Library
Jackson, Mississippi 39210

Lehman Engel Collection, consisting of 1000 scores and 2000 books, mostly post-1940; personal correspondence; memorabilia, including autographs and photographs of Broadway performers; and 1000 disc recordings of his musicals

—Laurie Brown

829
MISSISSIPPI DEPARTMENT OF   Ms-Ar
ARCHIVES AND HISTORY
Box 571
Jackson, Mississippi 39205

Sheet music, 900 popular-music items, mostly 1860s

Hymnals and school songbooks, 100 items, ca. 1880, and 20 vols. of other printed music

Manuscript music, including a Confederate music notebook with song texts, 1860–63, and 5800 song texts from the WPA Folk Music Tour, 1938–39, with photographs and transcribed interviews

Mrs. R. Lyon, papers, 1909–28, including a typescript article, "Writers and Musicians of Jasper County"

Organizational papers, including scrapbooks from the Mississippi Federation of Music Clubs, Century Theater, Jackson Opera Guild, and Grand Opera Association, all late 19th century

Programs and broadsides of local concerts, 125 items, 1870s

Other materials, including 9 music catalogues, 50 photographs of local musicians, and 25 recordings

—Linda Overman

830
Gayle Dean WARDLOW
1911 Fourteenth Street
Meridian, Mississippi 39301

Recordings, including 10,000 78-rpm discs and 25 piano rolls, strong in southern guitar blues and Mississippi blues, 1926–35, also postwar blues and Roy Acuff materials

Photographs of Mississippi performers

831
MISSISSIPPI STATE UNIVERSITY   MsSM
Mitchell Memorial Library
Box 5408
Mississippi State, Mississippi 39762

John O. Creighton (1915–40), papers, 70 linear cm. and 1 reel of microfilm, including letters about his music studies in New York City and St. Louis

Jimmie Rodgers (1897–1933, country-music singer), personal papers on 1 reel of microfilm, including sheet music, typed or ms lyrics, and biographical information

Margaret Valiant papers, 1926–76, 675 items, including correspondence, plays, interviews, newsletters, clippings, and tape recordings, relating to her work with the Resettlement Administration Special Skills Division (1935–39) and the National Youth Administration Music Program (1939–43), and including correspondence with Eleanor Roosevelt and Leopold Stokowski, also material on dramatic productions, folk music of migrant workers in California and Arizona, All-American Youth Orchestra, National Council of the Southern Negro Youth Congress, and East and West Association

Published sacred or secular songbooks, 1 linear meter, ca. 1850–1940; also broadsides and hymnals in various collections of personal papers

Published sheet music, 1400 items, also 3600 items of other printed music

Programs, 50 items, including some of local and University events

Recordings, including 50 78-rpm discs

—George Lewis

832
George W. BOSWELL
Department of English
University of Mississippi
University, Mississippi 38677

Folk Music Archive of Tennessee Folksongs, including 750 songs and musical works on 2 hours of wire recordings and tapes, from Tennessee, Kentucky, and Mississippi, collected ca. 1950–   , with typescript or ms transcriptions

833
UNIVERSITY OF MISSISSIPPI   MsU
University, Mississippi 38677

Music Library

Parks Grant, 6 items of music in ms or facsimile editions

Arthur Kreutz, 15 items of music in ms or facsimile editions

Recordings, including 12 linear meters of 78-rpm discs

—Beryl Fox

Archives and Special Collections, John Davis Williams Library

Mississippi Collection, including ms music by Mississippi composers

Manuscript music by other composers
Henry Bellamann, papers, 1911–45, including correspondence with Charles Ives, Bertram Shapleigh, Henry Houseley, Isidor Philipp, and other musicians; also mss of 300 published and unpublished literary poems
Sheet music, 300 items, predominantly 1910–30, and 1 Civil War item by Harry Macarthy
Kenneth S. Goldstein (University of Pennsylvania professor) Folklore Collection, comprising academic journals, 3000 published books on Anglo-American folksong, and 4500 disc recordings of folk music and oral folklore
Arthur Palmer Hudson Folklore Collection, including papers, and 8 78-rpm disc and 7 tape recordings, related to Mississippi (in the Archives)

—Frank N. Walker, Jr.

834
Stanley J. ROGAL
Department of English
Mary Holmes College
West Point, Mississippi 39773

Hymnals, 1734– , 105 items, emphasizing works of Isaac Watts and the Wesleys

---

In addition to the repositories listed above, the following have also reported holdings of the materials indicated:
Blue Mountain—Blue Mountain College, Music Library: songbooks, recordings
Carrollton—Carroll Society for the Preservation of Antiquities: sheet music, songbooks
Clinton—Mississippi Baptist Historical Commission: songbooks, programs
Clinton—Mississippi College, Leland Speed Library: songbooks, recordings
Hattiesburg—University of Southern Mississippi: songbooks, other printed music, catalogues, recordings
Holly Springs—Mrs. Hindman Doxey: recordings, miscellaneous
Holly Springs—Mrs. R. L. Wyatt: sheet music, songbooks
Vicksburg—Old Courthouse Museum: sheet music, miscellaneous

Missouri

835

TRINITY LUTHERAN CHURCH
Main and Church Streets
Altenburg, Missouri 63732

Johann F. F. Winter, ms sacred music arrangements for male voices, 36 works in 1 bound vol., 1848, with German words, in custody of the Perry County Lutheran Historical Society, Altenburg

—Vernon R. Meyr

836

STATE HISTORICAL SOCIETY   MoHi
OF MISSOURI
Hitt and Lowry Streets
Columbia, Missouri 65201

John W. "Blind" Boone (1864–1927), papers including the "Last Dream Waltzes," photocopies of 15 items published 1886–1961, obituary notices, a program of the Blind Boone Memorial Concert in Columbia, 1961, and a report of the Blind Boone Memorial Foundation, Inc.
Vance Randolph, "Unprintable songs from the Ozarks," 3 ms vols., including a preface by the collector
Scott Joplin, 9 sheet-music items and 1 compilation of his works, published 1899–1903
Missouri Federation of Music Clubs, materials including programs of annual meetings, 1900–1958
Songbooks, 40 popular items, 1849–1967, including songs of the American West and Southwest; also 30

hymnals of various denominations, 1842–1942, including some in German; and 1 copy of the *Missouri Harmony*, 1839
Sheet music, 1000 items for voice or piano, 1812–1954

—Laura Peritore

837

UNIVERSITY OF MISSOURI   MoU
Columbia, Missouri 65201

Joint Collection, University of Missouri Western Historical Manuscript Collection—Columbia and State Historical Society of Missouri Manuscripts (23 Elmer Ellis Library)

Adam Allendorf Collection, 3 folders, including songs and plays in German, n.d.
Hermann B. Almstedt (1872–1954), 80 folders and 18 vols. of papers, including programs of music groups directed by him, and material concerning music at the University
Boonville Turn and Gesang Verein Papers, 1 folder and 11 vols., 1852–1925, including a constitution, by-laws, secretary's reports, minutes, roster of members, and account books
James F. Davidson, of Chicago and of Hannibal, Mo., 5 folders and 15 vols. of papers, 1868–1917, including diaries, press clippings, and other materials concerning opera and theater
Hagerman–Hayden Family Papers, 51 folders, with correspondence and papers relating to the music-teaching career of Benjamin F. Hagerman in Alexandria, Mo., 1852–63, and music student P. C. Hayden of Oberlin, Ohio, 1879–86

Franz Schwarzer (1828–1904, Washington, Mo., zither manufacturer) Papers, 1840–1951, 14 folders and 5 vols., including family correspondence, factory records, catalogues, and photographs of instruments

Turner Society Pamphlets, 5 folders, 1912–45, including publications of St. Louis Turner groups, a history of the American Turnerbund, and an annual report of the National Executive Committee of American Turners

—Nancy Lankford

University Library—Special Collections Department

Songsters, 10 items, ca. 1870

Music pertaining to the University, including 5 songbooks, one of them compiled by James Thomas Quarles; 2 songsheets with words only, 1 published sheet-music edition of the school song, and music for 4 musical shows and operas, 1908–29

—Margaret Howell

838
Mrs. Floyd LaDUE

3200 Roosevelt Drive
Hannibal, Missouri 63401

Eleanor Davis (1889–1973, Hannibal composer), ms compositions for voice, organ, harp, flute, violin, or piano; 5 items of published music for voice or piano; and 3 scrapbooks compiled by her, containing programs, correspondence, clippings, and pictures

839
Mark TWAIN HOME & MUSEUM   MoHM

208 Hill Street
Hannibal, Missouri 63401

Hymnals and sacred songbooks, 5 items, 1850–67

Sheet music, 5 items, relating to Samuel Clemens's (Mark Twain's) writings

Aeolian Orchestrella of 58-note range, Model Y, bought by Clemens in 1904; also 150 tape rolls for orchestrella, mostly European classical music, bought by Clemens in 1904–10

Recordings of Ossip Gabrilowitsch, 6 RCA Victor discs, donated by Clemens's daughter, Clara Clemens Gabrilowitsch

—Henry Sweets

840
HISTORY COMMISSION OF THE   MoIRC
REORGANIZED CHURCH OF
JESUS CHRIST OF LATTER-DAY SAINTS

Library and Archives
Auditorium
Box 1059
Independence, Missouri 64051

Hymnals, 125 items, 1830– , mostly from the Latter-day Saints Church or the Reorganized Latter-day Saints Church, some with words only

—Patricia Roberts

841
JACKSON COUNTY HISTORICAL SOCIETY

Archives
Independence Square Courthouse
Room 103
Independence, Missouri 64050

Manuscript music, 25 items written or copied by Caroline Homassell (1795–1876), ca. 1815, in the Hudson Collection

Hymnals of various denominations, 25 items, ca. 1850–1925

Popular sheet music for voice and piano, ca. 1800–1925, 500 items, including some in bound vols., mostly in the S. Verdi Campbell, Chevis-Samuel, J. B. Wornall Family, Mary Mildred Zick DeWitt Sheet Music, and Hudson collections

Scrapbook of programs and clippings of local and national performers in the Kansas City area, 8 linear cm., compiled by Mrs. William J. Bland and her mother, Agnes Harris Johnson, ca. 1900–1940

—Nancy M. Ehrlich

842
R. Duane STEPHENS

First Presbyterian Church
100 North Pleasant Street
Independence, Missouri 64050

Hymnals and tune books, 800 items, arranged by denominations and publishers; also books concerning hymnology

843
Harry S. TRUMAN LIBRARY   MoIT

24 Highway and Delaware
Independence, Missouri 64050

See Jack L. Ralston, "Show-Me Songs in the Truman Library," *Whistle Stop*, 4/1 (1976), 1–3

Correspondence between Truman and his staff, and with music organizations, labor unions, musicians, and the general public, concerning music-related matters, ca. 30 linear cm., 1945–53 (in the Manuscripts Collections)

Photographs of the Truman family attending musical events, ca. 1945–53 (in the Audiovisual Collections)

Margaret Truman Daniel, 7 tape recordings of her singing, 1947–50 (in the Audiovisual Collections); 4000 items of sheet music given to her as gifts, 5 linear meters of public-opinion mail sent to her, and 60 linear cm. of correspondence, itineraries, scripts, publicity, programs, and clippings relating to her music career, 1945–54 (in the White House Office of Social Correspondence files, and Daniel papers)

Recordings, mostly popular, 550 discs presented to Truman as gifts during his presidential term (in the Audiovisual Collections)

Printed music, mostly sheet music, 6600 items, also 763 mss, mostly gifts to Truman during his presidential term, including Percy Wenrich, dedicatory ms copy of "Missouri, My State!", and "The Missouri Waltz" by Frederic Knight Logan, ms arrangement by A. C. Brill for calliope, to be used in the 1949 inaugural parade (in the Printed Materials Collection)

—Benedict K. Zobrist

844
Kenneth BIBLE
9406 McKinley Avenue
Kansas City, Missouri 64138

Hymnals, 400 items, 300 of them in English and 100 in German, also 100 books on hymnology, 1774– , mostly 19th century, including many Wesley collections

845
KANSAS CITY MUSEUM OF HISTORY
3218 Gladstone Boulevard
Kansas City, Missouri 64123

Sir Carl Busch (1862–1943, Danish-born composer, and conductor of the Kansas City Symphony, 1912–18), 30 linear cm. of papers, 1906–42, including ms and published music, correspondence, photographs, and awards

Photographs of Kansas City-area musicians and music groups, 1870–1960, 200 items, including group portraits of early minstrels, and the Mutual Musicians' Foundation collection on Kansas City jazz, 1920–60

Programs, 15 linear cm., ca. 1915–30

Hymnals, 6 items, 1849–1900

School and popular songbooks, 10 items, ca. 1840–1950

Popular sheet music, 500 items, ca. 1840–1950

—Beth Pessek

846
KANSAS CITY PUBLIC LIBRARY   MoK
311 East Twelfth Street
Kansas City, Missouri 64106

Joe Sanders (1896–1965), personal papers, including a ms book with 24 original songs; 3 other holograph mss; sheet music by Sanders, 1922– , 60 items; photographs, 148 separate items and others in 5 albums; association sheet music, 21 items; and 8 scrapbooks devoted to his career, also separate programs and press clippings of the "Night Hawks"

Hiner Band Collection, based on materials used by the Missouri 3rd Regiment National Guard, established by Dr. E. M. Himer (1872–1948), also including materials from Ben Kendrick, in all 11 boxes of marches (800 folders of parts for small band, with indexes), 1300 fox trots, 14 file drawers of "medium, large, and grand concert music," 2 drawers of orchestra music, and 3 boxes and 2 file drawers of salon music

Local programs and press clippings, in the Missouri Valley Room, as cited in James Milford Crabb, *A History of Music in Kansas City* (D.M.A. diss., University of Missouri—Kansas City, 1967), p. 194

847
UNIVERSITY OF MISSOURI—   MoKU
KANSAS CITY
Music Library
Conservatory of Music
4420 Warwick Boulevard
Kansas City, Missouri 64111

For reports on acquisitions involving the Institute for Studies in American Music, see *The Conservatory Clarion* (hereinafter cited as *Clarion*)

Songbooks, 200 catalogued and 50 uncatalogued community items, 1840– ; also 600 catalogued and 300 uncatalogued tunebooks and hymnals of various denominations, 1780–

Sheet music, 51,325 items uncatalogued, 55 bound vols. catalogued, 1000 piano rags, 500 catalogued and 100 uncatalogued items published pre-1826, and 300 items published by J. W. Jenkins' Sons, 1878–1973. The collection includes files of imprints and composers from Kansas City (Mo. and Kan.) and other midwestern states

Warner Brothers Orchestral Library, 13,000 items, comprising sets of parts with piano-conductor's scores for the accompaniment of silent films

Band Library, 1125 items, mostly sets of performance parts for Kansas City-area small bands, including the Missouri 3rd Regiment Band led by Robert Fraker, ca. 1930–45 (with a photograph of the band, and Fraker's uniform)

Isaac Baker Woodbury, tunebooks and hymnals from his personal library. See Robert M. Copeland, *The Life and Works of Isaac Baker Woodbury, 1819–1858* (Ph.D. diss., University of Cincinnati, 1974)

MacDowell Colony music, with items by composers resident at the colony, ca. 1920–50

Manuscript and holograph music, by Amy Cheney (Mrs. H. H. A.) Beach (1867–1944), 25 linear cm.; Walter Brenner (1906–69), 3 linear meters (*Clarion*, Jan. 1972); Francis Buebendorf (b. 1912), 30 linear cm.; Carl Busch (1862–1943), 2 linear meters, including some published items (*Clarion*, June 1969); Gladys Blakely Bush (b. 1898), 1 linear meter; Charles Wakefield Cadman (1881–1946), 30 linear cm.; Hans C. Feil (b. 1879, local organist and composer), 60 linear cm.; William Henry Humiston (1869–1923), 30 linear cm.; Eunice Lea Kettering (b. 1906), 35 items; Wiktor Labunski (1895–1974, pianist and composer), 2 linear meters, including some published items; Ernest Mannheim (sociologist), 155 pages; Clarence A. Marshall, 2 items; Ben Olson (Conservatory student), 3 items; Julius Ossier (1865–1939), 1 linear meter; Olive Nelson Russell (former faculty member), 8 linear cm.; Agnes M. Schaberg (St. Louis pianist and teacher), 4 items; George Eliot Simpson (1876–1958), 45 linear cm.; Charles Sanford Skilton (1868–1941), 9000 pages of scores and parts; N. Clark Smith (1873–1935), 25 linear cm.; Leith Stevens (1909–70, film composer and conductor), 1 linear meter (*Clarion*, April 1969); Powell Weaver (1870–1951, organist and composer), Mary Weaver (pianist and composer), and Thomas Weaver, in all 30 linear cm. (*Clarion*, June 1969); and Vincent Williams (1903–68), 100 items with parts (*Clarion*, June 1968)

Papers of musicians, including Edna Scott Billings (organist), Walter Brenner, Charles Wakefield Cadman, Katherine K. Davis (b. 1892, composer and arranger), Hans C. Feil, Charles E. Horn (1786–1849, 11 letters; *Clarion*, Oct. 1971), Wiktor Labunski, Geneve Lichtenwalter (1869–1951, local pianist, and teacher of Virgil Thomson), Clyde Neibarger (critic), Leith Stevens, Mary Weaver, and Powell Weaver

Papers of organizations, including the American Guild of Organists, Kansas City chapter; the University of Missouri—Kansas City Conservatory and its antecedents (Kansas City Conservatory of Music, Horner Institute, Kansas City—Horner Institute and Conservatory of Music, Conservatory of Music of Kansas City, and University of Kansas City Music Department), programs and scrapbooks; and Franz Schwarzer (Washington, Mo., zither manufacturer)

Programs of the University Conservatory of Music, 1906– ; the Kansas City Philharmonic and antecedents, 1933– ; and scrapbooks of programs compiled by Geneve Lichtenwalter and Archibald Gould (organist), documenting Kansas City musical events, ca. 1900–1920s

Catalogues of music publishers and dealers, 7.5 linear meters

Photographs of bands, orchestras, and musicians, some local, 300 items, ca. 1880s– , mostly from the collections of Wiktor Labunski and Willi Hoffman (violin repairer)

Books on music, periodicals, and method books, 300 items, pre-1914

—Jack L. Ralston

848
CLAY COUNTY MUSEUM ASSOCIATION
14 North Main Street
Liberty, Missouri 64068

Popular sheet music, 100 items in 1 bound vol., pre-1865, including Confederate songs; also 4 items, ca. 1900, published in Liberty and Excelsior, Mo.

Popular songbooks, including 1 item published by the Banner Buggy Co., St. Louis, ca. 1900

Hymnals of various denominations, 5 items, 1850–60

Programs, 15 items, ca. 1870– , of William Jewell College and of Clay Seminary in Liberty

Pictures of local bands, 5 items, ca. 1920–30

—Ron Fuenfhausen

849
William JEWELL COLLEGE   MoLiWJ
Liberty, Missouri 64068

Hymnals, chiefly English, but including scattered 19th-century U.S. imprints in the collection of Charles Haddon Spurgeon (1834–92, Baptist clergyman in England), acquired in 1905; see Donald C. Brown, "Spurgeon's Hymnals," *The Hymn*, 30 (1979), 39–48. Also 19th-century American hymnals and shape-note tunebooks, in the Missouri Baptist Convention Historical Collection

—Donald C. Brown

850
DeKALB COUNTY HISTORICAL SOCIETY
Route 3, Box 100
Maysville, Missouri 64469

Wilhelm F. Dieter, "Garden Prairie Waltz" for band with vocal solo, 1900, photocopy of the ms conductor's score

Mrs. I. H. Bloom, "Comrade Sleep," written in memory of her son who died in World War I, published 1938; and her "Missouri, Land of a Million Smiles," published 1939

Hymnals, 10 items, some used locally, ca. 1880–1925

School and popular songbooks, 5 items, some used locally, ca. 1865–1940

Programs of the local high school and of a local music-teacher's piano and vocal recitals, 2 items

Tape recording of Clara Canfield, 1971, performing "I Want to Go Back to Missouri" (1916), lyrics by Edna Pollard

—Lora R. Lockhart

851
VERNON COUNTY HISTORICAL SOCIETY
231 North Main Street
Nevada, Missouri 64772

J. Hurley Kaylor, 2 published works for piano, ca. 1900–1910, and 3 ms items by Kaylor and by Nellie E. High

—Patrick T. Brophy

852
John W. BAKER
First Baptist Church
Ninth and Cedar Streets
Rolla, Missouri 65401

Hymnals and songbooks, 250 items, 1850– , particularly strong in gospel songbooks, 1850–1900, also Baptist hymnals, especially the collections by Robert H. Coleman

853
BUCHANAN COUNTY HISTORICAL SOCIETY
Tenth and Edmond Streets
Saint Joseph, Missouri 64501

Hymnals of various denominations, 500 items, ca. 1860–1930, some in German, and some with words only

Sheet music, 5000 items, some in bound vols., ca. 1840–1900, mostly vocal

Photographs and colored lithographic posters (many formerly in the collection of Murphy Spair), 2000 items, ca. 1905–35, mostly of local theatrical productions and theaters, especially the Missouri Theater

Programs of local high-school groups, theaters, and concerts, including performances by Ernestine Schumann-Heink, Geraldine Farrar, and Harry Lauder, 150 items, 1876–1930

Music catalogues, 10 items, ca. 1900–1930, including 1 from the Victrola Company, and 1 of QRS player-piano rolls

Recordings of popular and classical music including 174 cylinders, ca. 1890–1940, and 78-rpm discs

—Richard T. Cameron

854

Janet E. PETERS
1701 South Twentieth Street
Saint Joseph, Missouri 64501

Agatha Pfeiffer (aunt of Janet Peters, and student of Pietro Yon), ms compositions, ca. 1905–50, including masses, children's music, and a work composed by her for a local pageant, 1936; compositions published ca. 1905–50; and personal papers, ca. 1870–1950, including programs of performances of her works, diaries, correspondence, photographs, and music catalogues of her publishers, McLaughlin & Reilly and G. Schirmer

Charles A. Pfeiffer (grandfather of Janet Peters), 3 scrapbooks containing clippings in German and English, programs, and letters, including materials concerning music in the St. Joseph area, ca. 1860–1900

Dorothy Gaynor Blake (1863–1921), printed music for children, including piano-instruction books and operettas; also photographs of her

Mary Elizabeth Pfeiffer Priebe (mother of Janet Peters, and producer of Dorothy Blake's operettas), personal papers, including staging materials for productions, and scrapbooks of programs and clippings about the productions

Katherine Wallace Davis, published compositions, ca. 1890–1910, and correspondence with Agatha Pfeiffer

Pietro Yon, various published works, ca. 1910–50

Other published music, including 100 hymnals of various denominations, ca. 1860–1940, some in German, and popular and semi-classical sheet music for voice or piano, ca. 1915–30

855

SAINT JOSEPH PUBLIC LIBRARY   MoStj
Tenth and Felix Streets
Saint Joseph, Missouri 64501

Constance Faunt Le Roy Runcie, ms opera *The Prince of Asturia*, 1894; also a Ditson edition of "Invocation to Love," for soprano or tenor with violin obligato

Sheet music of the Fortnightly Music Club, 3000 items, ca. 1890–1940, mostly classical, for piano, organ, or other instruments

Scrapbook of programs from St. Joseph theaters, including the Electric, Lyceum, and Tootle Lyric theaters, ca. 1890–1907

—Doris Finley

856

CONCORDIA HISTORICAL   MoSCH
INSTITUTE
Department of Archives and History
801 De Mun Avenue
Saint Louis, Missouri 83105

Manuscript music, 75 linear cm., 1893–1940, including sheet music for a concert given at the 1893 Lutheran Church—Missouri Synod Convention

Personal papers, of F. W. Herzberger (1859–1930), ms and printed music; Walter E. Buszin (1899–1973), notebooks and course syllabuses; W. G. Polack (1890–1950); F. R. Webber (b. 1887), correspondence, notebooks, sermons, and photographs; Walter Daib (1904–74), personal correspondence, and business correspondence including papers of the Historical Society of St. James, the Lutheran Liturgical Research Society, and the Lutheran Chaplains' Association; and Edmund Seuel (1865–1951), memorabilia

Organizational papers, 75 linear cm., including minutes of the Commission on Worship, Liturgics, and Hymnology, 1923–   , and the Historical Society of St. James

Hymnals, 1764–1940, 600 items, mostly Lutheran, including some in German, Swedish, or Norwegian

Songbooks, 400 items mostly for school use, including some in German, ca. 1830–1940

Sacred choral music, 1000 items, ca. 1800–1940; also, 100 other items of printed music, ca. 1800–1940

Programs, 500 items, including those of the Bach Society

Photographs of musicians and groups, ca. 1900–

Recordings, including 100 78-rpm discs, ca. 1900–1920, mostly sacred

—August R. Suelflow, Keith D. Boheim

857

CONCORDIA SEMINARY   MoSCS
Library
L. E. Fuerbringer Hall
801 De Mun Avenue
Saint Louis, Missouri 63105

Hymnals of various denominations, 200 items, 1750–

—W. Larry Bielenberg

858

LUTHERAN CHURCH, MISSOURI SYNOD,
NATIONAL HEADQUARTERS
Commission on Worship Library
500 Broadway Building
Saint Louis, Missouri 63102

Hymnals of various denominations including the Lutheran Church, 200 items, some of them in German or Scandinavian languages, ca. 1800–1940; also published material concerning hymonolgy

—Fred Precht

859

MERCANTILE LIBRARY   MoSM
510 Locust Street
Saint Louis, Missouri 63101

Sheet music, 3 bound vols. of mid 19th-century popular piano and vocal items

Programs, mostly of local concerts, including 7 performances of the St. Louis Philharmonic Society, 1845–63, in a loose-leaf vol.; also 40 programs, 1869–74, including concerts in the Mercantile Library Hall

Songbooks of popular songs and folksongs, 50 20th-century items

—Mary Mewes

860
MISSOURI HISTORICAL SOCIETY   MoSHi

Jefferson Memorial Building
Saint Louis, Missouri 63112

A. *Library*
B. *Personal Papers of Musicians*
C. *Other Personal Papers*
D. *Correspondence*
E. *Organizational Materials*
F. *Manuscript Music*
G. *Sheet Music*
H. *Scrapbooks*
J. *Programs*
K. *Other Materials*

A. Library

Hymnals, 2 linear meters of 19th-century vols., including German items

Tunebooks, 2.5 linear meters of 19th-century vols., including 10 early copies of Allen Carden, *Missouri Harmony*, 1820–57, and 1 of John B. Seat, *St. Louis Harmony*, 1831

Songbooks, 1 linear meter of 19th-century sacred and secular items

Sheet music, 11,000 items published ca. 1800– , vocal and instrumental, including sacred pieces, and opera arias, with some European publications but with major holdings of St. Louis and midwestern imprints; card index by title, with partial cross-index by lyricist, composer, publisher, dedication, arranger, cover, subject, advertiser, performer/performance, and date. Also 350 bound vols. of sheet music, 19th and 20th centuries, mostly from the collection of Ernst C. Krohn

Programs and playbills of theaters, operas, choral groups, colleges, and university clubs in the St. Louis area, ca. 1820–1970, in 12 legal-file drawers and 17 shelf boxes organized by theater or concert hall, including 2 drawers each of items from the Municipal Opera and the Grand Opera House; partial card index to theaters and concert halls

Programs and clippings of St. Louis musical performances, 1923–57, 49 shelf boxes, collected by Krohn

Apollo Club membership record, 1 vol., including programs, 1895–1913

—Catherine Barber

B. Archives: Personal Papers of Musicians

Robyn family papers, 100 ms items, ca. 1845–70, including the autobiography of William Robyn (1814–1905), with letters from musicians, clippings, and genealogical material; notes and a photocopy of a Central City (Colo.) Opera House program of Henry Robyn, 1878; and a sketch of Alfred G. Robyn (1860–1935), copies of news articles, and biographical notes furnished by the Kilgen Organ Co.

Charles Balmer (1817–92, music publisher and first musical director of the St. Louis Oratorio Society), papers, including a letter from James H. Comfort to Balmer, 1849; applications for naturalization of Charles (1852) and John Godfred Balmer (n.d.); and notes on the Balmer family by Charles' daughter, Lillie (Mrs. Charles) Unger, n.d.

Kroeger family collection, with translations of Minnesinger songs, clippings, and notes on the story of *Parsifal*, ca. 1877, by Adolph Ernst Kroeger (1837–82); an address by his son, Ernest R. Kroeger (1862–1934), on St. Louis musical history, 1927; and 12 letters from E. R. Kroeger to W. H. Pommer, 1891–1922

Charles Kunkel (1840–1923), autograph album, 1864–1909, signed by musicians including Ole Bull, Anton Rubinstein, Pablo Sarasate, Giuseppe Creatore, Victor Herbert, and John Philip Sousa; letters to Mrs. Kunkel from her husband's friends and associates, 1889; 4 letters from Sousa to Kunkel, 1904; letter to John H. Gundlach with a bill for Gundlach's daughter's music lessons, 1907; invitation to a St. Louis Conservatory of Music performance, 1870s; and a list of donors of commemorative panels in the Kunkel Collection, 1951

William H. Pommer (1851–1937, Columbia and St. Louis music teacher, composer, and supervisor of music in the public schools), clippings, programs, and 150 letters, 1881–1935; also genealogical material on the family in Philadelphia and Missouri, 1830s

Christian Charles Kunkel papers, with the marriage certificate of Kunkel and Mary Guthrie, 1853, and Kunkel's autograph typescript of a song performed by him, 1856

Adelaide Kalkman (1858–1929, St. Louis singer), correspondence, mementos, and notes, n.d.; also 2 account books, 1860–64, and 2 diaries of European tours, 1892–97

William Foden (1860–1947), notes on the history of the guitar, correspondence about arrangements by Foden, and ms compositions by him for guitar, (1890–1945)

Gecks family papers, with a letter from Frank Gecks to W. H. Pommer concerning a quintet written for him, 1913; a 1929 resolution of appreciation from the St. Louis Philharmonic Society to Frank Gecks; a sketch of Frank Gecks, Sr., by his son, Frank, Jr. (1865–1932), n.d.; recollections of Frank Gecks, Sr., by his son, John Gecks, 1948; and a letter on early St. Louis musicians, from John F. Gecks to Charles Van Ravenswaay, 1952 (see also under Ernst C. Krohn, below)

Samuel Bollinger (1871–1946), correspondence, clippings, and a calendar, 1908; also a typescript biography by Edward Eugene Briscoe, 1955

Carl Wilhelm Kern (1874–1945), scrapbook of programs, notices, and articles on music gathered while Kern was in Springfield, Ohio, ca. 1894–1901; also ms writings on music subjects, 1932–34

Rosalie Balmer Smith (Mrs. Charles Allan) Cale (1875–1958, composer and pianist, a descendant of Charles Balmer), collection including correspondence, programs, notes, and clippings on compositions and performances, ca. 1895–1955

Ottmar Moll (1877–1934), 5 account books for piano students, 1897–1927, and ms music notebooks and poems, 1904

Harry R. Burke (1885–1956, St. Louis critic), undated ms on music

Ernst C. Krohn (1888–1975), correspondence on musical activities in St. Louis, 1915–34; typescripts of correspondence, journals, and accounts of Frank Gecks (pianist), 1880–1928; typescripts and copies of letters of Richard Spamer (critic), 1930s; and a program of

"Music from Old St. Louis," prepared by Krohn and presented at the Missouri Historical Society, 1951

Guido B. Vogel (St. Louis musician), program notes, contracts, and correspondence, 1896–1940; also a scrapbook of concert programs of his military band, 1897–1921

C. Archives: Other Personal Papers

Amoureux–Langlois family papers, including an account book with several pages of Creole and French song lyrics, 1795–97; also a copybook of traditional and contemporary song lyrics in English, 1861–72

Ferdinand H. Walthers, ms and typescript notes and memoirs on music in St. Louis, 1830–1937

John H. Gundlach collection, with programs of St. Louis productions involving the Balmer & Weber Music Rooms, Ludlow & Smith's St. Louis Theatre, the St. Louis Choral Society, and the St. Louis Oratorio Society, 1847–65; programs of opera at the St. Louis Exposition Music Hall, 1885–1901; programs of the Amphion, Apollo, and Morning Choral clubs, 1903–27; and subscriptions for stock, box-office returns, and regulations for Ludlow & Smith's St. Louis Theatre and Mobile, Ala., theater, 1835–48

Samuel R. Curtis, diary mentioning St. Louis musical events and concerts involving Jenny Lind and others, 1850–52

Robert Herman Mueller, papers, with accounts of music binding and names stamped on covers, for work done by Mueller for Balmer & Weber, 1860

William B. Napton, journals and diaries mentioning St. Louis opera performances and the ballet *Black Crook*, 1867

Garesche family papers, 1877–?, including programs for St. Louis musical performances of August Waldauer, Robert Goldbeck, Eugenia Williamson, Marie R. Garesche, Lt. Col. Julius P. Garesche, and others

William G. B. Carson collection, including correspondence, clippings, play books, and programs, 1882–1927

George D. and Mary McKittrick Markham, 3 diaries with clippings and comments on the St.Louis Symphony Orchestra and the World's Fair, 1897–1943; also 2 scrapbooks of Mary McKittrick, with programs, 1891–95

D. R. Francis (Missouri governor) collection, with papers including a letter from L. A. Phillips concerning the St. Louis City Drummers' Association, 1892; a 1902 letter soliciting support for Weil's Band of St. Louis; and comments on St. Louis music in 1907

Shepard Barclay, papers, including programs, membership books, and other items of the Odeon Theatre, Apollo Club, Lyceum Theater, and other St.Louis organizations, 1902–25

James A. Reardon, papers, including the song "We All Love St. Louis" by Jessie Beattie Thomas, and a letter from Thomas to Reardon, 1912

Samuel Clemens, papers, including 1 item concerning Fritz Kreisler, 1930

Rice family papers, including 5 letters from Vladimir Golschmann to Mrs. May Rice concerning the St. Louis Symphony, 1932–38, and autographs and notes of musicians who performed in St.Louis

Luther E. Smith collection, including engraved letterhead and correspondence concerning the Municipal Theatre Association, 1940

Dorothy A. Neuhoff, alphabetical file with 1 item on the purchase of music mss of Philip Gottlieb Anton, Sr., 1952

Corinne Steele Hall collection, including songs and tunes used in St.Louis kindergarten instruction, n.d.

D. Archives: Correspondence

W. G. Wells, correspondence and legal papers, including documents relating to the construction of a music hall in St.Louis, 1839, in the Hamilton R. Gamble papers

J. L. Schnell, letter to General Stephen Watts Kearny concerning Schnell's music commemorating a western campaign, 1848, in the Kearny papers

Edward Chase papers, including letters to his wife concerning social life and the Philharmonic Society in St. Louis, 1849–66

Henry W. Williams, letterbook to his wife concerning St. Louis social life and the Concert Hall, 1849, in the Mesker Collection

Sallie Case, letter to Sue King, 1865, concerning a season of Italian opera at DeBar's Opera House in St. Louis, in the Case Family papers

John Green, 2 letters, 1868, to Hattie Jones (Templeton, Miss., singer), concerning performances in St. Louis, in the Green Collection

Theodore Spiering (1871–1925, violinist and conductor), letters received, 1872–1925, in the Spiering Collection

William H. Semsrott collection, including 1 letter from Albert Lutz to Cordilia Green concerning music teachers and publications, 1873, and 1 letter from L. E. Scott of St. Louis to Lizzie Bolduc of Ste. Genevieve, concerning music and social life, 1876

Lillie Balmer to William E. Buder, letters, 1877–80, concerning Charles Balmer and Henry Shaw, in the Shaw papers

Edward F. Goltra papers, including 4 letters concerning the San Carlo Opera Company, Herbert W. Cost and the Tetrazzini Concert Company, the Grand Opera season at the Odeon, and the Ellis Opera Company, 1908–16

W. K. Bixby, 2 letters concerning St. Louis musical events and Chaliapin's performance with the Grand Opera Association, 1925–26

Paul Robyn to Cyril Clemens, 1 letter, 1952, with a clipping on Robyn's ninety-ninth birthday, in the Clemens collection

Mrs. J. G. W. Schoenthaler to Charles Van Ravenswaay, 1 letter, 1959, with data on her father, Carl Froehlich (cellist), and his brother Egmont

Elizabeth Cueny, letter from Ernestine Schumann-Heink about the problem of German opera performances in America during World War I, 1918; 2 letters from Rudolph Vavpetich (concert manager) concerning Dusolina Giannini and the Daniel Mayer company of New York, 1925; and 1 form letter to Miss Cueny concerning the success of Lambert Murphy, 1926

Miscellaneous letters, including John T. S. Sullivan of St. Louis to Sir William Drummond Stewart, concerning the Missouri Musical Fund Society, 1838; Mary Atchison to Mrs. John F. Darby, concerning Jenny Lind and Charlotte Cushman, 1851; Jane Delany Lindsay to John O'Fallon Delany, on musicals, 1877; L. E. Rose to Ellen Magill, concerning Gilmore's Band, 1885; Lucy A. Wiggin to Miss Kohn, on music lessons and amateur concerts, 1891; Yvonne de Tre-ville, 1 item promoting her concert with the St. Louis Symphony Orchestra, 1912; George D. Markham to Edward F. Goltra, concerning box seats for the Symphony Orchestra, 1914; Lilburn A. Kingsbury to Miss Ida, concerning the Russian Ballet in St. Louis, 1916; William Clark Breckenridge to Mrs. Everett W. Pattison, concerning the rebec, 1922; Kathryn Meisle, 1 item on her St. Louis concert, 1925; W. C. Handy to J. Benoist Carton, concerning a recent composition, 1930; Vladimir Golschmann to Lt. Young, concerning the St. Louis Symphony, 1945; Alma Cueny (member of the Civic Music League of St. Louis, 1915–55), 1 item regarding her death in 1955; D. Carr, letter addressed to Mary, on a concert involving Balmer and Waldauer, n.d.

E. Archives: Organizational Materials

St. Louis Theatre, incorporation charter, stock certificates, lease, box-office returns, and letters, ca. 1836–50; also a clipping on the theater's history, 1930

St. Louis Oratorio Society, by-laws, 1839, and 2 letters, 1849–70

Polyhymnia Orchestra and Philharmonic Orchestra of St. Louis, catalogue of orchestra music, 1845–70

Miscellaneous items, including the St. Louis Musical Polyhymnia, constitution and by-laws, 1846; announcement of the Western Musical Convention in St. Louis, 1852; St. Louis Academy of Music, papers, minutes, and plans to build an opera house, 1864–69; Philharmonic Society, stock subscriptions and donations, 1869–70; St. Louis Musical Art Association, constitution and by-laws, 1870; St. Louis Musical Society, constitution, 1872; Rockspring Sängerbund papers, 1875–87; and an advertising song-card for J. Ellicock's Music Store in St. Louis, n.d.

St. Louis Philharmonic Society, minutes, constitution, and programs, 1860–69; other programs, 1860–99; and Homer Bassford, letter to Sylvia Walden concerning the Society, 1953

Chester Franz papers, with a letterhead of the St. Louis Piano Manufacturing Co., 1869, and a brochure of the St. Louis School of Musical Art, ca. 1900–1920

St. Louis Academy of Music papers, including programs of the Philharmonic Society and the Harvard Musical Association, 1870

Kunkel Brothers, bill for rent of the Temple, 1876

St. Louis Exposition & Music Hall Association, account books, stock certificate, letterbook, and other materials, 1880–1901, in various collections

St. Louis Choral Society, announcements, cash account, and clipping, 1888–92

Herwegh Sängerbund papers, including 8 record books, correspondence, programs, and printed and ms arrangements of music, 1889–1947

Kunkel's Music Review, credentials for their agent, G. W. McElhiney, 1889

Associated Music Committee, ms on choir salaries, 1896–1901

Missouri State Music Teachers' Association, rosters, minutes, convention records, and account books, 1907–26

Conrath's Conservatory of Music, circular, 1908

St. Louis Pageant and Masque, correspondence, register, and scripts, 1914

St. Louis Pageant and Drama Association, correspondence and notes on productions, 1915–16

St. Louis Pageant Choral Society, broadside for a *Messiah* performance, 1914; contract with the St. Louis Symphony, 1927; and correspondence, 1927–29

Strassberger Conservatories of Music in St. Louis, letterheads, n.d.

F. Archives: Manuscript Music

Phillip Gottlieb Anton (1839–96), 50 items, including arrangements and compositions for piano, chorus, chamber ensemble, or orchestra, also composition books and fragments

William Henry Pommer (1851–1937), 120 items, including operas, choral works, songs, orchestral and chamber music, and piano solos

Ernest R. Kroeger (1862–1934), 6 items, mostly for strings and piano

Samuel Bollinger (1871–1946), 30 items, including vocal, keyboard, and orchestral works

Carl Wilhelm Kern (1874–1945), 70 items, mostly piano music, with 2 operettas

Ottmar Moll (1877–1934), 4 ms notebooks, and a notebook of poems to be set to music, 1904 and n.d.

Ernst C. Krohn (1888–1975), 6 piano-music mss

Louis Moreau Gottschalk, "Nocturne" and "Valz" for piano, n.d.

Agnes M. Schaberg, 10 songs, n.d.

Confederate Civil War ballads, ca. 1861, in the Case Family papers

Other miscellaneous items, including a psalm book of Jane Dawson, 1821; a bound vol. of French songs, ca. 1841; Louis Conrath (1868–1927), *Concertstück* for piano and orchestra; cowboy songs copied from recordings made by Florence Hayward, 1897; M. I. Epstein (1855–1947), arrangements of Liszt's Second Hungarian Rhapsody n.d.; French folksongs, Negro songs, and dances, written from memory by Mrs. Amelia Noel, n.d. and 1951; and 5 songs and a 1956 script by Bert Baumgartner

G. Archives: Sheet Music

Miscellaneous items, including popular Union songs of the Civil War and 8 other items, 1861–1941; "The Kansas War and Other Matters," sung at Smith's Theatre by J. H. Thompson, ca. 1865; William Schuyler, "Wedding Music," 1890; victory songs of World War I, in the Dayton W. Canada collection; and Clara Tull Martin, "Dear Father Mine," in the Susan L. March collection

H. Archives: Scrapbooks

Thomas D. Day, 1 vol., ca. 1840–60, including tickets, programs, and other materials from music performances in New Orleans, St. Louis, and New York

Louis Hammerstein (1856–1918), scrapbooks with clippings, obituaries, and articles on St. Louis music clubs and musicians, including Emile Karst (1826–1917)

Letitia Fritch, 2 vols., 1876–86, with notices of concerts in which she appeared

Isaac L. Schoen (violinist and conductor), 2 vols., 1877–91

Florence Hayward, 1 vol., ca. 1899–1913, with Alfred G. Robyn's "Homage à Chopin" and his photograph

Herbert W. Cost, 1 vol., including opera and musical programs, 1907–42

Dr. Philip Skrainka, 2 vols. with pictures of actors, actresses, and opera singers, ca. 1900–1915

J. Archives: Programs

Miscellaneous items in envelopes, including the United Methodist Church, 1866; Adelina Patti, 1881; McCaull Opera Comique Company, 1885; Emma Dreyfus, 1887; YMCA, 1890; Kate J. Brainard, 1890; P. S. Gilmore and the St. Louis Exposition, 1891; Auditorium Concert, 1895; and the Thirty-eighth National Sängerfest of the North-American Sängerbund, 1934

Other St. Louis programs in various collections, including the Second Presbyterian Church, 1872; Grand Exposition concerts by the Cavalry Depot Band, 1884; St. Louis Exposition, 1886 and 1900; Grand Festival, 1900; Morning Choral Club, 1903–20; Music Supervisors' National Conference chorus and St. Louis Symphony Orchestra, 1919; St. Louis Symphony Orchestra with Helen Traubel and Lauritz Melchior, n.d.; and other miscellaneous events, 1897–1920

K. Archives: Other Materials

Music envelopes, containing a catalogue of the music library of Johann Weber, 1834; clippings on music, 1915–26; Negro spirituals sung by Mrs. M. Chapman Byers, 1928; a historical sketch of the Philharmonic Society, 1937; and a sketch of Severin Robert Sauter by Frank Gecks, Jr., n.d.

Printed and ms music, including the ballad "Come All You Good People," in the ms "Farmer's Day Book" kept by Galvin (William Richardson), 1788–1801, in the Ulysses S. Grant papers; I. B. Palmer, copybook with song lyrics and melodies, 1814; cover illustration of Julius Tenzler's "Benton Barracks Parade March," ca. 1861; Ernest R. Kroeger, "Aubade" for piano, ca. 1900; and French folksongs, in a genealogy of the Coleman and allied families

Biographical materials, including P. G. Anton, Jr. (1865–1935), clipping and biographical notes; Mathilde C. Gecks, biographical sketch, in the Jennie Wahlert papers; and recollections about Henry Rauth (musician), in the Mrs. Robert Lanlands Michie papers, 1953–

Legal items, including pension papers for the widow of Francis Gecks (musician in the Mexican War); receipts of J. B. Sarpy and Charles Balmer, 1842–45; a deposition by P. G. Anton on a piano transaction with B. H. Sale, 1877; letters on Charles Pommer's invention of a keyboard swell device, 1819, in the William H. Pommer papers; and a check from Philip Gottlieb Anton (d. 1935) to Tony Faust & Sons of St. Louis, 1899

Other items, including lists of sheet music published by D. McCartie in New York, 1870, and of sheet music published by D. Crawford and Co., St. Louis, n.d.; Academy of Music *Journal*, Chicago, 1874–75; clippings on musical instruments repaired by Frank H. Wood of St. Louis, 1888; subscriptions for a memorial for Julia Dean, Ben DeBar, Noah Ludlow, and Charles Balmer in the St. Louis Historical Building, 1890, and a booklet concerning the memorial; Enrico Caruso, pen-and-ink self-caricature, 1919; address on musicians of Missouri, for the Missouri Centennial Celebration of the DAR, 1921, by Mrs. Alfred F. Smith; a history and program of the Civic Music League of St. Louis, 1963; and other 19th- and 20th-century ephemera, including tickets, announcements, and invitations to musical events

—Beverly Bishop

861
NATIONAL MUSEUM OF TRANSPORT
3015 Barrett Station Road
Saint Louis, Missouri 63122

Sheet music and songbooks relating to railroads, ca. 1900–1945

—John P. Roberts

862
SAINT LOUIS PUBLIC LIBRARY   MoS
1301 Olive Street
Saint Louis, Missouri 63101

Manuscript music, including compositions by Alfred Robyn, 9 songs in pencil; Charles S. Skilton, autograph of his cantata *The Witch's Daughter*, 1919; Victor Herbert, orchestral score fragment, donated by Edward Menges, 1946; and Lewis Slavit, ms sketches, 1941

Sheet music, 2500 items of popular and classical instrumental and vocal music, ca. 1850– , including 1000 St. Louis imprints, and 50 items of instrumental music by Paul Tietjens, donated by his sister, Mrs. Dammert; also 21 linear meters of vocal and instrumental collections and individually bound items, European and American imprints, late 19th and 20th centuries

Hymnals, 3 linear meters, mid 19th and 20th centuries, including 10 in German

Photograph of the St. Louis Symphony Orchestra, ca. 1900

Engraved plates for 2 songs with words by Ora Hill of St. Louis

Recordings by Ovide Musin, 6 discs issued by the Belgian Conservatory of Music in New York

Periodicals, including a complete run of *Godey's Lady Book*

Card indexes of St. Louis music, 12 cm., indexing a portion of the library's sheet music, organized by publisher, then by composer and title; music—songs, 12 cm., indexing music printed in *Godey's Lady Book*, ca. 1830–80s; and programs, 3 linear meters, indexing composers and compositions in programs of 19 American orchestras, among them the St. Louis Symphony and the St. Louis Philharmonic, ca. 1910–70

863
SAINT LOUIS UNIVERSITY   MoSU
Department of Music—Library
221 North Grand Boulevard
Saint Louis, Missouri 63103

Sheet music, 200 items, 1910–40, mostly popular songs; also, 100 popular songs of the mid 19th century, in 1 bound vol.

Published songbook of works performed by the Rainer family of Tyrolese singers, 1829

Hymnals of various denominations, 10 items, ca. 1890–1920

Other published music, including piano music by Louis M. Gottschalk and other American composers, 200 items

Solo vocal scores by Chadwick, Foote, and others, 200 items; also 15 scores by Frederick S. Converse, mostly of orchestral music, 1895–1930

—Rev. Francis J. Guentner

864
Trebor Jay TICHENOR

3801 Federer Place
Saint Louis, Missouri 63116

Ragtime music and related documents, predominantly sheet music (including almost the entire catalogue of music published by John Stark in Sedalia, St. Louis, and New York, 1893–1922) and piano rolls (including the Hubert S. Pruett collection), also publishers' catalogues, trade publications, disc recordings, clippings, photographs, and biographical information. The collection formed the basis for the book by Tichenor and David A. Jasen, *Rags and Ragtime, A Musical History* (New York, 1978)

865
UNIVERSITY OF MISSOURI—   MoU-St SAINT LOUIS

Western Historical Manuscript Collection
8001 Natural Bridge Road
Saint Louis, Missouri 63121

Jazz musicians on Mississippi riverboats, 15 interviews, recorded on tape and transcribed

—Irene E. Cortinovis

866
WASHINGTON UNIVERSITY   MoSW

Washington University Libraries
Saint Louis, Missouri 63130

Gaylord Music Library

Some items, as designated, come from the gift of Prof. Lincoln B. Spiess, or from miscellaneous other sources. The remainder represents the vast collection of library materials, research files, and ephemera assembled by Ernst C. Krohn (1888–1975), specialist in a wide range of American music topics, most notably in St. Louis music and music bibliography. See his *Missouri Music* (1924, reprinted New York 1975)

Sheet Music

Sheet music, 50,000 items, mostly the Krohn collection and including materials from the St. Louis Public Library. See Krohn's article, "On Classifying Sheet Music," M.L.A. *Notes,* 26 (1970), 473–78. Materials are arranged in 6 groups:

1) Special collection, 5000 items (in the librarian's office), including files of and on ragtime (60 items), St. Louis newspaper music supplements (123 items), early Balmer & Weber imprints (60 items), coon songs (90 items), Bromo-Selzer editions (36 items), Civil War music (150 items), lithograph portraits of women (180 items), and other engraved or lithographic title pages (300 items), also 36 bound vols. of

vocal and solo piano music, 6 of them for piano and of early St. Louis provenance, including 1 from Amanda Phillipson, dated 1833

2) Imprint collection, 6000 items subdivided as St. Louis imprints (1800 items, including 550 Balmer & Weber, 500 Kunkel, 350 Shattinger), pre-1875 non-copyright editions (2400 items, arranged by city of publication), and pre-1875 copyright editions (2000 items, arranged by decade)

3) General post-1880 collection, American items intermixed with some European editions, including topical files (2000 items, mostly organized either by title, composer, or subject), songs (5000 items, arranged by composer), piano music (8000 items, by composer), instrumental music (3700 items, grouped by medium and arranged by composer), other vocal music (1500 items, grouped by medium or topic), and a file with editions of the Art Publication Society of St. Louis, ca. 1930 (500 items)

4) Miscellaneous materials, 1000 items, unsorted

5) Materials of other than Krohn provenance, 8500 items, unsorted

6) Popular music, 4500 items, arranged by title

Other Music

Tunebooks and hymnals, 10 linear meters, 1803– , rich in Lowell Mason-period editions and St. Louis imprints, gospel songs, and children's hymnals, some of Spiess provenance; partly catalogued

Other printed music, including 250 vocal scores of operas, operettas, cantatas, and oratorios; 100 songs and song collections; and 50 solo, chamber, and orchestra items

Manuscript music, including extensive holdings of materials by P. G. Anton, Hubert Bauersachs, Carl August Kern, Ernest Richard Kroeger, Ernst Krohn, Sr., Ernst C. Krohn, Ottmar Moll, Anna May Loewenstein Nussbaum, and Paul Tietjens; single or several mss of E. M. Berry, Fred G. Bowles, E. Marie Cooper, G. Marshall Cragin, Francis Gaal, A. Goring-Thomas, Seth Greiner, Elliott Griffis, David Jacobs, Cedric Lamont, Irvin Mattick, Charles Mayhew, Max Meyer, Fred Miller, Paul Amadeus Pisk, Mrs. Q. B. Rohland (early resident of Alton, Ill.), Louis Victor Sarr, and T. Carl Whitmer; also music books and fragments presumably from early St. Louis, including 1 book for bugle, 1839, and 1 small oblong 4-part tunebook, ca. 1840

Papers

Research notes and personal papers of Ernst C. Krohn, comprising 200 notebooks of research notes, 50 1-inch-thick notebooks with teaching materials and 29 2-inch-thick notebooks with materials for his published writings, 14 scrapbooks, 20 shelf boxes, 4 four-drawer file cabinets, 4 notebooks and 4 shelf boxes of typescripts for a book on local music publishing, and several linear meters of miscellanea. The topics include the subjects of his published writings, extending into all aspects of the history of St. Louis music, and ranging to matters of piano pedagogy and music bibliography, also to such Americana topics as Gottschalk, Nelson Kneass, Alexander Reinagle, Bernhard Ziehn, *Sacred Harp* singing, and Beethoven in America. There is an autobiographical sketch entitled "A Tale of Two Cities." The extensive personal correspondence file includes all the questionnaires returned from composers in connection with the *Missouri Music* book. Among the card files are an index to 19th-century sheet-music engravers, artists, and lithographers (300 cards); incipits from 19th-century tunebooks (2000 cards); obituaries of St. Louis musicians, 1930–50 (1 box of clippings); and the catalogue of his personal library (125 catalogue trays)

Programs, 7 linear meters, strong in St. Louis Symphony, Bach Society, and other St. Louis materials, also in Sängerbund and Sängerfest items

Pictures, including 1 linear meter of clipped photographs of musical subjects; 1 linear meter of scrapbooks with personal photographs, and 2 other boxes of miscellaneous photographs; and 150 picture postcards, mostly on musical subjects

Scrapbooks, 14 vols. plus loose gatherings, on St. Louis musical activity; also clippings, mostly on St. Louis composers, arranged by subject

Olin Library

Hymnals, 3 with music, 1822–79, and 5 with words only, 1791–1871, some of them from the Arthur C. Hoskins Collection of St. Louis and Missouri materials (in Rare Books and Special Collections)

Babette Deutsch (1921–66, poet), personal papers, including music references (in Rare Books and Special Collections)

Arthur W. Proetz, papers, 1901–63, including press clippings, programs, scripts, announcements, and published music by him and others for Washington University concerts, the Quadrangle Club, and the Snooper's City Club, also 1 ms fraternity song (in the Archives)

Quadrangle Club (University student organization for writing and producing musical comedies), 15 linear cm. of papers, 1910–63, including press clippings, photographs, scripts, programs, posters, music scores, correspondence, interviews, and a ms history of the Club by Sid Wallach (in the Archives)

Programs of University organ recitals, complete run, 1914–42 (in the Archives)

Music Department administrative archives, from its founding in 1947, including financial papers, appointment papers, and other business papers (in the Archives)

—Elizabeth R. Krause

867
DENT COUNTY HISTORICAL SOCIETY

1210 Gertrude Street
Salem, Missouri 65560

Printed music, including 150 hymnals, ca. 1820–1940; 20 school songbooks, ca. 1920–40; and 75 popular or sacred sheet-music items, ca. 1910–30

Tape recording of a local man singing 2 ballads, ca. 1975

—Ken Fiebelman

868
STATE FAIR COMMUNITY COLLEGE

Library
1900 Clarendon Road
Sedalia, Missouri 65310

Materials on ragtime music in Sedalia, ca. 1894–1900, including Scott Joplin, *Treemonisha* (1911 first edition, published by Joplin), donated by Rudi Blesh; photocopy of the first contract between Joplin and his publisher, John Stark; oral-history tapes collected 1978, of 2 local persons who had heard Joplin perform; 7 other oral-history tapes, including 3 with Eubie Blake, 1974–75; papers, music, and photographs of other ragtime musicians, including "Blind" Boone, Euday L. Bowman, George Thomas "Tom" Ireland (including his scrapbook), Arthur Marshall, James Scott, Percy Wenrich, and Walter Williams; Maple Leaf Club and Wood's Opera House mementos; 15 pianola and player-piano rolls of ragtime and popular music; and popular sheet music

Manuscript books of popular songs, probably copied by L. Burger (music teacher) for Clarence Koenig, 3 items, ca. 1885

Published popular songbooks, 4 items, 1880s; also 1 cabinet-organ instruction book, 1899

Printing plates for "Minnie Polka" and "Southern Comfort," Perry Music Co., 1886 and 1899

Photographs, including local bands and camp meetings, 11 items, ca. 1880–1910

—Berniece Craig, Virginia Wickliffe

869
SOUTHWEST MISSOURI STATE UNIVERSITY

MoSpS

Library
Springfield, Missouri 65802

Missouri Music Educators' Association archives, ca. 1931– , 1.5 linear meters, including minutes, clippings, programs, contest results, and the official journal, *Missouri Music*

—L. G. Blakely

870
SPRINGFIELD–GREENE COUNTY LIBRARY

Box 737
Springfield, Missouri 65801

Max Hunter Folk Song Collection, 50 tape recordings of Ozark folksongs recorded by Hunter 1960s–70s, with typescript lyrics and indexes of singers and titles; also 15 file folders of Hunter's personal papers

—Kay Madden

871
Mark TWAIN BIRTHPLACE

Mark Twain State Park
Stoutsville, Missouri 65283

Clara Clemens Gabrilowitsch, memorabilia including letters, photographs, and other documents, 1924–60, largely on non-musical topics

---

In addition to the repositories listed above, the following have also reported holdings of the materials indicated:

Carrollton—Carrollton Public Library: songbooks
Centralia—Centralia Historical Society: sheet music, songbooks, programs
Charleston—Mississippi County Library District: sheet music
Conception—Conception Seminary College, Library: sheet music, songbooks, other printed music, programs, catalogues, pictures, recordings, miscellaneous
DeSoto—DeSoto Public Library: sheet music, songbooks
Fayette—Central Methodist College, George M. Smiley Memorial Library: sheet music, songbooks, programs, pictures, recordings
Glasgow—Glasgow Public Library: songbooks, recordings
Graham—Graham Historical Society: programs
Hannibal—Hannibal–Lagrange College, Library: songbooks
Hermann—Historic Hermann: songbooks, pictures
Kansas City—Rockhurst College, Greenlease Library: recordings
Lexington—Lexington Historical Association: programs, pictures
Liberty—Frank Hughes Memorial Library: sheet music, songbooks

Marshall—Rodney Polson: sheet music, other printed music, miscellaneous
Maryville—Northwest Missouri State University, Wells Library: sheet music, songbooks
Mt. Vernon—Lawrence County Historical Society: sheet music, songbooks, other printed music, recordings, miscellaneous
Point Lookout—School of the Ozarks, Ralph Foster Museum: sheet music, songbooks, pictures, recordings
St. Joseph—Missouri Western College, Learning Resources Center: sheet music, songbooks, other printed music, recordings
St. Joseph—St. Joseph Museum: programs, pictures, recordings
St. Louis—General Daniel Bissell House: sheet music, songbooks, pictures
St. Louis—Seminex Library (Concordia Seminary in Exile, Library): songbooks
St. Louis—Covenant Theological Seminary, Library: songbooks, recordings
St. Louis—Missouri Baptist College, Library: songbooks, pictures, recordings
St. Louis—Webster College: sheet music, miscellaneous
Salem—Salem Public Library: sheet music, songbooks
Springfield—Assemblies of God, Graduate School Library: songbooks
Springfield—Drury College, Walker Library: songbooks

Montana

872
MONTANA STATE UNIVERSITY   MtBC
Library, Special Collections
Bozeman, Montana 59715

Gene Quaw, oral-history interviews, 1964, concerning the annual Sweet Pea Carnivals, in which he was involved, 1913–17, also other carnivals, 1906–64, for many of which he contributed such songs as "The Sweet Pea Girl," "Under the Banner of the Red Cross Nurse," and Miss Montana Centennial songs. See the article, "Opera House, Quaw Family, Bywords in Talent Shows," *Bozeman Chronicle*, 9 August 1964, p. B2

—Minnie Paugh

873
GREAT FALLS PUBLIC LIBRARY   MtGr
Third Street and Second Avenue North
Great Falls, Montana 59401

Tuesday Music Club, scrapbooks, including programs, clippings, and notes of meetings, 1930– , 3.6 linear meters
Sheet music, 10 items, mostly classical, 1920s–40s

—Kay H. Courtnage

874
MONTANA HISTORICAL SOCIETY   MtHi
225 North Roberts Street
Helena, Montana 59601

Ed M. Brown (army trumpeter), diary written during military expeditions in Montana, 1876–77
Archie Bray, 30 linear cm. of programs, playbills, brochures, and pamphlets concerning musical and theatrical events, mostly in Helena, ca. 1920–50
John H. Ming, 30 linear cm. of papers, 1852–87, including correspondence, financial records, and miscellaneous items pertaining to his theater in Helena
Typescripts on Montana theater history, ca. 1865-1920, 3 items. See Firman H. Brown, Jr., *A History of Theater in Montana* (Ph.D. diss., University of Wisconsin, 1963)
Published music scores and sheet music, 40 items, mostly popular, 1897–1964, chiefly about Montana or composed by Montanans; also published songbooks of western U.S. or Montana songs

—Bob Clark

875
PARK COUNTY MUSEUM ASSOCIATION
118 West Chinook Street
Box 1272
Livingston, Montana 59047

Printed sacred music for choir, 15 items, ca. 1920–40, and 1 in German, 1888; also 5 hymnals of various denominations, 1920–40, and 1 school songbook, 1891

Sheet music, 55 items, 1900–1920, mostly popular songs, including "On the Prairie" (1914) by Mark Fox (local composer)

Programs of local music groups, including Park County Pioneer programs, 1940–75

Photographs, 12 items of local bands and church choirs, ca. 1900–1950

Recordings of popular music, 100 78-rpm discs, 1920s–30s

—Doris Whithorn

876
Joseph MUSSULMAN
2318·Forty-third Street
Missoula, Montana 59812

William F. Apthorp (1848–1913, Boston music critic), published writings; also research files relating to a biographical study of Apthorp

877
VIRGINIA CITY–MADISON COUNTY HISTORICAL MUSEUM
Box 235
Virginia City, Montana 59755

Photographs of bands, mostly fraternal organizations, 10 items, 1890s; also several recordings

—J. H. Vanderbeck

In addition to the repositories listed above, the following have also reported holdings of the materials indicated:

Baker—O'Fallon Historical Society: sheet music
Cascade—Wedsworth Memorial Library: songbooks
Circle—Pioneer Historical Circle: sheet music
Crow Agency—Custer Battlefield Historical and Museum Association: songbooks, pictures, recordings
Dillon—Beaverhead County Museum: sheet music
Havre—Northern Montana College, Library: songbooks
Livingston—William and Doris Whithorn: recordings
Richey—Richey Historical Society: sheet music, songbooks, recordings
Sidney—Mondak Historical and Arts Society: songbooks, pictures

Nebraska

878
WASHINGTON COUNTY HISTORICAL ASSOCIATION
Fourteenth and Monroe South
Fort Calhoun, Nebraska 68023

Manuscript school song, n.d.
Published piano books and opera and operetta scores, 5 items
Hymnals and school songbooks, 25 items, ca. 1900–1940, including some in German or Danish
Popular vocal sheet music, 600 items, ca. 1910–40
Programs of local musical events and of traveling musicians in the Omaha area, 20 items, 1877–1978, and 30 in scrapbooks, ca. 1880–1940
Photographs, mostly of local bands, 25 items, 1888–1940

—Genevieve Slader

879
DOUGLAS COUNTY HISTORICAL SOCIETY
General Crook House
Thirtieth and Fort Streets
Fort Omaha, Nebraska 68111

Martin Bush (founder of and professor at the School of Music, University of Omaha), 4 scrapbooks of programs and clippings on music at the University of Omaha and in the Omaha area, ca. 1890–1940, also a printed oral-history study of him, 1960

Mozart Male Quartet, scrapbook of clippings, letters, programs, and 1 ms music composition, 1894–96

Hymnals and songbooks, 20 items, ca. 1890–1940

Popular sheet music, including songs about Omaha or Nebraska, 200 items, ca. 1890–1940

Programs of Tuesday Musicale concerts and other musical events in the Omaha area, 60 linear cm., ca. 1900–1940

Photograph album of a local church choir, ca. 1915

—Mary Jo Guinan

880
DODGE COUNTY HISTORICAL SOCIETY
Box 766
Fremont, Nebraska 68025

Otto Pohl (local composer), 3 items of printed sheet music for piano, ca. 1900–1910

Other published music, including 8 linear cm. of parts for dance orchestra, 1920–40; 15 hymnals of various denominations, ca. 1900–1920, some in German; 5 psalm books, ca. 1850; 5 popular songbooks; and 1 linear meter of sheet music, ca. 1870–1920, mostly popular works for piano

—Loell Jorgensen

881

NORTH PLATTE VALLEY HISTORICAL ASSOCIATION

Eleventh and J Streets
Box 495
Gering, Nebraska 69341

Estelle Laughlin, scrapbook, ca. 1930–60, containing music programs and other materials of the Golden Age Club
Hymnals of various denominations, 7 items, ca. 1930–40
Popular sheet music, 12 items, ca. 1910–40
—Jan Spencer, Charles H. Scott

882

ADAMS COUNTY HISTORICAL SOCIETY

Box 102
Hastings, Nebraska 68901

Matthew H. Shoemaker Collection, 1922–69, 2.7 linear meters of scrapbooks with clippings and programs, mostly of local high schools, Hastings College, and the Hastings Civic Symphony
Kerr Opera House, scrapbook, 1900–1901
Photographs of local music groups, 50 items, ca. 1870–
—Tom Isern

883

PHELPS COUNTY HISTORICAL SOCIETY

512 East Avenue
Holdrege, Nebraska 68949

Ole Vikoren (local composer and band director), 8 published marches for piano, ca. 1900–1915, 1 program of a band concert directed by him, ca. 1910, and 1 photograph of him, ca. 1910
—Don Lindgren

884

AMERICAN OLD TIME FIDDLERS ASSOCIATION

Fiddling Archive
6141 Morrill Avenue
Lincoln, Nebraska 68507

Material pertaining to fiddling in the U.S. and other nations, 20 linear meters, ca. 1800– , including personal correspondence of J. E. Mainer and other fiddlers, press releases of fiddle concerts by DeLores "Fiddling De" DeRyke (ca. 1929–) and others, photographs of fiddlers, ms music including original works and items copied on postcards (ca. 1920–), printed music for concerts and dances (ca. 1800–), and recordings of fiddle performances on discs and tapes (ca. 1920)
—DeLores DeRyke

885

LINCOLN CITY LIBRARIES   NbL

Bennett Martin Public Library
Fourteenth and N Streets
Lincoln, Nebraska 68503

Polley Music Reference Library

Carl-Frederic Steckelberg (violinist) and Ouida Steckelberg (pianist), 30 linear cm. of papers, ca. 1900–1940, including his ms studies for violin, programs of their concerts and of other organizations such as the Lincoln Symphony Orchestra and Lincoln high schools; also violin scores and orchestra parts and scores from his library, 8.5 linear meters, ca. 1900–1930
Sheet music for voice or piano, 3 linear meters, including items donated by Lillian Helms Polley, ca. 1900–1940
Popular songbooks and choral-music collections, 60 linear cm., ca. 1890–1940
Hymnals, 1 linear meter, ca. 1900–1940
Published music for piano, organ, orchestral instruments, or voice, 30 linear meters, ca. 1900–1940, from the libraries of various Lincoln-area performers

Heritage Room

Jim Fras, "Beautiful Nebraskaland," ms sheet music, n.d.
Programs of traveling music group in Lincoln, 2 items, 1920

—Kay Stenton

886

NEBRASKA CONFERENCE UNITED METHODIST HISTORICAL CENTER

Lucas Building
Fiftieth and Saint Paul Streets
Lincoln, Nebraska 68504

Hymnals and gospel songbooks, 600 items, 1800–
—C. Edwin Murphy

887

NEBRASKA STATE HISTORICAL   NbHi
SOCIETY

1500 R Street
Lincoln, Nebraska 68508

Materials are housed in various divisions of the Society, and in its branch museums throughout the state

Flora Bullock (1871–1962, Lincoln educator), 35 linear cm. of papers, 1913–62, including 15 linear cm. of her ms music
Alice Christine (Towne) DeWeese, papers, including 15 linear cm. of published popular songs in sheet music or songbooks, 1920s–30s
Gregory Family papers, 10 linear cm. of published music, including a GAR songbook and temperance songbooks, and sheet music containing patriotic and inspirational songs, ca. 1870–1900
Hazel Gertrude Kinscella (1893–1960, music educator), 30 linear cm. of papers, 1920–60, including her published original or arranged works, and materials concerning her piano-pedagogy correspondence course (1918) and the "Kinscella method" for teaching piano in the public schools
LaFlesche Family papers, 50 linear cm., 1859–1939, including correspondence and notes pertaining to

Charles W. Cadman's opera *Da-O-Ma,* based on an Omaha Indian legend, with a libretto by Francis LaFlesche and Nelle Richmond Eberhart; also clippings and programs relating to Cadman's performances and lectures on Indian music

Annie Louise Miller (1860–1945, Lincoln journalist), 25 linear cm. of music materials, with programs of Lincoln theatrical and performing-arts events, 1890s–1930s, and clippings regarding musical events in Lincoln, 1920s

Louise Pound (1872–1958, folklorist), 20 linear cm. of music-related materials, including folksong texts, mss for her articles on folksongs, and a bibliography of folksongs, ca. 1890–1958

Carl Frederick Steckelberg (1877–1960, teacher and violin-maker), 30 linear cm. of papers, 1900–1961, including correspondence, lecture notes, programs, clippings, a ms violin study course, and a prepared patent for a structural change in the violin, 1954

Lines West Band for the Burlington Railroad, 50 linear cm. of papers, 1928–67, including administrative correspondence, financial records and scrapbooks of programs and clippings (1929–52)

Lincoln Symphony Orchestra Association, 80 linear cm. of papers, 1926– , including programs and clippings relating to the Association

Nebraska Theater Programs collection, 70 linear cm., 1876–1966, including programs of Creighton and Farnam Street theaters, the Grand and Boyd's opera houses, the Orpheum, and other Omaha performances; the City Auditoriuum, New Stuart and Oliver theaters, Funkes Opera House, and other Lincoln performances; and various programs from other Nebraska communities

Songbooks and hymnals, 275 items, 1840–1940

Sheet music, 1150 items, mostly popular, 1854–1940

Catalogues and directories of Lyon and Healy, the National Music Association, and the Columbia Concerto Corp., 8 items, 1884–1941

—Anne P. Diffendal

888
UNIVERSITY OF NEBRASKA NbU
Lincoln, Nebraska 68588

Special Collections Department, Don L. Love Memorial Library

Excepting the hymnals and sacred songbooks, all materials are located in the University Archives in the Special Collections Department

Popular Music of the 1930s and 1940s Collection, mostly "swing" music, a collection of 80 78-rpm disc recordings, donated by Mrs. Willard M. Folsom

Theatre Programs Collection, ca. 1902–40, 5 scrapbooks and 20 linear cm. of programs and miscellaneous musical materials, mostly from theaters in New York, Los Angeles, Kansas City, Chicago, and Stamford, Conn.

Benjamin A. Botkin Collection of materials on folk music, jazz, and music of the 1930s, including 7 linear meters of disc recordings, 200 tape recordings of music and oral history, ms and printed scores, programs, and miscellaneous folk materials

University School of Music materials, 1 linear meter, ca. 1870–1940, including catalogues, announcements,

and a complete run of programs 1880– ; also 4 college songbooks, some of them from the University

Paul Stoeving (1868–1948, string teacher), 1 linear meter of materials related to music, including 11 ms compositions, mostly for violin or orchestra

Hymnals and popular songbooks, 20 items, ca. 1800–1920

—Joseph Svoboda, Susan Messerli

School of Music

Hymnals and sacred songbooks, ca. 1850–1950, 120 items received from the Cotner College of Religion, Lincoln, including some in German and some shapenote tunebooks

Sheet music, 500 vocal and 600 instrumental items

Recordings including 18 linear meters of 78-rpm discs, ca. 1890–1940

—Raymond Haggh

889
Janice CLEARY
412 North Elmwood Road
Omaha, Nebraska 68132

Popular sheet music for voice or piano, 10,000 items, ca. 1840–1940, including items from the collection of Harry Dichter; catalogued

890
OMAHA PUBLIC LIBRARY NbO
Special Collections Department
215 South Fifteenth Street
Omaha, Nebraska 68102

Programs of the Omaha Symphony Orchestra and of 5 Omaha theaters, in 44 bound vols., ca. 1870–1920; also programs, clippings, and other miscellaneous material on Omaha music, in 44 envelopes, ca. 1920–

Byron Reed (Omaha businessman), collection of 1029 autographs, including some of musicians (*NUCMC*, 62-3729)

—Tom Heenan

891
Elaine MILLER
Box 216
Orchard, Nebraska 68764

Hymnals, 15 items, ca. 1900– , mostly Methodist

Printed piano music, including instruction books, 30 linear cm., ca. 1900–

Popular sheet music for voice, 2000 items ca. 1900–

892
CASS COUNTY HISTORICAL SOCIETY
644 Main Street
Plattsmouth, Nebraska 68048

Liederkranz, (local organization), papers including a songbook, record book, and photographs, ca. 1860–1915

Hymnals, 15 items, ca. 1860–1940

—Alice Pollock Perry

893

Willa CATHER (NbRcW)
HISTORICAL CENTER
Nebraska State Historical Society
338 North Webster Street
Red Cloud, Nebraska 68970

Willa Cather, personal papers, including correspondence, 200 items, ca. 1890–1947, some containing references to music; programs of concerts in the Red Cloud Opera House, 5 items, ca. 1890; photographs of musicians associated with Cather, 15 items, ca. 1900–1940; and 20 cylinder recordings, ca. 1890–1910
Sheet music, 40 items, ca. 1900–1950, mostly classical, related to Cather's interests in music

—Ann Billesbach

894

Lloyd KUNKEL
202–204 West H Street
Weeping Water, Nebraska 68463

Personal collection relating to violin-making, including 8 press clippings, correspondence, and 4 violins made by Kunkel, ca. 1920
Manuscript fiddle music written in Denmark, brought to the U.S. and performed by Louie Anderson, 4 books, 1875
Weeping Water Little Symphony Orchestra, 2 photographs and 1 78-rpm disc recording, 1933
Weeping Water Municipal Band, 10 programs, 1932–40, and 2 photographs
Published theater music for an orchestra conducted by Kunkel, 25 conductor's scores with parts, ca. 1920
Hymnals, 2 items, ca. 1850–70
Sheet music, 25 vocal items, ca. 1885–1920, and 1 march for piano
Catalogues of musical instrument manufacturers, 4 items, ca. 1920–40

895

DVORACEK MEMORIAL LIBRARY NbWi
419 West Third Street
Wilber, Nebraska 68465

Printed music for band or piano, 9 linear meters, ca. 1920–40, mostly polkas and waltzes, by Czechs or their descendants

Hymnals of various denominations, 20 items, ca. 1920–40, including 2 in Czech
School songbooks, 10 items, ca. 1915, and popular songbooks, 10 items, ca. 1920–40, including several in Czech
Popular sheet music for voice, 15 linear cm., ca. 1900–1930

—Marjorie Kobes

In addition to the repositories listed above, the following have also reported holdings of the materials indicated:

Aurora—Hamilton County Historical Society: sheet music, songbooks, other printed music, programs, pictures, recordings, miscellaneous
Bancroft—Bancroft Public Library: songbooks
Burwell—Garfield County Historical Society; songbooks, pictures
Creighton—Creighton Public Library; songbooks
Gothenburg—Cozad Historical Society: songbooks, pictures, miscellaneous
Grand Island—Stuhr Museum of the Prairie Pioneer: sheet music, songbooks, other printed music, programs, pictures, recordings
Hay Springs—Sheridan County Historical Society: sheet music, songbooks
Howells—Howells Public Library: picture
Hyannis—Opal Bilstein: sheet music, songbooks
Hyannis—Grant County Historical Society: programs, pictures, recordings
Lincoln—Nebraska Library Commission: songbooks, other printed music, miscellaneous
Lincoln—Nebraska Wesleyan University, Cochrane–Woods Library: sheet music, songbooks, other printed music, programs, recordings
Loup City—Loup City Township Library: sheet music, songbooks
Norfolk—Norfolk Public Library: pictures
North Platte—Lincoln County Historical Society, Western Heritage Center: sheet music, songbooks, recordings
Omaha—College of St. Mary, Library: songbooks, recordings
Omaha—Jewish Federation of Omaha, Library: sheet music, songbooks, recordings
Omaha—University of Nebraska at Omaha: sheet music, songbooks, other printed music, pictures, recordings, miscellaneous
Red Cloud—Webster County Historical Society: sheet music, other printed music, recordings
York—York Public Library: sheet music, songbooks

Nevada

896

NEVADA HISTORICAL SOCIETY NvHi
1650 North Virginia Street
Reno, Nevada 89503

See the *Guide to the Manuscript Collections* (Reno, 1975; hereinafter cited as *Guide*)

Personal papers of G. Bruce Blair (*Guide,* 202), Wilhelm da Costa (*Guide,* 503), Margaret Lane (*Guide,* 1160), and Mrs. V. Vrooman (*Guide,* 2278)
Richard "Dickie" Jose (1869–1940, singer), 1 tape recording, 2 78-rpm discs, and photographs; also programs in scrapbooks of various individuals
Emma Wixom (pseud. Emma Nevada, 1859–1940,

singer), photographs and programs in scrapbooks of various individuals

Bertha Purdy, 2 tape-recorded songs about the pioneers, composed and performed by her, n.d. (*Guide*, 1747)

Nevada Musical Club, papers, including correspondence, 35 items, 1922–24 (*Guide*, 1504)

Stanford Club, papers, 1922, 4 items, including the Stanford University alumni song (*Guide*, 2079)

Nevada WPA, papers, 1935–40, 31 boxes of mss and typescripts, including materials on music (*Guide*, 2250)

Published orchestral, operatic, vocal, choral, and solo instrumental music, 400 items, ca. 1870–1940

Hymnals, 40 items, ca. 1860–1900

Popular and school songbooks, 80 items, ca. 1859–1930

Sheet music, 350 items, ca. 1875–1955, mostly popular vocal, some by Nevada composers Herman W. Albert (b. 1882), John P. Meder (1848?–1908), and Alrick G. Spencer; the autographed state song, "Home: Means Nevada" (1935), by Bertha Eaton Raffetto (1885–1952); and Kenneth Crouch's essay "The State Song of Nevada," and biographical notes on Bertha Raffetto (*Guide*, 485)

Programs of local and touring music groups, 150 items, ca. 1870–1930, mostly in scrapbooks of individuals

Photographs of Nevada musicians and groups, 50 items, ca. 1870–1930

Recordings, including 20 78-rpm discs and tapes

—Guy Louis Rocha

In addition to the repository listed above, the following have also reported holdings of the materials indicated:

Carson City—Nevada State Library: sheet music, songbooks

Carson City—Nevada State Museum: sheet music, songbooks, pictures, miscellaneous

Elko—Northeastern Nevada Society and Museum: sheet music, songbooks, pictures, recordings

Henderson—Southern Nevada Museum: recordings

Las Vegas—University of Nevada, Library: printed music, recordings

Reno—University of Nevada, Nobel H. Getchell Library: sheet music, songbooks

New Hampshire

897

SHAKER VILLAGE
Shaker Road
Canterbury, New Hampshire 03224

Manuscript songbooks containing hymns by Shakers, 40 items, late 1800s, including items by Dorothy Durgin (d. 1898)

Sheet music, 30 sacred titles, 1850–90

Sacred songbook, ca. 1908, 200 copies

Photographs of Shaker sisters singing, 2 items, early 1920s

—J. E. Auchmoody

898

NEW HAMPSHIRE HISTORICAL SOCIETY   NhHi
30 Park Street
Concord, New Hampshire 03301

Sheet music, 500 items, 1800–1920, including some printed for the Hutchinson and Baker family singers

Tunebooks, 33 late 18th- and early 19th-century vols. as cited by Louis Pichierri, *Music in New Hampshire, 1623–1800* (New York, 1960), pp. 279–81

Hymnals and songbooks, 100 19th-century items used in New Hampshire

Manuscript music, including Caleb Chase, copybook for fiddle, ca. 1800; Richard Kent, copybook for woodwind instrument, 1825; and Third New Hampshire Volunteer Infantry, 21 band books in ms used at

Port Royal, S.C., during the Civil War (other vols. are at the Library of Congress and the New Hampshire Antiquarian Society, Hopkinton)

Abraham Prescott (bass-viol manufacturer), account books, 1810–40

Musical instruments, 15 woodwinds, horns, violins, or melodeons made in New Hampshire 1820–1900, including some by Abraham Prescott

Concord Musical Society, minute books, 1799–1865

Campton Sacred Music Society, records, 1816–52

Programs for 19th-century concerts in New Hampshire, 500 items

Photographs of New Hampshire musicians, 50 late 19th-century items scattered in different collections

—Bill Copeley

899

NEW HAMPSHIRE STATE LIBRARY   Nh
20 Park Street
Concord, New Hampshire 03301

Amy Cheney (Mrs. H. H. A.) Beach, 33 sheet-music items, 19 autograph letters, 2 photographs, and 1 recording of her piano quintet

Hymnals, 100 items, 1782–1932

Music periodicals, including *Moore's Musical Record*, 1868–70; *New York Musical Pioneer and Chorister's Budget*, 1855–56; and *World of Music*, 1843–45

—Stella Scheckter

900
UNIVERSITY OF NEW HAMPSHIRE   NhU
Durham, New Hampshire 03824

Amy Cheney (Mrs. H. H. A.) Beach Collection, containing 10 ms and 75 published compositions, photographs, personal correspondence including letters from musicians and writers, and miscellanea

Robert Manton (1894–1967, University Music Department founder and faculty member), papers, including his ms and published compositions; also his collection of correspondence and 8 ms and 18 published compositions and sketches by Edward A. MacDowell

Musical celebrity recordings collection, tapes of 400 cylinders and vertical-cut discs of 200 performers, 1920–25

—Reina Hart

901
EXETER BRASS BAND
c/o Mr. Robert Curran
15 Cass Street
Exeter, New Hampshire 03833

Materials are located in the Town Office Building, Front Street, Exeter, New Hampshire 03833

Sheet music for band, 10 linear meters, 1847– , and other printed music, including 4 sets of march books, 1847–

Manuscript music for band, including 2 marches by Larry Wiley (d. 1976), and a ms copy of "Haverhill Commandry March," ca. 1920

Ledgers and record books, 10 vols., 1847– ; programs for band concerts, 12 items, 1940s; and photographs of band members, 25 items, 1847–

902
EXETER HISTORICAL SOCIETY
27 Front Street
Exeter, New Hampshire 03833

Tunebooks, 3 editions of the *Village Harmony* (Exeter, 1797, 1819, and 1821); also 2 19th-century songbooks

Programs of concerts given at the Town Hall, Exeter, 1860–70, 35 items

—Mrs. David D. Merrill

903
PHILLIPS EXETER ACADEMY   NhExP
Library
Exeter, New Hampshire 03833

Music published in Exeter, 1799–1850, 23 sacred and instrumental editions, in the collection of Exeter imprints

—William W. Chase

904
GOODWIN LIBRARY
Farmington, New Hampshire 03835

The papers of a musical association, 1866–70, as cited in *HRS*, p. 17, have not been located

905
William L. WARREN
Fitzwilliam, New Hampshire 03447

Samuel C. Jackson, of Stratford, Conn., 2 ms letters with musical notations, to Israel Godrich of Litchfield, Conn., 1810–1819

906
GOFFSTOWN HISTORICAL SOCIETY
14A Main Street
Goffstown, New Hampshire 03045

Printed music, including 2 sheet-music items by local composers, 1868 and 1909; 12 hymnals and sacred songbooks, 1814–98, some of them published in Montpelier, Vt., Haverhill, Mass., and Port Hope, N.C.; and 2 songbooks, 1847 and 1874

Programs of local concerts, a minstrel show, and recitals, 1905–24, 4 items

Photographs of Stark's Cornet Band, 2 items, 1875

—Mary Carroll Hillis

907
DARTMOUTH COLLEGE LIBRARY   NhD
Hanover, New Hampshire 03755

Material is in Special Collections, unless otherwise noted. See *A Brief Guide to the Principal Collections of the Rare Books Department* (Hanover, 1964; hereinafter cited as *Guide*), also the issues of the Dartmouth College Library *Bulletin* (1931– ; hereinafter cited as *DCLB*)

Music ms copybook, ca. 1790, with single-line tunes for reels, jigs, country dances, and other dances; also John and James Richard, 2 ms music copybooks, ca. 1796 and post-1800, with psalms, hymns, and anthems

James G. Huneker (1857–1921), personal papers, including literary mss, notebooks, photographs, and memorabilia; correspondence with Walter Damrosch, Enrico Caruso, Leopold Godowsky, Mary Garden, Yvette Guilbert, Victor Herbert, and others; 3 cases of press clippings by and about Huneker; and 175 vols. from his library (*Guide*, pp. 21–22)

Genevieve Taggard (1894–1948), personal papers, including 6 music scores set to her texts, by Henry Leland Clarke, Aaron Copland, Ruth Culbert, William Schuman, and others; also 23 concert programs. See *DCLB*, 4/6 (1947), 87–91

Werner Janssen, personal papers, 60 linear cm., including correspondence, ms and printed music (band arrangements in particular), programs, and scrapbooks

Burrill collection of sheet music, 12,000 items, ca. 1790–1960, also 1200 orchestrations of popular music, 1886–

1930s, mostly used by Bert Nash's Band. See Roger H. Burrill, "The Dartmouth Collection of American Popular Songs," *DCLB*, n.s., 14 (1974), 73–76; also his "For Me and My Gal: You Can Tell the Times from the Music," *Dartmouth Alumni Magazine*, 68 (Oct. 1976), 32–37

Other sheet music, including 8000 single items now combined with the Burrill collection and arranged chronologically by decade up to 1890, thereafter by year, with annual indexes through 1929, and a special subject index for important topics (i.e., Irish songs, coon songs) and lithographer; a comprehensive index is now in preparation. Also 22 bound vols. of 19th-century sheet music, mostly U.S. imprints, in the general library stacks

Sheet music relating to New Hampshire, in the White Mountains Collection, 132 items. See *DCLB*, n.s., 13 (1973), 124

Hutchinson Family, sheet music, 1843–92, 141 imprints of 91 different works; 1 box of clippings and notices, 1850s; family obituaries, and information on recent research concerning the family; and a second file devoted to correspondence regarding Hutchinson research

Baker Family, 1 box of sheet music, 1845–66, 59 imprints of 35 different works; also a separate file devoted to recent correspondence

Tunebooks and instrumental instructors, 35 items, late 18th and early 19th centuries; also 50 19th-century hymnals and tunebooks in the general library stacks

Isaiah Thomas (1749–1831), 470 vols. from his presses and bookstores, presented by Thomas in 1819, including many tunebooks. See *The Isaiah Thomas Donation* (Hanover, 1949); also the *Guide*, pp. 38–39

Dartmouth College Winter Carnivals and junior prom shows, ms and printed music, 26 items, 1903–30

Handel Society of Dartmouth College, 2 boxes of archives, 1807–1926; programs, 1922–29; 35 19th-century tunebooks; and 5 boxes of photographs, correspondence, and press clippings

New Hampshire Philharmonic Society, programs, 1889 and 1895–96

Prokofieff Society, ca. 1940– , 2 boxes of music, correspondence, membership lists, photographs, minutes, and press clippings

Kenneth Roberts (1885–1957), scrapbook of army songs, as cited in *NUCMC*, 65-1854

Abnaki (American Indian) music, 60 tape recordings "of more than 25 contemporary Indians conversing, singing, and narrating tribal legends." See *DCLB*, n.s., 5 (1962), 41–43

—Dale Cockrell, Kenneth Cramer

908
FULLER PUBLIC LIBRARY
Hillsboro, New Hampshire 03244

Amy Cheney (Mrs. H. H. A.) Beach (1867–1944), 1 ms notebook, 2 bound vols. of piano-solo and piano-vocal music, 1891, 5 sheet-music items for piano, ca. 1892, 2 scrapbooks containing clippings about her career, and 2 notebooks of minutes of the Beach Club (music group founded by her), 1920s–30s

—Rita Morgan

909
NEW HAMPSHIRE ANTIQUARIAN SOCIETY   NhHopA
Main Street
Hopkinton, New Hampshire 03301

Third New Hampshire Volunteer Infantry, 20 ms band books used at Port Royal, S.C., during the Civil War (other vols. are at the Library of Congress and at the New Hampshire Historical Society, Concord, q.v.)
Songbooks, 67 items, also several songsters, 1722–1893
Catalogues of music publishers, 58 items

—Rachael H. Johnson

910
Sylvia BOARDMAN
16 West Elm Street
Littleton, New Hampshire 03561

Howard Brockway (1870–1951, pianist, and father of Mrs. Boardman), materials including his Berlin diaries, 1891–96, also photographs and correspondence

911
LITTLETON AREA HISTORICAL SOCIETY
4 Merrill Street
Littleton, New Hampshire 03561

Frances A. J. Hancock (local composer), sheet-music song, "Old Man of the Mountain" (Littleton, 1936)
Littleton Opera House, 50 programs, 1900–
Music Lovers' Club, papers, in 10 scrapbooks compiled by Mrs. Ethel Wright, 1920s–30s

—Mary E. Heald

912
INSTITUTE OF ARTS AND SCIENCE
148 Concord Street
Manchester, New Hampshire 03104

Materials used at the Institute, 1898– , 3 linear meters, including sheet music, teaching materials, and choral songbooks, some in ms

—Angelo Randazzo

913
MANCHESTER CITY LIBRARY   NhM
405 Pine Street
Manchester, New Hampshire 03104

New Hampshire Collection

Manuscript music by New Hampshire composers, 1880–1929, including Mabel Claire Lewis, C. W. Hardy, Harland Bradford, Walter H. Lewis, Carl Goldmark, and Rudolph Schifler; also Alonzo ("Zo") Elliott, 5 ms songs, 9 published items, and 10 cm. of papers, letters, and press clippings, early 20th century

Other printed music, including works by Amy Cheney (Mrs. H. H. A.) Beach, Maurice Hoffman, Mabel Claire Lewis, C. W. Hardy, and Ida Mae Grombie, 1880–1929

Programs of New Hampshire concerts, late 1890s–1970, 700 items

Clippings concerning music and musicians in New Hampshire, 1 linear cm., 1920–78

Music and Art Collection

Sheet music, 7000 popular and classical items, 19th and 20th centuries

Hymnals and songbooks, 3.5 linear meters, 19th and 20th centuries

—Phyllis Endicott, Ann W. Frank

914
MANCHESTER HISTORIC ASSOCIATION

129 Amherst Street
Manchester, New Hampshire 03104

Sheet music, 18,000 popular and classical items, 1850–1920

Other printed music, including 35 music newsletters with songs and biographical notes, some published in Manchester, 1850–1900

Walter Dignam (1828–92, leader of the Manchester Cornet Band), ms copies of band music, 1 linear meter, 1850s, also a scrapbook of programs for the Band, and a photograph of the Harmonic Orchestra led by him, 1870s

Manchester Cornet Band, 94 sets of ms band music, 1850s, and portraits of individual band members with their cornets

William McAllister (music educator and church musician), 1 linear meter of papers, 1920–79

First Congregational Society of Manchester (church-music group led by E. T. Baldwin), papers, 60 linear cm., 1870s–1900

Manchester Institute of Arts and Sciences (music school organized by Rudolph Schiller), 60 linear cm. of papers, 1914–40

Harrison Collection, materials gathered by Peleg Harrison for his study, "The Stars and Stripes" (1906)

Recordings, including a 78-rpm disc by Roger Barrett (local organist), ca. 1930

—Elizabeth Lessard

915
WADLEIGH MEMORIAL LIBRARY

Nashua Street
Milford, New Hampshire 03055

Hutchinson Family Singers, scrapbook of pictures, playbills, and press clippings, partly contemporary

—Anna Kjoss

916
Mary Hoffman MacNAUGHT

Four Winds Road
Box 72
Peterborough, New Hampshire 03458

May Fiske (the "Scotch Nightingale," niece of "Jubilee" Jim Fiske and mother of Mary Hoffman MacNaught, actress and opera singer, and founder of a traveling company), personal papers, including 250 popular songs, ca. 1900–1918; letters from early 20th-century music critics; photographs of opera and theater productions, including those of Augustin Daly; 100 Chickering piano rolls, 1926–40, used by her as a Chickering concert mistress under her married name, May Fiske Hoffman; programs and clippings of the Weymouth (Mass.) Choral Society and the Massachusetts Federation of Music Clubs while she was president of the groups, 1920s–30s; invitations to the 1908 opening of the Boston Opera House (Miss Fiske was an original stockholder); and posters of the Stage Women War Relief program, including pictures of May Fiske, Lotta Crabtree, and Elsie Janis

Lowell Mason tunebooks, 2 items, 1850s

Oliver Ditson music catalogues, pre-1922

Programs of local music groups and of the Mariarden School of Drama, including 1 of Paul Robeson's first concert, 1922

Photographs of the Handel & Haydn Society in Boston; of the singer Vai Buell; and of the Josephine Durrell String Quartet, fl. 1915–40

917
PETERBOROUGH   NhPHi
HISTORICAL SOCIETY

Box 58
Peterborough, New Hampshire 03458

Henry Ware Dunbar (1822–92, blind amateur violinist), materials including a ms book of popular songs, mostly words only; 1 ms hymn written for the Peterborough Centennial, 1839; and a large folio of published song texts; also biographical information on the blind Dunbar brothers, James Munroe, Henry Ware, and Quincy Adams Dunbar, who performed as singers

Hymnals, several 19th-century items used locally

—Elizabeth C. Greenie

918
PETERBOROUGH TOWN LIBRARY

Main and Concord Streets
Peterborough, New Hampshire 03458

Edward A. MacDowell (1861–1908), 7 music mss, 23 linear cm. of sheet music, ca. 1898, and 10 early sheet-music items published under his pseudonym, Edgar Thorn

Stephen Collins Foster, 5 sheet-music items, 1854–64

Songbooks and hymnals, 3 items, 1832, 1835, and n.d.

Dance cards used in Peterborough, ca. 1910, 30 items

National Federation of Musical Clubs, Eleventh Annual Convention Program, Peterborough, 1919

—Ann Geisel

919
STRATTON LIBRARY

West Swanzey, New Hampshire 03469

George William Stratton (1830-1901, music publisher), 1 linear meter of music published or composed by him, including sections from his opera *The Buccaneer*, 1858

—Sandra Allen

In addition to the repositories listed above, the following have also reported holdings of the materials indicated:

Canterbury—Canterbury Historical Society: sheet music, songbooks, programs, pictures
Fitzwilliam—Fitzwilliam Historical Society: sheet music, songbooks
Hinsdale—Hinsdale Historical Society: songbooks
Keene—Keene State College, Wallace E. Mason Library: songbooks, other printed music

Kingston—Kingston Improvement and Historical Society: sheet music, songbooks, programs
New Hampton—Gordon–Nash Library: sheet music, songbooks
Plymouth—Plymouth State College, Lamson Library: songbooks, other printed music, recordings
Portsmouth—Portsmouth Athenaeum: sheet music
Raymond—Dudley–Tucker Public Library: songbooks
Rochester—Rochester Public Library: sheet music, songbooks, pictures, recordings
Salem—Salem Historical Society: recordings
Walpole—Bridge Memorial Library: songbooks

New Jersey

920
CAMDEN COUNTY   NjCaHi
HISTORICAL SOCIETY
Park Boulevard and Euclid Avenue
Camden, New Jersey 08103

Sheet music, 49 World War I songs and 27 early 20th-century songs, also 19 items composed or published locally
James Clayton Warhurst (Camden organist and choirmaster), 5 compositions, 1911–14
Popular songbooks, 3 early 20th-century items
Camden County Musical Society, minutes, programs, and other papers, 1920s, 9 linear cm.
Recordings, including 200 RCA Victor 78-rpm discs; also 5 RCA Victor catalogues and 10 photographs of RCA Victor performers, late 1920s

—Miriam Favorite

921
CLINTON HISTORICAL MUSEUM VILLAGE
56 Main Street
Box 5005
Clinton, New Jersey 08809

Published music, including 2 items for violin or piano, ca. 1874–1900; 10 songbooks, ca. 1883–1930; 3 hymnals, ca. 1873–1881; and sheet music, ca. 1880–1940
Programs of the Clinton Glee Club and the Blue Moon Orchestra, 2 items, ca. 1900–1940; also a book of New York theater programs, ca. 1910–50
Photographs of the Clinton Band and Clinton Minstrel Group, 7 items, ca. 1900–1940, and autographed photographs of theatrical stars, ca. 1900
Recordings, including 4 Edison cylinders, 30 Edison discs, and other 78-rpm discs

—Claire Young

922
COLLINGSWOOD FREE   NjCo
PUBLIC LIBRARY
Haddon and Frazer Avenues
Collingswood, New Jersey 08108

C. Austin Miles (organist at the First Methodist Church, Collingswood), 3 ms hymns, ca. 1910–40
Philadelphia Orchestra, 3 scrapbooks of clippings and concert schedules, ca. 1930s, and other programs, compiled by Hilda Radey (secretary to Eugene Ormandy)
Programs of local church concerts, 1910–40, 25 items
RCA Victor talking-machine catalogues, 5 items, 1900–1915, and a jigsaw puzzle forming a phonograph record with names of famous Victor recording artists

—Peter D. Childs

923
COLLEGE OF SAINT ELIZABETH   NjConC
Convent Station, New Jersey 07961

A. Louis Scarmolin (1890–1969, musician), papers, including printed and ms scores, letters, and memorabilia given by his widow to the College. See Helen Bermel, "Catalogue of the Scarmolin Collection at the College of Saint Elizabeth" (typescript, 1976)
Sheet music, 120 popular-music items, 1890–1920, mostly New York and Boston imprints
Other printed music, including sacred works by music-faculty members, 3 items, 1909–14, and banjo music, 1880s
Programs for New York musical comedies, 1920s–30s, 66 items

—Sister Marie Rousek

924
Paul KIERNEY
271 Old Bridge Turnpike
East Brunswick, New Jersey 08816

Recordings, including 3000 78-rpm discs, 1925–35, and 50 cylinders, mostly of popular, jazz, ethnic, and hillbilly music

925

UPSALA COLLEGE LIBRARY NjEoU

Prospect Street
East Orange, New Jersey 07019

Personal papers of Percy Aldridge Grainger, formerly in
the Library, are now in the Grainger Museum, Melbourne, Australia, q.v.

926

HUNTERDON COUNTY NjFlHi
HISTORICAL SOCIETY

114 Main Street
Flemington, New Jersey 08822

Materials relating to the Flemington Choir School,
1895–1958, organized by Elizabeth Van Fleet Vosseller
and Bessie Richardson Hopewell, including personal
papers of Miss Vosseller (1874–1939), a ms history of
the school, ca. 1937, children's choral music, programs from operas and school concerts, clippings,
financial papers, and an album of photographs of
children's performances

—Kathleen Schreiner

927

Frank MARE

2153 Center Avenue, Apt. 22
Fort Lee, New Jersey 07024

Recordings, including 5500 78-rpm discs of American
country music and rural blues

928

Albert F. ROBINSON

12 Kings Highway East
Haddonfield, New Jersey 08033

Published 19th-century American organ music, also
hymnals, including Canadian imprints
Research materials assembled and used in connection
with *The Tracker*, quarterly newsletter of the Organ
Historical Society

929

HOPEWELL MUSEUM NjHopM

28 East Broad Street
Hopewell, New Jersey 08525

Zacharias Stout (d. 1809), ms notebook of sacred songs
Hymnals, also school and popular songbooks, 10 items,
1793–1931
Published collections of organ, piano, and band music,
4 items, ca. 1856–73
Sheet music, mostly popular, 2 bound vols. and 20
separate items, ca. 1845–1931
Programs of local events, including those in Boggs
Seminary and Columbia Hall, ca. 1865–1940

—Beverly Weidl

930

LAWRENCEVILLE SCHOOL

John Dixon Library
Box 6128
Lawrenceville, New Jersey 08648

Robert Thiele (founder and owner of the Flying Dutchman Record Co., New York), collection of disc
recordings, primarily jazz and popular music, ca.
1930– , and several published books

—Marilyn Lutz

931

Margaret Hazelton (Mrs. Henry A.) BOORSE

338 Summit Avenue
Leonia, New Jersey 07605

Sir Carl Busch, papers, including 4 music mss, published cantatas, correspondence, notes, photographs,
clippings, and memorabilia, from the collection of
Maude V. Pepper (Mrs. John Morton Hazelton)

932

Robert C. HEATH

1828 Shore Road
Linwood, New Jersey 08221

Sheet music, 500 popular and classical items, 1860–
Manuscript music, ca. 30 items of popular, classical,
and sacred music, written by friends for Mr. Heath,
1900–1930
Recordings, including 200 78-rpm discs, 2 Edison cylinders, and 5 Edison discs

933

DREW UNIVERSITY NjMD-T

Library
Madison, New Jersey 07940

Creamer Hymnology Collection, 3000 hymnals and
tunebooks, particularly strong in Methodist, camp-meeting, and revival hymnody, late 18th and 19th
centuries, deposited at the University in 1869
Methodist Hymnology Collection, 500 20th-century
hymnals and tunebooks, updating the Creamer
collection
Frank Mason North (1850–1935, hymn writer), 1 file
drawer of papers and memorabilia

—Kenneth E. Rowe

934

MADISON TOWNSHIP NjMatHi
HISTORICAL SOCIETY

Route 1, Box 150
Matawan, New Jersey 07747

Sheet music, 600 items of popular piano and piano-vocal music, 1840 and 1890–1920
Other published music, including 16 vols. of organ
music, 1932–62, 5 hymnals, 1872–1920, and 2 songbooks, 1910 and 1947

Recordings, including 265 Edison cylinders with 1 Edison phonograph catalogue, 1911, and 60 78-rpm discs

—Alvia Martin

935

MORRISTOWN NATIONAL HISTORICAL PARK MUSEUM

NjMoHP

Morristown, New Jersey 07960

"A Carol for Christmas Day" and 5 other 3-voice works, in 17 ms pages, at the end of Tax Book A, County Collector Business, 1789, of J. Lewis (presumably Joseph Lewis, quartermaster in the Continental Army during Washington's encampment in Morristown)
Oliver Holden, *Sacred Dirges* (Boston, 1800)

—Margery Stomne Selden

936

Llewellyn WATTS

290 Morris Avenue
Mountain Lakes, New Jersey 07046

Gustav Hinrichs (1850–1942, conductor and composer, father of Mrs. Watts), papers, including 2 opera mss, letters from Edward A. MacDowell, and photographs

937

JOHNSTON HISTORICAL MUSEUM

Route 130
New Brunswick, New Jersey 08902

Music materials relating to the Boy Scouts of America, including 25 songbooks, 4 sheet-music items, 10 other music items, and 30 recordings

—Joan Delle Cave

938

NEW BRUNSWICK THEOLOGICAL SEMINARY

NjNbS

Sage Library
17 Seminary Place
New Brunswick, New Jersey 08901

Hymnals of various denominations, 300 items, 1613–
Archives of the Reformed Church in America, including all Reformed Church hymnals, 1767–1955, hymnals of various foreign missions of the Reformed Church, and a collection of Dutch and English psalters

—D. L. Englehardt

939

RUTGERS—THE STATE UNIVERSITY

NjR

New Brunswick, New Jersey 08901

Special Collections Department, Alexander Library

See H. F. Smith, *Guide to the Manuscript Collection of Rutgers University Library* (New Brunswick, 1964); Donald

A. Sinclair, *A Guide to Manuscripts Diaries and Journals in the Special Collections Department* (New Brunswick, 1979); and Oral S. Coad, "Songs America Used to Sing," Rutgers University Library *Journal*, 31 (1968), 33–45

Julia Colt Butler, diary mentioning concerts in Paterson, N.J., and music lessons in France, 1889–90
Abraham Harrison (d. 1851), music collected while he attended or taught at Princeton University
Emily L. Jarnagin, diary (in photocopy) of a visit with friends and relatives in the Cherokee Nation, 1850, mentioning music
Gerard Rutgers (1778–1848), papers, including sheet music of Catherine Rutgers, ca. 1840
Franz S. M. Schneeweiss (1831–88, music teacher), papers, 1849–72, also a diary of his sister (a singer). See F. Gunther Eyck, "Franz Schneeweiss: A '48er in New Brunswick," Rutgers University Library *Journal*, 19 (1955/56), 37–48
Jessie May Wendover, of Newark and Metuchen, diary, 1881–1953, mentioning music lessons
Jacob H. Ziegler (farmer of Lancaster County, Pa.), diary (in photocopy) mentioning organ music and singing, 1877
New Brunswick Band, 1 vol. and 1 folder of minutes, accounts, and letters, 1813–28
New Brunswick Musical Society (formerly the City Amateurs), minutes and constitution, 1830–32, and a tunebook attributed to Capt. John Holden (instructor of the Amateurs)
Vincentown Band, papers, 1 vol., including membership records, a constitution, an account ledger, and by-laws, 1829–30
Westwood Musical Club, scrapbook of clippings, programs, and ms records of the group compiled by William H. Hogg, 1910–17
Sheet music, 5000 items pre-1865, including songs, marches, dances, and sacred music, 400 song sheets, and 200 New Jersey imprints; also 4000 broadsides, 1620– , many of them serving as concert programs or containing musical materials
Hymnals, tunebooks, songbooks, and vocal method books, late 18th and 19th centuries
American music periodicals, 8 titles, 1835–52
Pamphlets relating to New Jersey and music, 1 box of 20th-century items

University Archives

Rutgers University Glee Club, 1 vol. of accounts and a list of engagements compiled by Jasper S. Hogan, 1889–91
Programs of University concerts, 400 items, 1866–

—Donald A. Sinclair, Charles A. Beck, Jr.

Douglass Library

Musical materials, including 50 mss, 200 sheet-music items, 30 songbooks, and 50 other items of published music

—Carleton Sprague Smith

American Studies Program, Douglass College

New Jersey Folklore Archive, including tape recordings of music presented at New Jersey Folk Festivals, ca.

1975– , and student term-papers and field tapes concerning folk music, largely of the New Jersey area and the Pine Barrens, indexed by subject

—Angus K. Gillespie

940
NEW JERSEY HISTORICAL SOCIETY   NjHi
230 Broadway
Newark, New Jersey 07104

See the *Guide to the Manuscript Collections of the New Jersey Historical Society* (forthcoming)

Sheet music, 15 items of early 20th-century popular music; also "They Shall Beat Their Swords into Plow-Shares," an anthem written by Mark Andrews (Montclair organist) and dedicated to William B. Dickson (1865–1942), industrialist
Hymnals, 12 items, 1800–1825
Manuscript transcriptions of dance music, 1800–1850, 14 items
Method books for piano and flute, 3 vols., ca. 1803
Stuart C. Smith Collection, including 2 subscription lists for military-band units, 1825–27
Joseph A. Fuerstman (Newark concert manager), correspondence and press clippings, 1920–21 and 1936–38, 1 linear meter
Idabelle Haughey Kress (soprano), journal of her European voyage and singing tour, 1881–83
Richard Bingham Davis (1771–99), ms "Book of Verse," ca. 1790–97, many of the poems set to music
William Robert Crawford (church organist), papers 1879–1931, 61 items
Sarah J. Churchill (New Jersey music teacher), 5-vol. diary, 1890–94
John H. Rothery (songwriter), papers, 1923–30, 30 linear cm.
New Jersey Music Collection, 8 music mss, ca. 1811–1930, including compilations of popular songs, dances, and marches by Sarah F. Cory (n.d.), Crowell Wilkinson (1811–30), and Sarah Cruser (1823)
Newark Handel and Haydn Society, 2 vols. of papers, 1831–40
Newark Sacred Music Association, record book, 1850–53
The Orpheus (Newark vocal music society), record book, 1868–72
New Jersey Militia, brigade record book, 1776–78, containing lyrics for "A Song of the Times"

—Don C. Skemer

941
NEWARK PUBLIC LIBRARY   NjN
5 Washington Street
Newark, New Jersey 07101

Sheet music, 2000 popular-music items, early 20th century
Songbooks, 200 vols. of 20th-century popular music
Edward O. Schaaf (1869–1939, New Jersey doctor and composer), 61 music mss for piano, military band, mixed voices, cello, or opera
John Tasker Howard (1890–1964), 1500 items of papers,

including clippings, biographical notes, and correspondence concerning his book *Our American Music* (New York, 1931)
Other ms materials, including 500 autographed New Jersey literary and musical letters and documents, 1880–1950
Programs of New Jersey concerts, 250 items, 1900–
Photographs of musicians and music ensembles, 400 items, 1880–1950

—Joan Burns, William J. Dane

942
RUTGERS UNIVERSITY   (NjR)
Newark, New Jersey 07102

Institute of Jazz Studies, an archival collection of jazz and jazz-related materials, comprising 50,000 recordings including piano rolls, cylinders, 78-rpm and LP discs, and tapes; sheet music and collections of jazz and popular music; solo transcriptions; arrangements by Muggsy Spanier (cornetist); 3000 books and numerous periodicals on jazz and popular music; vertical-file materials on musicians and topics, including clippings, letters, photographs, and promotional materials; original ledgers for some recording companies, and catalogues and discographies of record labels and artists. See *A Computerized Catalog of the Recorded Sound Collection of the Rutgers Institute of Jazz Studies*, register and indexes on microfiche (Newark, 1980–), compiled by Marie Griffin et al.
John Dale Owen, jazz recordings, 12,000 items, 1917–50s, including 7000 10-inch 78-rpm discs, 1300 "V-discs," 1100 transcriptions of radio broadcasts of jazz, and albums and other materials; on deposit from the University of Wisconsin, Milwaukee

—Dan Morgenstern

943
David WHITNEY
80 Hillside Avenue
Newark, New Jersey 07108

"Pealing Chord" collection of sacred music, verse, and dance books, 6000 items, including 4000 items of 28 pages or more, 500 items of 9 to 27 pages, and 1500 items of 1 to 8 pages, mostly 1775– , with an emphasis on metrical verse in English

944
PASSAIC COUNTY   NjPatPHi
HISTORICAL SOCIETY
Lambert Castle
Valley Road
Paterson, New Jersey 07503

John Goetchius Zabriskie (1869–1931, organist of St. Paul's Church, also active with the Paterson Opera House), personal papers, in storage in a trunk (ca. 2 linear meters), including mss of his compositions, mostly operettas and sacred choral music

—Helen D. Hamilton

945

PATERSON MUSEUM

268 Summer Street
Paterson, New Jersey 07501

Popular songbooks, 2 items, ca. 1890
Popular songs printed on silk ribbons in Paterson, ca. 1870–1940, 4 items
Programs of minstrel shows in Paterson, ca. 1936–37, 4 items
Phonographs, 6 items, 1886–1913, with 10 photographs and advertisements for Edison phonographs
Recordings, including 62 cylinders and 40 Edison discs

—John A. Herbst

946

SEVENTH DAY BAPTIST   NjPlaSDB HISTORICAL SOCIETY

Seventh Day Baptist Building
510 Watchung Avenue
Plainfield, New Jersey 07060

Julius Friedrich Sachse (1842–1919), music mss, including 8 vols. with material from the Ephrata community, containing works of Johann Conrad Beissel and others, as cited in *Hamer*, *NUCMC*, and elsewhere

947

HISTORICAL SOCIETY   NjPHi OF PRINCETON

158 Nassau Street
Princeton, New Jersey 08540

Thomas Lord, holograph music book of marches and waltzes, 12 pages, dated Ipswich, Mass., 1818
Herbert McAneny, "Some Notes on Princeton Amusements, Civil War to 1887," typed paper, for the Historical Society of Princeton, 1942
Dr. James Wikoff (physician) and family, 1 box of papers, 1887–1914, including invitations and programs of musical events at Princeton University
C. R. Arnheiter, 2 letters to (Louise?) Zapf, 1887–88, concerning music lessons and teaching
Farr's Band, 1 vol. of minutes, 1892–95
Princeton Athletic Club Band, 1 vol. of papers, including by-laws, membership lists, concert schedules, and receipts, 1918–31
Princeton Municipal Band, 1 vol. of minutes, 1920–38

—Joseph Felcone

948

PRINCETON THEOLOGICAL   NjPT SEMINARY

Robert E. Speer Library
Princeton, New Jersey 08540

Louis F. Benson (1855–1930) Collection of Hymnology, including 5000 vols. of religious music, many of them with U.S. imprints. Although the strength of the Reformed and Presbyterian works reflects a special interest of Benson, the collection also includes many gospel, Sunday-school, and children's music books. Among the several mss are a copy of Johannes Kelpius, *Die klägliche Stimme der verborgenen Liebe*, with an imprint note, "Pennsylvanien in America, 1705"; Caspar Weiss's Schwenckfelder text, entitled *Buch der christlichen Gesenge*, including Georg Weiss's "Gesenge auff alle erklert Evangelion," in a ms dated 1740; and 1 vol. of Ephrata Cloister hymn tunes. Particular titles are accessible through a separate dictionary catalogue, adjacent to the Library's main card catalogue. Benson's own author catalogue is kept with the collection. See Kenneth Gapp, "The Theological Seminary Library, " Princeton University Library *Chronicle*, 15 (1964), esp. pp. 10–11

—Barbara J. MacHaffie

949

PRINCETON UNIVERSITY   NjP

Princeton, New Jersey 08540

Music Collection

Sheet music, 60 bound vols., mostly U.S. imprints, pre-1860, with a separate dictionary catalogue

—Paula Morgan

Western Americana Collection

Mormon hymnals, 100 items, 1870s– , a nearly comprehensive collection

—Alfred Bush

Theatre Collection

Robert B. Sour Collection of Music of the Theatre, 308 vols. of piano-vocal scores and bound sheet music, collected by Sour (BMI music executive) and Milton K. Breslauer. See the Princeton University Library *Chronicle*, 23 (1971), 134
Sheet music, including the Louis E. Tilden Collection, 30 bound vols., 1920s–30s; Edward H. White Collection, 4 boxes, 1916–54; and 7000 other items
Tams–Witmark Collection, in 215 cartons, ca. 1895–1915, including vocal and full scores, vocal and instrumental parts, stage managers' guides, promptbooks, dialogue parts, and other musical materials
Fred D. Valva Collection, comprising 139 boxes of scores for silent-film accompaniments
Triangle Club, 50 linear meters of archival material, 1888– ; also recordings of musical-comedy productions on 270 cassette tapes
Arthur L. Friedman Collection, 57 scrapbooks of playbills, 1894–1973, including 2416 opera productions

—Mary Ann Jensen

Manuscripts Collection

See the Princeton University Library *Chronicle*, 18 (1967), 123

George Antheil (1900–1959), autograph score, Pleyela player-piano rolls, program materials for the first performance of the *Ballet mécanique* (1926), and photographs including a portrait by Man Ray (1924), from the collection of Sylvia Beach
Paul Hindemith, unpublished sonata for solo viola, written April 1937 on a train trip from New York to

Chicago, according to a letter from W. Oliver Strunk, to whom the composer presented the ms

Roger Sessions, autograph scores, 10 boxes, including his eight symphonies, *Montezuma*, and chamber-music works

Igor Stravinsky, *Requiem Canticles*, mss bound in 1 vol.

—Jean Preston

950
SCHEIDE LIBRARY (NjP)

Princeton University Library
Princeton, New Jersey 08544

See the Grolier Club exhibition catalogue, *Selections from the Library of William H. Scheide* (New York, 1967), pp. 7–11

Famous songs in holograph fair copies, including John Howard Payne, "Home, Sweet Home"; Samuel Francis Smith, "My Country, 'Tis of Thee" and "The Morning Light Is Breaking"; Ray Palmer, "Jesus, These Eyes Have Never Seen"; S. Fillmore Bennett, "Sweet By-and-By"; S. Dryden Phelps, "Savior, Thy Dying Love"; Robert Lowry, "Shall We Gather at the River?"; Phillips Brooks, "O Little Town of Bethlehem"; Jeremiah Eames Rankin, "God Be with You till We Meet Again"; Edward S. Ufford, "Throw out the Life Line"; Edgar Page Stites, "I've Reached the Land of Corn and Wine"; and R. H. McDaniel, "Come Ye Who Are Weary of Sin and Oppressed"

Several published books of and about music, 1767–1867

—Mina R. Bryan

951
WESTMINSTER CHOIR COLLEGE

Talbott Library
Princeton, New Jersey 08540

Choral music, sample octavo file, 20,000 titles in 16 file drawers

Choral music, formerly of the Tams–Witmark music rental library in New York, 300 published works, some with orchestrations but with few full conductor's scores, including works by Amy Cheney (Mrs. H. H. A.) Beach (3 items), Dudley Buck (11 items), George W. Chadwick (4 items), Arthur Foote (4 items), Henry Hadley (4 items), H. H. Huss (2 items), Ethelbert Nevin (1 item), and John Knowles Paine (1 item)

Sacred choral music, chiefly late 19th-century published anthems by American composers, including Dudley Buck and William H. Neidlinger, collected and donated by H. Earle Johnson

Leopold Stokowski collection of 200 miniature and full scores, donated mid 1950s. Six are presentation copies from composers to Stokowski, and some are marked by Stokowski for his use, including 3 vols. of J. S. Bach's organ works with notes about their orchestration. The collection also includes letters from Ralph Vaughan Williams and Darius Milhaud

Westminster Choir, Dayton, Ohio, programs and tour books, 1920s

—John G. Peck, Jr.

952
Evelyn N. OLSON

320 Gordon Street
Roselle, New Jersey 07203

Sheet music, 242 popular and religious items, 1870–

Other printed music, including choral and instrumental solos and duos, 344 items, 1846–

Recordings, including 81 78-rpm discs and 3 one-sided discs

953
TRENTON FREE PUBLIC LIBRARY NjT

120 Academy Street
Trenton, New Jersey 08608

Sheet music, 9000 items, mostly popular vocal works, 1920s–30s (in the Music Library)

Local music programs, 1921– , including those of the Trenton Symphony Orchestra (in the Trenton History Collection)

—James Kisthardt, Richard Reeves

954
EDISON NATIONAL HISTORIC SITE

Main Street and Lakeside Avenue
West Orange, New Jersey 07052

Thomas A. Edison (1847–1931), personal papers, including annual files for the "Phonograph Division," containing correspondence and contracts with musical performers

Business papers, including release sheets for cylinder and disc recordings, 1913–29, in 6 file drawers; also cash books, 1906–29, documenting payments to performers

Catalogues of Edison cylinder and disc recordings, 25 items, 1907–29

Periodicals, a complete run of the various Edison house publications, 1890s–1929, which include extensive information on Edison Co. music performers; also scattered holdings of other American and European journals devoted to recordings and sound equipment

Recordings, including complete holdings of the 2000 cylinders and 7000 discs released by the Edison Co.; also tapes of unreleased cylinder and disc recordings

Sheet music, 2000 popular songs, 1850s–1920s, mostly ca. 1890–1910, catalogued by title

Photographs of Edison Co. music performers, in 1 folder

—Arthur R. Abel, Leah Burt

955
GLOUCESTER COUNTY NjWdHi
HISTORICAL SOCIETY

17 Hunter Street
Woodbury, New Jersey 08096

Sheet music, 3 bound vols. for piano, 1833–50, and 12 early 20th-century popular items

Civil War song sheets, 6 items with words only

Andrew Law, *The Art of Singing in Three Parts . . . Musical Primer* (Cambridge, Mass., 1803)

James Bellak, method book for organ (Boston, 1876)
Method books for piano, 4 items, 1859 and 1910

—Edith Hoelle

956

WYCKOFF PUBLIC LIBRARY   NjWy
200 Woodland
Wyckoff, New Jersey 07481

A. Louis Scarmolin (1890–1969), 1 folder of materials with biographical information and 7 items of published music

—Louise H. Nelson

In addition to the repositories listed above, the following have also reported holdings of the materials indicated:

Barnegat—Barnegat Historical Society: sheet music, songbooks

Beach Haven—Long Beach Island Historical Association: sheet music

Blairstown—Blair Academy, Clinton Hall Museum: miscellaneous

Bloomfield—Bloomfield College, Library: sheet music, songbooks, other printed music, recordings

Bloomingdale—Bloomingdale Public Library: printed music

Bordentown—Bordentown Historical Society: sheet music

Califon—Califon Historical Society: programs

Cape May Court House—Cape May County Historical and Genealogical Society: sheet music, songbooks

Cedar Grove—Cedar Grove Public Library: sheet music, programs

Cinnaminson—Temple Sinai, Library: songbooks

Chatham—Chatham Historical Society: programs, pictures

Cranford—Union College, A. Johnson Memorial Library: songbooks, recordings

Delanco—Delanco Public Library: songbooks, recordings

Elizabeth—Elizabeth Public Library: sheet music, songbooks, recordings

Elmwood Park—Elmwood Park Public Library: songbooks

Essex Fells—Northeastern Bible College, Library: songbooks, recordings

Glen Ridge—Glen Ridge Congregational Church, Library: sheet music, songbooks, other printed music

Hackettstown—Centenary College, Taylor Memorial Library: programs

Haddon Heights—Haddon Heights Public Library: songbooks, recordings

Long Valley—Washington Township Historical Society: songbooks

Lyndhurst—Lyndhurst Free Public Library: sheet music, songbooks

Mahwah—Mahwah Historical Society: programs

Mahwah—Ramapo College of New Jersey, Library: recordings

Manasquan—Manasquan Public Library: songbooks, recordings

Maplewood—Margery Stomne Selden: songbooks

Moorestown—Historical Society of Moorestown: recordings

Morristown—Morris County Historical Society: sheet music, songbooks, other printed music

Neptune—Township of Neptune Historical Society: songbooks

Norwood—Norwood Public Library: songbooks, recordings

Ocean City—Ocean City Historical Museum: sheet music, songbooks

Park Ridge—Pascack Historical Society: songbooks, recordings

Passaic—Passaic Public Library, Julius Forstmann Memorial: songbooks

Piscataway—Piscataway Township Free Public Library: songbooks

Plainfield—Historical Society of Plainfield and North Plainfield: sheet music, other printed music

Plainfield—Plainfield Public Library: sheet music

Ramsey—Ramsey Historical Association: sheet music, songbooks, recordings

Roselle—Roselle Free Public Library: songbooks, programs

Roselle—Roselle Historical Society: recordings

Springfield—Springfield Historical Society: songbooks

South Amboy—South Amboy Historical Society: sheet music, songbooks, other printed music, pictures, recordings, miscellaneous

Summit—Summit Historical Society: programs, recordings

Trenton—New Jersey State Museum: sheet music, recordings

Union—Union Township Historical Society: songbooks

Upper Saddle River—Upper Saddle River Public Library: recordings

Ventnor City—Olga Licks: miscellaneous

Vincentown—Southampton Historical Society: sheet music

New Mexico

957

UNIVERSITY OF NEW MEXICO   NmU
Albuquerque, New Mexico 87131

Fine Arts Library

Eunice Lea Kettering (organist and composer), 4 linear meters of her complete ms and published composi-

tions, including chamber music, vocal and instrumental solos, choral anthems, cantatas, oratorios, and operettas

John Donald Robb (lawyer and composer), 6 linear meters of his complete ms compositions, including symphonies, concertos, operas, and electronic-music works, 1936–

New Mexico Symphony Orchestra (and its predecessors, the Albuquerque Symphony Orchestra and the Albuquerque Civic Symphony), papers, 1932– , 3 linear meters, including a complete run of bound programs, business correspondence, scrapbooks of clippings, and photographs

Bruce T. Ellis, collection of popular vocal sheet music, 800 items, ca. 1850–80, including William Billings's *Singing Master's Assistant* (1778) (in the Rare Book Room)

William H. Rohm, collection of hymnals, 25 items, ca. 1830–1900

Popular, school, and community songbooks, 25 items, ca. 1880–1910

Manuel Areu Collection of zarzuelas, performed in New Mexico and Arizona, ca. 1850–1920, ms and printed scores, lyrics, and dramatic prose for 200 titles

Other printed music, including 733 editions of string music, with ms indications of variant bowings, from the library of Charles Gigante

Archive of southwestern music, an on-going project with 3000 hours of recordings and several video tapes of Indian, Spanish, Anglo, Black, and Mexican cultures in the Southwest, including the John Donald Robb collection of 3900 recordings. See Ned Sublett, *A Discography of Hispanic Music in the Fine Arts Library of the University of New Mexico* (Albuquerque, 1973)

—James B. Wright

University Library, Special Collections Department

Thomas N. Pearce (folklorist), collection of New Mexico folklore, including 1 shelf meter of tape recordings, and a notebook of Spanish-American folksongs, 1938–66

—Don Farren

958
Peter WHITE

Department of English
University of New Mexico
Albuquerque, New Mexico 87131

Fiddle music, collected on 20 cassette recordings in New Mexico, ca. 1977– , including contests and 25 fiddlers

959
SAN JUAN COUNTY MUSEUM ASSOCIATION

Route 3, Box 169
Farmington, New Mexico 87401

Music box with metal disc recordings, purchased with funds raised by Katharine Hepburn (at age 11) for purposes of bringing music to the American Indians

960
NEW MEXICO STATE UNIVERSITY   NmLcU

Archives—University Library
Box 3475
Las Cruces, New Mexico 88003

Manuscript music, "The Rail-Road Cars Are Coming," ca. 1890

Elizabeth Garrett, 7 sheet-music items, 1916–21

Materials from University musical events, 50 linear cm., 1934– , including programs, playbills, and photographs; also a taped oral-history interview with Carl Jacobs (band director)

—Austin Hoover

961
HIGHLANDS UNIVERSITY   NmLvH

Music Department
Las Vegas, New Mexico 87701

Clarence Loomis (1889–1965), 300 ms compositions, also published copies and ms sketches, including teaching materials; and 150 popular sheet-music items, ca. 1900

—James Mark

962
MUSEUM OF INTERNATIONAL   (NmSM)
FOLK ART

Museum of New Mexico
Box 2078
Santa Fe, New Mexico 87501

Isidor Berger, 5 ms copies of instrumental or vocal music, including a New Mexico Pueblo cradle song, ca. 1916–18

Songbooks, 50 items of popular and folk music, including 2 Spanish-language hymnals published in El Paso, Tex.

Other published music, 50 items, including 20th-century *alabados* (hymns), and photocopies of masses

Recordings, including 25 78-rpm discs; music of Spanish-speaking people of the Southwest, including folksongs, *alabados*, and other sacred music, 93 tape reels collected by John D. Robb, 1939–63, duplicating his collection at the University of New Mexico, Albuquerque (q.v.), and 20 discs of field recordings by Juan D. Rael, 1940s; also music of Spanish folk plays, collected by Richard Stack, 1960s

—Judith Sellars

963
STATE RECORDS CENTER AND ARCHIVES

Historical Services Division
404 Montezuma
Santa Fe, New Mexico 87501

Dorothy Woodward, papers pertaining to New Mexico folk music, 1940s

WPA Writers' Project files, ca. 1933–40, 15 items concerning New Mexico folk music, and 25 programs of New Mexico musical events

Recordings of the state song, in English and in Spanish

—Myra Ellen Jenkins

964

WHEELWRIGHT MUSEUM OF THE AMERICAN INDIAN

704 Camino Lejo
Santa Fe, New Mexico 87501

Washington Matthews, 200 cylinder recordings, also research notes and other materials collected in the 1890s, relating to the Navajo and other American Indian ceremonial music

Mary Cabot Wheelwright, cylinder recordings of Navajo and Pueblo ceremonies, collected in the 1920s and 1930s, now on tapes

American Indian music tapes, 215 items from the Music Project

—Catherine Hewitt

In addition to the repositories listed above, the following have also reported holdings of the materials indicated:

Abiquiu—United Presbyterian Board, Christian Education, Ghost Ranch Conference Library: programs

Albuquerque—Menaul Historical Library: songbooks

Albuquerque—University of Albuquerque, St. Joseph's Library: recordings

Las Vegas—Las Vegas Carnegie Public Library: recordings (oral-history tapes)

Las Vegas—Rough Rider and City Museum: sheet music

Los Alamos—Los Alamos County Historical Museum and Society: programs, pictures

Portales—Roosevelt County Museum: recordings, miscellaneous

Roswell—Chaves County Historical Society: sheet music

Sante Fe—New Mexico State Library: sheet music, songbooks

Silver City—Western New Mexico University, Museum: sheet music, songbooks, programs, pictures, recordings

Truth or Consequences—Sierra County Historical Society: songbooks

New York

Entries for the boroughs of New York City are listed under New York in the following order: (1) New York (Manhattan); (2) Bronx; (3) Brooklyn; (4) Queens; and (5) Staten Island

965

JERICHO HISTORICAL SOCIETY

169 Main Street
Afton, New York 13730

Town Band, archives, including music performed by the Band with an inventory, and 10 photographs of the Band, its floats, and the bandstand, 1930s

—Charles J. Decker

966

ALBANY INSTITUTE OF HISTORY AND ART   NAll

125 Washington Avenue
Albany, New York 12210

Sheet music, 50 mid 19th-century popular and classical items published in Albany

Sacred songbooks, 25 19th-century items, scattered in various family collections

Songsters, 3 items published in Albany, 1828–52

Programs from the Albany Theater Collection, 60 linear cm., including 19th-century musical events

—Christine M. Ward

967

NEW YORK STATE LIBRARY   N

31 Washington Avenue
Albany, New York 12224

Sheet music, 20,000 popular-music items, late 18th to early 20th centuries; also 44 Confederate broadside ballads, as cited in *Rudolph*

Hymnals, secular songbooks, anthems, and other published choral music; also sacred and secular music mss, mostly early 19th century, including 9 Shaker hymnals, as cited in *Cook*, pp. 291–92

George Washington Doane (fl. 1824, hymn writer), personal papers, including correspondence and poems

Other materials, including theater programs and ephemera, mostly in the Severance Collection concerning Albany, ca. 1900–1930, 24 linear meters

—James Corsaro

968

NEW YORK STATE MUSEUM

Empire State Plaza
Albany, New York 12230

Sheet music, 1250 popular and classical items, 1840–1960, including Albany imprints

Cappelano's Band of Albany, account book, photographs, instruments, and uniforms, 1900–1925

Pictures, including a pen-and-ink sketch of Enrico Caruso by Arturo Toscanini

Herbert Sachs Hirsch collection, 4 scrapbooks of programs and playbills for New York City concerts and musical-theater productions, 1907–60

Programs for New York city concerts, 1900–1940, 100 items

Recordings, including 100 cylinders, 800 78-rpm discs, and 400 piano or organ rolls, mostly popular music; also 8 Edison cylinder phonographs, an autophone made in Ithaca, N.Y., and 2 early jukeboxes, ca. 1935

—John L. Scherer

969

Barrett G. POTTER

SUNY Technical College
Alfred, New York 14802

Sheet music, 300 items, 1900–1940s, mostly 1910s–20s; also hymnals and popular song collections; 100 78-rpm recordings, 1920s–40s; 75 books and periodicals; and other materials relating to the history of jazz and popular music

970

STATE UNIVERSITY OF NEW YORK NAlfUA

Western New York Historical Collection
Walter C. Hinkle Memorial Library
Alfred, New York 14802

Tunebooks, hymnals, and other music books, mostly 19th century, 10 items, including an edition of Little and Smith's *The Easy Instructor*, with extensive ms additions in round and shape notation, among them "Sylvia C. M., words and music by Dr. Wetmore on the death of his wife"

Willis Frederick Graves (1831–1908), scrapbook, probably compiled by a member of his family, ca. 1900, with biographical information, mostly press clippings, and pasted on the pages of an unidentified *Catalogue of Musical Merchandise, Edition K*

A. Neil Annas, ms music book, ca. 1900, containing 7 of his songs, some written expressly for the New York State School of Agriculture; also sheet music by Annas, with engraved plates

—Barrett G. Potter

971

John W. BEACH

300 McLain Street
Bedford Hills, New York 10507

John Parsons Beach (1877–1953, composer, and father of John W. Beach), mss and personal papers

972

BERGEN HISTORICAL SOCIETY

24 Clinton Avenue
Bergen, New York 14416

E. Richmond Mann (local composer), scrapbook with photographs and biographical information, ca. 1900; also 3 sheet-music songs

Songbooks, 7 items, 19th and 20th centuries

Programs of 12 local 20th-century musical events

—Virginia M. Barons

973

Philip CONOLE

Fine Arts Library
SUNY at Binghamton
Binghamton, New York 13901

Frances R. Conole Archive, 65,000 disc and 2000 tape recordings devoted to performance practice of opera and the human voice, 1900– , including many American performers, and early radio (1930–55); also a collection of sheet music emphasizing American war songs, ca. 1880–

974

Brice FARWELL

5 Deer Trail
Briarcliff Manor, New York 10510

Arthur Farwell (1872–1952, father of Brice Farwell), mss and memorabilia, as described in *A Guide to the Music of Arthur Farwell and to the Microfilm Collection of His Work* (Briarcliff Manor, 1972)

975

Sarah LAWRENCE COLLEGE NBronSL

Music Library
Bronxville, New York 10708

Edmund Haines (1914–74, composer), materials from his personal library, including 606 printed and ms scores, 291 books on music, 60 pamphlets, and 100 disc and 25 tape recordings

Hulda Lashanska (1891–1974, soprano), materials from her personal library, including 26 opera scores, 28 vols. of lieder, 14 cantatas or oratorios, 255 sheet-music items, ms letters, signed photographs, concert programs, and a pastel portrait

Printed music, including several boxes of sheet music and of songbooks and hymnals

Programs of College concerts and pictures of College music groups, 1928– (in the Archives)

—Margaret S. Protzman

976

Eunice D. WEBER

Whip-poor-will Lane
Brooktondale, New York 14817

Sheet music, 1 bound vol. of dance music for piano, mid 19th century, and 2 bound vols. of 19th-century piano and vocal items, including local imprints; also 28 mid-19th-century sheet-music items

Hymnals with words only, 5 items, 1819–68, and 49 sacred tunebooks, hymnals, sacred songbooks, and school songbooks, 1848–1941

Photographs and programs for concerts of the Ithaca Band School, Patrick Conway and his band, and the Ithaca College Band, ca. 1925–40

Recordings, including 60 linear cm. of 78-rpm discs and 50 cylinders

977

BUFFALO AND ERIE NBu, NBuG
COUNTY PUBLIC LIBRARY

Lafayette Square
Buffalo, New York 14203

The collections mostly consist of materials formerly in the Grosvenor Reference Library. All materials are in the Music Department, unless otherwise specified

Papers

Scrapbooks of local musicians, including John Lund (composer and conductor), 3 vols., 1887–97; Herman Schultz (organist, conductor, and composer), 1896–1930; Jeno Swislowski (pianist), 1923–41; and Harry Cumpson (pianist), 1928–43

Papers of local musical organizations, including the Buffalo Harmonic Club, constitution, reports, correspondence, and receipts, 1877–78, as cited in *HRS*; Buffalo Musical Association, minutes, 1885–97; Buffalo Symphony Orchestra, scrapbook of reviews and articles, 1921–27; Buffalo Chamber Music Society, 5 notebooks and ledgers of minutes, treasurers' reports, essays, and membership lists, also 1 box of programs, 1923–66; Buffalo Philharmonic Orchestra, 25 vols. of reviews and articles, 1932– ; Western New York Musical Association, scrapbook of papers, 1940–41; and Zorah Berry Concert Series, 5 scrapbooks of reviews and articles (1938–57), 1 file drawer of programs with composer, title, and performer indexes (1927–62), and 335 photographs of musicians (ca. 1920–60)

Programs, including orchestra concerts, 6 linear meters of boxes and 14 linear meters of bound vols., including complete runs for the major orchestras of Buffalo (1887–) and Boston (1892–), with a selective composer index, as well as title and performer indexes for local programs; miscellaneous local concerts, 1850– , 2 file drawers of items, indexed by composer, title, and performer; Helen Blackmon, "Concert Music Performed in Buffalo, New York, 1918–1927," analytical essay, with card indexes of composers, titles, performers, and dates for all concerts announced or reviewed in the *Buffalo Evening News*; and the *Music Calendar for Buffalo*, published 1931–75

Music

Manuscript music

A Gamut, or Scale of Music (Hartford, 1807), published instruction booklet with added ms music at the end (in the Rare Book Room)

Phebe Swan's book, Tunbridge, Mass., 1819, containing ms hymns copied from a hymnal (in the Rare Book Room)

Shaker songbook, ca. 1840–45, as cited in *Cook*, pp. 290–91 (in the Rare Book Room)

Josephine Gorton, *Aeroplane*, comic opera piano-vocal score, ca. 1902

Holograph music mss (in the Rare Book Room), 20th-century, including compositions by David Diamond, Lukas Foss, Livingston Gearhart, Alexei Haieff, William Leudeke (in photocopy), Darius Milhaud, Frederick E. Myrow (2 items), Ned Rorem, and Leo Smit (5 items)

Published Music

The sheet-music holdings comprise the former collections of Judge Louis Bret Hart, late 19th-century popular songs given while he was a trustee of the Grosvenor Library, 1914–39; 1500 19th-century minstrel and music-hall items from the estate of Frank Dumont, acquired 1923; the library of W. W. Nolen, 7200 separate sheets and 51 bound vols., with an emphasis on lithographed covers, acquired 1923; 13,000 items from William Delaney's music shop, including his series of 89 songbooks, acquired 1924; and 10,000 items purchased from the Plaza Music Co. of New York, 1930. The collections were the basis for 2 major illustrated bibliographies by Margaret M. Mott, "Sports and Recreations in American Popular Songs," M.L.A. *Notes,* 6 (1948), 379–418; 7 (1949), 522–61; and 9 (1951), 33–62; and "Transportation in American Popular Songs," Grosvenor Library *Bulletin*, 27/3 (1945). See also her article, "History Lives and Music Is Promoted," *Music Publishers Journal*, 4/3 (1946), 13 and 55–59

Special sheet-music collection, including campaign and presidential songs and piano pieces (1833– , 254 items), Confederate songs (1860–65, 24 items, in the Rare Book Room), "Star-spangled Banner" (19 early editions, in the Rare Book Room), and World War I songs (560 items)

Sheet music in 670 bound vols., containing 27,000 19th-century editions of songs and piano music, indexed by composer, title, and publisher. Also 74,000 separate sheet-music items, arranged alphabetically within 5 categories: (1) songs, 1790–1865, indexed by composer, title, first line, publisher, lithographer, subject, and publication date; (2) songs, 1866–90, similarly indexed; (3) songs, 1890– , indexed by title and partially by subject; (4) piano music, 1800–1865, partially indexed by subject; and (5) piano music, 1866– , partially indexed by subject

Art music, including cantatas, oratorios, and pageants, 13 items pre-1900, and 35 items 1901–40; chamber music, 10 items pre-1900, and 40 items 1901–40; musical comedies, 28 items pre-1900, and 82 items 1901–40; operas, 47 items pre-1901, and 26 items 1901–40; organ music, 19 items pre-1901, and 57 items 1901–40; piano music, 38 items pre-1901, and 41 items 1901–40; and symphonic music, 13 items pre-1901, and 73 items 1901–40

Broadsides, 2000 19th-century items

Songsters, 450 19th-century items (mostly in the Music Department), including 90 minstrel songsters (in the Rare Book Room)

Tunebooks, 17 18th-century items (in the Rare Book Room) and 170 19th-century items

Books on music, an extensive collection, including 159 instruction books and 16 music periodicals in 151 bound vols. The collection was enriched in 1924 with the purchase of Louis C. Elson's library of 400 vols. of books on music, scores, and libretti

—Norma Jean Lamb

978
QRS MUSIC ROLLS
1026 Niagara Street
Buffalo, New York 14213

Catalogues and sales literature of the Company, 1900– ; also their piano rolls, including masters, 1920–

—Bob Berkman

979
STATE UNIVERSITY OF NEW YORK AT BUFFALO
NBuU

Buffalo, New York 14214

Music Library, Baird Hall

Music librarianship in the U.S., source materials assembled in connection with Carol June Bradley, *The Genesis of American Music Librarianship, 1902–1942* (diss., Florida State University, 1978), extended to provide a comprehensive documentation of the history of music librarianship in the U.S., and of the first 50 years of the Music Library Association, 1931–81. Included are research correspondence, 1 linear meter; oral-history interviews with early music librarians and their associates, 50 hours; writings, many of them unpublished, by early music librarians, 2 linear meters; and other documents relating to music bibliography and librarianship (i.e., 3 linear meters of material in Library of Congress class ML 111), including photocopies from other repositories. Most of the material is catalogued as part of the Music Library collections, and there are supplemental card files of the bibliography of music librarianship and the history of music libraries in the U.S.

Arnold Cornelissen (1887–1953, Dutch-born composer active in Buffalo after ca. 1908), holograph scores and ms parts, 3 linear meters (with an inventory)

—Carol June Bradley

Center for Studies in American Culture (Buffalo 14260)

Folk-music collection, 400 hours of tape recordings by staff and students, ca. 1961– , some with transcriptions, emphasizing music of the South and including southern prison songs, Newport Folk Festivals, ca. 1963– , and songs from the Buffalo area and the Ozarks

—Bruce Jackson

980
SAINT LAWRENCE COUNTY HISTORY CENTER
Box 506
Canton, New York 13617

Manuscript music, including a "bass horn" partbook of the Wegatchie Band; and W. F. Sudds, autograph score of "The Convalescent Schottische," written in a New Orleans hospital during his recovery from battle wounds in the Civil War

Sheet music, 25 items, including works by local composers, 1860s?–

Songbooks, 25 items, including 1 for dulcimer accompaniment; also 12 Welsh hymnals, and other printed music for military and marching bands

Programs of local musical events, 35 items, including Musical Union programs, some in scrapbooks

Photographs and papers relating to local bands, choruses, mandolin clubs, and other music groups, 50 items

Recordings, including 25 78-rpm discs, 1910s–20s; 100 tapes of local fiddlers and Welsh singers, made at nearby Welsh festivals; and transcriptions of the fiddle tunes and of local country dances

—Mary H. Smallman

981
NEW YORK BARTÓK ARCHIVE
2 Tulip Street
Cedarhurst, New York 11516

Béla Bartók (1881–1945), personal papers, including autograph and copyists' mss and sketches, correspondence, research materials, books, periodicals, printed music, programs, press clippings, and recordings, as described in Victor Bator, *The Bela Bartok Archives: History and Catalogue* (New York, 1963)

982
SMITH MEMORIAL LIBRARY
Box 1093
Chautauqua, New York 14722

Music library, 11 linear meters, including materials from the collections of Julius Huehn (1909–71) and Josephine Antoine (1907–71), the latter collection including materials from Farrell Yancy. Included are 500 items of sheet music; 1 linear meter of opera libretti; books about music, with many opera scores; and 250 photographs, mostly of singers

Programs, scrapbooks of press clippings, printed announcements and pamphlets, and other materials relating to the Chautauqua Institution, as discussed in L. Jeanette Wells, *A History of the Music Festival at Chautauqua Institution from 1874 to 1957* (Ph.D. diss., Catholic University of America, 1957); Eugene W. Troth, *The Teacher Training Program in Music at Chautauqua Institution, 1905–1930* (Ph.D. diss., University of Michigan, 1959); and Robert H. Cowden, *The Chautauqua Opera Association, 1929–1958, an Interpretative History* (New York, 1974)

—Barbara B. Haug

983
NEW YORK STATE HISTORICAL ASSOCIATION   NCooHi
Cooperstown, New York 13326

Historical Association collections, including 5 music mss, n.d.; 700 popular sheet-music items, mostly 19th century; 50 songbooks, including hymnals and popular songbooks, 1795– ; 25 photographs of bands in parades, in a local-history collection, late 19th and early 20th centuries; and 270 78-rpm disc recordings, mostly of popular songs and folksongs

Archive of New York State Folklife, including field recordings, documentary films, and research papers on folklore and folk music, by students in the graduate program at the Association

—Marion Brophy

984
CORNING–PAINTED POST HISTORICAL SOCIETY
59 West Pulteney Street
Corning, New York 14830

Harry Linwood Tyler (Corning composer), personal

papers, including 2 music mss, 8 sheet-music songs, instrumental scores, 1 opera, 2 photographs, and a typescript biography by Celesta V. Dimitroff

—Celesta V. Dimitroff

985
CORTLAND COUNTY HISTORICAL   NCortHi SOCIETY

25 Homer Avenue
Cortland, New York 13045

William Austin Dillon (1877–1966) and family (vaudeville musicians), 45 linear cm. of papers, including sheet music, day books, ledgers, theater programs, press clippings, and photographs, 1880s–1940s
Civil War songs, 1 ms. vol.
Sheet music, 100 items, 19th to mid 20th centuries
Early 19th-century hymnals, 15 items, and 5 song books
American Federation of Musicians, Chapter 528, minutes, 1909–27
Programs of local concerts, 2000 items, 1860s–
Photographs of local music groups, late 19th century, 50 items, including the Amphions led by Alonso Blodgett
Recordings, including 30 78-rpm discs

—Shirley Heppell

986
GREENE COUNTY HISTORICAL   NCoxHi SOCIETY

Bronck House Museum
Route 9W
Coxsackie, New York 12051

Frederick Tours, ms vol. of marches and waltzes, possibly of German origin, 1835
Thomas Cole (founder of Hudson River School of Art), collection of flutes, and a harp-zither invented by him
Sheet music, 100 separate items and bound vols. of popular music, ca. 1850–1900; also sheet music of the Rip Van Winkle Outdoor Commercial Production, and of Catskill Mountain resorts
Songbooks, 6 items, 1799–1869, including sacred, temperance, political, and pedagogical collections
Thomas Brothers Musical Journal, several issues, 1880s

—Raymond Beecher

987
MUSICAL MUSEUM

Main Street
Deansboro, New York 13328

Sheet music, 2000 popular and classical vocal and instrumental items, 1880s–1930
Songbooks, 50 vols., including community and school songbooks, 1880s–98
Other printed music, including method books for violin and guitar, 1878 and 1880
Programs of concerts in Utica, 1910–18
Nel Blaich (singer), 45 linear cm. of papers, 1926–56, including photographs and press clippings related to performances in New York City and Syracuse, also published music

Music catalogues, 25 items, 1880–1910
Recordings, including 800 cylinders, 1890–1915, 3000 diamond and 78-rpm discs, and 1500 piano rolls

—Arthur H. Sanders

988
Clifford A. ALLANSON

126 Marlboro Road
Delmar, New York 12054

Sheet music, 15,000 popular-music items, 1850–1970
Hymnals, 2 linear meters, 19th and early 20th centuries
Other printed music, including 50 file drawers of popular-song and musical-comedy orchestrations, late 19th and 20th centuries
Recordings, including 600 wax cylinders, ca. 1900–1910s, and 5000 78-rpm discs, early 1930s
Musical instruments, 800 19th-century items, and a hammered dulcimer brought to the U.S. in 1750

989
Marty D'AMICO

5 Barnabas Drive
Depew, New York 14043

Hank D'Amico (1915–65, clarinetist with Big Bands, 1930s), personal papers, including commercial recordings by bands in which he played, photographs, a scrapbook of press clippings and photographs, and other memorabilia

990
ELMIRA COLLEGE   NElmC

Learning Center
Elmira, New York 14901

Charles T. Griffes, 2 vols. and 36 items of ms scores and other papers, 1884–1920, including 10 autograph music mss and 1 sketchbook, letters, and a list of his compositions. See Donna K. Anderson, *The Works of Charles T. Griffes: A Descriptive Catalogue* (Ph.D. diss., Indiana University, 1966)
Other printed music, including 50 songbooks, sheet music, and 200 other items

—John W. Berry

991
ESPERANCE HISTORICAL SOCIETY

Box 143
Esperance, New York 12066

Diaries of several persons, 1860–80, with mention of traveling choral groups in the Esperance area
Sheet music, several early 20th-century items; also hymnals
Photographs of the Esperance Band
Recordings, including cylinders

—Kenneth M. Jones

992
Milford H. FARGO

12 Park Circle Drive
Fairport, New York 14450

Ada Jones Memorial Collection, 500 cylinder recordings, 1000 78-rpm discs, photographs, taped interviews, and correspondence, 1894–1922

General collection of 2500 cylinder recordings and 6000 78-rpm discs, including musical, theatrical, and political personalities, 1889–1942

993
Darwin R. BARKER LIBRARY   NFred

Historical Museum
20 East Main Street
Fredonia, New York 14063

Sheet music, 10 items, 1868–1914
Songbooks, 15 items, including shape-note tunebooks, 1798–1890; also 2 singing-school songbooks, 18 and n.d., with inserted ms music and texts
Other printed music, 30 items, 1864–1915
Programs of 100 local musical events, mostly at Fredonia Normal School, mid 19th and early 20th centuries
Photographs and pictures of local bands and Fredonia Normal school groups, 50 items, late 19th and early 20th centuries

—Ann M. Fahnestock

994
STATE UNIVERSITY OF NEW YORK,   NFredU
COLLEGE AT FREDONIA

Fredonia, New York 14063

Reed Library

Sheet music, 3500 items, including popular songs and dance band arrangements, 1855–1953
Hymnals, 50 19th-century items and 5 Lowell Mason tunebooks. See Arlene E. Gray, *Lowell Mason's Contribution to American Church Music* (Master's thesis, Eastman School of Music, 1941), on file with the collection
Photographs relating to the early history of the College, including materials of musicians or music groups, 1 linear meter, 1867–

Archives Room

Robert Wiley Marvel (1918–74, faculty member and composer), 1 linear meter of papers, including music mss, correspondence, and published articles
Hillman Memorial Music Association, 1 file drawer of papers, including research on Jessie Hillman and her pupils
Fredonia Normal School (later SUNY College at Fredonia), 2 linear meters of archives relating to the music curriculum, including photographs, 1867–

—Joseph Chouinard, Yvonne Wilensky,
Joanne Schweik

995
ADELPHI UNIVERSITY   NGcA

Fine Arts Library
Garden City, New York 11530

Sheet music, 30 popular and classical items, ca. 1940
Hymnals and school and college songbooks, 2 linear meters, early 20th century
Americana collection, including an autographed copy of Walter Damrosch's *My Musical Life*; also 3 method books and 1 libretto, 1862–1976
Recordings, including 325 78-rpm discs of popular and classical music

—Gary E. Cantrell

996
GENEVA HISTORICAL SOCIETY

543 South Main Street
Geneva, New York 14456

Geneva Choral Society, 2 boxes of papers, including programs, minutes, membership lists, and photographs, 1894–1943
Smith Opera House (Geneva Theater), 2 boxes of papers, including programs, photographs, press clippings, and a history, 1894–1978
Songbooks, hymnals, bound sheet music, and published vocal works, ca. 60 items, 1801–1935
Programs and advertisements of local musical events, ca. 65 items, 1829– , mostly late 19th and early 20th centuries

—Mark S. Delluomo

997
Bernard KLATZKO

Box 306
Glen Cove, New York 11542

Recordings, of New Orleans jazz (1940–70), country blues, sanctified church music with instrumental accompaniment, ragtime and barrelhouse piano, jug bands, New Orleans musicians, and hillbilly music (1923–34), in all 2000 items including LP discs and tape copies of 78-rpm discs

998
GOUVERNEUR HISTORICAL SOCIETY

26 John Street
Gouverneur, New York 13642

W. F. Sudds (local composer), original sacred compositions in sheet-music editions, also books of his parlor-organ works, and letters and photographs scattered through various local personal collections
Documents of other local musicians, as cited in *The Centennial History of the Town of Gouverneur* (Watertown, N.Y., 1905), pp. 146–51, and in the publications of the St. Lawrence County Historical Association, Canton, N.Y.

—Eugenia M. Huntress

999

PEMBER LIBRARY AND MUSEUM
Granville, New York 12832

The autograph album, 1832–96, including signatures of singers (and others), as cited in *HRS*, cannot now be located

1000

HASTINGS HISTORICAL SOCIETY
Municipal Building
Hastings on Hudson, New York 10706

Programs and press clippings of local performances, including events featuring visiting musicians from New York City, 1910s– , in 4 folders
—Virginia McGuire

1001

HERKIMER COUNTY   NHerkCHi
HISTORICAL SOCIETY
400 North Main Street
Herkimer, New York 13350

Fort Dayton Fireman's Band, archives and photographs, 1898–1917
Remington Band (1890s–1930s, comprised of employees of the Remington typewriter factory), archives and photographs
Programs of musical performances at the Fairfield Academy and local opera houses, 1815– , uncatalogued and dispersed through the general collections
—Jane S. Spellman

1002

Keith C. CLARK
Route 1, Box 32
Houghton, New York 14744

American and British hymnology, 9654 items, including 1987 books about hymnology, 205 psalm books, 663 oblong tunebooks, 1214 denominational hymnals, and 788 gospel songbooks

1003

Franklin D. ROOSEVELT   NHpR
PRESIDENTIAL LIBRARY
Albany Post Road
Hyde Park, New York 12538

Music mss, 6 linear meters of materials, mostly proposed campaign songs sent to the president, 1933–45
—Donald B. Schewe

1004

William W. AUSTIN
Department of Music
Lincoln Hall
Cornell University
Ithaca, New York 14853

Personal research materials, including files on American composers and topics; 70 mss, photocopies, and ozalid prints of works by American composers; and other materials

1005

CORNELL UNIVERSITY   NIC
Ithaca, New York 14853

Music Library, Lincoln Hall

Sheet music, 11,000 items, 1850–1940, with a card index by title and composer
Printed music, including 114 tunebooks and hymnals, 1788–1921, mostly from the Harris Hymnal Collection (parts of this collection are in the Olin Library, cited below); 11 college and fraternity songbooks, 1860–1919; and 21 early editions of works by Louis Moreau Gottschalk
Music periodicals, extensive holdings, mostly 1834–
Recordings, including 10,000 miscellaneous 78-rpm discs

Olin Library, General Collections

Masonic songbooks, 5 items, 1818–98
Gilbert & Sullivan libretti, 9 items, 1878–92
Programs of miscellaneous Cornell musical events, 1917–22, collected by P. G. Gulley

University Archives, Olin Library

Personal papers, of Claire Alcée (Mrs. Andrew Strong White, concert singer), press clippings, posters, and programs documenting her career; Charles Hazen Blood (1866–1938, local lawyer), papers relating to his work as a trustee of the Ithaca Conservatory of Music; Laura Bryant (1895–1961, music teacher), professional correspondence, scrapbooks, scores, and Ithaca High School concert programs, 1901–50; Charles William Curtis, mss of University songs, ca. 1888; Alice Edwards Emerson (1862–1933, music teacher at Wellesley College, Ithaca Conservatory of Music, University of Chicago, Cornell University, and Hobart College), memoir of her career, written by her daughter, Edith Emerson, 1963; Donald Jay Grout, correspondence and research materials, 1929–67, 4 linear meters, also a transcript of an interview with Otto Kinkeldey; Vladimir Karapetoff (1876–1918, composer and Engineering College faculty member), recordings, early 1930s, and holograph music mss; Eudorus Catlin Kenney (1857–1918, teacher, author, and lecturer), ms and published editions of his musical works; Otto Kinkeldey (1878–1966), correspondence, research materials, and programs, 1902–66, 3.8 linear meters; Bert Lord, personal papers, including 20 letters on the funding of town-band concerts in Chenango County, N.Y., 1927–28; Elsie Murray (1878–1965, psychologist), personal papers reflecting her interests in music, also a journal kept while she was secretary of the Music Department, 1926–27; Ethel Newcomb (pianist), 55 letters to Mrs. Selma Marian Urband Pratt, 1935–57; and Robert Burns Reynolds (1834–1910), notebook of naval songs and folksongs

Organizational archives, including University Music Department records, correspondence of the chairman, 1927–44, 700 items, and papers and correspondence, 1884–1954, 24 linear cm.; Cornell Masque, scrapbooks, correspondence, and scores for their musical-theater productions, 1870–1900s; Lyceum Theatre and other Ithaca theaters, records of bookings, 1892–1924, in 10 vols.; account book of the Lyceum Theatre in Ithaca, 1893–1923, in the papers of Romeyn Berry, also specifications for the Lyceum Theatre building, erected ca. 1890, 15 items; records of the Lyceum Theatre in Rochester, N.Y., 1888–1934, including scrapbooks of press clippings, 1888–1934, and financial records, 1917–34, 4.5 linear meters; Ithaca Conservatory of Music, catalogue and announcement, 1903–ca. 1925; and correspondence and printed materials concerning the Ithaca Civic Opera Group, in the Alexander M. Drummond Papers

Programs of University musical events, including concerts sponsored by the Music Department, featuring visiting performers, 1890–1949, particularly 1910–40, also organ recitals, 1884–1954, and University Orchestra concerts, 1905–17, with historical sketches of the Orchestra; other musical organizations at Cornell, 1878–1958; Cornell Music Festivals, 1905–20; Glee, Banjo, and Mandolin Club, 1888– ; Sage Chapel services and organ recitals, 1878– ; and the Flonzaley Quartet, 1903–28

Other programs and related materials, for the Lyceum Theatre, Ithaca, 1894–1925, 1786 items; other Ithaca events, 1898–1954, as collected by Elizabeth Lyman; Diller's Cornet Septet, from New York, 6 concerts given on Norfolk Green, 1883; Rochester concerts, performed by Dr. Frederick Austin Mandeville and Mrs. Emma (Underhill) Mandeville, also programs for the Eastman and Lyceum Theatres, and a notebook of selections sung by the choir of St. Peter's Presbyterian Church, 1889–94, in all 25 linear cm.; and various Ithaca performances, including the Ithaca Harmonia Club, Mozart Club, and Choral Club of Ithaca, 1856–1904, 116 items. Other programs are to be found in the papers of Walter Buckingham Carver (mathematician) for performances ca. 1906–48; of Dr. and Mrs. Emerson Crosby Kelly, for 1885–1960; of Joseph Anthony Kohm, for 1917–38; of the Shanklin and Avery families, for 1848–1916; and of the Rawley family of Tioga County, for 1867–1938

Photographs of early University Music Department performances and ensembles, 42 items

Sheet music, 2 bound vols., mostly for piano solo

George Coleman, material collected toward a history of music at the University, including transcripts, memoirs, and programs, 1870–1939

Recordings, tapes collected by Ellen Stekert, 1956–57, of Ezra Barhight (b. 1875, lumberjack from Potter County, Pa.) singing 75 English, Irish, and American folksongs and popular tunes. See the *Report of the Curator and Archivist of the Collection of Regional History and University Archives* (Ithaca, 1954–58), p. 26

Rare Book Department, Olin Library

McKim family papers, including materials of Lucy McKim relating to black music in America, as cited in Dena J. Epstein, "Documenting the History of Black Folk Music," *Fontes artis musicae*, 23 (1976), 151–57

Catherwood Library, School of Industrial and Labor Relations

Labor and labor-related songbooks, 80 items, in the Labor Management Documentation Center

—Peggy E. Daub, Michael Keller, Kathleen Jacklin

1006
DeWITT HISTORICAL SOCIETY OF TOMPKINS COUNTY   NIHi
116 North Cayuga Street
Ithaca, New York 14850

Ithaca Music Collection, 1822–1971, including early 20th-century sheet music of minstrel shows, Cornell University songs, war songs, and popular tunes; sheet music formerly owned by Ann H. Utter of Ithaca; 30 bound vols. of Scottish songs, early 19th century; published religious music; arrangements of popular band music, ca. 1900–1930; organizational papers, including receipts, clippings, programs, and advertisements of the Choral Club, Harmonia Club, Mozart Club, Patsy Conway and the Ithaca Band, and the Westminster Choir School, also a constitution, by-laws, and directory of the Ithaca Musicians' Protective Union; and recordings, including 40 albums of 78-rpm discs with early 20th-century popular songs

Ithaca Conservatory of Music and Ithaca College Collection, 1908–67, including programs, pamphlets, catalogues, letters of the Conservatory recommending Nellie Allen, 1908, letters concerning institutional affairs, 1930–40s, minutes, financial papers, and school publications

Lyceum Theatre, 1 scrapbook of programs, 1892–1924, including programs of the Choral Club, 1892–97, and architectural specifications of the theater

Hattie Barnes Collection, including published gospel and sacred songbooks, ca. 1875–1907

William A. Dillon (vaudeville entertainer, and song writer) Collection, 1902–66, including correspondence, clippings, articles, biographical materials, and original songbooks and sheet music (some in photocopies)

Albert Force Collection, including programs of the Wilgus Opera House, Ithaca Conservatory of Music, and Ithaca Choral Club

Rodney W. Hanford Collection, including songbooks, and clippings concerning musical activities of Ithaca College, Cornell University, Ithaca High School, and the Ithaca community

Other published materials, including William Edson and Ephraim Reed, *The Musical Monitor* (Ithaca, 1822–33), 4 vols. of sacred music

Photographs, including glass-plate negatives of bands, in the Susie Jones Collection; also 25 photographs of bands, and 25 of bandstands

Recordings, including 60 Edison cylinders of popular songs, ca. 1885–1915, and 9 early 20th-century piano rolls of popular tunes

—Annita A. Andrick, Shari D. Comins

1007
ITHACA COLLEGE   NIIC
Library
Danby Road
Ithaca, New York 14850

Gustave Haenschen collection of radio-orchestra scores and performance parts, arrangements of classical and popular music, 1925–52, 50,000 items including 10,000 mss

Roberta Peters (Metropolitan Opera singer), papers, including 30 envelopes of clippings, 25 diaries, tape recordings and 225 disc recordings, 2 folders of correspondence, photographs, 35 scrapbooks, 200 programs, and other materials

Donald Vorhees collection, scripts and music used in the "Bell Telephone Hour" radio and television program, 1940–50, 150 file drawers

Ithaca College History Archives, including 3 file drawers of photographs, minutes, class lists, catalogues (1893–), scrapbooks (1922–), and other materials of the Ithaca Conservatory of Music and affiliated schools (including at various times the Patrick Conway Military Band School and the Westminster Choir School), and its successor, Ithaca College

—Betty Birdsey

1008
COLUMBIA COUNTY HISTORICAL SOCIETY
Broad Street
Kinderhook, New York 12106

Shaker ms music book, late 18th century
Manuscript lyrics to an anti-rent song, ca. 1840
Published music materials, 100 items, mid 18th to early 20th centuries, including 8 18th-century songbooks from the Hudson Valley, among them Dutch and German items; 1 Shaker music book; 1 Indian songbook; sheet music from the Civil War to World War I; and programs of local 19th-century musical performances

—Ruth Piwonka

1009
Marcella SEMBRICH MEMORIAL STUDIO
Bolton Landing
Lake George, New York 12814

Books, costumes, and memorabilia of Mme Sembrich (1858–1935), including her scores (except for 500 vols. given to the Juilliard School of Music), also photographs and portraits from her career, and dedicatory copies of music from her associates

—Philip L. Miller

1010
OLD VILLAGE HALL MUSEUM   NLin
Lindenhurst Historical Society
Box 296
Lindenhurst, New York, 11757

Frohsinn (local German singing society), annual concert journals and memorabilia
Pictures, 3 items
Published music, including 25 sheet-music items and 7 songbooks

—Lorraine S. Ryan

1011
June M. DICKINSON
2904 East Lake Road
Livonia, New York 14487

Autograph ms of John Alden Carpenter's *Adventures in a Perambulator;* also letters of European performers written during American visits. See the catalogue of the collection, by Ralph P. Locke and Jurgen Thym, in *Fontes artis musicae* (forthcoming)

1012
NIAGARA COUNTY HISTORICAL SOCIETY
215 Niagara Street
Lockport, New York 14094

Sheet music, 4609 19th- and early 20th-century popular songs, in original and photocopy, including 12 on local topics, 13 relating to Niagara Falls, and 23 by Chauncey Olcott

Songbooks and hymnals, 25 vols., 1890s–1920s

Organizational papers, including items of the Four Season Players, late 19th century; also 19th-century diaries and scrapbooks of local musicians

Hodge Opera House, posters and playbills, 1860s–1928

Photographs of local musicians, and a clipping file including materials on visiting musicians in Niagara County, 1865–

—John F. Krahling

1013
STEINWAY & SONS
Steinway Place
Long Island City, New York 11105

Archives of the piano-manufacturing firm, including the diary of William Steinway, 1861–96, minutes of the Board of Trustees of Steinway & Sons, and photographs, as cited in Theodore C. Russell, *Theodore Thomas: His Role in the Development of Musical Culture in the United States, 1835–1905* (Ph.D. diss., University of Minnesota, 1969)

1014
Millard CHAMBERLAIN
Lowville, New York 13367

Lowville Village Band, 300 arrangements of band music and 200 marches, late 19th and early 20th centuries, also minutes, press clippings, financial papers, and photographs, mostly early 20th century

1015
Carol Jane MOORE
Nanticoke Valley Historical Society
63 Main Street
Maine, New York 13802

Sheet music, 3 cabinets and 2 boxes of items, ca. 1900–1940s; also 30 songbooks, and printed music for guitar and mandolin

Programs of local musical events, several items
Catalogues of music dealers, several items, 1920s
Recordings, including 78-rpm discs, 1920s–30s

1016

HISTORICAL SOCIETY OF MIDDLETOWN AND THE WALLKILL PRECINCT

25 East Avenue
Middletown, New York 10940

Sheet music, including ballads, marches, and other piano music, 100 items, 1860–1920; also piano editions of popular songs with ukulele arrangements in professional copies, 55 items; and 1 bound vol., ca. 1850, containing instrumental works, many with lithographed covers
Hymnals and sacred-song collections, 3 items, 1840–61, and 4 items, 1913–17

—Charles L. Radzinsky

1017

MUSEUM VILLAGE IN ORANGE COUNTY

Museum Village Road
Monroe, New York 10950

Sheet music, 1100 popular and classical items, including some bound vols., ca. 1820– , mostly late 19th and early 20th centuries
Hymnals, tunebooks, and school songbooks, 45 early 19th-century items, including a Little and Smith *Easy Instructor* (Albany, n.d.), inscribed 1821, and Thomas Hartwell, *The New York & Vermont Collection* (Albany, n.d.)
Manuscript music, in 1 early 19th-century school notebook containing songs, and 1 vol. of ms copies of sheet music
Recordings, including 150 cylinders, 170 piano rolls, and 150 78-rpm discs
Musical instruments, including a Chickering–McKay piano shipped from New York, 1838, a Stanbrough piano built in Newburgh, N.Y., 1840s?, and an organ built by Healy & Bishop, Goshen, N.Y., mid 19th century

—Renee Klish Ginsberg

1018

AMERICAN ACADEMY AND INSTITUTE OF ARTS AND LETTERS   NNAL

633 West 155th Street
New York, New York 10032

Music mss and correspondence of members of the Department of Music. Among the composers whose music mss are present are Charles Wakefield Cadman, John Alden Carpenter, Frederick S. Converse, Henry K. Hadley, Howard Hanson, Edward Burlingame Hill, Philip James, Edgar Stillman Kelley, Douglas Stuart Moore, Horatio Parker, and Leo Sowerby. Among the officers, whose correspondence is extensive, are Elliott Carter, Walter Damrosch, Ross Lee Finney, Douglas Stuart Moore, Otto Luening, Quincy Porter, William Schuman, Virgil Thomson, and Hugo Weisgall. For references to the Con-

verse holograph mss and correspondence, see Robert J. Garofolo, *The Life and Works of Frederick Shepherd Converse* (Ph.D. diss., Catholic University of America, 1969). For references to the 200 letters by and to Harry Rowe Shelley, including 6 by Dudley Buck, see William K. Gallo, *The Life and Church Music of Dudley Buck* (Ph.D. diss., Catholic University of America, 1968)

1019

AMERICAN COMPOSERS ALLIANCE

170 West Seventy-fourth Street
New York, New York 10023

Library of 4000 scores and performance parts of compositions by the 230 active members, as well as of composers' estates retaining membership; also masters of scores by some non-members. Materials are predominantly mss, including nearly all the mss of members, except those held by publishers, and are represented in the Composers Facsimile Edition and American Composers Edition catalogues. See the Alliance's pamphlet, also its *Bulletin* (1951–65)
Papers of the Alliance, founded 1938, and of its first president, Aaron Copland, including business papers and legal documents

—Francis Thorne

1020

AMERICAN GUILD OF MUSICAL ARTISTS

1841 Broadway
New York, New York 10023

Archival records of the Guild, 1936– , including minutes, records, contracts, and memorabilia, available for consultation on special permission

—Joan Greenspan

1021

AMERICAN JEWISH CONGRESS

Library
15 East Eighty-fourth Street
New York, New York 10028

Research materials concerning Jewish instrumental and theatrical music, field recordings of (Ladino) Sephardic music, and Jewish family music; also tapes and reissues of 78-rpm discs of Yiddish music and tape-recorded interviews with Jewish immigrants, concerning Yiddish music and jazz

—Henry Sapoznik

1022

AMERICAN MUSEUM OF NATURAL HISTORY   NNM

Department of Anthropology
Central Park West at Seventy-ninth Street
New York, New York 10024

Recordings of American Indians, 2500 items, mostly field recordings of songs and dance music, including

Jane Belo and Zora Neale Hurston, field recordings of black spirituals, 1930s, also some commercial recordings. See the 115-page *Catalog of Phonograph Records* (New York, 1971)

1023
AMERICAN MUSIC CENTER
250 West Fifty-seventh Street, Room 626
New York, New York 10019

The Center is concerned with the promotion of contemporary American music. While its library is therefore strong in contemporary works, with 12,000 scores and 1100 recordings (in 1978), it annually transfers to other repositories all scores and recordings of music by composers who have been deceased for 25 years

Archives of the Center, dating from founding in 1940 by Marion Bauer, Aaron Copland, Howard Hanson, Otto Luening, Quincy Porter, and others
Biographical files on 1200 composers whose music is now or was formerly promoted by the Center. The files are mostly post-1950, and include clippings, reviews, programs, lists of works, publishers' brochures, and biographical survey forms

—Karen McNerney Famera

1024
AMERICAN SOCIETY OF COMPOSERS, AUTHORS AND PUBLISHERS
One Lincoln Plaza
New York, New York 10023

For general historical background, see Bennie DeWhitt, *The American Society of Composers, Authors, and Publishers, 1914–1938* (Ph.D. diss., Emory University, 1977); also the *New York Times*, 16 February 1964, special supplementary section XI

Archival records of the Society, including memorabilia of the founders, press clippings, an extensive file of photographs, 1914– , and official records
Sheet music, ca. 1914–30s, an extensive collection, uncatalogued
Raymond B. Hubbell, typescript history of the Society to ca. 1940, entitled "From Nothing to Five Million Dollars"
Oral-history interviews by Mike Whorf, for radio station WJR, Detroit, Mich., 1968– , of 150 ASCAP songwriters, among them Harold Adamson, Harold Arlen, Howard Dietz, E. Y. Harburg, Burton Lane, Arthur Schwartz, and Harry Warren

—Gerald Marks

1025
Leo BAECK INSTITUTE   NNLBI
129 East Seventy-third Street
New York, New York 10021

Robert Alexander (b. 1883), ms and printed music, 40 linear cm., including 43 piano sonatas and other works, with several ms lists of his works which serve as a partial inventory of the collection; also a bio-

graphical sketch by Julius Mattfeld, detailing some of Alexander's musical activities in the U.S., which began in 1938
Carl Goldmark Family Collection, including correspondence, 1850s–80s, mostly between Goldmark (1830–1915, Hungarian composer) and his brother, Leo Goldmark (cantor and teacher, active in the U.S. after 1867, manager with Heinrich Conried of the Authors' and Composers' International Agency in New York, and father of the composer Rubin Goldmark)
Otto Klemperer (1885–1973), 6 holograph music mss, correspondence, 7 photographs, and press clippings
Erich Wolfgang Korngold (1897–1957), letters and holograph music mss, mostly from his European career, 1902–28
Max Kowalski (1882–1956, lawyer and composer), correspondence with musicians, including 11 letters from Arnold Schoenberg, 1933–34 and 1948–49
Manfred Lewandowski (1895–1970, cantor, composer, and teacher in Germany and later in Philadelphia), personal papers, including letters from Harry Truman, Richard Tucker, Pablo Casals, and others; sheet music and recordings; and press clippings, genealogical records, and lists of music
Ludwig Misch (1887–1967, musicologist), personal papers, including letters from Wilhelm Furtwängler, Bruno Walter, and Max Unger
Bruno Walter (1876–1962), letters to Siegfried Altmann, mostly from his years in the U.S., also photographs and concert programs, 1919–55

—Sybil Milton

1026
Mary Louise BOEHM and Kees KOOPER
210 Riverside Drive
New York, New York 10025

Arne Oldberg, mss of unpublished piano works
Amy Cheney (Mrs. H. H. A.) Beach, mss of unpublished violin works
Henry Holden Huss, Violin Concerto in D Minor op. 12, reconstructed by Kees Kooper based on the holograph ms in the New York Public Library (q.v.)

1027
"The BOHEMIANS"
Brent Williams, Executive Director
200 West Fifty-fifth Street
New York, New York 10019

Minutes of the club, 1906– , also annual brochures relating to its activities and to those of its philanthropic arm, the Musicians' Foundation, Inc., established 1914

1028
CBS RECORDS   (NNCBS)
Archives
51 West Fifty-second Street
New York, New York 10019

Correspondence, office memoranda, and photographs of artists of the Columbia Broadcasting System,

1893– ; also recording information, 1903– , and pre-1900 recording catalogues

—Tina McCarthy

1029
Barton CANTRELL
345 East Seventy-seventh Street
New York, New York 10021

Research notes and correspondence concerned with the locations of documents relating to American composers, in 70 folders; also programs, papers, and sheet music, mostly late 19th- and early 20th centuries

1030
CITY COLLEGE OF THE CITY UNIVERSITY OF NEW YORK   NNR
New York, New York 10031

Music Library (138th Street and Convent Avenue)

Mark Brunswick (1902–71, faculty member), materials from his personal library, including 4 holograph mss (partly photocopies) by Roger Sessions, 1923–26, and an autographed study score of the Violin Concerto, 1937; also 5 copyists' mss (photocopies) of compositions by Brunswick

Frederick Jacobi (1891–1952), published scores from his personal library, including 6 of his own compositions, 1923–47, and Lazare Saminsky, *Symphonie des Sommets* (Paris, 1924), inscribed to Jacobi

Other printed music, a large general collection, including 6 scores by Rubin Goldmark, 1900–1923, 30 by Ernest Bloch, 1910–40, 8 by Aaron Copland, 1929–39, and 8 by Sessions, 1929–38

City College Archives (135th Street and Convent Avenue)

Mark Brunswick, papers, including correspondence related to the Placement Committee for German & Austrian Musicians, 1938–45, and 23 holograph mss, 1919–70

Samuel Baldwin (1862–1949, organist and faculty member), facsimile of his ms score, *Symphonic Rhapsody no. 4*, 1934; annotated catalogue of 60 organ recitals given by him at City College, 1912–13; syllabus of music-appreciation lectures; and 1 folder of clippings about him

Giovanni E. Conterno (faculty member, 1934–37), 9 mss arrangements and compositions, program of a concert conducted by him in Bridgeport, Conn., 1921, and biographical information

Programs and clippings of Lewisohn Stadium concerts at City College, 1920s–30s

—Melva Peterson

1031
COLUMBIA UNIVERSITY   NNC
New York, New York 10027

Rare Book and Manuscript Library, Butler Library

Frederick Barry (1876–1943, mathematician), personal professional papers, including his ms music scores, notably *The Alcayde*, 1890s

Béla Bartók, 3 mss (2170 pages) of his folksong books

Jacques Barzun, personal papers, including music correspondence, 1931–70, with letters to and from Cecil Hopkinson, 1939–52, and other research materials

Harold Bauer (1873–1951), 130 letters to Isabel Pelham Shaw (Mrs. Frederick) Lowell and Mrs. George Shaw, 1900–1935, mostly on personal subjects, such as his opinions on World War I; also 1 photograph and 35 concert programs of Bauer

Eleanor Robson (Mrs. August) Belmont, 4000 items, 1853–1960, including correspondence, working files, and reports concerning the Metropolitan Opera

Nicolai Berezowsky (1900–1953), 1250 letters, including correspondence with David Diamond (63 items), Serge Koussevitzky (22 items), Nicolai Lopatnikoff (72 items), and Eugene Ormandy (31 items), also concerning the WPA music program, League of Composers, Juilliard School of Music, and ASCAP

Augustin Daly (1838–99), 11 vols. of financial records of Daly's Theatre, Broadway, 1872–99, including cash account books, personnel rosters, salary accounts, attendance books, receipt books, and directions for stage settings. (Check stubs and bank books are in the Brander Matthews Dramatic Museum collection, below.)

Jessica Dragonette, 300 items, including photographs, clippings, programs, and mss

Ephrata Cloister Manuscript Collection, 12 items, ca. 1747–1800, including 6 printed editions of works by Conrad Beissel, some with extensive added ms musical notation; and 6 ms music books with texts based on printed editions

John Erskine (1879–1951), 41 boxes, 18 scrapbooks, 69 publications, and 1 box of photographs on educational, literary, and musical matters, including correspondence with Walter Damrosch (6 items, 1929–47), Ernest Hutchinson (8 items, 1929–48), Marian MacDowell (12 items, 1932–48), and Ernest Schelling (6 items, 1932–38)

Constance Hope (1908–77), 3400 letters and 2000 photographs, contracts, and printed items, 1931–75, relating to her work as a public-relations specialist and artists' representative for such musicians as Lotte Lehmann, Erich Leinsdorf, Lily Pons, Bruno Walter, and Grace Moore

Edward A. MacDowell (1861–1908), 78 items, 1876–1908, including letters to Arthur P. Schmidt, William Mason, and others; Mrs. Marian MacDowell's diary and letter book, with drafts of letters to Nicholas Murray Butler and others concerning his career at Columbia University; ms scores and sketches for the *Indian Suite* and the *Sonata Tragica;* and 2 original drawings of MacDowell by Orlando Rowland

Daniel Gregory Mason (1873–1953), 3276 items, 1894–1953, including 16 boxes of correspondence; 8 boxes of journals; 12 boxes of mss and published editions of Mason's music; 4 boxes of sketchbooks and miscellaneous documents; 3 boxes of Mason's published music, some items heavily annotated; 2 boxes of business papers; 1 box of Mason's phonograph recordings; 2 boxes of photographs; 7 boxes of scrapbooks; 12 boxes of books from his library; and 7 boxes of printed and ms music by other composers. See Sister Mary Justina Klein, *The Contribution of Daniel Gregory Mason to American Music* (Ph.D. diss., Catholic University of America, 1957), 137–44

William Mason (1829–1908), autograph album with

signed messages from 103 of his prominent musical associates

Brander Matthews Dramatic Museum collection, 1732–1902, including 4000 letters and mss from actors, actresses, and managers; business records of American and English theaters and agents, 64 items, 1864–1911; and Matthews' correspondence, along with research on Matthews. The ephemera collection comprises the Portrait File, with 30,000 cabinet photographs, *carte de visite* photographs, and prints; the Subject File, with 15,000 clippings, pamphlets, programs, prints, and photographs; the Program File, 23,000 items arranged by title of play and by actor's name, with a separate index to theaters; and the Scrapbook File, 18,000 items. Most of this material concerns the theater in the U.S., and includes many musical items

Douglas Stuart Moore (1893–1969), 5400 items, including ms music scores and sketches, also production materials relating to his works, records of his work for the Music Department at Columbia University and the MacDowell Association, and other personal and professional correspondence

George C. D. Odell (1866–1949), 700 items, including research materials for his *Annals of the New York Stage* (New York, 1927–49)

Solomon Pimsleur (1900–1962), 150 music mss, also recordings and related publications

Max Rabinoff (1877–1966, impresario and economist), 1000 items, 1908–61, including records of his work in founding the American Institute of Operatic Art, promoting the American career of Anna Pavlova, and producing opera in New York, Chicago, and Boston

Random House, Inc., 700,000 items, containing correspondence with playwrights and composers of Broadway musical comedies, including George Gershwin and Richard Rodgers

Eda Rothstein Rapoport (1890–1968), 407 music items, ca. 1915–68, including mss and photocopies of scores and parts for all her musical works, also the diary kept by her husband, Dr. Boris Rapoport, 1932–48

Anton Seidl (1850–98), papers and music mss, 1870–98, including correspondence, journals, diaries, and memorandums, also photographs, clippings, and 27 ms orchestrations

Frederick Schang, 1500 items, ca. 1800–1977, including visiting cards, photographs, and other memorabilia of composers, conductors, and singers, largely connected with his work as chairman of Columbia Artists Management, Inc. See his *Visiting Cards of Celebrities* (New York, 1972), *Visiting Cards of Violinists* (New York and Stuart, Fla., 1975), and *Visiting Cards of Prima Donnas* (New York, 1977)

Joseph Urban (1872–1933), 15,000 items, mostly drawings, sketches, paintings, and glass plates of his stage sets, many of them for operas and musical comedies, including 500 for the *Ziegfeld Follies*, 1915–31

Roger Wheeler (proprietor of Rare Old Programs, Inc., Newtonville, Mass.), theatrical memorabilia, 1770–1940, 12,800 items, including programs, playbills, photographs, engravings, and prints of operettas, musical comedies, revues, and concerts

Isidore Witmark (1869–1941), 121 items, 1903–39, including 8 ms scores by Victor Herbert and other composers, 43 dedicatory letters from authors, and 67 programs, clippings, prospectuses, and other printed documents

Frederick Zimmermann (1906–67, member of the New York Philharmonic-Symphony Orchestra), correspondence, mostly from artists of Der Blaue Reiter school, Munich

Miscellaneous letters of musicians, including Harold Bauer, Mordecai Bauman, Satis N. Coleman, Edward Dickinson, Carl Engel, Arthur Farwell, George Gershwin, Henry S. Gilbert, Douglas Stuart Moore, Adelina Patti, Paul Rosenfeld, Arnold Schoenberg, Arturo Toscanini, and Edgard Varèse

Hunt–Berol Collection

Assembled by Arthur Billings Hunt (1890–1971). See June Lord-Wood, *Musical Americana in the Hunt–Berol Collection at the Columbia University Libraries* (Master's thesis, Columbia University, 1975)

Sheet music, 50,000 items, being arranged and catalogued

Hunt's personal music library, 50 linear meters, strong in 18th- and 19th-century British and American hymnology

Miscellaneous ms materials collected by Hunt, as well as miscellaneous other music items presented to the Library. Catalogued correspondence includes letters from Clarence S. Brigham regarding Hunt's work with the American Antiquarian Society; Benjamin Carr, letter to Dr. Hays, 1829; Jessie F. Coleridge-Taylor, 11-page letter to Hunt, 1923, with enclosed photographs, also another letter, 1932; Frederick S. Converse, letter, 1917; John Tasker Howard, 4 letters, 1929–32; and Marian MacDowell, letter, 1926. Catalogued ms music includes Miss Broadhurst, operatic music, 1790s?, 179 pages, possibly for her use in the Philadelphia theater; Benjamin Carr, notebook, 84 pages; Theodore Chanler, *Sonate, piano et violon III*, n.d.; Samuel Coleridge-Taylor, "If I Could Love Thee," 5 pages n.d.; Richard Watson Gilder, "O Glorious Sabbath Sun," 1 page, n.d.; John Tasker Howard, "Intaglio" and "Waltzes in Miniature," 5 pages, ca. 1924; Lowell Mason, 2 autograph album leaves, 1857; Clement C. Moore, Psalm 150, 1 page, ca. 1839; Mordecai Quin, "Music Scores and Notes on Harmony," 56 pages ca. 1750 (possibly English); and other items, late 18th century, some of Philadelphia provenance including music for "The First Assembly, Philadelphia, 1783," 1 page. Catalogued ms vols. include Emma Webb, music book, 39 pages, 1858, also other British items. Catalogued autographs, compositions, and poems include items of George Washington Birdseye. Catalogued scores and vols. include works by George F. Bristow, Theodore Chanler, Frederick S. Converse, Reginald De Koven, Robert Delaney, Anthony Philip Heinrich, Edward A. MacDowell, Horatio Parker, and Virgil Thomson. Uncatalogued ms music includes fragments with theory exercises and short pieces, also several full scores, by Lowell Mason, Clinton H. Patterson, George Rittenhouse, George C. Stebbins, and others. Uncatalogued miscellaneous items include Bill Birch, gag book for minstrel shows, ca. 1870; Anne T. Flint, autograph book, ca. 1857–65; Sarah A. Root, unbound book, North Reading, Mass., ca. 1857; Arthur Weld, "History of Music," 5 lectures for the Wisconsin Conservatory of Music, 1900; and a scrapbook of hymn studies, "Chronological History of Christ's Life in Gospel Song," Des Moines, Iowa, 1900. Uncatalogued ms music books include vols. owned by Jane Allette Howells and Maria R. Vesey (Veazy), 18th to 20th centuries, mostly U.S. Miscellaneous materials include items relating to Stephen Collins Foster and Foster Hall, and correspondence relating to radio programs. Oversize scores include Frank Seymour Hastings (1853–1924), 11 scores; also Charles T. Nolan, "Dreaming of Love," and other items presented by Jacques Barzun

—Kenneth A. Lohf

Center for Studies in Ethnomusicology, Department of Music

Field and commercial recordings, photographs, films, and written documents concerning 210 ethnic groups in North America, also concerning New York City, the Caribbean, Central America (especially Mexico), and South America. Holdings include materials collected by University faculty and students, also the Laura Boulton Collection of Traditional and Liturgical Music

Oral History Collection, Butler Library

The Collection consists of transcriptions of oral-history interviews, as described by Elizabeth B. Mason and Louis M. Starr, eds., *The Oral History Collection of Columbia University* (New York, 1979)

Special projects, including Radio Pioneers, 4765 pages, documenting the early history of radio, with materials concerning Howard Barlow (1892–1972), Abram Chasins, and Arthur Judson (1881–1975); Jazz Project, concerning social conditions in south side Chicago, 1920s–30s, and a comparison of New York and Chicago jazz, with materials on Ralph E. Brown, Scoville Browne, Earl ("Fatha") Hines, Milton Hinton, Willie Randall, William E. Samuels, Red Saunders, and Leon Washington; Popular Arts in the 20th Century, including interviews with lyricists, orchestra conductors, music publishers, and song "pluggers," and materials concerning George Gershwin, Benny Goodman, Oscar Hammerstein II, Otto Harbach, Arthur Judson, Katherine Handy (Mrs. Homer) Lewis, Jeanette MacDonald, Mitch Miller, and Meredith Willson; Austrian Project, with information on Austrian immigrants' American careers in music, painting, and writing, including Felix Popper and Frederic Waldman; Hungarian Project, including personal recollections of Hungarian immigrants active in the arts, politics, and international relations, including Gabor Carelli, Béla Bartók, Beniamino Gigli [sic], George Feyer, Otto Herz, Zoltán Kodály, and Abel Lajtha; and American Cultural Leaders, materials collected by Joan Simpson Burns of Williamstown, Mass., studying patterns in American cultural life, including the views of Goddard Lieberson

Individual collections, including Rose Bampton; Aaron Copland, mentioning his childhood education, early compositions, studies with Nadia Boulanger, lectures, and the MacDowell and Yaddo Colonies; Henry Cowell, concerning his early compositions, tone clusters, folk music, and anecdotes of notable musicians including Charles Ives; Samuel Gardner, concerning Thomas Alva Edison; Saul Goodman, on his career as a silent-film accompanist, and impressions of Bruno Walter, Arthur Judson, Leonard Rose, Fritz Reiner, Leopold Stokowski, Arturo Toscanini, Dimitri

Mitropoulos, and Artur Rodzinski; Morton Gould, on his early musical activity, vaudeville, and the Radio City Music Hall; John Hammond; Goddard Lieberson (1911–77), on his early life in Seattle, and activities with the Eastman School of Music; Otto Luening, on composing in Chicago, the Eastman School of Music, Yaddo Colony, and the American Composers' Alliance; Dorothy Maynor, including information on music tours with the Hampton (Va.) Institute Choir; Mary Ellis Peltz, reflecting her career as music critic for the *New York Evening Sun* and her affiliation with the Metropolitan Opera Guild; Max Rabinoff (1876–1966, impresario), discussing the Boston National Opera, Chicago Opera Company, and the American Institute of Operatic and Allied Arts; John Davison Rockefeller III, including information on the development of Lincoln Center for the Performing Arts, the Metropolitan Opera, New York Philharmonic, and the Juilliard School of Music; Richard Rodgers, concerning his association with Lorenz Hart and Oscar Hammerstein II, and his impressions of George Balanchine, Gertrude Lawrence, Florenz Ziegfeld, and Billy Rose; Roger Sessions, on his New England background and early music training; Elie Siegmeister, including impressions of his studies with Nadia Boulanger, 1927–31; Madeline P. Smith, on her experience as private secretary to Cole Porter; Sigmund Spaeth, on his career as music critic for the *New York Evening Mail* and the *New York Times*, also reminiscences of broadcasts, and impressions of Woodrow Wilson and Fiorello LaGuardia; Virgil Thomson, discussions of his childhood in Kansas City, studies with Nadia Boulanger, and concerning filmmaker Robert J. Flaherty (in the Flaherty Project); and Vladimir Ussachevsky, concerning his musical education in the U.S.

Music Library (701 Dodge Hall)

Edward A. MacDowell, published music from his library, and editions of his music

Anton Seidl, library of orchestral performance scores and parts

Columbiana Collection (210 Low Library)

Richard Rodgers, scores of music written for college musicals during his student days

1032

COOPER UNION FOR THE ADVANCEMENT OF SCIENCE AND ART

NNCoo

41 Cooper Square
New York, New York 10003

Programs for and archival materials relating to concerts given by the Peoples Institute, early 20th century

1033

COUNTRY DANCE & SONG SOCIETY OF AMERICA

505 Eighth Avenue
New York, New York 10018

Sheet music, songbooks, and collections of dance music, late 18th century; a dance-tune index, pre-1820; 20 vols. of papers of the Society, 1915– ; photographs; and 50 78-rpm discs

—Sue Salmons

1034
DANCE FILMS ASSOCIATION
250 West Fifty-seventh Street
New York, New York 10019

Films on historical dance topics, among them ballroom dancing, square dancing, jazz, and American Indian dances, produced 1941–

—Susan Braun

1035
Carl FISCHER, Inc.
62 Cooper Square
New York, New York 10003

Archives of the publishing firm, 1872– , including all publications of Carl Fischer, catalogues, programs from Judson Hall during the period of its management by Carl Fischer, plate books for publications, copyright and other publication records, photographs, and memorabilia. See the centennial historical booklet, *Carl Fischer, Inc., 1872–1972: 100 Years of Progress* (New York, 1973?)
Music mss of unpublished works, in the Department of Serious Music

—Martha Tygrel

1036
James J. FULD
1175 Park Avenue
New York, New York 10028

> See his "Surrounded by One's Friends," M.L.A. *Notes*, 33 (1976), 479–90

Sheet music, 5000 items, including first editions of almost all the songs by Irving Berlin, George Gershwin, Jerome Kern, Cole Porter, and Richard Rodgers; also 155 first and early editions of Stephen C. Foster, as described in Fuld's *Pictorial Bibliography of the First Editions of Stephen C. Foster* (Philadelphia, 1957); first edition (the only one now in private hands), other early editions, and other source materials for "The Star-spangled Banner"; and first and early editions of Louis Moreau Gottschalk, Charles Ives, and Scott Joplin, and of other well-known works. Many of these are autographed copies, and many are cited or illustrated in Fuld's *American Popular Music, 1875–1950* (Philadelphia, 1955) and *The Book of World-Famous Music* (New York, 1966; 2nd ed., 1971)
Autographed letters and documents of major American composers, including Stephen Foster, George Gershwin, and Charles Ives, also of lyricists, performers, and scholars; also holograph fair copies of "Dixie," "America," and "God Bless America"

Tunebooks and other early American printed music, 1755– , including 20 pre-1801 editions, with a specialty of early patriotic music (i.e., "Yankee Doodle" and "Hail Columbia"); also a copy of Richard Storrs Willis, *Church Chorals and Choir Studies* (New York, 1850), owned by Lowell Mason, with extensive critical ms annotations
Early ms music, 3 items, including a sacred and secular tunebook signed by Philo Leeds, 1733; a secular song-book owned by James Pike, ca. 1785 (including the "Yankee Doodle" tune); and a secular tunebook signed by Susan Asshetan, 1789
Other special areas include Confederate patriotic music; works by black composers; American college songs; early U.S. songsters; music and cue sheets for silent films; programs, tickets, and other ephemera for important musical events, including U.S. premières of major European and American works, and events involving Enrico Caruso, Arturo Toscanini, and other celebrated performers; also Anton Bruckner, album leaf with dedication, "Hoch, Amerika!"

1037
Coe GLADE
170 West Seventy-third Street
New York, New York 10023

Personal papers relating to her career as a mezzo-soprano with the Chicago Opera and the San Carlo Opera, to her performances as Carmen, and to her career as a concert singer, 1920s– , also an unpublished libretto for the *Elf-Wife*, by Homer Moore, ca. 1917

1038
GRAND LODGE LIBRARY   NNFM
AND MUSEUM
Free and Accepted Masons of New York
71 West Twenty-third Street
New York, New York 10010

Masonic songbooks and sheet music, some 18th century, mostly 20th century
Biographical material on famous masons, including musicians

—Alan Boudreau

1039
Anna HAMLIN
50 West Sixty-seventh Street
New York, New York 10023

George Hamlin (1868–1923, tenor, and father of Miss Hamlin), materials including 4 scrapbooks of reviews, clippings, and programs; a ms piano score of the overture to Hugo Wolf's opera *Der Corregidor*, copied by Heinrich Potpeschnigg and given to Hamlin in 1918; and recordings, including numerous 78-rpm discs and 2 tapes of early recordings

1040
Carl HAVERLIN COLLECTION / BMI ARCHIVES

Broadcast Music, Inc.
40 West Fifty-seventh Street
New York, New York 10019

For general background, see the brochure for the U.S. bicentennial traveling exhibition, *The Carl Haverlin Collection/BMI Archives* (New York, 1976)

Autograph materials relating to famous American musical works, including George Cooper (1840–1927), autographed copy of the text of Henry Tucker's song, "Sweet Genevieve," dated 1917; Daniel Decatur Emmett, autographed copy of "Dixie's Land," dated 1893, with a photograph and signed statement by Emmett; Stephen C. Foster, autographed copy of the American Sunday School Union's *Union Hymns* (1845), with several bars of music added in Foster's hand; James Sloan Gibbons, autographed copy, n.d., of the text for "We Are Coming, Father Abraham"; John Hill Hewitt, autographed copy, n.d., of "All Quiet along the Potomac Tonight"; Francis Scott Key, autographed document, 1805; Robert Lowry (1826–99), autographed fragment of music for the hymn, "Shall We Gather at the River"; William Mason, autographed ms fragment of his Serenata op. 39, dated 1904; Ethelbert Nevin, autographed ms of "My Lady Sleeps," dated 1885; John Howard Payne, autographed copy, dated 1842, entitled "Sweet Home"; Eben E. Rexford (1848–1916), autographed copy of the poem for Hart P. Danks's song, "Silver Threads among the Gold"; Robert Cameron Rogers (1862–1912), autographed copy, dated 1907, of the poem for Ethelbert Nevins's song "The Rosary"; Samuel Francis Smith, autographed copy, dated 1895, of the text for "My Country, 'Tis of Thee"; and Septimus Winner, autographed copy, dated 1899, of "Listen to the Mocking Bird"
Sheet music, 4000 items, including first and early editions of the major U.S. patriotic songs; 100 early editions of music by Louis Moreau Gottschalk; and 80 Confederate and post-Confederate items, mostly published in Nashville, 1859–68
Col. Alexander Scammill (1747–81, U.S. Army bandmaster), letter to Col. Henry Jackson, dated 13 October 1778, requesting musicians and instruments
Autograph letters, of Louis Moreau Gottschalk to M. Benaccio, dated 1850; of Lowell Mason, dated 1858; and of Ernest Giraud, dated 1877
Recent letters and autograph mss of American composers, including Milton Babbitt, Elliott Carter, Henry Cowell, Lehman Engel, Peggy Glanville-Hicks, Henry K. Hadley, Roy Harris, Lou Harrison, Alan Hovhaness, Ulysses Kay, Edgar Stillman Kelley, Walter Piston, Wallingford Riegger, William Schuman, Roger Sessions, Stanley Silverman, Leopold Stokowski, and others
Songbooks, songsters, and programs, including a program for the first broadcast concert, a Maurice Strakosch performance in Philadelphia, 2 April 1877, transmitted by telephone and electrically amplified at Steinway Hall, New York

—William T. Stringfellow

1041
INSTITUTE OF THE AMERICAN MUSICAL

220 West Ninety-third Street
New York, New York, 10025

Research collection of materials from musical theater, ca. 1880– , including disc recordings of nearly all recorded American productions, cylinder recordings, recording manufacturers' catalogues, sheet music and vocal scores, libretti and scripts, playbills and programs, biographical material on performers, photographs of performers and productions, still photographs and publicity material for cinema productions, trade publications, correspondence with composers and performers, research notes, and reference works. The collection formed the basis of Miles Kreuger, *The Movie Musical from Vitaphone to 42nd Street* (New York, 1975) and other reference books on theater

1042
INTERNATIONAL LADIES' GARMENT WORKERS UNION

1710 Broadway
New York, New York, 10019

Sheet music, 75 labor-song texts, 1930s–50s, including some in Yiddish, also 3 ms libretti for related musical productions, 1930s

—Robert Lazar

1043
INTERNATIONAL PIANO LIBRARY

c/o Gregor Benko
215 West Ninety-first Street, Apt. 22
New York, New York, 10024

Recordings of piano music, almost all of them pre-1940 U.S. pressings, beginning with an 1898 recording of an unnamed pianist. See the *New York Times*, 20 July 1978, section 3, p. 13

1044
JEWISH THEOLOGICAL SEMINARY OF AMERICA   NNJ

Cantors Institute Library
3080 Broadway
New York, New York 10027

Max Wohlberg (b. 1909, cantor), materials from his personal library, including 300 sheet-music items, 2 linear meters of liturgical music mss, 600 vols. of Yiddish and Hebrew songs, liturgical music, and books on Jewish music, 1880–1970

—Judith E. Endelman

1045
JOHN STREET METHODIST CHURCH

44 John Street
New York, New York 10038

Hymnals and tunebooks, 1820– , 1.5 linear meters, uncatalogued

—George R. Hill

1046
JUILLIARD SCHOOL OF MUSIC   NNJu
Lila Acheson Wallace Library
144 West Sixty-sixth Street
New York, New York 10023

Holograph music mss of Henry Dreyfuss Brant, Violin Concerto; Eric De Lamarter, overture and intermezzo from *The Betrothal*, and Serbian folksong "O Girl That Singest," for viola and orchestra; Henry Eichheim, *Java*; Louis Gruenberg, *Jack and the Beanstalk*; Leopold Damrosch, Violin Concerto in D Minor, *Ruth and Naomi*, *Sulamith*, and Symphony in A Major; and Ernest Hutcheson, Caprice, for 2 pianos
Archives of the School and its forerunner, the Institute of Musical Art, 3.5 linear meters, including programs, catalogues, minutes, and reports, 1905–70
Psalm books and hymnals, 50 items, mostly 19th century, listed under "Psalters" in a file in the librarian's office
Correspondence and 100 photographs of prominent persons, 1910–40, indexed, including a separate file of Juilliard-related photographs
Sheet music, 31 bound vols., 1890–1935, indexed by title
Scrapbooks with clippings on Juilliard-related subjects, 1920s–40s, 3.5 linear meters
Musical editions, including the Edwards Collection of first and rare editions of chamber-music scores and parts (some reproduced from ms), which contains numerous American items after ca. 1860, notably 24 works for violin and piano, 10 piano trios, 25 quartets, 7 piano quartets and quintets and 6 other chamber works; also 17 vocal or instrumental works in the Reference Collection; 26 piano-vocal scores and 11 libretti from the Cage Collection; 100 Juilliard editions or commissions; music from the library of Marcella Sembrich and other faculty members; and nearly complete runs of the publications by New Music and by the Society for the Publication of American Music

—Nina Jo Davis-Millis

1047
Mrs. Frida KAHN
30 East End Avenue, Apt. 6-F
New York, New York 10028

Erich Itor Kahn (1905–56, pianist and composer), personal papers, including correspondence received, music mss and published music, programs, photographs, and his personal music library. See *Spalek*, p. 453

1048
W. Lloyd KEEPERS
New York, New York

William Lloyd Keepers (d. 1978), personal sheet-music collection, 200,000 items, ca. 1800– , not available for consultation

1049
Daniel B. ("Banjo Dan") McCALL
50 Grove Street, Apt. 3
New York, New York 10014

Sheet music, 1840s– , mostly 1890s–1920s, 50,000 items, arranged primarily by subjects; also 1000 songbooks, 4000 recordings, and 200 books relating to banjo music, vaudeville, minstrelsy, and other areas of American popular music. See Charles J. Jordan, "Collecting Those Old-Fashioned Melodies," *Yankee*, 431 (1979), 166–79

1050
MANNES COLLEGE OF MUSIC   NNMC
157 East Seventy-fourth Street
New York, New York 10021

Leopold Mannes (1899–1964), holograph music mss of piano, chamber, and orchestral works, 50 items
Carlos Salzedo (1885–1961) Collection, including annotated scores, transcriptions, and original compositions for the harp

1051
METROPOLITAN   NNMM
MUSEUM OF ART
Fifth Avenue and Eighty-second Street
New York, New York 10028

Crosby Brown Collection of Musicians' Portraits, 1500 items, mostly European, assembled in the U.S., mostly 1870s–80s. See the *Catalogue of the Crosby Brown Collection*, Metropolitan Museum of Art, Handbook no. 13/IV (New York, 1904)
Documents of American musical-instrument makers, including certificates of award, engravings, trade catalogues, and photographs. Among the makers are August Gemünder (violin-maker, 1814–95, in Springfield, Mass., and New York), Angelo Mannello (mandolin-maker, New York, ca. 1900), and Lars Jorgen Rudolf Olsen (20th-century violin- and bow-maker, New York and New Jersey)

—Laurence Libin

1052
METROPOLITAN OPERA ARCHIVES
Lincoln Center
New York, New York 10023

> Established and organized through the efforts of Mary Ellis Peltz, 1958–59. See her article, "The Metropolitan Opera Archives," *American Archivist*, 30 (1967), 471–75

Bound programs of the Metropolitan Opera, 1881– , including tour programs. These copies have ms corrections in the cast, entered mostly by the house manager, and thus supersede the generally available printed copies
Card files on performers, 1881– , 1 arranged by opera and subdivided according to roles and singers, and 1 arranged by singers and subdivided according to roles. Based on the corrected copies of programs (cited above), this file corrects and extends the lists in William

H. Seltsman, *Metropolitan Opera Annals* (New York, 1947; suppls. 1957 and 1968)

Financial records of the Metropolitan Opera, including box-office ledgers and day books, 1880– , 5 linear meters for the period to 1940; contracts with conductors and singers, 6 four-drawer cabinets; salary account books, by year and subdivided by performer, 1896– , 2.5 linear meters for the period to 1940; concert-artist contracts, 1909– , for special appearances by Metropolitan Opera artists under contract, negotiated by the company, 1 linear meter; and other miscellaneous records, including tour contracts and rental-property account books

Personal correspondence files of company officers, including John Brown and Giulio Gatti-Casazza, 1909–19, 60 linear cm.; Edward Ziegler, 1916–44, 4 linear meters; Giulio Gatti-Casazza, 1918–35, 4.5 linear meters; Frank Garlichs, 1924–41, 30 linear cm.; Paul D. Cravath, 1928–40, 1 linear meter; Cornelius Bliss, 1928–45, 30 linear cm.; Herbert Witherspoon, 1933–35, 1.2 linear meters; and Edward Johnson, 1935–49, 8 linear meters

Press releases, 1915– , mostly post-1940; also press clippings in 72 bound vols. for the period 1903–40, and a subsidiary file of press announcements and reports

Pictorial material, including sketches and designs, mostly of opera sets, 2 linear meters; general files of photographs, including conductors (1 four-drawer file cabinet), singers (6 cabinets), and miscellaneous (1 cabinet); blueprints, elevations, plans, production books, oversize photos of operas, and other materials (6 linear meters); and glass negatives (2 cabinets)

Scrapbooks, including vols. for Gladys Axman, Anna Bishop, Frieda Hempel, Clara Louise Kellogg, Berta Morena, Grace Moore, Adelina Patti (including extensive ms correspondence with Max Strakosch, 1864–66), Maurice Strakosch, Terese Tietjens, and Florence Wickham

Musical texts used by Giuseppe del Puente, in 1 folder; and by Lillian Nordica, 150 editions, including a dedicatory holograph copy of Charles Wakefield Cadman, *Three Songs to Odysseus*

Files of the Metropolitan Opera Guild, 1935– , 2.5 linear meters, and broadcast scripts, 1941– , 1.5 linear meters

—Mary Ellis Peltz

1053

Pierpont MORGAN LIBRARY NNPM
29 East Thirty-sixth Street
New York, New York 10016

John Pierpont, journal, including descriptions of music in South Carolina, ca. 1805, as discussed in Abe C. Ravitz, "John Pierpont and the Slaves' Christmas," *Phylon: The Atlanta University Review of Race & Culture,* 21 (1960), 383–86

Holograph music mss in the general collections, including Frederick S. Converse, 4 items, among them *The Pipe of Desire* (1910) and the Symphony no. 6 (1940); Victor Herbert, "The Nightingale and the Star"; Gian Carlo Menotti, 1 item; Randall Thompson, 1 item; and Virgil Thomson, Portraits for piano of Agnes Rindge and Minna Curtiss (1936–41)

Mary Flagler Cary Collection, including holograph mss of Marc Blitzstein, *Theater for the Cabaret;* Henry T.

Burleigh, "Deep River," dated 1926; John Cage, *Three Dances, for 2 pianos,* in 2 and sometimes 3 variant versions, including instructions for preparing the pianos; Paul Creston, "Picnic Waltz"; Vladimir Dukelsky, arrangement of Sergei Rachmaninoff's "Vocalise," with parts; Gian Carlo Menotti, 2 items; Roger Sessions, *Music for the Black Maskers;* and Virgil Thomson, "O, My Deir Hert," 1921. Also correspondence of musicians, as cited in *The Mary Flagler Cary Music Collection* (New York, 1970), pp. 53–101, much of it addressed to Harry Harkness Flagler or to Mrs. Cary, and including letters from Emma Albani (10 items, 1885–95), Frances Alda, Richard Aldrich, Winthrop Ames, Margaret Mary Anglin, Ugo Ara, Leopold Auer, Béla Bartók, Katherine Lee Bates (autograph fair copy of "America, the Beautiful"), Harold Bauer (9 items, 1914–34), Thomas F. Bayard, Amy Cheney (Mrs. H. H. A.) Beach, Rudolf Berger, David Bispham, Edwin Howland Blashfield, Lucrezia Bori, William A. Bradley (7 items, 1919–30), Frederick A. Bridgman, Dudley Buck, Ole Bull, Bryson Burroughs (6 items, 1907–15), Fritz Busch, Giuseppe Campanari, John Alden Carpenter, Albert Coates (19 items), Edward J. de Coppet, Royal Cortissoz, Leopold Damrosch, Walter Damrosch (124 items, 1889–1950), Reginald De Koven, Édouard Déthier, Gaston Déthier, Andreas Dippel, Olin Downes, Ruth Draper, Emma Eames, Florence Easton, Gervase Elwes, Blair Fairchild (6 items, 1924–29), Geraldine Farrar, Sir Johnston Forbes-Robinson, Olive Fremstad, Daniel Frohman, Johnna Gadski, Gottfried Galston, Fraser Gange, Mary Garden, Etelka Gerster Gardini, Alfred Gaul, Eva Gauthier, Maria Lawrence Gilman, Alma Gluck, Emilio de Gogorza, Percy A. Grainger, Heinrich Gudehus, James K. Hackett, Henry K. Hadley, Guy d'Hardelot, Sandor Harmati, Mack Harrell, Victor Harris, Minnie Hauk (10 items, 1879–94), Frieda Hempel, W. J. Henderson, Alfred Hertz, Dame Myra Hess, Ripley Hitchcock, Josef Hofmann, Ferdinand von Inten, Joseph Jefferson, James Howard Jenkins (materials on "John Brown's Body," Oshkosh, Wis., 1899–1910), Edward Johnson, Robert Underwood Johnson, Franz Kneisel, Paul Kochanski, Victor Kolar, Nina Koshetz, Henry Edward Krehbiel, Fritz Kreisler, Alexander Lambert, Hans Lange, Charles Martin Loeffler, Georges Longy, Edward A. MacDowell (7 items, 1890–1904), Maria (Garcia) Malibran, Nicolai Malko, David Mannes (7 items, 1912–43), Riccardo Martin, Daniel Gregory Mason, Aylmer Maude, Antonia Mielke, Ethelbert Nevin, Franz Ondricek, Ignace Jan Paderewski (6 items, 1897–1938), Attilio Parelli, Horatio Parker, Bliss Perry, Eugenio di Pirani, John Powell, Serge Prokofiev, Henri Rabaud, Sergei Rachmaninoff, Eduard Remenyi, Martin Roeder, Francis Rogers (12 items, 1927–31), Felix Salmond, Carlos Salzedo, Alexander Saslavsky, Rosario Scalero, Ernest Schelling (6 items, 1916–39), Kurt Schindler, Rudolph Schirmer, Arnold Schoenberg (43 items, 1893–1950), Friedrich Schorr, Anton Seidl, Arthur Seidl, Marcella Sembrich (34 items, 1913–34), Alexander Siloti (7 items, 1922–31), John Philip Sousa, Albert Spalding (15 items, 1920–50), Carl Stoeckel, Albert Stoessel, Sigismond Stojowski, Deems Taylor, Milka Ternini, Emma Thursby, Arturo Toscanini, Auguste Vianesi, Augustus Vogt, Bruno Walter, Arthur Whiting, Herbert Witherspoon, and Fannie Bloomfield Zeisler. Also testimonial materials honoring Mr. Flagler for his activity on behalf of the New York Philharmonic-Symphony Orchestra, 100 inscribed photographs from musicians, and Mrs. Cary's autograph book, 1914–36 (*ibid.,* pp. 87–103)

Dannie and Hettie Heineman Collection, including Adolf Busch, holograph ms of the *Nocturno für Saxophon und kleines Orchester über ein Negro Spiritual;* Jenny Lind, letter, 1849; and letters to Mr. or Mrs. Heineman from Adolf Busch, Mieczyslaw Horszowski, Bronislaw Hubermann, Lotte Lehmann, Darius Milhaud, Joseph Szigeti, and Bruno Walter, as cited in *The Dannie and Hettie Heineman Collection* (New York, 1978), pp. 105–9

—J. Rigbie Turner

Reginald Allen and Gilbert & Sullivan Collections, including materials in three sections—Gilbert; Sullivan; and Gilbert & Sullivan—each with major U.S. holdings, including the holograph score and other related matter for the world première of *The Pirates of Penzance,* New York, 1879; Sullivan's pocket diary for his first U.S. trip, 1879–80; letters from Sullivan written during this visit to America, and others from his second visit in 1885; vocal scores and sheet music with U.S. imprints; and programs, photographs, and colorful ephemera. For a general overview, see the Gallery Association of New York State's monograph exhibition catalogue commemorating the first D'Oyly Carte Opera Company American tour and *The Pirates of Penzance* première, entitled *Gilbert & Sullivan in America* (New York, 1979). For greater detail on specific items, see the Morgan Library exhibition catalogue, *Sir Arthur Sullivan: Composer & Personage* (New York, 1975), and the Grolier Club exhibition catalogue, *W. S. Gilbert, an Anniversary Survey and Exhibition Checklist* (Charlottesville, 1963)

—Reginald Allen

1054
MUSEUM OF BROADCASTING

1 East Fifty-third Street
New York, New York 10022

See the *Subject Guide to the Radio and Television Collection of the Museum of Broadcasting,* 2nd ed. (New York, 1979)

Recordings and scripts of radio and television broadcasts, including 250 musical-broadcast recordings, 1920s– , 983 radio programs on audiocassettes, 901 television programs on videocassettes, and 163 radio scripts on microfiche

1055
MUSEUM OF MODERN ART   NNMMA

11 West Fifty-third Street
New York, New York 10019

Department of Film collection, including 22 orchestral scores, 50 miscellaneous items of music for orchestra or piano, and 60 cue sheets to accompany silent films, 1915–26; 1500 scripts, 1900– ; silent and sound films, 8000 items; disc and tape recordings of film scores, 15 items, 1927– ; and 8000 books related to the film industry

—Charles Silver

1056
MUSEUM OF THE AMERICAN   NNMAI
INDIAN—HEYE FOUNDATION

Broadway and 155th Street
New York, New York 10032

Materials are dispersed between the Museum, the Research Annex (Bruckner Boulevard and Middletown Road, Bronx, N.Y. 10461), and the Huntington Free Library and Reading Room (9 Westchester Square, Bronx, N.Y. 10461)

Materials concerning American Indian music, including commercial recordings; films on American Indian music, some of them made by the Foundation staff, 1920s; photographs of musicians and musical instruments in a general photograph collection of 70,000 items, including prints, rare archival photographs, and negatives; and published material pertaining to music and performing arts of the American Indian. See the *Dictionary Catalogue of the American Indian Collection* (Boston, 1977)

—Nancy Henry

1057
MUSEUM OF THE CITY   NNMus
OF NEW YORK

Theater and Music Department
Fifth Avenue at 103rd Street
New York, New York 10029

Individual collections containing sheet music, ca. 1800– , also other printed and ms music, programs, catalogues, pictures, and memorabilia, emphasizing New York musical theater and including items by and relating to George M. Cohan, Betty Comden and Adolph Green, Howard Dietz, George and Ira Gershwin, Mary Martin, Ethel Merman, and others, also materials on Yiddish theater, and papers relating to the Theater Guild

—Mary C. Henderson

1058
NATIONAL GUILD OF COMMUNITY
SCHOOLS OF THE ARTS

570 Seventh Avenue, Seventeenth Floor
New York, New York 10018

Archives of the Guild and its predecessors, 1923–72, 3 linear meters, of which roughly one-fifth has been sorted and organized. Included are minutes, speeches, newsletters, and conference papers and programs, 1939– ; also extensive correspondence of Harold Bauer, Robert Egan (of Duquesne University), Ruth Kemper (of the Turtle Bay Music School, New York), Howard Whittaker (of the Cleveland Music School Settlement), and Herbert Zipper (of the Music Center of the North Shore, Winnetka, Ill.)

Archives of the National Federation of Settlements, including its Music Division (1920s–33), are at the University of Minnesota, Minneapolis (q.v.). Other predecessors of the Guild are documented in the

New York archives, including the New York Association of Music School Settlements, financial and personal records, 1930–33, comprising itemized accounts of 9 member schools, minutes, 1924–35, and summaries of minutes, 1923–35; the New York Association of Community and Settlement Music Schools, official documents, minutes, planning reports, and other papers, 1935–37; and papers relating to WPA music programs, 1934–37, 10 items, including speeches by Harold Bauer, I. A. Herschmann, Ernest Hutcheson, and Olga Samaroff, and annual reports of the Yorkville Music School, 1927–32

—Marcy Horwitz, Alice Hudson

1059
NEW-YORK HISTORICAL SOCIETY NHi
170 Central Park West
New York, New York 10024

See Arthur J. Breton, *A Guide to the Manuscript Collections of the New-York Historical Society* (Westport, Conn., 1972; hereinafter cited as *Breton*)

Sheet music and scores, 10,000 items, 18th to 20th centuries, strong in Confederate imprints and Spanish-American War music, and including materials from the collection of Belle C. Landauer. See her illustrated guides, *My City 'Tis of Thee* (New York, 1951), *Striking the Right Note in Advertising* (New York, 1951), and *Some Terpsichorean Ephemera* (New York, 1953)

Tunebooks and hymnals, 700 items, late 18th and 19th centuries, items pre-1801 fully catalogued

Music holographs, including mss of Micah Hawkins, Charles Edward Horn (1786–1849), and Richard Grant White (1842–85); also Fernando Andrillon, *The Evening Prayer* ("A Grand Melody for Voices and Piano"), dedication copy presented to Elizabeth T. Porter Beach, ca. 1880 (*Breton*, 3418)

Manuscript music collections, including John Bremner (British soldier, active in New York and Ontario), diary and memorandum book, with 10 pages of Scottish and other tunes (*Breton*, 343); a British fife-major's music book, post-1780, with 80 tunes, as presented to John Greenwood (former fife-major in Peterson's 15th Massachusetts Regiment) (*Breton*, 975); Henry Brown, book of romantic and patriotic poems and songs, many with music, ca. 1789 (*Breton*, 1244); Shaker music, in 3 vols., 1843, 1846, and n.d. (*Breton*, 2647); and Henry Haas (1802–72, German immigrant), personal papers, including 4 ms music books and 11 other music mss (*Breton*, 2303)

Vocal-music texts in ms, including William Darlington (scientist and political leader), personal papers, with 1 vol. of secular songs, copied 1807–31 (*Breton*, 1541); John Adams Dix (1789–1879), translations of Latin hymns, 58 pages (*Breton*, 2137); Edwin F. Hatfield, notes on psalms and hymns, 1864, 175 pages (*Breton*, 2813); Henrietta Hobart, ms notebook, of songs by Gen. John Burgoyne and other British authors, including a "Prologue wrote by Francis Lord Rawdon on the opening of the Theatre at New York, 6th June 1776" (*Breton*, 751); James Lewis, notebook, including 11 pages of his songs, ca. 1806 (*Breton*, 1086); Samuel Francis Smith (1808–95), correspondence and mss of his hymns and poems (*Breton*, 3300); Bernardus Swartwout (ensign in the 2nd New York Regiment), orderly books, 1781–83, including a song sung at Poughkeepsie, 4 July 1783, "Columbia, Columbia, to Glory Arise" (*Breton*, 1053); Bayard Taylor, personal papers, including ms of a song written for Jenny Lind (*Breton*, 2765); and Maria C. (Mrs. William W.) Todd, diaries, 1837–54, including hymn texts (*Breton*, 2495)

Personal papers with music references, including James Alexander (1691–1756), with steps for 12 popular dances (*Breton*, 123); John Anderson, Jr. (1773–98), diary, 1794–98, mentioning the theater and his playing of the violin (*Breton*, 1353); William Dunlap (theater manager), correspondence, 1826–37, 19 items, and diaries, 1797–98, 1819–20, and 1833–34 (*Breton*, 1468); William Hoffman, diary, 1847–50, mentioning Jenny Lind's New York visit (*Breton*, 2741); Jenny Lind, letters to and contracts with Phineas T. Barnum, 1850–51, 7 items; Aneas Mackay, diary, 1810–15, mentioning his activity as a flute player and the Apollo Society (*Breton*, 1817); Jenny Maude (daughter of Jenny Lind, in London), 14 letters to Leonidas Westervelt, 1926–33, regarding her mother's memorabilia (*Breton*, 3655); Julius Edward Meyer (singing teacher), record book, 1858–99, involving Emma Thursby and others of his students at the German Conservatory of Music (*Breton*, 2933); Herrmann Rannefeld (organist of Zion Evangelical Church, New York), correspondence, 1879–83, and diaries, 1883–1939, including accounts, expenses, and some ms music (*Breton*, 3404); Claudius W. Rider (Civil War fifer, Company C, 110th New York State Volunteers, active in Baltimore, Louisiana, and Florida), diaries, 1862–65, mentioning military and other music (*Breton*, 3136.1); Amanda L. Dunwell (Mrs. Benjamin Harvey) Streeter, personal papers, 1847–54, including references to music in the Dunwell family (*Breton*, 2726); George Templeton Strong, diaries, 1837–75, 4 vols., with extensive musical references, particularly concerning his presidency of the Philharmonic Society (*Breton*, 2488); Grant Thorburn, ms of "A Visit to Jenny Lind," 1851 (*Breton*, 2005); Emma Thursby (1854–1931, opera singer), personal papers, in 57 vols. and 7 boxes (*Breton*, 3323); Andrew C. Wheeler (1870–1922, music journalist), correspondence and lecture notes; and William Halsey Wood (organist and choirmaster), papers, 1855–97

Organizational records, including the Theatre Royal, New York, receipt book, 1779, kept by Thomas Barrows (treasurer), including entries for payments to musicians (*Breton*, 888); Italian Opera Association, New York, minutes of the Board of Trustees, 1832–35, also correspondence and papers, 1832–40, 1860, in all 66 items (*Breton*, 2375); Castle Garden, day book, 1843–51, with records of 1850 concerts by Jenny Lind, including entries for musicians; *Musical Review* (New York music journal), letterpress book, 1879–81, with correspondence involving its editors and publishers, José C. Rodrigues, F. J. C. Schneider, and Archibald MacMartin (*Breton*, 3406); and the MacDowell Club, New York, archives, 1905–45, including minutes, other official records, and scrapbooks (*Breton*, 3598)

Programs and playbills, including the Dr. Edward Titus collection for New York, 1852–75

Broadsides, many with song texts, 700 pre-1900 items

Photographs, including extensive holdings relating to New York City in the ragtime and swing eras

—Jean Bowen

1060

NEW YORK JAZZ MUSEUM

236 West Fifty-fourth Street
New York, New York 10019

This collection, as cited in *NHPRC* and elsewhere, is no longer accessible

1061

NEW YORK PUBLIC LIBRARY　　　　　　**NN**

Fifth Avenue and Forty-second Street
New York, New York 10018

Most of the divisions cited below have published their holdings in a G. K. Hall *Dictionary Catalog* series, as noted. These are now being updated in the annual *Bibliographical Guides* series, which include books, music, and other material catalogued during the year in question (i.e., some of which may have been copied or published and/or acquired considerably earlier)

Music Division (a part of the Performing Arts Research Center, 111 Amsterdam Avenue, New York 10023)

A. *Music Manuscripts*
B. *Personal and Organizational Papers*
C. *Sheet Music*
D. *Other Printed Music and Books*
E. *Programs*
F. *Scrapbooks*
G. *Pictorial Materials*
H. *Miscellaneous Other Materials*

Other Divisions of the Performing Arts Research Center

J. *Rodgers and Hammerstein Archives of Recorded Sound*
K. *Dance Collection*
L. *Billy Rose Theatre Collection*

Other Divisions

M. *Manuscripts and Archives Division (Fifth Avenue and Forty-second Street, New York 10018)*
N. *Schomburg Center for Research in Black Culture (103 West 135th Street, New York 10030)*

For general background on the Music Division see Frank C. Campbell, "The Music Division of the New York Public Library," *Fontes artis musicae*, 16 (1969), 112–19; Philip L. Miller and Frank C. Campbell, "How the Music Division of the New York Public Library Grew—A Memoir," M.L.A. *Notes*, 35 (1979), 537–55, and 36 (1979), 65–77 (Parts 1–3; Part 4 to follow); and the Division's 6-page brochure. Catalogued items are cited in the *Dictionary Catalog of the Music Division* (Boston, 1964, with suppls.; hereinafter cited as *DC*)

A. Music Manuscripts

Holograph materials may be either fully catalogued (see *DC*, vol. 2, pp. 68–174); processed and accessible through the shelf list (class *MNY-Amer in the Special Collections Reading Room); or uncatalogued and unprocessed, but usually described in a finding list

Early ms copies, including John Field (of Philadelphia, fl. ca. 1790), ms duets for piano 4-hands; Joseph Lewis, ms duets for 2 violins (ca. 1805); songs and piano music (ca. 1810); John Muenscher, 2 vols. of sonatas and other keyboard music (Providence, ca. 1810); Job Plimpton, ms of *The Universal Repository of Music* (New York, ca. 1808); and L. A. Townes, ms

harp music (Petersburg, Va., ca. 1832). For details, see *DC*, vol. 18, pp. 289ff

Among those composers whose mss are definitively or extensively represented in the collections are Samuel A. Baldwin, John J. Becker (see *DC*), Nicolai Berezowsky, Alberto Bimboni, Gena Branscombe, John Hyatt Brewer, George F. Bristow, Charles Wakefield Cadman, Henry Cowell, Frank Damrosch, Leopold Damrosch, Walter Damrosch, Francesco Fanciulli (see *DC*), Arthur Farwell, William Flanagan, Caryl Florio, Isadore Freed, Louis Moreau Gottschalk, Charles Tomlinson Griffes, Henry K. Hadley, Eugen Haile, Louis Horst, John Tasker Howard, Mary Howe, Henry Holden Huss, Chester Ide (see *Music of Chester Edward Ide, 1878–1944* [New York, 1976]), Noble Kreider, Sara Ida Liventhan, Frank Loesser, Daniel Gregory Mason, Courtland Palmer, Meyer Posner, Wallingford Riegger, Joseph Schillinger, Sholum Secunda, Joseph Strimer, Deems Taylor, Arthur Whiting, and Florence Wickham. (Material of Percy A. Grainger is now in the Grainger Museum, Melbourne, Australia, q.v.)

Smaller collections of holograph ms materials are also present for Homer N. Bartlett, Marion Bauer, Rick Besoyan, Seth Bingham, Marc Blitzstein, John Parsons Beach, Ernest Bloch, Carrie Jacobs Bond, Howard Brockway, Dudley Buck, George W. Chadwick, Theodore Chanler, John Cheshire, Louis Cheslock, Aaron Copland, Helen Crane, Reginald De Koven, Nathaniel Dett, Duke Ellington, Arthur Foote, Rudolf Forst, Sam Franco, William Henry Fry, Rudolph Ganz, Eva Gauthier, Philip James, Clayton Johns, Horace Johnson, J. Rosamond Johnson, Werner Josten, Erich Itor Kahn, Hershy Kay, Gail Kubik, Robert Korda, Edward Kurtz, Harvey Worthington Loomis, Edward MacDowell, Colin McPhee, Eduardo Marzo, Jan Meyerowitz, Albert Mildenberg, Leo Ornstein, Thorvald Otterström, Horatio Parker, Victor Pelissier, Walter Piston, Silas G. Pratt, Robert Prince, Sigmund Romberg, Carl Ruggles, Marthe Servine, Roger Sessions, Harry Rowe Shelley, Arthur Shepherd, Charles Stanford Skilton, Stefan Sopkin, John Philip Sousa, George Templeton Strong, Virgil Thomson, J. C. Viereck, Harriet Ware, Karl Wiegl, Emerson Whithorne, Septimus Winner, Benjamin Edward Woolf, and Edgard Varèse

R. H. Burnside (1870–1952, conductor, proprietor of the rental agency bearing his name, and musical director of the New York Hippodrome), working library of scores and parts, 1902–ca. 1925

Helen Tamiris Collection of 20th-century popular and serious music, 33 items

Elliott Carter, personal papers, including music mss and other correspondence, on deposit, as cited in the exhibition catalogue, *Elliott Carter Sketches and Scores in Manuscript* (New York, 1973)

Many of the items listed above were acquired through the efforts of Barton Cantrell, Mrs. Henry K. Hadley, and the National Association for American Composers and Conductors, and from the estates of David Bispham and Eva Gauthier

B. Personal and Organizational Papers

For further details on many of these items, see *DC*, esp. vol. 2, pp. 37–68 and 174–229. In addition, the shelf-list for class *MNY, maintained in the Special Collections Reading Room, contains 10,000 cards; considerably more than half of these are for American subjects, with many references to other single letters by persons cited below and by other American musicians. Major holdings include the following:

Carnegie Hall, New York, ledgers and cash books, 1891–1926

Walter and Leopold Damrosch, 6000 items, 1832–1950, including archival files of the Society of American Symphony Conductors, the Musicians' Emergency Fund, and the New York Symphony Orchestra, also correspondence with the Aeolian Company and relating to the Metropolitan Opera Contest, 1910. See the index to the collection, prepared by Fred Himmelein, 1972, 666 pages

Eva Gauthier, 1000 items, ca. 1900–1958, involving her work with contemporary art-song composers, and including 16 personal diaries, also 71 letters with Emma Albani, ca. 1905–10

Charles Tomlinson Griffes, 250 letters, 1903–22, also original drawings, watercolors, and etchings, ca. 1909–14

Henry K. Hadley, personal papers, including letters and his autograph address book

Mary Howe, personal papers, 1915–65, including 3000 letters and 30 folders of correspondence, also 11 folders of working records on various matters, and 4 folders relating to the National Federation of Music Clubs, the National League of American Pen Women, Sigma Alpha Iota, and *Who's Who in America*

Henry Holden Huss, 7 boxes, 1862–1933, including correspondence, research notes, and files relating to the Presser Foundation, with 20 letters from Daniel Gregory Mason

Otto Kinkeldey, personal papers, including correspondence, lecture and research notes, and mss of his scholarly publications

League of Composers, 800 letters received by Claire Reis, including 36 from Darius Milhaud, 14 from Arnold Schoenberg, and 45 from Leopold Stokowski; also 200 other letters to Claire Reis on other matters, 1932–78

Minna Lederman, collection of letters from Igor Stravinsky

Mailamm (American Palestine Music Association), 1000 letters, 1930s–40s, mostly addressed to Ethel S. (Mrs. Frank) Cohen and Miriam Shomer (Mrs. Charles) Zunser

Manuscript Society of New York, 5 vols. of minutes and reports, 1896–1912

F. F. Mueller, ms memorandum book of the Handel and Haydn Society, Boston, 1854

New Music Society, 26 cartons of archival materials

Gustave Reese, personal papers, including correspondence, lecture and research notes, and mss of his scholarly publications

Joseph Schillinger, personal papers, including 60 legal documents, 7 typescripts, 700 items of research materials, and 170 letters received, 1923–46

Town Hall, New York, archival records, including correspondence, account books, and programs

Bruno Walter, personal papers, including correspondence, scrapbooks, photographs, and memorabilia, as described in *Spalek*, p. 942, and comprising the archives of the Bruno Walter Memorial Foundation

Smaller collections of letters and documents, including the American Music Association, list of autographs of members, dated New York, 10 September 1856;

George Antheil, 125 items, 1931–55; John Parsons Beach, 5 letters from Arthur Farwell, 1903–4; Beethoven Choral Society, New York, account book, 1877–78; Seth Bingham, 80 items, 1935–72; Artur Bodanzky, 10 items, 1919–37; Gilbert Chase, 120 items, 1920–72; Composers Forum; Henry Cowell, 14 items, 1932–54; Howard Dietz; Rudolf Forst, 40 items, 1934–73; Nahan Franko, 101 items, 1857–1935; Sam Franko, 75 items, 1866–1917; Ossip Gabrilowitch, 20 items, 1902–33; Lawrence Gilman, 30 items, 1922–37; Charles Jerome Hopkins, 22 items, 1856–98; International Society for Contemporary Music, 90 items, 1923–58; Burl Ives, 1200 items of research notes for his publications; Charles Ives, 20 items; Henry E. Krehbiel, 33 items, 1890–1922, with research notes and letters to Frances Perkins; Carl V. Lachmund, 25 letters received, 1920s–30s; Edward A. MacDowell, 150 items, 1859–1906; Bob Maltz, 50 letters received from jazz and pop musicians, ca. 1940–60; Daniel Gregory Mason, 25 items, 1940–51; William Mason, 30 letters received, 1853–1906, his 1847 ms "Catalogue of Music," a scrapbook of "programmes of all concerts I have played in from Nov. 3rd, 1846," ca. 1879, and his "Anniversary" autograph album; Arthur H. Messiter (1834–1916), "The Literature of Music," 8-vol. ms bibliographic list, ca. 1900 (*DC*, 19:111); Adelina Patti, 88 letters and 86 other documents, 1880–1905; Henry Reyer, personal account book, New York, 1848–56; Deems Taylor, 17 letters, 1927–60, also scrapbooks of his criticism in the *New York World*, 1921–25, and the *New York American*, 1931–32; and Arthur Whiting, 100 items, 1884–1946, concerning his studies in Germany and his dealings with his music publisher, G. Schirmer

C. Sheet Music

Included are the extensive collections of Joseph Muller, Elliott Shapiro, and George Goodwin, and numerous smaller collections

The collections, numbering 400,000 items, consist of the following categories: (1) U.S. imprints to 1831, 5000 items, classed as AM-V (vocal) or AM-I (instrumental), each arranged by composer; (2) U.S. imprints, 1831–70, 35,000 items, classed as AM2-V or AM2-I, as above; (3) U.S. imprints, 1871–1900, 23,000 items, classed as AM3-V or AM3-I, as above, but not sorted; (4) U.S. popular songs, 1890–1977, 20,000 items in bound vols. and 250,000 unbound items, the latter arranged by title within each year; (5) vocal music from shows, 1890– , classified as M.C. (musical comedy) or T. ("talkies," i.e., sound films), 10,000 items arranged by show title; (6) popular instrumental music, 1890– , 14,000 items, classed as P. I. ("pop instrumental"), subdivided for Shows, Marches, General (e.g., piano "novelties"), and Ragtime; and (7) other uncatalogued sheet music, including foreign materials but largely U.S. imprints, classified as U-V (vocal, mostly songs, in folio size), 50,000 items, and U-O (uncatalogued octavos), 2000 items

Catalogues, as follows: (a) the Song Index, with entries for titles and first lines for groups 5 and 7 above, 1 and 2 in progress; (b) a chronological index, 1769–1853, with 5000 cards, maintained up to ca. 1960 for groups 1 and 2 above; (c) the "Medium" file in the Americana section, 50,000 cards, mostly items from groups 2, 5, and 7 above; (d) the subject file in the Americana section, 40,000 cards for song topics, references, and forms; (e) main-entry indexes for groups 1 and 2 above; (f) composer and show-title index for group 5 above; and (g) author and title file for the P. I. (ragtime) materials in group 6 above

D. Other Printed Music and Books

Materials are entirely catalogued and accessible through the *DC*. Quantitatively, the holdings of pre-1940 U.S. music are spread through the following general areas of the classification:

Form	Class	Items
Secular songbooks	*MP	1351
Books of national music	*MO	453
Tunebooks and hymnals	*MRA	1185
Sacred vocal works	*MR	82
Dramatic scores	*MS	212
Orchestral music	*MT/*MV/*MW	541
Chamber music	*MX	232
Instrumental solos	*MY	153
Songsters	*MPW	326
Libretti	*MZ	22

Included in the collections are extensive gifts and acquisitions from the music libraries of George Antheil, John J. Becker, David Bispham, Herter Bliss, Sophie Braslau, Henry Cowell, Julian Edwards, Eva Gauthier, Louise Homer, James G. Huneker, Henry E. Krehbiel, Arthur Mees, Horace W. Nicoll, Robert Haven Schauffler, Joseph Schillinger, Lawrence Tibbett, Paul Whiteman, Arthur Whiting, and Paul Wittgenstein. The nucleus of the rare-book holdings consists of the library of Joseph Drexel (d. 1880), one of the earliest major private collectors of music in America, his collection incorporating the music libraries of H. F. Albrecht and J. D. LaRoche. The Harry Schumer collection includes opera scores assembled by the librarian of the Metropolitan Opera Co. Among the organizations that have provided special funds for music are the American Guild of Musical Artists, ASCAP, Beethoven Association, BMI, Carnegie Foundation, Juilliard Foundation, National Association of American Composers and Conductors, and Society of the Friends of Music

E. Programs

General collection, 10 linear meters, in two series: (1) catalogued, in bound vols., and arranged by organization or performance site; and (2) uncatalogued, unbound, and mostly arranged by personal names of performers. The shelflist for the two series is merged into one alphabetical sequence

League of Composers, a presumably complete run of their programs, 1923–54

Joseph Schillinger, programs of his works, in Russian and English

F. Scrapbooks

Scrapbooks, with clippings, programs, and/or other materials. Scrapbooks listed below have been filmed (except as noted) and are available under the call number *ZAN-*M28. Items were collected by or devoted to the following: Paul Aron, 5 vols.; Carl Barus; Henriette Beebe, 1873–82; Flora Mae & Ruby Beeching (not filmed); the Birseck collection, 15 vols., 1883–1920; David Bispham, 58 vols., 1886–1917; Jussi Bjoerling, 1938–41; Marc A. Blumenberg, 1913–14; Bohemian Club of San Francisco, 1870; Alexander Borovsky, 1941–44; Sophie Braslau, 11 vols., 1913–34; John Lathrop Burdett, 7 vols., 1863–1922; Charles Wakefield Cadman, 1936–41; Henriette Cady, 1909–22, in the Joseph Raffaelli collection; Chicago opera and concert programs, 1914–17 (not filmed); Chicago Opera Co., ca. 1900–1925, in the Joseph Raffaelli collection; City Symphony, 3 vols., 1921–23; Robert Hall Collins; Marilyn Cotlow; Walter W. Clark; Stella Marek Cushing; Frank Damrosch, 5 vols., 1887–1912; Walter Damrosch, 39 vols., 1881–1946; Mary Alice Digriam on Philadelphia music, 1928–43 (not filmed); Don Cossack Chorus, 6 vols., 1939–49; Frank C. Dossert; Claire Dux, 1921–23; Mischa Elman, 1939–44; Wellington Ezekiel, 1939–45; Arthur Farwell; Kirsten Flagstad, 3 vols.; Elsa Foerster, 1920s–30s (not filmed); the Four Piano Ensemble; Leo Frank, 9 vols., 1884–93; Naham Franko, 2 vols., 1869–1906; Sam Franko, 5 vols., 1874–1917; John C. Freund, 6 vols., 1913–23; Walter C. Gale, 2 vols., 1888–95; William T. Gale, 1891–98; German-American collection, 3 vols., 1903–14; Nina Gordani; Joseph Hoffmann, in the Joseph Raffaelli collection; Mrs. Charles Homer, 12 vols., 1884–1906; International Society for Contemporary Music; Dorothy Jardon, 1916–25; E. M. Jenks, 1908; Allan Jones, 1939–40; Rafael Joseffy; the Juilliard scrapbooks, 3 vols., 1861–1913; Jan Kiepura, 2 vols., 1938–42; Alexander Kipnis, 2 vols., 1938–42; the Lehmann collection (not filmed); Ralph Leopold, 9 vols., 1894–1943; Harold Lindau (Aroldo Lindi), 1920–33 (not filmed); Jeanette MacDonald, 4 vols., 1939–42; Eduardo Marzo, 2 vols., 1868–1918; William Mason, 2 vols., 1851–67; James Melton, 1940–46; Metropolitan Opera Co. and Manhattan Opera Co., 3 vols., 1908–14 (not filmed); Metropolitan Opera Guild, 14 vols., 1936–50; Montclair, N.J., programs, 1906–12 (not filmed); miscellaneous musical necrology, 1942–50; H. W. Nancrede, 2 vols., 1867–92; New York Philharmonic-Symphony Orchestra, 3 vols., 1930–49, also official press books; the "New York Scrapbooks," 105 vols.; Jarmila Novotna; Ricardo Odnopossoff; Lina Pagliughi, 1939–40; the Philadelphia Opera Co., 3 vols., 1940–44; Gertrude Pitzinger, 1939; Maud Powell, 33 vols., 1883–1919; Joseph Raffaelli, 6 vols., devoted to Henriette Cady, the Chicago Opera Co., Il Trio Florentino, Josef Hoffmann, New York opera and concerts, 1904–10, and Guiseppe Verdi; William Saar, 1853–62; H. B. Satcher, 89 vols., 1910–66; the San Carlo Opera, 31 vols., 1930–50; Henry W. Savage, concerning Puccini's *Il Fianciullo del Oest*; Kurt Schindler, 1899–1904; John Philip Sousa, 5 vols., 1892–96; the Spivakovsky–Kurtz Trio, 1933; Noel Strauss; Richard Strauss in America, 1921–22; Alexander Sved, 1939–42; Giovanni Tagliapietra, 1875–85; Jean Tennyson, 1938–42; Mrs. Frances B. Thurber, 7 vols., 1886–92; Henry C. Timm, 2 vols., 1846–75; Arturo Toscanini, 3 vols., 1928–38; Yvonne de Treville, 3 vols., 1897–1901; Il Trio Florentino, 1891–92, in the Joseph Raffaelli collection; Rosalyn Tureck, 1937–41; Bruno Walter, 1939–41; Wesley Weyman, 2 vols., 1901–29; Lew White, 1927–29; and the *New York World-Telegram* scrapbooks, 26 vols., 1918–34

G. Pictorial Materials

There are two collections: materials of general provenance, and the Joseph Muller collection. Both are indexed and arranged for service, but in neither has the American character of specific materials been brought out

General iconography collection, 20,000 items, mostly portraits. See the iconography index in the Special Collections Reading Room

Muller collection, 5000 items, with several indexes in the Special Collections Reading Room. Entirely portraits, largely European, but a few American, notably famous early 20th-century musicians, and American lithograph portraits, ca. 1850

H. Miscellaneous Other Materials

Toscanini Memorial Archive, established 1964 in memory of Arturo Toscanini, consisting of microfilms of important source material of European master composers

American music publishers' and dealers' catalogues, including materials from Irving Lowens integrated into the collections

Reference indexes, including files compiled by Virginia Larkin Redway on Handel in America and on early New York musical life, also the "plate number" file containing information on American music publishers

—Richard Jackson

J. Rodgers and Hammerstein Archives of Recorded Sound

See the brochure on the Archives, also David Hall, "The Rodgers and Hammerstein Archives of Recorded Sound," A.R.S.C. *Journal*, 6/2 (1974), 17–31

Recordings, 400,000 items, of which 200,000 (including 50,000 duplicates) are 78-rpm discs. Of these, 30,000 are classified and catalogued, and 120,000 are uncatalogued, arranged by label numbers. Included are the collections of G. Lauder Greenway, 9000 items, mostly early vocal; Jan Holcman, 1000 historical piano items; A. F. R. Lawrence (1922–72, collector and archivist for Columbia Records); Benedict Stambler, 3000 Jewish folk and cantorial items; and radio station WNEW, 12,000 pop items, of which 4000 are pre-1940. Among the 500 cylinders are the 119 "Mapleson cylinders" of performances at the Metropolitan Opera, 1901–3. Among the 11,000 instantaneous lacquer discs and radio-broadcast transcriptions are many first performances of American works

Recording company catalogues, 30 linear meters, of which 15 meters are pre-1940

Program notes (removable items issued with recordings), 32 linear meters, of which 8 linear meters are for 78-rpm discs, keyed to the recording catalogue numbers

Thomas A. Edison, testimonial book assembled by J. H. Block in Russia and Central Europe, 1889–90 and 1904, with autographs of Tchaikovsky, Tolstoy, and others (in the custody of the Special Collections Department). See the A.R.S.C. *Journal*, 1/1 (1967–68), 2–5

Personal papers and working research materials of Stephen Fassett (Boston critic and vocal-music collector), dispersed through the collection; and of A. F. R. Lawrence, 5 linear meters

Victor Talking Machine Co., log books, 1920s, 1 linear meter, acquired from Steven Smolian

Josef Schillinger, acetate lacquer discs recorded by pupils in his studio, also broadcast materials including a performance of Henry Cowell's *Anthropos* by the WPA Orchestra conducted by the composer, and other items

Henry Cowell, acetate lacquer discs, including many of his own works never commercially recorded, rhythmicon demonstrations, and ethnographic field recordings

National Orchestral Association, recorded sound archives, 1939–68, mostly conducted by Leon Barzin and including many first performances of major American works

"The Railroad Hour" (radio series, 1940s, featuring adaptations by Jerome Lawrence and Robert E. Lee of 20th-century American musical-theater music), tapes and broadcast transcriptions

Margaret Fairbank (Jory), tapes and transcripts of oral-history interviews with 20th-century American composers, 1967. (Copies of the tapes are also at Yale University, New Haven, Conn., q.v.)

—David Hall

K. Dance Collection

While musical notation relating to the dance has been assigned to the Music Division, the Dance Collection has extensive materials relating to dance music, also incidental musical texts in books and other items concerned primarily with dance. See the *Dictionary Catalog of the Dance Collection* (New York and Boston, 1974), esp. vol. 7, pp. 4338–86, also related headings, such as the names of composers (e.g., Copland, Stravinsky) or subjects (e.g., "Opera ballet," vol. 7, pp. 4660–95; or "Square dance," vol. 9, pp. 6043–62)

L. Billy Rose Theatre Collection

For general background see Evelyn Hisz, *History of the Theatre Collection, New York Public Library at Lincoln Center* (Master's thesis, Long Island University, 1969). Catalogued items are cited in the *Dictionary Catalog of the Theatre and Drama Collections*, parts I-II for books, part III for non-books (Boston, 1967–76; hereinafter cited as *DC*). The reading-room card catalogue (photographed for the *DC*), with entries by title of work or name of person, extends to 420 drawers for clippings, programs, reviews, obituaries, photographs, scrapbooks, and promptbooks entered before 1975, and 28 drawers for items added 1975– ; 144 drawers for books on theater including musical theater and for typed libretti to 1967 (thereafter items are entered only in the *DC*); and 24 drawers of typed scripts. Letters, autographs, and some photographs are kept in a Cage File (see *DC*, Part III)

Personal papers of individuals active in the musical theater and of music-related persons, including extensive holdings from the papers of George Abbott (photographs, posters, scrapbooks, programs, and clippings), Boris Aronson (photographs and sketches for scenic designs), David Belasco (typescripts, photographs, scrapbooks, and set designs to 1931), Chamberlin and Lyman Brown (theatrical agency scrapbooks, clippings, photographs, correspondence, financial sheets, and programs, 1910–61), R. H. Burnside (press books), Jefferson De Angelis (photographs and programs to 1933), Nikki Eastman (designs and photographs for stage sets and costumes for Florenz

Ziegfeld, the Chicago and Metropolitan Opera companies, and others), A. L. Erlanger (117 scrapbooks of clippings and photographs related to Erlanger Amusement Enterprises to 1932), John Golden (press books of the producer and songwriter), Edward Harrigan (holograph promptbooks of musical plays), James G. Huneker (his library of 800 books and pamphlets on music and literature, also with scrapbooks including music criticism), Sol Hurok (photographs, press releases, and programs), Burl Ives (personal memorabilia), A. J. Jones and Morris Green (typescripts and prompt scripts of unpublished plays and musical comedies, 1920–33), Robert Edmond Jones (scenic design sketches and photographs including operas of Ferenc Molnar and others), Henry Edward Krehbiel (1936 vols. of books and 373 pamphlets and scrapbooks including sheet music and music criticism, to 1923), Bert Lahr, Gertrude Lawrence (annotated correspondence, play notices, photographs, and recordings), Joshua Logan (scripts), Brander Matthews (writings on New York dramatic history), Laura O. Norlin (scrapbooks, clippings, photographs, and programs tracing the career of Ziegfeld star Marilyn Miller), Lee Simonson (photographs of his settings and costumes, some of them for the New York Metropolitan Opera), Sophie Tucker, Carl Van Vechten (programs, scrapbooks, and photographs), Joseph M. Weber and Lew Fields (photographs, tintypes, and bound programs), Frances Williams (10 scrapbooks of photographs and reviews of the star of *George White's Scandals*), Peggy Wood (clippings, and writings to her husband, John Van Alstyne, to 1938), and Paul J. Woodward (88 scrapbooks of clippings, programs, and halftone illustrations of New York theater productions, and 55 scores of musical shows, mostly 20th-century American)

Robinson Locke Collection of Dramatic Scrapbooks, 800 bound vols. and 2500 portfolios of clippings, programs, correspondence, and photographs, 1870–1925, among them vols. on the operatic careers of Mary Garden and Geraldine Farrar. See the exhibit catalogue (New York, 1925)

M. Manuscripts and Archives Division

See the *Dictionary Catalog of the Manuscript Division* (Boston, 1967; hereinafter cited as DC); note especially the "Musical Resources Largely Transferred to the Music Division, November 1965," vol. 2, pp. 601–8

David Blakely (1834–96, manager and impresario, journalist, and printer), personal papers, 1862–1931, also those of Mrs. Blakely, in 18 boxes and 32 vols. Also business correspondence, mostly relating to tours, of the Gilmore Band, 1889–91; Theodore Thomas Orchestra, 1889–91; Edouard Strauss Orchestra, 1890; U.S. Marine Band, 1891–92; Sousa's Band, 1892–97; All Girl Orchestra, 1891–92; and Austro-Hungarian Juvenile Band, 1891–92. See Frank J. Cipolla, "The Business Papers of David Blakely," *Journal of Band Research*, 13/2 (1978), 2–7

Robert H. Burnside (1870–1952, theatrical producer), personal papers relating to his management of the Hippodrome, New York, and to early U.S. productions of Gilbert & Sullivan; also a scrapbook of Grace Greenwood Miles (pianist)

William Cosby (colonial governor of New York), 73 documents, 1732–36, relating to an incident over

satirical song texts and their suppression, as described in the New York Public Library *Bulletin*, 2 (1898), 249–55

Marcia von Dresser and Gertrude Norman, correspondence received from musicians, 1895–1956, including letters from Geraldine Farrar, Clara (Clemens) Gabrilowitsch, and Leopold Stokowski

Ferdinand Dunkley (b. 1869), personal papers, mostly from his activity in New Orleans, in 4 boxes

Julia Elizabeth Dunn (1851–87, music teacher and poet), letters received, 1876–82, many from Germany, also mss and press clippings of Percy McKaye

Geraldine Farrar, 47 letters to Lawrence and Alice Eyre, 1952–56, on musical matters

Karl Feininger (1844–1922, music teacher in New York and Stamford, Conn.), diary, 1911–13, describing music lessons, concerts, and musical life

Lucy (McKim) Garrison, personal papers, also the papers of the McKim family, with extensive references to music and her career in collecting black spirituals, as described in Dena J. Epstein, "Lucy McKim Garrison, American Musician," New York Public Library *Bulletin*, 67 (1963), 529–46

Augustine Post (1873–1952), personal papers, mostly letters concerned with his singing and speaking engagements, also relating to his interests in aeronautics, Boy Scouts, philanthropy, theosophy, and the National Association for Music in Hospitals, 1925–31

John Puring (b. 1872), ms songs and poems, and other personal papers, 1907–56, in 1 carton

Frederick Rausch (pianist, music dealer, and vice-president of the St. Cecelia Society), 65 (possibly 69) receipts, some of them for musical materials, from London and New York, 1797–1810

Constance Skinner (1877–1939), personal papers and 5 scrapbooks containing her criticism for the *Los Angeles Times* and *Los Angeles Examiner*, 1901–6, and 1 scrapbook of other Los Angeles music reviews, ca. 1902–6

Harman C. Westervelt, ms reports on "Musical Progress in the City of New York," 1826–27 (no. 28), and "Early Theatricals" (no. 30)

Revolutionary War ms music, including Absalom Blachly, 8 songs with music, ca. 1785, in the Wick–Blachly–Colles papers; "Colonel Gansevoorts Musick Book 1778," as cited in DC, vol. 2, p. 534; and Baron Steuben, "American March," ca. 1778, as cited in Evarts B. Greene and Richard B. Morris, *A Guide to the Principal Sources for Early American History*, 2nd ed. (New York, 1953)

Miscellaneous music materials in general collections, including references to the Handel and Haydn Society, New York, 1819, in the Armitage family papers; manuals concerning labor and socialism, 1787–1949, some with extensive discussions of music, as collected by Morris Onans; references to German singing-school activity in the Hudson–Fulton Celebration of 1909, also transcripts of German songs, and material on the visit of the German squadron to New York, 1912, in the papers of Gustav Scholer (b. 1851); and references to work as an usher at Crosby's Opera House, Chicago, in the diary of William Cumming Story (b. 1851, staff member of Lyon and Healy)

Song texts, including a ms book of English and American works, ca. 1800; and R. K. Sneden, Civil War diary with a scrapbook of songs, 1848–1905

Emergency Committee in Aid of Displaced Foreign Scholars, archives, 1933–45, including letters of or concerning Erwin Bodky, Manfred Bukofzer, Alfred Einstein, Karl Geiringer, Gerhard Herz, Ernest Kanitz, Ernst Krenek, Edward Lowinsky, Paul Nettl, and Karl Weigl. See *Spalek*, passim

Ephrata (Pa.) Cloister, 18th-century ms music book entitled "Geistliches Blumenfeld von Rosen und Lilien"

—Jean R. McNiece

N. Schomburg Center for Research in Black Culture

See the Center's *Journal*, 1/4 (1978). Printed music, books about music, and music recordings, 2000 items, as described in the collection's *Dictionary Catalog* (Boston, 1962), vol. 6, pp. 4784–4813, the *First Supplement* (Boston, 1967), vol. 3, pp. 137–61, and *Second Supplement* (Boston, 1972), pp. 152–58

Archival collections pertaining to 20 musicians and music-related groups, including holograph and published music, programs, correspondence, and personal papers. Major collections with pre-1940 materials are those of Lawrence Brown (accompanist to Paul Robeson and arranger of black spirituals and folksongs), Mary Caldwell Dawson (founder of the National Negro Opera Company), Ruby Shepperd Davis (poet and singer), W. C. Handy (composer and bandleader), Andy Razaf (lyricist and composer), Leigh Whipper (composer), and Clarence Cameron White (composer)

Sheet music, mostly published but including some ms items, 19th and 20th centuries, 4.5 linear meters, including spirituals, coon songs, marches, two-steps, banjo melodies, foxtrots, "plantation melodies" and minstrel songs, cakewalks, work songs, rags, operas, cantatas, and orchestral and band scores

Programs, posters, playbills, and other ephemera of musical events, 1 linear meter, 1930s– , including an extensive collection of playbills of New York musicals written or performed by blacks

Vertical file of clippings, booklets, and pamphlets, including musical subjects

Audio Visual Section, with disc and tape recordings of American, Caribbean, and African music, including field recordings, oral-history materials, commercial recordings, and non-commercial publications

Photographs, including music subjects

Index to Articles in Black Periodicals, on cards, with extensive music-subject coverage

Robert Rusch collection of jazz periodicals, with an index of articles on performers and composers

1062

NEW YORK UNIVERSITY   NNU

Washington Square
New York, New York 10003

Henry Barnard (1811–1900), personal papers (in the Fales Library), including materials relating to his extensive activity in the development of American music education (to be accessible through a major indexing project, in progress)

Minstrel entertainment, 11 items, 1863–1913, as described in the Fales Library *Checklist* (New York, 1974), 1st suppl., p. 278

Labor songs, 200 items, several of them pre-1940 (in the Tamiment Library)

New Music, two-thirds of the published editions, 1927–

—Ruth Hilton

1063

PHILHARMONIC-SYMPHONY SOCIETY OF NEW YORK

Lincoln Center
New York, New York 10023

Archival records of the New York Philharmonic Orchestra and its various related activities, as mentioned in Howard Shanet, *Philharmonic: A History of New York's Orchestra* (Garden City, N.Y., 1975), pp. 481–82 and passim. Included are copies of the *Constitution and By-Laws*, 1846–99, and other official publications; ms minute books, 1850–1932; *Annual Reports*, 1843– ; programs, 1842– ; correspondence, press clipping books (on microfilm), files, and other records; also materials relating to the Musical Society of the City of New York, Inc., 1922–23, the Philharmonic Society of New York, the Symphony Society of New York, and the Stadium Concerts, Walter Damrosch letters, scrapbooks, and programs, and Ernest Schelling correspondence and papers

1064

The PLAYERS   NNWC

Walter Hampden–Edwin Booth
Theatre Collection and Library
16 Gramercy Park
New York, New York 10003

Cabinet photographs of 19th-century opera singers, 400 items

Charles S. Callahan (1909–54, writer of burlesque-routine scripts), 36 music mss and notebooks, as cited in *NUCMC*, 69–556

—Louis A. Rachow

1065

SHUBERT ARCHIVE

Lyceum Theatre
149 West Forty-fifth Street
New York, New York 10036

Materials are collected as part of a program sponsored by the Shubert Foundation, documenting the history of the Shubert Organization, which was established in 1890 in Syracuse, N.Y. See the Archive's newsletter, *The Passing Show* (1977– ; hereinafter cited as *PS*)

Century Library, consisting of a rental collection of operettas, musical comedies, and musical revues, 1900s–1940s. Included are scores, parts, libretti, and other materials for 100 revues and 179 musical comedies and operettas, also sheet music and a small amount of silent-film music. See Susan Spector, "Music Unlimited," *PS*, 1/1 (1977)

Sheet music, 1870s–1930s, 2 file drawers, mostly related to Shubert productions. See Barbara Naomi Cohen, "Sheet Music," *PS*, 2/1 (1978)

Miscellaneous other materials, including technical drawings and sketches, photographs, piano rolls, correspondence, and memorabilia

Radio-broadcast transcriptions of Shubert musical productions, 50 items

—Brooks McNamara, Brigitte Kuppers

1066

SONG WRITERS HALL OF FAME

1 Times Square
New York, New York 10036

Songbooks, hymnals, song folios, and popular sheet music, 1850– ; also 100 ms songs, mostly 20th century

Papers and memorabilia of song writers, including signed photographs and clippings, 2 file drawers

Music publishers' catalogues, 1 file drawer

Programs of musicals, mostly in New York City, 40 items, 1920–40

Recordings, including 200 78-rpm discs and 500 piano rolls

—Frankie MacCormick

1067

Peter Pindar STEARNS

Mannes College of Music
157 East Seventy-fourth Street
New York, New York 10021

Theodore Stearns (1875–1935), holograph music mss, including his operas *Snowbird* and *Atlantis,* and many works in smaller forms; also scrapbooks of his press clippings as a critic for the *New York Morning Telegraph,* 1920s

1068

THIRD STREET MUSIC SCHOOL

235 East Eleventh Street
New York, New York 10003

Papers of the School (founded 1894), including annual reports, minutes, speeches, and photographs of student performing groups, 1901–

—Barbara Wong

1069

Ephraim TRUESDELL

133 Fifth Avenue
New York, New York 10003

Catalogue of harpsichords and clavichords manufactured by John Challis, of Detroit, ca. 1930–

1070

UNION THEOLOGICAL   NNUT
SEMINARY LIBRARY

3041 Broadway
New York, New York 10027

The Library's holdings in hymnology began in 1888 with Henry Day's donation of the Collection of Frederick M. Byrd (1838–1908), followed in 1908 by the donation of the Henry Day Collection of Hymnology, Linguistics, and Ecclesiastical Law. Also represented are vols. with ms annotations of Henry Richard Bird (1842–1915, English organist) and Daniel Sedgwick. The collection maintained by the Hymn Society of America (often cited as the Newman Collection) was acquired in 1925.

The catalogued collections of the Library are described in the *Shelf List of the Union Theological Seminary Library in New York City, in Classification Order* (Boston, 1960), and in the *Alphabetical Arrangement of Main Entries from the Shelf List* (Boston, 1960)

Hymnals, 2000 items, including English and American, German-American, and Amerindian hymns, hymnals for youth, gospel songbooks, Sunday-school hymnals, and books for the special use of missionaries, the Salvation Army, social workers, abolitionists, and temperance leaders; also published books of religious poetry used as sources for hymn texts; and published books on hymnology

Published secular music, including vocal anthologies, dramatic music including operas and operettas, and instrumental music; also 1 bound vol. of 19th-century sheet music

Miscellaneous programs and festival books

Theses and dissertations of the Seminary's School of Sacred Music, ca. 1930–73

Missionary Research Library, including hymnals with U.S. and foreign imprints

Baldwin Library of Organ Music, including 19th- and early 20th-century published organ music from the collection of Samuel Atkinson Baldwin (1862–1949, organist at City College of New York and founder of the American Guild of Organists)

Hymn Society of America, Committee on Hymn Origins, 2 scrapbooks of correspondence and writings by English and American composers and scholars, 1940–52; also clippings from the *Diapason,* 1937–

—Seth Kasten

1071

Mrs. Vally WEIGL

50 West Ninety-fifth Street
New York, New York 10025

Karl Weigl (1881–1949), personal papers, including correspondence, music sketches, printed articles, personal library, reviews, and photographs. See *Spalek,* p. 956

Vally Weigl, ms sketches, holographs, printed copies, and recordings of her chamber music; also poems, and articles and notes on her work as a composer and music therapist

1072

Lotte Lenya WEILL-DETWILER

404 East Fifty-fifth Street
New York, New York 10022

Kurt Weill (1900–1950), personal papers, including correspondence, scores to Broadway shows, programs, and photographs. See *Spalek,* p. 964

1073

Kurt WEILL FOUNDATION

160 West Seventy-third Street
New York, New York 10023

Kurt Weill (1900–1950), photocopies and microfilms of manuscripts, correspondence, scores of German and

American works, clippings, programs, photographs, and unpublished materials

—Lys Symonette

1074
Eric WERNER
900 West 190th Street
New York, New York 10040

Eric Werner, personal papers, including correspondence, reviews, literary mss, personal library, photographs, and memorabilia. See *Spalek*, p. 997

1075
Marianne WURLITZER
60 Riverside Drive
New York, New York 10024

Archival materials relating to the firm of Rembert Wurlitzer, 1948–74, also to the earlier work of the Rudolph Wurlitzer Co. in the field of string instruments, now in the possession of Mrs. Rembert Wurlitzer. The records include a file on all fine instruments sold by the Wurlitzer firm, arranged by serial number; an index of important instruments, in 80 binders arranged by instrument maker, covering those instruments which passed through the hands of the Wurlitzer firm or were called to their attention; a "history file" of information on important instruments which were sold by the firm, consisting mostly of duplicates of documents which were supplied to the purchaser; and a miscellaneous collection of photographs (many of them autographed), correspondence, and memorabilia

1076
YIVO INSTITUTE FOR JEWISH RESEARCH   NNYI
1048 Fifth Avenue
New York, New York 10028

Sholem Perlmutter Theatre Archives, 10 linear meters of ms performance parts and published sheet music, by composers including Joseph Brody, Abraham Goldfaden, and Joseph Rumshinsky; also programs, press clippings, photographs, and memorabilia, as discussed in Mark Slobin, "Yiddish Theater Music in the Yivo Archives," *Musica judaica* (forthcoming)

Lazar Weiner Archive, including ms and printed music performed in the U.S., 1920s– , also programs, press clippings, and photographs

Samuel Bugatch, musical mss, in 4 boxes, mostly cantorial works

Mikhl Gelbart, 3 boxes of music mss, printed music, and a clipping file

Leo Low, personal papers, including ms and printed music

Yiddish sheet music from the collection of Barbara Kirshenblatt-Gimblett, 300 U.S. imprints, 1897–1930s

Recordings, including 800 commercial 78–rpm discs, ca. 1908–30s; and the Ben Stonehill collection of field tapes of arriving Jewish immigrants, 1947

—Mark Slobin

1077
Morris N. YOUNG
270 Riverside Drive
New York, New York 10025

Barnard A. and Morris N. Young Library of Early American Popular Music, 20,000 items, mostly 1790–1910, containing 48,000 music titles, and comprising 10,500 sheet-music items, of which the black American collection of 3500 items is particularly important; 90 bounds vols. of sheet music, and other special sheet-music collections, including 165 patriotic items, 120 advertising items, 900 theater-music items, 1000 items in small format, and 175 items of college and organizational songs; 825 songsters; 300 song-text items, of which 50 are broadsides; 125 mss with texts, some with music as well; 150 music serials; 200 sets of orchestral parts; 800 songbooks and other vocal anthologies; 500 instrumental anthologies; 50 dance folios; 100 programs, circulars, and other items of memorabilia; 2000 photographs; 500 books about music and related subjects; and 1000 recordings

1078
TOSCANINI ARCHIVES
Villa Pauline
(New York/Bronx) Riverdale, New York 10471

Recordings of Arturo Toscanini, also published music with Toscanini's markings, programs, press clippings, photographs, and other memorabilia. See Walter Toscanini, "The Story of the Riverdale Project and My Father's Recordings," in *Arturo Toscanini: A Complete Discography* (New York, 1966); also Dorman H. Winfrey, "The Toscanini Archives," *American Archivist*, 30 (1967), 468–70. This material is not available for consultation

1079
ANTIQUE PHONOGRAPH AND RECORD SOCIETY
650 Ocean Avenue
(New York) Brooklyn, New York 11226

Cylinder recordings, 5000 items, 1892–1929, as discussed in Allen Koenigsberg, *Edison Cylinder Records, 1889–1912* (New York, 1969)

Materials relating to early sound recording, including 200 catalogues of phonograph manufacturers and recording companies, correspondence, posters and advertisements, 1000 pictures, programs, and 2000 patents

—Allen Koenigsberg

1080
BROOKLYN COLLEGE OF THE CITY UNIVERSITY OF NEW YORK   NBC
(New York) Brooklyn, New York 11210

Institute for Studies in American Music

Sheet music, including 700 items concerning Yiddish musical theater in the U.S., early 20th century, given by Edward Kunofsky; and 1800 additional items, 1890–1970, including early Stephen Foster editions

Henry Cowell (1897–1965), published musical editions, recordings, and writings about his music, a specially designated repository

Alfred de Voto (pianist), 24 early 20th-century works from his music library, including piano music of Leonard Bernstein, Arthur Farwell, Henry Franklin Belknap Gilbert, Charles Griffes, Edward MacDowell, Horatio Parker, Arthur Shepherd, and Arthur B. Whiting, also 16 issues of *New Music Quarterly* (1928–33), presented by Susan Williams Lyon

Other printed music for piano or voice, mid 19th and early 20th centuries, by George W. Chadwick, John A. Carpenter, Arthur Foote, Edward MacDowell, Edgar Stillman Kelley, Arthur B. Whiting, and others; also 19th-century tunebooks, piano anthologies, and method books

Oscar Sonneck (1873–1928), ms notes, on 5 reels of microfilm

Other materials, including concert programs, clippings, and biographical and bibliographical information on 20th-century composers

—Rita Mead

Brooklyn College Library, Manuscripts and Special Collections

Edward B. Wisely, "Music Hall and Vaudeville," his collections of 100 tape recordings of 78-rpm discs of musical theater and vaudeville in the U.S., Great Britain, and Ireland, 1875–1940, with printed descriptions of the contents

—Antoinette Ciolli

1081
BROOKLYN MUSIC SCHOOL AND PLAYHOUSE
126 Saint Felix Avenue
(New York) Brooklyn, New York 11217

Archival materials relating to the School, 1912– , including minutes of meetings, programs, and photographs

—Donna Morris

1082
BROOKLYN PUBLIC LIBRARY   NB
Art and Music Division
Grand Army Plaza
(New York) Brooklyn, New York 11238

Rafael Navarro (fl. 1910s), ms scores of his opera *Abelard, the Knight of Reason*, 1890, and the "Christmas Anthem," also a scrapbook of letters, clippings, and programs

Joseph Aviron (1899–1976), 1500 items of papers, including music notebooks, ms music for voice, violin, or piano, 1 published music edition, letters, programs and memorabilia

Sheet music, 100 bound vols. and several separate items of popular music, 1790s–

Songbooks and hymnals, 300 vols., 1820–

Other printed music, including 3 vocal works by

George Bristow, 1860–90, and several hundred orchestral, vocal, and chamber-music scores, early 20th century

Programs of Brooklyn concerts, 8 items, ca. 1900

—Sue Sharma

1083
LONG ISLAND HISTORICAL   NBLiHi
SOCIETY
138 Pierrepont Street
(New York) Brooklyn, New York 11201

Leopold Damrosch, 3 letters to George Hannah, 1877

Sheet music, 5 bound vols. of popular music, 1840–80

Hymnals used by Dutch settlers on Long Island, 1665–1800, many in Dutch

Programs and playbills of performances at the Brooklyn Academy of Music, 1859– ; also programs and clippings related to Dudley Buck, filed under the Apollo Club and Holy Trinity Church, as cited by William K. Gallo, *The Life and Church Music of Dudley Buck (1839–1909)* (Ph.D. diss., Catholic University of America, 1968)

Research notes for Harriet Stryker-Rodda, "Scott & Van Attena, Masters of the Song Slide," *Journal of Long Island History*, 5/3 (1965), 17–27

—Anne M. Gordon

1084
STRATHCLYDE COLLABORATIVE
50 Willow Street
(New York) Brooklyn, New York 11201

Early lantern slides, 85,000 items, including 900 items on musical subjects, among them late 19th- and early 20th-century song texts, also pictures of singing groups

—James Hamilton

1085
Tim BROOKS
1940 Eightieth Street
(New York/Queens) Jackson Heights, New York 11370

Recordings of U.S. popular music, 1890– , including 10,000 78-rpm discs and 800 cylinders; also recording catalogues, supplements, pamphlets, and trade literature

1086
David A. JASEN
40-21 155th Street
(New York/Queens) Flushing, New York 11354

Collection of popular American music and related documents, including 10,000 sheet-music items; 2500 78-rpm disc recordings of ragtime music, 1897–1950s, also other discs of popular music, mostly early jazz and ragtime; 1500 piano rolls; pictures, biographical files on composers and performers, and interviews; catalogues of recordings; and books and periodicals.

The collection has provided material for reissues of early jazz and ragtime recordings, as well as for the discography by Jasen, *Recorded Ragtime* (Hamden, Conn., 1973), and the book co-authored with Trebor Jay Tichenor, *Rags and Ragtime: A Musical History* (New York, 1978)

1087

QUEENSBOROUGH COMMUNITY COLLEGE OF THE CITY UNIVERSITY OF NEW YORK

NBsdQ

(New York/Queens) Bayside, New York 11364

Jimmy Lanin, library of popular stock dance-band arrangements, ca. 1920–40s, 24 linear meters, on deposit

—R. John Specht, Raoul F. Camus

1088

QUEENS BOROUGH PUBLIC LIBRARY   NJQ

89-11 Merrick Boulevard
(New York/Queens) Jamaica, New York 11432

Musical Society of Jamaica, N.Y., papers and 7 year-books, 1910–65 (in the Long Island Divison)
Published materials, including 4 Lowell Mason song-books, 1835–61; 9 late 19th-century operas and other scores; and American music periodicals, including 2 numbers of the *American Music Journal*, 1834–35 (in the Art and Music Division)

—Nicholas Falco, Dorothea Wu

1089

QUEENS COLLEGE OF THE CITY UNIVERSITY OF NEW YORK

NFQC

(New York/Queens) Flushing, New York 11367

Paul Klapper Library

Printed music materials, accessible through the Music Library card file, including 550 songbooks, mostly early 19th-century tunebooks; 200 items of sheet music, mostly mid 19th-century piano and solo vocal music; and George Gershwin's autographed published arrangement for solo piano of *Rhapsody in Blue*, 1927
Recordings, including 100 78-rpm discs of classical music

Music Library

Karol Rathaus (1895–1954, professor of music at the College), complete music scores in ms photocopy or published editions, 1.5 linear meters
Songbooks, 153 20th-century collections of popular music
Other published music by American composers, 1200 scores of vocal or instrumental works
Recordings, including 35 78-rpm discs of classical music

—Barbara R. Greener

1090

STATEN ISLAND INSTITUTE OF ARTS AND SCIENCES

NNSII

75 Stuyvesant Place
(New York) Staten Island, New York 10301

Historical recordings, 19th-century sheet music, and an index to Staten Island newspapers with references to local musical events

1091

Earl W. BRYDGES PUBLIC LIBRARY

NNia

Local History Department
1425 Main Street
Niagara Falls, New York 14305

R. Nathaniel Dett (1882–1943), personal papers, including 600 press clippings, programs, and brochures; printed sheet music, songbooks, and poems by Dett; 1 recording; a music ms; and letters to his mother. See Vivian Flagg McBrier, *The Life and Works of Robert Nathaniel Dett* (Ph.D. diss., Catholic University of America, 1967)

—Donald E. Loker

1092

D. DeWitt WASSON

213 Highland Avenue
North Tarrytown, New York 10591

Hymnals, 215 items, also handbooks and books on hymnology, 1837– , strong in contemporary editions

1093

CHENANGO COUNTY HISTORICAL SOCIETY

Rexford Street
Norwich, New York 13815

Sheet music, 2500 items, mostly early 20th-century imprints, including religious and local topical songs, some of them by John Prindle Smith; with an accessions list
F. W. Riesberg (b. 1863, music critic and pianist, a Liszt pupil), miscellaneous documents. See *Etude*, 54 (1963), 698ff
Programs of local opera houses, 1890s–1920s
Recordings, including 40 cylinders

—Mae Smith

1094

NYACK COLLEGE   NNyM

Library
Nyack, New York 10960

Hymnals of various denominations, 126 items with music (including 7 of the Christian and Missionary Alliance), and others with words only, 1850– ; also 30 nondenominational songbooks and hymnals, and 1 book of Shaker songs and dances

—Ruth Bailey

1095
Frank and Anne WARNER COLLECTION OF TRADITIONAL FOLKSONGS
Cedar Swamp Road
Old Brookville, New York 11545

Complete transcriptions of 1000 song texts from field recordings collected in the Appalachian Mountains, (Beech Mountain, Watauga County, N.C.), Outer Banks, N.C., Tidewater, Va., East Jaffrey, N.H., Dorset, Vt., the Adirondack Mountains, West Virginia singers in New York, and single songs collected in Ohio, Arkansas, and elsewhere, 1940–70. The original recordings, including only 2 verses for many of the songs, are in the Archive of Folk Song, Library of Congress (q.v.)

Folk songbooks and other folk-related books, 9 linear meters, plus 1.5 linear meters of Civil War items, including early 19th-century shape-note hymnals, songsters, ballad sheets, and 19th-century song collections, among them a first edition of W. F. Allen, C. P. Ware, and L. M. Garrison, *Slave Songs of the United States* (New York, 1867)

Warner family papers, 4 file drawers, including correspondence with Carl Carmer, William Rose Benét, and southern mountain singers, among them Frank Proffitt and Nathan Hicks; also concert programs, posters, ephemera, and folk-portrait photographs of singers

—Anne Warner

1096
SHAKER MUSUEM   NOcaS
Shaker Museum Road
Old Chatham, New York 12136

Music mss, including 70 vols. of Shaker songs, mostly in letter notation; also 2 items of sheet music, n.d.
Shaker hymnals, 84 items, published 1813–1908
Music instruction books, 25 19th-century items used in the Shaker community
Programs for holiday musical performances, 102 mss and printed items, 1895-

—Jean D. Anderson

1097
MADISON COUNTY HISTORICAL SOCIETY
435 Main Street
Oneida, New York 13421

Manuscript music, 1 vol., 1776
Hymnals and songbooks, 29 19th-century items
Photographs of musicians, 20 items, also 9 concert programs
Recordings, including 20 discs and 3 tapes of traditional musicians of the 1920s and 1930s, recorded 1979

1098
OYSTERPONDS HISTORICAL SOCIETY
Orient, New York 11957

George M. Vail, mss of 10 sacred songs
Manuscript songbook, 1884

Orient Cornet Band, papers, including 2 programs, 1888–1939
Songbooks, 60 items, mostly hymnals and sacred songbooks, 1814–1902, also including 2 temperance songbooks, 1890, 1 vol. of ballads and popular songs, 1863, and 1 children's songbook, 1842
Sheet music, 1 item, 1897

—Constance J. Terry

1099
STATE UNIVERSITY OF NEW YORK,   NOsU COLLEGE AT OSWEGO
Penfield Library
Oswego, New York 13126

Edward Austin Sheldon (music-faculty member), papers, including 4 Lowell Mason letters
Hymnals, 13 items, 1863–1907
Children's songbooks, 6 late 19th-century vols.
Programs of College and local concerts, 30 linear cm., 1913–
Photographs of College performing groups, 20 items, 1910–
Oral-history tape of William Gregway, singing early sea chanteys, recorded 1975

—Bruce Turner

1100
OLD OUAQUAGA HISTORICAL SOCIETY
Box 24
Ouaquaga, New York 13826

Ouaquaga Cornet Band, papers, ca. 1900
Hymnals, several early 20th-century items
Programs of 4 local band concerts, ca. 1900; and 3 photographs of the Harpursville Band, 1908

—Anne T. Herbert

1101
KENT–DELORD HOUSE MUSEUM
17 Cumberland Avenue
Plattsburgh, New York 12901

Manuscript music notebooks and exercise books, 4 19th-century items including many songs in French
Sheet music, 450 songs and dances
Hymnals, 9 items, 19th century
Other printed music, including 5 19th-century books of music, 1 of them owned by Frances Delord, ca. 1830

—Bruce Stark

1102
STATE UNIVERSITY OF NEW YORK,   NPlaU COLLEGE AT PLATTSBURGH
Benjamin F. Feinberg Library
Plattsburgh, New York 12901

Special Collections Department, including the Marjorie Lansing Porter Collection with 20 tapes of Adirondack folksongs made during the late 1940s, and 1200 early 20th-century popular and classical sheet music items; also archival materials on deposit from the Kent–Delord House Museum, Plattsburgh (q.v.), including Nathaniel Billings, *Republican Harmony* (Lansingburgh, N.Y., 1796)

—Bruce Stark

1103
Lawrence ASHLEY

Route 3
Potsdam, New York 13676

Recordings, including 950 cylinders, 1896–1926, mostly Edison Co. issues of popular vocals, catalogued; and 78-rpm discs, 1920s–40s, uncatalogued

1104
STATE UNIVERSITY OF NEW YORK,   NPotU
COLLEGE AT POTSDAM

Crane Music Library
Potsdam, New York 13676

Crane School of Music, papers, 1886– , including financial records, correspondence, programs, scrapbooks, address files, materials on the Spring Festival of the Arts, and essays by Julia Crane (founder and first director of the School), in 90 boxes, catalogued; also 16 boxes and 5.5 linear meters of uncatalogued materials, and tapes of School of Music performances
Helen Hosmer (director of the Crane School of Music), papers, 1922–66, 75 boxes
Hymnals and secular songbooks, 30 19th-century items

—David Ossenkop

1105
ADRIANCE MEMORIAL LIBRARY   NP

93 Market Street
Poughkeepsie, New York 12601

Manuscript music book of popular songs, copied by Hannah R. Morgan, 1853
Hymnals and sacred songbooks, 5 items, early 19th century
Charles Gilbert Spross (1874–1961), 11 leather-bound vols. of printed orchestral and chamber music, 1910–30s
Charles Hickok (d. 1920, Poughkeepsie music dealer), 6 scrapbooks of correspondence with booking agents, 1902–7
Papers of local music groups, 10 pamphlet boxes, including financial reports and correspondence of the Lyric Club, 1900–1960, and the Singers Club, 1915–30s
Programs of local 19th-century concerts by 18 performing groups, 300 items; also music and dramatic programs of the Collingwood Opera House, 1869–1924
Germania Singing Society, Poughkeepsie, *Sängerfest Zeitung*, nos. 1–10 (Troy, N.Y., 1930–31)
Bertha M. Round Collection of 40 framed and autographed photographs of musicians, 1920s–30s, including Jascha Heifetz, Pablo Casals, Roland Hayes, Ignace Jan Paderewski, Mischa Elman, and Sergei Rachmaninoff
Poughkeepsie Symphony Orchestra, 20 photographs, 1901

—Kevin J. Gallacher

1106
Robert HOE

Box 69
Poughkeepsie, New York 12602

Band music, comprising 3500 marches, in original published editions and copyists' mss, for use in Hoe's extensive program for promoting band music. See, for instance, George Toot, "Bob Hoe, Portrait of a Man Concerned," *School Musician*, 50/6 (1979), 58–59. Among the notable holdings are many U.S. published editions of the years after 1929, for which copyright depository copies were not transferred from the Copyright Office to the Music Division of the Library of Congress (q.v.), and including music by John Philip Sousa
Recordings of band music, including early recordings by the service bands, notably the U.S. Navy Band for the radio broadcasts of the "Navy Hour," also by the Long Beach Band

1107
VASSAR COLLEGE   NPV

Poughkeepsie, New York 12601

George Sherman Dickinson Music Library

See George S. Dickinson, "The Living Library," M.L.A. *Notes*, 3 (1946), 247-55, and Carol June Bradley and James B. Coover, "Vassar's Music Library: The First Hundred Years," M.L.A. *Notes*, 35 (1979), 819–46

The general music collection has incorporated the special gifts of string-quartet music presented by Gustav Dannreuther (1200 items, as listed in a separate card catalogue); piano music presented by Kate Chittenden; and recordings presented by Howard Barlow. Professor Dickinson's music-collecting activity was supported by special memorial funds in honor of Margaret Peabody and Soloman H. Kohn
Teresa Carreño, personal papers, including correspondence, 5 scrapbooks, loose photographs, and a diary kept during World War I
Vassariana collection, recordings of music performances at the College and of music by College composers
Manuscripts of composers associated with the College, including the complete works of Boris Koutzen, and many works of Jean Slater Appel, Martha Alter, Clair Leonard, and T. Carl Whitmer; also the holograph ms of a string quartet by Horatio Parker
Special catalogue of music by women composers
Programs of musical events at the College, 1861– , maintained in annual scrapbooks
Original music collection of Vassar College, ca. 1861, including European and American published editions, uncatalogued, 6 linear meters

Frederick Ferris Thompson Memorial Library

Although the large part of the library of Frédéric Louis Ritter (important early Vassar College professor of music) is at Tufts University, Medford, Mass., and the Newberry Library, Chicago (q.v.), some books from his collection are said to be in general collections
Pictures of College music-faculty members, in Special Collections

—Virginia Gifford

267

1108

STATE UNIVERSITY OF NEW YORK,   NPurU
COLLEGE AT PURCHASE
Library
Purchase, New York 10577

Oliver Daniel collection of scores and performance materials of 20th-century music, 1084 items (with a 46-page typescript inventory), integrated into the library's holdings, mostly post-1940 but with significant pre-1940 items. The scores are mostly published by firms affiliated with BMI, but there are also numerous black-line prints and photocopies of unpublished works. Among the composers extensively represented are Elliott Carter (12 items), Henry Cowell (180 items), Alan Hovhaness (160 items), Andrew Imbrie (11 items), Charles Ives (71 items), Daniel Pinkham (26 items), Walter Piston (41 items), Wallingford Riegger (80 items), and Carlos Surinach (12 items)

—Karl Van Ausdal

1109

AMERICAN BAPTIST   NRAB
HISTORICAL SOCIETY
Samuel Colgate Library
1106 South Goodman Street
Rochester, New York 14620

Baptist hymnals, 500 items, including 400 U.S. editions and 100 foreign editions
Personal papers of Baptist hymn-tune and -text writers, 7 boxes, 1850–1940, including papers of William H. Doane

—William H. Brackney

1110

COLGATE ROCHESTER /   NCRC
BEXLEY HALL / CROZER
THEOLOGICAL SEMINARIES
Ambrose Swasey Library
1100 South Goodman Street
Rochester, New York 14620

Hymnals with words only, 500 items, mostly in English, some in German, French, and other languages, 1745– ; also hymnals with music, 500 items of various Protestant denominations, for children, youth, and adults, in English, 1777–

—P. Vanden Berge

1111

EASTMAN SCHOOL OF MUSIC   NRU-Mus
Sibley Music Library
University of Rochester
26 Gibbs Street
Rochester, New York 14604

See Ruth Watanabe, "The Sibley Music Library of the Eastman School of Music, University of Rochester," M.L.A. *Notes,* 33 (1977), 783–802; her "Historical Introduction to the Sibley Music Library," University of Rochester Library *Bulletin,* 17 (1962), 43–48; and other articles in the *Bulletin* (hereinafter cited as *URLB),* mostly as cited in the *Notes* article, pp. 801–2

The general music collections include the personal libraries of Oscar Sonneck, consisting of 25 linear meters of scholarly musical literature, also materials on classification used in his preparation of the Library of Congress scheme for class M, acquired 1920–21; Henry E. Krehbiel, published folksong anthologies used in his studies of U.S. folksong; Samuel Belov, viola music, acquired 1949; Jacques Gordon (1899–1948), 2000 string and chamber music editions (*URLB,* 7 [1952], 25–27); virtually complete holdings of the published music of George W. Chadwick and Arthur Foote, acquired 1955; Composer Facsimile Editions and other facsimiles of contemporary works, presented by the American Composers' Alliance, 1957–61; John R. Slater, books and music; Phyllis Oster, 400 songs and piano works, bequeathed 1960; Theodore and Lorraine Noel Finley Fitch, 1000 scores and books about music; and Ben Dennof, violin music, bequeathed 1960

Holograph music mss in the classified collections, written before 1941, many of them acquired through the Festivals of American Music, 1930–71, and the American Composers' Concert series, 1925–54 (*URLB,* 17 [1962], 58–62), and including works by George Antheil, Ernst Bacon, Wayne Barlow, Russell Baum, Evelyn Berckman, William Bergsma, Jeanne Boyd, Gertrude Brown, Hoyle Carpenter, George W. Chadwick, Aaron Copland, Frederick Nichols Crouch ("Sheila, My Darling Colleen. The Marriage, revised for & inscribed to the Honorable Mrs. Folsom, Grovenor [sic] Cleveland, Washington, D.C. 1887"), Eric DeLamarter, Robert Delaney, R. Nathaniel Dett, David Diamond, Anthony Donato, Arthur Farwell, Theodore Fitch, Arthur Foote, Kent Gannett, Harold Gleason, Eugene Goossens, Parks Grant (27 holograph sketches and mss), Henry K. Hadley, Edmund Haines, Howard Hanson (26 items; *URLB,* 5 [1950], 21–24), Roy Harris, Weldon Hart (25 holograph scores, also performance parts; *URLB,* 19 [1964], 27–30), Edward Burlingame Hill, Walter Howe, Herbert Inch, Bernhard Kaun, Homer Keller, Ernst Krenek, Alfred Kroeger, Boris Levenson, Normand Lockwood, Otto Luening, Edward A. MacDowell, George F. McKay, Leopold Mannes, Douglas Stuart Moore, Harold Morris, Walter Mourant, Arthur Nevin, John Knowles Paine, Robert Palmer, Burrill Phillips, Quincy Porter, Gardner Read, Wallingford Riegger, Bernard Rogers, Edward Royce, Robert Sanders, Ludwig Schenck, Mark Silver, Christian Sinding, Nicolas Slonimsky, Gustave Soderlund, Leo Sowerby, Timothy Spelman, William Grant Still, Edwin Stringham, Randall Thompson, Virgil Thomson, Donald Tweedy, Vladimir Ussachevsky, David Van Vactor, Bernard Wagenaar, John Weinzweig, Adolph Weiss, Paul White, Alexander Wilder, and Frederick Woltmann. Material of Percy A. Grainger, formerly in the collections (see *URLB,* 19 [1964], 21–26), is now at the University of Melbourne, Australia, q.v.

Books of early ms music, including a vol. compiled ca. 1750–70, said to have been from the library of Robert Carter of Virginia; Betsy Danielson, book dated 1780; anonymous vol., 1784; Nancy Brown, book dated 1796; John Howe, book dated 1808; Mary McCulloch Shaw, 7 vols., 1810–15; Thomas Barron, book dated 1814; Henry Boller, 3 vols., 2 of them for piano, 1814–15; anonymous vols., ca. 1815 and 1830; John Carter (musician active in Canada after 1853), 5 vols., 1 of

Anglican chants, pre-1842, others of hymns, national airs, and original compositions, ca. 1860, also a ms Sonata in G Major and testimonial letters for him; and Orren N. Haskins, compilation of a "Collection of ancient tunes . . . commenced 1852"

Anthony Philipp Heinrich, 2 presentation vols. to Elizabeth, Empress of Austria, including his musical works in ms and printed editions, dated New York, 1856, and including an autograph letter to the empress from Heinrich, also 1 from Lucy Audubon (widow of John J. Audubon)

Dudley Buck, holograph ms list of his published and unpublished compositions

Miscellaneous Collection, of 19th- and 20th-century musical mss, unidentified

Autograph letters of musicians, 1000 items, including letters of William Armstrong, Harold Bauer, Anna Behrens, David Bispham, George F. Bristow, Dudley Buck, Cecil Burleigh, John Alden Carpenter, Teresa Carreño, Pablo Casals, George W. Chadwick, Henry Cowell, Walter Damrosch, Lorenzo DaPonte, William R. Dempster, Emmy Destinn, John Sullivan Dwight, Clarence Eddy, Louis C. Elson, Arthur Farwell, Adolph Martin Foerster, Arthur Foote, Myrta French, Ossip Gabrilowitsch, George Gershwin, Frederic Grant Gleason, Alma Gluck, Leopold Godowsky, Vladimir Golschmann, Eugene Goossens, Louis Moreau Gottschalk, Henry K. Hadley, Arthur Hartmann, Henry L. Higginson, Rafael Joseffy, Franz Kneisel, Henry Edward Krehbiel, Fritz Kreisler, Lilli Lehmann, Jenny Lind, Edward A. MacDowell, Lowell Mason, Arthur Nevin, Christine Nilsson, Ignace Jan Paderewski, John Knowles Paine, Horatio Parker, John Howard Payne, Johann Ernst Perabo, Rosa Ponselle, Maud Powell, Sergei Rachmaninoff, George F. Root, Pablo Sarasate (30 letters to his mother during his American tour, 1869–70), Ernestine Schumann-Heink, Christian Sinding, Oscar Sonneck, Igor Stravinsky, Theodore Thomas, Ernst Toch, Frank Van der Stucken, and Emerson Whithorne

Miscellaneous collections of personal papers, including Josephine Antoine, 7 scrapbooks with clippings, programs, playbills, photographs, and memorabilia documenting her career; Carlo Buonamici, ms score and parts for Rachmaninoff's First Concerto, which he premièred in the U.S.; R. Nathaniel Dett, 100 holograph scores, ms sketches, typescript items inscribed by or to him; Adelin Fermin, 30 holographs of works by Fermin and by others dedicated or inscribed to him; Theodore Fitch and Lorraine Noel Finley Fitch, holograph scores, parts, recordings, publications, and other materials of their compositions, singly or jointly; Howard Hanson, 27 scrapbooks documenting his career; Gustave Soderlund, 100 holograph scores, sketches, workbooks for class lectures, scrapbook, photographs, and letters; A. J. Warner (Rochester music and theater critic), scrapbooks, photographs, and personal papers; and Paul White, 100 holograph scores, sketches, photographs, and a caricature of White

Archives of musical organizations, including Enid Knapp Botsford, ballet scores and materials used in connection with her School of Dance and the Eastman Theatre Ballet; and Eastman Theatre, library of performance materials, now incorporated into the Ensemble Library, including 15,500 titles (8000 orchestra titles, 2000 theater-orchestra titles, 1600 large ensemble titles, 800 jazz ensemble titles, 1400 choral titles, and 1600 small ensemble titles)

Sheet music, 75,000 unbound items, 1790s–1940s, mostly pre-1900, with 500 pre-1825 imprints, 700 Civil War editions, and 1200 Rochester imprints; also 25,000 19th-century imprints in 600 bound vols.; and the Fanny and Julius Israel collection, including European and American illustrated editions (URLB, 29 [1974], 190–94)

Tuesday Musicale (local group), minute books, 1890s–1920s, in 4 vols.

Eastman School of Music archives, including official publications, 15 linear meters; and the Concert Office and Publicity Office, 18 linear meters (excepting financial and confidential documents)

Hymnals and tunebooks, 800 items, 300 of them pre-1850 imprints

Scrapbooks, 750 vols., including 17 vols. on the Eastman School of Music, and 50 other vols. of related materials; 200 vols. devoted to musical activity in Rochester; and 450 vols. devoted to other U.S. musical activities

Programs, including American orchestras, 39 linear meters of bound vols.; 1 linear meter of miscellaneous local performances; 9 linear meters of Eastman School of Music programs, singly and in bound vols.; and other local performances, by the Schenck Orchestra, the Dossenbach Orchestra, the Rochester Philharmonic Orchestra, the Rochester Civic Orchestra, and the Tuesday Musicale

Pictorial materials, 2000 photographs and 1000 other items, including U.S. subjects, being organized

Recordings, including transcriptions of local American-music performances, many for the Festivals of American Music and American Composers' Concerts, 1930s– ; also 700 piano rolls, ca. 1900–1930s

—Charles Lindahl, Neil Bunker

1112
Ann M. Pfeiffer LATELLA
70 Mariposa Drive
Rochester, New York 14624

Edward H. Pfeiffer (1868–1932, artist, and grandfather of Mrs. Latella), materials including 300 sheet-music items illustrated by him, 1907–24, a bibliography of 550 sheet-music titles, and photographs of him

1113
Ralph P. LOCKE
Eastman School of Music
University of Rochester
26 Gibbs Street
Rochester, New York 14604

William Garfield Paynter (Chicago piano teacher, pupil of Emil Liebling), collection including an autograph ms album of character pieces, songs, and duets by Liebling, dedicated to friends in Cincinnati and various Kentucky towns, 1867–70; an autograph ms orchestral score of Liebling's Gavotte moderne op. 11; ms orchestral parts of Liebling's Kensington Waltzes and Weber's Concertstück; ms choral parts for Flotow's Stradella, heavily marked, apparently used both in

Hamburg, Germany, and in Philadelphia; and 2 ms books of tunes for melody instrument and chordal accompaniment, titles mainly in German but copied in Chicago (from the Pipenhagen family)

1114
ROCHESTER MUSEUM AND   NRM SCIENCE CENTER
Library
657 East Avenue
Box 1480
Rochester, New York 14603

Sheet music, 8000 items; also 150 songbooks, mostly 19th century
Programs of local theatrical and musical performances, 2.5 linear meters

—Janice Wass

1115
UNIVERSITY OF ROCHESTER   NRU
Rush Rhees Library
Rochester, New York 14627

Herman Dossenbach (1868–1946, orchestral conductor in Europe and Rochester), correspondence and press clippings
William C. Gannett (1840–1923, Unitarian clergyman), hymnals and notes on the editing of hymns

1116
SAINT BONAVENTURE UNIVERSITY   NStBU
Friedsam Memorial Library
Saint Bonaventure, New York 14778

The ms hymnal of William F. Fahnestock, of Ephrata, Pa., cited in HRS, is not now locatable

1117
HISTORICAL SOCIETY OF SARATOGA SPRINGS
Box 216
Saratoga Springs, New York 12866

Programs of concerts in Congress Park, Saratoga Springs, 1870s–1910, 3 linear cm., also clippings related to the concerts, 3 linear cm.
Wooden piano rolls, 40 items, ca. 1885
Chautauqua roller organ

—Heidi Fuge

1118
UNION COLLEGE   NSchU
Schaefer Library
Schenectady, New York 12308

Robert Emmet Kennedy (1877–1941), ms music transcripts, 47 leaves, of black spirituals, street cries, and other songs, some with French Creole texts, some of them cited in Kennedy's Mellows: A Chronicle of Unknown Singers (New York, 1925)

—Ann M. Seemann

1119
SCOTIA HISTORY CENTER
4 North Ten Broeck Street
Scotia, New York 12302

Papers relating to the early history of Scotia, ca. 1903, including poems set to music and songs about the village, some in ms; also oral-history tapes mentioning early bands

—Michelle J. Norris

1120
SENECA FALLS HISTORICAL SOCIETY
55 Cayuga Street
Seneca Falls, New York 13148

Sheet music, 4 bound vols. and 46 separate items of popular music, 1832–1931
Hymnals and sacred songbooks, 10 items, 1816–76, and 6 popular songbooks, 1859–96
Other printed music, 7 items, 1849–1909, including method books and piano and orchestral music
Photographs of local music groups, 17 items, 1870–1950
Recordings, including 4 Edison cylinders and 50 78-rpm discs of popular music
Other musical materials listed in HRS are not located in the collections, notably the papers of Belle L. Palmer, including programs and personal papers, 1869 (p. 288); a music book, 1869–71 (p. 290); and the records of the Musical-Literary Society of Seneca Falls, 1897–1916, 8 vols. (p. 289; also Hamer, p. 449)

—Diana Wildemann

1121
Winona BIMBONI
Smallwood, New York 12778

Alberto Bimboni (1882–1960), personal papers, including holograph music mss of the operas Karin and Winona, the light opera In the Name of Culture, and 10 other works; 10 published songs, and other works in photocopy; incoming correspondence, 5 linear cm.; 50 photographs and 3 scrapbooks, mostly with programs

1122
SOUTHOLD HISTORICAL SOCIETY AND MUSEUM
Maple Lane and Main Road
Southold, New York 11971

Alan Glover Salmon (1868–1917, composer and pianist), performance library of 3000 vols., mainly by Russian composers, also a collection of autographs and photographs
Manuscript music, including 50 military marches and songs by 19th-century local composers
Sheet music, 5000 popular and patriotic 19th-century songs
Songbooks and hymnals, several 19th-century items, also 3 linear meters of popular Irish and patriotic songbooks owned by the Kuhn family of Brooklyn, ca. 1906

Programs of local and New York City concerts, 19th and early 20th centuries
Photographs of local musicians

—George D. Wagoner

1123
MUSEUMS AT STONY BROOK
Stony Brook, New York 11790

William Sidney Mount (1807–68, artist and composer), papers, including diaries, notebooks, 25 items of sheet music for solo voice or piano, 450 ms tunes, some bound in vols., including a book owned by his uncle, Micah Hawkins (1777–1825), and 2 vols. of published dance music by Higgins and by Septimus Winner. See Alfred V. Frankenstein, *William Sidney Mount* (New York, 1975); also Vera Brodsky Lawrence, "Micah Hawkins, the Pied Piper of Catherine Slip," *New-York Historical Society Quarterly*, 62 (1978), 138–65, esp. p. 146
Other published music, including sheet music and songbooks
Programs and photographs of local musical events

—Michiko Okaya Taylor

1124
STATE UNIVERSITY OF   NSbSU
NEW YORK AT STONY BROOK
Stony Brook, New York 11790

Hymnals and songbooks, 150 19th- and 20th-century items, maintained as a unit in the Department of Special Collections
Michael Edwards (1893–1962), personal papers, 1930–62, 952 items, including correspondence with publishers and musicians, among them Leroy Anderson, Robert Burns, Tommy Dorsey, Richard Franko Goldman, and Leonard B. Smith; scores and instrumental, band, orchestral, and choral arrangements; 23 scrapbooks, personal and historical; autographed sheet music and photographs; and other books and catalogues (with a register)

—Judy Kaufman

1125
ONONDAGA COUNTY   NSy
PUBLIC LIBRARY
335 Montgomery Street
Syracuse, New York 13205

Gerrit Smith (1859–1912, church organist and composer), papers, as cited in *Hamer*, p. 451 (in the Art and Music Department)
Published music, including 60 linear cm. of popular 19th-century sheet music, and a few 19th-century hymnals (in the Art and Music Department)
Programs for local concerts, 1880s– , 1 bound vol. (in the Local History Department)

—Beatrice Marble, William Cook

1126
ONONDAGA HISTORICAL   NSyOHi
ASSOCIATION
311 Montgomery Street
Syracuse, New York 13202

Syracuse Musical Institute, 1 vol. of minutes, 1849–57, as cited in *HRS*
Published music, including 19th-century sheet music, hymnals, and songbooks

—Richard Wright

1127
SYRACUSE UNIVERSITY   NSyU
Syracuse, New York 13210

George Arents Research Library

Ernst Bacon, personal papers, including holograph music mss, correspondence, literary works, and printed matter, mostly 1939–49, 1.6 linear meters
George Barati, music mss and correspondence, 30 linear cm.
William H. Berwald (1864–1948), mss and printed editions of his music, 1913–40, 2.7 linear meters
Adolf Bolm, materials relating to ballet, including sheet music
Arna Bontemps (1902–73), personal papers, 1936–67, including correspondence with Pearl Bailey and William Grant Still, music mss of songs, and materials for *Jubilee: A Cavalcade of the Negro Theater*
Grace Bush (b. 1884, poet and composer), personal and literary papers, 7.5 linear cm., including her music mss
Melville Clark (1884–1964, harpist and musical inventor), papers relating to his career and to the Clark Music Co. (music retailers in Syracuse), 1889–1960, in all 5 linear meters
Louis Gruenberg (1884–1964), mss of his journals (called "Conversations with Myself"), speeches, and published works, in all 15 linear cm.
Charles Huerter (1885–1974), personal papers, 1898–1970, including ms and printed music, incoming correspondence, programs, and biographical materials, in all 1.5 linear meters
Louis Krasner, printed music for and published writings relating to the violin, on deposit
Arthur Poister, personal papers, 1928–67, including correspondence, printed programs, and memorabilia, 1.5 linear meters
Andre Polah (d. 1949), personal papers, 1915–49, consisting of printed items, press clippings, and correspondence, including 26 letters from Rose O'Neill, in all 45 linear cm. (Polah's substantial library of orchestral scores and parts now belongs to the School of Music at Syracuse University.)
Bernard Rogers (1893–1967), personal papers, including correspondence, biographical material, ms music, programs, and other printed items, in all 50 linear cm.
Miklos Rozsa, holograph music mss, 75 linear cm.; also correspondence, published scores, photographs, memorabilia, and recordings, in all 4 linear meters
George B. Saul, materials relating to his literary career, 1912–68, including writings about music and 40 holograph music mss

Leo Sowerby (1895–1968), correspondence, literary mss, photographs, and other biographical material, 1917–63, some of it relating to his army band activity in World War I, in all 1 linear meter

Franz Waxman (1906–67), personal papers, 1922–68, 12.5 linear meters, including holograph music mss; correspondence, much of it with major conductors and composers; documents relating to the production and publication of his music; and speeches, program notes, and photographs

Paul F. Webster, personal papers, 1930–67, including correspondence, mss, and printed texts concerning his work as a lyricist for Hoagy Carmichael, Duke Ellington, Rudolf Friml, and Oscar Straus, in all 2 linear meters and 5 bound vols.

George W. Wilson (1870–1946), personal and financial papers relating to the Clyde (N.Y.) Opera House and his other activities in producing theatrical performances, mostly vaudeville and musical entertainments, in all 60 linear cm.

Methodist hymnals, 80 19th-century U.S. imprints

Shaker publications, 500 vols., including music texts

—Donald C. Seibert

Audio Archives

Joseph and Max Bell collection of recordings, including 150,000 items, 1888–1964, as partially listed in *The "A-Z" of Musical History* (n.p., n.d.). To this collection have been added original recordings as well as materials re-recorded—through the auspices of the Thomas Alva Edison Foundation Re-Recording Laboratory at Syracuse—from collections of Edison cylinders owned by L. Brevoort Odell of Branchville, N.J., and by Duane D. Deakins, also Bettini cylinders owned by Walter L. Welch

Recording catalogues and announcements, including cylinder catalogues from Duane D. Deakins

—Walter L. Welch

1128
SLEEPY HOLLOW RESTORATIONS   NTaI
Washington Irving House ("Sunnyside")
150 White Plains Road
Tarrytown, New York 10591

Sheet music, 1 bound vol. of ms solos and duets for treble instruments, ca. 1800, and 10 bound vols. of published piano-solo and piano-vocal music, 1820–1859, owned by Washington Irving's 3 nieces, Catherine Irving (1816–1911), Charlotte Irving van Wart (1824–1911), and Sarah Irving (1817–1900)

—Nancy B. Reich

1129
HISTORICAL SOCIETY OF THE TONAWANDAS
113 Main Street
Tonawanda, New York 14150

Christie Hayes, 15 scrapbooks of papers and photographs

American Legion, Post 264, National Championship Band, papers

Printed music, including sheet music and songbooks

Programs of local musical events, several items

Recordings, including Edison cylinders and Victor 78-rpm discs

—Willard B. Dittmar

1130
TEMPLE BETH EL
Library
2368 Eggert Road
Tonawanda, New York 14150

Samuel S. Luskin Memorial Collection, including printed vocal music and mss in original and in photocopy, written by or from the library of cantor Luskin (1881–1959, founder of the Jewish Choral Society of Buffalo)

—Gerald DeBruin

1131
Ron E. HAYDE
583 Leonard Avenue
Uniondale, New York 11553

Hymnals, 55 items, 1920–

1132
ONEIDA HISTORICAL SOCIETY   NUtHi
318 Genesee Street
Utica, New York 13502

Materials of local musical events, including 500 programs, 50 photographs, and papers of 3 organizations, among them the local Welsh Eisteddfod festivals

Published music, including 1000 sheet-music items and 25 songbooks, 19th and 20th centuries

Music mss by various composers, 15 linear cm.

Recordings, including 25 Edison cylinders

—Douglas M. Preston

1133
UTICA MÄNNERCHOR
10 Avert Avenue
Utica, New York 13502

Materials relating to the Männerchor (German-American singing society), including 8 file drawers of sheet music, 1900– , press clippings, awards for prize singing, and programs of early Sängerfests

—Eric J. Kresse

1134
MORNING MUSICALES
c/o Mrs. Byron Soper
Duffy Road
Watertown, New York 13601

Papers of the organization, including press clippings, sheet music, 100 songbooks, other printed music, and programs, 1907–

1135

U.S. MILITARY ACADEMY — NWM

West Point, New York 10996

Archives

Records of troops stationed at West Point, 1809–1941, including the Academy Band and Detachment of Field Music, 3 vols. of letters, some to musical-supply firms, 1889–1906; and 4 vols. of orders concerning organization of the units, instruction and practice, and dress requirements

Special Collections

Sheet music composed by West Point cadets, graduates, and bandmasters, or concerning West Point or the Army, 3 vols., also separate items, 1830s–60s

Other printed music, including scripts and programs with original music for the *Hundredth Night Show*, 1914–58; also music for the organ and the Cadet Choir (in Cadet Chapel), Cadet Glee Club (in the Cadet Glee Club Library), and band (in the West Point Band Library, also with files on bandsmen)

Manuscript music, including a composition book signed by Cadet James Foster Swift, 1824, containing marches, quick-step waltzes, and polkas by Richard Willis (first bandmaster at the Academy)

Programs for band, chapel, and other concerts at West Point, 1840s–

Col. Francis E. Resta (1894–1968, West Point bandmaster), 1 linear meter of personal papers

Photographs of West Point bands, and of bands at various army posts

—Marie T. Capps, Herbert Leventhal

West Point Museum

Military sheet music, 40 items; also 5 photographs of the Academy bands, and 5 military recordings

—Michael J. McAfee

1136

Percy GRAINGER LIBRARY SOCIETY

7 Cromwell Place
White Plains, New York 10601

Percy Grainger (1882–1961, composer and pianist), materials including 4 file drawers of ms photocopies, 200 boxes of published music (some with ms markings), 300 photographs of the composer and his colleagues, letters, financial records, memorabilia, and 24 early 78-rpm disc recordings of Grainger performing or of his works. See Thomas Carl Slattery, *The Wind Music of Percy Aldridge Grainger* (Ph.D. diss., University of Iowa, 1967), pp. 175–76

—Stewart Manville

1137

Charles W. HUGHES

28 Ralph Avenue
White Plains, New York 10606

American music collections, 6.5 linear meters, including published music by American composers, press clippings of criticisms of American music, photographs (mostly of American opera singers and of foreign singers who performed in 19th-century America), books about secular and folk music, 500 hymnals, 1 shape-note ms book, 1 ms book by Ferdinand Dunckley with original hymns, and books about hymnology for use in Hughes's *American Hymns Old and New* (New York, forthcoming)

1138

WOODSTOCK LIBRARY

5 Library Lane
Woodstock, New York 12498

Sheet music, 620 classical items for piano, voice, or chamber ensemble, 1900–

Programs of the Maverick Concerts, 1930s–

Photographs of local musicians, 50 items, 1920s–

—Ellen K. Roberts

1139

YONKERS PUBLIC LIBRARY — NY

70 South Broadway
Yonkers, New York 10701

William Wood Struthers Collection of Historical Recordings, 2000 78-rpm discs, mostly 1903–25, including 57 test pressings of recordings by Geraldine Ferrar

William J. Lenox collection, 774 33⅓-rpm discs of classical music, ca. 1940s–70s, with tape copies, catalogued

Sheet music, 7550 19th- and 20th-century

—A. Beggs

In addition to the repositories listed above, the following have also reported holdings of the materials indicated:

Albany—Albany County Historical Association: sheet music

Albany—Historic Cherry Hill: sheet music, songbooks, programs, catalogues, recordings

Amityville—Amityville Historical Society: sheet music, songbooks, other printed music, recordings, miscellaneous

Amsterdam—Guy Park Manor: miscellaneous

Angola—Town of Evans Historical Society: recordings

Auburn—Cayuga County Historian's Office: programs

Baldwin—Baldwin Historical Society: sheet music, songbooks

Ballston Spa—Saratoga County Historical Society: sheet music, songbooks, programs, pictures, recordings, miscellaneous

Batavia—Genesee County Historian: sheet music, songbooks, programs, pictures, miscellaneous

Bayville—Bayville Historical Museum: sheet music, songbooks, programs, pictures, recordings

Bemus Point—Bemus Point Library: sheet music, songbooks

Binghamton—Charles Semowich: sheet music, songbooks, programs, recordings, miscellaneous

Black River—Black River Free Library: songbooks

Bronxville—Concordia College, Scheele Memorial Library: songbooks, recordings

Buffalo—Buffalo and Erie County Historical Society: songbooks, programs, pictures, recordings

Buffalo—State University College at Buffalo, Edward H. Butler Library: songbooks, recordings

Buffalo—Temple Beth Zion, Library: songbooks, recordings

Camden—Queen Village Historical Society, Carriage House Museum: sheet music, songbooks, programs, pictures, miscellaneous

Canandaigua—Ontario County Historical Society: songbooks, programs, pictures, recordings

Canastota—Canastota Canal Town Museum: sheet music, songbooks

Carmel—Kent Free Public Library: songbooks, recordings, miscellaneous

Carthage—Carthage Free Library: miscellaneous

Clinton—Etude Club: programs, pictures, miscellaneous

Clinton—Hamilton-Kirkland College, Burke Library: sheet music, songbooks, other printed music, programs, catalogues, miscellaneous

Cold Spring—Putnam County Historical Society: sheet music, songbooks, programs, recordings

Cooperstown—Town of Middlefield Historical Association: sheet music

Corning—Corning Public Library: programs, miscellaneous

Delhi Delaware County Historical Association: sheet music, songbooks, programs

East Durham—Durham Center Museum: sheet music, songbooks, programs, pictures, recordings

East Meadow—Nassau County Museum, Reference Library: sheet music, songbooks

Eden—Eden Historical Society: sheet music, songbooks, pictures

Ellington—Farman Free Library: songbooks

Elmira—Chemung County Historical Society: sheet music, songbooks, other printed music, programs

Fonda—Heritage and Genealogical Society of Montgomery County: sheet music, songbooks

Fort Plain—Fort Plain Museum: sheet music, songbooks, programs

Geneseo—State University of New York, College at Geneseo, Milne Library: sheet music, songbooks, other printed music, programs, catalogues, miscellaneous

Geneseo—Wadsworth Library: songbooks, recordings

Gilbertsville—Gilbertsville Library: sheet music, songbooks

Gloversville—Fulton County Museum: songbooks, programs

Gravesend—Gravesend Historical Society: sheet music, programs

Great Neck—Temple Bethel Library: sheet music, songbooks, programs, miscellaneous

Haines Falls—Haines Falls Library: songbooks, programs, recordings

Haines Falls—Mountain Top Historical Society of Greene County: songbooks, recordings

Hammondsport—Glenn Curtiss Museum of Local History: sheet music, other printed music, pictures, recordings, miscellaneous

Hartwick—Town of Hartwick Historical Society: pictures, miscellaneous

Hempstead—Hempstead Public Library: songbooks

Hempstead—Hofstra University, Library: printed music

Hewlett—Hewlett–Woodmere Library: miscellaneous

Huntington—Huntington Historical Society: sheet music, songbooks

Interlaken—Interlaken Historical Society: pictures

Island Park—Island Park Public Library: songbooks

Ithaca—Hinckley Foundation: sheet music, songbooks, programs, pictures

Jamestown—Fenton Historical Society: sheet music, songbooks, other printed music, programs, pictures, recordings

Johnstown—Johnstown Public Library: songbooks

Lake Placid—Lake Placid–North Elba Historical Society: sheet music, recordings

Lakewood—Lakewood Memorial Library: sheet music, songbooks

Liberty—Frank Marion: sheet music, other printed music

Liberty—Liberty Public Library: songbooks, other printed music, recordings

Lyons—Wayne County Historical Society: sheet music, songbooks, programs, pictures, recordings

Lyons Falls—Lewis County Historical Society: sheet music, songbooks, recordings

Malone—Franklin County Historical and Museum Society: sheet music, songbooks, programs, pictures

Medina—Medina Historical Society: sheet music

Montour Falls—Schuyler County Historical Society: recordings

Mount Vernon—Society of the National Shrine of the Bill of Rights: sheet music

Mumford—Big Springs Historical Society: sheet music, songbooks, programs

New Lebanon—Shaker Community: ms music book, 1880

New Paltz—State University of New York at New Paltz, Sojourner Truth Library: songbooks, other printed music

New Rochelle—New Rochelle Public Library: sheet music, song books, pictures, recordings, miscellaneous

New York—American Bible Society, Library: songbooks

New York—Archives of Cooperative Lutheranism, Library of the Lutheran Council in the USA: songbooks

New York—City University of New York, Graduate Center Library: sheet music

New York—Federal Hall Museum: sheet music

New York—Mercantile Library Association: songbooks

New York (Bronx)—Fordham University, Duane Library: 5 music handbills, ca. 1800

New York (Brooklyn)—Harry T. Friedman: sheet music, other printed music

New York (Staten Island)—Wagner College, Horrmann Library: sheet music, songbooks, other printed music

Oneida—Oneida Library, Hand Barker Memorial: songbooks

Oneonta—Hartwick College, Library: songbooks, other printed music, recordings

Oneonta—State University of New York, College at Oneonta, James L. Milne Library: sheet music, songbooks

Oriskany Falls—C. W. Clark Memorial Library: programs

Ossining—Ossining Historical Society: sheet music, songbooks, other printed music, programs

Oswego—Oswego County Historical Society: sheet

music, songbooks, programs, pictures, recordings, miscellaneous

Owego—Tioga County Historical Society: sheet music, songbooks, other printed music, catalogues, pictures, recordings, miscellaneous

Oyster Bay—Friends of Raymhan Hall: songbooks

Oyster Bay—Oyster Bay Historical Society: songbooks, programs, pictures, miscellaneous

Palmyra—Historic Palmyra: sheet music, songbooks, pictures, miscellaneous

Penn Yan—Yates County Genealogical and Historical Society: sheet music, songbooks, programs, pictures, recordings

Port Chester—Port Chester Public Library: songbooks, recordings

Pultneyville—Pultneyville Historical Society: programs

Purchase—Manhattanville College, Library: sheet music, songbooks, other printed music

Richmondtown—Staten Island Historical Society: sheet music, songbooks

Ripley—Ripley Free Library: songbooks

Riverhead—Suffolk County Historical Society: sheet music, songbooks, programs, catalogues, pictures, recordings, miscellaneous

Rochester—St. John Fisher College, Library: recordings, miscellaneous

Rochester—Nazareth College of Rochester, Library: songbooks, recordings

Rochester—William T. Sherwood: pictures

Rochester—Margaret Woodbury Strong Museum: sheet music, songbooks, programs, catalogues

Rochester—Robert Wesleyan College, Keating Library: songbooks, other printed music

Rome—Historic Rome Development Authority: songbooks, miscellaneous

Rome—Rome Historical Society: sheet music, songbooks, programs, miscellaneous

Sinclairville—Sinclairville Free Library: songbooks

Somers—Somers Historical Society: sheet music, songbooks, miscellaneous

Springville—Concord Historical Society: miscellaneous

Springville—Concord Public Library: songbooks

Ticonderoga—Ticonderoga Historical Society: songbooks, programs

Tonawanda—Tonawanda–Kenmore Historical Society: recordings, miscellaneous

Troy—Rensselaer County Historical Society: sheet music, songbooks, miscellaneous

Troy—Troy Public Library: songbooks, programs

Utica—Utica Public Library: songbooks, programs, pictures

Waterloo—Waterloo Library and Historical Society: songbooks

Watertown—Roswell Flower Library: sheet music, songbooks, catalogues

Weedsport—Old Brutus Historical Society: sheet music, songbooks, programs, recordings

Wyoming—Middlebury Historical Society, sheet music, songbooks, other printed music, programs

Yonkers—St. Joseph's Seminary, Corrigan Memorial Library: songbooks, other printed music, recordings

North Carolina

1140
APPALACHIAN STATE UNIVERSITY
NcBoA

Boone, North Carolina 28608

W. L. Eury Appalachian Collection, 6 linear meters of folksong materials, including ms and typed transcriptions of texts and music collected by I. G. Greer (ca. 1912–30), W. Amos Abrams (ca. 1935–45), James R. York, and Virgil L. Sturgill (ca. 1920–60); 200 78-rpm disc field recordings collected by Abrams; the Jack Guy Collection, 30 hours of tape recordings of musicians in western North Carolina and eastern Tennessee, collected ca. 1950–60, and 1000 hours of other tape recordings, 400 33⅓-rpm discs, and 30 video tapes of musical performances of musicians and instrument-makers; published songbooks and sheet music containing Appalachian folksongs, ballads, and hymns, 100 items, ca. 1850–1950; and photographs and slides of Appalachian musicians, especially in Watauga County, N.C., 50 items, 1900–

—Eric J. Olson

1141
UNIVERSITY OF NORTH CAROLINA
NcU

Chapel Hill, North Carolina 27514

Manuscripts Department,
Louis Round Wilson Library

The Department includes the Southern Historical Collection and the Southern Folklore Collection. See Susan Sokol Blosser and Clyde Norman, Jr., *The Southern Historical Collection: A Guide to Manuscripts* (Chapel Hill, 1970; hereinafter cited as *Guide*)

Sarah Jane Bailey, 1 bound vol. of sheet music, ca. 1843–45, used at St. Mary's School, Raleigh, in the John L. Bailey papers (*Guide*, 39)

Henry Bradford (minister in Halifax County, N. C.), ms book of Methodist hymns and songs, copied by him, ca. 1804–11 (*Guide*, 3447)

Annabel Morris Buchanan (b. 1888), mss and photographs from her career as a composer, transcriptions of folksongs collected in the Appalachian Mountains, 3 unpublished books on folksong, materials relating to the White Top Folk Festival and the National Federation of Music Clubs, and correspondence

John Charles Campbell (1867–1919) and Olive Arnold Campbell (1882–1954), papers, 1865–1962, 3 linear meters, including ballads collected by her and materials of the John C. Campbell Folk School, which she founded at Brasstown, N. C. (*Guide*, 3800)

Frederick Mason Colston (Confederate officer), reminiscences of operas heard by him, 1853–1910, in the Campbell and Colston family papers (*Guide*, 135)

John Hamilton Cornish (1815–78, Episcopal minister), 1 linear meter of papers, 1833–1966, including a ms history of ritual music at the Episcopal church on Sullivan's Island, S. C., 1846 (*Guide*, 1461)

Abram Crabtree, Jr., of North Carolina, words for a religious ballad, 1848 (*Guide*, 190)

Moses Ashley Curtis (1808–72, Episcopal minister), personal papers, 1825–1929, including ms church music (*Guide*, 199)

Edward Dromgoole, papers, 1766–1871, including 1 handmade book entitled "Spiritual Songs," with words to a camp-meeting hymn and other hymns (*Guide*, 199)

Paul Eliot Green (b. 1894, radio and film writer), 14 linear meters of papers, 1917–75, including correspondence concerning symphonic drama (*Guide*, 3693; restricted)

Mrs. Ella (Goode) Hardeman, 8 scrapbooks, 1917–46, including World War I sheet music (*Guide*, 308)

Harmony Old Singers Association, 58 pages of minutes of annual meetings, 1912–62, including business records and membership lists (*Guide*, 3793; restricted)

Charles A. Hentz, of Columbus, Ga., ms "Autobiography" and diary, 1848–52

Roland Holt Collection of American theater materials, 1881–1931, including 15,000 clippings, programs, pictures, photographs, and articles, also 13 scrapbooks, 19 letter files, 250 photographs in albums, 100 opera libretti, and 60 books on drama

Edward Vernon Howell (1872–1931, pharmacist), personal papers, 1725–1929, including copies of ballads collected in Avery County, N.C., 1917–18 (*Guide*, 1060)

Hubard family papers, 1741–1907, including 2 ms music-score books, 1791 and undated, 68 sheet-music items, and correspondence between E. W. Hubard and the James Woodhouse Co. of Richmond, Va., concerning publication of music (*Guide*, 360)

William L. James (clarinetist), 2 ms music scores used by the band of the Confederate Army of Northern Virginia, led by William H. Neave, ca. 1860–65, also 1 photograph of James (*Guide*, 1519)

Drucy Lacy (1802–1884, Presbyterian minister), personal papers, 1823–1903, including 1 vol. containing records of literary and musical organizations in Charlotte, N.C. (*Guide*, 3641)

Penn School (Freedman's Bureau School, St. Helena Island, S. C.), papers, including ms texts of spirituals and photographs of ring shouts

Ebenezer Pettigrew (1783-1848), ms music-exercise book, 1792, in the Pettigrew family papers (*Guide*, 592)

Robert S. Phifer (professor of music at Virginia and North Carolina colleges), 170 items of papers, 1865–1901, including programs, clippings, correspondence, and scrapbooks (*Guide*, 593)

Hubert McNeil Poteat (North Carolina composer), letters, 1931–42, in the Frank P. Graham papers

James Ryder Randall (d. 1908, composer, poet, and author of "Maryland, My Maryland"), poems, diary, and correspondence, 1855–63, also clippings, ca. 1908 (*Guide*, 1506)

Lamar Stringfield (1897–1959, composer, conductor, and educator), 3 linear meters of papers, 1926–59, including ms and published music, correspon-

dence, typescripts and mimeographed writings, and 3 tape recordings (*Guide*, 3522)

Maude (Minish) Sutton (d. 1936, folklorist), 1 item and 3 vols. of microfilmed papers, including a notebook of ballads collected in the Blue Ridge Mountains, 1921–22 (*Guide*, 2681)

Nicholas Philip Trist, papers, including bills and correspondence with scattered references to music and the Jefferson family, 1820s–40s (*Guide*, 2104). See Helen Cripe, *Thomas Jefferson and Music* (Charlottesville, 1974), pp. 38–40, 60–63

John Thomas Wheat (1801–88), papers, 60 linear cm., including materials concerning his daughter, Leonidas Polk Wheat (1841–1915), who studied music in Europe (*Guide*, 1832)

Thomas J. Wilson, 2 ms books of violin tunes, n.d., and 1 copy of *The American Harmonist* (1821) (*Guide*, 2257)

Manuscript music books, 3 items from Mecklenburg County, N. C., 1 belonging to Archible Woodside with notes and instructions from his teacher, 1772 or 1785, 1 with sacred vocal music by John W. Herron used by the McDowell family of Mecklenburg County, 1813, and 1 from Pennsylvania, 1820s

—Richard A. Schrader

Music Library

Annabel Morris Buchanan Collection, including 44 19th-century tunebooks, mostly with shape notes, and 1 ms tunebook, probably of an itinerant preacher of Middletown, Ohio, ca. 1820; with a computer-based index of tune names, authors of tune texts, and arrangers

Songbooks, tunebooks, and hymnals, including 500 19th- and 20th-century tunebooks and gospel songbooks, and other vols. in reprint and microform, with an emphasis on southern and folk-related items, 1816–

Early American Sheet Music Collection, 4200 items of published sheet music bound in 100 vols., ca 1810– , mostly indexed by composer and title, with some ms items inserted

Programs of the University and Chapel Hill, 1930s–

—Margaret F. Lospinuso

Folk Music Archives

Recordings, including 2000 commercial, institutional, or private discs and tapes of authentic traditional music of the British Isles and the U.S., with a computer-based index by geographical region, genre, song-type, and performer

Field recordings, 2000 tapes, mostly collected by students and faculty at the University. Major emphases include black and white religious songs; black and white Primitive Baptists, including the Hartman–Sutton collection with log sheets and transcriptions; Shakers; fiddle tunes, principally from southwest Virginia and North Carolina, including the Carter–Owens collection with log sheets listing fiddle tunes, and recordings for a film on the white North Carolina fiddler Tommy Jarrell; black secular folksong, particularly for a film documentary of Arthur ("Peg Leg Sam") Jackson; and blues

—Daniel W. Patterson

1142

UNIVERSITY OF NORTH CAROLINA   NcCU
AT CHARLOTTE

J. Murrey Atkins Library
UNCC Rural Station
Charlotte, North Carolina 28223

Sheet music, 15 popular-music items, pre-1867, and 29 first editions of Stephen Foster songs, 1849–64

Songbooks, 2 vols. of popular songs, 1 vol. of slave songs, and 2 hymnals, all 19th century

John Tennant (1868–1957, editor), scrapbook of New York City concert programs, 1905–55

G. D. Russell & Co. (Boston music publisher), music catalogue, ca. 1868

—Robin Brabham

1143

DUKE UNIVERSITY   NcD

William R. Perkins Library
Durham, North Carolina 27706

Rare Book Room

Sheet music, 2250 catalogued and 2000 uncatalogued items, vocal or piano, as separate sheets or in bound vols., mostly late 19th and early 20th centuries; also 450 Confederate sheet-music imprints, some in the Crandall Collection (Flowers Room)

Broadside texts, 360 Civil War and 140 other items, catalogued by title or first line

Songbooks, late 18th and 19th centuries, including 100 hymnals, mostly Methodist and Confederate; 10 Confederate songbooks; 25 tunebooks; and popular songbooks, scattered through the collections

—Michael P. Harris, Laird Ellis

Manuscript Department

See the *Guide to the Cataloged Collections in the Manuscript Department* (Santa Barbara, Cal., 1980)

Sheet music, 8000 popular songs and piano pieces, arranged alphabetically by title within 4 categories: Antebellum (ca. 1830–60), Civil War—Confederate, Civil War—United States, and Postbellum (to ca. 1945); also 300 unsorted items

Manuscript songbook, 1861–62, containing lyrics to popular songs

Advertising Collection, including concert programs primarily from the southern U.S., 19th and 20th centuries

Z. W. Anderson (band member in a Georgia regiment of the Confederate Army), holograph vol. of band music, 1865

Frank Clyde Brown (folklorist), personal papers, including 63 cylinder and 150 78-rpm disc recordings, transcriptions of lyrics, and sheet music, ca. 1920–40, arranged chronologically by form. See Newman Ivey White, ed., *The Frank C. Brown Collection of North Carolina Folklore*, 7 vols. (Durham, 1952–64)

Les Brown, 342 holograph arrangements for his band, 1930s–1950s

Durham Savoyards (local Gilbert & Sullivan society), papers including organizational records, photographs, stage designs, and publicity materials, 1898– , 2000 items

Edward Harden (Georgia plantation owner and lawyer), papers, including an early 19th-century holograph vol. of music

Robert Preston Harriss (Baltimore novelist and music critic), personal papers, 1927–75, 3500 items

Charles Frederic Hartt (1840–78, zoologist), essay on music

Lenoir (N.C.) High School Band, scrapbooks of social activities and performances, 1927–73

Montrose Jonas Moses (theater historian), personal papers, 1789–1960, mostly 1900–1933, including programs and photographs of stage sets and actors, grouped by form, each arranged chronologically

Savannah (Ga.) Music Club, scrapbooks, 2 vols., 1895–1903

Laura Waldron (singer and actress, of Charleston, S.C.), personal papers, 1859–83, 97 items

George Frederick Williams (Boston politician and patron), 3800 items of papers and correspondence, some reflecting his social life in Boston musical circles, 1876–88

—Paul I. Chestnut, Robert L. Byrd

General Collections

The collections consist of unprocessed materials in the Department of Technical Services

Songbooks, 1840s–90s, 75 items, including sacred music, glee books, and choral music

Hymnals, 1000 vols. in the Baker Collection of Methodistica, with a partial list

Sheet music, 4000 19th- and 20th-century items, strong in southern U.S. imprints

—Bill Gosling

University Archives

Materials concerning the Music Department, including correspondence from Edward Hall Broadhead (Chapel organist) and others, 2 items, 1925 and 1935, in the papers of William Preston Few (president of the University, 1910–40) and Robert Lee Flowers (vice-president, Business Division); correspondence, 1936, personnel file, 1938, budget and curriculum, 1938–39, in the papers of William Hane Wannamaker (vice-president, Division of Education); 50 programs of campus musical events, 1920s–30s; reminiscences and reissued recordings of Big Bands at Duke, 1930s– ; rosters of the college orchestra and band, founded 1914 (materials date only post-1940), and a 1974 reminiscence by Walter W. Turrentine, Sr., of the beginnings of the Trinity College Band in 1920

Programs of 50 organ recitals and 50 carillon recitals, 1932–37, and of the University Service of Worship, 1932–

Music Study Club of the Woman's College of Duke University, papers, including a brief history, 1933–54

Trinity College and Duke University songbooks, 6 items, 1915–33

Photographs, including 10 of Les Brown, ca. 1936–40; 6 of Johnny Long, ca. 1940s; and several of bands at Duke University, including Jimmy Lunceford and Glenn Miller, ca. 1940

Biographical files of clippings concerning Les Brown and George E. ("Jelly") Leftwich

Miscellaneous materials on musical activities and alumni, in yearbooks, registers, and periodicals

—Mark C. Stauter

1144

AMERICAN THEATER ORGAN SOCIETY

NcElon

Elon College Library
Elon College, North Carolina 27244

Materials relating to silent-film music, including sheet music, 300 player rolls, and 12 tape-recorded interviews with organists and other authorities on silent-film music, 1900–
American Theater Organ Society, papers, late 1920s– , including letters, periodicals, and newsletters; also glass movie-slides used in sing-alongs

—Charles B. Lowry

1145

Carl SANDBURG HOME NATIONAL HISTORIC SITE

Box 395
Flat Rock, North Carolina 28731

Miscellaneous materials from Sandburg's personal library, partly pre-1940, including music mss, folk-music collections, programs and publicity materials for his lectures, photographs, and recordings

—Warren R. Weber

1146

GREENSBORO HISTORICAL MUSEUM

130 Summit Avenue
Greensboro, North Carolina 27401

Ann Morehead, 20-page ms music book for piano, copied mid 19th century
Sheet music, 102 items, 1840–1950, including World War I and II items; 1 bound vol. of 25 Confederate imprints, 1864; and 2 bound vols. of classical music and dances for the piano, 1830–60
Hymnals and sacred songbooks, 3 items, 1849–78; also 10 school songbooks used locally, 1850–1920
Other printed music, including Thomas Moore's *Irish Melodies* (Philadelphia, n.d.), donated in 1819; Elias Howe's *Young America's Instructor for the Flute* (Boston, 1858); an instruction book for banjo (1885); and a piano primer (n.d.)
Programs for concerts and musical-theater productions at the Grand Opera House, Greensboro, 1900–1925
Brockmann Music School & Orchestra, papers, and 1 photograph, 1895
Recordings, including Edison cylinders and 150 78-rpm discs

—Gayle H. Fripp

1147

GUILFORD COLLEGE

NcGG

Library
Greensboro, North Carolina 27410

Manuscript music, 3 items, 1 written in honor of Dolley Madison
Hymnals and songbooks, 14 vols., including Quaker items
Other printed music, 25 items

—Treva W. Mathis

1148

UNIVERSITY OF NORTH CAROLINA AT GREENSBORO

NcGU

Walter Clinton Jackson Library
Department of Special Collections
Greensboro, North Carolina 27412

Manuscripts of North Carolina composers, 110 items, including works by Mrs. Crosby Adams, Henry Hugh Altvater, Edward T. Cone, Martha Taylor Davison, Hermene Warlick Eichhorn, Herbert Hazelman, George E. Henry, Beverley E. Holmes, Hunter Johnson, Alma Lissow Oncley, Hubert McNeill Poteat, Lamar Stringfield, Carolyn Stearns Stroud, Christopher Joseph Thomas, Charles G. Vardell, Jr., and Elliot Weisgarber. See Hermene Warlick Eichhorn and Treva Wilkerson Mathis, *North Carolina Composers, as Represented in the Holograph Collection of the Library of the Woman's College of the University of North Carolina* (Greensboro, 1945); additions and corrections are available from the library, along with information on the mss acquired more recently through the "restful music" prizes established by Edward B. Benjamin
Ross Lee Finney, 4 autograph mss, ca. 1934–40
Wade R. Brown (1866–1950, educator, performer, and promoter of music in North Carolina), personal papers, including 3 folders of correspondence, 1886–94, and ephemera, 1910–77; programs of the Wade R. Brown Recital Series, 1940– ; and 12 photographs
Hermene Warlick Eichhorn, personal papers, including correspondence relating mostly to public school music in North Carolina, the state music contest-festival in particular, and several surveys and historical sketches of this topic, 1941–42
Luigi Silva (1903–61), personal library and research files, including his unfinished book on the history of the violoncello; also 300 books about music, 2000 scores, and ms copies of cello music, including works by such American composers as Josef Alexander, Ernst Bacon, Samuel Barber, Ernest Bloch, Henry Thacker Burleigh, David Diamond, Roy Harris, Walter Helfer, Herbert Inch, Fritz Kreisler, Otto Langey, George F. McKay, Joseph Malkin, Daniel Gregory Mason, Herman Sandby, Robert Sanders, Frederick Preston Search, Percy Such, and Paul White. See Barbara B. Cassell and Clifton H. Karnes III, *Cello Music Collections in the Jackson Library . . . , Part I: The Luigi Silva Collection* (Greensboro, 1978); also the Violoncello Society *Newsletter* (February, 1980)
Archives of the University's music department, 1902– , including programs of concerts and recitals, in 12 boxes and 6 bound vols.
Annual Conference of Music Teachers, programs, 1929–48, 14 items

—Emmy Mills

1149

EAST CAROLINA UNIVERSITY

NcGrE

Greenville, North Carolina 27834

Allen Taylor (b. 1874?, of Sealevel, N.C.), ms song texts of "The Battle of Gettysburg" and "Nora Darling," copied 1958 from childhood recollections for Mr. and Mrs. Frank C. Salisbury, in the J. Y. Joyner Library
American folklore materials prepared by students, 1000 collections containing 100,000 items, including tape

and disc recordings, research papers, photographs, and films, in the Folklore Archive, English Department. See D. J. McMillan, "ECU Folklore Archive," *North Carolina Folklore*, 19 (1971), 131–34

—Dennis R. Lawson, D.J. McMillan

1150

UNITED METHODIST CHURCH　　NcLjUM

Commission on Archives and History
39 Lakeshore Drive
Lake Junaluska, North Carolina 28745

Hymnals, 500 items, 1737–

—John H. Ness

1151

James C. HARPER

203 Norwood Street SW
Lenoir, North Carolina 28645

Lenoir High School Band library, 1924–77, including published editions and a few original arrangements of music for concert and marching band, with a 15-drawer card index by title, composer, and subject; also photographs, and the compiler's history, *The Lenoir High School Band*

1152

MARS HILL COLLEGE　　NcMhC

Memorial Library
Mars Hill, North Carolina 28754

Bascom Lamar Lunsford (1882–1973), collection of 2300 texts of folk ballads, folksongs, and popular songs from North Carolina and neighboring states; recordings of his performances, including 70 discs recorded at Columbia University, 1935, and 35 at the Library of Congress, 1949; video tapes of mountain folk festivals; and correspondence, memoirs, other recordings, photographs, and a 405-page scrapbook. A guide is in preparation

1153

HISTORICAL FOUNDATION OF　　NcMHi
THE PRESBYTERIAN AND
REFORMED CHURCHES

Montreat, North Carolina 28757

Tunebooks and hymnals, 1755– , 100 items, partly catalogued. Many of these are cited in Ruth D. See, *Historical Foundation Materials Concerning Early American Church Music* (Montreat, 1975)
Crosby Adams and Juliette Graves (Mrs. Crosby) Adams, personal papers, ca. 1895–1951, 6 linear meters, including correspondence, programs, sheet music, writings on music education, and memorabilia

—Ruth D. See

1154

MOUNT OLIVE COLLEGE　　NcMtC

Free Will Baptist Historical Collection
Moye Library
Mount Olive, North Carolina 28365

Hymnals of the Free Will Baptist Church, 18 items, 1832–1934, including several editions of *The Free Will Baptist Hymn Book* and *Zion's Hymns*

—Pam Wood

1155

NORTH CAROLINA DEPARTMENT　　NcAr
OF CULTURAL RESOURCES

Archives–Library Building
109 East Jones Street
Raleigh, North Carolina 27611

North Carolina Museum of History

Sheet music, 153 items, 1880s–ca. 1915
Recordings, including 471 cylinders and 272 78-rpm discs, mostly 1920s–50s; also 1200 78-rpm discs, 1915–45, as a separate collection

—Betty O. Tyson

North Carolina State Archives

North Carolina Federation of Music Clubs, archives, 1917–74, in 65 boxes and vols., with an inventory
North Carolina Symphony Orchestra, papers, 1932–73, in 53 boxes, also 2 microfilm reels of minutes, with a 25-page description
Black Mountain College Papers, 1933–56, 100 boxes of materials now on 2 microfilm reels, including programs, bulletins, photographs with a detailed finding aid, and correspondence of faculty members, among them Erwin Bodky, Ernest Krenek, Klaus Liepman, Edward Lowinsky, Paul Matthew, and Ray Toubman. See Anna M. Hines, *Music at Black Mountain College: A Study of Experimental Ideas in Music* (D.M.A. thesis, University of Missouri at Kansas City, 1973), and Martin Duberman, *Black Mountain, an Exploration in Community* (New York, 1972)
Music in the Private Collections, as cited in Beth G. Crabtree, *Guide to Private Manuscript Collections in the North Carolina State Archives* (Raleigh, 1964; collection numbers cited in parentheses below), including Salley D. Powell, ms songbook, 1814 (collection 1152); Stephen Graham, invoice for a piano, 1832 (collection 527); Nell Battle Lewis, personal papers, containing material for her newspaper series, 1920s–40s, entitled "Incidentally," and including articles on North Carolina music, such as the writing of "The Old North State," the first North Carolina State Symphony, activities of the State Federation of Music Clubs, and the "Gastonia Strike Song" of 1929 (collection 255); and William Henry Jones (1883–1963), personal papers, including press clippings, letters, and programs of the vocal career of his daughter, Carol Jones (collection 239). Other ms items, including song texts, programs, hymnals, and songbooks will be cited in the new edition of the *Guide*, being prepared by Barbara T. Cain, including 4 ballad texts copied for George Riggs, 1861–62 (collection 1499); Suson A.

Gary, bound vol. of sheet music for piano, 1850s, in the collection of Mrs. Sterling Stoudemire (collection 1602); and Cpl. Rudolph Nunn (of the 2nd North Carolina Infantry Band, A.E.F.), diary May 1918 to April 1919, describing war service and musical activities in France (collection 1308)

Microfilms of personal and family papers (originals are in private possession, as noted below, along with references to the *Guide*), including B. B. Brown, ms notes of lectures on music at the common school of Cabarrus County, ca. 1855, in the Beaver family papers (Mrs. Guy Beaver, Concord; *Guide*, MF.1); William Schaum, diary, 1865, with Civil War military recollections, including descriptions of Negroes playing banjos and band concerts (Mrs. Jack Jordan, Dunn; *Guide*, MF.40); and family correspondence with music references, press clippings of the singer Josie Dameron, songbooks, and other materials relating to opera in 1907, in the Williams–Dameron family papers (Mrs. Martha Scott Perry, Goldsboro)

Miscellaneous Collections, including ms music of the Swiss Bell Ringers, as performed in Raleigh in the 1830s, for which William Gaston wrote the text of the official state song, "The Old North State"; Lamar Stringfield, 10 ms transcriptions of folksongs collected in North Carolina, 1932; 100 items of sheet music, ca. 1849– ; and other published music for piano, guitar, and mandolin, 12 linear cm.

Music in the Military Collection, including 19 Confederate sheet-music items, 2 Confederate songbooks, and 12 World War I items

Recordings, 400 miscellaneous items, including Scottish songs and laments heard in North Carolina; "Bull City Blues: A Study of the Black Musical Community . . . , Durham, 1920s–1940s"; and other early transcription discs

—Barbara T. Cain

1156
FIRST PRESBYTERIAN CHURCH
125 South Third Street
Wilmington, North Carolina 28401

Tunebooks, 6 items, 4 of them pre-1860, mostly from the Howell family collection, as cited in Nancy R. Ping, *Music in Antebellum Wilmington and the Lower Cape Fear of North Carolina* (Ph.D. diss., University of Colorado, 1979)

—Nancy R. Ping

1157
Laura Howell Norden (Mrs. Wallace) SCHORR
1634 Country Club Road
Wilmington, North Carolina 28403

Howell collection of sheet music, 691 items, ca. 1825–1900, also 10 19th-century tunebooks, as listed in Nancy R. Ping, *Music in Antebellum Wilmington and the Lower Cape Fear of North Carolina* (Ph.D. diss., University of Colorado, 1979)

—Nancy R. Ping

1158
UNIVERSITY OF NORTH CAROLINA AT WILMINGTON   NcWU
William H. Randall Library
Box 3725
Wilmington, North Carolina 28405

Sheet music, 1 bound vol., ca. 1860, formerly owned by the Beery family of North Carolina

—Nancy R. Ping

1159
Mrs. Alfred Harding YOPP
Carolina Apartments, No. 1
420 Market Street
Wilmington, North Carolina 28410

Alfred Harding Yopp (1876–1973, composer, organist, and music-store proprietor, ca. 1915–70), personal papers, including holograph music mss and correspondence, notably a letter from his music teacher, George W. Chadwick

—Nancy R. Ping

1160
Estate of Vittorio GIANNINI
c/o Wachovia Bank & Trust Company
Box 3099
Winston-Salem, North Carolina 27102

Vittorio Giannini (1903–66), ms music

1161
MORAVIAN MUSIC FOUNDATION   NcWsMM
20 Cascade Avenue
Drawer Z, Salem Station
Winston-Salem, North Carolina 27108

The two major repositories of early Moravian music in America are the Moravian Archives in Bethlehem, Pa. (q.v.), and the present collection. Both are under the custody of the Moravian Music Foundation of Winston-Salem, except for several groups of material under the direct custody of the Moravian Archives in Bethlehem, as noted. In overview, the holdings consist of 14 "church and community" collections, and various "special" collections, located as follows (WS for Winston-Salem, B for Bethlehem):

Church and Community Collections

Bethania (N.C.) congregation	WS
Bethlehem (Pa.) congregation	B
Bethlehem collegium musicum	B
Bethlehem score collection	B
Dover (Ohio) congregation	B
Johannes Herbst score collection	WS
Lancaster (Pa.) congregation	B
Lititz (Pa.) congregation	B
Lititz collegium musicum	B
Nazareth (Pa.) congregation	B
Salem (N.C.) congregation	WS
Salem collegium musicum	WS
Salem "Lovefeast Ode" collection	WS
Watertown (Wis.) congregation	B

Special Collections

In Bethlehem: the Beckel, Detterer, Neisser, and Rau Collections; the music library of the Moravian Female Seminary; and other miscellaneous music and archival holdings

In Winston-Salem: the Erbe, Glen Plantation, Hagen, Kurth, Johanson, Lowens, Symington, and Vardell collections; the Salem ms copybooks, the Peter codex, and the Salem band books; and other miscellaneous music and archival holdings

See the issues of the Foundation's *Bulletin* (1956–). For related holdings in other repositories, see "Moravian music" in the index

Church and Community Collections

Bethania congregation, 150 works (1200 leaves), ca. 1780–1840, including some items from the community in Hope, N.J., disbanded 1805. The collection comprises ms parts for solo and choral music in German with instrumental accompaniment, for performance at regular and special church services. A catalogue, compiled by Frances Cumnock, is in preparation

Johannes Herbst (1735–1812), 1000 ms scores of anthems, and 45 scores with occasional parts for cantatas, oratorios, and other large-scale choral works. Most items were copied by Herbst himself, in England, Germany, or America; 120 are holographs. Of the items not in his hand, many are thought to be holographs of their composers. For this collection of scores, some of the parts are in the Moravian Archives in Bethlehem, in the Lititz congregation collection. See Marilyn Gombosi, *Catalog of the Johannes Herbst Collection* (Chapel Hill, 1970)

Salem congregation, 1500 titles, copied ca. 1772–ca. 1840, consisting of items acquired at first from other Moravian communities; mss copied 1780–90 mostly by Johann Friedrich Peter, including many of his own works not found in other collections; and mss after 1800 copied in Salem for the Home Moravian Church. The collection comprises ms parts, many in holograph, for sacred solo and choral music in German, with instrumental accompaniment. Most works are for mixed voices, but 500 vocal parts were copied for use by the choir or unmarried women (the "Single Sisters"). See Frances Cumnock, *Catalog of the Salem Congregation Collection* (Chapel Hill, 1980)

Salem collegium musicum, 600 titles, ca. 1780–ca. 1860, mss and published editions, comprising part of the personal library of Johann Friedrich Peter when he left Salem in 1790, with later additions copied locally or acquired from Baltimore, Philadelphia, or European music dealers. Included are 34 works thought to be unica, among them works by J. C. F. Bach, N. G. Gruner, Joseph Riepel, and J. D. Grimm. See Jeannine S. Ingram, "The Moravians in America: Preservers of a Musical Heritage," Moravian Music Foundation *Bulletin*, 22/2 (1977), 2–6; also her "Repertory and Resources of the Salem Collegium Musicum, 1780–1790," *Fontes artis musicae*, 26 (1979), 267–81. The present card catalogue will serve as the basis of a projected book-catalogue by Jeannine S. Ingram

Salem "Lovefeast Ode" (*Liebesmahl*) collection, 3500 ms and printed sheets, ca. 1740–ca. 1880, mostly 1770–1820. The collection comprises texts without music for special services, often 30 to 40 held each year, including congregational hymns, choir anthems, and

solo works. (See the comparable collection at the Moravian Archives in Bethlehem.)

Special Collections

Sheet music, 2000 items, mostly in 30 bound vols., from the libraries of Salem musicians and their associates, ca. 1795–1880; the Glen Plantation music collection, 300 items, ca. 1800–1860, mostly American popular songs and keyboard music; and 1000 titles, in 30 vols., assembled by Edith Symington in Baltimore, ca. 1780–1830, consisting mostly of London imprints

Irving Lowens collection, including 1000 tunebooks, 1764–1900, with many German and southern shape-note items; 200 hymnals, 1762–1960; and 200 other books, ca. 1820–1960, the latter of which will become part of the Peter Memorial Library. A catalogue of the tunebooks, compiled in 1971 by students of Prof. Robert John of the University of Georgia, is available as a computer printout

Salem ms copybooks, 89 vols. of sacred and secular songs and piano pieces, ca. 1790–ca. 1870. Most of the books come from the Salem area, but a few are from Bethlehem and Lititz. Most contain works copied from standard published sources, but a few are by Moravian composers such as Bechler, Herbst, Ricksecker, and Wolle. A catalogue is in preparation

Johann Friedrich Peter, ms music commonplace book, used for sketches of sacred and secular vocal and keyboard music by other composers, intended to be copied out later. An index is in preparation

Salem band books, 2 sets of part books for 4-voice trombone choir, mostly arrangements of Moravian chorales, the first 4 complete in the hand of J. F. Peter, ca. 1780, the other 4 belonging to 2 other sets, probably early 19th century

Twenty-sixth North Carolina Regiment, band books, 6 sets, containing 300 marches, popular-song arrangements, dance tunes, and chorales from the Civil War repertory. See the index by Donald McCorkle in Julius Leinbach, "Regimental Band of the Twenty-sixth North Carolina," *Civil War History*, 4 (1958), 234–36. A complete inventory is in preparation

Charles F. Kurth, Jr. (fl. 1864–1920s?, flautist with the New York Philharmonic Orchestra), mss, including original works, mostly chamber music, and arrangements of semi-classical and popular music

Charles Vardell (1893–1962, dean of the School of Music, Salem College), 100 holograph mss and published editions of his works in various mediums

Frances F. Hagen (1815–1907), personal papers, 50 items, including 4 diaries, commonplace books, music sketchbooks, and original works, printed and in ms

Ernst Immanuel Erbe (1854–1927, church musician in St. Louis, Mo.), holograph music, pedagogical texts, original published music, and correspondence, some of it involving his work for the Eden Publishing House, 1 linear meter

Rev. John H. Johanson (1916–79), hymnals and books about hymnology, 500 items, incorporated in the Peter Memorial Library

Miscellaneous letters of Moravian musicians, among them John Antes, Jeremias Dencke, Johannes Herbst, Johann Friedrich Peter, David Tannenberg, and Theodore F. Wolle, 30 items

—Karl Kroeger

1162

OLD SALEM

Drawer F, Salem Station
Winston-Salem, North Carolina 27108

Amy Van Black, ms sheet music "Centennial March,"
also 2 published sheet-music items
Hymnals, 12 18th- and 19th-century items, in German
Photographs of local 19th-century musicians, 3 items

—Miss Welshimer

1163

SALEM COLLEGE   **NcWsS**

Gramley Library
Salem Square
Winston-Salem, North Carolina 27108

Manuscript music books, 6 items copied by students at
the College (formerly Salem Female Academy), 19th-
century
Sheet music, 24 bound vols. owned by students and
teachers at Salem Female Academy, 1820s–50s
Hymnals, 12 vols. used at Salem Female Academy,
19th century
Programs for concerts at Salem Female Academy, 100
items, 1852–1900

—Susan S. Taylor

*In addition to the repositories listed above, the following have
also reported holdings of the materials indicated:*

Asheville—Blue Ridge Parkway: songbooks, programs,
recordings
Belmont—Belmont Abbey College, Abbot V. Taylor Li-
brary: songbooks, recordings
Boiling Springs—Gardner–Webb Junior College, Dover
Memorial Library: songbooks
Chapel Hill— Chapel Hill Public Library: songbooks,
other printed music
Cherokee—Qualla Boundry Public Library: songbooks,
programs, recordings
Greensboro—Bennett College, Thomas F. Holgate Li-
brary: songbooks, programs, pictures
Henderson—H. L. Perry Memorial Library: songbooks,
catalogues
Hendersonville—Fruitland Baptist Bible Institute, Li-
brary: sheet music, songbooks, recordings
High Point—High Point Historical Society: sheet music
Raleigh—Mordecai Historical Society and Raleigh His-
torical Properties: sheet music
Raleigh—North Carolina State University, Winston
Music Collection: miscellaneous
Shelby—Cleveland County Historical Association: sheet
music, songbooks, programs, recordings
Swannanoa—Warren Wilson College: sheet music,
songbooks, recordings, other printed music
Weldon—Weldon Public Library: songbooks
Wilmington—Lower Cape Fear Historical Society: pro-
grams, miscellaneous
Wilson—Atlantic Christian College, Hardy Library:
printed music
Winston-Salem—Museum of Early Southern Decorative
Arts: sheet music
Winston Salem—North Carolina Baptist Historical Col-
lection: songbooks
Winston-Salem—Wake Forest University, Wake Forest
Archives, Reynolds Library: pictures

North Dakota

1164

NORTH DAKOTA STATE   **NdFA**
UNIVERSITY

North Dakota Institute for Regional Studies
Fargo, North Dakota 58102

Published sheet music by a local Norwegian-American
composer, ca. 1920
University musicians' and groups' papers, 50 photographs, and programs, 30 linear cm.

—John E. Bye

1165

UNIVERSITY OF NORTH DAKOTA   **NdU**

Chester Fritz Library
Grand Forks, North Dakota 58202

W. P. Davies (1862–1944, journalist), papers, 1930–44,
including press clippings, notebooks, and programs
of early Grand Forks theater and opera

Edward J. Lander (1860–1953, local patron), personal
papers, including correspondence, records, and pam-
phlets relating to the Grand Forks Metropolitan
Opera House, 1890–1940, and the local Oratorio
Society
Grand Forks Metropolitan Opera House, notebook con-
taining a list of performances and dates, 1898–1903.
Other material is described in theses by Alan H.
Adair, *History of the Metropolitan Theatre of Grand
Forks, North Dakota, under Independent Management,
1890–1937* (University of North Dakota, 1970), and
Paul Tomasek, *The Metropolitan Opera House of Grand
Forks, N.D.* (University of North Dakota, 1971)
Grand Forks Oratorio Society, 8 programs, 1907–14, for
the annual spring music festival
Grand Forks Symphony Association, programs, clip-
pings, and other materials, 33 items, 1911–72
Grand Forks Municipal Band (founded 1918 by Com-
mercial Club members), typescript history
Carney Song Contest (University songwriting contest),
printed programs, 1 songbook, and 60 linear cm. of
ms songs submitted, 1910–53

—Bill Sherfey

1166

Fred WOLHOWE

Highway 52 East
Minot, North Dakota 58701

The collection is to be presented to Luther College, Decorah, Iowa

Sheet music, 40,000 items, ca. 1830–1960, mostly popular songs, including the collections formerly owned by Harry Victor and Johnny ("Crazy Otto") Maddox, also with some autographed items

Dance-band orchestrations of popular and semiclassical songs, 6000 items, 1890s–1930s

Gospel songbooks, 15 items, ca. 1880–1910

Song and dance folios, 200 items, ca. 1905–39

Catalogues of major recording companies, 20 items, ca. 1915–40

Recordings, including 25,000 78-rpm discs of hot jazz, blues, ragtime, humor, folk, and classical music, 1900–1945

In addition to the repositories listed above, the following have also reported holdings of the materials indicated:

Jamestown—Jamestown College, Raugust Library: recordings

Mayville—Mayville Public Library: songbooks, recordings

Regent—Hettinger County Historical Society: songbooks

Valley City—Barnes County Historical Society: sheet music, songbooks

Ohio

1167

OHIO UNIVERSITY   OAU

Athens, Ohio 45701

Music Library

Songbooks, including hymnals and school songbooks, 50 items, ca. 1860–1900

Popular sheet music, 500 items, ca. 1880–1930, mostly vocal; also 2000 other items in a general collection of scores

Recordings of music performances at the University, 200 78-rpm discs

—Dan O. Clark

University Library, Special Collections

Karl Ahrendt, 70 linear cm. of papers, including photocopies of all of his ms scores; papers of his term as conductor of vaudeville performances at the Toledo Paramount Theatre, 1929–30; and 5 tape recordings of local performances of his works

Eusebia Hunkins, 30 linear cm. of materials relating to her work in women's music clubs and music education, including workbooks and published operettas

Carr Liggett (1894–1977), 30 linear cm. of photocopies of his ms and published choral music, and 4.5 linear meters of music from his personal collection

—Gary Hunt, Dan O. Clark

1168

BALDWIN–WALLACE COLLEGE   OBerB

Berea, Ohio 44017

Riemenschneider Bach Institute

Albert Riemenschneider (1878–1950), 115 linear meters of papers, including lecture notes, scrapbooks, and correspondence

Hans T. David (1902–67, musicologist), personal library of his writings and of 1900 books and music

scores, primarily from the Renaissance and baroque periods, and including American tunebooks, hymnals, and Moravian music materials

Emmy Martin, 2 notebooks of materials describing her collection of first editions of musical compositions

Hymnals and secular songbooks, including 2 Mennonite hymnals, 1785, and 1 Mennonite psalter, 1804; 14 songbooks, 1870s, given by Mary Weld Coates; and 3 items, late 19th century, given by Jean Unnewehr

Vocal method books and collections, 17 items, 1896–1931

Bach festival programs, 1933–78

—Esther M. Hoose

Ritter Library

Methodist Historical Collection, materials of the Ohio district of the United Methodist Church, including 250 hymnals, songbooks, and psalm books, mostly 19th century, including German-language items

Harry L. Ridenour Collection of Ohio folksongs and books on folksongs, 500 items, ca. 1800– , mostly concerning Ohio

Programs of the Bach Festival, a complete run of bound vols., 1933–

—Richard Densmore

Fern Patterson Jones Memorial Music Library

Sheet music of American musical shows, 30 items, 1930s

Programs of College concerts, 1890s– , 40 vols.

—Kathleen L. Maciuszko

1169

BLUFFTON COLLEGE   OBlC-M

Mennonite Historical Library
Bluffton, Ohio 45817

Mennonite and Amish hymnals, 5 linear meters, including some in German, ca. 1650–

—Delbert Gratz

1170

BOWLING GREEN STATE UNIVERSITY

OBgU

Popular Culture Library and Audio Center
Bowling Green, Ohio 43402

Popular culture collection, including 3000 items of 19th- and 20th-century American sheet music, 300 song-books, 200 programs of music performances, 200 catalogues of recording dealers and manufacturers, 20,000 78-rpm recordings, a collection of pre-1940 radio broadcasts on tape, 75 cylinder recordings, field recordings, and song files and lists. The holdings emphasize commercial popular music, jazz, country and western, blues, gospel, folk, and classical music; they were acquired partly from private collections of Gerald Hughes, William Randle, and William L. Schurk

—William L. Schurk

1171

Richard B. GILBERT

248 South Summit Street
Bowling Green, Ohio 43402

Hymnals and tunebooks, 150 items, 1821– , including Anglican prayer books and liturgy books

1172

CINCINNATI HISTORICAL SOCIETY

OCHP

Eden Park
Cincinnati, Ohio 45202

Organizational Papers

Afternoon Orchestral Concerts, account book of Julius Dexter (treasurer), 1871–72

Baldwin Piano Co., 60 linear meters of materials, 1865–1964, in the Wulsin family papers, including documents concerning the sale and manufacture of pianos, publicity photographs and contracts with performers, and correspondence with orchestras; also papers of the Baldwin family, documenting their involvement in Cincinnati musical life, and of Lucien Wulsin (company president) and Lucien Wulsin II

Cincinnati Conservatory of Music, journal, 1885–90; articles of incorporation, by-laws, and minutes, 1920–30; and a report by the American Appraisal Company, 1930, 3 vols.

Cincinnati Grand Opera, scrapbook, 1883–1900

Cincinnati Literary and Musical Society, records and scrapbooks, 1933– , 6 vols. in 3

Cincinnati Männerchor, minute book, 1857–65, and a scrapbook of programs, 1873–83

Cincinnati Music Hall Association, lists of subscribers to the Guarantee Funds of the 6th and 7th Cincinnati Industrial Expositions, 1875 and 1878, with the subscription book used by Edmund H. Pendleton, also the bank book kept by John Shillito (treasurer) for the Cincinnati Music Hall Organ Association, 1878, minutes of the Organ Association Board of Directors, 1877–78, and clippings regarding the Hall and the organ, 1933–

Cincinnati Musical Club, correspondence between William N. Hobart and A. W. Chatfield concerning John Lund, 1891

Cincinnati Musical Festival Association, papers of the first meeting of the stockholders and board of directors, 1874, and official records, 1874–1968, in 31 boxes, with a register, including minutes, 1878–1946, in 5 vols.; prices paid for seats at auction, 3 vols. 1906–37; clippings from local newspapers regarding the May Festivals, 1910– , including the series by J. Herman Thuman, 1908–33; lists of ticket holders, 1912–44; 2 vols. of papers relating to the Endowment Fund, 1921–33; records of the chorus rehearsals, 1923–33; and financial statements, 1933–36

Cincinnati String Quartette, programs, biographical notes on musicians, clippings, and a history, 1939

Cincinnati Symphony Orchestra, 86 vols. of press clippings, 1902–64; also a policy memorandum from Arthur Judson, 1923; musicians' contracts (1200 items in 10 boxes), 1923–36, passim; programs, 1931– ; miscellaneous publicity notes, 1939–40; and a program noted by Donzella Cross Boyle for the Young People's Concerts, 1939–41

Clifton Music Club, 7 vols. of scrapbooks with clippings, correspondence, and programs, 1936–65

Deutschen Mandolin Club, a list of members and repertory, and sheet music, 1930s

Harmonic Society of Cincinnati, minutes and lists of members, 1874–80, 2 vols.

Ladies' Musical Club, constitution, by-laws, and original list of members, 1892

Mothersingers (music appreciation group), clippings and programs, 1925–51

Music Lovers' Club, constitution, 1924, and miscellaneous records, 1921–26

Ohio Mechanics Institute, press clippings, 1908– , with musical references

Orpheus Club of Cincinnati, programs, 1893– , and souvenir book, 1925

Pianist's Club, constitution, list of officers, descriptive leaflet, and letter from Susan D. D. M. (Mrs. Theodore) Bohlmann to Mrs. A. H. Chatfield, 1919

Universalist Sacred Music Society of Cincinnati, minute book maintained by E. Longley (secretary) with a constitution, list of members, and programs, 1844–48

Vaudeville Club, historical pamphlet, correspondence, and financial papers, ca. 1909

Zoo Opera, local press clippings, 1931–33

Personal Papers

Chapin family diaries, correspondence, and other materials, including 2 ms hymnals and 1 ms hymn by Lucius Chapin, in the Blinn papers, as described in James W. Scholten, *The Chapins: A Study of Men and Music West of the Alleghenies, 1797–1842* (Ed.D. diss., University of Michigan, 1972)

Wendell Phillips Dabney (1865–1952), 1 box of materials by and about him, 1905–64

George Elliston (1883–1946, club woman, newspaper woman, and poet), 6 boxes of papers, including correspondence, music, scrapbooks, manuscripts, and photographs

Aline Fredin, correspondence and recital programs, 1887–1934

Grace G. Gardner (dramatic soprano and voice teacher), programs and press clippings of her concerts, 1894–1907

Eugene Goossens, letter to Marie Dickore, 1940

Sherwood Kains (1904–57), biographical materials, including brochures and press articles, 1934–57

Kemper family papers, including early 19th-century American music (Box II, Folder 9)

Edward Rawson, letters to Miss Laws, 1905, and Henry L. Hobart, 1914, concerning Cincinnati music

Reuben Runyan Springer, letter to John Shillito, May 1875, offering a gift of $125,000 to be matched for the building of Music Hall

W. C. Tichenor, 6 letters to Dorothy Fulton, 1938–42, concerning the song "Glorious Ohio"

Other Materials

Scrapbooks, of Mrs. Davis Clark, 1 vol. on the May Festival and the Music Hall organ, 1878–80; Gaff Family, 1 vol., late 19th century; Mrs. Ruth Kinsey, 1 vol. with programs, 1904–9; Lawrence Maxwell (president of the May Festival Association) and Clara Maxwell, 3 vols., 1871–1931; John Melville, 7 vols., 1895–1955, relating to the careers of Dr. Karol and Marguerite Melville Liszniewski; George H. Mantel, 1 vol., 1887–90, on opera; G. W. Nichols, 2 vols., 1873–80; Lawrence Pike, 1 vol., ca. 1866, of clippings concerning Pike's Opera House; Lucie Russell Rawson, 1878–1913, 1 vol., including programs of the Unite Club; Emma L. Roedter, 1 vol., 1909–24; Ruth Hargrave (Mrs. Charles Wickham) Skinner, 2 vols., 1900–1912; William Clifford Smith, 1 vol., 1880–97; and August E. Wilde, 1 vol., 1857–70, with programs of the Cecilia Society

Music clippings collections, including materials assembled by Flora Mueller, 1870–97, mostly in German and also covering Cleveland, Indianapolis, Louisville, and Columbus; Lenore Spiering, 1870s, also in German; H. P. S. O., miscellaneous local music, 1877– ; and on local music clubs, 1947–

Writings relating to local music history, mostly unpublished, including texts prepared by Helena Herppich Adams on the Glendale Military Band, ca. 1906; Marie Paula Dickore on local Bach traditions, 1938; Joseph Donnelly on military music; Robert M. Fleming on the Musical Festival Association; Edwin Henderson on women and the early May Festivals; Earl R. Hoover on Ohio composers; George H. Katterhorn on the local Bach Society, 1938; Edward J. McGrath on Reuben R. Springer; Joseph W. Wagmaster on early local music; Anne Boyer Shepherd on the College Conservatory of Music; Harry Robert Stevens on early concert life, 1810–26, and on early folk music, 1788–1825, in Cincinnati; Ralph A. Van Wye on 19th-century activity; William S. Wabnitz on Ohio Valley songs; James Ritter Werner on early Cincinnati shape-note tunebooks; Mrs. Dell Kendall Werthner on the Woman's Music Club, 1908–44; and Herbert C. Zafren on the Hebrew Union College Library

Musical materials, including 4000 sheet-music items, 1840s–1930s, in 40 vols. and 15 boxes, arranged by publisher; 35 hymnals, mostly 19th-century shape-note vols.; Anita (O'Hara) Comfort Brooks, holograph of "Alice the Bride of the White House," ca. 1906; Walter H. Aiken, "Cincinnati Civic Song," words by Callie King Walls (printed privately, 1929); and words to the Franklin School Song

Other materials, including 5 boxes of programs, mostly for Cincinnati musical events, 1870s–1940s, arranged chronologically; a general collection of 250,000 photographs, mostly of metropolitan Cincinnati subjects, 1850s– , including some musical materials; and 5000 posters of circus, theater, and other events in Cincinnati, late 19th and early 20th centuries, arranged by subject

—Laura Chace, Ed Rider

1173
CINCINNATI SYMPHONY ORCHESTRA
Central Trust Tower
Cincinnati, Ohio 45202

Administrative records of the Orchestra, 1895– , including agreements, annual reports, cashbooks, contracts, correspondence, daybooks, financial statements, ledgers, minutes, proceedings, programs, and scrapbooks, as cited in David R. Larson, *Guide to Manuscript Collections and Institutional Records in Ohio* (Columbus, 1974). See also the Cincinnati Historical Society holdings

1174
HEBREW UNION COLLEGE   OCH
3101 Clifton Avenue
Cincinnati, Ohio 45220

Jewish Institute of Religion, Klau Library

Yiddish theater collection, including playbills, posters, photographs, and ephemera, in all 3100 items in 11 boxes, arranged alphabetically by location; also an extensive collection of music mss, arranged by composer or title, as well as scenarios and other materials, in all 1000 items in 13 boxes, including U.S. as well as foreign materials, mostly 1900–1920s

Sheet music, 2000 catalogued items

American Yiddish "penny" songs (i.e., broadside song-sheets with texts only), ca. 1890–1910, 240 items, including songs by Morris Rund

—Barbara Pomerantz

American Jewish Archives

See the *Manuscript Catalog* (Boston, 1971), esp. vol. 2, pp. 658–70, also the suppl. (1979), pp. 561–62

Personal papers and other ms materials, including Max Adler, correspondence relating to the Palestine Symphony Orchestra and Music Foundation, Chicago, 1936–54; Edward Bloch, biographical memoir, 1852–81; Ernest Bloch, correspondence and lecture, 1930–33; David A. Brown, scrapbook with press clippings, letters, and other documents relating to his philanthropic activities in Detroit and New York, 1894–1957; Albert Einstein, 3 letters to Dr. Ernest B. Zeisler, 1939–50, regarding the Palestine Orchestra Fund, Ernest Bloch, and other matters; Ephraim M. Epstein, musical libretti and other documents, 1880; Marcella Schiller (Mrs. Morris) Firestone, biographical notes and programs of Los Angeles-area music performances; Bianca Fleischmann, autobiography, describing her life and musical activities in Buffalo, also 2 of her musical compositions; Elias Hecht, letter to Arthur J. Sumner giving information on his family in San Francisco; James G. Heller, correspondence, press clippings, and other original writings, 1906–52, 6 boxes; Abraham Z. Idelsohn, correspondence and other documents, 1928–61, 1 box; Settie S. Kuhn, correspondence relating to music, 1903–48; Antoinette Brody (Mrs. Jacob R.) Marcus and Merle Judith Marcus, personal letters and papers, 1927–47, 1 box; Adolf Muhlmann, ms of *A Grobber Koll*, and letters in response to the publication of the book, 1931–32; Elkan Naumburg, booklet of eulogies, New York, 1924; Levi A. Olan, correspondence, press clippings, sermons, and addresses, from Worcester, Mass., and Dallas, 1927–70, 43 boxes; Julius Singer, pamphlet memorabilia, Cincinnati, ca. 1905; Jacob H. Schiff, personal and business correspondence, also a draft of Cyrus Adler, *Jacob Henry Schiff, 1847–1920;* Abraham de Sola, scrapbooks, 1890–1917, and songbook; Therese Abraham Strauss, personal correspondence, press clippings, and other documents, Cincinnati, 1897–1949; Elkan Voorsanger, correspondence and personal papers, with music references, 1914–70, 2 boxes; Eric Werner, correspondence and personal papers; and Fannie (Bloomfield) Zeisler, press clippings, programs, correspondence, and a biographical sketch by her husband, Sigmund Zeisler

Union of American Hebrew Congregations, archives, including minutes of the Committee on Synagogue Music, 1924–48, as maintained by Louis Wolsey

Personal documents of Irving Berlin, Abraham W. Binder, and Arnold Schoenberg

Musical materials, including Leopold Damrosch, albumleaf, n.d.; G. M. Cohen, "Musical Relaxations for the Family Circle, for the School and Public Service"; song-sheets of Henry Russell, 1830s; and recordings of Jewish popular and liturgical songs, 1920–25, as collected by Will Levy, Union City, Tenn., 1 reel of tape

Miscellaneous printed musical documents, including a subscription list for the Cincinnati Conservatory of Music, 1885; a libretto for Erwin Ledyard and Sigmund Schlesinger, *The Schoolmaster,* performed at a "benefit for Hebrew orphans," Mobile, Ala., 1885; a Brunswick recordings catalogue, 1927; and a collection of anti-Semitic soldiers' songs, n.d., in the Palestine collection

Historical studies relating to Jewish music in the U.S., including Edward P. Cohn, "Reform Jewish Hymnal Impulse from 1890–1914" (term paper, University of Cincinnati, 1973); Hillel Cohn, "The Life and Career of Fannie Bloomfield Zeisler" (term paper, University of Cincinnati, 1960); Joseph Drochotz, materials relating to country music in American Jewish musical life (Minneapolis, 1963–64); Jewish Club of Milwaukee, collection of songs, stories, history of recollections, and oral-history tape, 1955; Bertram W. Korn, letter to Judge Earl R. Hoover regarding Jewish music in the Civil War, dated Philadelphia, 1962; Harold Krantzler, *The Jewish Choral Movement in the United States* (Thesis, University of Cincinnati, 1953); Laurence Marton Lerner, *The Rise of the Impresario: Bernard Ullman and the Transformation of Musical Culture in Nineteenth-Century America* (Thesis, University of Wisconsin, 1970); and Howard B. Zyskind, "Felix Warburg's Interests in the Fine Arts, Principally Music and Painting, as Reflected in the Warburg Papers, 1926–1934" (term paper, University of Cincinnati, 1966)

—Fannie Zelcer

1175

MUSIC TEACHERS' NATIONAL ASSOCIATION

408 Carew Tower
Cincinnati, Ohio 45202

The archives of the Association are not known to have been preserved, and the extant records do not predate 1940. For the early history, see Henry S. Perkins, *Historical Handbook of the Music Teachers' National Association, 1876–1893* (Chicago, 1893?), and Homer Ulrich, *A Centennial History of the Music Teachers' National Association* (Cincinnati, 1976). The activities of the Association are documented in the *Proceedings,* and in the personal papers of its officers and active members

1176

PUBLIC LIBRARY OF CINCINNATI   OC
AND HAMILTON COUNTY

800 Vine Street
Cincinnati, Ohio 45202

Art and Music Department

See T. Kolmschlag, "The Cincinnati Public Library," M.L.A. *Notes,* 1st ser., 8 (August 1940), 6–9; also Alice S. Plaut, "A Promenade in the Art and Music Department," M.L.A. *Notes,* 13 (1956), 403–5

Sheet music, 28,500 items, including single items grouped by chronological periods and arranged by title, with Cincinnati imprints separated. The collection is particularly strong in Cincinnati music, and in music of the period 1910–40

Delta Omicron Composer's Library, 1500 items, maintained as a circulating collection. See Mrs. Edward G. Mead, *Catalog of Composer's Library* (Cincinnati, 1977)

Music mss and printed editions by Cincinnati composers, including pre-1940 holdings by Margaret Bronson (14 items, 1933–47), Walter A. Draper (1 item, 1924), Martin D. Dumler (75 items), Albino Gorno (2 items, 1898–99), C. Hugo Grimm (29 items, 1894–1958), James G. Heller (1 item, 1929), Ethel Glenn Hier (14 items, 1912–55), John N. Klohr (1 item, 1901), Mrs. E. Burke Kramer (1 item), George A. Leighton (51 items), L. F. Maschinot (2 items, ca. 1940), Lino Mattioli (1 item, 1939), Iva D. Moore (1 item, 1913), Augustus O. Palm (1 item, 1912), Lillian T. Plogstedt (1 item), Alfred Rosé (1 item, 1933), J. Alfred Schehl (17 items, 1930–54), Edward F. Schneider (5 items, 1897–1941), Emma Besser Scully (1 item, 1923), Louis Snodgrass (1 item, 1934), Jean Ten Hage (1 item, 1935), Frank van der Stucken (1 item, 1926), Emil Weigand (8 items, 1892–1901), and Frank A. Young (43 items, early 20th century)

Other printed music, 2500 pre-1940 items, including the choral library presented by the Orpheus Music Club; chamber music presented by Dr. Frederick Forchheimer; the Fink Collection of piano music; and general materials presented by Emma Rodetke Roedter

Programs, 2500 items, with Cincinnati material separated from that of other cities, each arranged by performing group or soloist; also 205 bound vols. for performances of the Cincinnati Symphony Orchestra, the Cincinnati Summer Opera, and the Cincinnati May Festival

William H. Doane (1832–1915), personal papers, 1 box
Organizational archives of the Cincinnati Haydn Society, Cincinnati College of Music (press clippings and programs, 1926–30), and Delta Omicron
Pictures, 186 envelopes containing press clippings, glossy prints, etc., on Cincinnati subjects, mostly portraits of musicians

—R. Jayne Craven

Rare Books and Special Collections Department

Billy Bryant, 4 typescript texts of showboat productions, as cited in Clyde N. Bowden, *Catalog of the Inland Rivers Library* (Cincinnati, 1968), p. 107; see also Bryant's *Children of Ol' Man River* (New York, 1936). Other materials in the Inland Rivers Library include showboat posters, 1930s; 100 photographs of showboats, many of them including musical subjects; the privately published diary of T. W. Scraggs (musician on the *New Sensation,* 1882–87); and recordings of calliope and other riverboat music, several of them produced in Czechoslovakia
Tunebooks and other printed music, 12 items, 1815– , mostly shape-note vols. and Cincinnati imprints

—Yeatman Anderson III

1177
UNIVERSITY OF CINCINNATI   OCU
Cincinnati, Ohio 45221

College-Conservatory of Music, Gorno Memorial Music Library

Henry Edward Krehbiel (1854–1923), scrapbook containing letters from musicians and statesmen, among them Walter Damrosch, Percy A. Grainger, Philip Hale, Josef Hofmann, Charles Martin Loeffler, Nellie Melba, Karl Muck, Horatio Parker, Maud Powell, Marcella Sembrich, and William Howard Taft
Leigh Harline (1907–67, film composer), ms sketches, full scores, and conductor's reduced scores for his works, beginning with animated short films for the Walt Disney studios in the 1930s, 23 items. See Ross Care, "The Film Music of Leigh Harline," *Filmmusic Notebook,* 3/2 (1977), 32–43
Composers' holograph mss, including John Powell, 1 item; Edward Burlingame Hill, 9 items; Ethel Glenn Hier, 25 items; Albino Gorno, 75 items; Eugene Goossens, 2 items; Chalmers Clifton, 2 items; W. S. Sterling, 1 item; and Walter Aiken, 3 items
Karol Liszniewski (1876–1958, piano professor), 100 letters received from famous musicians, among them Robert Casadesus, Karl Flesch, Ossip Gabrilowitsch, Hans Kindler, Wanda Landowska, and Olga Samaroff
Songbooks and hymnals, ca. 1840–90, 53 items, mostly Boston and Cincinnati imprints; also 53 instruction books, mostly vocal, ca. 1840–80

—Robert Johnson

University Archives

Cincinnati Conservatory of Music, minutes of meetings of the Board of Trustees, 1930–57, 1 vol.
College of Music of Cincinnati, annual reports, 1884–97, passim, and minutes of meetings of the Board of

Trustees, Executive Committee, and stockholders, 1878– , in 11 boxes

—Robert Johnson

Division of Broadcasting

Frederick W. Ziv Archive, including 20,000 electrical transcription discs from radio shows, 1939–50; business files, including contracts, sales books, and promotional materials of the F. W. Ziv Radio Co., 11.5 linear meters; and the Daniel Engel collection of popular sheet music, 1870s–1950s, 2500 items. See Morleen Getz-Rouse, *A History of the F. W. Ziv Radio and Broadcasting Companies, 1939–1960* (Ph.D. diss., University of Michigan, 1976)

—Morleen Getz-Rouse

1178
Ted LEWIS MUSEUM OF CIRCLEVILLE AND PICKAWAY COUNTY
Box 492
Circleville, Ohio 43113

Ted Lewis (Theodore Leopold Friedman, 1891–1971), papers and memorabilia, including music mss, sheet music, programs, 2 scrapbooks of pictures, recordings, and his top hat, canes, and clarinet

—Polly Miller

1179
AFRO-AMERICAN CULTURAL AND HISTORICAL SOCIETY
1839 East Eighty-first Street
Cleveland, Ohio 44103

Books, periodicals, music, programs, photographs, press clippings, and recordings of Afro-American music, including source materials on the Fisk Jubilee singers and hymnals for black church usage, as discussed in Martha Smith, "The Music Collection of the Afro-American Cultural and Historical Society," in the *1978 Internship Report* of the Immigrant Experience Project of the Greater Cleveland Ethnographic Museum (Cleveland, 1978), pp. 24–25

—Icabod Flewellen

1180
John CARROLL UNIVERSITY   OCIJC
Grasselli Library
University Heights
Cleveland, Ohio 44118

Louis L. Balogh (1895–1971), personal papers, including holograph mss of 3 major cantatas and 20 smaller choral works; programs and press clippings documenting his work and that of the University Glee Club; and 30 editions of choral music

—Marcella D. Milota

1181

CASE-WESTERN RESERVE UNIVERSITY   OClW

Cleveland, Ohio 44106

Music Library, Haydn Hall

Early printed music, including 15 tunebooks and hymnals, 1781–1876, and 275 sheet-music items, 1830s–60s, in 8 bound vols., as described in Theodore Albrecht et al., *An Annotated Bibliography of Rare Musical Materials in the Libraries of Case Western Reserve University*, preliminary ed. (Cleveland, 1978)

Robert E. Nelson, band-music library, 1 linear meter, including works by Herbert Elwell, whose ms scores are also present. A catalogue by Richard Latimer is in preparation

University Archives, Adelbert Hall

Dayton C. Miller (1887–1939, professor of physics), personal papers, 1 linear meter, including clippings and reprints of his articles, many on acoustics

F. Karl Grossman (1886–1969, conductor of the Cleveland Philharmonic Orchestra), full typescript of *A History of Music in Cleveland*, subsequently published in an abridged version (Cleveland, 1972)

1182

CLEVELAND FEDERATION OF MUSICIANS

2200 Carnegie Avenue
Cleveland, Ohio 44115

Archives of the union, 4.5 linear meters, including administrative records, minutes, directories, 1888– , and issues of the *Cleveland Musician*, 1928– , as cited in David R. Larson, *Guide to Manuscript Collections and Institutional Records in Ohio* (Columbus, 1974)

1183

CLEVELAND INSTITUTE OF MUSIC

11021 East Boulevard
Cleveland, Ohio 44106

Beryl Rubinstein (1898–1952), 1.6 linear meters of papers, including a holograph ms of *Le petite tambour*, 1923, sketches of the Second String Quartet, 1933, and 56 pages of ms sketches of music; reproductions of ms scores and parts for *The Sleeping Beauty* (opera written with John Erskine) and *The Pied Piper of Hamelin* (cantata for children); 55 published editions and 8 recordings; and scrapbooks, 1921–32

Victor Babin (1908–72), materials from his personal music library, including published editions and some ms reproductions, mostly for piano duet and piano 4-hands, in all 1 linear meter

—Karen Miller

1184

CLEVELAND ORCHESTRA

Severance Hall
11101 Euclid Avenue
Cleveland, Ohio 44106

Cleveland Orchestra pressbooks and public-relations material; also programs of the Orchestra and of other major U.S. orchestras, indexed

George Szell (1897–1970) Memorial Library, 40 linear meters, containing his scores, performance parts, chamber music, and books

1185

CLEVELAND PUBLIC LIBRARY   OCl

325 Superior Avenue
Cleveland, Ohio 44114

Fine Arts Department

Sheet music, 18,000 items, arranged by composer, with partial index and a shelflist

Orchestral music parts, begun with a donation by Emil Ring (1863–1922) in the 1920s, extended by materials prepared by the WPA Federal Music Project, and used in concerts sponsored by the city of Cleveland (known as the "CM" collection)

Musical editions, including 500 vols. from the personal library of Charles Rychlik (1875–1962, local violinist)

Johann H. Beck (1856–1924, local conductor), personal papers, including holograph music mss, press clippings, scrapbooks, his personal library, memorandums, programs, and memorabilia, 1872–1939

Literary and musical holograph mss of Clarence Metcalf (1878–1961), 10 items, and F. Karl Grossman (1886–1969), 4 items

—Joan Hoagland, Russell Hehr

John G. White Collection

Books, music, and other materials relating to folksong, 2500 items, as listed in the Collection's *Catalog of Folklore, Folklife and Folksongs*, 2nd ed. (Boston, 1978), esp. the headings, "Folk-Music and Folk-Song," vol. 2, pp. 418–526; "Ballads, American," vol. 1, pp. 126–27; "Ballads and Songs, American," vol. 1, pp. 133–37; and various specific occupations, e.g., "Lumbermen—Songs and Music"

Field recordings by Newbell Niles Puckett, including 20 tapes of Canadian lumberjack songs, made 1956–63 at Bobcaygeon; 3 tapes of "Mountaineers—Mountain Songs," 1956–63; and 10 tapes on "Religious Beliefs of the Southern Negro," including hymns, 1957–63

Mary Olive Eddy, typed transcriptions of Ohio folksongs and ballads, ca. 1935

—Alice N. Loranth

1186

CLEVELAND STATE UNIVERSITY   OClU

Music Library, Monuments Section
1860 East Twenty-second Street
Cleveland, Ohio 44114

Herbert Elwell (1898–1974), personal papers, including scrapbooks containing honors and awards, programs, and press clippings, 1929–60s; also memorabilia, and 60 scores of his music

Published music by local composers J. D. Bain Murray and Rudolph Bubalo

1187

Zelma Watson GEORGE

13800 Shaker Boulevard, Apt. 308
Cleveland, Ohio 44120

Published editions of music by black composers, mostly late 19th- and early 20th-century popular and Broadway-show music, also spirituals by R. Nathaniel Dett, Hall Johnson (his complete published works), Harry T. Burleigh, and Samuel Coleridge-Taylor; also research notes, including interviews with Dett, which were partly the basis for the collector's *A Guide to Negro Music* (Ed.D. diss., New York University, 1953)

1188

GREATER CLEVELAND ETHNOGRAPHIC MUSEUM

137 The Arcade
Cleveland, Ohio 44114

Ethnic music from the Cleveland area, collected mostly in spring 1979, 110 cassettes and reel-to-reel tapes, including a "Burying of the Fiddle" Hungarian Easter ritual, traditional in Cleveland; liturgy and singing of Greek Orthodox, Slovenian (Catholic), Ukrainian, Hungarian (Catholic), and Syrian/Lebanese Orthodox churches, particularly of Lenten and Easter music; Italian and Yiddish singers; and disc recordings and films of Serbian, Croatian, and Macedonian music, a Cretan band, an Irish fiddler and band, and Frankie Yankevich's polka band

—Annette Fromm

1189

Earl R. HOOVER

3356 Grenway Road
Cleveland, Ohio 44122

Research materials relating to studies of Civil War music, the biographies of Benjamin R. Hanby (1833–67), Jonathan E. Spilman (1812–96), and Ernest R. Ball (1878–1927), and early Cleveland composers, as reflected in his "Famous Cleveland Musicians and Song-Writers," in *Annals of the Early Settlers Association of the Western Reserve* (1967–71), pp. 82–86

1190

WESTERN RESERVE HISTORICAL SOCIETY   OClHi

10825 East Boulevard
Cleveland, Ohio 44106

> See Kermit Pike, *A Guide to the Manuscripts and Archives of the Western Reserve Historical Society* (Cleveland, 1972; hereinafter cited as *Pike*)

Shaker music, a preeminent collection, including 507 ms items and 16 published eds., mostly 19th century, as cited in *Cook*, pp. 252–85 and 299–302. See also *A Guide to Shaker Manuscripts in the Library of the Western Reserve Historical Society* (Cleveland, 1974)

Personal papers with music references, including Louis Balogh (1898–1971), 4 folders of speeches and writings, 1925–70; Robert Barnes, songbook, 1768; Robert Jones Buckley (1886–1957, local lawyer and banker), materials on the Northern Ohio Opera Association (*Pike*, 791); Jonathan Hale (1777–1854), 4 songbooks; Henry Holcomb (1830–1919, furnace manufacturer in Painesville, Ohio), autobiographical scrapbooks with references to his experiences as a band musician in the 2nd Brigade, 3rd Division, 23rd Army Corps, 1864–65 (*Pike*, 791); Adella Prentiss Hughes (1869–1950, founder and manager of the Cleveland Orchestra, and local impresario), correspondence, programs, press clippings, printed ephemera, and photographs of her career (*Pike*, 609); John Kerr (d. 1823, surveyor), arithmetic and music books, 1788–92 (*Pike*, 52); Edwin Arthur Kraft (1833–1962), correspondence and programs, 1901–64, in 5 boxes; Charles H. Merrick (Civil War musician, 8th Ohio Infantry Regiment), letters to his wife, 1861–64, 1862 pocket diary, and other documents (*Pike*, 650); Dayton C. Miller (1887–1938, physicist), research notes and clippings, including photographs of sound waves, notes on flute construction, and musical compositions; William H. Richardson (Civil War drummer, 104th Regiment, Ohio Volunteer Infantry), 4 vols. of diaries, 1862–65, mentioning his band duties (*Pike*, 457); James Hotchkiss Rogers (1857–1940, music ed. of the *Cleveland News* and the *Cleveland Plain Dealer*, 1913–32), 2 folders of his music, mostly in printed editions, 1910–20 (*Pike*, 672); John Philip Sousa, ms of the "Black Horse Troop March"; Mabel Hope Stuntz (1901–36, of East Orange, N.J.), 8 items relating to musical studies in New York; and Marie Weissheimer, music notebooks, 1890s (*Pike*, 750). Personal papers of Arthur Shepherd, formerly in this collection, are now at the University of Utah, Salt Lake City, q.v.

Organizational archives, including the Beethoven Society and Seville Musical Association of Seville, Ohio, membership lists, regulations, and minutes, 1845–48 and 1860–75 (*Pike*, 257); Cleveland Federation of Musicians, records, 1888–1965, 4 linear meters, also records of the East End Neighborhood House, 1911–64, in 30 boxes; Cleveland Institute of Music, documents as part of the files of the Cleveland Conference for Educational Cooperation, 1924–30 (*Pike*, 54); Cleveland Philharmonic Orchestra, miscellaneous items (*Pike*, 948); Euclid Avenue Opera House, records, including a list of productions, 1869–78 (*Pike*, 554, 948); Fortnightly Music Club, minutes, notices, programs, and guestbooks, 1894–1971, in 6 boxes and 18 vols., as listed in Joyce E. Taipale, *The Fortnightly Musical Club: A Register of Its Records, 1894–1971* (Cleveland, 1977) (*Pike*, 934); Goodrich Social Settlement, material relating to the Music Settlement, 1897–1960, in 10 boxes, with a register by Dennis Harrison; the Grange, Shakersville, Ohio, records of meetings, 1900–1903, including musical entertainments (*Pike*, 291); Morning Music Club of Cleveland, 3 vols. of programs, notes, minutes, and regulations (*Pike*, 97); Rubinstein Club, 1 vol. of records, including minutes, membership lists, and financial accounts, 1909–12 (*Pike*, 439); University Settlement Records, 1926–70, in 33 boxes, with a register; and Zoar (Ohio) Gesang-Verein, 2 ms vols. of songs, ca. 1840, 1 copied in England, the other belonging to Solomon Ackerman (tenor), with German text (*Pike*, 360), also a hymn book (*Pike*, 366)

Sheet music, 6500 mid-19th-century items; shape-note

songbooks and tunebooks, with midwestern imprints; and a complete run of *Brainard's (Western) Musical World* (1864–95)

1191
Paul E. BIERLEY
3888 Morse Road
Columbus, Ohio 43219

Research materials concerning Henry Fillmore and John Philip Sousa, including published music, recordings, photographs, programs, photocopies of correspondence, clippings, day-by-day logs of the composers' careers, route sheets and rosters of Sousa's Band, periodicals, and other items, as represented in Bierley's *John Philip Sousa: A Descriptive Catalog of His Works* (Urbana, 1973) and *Henry Fillmore* (forthcoming)

1192
GUITAR FOUNDATION OF AMERICA
c/o Thomas F. Heck, Archivist
Music Library, Sullivant Hall
Ohio State University
Columbus, Ohio 43210

The collection is maintained in two locations: books, microfilms, and periodicals at the above address in Columbus; and sheet music through the offices of Calvin Elliker, Assistant Librarian, Wisconsin Conservatory of Music, 1584 North Prospect Avenue, Milwaukee, Wis. 53202. See the *Checklist of Music in the Archive of the Guitar Foundation of America and at Cooperating Collections* (Cypress, Cal., 1977); also the continuing feature, "Archivist's Report," supplemented by a "New Acquisitions" list, in the Guitar Foundation of America *Soundboard* (1973–)

Guitar music, including guitar solos, songs with guitar accompaniment, and chamber music, 300 items published in the U.S., ca. 1840–1930, mostly by U.S. composers or arrangers, in original and photocopy

1193
OHIO HISTORICAL SOCIETY   OHi
1982 Velma Avenue
Columbus, Ohio 43211

A. Beuter (Bloomington, Ill., music teacher), 2 vols. of ledgers, 1875–81

George W. Botkin, diary with 2 ms songs, 1863, in the Sidney C. Baker papers

Columbus Beethoven Association, minute book, 1855–62, 1 vol.

Carlos Curtis, 2 items of papers, 1825, concerning a singing school in Worthington, Franklin County

Paul Laurence Dunbar, ms song texts, literary mss, notebooks, scrapbooks, correspondence, and financial records, 1873–1942, 3 linear meters, with a published guide

Heinrich J. G. Düring (composer), 1 vol. of letters, memoirs, and notes on music, 1850–1906, in the Charles A. A. Düring papers

Daniel Decatur Emmett (1815–1904), 5 boxes of papers, 1830–1900, including song mss, drafts, and published editions, also instrumental compositions and correspondence. See Hans Nathan, *Dan Emmett and the Rise of Early Negro Minstrelsy* (Norman, Okla., 1962, 1977), also the supplement (available from the author)

William Gallagher, of Cincinnati, ms poem "The Spotted Frog," and song "Be Sure That We Girls Never Mean Half We Say," n.d.

Jesse B. Gordon, illustrated ms Civil War songster, including songs by Flora March, 1875 and 1880

"The Hero of Tippecanoe," ms campaign song, 1840

James Johnson, ms song, "The Old Sixth Corps," ca. 1865, with the papers of the Ohio Infantry, 122nd Regiment

Thomas W. Lewis, typescript article, "Campaign Songs Had Their Origin in Zanesville," 1928, concerning Alexander Coffman Ross (songwriter)

Jacob Maurer, letters and ms military-music books, 1834–76, 22 linear cm.

Grace Hamilton Morrey (1877–1962, pianist), 30 linear cm. of papers, 1890–1932, including scrapbooks, programs, Morrey School of Music calendars, 1916–35, biographical information, and correspondence with John Porter Lawrence, Emil Paur, Vladimir De Pachmann, Joseph Stransky, and Mana-Zucca (Cassell)

Pearl R. Nye (1872–1950, canal-boat captain, of Akron), 8 linear cm. of ms canal songs and folksongs, written or collected by him, 1870–1937

Ezra E. Rickett, 29 items of papers, 1860–1920, including Civil War songs he composed or copied

Karl Schneider (music teacher, organist in Lancaster, and founder of the Columbus Männerchor, 1848), ms music books and photographs, and a scrapbook of clippings, 1879–1883, in all 30 linear cm.

Noah Haynes Swayne (singer), 1 box of papers, 1823–62

Jeannette Bell Thomas (founder of the American Folksong Society), 1.2 linear meters of correspondence and clippings related to the Society, 1926–40; galley proofs and mss for her books, *Ballad Makin' in the Mountains of Kentucky* and *The Singin' Gatherin'* (both 1939); and 25 78-rpm discs of folksongs

Union Brass Band, Marysville, Ohio, articles of agreement with subscribers, including lists of members and subscribers (photocopy), 1863

Walker family (1744–1956), 3.4 linear meters of papers, including an address on the "Beauties of Music"

Sheet music, 30 boxes and 20 bound vols. of popular instrumental and vocal music, 1840–70, and 100 Civil War broadsides

Hymnals, 300 19th-century items, including 9 Shaker vols.

Songbooks, 200 vols., 1829– , also 46 campaign songsters, 1840–1924, and 60 temperance songbooks

Other printed music, including 25 19th-century instruction and study songbooks used in Columbus public schools

Programs of Ohio concerts, 1000 items, 1850s–80s

Music catalogues of late 19th- and early 20th-century Ohio music dealers

Photographs of local bands and musicians, including Daniel Decatur Emmett and Paul Laurence Dunbar, in various collections

Recordings, 3000 discs, including 167 shellac discs of popular, classical, and religious music, 1910–20; also 200 cylinders of popular and classical music, 1900–29, numerous temperance and prohibition songs, and 2589 LP and 45-rpm discs of popular music, 1924–55

—Priscilla Hewetson, William G. Meyers

1194
OHIO STATE UNIVERSITY   OU
Columbus, Ohio 43210

Music Library, Sullivant Hall

> See Bill Ellis, "An Evaluation of the Popular Music Holdings in the Music Library, Ohio State University" (unpublished 84-page report, 1977)

Sheet music, including 8 bound vols., 1845–85, and 3000 unbound items, mostly 1881–1940, the latter including 60 Irving Berlin editions; unsorted sheet music, ca. 1900–1930, 3000 vocal and 1000 instrumental items; and the Fanny Arms Collection, 7000 items, 1850–1910, arranged by title with a card catalogue for composers, titles, and publishers (the latter in the Rare Book Room, University Library)

American Broadcasting Company, Chicago, music library, originally at radio station WENR, including sheet music, 13,000 popular songs, 1900–1968, mostly post-1945; 400 popular and gospel song folios; and 5000 instrumental and vocal arrangements (medleys, instrumental "openers," show tunes, polkas, and dance orchestrations), mostly in ms, catalogued by composer, title, and subject

Songbooks, including 15 tunebooks, 1809–70, mostly post-1850; 15 gospel songbooks, 1867– ; 30 hymnals; and 125 public-school songbooks, mostly early 20th century

Operas, operettas, and secular cantatas in piano-vocal score, 70 items published before 1941, by U.S. composers

Recordings, including 10,000 78-rpm discs, mostly post-1925, arranged by label number

—Lois Rowell, Thomas F. Heck

Archive of Published Primitive, Ethnic, and Folk Music

Recordings, mostly of American music, including 2000 78-rpm discs and 4000 other discs, as cited in *Briegleb*, no. 92

1195
STATE LIBRARY OF OHIO   O
65 South Front Street
Columbus, Ohio 43215

Daniel Decatur Emmett (1818–1904, composer), 1000 items of papers, including biographical materials, correspondence, and scores. See Hans Nathan, *Dan Emmett and the Rise of Early Negro Minstrelsy* (Norman, Okla., 1962, 1977), also the supplement (available from the author)

—Shirley Courtright

1196
TRINITY LUTHERAN SEMINARY
2199 East Main Street
Columbus, Ohio 43209

Hymnals, 200 items, 1820– , including many in German and some with words only. (The collection was formed on the consolidation of holdings of the former Evangelical Lutheran Theological Seminary, Columbus, and of the Hamma School of Theology of Wittenberg University, Springfield, Ohio.)

—Donald L. Huber

1197
ROSCOE VILLAGE FOUNDATION
381 Hill Street
Coshocton, Ohio 43812

Capt. Pearl R. Nye (1872–1950), texts to 50 canal songs, in ms or typescript; also personal papers, 1900–1930

—Nancy Lowe Lonsinger

1198
U.S. AIR FORCE MUSEUM
Wright–Patterson Air Force Base
Dayton, Ohio 45433

Glenn Miller, memorabilia relating to his military band, 1942– , including instruments and uniforms, also tapes (restricted), photographs, and personal correspondence

—Royal Fry

1199
DAYTON AND MONTGOMERY   ODa
COUNTY PUBLIC LIBRARY
215 East Third Street
Dayton, Ohio 45402

Dayton Collection, including music-related materials of the local opera association and theaters

Programs of local musical events, including a complete set of the Dayton Symphony Association, 1910–31, and a partial set of the Dayton Philharmonic, 1939–

Songbooks, 500 sacred, popular, folk, or school items, ca. 1860–

Sheet music, including popular songs and classical organ or piano compositions, 22,000 items, ca. 1880–1940

—Don Paul

1200
Ellen Jane LORENZ (Mrs. James B. Porter)
324 Oak Forest Drive
Dayton, Ohio 45419

Edmund Simon Lorenz (1854–1942, Toledo and Dayton music publisher, active after 1873) Collection, including 170 Sunday-school and gospel songbooks, 1857–94; 25 anthem books, and 110 hymnals, tunebooks, and hymn books without music, 1825–80; and 40 secular chorus books for children's, men's, and mixed voices. See Ellen Jane Lorenz, *A Critical Bibliography of the E. S. Lorenz Collection of Nineteenth-Century American Songbooks* (Master's thesis, Wittenberg University, 1971). For other material from the Lorenz collection, see Samford University, Birmingham, Ala.

Sheet music, 1 bound vol. of 46 vocal and 14 piano pieces, mostly 1856–64, probably bound in the South

Sacred and secular chamber music, ms or published, for chorus, solo, handbells, or organ, by Ellen Jane Lorenz (pseud. Allen James and others), ca. 1950–

1201
UNITED THEOLOGICAL SEMINARY   ODaTS
1810 Harvard Boulevard
Dayton, Ohio 45406

A library supporting graduate professional studies of the United Methodist Church, with extensive hymnology materials, as well as 250 hymnals of the United Methodist Church and its predecessors (the Evangelical United Brethren Church, Evangelical Church, and United Brethren in Christ), also of other denominations, including hymnals with words only and tunebooks, 18th to 20th centuries; 14 vols. of anthems and cantatas, late 19th and 20th centuries; 4 sacred sheet-music items, 20th century; 4 boxes of programs of musical events at the Seminary or of Seminary groups on tour, 1940– ; and 210 recordings, including several 78-rpm discs. The library is designated to receive the Edmund S. Lorenz Collection of hymnals (see Ellen Jane Lorenz, above)

—Richard R. Berg

1202
UNIVERSITY OF DAYTON   ODaU
Dayton, Ohio 45469

University Library

Urban Deger Collection of printed music, mostly for piano or organ, including some used for silent films, 15 linear cm., ca. 1900– (in the University Archives)
Urban Schnurr Collection of programs, including items of the Dayton Civic Music Association, Dayton Symphony Orchestra, Chicago Symphony Orchestra, Milwaukee Symphony Orchestra, and the Metropolitan Opera, New York, in all 2.5 linear meters, ca. 1890–1965 (in the Special Collections)

—Linda Keir Hinrichs

Marian Library

Hymnals, including the St. Cecilia hymnal (1929)
Published sacred music pertaining to the Virgin Mary, mostly 1950s–60s

—Rev. William Fackovec

1203
METHODIST THEOLOGICAL   ODM
SCHOOL IN OHIO
Library
3081 Columbus Pike
Delaware, Ohio 43015

Magnificat collection, including 175 printed scores by 19th- and 20th-century U.S. and European composers
Hymnals, 125 items of the United Methodist Church and its antecedents, ca. 1800–1964

—John McTaggart

1204
DOVER HISTORICAL SOCIETY
325 East Iron Avenue
Dover, Ohio 44622

Sheet music, 500 items, mostly early 20th century; also 25 early 20th-century songbooks
Music mss, 2 anonymous items, n.d.
Photographs, 20 items, mostly of early 20th-century local marching bands
Recordings, including 60 cylinders, 47 78-rpm discs, and 43 metal discs for a Regina music box

—Thomas H. Conwell

1205
Theodore J. ALBRECHT
14060 Superior Street, Apt. 14
East Cleveland, Ohio 44118

Scores and parts owned by early Cleveland conductors, including 15 items from Alfred Arthur, among them a score of the Violin Concerto in G Minor, inscribed to Arthur by Max Bruch during Bruch's visit to Cleveland, 1883; also 50 items from J. Garfield Chapman
Scores owned by Carl Beck (1850–1920, conductor in San Antonio, Tex., 1884–1904), 12 items
Research files, including original and photocopied materials relating to musical activities in Texas and in Cleveland, including minutes of Texas singing societies, 1850–60; programs of Texas singing festivals, 1853–1916; songbooks, programs, and press clippings relating to early Texas singing groups, pre–World War I, in all 3 linear meters; music holographs (in photocopy) of Wilhelm Carl August Thielepape (1814–1904), including *Ein- und mehrstimmige Lieder*, 1840–99, with incidental music for Ludwig Anzengruber's play, *Der Meineidbauer*, produced at the Casino Theater, San Antonio, in 1873; also a list of 280 entries in the library of the Cleveland Vocal Society, 1874–1902

1206
June and Ernest F. DUFFIELD
118 West Center Street
Fostoria, Ohio 44830

Fostoria High School Band and early local community bands, materials including 2 scrapbooks of photographs and clippings, ca. 1920–
Printed and ms arrangements for dance band, 1000 items used by Mr. Duffield, ca. 1920–
Songbooks, 100 secular and sacred items, ca. 1920–40
Sheet music, 1000 items, ca. 1850–1940
Recordings, including 20 cylinders and 78-rpm discs

1207
Rutherford B. HAYES LIBRARY   OFH
1337 Hayes Avenue
Fremont, Ohio 43420

Josephine McCulloch (music teacher), family papers, including ms and published sheet music, programs, and personal documents, late 19th and early 20th centuries, 3 linear meters

Harriet Billau (1896–1948), programs, souvenir cards, and materials relating to art and music, also programs, yearbooks, and minutes of the Matinee Musical Club, 1903–35, in all 2 linear meters

Robinson Locke (1856–1920, author and lecturer), 1.2 linear meters of papers, some concerning the Toledo Symphony Orchestra

Charles E. Frohman, 25 programs relating to late 19th-century musical theater produced in New York by his uncles, Charles E. and Daniel Frohman

Hayes family papers, including sheet music used by the president's daughter, Fanny Hayes, and waltzes and marches written in honor of President and Mrs. Hayes; 30 linear cm. of campaign music; and correspondence from Joseph Snelling about church music

Hymnals, choir books, and popular songbooks, late 19th and early 20th centuries, 2.5 linear meters

Other printed music, including 1 linear meter of piano and organ music owned by Virginia Marchman (wife of the Hayes Library director)

Brahms Choral Club, 15 linear cm. of papers, including yearbooks, programs, and minutes, 1880s

Photographs of local musicians, 15 late 19th-century items

Music catalogues from late 19th-century Boston and New York music publishers and dealers, 15 linear cm.

—Linda C. Hauck

1208
DARKE COUNTY HISTORICAL SOCIETY

Garst Museum
205 North Broadway
Greenville, Ohio 45331

"Western Girl" by Ixion, 1912, parts of the ms score for the Broadway musical in which Annie Oakley starred

Bob Jobes, scrapbook with clippings and photographs pertaining to his career in Big Bands and orchestras, including a traveling band with Sophie Tucker, ca. 1920–30s

Civil War and World War I songbooks, ca. 1860–1918, 10 items

Popular vocal sheet music, ca. 1880–1920, 50 items, including some by Carl and Frank Wilson of Greenville

—Toni Seiler

1209
HIGHLAND COUNTY HISTORICAL SOCIETY

154 East Main Street
Hillsboro, Ohio 45133

Bells Opera House, booking and management records, 1920–22, 10 linear cm., as cited in David R. Larson, *Guide to Manuscript Collections and Institutional Records in Ohio* (Columbus, 1974)

1210
HIRAM COLLEGE   OHirC

Geidlinger Music Room
Teachout–Price Memorial Library
Hiram, Ohio 44234

Sheet music, 1200 classical items, 1864–1948

School and community songbooks, 20 early 20th-century items

Other printed music, including 50 opera libretti, 1888–1927, from the library of Marcia Bissell (singer, and Hiram College faculty member, 1929–64); also early 20th-century instrumental-music scores

Manuscript music, 3 college songs, early 20th century

Programs for College concerts, 1857– , 15 linear cm.; also photographs of College music groups, including loose items in archival papers, and a complete run of College yearbooks, 1850–

Recordings, including 5.5 linear meters of 78-rpm discs of classical or children's pedagogical music

—Marjorie Adams

1211
KENT STATE UNIVERSITY   OKentU
LIBRARIES

Kent, Ohio 44242

Miscellaneous holdings of sheet music, hymnals, periodicals, and books about music, also many octavo editions of sacred choral music, much of this material acquired with the *en bloc* purchase in 1967 of Wright's Book Shop, Madison, Wis.

—Ruth C. Main

1212
Terry E. MILLER

717 Avondale Street
Kent, Ohio 44240

Songbooks, 1820– , 250 items, many of them shape-note tunebooks; also 50 hymnals with words only, mostly used by rural Baptist groups, 1830–

Materials concerning Old Baptist singing, including books, articles, minutes of associations, and tape recordings

1213
LAKEWOOD HISTORICAL SOCIETY

14710 Lake Avenue
Lakewood, Ohio 44107

Wilson G. Smith (fl. 1926, music teacher), papers, including letters and curriculum materials

Sheet music, 4 mid 19th-century items of popular music

Songbooks and school songbooks, 28 vols., 1798–1893, some with words only

Programs of local concerts, 5 items, 1880s

—Lucy Sekerka

1214
WARREN COUNTY HISTORICAL   OLeWHi
SOCIETY MUSEUM

105 South Broadway
Box 223
Lebanon, Ohio 45036

Collection of Shaker Music, partly from Union Village, Ohio, including 3 ms hymnals, ca. 1800, accompanied by descriptions in printed booklets; 10 printed hymnals, ca. 1800–1850; and 6 disc recordings of Shaker music, including performances by Shakers of Sabbath-Day Lake

—Elva Adams

1215
ALLEN COUNTY HISTORICAL SOCIETY
620 West Market Street
Lima, Ohio 45801

Faurot Opera House, pamphlets and programs, 1889–1921, 12 linear cm., as cited in David R. Larson, *Guide to Manuscript Collections and Institutional Records in Ohio* (Columbus, 1974)

1216
UNION COUNTY HISTORICAL SOCIETY
246 West Sixth Street
Marysville, Ohio 43040

Marysville Choral Union, 1 vol. of records, 1894, as cited in David R. Larson, *Guide to Manuscript Collections and Institutional Records in Ohio* (Columbus, 1974)
Printed music, including 50 early 20th-century popular songs in sheet-music form, and school and church songbooks

—W. S. Kennedy

1217
MASSILLON MUSEUM
212 Lincoln Way East
Massillon, Ohio 44646

Manuscript class song by a local composer, 1902
Programs of local musical events, 10 items, including those of the opera house, 1880s; also 12 photographs of local musical events, ca. 1880–1910
Printed music, including 40 hymnals, ca. 1831–1930; 2 political songbooks, ca. 1842–92; and 20 popular vocal sheet-music items, ca. 1870–1930, some of them by local composers
Recordings, including 40 78-rpm discs and cylinders

—Margaret Vogt

1218
LAKE COUNTY HISTORICAL SOCIETY
8095 Mentor Avenue
Mentor, Ohio 44060

Sheet music, 1870s–1900, vocal and instrumental items in bound vols., 2 of the vols. devoted to campaign music for the 1880 presidential election, from the library of James A. Garfield

—Carl Thomas Engel

1219
NAVARRE–BETHLEHEM HISTORICAL SOCIETY
Box 491
Navarre, Ohio 44662

Village band, ledger and picture, n.d.

—Mrs. Robert Cook

1220
TUSCARAWAS COUNTY HISTORICAL SOCIETY
Box 462
New Philadelphia, Ohio 44663

Reidenbaugh (or Reidenbach, local composer), 4 ms organ compositions in 1 bound vol., ca. 1840, personal correspondence, and a photograph
Tunebook, ca. 1795, in shape notation
Popular vocal sheet music, 600 items, ca. 1880–1900, including 1 by a local composer
Trombones made locally and used at a local Moravian church, 5 items, 1792

—Paul A. Goudy

1221
FIRELANDS HISTORICAL SOCIETY MUSEUM
4 Case Avenue
Norwalk, Ohio 44857

Notebook with ms music, early 19th century
Bert Webster, collection of programs, photographs, scrapbooks, and other memorabilia pertaining to local bands, ca. 1860–1920; also other programs and photographs of local events
Published music, including hymnals, ca. 1880–1910, and 70 linear cm. of popular vocal sheet music, ca. 1880–1920
Recordings, including 50 cylinders and 50 78-rpm discs

1222
OBERLIN COLLEGE   OO, OOC
Oberlin, Ohio 44074

Mary M. Vial Library (Conservatory Library)

Mr. and Mrs. C. W. Best Collection of Autographs, containing photographs and 110 letters of musicians, some with ms music fragments, mostly European but also including single American items of Juliette Graves Adams, Amy Cheney (Mrs. H. H. A.) Beach (1867–1944), Carrie Jacobs Bond (1862–1946), Dudley Buck (1839–1909), Charles Wakefield Cadman (1881–1946), Enrico Caruso (1873–1921), Emma Eames (1865–1952), Alfred Robert Gaul (1837–1913), Louis Moreau Gottschalk (1829–69), Otto Hegner (1876–1907), Victor Herbert (1859–1924), Jenny Lind (1820–87), Edward A. MacDowell (1861–1908), Nellie Melba (1861–1931), Ethelbert Nevin (1862–1901), Adelina Patti (1843–1919), Moriz Rosenthal (1862–1946), Ernestine Schumann-Heink (1861–1936), Alexander Siloti (1863–1945), Henriette Sontag (1806–54), John Philip Sousa (1854–1932), Albert Spalding (1888–1953), Theodore Thomas (1835–1905), and Fannie Bloomfield Zeisler (1863–1927); also postage stamps commemorating musical personages and events of various countries. See the published catalogue (Oberlin, 1967)
Karl W. Gehrkens (b. 1882) Music Education Library, 35 linear meters of vols. collected by him, including song collections, mostly American, now dispersed in the general holdings

Gustave Langenus (b. 1883), library of clarinet and chamber music, mostly European; also his ms book, and memorabilia of the New York Chamber Music Society

Published music, music-instruction books (mostly for keyboard or music theory), and books on music, 1500 items by Americans or with American imprints ca. 1820–1940. Composers represented by 10 or more published works include George Whitfield Andrews, Ernest Bloch, Aaron Copland, Edward A. MacDowell, and Walter Piston. Uncatalogued materials fill 24 file drawers, including some published music by Americans or with American imprints

Recordings, including 4000 78-rpm discs, mostly classical music

Seeley G. Mudd Library

Manuscript music, including compositions by Igor Stravinsky, G. W. Andrews, William Grant Still, and R. Nathaniel Dett

Oberlin Musical Union, papers, 1 linear meter, including minutes, membership lists, and programs

Songbooks, including 450 tunebooks or hymnals of various denominations and 175 hymnals with words only, ca. 1820– ; also 300 secular songbooks for singing schools, community singing, and public schools

Sheet music, 65 letter boxes of separate items, ca. 1890–1940, mostly vocal, and indexed by composer, title, and lyricist

Programs of Oberlin recitals; also 6 scrapbooks of opera programs, pictures, and reviews compiled by Prof. Laurel Yeamans, includings 4 vols. of American items, 1915–26

Books and monographs on music, 1000 items, 1821–1919

—Linda Fidler

Archives

George N. Allen (1831–94), papers, 1830–95, including correspondence and photographs

George W. Andrews (organist), papers, 1870–1935, including 2 scrapbooks, several letters, biographical and bibliographical materials, and music

William K. Breckenridge (pianist), classbooks, 1893–1933, and a scrapbook kept in Leipzig, 1885–86

William C. Cochran, papers, including sheet music by G. N. Allen, John P. Moran, and others, ca. 1850–90; also a scrapbook of Cincinnati musical events, 1860–90

Edward Dickinson, 20 linear cm. of notebooks and mss, 1876–1934

Karl Wilson Gehrkens, 5 linear cm. of short essays, 1915–67

James H. Hall, papers, 3 folders and 1 scrapbook, with correspondence and printed materials, ca. 1907–53

Daniel Harris (singer), papers, 3 folders of printed materials concerning him and his students, ca. 1939–67

Edwin M. Hoffman, papers, 1917–44, 30 linear cm., including music of Russian songs collected in Manchuria, 1919–20

Irving W. Metcalf, papers, including a scrapbook of opera and musical programs in Germany, 1906

George C. Westervelt, scrapbook of programs, clippings, and other materials, mostly concerning town bands, 1880s–1930s

Arthur L. Williams, 10 linear cm. of papers, ca. 1913–70

Conservatory of Music programs, 1867–

Oberlin Musical Union, papers, 1860–1929, including programs, correspondence, contracts, clippings, and membership lists

—William E. Bigglestone

1223
MIAMI UNIVERSITY   OOxM
Oxford, Ohio 45056

Western College Archives

Edgar Stillman Kelley (1857–1944), 5 music mss, 16 published scores, pictures, biographical and genealogical information about the Kelley family, and an award certificate to Kelley; also 33 items of sheet music, 63 scores, and 3 books on music from his personal library

John Knowles Paine (1839–1906), ms score to Azara, also a piano-vocal score of his Mass in D

Frederick Ayres (1876–1926), photocopies of mss of his Quartet in E Minor and Sonata for Cello

School songbooks, 10 vols. of college songs, 1897–1930

Scrapbooks, 10 vols. of press clippings and programs of college concerts, 1880–1930

Archive of Ohio and International Folklore and Music

The music section includes 150 books and 2000 recordings, many relating to Appalachian music, protest songs, slave songs, spirituals, jazz, and blues

Special Collections

Sheet music, 2000 items of late 19th- and early 20th-century popular music

Songbooks, 2.4 linear meters of popular songsters, late 19th and early 20th centuries

Recordings, including 8000 78-rpm discs of popular and classical music, also several Edison cylinders

—Jane Fryman, Stacie Williams

1224
FIRST CONGREGATIONAL CHURCH
22 Liberty Street
Painesville, Ohio 44077

Church-choir records, ca. 1900, 1 vol., as cited in David R. Larson, Guide to Manuscript Collections and Institutional Records in Ohio (Columbus, 1974)

1225
David C. THOMAS
6700 Olde Eight Road
Peninsula, Ohio 44264

Amzi Chapin, Sr. (1768–1835), papers, including his 116-page ms tunebook; his journal (1791–1835), listing singing schools held in Virginia, North Carolina, Kentucky, and Pennsylvania, 1792–1810; his account book, 1800–1835; an 1812 letter from Robert Patterson of the House of Patterson and Hopkins Music Publishers, Pittsburgh; numerous receipts, deeds, and letters, some from his brothers Lucius, Calvin, and Aaron; and papers formerly of the Sherrill family, descendants of the Chapin family

1226
Leonard RIVENBURG

8400 Riverside Drive
Powell, Ohio 43065

John Andrew (Van) Broekhoven (1852–1930), personal papers, consisting mostly of music mss and speculative writings on music, held on deposit. Included are ms libretti, books about music, published music, notebooks, and memorabilia. See the 11-page inventory

1227
PORTAGE COUNTY HISTORICAL SOCIETY

6549–6551 North Chestnut
Ravenna, Ohio 44266

Loudin Jubilee Singers, framed photograph and memorabilia, ca. 1880s
Sheet music, 300 popular items, ca. 1918

—Ruth Engelhardt

1228
GRACE EPISCOPAL CHURCH

315 Wayne Street
Sandusky, Ohio 44870

Typescript history, "100 Years of Music in Grace Church," ca. 1935?, as cited in David R. Larson, *Guide to Manuscript Collections and Institutional Records in Ohio* (Columbus, 1974)

1229
SANDUSKY LIBRARY ASSOCIATION   OSand

114 West Adams Street
Sandusky, Ohio 44870

Hugo F. Engles, scrapbook on Sandusky history, including materials relating to local opera performances, 1882–92, as cited in David R. Larson, *Guide to Manuscript Collections and Institutional Records in Ohio* (Columbus, 1974)

1230
SHAKER HISTORICAL SOCIETY

16740 South Park Boulevard
Shaker Heights, Ohio 44120

Alma McGill, ms collection of songs, hymns, and anthems in letter notation, 1 vol., 1870–80
Shaker hymnals and books on music, 28 published items, 1813–93

—Jane Piwonka

1231
Jack SAUL

3924 Eastway Road
South Euclid, Ohio 44118

Recordings, including all recordings made by the Cleveland Orchestra, 1924– , and tapes of live performances

—Theodore J. Albrecht

1232
CLARK COUNTY HISTORICAL SOCIETY

300 West Main Street
Springfield, Ohio 45504

Manuscript lyrics of a "Song on Politics," 1840, for the presidential campaign of William Henry Harrison, sung to the tune "Sitting on a Rail"
Gen. J. Warren Kelfer, 2 letters concerning the 110th Ohio Volunteer Infantry Band, 1860s
Published songbooks of the GAR, Spanish-American War, and World War I, and a fragment of a published songbook for the Rutherford B. Hayes campaign; also a sacred songbook, 1810, and a vocal instruction book, 1813
Song sheets, 2 printed items, including "Old Tom," by W. S. F. (probably the local Republican leader in 1860, W. S. Furay), and "Republican Song of Freedom," written for the Springfield Fremont Club, 1856; also 8 popular sheet-music items, ca. 1880–1900, and W. T. Porter's song "McKinley is the Man"
Programs of local musical events, including those of Black's Opera House and the Grand Opera House, in all 25 items, ca. 1870–1920; 10 photographs of musicians at Memorial Hall in Springfield, ca. 1920–1930; and 23 clippings on local music
Histories of local music groups, 3 typescripts by a Wittenberg College professor, 1930s

—G. H. Berkhofer

1233
HYMN SOCIETY OF AMERICA

Wittenberg University
Springfield, Ohio 45501

Hymnals, 16.5 linear meters of 19th- and 20th-century vols. of various denominations, including some with words only; 2 linear meters of foreign-language hymnals, mostly 20th century; and 150 other 19th-century hymnals, psalm books, and Sunday-school books
Papers of the Society, from its founding in 1922, 4 file drawers of materials concerning prominent members of the Society, hymn contests, and other subjects, including clippings, correspondence, printed and typescript articles, pictures and photographs, programs, ms music and hymn texts, and copies of the Society's publications
List of public and private collections of hymnals in the U.S. and Canada, compiled by questionnaire, 1977–78

—W. Thomas Smith

1234
Reuben POWELL
1361 Thomas Drive
Springfield, Ohio 45503

Early country music recorded or duplicated on tape, comprising 12,000 songs duplicated from 78-rpm discs, mostly 1920s–30s, including the recording collection of Robert O. Hyland of Springfield; 350 hours of electrical transcriptions; 450 hours of recordings of festivals and the Renfro Valley Barn Dance; 250 hours of interviews with performers, some of them broadcast on radio or television; 1200 hours of subject collections, concerning the hammered dulcimer, train songs, prison songs, fiddle contests, WLS "National Barn Dance" shows, Renfro Valley Bluegrass Festivals, and others; and over 3000 hours of other collections, mostly of Renfro Valley programs and radio and television country-music broadcasts. The entire tape collection is designated for deposit at Berea College, Ky.

1235
WITTENBERG UNIVERSITY   OSW
Springfield, Ohio 45501

> Materials are located as noted, in the Thomas Library, Music Library, Music School, University Archives, and Lutheran Studies Center

Hymnals, a collection of 16th- to 20th-century vols., largely Europen but including 2000 American imprints, among them German-language liturgies and hymnals, American Lutheran liturgies and hymnals, English-language hymnals, psalm books, and tunebooks, and hymnals and liturgies in Danish, Finnish, German, Norwegian, Swedish, and other languages (in the Lutheran Studies Center). See the catalogue by Louis Voigt, *Hymnbooks at Wittenberg* (Springfield, 1975)

Songbooks, 500 American publications of pedagogical, patriotic, social, and folk songs, 19th and 20th centuries (in the Lutheran Studies Center)

Sheet music including anthems, many by Lutheran composers, used by the Wittenberg Choir, conducted by John Thomas Williams, 1920s–30s, 3.5 linear meters, of which one-third is by American composers (in the University Archives and the Music School)

Other printed music, including scores and performance parts for University bands, choruses, and other groups, 7.5 linear meters of items with American imprints or by American composers, 19th and 20th centuries (in the Music Library)

Recordings, including 500 78-rpm discs (in the Thomas Library)

School of Music papers, 1922– , 15 linear cm. (in the University Archives)

Volunteer Band record books, 1897–1905, 3 linear cm.

—Louis Voigt

1236
TALLMADGE HISTORICAL SOCIETY
1 Tallmadge Circle
Tallmadge, Ohio 44278

Hymnals, 3 items, 1850s

Charles Bronson (fl. 1850s, bassoonist), ms band music written ca. 1854, in an 1814 preceptor for cornet

Tallmadge papers, 1806–1962, including minutes and papers of the Tallmadge Cornet Band, 1854–66, and of the Lyceum Association; a contract for a singing school held by John Wright, Jr., 1809; and a record of subscriptions to purchase a band wagon, n.d.

—Miriam Everhart

1237
TOLEDO–LUCAS COUNTY   OT
PUBLIC LIBRARY
325 Michigan Street
Toledo, Ohio 43624

Fine Arts Department

Sacred and secular songbooks, ca. 1890– , 7 linear meters

Sheet music, mostly popular songs, 5.5 linear meters, ca. 1910–50, including some by local composers

Local History Department

Mary Willing Collection, including 1000 programs, ca. 1895–1965

Theatre and Auditorium Collection, including 1600 programs, ca. 1870–1970

Toledo Orchestra, programs, 1920–26

—Roxanne Emerson

1238
TOLEDO MUSEUM OF ART   OTM
2445 Monroe Street
Box 1013
Toledo, Ohio 43697

Francis Hopkinson, *Seven Songs for the Harpsichord or Forte Piano* (Philadelphia, 1788) (in the Print Department)

Programs of the Cleveland, Chicago, and Minneapolis symphony orchestras and the New York Philharmonic, 1 linear meter of bound vols., ca. 1920–35

Photographs of music groups that performed in the Museum, 25 items, ca. 1920–40

—Joyce Smar

1239
TOLEDO SYMPHONY ORCHESTRA
1 Stranahan Square
Toledo, Ohio 43604

Papers of the Orchestra, 6 linear meters, ca. 1919– , including minutes, correspondence, programs, news releases, publications, and photographs

—Teri Taylor

1240
Louis BERTONI
Box 228
Vermilion, Ohio 44089

Hymnals and related books, 250 items, also 2000 published music editions, some 19th century, mostly 20th century

1241
GREAT LAKES HISTORICAL SOCIETY
Clarence S. Metcalf Research Library
480 Main Street
Vermilion, Ohio 44089

Sheet music and clippings, 6 items concerning Great Lakes shipping, including S. J. Monk, "On the Boat Eastland" (1911), and Dwight L. Moody, "Let the Lower Lights Be Burning" (1871)

—A. N. O'Hara

1242
HANBY HOUSE
Main Street
Westerville, Ohio 43081

Music by Benjamin R. Hanby or formerly belonging to his family, all mid 19th century, including 10 hymnals (some with words only), 1 method book each for piano and voice, 5 popular songbooks, 2 piano anthologies, 8 sheet-music songs, and the engraved plates for "Darling Nellie Gray"

1243
OTTERBEIN COLLEGE   OWeO
Westerville, Ohio 43081

Benjamin R. Hanby (1833–67, composer and faculty member), published scores and biographical materials, 60 linear cm.
Paul Frank (faculty member, 1946–65), 10 music mss for piano, 1930s
Sheet music, 40 items of classical music, 1860–1965
Hymnals, 100 vols. published by E. S. Lorenz, 1880s
Programs for College concerts, 200 items, 1858–

—John Becker

1244
ORGAN HISTORICAL SOCIETY
Box 209
Wilmington, Ohio 45177

> Materials are located in the Ohio Wesleyan University Library, Delaware, Ohio 43015

Sheet music for organ, 100 19th-century items
William H. Barnes (organ consultant), 2 scrapbooks of programs and clippings, late 1920s–70
Samuel Prowse Warren (1841–1915, organist), 3 scrapbooks, including concert programs from New York City
Everett E. Truette (1861–1933, organist), scrapbooks of programs, organ stoplists, and clippings (on microfilm)
Organ stoplists, several thousand items, partially indexed by city and organ builder; also numerous organ-builders' lists and organ-layout blueprints

Brochures of various organ builders, 1888–
Photographs of organ builders and instruments, 1870s–
Recordings, including 40 78-rpm and LP discs of organ music, and master tapes of recordings made at Society conventions

—Homer D. Blanchard

1245
WORTHINGTON HISTORICAL SOCIETY
Box 355
Worthington, Ohio 43085

Julia P. Strong, 24-page ms handmade tunebook, 1815
Manuscript music for quartet, "Book Agent," 1875
Songbooks, 10 late 19th-century, popular items, and a Lowell Mason vocal method book, 1856
Programs of local concerts, 1850–1900
Regina music box built in Cincinnati, with several dozen metal discs

—Marjorie Kaskey

1246
MAHONING VALLEY HISTORICAL SOCIETY
Arms Museum
648 Wick Avenue
Youngstown, Ohio 44502

Monday Music Club, papers, including programs and minutes, ca. 1912–
Youngstown Symphony Society, papers, including minutes
Programs of local musical events, including those of the Youngstown Symphony and the Youngstown Opera House, 25 linear cm., ca. 1900– ; also photographs of local musical events
Hymnals of various denominations, 10 items, ca. 1880–1930
Popular vocal sheet music, 200 items, ca. 1880–1930
Recordings, including 25 78-rpm discs, and 10 Edison cylinders in the Thomas A. Edison exhibit

---

In addition to the repositories listed above, the following have also reported holdings of the materials indicated:

Alliance—Mount Union College, Library: sheet music, songbooks, other printed music, recordings
Amherst—Amherst Public Library: songbooks, recordings
Ashland—Ashland College, Library: sheet music, songbooks, other printed music, recordings
Ashland—Ashland Public Library: songbooks
Ashtabula—Ashtabula County District Library: songbooks
Ashtabula—Ashtabula County Historical Society: sheet music, songbooks, other printed music, programs
Avon—Avon Historical Society: sheet music
Batavia—Clermont County Public Library: songbooks, recordings
Bellaire—Bellaire Public Library: recordings
Bellevue—Bellevue Public Library: sheet music, recordings

Burton—Geauga County Historical Society: sheet music, songbooks, programs, pictures, recordings
Canal Fulton—Canal Fulton Heritage Society: pictures
Canton—Malone College, Library: songbooks
Cedarville—Cedarville College, Library: songbooks
Centerville—Centerville Historical Society: sheet music, songbooks, miscellaneous
Chillicothe—Adena State Memorial: sheet music
Clyde—Clyde Public Library: songbooks
Columbus—Bexley Public Library: songbooks
Columbus—Capital University, Library: sheet music, songbooks, other printed music, programs, recordings
Columbus—Trinity Episcopal Church, Library: songbooks, other printed music, programs
Dayton—Wright State University, Library: sheet music, songbooks, other printed music
Defiance—Defiance County Historical Society: songbooks, pictures, recordings
Dublin—Robert V. Reinhard: sheet music, songbooks, other published music, miscellaneous
Eaton—Preble County Historical Society: sheet music, songbooks, programs, pictures, recordings
Findley—Hancock Historical Museum Association: sheet music
Fostoria—Fostoria Area Historical Society: pictures
Franklin—Franklin Public Library: sheet music
Fremont—Sandusky County Historical Society: sheet music, songbooks, programs
Gambier—Kenyon College: printed music, pictures
Granville—Denison University, Music Library: songbooks, other printed music, programs
Harrison—Eugene B. Woefel: sheet music, songbooks, recordings
Hubbard—Hubbard Public Library: songbooks
Kent—Kent Free Library: songbooks
Lithopolis—Wagnalls Memorial Library: songbooks, pictures, recordings
Marysville—Marysville Public Library: songbooks, recordings
Massillon—Massillon Public Library: sheet music, songbooks
Maumee—Maumee Valley Historical Society: sheet music

Medina—Medina County Historical Society: songbooks, programs, pictures, recordings, miscellaneous
Middleport—Meigs County Pioneer and Historical Society: songbooks, programs, pictures
Middletown—Middletown Public Library: miscellaneous
Milan—Edison Birthplace Association, Thomas Edison Museum: recordings, miscellaneous
New Concord—Muskingum College, Library: songbooks
Newark—Licking County Historical Society: songbooks, recordings
Newark—Newark Public Library: songbooks, recordings
Oregon—Oregon Jerusalem Historical Society of Ohio: sheet music, songbooks, recordings
Oxford—William Holmes McGuffey Museum: sheet music, songbooks
Perry—Perry Public Library: songbooks, recordings
Salem—Salem Historical Society: songbooks
Salem—Salem Public Library: sheet music, songbooks, programs, pictures
Tiffin—Kathryn T. Kay: sheet music, songbooks, programs, recordings
Upper Arlington—Upper Arlington Public Library: sheet music, songbooks
Van Wert—Brumback Library: sheet music, songbooks, pictures
Van Wert—First United Methodist Church: songbooks, programs, pictures
Van Wert—Van Wert County Historical Society: songbooks, programs, recordings
Vermilion—United Church of Christ, E and R Library: sheet music, other printed music, pictures
Waynesville—Mary L. Cook Public Library: sheet music, songbooks, pictures, miscellaneous
Wilmington—Wilmington College, Library: sheet music, songbooks, recordings
Youngstown—William K. Miller: songbooks
Youngstown—Public Library of Youngstown & Mahoning County: songbooks
Youngstown—Youngstown State University, Library: songbooks, other printed music.

Oklahoma

1247
DUNCAN PUBLIC LIBRARY
815 Ash Street
Duncan, Oklahoma 73533

Songbooks of popular folk songs, 50 items, ca. 1920–
—Mrs. Velma Lake

1248
STEPHENS COUNTY HISTORICAL MUSEUM
Fuqua Park, Box 1294
Duncan, Oklahoma 73533

Sheet music, 400 items, mostly 1920s
Cylinder recordings, 100 items, mostly ca. 1900–1910s; also 100 player-piano rolls
—Charlotte D. Jenkins

1249
CANADIAN COUNTY HISTORICAL SOCIETY
600 West Wade Street
El Reno, Oklahoma 73036

Instruction book for mandolin and harp, n.d.
Hymnals in German, 4 items, ca. 1900, including 3 used in a local Mennonite community; also 2 songbooks of popular and sacred songs, ca. 1880

Popular sheet music, 10 items, ca. 1890–1940, including Charles Buchbaum (local composer), "El Reno Waltz," 1894

Programs of local school and community events, 10 items, ca. 1900–1950

Catalogue of music published by the American Music Co. for harps, celestephone, and Marxophone, n.d.

Recordings, including 100 78-rpm discs, ca. 1920–40

—Mrs. F. C. Ball

1250
EL RENO CARNEGIE LIBRARY

215 East Wade
El Reno, Oklahoma 73036

Hymnals of various denominations, 75 items, ca. 1900–1940

Popular vocal sheet music, 171 items, ca. 1900–1940

Programs of the Beethoven Music Club, 1907–17, and of the Damrosch Music Club, 1931–74

—Martha Mulanax

1251
PHILLIPS UNIVERSITY   OkEP, OkEG

University Station
Enid, Oklahoma 73701

Zollars Memorial Library

Tri-State Musical Festival, pre-festival program and festival manual for each annual event, 1932–

—Marjorie Webber

Graduate Seminary Library

Hymnals of various denominations, ca. 1830– , 400 items, including titles in German, French, Swedish, and Japanese

—John Sayre

1252
Eugene J. ULRICH

Music Department
Phillips University
Enid, Oklahoma 73701

Orchestral, band, choral, instrumental, and vocal works by Ulrich, 58 original works and 5 transcriptions

Printed music, including 20 hymnals, ca. 1913–39; a book of dance music arranged for the piano, 1932; and 5 popular sheet-music items, 1909–38

1253
NO MAN'S LAND HISTORICAL MUSEUM

Sewell Street
Box 278
Goodwell, Oklahoma 73939

Hymnals, ca. 1870–1940, 50 items, including 1 in German

Popular vocal sheet music, 100 items, ca. 1890–1940

Programs, 15 linear cm., mostly of Panhandle State University, ca. 1915–

Catalogues of violin manufacturers, 2 items, 1910–13

Musical instruments, with documentation of their arrival and use in the community

Recordings, including 30 cylinders, ca. 1890–1910, and 30 78-rpm discs, ca. 1900–1930

—Joan Kachel, Harold S. Kachel

1254
Will ROGERS LIBRARY

Box 186
Marshall, Oklahoma 73056

Sheet music of popular songs, 30 items, 1912–30

Hymnals, 3 items, ca. 1917–40

Photographs of local bands, 3 items, ca. 1900–1915

—Mrs. J. L. Branen

1255
FIVE CIVILIZED TRIBES MUSEUM

Agency Hill—Honor Heights Drive
Muskogee, Oklahoma 74401

Hymnal with words only, in Creek and Choctaw, compiled by Rev. R. M. Loughridge and Rev. David Winslett, 5th ed., 1937; also 2 hymnals in Cherokee and 2 in Creek, ca. 1860–1940

S. J. Oslin, "My Indian Territory Home," printed sheet music (1902), dedicated to Green McCurtain (chief of the Choctaw Nation)

Tribal hymns and chants, 6 cassette tapes recorded ca. 1960–78, including vocal quartets and solos sung in Cherokee, Creek, and Choctaw, and flute solos

—Peggy Denton

1256
UNIVERSITY OF OKLAHOMA   OkU

Norman, Oklahoma 73069

Music Library

Printed scores, 4250 items in the general collection

Western History Collections, Division of Manuscripts

Spencer Norton, 20 holograph music mss

Mrs. O. R. Hisel (1890–1950), historical studies, including materials toward a history of the Oklahoma Federation of Music Clubs

Wilbur K. Bevan (1907–42, World War I soldier), scrapbook, diary, poetry, and song texts of the American Expeditionary Forces

Paul S. Carpenter (1870–1956, University professor and conductor), papers, including correspondence, ms and printed music, 2 scrapbooks, and programs, in all 1.2 linear meters

Muskogee Musical Arts Society, papers

Guy Fraser Harrison, personal papers, including materials from his music library, in 12 boxes, unsorted

Fredrik Holmberg (pioneer leader in music and art), 125 items of papers, including correspondence, speeches, clippings, lecture notes, and a scrapbook, 1903–35

Historic Oklahoma collection, 18 linear meters, including materials on music and musical organizations in Oklahoma

Walter Price, 4 theater playbills for productions in which he appeared, 1935

Tulsa Chamber of Commerce, 6 recordings of speeches and songs in Indian languages, made for the Tulsa Indian Exposition, 1938

Gerald M. Van Dyke, 5 songs written and published by him

Wichita Mountain Easter Pageant materials, including 67 scripts, programs, photographs, and memorabilia, 1935–47

Bill York, 13 southwestern U.S. folk-music books, 1936–48

—Jan Seifert

1257
FORTY-FIFTH INFANTRY DIVISION MUSEUM

2145 Northeast Thirty-sixth Street
Oklahoma City, Oklahoma 73111

Photographs of bands of the National Guard, 45th Division, 50 items, 1919–

—Ralph Jones

1258
McCLAIN COUNTY HISTORICAL SOCIETY

Box 255
Purcell, Oklahoma 73080

Piano-instruction books, 2 items, 1896–1910

Printed music, including 4 hymnals, 1858–1909; 1 children's songbook, 1897; 1 patriotic songbook, 1919; and 150 sheet-music items, mostly popular for voice or piano, ca. 1894–1930

Photographs of performers at Brown's Opera House in Purcell, 3 items, 1892–1902

—Marjorie P. Hesse

1259
OKLAHOMA BAPTIST UNIVERSITY   OkShB

University Library
Shawnee, Oklahoma 74801

B. B. McKinney (1886–1952, music and hymnal editor for the Broadman Press), correspondence, photographs, 25 ms works, and his complete published compositions, including choral settings of hymns and hymns published in hymnals

Hymnals and tunebooks, 7.5 linear meters, mostly Baptist, ca. 1850–1940

—Jack Pearson, Patty Sue Smith

1260
OKLAHOMA STATE UNIVERSITY   OkS

Stillwater, Oklahoma   74074

University Library

Angelo Cyrus Scott (1857–1949, founder of Oklahoma City, president of the Oklahoma Agricultural and Mechanical College, 1899–1908, and composer), 6 ms songs composed by him, some with his own lyrics

Songbooks, 150 items, ca. 1900–1940, including many of folk and western songs

Programs of University musical and theatrical events, 1898–

—Anita Evans

Band Library

Boh Makovsky (1878–1949, founder of the University Music Department and the Kappa Kappa Psi band fraternity), collection of band music, ca. 1915–50, 12 linear meters

—Andrew Harper

1261
Evelyn DAVIS

7106 East Fifty-third Place South
Tulsa, Oklahoma 74145

Arthur Farwell (1872–1952), personal papers, including holograph and published scores with sketches; correspondence, including 25 letters from Roy Harris; diaries, 1 of his mother, 1865–68, and 2 of his own dealing with his early musical training and later studies at the Massachusetts Institute of Technology and in Europe, 1893 and 1896–98; programs mostly featuring works by Farwell and other American composers; organizational records, including documents relating to the Wa Wan Society of America and the American Pageant Association, both of which he founded; research notes on cowboy, Spanish-American and American Indian songs; lectures and essays; photographs, many of early pageants including his *Pilgrimage Play* at the Hollywood Bowl; and drawings referring to his symbolic dreams. See Evelyn Davis, *The Significance of Arthur Farwell as an American Music Educator* (diss., University of Maryland, 1972), and Brice Farwell, *A Guide to the Music of Arthur Farwell and to the Microfilm Collection of His Work* (Briarcliff Manor, N.Y., 1972)

1262
TULSA COUNTY HISTORICAL SOCIETY

400 Civic Center
Tulsa, Oklahoma 74103

Tom Wickizer, mss and charts of a musical scale containing no accidentals, devised ca. 1920; also ms instrumental parts he used while playing with the Oklahoma City and Tulsa Symphony orchestras, 1920s

—Greta Faith

1263
Paul W. WOHLGEMUTH

8218 South Louisville Street
Tulsa, Oklahoma 74136

Hymnals, 1400 items, ca. 1800– , with emphasis on 19th-century gospel songbooks

1264

EASTERN TRAILS MUSEUM

Box 437
Vinita, Oklahoma 74301

Ballad lyrics, ca. 1870–1900, 25 typewritten texts collected from homesteaders who entered Oklahoma or Indian Territory from Texas
Hymnals, 3 items, including 1 in Cherokee with words only, and 2 used by missionaries, 1847–83
Vinnie Ream (1847–1914), 4 published songs
James A. Kenreigh, "I Dream of Childhood," sheet music, 1914
Fannie Blythe Marks Collection of sheet music, 1874–1903, 40 items, mostly popoular, including 10 for piano

—O. B. Campbell

1265

SEMINOLE NATION HISTORICAL SOCIETY

Box 1079
Wewoka, Oklahoma 74884

Wewoka Music Club, scrapbook, ca. 1930–40
Sheet music, 200 items, ca. 1850–1930
Programs of local musicians and groups, 5 items, 1930s
Photographs of musicians and groups including local bands, 30 items, ca. 1900–1940, and 1 of the Junior MacDowell Club, ca. 1930–33

—Idabel Bishop

In addition to the repositories listed above, the following have also reported holdings of the materials indicated:

Bethany—Bethany Nazarene College, R. T. Williams Library: songbooks, programs, recordings
Boise City—Soutar Memorial Library: sheet music, songbooks, recordings
Dewey—Herbert F. Tyler Memorial Library: songbooks
Goodwell—Panhandle State College, Marvin E. McKee Library: songbooks
Kingfisher—Chisholm Trail Museum: programs
Lawton—Institute of the Great Plains: sheet music, songbooks, programs, catalogues, recordings
Medford—Grant County Historical Society: songbooks
Norman—Cleveland County Historical Society: sheet music, songbooks, programs
Oklahoma City—Midwest Christian College, Library: songbooks
Oklahoma City—Oklahoma Christian College, Library: songbooks
Oklahoma City—Oklahoma Historical Society: miscellaneous
Sapulpa—Sapulpa Historical Society: sheet music, songbooks, other printed music, programs, catalogues, pictures, recordings, miscellaneous
Stillwater—IOA Youth Domain, Donnelley Memorial Fund: recordings
Tahlequah—Northeastern State College, John Vaughan Library: sheet music, songbooks
Tulsa—Oral Roberts University, Learning Resources Center: songbooks
Tulsa— University of Tulsa, McFarlon Library: sheet music, songbooks, other printed music, programs, pictures, recordings
Vinita—Vinita Public Library: songbooks, recordings

Oregon

1266

W. Bernard WINDT

1033 Clay Street
Ashland, Oregon 97520

Published songbooks, 50 mostly sacred items, ca. 1833–1920, including some advertising the issuing company's products
Published collections of instrumental music, 7 items for organ, flute, or banjo, 1851–89, and 25 bound items for piano, 1831–56
Sheet music for voice or piano, 500 items, including popular songs and songs about the Oregon Trail, 1825–1940
Programs, including 2 of recitals for the Ashland Centennial Exposition, 1876

1267

AURORA COLONY HISTORICAL SOCIETY

Oxbarn Museum
Box 202
Aurora, Oregon 97002

See Deborah M. Olsen and Clark M. Will, "Musical Heritage of the Aurora Colony," *Oregon Historical Quarterly,* 79 (1978), 232–67

Manuscript copybooks, 1856–77, containing dance songs, march tunes, and patriotic airs for band, composed or copied by Aurora Colony musicians including Henry Conrad Finck, Dr. William Keil (leader of Aurora Colony, 1856–77), his son Frederick Keil, Conrad Yost, and Henry C. Ehlen; miscellaneous orchestral music mss; and printed band books from the 19th and early 20th centuries

Manuscript songbooks, 5 items, ca. 1860–80, including words to German chorales; a hymn with text attributed to Dr. Keil, 1855; 2 song texts, probably by Dr. Keil; unsigned songs and poems, many probably written by Aurora Colony musicians; and American patriotic airs

Printed arrangements of popular opera tunes, for chamber orchestra, used in the Colony 1856–77

Hymnals, including 4 items in German with words only, printed in the 19th century; 1 German hymnal, 1890; and 4 19th-century hymnals in English

Printed books of German, Austrian, and Swiss folksongs, 3 items, used in the Colony 1856–77

Frederick Keil, account book from his general store, 1876–78, with orders for musical supplies

Musical instruments used by Aurora musicians, 24 items, many of them restored, including an ophicleide, 4 back-fire instruments (cornet, baritone, tuba, and tenor horn), and a Schellenbaum; also a demonstration recording of the re-created Aurora Pioneer Band, 1977, with original Aurora Colony music and instruments

—Deborah M. Olsen

1268

OREGON STATE UNIVERSITY   OrCS
Corvallis, Oregon 97331

Horner Museum

Harold A. Wilkins, ms song "Hail to O.A.C." (Oregon Agricultural College), 1914

Davis Entertainers of the DeMoss Family Bards of Oregon, 1872–1933, ms music written by the DeMoss family, published sheet music used by the Bards, journals, diaries, date books, scrapbooks, logs, posters, programs, contracts, 150 photographs, and other memorabilia; Edison discs and cylinders used by James DeMoss in his concerts, ca. 1905; a chart by James M. DeMoss, "The key to music—for the school room and family circle," 1873; and 20 musical instruments used by the Bards

Papers of local organizations, including the Pythian Society, Women's Literary Society, and various University organizations, ca. 1870–1920

Programs, 500 items, 1880–1930, including those of University groups and the Corvallis Opera House; also 400 photographs of University and Corvallis musicians and groups, ca. 1890–1930

Sheet music of popular or college songs, ca. 1870–1953, 126 items, including 2 by local musicians

Hymnals of various denominations, 25 items, ca. 1845–80

Printed vols. of popular and classical piano music, 25 items, ca. 1850–1910

Recordings, including 540 78-rpm discs and 47 cylinders

—Carl Weltzin, Lucy Skjelstad

University Archives

Theodore Lawrence Mesang (1902–67), 30 ms marches, ca. 1930–60

Photographs of musical activities at the University, 250 items, 1887–1940

University music materials, ca. 1887–1940, 15 linear cm., including correspondence, catalogues of the Music Department, recital programs, and a typed history of the Music School prepared for the University centennial, 1968

—Rolf Swensen

1269

LANE COUNTY MUSEUM
740 West Thirteenth Avenue
Eugene, Oregon 97402

W. F. Goodwin Thacher (author and scriptwriter for Oregon Trail pageants), 30 linear cm. of papers, 1926–50, including correspondence about pageant music

Jane Scotford Thacher (1885–1978, concert pianist, head of piano department at the University of Oregon, and wife of W. F. Goodwin Thacher), 12 linear cm. of papers, including clippings, reviews, scores, and photographs; also an oil painting of her in concert gown, along with 2 of her gowns, and 2 recordings of her playing the piano

Oregon state-song competition, 1924, 10 ms works by area composers.

Hymnals of various denominations, 12 items, 1850–80

Sheet music, 500 popular works for voice or piano, including some by local composers, 1840–1930

—Ed Nolan

1270

UNIVERSITY OF OREGON   OrU
Eugene, Oregon 97403

General Collections

Sheet music, 200,000 items, including materials from the collections of Evelyn Calbreath, Lucile Cummins, Leonard Friendly, and Oscar Hoch. See Edmund F. Soule, "Tutta la forza imaginevole," in the Library's *Call Number*, 28 (Spring 1967), 4–20

Music of Oregon composers, including published editions and ms photocopies of works by Francis W. Bittner, Carlton C. Buck, Edmund A. Cykler, Milton Dieterick, Sister M. Teresine Fouder, L. Stanley Glarum, Homer Keller, June Caldwell Kirlin, Edmund F. Soule, Robert H. Stolze, S. Clarence Trued, and Jean Elizabeth Williams (1876–1965). See the 254 items listed in Edmund F. Soule, "Contemporary Oregon Composers: A List of Works" (typescript, 1976)

Department of Special Collections

Frank J. R. Adams (1883–1963), lyrics and texts of his musical comedies, 1908–55

William Alderson, recordings of Karl Hutchinson (fiddler) and Mrs. Don Slocum (ballad singer)

Henry J. Beau (performer in dance bands, 1930s, later an arranger), 1100 stock arrangements, organized by song title, with an inventory

DeWitt C. Burton, documents relating to the Portland Civic Orchestra Association, 1940–

Harry Carroll (1892–1962), ms and published music, autobiography, and correspondence with ASCAP, 1 box, with an inventory

DeMoss Concert Entertainers, of DeMoss Springs, Ore., archival records, 1872–1932, 1.5 linear meters, including journals, engagement books, contracts, correspondence, ms and printed music, handbills, and memorabilia

Leonard Friendly, personal papers, including 2 music mss, miscellaneous correspondence, and a set of his Hammond Organ Stylings

Robert Winslow Gordon (1881–1961, English professor, folklorist, and founder of the Archive of American Folk Song in the Library of Congress), personal papers, 1909–34, 2 linear meters, including transcripts from published sources, notes on private collections and on special subjects and specific titles, course notes from his studies at Harvard University, and documents relating to the case of *Victor* v. *George*, involving copyright of the song "Wreck of the Old 97." See the typescript inventory, also the index to the collection maintained in the University's Department of English

Hans Ewald Heller (1894–1966, composer and critic), 45 mss and various published editions of his works, also tape recordings

Hoch family papers, ca. 1910–45, including dance-band arrangements, family memorabilia, and papers of the Multnomah School of Music, Portland

Alexander Hull (1887–1953), 1 linear meter of personal papers, including holograph music mss in 1 notebook, personal correspondence, and published literary material

Stoddard King, personal papers, including the holograph ms of "There's a Long, Long Trail A-Winding," correspondence with Vachel Lindsay, and other documents

Alexander Merovich (1895–1965, impresario), mss of original piano music, and correspondence with musicians; also sketches of Samuel Barber's Cello Concerto op. 23

Ernest Loring ("Red") Nichols (1906–50), personal papers, 1935–60, 3000 items, in 66 boxes, including performance materials for his band, with an inventory

Lowell Patton (1893–1961, organist of the First Presbyterian Church, Hempstead, N.Y.), ms and published music, personal papers, and memorabilia

Avery Robinson (1878–1965, composer and treasurer of the Royal Philharmonic Society, London), 59 holograph music mss, and published editions of his music; correspondence with his daughter, Charley Dawson, and with his music publishers, in all 132 items; and 2 notebooks with ms transcriptions of black hymns, collected by Mildred J. Hill of Louisville and Vagabondia, Ky., ca. 1893

Gustav M. Schuster (1896–1939), 3 scrapbooks relating to music and musicians in Salt Lake City and in Portland; also music mss and clippings in 1 box

George Steiner (1900–1967, composer and performer for Paramount Studios, New York), music mss, 1914–64, including original works, and mood and background music for radio, films, and other media, in all 1.8 linear meters

Henry R. Stern (1874–1966), professional papers, 1906–67, including business correspondence of Joseph W. Stern & Co., involving composers and lyricists, other music publishers, and ASCAP; also music, in ms and published editions, including some of his own works under the pseudonym of S. R. Henry, in all 1.5 linear meters

Axel Stordahl (1913–63, trumpeter for the Bert Block and Tommy Dorsey orchestras, and composer for the "Hit Parade" and for Frank Sinatra), scores and arrangements, mostly vocal with orchestra, many for specific performers, in all 1500 items covering 43 linear meters, with an inventory

Harriet Lucia Ward (1898–1968, music educator and composer), 1 box of ms music for string instruments and ensembles, and other memorabilia, 1928–42

—Edmund F. Soule

Randall V. Mills Memorial Archive of Northwest Folklore

Oregon folksongs, 200 taped field recordings

—Barre Toelken

1271
PACIFIC UNIVERSITY   OrFP
Music Library, School of Music
Forest Grove, Oregon 97116

Hymnals, 10 items, ca. 1915–40; also 10 popular songbooks, ca. 1895–1930, and 3 school songbooks, ca. 1900

Sheet music, ca. 1826–1976, 275 items, mostly by Stephen Foster

Recordings, including 150 78-rpm discs

—Norma M. Cooper

1272
JACKSONVILLE MUSEUM   OrJM
Southern Oregon Historical Society
Box 480
Jacksonville, Oregon 97530

Fred Alton Haight, 4 sheet-music items, ca. 1915–30; a diary, "One Year in the Book of Life," 1915–20; and a press clipping including a line drawing of him

Silver Cornet Band, 3 linear cm. of clippings, photographs, and notes about performances, 1860s–1920s

Manuscript music by unidentified composers, 1 linear meter, ca. 1860–1900, comprising copies or arrangements for piano or band

Printed band and orchestra parts used by local groups, including the Silver Cornet Band, 30 linear cm., ca. 1880–1920

Hymnals, mostly Methodist or Presbyterian, 1860s–1900s, 1 linear meter, including 5 ms vols.

Popular songbooks, 1 linear meter, 1880s–1920s, and 4000 items of popular sheet music, 1890s–1930s

Programs of the Andrews Opera Company in Medford, Ore., Chautauqua events, Sousa's band, and school and community concerts in the Jacksonville area, in all 30 linear cm., ca. 1850–

Music catalogues, 35 items, ca. 1880–1910, including some from wholesale distributors in San Francisco and Portland

Photographs, 80 items, ca. 1860–1930, including many of string-instrument performers

Recordings, including 55 Edison and Columbia cylinders of popular music, ca. 1910–20, 125 78-rpm discs and 45 piano rolls

—Richard H. Engeman

1273

LIBRARY ASSOCIATION
OF PORTLAND   OrP

Tenth Street at Yamhill
Portland, Oregon 97205

Papers of 6 local music organizations, including minutes and programs, ca. 1890–
Programs of local and visiting performers, including the Portland Symphony Orchestra (now the Oregon Symphony Orchestra), scrapbooks, ca. 1890– ; and 50 framed photographs of visiting performers, 1920s–40s, donated by the Concert Bureau manager
Classical and popular sheet music, 18,000 items; also songbooks and other published music

—Barbara J. Kern

1274

OREGON HISTORICAL SOCIETY   OrHi

1230 Southwest Park Avenue
Portland, Oregon 97205

Music mss, including Mary Evelene Calbreath, holograph of the Sonata for Violin and Piano in B Minor, also diaries, 1900–1902, programs, and press clippings; Frederick W. Goodrich (1867–1942, Portland composer and organist), 55 scores and arrangements used in local churches, ca. 1895–1930; Frederick Keil, singing book, mostly in German, 1868–71, used at the Aurora Colony; and Leland Smith, ms of "Stardust," ca. 1900
Personal papers of musicians, including Carl Denton (conductor of the Portland Symphony Orchestra, 1919–25), 71 items, including correspondence, papers, and constitution and by-laws of the Orchestra; Mabel Bourne Thompson Dodge, correspondence, 1916–46, also programs and other documents of the Harney County Sagebrush Orchestra and the Portland Junior Symphony Orchestra; John Stark Evans (organist and choirmaster of the First Presbyterian Church, Portland, and music administrator at Lewis and Clark College, later at the University of Oregon), personal papers, 1918–58, 1 box; Herman Kenin (1901–70, president of the American Federation of Musicians), correspondence, writings, and press clippings, 21 items, 1935–70; Harriet (Tibbetts) Kennedy, 31 songs and song texts; Clarence Olmstead, 2 boxes of correspondence, music scores, poems, and plays, 1929–69; Lois Steers (theatrical manager of the Portland firm, Steers & Coman), memorabilia, 1908–45, including correspondence, press clippings, autographed musical portraits, and a scrapbook of the 1933–34 theatrical season; Mae Ross Walker (1876–1970, Portland musician and teacher), 132-page autobiography; Julius Walter (1903–71, musician with the KOIN radio staff orchestra), scrapbooks, 1924–28, press clippings and other papers relating to stations KGW and KOIN, ca. 1930–62, scrapbooks of the Young Oregonians Accordion Club, 1935–36, photographs, and other papers; Harold A. Webber (d. 1934, Portland children's-orchestra leader), correspondence, press clippings, programs, music, account books, and other papers relating to Webber's Juvenile Orchestra, Webber's Melodyphiends, Webber's Juvenile Wranglers, and the Webber Academy of Music, in 3 boxes
Organizational archives, including the Apollo Club of Portland (men's singing group), program book and songbooks, 1909–14, 4 vols.; Oregon Music Teachers' Association, records and scrapbooks, 1915– , including minutes, membership information, reports, press clippings, and programs; Portland Philharmonic Society, journal and ledger, 1866–67, maintained by Edward Quackenbush, also concerned with the management of Oro Fino Hall; Society of Oregon Composers, correspondence, music scores, lists, programs, and ephemera, 1925–35, 1 box; music and programs of the Albany Conservatory of Music, ca. 1890, in the Brown–Clawson–Parvin family papers; programs of the Portland Flute Club, 1921–26, in the papers of John C. Abbett; and records of the Silverton Trombone Band and the Silverton Marine Band, 1877–1911, in the papers of James M. Brown
Additional references to music at the Aurora Colony, 1850s–80s, including a scrapbook of S. A. Clarke, mentioned in Deborah M. Olson and Clark M. Will, "Musical Heritage of the Aurora Colony," *Oregon Historical Quarterly*, 79 (1978), 232–67
Local music-history studies, including Robert Hirtzel, "A History of Music in Vancouver, Washington," 48-page typescript, 1948; Loisevelyn Scifers, "History of Music in Oregon," 15-page typescript, ca. 1940; Judy Cerveto, "Music in Portland before 1920," 48-page term paper, 1966; Linda Besant, "Opportunities for Higher Music Education in Oregon before 1900," 31-page term paper, 1968; and minutes and letters of the Music History Resources Committee of Portland, 1966–68, by Arthur C. Spencer (secretary)
Musical materials of various provenance, 10 linear meters, including programs, announcements, and other documents, gathered under the categories of histories and directories; schools and institutions, including their recitals; festivals, including religious, fraternal, ethnic, and other events; bands, orchestras, choral groups, and other ensembles, 2.5 linear meters, mostly programs; musicians; general sheet music, 3200 items arranged by title; songbooks, hymnals, and other music books, arranged by title, 2 linear meters; sheet music for specific instruments, arranged by instruments, 700 items; materials relating to musical instruments, 2.2 linear meters; and information on booking agents
Miscellaneous music documents in an Americana file

—Cathy de Lorge

1275

CROOK COUNTY HISTORICAL SOCIETY

246 North Main Street
Prineville, Oregon 97754

Children's operetta, 1904; also the first violin part for *White's Home Circle Orchestra*, 1887
Hymnals, 7 items, 1845–1909, and 1 popular songbook, 1921
Sheet music, 7 items, 1896–1917, and 2 for piano by Warren Glaze (local composer), ca. 1940
Recordings, including 50 Edison cylinders and 50 78-rpm discs

—Irene Helms

1276
Frances JURIS
330 West First Street
Prineville, Oregon 97754

Tillman Glaze, ms music for violin in a bound copybook, ca. 1874; and his son, Warren Glaze (1880–1972, band director), 4 notebooks of ms music for banjo or violin, ca. 1900–1930, published music for piano, and clippings; also photographs of both men

1277
OREGON STATE LIBRARY   Or
State Library Building
Summer and Court Streets
Salem, Oregon 97310

Eugene Bruce Knowleton (1875–1940), 3.5 linear meters of papers, including original ms and published compositions and choral or instrumental arrangements; also clippings, programs, and libretti
Sheet music, 300 items, including mss by Oregon composers, ca. 1859–
Songbooks and hymnals, 7 linear meters, about half by Oregon composers

—Candy Morgan, J. Glenn Hartwell

1278
TILLAMOOK COUNTY PIONEER MUSEUM
2106 Second Street
Tillamook, Oregon 97141

Monday Musical Club, 2.5 linear meters of papers, including programs
Hymnals and popular songbooks, 100 items
Sheet music, 6 portfolios
Music catalogues, 2 items
Photographs of early bands in the county, ca. 1900–1920
Recordings, including Edison metal discs and wooden piano rolls

—M. Wayne Jensen

In addition to the repositories listed above, the following have also reported holdings of the materials indicated:

Albany—E. R. Trout: sheet music, songbooks, other printed music
Ashland—Southern Oregon College, Library: songbooks, programs, recordings
Baker—Baker County Library: sheet music, songbooks
Brookings—Chetco Community Library: recordings
Clackamas—Oregon National Guard Military Museum and Resource Center: songbooks, pictures
Coquille—Coquille Public Library: songbooks
Corvallis—Corvallis Public Library: recordings
Eugene—Eugene Bible College, Library: songbooks
Eugene—Eugene Public Library: songbooks, catalogues
Eugene—Northwest Christian College, Library: songbooks
Glenwood—Oregon Electric Railway Historical Society: recordings
Hillsboro—Hillsboro Public Library: songbooks
Hillsboro—Washington County Historical and Pioneer Museum: sheet music, songbooks, programs
Joseph—Wallowa County Museum: sheet music, songbooks, programs, pictures, recordings, miscellaneous
Klamath Falls—Klamath County Museum: sheet music, recordings
Lakeview—Lake County Library: songbooks
Lakeview—Schminck Memorial Museum: songbooks, catalogues, recordings
Marylhurst—Marylhurst College, Shoen Library: sheet music, songbooks, other printed music, programs
Newberg—George Fox College, Shambaugh Library: sheet music, songbooks, other printed music, recordings
Newport—Lincoln County Historical Society: sheet music, songbooks
Pendleton—Umatilla County Library: songbooks, programs, miscellaneous
Portland—Concordia College, Library: sheet music, songbooks, other printed music
Portland—Georgia–Pacific Historical Museum: recordings, miscellaneous
Portland—Multnomah School of the Bible, Library: songbooks
Portland—Western Evangelical Seminary, G. Hallauer Memorial Library: songbooks, programs, recordings, miscellaneous
St. Helens—St. Helens Public Library: songbooks
Salem—Western Baptist Bible College, Library: songbooks, other printed music, recordings

Pennsylvania

1279
ALLENTOWN BAND
Box 1142
Allentown, Pennsylvania 18102

Archival materials of the oldest surviving concert band in the U.S., 1828– , including performance materials, official records, programs, photographs, and memorabilia. See the "Abridged History" in the sesquicentennial anniversary concert program, 30 June 1978, and elsewhere

—Henry J. Crespi

1280
LEHIGH COUNTY HISTORICAL SOCIETY   PAtL

Old Court House
Fifth and Hamilton Streets
Allentown, Pennsylvania 18101

Euterpian Society (19th-century choral group), 200 items of papers, also 50 concert programs and 25 photographs

Sheet music, 150 19th-century items, including 1 published in Allentown, 1864

Other published music, including 5 hymnals and songbooks, and 30 vols. of 19th-century classical piano music

—Maureen Stilwell

1281
HARMONY ASSOCIATES

Old Economy Village
Fourteenth and Church Streets
Ambridge, Pennsylvania 15003

Harmony Society papers, 1790–1950, 500,000 items, including 6000 mss, published band and orchestra music, 1880–1905, receipts, accounts, and letters. See Richard D. Wetzel, *Frontier Musicians on the Connoquenessing, Wabash, and Ohio: A History of the Music and Musicians of George Rapp's Harmony Society (1805–1906)* (Athens, Ohio, 1976), pp. 239–85

—Ruth S. Hahn

1282
TIOGA POINT MUSEUM

Box 143
Athens, Pennsylvania 18810

Stephen Collins Foster (1826–64), ms "Tioga Waltz," arranged for 3 flutes, 1841; 100 sheet-music items, ca. 1880s–90s; and songbooks

Other printed music, including songbooks with Foster's music

Photographs of local bands, 45 late 19th-century items

— Loreita M. Jackson

1283
BETHLEHEM STEEL CORPORATION   PBSteel

Charles M. Schwab Memorial Library
Bethlehem, Pennsylvania 18016

Bethlehem Steel Company Band, 1910–25, press clippings and photographs

—Ann Streiff

1284
LEHIGH UNIVERSITY   PBL

Department of Music
Bethlehem, Pennsylvania 18015

Bethlehem Steel Company Band, performance parts and scores of concert and marching music, 1910–25

—Kathryn L. Reichard

1285
MORAVIAN ARCHIVES   PSMCA

41 West Locust Street
Bethlehem, Pennsylvania 18018

The two major repositories of early Moravian music in America are those of the Moravian Music Foundation in Winston-Salem, N.C. (q.v.), and the present collection. In overview, the holdings of the two repositories consist of 14 "church and community" collections, and various "special" collections, located as follows (WS for Winston-Salem, B for Bethlehem):

Church and Community Collections

Bethania (N.C.) congregation	WS
Bethlehem (Pa.) congregation	B
Bethlehem collegium musicum	B
Bethlehem score collection	B
Dover (Ohio) congregation	B
Johannes Herbst score collection	WS
Lancaster (Pa.) congregation	B
Lititz (Pa.) congregation	B
Lititz collegium musicum	B
Nazareth (Pa.) congregation	B
Salem (N.C.) congregation	WS
Salem collegium musicum	WS
Salem "Lovefeast Ode" collection	WS
Watertown (Wis.) congregation	B

Special Collections

In Bethlehem: the Beckel, Detterer, Neisser, and Rau Collections; the music library of the Moravian Female Seminary; and other miscellaneous music and archival holdings

In Winston-Salem: the Erbe, Glen Plantation, Hagen, Kurth, Johanson, Lowens, Symington, and Vardell collections; the Salem ms copybooks, the Peter codex, and the Salem band books; and other miscellaneous music and archival holdings

See the issues of the Moravian Music Foundation's *Bulletin* (Winston-Salem, 1956–). For related holdings in other repositories, see "Moravian music" in the index

While all of the items reported below are owned by and located at the Moravian Archives in Bethlehem, most of them are under the administrative custody of the Moravian Music Foundation, Winston-Salem, N.C. (q.v.). Certain items, however, are under the direct custody of the Moravian Archives in Bethlehem, as noted. Most of these involve musical materials which are an integral part of the general collections of the Moravian Archives, or which are uniquely appropriate to the historic revival in Bethlehem of the Moravian musical tradition. The various card catalogues and projected publications, as noted below, supersede Albert G. Rau and Hans T. David, *Catalogue of Music by American Moravians, 1742–1842* (Bethlehem, 1938), concerned with several of the church collections

Church and Community Collections

The church collections, identified with particular congregations, consist of mss of concerted sacred solo vocal and choral works, with instrumental accompaniment, set to German texts and for Moravian service usage, unless otherwise noted. The community collections, identified with collegium musicum groups, include both instrumental and vocal music, both mss copied by members and published editions acquired from music dealers, mostly in Baltimore, New York, and Philadelphia, as attested by their stamps. The collegium musicum repertories are more likely to contain works by European composers who were not necessarily Moravians

Bethlehem congregation, 1800 works, 600 of them by American composers, copied mostly in Bethlehem, ca. 1765–1885. Entries in the Rau–David *Catalogue* are superseded by a card catalogue, which will serve as the basis of a projected book catalogue by Robert F. Steelman

Philharmonic Society of Bethlehem (1820–ca. 1885, successor to the Bethlehem collegium musicum, 1744–1820), 1000 works, ca. 1765–ca. 1880, including 20 works by American composers, notably the holograph score and parts for Johann Friedrich Peter's 6 string quintets. Also included are 48 printed programs and libretti for 19th-century Bethlehem performances. See Richard D. Claypool, "Archival Collections of the Moravian Music Foundation and Some Notes on the Philharmonic Society of Bethlehem," *Fontes artis musicae*, 23 (1976), 177–90. The present card catalogue will serve as the basis of a projected book catalogue by Claypool

Dover (Ohio) congregation, 175 works, 60 of them by American composers, comprising a gift from the Bethlehem congregation, ca. 1850, augmented by mss copied in Dover, ca. 1845–ca. 1875. The present card catalogue will serve as the basis of a projected book catalogue by Robert F. Steelman

Lancaster congregation, 350 works, 70 of them by American composers, copied ca. 1770–1850, including many 19th-century hymn tunes, some by Johann Christian Bechler and Peter Ricksecker. The parts are mostly vocal; the instrumental parts may never have been present. The present card catalogue will serve as the basis of a projected book catalogue by Robert F. Steelman

Lititz congregation, 1300 titles, copied ca. 1770–1900, 325 of them by American composers, including works by Matthäus Hehl and Bernhard Grube. Many of the mss belonged to Johannes Herbst, who presumably left them when he moved to Salem in 1811; the material thus complements the Johannes Herbst score collection at the Moravian Music Foundation in Winston-Salem, N.C. (q.v.). Entries in the Rau–David *Catalogue* will be superseded by the projected book catalogue by Robert F. Steelman

Lititz collegium musicum (ca. 1765–1815, and its successor, the Philharmonic Society, 1815–ca. 1900), 300 works, ca. 1775–ca. 1880, 25 of them by American composers, including 13 (of the 14) *Parthien* for wind ensemble by David Moritz Michael. See Theodore M. Finney, "The Collegium Musicum at Lititz, Pennsylvania, during the Eighteenth Century," *Papers Read by Members of the American Musicological Society* (Pittsburgh, 1937), pp. 45–55. The present card catalogue will serve as the basis of a projected book catalogue by Richard D. Claypool

Nazareth congregation, 850 titles, copied ca. 1770–1900, including 175 works by American composers. Entries in the Rau–David *Catalogue* are superseded by a card catalogue, which will serve as the basis of a book catalogue by Robert F. Steelman

Watertown (Wis.) congregation, 4 partbooks, 1858–95, including 24 sacred works; also a minute book of the choir, 1875–77, citing other works performed (in custody of the Moravian Archives)

Bethlehem score collection, 52 vols. containing 225 works, 75 of them by American composers, including 41 works by Jeremias Dencke (1725–95). Most are in the hand of Johann Friedrich Peter (d. 1813), and from his personal library. Entries in the Rau–David *Catalogue* are superseded by a card catalogue, which will serve as the basis of a projected book catalogue by Robert F. Steelman

Special Collections

Bethlehem Moravian Female Seminary, music library and collection of programs (in custody of the Moravian Archives). Included are 500 music items, 125 mss and 375 published eds., mostly by 18th- and 19th-century European composers, with some American works, a few of them Moravian; most of the items are songs and piano solos, but some are keyboard parts for chamber music (see the accessions list). The programs, 100 items in 2 boxes, are chiefly of the "Musical Entertainments of the Young Ladies Seminary," ca. 1830–ca. 1900, mostly 1870s, with several of other Bethlehem events

Pauline Detterer (performer with the Bethlehem Bach Choir), 115 sheet-music items in 4 bound vols. mostly 19th-century U.S. popular songs; 2 19th-century Moravian tunebooks; and 1 vol. of English and German songs in ms, ca. 1800 (in custody of the Moravian Archives)

Clarence E. Beckel (1880–1954) Collection, including 25 fragmentary ms books, devoted to songs, band music, and music instruction; 5 printed band part books, incomplete, and 200 loose sheets of band parts; 250 programs, printed and ms, 19th century, almost all for Bethlehem events, others mostly from other Moravian communities; 15 receipts pertaining to the Bethlehem collegium musicum; and 8 programs with 22 clippings pertaining to the Bethlehem Bach Choir, early 20th century

Georg Neisser (1715–83), 39 vols. of ms music, 1740s–84, comprising the earliest extant art music of the renewed Moravian church. The vols. contain mostly vocal music with keyboard accompaniment, largely Moravian hymnology, but also cantatas, arias, chorales, and instrumental pieces as well. See Robert F. Steelman's articles in the Moravian Music Foundation *Bulletin:* "A Cantata Performed in Bethlehem in the 1740s," 20/2 (1975), 2–7; "A Source of Some Early Moravian Chorale Melodies," 21/2 (1976), 7–9; and "The Origin of Gregor's *Art* 337a," 23/1 (1978), 14–16

Programs and libretti, 500 items, mostly printed, for secular and liturgical performances by Bethlehem musical organizations, ca. 1830–ca. 1900 (in custody of the Moravian Archives)

Odes and psalms, 24 boxes of ms and printed sheets, 1739– , mostly 1760–1850, from Bethlehem, Nazareth, Lititz, and Salem, including a few European items (comparable to the collection of Salem "Lovefeast Odes" in the Moravian Music Foundation, Winston-Salem, N.C., q.v.)

Early catalogues of Moravian music ms collections, 7 items, including the holdings of the Philharmonic Society of Bethlehem, 1873, prepared by Rufus A. Grider; the Bethlehem congregation, ca. 1805, copied by Hannah Weber; the Bethlehem congregation, ca. 1849, extended to 1900 in several hands; the Lititz congregation, begun in 1795 by Johannes Herbst and extended to ca. 1860; the Graceham (Md.) congregation, 1831, with 251 items (a collection no longer extant); the Lancaster congregation, 1830; and the Schoeneck (Pa.) congregation, post-1762 (the latter item in custody of the Moravian Archives)

Archives of the Bethlehem collegium musicum and the Philharmonic Society of Bethlehem, 1807–77 (in custody of the Moravian Archives), including account books, 1807–24 and 1869–73; constitutions of 1820, 1858, and 1869; and minutes of meetings, 1858–63 and 1869–74. See Richard D. Claypool, "Sources for the History of the Philharmonic Society of Bethlehem," *Moravian Music Foundation Bulletin*, 19/2 (1974), 6–8

Nazareth collegium musicum, ms notebook, 1796–1845, containing an index to local concerts, from the estate of Frederick B. Hartman (in custody of the Moravian Archives). See Barbara Jo Strauss, "The Concert Life of the Collegium Musicum, Nazareth, 1796–1845," *Moravian Music Foundation Bulletin*, 21/1 (1976), 2–7; also her *Register of Music Performed in Concert, Nazareth, Pennsylvania, from 1796 to 1845: An Annotated Edition of an American Moravian Document* (Thesis, University of Arizona, 1976)

List of choir performances by the Bethlehem and Nazareth church choirs, 1811–85 (incomplete), mss in 2 boxes

Robert Rau (1844–1906), mss on local history, collected mostly from church records and from newspapers, 6 notebooks of which include material on church music, 1742–1895 (in custody of the Moravian Archives)

Trombone Choir of Bethlehem, 150-page scrapbook, ca. 1900–ca. 1940, with pictures, programs, pamphlets, and press clippings relating to this and other local music groups

Miscellaneous vocal and instrumental music, printed and ms, from Bethlehem and Lititz, ca. 1750–ca. 1900, 24 boxes and 150 bound vols. The collection consists mostly of privately-owned vols. for use at Moravian schools or at home, including 7 boxes from the Tietze family. While most of the published material is European, there are U.S. imprints of songs and piano pieces by American Moravian composers, among them Jacob Till, F. F. Hagen, C. A. van Vleck, and Peter Wolle; also 1 box of mss by Massah Warner (1836–1900)

Rufus A. Grider (1817–1900), ms copy of *Historical Notes on Music in Bethlehem*, with notes, programs, and illustrations not in the published edition (Philadelphia, 1873)

—Richard D. Claypool, Robert F. Steelman

1286
BRYN MAWR COLLEGE   PBm
Canady Library
Bryn Mawr, Pennsylvania 19010

Theresa Helburn (1887–1959, theatrical producer), materials from her personal library, including programs, scripts, photographs, and published books relating to *Porgy and Bess* and other musical-theater performances produced by her for the Theatre Guild (in the Rare Book Room)

Printed music, including 30 songbooks, 10 sheet-music items and 20 other items

—John Dooley

1287
DICKINSON COLLEGE   PCarlD
Library
West High Street
Carlisle, Pennsylvania 17013

See Charles C. Sellers and Martha Slotten, *Archives and Manuscript Collections of Dickinson College* (Carlisle, 1972)

Germania Orchestra of Philadelphia, 7 vols. of papers, including a constitution, 1856, membership list, and minutes of meetings, 1857–96

Dickinson College Music Department, papers, including programs and a College songbook

Archives of the Evangelical United Brethren Church, Central Pennsylvania Conference, including 19th- and 20th-century hymnals, and a tuning fork used by Francis Scott Key

—Martha Slotten

1288
U.S. ARMY MILITARY   PCarlMH
HISTORY INSTITUTE
Carlisle Barracks, Pennsylvania 17013

Papers of drummers, buglers, and other bandsmen, 15 collections, including diaries, letters, and memoirs, 1861–

Giuseppe Savoca, ms conductor's score of "27th Infantry March," n.d.

Sheet music, 232 items, and 25 songbooks, some of them formerly at the Ft. Sheridan (Ill.) Museum

Programs of military band concerts; also photographs of military bands, including 20 items of the 181st U.S. Army Band, Ft. Sheridan, ca. 1900–

Recordings, including 1000 items of military songs and marches

Military manuals on bands and instruments

—Laszlo M. Alfoldi

1289
COLUMBIA PUBLIC LIBRARY
24 South Sixth Street
Columbia, Pennsylvania 17512

Chester Wittell, holograph mss of his chamber, piano, and vocal music, as listed in *Chester Wittell, Composer-Pianist* (Lancaster, 1976)

1290

EASTON AREA PUBLIC LIBRARY   PE

Sixth and Church Streets
Easton, Pennsylvania 18042

Sheet music, 3500 items, 1850–1930, mostly owned by
Richard N. M. Snyder (d. 1951, orchestra leader), also
a few items by local composers

—Barbara L. Wiemann

1291

NORTHAMPTON COUNTY
HISTORICAL SOCIETY

101 South Fourth Street
Easton, Pennsylvania 18042

Thomas Coates (local bandmaster), ms compositions for
band, including some for Pomp's Cornet Band; typescript biography, ca. 1920; clippings, including an
obituary; and programs of bands directed by him;
also diaries and programs of other early musicians
Männerchor programs, ca. 1870– ; and programs and
photographs of other local musicians or music
groups, 19th and 20th centuries
Published music, including hymnals and tunebooks, ca.
1840–1940, many in German, and sheet music for
piano, including the "Lehigh Valley Waltz" (ca. 1920)

—Jane S. Moyer

1292

Carl N. SHULL

Department of Music
Elizabethtown College
Elizabethtown, Pennsylvania 17022

Sheet music, 600 piano and vocal items, 1850–1930s;
also 1 bound vol. with Baltimore imprints, ca. 1810
Hymnals, 115 18th- and 19th-century items, including
some published by the Sauer press, Germantown, Pa.
Tunebooks, 150 19th-century items, including Andrew
Law's *Harmonic Companion* (1811)
Research notes, including letters from American composers such as Abram Chasins, Ernst Krenek, Douglas Stuart Moore, Leo Sowerby, Randall Thompson,
and Ernst Toch
Recordings, including 25 cylinders, some by John Philip
Sousa, and also 50 piano rolls

1293

EPHRATA CLOISTER

632 West Main Street
Ephrata, Pennsylvania 17522

Hymnals in ms, including 5 vols. from the 1740s, and 2
vols. ca. 1850 from the community at Snow Hill in
Franklin County, Pa. See Betty Jean Martin, *The
Ephrata Cloister and Its Music: The Cultural, Religious,
and Biographical Background* (Ph.D. diss, University of
Maryland, 1974)

—John L. Kraft

1294

ERIE COUNTY HISTORICAL SOCIETY

417 State Street
Erie, Pennsylvania 16501

Henry Thacker Burleigh (1866–1949), 40 linear cm. of
sheet music, programs, and personal papers

—John Claridge

1295

GETTYSBURG COLLEGE   PGC

Schmucker Memorial Library
Gettysburg, Pennsylvania 17325

Jacob Gundrum (music teacher), 21 mss and 4 published dances for piano, 1871–74
Claire Coci (1912–78), published organ music from her
personal library, with ms markings
Civil War songbooks, 5 items

—David T. Hedrick, J. H. Richards

1296

LUTHERAN THEOLOGICAL SEMINARY   PGL

Abdel Ross Wentz Library
Gettysburg, Pennsylvania 17325

Hymnals and liturgy books issued in the U.S., 260 pre-
1940 items, mostly Lutheran, slightly over half of
them without music. It has not been possible to
establish whether the collection includes the "materials purchased by J. Harter, of Canton, Ohio, for the
use of a committee to prepare a Common Service for
the English Lutheran churches in the U.S.," as mentioned in William Coolidge Lane and Charles
Knowles Benton, *Notes on Special Collections in American Libraries* (Cambridge, Mass., 1892), p. 28

1297

MENNONITE HISTORIANS OF
EASTERN PENNSYLVANIA

Route 1, Box 64
Harleysville, Pennsylvania 19438

Mennonite and Amish hymnals and singing books,
1803– ; also 4 European and American editions of
the Amish *Ausbund* hymnal, 16th to 20th centuries
Sheet music, several German sacred songs used by
Mennonites, mostly 19th century
Manuscript singing books, 4 shape-note items, written
in fraktur letters with illuminations, including original compositions and copies, 18th and 19th centuries
Papers of Vorsängern, including letters and diaries
Recordings, 200 hours of oral-history interviews and
field recordings of Mennonites with Vorsängern,
collected by Isaac Clarence Kulp and Dr. Beauveau
Borie IV, in southeastern Pennsylvania

—Joseph S. Miller

1298

PENNSYLVANIA HISTORICAL AND MUSEUM COMMISSION　　PHarH

William Penn Memorial Museum Building
Box 1026
Harrisburg, Pennsylvania 17120

Henry Thacker Burleigh (1895–1925), 18 items of papers, including mss of his "Deep River," "Go Down, Moses," and "Little Mother of Mine," a published collection of Negro spirituals (1917), photographs, and a biography by Melville Charlton
Will George Butler, 86 items of papers, 1917–32, including 8 ms works, a published composition conducted by John Philip Sousa, 5 photographs, and 6 press clippings
Charles Wakefield Cadman, 18 items of papers, 1906–40, including mss of "Before the Dawn" from *Thunderbird Suite*, "The Passing of the Nuwana," the opera *Shanewis*, and other compositions, also letters, and 3 photographs
John F. Duss (1894–1924), 11 items of popular vocal sheet music, 1894–1924
A. F. Hogan Collection, including a published opera (1901), 1 sheet-music item, and 4 photographs
Lois Miller, song, "The Rolling Hills of Pennsylvania" (1939)
Ethelbert Nevin (1862–1901), published polka (photocopy), 9 items of vocal sheet music, and a published biography
George Balch Nevin (1859–1933), 6 published sheet-music items, 2 letters, portraits, and an agreement with the Oliver Ditson Co., 1880–1920

—John E. Shelly

1299

STATE LIBRARY OF PENNSYLVANIA　　P

Rare Books Section
Box 1601
Harrisburg, Pennsylvania 17126

For holdings of early published works, see the Library's *Pennsylvania Imprints, 1689–1789* (Harrisburg, 1972)

Songbooks and hymnals, 170 items, mostly pre-1850 Pennsylvania imprints in English or German, also shape-note books and secular anthologies, including slave-song books
Broadsides of hymn and song texts, including several Ephrata imprints, 1768–84, and 4 William Gross imprints, Fountainville, Pa., ca. 1850
Hymnals in ms, 7 items, including 3 from the Ephrata community, 1740s, 1 from the Snow Hill settlement, dated 1844, and others of the mid 18th century, among them 2 by Balzer Hoffman
Caroli Anthoni Heine, *Unterricht im Klavier Spielen, für junge Anfänger geschrieben*, ms instruction book, dated 1788
Sheet music, including 2 guitar anthologies, Philadelphia, 1824–29; 1 bound vol. of songs, ca. 1850; and 1 bound vol. of Confederate imprints
Minstrel shows, 17 vols., 1920s, some with musical notation

—Barbara E. Deibler

1300

BIBLICAL THEOLOGICAL SEMINARY　　PHatfB

200 North Main Street
Hatfield, Pennsylvania 19440

Hymnals and sacred songbooks, 250 items representing various denominations, 1900–1950; 102 miscellaneous pre-1940 hymnals collected by Runyon G. Ernst: and 100 books about musicians and hymnology, 1900–1950

—James Pakala

1301

HAVERFORD COLLEGE　　PHC

Library
Haverford, Pennsylvania 19041

Collection of autograph letters, including items of David Bispham, Henry Cowell, Fred W. N. Crouch, Walter Damrosch, Francis Darley, Eugene Ormandy, John Howard Payne, Walter Piston, Leopold Stokowski, and Randall Thompson
Sir Francis Joseph Campbell (musician and teacher of the blind), correspondence relating to the Perkins School for the Blind

1302

JUNIATA COLLEGE　　PHuJ

L. A. Beeghly Library
Eighteenth and Moore Streets
Huntingdon, Pennsylvania 16652

Hymnals, 100 items, including Ephrata and Germantown imprints, 1739–62; ms tunebooks, including 1 by Johann Conrad Beissel; and Brethren Church hymnals, some printed in Huntingdon, 1877
Tunebooks used by 19th-century singing societies and schools, including some Pennsylvania imprints

—Katherine Rockwell

1303

HISTORICAL AND GENEALOGICAL SOCIETY OF INDIANA COUNTY

Sixth Street and Wayne Avenue
Indiana, Pennsylvania 15701

John McCormack, several music mss
Popular sheet music, 300 items
Photographs of local bands

—Richard Buskert

1304

INDIANA UNIVERSITY　　PInU

Cogswell Music Library
Indiana, Pennsylvania 15701

Sheet music, 5 boxes of published items; also 20 songbooks, and 3 boxes of other published music
Music mss, several scores
Recordings, including 1.5 linear meters of 78-rpm discs

—Suzanne T. Perlongo

1305
Bayard TAYLOR MEMORIAL LIBRARY

East State Street
Kennett Square, Pennsylvania 19348

Bayard Taylor (1825–78), holograph music mss of 5 songs with texts by Taylor (the music may be his as well; they may have been written for Jenny Lind), also 15 printed copies of the songs

—Joseph A. Lordi

1306
EVANGELICAL AND REFORMED   (PLT)
HISTORICAL SOCIETY

Lancaster Theological Seminary
555 West James Street
Lancaster, Pennsylvania 17603

Hymnals, 400 items, mostly in German

—George H. Bricker

1307
FRANKLIN AND MARSHALL COLLEGE   PLF

Fackenthal Library
College Avenue
Lancaster, Pennsylvania 17604

German-American imprints collection of 3375 books, including 120 hymnals in German, published in Pennsylvania, 1747–1900

—Renate Sachse

1308
LANCASTER COUNTY HISTORICAL   PLHi
SOCIETY

230 North President Avenue
Lancaster, Pennsylvania 17603

Chester Wittell, holograph mss of his musical works, 200 items, also 110 ms transcriptions and arrangements, as listed in *Chester Wittell, Composer-Pianist* (Lancaster, 1976)
Sheet music, 300 items, including S. Becker von Grabill, *Het Klaverack*
Songbooks, 25 19th-century items, including books by John P. McCaskey
Fulton Opera House, complete run of printed programs, 1894–1913, in bound vols. See Tyler L. Greiner, *A History of Professional Entertainment at the Fulton Opera House in Lancaster, Pennsylvania, 1852–1930* (Master's thesis, Pennsylvania State University, 1977)

—John Ward Willson Loose

1309
LANCASTER MENNONITE   PLMHi
CONFERENCE

Historical Society Library
2215 Millstream Road
Lancaster, Pennsylvania 17602

Manuscript Mennonite songs in German script, mid 18th century, 10 linear cm.
Hymnals and sacred songbooks, 1720– , 55 linear meters, including some facsimiles and European imprints, and incorporating 2000 vols. from the collection of Wilmer D. Swope, Leetonia, Ohio

—Carolyn Charles

1310
PENNSYLVANIA FEDERATION
OF MUSIC CLUBS

c/o Mrs. Robert E. Humphreville
160 North School Lane
Lancaster, Pennsylvania 17603

Papers of the Pennsylvania Federation of Music Clubs, from its founding in 1916 to the present, including scrapbooks, minutes of meetings, committee-chairmen's reports, programs of regional and state conventions, treasurer's records, copies of the state publication, the *News Sheet*, and other materials; in storage, available by permission

1311
PHILADELPHIA COLLEGE OF BIBLE   PPPSB

Scofield–Hill Memorial Library
Langhorne Manor, Pennsylvania 19047

Hymnals, 1000 19th-century American items, including duplicates formerly owned by the Free Library of Philadelphia

1312
SAINT VINCENT COLLEGE AND   PLatS
ARCHABBEY

Latrobe, Pennsylvania 15650

Wimmer Music Collection, 2500 items, many of them mss, 1750–1900, acquired or performed by the monks during the early days of the monastery. One-third of the materials are sacred; two-thirds are secular, including 538 keyboard items, 219 solo instrumental items, 125 string quartets, and 177 instrumental ensemble works. Many are listed in Joseph Maurice Schwab's ms catalogue of music holdings at the Archabbey, ca. 1860; see also F. J. Moleck, *Nineteenth Century Musical Activity at St. Vincent Archabbey, Latrobe, Pennsylvania* (Ph.D. diss., University of Pittsburgh, 1970)

—F. J. Moleck

1313
BUCKNELL UNIVERSITY   PLeB

Ellen Clarke Bertrand Library
Lewisburg, Pennsylvania 17837

Ignace Jan Paderewski, autograph ms music sketch, inscribed to Mrs. D. Hill, in a scrapbook of 1907 (in the David J. Hill collection)
Printed music, 20 items, ca. 1818–1922, including 15 songbooks and hymnals

—George M. Jenks

1314

LINCOLN UNIVERSITY PLuL

Langston Hughes Memorial Library
Lincoln University, Pennsylvania 19352

Langston Hughes (1902–67), personal library, 3300 items

1315

LINDEN HALL

Lititz, Pennsylvania 17543

The collection consists mostly of music used at the Linden Hall girls' school. See the typed guide to music books at Linden Hall (1973), and the 8-page access list

Manuscript music, including 6 piano-music notebooks of Eliza Ewing Jacobs (Mrs. E. E. Haldeman), of Colebrook, Pa., 1800–1802; a music notebook of Hanna Matlack, 1810; 1 vol. of piano-music copies, dated "Litiz Seminary, 1837"; 8 copies of instrumental scores and parts, ca. 1860–1900; and 3 copies of 4- to 8-hand piano music, ca. 1865
Sheet music, ca. 1800–1930, mostly for piano, 86 separate items and 5 bound vols., 2 of them collected by Eliza Jacobs, ca. 1802–28
Other printed music, including 3 hymnals, 1803–25; instrumental and vocal music, 22 items including some fragments, ca. 1820–1912; 2 keyboard instruction books, 1839–53; choral-music scores and songbooks, 20 items published 1850–1952; 1 secular songbook, 1878; and 11 secular songbooks from the personal collection of Jean Whitney, 1904–23
Eliza Jacobs, letterbook, 1802, transcribed in typescript copies

—Joan A. Fyock

1316

LITITZ MORAVIAN CHURCH

Church Square
Lititz, Pennsylvania 17543

Hymnals, 100 items used at the Church, or used in Germany by persons who later emigrated to Lititz, ca. 1720–1930
Abraham R. Beck, several mss including the holograph "Just as I Am," and miscellaneous material about his life; also several ms compositions by other Moravian composers
Programs of musical events at the Church, including oratorio presentations and love-feasts, ca. 1820– ; also photographs with musical subjects, including early orchestras and the Moravian trombone choir

—Byron K. Horne

1317

MANSFIELD STATE COLLEGE PManM

Mansfield, Pennsylvania 16933

Music Library

Printed music, including 200 popular sheet-music items, 1920s–30s; 7 sacred songbooks, 1843–91, and 102 vols. of popular songs, 1920s–30s; and 20 hymnals of various denominations, 1843–1972
Benjamin Husted (Mansfield State College professor), ms op. 10, 1920
Programs of College concerts and musicals, a complete run, 1920s–
Recordings, including 700 78-rpm discs, mostly jazz

Archives

Will George Butler (b. 1876), 2.5 linear meters of letters, mss, programs, Chautauqua tour contracts, sheet music, catalogues, pictures, poems (later set to music), and sketches for later compositions; also miscellaneous materials relating to Elbert Hubbard (1856–1915) and an oil painting of Ole Bull by Butler, 1920s

—Pauline Borodkin, Robert W. Unger

1318

JUANITA COUNTY HISTORICAL SOCIETY

Star Route
Mifflintown, Pennsylvania 17059

James Patterson (saddler), accounts ledger including ms clarinet music, ca. 1830
Programs for local concerts and recitals, 5 items, mid to late 19th century

—David A. Shellenberger

1319

MILLERSVILLE STATE COLLEGE PMilS

Ganser Library
Millersville, Pennsylvania 17551

Songbooks, 50 items used in local schools, including some by local composers, 1875–1920
Programs for College concerts, 100 items, 1930s– ; also photographs of College choirs, bands, and other musical performers, 35 items, ca. 1915–30s
Pennsylvania History and German-American Collection, including 50 books on music at Ephrata, Bethlehem, and Philadelphia; also miscellaneous hymnals from local congregations

—Robert E. Coley

1320

Karl MOYER

Music Department
Millersville State College
Millersville, Pennsylvania 17551

Hymnals, 40 German Lutheran and German Reformed items, mid 19th century
Songbooks, 12 items used by a secular singing society in Lititz, Pa., mid 19th century

1321

Robert S. WILSON

204 West Franklin Street
Myerstown, Pennsylvania 17067

Hymnals, 200 items, mostly 1890– ; also 3 file drawers of press clippings and other materials on particular hymns

1322
C. F. MARTIN ORGANIZATION
Box 329
Nazareth, Pennsylvania 18064

Archives of the Organization, containing catalogues, sales records, production records, photographs, and publicity materials of the guitar manufacturer and music shop in New York City, 1833–39, and in Nazareth, 1839– . See Mike Longworth, *Martin Guitars: A History* (Cedar Knolls, N.J., 1975)

—Mike Longworth

1323
MORAVIAN HISTORICAL SOCIETY   PNazMHi
Whitefield House
214 East Center Street
Nazareth, Pennsylvania 18064

Printed and ms music, 26 items, mostly sacred vocal and keyboard anthologies, 1800–1880, including European imprints; 2 U.S. publications by T. R. Weber; ms score of Francis Florentine Hagen (1815–1907), Overture in F Major; Peter Ricksecker (1791–1873), ms accordion book, said to have been used by him to teach blacks in the West Indies; ms copy from the Kühnel (Leipzig) edition of Antonio Bagatello's treatise on constructing string instruments, in the translation by J. O. H. Schaum; and 2 printed programs of the Philharmonic Society of Bethlehem, 1850–54

—Richard D. Claypool

1324
AMERICAN CATHOLIC HISTORICAL SOCIETY   PPACHi
Saint Charles Borromeo Seminary
Overbrook, Pennsylvania 19151

Filippo Trisobio, published sheet music, Philadelphia, 1790s, 22 items, most of them reportedly unique; also other Philadelphia imprints, ca. 1800. See Jane Campbell, "Notes on a Few Old Catholic Hymn Books," *American Catholic Historical Society Records*, 31 (1920), 129–43; also other articles in this journal by Hugh T. Henry, 26 (1915), 208–23, 311–27; 27 (1916), 296–99; and 28 (1917), 189–96

1325
SCHWENCKFELDER HISTORICAL LIBRARY   PPeSchw
1 Seminary Avenue
Pennsburg, Pennsylvania 18073

Mennonite and Schwenckfelder hymnals, 60 early 19th-century mss; also 1 vol. each by Christopher Hoffman (1727–1804), Christopher Kriebel (1724–1800), Abraham Wagner (1715–63), and Georg Weiss (1689–1740)
John Krauss (1770–1819, organ builder), 1 vol. of ms notes and plans for organ construction
Songbooks and printed hymnals, 35 vols., early 1800s–1850

Photographs of local bands, 10 items, 1910s
Programs of local church concerts, 20 19th-century items; also 1 program of the installation of a church organ in Philadelphia, 1790

—Dennis K. Moyer

1326
Otto E. ALBRECHT
463 West Ellet Street
Philadelphia, Pennsylvania 19119

Personal papers, including correspondence and research notes on Philadelphia music and on music holdings in American libraries, notably composers' mss and pre-1800 materials; also 3500 opera and concert programs

1327
AMERICAN PHILOSOPHICAL SOCIETY   PPAmP
105 South Fifth Street
Philadelphia, Pennsylvania 19106

The institution was established by Benjamin Franklin, and includes archives of the Society and a library relating to its own history and research activity. Items listed below are partly noted in Whitfield J. Bell and Murphy D. Smith, *Guide to the Archives and Manuscript Collection of the American Philosophical Society* (Philadelphia, 1966; hereinafter cited as *Guide*), in the Society's annual *Proceedings* (hereinafter cited as *Proc.*), and in the *Catalog of Books in the . . . Library* (Westport, Conn., 1970; hereinafter cited as *Catalog*)

Philadelphia Assembly (dancing association), expense book, 1748–49, maintained by John Swift (*Guide*, 583; *Proc.*, 41 [1902], 260)
Brillon mss, 26 instrumental and vocal pieces, in 3 unbound "volumes," mostly works by Mme Anne Louise Boyvin d'Hardancourt Brillon de Jouy (1744–1824, Parisian hostess and friend of Benjamin Franklin) (*Guide*, 160; *Proc.*, 100 [1956], 331)
Musical materials relating to Benjamin Franklin (*Catalog*, vol. 11, pp. 205, 282–83)
Peale's Museum, account book, 1785–95, maintained by Charles Willson Peale, and including a few itemizations "for Musick" (*Guide*, 529)
Franklin Peale (1795–1870), ms music book copied mostly by him or by his wife, 1822–23, containing songs for guitar and piano in 1 vol., and works for solo guitar in a second vol. (*Guide*, 536; *Proc.*, 11 [1870], 597–604)
Robert Maskell Patterson (1787–1854, professor of natural philosophy at the University of Pennsylvania), miscellaneous notes and papers on various topics, including music (*Guide*, 520; *Proc.*, 6 [1854], 60–64)
Samuel Rush (1795–1859, lawyer, and son of Benjamin Rush), notebook, 1859, with short and "generally splenetic" essays on subjects including songs and public singers ("the mountebanks of the voice") (*Guide*, 629)
William F. G. Swann (1884–1962, physicist and researcher in the Franklin Institute), personal papers, ca. 1900–1962, including correspondence relating to his activity as a cellist in and conductor of the Swarthmore Symphony Orchestra; also articles on subjects including music (*Guide*, 719)

John Frederick Lewis (1860–1932, lawyer), personal papers, involving his activity as a music patron (*Guide*, 408)

Sheet music, 9 items, ca. 1800, in the Elizabeth F. Dawes collection (*Guide*, 221)

Funeral marches written on the death of Elisha Kent Kane

Other sheet music, some from the early 19th century, also books about music and instruction books, in all 250 items (*Catalog*, vol. 19, pp. 767–77, also vol. 24, pp. 682–84)

American Indian folksong and dance materials, based on research sponsored by the Society. See John F. Freeman, *A Guide to Manuscripts Relating to the American Indian in the Library of the American Philosophical Society*, A.P.S. Memoirs, vol. 65 (Philadelphia, 1966); suppl. ed. by Daythal L. Kendall (forthcoming). Among the citations in the Bell & Smith *Guide* are Franz Boas (*Guide*, 101); Charles Marius Barbeau, Robert A. Black, Gertrude Kurath, and Joel Maring (*Guide*, 102); Barbeau (*Guide*, 169); Jesse Cornplanter (*Guide*, 204); Frederica de Laguna (*Guide*, 225–26); Elsie Clews Parsons (*Guide*, 517); Paul Radin (*Guide*, 615); Helen H. Roberts (*Guide*, 630); and Frank Goldsmith Speck (*Guide*, 709)

1328

AMERICAN SWEDISH HISTORICAL MUSEUM   PPAmSwM

1900 Pattison Avenue
Philadelphia, Pennsylvania 19145

Jenny Lind, 300 letters and other documents, 1840–87, relating to her career and to that of her husband, Otto Goldschmidt

1329

ATHENAEUM OF PHILADELPHIA   PPA

219 South Sixth Street
Philadelphia, Pennsylvania 19106

Sheet music, 15 items for piano, and 2 vols. published in London containing autographed items by G. P. Christy and Stephen Foster

Songbooks, several 19th-century items with political songs, children's songs, and hymns, some vols. containing words only

Playbills (broadsides), 6 items from Philadelphia theaters, 1846–52

Catalogues, 1 item each of Birgfeld & Ramm (Philadelphia piano manufacturers), 1856, and of J. Estey & Co. (Brattleboro, Vt., cottage-organ manufacturers), 1874

—Jean Lenville

1330

BALCH INSTITUTE   PPBI

18 South Seventh Street
Philadelphia, Pennsylvania 19106

Sheet music, 1 linear meter, by or about southern- and eastern-European immigrants, 1920s

—Pat Proschino

1331

CURTIS INSTITUTE OF MUSIC   PPCI

Rittenhouse Square
Philadelphia, Pennsylvania 19103

Archives of the Institute, including 2 linear meters of scrapbooks and clippings, 2.3 linear meters of programs, 1 linear meter of catalogues, a complete run (1929–40) of the Institute's periodical, *Overtones*, and recordings of recitals, 1930s–40s, on 350 78-rpm discs

Mary Louise Curtis Bok Zimbalist (1876–1970), personal papers, including correspondence, photographs, press clippings, and memorabilia

Carlos Salzedo (1885–1961), music for harp, including holograph mss of his compositions and arrangements, 87 items

Anton Torello (1884–1959), music for contrabass, much of it edited by Torello, 56 items. See Gordon Mapes, "Music Manuscripts in the Anton Torello Bequest" (typescript)

William Strasser (1875–1944), holograph mss of his original compositions and sketches, 120 items

Lynnwood Farnam (1885–1930), scrapbooks and other memorabilia, 2 linear meters

Charles H. Jarvis (1837–95, pianist), personal library, strong in 19th-century printed books, 27 linear meters

Holographs and memorabilia of composers associated with the Institute, including George Antheil, Samuel Barber, Sylvan Levin, Gian Carlo Menotti, and Efrem Zimbalist

—Ann Viles

1332

Charlotte CUSHMAN CLUB

Theatre Research Library
239 South Camac Street
Philadelphia, Pennsylvania 19107

Books pertaining to the theater, mostly plays, biographies, and histories; also scripts, programs, posters, photographs, and letters, singly and in scrapbooks, of which a portion—not separated or catalogued, and probably not large—relate to musical theater

—Mrs. Hendrika McElroy

1333

FREE LIBRARY OF PHILADELPHIA   PP

Logan Square
Philadelphia, Pennsylvania 19103

Music Department

See Bernice B. Larrabee, "The Music Department of the Free Library of Philadelphia," *Library Trends*, 8 (1960), 574–86

Manuscript music, mostly uncatalogued, as well as items in the (catalogued) general collection. Major holdings include 4 boxes of anonymous works, and compositions by Amy Cheney (Mrs. H. H. A.) Beach (2 items), Domenico Brescia (37 items), Benjamin Carr (3 items), Michael Hurley Cross (6 items), W. W. Gilchrist (2 drawers), Arthur Hartmann (2 drawers), Charles Hommann (3 items), Frances McCollin (4 drawers), Hermann Parris (2 drawers), and Herbert Tiley (4 boxes)

Printed scores and parts, an extensive collection of American and European scores catalogued along with books in a general collection of 100,000 vols.; chamber-music parts, particularly rich in 20th-century works; and the Hopkinson Collection of 19th-century chamber-music parts, on loan from the Musical Fund Society of Philadelphia

Drinker Library of Choral Music, 700 items in multiple copies, mostly German baroque sacred music with orchestral parts, translated into English by Henry S. Drinker (1880–1965), catalogued

Hymnals, tunebooks, songsters (partly indexed), and school and community songbooks, 400 items, 18th to 20th centuries, including important holdings of works by William Billings, Andrew Law, Isaiah Thomas, and John Wyeth

Civil War broadsides, 200 items

Sheet music, 190,000 items, singly and in 1000 bound vols., 18th century to the present, including songs and instrumental works, and incorporating the major collections assembled by Harry Dichter, Josephine A. McDevitt and Edith A. Wright, and the Musical Fund Society. Vocal music is filed alphabetically by title, instrumental music by composer; indexes are available for the bound vols., for music from shows and films, and for portraits (incomplete). Early Philadelphia music is represented with works by Francis Hopkinson, Raynor Taylor, Benjamin Carr, and Francis Johnson

Edward I. Keffer collection of early American sheet music, mostly ca. 1800–1830, on loan from the Musical Fund Society, 1000 items, catalogued, with an index to lithographers

Organizational papers, including 60 linear cm. of business records of the Metropolitan Opera House in Philadelphia, 1920s–40s, and 1 scrapbook of invoices for Willow Grove band concerts, 1907–23

Jean Sinclair Buchannan papers, containing correspondence with a typescript biography of Arnold Dolmetsch, 1913–60; 1 box of legal papers of Enrico Caruso; business records of Arthur Hartmann and Frances McCollin; and 1 drawer of musicians' letters to Hartmann

Scrapbooks, including 3 items containing programs of C. W. Zeckwer and the Philadelphia Musical Academy, 1891–1922

Programs of 19 major American orchestras, 43 linear meters (catalogued); also miscellaneous programs and announcements of Delaware Valley music performances, 24 drawers (indexed), including programs of the Academy of Music, 1850–1910; programs of Musical Fund Society public performances, 1896–1905, 3 drawers (on loan); 5 scrapbooks of the Philadelphia Civic Opera, 1923–30; and 5 vols. of clippings concerning the Music Project of the Philadelphia Local Works Division of the WPA, 1934–35

Music catalogues, including current music-publishers' and dealers' catalogues, 5 drawers; recording-dealers' and publishers' catalogues, 5 drawers, including 2 drawers of RCA numerical catalogues, 1925–65, 1969; miscellaneous items in the general collection (catalogued), including early 20th-century catalogues of Oliver Ditson and Theodore Presser, and 10 catalogues of piano rolls published by Aeolian, Ampico, Duo-Art, Melodant, Universal, and Welte-Mignon

Pictures of musicans and music subjects, removed from printed sources, in 19 drawers in the press file; also 4 oil portraits of past members of the Musical Fund Society, on loan from the Society

Recordings, including 21,000 78-rpm discs (indexed); deposit copies of the RCA Masterworks series, 1925–52; 6 cartons of 10-inch jazz discs from the Harvey Husten collection; and 18 linear meters of classical and popular albums and discs (unsorted)

Books and periodicals, extensive holdings, including many periodicals and uncatalogued vocal and instrumental tutors, late 19th and early 20th centuries

—Frederick Kent

Edwin A. Fleisher Collection of Orchestral Music

Begun in 1929 with a donation by Mr. Fleisher of over 4000 orchestral compositions, by 1978 the collection contained 13,000 compositions with conductor's scores and instrumental parts, as described in the *Cumulative Catalog, 1929–1977* (Boston, 1979), and 1000 scores without performance parts. For the American items, which include printed works and composers' mss, there is a partial catalogue on cards, divided pre-1861 (100 titles) and 1861– (900 titles). The collection includes 2000 WPA-sponsored ms copies of 20th-century compositions, programs of performances of materials borrowed from the collection, recordings, and 17 file drawers of clippings, reviews, photographs, correspondence, and biographical files on composers. Materials on black bandleaders were used in Arthur Milner, "Live from the Library," *American Libraries*, 8/2 (1977), 75–76. Other specific holdings are cited in the *Music of Chester Edward Ide, 1878–1944* (New York, 1976), and the brochure listing the works of Chester Wittell

—Sam Dennison

Rare Book Room

Pennsylvania German Collection, mostly purchased from Henry S. Borneman in 1955, including 10 music mss of hymns from Ephrata, Pa., 1745–62; 3 music mss from Snow Hill Cloister, Franklin County, Pa., ca. 1830–80; and 40 ms singing-school books, 1 of them (non-German) by Thomas Collins, 1774, the others mostly Mennonite items from Bucks, Lehigh, Northampton, Chester, and Montgomery counties, 1780–1856

Early American children's books, including 30 early 19th-century printed songbooks

—Howell J. Heaney

Theatre Collection

The holdings incorporate and interfile materials from three private collectors: Mark W. Wilson of the Shubert Theatres in Philadelphia (acquired 1951); Paul E. Glase, a Reading, Pa., theater manager (1956); and Lawrence Shubert Lawrence, of the Shubert organization in Philadelphia

Scrapbooks and memorabilia, including the J. Parker Norris collection of 17 scrapbooks on theater in Philadelphia, 1885–1930, programs of the Chestnut Street Theatre, 1803–1910, and programs, posters, and promptbooks of Dumont's Minstrels, 1895–1911; 5 personal scrapbooks of Helen Morgan; 18 scrapbooks of theater and film reviews by Henry T. Murdock for the *Philadelphia Inquirer*, 1926–44; 8

scrapbooks of theater and film reviews by Lewis Devon for the *Philadelphia Evening Ledger*, 1924–42; and 35 scrapbooks of film reviews by Mildred Martin for the *Philadelphia Inquirer*, 1941–61

Biographical files, arranged alphabetically by surname, with information on persons active in theater, film, radio, television, circus, and minstrel productions, containing press clippings, magazine articles, photographs, and publicity releases from television and film studios

Theater production files, with information on musical shows, containing playbills, newspaper and magazine articles and reviews, photographs, and other publicity items arranged alphabetically by title of production. Emphasis is on Philadelphia, but material on out-of-town productions is also collected. Broadsides and programs pre-1900 are arranged chronologically by theater

Philadelphia Theatre Index, listing productions at the major local theaters by title of play, theater, and date, 1855–

Programs and playbills, 7000 items, including minstrel performances (particularly the Carncross & Dixie troupe, 1862–78, and the Dockstader troupe), Philadelphia theaters, 1803– , and other American cities

Motion picture files, with materials from the beginning of the industry to the present, containing newspaper and magazine articles, reviews, programs, posters, and 30,000 film stills, all arranged alphabetically by title of production

—Geraldine Duclow

Print and Picture Department

Portraits of European and American musicians, 18th century to the present, 10,000 photographs, engravings, lithographs, and other forms including some copies, arranged alphabetically

Pictures of music in art, musical instruments, and opera, mostly photographic copies and clippings of European subjects but also including American items, 18th century to the present, 4000 items arranged alphabetically by instrument, title of opera, or country

—Robert F. Looney

1334
GERMAN SOCIETY OF PENNSYLVANIA   PPG

Joseph Horner Memorial Library
611 Spring Garden Street
Philadelphia, Pennsylvania 19123

German hymnals, with or without music, 150 items, 1741– , including 30 imprints of Christopher Saur and other 18th-century local printers

Ephrata ms book, *Paradisisches Wunder-Spiel*, 1766

Harmonie Gesangverein of Philadelphia, miscellaneous materials, including programs and a historical sketch

—Christine E. Richardson

1335
GERMANTOWN HISTORICAL SOCIETY

5208 Germantown Avenue
Philadelphia, Pennsylvania 19144

Early American imprints, 5 items, including 4 18th-century German hymnals printed in Germantown

1336
GRATZ COLLEGE   PPGratz

Abner & Mary Schreiber Jewish Music Library
Tenth Street and Tabor Road
Philadelphia, Pennsylvania 19141

Edward Bernard, holograph music mss, including 60 symphonies, 40 suites for strings, 100 instrumental solos, and other musical works; also theoretical writings, particularly on mirror-fugue form

Eric Mandell Collection of Jewish Music, including sheet music that reflects events in the life of American Jewry, also popular songs from the immigrations, 1890s– ; scores of musical productions in New York Yiddish theater; ms scores for the radio series "Molly Picon," 1920s; Mischa Portnoff, holograph of the Variations on "Hatikva"; printed editions of works by Jewish composers; and files of press clippings on composers and performers. See his "A Collector's Random Notes on Bibliography of Jewish Music," *Fontes artis musicae*, 10 (1963), 34–39; also the guide to the exhibition in the Free Library of Philadelphia, 1947 (mimeographed)

—Shalom Altman

1337
Peter HESBACHER

5533 Pulaski Avenue
Philadelphia, Pennsylvania 19144

Hesbacher Collection for studies of popular music, 42,000 disc recordings, including 2000 pre-1940, comprising a complete collection of single discs on the *Billboard* magazine weekly charts, and other recordings of special interest; filed alphabetically by label or chronologically, and indexed

1338
HISTORICAL SOCIETY OF PENNSYLVANIA   PHi

1300 Locust Street
Philadelphia, Pennsylvania 19107

The collections of the Society are divided between the Library and the Manuscripts Department, each of which has various general and special catalogues, as well as uncatalogued material. Many of the printed books in the Library, particularly those before 1820, are now maintained and serviced by the Library of Company of Philadelphia (q.v.), and accessible through its catalogues. The Manuscripts Department holdings are partially described in the Society's *Guide to the Manuscript Collections* (Philadelphia, 1949; hereinafter cited as *Guide*), which is being revised. The Manuscript Department also maintains the collections of printed material in particular forms—e.g., broadsides, sheet music, hymnals, programs, playbills, and maps—which may also be found in the various manuscript collections noted below

Large General Manuscript Collections

These collections—one of the distincitve strengths of the Society's holdings—often include music, usually accessible only through the personal name of a creator, as it may be found in the Society's card catalogue. Among the musicians represented are William B. Bradbury, Frederick S. Converse, Leopold Damrosch, Reginald DeKoven, Otto Dresel, Arthur Foote, Stephen Foster, William Henry Fry, Thomas Hastings, Anthony Philip Heinrich, Gustav Henschel, Victor Herbert, Charles E. Horn, Clara K. Kellogg, Francis Scott Key, Andrew Law, Edward A. MacDowell, Lowell Mason, Lillian Nordica, John Knowles Paine, Horatio Parker, Alexander Reinagle, and Raynor Taylor

Abraham Cassel Collection of 18th-century Pennsylvania German materials, 41 vols., many concerning the Ephrata Cloister and Conrad Beissel, with ms and printed music books, hymnals, chronicles, a death register, letters, and other documents, also copied materials of John Kelpius including his journal (*Guide*, 1610)

Ferdinand Julius Dreer Collection, including 3 vols. of autographs of actors, singers, dancers, and musicians, 1664–1915 (*Guide*, 175)

Simon Gratz Collection, 320,000 items (*Guide*, 250). Most of the musical materials are in a box marked "Musicians and Composers" (Case 13, Box 14); in 7 boxes on American actors and actresses, 1794–1928; and in 2 boxes on hymn writers, 1753–93

Claude W. Unger Collection, 10,000 items, including 31 statements of payment for musical instruction by Philadelphia music teachers, 1795–1829

Individual and Smaller Groups of Manuscripts

American Negro Historical Society Papers, including 9 music books in 6 vols., 1800–1865 (*Guide*, 8)

Amphion Amateur Musical Association, minutes, 1849–68 (*Guide*, 756)

Robert Ashton, ms hymns, 1795–1832 (*Guide*, 18)

Michael Billmeyer (Philadelphia book- and music-dealer), ledger, 1809–15 (*Guide*, 108)

Eliza Boller, ms music book, ca. 1810–13, containing Moravian secular and sacred music (*Guide*, 62)

Benjamin C. Calhoun, receipt book, 1807–12, with ms vocal music (*Guide*, 112)

Matthew Carey, papers concerning his Philadelphia publishing firm established in 1792, with biographical materials and correspondence, in the Edward Carey Gardiner Collection (*Guide*, 277a), also letterbooks in the Lea and Febiger Collection (*Guide*, 227b)

John Curtis, typescript 7-vol. ms, "One Hundred Years of Opera in Philadelphia (1820–1920)" (*Guide*, 1423)

Jenö de Donath, autograph compositions, mostly unpublished

Doran Collection, 1797–1880, including a music book of Lydia C. Warner (*Guide*, 1394)

Isaac Fox, papers, including 2 Civil War song sheets and a copy of a Confederate song, 1863–69 (*Guide*, 1502)

Mary Hallock Greenwaldt, papers relating to the invention of a color organ, 1936, and a brief on her lawsuit with the Musical Art Association (*Guide*, 867)

Henderson-Wertmüller Papers, including a list of subscribers for the purchase of an organ for St. Paul's Church, 1783 (*Guide*, 277)

Betsy and Eliza Henry, 6 ms vols. of English and German secular songs, 1796–1823 (*Guide*, 279)

Michael Hillegas (Philadelphia merchant), letter books, with references to his musical-instrument trade, 1757–60 (*Guide*, 287)

Hopkinson family archives, including correspondence of Francis and Joseph Hopkinson on musical topics

Jacob Hubley, 2 music books, 1776, in the Shippen family papers (*Guide*, 595)

Francis Jennings, 1-vol. index to authors of hymns, 1870 (*Guide*, 321)

Col. John Jones (of the Pennsylvania militia), papers, 1814–64, including army music requisitions (*Guide*, 888)

George May Keim, mss of the national anthem and "Home, Sweet Home," ca. 1814 and 1841 (*Guide*, 1304)

Johannes Kelpius (1663–1708), ms book of hymns, ca. 1707–12, including "The Lamenting Voice of the Hidden Love," presented by Samuel W. Pennypacker (*Guide*, 336)

Thomas McKean, book of poetry and songs, ca. 1800? (*Guide*, 405)

William Man, ms book of piano music, 1829 (*Guide*, 394)

J. Hill Martin, historical sketch of music at Bethlehem, Pa., 1742–1870, based on notes of Rufus Grider (*Guide*, 947)

T. Chalkley Matlack, literary and musical notes in ms, including 160 composers' biographies, also 4 Aeolian recording catalogues, 1916–22 (*Guide*, 401)

Musical Fund Society, 9 vols. of papers, 1820–

Philadelphia Dancing Assembly, papers 1749–1916, 100 items (*Guide*, 1015)

Gen. August Pleasanton, diary, 1838–44, with musical accounts (*Guide*, 511)

Fred Perry Powers Papers, 600 typescripts of lectures on "Songs of the Revolution" and "War songs " and research notes (*Guide*, 1367), also modern sources for a study of Revolutionary War songs (*Guide*, 618)

Ringgold Brass Band Papers, 150 music scores used ca. 1870–80 (*Guide*, 1477)

Albertus Shelley family papers, 1882–1905, relating to his musical studies in Germany and his activity as a violinist in Philadelphia, also with musicians' autographs (*Guide*, 592)

David McNeely Stauffer Collection, unbound materials, formerly part of an extra-illustrated copy of Thompson Westcott's *History of Philadelphia*, as printed in the *Sunday Dispatch* (*Guide*, 1095)

Filippo Trajetta (1777–1854), 3 boxes of vocal and instrumental music mss

U.S. Constitutional Centennial Commission, 1886–87, official papers, including songs, programs, and broadsides (*Guide*, 676)

James G. Whiteman, miscellaneous writings, 1849–55, including a burletta and opera libretti (*Guide*, 712)

John Greenleaf Whittier, hymn for the Philadelphia Centennial Exhibition, 1876, copy illuminated by Annie L. Wiley (*Guide*, 713)

Septimus Winner (1827–1909), papers, including diaries, letters, music notebooks, and songs, among them a ms of "Listen to the Mocking Bird" (*Guide*, 1536)

Miscellaneous music books, 6 vols., 1800–1865 (*Guide*, 948)

Printed and Other Materials

Tunebooks and hymnals, 40 items, mostly 19th century; also other items in various families' papers, i.e. Dickinson, Drinker, Peters, and Harris

Sheet music, 3000 items, mostly 19th century, accessible by composer, title, first line, or publisher through a card catalogue; also illustrated lithograph covers, maintained in the collection of early lithographs, with no access by musical content

Programs, including a nearly complete run of the Academy of Music concerts, 1852–

Oil portraits, early prints, and photographs of persons and places connected with music

—Peter J. Parker

1339
KEAN ARCHIVES
1320 Locust Street
Philadelphia, Pennsylvania 19107

Sheet music, 225,000 items, 1790s– , including some materials acquired from Harry Dichter. The collection is arranged by subjects, including ragtime, hit songs, musical-comedy scores, recreational topics, illustrations (by subject or artist), Biblical texts set to music, and composers

Biographical files, including photographs, press clippings, and other ephemera, 100 folders, many of them devoted to composers and other musicians

—Manny Kean

1340
LIBRARY COMPANY OF PHILADELPHIA   PPL
1314 Locust Street
Philadelphia, Pennsylvania 19107

Manuscript materials in the collection are accessible through special arrangements with the Historical Society of Pennsylvania, q.v.

Pierre Eugène du Simitière (1736–84), personal papers, including song texts, an opera libretto, and references to American Indian musical instruments and dance, as cited in the Historical Records Survey, *Descriptive Catalogue of the du Simitière Papers in the Library Company of Philadelphia* (Philadelphia, 1940)

Francis Johnson (Philadelphia black musician), ms book of songs, ca. 1820, and printed sheet music

William Henry Fry (1813–64), 45 holograph music mss, as cited in William Treat Upton, *The Musical Works of William Henry Fry* (Philadelphia, 1946). See also Byron Kauffman, *The Choral Works of William Henry Fry* (D.M.A. diss., University of Illinois, 1975)

Sheet music, 2000 U.S. imprints, 1790s–1870s; also sheet music including some U.S. imprints, bound organ music, and other original published theoretical works from the library of Albert G. Emerick (1817–98), as well as original ms compositions; and sheet music, including some U.S. imprints, and other printed musical works from the library of James Rush (1786–1869), in 15 vols. used for his studies of the human voice, and 15 vols. of piano music

John A. McAllister (1813–83), books from his personal library, including hymnals and related works; also scrapbooks containing notices and programs of the Musical Fund Society, 1824–73, and of the Philadelphia American Musical Academy (Academy of Music)

Musical broadsides, 2900 items, mostly mid 19th century, including 200 Confederate imprints, as shown in Edwin Wolf II, *American Song Sheets, Slip Ballads, and Poetical Broadsides, 1850–1870* (Philadelphia, 1963)

Other scattered U.S. music imprints to ca. 1876, including songsters, libretti, hymnals, instruction books, and other musical editions

—Lillian Tonkin

1341
LUTHERAN CHURCH IN AMERICA
Board of Publication
2900 Queen Lane
Philadelphia, Pennsylvania 19129

Hymnals and related publications, 150 items; also sheet-music publications of the Fortress Press

Programs of church services, pageants, and similar musical events, 200 items

—Charlotte Odman

1342
LUTHERAN THEOLOGICAL   PPLT
SEMINARY
Krauth Memorial Library
7301 Germantown Avenue
Philadelphia (Mount Airy), Pennsylvania 19119

Lutheran hymnals and related publications, including Germantown imprints, many from the library of St. Michael-Zion Church in Philadelphia, and many as cited in Edward C. Wolf, "Lutheran Hymnody and Music Published in America, 1700–1850: A Descriptive Bibliography," *Concordia Historical Institute Quarterly*, 50 (1977), 164–85

—David Wartluft

1343
MUSICAL FUND SOCIETY OF PHILADELPHIA
c/o Rev. James C. Dorsey, Archivist
Saint Albans Church
Second Street and Tabor Road
Philadelphia, Pennsylvania 19120

Music library, 1790–1840, including ms and published music, mostly European but also with works by Antonio Bagioli (1795–1871), Benjamin Carr, Francis T. S. Darley (1833–1914), Henri-Noel Gilles, (1778–1834), Charles Hommann, Leopold Meignen (1793–1873), E. Phelps, and Charles Zeuner (1795–1857), also with arrangements. See the *Catalog of Orchestral and Choral Compositions Published and in Manuscript between 1790 and 1840* (Philadelphia, 1974). This material is now on deposit in the Free Library of Philadelphia (q.v.)

Archives of the Society, founded 1820, including constitutions and by-laws, minutes, financial records of the Society and relating to Musical Fund Hall, programs, and publications. See Louis C. Madeira, *Annals of Music in Philadelphia and Hisory of the Musical Fund Society* (Philadelphia, 1896)

Holograph music mss of compositions that received prizes awarded by the Societs through the McCollin Memorial Fund, 1925–

1344
NEW SCHOOL OF MUSIC

Alice Tully Library
301 South Twenty-first Street
Philadelphia, Pennsylvania 19103

Curtis String Quartet, scrapbook containing press clippings, photographs, and programs, mid 1930s

—Virginia B. Emerson

1345
PHILADELPHIA COLLEGE OF THE PERFORMING ARTS

250 South Broad Street
Philadelphia, Pennsylvania 19102

Archival records of the College (formerly the Philadelphia Musical Academy, and the Philadelphia Conservatory of Music), 3 boxes

—Kent Christensen

1346
PHILADELPHIA ORCHESTRA

230 South Fifteenth Street
Philadelphia, Pennsylvania 19102

Scrapbooks, 1900– , and other records and memorabilia, as cited in Herbert Kupferberg, *Those Fabulous Philadelphians: The Life and Times of a Great Orchestra* (New York, 1969), p. vii

1347
PRESBYTERIAN HISTORICAL SOCIETY   PPPrHi

425 Lombard Street
Philadelphia, Pennsylvania 19107

Hymnals and tunebooks, 1400 items, mostly in the Hood Collection

Louis F. Benson (1855–1930), personal papers, 145,000 items in 11 boxes, including research notes, incoming correspondence, music scores, sermons, book reviews, articles, hymns, poems, press clippings, printed ephemera, and research notes on composers and hymn writers

Hymnals of the Presbyterian and Reformed churches in the U.S., 500 items, including many editions of Isaac Watts hymns

Francis Hopkinson, music from his personal library

—Gerald W. Gillette

1348
Phillip H. and A.S.W. ROSENBACH   PPRF FOUNDATION

2010 DeLancey Place
Philadelphia, Pennsylvania 19103

Collection of rare books, including 4 music books printed 1722–81

1349
SAVOY COMPANY

1009 Western Savings Bank Building
Philadelphia, Pennsylvania 19107

Programs and other documents of the Company, 1901– , as used in William Cramp Ferguson, *A History of the Savoy Company*, 1950 ed. (Philadelphia, 1951), and other historical studies

—Daniel S. Knight

1350
Donald J. STUBBLEBINE

318 South Fawn Street
Philadelphia, Pennsylvania 19107

Sheet music, 50,000 items, including extensive holdings of materials from Broadway musicals, 1895– , Hollywood films 1930s– , British productions of musicals, 1930s– , dance bands, 1930s–50s, Frank Sinatra, 1930s– , and popular tunes, 1930s–50s

Playbills of musicals and dramatic productions, nearly all in New York, 5000 items, 1920s–

Miscellaneous songbooks and other printed music, classical and popular, mostly 20th century, in 20 cartons

1351
TEMPLE UNIVERSITY LIBRARIES   PPT

Special Collections Department
Philadelphia, Pennsylvania 19122

University Archives

William Benson Richter (1901–73, composer and dentist), ms and published scores, correspondence, biographical materials, and recordings

Temple University Theatre productions, 1930–69, papers including photographs, programs, handbills, press clippings, and scrapbooks

Temple University, papers concerning music activities, 1900– , including press clippings, articles, photographs, press releases, and other materials, scattered in various collections

Urban Archives Center

Philadelphia Settlement Music School, papers, 1910–66, 1 linear meter, including executive and financial records, publications, programs, correspondence, photographs, scrapbooks, and notebooks

Rare Book and Manuscript Collection

Sheet music, 1000 18th- and 19th-century titles, including early lithographed covers

—Thomas M. Whitehead

1352
UNIVERSITY OF PENNSYLVANIA PU
Van Pelt Library
Philadelphia, Pennsylvania 19104

Albrecht Music Library

The general collections include materials from the personal collections of Prof. Otto E. Albrecht; Horatio Connell (1876–1936), strong in vocal music; Carl Pfatteicher (1882–1957), mostly Protestant church music; A. Carson Simpson (1895–1965), mostly opera scores; Owen Wister (1860–1938), including the collections of his grandparents, Pierce Butler (1807–67) and Fanny Kemble (1809–93); and of the Philadelphia Art Alliance

Sheet music, 3000 items, uncatalogued
Recordings, including 1000 acoustical 78-rpm discs
Hugh A. Clarke (1876–1919, music professor at the University), oil portrait

Rare Book Collection

Francis Hopkinson (1737–91), music library, including 4 holograph music mss as discussed in Otto E. Albrecht, "Francis Hopkinson, Musician, Poet, and Patriot," University of Pennsylvania *Library Chronicle*, 6 (1938), 3–15; also Caroline Richards (Davidson), *An Eighteenth-Century Music Collecction* (Master's thesis, University of Pennsylvania, 1968)

John Rowe Parker, correspondence maintained in connection with his editorship of the *Euterpiad*, and his management of the Franklin Music Warehouse, Boston, 1000 items, ca. 1800–1840

John Durang, extra-illustrated presentation copy of his "Account of the Philadelphia Stage," as used in Alan S. Donner, *The Memoirs of John Durang, American Actor, 1785–1816* (Pittsburgh, 1966)

Materials from the Yarnall Library of Theology of St. Clement's Church, formerly housed at the Protestant Episcopal Church in Philadelphia Divinity School, and including liturgical items, some of them described in Joseph Cullen Ayer, *Yarnall Library of Theology of St. Clement's Church* (Philadelphia, 1933); also portions of the library of Bishop William Bacon Stevens (1815–87). See Joyce L. White, "Biographical and Historical Background of the Yarnall Library of Theology," University of Pennsylvania *Library Chronicle*, 43 (1979), 134–58

Alma Mahler Werfel (1879–1964), 25 cartons of letters and journals, including extensive correspondence with musicians in Europe and the U.S. See Adolph Klarmann and Rudolf Hirsch, "Note on the Alma Mahler Werfel Collection," University of Pennsylvania *Library Chronicle*, 35 (1969), 33–35

Marian Anderson, personal papers, including letters and memorabilia, photographs, and music from her personal library, with a preliminary inventory

Theodore Dreiser, personal papers, including scrapbooks, sheet music, photographs, and letters from his brother, Paul Dresser (1857–1911), in all 20 linear cm.

Book of ms and printed music, ca. 1800, as discussed in Otto E. Albrecht, "Eighteenth-Century Music in the University Library," University of Pennsylvania *Library Chronicle*, 5 (1937), 13–24; also other materials from the Charles J. Nagy collection, as listed in the Samuel T. Freeman & Co. auction catalogue (Philadelphia, 1938)

Folklore Archives

Located in the Folklore–Folklife Department, 415 Logan Hall

MacEdward Leach (folklorist), papers, including field notes on research in Jamaica, field diaries, and correspondence with ballad scholars D. K. Wilgus, Archer Taylor, and others

American Folklore Society, records, including correspondence, 1914–60

Wise County, Va., transcriptions of several hundred songs and other folklore collected partly by the WPA, Emory L. Hamilton, and MacEdward Leach, 1930s–60s

West Virginia and southwestern Pennsylvania folk music, tape copies of 30 recordings by Samuel Bayard, 1930s–40s, including fife music, ballads, religious music, and Irish-American music

Eastern Pennsylvania and Philadelphia collection, including tape recordings and transcriptions of songs, riddles, jump-rope rhymes, and games of Afro-American, Czech, Greek-American, Irish-American, Ukrainian, and other groups of children

West Indies collection, including 40 tape recordings of songs, tales, and other materials recorded by MacEdward Leach in Jamaica, 12 tapes of songs recorded by Horace and Jane Beck in Antigua, and 40 tapes of songs recorded by Jacob D. Elder in Trinidad, some of the materials in Gullah dialect

Newfoundland and Labrador collection of monologue songs and tales, including 40 tape recordings collected by Kenneth Goldstein, 4 tapes recorded by Ralph Rinzler, and other tapes recorded by Leach

—Jim Couza

1353
Frederick P. WILLIAMS
8313 Shawnee Street
Philadelphia, Pennsylvania 19118

Military band recordings, 1888– , including 22,000 78-rpm discs, 1000 cylinders, and 4000 LP discs, representing Victor, Columbia, Brunswick, Paramount, Capitol, and other labels; also 350 recording catalogues

1354
BACH CHOIR OF PITTSBURGH
476 Broadmoor Avenue
Pittsburgh, Pennsylvania 15228

A volunteer, non-profit group founded in 1934 as the Bach Festival Choir

Official archival records of the Choir, including minutes, correspondence, membership lists, and newsletters, 1944– ; also the constitution and by-laws. While the file of concert programs does not begin until 1948, those for earlier years may be found at the Carnegie Music Hall (q.v.) and the Carnegie Library of Pittsburgh (q.v.)

A brief written history of the choir, 1934–60, summarized with minor additions, 1978

1355
Mrs. William E. BENSWANGER
5429 Aylesboro Avenue
Pittsburgh, Pennsylvania 15217

William E. Benswanger (1892–1972, organizer of local musical activities, program annotator for the Pittsburgh Symphony Orchestra, and correspondent to *Musical America*), personal papers, ca. 1926–44, 50 linear cm., including correspondence with performers who appeared in Pittsburgh and contemporary composers whose works were performed in Pittsburgh; programs, directories, minutes, and other documents of the Pittsburgh Symphony Orchestra, Musician's Club, Fine Arts Society, Pittsburgh Chamber Music Society, and Irene Kaufmann Settlement Music School; and articles and reviews by Benswanger, in the form of clippings and typescripts

1356
Mrs. Marshall BIDWELL
14 McKelvey Avenue
Pittsburgh, Pennsylvania 15218

Marshall Bidwell (organist and director of music at the Carnegie Institute, 1932–64), personal papers, including correspondence with composers, organists, churches with whom he worked on matters of organ design and installation, and others, 80 linear cm.; programs of his recitals outside Pittsburgh, 200 items, those before 1930 in 3 scrapbooks; annotated programs of his recitals and lectures at the Carnegie Music Hall, 1932–64; typescripts of his lectures, 20 linear cm.; 40 pocket diaries; and mss of organ works dedicated to him, composed by Garth Edmundson and John Tasker Howard

1357
BYZANTINE CATHOLIC SEMINARY LIBRARY
3605 Perrysville Avenue
Pittsburgh, Pennsylvania 15414

Carpatho-Rusin liturgical music books, 9 items, some with U.S. imprints

—Joseph W. Bertha

1358
CALVARY EPISCOPAL CHURCH
315 Shady Avenue
Pittsburgh, Pennsylvania 15206

Musically an active church, which ca. 1890 instituted musical services in poverty neighborhoods. Harvey Gaul was organist and choirmaster, 1910–45; in 1921 the Church made the first-ever radio broadcast of a religious service, with considerable music; in 1923 a "Seaman's Service" was broadcast over KDKA; and the Nathaniel Holmes Fund was established in 1929 for "the support of music." Special concerts have been devoted to Pittsburgh composers, Negro spirituals, the Old Harp Singers, the Pittsburgh Savoyards, and other special groups

Minutes of the vestries, 1855–
Annual vols. of church bulletins, weekly calendars, and special music programs, 1917–

1359
CARNEGIE LIBRARY OF PITTSBURGH   PPi
Music and Art Department
4400 Forbes Avenue
Pittsburgh, Pennsylvania 15213

The general music collections began with 1300 vols. from the library of Karl Merz (1836–90, founder and director of the Conservatory of Music, University of Worcester, Ohio), as described in the *Catalog of the Karl Merz Music Library* (Pittsburgh, 1892), supplemented by 500 vols. from the library of Charles C. Mellor (1836–1909, local music dealer). Other personal collections now in the Library include chamber music from Carl Braun, choral music from Henry Ringwalt, organ music from Marshall Bidwell (1895–1966, organist of the Carnegie Institute) and William K. Steiner, piano music from Mrs. Beveridge Webster, operas and oratorios from Alphonse Zinsmeister, and violin music from Gaylord Yost. Special music endowment funds were established by Edward C. Bald, Jr., David H. Light, and the Friends of the Music Library. The latter, established in 1938 with Will Earhart as president, helped in acquiring the 3000 vols. of the personal library of Charles N. Boyd (1875–1937, organist, scholar, and Associate Editor [with Waldo Selden Pratt] of the *American Supplement* to *Grove's Dictionary of Music and Musicians*, New York, 1920); see Sara Ellen Germon, *The Boyd Memorial Collection in the Music Division of the Carnegie Library of Pittsburgh* (Thesis, Carnegie Library School, 1951). For general background see Irene Millen, "Andrew Carnegie's Music Library," *M.L.A. Notes*, 22 (1965), 681–90

Music mss, including Harvey Gaul (1881–1945), holographs of 131 works, in 11 vols.; Adolph M. Foerster (1854–1927), holographs, in 8 vols.; William Middelschuelte, holograph of the "Perpetuum mobile" for organ pedals alone, from the *Concerto on a Theme by Johann Sebastian Bach* (1903), with later ms corrections by the composer, presented by Caspar P. Koch; J. Vick O'Brien (1876–1953, first head of the Music Department, Carnegie Institute of Technology), 25 holographs; T. Carl Whitmer (1873–1959), 51 items; Gaylord Yost (1888–1958), 48 items; and Emil Paur (1855–1932), sketches for his Symphony *In der Natur* (1909), written for the Pittsburgh Orchestra
Personal papers of T. Carl Whitmer, 5 boxes, 1899–1958), including his David Bispham Medal; also autograph letters of Charles Wakefield Cadman, William C. Carl, George W. Chadwick, Walter Damrosch, Edward Dickinson, Olin Downes, Arthur Foote, Victor Herbert, Charles Ives, Ernst Krenek, Waldo Selden Pratt, Victor de Sabata, Oscar Sonneck, Leopold Stokowski, Beveridge Webster, and Isidore Witmark
William Evens (1783–1854, Pittsburgh singing-school teacher), letter to John Rowe Parker in Boston, 1819; also 4 scrapbooks of press clippings
Pittsburgh Orchestra, archives, 1896–1910, including 26 vols. of letterpress copies of correspondence, indexed by subject, personal name, and musical work; also letters, papers, clippings, documents, and memorabilia, in all 68 items
Tuesday Musical Club, archives, including 17 vols. of scrapbooks and 65 vols. of membership directories, 1909–
Art Society of Pittsburgh, archives, including minutes, financial records, correspondence, regulations, programs, and memorabilia, 1891–1943

Charles N. Boyd, 9 scrapbooks, including 2 vols. of press clippings on Music Week in Pittsburgh, 1924; 15 vols. of press clippings and programs of events in which Boyd participated; and 100 vols. of press clippings, ca. 1900–1937, of which vols. 5–6 are devoted to the Kunits String Quartet, vols. 7–8 to recital series, and vol. 9 to the People's Singing Classes. See the index to this collection, on 80,000 cards

George H. Wilson (1854–1908, annotator for the Boston Symphony Orchestra, manager of music for the World's Columbian Exposition of 1893, and manager of the Pittsburgh Orchestra, Carnegie Music Hall, and the Art Society of Pittsburgh), 23 scrapbooks, including press clippings and programs of the Pittsburgh Orchestra, 1896–1910; other music clippings from Pittsburgh newspapers, 1895–97; and press clippings on opera in Pittsburgh and other cities, 1903

Other scrapbooks, including Adolph M. Foerster, 6 vols. of musical and literary programs and press clippings; Charles C. Mellor, 4 vols. of articles, programs, and press clippings concerning Pittsburgh music, 1850–1900; Carl Retter, 1 vol. of programs and press clippings of performances in which he participated, 1875–86; and Victor Saudek, 1 vol. of programs and press clippings for the Saudek Ensemble, 1912–27

Programs of local musical events, in bound vols., including the Alvin Theatre, 1899–1902; Apollo Club of Pittsburgh, 1897–1901; Art Society of Pittsburgh, 1891–1905, in 5 vols.; Brahms Musical Club of Pittsburgh, with their constitution; Charles Wakefield Cadman, testimonial concert, 1910; Carnegie Music Hall, 1896– , in 21 vols. to 1940; the Ellis concerts, Carnegie Music Hall, 1913–23; Gounod Club of Pittsburgh, 1875–78; Heyn recitals, 1914–22, in 3 vols.; concerts by Fritz Kreisler, 1913–39; May–Beegle concerts, 1913–51, in 12 vols.; Ignace Jan Paderewski concerts, 1893–1923; Pittsburgh Bach Choir, 1934– ; Pittsburgh May Musical Festivals, 1879–91 passim, in 3 vols.; Pittsburgh Mendelssohn Choir, 1909– , in 2 vols. to 1940; Pittsburgh Mozart Club, 1891–1917, in 6 vols.; Pittsburgh Musical Institute, 1915–55, in 25 vols. to 1940; Pittsburgh Orchestra, 1896–1910, in 15 vols.; Pittsburgh Orchestra Association, 1910–50, in 9 vols.; Pittsburgh String Orchestra, 1934–35; Pittsburgh String Symphonic Ensemble Society, 1934–37; Pittsburgh Symphony Orchestra, 1926– , with 5 vols. to 1940; and Ringwalt Choral Union, 1894–1931; also programs of visiting orchestras; and of operas presented in Pittsburgh, 1909–47, in 2 vols. In addition to the above, there are 2 file drawers of programs of miscellaneous local concerts; also scattered holdings of programs of concerts elsewhere

Indexes to programs, through the Performers in Pittsburgh Index (PIPI), and the Analysis Index (AI) of musical works, providing access to the programs listed above, also to those included in the bound scrapbooks

Sheet music, including 6000 unbound items, 1875–1950, with access by title, composer, and author in the "Sheet Music Index"; 100 bound vols., with access through the "Vocal Anthology Index" and the "Piano Anthology Index"; and 364 sets of dance-band music, 1910–30, indexed by composer and title

Music periodicals, as cited in Irene Millen, *American Musical Magazines, 1786–1865* (Thesis, Carnegie Library School, 1949), and Carol Stephen, *Descriptive Bibliography of American Musical Magazines, 1866–1886, in the Carnegie Library of Pittsburgh* (Thesis, Carnegie Library School, 1954)

Pictures, including the Mounted Picture Collection in the Music and Art Department, 300,000 items, of which several hundred depict musical subjects, arranged by personal name and by subject; and the Pittsburgh Photographic Library, in the Pennsylvania Division of the Library, including 200 items on musical subjects

—Ida Reed

1360
CARNEGIE–MELLON UNIVERSITY   PPiC

Hunt Library
Schenley Park
Pittsburgh, Pennsylvania 15213

Published and ms compositions by American composers, including Roland Leich mss, Nikolai Lopatnikoff items, Philip Catelinet band mss, and Leonardo Balada works, all in the Music Division

Walter Van Dyke Bingham (professor of applied psychology), papers, 1852–1965, with materials concerning Thomas A. Edison, and Bingham's research on the emotional influences and practical effects of music, including the Seashore tests

—Myrtle Nim

1361
CARNEGIE MUSIC HALL

Carnegie Institute
4400 Forbes Avenue
Pittsburgh, Pennsylvania 15213

Scrapbooks, 55 items, containing every program given in the Hall since the dedication, 5 November 1895, including those of the first Pittsburgh Symphony Orchestra, 1896–1910

Programs for organ recitals sponsored by the Carnegie Institute, beginning 6 November 1895, in bound vols.

1362
CHATHAM COLLEGE   PPiCC

Mellon Library
Woodland Road
Pittsburgh, Pennsylvania 15232

Published books relating to the College, with music and music references, including 4 student songbooks, 1900–1928; programs and music references in the 2 student literary magazines, *Sorosis* (1895–1921) and *Arrow* (1921–59); and yearbooks and College catalogues. The books are in the College Archives, along with minutes of the Board of Trustees, 1869– , and of the faculty, 1900– , which also include music references

1363
FIRST BAPTIST CHURCH OF PITTSBURGH
Bayard and Bellefield
Pittsburgh, Pennsylvania 15213

Church weekly calendars, 1841– , bound vols. of
weekly church bulletins, 1927– , and other miscellaneous publications, 1885– , with references to
music
List of organists and members of the vocal quartet,
1912–
H. Alan Floyd (d. 1958), anthems and musical pageants
to texts by Bernard Clausen (pastor of the Church),
20 items in ms and published editions

—Mary Louise Wright

1364
HISTORICAL SOCIETY OF WESTERN   PPiHi
PENNSYLVANIA
4338 Bigelow Boulevard
Pittsburgh, Pennsylvania 15213

Manuscripts, including James Krepps, 7 books of fiddle
tunes, also keyboard music for two or more hands,
including "A Collection of Instrumental Music
Arranged for the Monongahela Musical Association,"
signed William Taylor Krepps, 1858; also 3 bound
vols. (16, 156, and 300 pages) of vocal and instrumen-
tal music for the Harmony Society, the first entitled
"Sing & Spielstücke für Clavier & Piano Forte.
Harmonie, 1819"; and a fife book, ca. 1800
Tunebooks, 19 items, 1807–79, including 3 Pittsburgh
imprints, 1816–46
Sheet music, including 374 items, 1843–1921, from the
collection of Marie Cyphers, with a special inventory;
also 2 bound vols., ca. 1825–40, owned by Martha M.
McCook
W. A. Solomon, collection of 100 items from *The Daily
Programme*, official playbills and programs for the
Opera House in Pittsburgh, 1869–71, including per-
formances by minstrel groups and by Lisa Weber's
Burlesque Opera Troupe
George Scully, 4 vols. of scrapbooks, 1874–1903, includ-
ing theater and concert programs and portraits, most-
ly from Pittsburgh but some from east-coast cities

1365
Paul KOCH
5 Ellsworth Terrace
Pittsburgh, Pennsylvania 15213

Materials relating to music at St. Paul's (Roman Catholic) Cathedral, Pittsburgh, ca. 1850–65 and 1900–
Caspar P. Koch (organist at Carnegie Music Hall, North
Side, 1904–1954), personal papers, including letters
from Andrew Carnegie, contracts for organs and
pianos, and programs

1366
Mrs. J. Fred LISSFELT
1515 Shady Avenue
Pittsburgh, Pennsylvania 15217

J. Fred Lissfelt, 9 scrapbooks of his music criticism, for
the "Musical Forecast" of the *Pittsburgh Dispatch*,
1922–27, and for the *Sun-Telegraph*, 1927–61

1367
MENDELSSOHN CHOIR OF PITTSBURGH
404 Duquesne Drive
Pittsburgh, Pennsylvania 15243

Archives of the Choir, 1908– , including a charter and
by-laws, financial reports, board minutes, correspondence, membership lists, budgetary documents,
and a 1938 history of the Choir by R. B. Watkins

—Barry K. Miller

1368
PITTSBURGH OPERA
Heinz Hall for the Performing Arts
600 Penn Avenue
Pittsburgh, Pennsylvania 15222

Archival records, 1940s–60s, including programs, chorus rosters, scrapbooks of press clippings, financial
records, minutes of the board of directors, contracts,
and photographs. Earlier records are held by Mrs.
Arthur J. Kerr, Jr., 100 Crofton Drive, Pittsburgh
15238, along with a chronicle of the founding of the
company in 1938

1369
PITTSBURGH THEOLOGICAL   PPiPT
SEMINARY
Clifford E. Barbour Library
616 North Highland Avenue
Pittsburgh, Pennsylvania 15206

James Warrington Collection of hymnals and tunebooks, mostly 19th-century U.S. items, supplemented by material from Theodore M. Finney and
other sources, in all 5000 items, also 1200 books on
related fields of music and literature
James Warrington, research files, including indexes to
his collection, by composer, meter, tune, and other
access points, in all 300,000 cards; also 40 cartons of
indexes to the collection, formerly with the Hartford
(Conn.) Seminary Foundation collection

—Dikran Y. Hadidian

1370
REFORMED PRESBYTERIAN THEOLOGICAL
SEMINARY
7418 Penn Avenue
Pittsburgh, Pennsylvania 15208

Psalm books and books about psalmody, 200 vols., of
which many are U.S. imprints, including 2 editions of
works by Gilbert McMaster, 1818–25

—Rachel George

1371
RODEF SHALOM TEMPLE
4905 Fifth Avenue
Pittsburgh, Pennsylvania 15213

Minute books of the congregation, 1880–1902, with notations pertaining to music, as cited in Maurice Strambler, *The Jewish Community of Pittsburgh: An Ethnomusicological Study* (Master's thesis, University of Pittsburgh, 1975). See also the *Temple Bulletin* (13 March 1974)

1372
TAMBURITZANS OF DUQUESNE UNIVERSITY
Tamburitzan Institute of Folk Arts Building
1801 Boulevard of the Allies
Pittsburgh, Pennsylvania 15219

Library and archival materials on east-European folk music in the U.S. and elsewhere, comprising 12,000 books, 200 films, 24,000 recordings, and 50,000 sheet-music items, including the library of Rudolph Cernkovic, as described in "The Museum that Music Built," *Pittsburgh Press*, roto section, 15 June 1975

Elizabeth Burchenal (folk-dance scholar, 1920s–30s), papers, including music, films, and illustrative materials, mostly pertaining to folk dance in Europe and the Appalachians

—David René Kolar

1373
THIRD PRESBYTERIAN CHURCH
Fifth Avenue at South Negley Street
Pittsburgh, Pennsylvania 15232

Church archives with music references, including minutes of the Session, 1900– , discussing financial aspects of the music program; weekly bulletins, 1932– , including programs of special musical performances; and *Dedicatory Services of the New Edifice* (Pittsburgh, 1900), a book including a history of the Church, with details on the organ, organists, and music program

—John R. Lively

1374
TUESDAY MUSICAL CLUB   (PPiU-SF)
Stephen Collins Foster Memorial
University of Pittsburgh
Pittsburgh, Pennsylvania 15260

Historical records of the Club (founded 1889), including 24 scrapbooks, called "Presidents' Books," containing programs, clippings, and photographs, 1903– ; an album of studio photographs of the presidents (called the "Book of the Presidents"), 1889– ; yearbooks, including membership rosters, 1921– ; by-laws, revisions, and related records, 1921– ; materials pertaining to scholarship awards, 2½ vertical file drawers; archival files concerning the Stephen Collins Foster Memorial; other financial and operational records, 6 vertical file drawers; and typescript histories of the Club, prepared 1909, 1914, and 1939

1375
UNIVERSITY OF PITTSBURGH   PPiU
Hillman Library
Pittsburgh, Pennsylvania 15260

Theodore M. Finney Music Library

See Theodore M. Finney, *A Union Catalogue of Music and Books on Music Printed before 1801 in Pittsburgh Libraries* (Pittsburgh, 1959; 2nd ed., 1963)

Adolph M. Foerster (1845–1927), music compositions, 1874–1923, including 200 holographs, 25 other mss, and 100 printed editions, 10 of the latter being proof-sheets. See S. Philip Kniseley, *Catalogue of the Manuscripts and Printed Music of Adolph M. Foerster in the Music Library, University of Pittsburgh* (Pittsburgh, 1960)

Ethelbert Nevin (1862–1901), papers, including 80 ms compositions, some of them holographs, 1 holograph notebook of melodies (1880), also letters, photographs, sheet music, books, and memorabilia

Pittsburgh Symphony Society, campaign material, newsletters, brochures, advertisements, and season-ticket information

William Steinberg (1899–1978, conductor of the Pittsburgh Symphony Orchestra, 1952–76), collection of 800 musical scores, facsimiles, recordings, and presentation copies of symphonic works

Sheet music, 10,000 items, mid 19th to early 20th centuries, including piano, vocal, and chamber works, uncatalogued

Songbooks, 1600 items, early 19th century to the present, including hymnals, tutors, and anthologies

Other printed music, 5000 items, late 19th and early 20th centuries, including piano, vocal, orchestral, and chamber works, with many first and early editions of works by Edward A. MacDowell

Programs, 86 bound vols., including major U.S. orchestras; Carnegie Hall, Pittsburgh (North Side) organ recitals, 1948–52; Carnegie Music Hall, Pittsburgh (Oakland), organ recitals, 1934, 1952–66; and University of Pittsburgh Heinz Memorial Chapel Services, 1938–63; also unbound vols. of programs of the May Beegle Concerts, 1923–55, and the Pittsburgh Opera, 1955–

Photographs of local performing groups and individuals, 10 items, ca. 1900

Recordings, including 1000 78-rpm discs, mostly popular songs, 1920s–30s

Archives Service Center

Pittsburgh Symphony Society, archives, 1927–60, with organizational records, including those of its committees (i. e., Women's Association, Men's Committee), financial records, contracts (for conductors, soloists, AFM Local 60, the Pittsburgh Opera, program advertisers), operational records, active and inactive membership cards, campaign material, and scrapbooks with clippings, brochures, and advertisements

Teutonia Männerchor (German singing society of northern Pittsburgh, affiliated with the North American Singers' Union), records, 1880–1976, including history, by-laws, minutes, constitution, financial records, contracts, correspondence, programs, and photographs

Abraham L. Wolk (b. 1891), materials on the Civic Light Opera in Pittsburgh, 1940s–50s, including correspondence, photographs, miscellaneous documents, and 7 scrapbooks

Special Collections Department

Ford E. and Harriet R. Curtis theater collection, 750,000 items, 1860– , including programs primarily from New York and Pittsburgh, also from other U.S. cities as well as from principal university theaters; also several collections maintained separately as acquired, containing scrapbooks, programs, clippings, photographs, posters, and reviews

Oliver Paxton Merriman (1866–1942) scrapbook collection, 142 scrapbooks in 34 boxes, containing materials on Pittsburgh and New York theaters, 1865–1942. See Ned A. Bowman, *Comprehensive Index to the Merriman Scrapbook Collection on Pittsburgh and New York Theatre* (Pittsburgh, 1966)

Anna Pavlowa (1881–1931)–Karl Gottlieb Heinrich (1886–1966) ballet collection, including photographs, films, and scrapbooks on the Pittsburgh Civic Ballet, 1912–50, and other posters, programs, and annotated music. The Pavlowa collection contains 135 printed books on dancing and ballet; the Heinrich collection contains papers, 1915–62, 85 letters, 21 folders, 7 scrapbooks, and 5 boxes of miscellaneous materials

Henry Sterling (1810–63), minutes of the Associated Singing Society, with the treasurer's report, list of subscribers, and rules and regulations for 1829

Fidelis Zitterbart, Jr. (fl. ca. 1900), 1500 ms compositions, mostly holographs, including popular tunes, overtures, chamber music, symphonies, and an opera

—Norris L. Stephens

Foster Hall Collection—Stephen Collins Foster Memorial

See Fletcher Hodges, Jr., "A Pittsburgh Composer and His Memorial," *Western Pennsylvania Historical Magazine,* 21/2 (1938), and "The Research Work of the Foster Hall Collection," *Pennsylvania History,* 15/3 (1948). The museum and research library were founded by Josiah Kirby Lilly

Stephen Foster collection, 10,000 items, including holographs and other mss of compositions, verses, inscriptions, and cartoons, 200 pages; 6 publisher's mss; facsimiles of mss in other repositories; a complete collection of first and early editions of his music, as represented in the *Foster Hall Reproductions of the Songs, Compositions and Arrangements by Stephen Collins Foster* (Indianapolis, 1933), also modern editions; songbooks with his music; broadsides; personal effects, including his account book and correspondence, 4 photographs; his flute and melodeon; books on him, periodicals, clippings, and recordings of his music; Foster family records, scrapbooks, account books, and other papers; and minutes of the Buchanan Glee Club directed by him

—Fletcher Hodges, Jr.

1376
Martin E. RESSLER
Route 2, Box 173
Quarryville, Pennsylvania 17566

Mennonite and other hymnals, tunebooks, and hymnological works, 3400 items, 1742–1940. See his *Bibliography of Mennonite Hymnals and Songbooks, 1742–1942* (Quarryville, 1973). Of the total, the vols. in English include 400 hymnals with music; 200 with words only; 600 gospel songbooks; 100 Sunday-school songbooks in small oblong format, 1850–1900, and 600 in upright format, 1875–1925; 200 oblong tunebooks; 250 books on hymnology, music history, and music pedagogy; and 600 paperbound vols. The vols. in German include 550 hymnals, including 7 editions of *Zions Harfe,* 1803–1904, and all 32 known editions of *Ein unpartheyisches Gesangbuch,* 1804–1978

Music books in ms, 9 vols., including a book of secular songs in German script, ca. 1815, signed by Josephan Schlienman (?); and a soprano part book of religious songs in German, ca. 1840 (?), signed by Roy Huppert (?), also instrumental parts for "clarinetto" and "tromba"

1377
ALBRIGHT COLLEGE　　　　　　　　　PRA
Alumni Memorial Library
Reading, Pennsylvania 19604

Manuscript music for "Greek" festivals held at the College after 1890, as cited in *HRS*
Programs of College musical events

—Arlene Breiner

1378
HISTORICAL SOCIETY OF BERKS　　PRHi COUNTY
Third and Spring Streets
Reading, Pennsylvania 19601

Music books in ms, 1790–1820; also holograph piano-music mss of Howard Kuehn
Materials on early musical theater in Reading, including press clippings in the scrapbooks of A. S. Jones, and references in the diary of James Morris, 1841–42, as cited in Richard Byron Rosewall, *Singing Schools of Pennsylvania, 1800–1900* (Ph.D. diss., University of Minnesota, 1969)

1379
ELK COUNTY HISTORICAL SOCIETY
Box 361
Ridgway, Pennsylvania 15853

Miscellaneous documents relating to P. P. Bliss and the music of Elk County, as reflected in the articles by Alice L. Wessman in the Society's journal, *The Elk Horn,* 2/3 (1966), 2–3; 6/1 (1970), 1–8; and 6/2 (1970), 3

—Mary C. McMahon

1380
P. P. BLISS MUSEUM
Rome, Pennsylvania 18837

Philip Paul Bliss (1838–76, composer, hymnodist, and singer), personal papers, including 50 letters, 14 hymnals, 35 sheet-music editions of his songs, photographs, and memorabilia

—George L. Abell

1381
LACKAWANNA HISTORICAL SOCIETY

232 Monroe Avenue
Scranton, Pennsylvania 18510

Jones Musical Collection, containing the programs, press clippings, and other professional materials used by Dr. David E. Jones (1867–1947, music critic for the *Scranton Tribune*), in 10 scrapbooks; also his personal music library, 6 linear meters

—William P. Lewis

1382
AMERICAN GUILD OF ORGANISTS—PITTSBURGH CHAPTER

c/o Lee Kohlenberg, Jr., Dean
309 Walnut Street
Sewickley, Pennsylvania 15143

Archives of the Chapter (formerly known as the Western Pennsylvania Chapter), including the charter, constitution and by-laws, minutes from 1921– , and other documents, in all 1 linear meter

1383
SEWICKLEY PUBLIC LIBRARY

Thorn and Broad Streets
Sewickley, Pennsylvania 15143

Stephen Collins Foster (1826–1864), 6 sheet-music items, 1850s, biographical materials, and 5 Foster Hall *Bulletins*
Hymnals, 10 late 19th-century items
Alexander C. Robinson Collection of Western Pennsylvania, including Freeman Lewis, *The Beauties of Harmony* (Pittsburgh, 1816)
Sewickley Music Club, 6 vols. of minutes, 1922–73

—Ruth Fondi

1384
TOWANDA MUSEUM

Bradford County Historical Society
21 Main Street
Towanda, Pennsylvania 18848

Philip P. Bliss (1838–76, gospel-song writer), tape recording documenting his career, as described in Sylvia Wilson, "Philip P. Bliss," *The Settler*, 16/4 (1978), 1–16
Towanda Musical Society (1878–), archives, as described in *The Settler*, 16/4 (1978), 17–23

—Mrs. A. Carlton Wilson

1385
PENNSYLVANIA STATE UNIVERSITY
PSt

Fred Lewis Pattee Library
University Park, Pennsylvania 16802

Penn State Room

See Leon J. Stout, "The Arts at Penn State: A Preliminary Guide to . . . Holdings" (typescript, 1979)

Local theater materials, 1897–1974, 16 linear meters, including photographs, programs, posters, scrapbooks, correspondence, and financial records of the Penn State Players and other groups
Vertical file materials, including a general file containing programs, sheet music, announcements, minutes, and other records of local and University music groups, 1900– , 60 linear cm.; pictures, ca. 1890– , 110 items, of the State College Women's Club, Music Section (now the State College Choral Society), and other music groups; and programs, ca. 1898– , 3.2 linear meters

Special Collections

Sheet music, including 5 bound vols.; 200 miscellaneous single items; and 200 minstrel songs, the latter accessible through a typescript list of titles
Songbooks, including 30 tunebooks, 1780s–1870s; also 20 18th-century and 75 19th-century Pennsylvania imprints
Posters of Philadelphia musical and other events, 1836–1900, collected by William Seddinger Dye and presented by his grandson, William S. Dye III
Century-Strand Theatre Lighting Archive, including materials relating to the development of equipment specially designed for music auditoriums

Arts Library

Piano manufacturers' catalogues and brochures, 10 items; also a brochure of the "Great Organ" at Wanamaker's department store, Philadelphia

Music Department Collections

Charles Wakefield Cadman, personal papers, including sheet music and other published music; holograph music mss and ms copies; 140 personal letters; scrapbooks, programs, and photographs; cylinders of his recordings of American Indian music; 78-rpm discs and tape recordings of his songs and arrangements; and 8-mm. films made by him. See Harry Perison, *Charles Wakefield Cadman: His Life and Works* (Ph.D. diss., University of Rochester, 1978), pp. 438–39, passim, and pp. 452–74 of the "Bibliography"

—Carole Franklin

1386
AMERICAN BAPTIST CHURCHES EDITORIAL LIBRARY

Valley Forge, Pennsylvania 19481

Judson Press Collection, containing all books and materials printed and published by the American

Baptist Publication Society, 1840– , 2000 vols., including 100 hymnals and songbooks

—Dorothy Martin

1387
WARREN COUNTY HISTORICAL SOCIETY
Box 427
Warren, Pennsylvania 16365

Manuscript and published music by local composers, 10 linear cm., mostly for band
Leroy B. Campbell (founder and director of the Warren Conservatory of Music), 5 linear cm. of ms music
Warren Conservatory of Music, 15 linear cm. of papers, ca. 1908–62, including programs, clippings, and announcements
Philomel Club, annual programs, ca. 1925–77, 55 items
Programs of other local or regional musical events, 8 linear cm., ca. 1875– ; also theater programs of Library Hall (later Library Theater), in scrapbooks of the manager, ca. 1881–1926
Printed sheet music, 500 separate items, ca. 1890–1930, and 10 linear cm. of bound music books, ca. 1835–67
Photographs of local musicians and music groups, 50 items

—Chase Putnam

1388
WARREN PUBLIC LIBRARY   PWa
205 Market Street
Warren, Pennsylvania 16365

Hugh Robertson (1899–1966, local physician), sheet-music collection, 3600 items, 1934–55, particularly strong in imprints of the 1850s, 1890s, and 1904–40, with a card index for titles and show names

—Ann Lesser

1389
WAYNESBURG COLLEGE   PWayC
Waynesburg, Pennsylvania 15370

Sheet music, 600 popular items, from the Civil War to World War I
Presbyterian hymnals and school songbooks, 40 items, late 19th and 20th centuries
Songbooks, 100 items used by local singing societies, including several vols. in shape notation, 1816–
Waynesburg College Music Conservatory, concert programs, 1880– , 50 items
Recordings, including 600 78-rpm discs, partly of Caruso and early jazz; and an archive of local folk music, mostly vocal and fiddle music, 30 tapes, 1930–

—James D. Randolph

1390
CHESTER COUNTY   PWcHi
HISTORICAL SOCIETY
225 North High Street
West Chester, Pennsylvania 19380

Music mss and sheet music by Chester County composers, also miscellaneous published songbooks
Information on 19th-century singing schools in Pennsylvania, in diaries of Mary Ann Charlton, 1844–49, and Alice Cheney, 1863, and in a letter from David Parry to Peter Smedley, as cited by Richard Rosewall, *Singing Schools of Pennsylvania, 1800–1900* (Ph. D. diss. University of Minnesota, 1969)
Newspaper clipping file, 1808– , with materials relating to Samuel Barber (who was born in West Chester)

—Kathy Shady

1391
WEST CHESTER STATE COLLEGE   PWcS
West Chester, Pennsylvania 19380

Music Library collections, including popular sheet music, 1900–1930, and 20 hymnals and school songbooks, 1850–80
Francis Harvey Green Library, Special Collections, including 75 linear cm. of ms band and orchestral music by Edward Zimmer (College faculty member), ca. 1920s, and 30 linear cm. of College concert programs, 1880–

—Allison Carmichael, Gerald Schoelkopf

1392
KING'S COLLEGE   PWbK
D. Leonard Corgan Library
Wilkes-Barre, Pennsylvania 18702

George Korson (1899–1967) Folklore Archive, including personal papers and research notes on his studies of Pennsylvania coal-mine folklore and folksong, 13 linear meters; field recordings of interviews with miners, 107 tapes and 40 discs; and photographs and clippings. See Judith Tierney, *A Description of the George Korson Folklore Archive* (Wilkes-Barre, 1973), and her summary, "The George Korson Folklore Archive," *Keystone Folklore Quarterly*, 16 (1971), 108–11

—Judith Tierney

1393
LYCOMING COUNTY
HISTORICAL SOCIETY
858 West Fourth Street
Williamsport, Pennsylvania 17701

Sheet music, 100 items printed in Williamsport, 1900–1920
Elks Pepasz Band (local marching band), 50 items of papers, photographs, and instruments, 1831–
Moravian Symphony Orchestra, Bethlehem, 100 items of photographs, lists of players, and miscellaneous materials, ca. 1930s
Programs of Williamsport opera houses, 1000 items, including the Ulman Opera House, 1868–74, Elliot's Academy of Music, 1870–93, Lycoming Opera House, 1892–1915, Vallamont Park Pavilion, 1895–1915, and Majestic Theater, 1917–37

—Andrew K. Grugan

1394

GOSPEL SONGWRITERS MUSEUM

P. P. Bliss Homestead
Rome Village
Wysox, Pennsylvania 18854

Philip Paul Bliss (1838–76), 35 editions of his sheet music, 14 songbooks, and 1 journal, as preserved with other personal effects in the home he built for his parents in 1863

Letters from Bliss to members of his family, 50 items, some cited in Victor Chalres Detty, *P. P. Bliss: A Centennial Sketch of His Life and Work* (Wysox, 1938). See also Bobby Joe Neil, *Philip P. Bliss (1838–1876): Gospel Hymn Composer and Compiler* (Ed.D. diss., New Orleans Baptist Theological Seminary, 1977)

Daniel B. Towner (1850–1919, gospel-song composer, of Wysox), 10 published songbooks

—George L. Abell

1395

Mark and Susan OSTERMAN

26 Penn Valley Drive
Yardley, Pennsylvania 19067

Collection of early American banjo music, including 40 music mss, ca. 1880–1900; 30 books of banjo solos, mostly 1870s–80s, and including a 1st edition songbook of Christy's Minstrels (ca. 1840); and 78-rpm disc and cylinder recordings of banjo music

Miscellaneous papers of musicians, many not connected with the U.S., but including material relating to Joseph Rogers (drum maker) and Peter Conway ("Father of the U.S. band")

Victrola (Camden), 200 original or copied ms scores and parts for works recorded on this label ca. 1900

Published sheet music, 400 items, ca. 1800–1850, including a Stephen Foster autograph

Programs, mostly from New York City and Pennsylvania, 50 items

Catalogues of antique musical instruments and sheet music, 15 items, ca. 1850–1900

Recordings of Big Band music, 60 78-rpm discs

1396

HISTORICAL SOCIETY OF YORK COUNTY   PYHi

250 East Market Street
York, Pennsylvania 17403

John Durang, diary, including operatic references, as cited in Alan S. Downer, *The Memoirs of John Durang, American Actor, 1785–1816* (Pittsburgh, 1966)

James Warren Shettel, materials relating to the theater and circus, including correspondence, route books, playbills, broadsides, and photographs, in all 1.5 linear meters

Matinee Musical Club of York, scrapbook, "Old Time Music of York," as cited in Richard Byron Rosewall, *Singing Schools of Pennsylvania, 1800–1900* (Ph.D. diss., University of Minnesota, 1969)

Materials relating to early American organs, including file 430-5, "Barbara Schmidt Organ," as cited in Tal-

mage Whitman Dean, *The Organ in Eighteenth-Century English Colonial America* (Ph.D. diss., University of Southern California, 1960)

In addition to the repositories listed above, the following have also reported holdings of the materials indicated:

Aliquippa—B. F. Jones Memorial Library: sheet music, songbooks, programs

Allentown—Muhlenberg College, John A. W. Haas Library: songbooks

Annville—Annville Free Library: songbooks

Bala-Cynwyd—Bala-Cynwyd Memorial Library: sheet music

Bedford—Bedford Historic Village: songbooks, pictures, miscellaneous

Bethlehem—Christ Church, United Church of Christ, Library: songbooks

Brookville—Jefferson County Historical and Genealogical Society: sheet music, songbooks, other printed music, programs, catalogues, pictures, recordings, miscellaneous

Bryn Athyn—Academy of the New Church, Library: songbooks, other printed music, recordings

Chambersburg—Coyle Library: sheet music, songbooks

Clarks Summit—Baptist Bible College, Murphy Memorial Library: songbooks

Collingdale—Mrs. John Hutchinson: sheet music, songbooks

Connellsville—Connellsville Carnegie Library: sheet music, other printed music, programs

Darby—Collingdale Public Library: songbooks, catalogues, pictures

Doylestown—Bucks County Historical Society Library: sheet music, songbooks, programs, pictures, miscellaneous

Doylestown—Delaware Valley College of Science and Agriculture, Krauskopf Library: songbooks

Easton—Lafayette College, David B. Skillman Library: sheet music, recordings

Ebensburg—Ebensburg Public Library: songbooks

Elizabethtown—Elizabethtown College, Zug Memorial Library: programs

Emmaus—Emmaus Public Library: songbooks

Ephrata—Pennsylvania Federation of Junior History: songbooks

Gettysburg—Adams County Historical Society: sheet music, songbooks, other printed music, programs, pictures, recordings

Harmony—Harmonist Historic and Memorial Association: sheet music, songbooks

Honesdale—Wayne County Historical Society: songbooks

Huntingdon—Huntingdon County Historical Society: sheet music, songbooks, programs

Jenkintown—Abington Library Society: songbooks, catalogues

Johnstown—Johnstown Flood Museum Association: sheet music, songbooks, pictures, recordings, miscellaneous

Kingston—Wyoming Seminary, Kirby Library: songbooks, recordings

Lancaster—Lancaster Bible College, Library: songbooks, catalogues

Lancaster—Lancaster Theological Seminary: songbooks

Lancaster—Trinity Lutheran Church: miscellaneous

Lebanon—Lebanon Community Library: recordings

Lenhartsville—Pennsylvania Dutch Folk Culture Society: songbooks

McEwensville—Montgomery House, Library: songbooks

Meadville—Ralph E. Luker: songbooks

Montrose—Susquehanna County Free Library: sheet music, songbooks

Mt. Pleasant—Mt. Pleasant Public Library: sheet music, pictures, recordings, miscellaneous

New Castle—New Castle Public Library: sheet music, songbooks

Penn Hills—Penn Hills Library: songbooks, programs

Philadelphia—INA Corporation Museum and Archives: sheet music, programs, pictures, miscellaneous pertaining to firemen

Phoenixville—Public Library: sheet music, songbooks

Pittsburgh—Duquesne University, Library: sheet music, other printed music

Pittsburgh—Northland Public Library: songbooks, other printed music, recordings

Pittsburgh—Pittsburgh History and Landmarks Foundation: sheet music, songbooks, programs, recordings, miscellaneous

Pittsburgh—Polish Historical Commission of Central Council of Polish Organization: programs, pictures

Red Lion—Kaltreider Memorial Library: songbooks, recordings

St. Marys—Historical Society of St. Marys and Benzinger Township: recordings

Selinsgrove—Susquehanna University, Blough Learning Center: sheet music, songbooks, recordings

Smethport—McKean County Historical Society: sheet music, recordings

Tionesta—Sara Stewart Bovard Memorial Library: sheet music, songbooks

Troy—Bradford–Wyoming County Libraries: sheet music, songbooks, other printed music

Waterford—Waterford Public Library: songbooks

Waynesburg—Greene County Historical Society: songbooks, Miscellaneous

Wilkes-Barre—Wyoming Historical and Geological Society: sheet music, programs, pictures, recordings

York—York College of Pennsylvania, Library: sheet music

Rhode Island

1397

BARRINGTON COLLEGE RBaB

Library

Middle Highway

Barrington, Rhode Island 02806

Sheet music, including late 19th- and early 20th-century piano music comprising the performance libraries of Avis Vliben Charbonnel, Ruth Tripp, and Margaret Mason

Manuscript music by College composers, 1930s

Hymnals, 125 items of various denominations, ca. 1900

School songbooks, 12 early 19th-century items

Photographs of College music groups and concerts, 1900–1930, 150 items

—Donald E. Brown

1398

Lionel D. WYLD

Rolling Acres

20 Countryside Drive

Cumberland, Rhode Island 02864

Archival materials concerning Erie Canal folksongs of the 19th century, as reflected in Wyld's *Low Bridge! Folklore and the Erie Canal* (Syracuse, 1962)

1399

NEWPORT HISTORICAL SOCIETY RNHi

82 Touro Street

Newport, Rhode Island 02840

Sheet music, 40 items, with specific reference to Newport

Tunebook in ms, ca. 1810, entitled "The Singers Assistant, Containing a Number of Psalm Tunes, The Property of Miss L. W. Morris, Newport"

Theatrical scrapbooks, 10 vols., 1885–1933, including programs of musical events

—Mrs. Peter Bolhouse

1400

REDWOOD LIBRARY AND ATHENAEUM RNR

50 Bellevue Avenue

Newport, Rhode Island 02840

Songbooks, 20 items of 19th-century popular music, including *Slave Songs of the United States* (1867)

—Donald T. Gibbs

1401

Thomas E. GREENE

119 Olney Avenue

North Providence, Rhode Island 02911

Materials concerning the guitar, including 11 separate sheet-music songs and 1 bound vol. of miscellaneous solos and songs, 1820s–60s; 5 method books, 1838–63; and ms guitar lessons by James Garcia for Miss Maria McCormick, ca. 1850

1402
BROWN UNIVERSITY   RPB

John Hay Library
Department of Special Collections
Providence, Rhode Island 02912

This report was coordinated by John Stanley

Harris Collection

Catalogued materials in the collection are cited in the *Dictionary Catalog of the Harris Collection of American Poetry and Plays* (Boston, 1974; suppl. 1977). The collection originally assembled by C. Fiske Harris has been partially dispersed through other units of the John Hay Library, the sheet music collection in particular, as noted below

Songsters, 1100 items, 1779– . Early titles are cited in *Lowens*, including 40 copies not located elsewhere. For later holdings, see Rachel Young, "American Songsters up to 1860" (typescript, 1950s–), and "Songsters, 1860–90" (typescript, 1950s–), both of which list materials in the American Antiquarian Society, Worcester, Mass., as well. See also Alice Louise Thorpe, *American Songsters of the 18th Century* (M.A. thesis, Brown University, 1935); Arthur Ansel Lewis, *American Songsters, 1800–1805* (M.A. thesis, Brown University, 1937); George John Devine, *American Songsters, 1806–1815* (M.A. thesis, Brown University, 1940); and Thomazia Dube Roy, *A Study and Catalog of Presidential Campaign Songsters in the Harris Collection . . . and the McLellan Lincoln Collection* (M.A.T. thesis, Brown University, 1964)

Hymnals, 5500 items, 3175 with music and 1375 with texts only, including many periodical publications and editions of Isaac Watts, also editions of William Billings and Andrew Law

Folk and popular music, 6800 items, mostly songbooks, but also including libretti and musical plays. Areas of strength include sentimental songs, Civil War songs, anthologies of art songs by 20th-century U.S. composers, and American operas and operettas

Henry S. Saunders Collection of Whitmaniana, including 100 songs in 4 bound vols. with words by Walt Whitman. See Saunders' "Whitman Music List" (typescript, 1920s?)

Yiddish musical theater collection of Menache Vaxer, including 10 ms and 40 published operettas, some of them to texts by J. Rumshinsky and Peretz Sandler

Hugh Frederick MacColl (1885–1953, local composer), 46 vols. of ms music, mostly songs but also operas and instrumental works; also miscellaneous printed editions, ms photocopies, and recordings

Other miscellaneous materials, including books and other writings pertaining to dance, particularly square dancing of the 19th and early 20th centuries; also scrapbooks and playbills with scattered musical materials and references

—Rosemary L. Cullen

Sheet Music

The collection, developed out of the Harris Collection largely through the efforts of S. Foster Damon, comprises 150,000 vocal items arranged by title; 100,000 instrumental items arranged by composer or title; 300 bound vols.; 100,000 folio orchestrations; and 100,000 miscellaneous items. See Damon's *Series of Old American*

Songs (Providence, 1936); his "The Harris Collection of Sheet Music," *Books at Brown*, 13 (May 1951), 1–4; and his booklet on *Yankee Doodle*, "issued . . . for the annual meeting of the Bibliographical Society of America" (Providence, 1959); also Ann Banks, "They're Not Writing Songs Like That Anymore," *Brown Alumni Monthly* (March 1973), 24–29. Included in these totals are various specialty areas, as described below

U.S. imprints to 1825, including 150 pre-1801 items arranged by *Sonneck–Upton* entries; and 3000 titles, 1801–25, arranged by *Wolfe* numbers

Lithographed music covers, mid 19th century, including 800 items from the New York firm of Endicott, a bequest of F. Monroe Endicott, 1935; also 600 items from other New York firms, and 1000 from Boston firms

Confederate imprints, 170 items, arranged by *Crandall* and *Harwell* numbers

Yiddish sheet music, 700 items, mostly 1900–1930, from the Vaxer collection

World War I titles, 3000 items, and World War II titles, 1000 items

Music by black composers or on black subjects, 5000 items

Rhode Island music, 2000 items by Rhode Island composers or with Rhode Island association

—John Stanley

Broadside Collection

Song sheets, 5000 loose items and 2200 items in bound vols., mostly 1830–70, and including many Civil War items, mostly issued by A. W. Auner and J. H. Johnson in Philadelphia, and by H. de Marsan, Charles Magnus, and J. Wrigley in New York. The collection is being catalogued and arranged by the system used in Edwin Wolf II, *American Song Sheets, Slip Ballads, and Poetical Broadsides* (Philadelphia, 1963), where many of these particular copies are cited

—Mary T. Russo

McLellan Lincoln Collection

Abraham Lincoln music, 325 items, 1860s–1900s, mostly sheet music, but with some broadsides and a few songbooks; also campaign songsters, other editions of printed music, programs, and recordings. See Esther Cowles Cushman, *Lincoln Sheet Music* (n.p., 1932), prepared by the first curator of the Charles W. McLellan Collection; also her later bibliography of Lincoln music (unpublished typescript)

John Hay Collection, including 7 songs with texts by Hay

—Mrs. Virginia M. Trescott

Manuscript Collection

Johann Christian Gottlieb Graupner (1767–1836), personal papers, 58 items collected by Horace M. Reynolds, including ms music, account books, and ledgers, 1802–38, concerning Graupner's music-publishing activity, as well as that of the Franklin Music Warehouse, which he operated with John Rowe Parker

Mellinger Edward Henry (1873–1946, folklorist), personal papers, 1910–42, 1000 items, including correspondence, songs, mss and drafts of speeches and articles, and various typescripts and proofsheets of his folksong books

S. Foster Damon (1893–1971, professor of English, poet, William Blake scholar, and curator of the Harris Collection), personal papers, 24 linear meters, including music, correspondence, and research notes relating to his work with American sheet music and other topics

American popular verse, 1762– , 800 items, some with specific musical reference, arranged by subject of text'

Harris Miscellaneous Manuscripts, 500 letters and other ms items, 1740– , including anonymous and unpublished verse, music, hymns, operas, songbooks, commonplace books, and scrapbooks. Among the holdings are vols. of Eunice Carew, Norwich, Conn., 1790; Ellen Maria Byrne, Philadelphia, ca. 1797; and Susanna Mueller (Susan Miller?), Lititz, Pa. (?), ca. 1800. See William Dinneen, "Early American Manuscript Music-Books," *Musical Quarterly*, 30 (1944), 50–62

—Clifton H. Jones

University Archives

Programs of concerts, operas, and other musical events at Brown University, 1377 items, including 17 items pre-1890, 25 items 1890 through the 1899–1900 season, 40 items through 1909–10, 27 items through 1919–20, 47 items through 1929–30, 133 items through 1939–40, and other items post-1940 or undated

—Martha L. Mitchell

Miscellaneous Holdings

Hamilton C. MacDougall (1858–1945), 3 vols. of research notes relating to his studies of early New England psalm-singing

Sidney Smith Rider, "Rhode Island Scrapiana," mostly 19th-century printed ephemera with scattered music materials and references, not analyzed by content, in 60 vols.

William Dinneen, "William Billings, 1746–1800: The Psalm-Tunes and Fuging Pieces" (typescript, 1950)

1403
JOHN CARTER BROWN LIBRARY   RPJCB
Brown University
Providence, Rhode Island 02912

> A special collection of materials on the discovery and early history of the New World, to 1800. See the Library's various catalogues, entitled *Bibliotheca Americana*, which however have no subject access to music; also the exhibition catalogue, *Music in Colonial America* (Providence, 1975; hereinafter cited as *MCA*)

Sacred music books, 40 pre-1800 items, including major works as cited in *MCA*, pp. 4–12

Sheet music, 100 items, mostly pre-1800, including major items as cited in *MCA*, pp. 11–12, 25–33

Music in periodicals, separate announcements and programs, and miscellaneous printed musical ephemera, including major items as cited in *MCA*, passim

Music mss, including Mary B. Steller's piano exercise book, Philadelphia, 1784 (*MCA*, p. 16); Captain Megee's tunebook, shipboard, pre-1809 (*MCA*, p. 16); and Providence theater programs, 1811–12 (*MCA*, p. 17)

—Samuel J. Hough

1404
Arlan R. COOLIDGE
88 Meeting Street
Providence, Rhode Island 02906

Tunebooks and hymnals, 367 items, mostly 1818–75, a few later, and miscellaneous other music books, as listed in a 29-page inventory

Sheet music, 2000 items, 1790s–1930s

Personal papers, containing correspondence and research notes relating to Rhode Island music history, including studies of Francis H. Brown and Harrison Millard

1405
PROVIDENCE PUBLIC LIBRARY   RP
150 Empire Street
Providence, Rhode Island 02903

Art and Music Department

Sheet music, 4000 items, mid 19th and 20th centuries

Hymnals and school and popular songbooks, 500 published items, 1875–

Programs of local concerts, 1850–

Scrapbooks of press clippings concerning music, 1929–

Herbert Chandler Thrasher, "Two Hundred and Fifty Years of Music in Providence, Rhode Island, 1636–1886" (typescript, 1937)

Pictures of musicians and musical instruments in Providence, 1000 items, in a general photograph collection of 160,000 items

Recordings, including 1300 78-rpm discs of popular and classical music

Special Collections

David Wallace Reeves (1838–1900), 130 band mss, 3 operettas, photographs, correspondence, 1891–94, and a minute book of the American Brass Band, 1859–1906

Harris Collection, including 700 Confederate broadside ballads, and 100 items of Civil War sheet music

—Susan R. Waddington, Virginia M. Adams

1406
RHODE ISLAND BLACK
HERITAGE SOCIETY
45 Hamilton Street
Providence, Rhode Island 02907

Sheet music, 24 popular items, ca. 1920

Hymnals, 24 Episcopal and Baptist items, 1880s to early 1900s

Brockholst Livingston (poet), 3 music mss, 1920s, and 5 linear cm. of personal papers

African Union Society, Newport, 30 linear cm. of papers, 1680

Programs of local church organists, 1859 to early 20th century

Recordings, including 700 78-rpm discs of early jazz and blues, 1920s

—Leon Brody

1407
RHODE ISLAND   RHi
HISTORICAL SOCIETY
52 Power Street
Providence, Rhode Island 02906

Manuscripts and Special Collections

Kentish Guards, East Greenwich, R.I., 2 contracts for a drummer and fifer, 1774

Sally Brown's music book, Providence, ca. 1780, including ms exercises for keyboard. See *Music in Colonial America: An Exhibition at the John Carter Brown Library* (Providence, 1975)

Herreshoff Music Collection, including 10 linear cm. of vocal and keyboard music, copied or collected by members of the Herreshoff family of Providence, and including a ms text of "A New Song of Liberty," ca. 1776; also commonplace books of A. M. Blodgett and Sarah Brown Herreshoff (1773–1846; cf. the above entry). See Arlan Coolidge's preliminary inventory to the collection, 1975

Psallonians (local singing society), 4 vols. of minutes, ca. 1816

Music books, 6 19th-century ms vols., including a vol. of songs with guitar or keyboard accompaniment compiled by Luigia Bartolini, and a vol. owned by John R. Bartless (1805–86)

Jean (Browning) Madeira (1918–72, operatic contralto), personal papers, 4 linear meters

Printed Materials

Sheet music, songbooks, and other printed music by Rhode Island composers or related to Rhode Island, 1500 items

David Wallace Reeves (1838–1900), sheet music and memorabilia, also brass instruments used by him

Programs, including theater and vaudeville playbills, 1800–1815 and 1880s–1930s

      —Nancy Chudacoff, Nathaniel Shipton

1408
WESTERLY HISTORICAL SOCIETY
c/o Dorothy W. Benson
36 Newton Avenue
Westerly, Rhode Island 02891

Hopkinton (R.I.) Singing School, 2 membership lists, 1852

Lantern color-slides, 54 items, containing words and illustrations for 5 early 20th-century popular songs

1409
WESTERLY PUBLIC LIBRARY   RWe
Box 356
Westerly, Rhode Island 02891

Sheet music, 600 popular items, 1920s–30s

Songbooks, 50 vols. of popular and sacred music, 1920s–

Westerly Music Club, 1 folder of papers, 1920s–30s

Programs of local concerts, 1920s– , scattered in local-history vertical files

      —Karen M. Light

1410
WOONSOCKET HISTORICAL SOCIETY
c/o Phyllis Thomas
563 South Main Street
Woonsocket, Rhode Island 02891

Sheet music, 600 popular piano and piano-vocal works, late 19th and early 20th centuries

Protestant hymnals, 8 early 20th-century items

Songbooks of popular and classical music, 24 early 20th-century items

Programs of local school concerts, 30 linear cm., 1900–1920

Recordings, including 6 Edison discs, ca. 1890s, 75 78-rpm discs of popular and classical music, and 10- and 12-inch discs, ca. 1910–20

In addition to the repositories listed above, the following have also reported holdings of the materials indicated:

Cumberland—Sisters of Mercy Provincialate Religious Archives: songbooks

Kingston—Pettaquamscutt Historical Society: sheet music, songbooks, pictures, recordings

Newport—International Tennis Hall of Fame and Tennis Museum: programs

North Smithfield—Beethoven Club: programs, pictures, miscellaneous

Providence—First Baptist Church in America: sheet music

Providence—Rhode Island School of Design, Museum of Art: sheet music, songbooks

Woonsocket—Burrillville Historical and Preservation Society: songbooks

Woonsocket—Harris Institute, Library: songbooks

Woonsocket—Union St. Jean Baptiste, Mallet Lobrary: French and French-Canadian songbooks

South Carolina

1411
ANDERSON COLLEGE
316 South Boulevard
Anderson, South Carolina 29621

Lily Strickland Anderson (1884–1958), 115 vocal scores, 25 piano scores, photographs, paintings, poems, and memorabilia

      —Annie Francis Blackman

1412
Helen BURRISS

1806 Holly Street
Anderson, South Carolina 29621

Materials relating to Lily Strickland Anderson (the collector's music-teacher), including letters, published scores, and pamphlets

1413
CENTRAL WESLEYAN COLLEGE

Library–Learning Center
Wesleyan Station
Central, South Carolina 29630

Wesleyan Methodist Church of America, 25 hymnals, 1863–1976
Frank M. Graham (1859–1931, gospel-song writer), biographical files, also editions of his *Songs of Jesus*, in the Wesleyana Collection
—Martha Evatt, Joel F. Reed

1414
CHARLESTON COUNTY LIBRARY ScCF

404 King Street
Charleston, South Carolina 29403

Theodore Wichmann (Charleston Symphony Orchestra conductor), papers, 1920s–60s
Eola Willis (arts patron), personal papers
Sheet music and songbooks, 12 boxes, early 20th century
Programs of Charleston concerts, 1930s–
—Jan Buvinger

1415
CHARLESTON MUSEUM LIBRARY ScCMu

121 Rutledge Avenue
Charleston, South Carolina 29401

Music book in ms, ca. 1810
Sheet music, 6000 items, mostly 1820–85; also 5000 items in the family collection of Gov. William Aiken (in his home)
—Donald G. Herold

1416
COLLEGE OF CHARLESTON ScCC

Library
66 George Street
Charleston, South Carolina 29401

Charles Henry Meltzer (1873–1936, New York dramatist and critic), collection of musicians' autographs, 19th and 20th centuries, including a letter to Meltzer from George Gershwin, 1928, concerning *Porgy and Bess*
—Ralph Melnick

1417
Donald G. HEROLD

778 Jim Isle Drive
Charleston, South Carolina 29412

Sheet music, 1500 items, 1835– , mostly 1870–1940, arranged largely by subject

1418
SOUTH CAROLINA ScHi
HISTORICAL SOCIETY

100 Meeting Street
Charleston, South Carolina 29401

See *South Carolina Historical Society Manuscripts*, suppl. to the *South Carolina Historical Magazine* (July, 1979)

Personal Papers and Correspondence

Bacot–Huger Collection, 1754–1927, including correspondence and a receipt book of Daniel Huger (1779–1858, plantation owner), with receipts to Charleston music teachers, 1804–18
Porcher Family Papers, 1771–1940, including a notebook of spirituals and clippings relating to the Society for the Preservation of Spirituals
Allston–Pringle–Hill Papers, 1812–1929, including a letter from Adele Allston to C. P. Allston regarding a concert by Adelina Patti, 1860, and a diary of Elizabeth W. Allston mentioning music, 1905
Barbot Family Papers, 1820–1960, 75 linear cm. of clippings, correspondence, notebooks, scrapbooks, and photographs, including materials of Mrs. P. J. Barbot (Charleston musician) and Blanche Hermine Barbot (1882–1966, music teacher, and master of the Charleston Musical Association)
G. H. D. Cramer, ms vol. of dance instructions, ca. 1880
Bacot–Rhett Papers, including a program of Rossini's *Stabat Mater* at St. Mary's Church, Charleston, 1869
John Bennett (1865–1956, folklorist), collection of research notes on the cries of Charleston street vendors, black music, and folksongs, also 100 transcriptions of spirituals, with words and music

Organizational Records

Siegling Music House (Charleston music firm, founded 1819 by John Siegling) Collection, 1820–1955, 105 papers and 52 vols. of business records, 3 bound vols. of music, and 24 sheet-music items
Trinity and Cumberland Methodist Church, Charleston, 4 ms and published hymnals, 1860–1903, and 1 folder of ms and published sheet music
Charleston Musical Society, 1 vol. of papers, ca. 1919–22, and 1 folder of miscellaneous materials
Society for the Preservation of Spirituals, 1.4 linear meters of papers, 1923– , including notebooks of spirituals, minutes, correspondence, scrapbooks of clippings, and programs
Clippings, pamphlets, and papers, 1 folder each for the Charleston Symphony Orchestra, Musical Arts Club, and Academy of Music; also 1 photograph of the Charleston Festival Chorus, 1909; and correspondence on music in Charleston
Charleston String Symphony, brochure, n.d., and program, 1937

Other Materials

Sheet music, 9 separate items and 6 bound vols. of 19th- and early 20th-century music, published in Charleston and New Orleans

Songbooks, 2 popular items, 1941 and 1901; also 1 Methodist Episcopal hymnal, 1828

Jacob Eckhard (1715–1833, organist), choirmaster's book used in St. Michael's Church, Charleston, as reproduced in George W. Williams, *Jacob Eckhard's Choirmaster's Book of 1809* (Columbia, 1971), on deposit from St. Michael's Church; also ms music in a vol. of published piano music. See also materials in the University of South Carolina, Columbia

"Instructions for the Kent Bugle," ms copy from Logier's *Art of Playing the Kent Bugle*, 1813

Desire Ikelheimer (Charleston violinist), copy of a lithograph, 1849

"The World Turned Upside Down," ms copy for septet, 1908

Elizabeth P. Simons, a history of *Music in Charleston from 1732 to 1919* (Charleston, 1927)

—Sallie Doscher

1419
LUTHERAN THEOLOGICAL SOUTHERN SEMINARY   ScCoT

Lineberger Memorial Library
4201 Main Street
Columbia, South Carolina

Lutheran hymnals, 500 items, 1760– , including many 18th-century U.S. and German imprints

—W. Richard Fritz

1420
UNIVERSITY OF SOUTH CAROLINA   ScU

Columbia, South Carolina 29208

South Caroliniana Library

James Edward Calhoun (1798–1889), 28 ms copies of music, songs, and Spanish-guitar pieces, some composed by Joseph Watson, 1820s

Jacob Eckhard, Jr., ms score of *Blucher's Triumph*, 1832; also portions of a choirmaster's book used at St. Michael's Church Charleston, 1809–33, attributed to Eckhard. See also the South Carolina Historical Society, Charleston

Darius Gandy (1838–82, of Darlington District, S.C.), records of tuition for school and music lessons

Annie J. Hart (1884–1931), 7 music mss

James C. Janney (1856–80, hotel proprietor, Columbia), playbills for minstrel shows and concerts

Lily Strickland Anderson (1887–1958), 46 items of papers, including letters and articles describing her career, and an incomplete ms of "Mah Lindy Lou," 1920

Fud Livingston (1906–57), 100 items of papers, including published music, pictures, and memorabilia

Maurice Jefferson Matteson (1893–1964, singer, teacher, and folksong collector), 458 items of papers, 1917–70, relating to American folksong and black music, including correspondence and 5 vols. of unpublished ballads

Hugh Philips Williamson and Evelyn Potter Williamson (music teachers and performers), 2330 items of papers, 1907–75, including recital and concert programs, clippings, photographs, correspondence, and records of the University Music Department and the South Carolina Opera Workshop Guild

Sheet music, 500 items, including songs by South Carolina composers or about South Carolina, 1800–

Hymnals, 14 19th-century South Carolina imprints

Other printed music, including a collection of Confederate music, entitled *Shelby's Lost Cause Music*, 1860s; and 15 vols. of popular music, 1830s–60s

Columbia Music Festival, 26 programs, 1909–52

Stateburg Literary and Musical Society, historical sketch, 1885–1949

Recordings, including 9 78-rpm discs

Rare Book Room, Cooper Library

Edwin Hughes (1884–1965, pianist, editor for G. Schirmer Co.), 642 published scores, 3 mss by Henry Cowell written for Hughes, 118 books on music and American history, scrapbooks, programs, and magazine articles

American music periodicals, 2 titles, 1829–86

Music Library

A general collection of 12,000 books, scores, and recordings, 20th century

—Eleanor M. Richardson

1421
DARLINGTON COUNTY HISTORICAL COMMISSION

Court House, Room 307
Darlington, South Carolina 29532

J. D. Smithdeal, "Darlington Guards March" (Columbia, S.C., and Columbus, Ohio, 1897)

Manuscript music (photocopies), 2 items, 1796, owned by Ezra Pugh

Darlington Music Club, papers and yearbooks, 1916–63

Early School of Music (Darlington-area music school), papers, including sheet music, exams, and student rosters, 1924–25

Programs of local concerts, 4 items, 1889–1901

Clippings and letters concerning Darlington County musicians and brass bands, 12 items, ca. 1858–1950

—Horace F. Rudisill

1422
FURMAN UNIVERSITY   ScGF

James B. Duke Library
Greenville, South Carolina 29613

William Walker (1809–75), ms music book containing 73 songs and anthems, 1832–33. See Milburn Price, "Miss Elizabeth Adams' Music Book: A Manuscript Predecessor of William Walker's *Southern Harmony*," *The Hymn*, 29/2 (1978), 70–75

Hymnals, 10 19th-century Baptist items

Basil Manley, Jr., personal papers, 1838–91, including original hymns, as cited in *Howell*, p. 254

—J. Glen Clayton

1423

WINTHROP COLLEGE ScRhW

Dacus Library
Rock Hill, South Carolina 29733

See the published guides to the ms and oral-history collections, and to the records relating to the College

Winthrop College Music Department (later the School of Music), a complete run of programs, 1896– , official archives, and a photographic file of musical events and organizations at the College, 1910–
Research materials for J. E. Walmsley and Nancy G.Campbell, *The Making of South Carolina: A Historical Pageant* (1921)
Juvenile Music Club of Rock Hill, scrapbook, 1936–
Haasis family papers, including programs of New York musical events, 1880s
College songbooks, 1915–

—Ronald J. Chepesiuk

1424

CALHOUN COUNTY MUSEUM

303 Butler Street
Saint Matthews, South Carolina 29135

Printed music, including 2 scrapbooks of half-guitar music used locally, ca. 1840
St. Matthews Spirit Band, 2 photographs, ca. 1900
Programs of late 19th-century local musicals, 12 items
Recordings, including 60 Edison discs and several cylinders, 1904

—Jeanne W. Ulmer

1425

CONVERSE COLLEGE ScSpC

Gwathmey Library
East Main Street
Spartanburg, South Carolina 29301

Sheet music, 2600 early 20th-century classical items, some of them donated by Walter Spry (1868–1953, Chicago music teacher)
William Walker, *Southern Harmony* (1835), initialed by him
Ernst Bacon, 2 music mss, "A Tree on the Plains" and "Ten Songs for Women's Chorus to Poems by Emily Dickinson"
Edwin Gerschefski (Converse College faculty member), 2 ms and 3 published scores
Lily Strickland (1884–1958), 1 box of published songs, piano music, and vocal music from her personal library
Radiana Pazmor (New York singing teacher), 12 letters to her from composers, including Charles Ives, Aaron Copland, Darius Milhaud, and William Grant Still; also several early 20th-century popular songbooks
Scrapbooks containing press clippings, 100 photographs, and programs of local concerts, 20 vols., 1890–1941
Spartanburg Symphony Orchestra, clippings, 1927–

Recordings, including 2 linear meters of 78-rpm discs of classical music, also Converse College Chorale concerts on tape

—Lenore Mack

1426

WOFFORD COLLEGE ScSpW

Sandor Teszler Library
Spartanburg, South Carolina 29301

Hymnals, 400 items, ca. 1850– , including gospel songbooks, books in small format with words only, and southern folk-hymnody works. The original collection of 168 items is described in Frank J. Anderson, *Hymns and Hymnody*, Wofford College Library, Special Collections Checklists, 1 (Spartanburg, 1970); to this material have been added vols. from the personal collection of Pierce Gault, Washington, D.C.

—Frank J. Anderson

1427

OLD SLAVE MART MUSEUM
AND LIBRARY

Miriam B. Wilson Foundation
Box 446
Sullivans Island, South Carolina 29482

Sheet music, songbooks, programs, photographs, and recordings, partly described in the *Catalog of the Old Slave Mart Museum and Library* (Boston, 1978)

—Judith Wragg Chase

In addition to the repositories listed above, the following have also reported holdings of the material indicated:

Allendale—University of South Carolina, Salkehatchie Regional Library: songbooks, recordings
Camden—Camden Archives: songbooks
Columbia—Confederation of South Carolina Local Historical Societies: songbooks
Columbia—South Carolina Confederate Relic Room and Museum: sheet music, songbooks
Due West—Erskine Theological Seminary, Library: songbooks
Florence—Florence Museum: sheet music, pictures, recordings, miscellaneous
Ft. Jackson—Ft. Jackson Museum: sheet music, songbooks
Hilton Head Island—Hilton Head Island Historical Society: sheet music, songbooks, other printed music
Orangeburg—South Carolina State College, Whittaker Library: printed music
Spartanburg—Spartanburg County Historical Association: sheet music, songbooks, pictures, recordings
Winnsboro—Fairfield County Historical Society: sheet music, songbooks

South Dakota

1428
DACOTAH PRAIRIE MUSEUM
Box 395
Aberdeen, South Dakota 57401

Ivor Thomas, "In Flanders' Field," ms vocal solo written in memory of his son, ca. 1919
Merritt Johnson (1904–78, organist), 5 published organ compositions, ca. 1925–60
Published organ-music books and piano-instruction books, 5 items, ca. 1920
Hymnals, 50 items, ca. 1900, mostly Lutheran, including some in German, Norwegian, and Swedish
School and community songbooks, 50 items, ca. 1900–1940
Sheet music, 1000 mostly popular items, ca. 1875–1950, including some by local composers
Programs of local Chautauqua presentations, theaters, community concert series, Northern State College (Aberdeen) performances, and traveling performers and groups
Recordings, including 100 cylinders and 450 78-rpm discs

—Helen J. Bergh

1429
SMITH–ZIMMERMAN HISTORICAL MUSEUM
Dakota State College
Madison, South Dakota 57042

F. M. Halstead (army bandmaster), sheet-music march, 1899
Programs, mostly of Chautauqua meetings and Dakota State College musical events, 30 items, ca. 1882–1932
Photographs of local town bands and of Norwegian singing groups from South Dakota, 20 items, ca. 1900
Recordings, including 100 78-rpm discs and 15 Edison cylinders

—Deborah Strahan

1430
George B. GERMAN MUSIC ARCHIVES
Siouxland Heritage Museum
200 West Sixth Street
Sioux Falls, South Dakota 57105

Charles Badger Clark, poems and songs in 10 published collections, ca. 1920
Ben Stoller, 50 ms compositions, ca. 1920–
George B. German (radio cowboy-singer and composer), ms compositions, clippings, promotional photographs, 3 hours of tape recordings, and film clips of him singing
Clifford Spurlock Collection, including master tapes of Carter Family recordings for Acme Records, 120 titles; also several hours of tapes of country and western music, ca. 1930–
Virgil Smith Collection of jazz, 500 78-rpm disc recordings and 2000 sheet-music items, 1923–

Mining songs and folksongs of the Black Hills, 10 hours of tape recordings of singing and oral-history interviews, also 6 copies of mining songs, and 30 ballads photocopied from Black Hills-area newspapers, ca. 1900–1910, collected in 1976 and documented by David Kemp
Songs relating to the Populist movement, copied from midwestern Populist newspapers

—David Kemp

1431
Freda HOSEN
108 East Thirty-fifth Street
Sioux Falls, South Dakota 57105

Popular sheet-music collection, 15,000 items, ca. 1830– , emphasizing social and historical topics, and including items by South Dakota composers or publishers
Recordings, 2000 items, including 78-rpm discs, Edison discs, and Edison cylinders

1432
W. H. OVER MUSEUM
University of South Dakota
Vermillion, South Dakota 57069

Hymnals in English or Norwegian, 5 items, ca. 1880–1920
Photographs, including a Civil War band at Point Lookout, Md., ca. 1863 (in the Stanley Morrow Collection), a Chautauqua band at Madison, S.D., and several Indian drummers

—June Sampson

1433
UNIVERSITY OF SOUTH DAKOTA   SdU
Vermillion, South Dakota 57069

Shrine to Music Museum

"Golden Age of Bands" collection, 170 linear meters of printed band and dance-orchestra arrangements, organized by title, and being catalogued
Manuscript parts used in the Midwest by dance bands of Central European origin, mostly Czech, in all 4 linear meters, ca. 1900
Sheet music, 20,000 items, ca. 1880– , unsorted and uncatalogued, including the stock of several music stores in South Dakota, Nebraska, Iowa, and Minnesota; also other printed music, hymnals, and songbooks, 3 linear meters
Personal papers, of Arne B. Larson relating to his professional career and the founding of the Shrine to Music Museum; and of early music graduates of the University
Programs of University concerts, 1900– , 3 linear meters
Pictures, mostly of midwestern bands and musicians, 1875– , 300 items
Recordings, 10,000 items, including 78-rpm discs, mostly midwestern popular music but also including classical items; 1000 cylinders; and 300 piano rolls

—André P. Larson

Oral History Center

James Jurren collection of American Indian music, mostly of South Dakota tribes, 44 tape recordings collected by him, ca. 1963, as part of the American Indian Research Project

Folk music of South Dakota, 34 tape recordings, collected mostly by Bernard Hagerty and David Kemp

Tape recordings concerning northern Great Plains music and the making and use of musical instruments, 156 items

—Judy Zabdyr

1434

MOUNT MARTY COLLEGE   **SdYM**

Sacred Music Resource Center
Yankton, South Dakota 57078

See Mary Jane Klimisch, *A Cumulative Index of Gregorian Chant Sources* (Yankton, 1975)

Published collections of Gregorian chant in the Solesmes tradition, 250 items published or used in the U.S. since the late 19th century

— Sister Mary Jane Klimisch

1435

Villiet VINATIERI

701 East Seventeenth Street
Yankton, South Dakota 57078

Felix Villiet Vinatieri (1834–91, composer, and army bandmaster for Gen. George Custer), 2 boxes of ms scores and parts for operas, marches, and dances, also notes and drawings

1436

YANKTON COLLEGE   **SdYC**

Yankton, South Dakota 57078

Lloyd Library

Recordings, including the Alice Pihl Hohf collection of 200 78-rpm discs, the Lawrence Riggs collection of 200 78-rpm discs, and the libraries of radio stations WNAX, Yankton, and KSCJ, Sioux City, Iowa

Conservatory of Music

Felix Villiet Vinatieri, music, including a piano-vocal score for the opera *The American Volunteer*. See Robert Marek, "Felix V. Vinatieri (1834–1891); Dakota Musi-

cian," *South Dakota Musician*, 10/2 (Winter 1976), 14–16

William Warville Nelson (silent-film orchestra conductor, of Minneapolis), published and ms scores used by him

Programs of local musical events, 6 vols., 1888–

Recordings, including 25 Duo-Art piano rolls

—J. Laiten Weed

1437

YANKTON COUNTY HISTORICAL SOCIETY

1012 West Ninth Street
Yankton, South Dakota 57078

Felix Vinatieri, photographs, army personnel records, and memorabilia

George B. German (cowboy singer and radio entertainer), songs, recordings, and memorabilia, 1928–45

—Don Binder

_____

In addition to the repositories listed above, the following have also reported holdings of the materials indicated:

Brookings—South Dakota State University, H. M. Briggs Library: songbooks, other printed music

Custer—Custer County Library: songbooks

Ipswich—P. Beebe Memorial Library: songbooks, recordings

Kadoka—Jackson–Washabaugh County Library: sheet music

Lead—Hearst Free Library: sheet music, songbooks, recordings

Mitchell—Friends of the Middle Border: sheet music, songbooks, recordings

Pierre—Office of Cultural Preservation: sheet music

Pierre—South Dakota State Library: sheet music, songbooks, pictures

Scotland—Scotland Historical Society: songbooks, pictures

Sioux Falls—Augustana College, Center for Western Studies: sheet music, songbooks, recordings

Sioux Falls—Minnehaha County Historical Society: sheet music, songbooks, programs, pictures, miscellaneous

Spearfish—R. R. Oedekoven: songbooks

Volga—Brookings County Historical Society: recordings

Wagner—Charles Mix County Historical Society: sheet music, recordings

Wolsey—East River Genealogical Forum: songbooks, recordings, miscellaneous

Tennessee

1438

Jerry W. PEVAHOUSE

10942 Highway 64
Arlington, Tennessee 38002

Anglo-American folk music and commercial country music, 100 sheet-music items, ca. 1920–60, and songbooks, 1916–40s

Other printed music, including 3 method books for 5-string banjo, 1884–93

Manuscript music, 10 traditional folksongs
Photographs of folk musicians, 20 items, ca. 1895–1945
Recording-company catalogues, 4 early 20th-century items
Recordings, including 1000 78-rpm discs and tape recordings of Anglo-American folk music, rock-a-billy, and rhythm and blues, 1923– , also 6 privately recorded discs, 1940s

1439
CHATTANOOGA–HAMILTON COUNTY   TC
BICENTENNIAL LIBRARY

Local History Department
1001 Broad Street
Chattanooga, Tennessee 37402

Cadek Conservatory of Chattanooga, 46 scrapbooks of papers and 1 box of photographs, 1887–1946
Papers on cultural life in Chattanooga, 1886–1957, including Will Seward Albert, scrapbooks of Opera House clippings and programs, 1902–8; Chattanooga Music Club, scrapbooks of clippings, programs, and photographs, 1899–1957; William Edgar Herron, scrapbooks of concert and theater programs, and materials on the history of the Chattanooga Spring Festival, 1893–1900; and M. B. Music Club, scrapbook of clippings and programs, 1907–57

—Clara Swann

1440
TENNESSEE MUSIC AND
PRINTING COMPANY

Church of God Publishing House
Box 850
Cleveland, Tennessee 37311

Music materials acquired through the purchase of publishing rights from the Hall, Parris–Denson, George W. Sebran, A. J. Showalter, and James D. Vaughn music companies, 20,000 copyright items, ca. 1900– , mostly paperback shape-note songbooks for sacred singing conventions, also original mss, correspondence, and business papers

—Connor B. Hall

1441
TENNESSEE TECHNOLOGICAL   TCooP
UNIVERSITY

Cookeville, Tennessee 38501

Charles Faulkner Bryan (1911–55), personal papers, including holograph music mss, personal and official correspondence relating to his work in Tennessee music education, and materials relating to his work in constructing folk-music instruments

—James Wattenbarger

1442
David H. and Cheryl T. EVANS

8566 Ericson Cove
Cordova, Tennessee 38018

Recording collection, 30,000 items, including 200 cylinders of popular music and the spoken word, ca. 1898–1925; 78-rpm discs including 1850 recordings of blues, 1920–59, 800 of black gospel music, ca. 1920–59, 800 of international and American ethnic music, ca. 1915–59, 2000 of country and western, 1923–59, 1250 of rock and roll and rhythm and blues, 1945–59, and 3000 of popular music (including jazz) and the spoken word, ca. 1901–45, also 5000 blues songs dubbed on tape from 78-rpm discs; 45-rpm discs including 1650 items of rock and roll and rhythm and blues, 500 of blues and gospel, and 350 of country and western, all 1950– ; and LP discs, 1955– , some of them reissues, including 700 discs of blues, gospel, and black folk music, 350 of international folk music, 100 of jazz, 300 of country and western, and 350 of rock and roll and rhythm and blues

1443
Doug SEROFF

Route 3, Box 506
Goodlettsvillle, Tennessee 37072

Collection of recordings, as part of a mail-order dealership, including discs and radio transcriptions, mostly 78-rpm discs of race music, rhythm and blues, gospel music, and jazz; also 2000 tapes of black gospel quartets, 1902–60

1444
LINCOLN MEMORIAL   THaroL
UNIVERSITY

Abraham Lincoln Library and Museum
Harrogate, Tennessee 37752

Sheet music, 4500 items, including 1500 Union and Confederate works, Stephen Collins Foster songs, and 444 items in the M. F. Savage Collection of Lincoln Sheet Music, 1850s–60s. See "The M. F. Savage Collection of Lincoln Sheet Music," *Lincoln Herald*, 53 (Fall 1951), 38–40
Songbooks, 150 Union and patriotic items, 1860s
Music publishers' catalogues, 20 items from New York and Chicago, 1870s–80s
Programs and playbills of concerts attended by Lincoln or about him, 150 items, 1860s
Photographs of regimental bands and musicians, ca. 1860, 250 items in a general collection of 5000 items
Recordings, including 75 78-rpm discs, mostly military music

—Edgar G. Archer

1445
EAST TENNESSEE   TJoS
STATE UNIVERSITY

Archives of Appalachia
Sherrod Library
Johnson City, Tennessee 37601

See reports of acquisitions and holdings, in the *Archives of Appalachia Newsletter* (1979–)

Materials documenting the history and development of southern Appalachia, including the Thomas G. Burton–Ambrose N. Manning Collection, 3.4 linear meters and 1 folder of papers; also 158 tape recordings and 6 video tapes of folksongs, ballads, tales, and other folklore pertaining to the Appalachian area of North Carolina, collected 1960–72

Broadside Television, Inc., 8 linear meters of papers and 600 hours of video tapes, 1970s, including folksongs of central and southern Appalachia and video tapes of the Southern Appalachian Video Ethnography Series (SAVES). Among the subjects covered are mining songs, the Industrial Workers of the World (Wobblies), and mountain music. Performers include Charles Beverly, Elizabeth Cotten, Hazel Dickens, Ernest East, the Ferrum Blues Festival, Claude Grant, Blaine Green, Sarah Ogan Gunning, Tommy Jarrell, Malcolm Johnson, Grandpa Jones, Taylor and Stella Kimble, Eunice McAlexander, the Morris brothers, Utah Phillips, the Fiddlin' Powers family, Florence Reece, George Tucker, Doc Watson, and Hedy West

—Richard Kesner

1446
KINGSPORT PUBLIC LIBRARY   TKi
J. Fred Johnson Memorial
Broad and New Streets
Kingsport, Tennessee 37660

Sheet music, 4056 items, 1900–   , mostly vocal, indexed and arranged by composer, with additional indexing by medium

Kingsport Music Club, archives, 1927–   , 50 linear cm.

—T. C. Hendrix

1447
PUBLIC LIBRARY OF KNOXVILLE   TKL
AND KNOX COUNTY
500 West Church Avenue
Knoxville, Tennessee 37902

Carrie Stakely (pianist), correspondence about music lessons, and 1 vol. of published songs, including her compositions, 1860s–   , in the Hall–Stakely family papers

George Pullen Jackson collection, including 71 vols. of sacred music and instruction books, late 18th to early 20th centuries, and a typescript of "Early Musical Activities in Tennessee," which he read before the East Tennessee Historical Society, 1932

Programs for local musical and theatrical events, in bound vols. and folders, 1875–1925

Knoxville Male Chorus, scrapbook, 1930s–40s

—Linda Posey

1448
UNIVERSITY OF TENNESSEE   TU
Knoxville, Tennessee 37916

James D. Hoskins Library

Gottfried Galston (1879–1950, pianist and teacher at the St. Louis Institute of Music) Music Collection and Galston–Busoni Archive, including letters, photographs, literary and music manuscripts, and memorabilia of Ferruccio Busoni and Galston, 450 items, 1879–1927; also 1500 items of piano music, ca. 1890–1945. See Pauline S. Bayne, *The Gottfried Galston Music Collection and the Galston–Busoni Archive* (Knoxville, 1978)

Songbooks, 23 shape-note tunebooks and 2 sacred songsters, many published in Tennessee in the 19th century; also 12 secular items, including minstrel songbooks, ca. 1872–1927

Sheet music, 10 items published ca. 1900, with Tennessee or minstrel subjects

Music-instruction book for keyboard, 1874, and for guitar, 1881

—Pauline S. Bayne

Frank H. McClung Museum

Grace Moore (1898–1947), materials documenting her career, including photographs, programs, letters of commendation, awards, costumes and other memorabilia, and the ms of her book, *You're Only Human Once* (New York, 1944)

—Joe Hopkins

1449
CENTER FOR SOUTHERN FOLKLORE
Archives
1216 Peabody Avenue
Memphis, Tennessee 38104

Recording of folk music in a general collection of 20,000 hours of tapes, collected 1970s, mostly music of Tennessee, Mississippi, and Arkansas, partly transcribed; also 2000 78-rpm commercial discs, including blues and race records

Published sheet music, especially pertaining to blacks and to Beale Street in Memphis, ca. 1900–1940

Photographs and photographic slides of folk musicians; also a collection of folk instruments

Other materials, including 10 songbooks and 25 programs

—Deck Reeks

1450
Harry GODWIN
796 Reddoch Street
Memphis, Tennessee 38117

Sheet music, several hundred items of jazz and blues, including 20 by Jelly Roll Morton, 20 by W. C. Handy, and some by Clarence Williams, ca. 1910–25

Scrapbooks, 6 items, containing photographs and correspondence of jazz and blues musicians, including interviews with Louis Armstrong

Photographs of Louis Armstrong and other New Orleans jazz musicians, early 20th century; also 30 paintings and collages of jazz musicians by Stephen Longstreet, and 3 of his books with ms illustrations

Recordings of jazz and blues, including radio and television retrospective programs; 50 tapes of interviews or private performances with jazz musicians, including Frank Assunto, Billie and Dede Pierce, Edmond

Souchon, Johnny St. Cyr, Phil Napoleon, Mahalia Jackson, W. C. Handy (also with memorabilia), and Louis Armstrong; 200 78-rpm discs, 1910–25, and 1200 other discs of jazz and blues; and unpublished master tapes of Johnny Wiggs, Muggsy Spanier, Bing Crosby, and Turk Murphy

1451
MEMPHIS–SHELBY COUNTY   TM
PUBLIC LIBRARY
1850 Peabody Avenue
Memphis, Tennessee 38104

Naomi Carroll Haimson (Memphis composer, fl. 1920s–70s), 5 music mss, some published works, and personal papers
Printed music, including 1000 radio-orchestra scores from station WMC, Memphis, early 1940s
Photographs of or relating to W. C. Handy, Beale Street, the blues, and music in Memphis, 200 items, 1910–
Oral-history materials concerning the development of blues, including interviews with Furry Lewis, Bukka White, Fred McDowell, W. C. Handy, Nat Williams, and Sterling Brown

—Lyndal Grieb

1452
MEMPHIS STATE UNIVERSITY   TMM
Memphis, Tennessee 38152

John Brister Library, Special Collections

Sheet music, 3000 items, mostly popular, early 19th century to 1930s, with a composer and title index
Songbooks, 30 items, mostly tunebooks of the southern U.S., 19th century
Johannes Smit (1913–72, theorist and composer), papers, including 50 ms compositions
Programs, 104 boxes of theater programs, including opera and musical productions
Photographs, including items of W. C. Handy, also the newspaper photograph morgue of the *Memphis Commercial Appeal*, 1900–1978
Oral History Research tapes and transcribed interviews, including series on blues in Memphis and on folk music of the Ozark Mountains

—Eleanor McKay

Southern Music Archive, Department of Music

Published theater orchestrations, 2000 titles, donated by a member of a Memphis orchestra that performed for silent films, radio, dinner clubs, and other social events from World War I to the 1930s; indexed
Recordings of black folk music from Memphis and the mid-South, 50 tapes and 20 video tapes, recorded 1978–79

—David H. Evans

1453
SOUTHWESTERN AT MEMPHIS   TMSC
Burrow Library
2000 North Parkway
Memphis, Tennessee 38112

Burnet Corwin Tuthill (b. 1888, Southwestern faculty member), 100 ms and published instrumental works, also personal papers

—Bill Short

1454
Charles WOLFE
Middle Tennessee State University
Box 201
Murfreesboro, Tennessee 37132

Shape-note convention books and hymnals, 200 items published in the South, 1900–1950
Sheet music, 200 19th-century items
Photographs of early country- and traditional-music performers, 400 items
Research files of notes and printed ephemera on early country musicians and southern traditional music
Oral-history interviews with early country musicians and with performers of traditional music, 200 reels, being transcribed
Commercial recordings, including 500 78-rpm discs of country music, 1920s–30s

1455
COUNTRY MUSIC FOUNDATION   TNC
4 Music Square East
Nashville, Tennessee 37203

Library and Media Center

The holdings, housed in the Hall of Fame building, incorporate the extensive miscellaneous collection assembled by Joe Nicholas of Palmer, Mich., also the Roy Acuff collection of various materials assembled by Elizabeth Schlappi

Sheet music, 5000 items, half of them from the period 1860–1942, most of these post-1920, partially catalogued
Song folios and other songbooks, 4000 country-, gospel-, and folk-music items, 1000 of them pre-1942 but mostly post-1935; partially indexed by composer, performer, and song title
Programs and posters, 250 items before 1942, strongest in posters advertising films with country-and-western music subjects or performers. There is an inventory of the Roy Acuff materials
Manufacturers' catalogues, 380 items before 1940, mostly of recordings but some for instruments and phonographs
Correspondence and memorabilia of performers, some pre-1940, including letters of Jimmie Rodgers (1897–1933)
Recordings, including 9200 78-rpm recordings and 50 radio-transcription discs, 1920s–40s

—Danny R. Hatcher

Hall of Fame and Museum

Permanent songwriters' exhibit, including 15 ms documents, 1920s– ; also 48 pictures and photographs of performers in the artists' gallery exhibit
Johnny Bond, ms songbook

—Diana Johnson

1456

DISCIPLES OF CHRIST   TNDC
Historical Society Library
1101 Nineteenth Avenue South
Nashville, Tennessee 37212

Frank C. Huston (fl. 1900, hymn writer), 1 folder of music mss and personal papers

Irving Wolfe (fl. 1930s– , music educator and composer), 10 items of papers and 3 boxes of published children's-music texts

Sheet music, 1200 published works, 1878–1969, by church members including Hoagy Carmichael

Hymnals, 400 19th- and early 20th-century vols., some with words only

—David I. McWhirter

1457

FISK UNIVERSITY   TNF
Library
Seventeenth Avenue North
Nashville, Tennessee 37203

See the library's shelflist for each collection

George Gershwin Memorial Collection, containing 2000 books on music, printed music, and music scores formerly in Gershwin's personal library; 516 items of correspondence, musical mss, printed items with Gershwin's ms notes, and memorabilia; also scrapbooks of music criticism by Carl Van Vechten

Special Collections (Negro Collection), a general collection of books by or about blacks, including books on music, published music scores and collections, sheet music, handbills, programs, and memorabilia. See the Collection's *Dictionary Catalog* (Nashville, 1974)

Jubilee Singers Collection, 15 ms boxes and 1 carton, including personal papers, programs, pictures, scrapbooks, memorabilia, correspondence about invitations to perform, and 23 vols. of autographs given to the group during an early European tour, 1865–

Papers of the University, including minutes of the Mozart Society (forerunner of the Fisk University Choir), 1881–93; minutes of the music faculty, 1885–1915; and scrapbooks of music programs and examinations, 1884–88

Ernest R. Alexander, 7 boxes of books, sheet music, and personal papers

Howard J. Angel, jazz and ragtime recordings, 550 78-rpm discs

George Washington Cable (author on folk music), 49 letters, 1889–1921, in the Jean Toomer Collection

Carrie B. H. Collins, 1 box of sheet music

Ludie Collins, 1 box of materials concerning the Jubilee Singers, including personal papers, sheet music, pictures, and programs

Countee Cullen (1903–46), 1 box of sheet music, scrapbooks, handbills, programs, clippings, and photocopies

Arthur Cunningham, 1 box of sheet music, ms music, and personal papers

W. C. Handy (1873–1958), 1 box of sheet music, articles, correspondence, pictures, and other personal papers

James Weldon Johnson (1871–1938), 2 boxes of sheet music and personal papers

Scott Joplin (1868–1917), 2 boxes of sheet music, photographs, and correspondence

Eileen Southern, 1 box of personal papers, including articles and speeches

John W. Work (1901–67, chairman of the Department of Music), ms and published music, sheet music, correspondence, personal papers, programs, and pictures, in all 18 boxes, 1915–71

—Darius Thieme

1458

Joseph F. GREEN
419 Barrywood Drive
Nashville, Tennessee 37211

Hymnals and books on hymnology, 200 items, mostly 19th- and 20th-century American and British works

1459

JOINT UNIVERSITY LIBRARIES   TNJ
Nashville, Tennessee 37203

Special Collections

Cyrus Daniel (organist), ms and published compositions, programs of Nashville concerts and recitals and a scrapbook and papers of the Vanderbilt University A Cappella Choir

Grand Ole Opry, papers, 1928–67, 90 linear cm., including sheet music, correspondence, programs, clippings, songbooks by Opry performers, photographs, and other materials

Mildred Haun (1911–66, editor), 8 boxes of papers, including research notes on folksongs and folklore, 350 holograph and typescript folksongs arranged alphabetically by title, and her *Cocke County Ballads and Songs* (Master's thesis, Vanderbilt University, 1937)

Isabell Howell Collection, including 24 choral-music items, 1887–1919, 8 items of Vanderbilt University music, 1900–1938, and 250 popular sheet-music items, 1840–1956

George Pullen Jackson, papers, 1901–65, comprising his research notes on folksongs; published and unpublished writings; ms songs and transcriptions; correspondence; photographs; card indexes of tunebooks and songs; recordings of the Old Harp Singers of Nashville, the Denson–Parris Sacred Harp Singers, and other religious folksongs; and books and articles on folksong

Charles S. Mitchell (1873–1952), collection of theatrical playbills, 1866–1952, including miscellaneous programs of opera and recitals in Nashville, Chicago, and New York; also libretti

John Lark Taylor (member of the Sothern and Marlowe Shakesperean Company), papers, 1879–1944, including 33 items of published sheet-music songs and arrangements

Warren Taylor collection, including 55 music programs, 1922–31, mostly of the Ryman Auditorium and Ward–Belmont Conservatory of Music, Nashville, also 16 programs of the Nashville Symphony Orchestra, 1921–27

W. F. Tillett, collection of papers on Methodist doctrine, including the ms of W. F. Tillett and Charles S. Nutter, "Hymns and Hymn Writers of the Church," an annotated edition of the Methodist hymnal prepared for the hymnal revision commission, 1905; also 2 songs for which Tillett wrote the words, "My Father Knows" and "O Vanderbilt! Dear Vanderbilt!"

—Jo Anna Kessler, Marice Wolfe

Peabody Division—Music Library

Eldon J. Gattwood, song, "Pillars of Peabody," 2 photocopies of the ms, 1926

Music method books, school-music series, and songbooks, 60 vols., late 19th century to 1940

Hymnals of various denominations, 25 items, late 19th century to 1940

Recordings, including 800 78-rpm discs of classical music

—Shirley Marie Watts

1460
Mrs. Clifton McPHERSON, Jr.

1700 Tyne Boulevard
Nashville, Tennessee 37215

Tennessee Federation of Music Clubs, materials including 8 file drawers of sheet music, programs, papers, pictures, yearbooks, and recordings, 1900–1979

1461
PUBLIC LIBRARY OF NASHVILLE   TN
AND DAVIDSON COUNTY

Eighth Avenue North and Union Street
Nashville, Tennessee 37203

Sheet music, 50 popular-music items, 1850–1930

Other printed music, including 5 bound vols. of piano music used or published in Nashville, 1850–

Naff Collection of materials concerning professional theater in Nashville, 1900–1960, including programs of musical comedies, operas, operettas, concerts and recitals, also letters, libretti, press clippings, photographs, posters, and scripts

Jetter Collection of dance memorabilia, mostly 1920s–30s

Music catalogues, 12 items

—Mary Hearne

1462
SOUTHERN BAPTIST   TNSB
CONVENTION HISTORICAL COMMISSION

Dargan–Carver Library
127 Ninth Avenue North
Nashville, Tennessee 37234

Hymnals of Baptist and other denominations, 500 vols., 19th and 20th centuries

Other printed music, including 200 sacred-music collections, 19th and 20th centuries

Isham E. Reynolds (1879–1949, music educator), papers, including writings on church music. (See also his papers at the Southwestern Baptist Theological Seminary, Fort Worth, Tex.)

R. H. Coleman (Dallas music publisher), complete collection of his published songbooks, 1909–39

Baylus Benjamin McKinney (d. 1952, songwriter and evangelist singer), ms and printed gospel songs, on microfilm

Recordings, including several 78-rpm discs, and oral-history tapes of Southern Baptist church musicians

Collection of dissertations concerning church music, written at Southern Baptist seminaries

—William J. Reynolds, A. Ronald Tonks

1463
TENNESSEE STATE LIBRARY   T
AND ARCHIVES

403 Seventh Avenue North
Nashville, Tennessee 37219

Archives and Manuscripts Section

Manuscript music, including a book prepared by Mr. Little for Robert Wilson of Williamsburg District, S.C., 1775, and a copy of "Our Risen Savior" by Mrs. E. L. Ashford, 1917

Campbell Brown and Richard Stoddert Ewell Papers, including correspondence of Elizabeth S. Ewell on music, 1869

Chapman Family Papers, including 2 ballads, 1864

James Clitherall (fl. 1770–76), journal, 1776, with 2 songs of the First Regiment of Provincial Infantry at Charlotte, N.C., "New Song for Liberty" and "Liberty Song"

Cooper Family Papers, with a letterbook of William F. Cooper mentioning Jenny Lind's performance in Nashville, 1851

Jane and Lydia Cravens, 3 Civil War ballads, words only, 1861

Darden Family Papers, 1832–1944, including music books for Minnie Graves Allensworth, programs and a scrapbook of the Ward–Belmont Conservatory of Music, and programs of students of Emil Winkler

Henry Melvil Doak Papers, 1921–29, including his typescript article, "National Airs—'Little Griffin,'" 1925

Mamie Frances (Moser) Dyche Papers, including W. C. Hafley's sheet music, "Only a Brakeman" (1893) and "No One to Kiss Her for Mother" (1894)

Fergusson Family Papers, 1784–1927, including William Wallace Fergusson's diary mentioning Jenny Lind's 1851 concert in New Orleans, and materials of his 8 children who were musicians

Frank Searcy Green, scrapbook of programs of music and drama, 1904–8

Lenamay Green (1869–1952, Nashville socialite) Papers, 1886–1958, including scrapbooks with songs

William C. Handy (1873–1958), 2 letters, 1948, concerning his music-publishing company in New York and his books

Miss Frank Hollowell (1880–1962, Nashville organist) Papers, 1834–1961, including biographical sketches, clippings, correspondence, diaries, photographs, and teaching and recital notes and materials, documenting her career at the First Baptist Church and with radio station WSM. See the register

Zilphia Horton (1910–56) Folk Music Collection, 1935–56, 1000 items in 90 linear cm., including correspondence, labor-union songbooks, picket-line song sheets, tape recordings, field notes, and other material mostly concerning social-protest songs, Anglo-American folksongs, and popular songs; also several clippings and programs of the Highlander Folk School. See the register

George Pullen Jackson, scrapbook of clippings from throughtout Tennessee, concerning grand opera in Nashville, 1919–29

John Trotwood Moore (1858–1929) Papers, 1781–1957, with materials for his book, *A Summer Hymnal*, 1901, and Mrs. Moore's scrapbook of programs of Nashville musical societies including the MacDowell Club, Wednesday Morning Musicale, and Chaminade Musical Club, 1896–1910

Mary Hamilton (Thompson) Orr Papers, including 2 letters describing Jenny Lind's performance in Nashville, 1851

Ransom Family Papers, 1833– , including correspondence of Ann P. Ransom (b. 1887, music teacher), and clippings and programs of Nashville musical events, 1900–1943

Kenneth Daniel Rose (1888–1960, violinist and sheet-music collector) Papers, 1879–1957, with programs, reviews, a scrapbook of materials from European study, writings including mss of his 3-vol. study, "Pioneer Nashville: Its Songs and Tunes, 1780–1860," and materials of the Ward–Belmont Conservatory of Music, Friends of Chamber Music (Nashville), and the Nashville Symphony Orchestra. See the register

Samuel Robert Simpson (1823–1906) Papers, 1862–1906, including a broadside announcing the Fiddlers Carnival at Gallatin, Tenn., 1899

Tennessee Electric Power Company, Historical Source Materials, mentioning 2 songs sung in the Caney Fork (Kenneport River, Cumberland Mountain) region before the advent of radio

Tennessee Historical Society collections, including Bettie Mizell Donelson (1862–1939) Papers, 1787–1938, with sheet music; the Dyas Collection with the John Coffee Papers, 1770–1917, including poetry and writings, and an 1851 letter mentioning Jenny Lind's performance in New Orleans; and a broadside for a Tennessee Historical Society concert at the Nashville Female Academy, 1858

Frances (Hannah) Trannum (composer of "My Tennessee," official school song of the state), typescript autobiographical sketch

Weber Family Papers, including 1 sheet-music song, "Fair Tennessee," by Henry Weber

Winston Family Papers, with 3 tape recordings by Nat Winston on Appalachian folk music, including songs performed by the Gragg family of North Carolina, 1963, oral history and folklore of Sam and "Happy" John Coffey of North Carolina, 1963, folk tunes performed by Earl Scruggs and Nat Winston, Jr., 1956, and a history of the 5-string banjo. See the register

Yeatmann–Polk Collection, 1900–1970, including a letter concerning music in Columbia, Tenn., by Eliza E. Polk, of Mulberry Hill, n.d.

—John H. Thweatt

Library

Kenneth D. Rose Sheet Music Collection, 10,000 items, including 70 bound vols., 18th to 20th centuries, with 2400 items before 1836, also with a few ms items. The collection includes 500 19th-century Tennessee imprints and 165 Confederate imprints, others printed in Nashville, 1862–65. Subjects strongly represented include minstrel music, coon songs, comic songs,

ships and shipping, U.S. presidents, early editions of the national anthem, political songs, war songs, sentimental ballads, and sports. The collection is indexed by author, composer, and title, as well as by selected subjects. See Kenneth D. Rose, "The Story of a Music Collection," *Tennessee Historical Quarterly*, 15 (1956), 356–63

Songbooks, including English-language hymnals, war songs, patriotic songs, and folksongs, 100 items, 19th and 20th centuries

Programs of the Nashville Symphony Orchestra, 1920–30 (in Special Collections)

—Fran Schell

1464
UNITED METHODIST PUBLISHING HOUSE
Library
201 Eighth Avenue South, Room 122
Nashville, Tennessee 37202

Methodist hymnals, 1200 items, 1739–

Other printed music, mostly religious, in 2 file drawers

Methodist Book Concern (publishing house), records, including letters from hymn writers regarding music copyright, 1885–92

—Carolyn Wilson

1465
UPPER ROOM DEVOTIONAL   TNU
LIBRARY AND MUSEUM
1908 Grand Avenue
Nashville, Tennessee 37203

Hymnals, 25 ms vols.

Songbooks, 21 linear meters of religious and gospel items, late 19th and early 20th centuries

Correspondence of writers of sacred songs, including John Bowring (1792–1872), 1 letter dated 1831; Fanny Crosby (1823–1915); Mary Lee Demarest, 1 letter dated 1876; Philip Dodridge (1702–1751); George Duffield, 1 letter dated 1866; Charles H. Gabriel, 1 letter dated 1922; Joseph H. Gilmore, 1 letter dated 1888; Eliza Edmunds Hewitt, letters, 1900–1907; James Montgomery (1771–1854); John Newton (1725–1807); Ray Palmer; Isaac Watts (1764–1748); Samuel Wesley (1766–1837); and Francis Wrangham, dated 1817 and 1822

—Dale Bilbrey, Brooks B. Little

1466
HIGHLANDER RESEARCH AND EDUCATION CENTER
Route 1, Box 245A
New Market, Tennessee 37820

Recordings, including tapes of Zilphia Horton singing at a Farmers' Union meeting in Montana; several tapes of Appalachian workshops on music, with 1 series of video tapes on coal mining and music; and related materials, among them songbooks from the civil-rights movement

—Sue Thrasher

1467
UNIVERSITY OF THE SOUTH   TSewU
Sewanee, Tennesee 37375

Saint Luke's Library

Hymnals, 150 items, including those of the Episcopal Church, ca. 1840–
Jones Liturgical Library, including published chant books and other music

—Grace Harvey

DuPont Library

Thomas ("Blind Tom") Bethune, comments on his playing and on his master, in the 1864 diary of Charles Todd Quintard (Civil War chaplain)

—Trudy Mignery

1468
W. Porter WARE
Plum Tree Cottage
Sewanee, Tennessee 37375

Jenny Lind collection, with 250 letters from her, including those to the Wichmann family in Berlin, and to Mme Birch-Pfeiffer; other letters to her; programs of concerts in the U.S., Canada, and Europe; newspapers containing articles about her; published books; 150 pictures and 1 oil painting; and other memorabilia

1469
Walter Darrell HADEN
Route 5, Box 409
South Fulton, Tennessee 42041

Collection of recordings, including 1500 78-rpm 12-inch discs of classical music, 1930s–40s; 150 78-rpm 10-inch discs of ethnic music, 1930s–50s; 8000 78-rpm 10-inch discs of country music, 1923–56; 11,000 78-rpm 10-inch discs of popular music, 1914–56. Post-1940 materials include country music (7000 45-rpm 7-inch discs and 5000 LP discs); popular music (11,000 45-rpm 7-inch discs and 6000 LP discs); German, Swedish, Spanish, Mexican, and Japanese ethnic music (100 45-rpm 7-inch discs and 100 LP discs); classical music (3500 LP discs); 500 popular, country, classical, and ethnic radio transcriptions, 1940s to early 1950s, representing the Standard Program Service, World Program Service, and Keystone Broadcasting Sustaining Program Service; and 500 10-inch and 12-inch transcriptions of recruiting-service, religious, and classical-music radio programs
Lewis Elliot and Associates of Martin, Tenn., 3500 unpublished popular, country, and religious-music mss, 1930s–late 1960s

Sheet music, including 500 popular and country songs for piano and voice, and 2000 published lead sheets of popular songs
Songbooks, including 50 hymnals and paperback gospel-music convention songbooks, and 50 country-and-western song folios
Original published and unpublished country, popular, and religious songs by Haden, 800 items

1470
GIBSON COUNTY PUBLIC LIBRARY
303 South High Street
Trenton, Tennessee 38382

Thomas Ingram (1918–53, pianist), papers, including letters from Josef Hofmann and Olga Samaroff; programs, clippings, diplomas, and photographs; and tape recordings of his performances

—Vivian Barber

In addition to the repositories listed above, the following have also reported holdings of the materials indicated:

Cleveland—Lee College, Lee Memorial Library: sheet music, songbooks, other printed music, recordings
Collegedale—Southern Missionary College, Mickee Library: songbooks
Dayton—William J. Bryan College, H. A. Ironside Memorial Library: songbooks
Greenville—Tusculum College, Library: songbooks, programs
Hermitage—Ladies Hermitage Association: songbooks (*see* Stanislaw)
Jackson—Lambuth College, Luther L. Gobbel Library: songbooks, other printed music, recordings
Jackson—Lane College, J. K. Daniels Library: songbooks, recordings
Jamestown—Fentress County Historical Society: songbooks
Knoxville—Knoxville Heritage: programs
Lebanon—History Associates of Wilson County: songbooks, programs
Memphis—Memphis Theological Seminary, Library: songbooks
Nashville—American Baptist College, T. L. Holcomb Library: songbooks
Nashville—David Lipscomb College, Crisman Memorial Library: songbooks
Nashville—Scarrit College, Library: printed music
Nashville—Southern Publishing Association of Seventh-Day Adventists, Editorial Library: songbooks
Nashville—Tennessee State Museum: sheet music, songbooks
Trenton—Isabel Smith: sheet music, songbooks, miscellaneous

Texas

1471

Nessye Mae ROACH

609 North Tenth Street
Alpine, Texas 79830

Manuscript orchestral part books, 6 items containing original and copied works, ca. 1850, used by the Ft. Davis (Tex.) String Band in the Civil War period

Personal papers of Mrs. Roach, including a ms family history, and typed lyrics and ms music to 20 folksongs sung by her family

Hymnals, ca. 1900–1930, 15 items, including Baptist and Christadelphian vols.

School songbook, ca. 1925

Sheet music, ca. 1900–1940, 25 items, including Irish songs

Recordings, including 45 linear cm. of 78-rpm Edison discs, and 62 brass records for a Stella music box

1472

SUL ROSS STATE UNIVERSITY TxAlpS

Alpine, Texas 79830

Sheet music, 500 popular and classical items, 1855–1943 (in the Archives)

Piano music and piano-instruction books, 50 items, 1880–1931, and 200 78-rpm disc recordings, donated by Ethel Schwalbe (local music teacher) (in the Archives)

Wilson Collection of Folk Music and Folk Traditions, 21 tape recordings of folk, western, and early popular music, ca. 1890–1940, including 9 of the Roach family, and oral history of folk musicians; also 11 folders of transcriptions and analytical commentaries. Taped and compiled by Rex Wilson, 1977 (in the Music Department)

—Pat Finnell, Rex Wilson

1473

AMARILLO PUBLIC LIBRARY TxAm

Box 2171
Amarillo, Texas 79189

Radie Britain, 9 music mss and 5 printed sheet-music items, mostly songs, ca. 1939–40

H. B. Martin, sheet music of "Take Me Home," 1939

Programs, 1930–40, 65 items, including those of the Panhandle Music Festival, Musical Arts Conservatory (Amarillo), and Amarillo College of Music Expression; also 25 programs of the Amarillo Symphony

Esther Johnssohn (local composer, teacher, and publisher), photograph, 1931

—Mary Kay Snell, Greg Thomas

1474

ARCHIVES AND HISTORICAL TxAuCH
COLLECTIONS—EPISCOPAL CHURCH

Historical Society—Episcopal Church
Box 2247
Austin, Texas 78767

Hymnals, 1800– , 7.5 linear meters, mostly Episcopal, including some in German and some with words only

Commission on Church Music, correspondence regarding hymnal and hymn publication, 5 linear cm., 1922–30

—Elinor S. Hearn

1475

SAINT EDWARD'S UNIVERSITY TxAuSE

3001 South Congress Avenue
Austin, Texas 78704

Silvestre Revueltas (1899–1940, Mexican composer and violinist), papers, 8 items, including programs, an article on him, personal correspondence, and 2 tape recordings (in the Archives)

Hymnal published for Mexican-Americans (El Paso, 1916) (in the Library)

—Philip Odette, Joseph Sprug

1476

TEXAS STATE LIBRARY Tx

Archives Division
Box 12927, Capitol Station
Austin, Texas 78711

Fannie M. Wilcox collection, 1923–45, 30 linear cm. of papers of the Wednesday Morning Music Club of Austin, including scrapbooks, programs, papers delivered at meetings, and issues of *Texas Music News* (1928–35, incomplete)

Oscar Haas collection, 15 linear cm. of materials, including minutes of the New Braunsfelser Männerchor, 1876–89, constitution and minutes of the Gesangverein Germania, 1850–60, and Haas's "A Chronological History of the Singers of German Songs in Texas" (typescript, 1948)

Sheet music, 90 linear cm. of bound and separate items, 1836–1950, mostly on Texas subjects or published in Texas, including popular and classical music for voice or piano

—Michael J. Dabrishus

1477

UNIVERSITY OF TEXAS TxU

Austin, Texas 78712

Fine Arts Library, General Library

Vocal anthologies, including 6 linear meters of sacred and secular books, catalogued, mostly 19th century; also 80 uncatalogued anthologies, 1804–90; and 300 uncatalogued hymnals and related texts, 1800–1960

Adolfo Betti (1875–1950, violinist with the Flonzaley Quartet), instrumental chamber music, incorporated into the general collection as described in Donald Bemis Jones, *The Adolfo Betti Music Collection at the University of Texas* (Master's thesis, University of Texas, 1956)

Humanities Research Center

George and Ira Gershwin, autograph layout of songs and themes for *Porgy and Bess*; mss, galley proofs, and correspondence relating to Edward Jablonski's books, *The Gershwin Years* and *The Gershwin Years in Song*; and a typescript with printer's annotations of DuBose Heyward's play *Porgy*, 1925

David Guion, 100 holograph music mss, a definitive collection of his compositions to 1960

Katherine S. Diehl collection of hymnals, 1920–40, 113 items

Hoblitzelle Theatre Arts Library

Minstrel collection, 10,000 items, 1830s–1930s, including mss, sheet music, photographs of composers and performers, other pictorial materials, songsters, playbills, and programs, comprising the special collections assembled by Harry Houdini, Albert Davis, and Messmore Kendall

W. H. Crain Collection, comprising sheet music of Broadway musicals and revues, 1880–1940, 400 items; and sheet music for *Ziegfeld Follies* performances, 1907–33, 350 items assembled by Robert Baral

Hoblitzelle Interstate Orchestral Music Collection, 75,000 printed and ms items, including sheet music for vaudeville performances, and a score and parts for music used for the D. W. Griffith film *America*

Historical Sheet Music, 30,000 items, late 18th to early 20th centuries, with an alphabetical title catalogue

Harry B. Smith Operetta Collection, 150 vocal scores, songs, and playbills, including his own works written in collaboration with Victor Herbert and others

Hoblitzelle Theatre Arts Playbill Files, 300,000 items, mid 18th to 20th centuries, including a separate section devoted to operas and musicals

Biographical Performer Files, including press clippings, pictorial materials, mss, and printed materials for musical performers of all kinds; also a Musicians Photograph File of 2000 items, and a Musicians Engraving File with 2000 items of American composers and performers, arranged alphabetically

Recordings, including the Dan Laurence Musical Comedy Collection and the W. H. Crain Record Collection, 1890s– , re-recorded, particularly strong in musical comedy of the 1940s

Joe E. Ward Collection, devoted to American circuses, 1850–1950, including photographs of marching bands, circus bandwagons, and other circus music; 500 letters between J. G. Sims and members of the John Philip Sousa Marine Band, 1911–31; and memorabilia

Barker Texas History Center

See Chester V. Kielman, *The University of Texas Archives* (Austin, 1967; hereinafter cited as *Kielman*)

Julien Paul Blitz, personal papers, 1852–1941, 8 items relating to the history of music in New Mexico and Texas (*Kielman*, 212)

Horace Clark (ca. 1862–1946, music teacher in Altavista, El Paso, and Houston), personal papers, 1884–1945, 10 linear cm., including correspondence, diaries, programs, press clippings, and other materials (*Kielman*, 441)

Mary Inglehart Crosby, ms music book, 19th century (*Kielman*, 535)

Mary Dunn (music educator in Lubbock), personal papers, 1910–46, 1.5 linear meters, including correspondence, music, press clippings, and documents pertaining to accreditation matters, also to the activities of the South Plains Music Association, the Texas State Music Teachers' Association, the Applied Music Division of the Texas Department of Music Education, the Texas Federation of Music Clubs, and the Texas State Music Festivals (*Kielman*, 646)

David Guion, ms and printed music, also a biographical file of press clippings

Oscar Haas, personal papers, 1844–1955, 18 linear cm., including research materials relating to the Singers' League in Texas, the Comal Singers' League, the West Texas Hill Singing Society, the Sängerfest Centennial Celebration, and other Texas singing societies (*Kielman*, 905)

John A. Lomax (1867–1948), personal papers, 1896–1948, 6 linear meters (*Kielman*, 1279)

Harold Morris, literary and music mss, 4 linear meters (*Kielman*, 1518)

Paul Amadeus Pisk, personal papers, 1914–63, 1 linear meter, including ms and printed music, also correspondence and research materials

Lota Mae (Mrs. Jefferson Rea) Spell (1885–1972, Texas music historian), personal papers, 1923–35, 80 linear cm., including letters, music, research materials, printed matter, and press clippings (*Kielman*, 2019)

Carl Venth, personal papers, 1923–59, 6 linear meters, including press clippings, music, and other mss, among them "My Memories," 1939

Mrs. R. Leon White, personal papers, 1927–63, 22 linear cm., including programs, and other materials relating to music in Austin (*Kielman*, 2337)

Ray Wood (journalist), papers, 1847–48, including folksongs and ballads (*NUCMC*, 71-481)

Correspondence and music mss of Texas composers, 1840–1950, 60 linear cm., including documents of Victor Alessandro, Samuel E. Asbury, E. L. Ashford, Karle Wilson Baker, Charles von Boeckman, Harry and Mildred Bell, Julia Booth, Ida Bassett Botts, Radie Britain, Pearl and Sterling Bunch, Francis de Burgos, Ulala Howard Burnet, W. Glen Darst, William Dressler, Virgean England Estes, Louise D. Fischer, Bernard Fitzgerald, Millie Moore Gadbold, Mamie Gaffney, Eva R. Garcia, Camille Gillmour, William C. Glynn, Hugh Gordon, William Parker Grant, L. R. Hamberlin, Clara May Russell Hamilton, Lee C. Harby, Oswald Payne Harrison, Chauncey Marion Hendershott, Mary Austin Holley, William Iucho, Floyd Duke James, Dyna Jones, Frederick King, Rudolph Kleberg, Theodore von La Hache, Annie Lamb, Augusta Laughry, Lena Dancy Ledbetter, Sam Leigh, Harry Macarthy, Ruby McKinnon, Emily Harris Maddox, Alice Mayfield, Edwin Meyrick, Evelyn Mims, S. T. Moore, Harold Morris, Eitel Allen Nelson, Mrs. Walter Nix, A. Noir, Olle Naomi Ocker, Laura Bryan Parker, Lois Pinson, Minnie Stevens Piper, Francis Prentiss, George May Randolph, William Ratel, Charles H. Rondeau, Belle Schrag, Marvin B. Shannon, J. Emory Shaw, C. T. Sisson, LaUna De Cordova Skinner, William Spross, John M. Steinfeldt, Austin Storie, J. Meredith Tatton, Jessie Beattie Thomas, Annie Lauri Trousdale, W. V. Wallace, Florence Birdwell Williams, W. J. Wilson, and Virginia Bassett Young (*Kielman*, 2127)

North Texas Music Teachers' Association, and Panhandle Music Teachers' Association, 17 brochures of programs and contests, 1928–36 (*Kielman*, 1589)

South Plains Music Teachers' Association, archives, 1923–42, 20 linear cm., including correspondence, official records and history, press clippings, and other materials (*Kielman*, 2010)

Texas Federation of Music Clubs, archives, 1915–62, 4 linear meters, including correspondence, minutes, reports, scrapbooks, songbooks, and press clippings (*Kielman*, 2131)

Texas Folklore Society, archives, 1911–24, 3 linear cm., including programs and press clippings of John A. Lomax and L. W. Payne, Jr. (*Kielman*, 2132)

Texas Music Educators' Association, archives, 1922–60, 1 linear meter, including correspondence, other documents, and press clippings related mostly to band music (*Kielman*, 2137)

Texas Music Teachers' Association, archives, 1888–1929, 25 linear cm., including correspondence, receipts, minutes, and a scrapbook (*Kielman*, 2138)

Tri-State and Texas Music Festivals, archives, 1933–40, 1 vol. (*Kielman*, 1533)

Texas music scrapbook, 1933–40, 1 vol. (*Kielman*, 1911)

Other miscellaneous music items, in the papers of Lizzie Scott Neblett (1849–1928); in the Glasgow family papers, including Civil War songs; cowboy songs in the papers of James Frank Dobie, 1930–46; and rabbinical music in the papers of Henry Cohen (1884–1951)

Miscellaneous references to German music in Texas, in the papers of Adolf Douai (1819–88, writer, theologian, politician, and composer) (*Kielman*, 622); and in the Solm-Braunfels archives, 1842–92, 70 vols., including the Verein zum Schutze deutscher Einwanderer in Texas (*Kielman*, 2007)

Center for Intercultural Studies in Folklore and Ethnomusicology

Field recordings on tape, 345 reels, including Francis E. Abernathy, 4 reels of fiddle tunes recorded in Texas; Roger Abrahams, 5 reels of Anglo-American ballads and fiddle tunes recorded in Texas, 8 reels of Anglo-American songs recorded in Virginia, and 6 reels of hillbilly songs and fiddle tunes recorded in North Carolina; Stan Alexander, 6 reels of fiddle tunes recorded in Texas; John H. Faulk, 69 reels of black church services recorded in Texas; George Foss, 9 reels of Anglo-American songs, recorded in Kentucky, North Carolina, and Virginia, and 1 reel of Anglo-American songs recorded in Virginia; Texas Gilmer, 7 reels devoted to the Old Timer's Fiddle Contest; Hally Wood Gordon, 4 reels of black and Anglo-American songs recorded in North Carolina and Texas; John A. Lomax and others, 41 reels of black, Anglo-American, and Mexican songs recorded in Arkansas, Louisiana, New Mexico, South Carolina, Texas, and the District of Columbia; Mack McCormick, 13 reels of Anglo-American, black, Cajun, and bawdy songs recorded in Texas; Normal L. McNeill, 4 reels of Mexican songs: Marion Michael, 7 reels of black, religious, and Anglo-American songs recorded in Texas; Tarry Owens, 54 reels of black, Anglo-American, country and western, blues, fiddle tunes,

and Spanish-American songs recorded in Texas; William A. Owens, 20 reels of Cajun, Anglo-American, and Mexican songs, blues, black sermons and spirituals, and fiddle tunes, recorded in Louisiana, Missouri, and Texas; Américo Paredes, 55 reels of Texas-Mexican border songs; Harry Schmidt, 17 reels of fiddle music; and Rudolph Willard, 15 reels of Taos Indian songs recorded in New Mexico, and black religious music recorded in Texas

—Olga Buth

1478
BASTROP COUNTY MUSEUM
Bastrop, Texas 78602

Mary Ann N. McDowall (1848–1935, music teacher and innkeeper), papers relating to Houston and Bastrop, including correspondence and an autobiography, as cited in *NUCMC*, 75-1916

1479
BELTON CITY LIBRARY
301 East First Avenue
Box 89
Belton, Texas 76513

Popular and classical sheet music for voice or piano, ca. 1860–80, collected locally, in 1 bound vol.

Belton Opera House, 3 account books listing performers and finances, 1889–99; also 11 photographs of traveling performers and groups that appeared at the Opera House, ca. 1880–1910

—Lena Armstrong

1480
PANHANDLE–PLAINS HISTORICAL MUSEUM
Historic Research Center
Box 967, W. T. Station
Canyon, Texas 79016

Bob Wills (1905–1975) Memorial Archive of Popular Music, including materials donated by Charles Townsend, Walter Juniper, Esther Klinke, and others, and containing published sheet music, 1.2 linear meters, ca. 1915– ; 4000 recordings, including 3900 78- and 33⅓-rpm discs; 33 reference books and discographies on popular music; 57 ms band arrangements for Billy Byron and his band, ca. 1938–50; 21 photographs of Wills and his band; and the Glenn White collection concerning Wills, 60 linear meters of microfilm reproductions of materials, 1935–70, including correspondence regarding western bands, a scrapbook of press clippings, contracts and payroll records of Johnnie Lee Wills and Band, discographies and listings of booking agents, and lists from the AFM

Wallace R. Clark (music educator at West Texas State University), 1.2 linear meters of papers, ca. 1900–1970, including personal and business correspondence, and photographs of the Clark family and of University music groups

Hymnals, ca. 1870–1900, 25 items, including a chapel hymnal used at West Texas State University in 1910

Tunebooks, 2 items, ca. 1875
Sheet music, ca. 1887–1958, 500 mostly popular items, including 2 by Charlotte Ingham Word
Photographs of traveling performers, 3 items before 1940

—Claire Kuehn

1481
WEST TEXAS STATE UNIVERSITY   TxCaW
Music Library
W. T. Station
Canyon, Texas 79016

Ruth Crawford, photocopies of mss of most of her works, 40 linear cm., also recordings of performances
Houston Bright, 2 linear meters of papers, including his complete ms compositions, especially choral compositions and arrangements, also correspondence, a dissertation, and a scrapbook
David A. Clippinger Collection of published early madrigals, formerly used by the Madrigal Club, University of Chicago
Texas Music Educators' Association, 10 linear cm. of photocopied papers, including minutes and financial records, 1924–61
Songbooks, 13 items, mostly published collections of folk or popular songs, 1930s
Popular sheet music, 34 items, 1930s

—Martha Morris

1482
HOUSTON COUNTY HISTORICAL COMMISSION
629 North Fourth Street
Crockett, Texas 75835

Yearbooks of the Cadman Club, 2 items, and of the Junior Cadman Club, 7 items, ca. 1930–40
Hymnals, 3 items, 1832–1920, of the Methodist, Episcopal, and Baptist denominations
Programs of 13 local musicals and operetta performances, 1928–38

—Eliza H. Bishop

1483
DALLAS HISTORICAL SOCIETY   TxDaHi
Box 26038
Dallas, Texas 75226

H. L. Hanks, 2 autograph ms songs, 1862–63
William J. Marsh, ms and published versions of the state song, "Texas, Our Texas," and miscellaneous items pertaining to him
Margaret Scruggs Carruth, papers, ca. 1924–42, including letters, programs, and playbills relating to the Civic Music Association (1925–42), Southern Methodist University Music Festival, Metropolitan Opera (New York), Dallas Symphony Orchestra, and other Dallas and New York musical events
Sudie L. Williams (supervisor of Dallas public-school music), 5 scrapbooks, including correspondence, clip-

pings and photographs pertaining to music education in Dallas, 1920–22 and 1939
Jack Frederick Kilpatrick, catalogue of his published music, compiled by the Kilpatrick Society, 1959
Dallas Civic Opera, Dallas Theater Center, and Dallas Symphony Orchestra, 15 linear cm. of clippings and minutes, 1900–
Dallas Pen Women, papers, including music and papers of Texas composers or pertaining to Texas, 1925–40
Programs and clippings of local musical events, 15 linear cm. plus scattered items in personal collections, ca. 1870– , including some of the Dallas Symphony Orchestra, Southern Methodist University, the Vivaldi Orchestra, and 1 of Victor J. Erhart's Grand Juvenile Orchestra, 1892
Songbooks, 5 items, mostly popular, ca. 1880–1920; also *Patriotic Texan Hymns from the Fall of the Alamo* (1836) and *Songs of the Confederacy*
Popular vocal sheet music with works by Texas composers or on Texas subjects, 100 19th- and early 20th-century items, including items from the collections of Mrs. D. R. P. McDermott, the Dallas Federation of Music Clubs, and the Winnie family.
Bywaters Cochran collection, including 100 sheet-music items, 1870–1900; 20 songbooks and 20 hymnals, ca. 1900–1940; and 78-rpm discs
Photographs of local music groups including the Erhart Juvenile Orchestra, 10 items, ca. 1870–1950
Recordings, including 50 music-box cylinders

—Peggy Riddle

1484
DALLAS PUBLIC LIBRARY   TxDa
1954 Commerce Street
Dallas, Texas 75201

Papers of Marion Flagg (music educator), and of John Rosenfield (Texas music critic)
William E. Hill (1886–1962, artist) Theater Collection, several hundred thousand items, including playbills, programs, holograph letters, autographs, portraits, engravings, production photographs, and miscellaneous scrapbooks pertaining to personalities and performances of the theater, vaudeville, minstrel shows, the circus, and pop concerts. Subjects include T. D. Rice, Christy's Minstrels, Lillian Russell, Florenz Ziegfeld, Jr., Francis Scott Key, Ole Bull, Jenny Lind, Nellie Melba, Ernestine Schumann-Heink, Enrico Caruso, and Josef Hofmann. See the exhibit catalogue (April–May, 1966)
Dallas Theatre History collection, including theater programs, clippings, and photographs
Published sheet music, 4200 items

1485
DALLAS THEOLOGICAL SEMINARY   TxDaTS
Mosher Library
3909 Swiss Avenue
Dallas, Texas 75204

Hymnals of various denominations, 250 items, ca. 1880–

—John A. Witmer

1486

Richard P. DeLONG

7159 Wildgrove
Dallas, Texas 75214

Hymnals, 200 items, 1853–

1487

SOUTHERN METHODIST   **TxDaM**
UNIVERSITY
Dallas, Texas 75275

Music Library

Items are in the Special Collections Room

Music mss from German settlements in southern Texas, 14 items including bound vols., for solo voice and guitar, instrumental ensemble, or choir
Letters to John Wakefield Cadmen and Constance Eberhart (librettist and poet) from composers, conductors, film stars, politicians, and others, 102 items
Sheet music, ca. 1890–1940, including Texas imprints
Concert programs, especially from the Dallas area, several hundred items, mostly 1910–30
Southern Methodist University Music Division concert and recital programs, ca. 1920–
Recordings, 4000 78-rpm discs donated by Milton J. Kuser, emphasizing jazz and Big Bands
Clippings from Dallas and University newspapers concerning musical activities at the University, 2 boxes, collected by Paul van Katwijk (dean of the Music School, 1919–49)

Fondren Library West

Ferde Grofé collection, 5000 items from his personal library, comprising mss, orchestrations including the complete Schirmer's Galaxy Library and the E. B. Marks Printed Concert Music Collection, and recordings
Zeta McCord Theatre Collection, comprising theater programs, scrapbooks of press clippings, photographs, including the Eli Sanger collection on visiting companies in Texas, 1892–1945, and 200 sheet-music items, 1890–1930

—Robert Skinner

Bridwell Library, Perkins School of Theology

Hymnals, including those of the United Methodist Church and its antecedents, 15 linear meters, ca. 1737– , also related published materials on hymnology, including 6 linear meters of materials concerning the interests of the Hymn Society of America
Papers and working files used in preparing the *Hymnbook of the Methodist Church* (1935), 3.3 linear meters, and the *United Methodist Book of Hymns* (1964), 8 linear meters
Stephen Ayres, personal hymnal collection, 750 items

—Richard Heitzenrater

DeGolyer Foundation Library

Colorado opera-house programs, 1876–1900

—James W. Phillips

DeGolyer Institute for American Studies

Oral History Collection, including interviews with Mrs. John Q. Adams, Robert Alda, Don Ameche, Fred Astaire, Ray Bolger, Sammy Kahn, Saul Chaplin, James O. Cherry, Dan Dailey, Carl ("Pappy") Dolson, Arthur Fiedler, Jerry Gray (1915–76), Lynn Harris, May Higgins (b. 1888, secretary to Claudio Muzio), Gene Kelly, Frankie Laine, Mance Lipscomb (1895–1976, on country blues singing), Harold Minsky, William E. Mitchell, William O'Donnell, Ted Parrino, LeRoy Prinz, David Raksin, Ligon Smith, Rudy Vallee, Harry Warren, and others. See the descriptive inventory, *Oral History Collection on the Performing Arts* (Dallas, 1978)

—Ronald L. Davis

1488

NORTH TEXAS STATE   **TxDN**
UNIVERSITY
Denton, Texas 76203

Music Library

Arnold Schoenberg and Hans Nachod, correspondence, including 62 letters and other documents, 1909–49; also music mss of Schoenberg, including original works, sketches and exercises, and arrangements, in all 19 complete items and 14 fragments. See Dika Newlin, "The Schoenberg–Nachod Collection: A Preliminary Report," *Musical Quarterly*, 54 (1968), 31–46; also John A. Kimmey, Jr., *The Arnold Schoenberg–Hans Nachod Collection*, Detroit Studies in Music Bibliography, 41 (Detroit, 1979)
Lloyd Hibberd (1904–65), personal research library, 10,000 vols., particularly strong in historical musicology and bibliography materials
Helen Hewitt (1900–1977), personal papers, including extensive correspondence with musicologists relating to Renaissance topics, also printed music and research notes and photocopies
Don Gillis (1912–78), personal papers, including 50 reels of tape and other commercial and non-commercial recordings; holograph music mss, also photocopies and published editions; extensive correspondence relating to his work with Arturo Toscanini and NBC; autobiographical materials, program notes; and other items
Radio station WFAA, Dallas, music library of 60,000 sheet-music items and 80,000 stock and original orchestrations, in 175 boxes, 1920s–60s, with title index
Radio station WBAP, Fort Worth, music library of sheet music and performance materials, 260 boxes, 1920s–60s, with title index
Edward Kennedy ("Duke") Ellington (1889–1974), recordings on discs and tapes, discographies, and other biographical sources, in all 1000 items, 1920s–60s
Jazz recordings, a general collection of 78-rpm discs, 80 linear meters
North Texas Composers Archives, including works of Violet Archer and other composers, in holograph or ms photocopy
Stan Kenton, 67 charts for use with lab bands, mostly 1940s

—Morris Martin

Folklore Archive, Media Library

Recordings of southwestern folk music and folklore, 89 reels collected by George D. Hendricks, 1962–76

—John Brewster

Historical Collection

North Texas State University materials, including 600 programs from University music performances, ca. 1900– ; papers of University music or performing-arts organizations; and 230 photographs of music groups and musicians of the University, including those in University yearbooks
Recordings, including 140 78-rpm discs or cylinders

—Barbara H. Butler

1489

EL PASO PUBLIC LIBRARY   TxE

Southwest Collection
501 North Oregon Street
El Paso, Texas 79901

> See Robert M. Stevenson, *Music in El Paso, 1919–1939,* Southwestern Studies, Monograph 27 (El Paso, 1970)

Francis Moore, collection of published music, clippings, and other miscellaneous items
El Paso Symphony programs, ca. 1890–
Vertical-file materials on music, including clippings of local interest, and sheet music by local composers
Photographs, including local music-related items, 1890s–
Index to El Paso Newspapers, 1881– , including music references

—Mary Sarber

1490

Franklin G. SMITH

1364 Backus Street
El Paso, Texas 79925

Collection of military songs, ca. 1750– , mostly post-1865, with 400 published vols. of music or songbooks; also the Cullinane Collection of texts, 1900–1945; and 5000 pages of photocopied material (index in progress)

1491

FORT DAVIS NATIONAL HISTORIC SITE

Fort Davis, Texas

Benjamin H. Grierson collection, mostly military music, including ms and printed sheet music, parts, and scores, largely composed or arranged by Grierson, 1849–98, 100 items

—David H. Wallace

1492

FORT WORTH PUBLIC LIBRARY   TxF

Arts and Recreation Department
Ninth and Throckmorton Streets
Fort Worth, Texas 76102

Published sheet music and scores, 20,000 items, also including tune cards, pamphlets, articles, and clippings, with sections on Forth Worth or Texas composers, and folk music

1493

SOUTHWESTERN BAPTIST   TxFS
THEOLOGICAL SEMINARY

Music Library
Box 22000-D4
Fort Worth, Texas 76122

Manuscript music by various composers, mostly associated with the Seminary, 20 20th-century items
Henry E. Meyer (music educator at Southwestern University, Georgetown, Tex.), papers, including his personal notes on sacred music, also 250 published editions of American music
Published hymnals, gospel songbooks, and tunebooks, 1000 items, including some in foreign languages, ca. 1780–1940; also a general collection of scores for solo voice or instrument, choir, or orchestra
Programs of the Seminary, other local schools, and local musical events, 2500 items, ca. 1925–
Recordings, including 100 78-rpm discs, ca. 1900–1940

—Phillip Sims

1494

TEXAS CHRISTIAN UNIVERSITY   TxFTC

Music Library
Fort Worth, Texas 76129

Manuscript music, 10 items, mostly by faculty or Fort Worth composers, including Don Gillis, Ralph Guenther, and Julia Smith; also published compositions by local or University composers
Grace Ward Lankford (local piano teacher, initiator of the Van Cliburn International Piano Competition) Collection of scores and sheet music, including piano works used by her
Published scores and songbooks in a general collection of 19,000 vols.
Programs of University music performances, 1939–

—Anna Harriet Heyer

1495

ROSENBERG LIBRARY   TxGR

2310 Sealy Avenue
Galveston, Texas 77550

Sheet music, 800 late 19th- and early 20th-century imprints, including 300 items relating to Galveston
American Guild of Organists, Galveston Chapter, official archives, 1941–76, 13 linear cm.
Thomas G. Rice (d. 1962, church organist and historian of Galveston), scrapbooks

—Jane A. Kenamore

1496

HOUSTON PUBLIC LIBRARY   TxH

500 McKinney Avenue
Houston, Texas 77002

Fine Arts Department

Collection of parts for symphony or salon orchestra
Pre-1900 Sheet Music Collection, mostly popular items; also other published sheet music, scores, and songbooks in the general music collection, including classical, popular, and folk items
Houston Symphony Orchestra, bound vols. of programs
Recordings, including 5 linear meters of 78-rpm discs

—Jeff Earnest

Texas and Local History Library

Scrapbooks and clippings concerning Texas musical events, including 3 vols. compiled by Adele Looscan
Sheet music, 550 published items relating to Texas, ca. 1833–1974
Confederate broadside ballads, 3 items
Programs of musical events in Houston, 1901–

—Dorothy Glasser

1497
RICE UNIVERSITY   TxHR
Fondren Library
Houston, Texas 77001

Stephen A. Sylvester, music collection, including sheet music printed from lithograph stones, 1840s–90s; 400 acoustical recordings, ca. 1900–1925; also books and periodicals on piano restoration and tuning, and on ragtime piano music
Sheet music, including 5576 items in the Music Library, singly and in 16 bound vols., of which 165 are Texas imprints, 55 are Civil War imprints, and 900 are pre-1900 imprints; and 970 items in 26 bound vols. in the Woodson Research Center, of which 42 are Texas imprints and 66 are Confederate imprints, in addition to 22 other items in the separate Civil War Imprints Collection
Works by present and former faculty members of the Shepherd School of Music, in the form of published, ms, and photocopied music and recordings, including works by Arthur Edwin Hall (1902–78)

—Ralph Holibaugh

1498
UNIVERSITY OF HOUSTON   TxHU
M. D. Anderson Library
Houston, Texas 77004

Bayard Turner Gross Dudley Collection, including 4450 scores, program notes of the Boston and Philadelphia orchestras, and published books on music (in the Music Library)
Ima Hogg collection, including 6 scrapbooks of programs, clippings, and photographs, with her commentary on musical and theatrical performances, 1899–1938; also press clippings pertaining to the Houston Symphony Orchestra (in the Department of Special Collections)

1499
KARNES COUNTY LIBRARY SYSTEM
303 West Main Street
Kenedy, Texas 78119

Scrapbooks containing press clippings, programs, and photographs of local school and community events, 4 vols. compiled by Sykes S. McClane, ca. 1897–1961, and 7 vols. by Bess Holchak, ca. 1962–75

—Darlene Nichols

1500
TEXAS A & I UNIVERSITY   TxKT
John E. Conner Museum
805 West Santa Gertrudis Street
Kingsville, Texas 78363

Manuscript music, 2 items for a Spanish play, *Los Pastores*
Organizational papers, including a history of the local Community Concert Association, and yearbooks and presidents' personal papers of a local club, 1914–70
Corridas (folk ballads of the Mexican border), 70 linear cm. of texts and musical transcriptions by Norman L. McNeil, 1930s–40s, complementing recordings in the Library of Congress; also 70 linear cm. of 78-rpm discs of *corridas*, and 9 songbooks
Programs of local musical events, including those at the Opera House, ca. 1914
Recordings, including 70 linear cm. of discs, ca. 1890–1916

—Mrs. Jimmie R. Picquet

1501
TEXAS TECH UNIVERSITY   TxLT
Box 4090, Tech Station
Lubbock, Texas 79409

Southwest Collection

Personal papers, 26,165 items and 43 linear meters, 1837–1975, including musical materials of Raymond T. Bynum (microfilm copies), Mary Dunn, David Guion, Julia Duggan Hart, Jeanette Ramsey Olive, Mrs. Frank E. Wheelock, and Dewey O. Wiley
Papers of the South Plains Music Teachers' Association and the Texas Music Educators' Association, 400 items, 1924–61
Hymnals, 40 items, 1877–1952
Secular Music Collection, including popular songbooks and vocal sheet music, 210 items, 1877–1939, and 15 linear meters on microfilm, 1905–35
Radio station KRLD, Dallas, music library of 40,000 items, including sheet music and orchestra parts, ca. 1930–60
Programs of Lubbock musical performances, 100 items, 1926–63
Recordings, including 500 78-rpm discs or tapes, ca. 1930–40, mostly classical; also 80 oral-history tapes about music in Texas and the western U.S., including Bob Wills and the Big Band Era, collected 1952–75

—David Murrah, Michael Q. Hooks

Museum of Texas Tech University

Sheet music, several hundred items, also 12 songbooks, mostly late 19th and early 20th centuries

—Bill Green

1502
HARRISON COUNTY HISTORICAL SOCIETY
Old Courthouse
Marshall, Texas 75670

Mrs. W. G. Twyman, 6 printed sheet-music items, ca. 1910–25, and a press clipping with her photograph, ca. 1920

Ernest Powell, ms song, "Marshall, Old and New," written for the Texas State Centennial, 1936; also 15 recital programs of his students, ca. 1908–51, and 12 photographs of his family, 1876–1951

Charles Robert Aber, 12 ms or published symphonic works, ca. 1930–60

Anna Craig Bates (1881–1977), 4 published songs

Autographed published music by Texas composers Ella Hudson Day, Alice Sheppard Shillman, J. I. Ayres, and David W. Guion, 1909–23

Printed music, including 40 school songbooks, ca. 1910–40, donated by Dana Boone Taylor (elementary-school music teacher); 10 hymnals of various denominations, 1882–1923; a piano instruction book, 1869; and 180 sheet music items, 1848–1960, mostly popular vocal music

Programs of local musical and theatrical events, 10 items, 1909–50

Photographs, 16 items, 1885–1940, including the local Light Guard Band (1885); Maud Powell (1915), José Iturbi, Alma Milstead, and Vincent Lopez (each autographed); and a local production of *The Mikado*, 1909, with a program; also 1 oil painting each of Jenny Lind and Edward A. MacDowell

Recordings, including 150 Edison cylinders, ca. 1890–1910, and 40 78-rpm discs

—Mrs. Solon G. Hughes

1503
MIDLAND COUNTY PUBLIC LIBRARY   TxMM
301 West Missouri Street
Midland, Texas 79701

Music and books about music from the personal library of Lloyd Hibberd (1904–65, musicologist), as cited in *Ash*, p. 712

1504
Stephen F. AUSTIN STATE UNIVERSITY   TxNacS
Ralph W. Steen Library
Box 3055, SFA Station
Nacogdoches, Texas 75962

Hymnals and popular songbooks, 200 items, ca. 1880–1940; also 25 other items of printed music, ca. 1900–1940

Sheet music, 140 items, ca. 1854–1920 (in the Special Collections Department)

Programs of the University and of other local musical performances, 35 items, ca. 1928–40

Recordings, including 100 78-rpm discs

—David Vancil

1505
Oscar HAAS
329 East Zink Street
New Braunfels, Texas 78130

Research files, including programs and press clippings of the West Texas Gebirgs-Sängerbund, 1881– , also photographs, press clippings, and other documents relating to German singing societies in New Braunfels, Comal County, and the German hill-country of Texas, as reflected in Haas's *History of New Braunfels and Comal County, 1844–1946* (New Braunfels, 1948) and *Chronological History of the Singers of German Song in Texas* (New Braunfels, 1948), in all 3 linear meters

—Theodore J. Albrecht

1506
SOPHIENBURG MEMORIAL MUSEUM
New Braunfels, Texas 78130

Materials used by local performing groups, including the Germania (singing society, 1850–60), songbooks and sheet music; and the Liedertafel (1855–60), songbook

—Theodore J. Albrecht

1507
CARSON COUNTY SQUARE HOUSE MUSEUM
Fifth and Elsie Streets
Box 276
Panhandle, Texas 79068

Radie Britain, 2 ms songs, after 1928

Hymnals, 4 items, 1880–1902

Sheet music, ca. 1876–1928, 25 items, including 2 by Mrs. F. H. Hill (local composer), 1915

Programs of 10 opera performances, ca. 1920–30, and 1 of the Pampa Band led by Alex Schneider, 1914

Photographs of local musicians, in a general collection of 1500 items

Recordings, including 13 cylinders and 47 78-rpm discs

—Jo Stewart Randel

1508
RICHARDSON PUBLIC LIBRARY
900 Civic Center Drive
Richardson, Texas 75080

Hymnals of various denominations, 10 items, ca. 1930–

Sheet music, 100 items, mostly classical and popular works for piano, ca. 1900–1940

—Peter Fekety

1509
BEETHOVEN MÄNNERCHOR
422 Pereida Street
San Antonio, Texas 78212

San Antonio Männergesang-Verein (1851–55) and Beethoven Männerchor (1876–), minutes, record books, membership lists, and other archival records, in all 1 linear meter (W. C. A. Thielepape, first conductor of the group, kept no minutes, 1865–74); also early songbooks, press clippings, programs, and framed photographs. See the 2 historical studies by Theodore J. Albrecht, *History of the Beethoven Männerchor* (1975) and *San Antonio's Singing Mayor, W. C. A. Thielepape, 1814–1904* (1976)

Music materials for performance, ca. 1900– , in all 5 linear meters

—Theodore J. Albrecht

1510

DAUGHTERS OF THE REPUBLIC   TxAuDR
OF TEXAS

Library
The Alamo
Box 2599
San Antonio, Texas 78299

Manuscript music by Edwin W. Sooladey, "Lelia" for violin and piano, 1898, and Lilla Seeligson Whitaker, "There You Are" and "Prettiest Ever," n.d.

Published music including a musical comedy by E. J. Smith and A. R. Kelle, *San Antonio, Texas*, n. d.; 10 popular songbooks, 1918–39; 2 piano-instruction books, ca. 1920–40; 3 hymnals, 1891–1900; and 158 vocal sheet-music items, 1886–1950

Programs, 2 items, of a student recital and of the 1916 San Antonio Music Fesitval

Vertical files of clippings on Texas music, 12.5 linear meters, ca. 1900–

—Mary Tausch

1511

SAN ANTONIO PUBLIC LIBRARY   TxSa

203 South Saint Mary's Street
San Antonio, Texas 78205

Art, Music, and Films Department

La Meri (ethnic dance teacher), papers, ca. 1935–75, including business correspondence, programs, scrapbooks and photographs

Theater Archives with 9 linear meters of local programs, clippings, and photographs, ca. 1920– , including Majestic Theater vaudeville performances, San Antonio Choral Society, San Antonio opera season festivals, San Antonio Symphony Orchestra, and local youth orchestras

Popular sheet music, 300 items, ca. 1880–1940, indexed

—Kathy Ley

Harry Hertzberg Circus Collection

Albert Smith, ms orchestra parts for "Hop on My Thumb" and other printed or ms music used by Gen. Tom Thumb and his wife; also other published music used by circuses

Jenny Lind materials, including published books on music, programs, and texts of Scandinavian folksongs

—Betty King

1512

UNIVERSITY OF TEXAS, INSTITUTE OF
TEXAN CULTURES AT SAN ANTONIO

801 South Bowie Street
San Antonio, Texas 78205

Photographs of Texas musicians and groups, ca. 1864–1940, 250 items, including German, Polish, and Czech bands, blues singers, and musicians with homemade instruments

Manuscript music, 3 items used in an annual local miracle play

—Judy Ranney, Tom Shelton

1513

AUSTIN COLLEGE   TxShA

Library—Archives
Grand Avenue
Sherman, Texas 75091

Ollie Kidd Key (president of Kidd Key College and Conservatory of Music, Sherman, formerly North Texas Female College), 10 letters, 1896

—Martha Cox

1514

TARLETON STATE UNIVERSITY   TxSvT

Library
Tarleton Station
Stephenville, Texas 76402

Papers of University music groups, ca. 1910– , 50 items, including programs, clippings, and photographs

Published choral music used by the University choir, 200 American titles, ca. 1920–50

Popular sheet music, including Broadway show tunes, 200 items, ca. 1920–50

Songbooks, 50 popular items, ca. 1920–50

Recordings, including 200 78-rpm discs

—Christine E. Thompson

1515

RAILROAD AND PIONEER MUSEUM

710 Jack Baskin Street
Box 5126
Temple, Texas 76501

Programs of local concerts of the Music Club of Temple, Self-Improvement Club, and Chautauqua series, 10 items, 1888–1910, also of *Parsifal*, 1907

Popular songbooks, 25 items, ca. 1880–1920

Popular sheet music, 200 items, mostly for voice, ca. 1880–1940

Photographs of a local band, chorus, and the Temple and Belton opera houses, 4 items, ca. 1885–1900

—Mrs. Richard D. Haines

1516

TEXARKANA HISTORICAL SOCIETY AND
MUSEUM

Box 2343
Texarkana, Texas 75501

Hymnals, 10 items, 1894–1931, including 2 written or published in Arkansas

Programs of local musical events, 75 items, representing the Texarkana School of Music, Texarkana School of Fine Arts, students of Louise Stuart Holman, Marshall–Wood Studios, and the "Hour of Charm" All-Girl Orchestra directed by Phil Spitalny

Sheet music, 50 items of popular songs, 1920s–30s, and 40 items for mandolin, violin, and piano

Recordings, including local performances of Scott Joplin compositions (in the Oral History Department)

—Tommy O'Keefe

1517
BAYLOR UNIVERSITY   TxWB
Waco, Texas 76706

Crouch Music Library

> See John Mohr Minniear, *An Annotated Catalog of the Rare Music Collection in the Baylor Unversity Libraries* (M.Mus. thesis, Baylor University, 1963); George G. Townsend, Jr., *First Supplement to An Annotated Catalog* (M.Mus. thesis, Baylor University, 1966); Alberteen Ratliff, *Second Supplement to An Annotated Catalog* (M.Mus. thesis, Baylor University, 1969); and Anne Lea Donaldson, *Third Supplement to An Annotated Catalog* (M. Mus. thesis, Baylor University, 1972)

David Guion, 17 music mss, mostly folksongs, and 81 published editions, ca. 1920–40; 40 reproductions of mss; and 7 linear meters of correspondence and programs. See Shirley McCullogh, *David Guion and the Guion Collection* (M.Mus. thesis, Baylor University, 1975)

Francis G. Spencer Collection of American Printed Music, 18th to 20th centuries, 30,000 items, including songsters, light-opera and musical-comedy scores, early editions of "The Star-spangled Banner," minstrel-show music, and silent-film music

Baylor Collection, 1744 items, ca. 1753–1920, including James Lyons's *Urania* (1761), 18th-century chamber-music scores, and early 19th-century bound music books

—Bessie H. Smith

Armstrong Browning Collection

Musical settings of poetry by Robert and Elizabeth Barrett Browning, many with U.S. imprints, as cited in Sally Keith Carroll East, *Browning Music* (Waco, 1973)

—Jack Herring

Texas Collection

Music by Texas composers or on regional subjects, including 1 linear meter of music mss, 300 sheet-music items, 12 songbooks, 30 linear cm. of photographs, and personal papers of 6 Texas musicians

Programs of Texas musical events, 1850– , in various collections of personal papers, and of Baylor University musical events, ca. 1850–

Oral-history tapes of Texas musicians

—Ellen Kuniyuki Brown

In addition to the repositories listed above, the following have also reported holdings of the materials indicated:

Abilene—Abilene Public Library: songbooks, recordings

Abilene—Abilene Christian College, Brown Library: sheet music, songbooks

Alpine—Alpine Public Library: songbooks

Arlington—University of Texas at Arlington, Library: songbooks

Austin—Austin Public Library, Austin–Travis County Collection: sheet music, programs, pictures

Austin—Texas Catholic Historical Society: songbooks

Azle—Azle Public Library: songbooks

Beaumont—Lamar University, Spindletop Museum: sheet music, programs, pictures

Canadian—Hemphill County Library: sheet music, songbooks, pictures, recordings

Corpus Christi—Corpus Christi Museum: sheet music

Corpus Christi—Corpus Christi State University, Library: sheet music

Crockett—Crockett Public Library: sheet music, programs

Cuero—Cuero Public Library: recordings

Dallas—Philip E. Baker: songbooks

Dallas—Dallas Christian College, Library: songbooks

Decatur—Wise County Historical Society: sheet music, songbooks, recordings

Deer Park—San Jacinto Museum: sheet music

Denton—Emily Fowler Public Library: songbooks, recordings

El Paso—El Paso County Historical Society: sheet music, programs

El Paso—University of Texas at El Paso, Library: sheet music, songbooks, other printed music

Fairfield—Fairfield Library: songbooks, recordings

Ferris—Ferris Public Library: songbooks

Fredericksburg—Gillespie County Historical Society and Commission: songbooks

Galveston—Ashton Villa: sheet music

Hereford—Deaf Smith County Historical Museum: miscellaneous

Hillsboro—Confederate Research Center, Hill Junior College: sheet music, programs

Junction—Kimble County Library: songbooks, programs

Keene—Southwestern Union College, Findley Memorial Library: songbooks, other printed music

Levelland—South Plains Museum Association: sheet music, programs, miscellaneous

Liberty—Atascosito Historical Society: sheet music, songbooks, other printed music

Lubbock—Lubbock Christian College, Moody Library: sheet music

Marshall—East Texas Baptist College, Library: sheet music, songbooks, other printed music, programs, recordings

Midland—Midland County Historical Society: sheet music, songbooks, programs, pictures, recordings, miscellaneous

San Antonio—Our Lady of the Lake College, Library: songbooks

San Antonio—San Antonio Museum Association: sheet music, songbooks, programs, recordings

San Antonio—Travis Park United Methodist Church: songbooks, programs, pictures

San Marcos—Southwest Texas State University, Library: songbooks, other printed music, catalogues, recordings
Victoria—University of Houston, Victoria Campus, Victoria College Library: sheet music, songbooks, recordings
Washington—Star of the Republic Museum: sheet music, songbooks

Waxahachie—Southwest Assembly of God College, Nelson Memorial Library: songbooks
Wellington—Collingsworth County Historical Commission: songbooks, programs, pictures, recordings
Witchita Falls—Midwestern University, George Moffett Library: sheet music, songbooks, recordings
Wichita Falls—Wichita Falls Museum and Arts Center: pictures

Utah

1518

SOUTHERN UTAH STATE COLLEGE UCS
Library
351 West Center Street
Cedar City, Utah 84720

John Laurence Seymour (composer, and professor of English at Sacramento Junior College), 20 ms and 50 published compositions, including operas, vocal solos, and works for strings; also 25 linear meters of U.S. and European opera scores and libretti, and 2.5 linear meters of disc recordings of opera music
Carter theater music (in the Seymour Collection), 70 linear cm. of materials, ca. 1890–1920, including popular sheet music of Broadway show tunes, programs, handbills, and photographs of performers and stage settings, from the collections of Mrs. Leslie Carter and her nephew, Leslie Carter (Broadway performers)
Hymnals, mostly of the Latter-Day Saints Church, 70 linear cm., 19th and 20th centuries
Canonza (local women's choral organization) and Music Arts Association, minutes and programs, 70 linear cm., ca. 1930–
Photographs of College and community musical and theatrical events, 30 linear cm., ca. 1898–1940
Recordings, including 2 linear meters of 78-rpm discs; and 1 tape recording of American Indian music, collected in 1978 by O. V. Deming

—Inez S. Cooper

1519

UTAH STATE UNIVERSITY ULA
Merrill Library
Logan, Utah 84322

Rare Books and Special Collections Department

Evan Stephens (1854–1930, Mormon hymn writer, and member of the Salt Lake Tabernacle Choir), papers, including ms hymns, published music, including early Utah imprints; scrapbooks and programs, mostly of Choir performances; and a portrait
Published dance-band music, 4.5 linear meters of scores and parts used by a band in northern Utah, ca. 1930–45
Blanche Browning Rich Collection of Edison recordings, 50 linear meters of cylinders and discs, mostly popular or World War I songs, 1903–23, indexed

Brigham Young College (Logan) archives, 1877–1926, including a ms and printed score and programs for the drama *Corianton*, which toured the U.S., with music by G. W. Thatcher, Jr.

University Archives

Programs of University and local theatrical and musical events, ca. 1890– ; also Music Department papers, photographs, and scores used in local productions

—Jeff Simmonds

Fife Folklore Archive

Austin E. Fife and Alta Fife Collections of Mormon and American folklore materials, collected ca. 1930–70, including disc recordings (many acetate), tape copies, transcriptions, data from ms diaries and scrapbooks and from published sources, and a card index to published sources and themes for 225 American folksongs, in all 120 linear meters

—William A. Wilson

1520

BRIGHAM YOUNG UNIVERSITY UPB
Provo, Utah 84602

Harold B. Lee Library

Manuscript Music

John Laurence Seymour Collection, with 3 linear meters of mss and some published items, including operas, ballet, and chamber music. See Larry Childs, *A Register of the John Laurence Seymour Archives* (Provo, 1979)
Brigham Young University faculty, 6 folders of ms music, including works by Gerritt DeJong, Jr., William F. Hanson, J. J. McClellan, Harrison R. Merrill, and Robert Sauer, ca. 1920–40
Republic Pictures Music Collection, 15 linear meters of ms music and acetate recordings of Republic Pictures film soundtracks, 1935–59
Josef Bonime Sheet Music Collection, comprising 25,000 ms and published orchestrations for orchestra, stage band, chorus, and radio broadcasts
Percy Faith (orchestra leader), 29,747 pages of original ms compositions and arrangements

Personal Papers

Emma Lucy Gates Bowen (1880–1951, Utah musician), papers, including correspondence, programs, pictures, libretti, and press clippings relating to her concerts in the U.S. and abroad, and pictures of the Lucy Gates Opera Company

Mortimer Browning (1892–1953, organist, pianist, composer, and teacher), papers, including ms and published music, correspondence, programs, clippings, teaching materials, photographs, and ASCAP correspondence

William King Driggs (musician, music teacher, showman, and father of the King Sisters), 34-page holograph autobiography, 1909–29, also his letter of 1961 to Harold Laycock regarding Music Departments in Latter-Day Saints Church academies, 1909–21

Elbert H. Eastmond (1876–1936, art professor), papers, including clippings, notes, and miscellaneous materials from his and other persons' pageants on Mormon, patriotic, and western themes

William Grant (1838–1916, Utah musician and composer), 298-page holograph journal, 1838–1910

Harold I. Hansen, papers relating to the annual Hill Cumorah Pageant at Palmyra, N.Y., 1937– , 3.6 linear meters

William F. Hanson (1913–62, ethnomusicologist), papers, including scores for his American Indian operas, and research material, scrapbooks, and photographs pertaining to music of the Ute Indians

Joel Hills Johnson (1802–84, composer), microfilm of his diary, 1860–82, and an autobiographical sketch

Ted Mack (1904–77), papers, including correspondence, financial records, photographs, and memorabilia, 1930s–

Florence J. Madsen (1886–1977) and H. Franklin Madsen (1887–1971), papers, including mss of published and unpublished compositions, correspondence, and photographs

Charles Ludwig Olsen (1856–1923, Utah musician), microfilm of his 349-page holograph autobiography, including discussion of the Latter-Day Saints Church leaders' attitudes toward music and dance

Jules Stein (founder of the Music Corporation of America), 2 folders of papers, including historical information on the MCA, and printed sheet music, 1930s

Margaret Summerhays (b. 1884, voice teacher at the University), papers, including programs, correspondence, and press clippings

Lotta van Buren (1877–1960, restorer of and performer on early instruments), papers, including scrapbooks, programs, research notes, lectures, press clippings, photographs, published sheet music, and memorabilia; also her collection of early instruments (in the Music Department)

Organizational Archives

Mormon Tabernacle Choir and Tabernacle Organ, 4 folders of photographs, 1880s–

University Opera Company, 1 scrapbook of press notices for the production of William Vincent Wallace's *Maritana*, 1910

Herald R. Clark (1890–1966, chairman of the University's Community Concerts and Forum Assemblies), 13 boxes of papers, including correspondence and programs, 1929–65

Susa Young Gates, 4-page history of the University Music Department, 1892

Recordings

Victor, Brunswick, and Columbia 78-rpm discs, 41 items of various popular pieces, early 1900s; also piano rolls

University Archives collection of tapes, 2500 hours, including Ute Indian Reservation music and chants, and Polynesian and Hawaiian Club assembly programs with songs and dances

Sheet Music

Harry F. Bruning collection, 14,500 items, partly in 145 bound vols., catalogued by composer and title, and partly unbound and uncatalogued, arranged by title

Radio–Keith–Orpheum (RKO) Vaudeville Collection, 6000 published arrangements, early 20th century. See the typescript history and description of the collection, prepared by its donor, Willard Gleeson

Miscellaneous sheet music, mostly 1930s, 2000 items, arranged by title

Printed Music

Mormon hymnals, 1835– , 200 items, a virtually complete collection

Programs, Clippings, and Scrapbooks

Brigham Young University Concert and Lyceum programs, 1926–40, 45 linear cm.

Miscellaneous vaudeville and minstrel-show programs, handbills, and broadsides, ca. 1900–1940, 25 linear cm.

Maddox Performing Arts collection, including a scrapbook of concert and theater programs from Rouse's Hall, Peoria, Ill., 1875–1912; 6 scrapbooks of press clippings concerning music and musicians, especially singers and pianists, collected by Edward Gleason, 1912–13; a scrapbook of articles, 1925–37, concerning Ignace Jan Paderewski, 2 scrapbooks of articles and pictures of pianists and opera singers, 1920s; 12.5 linear cm. of clippings, 1898–1908, concerning Kathleen Parlow (child prodigy violinist); a folder of silent-film cue sheets; and photocopied press clippings of reviews by Karleton Hackett (*Chicago Evening Post* music critic, 1914–33)

—Beth R. Webb

Folklore Archives, Department Of English

Field recordings of Utah folk music, 20 hours on tape, including American Indian music, Child and broadside ballads, and nonsense songs, collected by University students, ca. 1965–79; also partial ms and typescript transcriptions of the music

—Richard Poulsen

1521
CHURCH OF JESUS CHRIST OF LATTER-DAY SAINTS USIC
Library—Archives Division,
Church Historical Department
50 East North Temple Street
Salt Lake City, Utah 84150

Manuscript music by George Edward Percy Careless (director of the Salt Lake Tabernacle Choir), vocal and instrumental works in 1 vol.; William C. Clive; John Crook, 2 vols. of anthems and hymns, mostly without words; Joseph John Daynes (Salt Lake Tabernacle organist), Tabernacle organ book; Henry Gardner; Irene H. Hansen, 4 original hymns arranged for piano; Samuel Bailey Mitton (director of the Logan Tabernacle Choir), diaries and music, 1889–1951; Charles John Thomas, 2 music books, mostly for choir and organ, ca. 1900–1914; and C. F. Tollestrup, oratorio, n.d.

Alexander Ferdinand Schreiner (Salt Lake Tabernacle organist, 1924–), 1 linear meter of materials, including ms and published works for organ, and scrapbooks of clippings, programs, and photographs, ca. 1954–75

Papers of musicians, including Frank Wilson Asper (Salt Lake Tabernacle organist), 8 items, including a score, letters, programs, and news releases, 1932–54; Joseph Barton (Kaysville, Utah, brass-band member), biographical sketch (photocopy); Joseph Beecroft (1811–83, author, singing leader, and educator), holograph 11-vol. journal, also a typescript copy; Harry Arnold Dean (Utah music educator and hymnologist), journals, 1912–76 (microfilm); Joseph H. Dean (father of Harry Arnold Dean; composer and church musician), 66-vol. diary, 1876–1944, including discussion of his work shipping hymnals to Samoa, with an annotated Hawaiian hymnal included as vol. 66; Heber Sutton Goddard, scrapbook pertaining to Utah music, 1882–96; William Grant (Utah musician), autobiographical diary including some of his compositions, 1882–1911 (photocopy); Thomas Cott Griggs (Salt Lake Tabernacle Choir member), 20 vols. of diaries, 1861–1903 (microfilm); George Kirkham (1852–1923, member of a traveling orchestra and of the Salt Lake Tabernacle Choir), 64 vols. of diaries, 1876–1923 (microfilm); Thomas McIntyre (Utah band and orchestra member), diary, 1854–1913; William Hart Manning (music educator), ms memoires, ca. 1956–59; Laura Shepherd Miner, description of early Utah musical activities, appended to the Robert Stoney journal (photocopy); Eli Harvey Peirce, Jr. (Salt Lake Tabernacle Choir member, diary, 1897–1901; Tom Wright Pinder, 3 letters regarding the Salt Lake Tabernacle organ, 1895; Charles Isaac Robbins, typescript history (1965) of the Provo Marshal Band, ca. 1849– ; Evan Stephens (conductor of the Salt Lake Tabernacle Choir), 8 items, including letters concerning Choir business, 1892–1906; William Ray Van Noy (secretary of the Salt Lake Tabernacle Choir), scrapbook of Choir materials, including programs, itineraries, and clippings, ca. 1939–73; and William Willes, papers, including his music compositions, ca. 1855. See Davis Bitton, *Guide to Mormon Diaries and Autobiographies* (Provo, 1977)

Salt Lake Tabernacle Choir papers, 1847– , including 3 linear meters of financial records, tour itineraries, scrapbooks, minutes, and a repertory list; 1 linear meter of printed music used by the Choir; a complete run of programs (indexed); photographs; and other materials about the Choir and the Salt Lake Tabernacle Organ, in various collections of personal papers

Salt Lake City Bands, financial and legal papers, 1850–55

Church Music Department of the Latter-Day Saints Church, 2 linear meters of papers, 1920–

Printed music used in dramatic productions of the Church, ca. 1900– , 30 linear cm., and programs (indexed) and photographs of the productions; also programs of musical productions of other Latter-Day Saints churches in the U.S.

Hymnals, ca. 1830– , 6 linear meters, including every edition of the Latter-Day Saints hymnal, also the hymnal in 18 translations, and non-Latter-Day Saints hymnals

Typed transcripts of oral-history interviews with musicians, including items in the Historical Department Oral History Program Collection, James Moyle Oral History Collection, and the Music Division Oral History Collection. Subjects include Alvin Harold Goodman (chairman of the Brigham Young University Music Department and member of the Latter-Day Saints Church Music Committee) and Maurice Abravanel

Photographs of musicians, bands, choirs, orchestras, and musical performances, 40 items, ca. 1868–1940

Recordings of the Salt Lake Tabernacle Choir and other Latter-Day Saints music groups and soloists, 70 discs, ca. 1900–1950

Miscellaneous published material concerning music in the Church, 12.5 linear meters

—Glenn N. Rowe

1522

SALT LAKE CITY PUBLIC LIBRARY　　　USI

209 East Fifth Street South
Salt Lake City, Utah 84111

Printed orchestral, choral, vocal, and solo instrumental music, 50 items, ca. 1870–1940

Hymnals, 1 linear meter, ca. 1870–1940, including Mormon hymnals compiled by Utah musicians

Popular, folk, and school songbooks, 300 items, ca. 1870–1940

Popular vocal sheet music in 15 bound vols., ca. 1890–1920

Programs of local musicians and groups, 35 items, ca. 1900–1940

Photographs of local musicians and groups, 150 items, ca. 1900–1940

Recordings, including 750 78-rpm discs, mostly classical

—Bruce Ludwig

1523

UNIVERSITY OF UTAH　　　UU

University Libraries
Salt Lake City, Utah 84112

Special Collections Department

Austin and Alta Fife Collection of folksong recordings, 2 linear meters of discs, including Mormon and Utah folk music collected ca. 1948–

Lester Hubbard Collection of folksong recordings, including Mormon and Utah folk music, 2 linear meters of tapes and discs

Hugo Leichtentritt (1874–1951), 30 linear cm. of papers, including his "History of the Motet," an autobiography, and correspondence; also his personal library of books and music scores. See Carol E. Shelby, *A Cata-*

logue of Books and Music Acquired from the Library of Dr. Hugo Leichtentritt (Salt Lake City, 1954)

George D. Pyper (1860–1943, manager of the Salt Lake City Theatre), 6.4 linear meters of papers, including programs, playbills, promptbooks, photographs, clippings, and record books from his theater, 1862–1904; also materials on music in Salt Lake City, including the Latter-Day Saints Tabernacle Choir and the Salt Lake Symphony Orchestra

LeRoy J. Robertson (1896–1971, professor and composer), 5.7 linear meters of papers, including his complete ms compositions, disc and tape recordings, biographical information, correspondence, and photographs of musicians

Arthur Shepherd (1892–1958), 10 linear meters of papers, including ms compositions, recordings, biographical materials, and correspondence

University of Utah Collection of Folk Songs, 1 linear meter of disc recordings collected 1945–47

Published music by 79 Utah composers, 170 items; also 5 music mss bound in 1 vol. entitled "Emma Lucy Gates Bowen Song Collection"

Hymnals, mostly of the Latter-Day Saints Church, 150 items, ca. 1850–1958

—Della L. Dye

Fine Arts Department

Popular sheet music and published choral and band music, 15,000 items, ca. 1890–1940

—Laird Rodet

1524

UTAH STATE HISTORICAL SOCIETY UHi

Crane Building, Suite 1000
307 West Second South
Salt Lake City, Utah 84101

Emma Lucy Gates Bowen (1880–1951, opera singer), 75 linear cm. of papers, including scrapbooks, diaries, correspondence, programs, and photographs

Biographical files on Utah musicians, including Becky Almond (b. ca. 1900), John Wesley Bush (ca. 1887–1962), Lucy A. Rice Clark (1850–ca. 1925), Thomas E. Giles (1881–1959), Edna (Evans) Johnson (ca. 1900–1972), and Samuel Bailey Mitton (1863–1954)

Hymnals, 70 items, mostly Mormon, ca. 1830–

Popular vocal sheet music, 15 items, mostly by Utah composers, ca. 1890–

Programs of the Salt Lake Theatre and musical events, 75 linear cm., ca. 1900–

Photographs of local musical events, 50 items, late 19th and 20th centuries

—Linda Thatcher

In addition to the repositories listed above, the following have also reported holdings of the materials indicated:

Richfield—Richfield City Library: songbooks
St. George—Washington County Library: songbooks

Vermont

1525

UNIVERSITY OF VERMONT VtU

Guy W. Bailey Memorial Library
Burlington, Vermont 05401

Manuscripts and Special Collections, Wilbur Collection of Vermontiana

Sheet music, 150 popular-music items, 1915–30

Songbooks, 15 19th-century vols., including some from Vermont and elsewhere in New England

Alan Carter (1904–75, composer, and faculty member at Middlebury College), 5.2 linear meters of papers, including music mss, correspondence, teaching materials, and papers of the Vermont Symphony Orchestra, 1935–75

Ernest Jores (1873–1948?, Montpelier organist), 60 linear cm. of papers, 1900–1945, including his published scores, scrapbooks of press clippings, letters, and recital programs

Programs of Vermont concerts, 1850–   , 100 items

Archives

Samuel Lysander Bates, scrapbook, 1821–1941, including material on hymnology

Joseph Lechnyr (University faculty member, and direc-

tor of local music groups), 1 linear meter of papers, 1920–55

—John Buechler, Connie Gallagher

Archives of Folklore and Oral History, Department of English

Recordings of folk music, mostly country and western and traditional ballads, also interviews with musicians, in all 10 hours of tape recordings, collected by Richard Sweterlitsch and students, ca. 1975–

—Richard Sweterlitsch

1526

ROKEBY MUSEUM

Rowland E. Robinson Memorial Association
Route 1
Ferrisburg, Vermont 05456

Sheet music, 15 19th-century items
Songbooks, 30 19th-century items
Vergennes City Band, letters, 19th century
Programs of local 19th-century concerts, 20 items

—Chris Morgan

1527
W. Dale COCKRELL
3 Storrs Avenue, Apt. 1
Middlebury, Vermont 05753

Research notes and materials relating to secular songsters and to New England composers and performers of mid 19th-century popular music, including the Baker, Barker, and Hutchinson families, Ossian E. Dodge, and Bernard Covert
Tunebooks and hymnals, 1818–   , including 67 sacred items, some of them in shape notes, 21 secular items, and 12 juvenile tunebooks; also 3 vols. of piano music, 2 piano-instruction books, 2 reed- or parlor-organ instruction books, and 110 sheet-music items, 19th and early 20th centuries

1528
MIDDLEBURY COLLEGE   VtMiM
Egbert Starr Library
Middlebury, Vermont 05753

Helen Hartness Flanders Ballad Collection, mostly collected ca. 1930–63 by Mrs. Flanders and Marguerite Olney. See Flanders, *Ancient Ballads Traditionally Sung in New England,* 4 vols. (Philadelphia 1960–65), and earlier writings by her. The archival collection of 3500 items on field recordings comprises 254 wax cylinders of ballads, songs, fiddle tunes, and commentary, mostly recorded in Vermont, 1930s, as well as the wax-cylinder recorder; 1214 discs of ballads, songs, and commentary, 22 discs of fiddle tunes, and 5 discs of fife tunes, mostly from New England, 1940s; and 53 tapes of ballads, songs, fiddle tunes, commentary, and oral history, mostly from New England, late 1940s and early 1950s. There are also tape copies of the recordings, and notebooks and filing boxes of transcriptions. Songs and ballad texts total 5000 items, comprising 578 broadsides (among them Irish street ballads and U.S. imprints); 16 mss and ms collections of ballads, an opera, and instrumental tunes, from Vermont and New England, late 18th to mid 19th century. Other printed materials include 125 tunebooks and hymnals, late 18th and 19th centuries; also 11 sacred and 2 secular juvenile tunebooks, 45 glee books, 17 instrumental books for fiddle, flute, and piano, 50 songsters (1767–1901), 27 hymnals without music, 3 vols. of loose sheet music including an autograph of E. P. Christy, and other materials concerning sea songs, Shaker music, American Indian music (including some field recordings), and 18th- and 19th-century English, Irish, and Scottish music. Other materials include 25 photographs of informants and ballad singers; files of papers, correspondence, clippings, and memorabilia of Flanders and Olney; and a library of 2000 vols. on North American folklore and folk music

—W. Dale Cockrell

1529
SHELDON ART MUSEUM   VtMiS
Middlebury, Vermont 05753

Henry L. Sheldon (1821–1907, founder of the Museum, piano and organ dealer, and organist of the local Episcopal church), 1.2 linear meters of papers, including materials on Addison County history
Western Vermont Musical Association, 2 record books, 1857–74
Middlebury Choral Society, scrapbook of programs, record book and cash book, 1872–78
Middlebury Musical Institute, book of records of meetings, 1840–42
Music mss, 30 linear cm. of items by local composers and copyists, mostly 19th century but including a book of instrumental accompaniments to hymns, owned by Eliakim Weeks, dated 1786
Songbooks, 3 linear meters of items, mostly 19th century
Sheet music, 1200 items, mostly 19th century
Scrapbooks, 5 items containing programs of local performances including music, mostly 19th century
Catalogues of piano and organ dealers, mostly 19th century
Photographs of the Middlebury Band, 3 items, 1900–1912; the Vergennes (Vt.) Band, 1 item, ca. 1905; and the Bristol (Vt.) band, 1 item, ca. 1905

—Polly C. Darnell

1530
VERMONT HISTORICAL SOCIETY   VtHi
Pavillion Office Building
109 State Street
Montpelier, Vermont 05602

Justin Morgan, "Judgment Anthem," ms treble part, copied 1805
Londonderry Cornet Band, ms music notebook, 1802
Eleazer Dexter, ms songbook from Reading, Vt., 1849–74
Joseph Tenney, *The Gamut or Scale of Music* (1795), containing ms music, owned by Josiah Badcock of Hartland, Vt.
Nelson A. Chase, 24 ms letters to Marsh & Chase about the manufacture and sale of musical instruments, 1837–40
Charles M. Cobb (Reading, Vt., musician), diaries 1851–62; also his *Universal Musician* (1849–50), 737 pages of printed band and dance music, with a ms list of dances and concerts in Weston, Springfield, and Chelsea, Vt.
Sacred songbooks, 1804–79, and hymnals, 1796–1926, 1.2 linear meters
Sheet music, 600 items, 1845–1937
Organizational papers, including record books of the Black River Music Association, 1867–73; Windsor County Musical Association, journal, 1858–68; St. Albans Brigade Band, 1874–99; Hartland Brass Band, 1853–69; and Northfield Singing Society, 1836–42; also press clippings relating to the Central Vermont Music Association, 1870–71; a convention program of the Northern Vermont Musical Association, 1872; and a constitution and by-laws of the Musicians' Association of Vermont, 1921
Broadsides for late 19th-century concerts in Vermont, 200 items
Music periodicals, including the *Vermont Music Journal,* vol. 1, no. 9 (1867); *Vermont Musical Bulletin,* vol. 1, no. 1 (1868), and vol. 3, nos. 8 and 11 (ca. 1870); *World of Music,* published in Bellows Falls, Vt., mis-

cellaneous issues (1840–45); and *New York Musical Review* (1854–56)

Recordings, including 52 Edison blue amberol cylinders

—Laura P. Abbott

1531
GOODRICH LIBRARY
Main Street
Newport, Vermont 05855

Robert Bickford collection of recordings, including 1400 cylinders, 1026 Edison diamond discs, and 1000 regular Victor discs

—Gertrude Drown

1532
PUTNEY HISTORICAL SOCIETY
Main Street, Town Hall
Putney, Vermont 05346

Putney Musical Society (organized to promote "substantial music" of Handel, Arne, Croft, and "such other European and American productions as are written in a similar style and . . . totally discard those airy fuging tunes which are calculated rather to excite levity than the spirit of true devotion"), booklet of ms records, 1817

—Elaine Dixon

1533
RUTLAND HISTORICAL SOCIETY
101 Center Street
Rutland, Vermont 05701

Sheet music by George A. Mietzke, Harry F. Stafford, Josephine Hovey Perry, and J. W. Wheeler, 7 items, 1867–1938

Harry Engles (ca. 1840–1900, local organist), ms notebook of lectures

Programs of local concerts, 200 items, 1860–

Papers of local music organizations, including the Philharmonia Club, Rutland Choral Society, and Rutland Music Festival, ca. 1880– , 13 linear cm.

Photographs of local bands and orchestras, 5 items, ca. 1880–

—Frederick P. Elwert

1534
THETFORD HISTORICAL SOCIETY
Box 25
Thetford, Vermont 05074

Manuscript music, including 10 band books used by local musicians, ca. 1865; 1 shape-note hymnal, ca. 1840–50, containing 50 hymns, owned by Elizabeth Sanborn; music for the Thetford Pageant, 1911, including preludes, dances, and choruses; and John Huntington's book of country fiddle tunes, ca. 1890

Thetford and Lyme Musical Society (founded 1781), ms constitution

Cheney Singers (Vermont performing group), 9 letters, 1878–91

Charles H. Farnsworth (1859–1947, music eduator), correspondence, photographs, and course outlines, in 2 file drawers

Sheet music, 3000 popular songs, ca. 1840–1900

Protestant hymnals, mid 19th century, 9 linear meters

Method books for reed organ, bass viol, and other instruments, 60 linear cm., 1850–80

Anthem collections, cantatas, and operas by Dudley Buck, George Whitfield Chadwick, and others

Programs of concerts in Thetford and South Royalton, mid 19th and early 20th centuries, 100 items; also music and programs of the National Peace Jubilee, Boston, 1869

Photographs of 19th-century local musicians, 12 items

Recordings, including 100 wax and early Edison cylinders, and 3 linear meters of 78-rpm discs

—Charles W. Hughes

1535
SAINT MICHAEL'S COLLEGE   VtWinoS
Library
Winooski, Vermont 05404

Richard Stoehr (1874–1968, composer and theorist), 120 ms scores and sets of parts for his compositions and arrangements, 1880–1964; published scores and parts for 80 works, many in multiple copies, ca. 1900–1951; and copies of his writings on music theory, mostly published in Europe before 1939. See the Library's 22-page typescript guide

—Rev. Henry Nadeau, S.S.E.

1536
WOODSTOCK HISTORICAL SOCIETY
26 Elm Street
Woodstock, Vermont 05091

Printed music, including 20 popular and classical sheet-music items, late 19th and early 20th centuries; 15 19th-century hymnals of various Protestant denominations, and 10 Isaac Watts collections; and 6 songbooks of 19th-century parlor music

Programs of local theatrical and musical events, 20 late 19th-century items

Photographs of local bands, 6 items, 1880–1920

Recordings, including 30 78-rpm discs of popular music

—Jan Hathorn

In addition to the repositories listed above, the following have also reported holdings of the materials indicated:

Arlington—Russell Vermontiana Collection, Martha Canfield Memorial Free Library: songbooks, programs

Bellows Falls— Bellows Falls Historical Society: sheet music, recordings

Bellows Falls—Rockingham Free Public Library: sheet music, songbooks, other printed music

Bellows Falls—Albert J. Tidd: sheet music, miscellaneous

Bethel—Bethel Historical Society: songbooks

Bradford—Bradford Public Library: songbooks
Brattleboro—Cathy Stockman: sheet music, songbooks
Burlington—Vermont Symphony Orchestra: printed music, programs, pictures, recordings, miscellaneous
Dorset—Dorset Historical Society: printed music, programs, pictures
Orleans—Orleans County Historical Society: printed music, pictures, miscellaneous
Peacham—Peacham Historical Association: sheet music, songbooks, programs

Randolph—Randolph Historical Society: songbooks, programs
St. Albans—St. Albans Historical Society: sheet music, programs, recordings
Shaftsbury—Shaftsbury Historical Society: songbooks
Strafford—Strafford Historical Society: songbooks, programs, pictures, miscellaneous
Warren—Warren Town Library: songbooks
Westminster—Westminster Historical Society: sheet music, other printed music

Virginia

1537
George WASHINGTON MASONIC MUSEUM
Alexandria, Virginia 22301

Collection of music owned by Anne Washington, representing music at Mount Vernon in the early 19th century, including 350 published and ms items of European and American music in 8 bound vols. See James R. Heintze, "Music of the Washington Family," *Musical Quarterly*, 56 (1970), 288–93

1538
RANDOLPH–MACON COLLEGE ViAsR
Walter Hines Page Library
Ashland, Virginia 23005

Methodist Collection of 2400 printed books and 500 other items, including 23 published hymnals, the earliest compiled in 1807 by Stith Mead of Richmond, also ms dairies of itinerant ministers

—Flavia R. Owen

1539
BRIDGEWATER COLLEGE ViBrC
Alexander Mack Memorial Library
Bridgewater, Virginia 22812

Diaries of Joseph Funk (1777–1862, local composer and music publisher), covering 1816 and following years, and of John W. Wayland (local author), covering 1901–62
Hymnals and songbooks, 105 items, mostly with imprints of Joseph Funk, Ruebush & Kieffer, and other publishers in Mountain Valley, Singers Glen, and nearby communities
Sheet music, 350 items, mostly popular songs, 1900–1925

—Orland Wages

1540
MONTICELLO
Curator's Office
Box 316
Charlottesville, Virginia 22902

Sheet music and ms music of the Jefferson family in 11 folders, mostly vocal with piano accompaniment but also including items for violin, flute, guitar, or piano solo, published in the U.S. or London, late 18th and early 19th centuries. See Helen L. Cripe, *Thomas Jefferson and Music* (Charlottesville, 1974); also Roger Paul Phelps, *The History and Practice of Chamber Music in the United States* (Ph.D. diss., University of Iowa, 1951). Also 4 items and 2 fragments of sheet music for piano, published in London, ca. 1800

—Jean Bonin

1541
UNIVERSITY OF VIRGINIA ViU
Charlottesville, Virginia 22903

Alderman Library

All materials are in the Rare Book Department, unless otherwise stated. See the Library's *Annual Reports*

Published Music

Tracey MacGregor collection, including a 1786 song sheet, 1811 Protestant Episcopal hymnal, 1816 songster, 1857 minstrel songbook, 1862 Confederate hymnal, 1863 Confederate psalm book, 1880 Republican campaign songbook, Joel Chandler Harris's 1881 *Uncle Remus* songbook, and Robert Charles Winthrop's 1908 essay, "Music in New England"; also the Mather Collection, with 9 editions of the *Bay Psalm Book*, 1698–1773, mostly with musical notation, and John Cotton's *Singing of Psalmes* (London, 1647)
Tunebooks, hymnals, and psalm books, 1744–1915, 75 items, including Ruebush & Kieffer imprints
Songsters, 15 items pre-1820, and several items 1820–
Vocal anthologies and method books, 100 items, mostly 19th century
Printed opera, oratorio, and cantata piano-vocal scores, including 250 vols. donated by Iredell Jenkins in 1925
Sheet music, 16,000 19th-century vocal and instrumental titles, in boxes and bound vols., entirely catalogued, partly on cards and partly on a computer data-base. See Lynn T. McRae, *Computer Catalog of 19th-Century American Imprint Sheet Music* (Charlottesville, 1977). Also 1200 20th-century items of parlor music and show tunes

Alexander MacKay-Smith collection of European chamber music and music treatises, 1000 items

Daniel D. Emmett, *Songs of the Virginny Banjoist* (London, 1843), songbook of 13 songs published for the Virginia Minstrels' tour of Britain

Monticello Music Collections

See Helen L. Cripe, *Thomas Jefferson and Music* (Charlottesville, 1974)

Monticello Music Collection (in the Manuscripts Department), 6 boxes and 1 oversize box of music that belonged to the Jefferson family, including published vocal and instrumental works and ms fragments; ms book of songs and pieces thought to have belonged to Martha Jefferson Randolph; and a ms music notebook, ca. 1770, thought to have belonged to Martha Wayles Skelton Jefferson

Music from the library of Thomas Jefferson, chiefly 18th-century published vocal music, with the autograph of Jefferson's father-in-law, John Wayles

Jefferson music, 11 folders of photocopies of published music contemporary with and associated with Thomas Jefferson

Triste-Burke mss (in the Manuscripts Department), by descendants of Thomas Jefferson, 1832–1928, with a list of memorabilia from Monticello and of nursery songs sung by Martha Jefferson Randolph

Scrapbook, "Jefferson Music 1723–1790," with European songs and poems collected by Thomas Jefferson's granddaughters

Manuscript Materials

Arthur Fickenscher (1871–1954, composer and first head of the University Music Department), personal papers, 200 items, mostly ms compositions and arrangements, also papers on his invention of the polytone, 1912–41, correspondence, 1920–51, clippings, programs, and biographical and bibliographical notes (in the Manuscripts Department); also an oil portrait and polytone (in the Music Department)

John Powell (1882–1963, composer and pianist), ms and published music, his personal library of books and music, an oil portrait, correspondence, programs, clippings, collection of traditional melodies, and tapes and recordings, 17 linear meters, catalogued (in the Manuscripts Department), and 12 boxes (in the Rare Book Department). See Carol Taylor, "A Catalog of the John Powell Collection Housed in the Rare Book Division" (typescript, 1975); Phillip L. Williams, *Music by John Powell in the John Powell Music Collection* (Master's thesis, University of Virginia, 1968); and James Michael Foster, *An Audiography of and an Investigation into the Recorded Performances of John Powell* (Master's thesis, University of Virginia, 1978)

John Powell Foundation archives, 300 items (in the Manuscripts Department)

Harry Rogers Pratt, 125 ms compositions, also students' works, and arrangements of 19th-century European works for teaching purposes; ms scores for dramatic-musical presentations at the University, 1930s; papers including music fragments, ms notes, and stage directions from Pratt's tenure as director of the Virginia Players, and 1 box of programs and correspondence related to his work as director of the University Glee Club, 1930s; 3 letters from Percy

Goetschius, 1902–3; 3 boxes of clippings, programs, scores, and scripts of theater productions in America and Europe collected during his travels; and 6 boxes of photographic negatives and prints from his European trips (in the Manuscripts Department)

Alfred Swan (1890–1970), 800 printed music scores, books, and periodicals (dispersed through the Library's collection); also correspondence, notes, photographs, press clippings, and typescripts of studies of Russian music (in the Manuscripts Department)

Randall Thompson, personal papers, 300 items, including drafts, corrections and printed copies of the "Testament of Freedom," correspondence, clippings, programs, portraits, and an oral-history interview (in the Manuscripts Department)

Lafcadio Hearn, ms notes, songs, and other materials concerning Arabian and Japanese music, 1850–1942 (in the Manuscripts Department)

Blackford Family of Lynchburg, ms poems and song texts concerning the Civil War, ca. 1862–80 (in the Manuscripts Department)

Nevil Gratiot Henshaw (b. 1880), clippings, typescripts, and a piano-vocal score of *The Visiting Girl*, with words by Henshaw and music by Jesse B. Hull, performed by University students, 1907 (in the Manuscripts Department)

George Harris, Jr. (b. 1884), 3 ms songs (in the Manuscripts Department)

Edwin Morris Betts (1892–1958), 16 items relating to a lecture-performance, "Jefferson: Gardening and Music" (in the Manuscripts Department)

E. Linwood Lehman (1895–1953), ms piano-vocal score and typescript of his opera *The Visit of Balkis*; also 50 ms scores, sketches, and songs, and copies of printed music, ca. 1930 (in the Manuscripts Department)

Kenneth Elwood Crouch, research materials for his unpublished study, "Our Singing Land: The State Songs of the United States," 180 items, 1900–1960, including published sheet music, scores, journals, pictures, photocopies, and correspondence (in the Manuscripts Department)

Amy Cheney (Mrs. H. H. A.) Beach, 3 letters to Abbie F. Brown, 1914–19 (in the Manuscripts Department)

David W. F. Guion, "Turkey in the Straw," ms arrangement for violin and piano by Hilton Rufty, n.d. (in the Manuscripts Department)

Folklore Materials

WPA Folklore Collection, including 2700 ballads, dance tunes, and folksongs, and 37 78-rpm discs, collected in Virginia, 1938–42 (in the Manuscripts Department). See Bruce A. Rosenberg, *The Folksongs of Virginia: A Checklist of the WPA Holdings* (Charlottesville, 1969)

Virginia ballads, folksongs, and dance tunes, 1 linear meter of materials collected by Winston Wilkinson, 1932–41, through the WPA Federal Music Project (in the Manuscripts Department)

WPA Federal Writers Project, notes on folklore and ballads, compiled 1936–40 (in the Manuscripts Department)

Kentucky folk music, 30 ms transcriptions and 50 mimeographed sheets of texts, prepared ca. 1938 by the WPA Federal Music Project, under the direction of F. Brandeis (in the Manuscripts Department)

—Jean Bonin

Virginia Folklore Society Archives, Department of Anthropology

Materials relating to folk music in Virginia, 1913– , including a collection of variants of Child ballads; see Arthur Kyle Davis, Jr., *Traditional Ballads of Virginia* (Charlottesville, 1969). Also 3000 folksongs and 340 recordings of folksongs collected by Davis and Fred F. Knobloch, 1932–33, on tape, and 1 linear meter of WPA song texts, late 1930s

—Charles L. Perdue, Jr.

1542

DANVILLE HISTORICAL SOCIETY

Box 2291
Danville, Virginia 24541

Danville Music Study Club, 3 scrapbooks, 1890–1978, including photographs, clippings, and minutes

—Ella Weber

1543

FAIRFAX COUNTY PUBLIC LIBRARY ViF

3915 Chain Bridge Road
Fairfax, Virginia 22030

Alma Grayce Miller (ca. 1900–1970, local composer), 25 ms chamber, opera, piano, band, and choral works
Sheet music, 1500 popular and classical items, early 20th century
Hymnals and songbooks, 100 early 20th-century items
Other printed music, including 200 choral works and 2880 dance-band arrangements, 1900–1960
Programs and playbills of local concerts, 15 items, 1917–45

—Anita Lamkin

1544

George MASON UNIVERSITY ViFGM

Fenwick Library, Special Collections
4400 University Drive
Fairfax, Virginia 22030

American Symphony Orchestra League, archives, including correspondence, official records, programs of member organizations, and other materials, mostly post-1947
WPA Federal Theatre Project, 1935–39, archival records, 32 linear meters and 12 file drawers, including ms music scores and parts in 7 file drawers, containing works by Lehman Engel, Max Hirschfeld, Earl Robinson, and 3 "living newspaper" productions, also the *Dr. Faustus* of Paul Bowles and Orson Welles, and Andrew Barton's *The Disappointment* (as performed under the title *Treasure Hunt*); also sheet music and published materials, 7 linear meters; 2500 radio scripts, many on musical topics such as black music, madrigals, and Gilbert & Sullivan; 800 production notebooks; 4 boxes of programs, 1500 posters, and

40,000 photographs, all catalogued by play title; 220 oral-history interviews with participants, including Eubie Blake, Leonard DuPaur, Lehman Engel, Earl Robinson, Ben Russak, and Virgil Thomson; research files of correspondence, memorandums, and other research materials, 15 file drawers, catalogued; and a general index, in 10 file drawers. See the various announcements of the Research Center for the Federal Theatre Project, notably the occasional newsletter, *Federal One*, 1976–

1545

FERRUM COLLEGE

Blue Ridge Institute
Ferrum, Virginia 24088

Songbooks, 100 vols., 1850–
Manuscript music, including native Virginia ballads, 1930s–40s
Photographs of local musicians, 100 items, 1890–
Field recordings of folksongs, blues, other music of blacks, string bands, religious music, and ballads, 1930– , in all 700 hours

—J. Roderick Moore

1546

HAMPTON INSTITUTE ViHaI

Hampton, Virginia 23668

Archives

See the *Guide to the Records at the Hampton Institute Archives* (forthcoming)

R. Nathaniel Dett (1882–1943), 1.8 linear meters of papers, including correspondence, curriculum materials, ms and published music, photographs, pamphlets, and poems
Manuscript music by faculty members, 1870– , 50 items
Hampton Singers, 7 linear meters of papers, including correspondence, reports, and announcements, 1870–1960
Archival papers of the Institute, 1.5 linear meters, 1870– , including items related to the school's musical activities and choir trips
Photographs of musicians, including Thomas Ferrer, R. Nathaniel Dett, Dorothy Maynor, and Cameron White, 200 items, 1870–1960
Recordings, including cylinders of work songs and folklore materials, 1880s (taped copies in preparation, to be available at the Library of Congress)

George Peabody Collection

Scrapbooks relating to black music and musicians, 4 vols., 1894–1921

—Cynthia Chapman, Mrs. McGee

1547

MENNONITE HISTORICAL (ViHarEM) LIBRARY

Eastern Mennonite College
Harrisonburg, Virginia 22801

Menno Simons Historical Library and Archives, including 670 sacred-music books, particularly strong in Mennonite hymnody, especially Ruebush & Kieffer imprints, with extensive holdings of *The Musical Million* and other materials relating to Joseph Funk. See Grace I. Showalter, *The Music Books of Ruebush and Kieffer, 1866–1942: A Bibliography* (Richmond, 1975); Martin E. Ressler, *A Bibliography of Mennonite Hymnals and Songbooks, 1742–1972* (Quarryville, Pa., 1973); and Irvin B. Horst, "Singers Glen, Virginia, Imprints, 1847–1878: A Checklist," and other articles comprising the Eastern Mennonite College *Bulletin*, 44/2 (1965)

—Grace I. Showalter

1548
ROCKINGHAM PUBLIC LIBRARY   ViHar
45 Newman Avenue
Harrisonburg, Virginia 22801

Shape-note hymnals and music books, 80 imprints of Ruebush & Kieffer and Joseph Funk

1549
HOLLINS COLLEGE   ViHo
Fishburn Library
Hollins College, Virginia 24020

Marian MacDowell, correspondence with Erich Rath, including a holograph ms of Edward A. MacDowell's "Song" from *Sea Pieces*
Sheet music, 500 catalogued items and 2000 unsorted and uncatalogued items; also published music by College faculty members William E. Haesche (1867–1929), Erich Rath (1866–1949), and Wilmar R. Schmidt (late 19th century), and published music by alumni
Programs of local recitals and of College groups on tour, 1900s–1920s, and bound vols. of programs of local performances, late 1930s–
Local archival materials, including correspondence regarding the construction of the Theodore Presser Music Building (Presser was on the faculty, 1880–83); catalogues and other publications; minutes of meetings; a scrapbook of photographs and autographs of visiting performers, 1900s–1910s; and press clippings concerning campus musical events

—Thelma C. Diercks

1550
Stonewall JACKSON HOUSE
8 East Washington Street
Lexington, Virginia 24450

Sheet music, 25 dance pieces, 1850s–60s, mostly waltzes and polkas and including some marches, in 1 bound vol. owned by Minnie Mosely Hurlbutt and J. L. Hurlbutt

—Katharine L. Brown

1551
James R. HINES
8 Willis Drive
Newport News, Virginia 23606

Charles Dacosta, ms music, ca. 1820s
Sheet music, 500 19th-century items
Programs of local concerts, 10 items, late 19th century
Photograph of a string class at Norfolk (Va.) Conservatory, 1903

1552
Moses MYERS HOUSE
Bank and Freemason Streets
Norfolk, Virginia 23510

Sheet music, 900 unbound items and 31 bound vols., early and mid 19th century, with extensive indexes. (Microfilms of this material are at Old Dominion University, Norfolk, and at the Norfolk Public Library.)

—Dorothy McNeil

1553
NORFOLK PUBLIC LIBRARY   ViN
301 East City Hall Avenue
Norfolk, Virginia 23510

Manuscript and published music by Virginia composers, including Sara Elliot Bostwick (1918–78), Friedrich Ludwig Diehn, Johann Henri Gustave Franco, Undine Moore, Jean Pasquet (1896–1977), and Charles E. Vogan (in the Archives)
Sheet music relating to Norfolk or to Virginia, 1857–1921, 15 items, and microfilms of materials at Myers House (q.v.) (in the Sargeant Memorial Room). See James R. Hines, *Musical Activity in Norfolk, 1680–1973* (Ph.D. diss., University of North Carolina, 1974)

—Audrey Hays, Lucille Portlock

1554
OLD DOMINION UNIVERSITY   ViNO
Library
Norfolk, Virginia 23508

Programs of concerts and recitals at the University (formerly the Norfolk Division of The College of William and Mary, and the Virginia Polytechnic Institute and State University), 1930s– , in 3 vols.
Recordings, including 8000 78-rpm discs from the collection of Dr. George Gay III, 1910s– , and 2000 78-rpm jazz discs from the collection of Clarence Walton, 1920s–

—Vernon A. McCart

1555
VIRGINIA STATE UNIVERSITY   ViPetS
Box J J
Petersburg, Virginia 23803

Papers and memorabilia of early 20th-century faculty members, including Anna L. Lindsay, Altona Trent Johns, Cleota Collins, and Undine S. Moore
Sheet music, 100 items

—Catherine Bland

1556

MUSEUM OF THE CONFEDERACY ViRC
LITERARY SOCIETY
1201 East Clay Street
Richmond, Virginia 23219

Confederate imprints, 1858–64, including 450 sheet-music titles, 7 songsters, 70 broadside sheets with words only, and 6 programs

—Kip Campbell

1557

RICHMOND PUBLIC LIBRARY ViR
101 East Franklin Street
Richmond, Virginia 23219

Sheet music, 15,000 popular 20th-century piano and vocal music items, including Confederate imprints

Other printed music, including 200 scores and parts used in Richmond for silent films, and 1000 dance-band arrangements from the library of Jack Kaminsky, 1930s–40s

Clippings related to music in Richmond, late 19th century to the present, 7 linear meters

Pictures of musicians, included in a general collection of 19 linear meters

Recordings, including 2900 78-rpm discs of popular and classical music

—Myra Kight

1558

UNIVERSITY OF RICHMOND ViRU
Richmond, Virginia 23173

Music Library, Modlin Fine Arts Center

Jacob Reinhardt (1845–1919), personal papers, including correspondence, photographs, 8 holograph music mss, and 5 sheet-music editions

Hilton Rufty (1909–74), photographs, and 26 holograph music mss

F. Flaxington Harker (1876–1936), musical works, including a holograph ms and 5 bound vols. of his published music

Published music, including 150 sheet-music items, 77 of them from the period 1830–70; also 50 songbooks and a violin method book with dances, 1850

Virginia Baptist Historical Society

Andrew Broadus (b. 1770, in Caroline County, Va.), ms hymnal with words only, dated 1790

Hymnals, 187 vols., mostly mid 19th century but including 2 18th-century items, also including Richmond imprints, and many Sunday-school hymnals

—Homer Rudolf

1559

VALENTINE MUSEUM ViRVal
1015 East Clay Street
Richmond, Virginia 23219

Published music, including 700 sheet-music items and 50 songbooks; also works by Richmond composers Frederick C. Hahr and John Powell

Edward Valentine, memoirs and papers relating to public-school music in Richmond, 1782–1902

Programs of 19th-century musical and theatrical performances in Richmond, 300 items; also 200 photographs of local musicians, mostly 19th-century, and including papers of local music groups

Recordings, including 500 discs

—E. M. Saavedra

1560

VIRGINIA HISTORICAL SOCIETY ViHi
428 North Boulevard
Box 7311
Richmond, Virginia 23221

Sheet music, 2400 items of 19th-century popular music, emphasizing Confederate and Virginia imprints; also sheet music in a drawing book of Robert Matthew Sully, 1824–42

Tunebooks, 100 early 19th-century items

Broadsides, 16 items in the Allen family papers, 1850–1910, mostly political or commercial, some of them issued at Petersburg or Richmond, or by the Virginia Normal Music School, New Market

Manuscript song, sung at the funeral of J. A. C. Chowning, copied by George Northern, n.d., in the Harrison family papers

Programs of Richmond-area concerts, 600 items, 1844–

"Music and the Theatre," anonymous 20-page typescript, 1937

Philip Barbour Ambler, of Lynchburg, notes on literature and music made while attending the University of Virginia, 1861–76, in the Barbour family papers

Richard Bache, letter to Henry Lee, dated 1825, concerning a piece of music being sent to Ann R. (McCarty) Lee and Henry Lee

Baylor family papers, 319 items, 1800–1925, including poetry and music

Beverley family papers, including a ms song, "Sweet Marie," copied by Ida Dulaney (Beverley) Wellford, n.d.; Richardetta Earle (Carter) Beverley (1856–1945, of Essex County), accounts concerning the purchase of a piano, 1891, and music, 1907; Fanny Scott (Beverley) Osborn, accounts concerning music, 1910–13; and Richardetta (Beverley) Killey (1885–1965, of Essex County), accounts concerning music, 1912–13

George Washington Parke Custis (1781–1857), letter dated 1854, to Benson John Lossing, concerning musical interests (photocopy; original not extant)

Gesang Verein Virginia, of Richmond, papers, 1854–1963, including minute books, account books, and membership lists

Gray family papers, including music and lines of verse, n.d.

Octavia (Robinson) Haxall, account book, 1830, concerning guitar instruction by Mrs. A. Colonna d'Orano of Richmond, in the Robinson family papers

Joseph Holladay (d. 1795, of Spotsylvania County), holograph psalm book, 1769

George Watson James (1887–1971), 2 letters dated 1871 and 1900, from or to William Hand Browne (with musical notation) and Sidney Lanier

C. J. H. Kehr, of Fredricksburg, 1852 ms report card and receipt concerning the musical study of Judith Williantina (Temple) Harrison, in the Temple family papers

Philip Ludwell Lee, 15 letters dated 1769–74, concerning music, in the Lee family papers

Robert Edward Lee (1807–70, of Lexington, Va.), 2 letters, dated 1857 and 1860, to Mildred Childe Lee of Winchester, concerning music lessons; also an 1869 letter to the Philip Hante Gachles (Gachle) piano manufacturing company of Baltimore, concerning sheet music

William Lee (1739–95), letterbook dated 1779, including correspondence with Samuel William Stockton concerning music

John Brown Patterson (1786?–1811, of Richmond and Matthews County), notebook, 1810–47, partly concerning the study of music, in the Minor family papers

Pitts family papers, including notes about a concert to benefit the North Farnham Protestant Episcopal Church, Richmond County, also some lines of verse, 1860–1922

Reed family papers, with 10 items related to the Richmond Musical Association and the Richmond Symphony Orchestra, 1930–33

Richmond Female Institute, papers, 1856–1937, including programs and invitations to musicals

Richmond Mozart Association, ms announcement by William Upshur Bass, 1880, concerning admittance to activities of the Association, in the Clarke family papers

Scott family papers, including invitations to a musicale of the Hahr Musical Society of Richmond, 1886, and a dance of the Batchelors Cotillion Club, n.d.

Second Presbyterian Church (Covenanters) of Richmond, scrapbook, 1896–1953, including sheet music, a hymnal, 1898, and membership pins of the choir

Thomas J. Spencer & Co., of Charlotte Court House, Va., account book, 1860 with an advertisement for James Woodhouse & Co. (Richmond music dealer)

T. W. H., 2 ms copies of popular songs, 1863

Virginia State Committee for Rural School Music, minutes of the 1932 Richmond meeting, in the Hannah family papers

Richard Ross White, unexecuted agreement to study music with Henry C. Roberts at the Mount Zion (Baptist) Church in Buckingham County, 1878

—Elizabeth Ayers Berry, Howson W. Cole

1561
VIRGINIA STATE LIBRARY   Vi
Twelfth and Capitol Streets
Richmond, Virginia 23219

Sheet music, 4500 items, singly and in 46 bound vols., mostly 19th-century popular works, including Confederate imprints

Hymnals and tunebooks, including Shenandoah Valley imprints

Programs of Richmond concerts

—Toni Waller

1562
Frank HOLT
310 Greenway Road
Staunton, Virginia 24401

Stonewall Brigade Band, 2 scrapbooks, ca. 1880s– , containing programs, photographs, press clippings, and other documents

1563
STONEWALL BRIGADE BAND ROOM
3 Gypsy Hill Park
Staunton, Virginia 24401

Archives of the Band, including minutes, correspondence, and press clippings, 1867– , mostly 1884– , as described in Marshall Moore Brice, *The Stonewall Brigade Band* (Verona, Va., 1967), pp. 199–203. Included is a photocopy of the muster roll for the Band in the Fifth Regiment of Virginia Infantry, 1862–64 (the original is in the Virginia State Library, Richmond); also documents relating to the Staunton Federal Band and the Staunton Musical Association

—Frank Holt

1564
SWEET BRIAR COLLEGE   ViSwC
Library
Sweet Briar, Virginia 24595

Sigrid Onegin (1889–1943), music library of 200 opera scores, mostly 18th- and 19th-century European published editions, with annotations, including ms cadenzas, stage directions, cast lists, and performers' autographs; also 9 boxes of art songs, mostly European published editions; and photographs of Onegin

—Allen W. Huszti

1565
William W. ENRIGHT
Box 44
Wattsville, Virginia 23483

Hymnals, 850 items, 1865– , mostly 1900–1935, including many Sunday-school texts; also writings about hymnology

1566
COLLEGE OF WILLIAM AND MARY   ViW
Earl Gregg Swem Library
Williamsburg, Virginia 23185

Sheet music, 60 bound vols., mostly 19th century, uncatalogued

—Margaret Cook

1567
COLONIAL WILLIAMSBURG   ViWC
FOUNDATION
Box C
Williamsburg, Virginia 23185

Chamber music, in European editions, known or likely to have been performed in Colonial America, 500 items. See the partial listing in Roger P. Phelps, *The*

History and Practice of Chamber Music in the United States (Ph.D. diss., University of Iowa, 1951), pp. 551–58

Miscellaneous ms materials, occasionally of musical interest. See Marylee G. McGregor, *Guide to the Manuscript Collections of Colonial Willamsburg*, 2nd ed. (Williamsburg, 1969), esp. item 78, an undated ms music book

Jane L. and Mary S. Rose, 2 ms music books, from Rosehill (near Geneva), N.Y., 1831

Miscellaneous transcripts of Colonial source materials, including Helen Bullock, "On Music of Colonial Williamsburg," 54 pages, containing transcripts of Williamsburg and related Virginia records, and music references from the journal of Philip Vickers Fithian, 1767–74, 6 pages; Harold B. Gill, "The Music Master in Colonial Williamsburg," 13 pages; Mary R. M. Goodwin, "Musical Instruments in Eighteenth-Century Virginia," 133 pages; and John Molnar, "Music in the Colonial Period," 206 pages, and "Music in the Colonial Theater," 214 pages

—David J. Martz, Jr., John E. Ingram

1568

CLINCH VALLEY COLLEGE   ViWisC

University of Virginia
John Cook Wyllie Library
Wise, Virginia 24293

James T. Adams, transcripts of the words of folksongs collected through WPA auspices, and related to recordings now in the Archive of Folk Song, Library of Congress (q.v.)

—Rosemary P. Mercure

In addition to the repositories listed above, the following have also reported holdings of the materials indicated:

Arlington—Arlington County Library: programs, recordings
Ashland—Mrs. W. C. Wickham, Jr.: sheet music
Axton—N. G. Payne: sheet music, songbooks, other printed music
Bristol—Virginia Intermont College, Hicks Memorial Library: sheet music, songbooks, other printed music
Courtland—Walter Cecil Rawls Library and Museum: recordings
Fort Lee—U.S. Army Quartermaster Museum: songbooks, miscellaneous
Harrisonburg—Madison College, Memorial Library: songbooks, other printed music
Lexington—Rockbridge Historical Society: sheet music, songbooks, other printed music, programs
Lynchburg—Lynchburg Museum System: sheet music, songbooks, programs, pictures
Newport News—Christopher Newport College, Capt. Smith Library: songbooks
Norfolk—MacArthur Memorial Foundation: sheet music, songbooks, recordings
Radford—Radford College, John P. McConnell Library: sheet music, songbooks, programs, pictures
Richmond—Union Theological Seminary, Library: songbooks
Richmond—Virginia Baptist Historical Society: songbooks
Richmond—Virginia Commonwealth University, Cabell Library: songbooks, recordings
Spotsylvania—Spotsylvania Historical Association: sheet music, songbooks, other printed music, catalogues, recordings
Williamsburg—Abby Aldrich Rockefeller Folk Art Collection: songbooks, pictures
Winchester—Handley Library: songbooks

Washington

1569

WESTERN WASHINGTON UNIVERSITY

Music Library
Bellingham, Washington 98225

Bellingham Women's Music Club, archives, 1917–72, 1 linear meter, with scrapbooks containing minutes, programs, yearbooks, and clippings

—Marian Ritter

1570

SNOQUALMIE VALLEY HISTORICAL SOCIETY

Box 179
North Bend, Washington 98045

Papers of a local music club, 1 box, including a scrapbook and clippings

Sheet music, 40 World War I items
Songbooks, including 2 vols. for organ, late 19th century

—Mrs. Farrell

1571

STATE CAPITOL HISTORICAL ASSOCIATION

211 West Twenty-first Avenue
Olympia, Washington 98501

K. Theil (local musician), personal papers and sheet music
Manuscript music by Washington composers
Papers of local theatrical companies, ca. 1880–1920, including the Olympia Opera House (1892–), comprising financial records, minutes, notes, and related programs and posters; also photographs, including 30 of Olympia Opera House productions, 1892–1920, and 30 of the Olympia Band and other local musicians, 1880–1900

Printed music, including 20 hymnals of various denominations, 1820–1920, 2 of them in Latin; 20 school songbooks, 1900–1940; and 200 sheet-music items, 1885–1940, mostly popular songs
Recordings, including 90 Edison cylinders, ca. 1910, and 75 78-rpm discs, ca. 1920–40

—Derek R. Valley

1572
JEFFERSON COUNTY HISTORICAL SOCIETY
City Hall
Port Townsend, Washington 98368

Nell Frances Willison (1882–1965, local violinist and teacher), personal papers, including correspondence, programs, and press clippings
Tuesday Musical Club, archives, 1901–
Manuscript band music, including the "Port Townsend Centennial March" by Sgt. Eugene D. Vacher (Fort Worden bandmaster)
Sheet music, 30 items, ca. 1900–1930, including Carrie Jacobs Bond editions
Hymnals, 13 items, ca. 1880–1940
Programs of local musical events, including Gilbert & Sullivan operettas, 6 items, ca. 1860–1930; also 10 photographs, ca. 1880–1930
Learned Opera House, 5 posters advertising musical events, ca. 1885–95

—Helen D. Burns

1573
WASHINGTON STATE UNIVERSITY   WaPS
Pullman, Washington 99163

Manuscripts, Archives and Special Collections, University Libraries

Mrs. John L. Metsker, diary, 1889–94, including words to 9 songs
Phoebe Bloom Taylor (b. 1879), personal papers, 1874–1964, including her music compositions, reminiscences, and family records
Pullman Music Club, 1 vol. of records, 1933–46
University Department of Music, administrative records, brochures, announcements, and programs, 1897–
Autograph collections, including that of Professor Paul P. Kies, containing signatures, letters, or scores of Amy Cheney (Mrs. H. H. A.) Beach, Robert Russell Bennett, Ernst Blank, Howard Brockway, Henry T. Burleigh, Noble Cain, J. DeForest Cline, Joseph W. Clokey, Mabel Daniels, Reginald De Koven, Peter William Dykema, Granville English, Geraldine Farrar, Maurice Grau, Howard Hanson, Josef Hofmann, Louise Homer, Philip James, Max T. Krone, Margaret Ruthven Lang, Don Malin, F. R. Patek, Maud Powell, Rudolph E. Reuter, Ernestine Schumann-Heink, Joseph Sisler, Charles Gilbert Spross, Frederick Stock, Alec Templeton, C. A. Veasy, Jr., and Reinald Werrenrath
Robert Cushman Butler Collection of Theatrical Illustrations, containing 450 sheet-music covers, 1827–80, other illustrations of singers and dancers, and songbooks

—Terry Abraham

Holland Library

Published songbooks, including hymnals with American Indian texts
Sheet music, 12,000 items

—P. Dean Vanderwall

1574
Ezra MEEKER HISTORICAL SOCIETY
Box 103
Puyallup, Washington 98371

Ezra Meeker (1830–1928, violinist and singer) and family, papers, including 1 songbook, correspondence, pictures, and a family history

—Dorothy Meredith

1575
SEATTLE HISTORICAL SOCIETY
2161 East Hamlin Street
Seattle, Washington 98112

Alexander Myers, scrapbook relating to the Amphion Society of Seattle, and other materials relating to male choruses, collected by former members, as cited in Wallace John Golleke, *A History of the Male Chorus Singing Movement in Seattle* (Ph.D. diss., University of Washington, 1969)
Programs of Seattle-area theaters, including the Moore, Orpheum, and Metropolitan theaters, 1.2 linear meters, ca. 1900–1968
Sheet music, 650 items, ca. 1900–1940s, including 30 by Seattle and Pacific Northwest composers, and several written for the Alaska–Yukon–Pacific Exposition, 1909
Hymnals and popular songbooks, 40 items, ca. 1851–1940
Photographs of local musicians, ensembles, and theatrical productions, 90 items, ca. 1900–1930

—Mary-Thadia d'Hondt

1576
SEATTLE PUBLIC LIBRARY   WaS
1000 Fourth Avenue
Seattle, Washington 98104

All items are in the Art & Music Department, except as noted

Manuscript and printed music by 50 Seattle-area composers, 200 items, 1900–1970, with an index, including works by William Bergsma, Lockrem Johnson (1924–76), George McKay (1899–1970), Irene Rogers, John Verrall (b. 1908), and Amy Worth
Scrapbooks of press clippings, 2.4 linear meters, including the Seattle Symphony Orchestra, 1904– , and Seattle opera companies, musicians, and dancers and dance companies, 1934–
Sayre's Theater Collection, 8.5 linear meters, comprising programs of local and visiting groups in Seattle-area theaters including the Civic Auditorium, Moore, and Metropolitan, 1870s–1950s, arranged by theater and indexed (in the History Department)
KOMO Radio Music Library, 30,000 sheet-music items, mostly popular songs, and 8000 dance-band and

369

theater-orchestra arrangements, 1920s–40s, with an index

Hymnals, 150 items, 1920– , including vols. in German and Scandinavian

Songbooks, ca. 1880–1934, 400 items, mostly collections of songs indexed in Minnie Sears, *Song Index* (New York, 1926; suppl., New York, 1934)

Recordings, including 300 78-rpm discs, 1910–25, mainly of opera, and 44 78-rpm discs, 1945–50, of local musicians

Catalogues of U.S. and foreign music publishers, ca. 1945– , in 6 file drawers

—W. J. Skinner

1577

UNIVERSITY OF WASHINGTON WaU

Seattle, Washington 98195

Suzzallo Library

All materials are in the Archives and Manuscripts Division, except as noted

American Union of Swedish Singers, Pacific Coast Division, 1 program, 1926

Eleanor Nordhoff Beck (d. 1962), 2 linear meters of papers, partly concerning her volunteer work with the Cornish School of Allied Arts, 1920–66

Cornish School (later Cornish Institute) of Allied Arts, papers, 1893–1969, in 30 vols., including organizational materials, correspondence, legal and financial records, registrar's records, newsletters, programs, and scrapbooks, also personal papers and other materials collected for the autobiography of Nellie C. Cornish, founder

Reginald De Koven, ms song "Washington Beloved," 1907, written as the Washington state anthem for the Alaska–Yukon–Pacific Exposition

Geraldine Farrar, letter to the La Boheme Music Club, Seattle, 1941

Maxine Cushing Gray (poet and music critic), papers, 1930–77, including ms poems, copies of her *Northwest Arts*, and a tape-recorded interview concerning arts and the Northwest

Henning Holstrom, 5 items of papers, 1935–39, including ms songs and poems

Melville Jacobs (anthropologist), 18 linear meters of field recordings of northwest-coast Indian music and linguistic materials

LeEtta Sanders King (pianist), 1 linear cm. of papers, 1924–45, including correspondence, clippings, sheet music, and a tape-recorded interview

Sugi Machi (Mrs. Goro Yorita, Japanese-American soprano), 30 linear cm. of papers, 1925–68, including scrapbooks and a tape recording documenting her career with the Seattle Civic Opera, and as founder of the Japanese Cultural Broadcasting Co. over radio station KRKD, Los Angeles

George Frederick McKay (1899–1970), 2.7 linear meters of ms and published music, also the ms text and galley proofs for his *Creative Orchestration* (Boston, 1969)

Music and Art Foundation, Seattle, 4 linear meters of papers, 1923–76, including minutes, correspondence, financial records, and scrapbooks

John Nordeen, 60 linear cm. of papers, 1920–68, including scrapbooks of press clippings, mss, and printed sheet music

Elfrida J. Pedersen (Danish-American actress), 1.7 linear meters of papers, including songs and items related to her activities as leader of the Danish Dramatic Club (Harmonien) in Seattle

Edouard Potjes (pianist), 30 linear cm. of papers, 1917–31, including ms symphonic scores, and published songs, also biographical and autobiographical materials, a scrapbook, and ephemera reflecting his career in Belgium and Seattle

Edgar Rotschy, 60 linear cm. of music mss, 1920–45, an autobiography, 1938, and miscellaneous notes about composing, n.d.

School of Music archives, including 10 letters from Béla Bartók

Seattle Turnverein, 60 linear cm. of records, 1889–1928, including songbooks, minutes, legal and financial documents, and correspondence

Anna Louise Strong (political activist), 5 linear meters of papers, including 2 folders of original songs and sheet music

Vilma Sundborg (Swedish-American actress and lyricist), 60 linear cm. of papers, 1900–1940, including correspondence, published music, clippings, photographs, programs, and a scrapbook

Gerard Tonning (1860–1940, composer), 1.4 linear meters of music mss and memorabilia

United Swedish Singers of the Pacific Coast, 1 program, 1924

Vasa Glee Club, Seattle, 4 items of papers, 1924–28

Walter B. Whittlesey (1886–1956, University faculty member, organist, and composer), 15 linear cm. of music mss

Carl Paige Wood (composer and University faculty member, ca. 1915–1940), 60 linear cm. of papers, including ms and published music, and writings about music

Programs and press clippings of local musical events, 1892– , 1.2 linear meters, in the Pacific Northwest Collection

—Eve Lebo, Richard Berner

Music Library (113 Music Building)

Hazel Gertrude Kinscella (1893–1960) Collection (formerly the American Music Center), including 275 early tunebooks, hymnals, and other printed music books; Edward A. MacDowell materials, comprising 3 MacDowell autographs including a draft of the "Etude novelette" and a sketchbook, 3 letters from Mrs. Marian MacDowell written to or concerning Kinscella, 14 photographs of or relating to the MacDowells, 6 printed items by Edward A. MacDowell or from his library, and 20 press clippings relating to the MacDowell Colony; also personal research materials of Kinscella, 30 linear cm., including typescripts of published and unpublished books and articles, correspondence mostly with William Bergsma, photographs, and photocopies of research materials

Sheet music, 10,000 items, 1790– ; also other printed music dispersed through the general collections

—David Wood

Archives of Ethnic Music and Dance, School of Music and Center for Asian Arts

Collection of world-music recordings, including materials on American Indians of the Northwest, Afro-American blues, early jazz, ragtime, and other early popular piano music, in all 1000 tape recordings and 50 films

—David Wood, Fred Lieberman

1578

EASTERN WASHINGTON STATE HISTORICAL SOCIETY WaSpHiE

West 2316 First Avenue
Spokane, Washington 99204

Pearl Hutton Shrader (1878–1964, Spokane singer and music educator), scrapbook of clippings, programs, and photographs
Bel Canto Club, Spokane, 2 scrapbooks containing photographs, programs, and clippings, ca. 1930–51
Sheet music, 564 items, mostly 1920s–30s, also 65 sacred and secular songbooks, mostly 1910s–20s, with a typed inventory of items acquired before 1979
Programs of musical events, mostly in Spokane, ca. 1924– , including Sophie Braslau, the San Carlo Grand Opera Company, Spokane Opera Association, Spokane Symphony Society, and Spokane Symphony Orchestra
Recordings, including 70 cylinders and 460 78-rpm discs; also a music box and 24 discs, 1880s, in Campbell House
Press clippings of local musical activities, ca. 1940– , in a vertical file collection, accessible by subject

—Doug Olson

1579

GONZAGA UNIVERSITY WaSpG

Crosby Library
East 502 Boone Avenue
Spokane, Washington 99258

Bing Crosby Collection, including 73 sheet-music songs, 9 songbooks, 831 78-rpm recordings of Crosby, 1000 radio transcriptions of the "Kraft Music Hall" program, ca. 1935–55, 100 33⅓-rpm discs, and 20 gold-record and 2 platinum-record awards
Jimmy Van Heusen, 7 holograph mss of popular songs, 1940s, some of them written for Crosby
Hymnals, 15 items, ca. 1890–1920, mostly Roman Catholic, including some in Latin
Songbooks of folk music, 20 items, 1920s–70s

—Evelyn Haynes

1580

MOLDENHAUER ARCHIVES

Rosaleen Moldenhauer, Executive Director
1011 Comstock Court
Spokane, Washington 99203

Musical estates of Charles Haubiel, Otto Jokl, Verne Kelsey, Kurt Manschinger, Karl Weigl, and Adolph Weiss; definitive or extensive collections of musical

mss of Dinos Constantinides, Wolfgang Fraenkel, Paul A. Pisk, David Tamkin, and Jaromir Weinberger; and extensive correspondence and musical documents of Arnold Schoenberg, some materials in connection with the Webern Archive
Major holograph music mss of Leopold Auer, Jacob Avshalomov, Béla Bartók, Marion Bauer, Arthur Berger, Abraham W. Binder, Ernest Bloch, William Brandt, Carl Bricken, Radie Britain, John Cage, Mario Castelnuovo-Tedesco, Louis Coerne, Roqué Cordero, Ingolf Dahl, Frederick Delius, Norman Dello Joio, Ross Lee Finney, Rudolph Ganz, George Gershwin, Morton Gould, Percy A. Grainger, Elliot Griffis, Ferde Grofé, Roy Harris, Herbert Klyne Headley, Bernhard Heiden, Paul Hindemith, Alan Hovhaness, Erich Itor Kahn, Ernest Kanitz, Walter Kaufmann, Ulysses Kay, Kent Kennan, Ernst Krenek, Charles Martin Loeffler, Otto Luening, George F. McKay, Bohuslav Martinů, Jan Meyerowitz, Douglas Stuart Moore, Joaquin Nin-Culmell, Paul Nordhoff, Juan Orrego-Salas, Harry Partch, George Perle, Vincent Persichetti, Solomon Pimsleur, Gardner Read, Wallingford Riegger, George Rochberg, Miklos Rozsa, Leo Sowerby, Frederick Preston Search, Halsey Stevens, Gerald Strang, Alexander Tcherepnin, George Tremblay, Edgard Varèse, Eugene Weigel, Vally Weigl, and others
Shorter holograph music materials of Harold Bauer, John J. Becker, Leonard Bernstein, Mark Brunswick, John Alden Carpenter, Elliott Carter, George W. Chadwick, Henry Leland Clarke, Aaron Copland, Henry Cowell, Paul Creston, Desiré Defauw, Ernö Dohnányi , Arnold Elston, Johan Franco, Leopold Godowsky, Eugene Goossens, Howard Hanson, Edward Burlingame Hill, Karel Jirak, Homer Keller, Erich Wolfgang Korngold, Nikolai Lopatnikoff, Leo Ornstein, Burrill Phillips, Walter Piston, Ernest Schelling, William Schuman, Tibor Serly, Nicolas Slonimsky, John Philip Sousa, Eduard Steuermann, William Grant Still, Igor Stravinsky, Virgil Thomson, Ernst Toch, Burnet Tuthill, Hugo Weisgall, Stefan Wolpe, and others
Autograph letters of Samuel Barber, Béla Bartók, Harold Bauer, John Parsons Beach, John J. Becker, Ernest and Suzanne Bloch, Artur Bodanzky, Felix Borowski, John Cage, John Alden Carpenter, Gilbert Chase, Henry Leland Clarke, Aaron Copland, Henry Cowell, Paul Creston, Ingolf Dahl, Frank and Leopold Damrosch, Desiré Defauw, Reginald De Koven, Richard Donovan, Alfred Einstein, John Erskine, Ross Lee Finney, Ossip Gabrilowitsch, George Gershwin, Leopold Godowsky, Vladimir Golschmann, Morton Gould, Charles T. Griffes, Louis Gruenberg, Howard Hanson, Roy Harris, Roland Hayes, Bernhard Heiden, Jascha Heifetz, Frieda Hempel, Paul Hindemith, Josef Hofmann, Vladimir Horowitz, Mieczyslaw Horszowski, Charles Ives, Frederick Jacobi, Edward Johnson, Thor Johnson, Oswald Jonas, Werner Josten, Arthur Judson, Ernest Kanitz, Louis Kaufman, Walter Kaufmann, Otto Kinkeldey, Rudolf Kolisch, Erich Wolfgang Korngold, Serge Koussevitzky, Ernst Krenek, Gail Kubik, Mischa Levitzki, Normand Lockwood, Charles Martin Loeffler, Nikolai Lopatnikoff, Otto Luening, Edward and Marian MacDowell, George F. McKay, Bohuslav Martinů, Dimitri Mitropoulos, Pierre Monteux, Douglas Stuart Moore, Karl Muck, Joaquin Nin-

Culmell, Eugene Ormandy, Leo Ornstein, Harry Partch, George Perle, Vincent Persichetti, Burrill Phillips, Paul A. Pisk, Walter Piston, Quincy Porter, Serge Rachmaninoff, Gardner Read, Fritz Reiner, Wallingford Riegger, George Rochberg, Carl Ruggles, Olga Samaroff, Ernst Schelling, Harold Schonberg, William Schuman, Ruth Crawford Seeger, Arthur Shepherd, Nicolas Slonimsky, Carleton Sprague Smith, Albert Spalding, Edward Steuermann, William Grant Still, Frederick Stock, Leopold Stokowski, Gerald Strang, Igor Stravinsky, Alexander Tcherepnin, Randall Thompson, Virgil Thomson, Ernst Toch, George Tremblay, Godfrey Turner, Bruno Walter, Herbert Witherspoon, and others

1581

OREGON PROVINCE OF THE SOCIETY OF JESUS — ARCHIVES

WaSpJ

Gonzaga University
502 East Boone Avenue
Spokane, Washington 99258

Manuscript hymnals, songbooks, and music scores in Indian languages of the Pacific Northwest and Alaska, 30 items, ca. 1889–1940
Rev. Frank Meneger, recorded adaptations of 6 Eskimo tunes, 11 78-rpm discs, 1948–52
Programs, 30 linear cm., of Gonzaga University Glee Clubs, 1935–50, and of mission-school graduations, 1890–

—Clifford Carroll

1582

SPOKANE PUBLIC LIBRARY

WaSp

Comstock Building
West 906 Main Avenue
Spokane, Washington 99201

Scrapbooks of clippings and programs of Spokane-area cultural events, 50 linear cm., ca. 1900–1960, containing programs of the Spokane Symphony Orchestra and the Spokane Opera House, 1915–30, including performances by Enrico Caruso
Programs of the Boston Symphony Orchestra, 1920s–50s, and the New York Philharmonic, 1920s– , 1.8 linear meters of bound vols.
Printed music, including 50 hymnals, 1803–1940, some of them in German and some with words only; 60 popular songbooks, 1784–1940; and 700 20th-century sheet-music items

—Janet Miller

1583

TACOMA PUBLIC LIBRARY

WaT

1102 Tacoma Avenue South
Tacoma, Washington 98402

Tacoma and Northwest Archives, including biographical information on local musicians
Sheet music, 2000 items, 1880s–1920s
Songbooks, 30 19th-century collections
Recordings, including 80 78-rpm albums of Bing Crosby

—Clayton Kirking

1584

WASHINGTON STATE HISTORICAL SOCIETY

WaHi

315 North Stadium Way
Tacoma, Washington 98403

Olof Bull (1852–1933, violinist and conductor), 3.6 linear meters of papers, including music scores, correspondence, and photographs
Grand Lodge of the State of Washington, Sons of Herman (German singing society in Tacoma), 1 linear meter of papers, including membership lists, programs, minutes, and songbooks, 1897–1920
Ralph Chaplin (1887–1961, artist, poet, and labor activist), papers, including a folder of labor songs. See the Society's *Inventory of the Ralph Chaplin Collection* (Tacoma, 1967)
Popular music, including 104 bound vols. of sheet music, ca. 1880–1940, and 22 linear meters of 78-rpm disc recordings, donated by I. I. Munch
Programs, mostly of Tacoma theaters, 50 linear cm., ca. 1900–1940
Photographs of musicians and theatrical productions in the Tacoma area, 25 items, ca. 1920–

—Frank L. Green

1585

WAITSBURG HISTORICAL SOCIETY

Fourth and Main Streets
Waitsburg, Washington 99361

Waitsburg Choral Group, papers, including a scrapbook of programs, and documents concerning the Group's founding, 1930–
Songbooks, 8 items, ca. 1880–1940; also 15 sheet-music items, late 19th century to ca. 1930
Pictures of a local band, several items; also 10 programs of local music performances, 1880s–
Recordings, including 24 78-rpm discs

—Roberta Broom

1586

AMERICAN POLITICAL ITEMS COLLECTORS

Education Division
1008 Bonsella
Walla Walla, Washington 99362

Materials relating to political campaigns (especially presidential campaigns) and special-interest groups, including recordings, songs, and other musical items, as cited in *NHPRC*, p. 671

1587

YAKIMA VALLEY MUSEUM AND HISTORICAL ASSOCIATION

2105 Tieton Drive
Yakima, Washington 98902

Programs, clippings, and photographs of events at Yakima theaters, 75 items, including materials of Mason's Opera House, ca. 1889–99, Switzer's Opera House, ca. 1889–1900, Larson's Theater, ca. 1900–1920, and the Capitol Theater, ca. 1920–75

—Frances A. Hare

In addition to the repositories listed above, the following have also reported holdings of the materials indicated:

Bellingham—Whatcom Museum of History and Art: sheet music, songbooks, recordings

Bremerton — Kitsap Regional Library: songbooks

Camas—Camas Public Library: songbooks, recordings

Cheney—Eastern Washington State College, John F. Kennedy Library: sheet music, songbooks, other printed music

Ellensburg—Central Washington State College, Victor J. Bouillon Library: songbooks, recordings

Fox Island—Fox Island Historical Society: sheet music

Gig Harbor—Peninsula Historical Society: songbooks, pictures

Kelso—Kelso Public Library: songbooks

La Conner—Skagit County Historical Museum: sheet music, songbooks, programs, pictures, recordings

Morton—Eastern Lewis County Historical Society: songbooks, recordings

Mount Vernon—Mount Vernon Public Library: songbooks, catalogues, pictures, recordings

Odessa—Odessa Public Library: songbooks, recordings

Olympia—Timberland Regional Library Headquarters: songbooks

Renton—Renton Historical Society: pictures, recordings

Renton—Renton Public Library: songbooks

Seattle—Seattle Pacific College, Weter Memorial Library: songbooks

Silverdale—Kitsap County Historical Society: sheet music, songbooks, pictures, recordings

Stevenson—Skamania County Historical Museum: recordings, miscellaneous

Tacoma—Faith Evangelical Lutheran Seminary, Library: songbooks

Tacoma—Salmon Beach Historical Committee: programs, pictures

Vancouver—Fort Vancouver Historical Society: sheet music, songbooks, programs, pictures, recordings

West Virginia

1588

CHESAPEAKE & OHIO HISTORICAL SOCIETY

Box 417
Alderson, West Virginia 24910

Materials concerning the history of folksongs about the C & O Railway, 1890–1930s, including sheet music, photographs, essays, recordings, and press clippings, many held privately by members of the Society

—Thomas W. Dixon, Jr.

1589

BETHANY COLLEGE   WvBC

Phillips Memorial Library
Bethany, West Virginia 26032

Alexander Campbell (1788–1866, founder of Bethany College), *The Christian Hymnbook,* 28 editions of the text, issued 1840–76

—Larry J. Frye

1590

WEST VIRGINIA DEPARTMENT OF   WV-Ar CULTURE AND HISTORY

Division of Archives and History
The Center
Charleston, West Virginia 25305

Sheet music, 2500 items, 1860–1920s, mostly comprising the Boyd Stutler collection, specializing in materials related to John Brown, Abraham Lincoln, the Civil War, and West Virginia, also early 20th-century songs on military topics

Books about music, 75 items, including reference works and sacred-music collections

—Ellen Hassig

1591

WEST VIRGINIA UNIVERSITY   WvU

West Virginia and Regional History Collections
University Library
Morgantown, West Virginia 26505

See Charles Shetler, *Guide to Manuscripts and Archives in the West Virginia Collection* (Morgantown, 1958; hereinafter cited as *Shetler*), and later eds. by F. Gerald Ham (1965) and James W. Hess (1974) (hereinafter cited as *Ham* and *Hess*, respectively)

Barns family papers, 1816–1929, 79 items, including Civil War ballads printed on stationery (*Hess*, 36)

Arthur I. Boreman (political leader and jurist), personal papers, including account books of the Parkersburg Musical Academy listing companies, play titles, and financial details (*NUCMC*, 60-1210)

Mary Vinson Clark, ms compilation "Mountain Ballads and Hymns," with a foreword by John W. Davis, and other miscellaneous ballads and notes, on microfilm (*Hess*, 153)

Mahala Chapman Mace Gregory, ms bound copybook of poems, hymns, drawings, and an autobiographical sketch, 1940 (*Hess*, 342)

Anna Jarvis (1864–1948), 70 cm. of personal papers, including papers of William Lynett (songwriter, of Fairmont, W. Va.) (*Hess*, 455)

Walter A. Mestrezat (military musician, 1898–1915), family papers on microfilm, 1862–1946, including his military papers and correspondence (*Hess*, 583)

Henri Jean Mugler (chief musician in the 13th Virginia Infantry, 1861–62?), diary and memoir, 1838–99, on microfilm (*Hess,* 657)

Jack W. Preble, personal papers, 1872–1956, in 1 vol., 1 folder, and microfilm, including materials concerning the Maryland folk-music festival at Mountain Lake (*Hess,* 740)

Scott–Palmer family papers, 1 linear meter, 1829–1917, including the papers of Saida Scott Palmer (music teacher), containing correspondence, school papers, clippings, programs, and a register, 1862–83 (*Hess,* 820)

Musicians' Mutual Protective Union of the Ohio Valley, Wheeling Local 142, AFM, 8 vols. and 1 folder of records, 1894–1922, including minute books, dues ledgers, cash books, and membership applications (*Hess,* 664)

West Virginia Music Educators' Association, 3 vols. of minute books, 1925–50 (*Hess,* 978)

West Virginia University, 2 vols. of bound typescripts regarding Student Night literary and musical productions, 1920–21 (*Shetler,* 714); a student register of the School of Music, 1 vol., 1903–25 (*Ham,* 414); and press clippings regarding the University Women's Glee Club, 1932–54, in 1 folder (*Ham,* 418)

Musical programs, press clippings, and miscellaneous materials pertaining to West Virginia musical events, 13 items, 1912–19 (*Hess,* 663)

"West Virginia," words and music of the prize-winning song written for the State's Jubilee, 1913, as published in the *Wheeling Sunday News* (*Shetler,* 581)

West Virginia Folklore Society, 2.5 linear meters of folk music and folklore, 1915–26, including published songbooks and ms and typescript folk tales and ballads collected by John Harrington Cox (*Hess,* 966), also ms texts of songs in a compilation of folklore from Lewis County by Opal Jones and Beth Curry (*Hess,* 291)

Sound Archives, 1000 tape recordings, mostly of 250 West Virginia and Appalachian folk-music performers, in-cluding recordings collected by Thomas S. Brown and his students, ca. 1971– , 600 discs recorded by Louis Watson Chappell, 1930s–40s, the C. D. Reece collection of black American songs from southern West Virginia, ca. 1950, and a tape of ballad singers at the West Virginia State Fair, 1961 (*Hess,* 290)

Miscellaneous materials, including the words and music of a song about the West Virginia counties (*Hess,* 593), and bills, broadsides, clippings, and photographs (*NUCMC,* 62-1252)

—George Parkinson, John A. Cuthbert

In addition to the repositories listed above, the following have also reported holdings of the materials indicated:

Athens—Concord College, J. Frank Marsh Library: sheet music, songbooks, other printed music, recordings

Bradley—Appalachian Bible Institute, Library: song-books

Charleston—First Presbyterian Church of Charleston, Library: songbooks, other printed music

Charleston—Morris Harvey College, A. S. Thomas Memorial Library: sheet music, songbooks, other printed music

Hamlin—Hamlin Public Library: songbooks, recordings

Huntington—Marshall University, Morrow Library: sheet music, programs, pictures, recordings, miscellaneous

Marlinton—Pocahontas County Historical Society: sheet music, songbooks, programs, recordings

Moorefield—Hardy County Public Library: sheet music, songbooks

New Martinsville—New Martinsville Public Library: songbooks, recordings

Vienna—Vienna Public Library: sheet music

Wisconsin

1592

OUTAGAMIE COUNTY HISTORICAL SOCIETY

320 North Durkee Street
Appleton, Wisconsin 54911

Irving Schwerke (1893–1975), personal papers, including unpublished memoirs and other documents relating to his work in Paris as a music critic and promoter of jazz, 1920s–30s, 30 linear cm.

Harmonie (local music club), minute book and 1 folder of records, ca. 1900–1920

Small collections of sheet music, programs, and recordings

—Mary Grogan

1593

Marion (Mrs. Henry) SPENCER

102 First Avenue North
Balsam Lake, Wisconsin 54810

Henry Spencer (1891–1977, member of the Sousa Band), 1.5 linear meters of original ms and published music for band, chamber ensemble, and chorus, also correspondence, photographs, and programs of performances of his music

1594

CIRCUS WORLD MUSEUM   WBaraC

Library and Research Center
Baraboo, Wisconsin 53913

See the descriptive brochure (Baraboo, 1973)

Archives of circus materials, including 5000 newspaper advertisements, 1793– ; handbills ("heralds"), 1797– ; 6000 lithographs (posters), 1835– ; couriers (circus magazines), 1839– ; 385 route books, 1863– ; route cards; letterheads; films, 1927– ; programs, 1870– ; libretti, 1889–1915; 55,000 negatives and photographs; 340 oil paintings and litho-graph watercolors; trade journals; 1100 circus books; 65 recordings of circus bands; and an index of 400,000 references to circus people, 1769– . Music collections include 50 circus-clown songsters, 1850–1905; manu-script music, 1898–1917; and 8200 published circus-band orchestrations, incorporating the performance library of circus bandleader Merle Evans

—Greg T. Parkinson

1595
SAUK COUNTY HISTORICAL SOCIETY
WBaraHi

133 Eleventh Street
Baraboo, Wisconsin 53913

Guy Holmes (1873-1945, composer for the Ringling Cir-cus band, ca. 1905–30, and orchestra director), 10 linear cm. of papers, including scrapbooks, photo-graphs, and 10 published music items
Haskell Harr (music educator), 10 linear cm. of papers, including scrapbooks and programs, ca. 1920–65
Hymnals, ca. 1860–1920, 12 items, including 2 in Ger-man; also 1 with words only, for Civil War soldiers
Programs of local and traveling musicians, 30 items, ca. 1900–1940

—Gordon L. Willson

1596
JACKSON COUNTY HISTORICAL SOCIETY

c/o Carol Kinley
223 North Fourth Street
Black River Falls, Wisconsin 54615

Verna Keefe (local voice teacher, ca. 1920–70), personal papers, including programs, financial records, photo-graphs, and published music used by her in teaching and in conducting local concerts
Schubert Club (local male chorus), clippings and photo-graphs, ca. 1930–40; also 25 programs, ca. 1900–40, including items of the Schubert Club and other local music groups
Pauline Lolliman (opera singer), 1 autographed bound copy of her published opera *Di Capi de Confucius*, 1911; also photographs of her and her son, Edgar Lol-liman (violinist)
Hymnals and popular and school songbooks, 25 items, ca. 1900–1920, including some in Norwegian and Ger-man, and a book of ms hymns and songs copied by a local musician, ca. 1900
Sheet music, 100 popular items, ca. 1900–1930, and 1 bound vol. of Civil War music
Photographs of local choruses, minstrel shows, and other musical events, 60 items, ca. 1880–1930
Clippings, including 1 folder on local musical events, ca. 1880–1930
Recordings, including 18 78-rpm discs, some of them by Harry Lauder; and 8 78-rpm discs of local ethnic music, recorded by Helen S. Thomas, ca. 1945

—Frances R. Perry

1597
Peter A. GRENDYSA

9708 Caddy Lane
Caledonia, Wisconsin 53108

Recordings of black vocal groups and soloists, 3000 discs, 1921–65, emphasizing products of the Atlantic Recording Co.; also miscellaneous taped interviews, oral histories, catalogues, master lists, photographs, sheet music, and discographies

1598
CEDARBURG PUBLIC LIBRARY

West 63 North 583 Hanover Avenue
Cedarburg, Wisconsin 53012

Hymnals of county churches, ca. 1880– , including some in German; also 50 popular songbooks, ca. 1900–1940, and 20 sheet-music items for piano, ca. 1900–1940, mostly semi-classical
Drum and bugle corps annual music festival, programs, ca. 1920–
Photographs of local music groups, in 2 notebooks in the Edward Rappold collection, ca. 1880–1920

—Mrs. George Loepfe

1599
OZAUKEE COUNTY HISTORICAL SOCIETY

West 61 North 619 Mequon
Box 206
Cedarburg, Wisconsin 53012

Port Washington (Wis.) Gesang-Verein, 3 concert pro-grams, 1906–7
Instruction books for mandolin, guitar, reed organ, and general musicianship, 4 items, 1892–97
Songbook of comic songs, 1858

—Alice Wendt

1600
CHIPPEWA VALLEY HISTORICAL MUSEUM

Box 1204
Eau Claire, Wisconsin 54701

Grand Opera House of Eau Claire, archives, 1883–1930, in 2 vols., also 50 posters, 1874–1929
Photographs of local bands and orchestras, 20 items, late 19th century
Sheet music, 721 items, 1888–1940s; also 91 songbooks, ca. 1860–
Recordings, including tapes of Mississippi River-area folk music and of Norwegian fiddle music, and 35 78-rpm discs

1601
UNIVERSITY OF WISCONSIN—EAU CLAIRE
WEU

Area Research Center
Eau Claire, Wisconsin 54701

Ku Klux Klan songbooks used by the Women's Auxil-iary of the Klan in Chippewa Falls, Wis., 1926–31, 2 photocopies
Jacob Miller (band musician), 1 folder of memorabilia, including photographs, clippings, and programs, ca. 1900

Chippewa Valley Musicians' Association, Local 345, AFM, 6 items of records, 1903

Scrapbooks of the University A Capella Choir, 1930s, 15 linear cm.; also photographs of University music groups, ca. 1916

—Richard Cameron

1602
WALWORTH COUNTY HISTORICAL SOCIETY

9 East Rockwell Street
Elkhorn, Wisconsin 53121

Joseph Philbrick Webster (1819–75) collection, including 25 published sheet-music items, mostly popular or patriotic, among them the first edition of "Lorena," and "Sweet By and By"; ms lyrics to "Sweet By and By" by Sanford Fillmore Bennett of Elkhorn, 1867; 10 hymnals, ca. 1865–1900, with hymns by Webster; personal papers, including scrapbooks, letters, personal and business correspondence of the family, 3 daguerreotypes of Webster, and a diary of his son, Frederick; and Webster's melodeon and piano

Community songbooks, 5 items, ca. 1865–1920
Sheet music, 50 mostly popular items, ca. 1865–1920

—Helen Kluge

1603
HOARD HISTORICAL MUSEUM— FORT ATKINSON HISTORICAL SOCIETY

409 Merchants Avenue
Fort Atkinson, Wisconsin 53538

School and Sunday-school songbooks, ca. 1850–1930, 200 items, including some in German and Scandinavian languages, and 1 used in local singing school directed by William Dempster Hoard (governor of Wisconsin), ca. 1850

Sheet music, 2000 items, ca. 1900–1940, including works by Halbert Hoard (son of W. D. Hoard) and ms music for the Ft. Atkinson centennial pageant, 1936

Papers of the Music Study Club, 1882–1950, and of local bands, ca. 1860–1940, including club records, minutes, and clippings

Programs of local events including Lyric Theater operas, and of Jenny Lind, Ole Bull, and other touring performers, ca. 1880–1940

Photographs of local bands, an orchestra, and Maddie and Lila Snell and their music school and orchestra, 50 items, ca. 1880–1940

—Hannah Swart

1604
JANESVILLE PUBLIC LIBRARY

316 South Main Street
Janesville, Wisconsin 53545

Louise Fulcher Collection of Sacred Choral and Organ Music, containing 350 items of published music for solo voice or choir, and 730 items of published music for organ

1605
ROCK COUNTY HISTORICAL SOCIETY

Box 896
Janesville, Wisconsin 53545

Carrie Jacobs Bond (1862–1946, Janesville composer), personal papers, including a ms of "A Perfect Day," 1909; 31 printed works, ca. 1890–1910, including 8 autographs; a scrapbook of clippings and photographs to 1939; 26 programs; letters; a financial agreement, 1922; poems by her; other clippings; a family genealogy; photographs; a catalogue of Roycroft Co. books; Victor Sincese's essay "Carrie Jacobs Bond" (12-page typescript, n. d.); and a list of songs by Bond, compiled by F. J. A. Forsters, 1907

—Ruth Widdicombe

1606
KENOSHA COUNTY HISTORICAL SOCIETY   WKenHi

6300 Third Avenue
Kenosha, Wisconsin 53140

Don Fina (1888–1957, local composer), personal papers, including several of his songs in editions from the Key City Music Publishing Co., a ms biographical sketch, photographs, press clippings, and letters of acknowledgment from Al Jolson, Kay Kaiser, Guy Lombardo, and other musical and political figures

—Lois Stein

1607
SOCIETY FOR THE PRESERVATION AND ENCOURAGEMENT OF BARBER SHOP QUARTET SINGING IN AMERICA

Harmony Hall
6315 Third Avenue
Kenosha, Wisconsin 53141

"Old Songs Library," comprising 36,000 sheet-music items, mostly 1895–1945, consisting mostly of copies presented by members of the Society, including the large collections of Ken Grant, Cleveland; Walter Wade, Chicago; and William F. Spengler, Colorado Springs. The collection was organized by Prof. Robert F. Brooks of Columbia, Mo., in one alphabet by song title. See the articles in *The Harmonizer*, 16/3 (1956), 2–3, and 25/1 (1965), 4; also D. W. Krummel, "Quantitative Evaluation of a Sheet-Music Collection (American Music Bibliography, 3)," *Yearbook for Inter-American Musical Research*, 9 (1973), 177–81

Archives of the Society (founded 1938), arranged by prominent early leaders such as Owen C. Cash, Deac Martin, and Frank H. Thorne (restricted access)

1608
KEWAUNEE PUBLIC LIBRARY

822 Juneau Street
Kewaunee, Wisconsin 54216

"Music in Kewaunee County," a set of 5 scrapbooks assembled by members of the Kewaunee County Historical Society, with photographs of local bands and orchestras, mostly German and Czech groups, 1856–1970s

—Catherine Hanrahan

1609

CLARK COUNTY HISTORICAL SOCIETY

Route 2, Box 117
Loyal, Wisconsin 54446

Listemann family collection, containing papers of Bernhard (1841–1917, violinist), his wife Sophia, their sons Paul (1871–1950, violinist), Franz (1873–1930, cellist), and Freddy, their daughter Virginia (singer), and Bernhard's brother Fritz (1839–1909, violinist). The collection includes 100 diaries of concert tours, 1868–1925; 100 letters, ca. 1860–1925; 10 scrapbooks of press clippings, ca. 1880–1920; 2 violin method books by Bernhard Listemann, 1868 and 1869; 500 classical sheet-music items, ca. 1870–1910; 50 tour programs, ca. 1880–1920; 5 string-music catalogues; 3 bound vols. of pencil drawings by Sophia Listemann, ca. 1850–1900; 10 oil paintings of family members, ca. 1870–1920; 30 photographs of family members, ca. 1880–1930; a marble bust of Bernhard Listemann; and an inscribed loving cup given to Bernhard Listemann by the Chicago Musicians' Union
Hymnals of the Methodist Episcopal Church, 10 items, 1890s–1920s

—Florence Garbush

1610

Lewis A. BOSWORTH

2829 Barlow Street
Madison, Wisconsin 53705

Hymnals, 350 vols., 1855– , including foreign-language hymnals

1611

STATE HISTORICAL SOCIETY OF WISCONSIN   WHi

816 State Street
Madison, Wisconsin 53706

See Steven L. Sundell, "An Index to Selected Music in the State Historical Society of Wisconsin" (typescript, 1977)

Archives Division: Archives–Manuscripts

William F. Allen (1830–89), 1 box of papers, 1775–1934, including a ms diary, 1863–64, documenting black folk music in the U.S.
Calvin P. Alling (1840–1928, Civil War musician in the Wisconsin Volunteer Army), 21-page typescript reminiscences
American Federation of Musicians, Local 59, Kenosha, 8 boxes and 13 vols. of papers, 1897–1940, concerning musicians' salaries, contracts, minutes, membership rolls, and accounts

Adolph Kornelius Austin (1876–1954, musician in Chetek), typescript biographical material
Wade Barnes (b. 1917), 1 box of radio scripts for music and drama programs with NBC station WTAM in Cleveland, Ohio, 1938–41
Marc Blitzstein (1905–64, composer), personal papers, 1905–70, 99 boxes, including ms scores, texts, correspondence, notebooks, writings, scripts, programs, clippings, and disc and tape recordings
Rev. Florimond J. Bonduel (b. 1801, parish priest in Winnebago County), 1 song and 2 letters to Charles Grignon
Ole Bull (1810–80), 1 letter, 1872, concerning concert arrangements
Cecil Edward Burleigh (1885–1980, composer and violinist), 1 box of correspondence and biographical materials, and 4 cartons of unprocessed papers including ms and published music
Irving Caesar, personal papers, 1905–72, in 3 boxes, including ms songs, correspondence, and writings, also clippings and disc recordings
Clarence Caldwell (LaCrosse and West Salem music teacher), 3 boxes of papers, 1832–1925, including correspondence, programs, and clippings
Vera Caspary (composer), 13 boxes and 3 vols. of papers, 1929–63, with drafts or copies of her musicals and other writings
J. Fred Coots (composer), 9 boxes of papers, 1912–60, including sheet music by him and others, royalty contracts, 200 playbills, and 228 recordings
Frank M. Crandall (1843–64, Civil War musician in the Wisconsin Infantry), correspondence, 1855–65, on microfilm
Albert Stevens Crockett (b. 1873), papers, 1903–61, including 2 ms songs
William Donahey (1883–1970, cartoonist), 9 boxes of papers, 1914–69, including ms music for 16 songs with words by him
Nathan Dye (Kenosha voice teacher), 9 items of papers, 1835–63, including recommendations for him as a teacher
Don Fina (1888–1957), 1 box of papers, 1947–54, including correspondence, work sheets, and autobiographical material
Ella Fitzgerald, 53 holograph orchestrations by Nelson Riddle of songs by Ira Gershwin, each signed by Fitzgerald, Riddle, and Gershwin, n.d.
Ernest Gold (composer), 40 boxes of papers, 1935–69, including ms sketches and scores for orchestral, stage, and film music
Edgar B. Gordon (1875–1963, professor of music at the University of Wisconsin), 3 boxes of papers, 1906–61, including correspondence, articles on music education, news releases, and reminiscences
Wendell Hall (1896–1969, ukulele player and radio singer), 3 boxes of correspondence, clippings, and scrapbooks, 1915–62, and 4 disc recordings of him singing
Ethwell (Eddy) Hanson (organist and composer in Chicago and with John Philip Sousa's band), 1 folder of sheet music and 5 tape recordings of interviews, 1972–75; also an interview with Dan Barton of Oshkosh, inventor of the Bartola and the Barton Pipe Organ
Sheldon Harnick (b. 1924, composer), 7 boxes of papers, 1937–68, including ms correspondence, scripts, and production materials for musical shows
Moss Hart (1904–61, author), papers, 1922–62, including correspondence to Hart and his wife, Kitty Carlisle,

from composers and playwrights, also playbills, scrapbooks, and photographs

Skitch Henderson (composer and bandleader), 1000 ms scores or arrangements and orchestral parts, in 25 file drawers (owned by the University of Wisconsin School of Music, on deposit with the Society)

Highlander Research and Education Center, New Market, Tenn., papers, 1917–73, including music clippings and programs, 20 songbooks, song sheets, correspondence, and tape recordings, concerning southern folk music and labor songs

Halbert L. Hoard (1861–1933, Fort Atkinson newspaper editor and composer), papers, 1872–1933, including ms and printed songs

Edith J. R. Isaacs (1878–1956, journalist), 1 box of papers, 1889–1957, including scripts and notes for 2 operas by her and her husband, and correspondence with Martha Graham

Alice Keith (1890–1962), papers, 1906–62, concerning the founding of the National Academy of Broadcasting (NAOB), NAOB memorabilia, and scripts for "Music in the Air" programs

Edwin O. Kimberley (d. 1919), 1 box of papers, 1850–82, including letters from his son in Gen. Sherman's army-brigade band

John Knell (1831–73, German immigrant in Wisconsin) papers, 1851–83, including 1 box of ms music

Thure L. Kumlein (1819–88, naturalist), papers, 1832–1946, including ms songs and poems

Grace Garrison Lincoln (1871–1970, music teacher in Richland Center), 1 box of papers, ca. 1899–1965

Madison Männerchor, 102 items of papers, including accounts and advertisements for a Sängerfest, 1881

Cyrus H. McCormick, Jr. (1859–1936), papers, 1840–1942, including correspondence with musicians, clippings on music in Chicago, and his own published music

Harold Fowler McCormick (1872–1941, music patron), papers, 1892–1947, including items relating to opera and symphony activities in Chicago

MacDowell Music Club, River Falls, 1 folder of papers, 1915–19, with minutes and programs

Mrs. Aubertine Woodward Moore (1841–1929, author and musician in Philadelphia and Madison, pseud. Auber Forestier), 10 boxes and 5 vols. of papers, 1781–1928, including articles on music; biographies; reminiscences of Ole Bull by his son, Alexander Bull, and letters written by Alexander Bull during concert tours of the northwestern U.S.; letters from publishers, musicians, and music critics, including James G. Huneker; and materials for her Scandinavian songbook, *Songs from the North*

Richard Nathan Nash (producer), 24 boxes of papers, 1937–61, including drafts and typescripts of musicals, and correspondence

National Broadcasting Company, 464 boxes and 1 vol. of archival papers, 1923–60, including materials relating to music performances, radio scripts, and 3211 disc recordings

May Peterson (Mrs. Thompson, 1880–1952, singer), unfinished biography with 2 photographs, n.d.

Playbill collection of miscellaneous theater, concert, and opera productions in New York City and Wisconsin, ca. 1861–   , arranged by city and title, in 2 file cabinets

Henry H. Rader (bandsman in the Indiana Volunteers, 1862–80), 1 folder of letters and 1 ms song

Neil Reed (Wisconsin bandleader), 1 vol. of sheet music and ms songs, 1920–45

Franz Lee Rickaby (1889–1925), 2 vols. of papers, including the journal of his ballad-collecting trip in 1919 through Michigan, North Dakota, northern Wisconsin, and Minnesota

Katherine A. Rood (1861–1948), papers, 1826 and 1872–1945, including scrapbooks on the First Presbyterian Church of Stevens Point, and 1 vol. of ms music including folk tunes

Jerry Ross (1926–55, composer), 2 boxes of papers, 1934–55, including published and holograph music scores and contracts

Harry Ruby (1895–1974, composer and playwright), 1 box of papers, 1926–51, including scripts and music scores

Arthur Schwartz (composer), 1 box of papers, ca. 1930–61, including ms scores of songs and musical shows

Bernard Sobel (1888–1964), 2 boxes of papers, 1923–61, including correspondence, clippings, photographs, and mss of his studies, *A Pictorial History of Burlesque* and *A Pictorial History of Vaudeville*

Harry Sosnik (conductor and composer), 75 boxes of materials, including air checks from radio and television broadcasts of music, also 78–rpm disc recordings, 1936–45

Theodore A. Steinmetz, ms "32nd Division Marching Song," 1917

George W. Stoner (1830–1912), 6 vols. of papers, 1849–1911, including clippings of songs and memoirs of early Madison

Tams–Witmark Music Library, Inc., 186 cartons of mss and typescript or printed music–rental materials, including European and American scores, orchestrations, stage-managers' guides, and dialogue parts of musical comedies and operas, ca. 1790–1925

Ada Alice Tuttle (1886–1936), 1 box of papers, 1896–1935, including letters concerning her musical activities and her work with the YMCA entertainment corps in France and Germany, 1918–19

WJR, Detroit radio station, 1 disc recording of broadcast selections, 1922–57

WPA Wisconsin Federal Music Project records, 1936–41, microfilm of monthly and final reports, programs, correspondence, and clippings

Watertown Musical Society, Concordia, Wis., 2 vols. of minutes, accounts, and printed programs, 1880–97

Joseph P. Webster (1820–75, songwriter), 1 box of papers, 1850–1921

William Wegener (b. 1867, opera tenor), 1 box of papers, 1897–1958, with an autobiography and 3 scrapbooks; also 2 tape recordings of reminiscences, 1958–59, and 1 tape of songs performed by him, 1959

Dwight Deere Wiman (1895–1951, producer), papers, 1925–50, including musical-comedy scripts, programs, photographs, sheet music, orchestrations, and 47 vols. of scrapbooks with press clippings

John M. Winterbotham (d. 1940), autograph collection, including correspondence of Arthur Weld (*Milwaukee Journal* music editor), 1887–98

Wisconsin Federation of Music Clubs, 13 boxes of papers and 3 tape recordings, 1926–64, including minutes, correspondence, reports, scrapbooks, and folk-music materials

Wisconsin State Musicians' Association, 3 boxes of papers of local AFM chapters, 1932–46, including correspondence, minutes, and financial records

Archives Division: Iconography, Film, and Recorded Sound

Sheet music, 350 popular items with illustrated covers, ca. 1900–1945

Come and Sing, 40-page songbook composed by first- to third-grade students of Milwaukee State Teachers' College, illustrated with 12 silk-screen prints by Ludwig Cinatl, sponsored by the WPA, ca. 1935–41

Advertising booklet of Edmund Gram (Milwaukee music dealer), including music of national anthems, 44 pages, ca. 1895

Jackson Piano Company trade catalogue, *The Miessner Piano* (Milwaukee, 1921)

—Myrna Williamson

Archives Division: Wisconsin Center for Film and Theater Research

All materials are housed with the State Historical Society of Wisconsin, and administered jointly with the Wisconsin Center for Film and Theatre Research, University of Wisconsin, 6039 Vilas Communication Hall, Madison, Wis. 53706. See the guide by Janice O'Connell, "The Collections of the Wisconsin Center for Theatre Research" (mimeographed, 1974)

Kermit Bloomgarden (Broadway producer), 112 boxes and 31 items of papers, 1935–65, including financial statements, files, contracts, production records, and 9 tape and 11 disc recordings

C. P. Bronson, published article, "The Self-Taught Reader, Orator, and Singer, or the Diatonic Scale and Illustrations of the Principles of Elocution and Music" (Cincinnati, 1836)

Charles R. Codman, 3 boxes of papers, 1904–37, including 1 holograph song by George and Ira Gershwin, also playbills and clippings from New York theater productions

John Cromwell (Broadway and film producer), 8 boxes of papers, 1902–72, including correspondence, scrapbooks, and scripts

Edna Ferber, papers, 1913–63, including materials concerning productions of *Show Boat*, and 4 disc recordings

Ira Gershwin, correspondence, in the Arthur Kober papers, 1924–59

Ruth Goodman Goetz, papers, 1916–59, including letters to Philip Goodman (producer) from Jerome Kern, Oscar Hammerstein II, and others

Francis Goodrich and Albert Hackett (playwrights), papers, 1927–61, including scripts and correspondence concerning musical films

Albert Johnson (set designer), 37 boxes of papers, 1910–67, including programs, clippings, photographs, production plans, and music for New York theater productions

George S. Kaufman (writer and producer), 2 boxes and 6 vols. of papers, 1918–51, including notes on *Of Thee I Sing*

Walter Kerr (critic and playwright) and Jean Kerr (playwright), papers, 1929–69, including correspondence from Oscar Hammerstein II, Joshua Logan, and Richard Rodgers, also musical scores and production materials for theatrical works, with 15 tape and 16 disc recordings

Millard Lampell (writer), 19 boxes and 14 items of papers, 1936–66, including correspondence, clippings,

music, and other ms or published materials from radio, theater, and film productions

Isabella W. Lewis, 4 scrapbooks of New York theater and opera programs, 1878–1944

Howard Lindsay and Russel Crouse (playwrights), 12 boxes of papers, 1918–68, including correspondence and production materials for musical plays

Michael Myerberg (artists' manager), 10 boxes of papers, 1937–49, including correspondence, files, and financial papers of theatrical productions and of the Westminster Choir and the Ensemble of the Red Army

Ernest Pett (performer), 1 folder of papers, 1926–33, concerning 3 minstrel shows in Madison, including 1 orchestral cue sheet

Nadonis Shawa (Ojibwa Indian poetess and performer of music), 1 folder of papers, 1921–51, including correspondence, playbills, brochures, and performance outlines

United Artists Corporation, 300 linear meters of papers, 1919–51, including corporate records, legal files, press books, photographs, and mss. Notable holdings within the collection include materials of Warner Brothers Films, 800 films and related materials, 1913–50; RKO Films, 708 films, 1929–54; and Monogram Films, 182 films, 1931–46, with dialogues, still negatives, and advertising materials

Library

Songbooks and songsters, including hymnals of various Protestant denominations, also hymnals written by missionaries for American Indians, ca. 1800–1890

Books and pamphlets on music, mostly 19th century, including 150 items of sheet music, programs, and song texts, 1860–1920

—James Hansen

Museums Division

Howard Kanetzke sheet-music collection, 150 items by Wisconsin composers or on Wisconsin subjects, ca. 1860–1940

Piano rolls, 600 items of popular and classical music, with ms inventory by title

Recordings, including cylinders, 114 Edison quarter-inch discs, and Regina music boxes with steel discs

—Howard Kanetzke

1612
UNIVERSITY OF WISCONSIN—MADISON   WU

Mills Music Library
Madison, Wisconsin 53706

Cecil Burleigh (1885–1980, professor of music), 42 items and 7 vols. of published music

Helene Stratman-Thomas Blotz (1896–1973), 5 boxes of papers, notes, and field recordings of Wisconsin folk music collected in the 1940s, including German, Polish, French-Canadian, Cornish, Scandinavian, and American Indian materials

John Knowles Paine, holograph score of his symphonic poem, *Shakespeare's Tempest*, and published music from his personal library

Brodhead (Wisc.) Silver Cornet Band, which served

under Gen. Sherman in the Civil War, 12 ms band books, 7 miscellaneous mss, and 17 photographs (in Special Collections, Memorial Library)

Tams–Witmark collection, musical-theater materials formerly of the Tams–Witmark rental library, New York, in 28 cartons, containing conductor's scores, 170 sets of orchestral parts, 70 vocal scores of operas and operettas by American composers (including Victor Herbert, John Philip Sousa, and Reginald De Koven), and 4000 vocal scores of European operas and operettas performed in the U.S.; with a title inventory

Leo Kissel Collection of Theater Orchestrations, 907 published sets of orchestrations of European and American music used in Milwaukee theaters, including some by Milwaukee composers, 1881–

Americana collection, 1200 items of music, incorporating the collection of Joseph P. Webster, and including 2 boxes of Webster mss; 1500 vocal and instrumental sheet-music items, mostly 1840–80; 57 19th-century hymnals, including 1 in Welsh (Rome, N.Y., 1857); and other vocal scores, songbooks, piano music, and libretti, ca. 1870-1900

Sheet music, 1100 items of 19th- and 20th-century popular music, with a partial computer-based catalogue by title, lyricist, composer, publisher, copyright date, and first line

Recordings, including 9500 78-rpm discs, mostly classical, made in the U.S.

—Lenore Coral

1613
MAYVILLE HISTORICAL SOCIETY

Box 82
Mayville, Wisconsin 53050

Printed music, including 3 hymnals, 1873–1905, 2 of them in German; 6 community songbooks, 1870s; and 2 file drawers of sheet music of the local Damenchor and Männerchor, mostly in German

Programs of town festivals, local concerts, and theatrical productions, 15 items, ca. 1900–1935

Photographs of local bands and a chorus, 35 items, ca. 1880–1950

Recordings, including 250 popular and classical 78-rpm discs

—Mrs. Evaline Boeck

1614
WISCONSIN STATE HISTORICAL SOCIETY (WMenU)

Area Research Center
University of Wisconsin—Stout
Menomonie, Wisconsin 54751

Mabel Tainter Literary, Library & Educational Society, Menomonie, 1 linear meter of papers, 1890–1965

George O'Brien Collection, with 11 pages of song texts, including published song sheets by H.J. Wehrman of New York, 19th century

Women's Christian Temperance Union, Chetek, Wisc., 1 linear meter of papers, 1907–61, including temperance songs

University of Wisconson—Stout, papers of the band, music, and other related faculty committees, also of the Music Department and music organizations, in all 13 linear meters, ca. 1920–64 (in the University Archives)

Photographs of the Stout Institute Band and Stout Institute Orchestra, 4 items, 1924–35 (in the University Archives)

—Gayle Martinson

1615
Mary Elizabeth DALAND

314 Davis Street
Milton, Wisconson 53563

William C. Daland (president of Milton College, 1902–21, and grandfather of M. E. Daland), ms and published music for piano, organ, voice, or choir; also photographs, 2 programs of his performances or performances of his compositions, and a printed Seventh Day Baptist hymnal, We Glorify Thy Name, containing one of his hymns

1616
MILTON HISTORICAL SOCIETY

18 South Janesville Street
Box 245
Milton, Wisconsin 53563

Alberta Crandall (1879–1975, faculty member at Milton College, 1903–50), ms music including songs, and published items including a college song printed in the Milton College songbook, Carmina (1928); also a collection of programs and clippings compiled by her, from College and other local musical events of the Choral Union, Treble Clef (girls' glee club), and Milton College Civic Orchestra, partly in scrapbooks, ca. 1898–1970

Jairus M. Stillman (chairman of the Milton College Music Department, ca. 1900), 3 hymnals and songbooks compiled by him and published 1873–82; also his "Badger Song" (1895)

—Lois K. Westlund

1617
Bernhardt H. WESTLUND

Milton College
Milton, Wisconsin 53563

Manuscript and published music composed or edited by Westlund for chorus, orchestra, or solo instruments, 1936–79

Programs of Milton College and local music organizations with which he was associated, ca. 1940–79; also annual programs of the Wisconson Composers Concert at Milton College, 1950s–60s

Recordings of his compositions, on 33⅓-rpm discs and tapes

—Lois K. Westlund

1618
HERITAGE MILITARY MUSIC FOUNDATION

Box 1864
Milwaukee, Wisconsin 53201

Band music, 1 linear meter of published or photocopied parts from band books of Civil War musicians, including works by Stephen Foster, W. E. Gilmore, Claudio Grafulla, Francis Scala, and Henry Clay Work; also 60 linear cm. of band parts, ca. 1870–1920

—Audrey B. Heckner

1619
HOPE LUTHERAN CHURCH

Library
1115 North Thirty-fifth Street
Milwaukee, Wisconsin 53208

Lutheran and Methodist hymnals, 9 items, 1894–1939, including 1 in German
Printed choral music, mostly anthems, 60 linear cm., 1908–38

—William H. Bopf

1620
John A. JAEGER

1507 North Fifty-second Street
Milwaukee, Wisconsin 53208

Scrapbook containing clippings and programs of elementary schools where Jaeger taught music, ca. 1930–70; also photographs of his school groups
Sheet music, ca. 1820–1900, 7500 items, mostly popular vocal music and dances for piano, organ, accordion, or banjo, including theater music for piano, and containing many works by local composers, with an index; printed music for organ, several hundred 19th- and 20th-century items; other printed music, including popular songs arranged as dance folios, 644 19th- and 20th-century items; 31 film-music books, 1920s, 17 cue sheets for silent-film piano accompaniment, 1930s; 80 popular songbooks, 19th and 20th centuries; and 30 hymnals of various denominations, ca. 1850–1920
Clippings on musical humor, 8136 items, ca. 1900–
Photographs of local musicians and groups

1621
MARQUETTE UNIVERSITY   WMM

Memorial Library Archives
1415 West Wisconsin Avenue
Milwaukee, Wisconsin 53233

Christopher Bach (1835–1927), 14 ms and published compositions for orchestra or chamber orchestra
Gustave Bach (son of Christopher Bach), 4 compositions for strings or violin solo, ca. 1882–96, including 1 ms
Hugo Kaun (1863–1932), ms and published orchestral parts for 2 works, ca. 1890–1906, and 8 printed works for piano or orchestra, ca. 1888–1902
Alexander MacFadyen (1879–1936), 3 works, ca. 1906–7, including a ms vocal solo with ms orchestral parts arranged by Christopher Bach
Printed works by Wisconsin composers John F. Carre, Lilorious Semman, and Harriet Ware, 3 items, 1910–21; also 8 songs and piano pieces with Milwaukee imprints, ca. 1896–1903, and 75 glee and school

songbooks, 1910–30, including some in German, and several with Milwaukee imprints
Printed music used for performance or study at Marquette College of Music, 600 items, 1910–30, including classical music for band, orchestra, piano, or chorus, and works by 20 Wisconsin composers
Marquette University Players, program and clippings, 6 linear meters, 1904–

—Robert Callen

1622
MILWAUKEE COUNTY   WMCHi
HISTORICAL SOCIETY

910 North Third Street
Milwaukee, Wisconsin 53203

Manuscript music, 1 linear meter, including holograph scores by Christopher Bach (1835–1927), also published works and personal papers; and mss by Henry A. Bokelman, Charles K. Harris (1865–1930), and Alexander McFadyen
Papers of 20 Milwaukee-area music organizations, 4 linear meters, including scrapbooks and programs of the Milwaukee Musical Society (Der Musikverein), Arion Music Club, Cadman Choral Club, Lyric Glee Club of Milwaukee, Lyric Male Chorus, McFadyen Club, Milwaukee Liedertafel, and Milwaukee Symphony Orchestra
Personal papers of musicians, 70 linear cm., including materials of Robert Adams-Buell, Rafael Baez, Heinrich Bartel, Gertrude Meyne Bates, Henry A. Bokelman, Joseph H. Chapek, Alice O. Hastings, and William R. Pfeil
Printed music, 6 linear meters, including sheet music
Programs, 1.2 linear meters
Photographs of musicians and groups, 30 linear cm.
Recordings, including 300 cylinders and 700 78-rpm discs

—Robert G. Carroon

1623
MILWAUKEE MUSIC CENTER

2432 West Kilbourn Avenue
Milwaukee, Wisconsin 53233

Sheboygan Theater, 8.5 linear meters of printed and ms silent-film scores for piano, organ, or orchestra, ca. 1910-30
Hymnals, 20 items, ca. 1850–1940, including some in German
Sheet music, 3000 items, including some by local composers or with local references, ca. 1820–1940, for solo piano or voice
Photographs of local musical events, 20 items, ca. 1910
Programs of local musical events, 20 items, ca. 1890–1930, including those of the Pabst Theatre and the Auditorium
Recordings, including many for mechanical instruments, with 6000 discs and 8000 piano or organ rolls; also 40 catalogues of discs and piano rolls, ca. 1900–1930

—Gregory K. Filardo

1624

MILWAUKEE PUBLIC LIBRARY   WM
Art and Music Department
814 West Wisconsin Avenue
Milwaukee, Wisconsin 53233

> Portions of the materials below, while assigned to the Local History Department, are also accessible through the Art and Music Department

Carl Eppert (composer and conductor), personal papers, 1907–61, including scores, correspondence, photographs, programs, and scrapbooks, 2.4 linear meters

Joseph Gigante (bandleader, composer, and teacher), personal papers, including 18 original works, 1929–47

Uno A. Nyman (Wisconsin dentist and composer), personal papers, 1915–58, including correspondence and mss of 248 original works

Music mss, including Christopher Bach, *Prinz Eugenius*, n.d.; Hugo Kaun, 3 works, 1895–1902; and 2100 scores and parts copied through the WPA Federal Music Project

Historic Popular Song Collection, 23,000 sheet-music items, 1890–1950, including works by Christopher Bach, Edward Sobolewski, and Alfred Bergen; also 35 American vocal anthologies, 1788–

Playbills, programs, posters, and other papers, including materials of the Milwaukee Musikverein, photographs, 1850s, and *Repertorium*, 1857–60; Milwaukee People's Theatre, 1887–89; Arion Music Club, scrapbook, 1930–34; Davidson Theatre, scrapbook, 1890–91, and programs, 1890–1954; Pabst Theatre, programs, 1893–1940; Milwaukee Symphony Orchestra, programs, 1890–91, 1924–34, and 1940– ; Chicago Symphony Orchestra, Milwaukee series, programs, 1915– ; Milwaukee Auditorium, extensive runs of programs, 1895–1967; and Milwaukee Grand Opera House, programs, 1888–90

Posters of theatrical, minstrel, and other events, 700 items

Recordings, including 73,000 discs, also wax cylinders and piano rolls

—June Edlhauser

1625

John STEINER
2748 South Superior Street
Milwaukee, Wisconsin 53207

Materials concerning ragtime, jazz, and blues, including 10,000 sheet-music items, 1860s– , 35,000 recordings, 1900– , letters of Chicago musicians, ca. 1940, and photographs and posters relating to music in Chicago

1626

UNIVERSITY OF   WMUW
WISCONSIN—MILWAUKEE
2311 East Hartford Avenue
Milwaukee, Wisconsin 53201

William Wegener (b. 1867, tenor), 3 vols. of personal papers, 1897–1958, including reminiscences and other autobiographical materials, reviews, and notes on opera in Oconomowoc, Wis.

Nellie Hobbs Smythe (d. 1940, pianist), 6 vols. of personal papers, 1887–1939, including correspondence with American and European musicians, writers, and artists; programs of concerts and recitals in Milwaukee and Berlin, 1889-90; and personal observations concerning musical life in Wisconsin, Minnesota, and Chicago

The John Dale Owen Collection of recordings of early jazz is now on deposit at the Institute of Jazz Studies, Rutgers University, Newark, N.J., q.v.

—Richard E. Jones

1627

Jacque D. VALLIER
7817 North Club Circle
Milwaukee, Wisconsin 53217

> The collection is designated for deposit with the Menominee Logging Camp Museum, Keshena, Wis. 54135, which is the property of the Menominee Indian Historical Foundation, Milwaukee

Books containing logging songs, 50 items, 1880–1940

Photographs of logging-camp scenes, portraying lumberjacks with various musical instruments, 400 items, 1858–1940

1628

WISCONSIN CONSERVATORY OF MUSIC
Library
1584 North Prospect Avenue
Milwaukee, Wisconsin 53202

James Hatzi Collection of Violin Music, containing 2000 scores for violin and 6000 scores for orchestra

Sheet music, 2000 mostly popular items, ca. 1890–1950; also 10 published songbooks

Catalogues of the Wisconsin College of Music and the Wisconsin Conservatory of Music (which later merged to become the Wisconsin College–Conservatory of Music, now the Wisconsin Conservatory of Music), a complete set, ca. 1920–

—Brian J. Gerl

1629

Stephen L. ADAMS
537 East Wisconsin Avenue
Neenah, Wisconsin 54956

Arthur Shattuck, letters to members of the Adams family, 12 items, 1890s–1940s

Songbooks, 6 items, ca. 1900–1920s, including Presbyterian hymnals, a World War I songbook, and a popular songbook

Sheet music, 400 popular and semi-classical items for piano, 1900–1930

Catalogues of mechanical music-instrument manufacturers, 5 items, 1918–29, and of pipe-organ builders, 6 items, 1918–29

Pictures of film theaters in Minneapolis, Milwaukee, Chicago, San Francisco, and New York, 350 slides and 150 photographs, 1915–

Recordings, including 40 78-rpm discs of popular and classical works, 1917–40

1630
Mrs. S. F. SHATTUCK
Box 645
Neenah, Wisconsin 54956

Arthur Shattuck (1881–1951, concert pianist), papers and memorabilia, as used in S. F. Shattuck, ed., *The Memoirs of Arthur Shattuck* (Neenah, 1961), with an account of his career by Willard Luedtke

1631
SHEBOYGAN COUNTY HISTORICAL SOCIETY
3110 Erie Avenue
Sheboygan, Wisconsin 53081

Programs of local musical events at Concordia Hall, the Sheboygan Opera House, and elsewhere, 12 items, 1891–1924; also 5 photographs of local music groups, 1890–1929
Hymnals and school songbooks, 9 items, ca. 1863–1894, including hymnals in German
Sheet music, 4 items for piano, 1897–1922, including "The Mail Carrier March" by W. D. Sanford (local composer)
Recordings, including 97 Edison cylinders, 9 music rolls for the Gately automatic organ, and 98 78-rpm discs
—Betty Potter

1632
UNIVERSITY OF WISCONSIN— STEVENS POINT   WSpU
Music Library
Stevens Point, Wisconsin 54481

Orchestral music, mostly popular arrangements, 2.7 linear meters, ca. 1898–1940
Music for men's and women's glee clubs, 10 linear meters, ca. 1920–40
Popular sheet music for voice, 250 items, ca. 1900–1940, including some by Wisconsin composers
Recordings, including 7 linear meters of 78-rpm discs
—Steve Sundell

1633
DOUGLAS COUNTY HISTORICAL MUSEUM
906 East Second Street
Superior, Wisconsin 54880

Printed music, including 4 hymnals of the United Lutheran Church of America, 1930s; 30 community songbooks, 1910–30; and 100 popular sheet-music songs, 1890–1930
Research notes on newspaper references to musical activities in the Twin Ports area (Superior, Wis., and Duluth, Hibbing, and Virginia, Minn.), 1857–1931, compiled by Louis Meier, on 35,000 cards, and arranged chronologically

Programs and playbills of the Lyceum Theatre, Superior, a complete run, 1896–1920; also 60 programs and playbills, 1900–1925, of theaters and opera houses in St. Paul, Duluth, St. Louis, and Chicago
Photographs of local theaters, bands, orchestras, and musicians, 1900–1940, indexed
Recordings, including 80 Edison cylinders, 1890s, and 100 78-rpm discs, 1910–30
—James E. Lundsted

1634
WATERTOWN HISTORICAL SOCIETY
919 Charles Street
Watertown, Wisconsin 53094

Richard Hardege (1853–1922, violinist and teacher), 1 published and 3 ms compositions for violin, also 3 letters, 5 programs, 20 photographs, and biographical information
Kindergarten songbooks, 5 items in German, ca. 1850–1900
Popular sheet music, 100 items, ca. 1920–40
Watertown Opera House programs, mostly of traveling performers, 6 items, ca. 1860–80
Photographs of local musical events, including 10 photographs of the Sangenfest annual festival, ca. 1870–90
Recordings, including 25 78-rpm discs
—Richard Berndt

1635
WATERTOWN PUBLIC LIBRARY   WWat
201 West Main Street
Watertown, Wisconsin 53094

Sproesser collection of music mss and sheet music, 113 vols., presented by the family of a local jeweler and music merchant, uncatalogued
—Mary Carol Powers

1636
NEW TRIBES MISSION BIBLE INSTITUTE
Library
915 North Hartwell Street
Waukesha, Wisconsin 53186

Hymnals of various denominations, 1 linear meter, ca. 1880–1940
Printed sacred choral music, 20 linear meters, ca. 1920–40
—Jim Ostewig

1637
WAUKESHA COUNTY HISTORICAL MUSEUM   WWauHi
101 West Main Street
Waukesha, Wisconsin 53186

Waukesha Musicale, 1 box of scrapbooks, 1899–1948
Local bands, 4 photographs, pre-1940; also vertical-file

materials on the history of music in Waukesha County

Sheet music, 750 items, uncatalogued

—Terry Biwer

1638
MARATHON COUNTY PUBLIC LIBRARY

400 First Street
Wausau, Wisconsin 54401

Printed music, including 10 hymnals of various denominations, 2 of them in German, 1920–40, 100 folksong books, ca. 1920–50; and 1000 popular sheet-music songs, 1920s–40s

—Elizabeth Scully

1639
Fred BENKOVIC

2117 North Eighty-ninth Street
Wauwatosa, Wisconsin 53226

Research collection of Civil War-era military-music materials, including mostly photocopies of music and documents, also with original editions of 4 bound vols. of piano sheet music, 1830s–60s, the *Fifer's and Drummer's Guide* (1862) by George Bruce and Dan Emmett, and 1 method book each for clarinet (1838) and drum (1860)

1640
Lawrence A. SCHLICK

1865 North Seventy-third Street
Wauwatosa, Wisconsin 53213

Catalogues of recording and phonograph manufacturers, ca. 1895–1925, including early issues of the Berliner Company and Eldridge R. Johnson (later Victor), North American Phonograph Company (Edison), and American Graphophone Company (Columbia)

Recordings, several thousand items, including 5000 cylinders, ca. 1895–1905, some of them wax; and early discs by Edison, Berliner, Johnson, Zonophone, and Columbia, ca. 1885–1925

1641
WASHINGTON COUNTY HISTORICAL ASSOCIATION

Fifth Avenue and Chestnut Street
West Bend, Wisconsin 53095

Manuscript songs written for local public schools, 2 items, ca. 1910

Printed music, including 3 hymnals, ca. 1900–1920s, 1 of them a liturgical work in German; 10 community songbooks, 1910s–20s, and 5 songbooks used for Little Theatre plays in West Bend, 1930s; and 20 popular sheet-music songs, ca. 1900–1920s

—Zella Loomer

1642
WEST SALEM HISTORICAL SOCIETY

357 West Garland Street
West Salem, Wisconsin 54669

Songbooks, 8 items, including 3 popular songbooks partly with lyrics by Hamlin Garland (local author), ca. 1915, 3 school songbooks, 1890–1930, and 2 early 20th-century hymnals

Sheet music, 60 popular items for voice or piano, ca. 1880–1915

Scrapbooks of clippings and letters pertaining to local musical events, 2 items, 1900–1940, 1 owned by Ida Tilson

Programs of high-school concerts in West Salem and of touring groups in La Crosse, 25 items, ca. 1890–1915

Photographs of a local military band, ca. 1880–1910, and of a local orchestra, ca. 1890–1920, 10 items

Edison cylinders, 15 items, 1898–1910

—Errol Kindschy

In addition to the repositories listed above, the following have also reported holdings of the materials indicated:

Appleton—Lawrence University: songbooks, other printed music, miscellaneous

Balsam Lake—Balsam Lake Public Library: songbooks

Barron—Barron County Historical Society: sheet music, songbooks, pictures, recordings

Benet Lake—St. Benedicts Abbey, Benet Library: sheet music, songbooks

Berlin—Berlin Historical Society: sheet music

Colfax—Colfax Public Library: songbooks

Delafield—Hawks Inn Historical Society: sheet music, songbooks, pictures, miscellaneous

Eagle River—Eagle River Public Library: songbooks

Exeland—Helen Aspseter: sheet music, other printed music

Fennimore—Southwest Wisconsin Library System: songbooks

Fond Du Lac—University of Wisconsin, Fond Du Lac Campus, Library: songbooks, other printed music

Germantown—Germantown Historical Society: sheet music, songbooks

Green Bay—Neville Public Museum: sheet music, programs, recordings

La Crosse—Viterbo College, Fine Arts Library: sheet music, songbooks

Loganville—Friendship Rural School Historical Society: songbooks, other printed music

Madison—GAR Memorial Hall Museum: recordings

Madison—Madison Public Library: sheet music, songbooks

Manitowoc—Manitowoc Public Library: sheet music, songbooks

Manitowoc—Silver Lake College, Library: miscellaneous

Mequon—Wisconsin Lutheran Seminary, Library: songbooks, programs

Mercer—Mercer Public Library: songbooks, recordings

Middleton—Cross Plains–Berry Historical Society: pictures

Milwaukee—Alverno College, Library: sheet music, songbooks, other printed music, recordings

Mineral Point—Mineral Point Historical Society: pictures

Muskego—Muskego Public Library: sheet music, recordings

Neenah—Neenah Public Library: recordings

Oak Creek—Oak Creek Historical Society: catalogues, miscellaneous

Platteville—University of Wisconsin at Platteville, Elton S. Karrmann Library: songbooks, programs, recordings

Platteville—Mrs. H. C. Zeigert: sheet music, songbooks

Plymouth—Plymouth Public Library: pictures

Portage—Columbia County Historical Society: sheet music

Reedsburg—Reedsburg Area Historical Society: sheet music, songbooks, pictures

Rib Lake—Taylor County Historical Society: sheet music, songbooks, recordings

Shawano—Shawano City–County Library: sheet music, songbooks, catalogues, recordings

Shawano—Shawano County Historical Society: sheet music, songbooks, programs, pictures, recordings

Sheboygan—Lakeland College, Community Memorial Library: songbooks, other printed music, recordings

Sheboygan Falls—Sheboygan Falls Memorial Library: recordings

Sparta—Monroe County Local Historical Room and Library: songbooks

Stanley—Stanley Area Historical Society: sheet music, songbooks

Stevens Point—Portage County Historical Society: sheet music

Three Lakes—Three Lakes Public Library: sheet music, songbooks, miscellaneous

Union Grove—Graham Memorial Library: songbooks

Wautoma—Waushara County Historical Society: sheet music, songbooks, programs, pictures

Webster—Burnett County Historical Society: sheet music, songbooks

Whitewater—University of Wisconsin at Whitewater, H. Anderson Library: sheet music, songbooks, other printed music, recordings

Wyoming

1643

WYOMING STATE ARCHIVES, MUSEUMS, AND HISTORICAL DEPARTMENT

Wy-Ar

Barrett Building
Cheyenne, Wyoming 82002

Sheet music, including Charles Earl Cady, original Wyoming songs; B. F. Coolidge, 10 original songs, ca. 1940, mostly on Wyoming subjects; Mrs. Leslie Lewis, sheet-music collection of 147 items, 1898–1952; a vertical-file folder of western state songs; and other sheet music, as indexed under "Music" and "Wyoming songs"

Music collections and personal papers of John Brueggemann (music teacher of Rock Springs), 45 folders; and Warren Richardson and his family, 500 items, mostly sheet music with some books and scores, mostly early 20th century

Music mss of Allan Arthur Willman and Regina Willman, as listed in a special inventory

"The Invasion Song," ms copy of the ballad of the Johnson County War, 1892

Col. Jay L. Torrey, personal papers, including sheet music, also a ms copy of "While We Go Riding with Torrey," possibly the regimental song of the 2nd Regiment, U.S. Volunteer Cavalry ("Torrey's Rough Riders"), 1890s

Wyoming Federation of Music Clubs, 16-page report on "Wyoming Composers," 1941

WPA oral-history transcripts, including Samuel E. Bailey on Natrona County music, Orville S. Johnson on music in Big Horn County, Ludwig Stanley Landmichl on Indian dances of Fremont County, and William Marquardt on early Laramie music; also subject files on early music, opera, and amusements

—William H. Barton

1644

Carroll HIGHFILL

Converse County Library
Box 570
Douglas, Wyoming 82633

Popular sheet music, 1000 items, ca. 1900–1960
Recordings, including 200 78-rpm discs

1645

LARAMIE PLAINS MUSEUM ASSOCIATION

603 Ivinson Avenue
Laramie, Wyoming 82070

Hymnals of various denominations, ca. 1900–1920, 10 items, including 1 in Swedish; also a college songbook, ca. 1920

Sheet music, 12 mostly popular vocal items, ca. 1920–30, including 1 each by Charles Earl Cady and John L. Hunton

Programs of local schools and of the University of Wyoming, 10 items, 1920s

Photographs of local children's bands and of high-school and University musicians, 12 items, 1900–1930

Recordings, including 25 cylinders and 12 78-rpm discs

—Mrs. J. S. Wright

1646

UNIVERSITY OF WYOMING

WyU

American Heritage Center
Laramie, Wyoming 82071

Twentieth Century Music Collections

Materials cited below relating to films are part of what has been identified as the Archive Collections of Film

Music. See the report by Edgar J. Lewis, Jr., "The Archive Collections of Film Music at the University of Wyoming: A Descriptive Guide for Scholars" (Laramie, 1976)

William Axt (b. 1888), 12 boxes of scores for film background music.

Rude Bloom, contracts, correspondence, and song lyrics, in 9 boxes

Perry Botkins, 17 boxes of scores, correspondence, press clippings, biographical materials, and tape recordings

Radie Britain, 2 boxes of orchestral music and biographical materials

Les Brown, 5 boxes of band-music recordings and other materials

Darrell W. Calker (1905–64), 11 boxes of scripts and music mss

Frankie Carle, 2 boxes of photographs, awards, and memorabilia

Irwin Cassel (b. 1886), 1 box of sheet music

Saul Chaplin, 4 boxes of correspondence and music mss

Larry Clinton, 5 boxes of scores, arrangements, and miscellaneous materials

Bob Crosby, 20 boxes of scores and arrangements, sheet music, photographs, press clippings, and recordings, 1932–73

Adolph Deutsch, 12 boxes of music mss, scores, correspondence and photographs

Frank Devol, 74 boxes of music mss

Robert Emmett Dolan, 12 boxes of correspondence, scores, sheet music, books, and awards

Carmen Dragon, 9 boxes of music mss

Eddy Duchin, correspondence, orchestrations, programs, and scrapbooks, 1932–51

L. Gilbert Wolfe (1886–1940), 49 boxes of scores, books, photographs, and recordings

Walter Gross, 8 boxes of correspondence, music mss, photographs, and recordings

Charles Haubiel, 2 boxes of music mss

Edward Heyman, 10 boxes of awards, correspondence, and recording albums, and 12 boxes of scores for Broadway stage productions and film music

Loretta Hildegarde, 2 boxes of press clippings and biographical materials

Harry James, 46 boxes of music mss

Jerome Jerome (1906–64), 13 boxes of music mss, sheet music, and press clippings

Bronislaw Kaper, 2 boxes of film-music scores

Hal Kemp (1905–40), 14 boxes of scores and dance-band arrangements, programs, and rehearsal records, 1929–39

A. Walter Kramer (1890–1969), 28 boxes of his music library of sheet music and symphonic scores

Gail Kubik, 4 boxes of scores for orchestral music

Alexander Laszlo, 12 boxes of film-music scores

William Lava, 17 boxes of sheet music and film scripts

Edgar Leslie (b. 1885), 2 boxes of music scores and scrapbooks

Lyn Murray, 12 boxes of music for films and Broadway musicals

Ben Oakland, 2 boxes of musical works

Eleanor Powell (dancer, singer, and actress), 25 boxes, comprising her recording library

Heinz Roemheld, 1 box of film-music scores

Harry Ruby, 49 boxes of books, photographs, and recordings

Hans J. Salter, 6 boxes of film-music scores

Walter Scharf, 15 boxes of music scores

Joseph Schillinger, 1 box of photographs and orchestral music

Walter Schumann, 44 boxes of scores for radio shows

Raymond Scott, 6 boxes of music scores and arrangements

Marlin H. Skiles, 9 boxes of music scores

David L. Snell, 2 boxes of music scores and biographical materials

Jack Stern, 4 boxes of music scores

William Grant Still, 2 boxes of photographs, programs, and biographical materials

Deems Taylor, 2 boxes of operatic materials

Henry Tobias, 2 boxes of music scores

John Scott Trotter, 10 boxes of music scores and arrangements

Nathan Van Cleave, 16 boxes of music scores and orchestral arrangements

Hugo Winterhalter (1909–73), 28 boxes of music scores and other works

Eugene Zador (1894–1977), music mss, as cited in *Eugene Zador: A Catalogue of His Works* (Los Angeles, 1977)

Other Collections

Western History Research Center, including materials of Owen Wister, notably his journals and notebooks, with occasional music references

Howard F. Greene Transportation Historical Collection, including songbooks and sheet music relating to railroads, accessible through a special finding aid

—Emmett D. Chisum

1647

Anna MILLER MUSEUM

Delaware Street and Washington Park
Box 698
Newcastle, Wyoming 82701

Manuscript notebook of popular songs and ms notebook of popular-song lyrics, copied ca. 1890

Printed music, including hymnals, 10 school and popular songbooks, ca. 1880–1930, and 185 sheet-music items, mostly popular vocal music, ca. 1900–1930

Local materials, including 15 programs of the Cambria (Wyo.) Opera House and band concerts directed by Waldemar Söllers, ca. 1890–1905; 10 photographs of ensembles and musicians including Söllers; and a scrapbook of the Treble Clefs

Recordings, including 60 linear cm. of 78-rpm discs

—Mabel E. Brown

In addition to the repositories listed above, the following have also reported holdings of the materials indicated:

Douglas—Converse County Library: songbooks

Douglas—Wyoming Pioneers Memorial Museum: sheet music, pictures

Fort Laramie—Fort Laramie National Historic Site: sheet music, songbooks

Newcastle—Wyoming State Historical Society, Weston County Chapter: sheet music, songbooks, catalogues, recordings

Riverton—Riverton Museum: sheet music, songbooks, recordings

Sheridan—Sheridan County Historical Society: recordings

Thermopolis—Richard Flood: sheet music, songbooks, recordings

Thermopolis—Hot Springs County Library: songbooks

Torrington—Goshen County Public Library: sheet music, recordings

U.S. Territories

1648
Jesús María SANROMÁ

Condominio Garden Hills Tower
Penthouse No. 1
Calle Miramonte, Garden Court
Guayanabo, Puerto Rico 00657

Holograph music mss of Edward Burlingame Hill, Ferde Grofé, and Walter Piston, also a general collection of piano and orchestral music by Puerto Rican composers, including all works by Juan Morel Campos, with a catalogue of his music, as cited in Catherine A. Dower, "Libraries with Music Collections in the Caribbean Islands," M.L.A. Notes, 34 (1977), 37

1649
MORLÁ COLLECTION

Llorens Torres 400
Hato Rey, Puerto Rico 00657

Ramón Morlá Trenchs (1876–1953), mss and printed music for church, band, piano, secular songs, and choruses. See Catherine A. Dower, "Libraries with Music Collections in the Caribbean Islands," M.L.A. Notes, 34 (1977), 37

1650
UNIVERSITY OF PUERTO RICO   PrU

Music Library
Río Piedras, Puerto Rico 00931

Sheet music, 70 items, mostly Puerto Rican imprints by Puerto Rican composers, 1910s–40s, largely piano music but including some songs

Music mss of José M. Franco (1935), Juan Rios Ovalle (2 items, 1907), José I. Quintón (2 items, n.d.), and Juan Urteaga (4 items, n.d.)

Monserrate Deliz, 41 scrapbooks, ca. 1927– , containing programs, press clippings, and photographs documenting music in Puerto Rico and the activities of Puerto Rican composers at home and abroad

Balbino Trinta, collection of 41 photographs relating to musical life in the community of Mayagüez

—Annie F. Thompson

1651
ARCHIVO GENERAL DE PUERTO RICO

Sección de musica
500 Avenida Ponce de León
Apartado 4184
San Juan, Puerto Rico 00901

Music mss, 5000 items, 1859– , also first editions of music by Puerto Rican composers, as cited in Catherine A. Dower, "Libraries with Music Collections in the Caribbean Islands," M.L.A. Notes, 34 (1977), 34–35. Among the collections with musical materials are those of Ernesto Ramos Antonini (works of Heraclio Ramos), Juan F. Acosta (150 of his danzas), José Hernández Bosch (works of Juan Rios Ovalle), Herminio Brau (700 mss and published editions of the Puerto Rico modernist period, 1880–1930, also waltzes, cancions, and danzas), Alfredo Romero Bravo (works of Alfredo Romero and Braulio Dueño Colón, 400 items), Braulio Dueño Colón (200 musical and literary mss), Monsita Ferrer (works of Luis R. Miranda), Eduardo Franklin (works of José I. Quintón), Antonio Otero (works of Quintón and R. Retana), Carlos R. Gadea Picó, Maria Teresa Picó (both with works of Quintón), and Elisa Tavárez (works by Juan Morel Campos, Ovalle, Quintón, and herself)

1652
ATENEO PUERTORRIQUEÑO

Avenida Ponce de León
Apartado 1180
San Juan, Puerto Rico 00901

Printed music editions and music mss of works by Puerto Rican composers, among them Jose Agullo y Prats, Rafael Balseiro Dávila, Monsita Ferrer Otero, Juan Morel Campos, and Manuel Gregorio Tavárez, as cited in Catherine A. Dower, "Libraries with Music Collections in the Caribbean Islands," M.L.A. Notes, 34 (1977), 35

1653
ESTUDIOS DE MÚSICA GUSTAVO BATISTA

Box 3104
San Juan, Puerto Rico 00936

Felipe Gutiérrez y Espinosa (1825–99), 30 mss of masses for chorus and instrumental ensemble, as well as other sacred works. See Catherine A. Dower, "Libraries with Music Collections in the Caribbean Islands," M.L.A. *Notes*, 34 (1977), 37

1654
MUSEO DE LA MÚSICA PUERTORRIQUEÑA
Casa Blanca Compound
Calle de San Sebastian
San Juan, Puerto Rico 00901

Original documents, photocopies, and memorabilia relating to music in Puerto Rico, as cited in Catherine

A. Dower, "Libraries with Music Collections in the Caribbean Islands," M.L.A. *Notes*, 34 (1977), 36

In addition to the repositories listed above, the following has also reported holdings of the materials indicated:

Pago Pago, Samoa—Library of American Samoa, Department of Education: songbooks, pictures, recordings

Canada

1655
Eugene MILLER
90 Prince George Drive
Islington, Ontario
Canada M9B 2X8

Recordings of jazz, blues, and ragtime, and by particular entertainers, 20,000 items, including 500 cylinders and Canadian Berliner recordings
Sheet music, 1500 items, specializing in jazz, ragtime, illustrated covers of E. T. Paull and on black subjects, and vaudeville covers

1656
Ray LA COURSE
658 Simcoe Street North, Apt. 10
Oshawa, Ontario
Canada L1G 4V4

Commercial recordings of Hawaiian music, 1900–ca. 1950, 650 78-rpm discs, 50 33⅓-rpm discs, and 100 related items including sheet music, post cards and stereo cards from the 1920s, and songbooks, 1890–

1657
Roger MISIEWICZ
742 Simcoe Street North
Oshawa, Ontario
Canada L1G 4V8

Recordings of 13,000 performances, 1902–42, including gospel, classic blues, country blues, and city blues, entirely on discs and copied on tape, with an index; also several unissued test pressings

1658
Stanley L. OSBORNE
705 Masson Street
Oshawa, Ontario
Canada L1G 5A6

Hymnals, 300 items, mostly English-language vols. 1920– ; also 21 hymnal companions, 70 books on

church music and hymnology, and pamphlets and journals; holographs of sacred works based on hymns; and other editions of sacred music

1659
NATIONAL LIBRARY OF CANADA   CaOONL
Music Division
395 Wellington Street
Ottawa, Ontario
Canada K1A 0N4

Personal papers, including those of musicians who were active both in Canada and in the U.S., among them Mme Albani (Emma Lajeunesse, 1847–1930), 15 letters, photographs, and other documents, including photocopies; Gena Branscombe (1881–1977), 2 holograph music mss, correspondence, biographical materials, and published music, in all 50 linear cm.; Rosy Geiger-Kullmann (1886–1964, German composer active in the U.S. after 1939, mostly in Los Angeles), music scores and parts in holograph ms and photocopies, memoirs, and other biographical materials, in all 7 linear meters; Luigi von Kunits (1870–1931), holograph music mss from his career in Pittsburgh and in Canada, 50 linear cm.; John W. Love, Jr. (1892–1969, amateur composer from Mount Vernon, N.Y., and Nova Scotia), holograph music ms scores and ms parts, 1 linear meter; and Lynnwood Farnam (1885–1930), scrapbook
Percy A. Scholes (1877–1958, British musicologist), personal research notes and library, the former arranged by subject and including materials on U.S. topics (i.e., Edward A. MacDowell, 500 slips; ragtime and jazz, 600 slips; U.S. in general, 200 slips, each slip containing references to information, or in some instances clippings or other printed materials); also correspondence with U.S. scholars, among them Carl Engel, Henry Wilder Foote, and Edwin Franko Goldman
Sheet music, including U.S. imprints, 1790s– ; also 40 bound vols. including Canadian, U.S., and British imprints intermixed
Recordings, including 64 Emile Berliner discs, 1894–99; 40 cylinders, mostly U.S. labels; 7200 78-rpm discs of

Canadian performers, many on U.S. labels; and 25
player-piano rolls, mostly on U.S. labels

—Helmut Kallmann

1660
UNIVERSITÉ LAVAL   CaQQLa
Faculté des Lettres
Quebec, Quebec
Canada G1K 7P4

Harry Oster collection of 300 songs with violin, guitar,
or accordion accompaniment, recorded in Louisiana

—Carole Saulnier

1661
Edward BRAKE
437 Sackville Street, Apt. 27
Toronto, Ontario
Canada M4X 1T1

Collection of music of U.S. blacks, 1920– , mostly blues
and rhythm and blues, 1948–58, including 3000 78-
rpm discs, 3500 45-rpm discs, 3000 LP discs, and 200
tape recordings, also 1000 related items, among them
books, magazines, photographs, posters, and postcards

1662
METROPOLITAN TORONTO   CaOTMCL
LIBRARY
789 Yonge Street
Toronto, Ontario
Canada M4W 2G8

Theatre Department

> See the department's *Selected List of Reference Acquisi-
> tions*. Collections cover all areas of the performing arts
> (except opera and music), including theater and drama,
> film, dance, radio, circus, music hall, and vaudeville,
> with special emphasis on Canadian materials

The Dumbells (World War I theatrical troupe), programs, photographs, correspondence, scripts, and
sheet music, 1917–76
Mae Edwards Collection, including photographs, correspondence, programs, clippings, and sheet music
used by her touring company in the Maritime Pro-
vinces and the eastern U.S., 1917–32
Marks Brothers (Canadian touring company), scripts,
photographs, programs, and sheet music, 1897–1929
George Summers (Canadian actor and manager), papers, including route books, business correspondence, clippings, play scripts, photographs, and
sheet music, 1889–1947
Taverner Company, papers of Albert Taverner and his
wife, Ida Van Cortland, for tours of eastern Canada
and the U.S., including photographs, promptbooks,
correspondence, account books, programs, and sheet
music, ca. 1873–1918
Boris Volkoff (dancer), scrapbooks, photographs, stage
designs, correspondence, programs, choreographic
notebooks, and music scores, 1924–73

—Heather McCallum

Music Department

Community songbooks and hymnals, 50 items, late
19th and early 20th centuries
Sheet music, 2000 items, mid 19th and early 20th
centuries
Programs, mostly of U.S. concerts, 100 20th-century
items

—Isabel Rose

1663
UNIVERSITY OF TORONTO   CaOTU
Edward Johnson Music Library
Toronto, Ontario
Canada M5S 1A1

Edward Johnson (1878–1959, manager of the New York
Metropolitan Opera, 1935–50), papers, including his
personal performance library of songs and operas, 1
linear meter; tape recordings of all his recorded performances, 4 reels; and other materials, among them
a few letters, 50 photographs, and memorabilia
General music holdings, a strong collection of 20th-cen-
tury publications, including representative holdings
of U.S. sheet music, tunebooks (12 early 19th-century
items), concert music, programs, and 78-rpm disc
recordings

—Kathleen McMorrow

1664
VICTORIA UNIVERSITY   CaOTV
Library
71 Queen's Park Crescent East
Toronto, Ontario
Canada M5S 1K7

Hymnals and tunebooks, 1200 items, mostly 19th and
20th centuries, with emphasis on Methodist and
North American materials

1665
UNIVERSITY OF VICTORIA   CaBViV
Music and Audio Collection
McPherson Library
Victoria, British Columbia
Canada V8W 2Y3

William Fletcher Tickle, 1500 sets of music scores and
parts for dances, marches, and medleys of popular
and show tunes, used by him for accompanying silent films in local theaters, 1919–26, leading the
orchestra at the Crystal Gardens, 1926–28, and leading the salon orchestra at the Empress Hotel, 1928–60
Annie Radford (1881–1959, violinist), performing library
of popular and classical music for violin and piano or
for small orchestra, and copies of press clippings and
photographs
Sheet music, including 2000 popular songs, ca. 1860s–
1910s; 200 items for piano, mostly early 20th century;
and 300 sets of 20th-century choral music and religious songs
Autographs of musicians, individually and included in
LP recordings from the collection of Kenneth G.
McKenzie

Recordings, 1500 popular and classical 78-rpm discs, mostly Victor and Columbia labels, many of them Canadian pressings, including Chinese-language items.

—Sandra Benet

In addition to the repositories listed above, the following has also reported holdings of the materials indicated:

Weston, Ontario—Ragtime Society of Canada: sheet music, recordings (mostly reprints of materials in the personal collections of its members)

Other Countries

1666

GRAINGER MUSEUM   (AuMU)

University of Melbourne
Parkville, Victoria 3052
AUSTRALIA

The Museum was established 1934–38 by Percy Aldridge Grainger (1882–1961), based on his personal collection of materials documenting his career and the careers of selected other composers. The original holdings are being supplemented by Grainger holographs presented to the Museum in his will, including materials formerly in the Library of Congress (see the *Annual Report of the Librarian of Congress*, 1938, p. 161; and the *Library of Congress Quarterly Journal*, 16:15 and 20:35); the New York Public Library; the Sibley Music Library of the Eastman School of Music, Rochester, N.Y. (see the University of Rochester Library *Bulletin*, 19 [1964], 21–26); and the library of Upsala College, East Orange, N.J. See A. M. Prescott, *A Guide to the Grainger Museum* (Melbourne, 1975); Kay Dreyfus, "The Adelaide Grainger Collection Transferred to the Grainger Museum," *Miscellanea musicologica*, 9 (1977), Australian Musicological Commission, Source Report no. 3; also her "Varsity's Grainger Museum History," *A.R.P.A. Journal*, 2 (1976), 56–59; and Thomas Carl Slattery, *The Wind Music of Percy Aldridge Grainger* (Ph.D. diss., University of Iowa, 1967)

Holograph and published music by Grainger, as described in Kay Dreyfus, *Music by Percy Aldridge Grainger*, Grainger Museum Catalogue, no. 1, Percy Grainger Music Collection, pt. 1 (Melbourne, 1978)

Holograph music by other composers associated with Grainger, among them Felix Borowski, Storm Bull, John Alden Carpenter, Henry Cowell, Natalie Curtis, Fannie Charles Dillon, Arthur Fickenscher, Eugene Goossens, Howard Hanson, Ernest Hutcheson, Daniel Gregory Mason (sketchbooks, as cited in Sister Mary Justina Klein, *The Contribution of Daniel Gregory Mason to American Music* [Ph.D. diss., Catholic University of America, 1967]), Orvis Ross, and Leo Sowerby

Grainger's music library, including many presentation copies. Special strengths include band music, 60 linear cm.; popular music, 30 linear cm.; and traditional music. For further details on this material, see especially Kay Dreyfus, "The Adelaide Grainger Collection" (1977), as cited above. Of the library's 2700 items, 550 are by American composers, among them Howard Brockway, Mortimer Browning, Charles Wakefield Cadman, John Alden Carpenter, Henry Cowell, Natalie Curtis, R. Nathaniel Dett,

Fannie Charles Dillon, Harvey Enders, Carl Engel, Arthur Fickenscher, George Gershwin, Richard Franko Goldman, Rubin Goldmark, Morton Gould, Charles Tomlinson Griffes, David Guion, Howard Hanson, Charles Martin Loeffler, Edward A. MacDowell, Daniel Gregory Mason, Ethelbert Nevin, Leo Ornstein, Orvis Ross, Lewis Slavit, Leo Sowerby, Albert Stoessel, Lamar Stringfield, Samuel Coleridge-Taylor, Deems Taylor, David van Vactor, and Arnold Volpe

Personal papers, including 11,000 letters sent or received by Grainger, his mother Rose, and his wife Ella, 1895–1961, many from U.S. associates; personal and business papers, 5 linear meters, including diaries, daybooks, and address books, also unpublished writings, including the autobiographical "Anecdotes," "The Love Life of Paris and Helen," and "Bird's-Eye View of the Together-Life of Rose Grainger and Percy Grainger"

Programs, 7.5 linear meters, mostly of Grainger's concerts, 1894–1960, those in the U.S. dating after 1914; programs of the Goldman Band, 1937– , and of Russell Ames Cook, 1925–54, also promotional material, 4.5 linear meters of press clippings, and 2 linear meters of scrapbooks of press clippings and programs of Grainger's musical activities

Photographs, 1300 items, some from the U.S., 1914–61, including inscribed portraits

Original paintings and drawings by Grainger, 200 items, 1886–1954, as described in Kay Dreyfus, *Objects, Documents, and Pictures to Reflect upon*, University of Melbourne, University Gallery Catalogue, Pt. 2 (Melbourne, 1978)

Recordings, including 150 piano rolls, mostly by Grainger, some in proof and ms

—Kay Dreyfus

1667

Max E. VREEDE

23, Avenue des Cerfs
B-1950 Kraainem
BELGIUM

Collection of 2400 recordings, emphasizing the Paramount 12000/13000 series of 900 race records, which formed the basis of Vreede's published discography (Storyville, England, 1971). Other holdings include non-race Paramount and related labels, 600 items, 1917–32; non–New York jazz, emphasizing collective improvisation before 1930, 500 items; and non-commercial, personal, or special recordings, black vaudeville, and rare labels before 1930, 200 items

1668
Det KONGELIGE BIBLIOTEK   Dn
Christians Brygge 8
DK-1219 København K
DENMARK

Autograph book with holograph mss of European master composers, formerly in the possession of Arthur Corning Clarke, Cooperstown, N.Y.

Letters and photographs of Carl Busch (1862–1943), as cited in Donald Robert Lowe, *Sir Carl Busch: His Life and Work as a Teacher, Conductor, and Composer* (D.M.A. diss., University of Missouri at Kansas City, 1972)

1669
NATIONAL LIBRARY OF IRELAND   IreDNL
Kildare Street
Dublin 2
EIRE

Percy A. Grainger, holograph music mss concerned with Irish culture, as cited in Thomas Carl Slattery, *The Wind Music of Percy Aldridge Grainger* (Ph.D. diss., University of Iowa, 1967), pp. 225–26

1670
BRITISH LIBRARY   Uk
Great Russell Street
London WC1B 3DG
ENGLAND

Department of Manuscripts
See Augustus Hughes-Hughes, *Catalogue of Manuscript Music in the British Museum* (London, 1906–9), and Pamela J. Willetts, *Handlist of Music Manuscripts Acquired, 1908–67* (London, 1970; hereinafter cited as *Willetts*)

Edward A. MacDowell, holograph mss of the full score and piano-duet arrangement of the *Ländliche Suite* op. 37, as cited in *Willetts*, p. 12

Ernö Dohnányi, holograph mss from his years at Florida State University and earlier, as cited in *Willetts*, pp. 48–50, 57. See also Marion Ursula Rueth, *The Tallahassee Years of Ernst von Dohnányi* (Master's thesis, Florida State University, 1962)

Percy A. Grainger, 21 holograph musical and literary mss, as cited in *Willetts*, pp. 32–33. See also her "The Percy Grainger Collection," British Museum *Quarterly*, 27/3–4 (1963–64), 69–71, and Thomas Carl Slattery, *The Wind Music of Percy Aldridge Grainger* (Ph.D. diss., University of Iowa, 1967), pp. 220–22

Edward Clark (BBC executive), correspondence from Béla Bartók, Paul Hindemith, Ernst Krenek, Serge Koussevitzky, Darius Milhaud, Arnold Schoenberg, Eduard Steuermann, Igor Stravinsky, and others, mostly during their European careers, as cited in *Willetts*, pp. 57–58

Johann Ernst Perabo (1845–1920), music mss of European master composers, from his music library. See Hughes-Hughes's *Catalogue*, vol. 3, p. 145; also *Willetts*, p. 15

Music Library (Department of Printed Books)
Queen Liliuokalani of Hawaii, letter to Queen Victoria, 1897, in the Royal Music Library, as cited in *Willetts*, p. 92

Ernst Toch, holograph ms of the *Burlesken* op. 31 (1923), in the Hirsch collection, as cited in *Willetts*, p. 97

1671
DELIUS TRUST
16 Ogle Street
London W1P 7LG
ENGLAND

Frederick Delius, holograph music mss in 49 vols., including works composed during his years in the U.S., 1884–86, as cited in Rachel Lowe, *Frederick Delius, 1862–1934: A Catalogue of the Music Archives of the Delius Trust* (London, 1974). See also Robert Threlfall, *A Catalogue of the Compositions of Frederick Delius: Sources and References* (London, 1977)

1672
UNIVERSITY OF LONDON   UkLU
Music Library
Senate House
Malet Street
London WC1E 7HU
ENGLAND

American music materials, including 600 published scores, 150 books on music, and 1500 recordings, transferred in 1966 from the library formerly maintained by the United States Information Service in London. See the *Catalogue of Scores in the Music Section of the American Library* (London, 1950)

—M.A. Baird

1673
BODLEIAN LIBRARY   UkOxU
Department of Printed Books, Music Section
Oxford University
Oxford OX1 3BG
ENGLAND

The Library's American music is mostly from the collection bequeathed by Walter N. H. Harding (1883–1973), as described in Jean Geil, "American Sheet Music in the Walter N. H. Harding Collection at the Bodleian Library, Oxford University," M.L.A. *Notes*, 34 (1978), 805–13. For materials so acquired, the library has maintained Harding's categories and arrangement. Items listed below are in the Harding Collection, except as noted

Sheet music, 80,000 items in 600 boxes and 12 bound vols., ca. 1790–1960, mostly piano solo or vocal with piano accompaniment. Special topics include Chicago imprints, ragtime, Irish songs, minstrel music, war songs (particularly Union imprints of the Civil War), American comic-opera selections, songs performed by singing families or other ensembles (including 100 Hutchinson Family items), patriotic music, works relating to presidents and presidential candidates, marches, waltzes, and performers' portraits. Harding arranged this collection variously by name of publisher, name of lithographer, place of imprint, subject or musical form, name of composer, title of song, title of stage production, or performance medium. The Library has an unpublished guide to the subject categories. Harding also compiled an incomplete title catalogue, on cards, for songs to ca. 1918

Opera and musical-comedy vocal scores, 150 items, ca. 1850–1930, with a separate composer catalogue, representing 100 composers and 13 university productions at Princeton, Northwestern, University of Wisconsin, and elsewhere

Psalm books and hymnals, 7 18th- and 19th-century items; also a first edition of the *Bay Psalm Book* (1640), in the general Bodleian Library collections

Secular songbooks and songsters, 50 items, ca. 1790–1940, including temperance collections, Masonic anthologies, college and university collections, school or juvenile songbooks, and miscellaneous anthologies

Song folios, 125 20th-century items

Serial publications of song texts, several late 19th- and 20th-century runs

Instrumental instruction books, 10 19th- and early 20th-century items, in the Harding collection and in the general Bodleian Library collections

—Jean Geil

1674
Robert LAUGHTON

39 Bexley Lane
Sidcup, Kent
ENGLAND

Recordings, several thousand items on tape and disc, emphasizing preachers and gospel quartets from before World War II to the late 1950s

1675
Kenneth ROBERTON

The Windmill
Wendover, Aylesbury
Bucks HP22 6JJ
ENGLAND

Glasgow Orpheus Choir (Sir Hugh Roberton, conductor), programs of their 1926 tour of the U.S. and eastern Canada

1676
BIBLIOTHÈQUE DU CONSERVATOIRE

2, rue Louvois
F-75002 Paris 2e
FRANCE

Quatuor pour trois violons et violoncelle, ms attributed to Benjamin Franklin, as transcribed by Guillaume de Van and issued in facsimile edition (Paris, 1946)

1677
VEREINIGUNG FÜR VOLKSTUM UND HEIMAT

Heimatsmuseum
Am Kirchplatz 4/5
D-3220 Alfeld/Leine
GERMANY (B.R.D.)

Documents concerning relationships with musicians and others in the U.S., as cited in *Americana in deutschen Sammlungen* (n.p., 1967), vol. 4, p. 225

1678
STAATSARCHIV UND PERSONENSTANDSARCHIV DETMOLD

Willi-Hofmann-Strasse, 2
D-493 Detmold
GERMANY (B.R.D.)

Correspondence of the German consulate in New York, involving visiting performances by the Deutschen Operngesellschaft, 1923, as cited in *Americana in deutschen Sammlungen* (n.p., 1967), vol. 6, p. 14

1679
Paul HINDEMITH INSTITUT

Untermainkai 14
D-6 Frankfurt
GERMANY (B.R.D.)

Music mss, correspondence, and other documents of Paul Hindemith (1895–1963), many of them from his career in the U.S., 1940–53

—Luther Noss, Dieter Rexroth

1680
STAATSARCHIV

Rathaus
Rathausmarkt 1
D-2 Hamburg 1
GERMANY (B.R.D.)

Schwäbisches Sängerbund of Brooklyn, press clippings of their 1910 European tour, as cited in *Americana in deutschen Sammlungen* (n.p., 1967), vol. 2, pp. 62, 362

1681
KREISARCHIV LAND HADELN

Hinter der Apotheke
D-2178 Otterndorf
GERMANY (B.R.D.)

Brochure entitled *Aufruf und Warnung an Auswanderunglustige in Deutschland*, dated Boston, 1864, under the name of 3 authorizing organizations, including the Gesang-Verein "Orpheus" and the Turn-Verein, as cited in *Americana in deutschen Sammlungen* (n.p., 1967), vol. 4, p. 304

1682
STADTARCHIV SALZGITTER

Rathaus (Postfach 1000)
D-3320 Saltzgitter-Lebenstedt
GERMANY (B.R.D.)

Materials involving communications between local
musicians and associates in America over nearly 180
years, as cited in *Americana in deutschen Sammlungen*
(n.p., 1967), vol. 4, p. 330

1683
HESSISCHES HAUPTSTAATSARCHIV

Mainzerstrasse 80
D-62 Wiesbaden
GERMANY (B.R.D.)

Documents concerning the kidnapping of children from
the community of Usingen by tinkers and musicians,
for shipment to Russia, England, France, and America, 1848–55, as cited in *Americana in deutschen Sammlungen* (n.p., 1967), vol. 7, p. 136

1684
INTERNATIONALE MUSIKBIBLIOTHEK

Leipzigerstrasse 26
D-108 Berlin
GERMANY (D.D.R.)

Materials from the Interaliierten Musik-Leihbibliothek,
with U.S. holdings as cited in the catalogue, *98 amer-
ikanische Komponisten und ihre Werke* (Berlin, 1947)

1685
HAIFA MUSIC MUSEUM AND LIBRARY

Box 5111
Haifa
ISRAEL

Yiddish folksongs and folklore of the U.S. and Canada,
139 tape recordings collected by Ruth Rubin of New
York City, as cited in *Briegleb*, no. 83. The materials
are also in the Motion Picture, Broadcasting, and Recorded Sound Division of the Library of Congress,
Washington, D.C. (q.v.)

1686
HEBREW NATIONAL AND IsJJNL
UNIVERSITY LIBRARY

Box 503
Jerusalem
ISRAEL

Jakob Michael (New York music collector), 10,000
printed editions and 15,000 mss of Jewish secular and
sacred music, from various countries including the
U.S. See Otto E. Albrecht, "Collections, Private," in
The New Grove Dictionary of Music and Musicians (London, 1980), vol. 4, p. 551

1687
NATIONAL LIBRARY OF UkENL
SCOTLAND

George IV Bridge
Edinburgh 1
SCOTLAND

Percy A. Grainger, holograph music mss, as cited in
Thomas Carl Slattery, *The Wind Music of Percy Aldridge Grainger* (Ph.D. diss., University of Iowa, 1967),
pp. 181–82, 226–27

1688
UNIVERSITY OF NATAL

King George V Avenue
Durban
SOUTH AFRICA 4001

Sheet music, 200 items, mostly early 20th-century
popular music, including selections from musical
shows and films
Songbooks, 15 items, ca. 1896– , including college
songs and other popular songs; also 4 hymnals by
Ira D. Sankey
Other printed music, 200 items, ca. 1850– , mostly early 20th-century, largely piano music, with orchestral
arrangements of 30 American musical shows
Alfred Scott Gatty, ms "Plantation Songs," n.d.

—Susan Hoeksema

1689
BIBLIOTHÈQUE CANTONALE SzLaCU
ET UNIVERSITAIRE

Département de la musique
Place de la Riponne
CH-1005 Lausanne
SWITZERLAND

George Templeton Strong (1856–1948), personal papers,
including 163 holograph scores of his music; 143 published editions of his music, ca. 1883–1940; 37 programs of concerts featuring his works, in Europe and
America, 1892–1963; 39 articles and clippings, 1912–
61; 148 letters, 1879–1948, from Ernest Bloch, George
Gershwin, Edward A. MacDowell, Gustav Mahler,
Igor Stravinsky, and Joseph Szigeti, as well as other
major European composers and performers; 7 of his
water-color paintings; 52 photographs; and miscellaneous materials relating to MacDowell and the
Geneva Conservatory. See Jean-Louis Matthey, *Inven-
taire du fonds musical: George Templeton Strong*, Inven-
taire des fonds manuscrits, 3 (Lausanne, 1973). Also
correspondence with Alfred Pochon, in the Pochon
papers (inventory forthcoming)

---

*In addition to the repositories listed above, the following have
also reported holdings of the materials indicated:*

University of Exeter (England), Library: sheet music,
other printed music, recordings, miscellaneous
University of York (England), Library: sheet music,
other printed music

⌇ INDEX ⌇

Most personal and institutional names appear below in the form reported by the repositories, since they are not recorded in standard scholarly reference works. For this reason, readers should not consider the name forms in the index as tantamount to an authority file. In general, readers looking for materials on a particular person will want to look not only under the name of the person, but also under the names of the person's associates and correspondents, as well as the relevant institutional names, professional activities, and geographical headings. Since many institutions and collections named for individuals are not always known best by their full titles, these are alphabetized according to the person's last name, such as "Huntington, Henry E., Library" rather than "Henry E. Huntington Library."

The names of all repositories with numbered entries, as well as of their component collections, are included in the index. But the names of organizations beginning with a city name are omitted when the materials are to be found in a repository in the city itself, except in instances of very large cities with many repositories. Since the alphabetical arrangement of the directory itself provides access by geographical location, the names of cities and states are listed in the index only for materials located elsewhere.

Lacking any extensive studies of American musical terminology as models, the subject headings for the index have been largely developed out of information supplied by the respondents. Specific terms at the fieldwork stage of the project would have been counterproductive. Few respondents

would have been prepared to work through their collections and tell us, for instance, whether they have "hymnals" or "tunebooks," since our request would have needed to specify (a) that hymnals were for service use and tunebooks for singing-school or personal use (a distinction generally but not universally accepted, and very difficult to apply in either the library catalogue or the stacks), or (b) that hymnals were usually upright and tunebooks oblong (an altogether more convenient but less generally accepted distinction). The difference between a band and an orchestra *may* depend on the absence or presence of strings; but when a leader (or director, or conductor, or bandmaster) called the group one or the other we chose to accept the designation as reported, rather than ask the repository to go to the trouble of looking for evidence of strings.

Prolific subject and form headings will tend necessarily to favor middle-size repositories, unless specific quantities are stated. Under the heading "programs," for instance, most large repositories have some holdings, whether mentioned or not, while many small repositories with one or two items will have been passed over by the indexers, and still others will have been consigned to the supplementary lists at the end of each state.

For such reasons, users are encouraged to view the index as a first step, continuing further by using relevant name and subject entries in the index, or through browsing. The headings should be viewed as suggestive rather than definitive, providing some overview of the deployment of materials.

A

A Capella Choir, 509
A capella music, 334
Aakhus, Daniel, 800
Abbe, Mrs., 84
Abbett, John C., 1274
Abbott, George, 1061-L
Abbott, John C., 712
ABC (American Broadcasting Company), 1194, 1646
Aber, Charles Robert, 1502
Abernathy, Francis E., 1477
Abnaki Indian music, 907
Abolitionist songs, 320, 398, 658, 729, 1070. *See also* Slave songs
Abrahams, Roger, 1477
Abrams, Samuel, 398
Abrams, W. Amos, 1140
Abravanel, Maurice, 1521
Academy of Motion Picture Arts and Sciences, 51
Academy of Music (Baltimore), 612

Academy of Music (Brooklyn, N.Y.), 1083
Academy of Music (Charleston, S.C.?), 1418
Academy of Music (Chicago), 315; *Journal*, 860-K
Academy of Music (Haverhill, Mass.), 671
Academy of Music (Kalamazoo, Mich.), 761
Academy of Music (Northampton, Mass.), 688, 689
Academy of Music (Philadelphia), 1333, 1338, 1340
Academy of Music (Redlands, Cal.), 103
Academy of Music (Saginaw, Mich.), 763
Academy of Music (St. Louis), 860
Academy of Music (Salem,

Mass.), 701
Acadian music, 545, 563. *See also* Cajun music
Accooe, Will, 226
Accordion, 271, 545, 800, 1274, 1323, 1620, 1660
Ackerman, Solomon, 1190
Ackley, B. D., 442
Acme Records, 1430
Acosta, Juan F., 1651
Acoustics, 1181, 1190. *See also* Music theory
Acuff, Roy, 830, 1455
Adams family (of Wisconsin), 1629
Adams, Crosby, 1153
Adams, Frank J. R., 1270
Adams, Helena Herppich, 1172
Adams, James. T., 1568
Adams, John Quincy (U.S. president), 643
Adams, John Quincy (fl. 1890), 127

Adams, Mrs. John Quincy (1775-1852), 234
Adams, Mrs. John Q. (b. 1912), 1487
Adams, John S., 226
Adams, Juliette Graves (Mrs. Crosby Adams), 227-F, 1148, 1153, 1212
Adams, Milward, 334
Adams, O. D., 815
Adams, Stephen L., 1629
Adams, William O., 227-G
Adams-Buell, Robert, 1622
Adams Clement Collection, 234
Adams County (Neb.) Historical Society, 882
Adamson, Harold, 1024
Addams, Jane, Hull House, 341
Addison County (Vt.), 1529
Ade, George, 443
Adelphi University, 995
Adirondack Mountains, 1095, 1102

Adler, Clarence, 227-F
Adler, Cyrus, 1174
Adler, Guido, 265
Adler, Max, 1174
Adler, Samuel, 195-C
Adriance, Jacob, 157
Adriance Memorial Library, 1105
Adventist hymnals, 297, 732
Adventure (magazine), 227-K
Advertisements. *See* Commercials and advertising songs; Programs
Advertising Collection, 1143
Advertising songs. *See* Commercials and advertising songs
Aeolian Band & Orchestra Library, 326
Aeolian Choral Series, 326
Aeolian Company (New York?), 1061-B, 1333
Aeolian Hall (New York), 803
Aeolian Orchestrella, 839
Aeolian Organ Series, 326
Aeolian Skinner Co., 700
Aeolian Vocalion, 471
Aeronautical songs, 195-B, 234, 411, 977, 1198
AFM. *See* American Federation of Musicians
Afon (Minn.), 815
African Methodist Episcopal (AME) Church, 398
African Union Society (Newport, R.I.), 1406
Africana, 357, 406, 1061-N
Afro-American Arts Institute, 406
Afro-American Cultural and Historical Society, 1179
Afro-American music, 6, 12, 13, 36, 73, 82, 84, 122, 129, 142, 184, 195-A, 195-B, 213, 226, 227-H, 227-K, 227-M, 230, 239, 244, 245, 265, 266, 267, 268, 269, 271, 282, 283, 305, 308, 315, 334, 340, 355, 357, 391, 398, 406, 414, 512, 544, 556, 558, 573, 618, 654, 692, 712, 729, 739, 741, 771, 827, 831, 860-F, 860-K, 957, 1005, 1022, 1036, 1053, 1061-M, 1061-N, 1077, 1095, 1111, 1118, 1127, 1141, 1155, 1179, 1185, 1187, 1193 1195, 1223, 1270, 1298, 1323, 1333, 1338, 1340, 1352, 1402, 1406, 1418, 1420, 1427, 1442, 1443, 1449, 1452, 1457, 1477, 1544, 1545, 1546, 1591, 1597, 1611, 1655, 1661, 1667
AFSCME (American Federation of State, County, and Municipal Employees), 742
Afternoon Orchestral Concerts (Cincinnati), 1172
Agard, Arthur, P., 50
Agents. *See* Impresarios
Agnes Scott College, 278
Agullo y Prats, Jose, 1652
Ahrendt, Karl, 1167
Aides, H., 227-D
Aiken, Walter H., 1172, 1177

Aiken, Gov. William, 1415
Air Force Museum, 1198
Airplanes: songs·about, 195-B 234, 411, 977, 1198
Aitken, Hugh, 227-E
Aitkin, John, 217
Akeley (minn.), 227-K
Akerman, Joseph, 707
Akker, Nancy C. Van den, 570
Akron (Ohio), 1193
Alabados, 142, 162, 962
Alabama, 266, 308, 398, 568, 1174
Alabama Department of Archives and History, 11
Alabama Federation of Music Clubs, 11, 15
Alabama, University of, 15
Alameda (Cal.), 354
Alamo, 1483, 1510
Alaska, 1031, 1581
Alaska, University of, 16
Alaska Historical Library, 18
Alaskan Native Literature Tapes, 16
Alaska-Yukon-Pacific Exposition (1909), 1575
Albani, Emma, 1053, 1061-B, 1659
Albany (N.Y.) Institute of History and Art, 966
Albany (Ore.?) Conservatory of Music, 1274
Albee Theater (Providence, R.I.), 476
Albee vaudeville circuit, 476
Albersheim, Gerhardt, 68
Albert, Eugène d', 195-A
Albert, Herman W., 896
Albert, Will Seward, 1439
Albert Lea (Minn.), 815
Albion (Mich.), 729-B
Albion College, 725, 730
Alboradas, 152
Albrecht, H. F., 1061-D
Albrecht, Otto E., 1326, 1352
Albrecht, Theodore, J., 1205
Albrecht Music Library, 1352
Albright College, 1377
Alcée, Claire, 1005
Alcott, Louisa May, Memorial Association, 657
Alcott, May, 657
Alda, Frances, 1053
Alda, Robert, 1487
Alderdice, Catherine, 729-A
Alderman, Pauline, 68
Alderman Library, 1541
Alderson, William, 1270
Aldrich, Richard, 227-F, 654, 1053
Aldridge, Amanda Ira, 226
Alessandro, Victor, 1477
Aleutian music, 195-B, 760
Alexander, Ernest R., 1457
Alexander, James, 1059
Alexander, Josef, 1148
Alexander, Robert, 1025
Alexander, Stan, 1477
Alexander, William Audley, 68
Alexander Library, 939
Alexandria (La.), 544, 573
Alexandria (Mo.), 837
Alford, H. L., 398

Alice Lloyd College, 539
"Alice the Bride of the White House," 1172
All-American Youth Orchestra, 831
Allanson, Clifford A., 988
Allegany Academy of Music, 815
Allegany County (Md.) Historical Society, 619
Allen family, 1560
Allen, Chester, 195-B
Allen, Dan, 142
Allen, George N., 1222
Allen, Heman, 334
Allen, Joel, 180
Allen, Mildred P., Memorial Library, 206
Allen, Nathan Henry, 185, 206
Allen, Nellie, 1006
Allen, Reginald, 1053
Allen, Stewart, 709
Allen, Warren D., 142, 260
Allen, Wilkes, 227-G
Allen, William F., 1095, 1611
Allen County-Fort Wayne (Ind.) Historical Society, 410
Allen County (Ohio) Historical Society, 1215
Allendorf, Adam, Collection, 837
Allensworth, Minnie Graves, 1463
Allentown (Pa.) Band, 195
Aller, Victor, 68
All Girl Orchestra, 1061-M
Alliance (N.C.), 227-K
Allied Artists, 340
Allied Arts Foundation (Denver), 157
Alliger, Newton Ingram, 195-A
Alling, Calvin P., 1611
Allison, Young Ewing, 531
Allmendinger, David F., 729-B
Allmendinger, Helene, 729-B
Allmendinger organs, 729-B
Allston, Adele, 1418
Allston, C. P., 1418
Allston, Elizabeth W., 1418
Allston-Pringle-Hill Papers, 1418
Almanac Singers, 742
Almand, Claude Marion, 535
Almond, Becky, 1524
Almstedt, Hermann B., 837
"Aloha Oe," 285
Alspaugh, Hannah Ditzler, 376
Alstyne, John Van, 1061-L
Altavista (Tex.), 1477
Alter, Martha, 1107
Altmann, Siegfried, 1025
Alton (Ill.), 866
Altschuler, Modest, 227-F
Altvater, Henry Hugh, 1148
Alverson, Margaret (Blake), 106
Alvin Theatre (Pittsburgh), 1359
Amana (Iowa) Heritage Society, 453
Amarillo (Tex.) College of Music Expression, 1473
Amarillo (Tex.) Public Library, 1473

Amateur Musical Club (Battle Creek, Mich.), 730
Amateur Musical Club (Bloomington, Ill.), 302
Amateur Musical Club (Chicago), 314
Amateur Musical Club (Peoria, Ill.), 381
Amateur Theater (Chicago), 25
Amato, Pasquale, 544
Amberol cylinders, 170, 300
Ambler, Philip Barbour, 1560
AME (African Methodist Episcopal) Church, 398
Ameche, Don, 1487
Amelia Gayle Gorgas Library, 15
"America," 314, 685, 1036
American Academy and Institute of Arts and Letters, 1018
American Antiquarian Society, 205, 398, 721, 1031
American Appraisal Company, 1172
American Ballet, 122
American Bandmasters Association, 398, 618
American Baptist Churches Editorial Library, 1386
American Baptist Historical Society, 1109
American Baptist Publication Society, 1386
American Brass Band, 1405
American Broadcasting Company, 1194, 1646
American Catholic Historical Society, 1324
American Composers Alliance, 195-A, 1019, 1031, 1111
American Composers' Concert Series, 1111
American Composers Edition, 1019
American Congregational Association, 634
American Conservatory of Music, 309
American Cultural Leaders, 1031
American Expeditionary Force (in Russia), 761
American Expeditionary Force (World War I), 1256
American Federation of Musicians, 136, 227-H, 227-L, 529, 568, 729-B, 737, 985, 1274, 1375, 1480, 1601, 1611
American Federation of State, County, and Municipal Employees, 742
American Folklife Center, 227-K
American Folklore Society, 1352
American Folksong Society, 1193
American Graphophone Co., 234, 1640
American Guild of Music Teachers, St. Paul and Minneapolis, 815

American Guild of Musical Artists, 1020, 1061-D
American Guild of Organists, 105, 603, 847, 1382, 1495
American Heritage Center, 1646
American Indians, 16, 24, 27, 28, 29, 30, 31 33, 50, 82, 84, 116, 129, 133, 156, 162, 190, 195-B, 213, 225, 227-L, 230, 234, 239, 271, 274, 291, 334, 355, 391, 398, 406, 502, 654, 729-B, 766, 805, 815, 887, 907, 939, 957, 962, 964, 1008, 1022, 1034, 1056, 1070, 1255, 1256, 1261, 1327, 1340, 1385, 1432, 1433, 1477, 1518, 1520, 1528, 1573, 1577, 1581, 1611, 1612, 1636, 1643. See also names of specific tribes
American Indian Research Project, 1433
American Institute for Exploration, 760
American Institute of Normal Methods, 618
American Institute of Operatic and Allied Arts, 1031
American Institute of Operatic Art, 1031
American Jewish Archives, 1174
American Jewish Congress, 1021
American Jewish Historical Society, 711
American Kantorei, 305
American Legion (Post 264), National Championship Band, 1129
American Liszt Society, 535
American Lutheran Church, Archives (St. Paul), 808
American Lutheran Church Archives (Dubuque, Iowa), 466
American Museum of Natural History, 1022
American Music Association, 1061-B
American Music Center, 195-A, 1023, 1577
American Music Co., 1249
American Music Research Center, 129
American Music Society, 334
American Musical Academy (Philadelphia), 1340
American Musical Theatre Collection, 195-B
American Musicological Society, Southern California Chapter, Archive, 68
American Negro Historical Society, 1338
American Newspaper Guild, 564
American Old Time Fiddlers Association, 884
American Opera Co. (New York), 636
American Opera Co. ballet, 314
American Pageant Association, 1361

American Palestine Music Association ("Mailamm"), 1061-B
American Philosophical Society, 1327
American Piano Society, 4
American Political Items Collectors, 1586
American Radicalism Collection, 743
American Revolution. See Revolutionary War
American School Band Directors Association, 398
American Society of Composers, Authors, and Publishers (ASCAP), 230, 360, 636, 1024, 1031, 1061-D, 1270, 1520
American Sunday School Union, 1040
American Swedish Historical Museum, 1328
American Swedish Institute, 794
American Symphony Orchestra League, 1544
American Theater Organ Society, 1144
American Theatre Band (Columbus, Ind.), 434
American Turnerbund, 837
American Union of Swedish Singers, 310, 388, 1577
American University, 218
Amerindians. See American Indians
Ames, Ruby, 349
Ames, Russell, 349
Ames, Winthrop, 1053
Ames (Iowa) Glee Club, 465
Amfitheathof, Daniel, 68
Amico, Hank d', 989
Amish music, 398, 509, 1297
Amoureux-Langlois family, 860-C
Amphion Amateur Musical Association (Philadelphia), 1338
Amphion Club (St. Louis), 860-C
Amphion Club (San Diego, Cal.), 114
Amphions (Cortland, N.Y.), 985
Amphion Society (Seattle), 1575
Amphitheatre Auditorium, 531
Ampico piano rolls, 1333
Anabaptist hymnals, 415
Anacreontic Society (Baltimore), 612
Ancient Free and Accepted Masons, Grand Lodge of Iowa, 458
Anderson, Carl E., 310, 388
Anderson, Clarence, 779
Anderson, Dwight, 535
Anderson, Gillian B., 219
Anderson, Harry, 68
Anderson, John Jr., 1059
Anderson, Leroy, 654, 1124
Anderson, Lily Strickland, 227-D, 1411, 1412, 1420, 1425

Anderson, Louie, 894
Anderson, M.D., Memorial Library, 1498
Anderson, Marian, 226, 230, 268, 1352
Anderson, Martha J., 729-E
Anderson, Z. W., 1143
Anderson House: Museum of the Society of the Cincinnati, 220
Anderson (Ind.) College, 405
Anderson (Ind.) School of Theology, 405
Anderson (S.C.) College, 1411
Andover-Harvard Theological Library, 654
Andover (New Center, Mass.) Theological Seminary, 685
Andover (Mass.) Historical Society, 628
Andover Newton Theological School, 685
Andrews family, 815
Andrews, Clifton, 606
Andrews, Edward Deming, 217
Andrews, George Whitfield, 1222
Andrews, Helen Armstrong, 36
Andrews, Mark, 940
Andrews Opera Company, 815, 1272
Andrews University, 732
Andrillon, Fernando, 1059
Angel, Howard J., 1457
Angelis, Jefferson de, 1061-L
Anglican church music. See Episcopalian music
Anglin, Margaret Mary, 1053
Anglo-American music, 21, 27, 32, 33, 34, 50, 73, 84, 227-K, 271, 291, 398, 406, 522, 833, 957, 1438, 1463, 1477, 1612
Anglo-American Music Conference (Lausanne, Switzerland, 1931), 618, 800
Anna Miller Museum, 1647
Annapolis (Md.), 606
Annas, A. Neil, 970
Annual Conference of Music Teachers, 1148
Antes, John, 1161
Antheil, George, 227-B, 227-H, 227-L, 265, 535, 949, 1061-B, 1061-D, 1111, 1331
Anthony, J. H., 477
Antigua (West Indies), 1352
Antique Phonograph and Record Society, 1079
Antoine, Josephine, 982, 1111
Anton, Philip Gottlieb, Jr., 860-K
Anton, Philip Gottlieb, Sr., 860-C, 860-F, 860-K, 866
Antonini, Ernesto Ramos, 1651
Anzengruber, Ludwig, 1205
Apache Indians, 31
Apel, Willi, 68
Apollo Boys Choir, 15
Apollo Club (Minneapolis), 798, 815
Apollo Club (New Haven, Conn.?), 195-A

Apollo Club (New York?), 1083
Apollo Club of Pittsburgh, 1359
Apollo Club (Portland, Ore.), 1274
Apollo Club (St. Louis), 860-A, 860-C
Apollo Club (Winfield, Kans.), 520
"Apollo" collection (1790), 227-G
Apollo Musical Club Directory (Chicago), 315
Apollo Quartette (Waukegan, Ill.), 400
Apollo Society (Boston), 636
Apollo Society (New York), 1059
Appalachian Ballad Collection, 522
Appalachian Center, 522
Appalachian Folk Music Collection, 1591
Appalachian Mountains, 42, 211, 227-K, 227-L, 522, 535, 537, 539, 1095, 1140, 1141, 1223, 1372, 1445, 1463, 1591
Appalachian Oral History Program, 539
Appalachian State University, 1140
Appalachian Studies Center, 537
Appel, Jean Slater, 1107
Appel, Richard, 636
Apthorp, William Foster, 636, 639, 876
Ara, Ugo, 227-F, 1053
Arabian music, 1477, 1541
"Arabian Nights," 167
Arant, Percy Button, 227-D
Arcadia (Cal.) Public Library, 44
Archdiocese of Los Angeles, 71
Archer, H. Richard, 719
Archer, Sarah E., 568
Archer, Violet, 1488
Archive Collections of Film Music, 1646
Archive of (American) Folk Song, 227-K, 227-L, 1270. See also Library of Congress
Archive of California and Western Folklore, 84
Archive of California Folk Music, 50
Archive of New York State Folklife, 983
Archive of Ohio and International Folklore and Music, 1223
Archive of Popular American Music, 84
Archive of Published Primitive, Ethnic, and Folk Music, 1194
Archive of Recorded Sound, 142
Archive of Southwestern Music, 957
Archive on Historic Tunings and Temperaments, 68

Archives of American Art, 234
Archives of Appalachia, 1445
Archives of the American
  Lutheran Church, 466, 808
Archives of the Performing
  Arts, 122
Archives of Traditional Music,
  522
Archivo General de Puerto
  Rico, 1651
Arents, George, Research
  Library, 1127
Areu, Manual, Collection of
  Zarzuelas, 957
La Argentina, 636
Arimondi, Vittorio, 122
Arion Club (Birmingham,
  Ala.), 2
Arion Music Club
  (Milwaukee), 1622, 1624
Ariontic Sodality, 642
Arizona, 831, 957
Arizona, University of, 31, 33
Arizona Friends of Folklore, 21
Arizona Historical Society, 30
Arizona State Museum, 31
Arizona State Parks Board, 22
Arizona State University, 28
Arkansas, 84, 398, 544, 815,
  1095, 1449, 1477, 1516
Arkansas, University of, 36
Arkansas Arts Center, 38
Arkansas Authors and Com-
  posers Society, 39
Arkansas College, 34
Arkansas State Library, 39
Arkansas State Music
  Teachers' Association, 36
Arkansas State University, 43
"Arkansas Traveller," 36
Arkas, M., 800
Arlen, Harold, 1024
Arlington Hills (Minn.)
  Mother's Club, 815
Armistead, Adelina Marie, 636
Armitage family, 1061-M
Armitage, Merle, 227-B,
  227-F
Arms, Fanny, Collection, 1194
Arms Museum, 1246
Armstrong, Alexander, 215
Armstrong, Grace, 391
Armstrong, Harry, 227-D
Armstrong, Louis, 406, 556,
  1450
Armstrong, William, 1111
Armstrong, William D., 348
Armstrong Browning Collec-
  tion, 1517
Army. See United States Army
Arndt, Felix, 36
Arndt, Nola Locka, 36
Arne, Thomas A., 1532
Arnett, Trevor, Library, 268
Arnheiter, C. R., 947
Arno, May, 157
Arnold, Byron, 15
Arnold, Frazer, 815
Arnold, Herman, 11
Arnold's Archives, 747
Arnold Schoenberg Institute,
  81
Aron, Paul, 1061-F
Aronson, Boris, 1061-L

Art Club (Chicago), 314
Art Hall, 241
Art Publication Society, 866
Art Society of Pittsburgh, 1359
Arthur, Alfred, 1205
Arthur, J. D., 227-K
Arvey, Verna (Mrs. William
  Grant Still), 68
Asbury, Samuel E., 1477
ASCAP. See American Society
  of Composers, Authors, and
  Publishers
Ascherfeld, Clara, 614
Ashford, E. L., 1477
Ashford, Mrs. E. L., 1463
Ashland (Ky.), 27
Ashland (Ore.) Centennial
  Exposition, 1266
Ashland Times, 314
Ashland (Wis.), 786
Ashley, Lawrence, 1103
Ashton, Fred T., 302
Ashton, Robert, 1338
Askov (Minn.), 396
Asmann, Edwin N., 366
Asper, Frank Wilson, 1521
Asshetan, Susan, 1036
Associated Music Committee
  (St. Louis), 860-E
Associated Music Publishers, 50
Associated Singing Society,
  1375
Association for the Humanities
  in Idaho, 295
Association of Junior Leagues
  of America, 800
Association of Music Schools
  (New York), 800
Assunto, Frank, 1450
Astaire, Fred, 1487
Astor, 935
Astroth, Margareta
  Liljenstope, 794
Atchison, Mary, 860-D
Atchison (Kan.) Library, 494
Ateneo Puertorriqueño, 1652
Athenaeum (Minneapolis),
  798
Athenaeum of Philadelphia,
  1329
Atherton, Percy Lee, 227-D,
  227-F, 268, 646
Atherton Center (Holt-
  Atherton Pacific Center for
  Western Studies), 145
Atkins, J. Murrey, Library,
  1142
Atkinson, Anna Louisa Tufts
  (Mrs. Theodore), 707
Atkinson, Buena Vista, 475
Atkinson, Fred W., Collection
  of American Drama, 340
Atkinson, Wallace E., 475
Atlanta Historical Society, 266
Atlanta Public Library, 267
Atlanta University, 268
Atlantic Recording Co., 1597
Attebery, Louie, 291
Atwill, Joseph F., 721
Auburn University, 1
Auditorium Concert
  (St. Louis), 860-J
Auditorium Theatre (Chicago),
  334

Audubon, John J., 1111
Audubon, Lucy, 1111
Auer, Leopold, 1053, 1580
Auernheimer, Raoul, 104
Augsburg College, 795
Augsburg Publishing House,
  797
Augusta (Me.), 707
Augustana College, 386
Augustana (Lutheran Church)
  Synod, 330, 815
Aumann, Elinor, 742
Auner, A. W., 1402
Aurora College, 297
Aurora Colony (Ore.), 1267,
  1274
Aurora Colony Historical
  Society, 1267
Aurora (Ill.) Historical
  Museum, 298
Austin, Adolph Kornelius,
  1611
Austin, Stephen F., State
  University (Tex.), 1504
Austin, William W., 1004
Austin-Ball, Thomas, 364
Austin College, 1513
Australia, 925
Austria, 1030, 1031, 1061-M,
  1267
Austrian Project, 1031
Austro-Hungarian Juvenile
  Band, 1061-M
Autenrieb, Max, 349
Authors' and Composers'
  International Agency, 1025
Authors and Composers
  Society, Arkansas, 39
Autograph collections, 798,
  860-B, 890, 941, 999, 1031,
  1036, 1040, 1053, 1061-B,
  1061-L, 1111, 1222, 1301,
  1338, 1359, 1416, 1457, 1573,
  1580, 1611, 1665. See also
  Collections of music,
  bibliophilic
Autoharp, 787
Automobile songs, 411, 736,
  739
Avakian, Anne, 50
Avery family, 1005
Avery, Stanley R., 798, 800
Avery County (N.C.), 1141
Aviron, Joseph, 1082
Avshalomov, Jacob, 1580
Awards. See Contests and
  awards
Axman, Gladys, 1052
Axt, William, 1646
Ayer, Edward E., Collection,
  334
Ayres, Frederic, 101, 227-D,
  227-F, 1223
Ayres, J. I., 1502
Ayres, Stephen, 1487
Ayres-Alumni Memorial
  Library, 451

B

Babbitt, Milton, 68, 227-D,
  1040
Babin, Victor, 227-B, 1183

Bach, Christopher, 1621, 1622,
  1624
Bach, Gustave, 1621
Bach, J. C. F., 1161
Bach, J. S., 398, 637, 951, 1359
Bach Choir (Bethlehem, Pa.),
  1285
Bach Choir (Pittsburgh), 1354,
  1359
Bach Festival, 1168
Bach Festival (Grand Rapids,
  Mich.?), 748
Bach Festival Choir, 1354
Bach (i.e., Riemenschneider
  Bach) Institute, 1168
Bach Society (Cincinnati),
  1172
Bach Society (St. Louis), 856,
  866
Bache, Richard, 1560
Bachmann, Charles William,
  815
Bacigalupi, Remo, 50
Backert, Fanny Kellogg, 465
Bacon, Emma Waleska
  Schneeloch, 195-A, 195-B
Bacon, Ernst, 1111, 1127, 1148,
  1425
Bacon, Leonard Woolsey,
  195-A
Bacon, Leonard Woolsey, Jr.,
  195-B
Bacon, Rev. Thomas, 612
Bacot-Huger Collection, 1418
Bacot-Rhett Papers, 1418
Badcock, Josiah, 1530
Badin, Norbert, 544
Baeck, Leo, Institute, 1025
Baermann, Carl, 646
Baermann Society, 646
Baez, Rafael, 1622
Bagatello, Antonio, 1323
Bagioli, Antonio, 1343
Bahr, Donald, 28
Bailey, Eben Howe, 227-F
Bailey, Guy W., Memorial
  Library, 1525
Bailey, John L., 1141
Bailey, Parker, 227-D
Bailey, Pearl, 1127
Bailey, Samuel E., 1643
Bailey, Sarah Jane, 1141
Bain, Wilfred, 406
Baird Hall, 979
Baker family, 898, 907, 1527
Baker, Addison, 157
Baker, John W., 852
Baker, Karle Wilson, 1477
Baker, Laura, 349
Baker, Sidney C., 1193
Baker, Theodore, 227-F
Baker, Timothy Minot, 721
Baker, W. Henry, 603
Baker Collection of
  Methodistica, 1143
Baker Library, 654
Balada, Leonardo, 1360
Balamos, John Epanimontas,
  227-D
Balanchine, George, 1031
Balatka, Hans, 398
Balch Institute, 1330
Bald, Edward C., Jr., 1359
Baldini, Marie (Alexandra), 122

Baldishol Committee
(Minneapolis), 815
Baldwin family, 1172
Baldwin, Anita A., 44, 127
Baldwin, E. T., 914
Baldwin, Ralph Lyman, 181
Baldwin, Samuel Atkinson,
1030, 1061-A, 1070
Baldwin, Simon Eben, 195-B
Baldwin Library of Organ
Music, 1070
Baldwin Piano Co., 1172
Baldwin-Wallace College, 1168
Balin, Isidore. *See* Berlin,
Irving
Ball, Ernest R., 747, 1189
Ball, Thomas, 648
Ball State University, 433
Ballads, 21, 34, 65, 75, 84,
107, 196, 213, 227-K, 227-L,
227-M, 271, 293, 366, 406,
476, 522, 523, 531, 538, 545,
592, 612, 614, 625, 630, 654,
687, 707, 721, 761, 787, 789,
860-F, 860-K, 867, 967, 1016,
1095, 1098, 1140, 1141, 1152,
1155, 1185, 1193, 1264, 1270,
1340, 1352, 1402, 1405, 1420,
1429, 1445, 1459, 1463, 1477,
1496, 1500, 1520, 1525, 1528,
1541, 1545, 1591, 1611, 1643.
See also Broadsides
Ballantine, Edward, 317, 646
Ballard, Charles E., 302
Ballet, 2, 84, 115, 122, 244,
314, 315, 319, 631, 860-C,
860-D, 1031, 1061-K, 1111,
1127, 1375, 1520. *See also*
Dance
Ballet Caravan, 122
Ballet Russe, 631, 860-D
Ballet Theatre, 122
Ballet West, 122
Ballman's Orchestra and
Symphonic Band, 314
Ballou, Esther Williamson, 218
Ballroom dance. *See* Dance
Balmer family, 860-B
Balmer, Charles, 860-B, 860-D,
860-K
Balmer, John Godfred, 860-B
Balmer, Lillie (Mrs. Charles),
860-B, 860-D
Balmer & Weber (firm), 544,
860-C, 866
Balogh, Louis L., 1180, 1190
Balseiro Dávila, Rafael, 1652
Baltimore, 227-H, 235, 1059,
1143, 1161, 1285, 1292, 1560
Baltimore Harmonic Society,
612
Baltimore Music Club, 604
Baltimore Musical Association,
612
Baltimore Musical Thieves,
613
Baltimore Oratorio Society,
612
Baltimore Symphony
Orchestra, 613
Baltimore Symphony
Orchestra Association, 605
Balzer, William, 490
Bampton, Rose, 227-L, 1031

Bancroft Library, 50
Band music, 9, 11, 14, 28, 54,
84, 114, 115, 136, 146, 150,
168, 190, 194, 195-C, 209,
227, 228, 229, 232, 234, 237,
239, 261, 278, 286, 304, 315,
326, 340, 342, 343, 349, 370,
377, 379, 389, 391, 396, 398,
401, 442, 457, 463, 465, 476,
482, 486, 487, 490, 500, 504,
511, 568-B, 576, 589, 618,
623, 665, 681, 701, 708, 721,
730, 746, 778, 798, 800, 815,
819, 821, 846, 847, 850, 895,
898, 901, 907, 909, 914, 965,
980, 1006, 1061-N, 1106,
1135, 1143, 1151, 1161, 1180,
1181, 1235, 1236, 1252, 1260,
1267, 1272, 1279, 1281, 1284,
1285, 1291, 1338, 1360, 1387,
1391, 1405, 1433, 1480, 1488,
1523, 1530, 1534, 1543, 1572,
1593, 1594, 1611, 1612, 1618,
1621, 1646, 1649, 1666. *See
also* Dance band music;
Military music
Banda Mexicana, 618
Bands (materials about), 2, 9,
19, 26, 30, 41, 43, 98, 136,
138, 139, 141, 146, 147, 150,
153, 154, 156, 157, 163, 188,
190, 209, 214, 227-E, 227-G,
228, 229, 230, 234, 237, 239,
242, 244, 245, 251, 253, 266,
278, 285, 286, 302, 304, 305,
314, 315, 340, 353, 354, 370,
374, 377, 379, 389, 391, 398,
419, 425, 430, 431, 434, 442,
443, 446, 462, 465, 470, 472,
475, 476, 478, 480, 486, 500,
502, 503, 514, 518, 529, 544,
568-B, 576, 577, 579, 586,
587, 589, 602, 618, 619, 621,
625, 633, 636, 654, 665, 668,
672, 673, 680, 681, 689, 701,
703, 720, 729-B, 730, 737,
739, 743, 746, 748, 749, 750,
761, 762, 763, 768, 773, 776,
777, 778, 779, 784, 787, 795,
802, 803, 807, 815, 821, 823,
846, 847, 848, 860-C, 860-D,
868, 875, 877, 878, 883, 887,
894, 901, 906, 907, 909, 914,
921, 939, 947, 960, 965, 968,
976, 980, 983, 991, 993, 1001,
1005, 1006, 1007, 1014, 1040,
1061-M, 1061-N, 1098, 1100,
1119, 1129, 1135, 1143, 1151,
1161, 1165, 1188, 1190, 1191,
1193, 1204, 1206, 1219, 1221,
1222, 1235, 1236, 1254, 1260,
1265, 1267, 1270, 1272, 1274,
1276, 1278, 1279, 1282, 1283,
1284, 1288, 1303, 1319, 1325,
1333, 1338, 1393, 1395, 1405,
1421, 1424, 1429, 1432, 1444,
1471, 1477, 1480, 1502, 1507,
1512, 1515, 1521, 1526, 1529,
1530, 1533, 1536, 1545, 1562,
1563, 1571, 1572, 1585, 1593,
1594, 1595, 1600, 1601, 1603,
1608, 1611, 1612, 1613, 1614,
1624, 1633, 1637, 1645, 1666.
See also Dance bands;

Military bands; School
bands and orchestras
Bandurist Chorus, 800
Bangor (Me.) Historical
Society, 578
Banjo and Mandolin Club
(Cornell University), 234
Banjo Club (Yale University),
195-B
Banjo music, 195-A, 195-B,
213, 271, 278, 510, 522, 630,
654, 923, 1005, 1049, 1061-
N, 1155, 1266, 1395, 1438,
1463, 1541, 1620
Banjos, 195, 234, 522, 630,
654, 1005, 1061-N, 1146,
1276, 1395, 1463
Banks, Mrs. Will C., 227-H
Banner Buggy Co. (St. Louis),
848
Baptist music, 273, 306, 380,
522, 523, 534, 559, 673, 849,
852, 946, 1109, 1154, 1212,
1259, 1363, 1386, 1406, 1422,
1462, 1463, 1471, 1482, 1493,
1558, 1560, 1615. *See also*
names of particular Baptist
denominations
Baptist Theological Seminary
(New Orleans), 559
Bar Harbor (Me.) Historical
Society, 579
Baral, Robert, 1477
Barati, George, 227-F, 1127
Barbeau, Charles Marius, 1327
Barber, Samuel, 227-B, 247,
1148, 1270, 1331, 1390, 1580
Barbot family, 1418
Barbot, Blanche Hermine, 1418
Barbot, Mrs. P. J., 1418
Barbour family, 1560
Barbour, Clifford E., Library,
1369
Barbour, J. Murray, 227-D
Barbour, Lyell, 646
Barclay, Shepard, 860-C
Bares, Basile, 555
Barhight, Ezra, 1005
Barili family, 270
Barili, Alfredo, 270
Barili, Emily Vezin, 270
Barili School of Music, 270
Baritone horn, 1267
Barker, Darwin R., Library,
993
Barker family, 1527
Barker Texas History Center,
1477
Barkin, Rev. Jacob, 254
Barlow, Howard, 1031, 1107
Barlow, Samuel L. M., 142
Barlow, Wayne, 1111
Barnard, Henry, 1062
Barndt-Webb, Miriam, 584
Barnes, Edward Shippen,
227-D, 730
Barnes, Hattie, Collection,
1006
Barnes, Raymond F., Collec-
tion, 78
Barnes, Robert, 1190
Barnes, Wade, 1611
Barnes, William H., 1244
Barnett, John, 227-G, 636

Barnhouse, C. L., 465
Barns family, 1591
Barnum, Phineas T., 335, 1059
Baron, John H., 549
Barras, Charles M., 654
Barrelhouse piano music, 997
Barrell, Edgar, 682
Barrère, Georges, 227-F
Barrett, Abby B., 642
Barrett, Charles, 642
Barrett, Roger, 914
Barrington (Ill.) Historical
Society, 299
Barrington (R.I.) College, 1397
Barrois, Raymond, 550
Barron, Thomas, 1111
Barrow, Bartholomew, 544
Barrows, Thomas, 1059
Barrus, Ruth H., 295
Barry, Frederick, 1031
Barrymore, Lionel, 84, 227-F
Barta, Bessie, 396
Bartel, Heinrich, 1622
Bartholomew, Hope Leroy,
195-A
Bartholomew, Marshall,
195-A, 195-C
Bartholomew County (Ind.)
Historical Society, 409
Bartless, John R., 1407
Bartlett, Homer N., 1061-A
Bartlett, Ida Work, 465
Bartlett, Maro Loomis, 465
Bartlett Memorial Library of
Exploration, 760
Bartlett's Brass Band, 681
Bartók, Béla, 227-B, 981, 1031,
1053, 1577, 1580, 1670
Bartola, 1611
Bartolini, Luigia, 1407
Barton, Andrew, 1544
Barton, Dan, 1611
Barton, Joseph, 1521
Barton, Richard J., 815
Barton, William E., 340
Barton Pipe Organ, 1611
Bartsch, William, 776
Barus, Carl, 1061-F
Barzin, Leon, 1061-J
Barzun, Jacques, 1031
Bass, William Upshur, 1560
Bass viol music, 281, 1331,
1534
Bass viols, 180, 898
Bassett, George S., 465
Bassett, Joseph A., 656
Bassford, Homer, 860-E
Bassoon, 1236
Bastrop County (Tex.)
Museum, 1478
Batchelder, Alice Coleman,
Music Library, 100
Batchelder, Mrs. Charles F.,
313
Batchelors Cotillion Club
(Richmond, Va.?), 1560
Batelle-Tompkins Library, 218
Bates, Anna Craig, 1502
Bates, Gertrude Meyne, 1622
Bates, Joshua, 636
Bates, Katherine Lee, 1053
Bates, Lucy, 265
Bates, Samuel Lysander, 1525
Bates College, 585

Bates Conservatory of Music, 409
Baton Rouge (La.), 406
Battell family, 195-B
Battell, Robbins, 195-A
Battle Creek (Mich.), 729-B, 761
"The Battle of Gettysburg," 1149
Bauer, Harold, 206, 227-E, 568, 1031, 1053, 1058, 1111, 1580
Bauer, Marion, 227-D, 227-F, 1023, 1061-A, 1580
Bauer, Phyllis, 195-C
Bauersachs, Hubert, 866
Baughman Family Collection, 544
Baum, L. Frank, 314
Baum, Russell, 1111
Bauman, Mordecai, 1031
Baumgartner, Bert, 860-F
Baumgartner, H. L., 195
Bawdy songs, 227-M, 407, 612, 1477
Bay City (Mich.), 729-B
Bay City (Mich.) Branch Library, 731
Bay County (Mich.) Library System, 731
Bay Psalm Book, 195-B, 636, 1541, 1673
Bayard, Samuel, 1352
Bayard, Thomas F., 1053
Baylor family, 1560
Baylor University, 1517
BBC, 1670
Beach, Amy Cheney (Mrs. H. H. A.), 221, 227-B, 227-H, 317, 547, 606, 646, 847, 899, 900, 908, 913, 951, 1026, 1053, 1222, 1333, 1541, 1573
Beach, Elizabeth T. Porter, 1059
Beach, John Parsons, 227-F, 502, 646, 971, 1061-A, 1061-B, 1580
Beach, John W., 971
Beach, Kay H., 496
Beach, Sylvia, 949
Beach Club, 908
Beacham, William C., 612
Beale, Frederick Fleming, 291
Beale Street (Memphis), 1449, 1451
Beals Memorial Library, 720
Beardslee Library, 759
Beaton, Isabella, 465
Beaton, Loretta M. Hubbard (Mrs. William), 465
Beattie, John Walter, 357
Beattys, Adele M., 190
Beau, Henry J., 1270
Beauregard, P. G. T., 544
Beaver family, 1155
Beaver, Mrs. Guy, 1155
Beaver Falls (Pa.), 679
Beaver Island (Mich.), 727
Beaver Island (Mich.) Historical Society, 768
Bechler, Johann Christian, 1161, 1285
Beck, Abraham R., 1316
Beck, Carl, 1205

Beck, Conrad, 465
Beck, Cora, 465
Beck, Earl C., 766
Beck, Eleanor Nordhoff, 1577
Beck, George V., 19
Beck, Henry, 227-G
Beck, Horace, 1352
Beck, Jane, 1352
Beck, Johann H., 1185
Beck & Lawton, 721
Beckel, Clarence E., Collection, 1285
Becker, Edna, 498
Becker, Eugene, 195-C
Becker, Mrs. John, 195-C
Becker, John J., 1061-A, 1061-D, 1580
Beckett, Ferol, 171
Beckett, Wheeler, 227-F
Beckman, Irja Wilhelmina Laaksonen, 815
Bedford (Mass.) Historical Society, 633
Beebe, Henriette, 1061-F
Beech Mountain (N.C.), 1095
Beecher, Lyman, 184
Beeching, Flora Mae, 1061-F
Beeching, Ruby, 1061-F
Beecroft, Joseph, 1521
Beef Steak Club, Tremont, 642
Beeghly, L. A., Library, 1302
Beegle (May Beegle) Concerts, 1359, 1375
Beery family, 1158
Beeson, Jack, 239
Beethoven, Ludwig van, 866
Beethoven Association (Columbus, Ohio), 1193
Beethoven Association (New York?), 1061-D
Beethoven Centenary (1927), 636
Beethoven Choral Society (New York), 1061-B
Beethoven Männerchor (San Antonio, Tex.), 1509
Beethoven Music Club (El Reno, Okla.?), 1250
Beethoven Society of Chicago, 334
Beethoven Society (Seville, Ohio), 1190
Beethoven Society (Yale Univ.), 195-B
Begnis, Giuseppe de, 636
Behrens, Anna, 1111
Behymer, Lynden Ellsworth, 79, 127
Beiderbecke, Bix, 463, 719
Beinecke Rare Book and Manuscript Library, 195
Beissel, Johann Conrad, 946, 1031, 1302, 1338
Bekker, Paul, 227-E
Bel Canto Club (Spokane, Wash.), 1578
Belasco, David, 227-B, 1061-L
Belasco Theater (Los Angeles), 77
Belcher, Supply, 660
Belcour, F. B., 632
Belden, Louis, 33
Belding collection, 667
Belfast (Me.) Museum, 580

Belgian Conservatory of Music (New York), 862
Belgium, 1577
Belknap, Elisha, 654
Belknap (Davison-Belknap) Collection, 531
Belknap Collection of the Performing Arts, 244
Bell, Aaron, 195-C
Bell, Harry, 1477
Bell, Joseph and Max, Collection, 1127
Bell, Mary, 195-C
Bell, Mildred, 1477
"Bell Telephone Hour," 1007
Bell-Ringers Guild of Boston, 635
Bellak, James, 955
Bellamann, Henry, 833
Bellamy Band, 227-G
Belleville (Ill.) Band, 305
Bellingham (Wash.) Women's Music Club, 1569
Bellows, Henry A., 815
Bellows Falls (Vt.), 1530
Bells and carillons, 195-B, 202, 247, 635, 636, 703, 752, 1155, 1200. See also Carillon music
Bell's Opera House, 1209
Bellstedt, Herman, 398
Belmont, Eleanor Robson (Mrs. August), 1031
Belmont, Ward, Conservatory of Music, 1463
Belo, Jane, 1022
Belov, Samuel, 1111
Belsom, Jack, 551
Belt, Delight, 372
Belt, Gerald, 372
Belton (Tex.) City Library, 1479
Belton (Tex.) Opera House, 1479, 1515
Beltzhoover, Daniel Melchior, 227-D
Benaccio, M., 1040
Bend, J. G. J., Rev., 612
Benét, William Rose, 1095
Benjamin, Edward B., 1148
Benko, Gregor, 1043
Benkovic, Fred, 1639
Bennard, George, 729-B
Bennett, David D., 389
Bennett, Ella, 156
Bennett, John, 1418
Bennett, Robert Russell, 227-B, 1573
Bennett, Sanford Fillmore, 950, 1602
Benoit, Paul, 227-D
Benson, Dorothy W., 1408
Benson, Louis F., 1347
Benson, Louis F., Collection of Hymnology, 948
Benswanger, William E., 1355
Benswanger, Mrs. William E., 1355
Benteen, Frederick D., 612
Bentley, Dr. William F., 391
Bentley Historical Library, 727, 729-B
Berckman, Evelyn, 1111
Berdahl, Arthur C., 60

Berea (Ky.) College, 522, 1234
Berezowsky, Nicolai, 227-D, 227-F, 1031, 1061-A
Berg, Alban, 68, 654
Berg, Helene, 654
Berg, Lina Sandell, 325
Bergen, Alfred, 1624
Bergen (N.Y.) Historical Society, 972
Berger, Arthur, 195-C, 227-D, 227-F, 1580
Berger, Edouard Nies, 227-F
Berger, Henri, 285, 286
Berger, Isidor, 962
Berger, Kenneth, Band Collection, 800
Berger, Rudolf, 1053
Berger, Wilhelm, 817
Bergquist, J. Victor, 819
Bergsma, William, 227-B, 1111, 1576, 1577
Bergstrom, L. P., 808
Beriot, Charles-Wilfride de, 227-F
Berks County (Pa.) Historical Society, 1378
Berkshire Athenaeum, 696
Berkshire Christian College, Library, 675
Berkley, Miss, 502
Berlin, Irving, 142, 185, 225, 227-D, 227-F, 527, 624, 747, 1036, 1174, 1194
Berlin (Germany), 910, 1468
Berliner, Emile, 1659
Berliner Co., 1640, 1655
Berlisg, John, 800
Bernard, Edward, 711, 1336
Berneri, Mrs. Samuel, 195-C
Bernhardt, Sarah, 84, 227-B, 395
Bernheimer, Elmer, 68
Bernstein, Leonard, 227-B, 1080, 1580
Berol (Hunt-Berol) Collection, 1031
Berquist, John W., 781
Berry, E. M., 866
Berry, Romeyn, 1005
Berry, Zorah, Concert Series, 977
Bertini, Henri, 315
Bertoni, Louis, 1240
Bertrand, Ellen Clarke, Library, 1313
Berwald, William H., 1127
Besoyan, Rick, 1061-A
Bessesen, Beatrice Gjertsen, 815
Best, Mr. and Mrs. C. W., Collection of Autographs, 1222
Bestor, Arthur E., Sr., 398
Bethania (N.C.), 1161
Bethany and Northern Baptist Theological Seminaries, 380
Bethany College, 505, 1589
Bethany Lutheran College, 790
Bethany Lutheran Theological Seminary, 791
Bethany Oratorical Society, 505
Bethel AME Church (Champaign, Ill.), 398
Bethel College, 509

Bethel (Me.) Historical Society, 581

Bethel Theological Seminary, 809

Bethlehem (Ohio) Historical Society, 1219

Bethlehem (Pa.), 1161, 1319, 1338, 1395

Bethlehem (Pa.) Bach Choir, 1285

Bethlehem (Pa.) Steel Corporation, 1283, 1354

Bethlehem (Pa.) Steel Company Band, 1283, 1284

Bethune, Mary McLeod, 226

Bethune, Thomas B. ("Blind Tom"), 544, 636, 714, 741, 1467

Betti, Adolfo, 227-F, 1477

Bettini cylinders, 1127

Betts, Edwin Morris, 1541

Beuter, A., 1193

Bevan, Wilbur K., 1256

Beverley family, 1560

Beverley, Fanny Scott, 1560

Beverley, Ida Dulaney, 1560

Beverley, Richardetta Earle (Carter), 1560

Beverly, Charles, 1445

Beverly Hills (Cal.) Public Library, 52

Bexley Hall, 1110

Beyer, Johanna M., 227-F

Beyerstedt, Bert, 823

Beyerstedt Theater Orchestra, 823

Bezanson, Philip, 476

Bible, 1339

Bible, Kenneth, 844

Biblical Theological Seminary, 1300

Bibliothèque Cantonale et Universitaire (Lausanne, Switzerland), 1689

Bibliothèque du Conservatoire (Paris), 1676

Bibo, Irving, 84

Bickford, Robert, 1531

Bickford, Vahdah, 68

Bidwell, Eondias, 180

Bidwell, Marshall, 1356, 1359

Bidwell, Mrs. Marshall, 1356

Bierley, Paul E., 1191

Big Horn County (Wyo.), 1643

Bigelow, Frederick E., 701

Bigelow, Thomas, 707

Biggle, Lloyd E., 729-B

Biggs, E. Power, 227-F, 227-L, 340

Biglow, Glenn, 163

Biglow and Main, 555

Bijou Opera House (Minneapolis), 815

Bilhorn organ, 356

Billau, Harriet, 1207

Billin, Maude, Collection, 575

Billings, Edna Scott, 847

Billings, Nathaniel, 1102

Billings, William, 127, 219, 227-D, 651, 729-A, 957, 1333, 1402

Billmeyer, Michael, 1338

Biltmore Theatre (Los Angeles), 78

Bílý, Jan (John F.), 815

Bimboni, Alberto, 227-D, 1061-A, 1121

Bimboni, Winona, 1121

Binder, Abraham W., 1174, 1580

Bing, Rudolf, 637

Bingham, Hiram, 195-B, 288

Bingham, Seth, 227-D, 1061-A, 1061-B

Bingham, Walter Van Dyke, 1360

Binghamton (N.Y.), 721

Birch, Al, 156

Birch, Bill, 1031

Birch, Phoebe, 156

Birch-Pfeiffer, Madame, 1468

Birchard, C. C., & Co., 357

Birchard, Clarence C., 227-F

Birckhead Civil War scrapbook, 612

Bird, Arthur, 227-B, 227-F, 272

Bird, Henry Richard, 1070

Birdsall, Sylvester H., 164

Birdseye, George Washington, 1031

Birge, Edward Bailey, 398

Birgfeld & Ramm pianos, 1329

Birmingham (Ala.), 2, 15, 266, 341

Birmingham (Ala.) Public Library, 2

Birmingham (Ala.) Jefferson Historical Society, 3

Birseck collection, 1061-F

Biscaccianti, E., 36

Bishop, Anna, 314, 636, 1052

Bishop, Bernice P., Museum, 285

Bispham, David S., 84, 227-F, 1053, 1061-A, 1061-D, 1061-F, 1111, 1301

Bispham, David, Medal, 1359

Bissell, Marcia, 1210

Bissell, Thomas, 334

Bisttram, Emil, 68

Bitgood, Roberta, 739

Bittner, Francis W., 1270

Bixby, W. K., 860-D

Bjoerling, Jussi, 420, 819, 1061-F

Björling Concert Hall, 819

Blachly, Absalom, 1061-M

Blachly (Wich-Blachly-Colles) papers, 1061-M

Black, Amy van, 1162

Black, Frank J., 815

Black, Robert A., 1327

Black, William, 391

The Black Crook, 142, 654, 860-C

Black Hills, 1430

Black music. See Afro-American music

Black Music Center, 406

Black Music Collection, 406

Black Mountain College, 1155

Black River Music Association, 1530

Blackface. See Minstrelsy

Blackfoot Indians, 227-L, 398

Blackford family, 1541

Blackfriars (University of Chicago), 340

Blackman, Orlando, 314, 332

Blackmar, Armand Edward, 555, 568

Blackmar, Dorothy, 568

Blackmar imprints, 556

Blackmon, Helen, 977

Black's Opera House, 1232

Blaich, Nel, 987

Blaine, James G., 227-M

Blair, G. Bruce, 896

Blake, Dorothy Gaynor, 854

Blake, Eliza Sprole (Mrs. James), 425

Blake, Eubie, 195-C, 226, 227-C, 564, 729-C, 868, 1544

Blake, Maj. Henry, 721

Blake, Isaac Elder, 50

Blake, J. Hubert, 26

Blake, John Henry, 227-F

Blake, Samuel, 658

Blakely, David, 1061-M

Blakely, Mrs. David, 1061-M

Blakely, Sara, 314

Blakeney, Andrew, 68

Blanchard, Amos, House, 628

Blanchet, Catherine B., 542

Bland, James A., 226, 283

Bland, Mrs. William J., 841

Blane, Ralph, 227-D, 227-F

Blank, Ernst, 1573

Blashfield, Edwin Howland, 1053

"Der Blaue Reiter" school, 1031

Blesh, Rudi, 868

Blind musicians, 227-M, 268, 513, 544, 636, 695, 741, 836, 917, 1301, 1467

Bliss, Cornelius, 1052

Bliss, Herter, 1061-D

Bliss, P. P. (Philip Paul), 235, 333, 1379, 1380, 1384, 1394

Bliss, P. P., Homestead, 1394

Bliss, P. P., Museum, 1380

Blitz, Julien Paul, 1477

Blitzstein, Marc, 227-D, 227-F, 1053, 1061-A, 1611

Bloch, Don, 334

Bloch, Edward, 1174

Bloch, Ernest, 33, 50, 63, 91, 121, 142, 206, 227-B, 317, 1030, 1061-A, 1148, 1174, 1222, 1580, 1689

Bloch, Ernest, Society, 50, 63

Bloch, Lucienne (Dimitroff), 63

Bloch, Suzanne, 1580

Block, Bert, 1270

Block, J. H., 1061-J

Blodgett, A. M., 1407

Blodgett, Alonso, 985

Blood, Charles Hazen, 1005

Bloom, Mrs. I. H., 850

Bloom, Rude, 1646

Bloom, Sol, 227-D, 314

Bloomgarden, Kermit, 1611

Bloomington (Ill.), 379, 398, 1193

Blotz, Helene Stratman-Thomas, 1612

Blow, Maria, 729-E

Blucher's Triumph, 1420

Blue Earth County (Minn.) Historical Society, 792

Blue Moon Orchestra, 921

Blue Ribbon Record Co., 394

Blue Ridge Institute, 1545

Blue Ridge Mountains, 1141

Blue River (Wis.), 396

Bluebird label (RCA), 545

Bluebirds, songs about, 565

Bluegrass music, 211, 213, 523, 733, 1234

Blues, 6, 49, 73, 74, 107, 185, 226, 245, 264, 265, 267, 268, 271, 278, 322, 389, 406, 654, 747, 750, 771, 830, 927, 997, 1155, 1166, 1170, 1223, 1406, 1442, 1449, 1450, 1451, 1452, 1477, 1512, 1545, 1577, 1625, 1655, 1657, 1661

Bluffton (Ohio) College, 1169

Blumenberg, Marc A., 1061-F

BMI. See Broadcast Music, Inc.

BMI Archives, 1040

Boardman, Frances, 815

Boardman, Sylvia, 910

Boas, Franz, 1327

Boat songs, 1241. See also Canal songs; Naval songs; Steamships

Boatwright, Howard, 195-C

Bochsa, C. M., 314

Bodanzky, Artur, 227-F, 729-E, 817, 1061-B, 1580

Bodky, Erwin, 713, 1061-M, 1155

Bodleian Library, 1673

Bodman, John Morgan, 199

Bodueau, Jessie L., 344

Boeckman, Charles von, 1477

Boehm, Mary Louise, 1026

Boggs Seminary, 929

La Boheme Music Club (Seattle), 1577

Bohemian Club, 227-H

Bohemian Club (San Francisco), 1061-F

Bohemian Musicians Club of Detroit, 731

"The Bohemians," 1027

Bohlman, Philip V., 396

Bohlmann, Susan D. D. M. (Mrs. Theodore), 1172

Boicourt, Blaine, 361

Boise, O. B., 614

Bojanowsky, Jerzy, 336

Bok, Edward W., 227-D

Bok, Mary Louise Curtis, 227-B, 227-F, 1331

Bok Singing Tower, 247

Bokelman, Henry A., 1622

Bolduc, Lizzie, 860-D

Bolger, Ray, 1487

Boller, Eliza, 1338

Boller, Henry, 1111

Bollinger, Samuel, 36, 227-D, 860-B, 860-F

Bolm, Adolf, 1127

Bolton Landing (N.Y.), 1009

Boltwood, Edward, 696

Bonaventura, Sam di, 195-C

Bond, Carrie Jacobs, 391, 442, 528, 734, 1061-A, 1222, 1572, 1605

Bond, Johnny, 1455

Bonds, Margaret, 195-B

Bonduel, Rev. Florimond J., 1611

Bonime, Josef, Sheet Music Collection, 1520
Bonner, Eugene, 227-D
Bonner, Pat, 727
Bonner County (Idaho) Historical Society, 296
Bonnet, Joseph, 227-D, 227-F
Bonstelle Theatre, 738
Bontemps, Arna, 268, 1127
Booker, Elmer, 349
Bookmyer, Rev. Edwin H., 227-A
Boone, Anne R., 8
Boone, John W. ("Blind"), 836, 868
Boonville (Mo.) Turn and Gesang Verein, 837
Boorse, Margaret Hazelton (Mrs. Henry A.), 931
Booth, Edwin, Theatre Collection, 1064
Booth, Julia, 1477
Booth, Rachel, 227-H
Boott, Francis, 227-D
Boreman, Arthur I., 1591
Bori, Lucrezia, 227-B, 227-F, 1053
Borie, Dr. Beauveau, IV, 1297
Borneman, Henry S., 1333
Bornschein, Franz, 612, 614
Borovsky, Alexander, 1061-F
Borowsky, Felix, 227-D, 227-F, 317, 334, 1580, 1666
Bos, Coenraad V., 227-F
Bosch, José Hernández, 1651
Boscobel (Wis.), 396
Boston, 83, 84, 129, 185, 227-H, 234, 252, 270, 334, 379, 523, 544, 577, 618, 654, 660, 679, 681, 686, 701, 702, 706, 707, 712, 721, 800, 876, 916, 923, 955, 977, 1031, 1061-B, 1061-J, 1142, 1143, 1177, 1207, 1352, 1359, 1402, 1534, 1682
Boston Academy of Music, 315, 636
Boston Athenaeum, 635
Boston Cathedral, 334
Boston Chamber Music Society, 636
Boston Conservatory of Music, 636
Boston Dining Club, 636
Boston Museum, 226
Boston Music Hall, 636
Boston Music Week, 636
Boston National Opera, 1031
Boston, National Peace Jubilee (1869), 646, 681, 701, 1534
Boston Opera Co., 636
Boston Opera House, 647, 916
Boston Orchestra, 636
Boston Orchestral Club, 636
Boston Philharmonic Orchestra, 636
Boston Public Library, 636, 721
Boston Singing Club, 636
Boston Symphony Music Club, 99
Boston Symphony Orchestra, 227-L, 260, 613, 637, 654, 682, 694, 1359, 1375, 1498, 1582

Boston Transcript, 636
Boston University, 637
Boston Woman's Symphony Orchestra, 636
Boston, World's Peace Jubilee (1872), 646
Bostonian Society, 638
Bostwich, Frank, 68
Bostwick, Sara Elliot, 1553
Boswell, George W., 523, 832
Bosworth, Lewis A., 1610
Botkin, Benjamin A., 84, 888
Botkin, George W., 1193
Botkins, Perry, 1646
Botsford, Enid Knapp, School of Dance, 1111
Botts, Ida Bassett, 1477
Boucher, Anthony, Archival Record Collection, 131
Boulanger, Nadia, 195-C, 636, 729-E, 1031
Boulder (Colo.) Musical Society, 150
Boulton, Laura, 227-L
Boulton, Laura, Collection of Traditional and Liturgical Music, 1031
Boutelle, Sara, 134
Bowdoin College, 585
Bowen, Abel, 638
Bowen, Catherine (Drinker), 227-F
Bowen, Emma Lucy Gates, 1520, 1523, 1524
Bowers, Q. David, 53
Bowes, Major, Amateur Hour, 227-L
Bowles, Fred G., 866
Bowles, Paul, 227-D, 227-F, 265, 1544
Bowling Green State University, 1170
Bowman, Euday L., 868
Bowring, John, 1465
Boxford (Mass.), 701
Boy Scouts of America. See Scouting
Boyd, Charles N., 1359
Boyd, Jeanne, 1111
Boyd, John Scudder, 195-A
Boyd, T. B., 227-K
Boyd Stutler Collection, 1590
Boyd's Opera House, 887
Boykan, Martin, 195-C
Boyle, Donzella Cross, 1172
Boyle, George F., 227-D, 614
Boylston Club, 636
Boylston Congregational Church, 656
Boynton, Sally, 197
Boys' choirs, 15, 132
Bozrah (Conn.), 180, 729-A
Bozyan, Frank, 195-A
Bozyan, Mrs. Frank, 195-C
Bozyan, H. F., 195
Braathen, Sverre O., 379
Bradbury, William B., 227-D, 227-F, 1338
Bradford, Harland, 913
Bradford, Henry, 1141
Bradford, Perry, 564
Bradford, Phoebe George, 215
Bradford County (Pa.) Historical Society, 1384

Bradlee imprints, 334
Bradley, Carol June, 979
Bradley, William A., 1053
Bradley University, 381
Bradshaw, Sam, 517
Bragdon, Rufus, 601
Brahms, Johannes, 583
Brahms Choral Club (Fremont, Ohio?), 1207
Brahms Musical Club of Pittsburgh, 1359
Braille music, 531, 714, 1301. See also Blind musicians
Brailowsky, Alexander, 637
Brainard, G. W., 535
Brainard, Kate J., 860-J
Brainard, S., 721, 1190
Brake, Edward, 1661
Brandeis, F., 1541
Brandeis University, 712
Brandon, George, 58
Brandt, Henri S., 398
Brandt, Marianne, 227-F
Brandt, William, 1580
Brandywine Valley Friends of Old Time Music, 211
Branscombe, Gena, 227-B, 227-D, 227-F, 338, 1061-A, 1659
Brant, Henry Dreyfus, 227-D, 1046
Braslau, Sophie, 1061-D, 1061-F, 1578
Brass Band (Foxborough, Mass.), 668
Brass instruments. See specific instruments; Instructional materials
Brasstown (N.C.), 1141
Brattleboro (Vt.), 270, 1329
Brau, Herminio, 1651
Braun, Carl, 1359
Bravo, Alfredo Romeró, 1651
Bray, Archie, 874
Bray, Oliver, 595
Brecht, Bertold, 195-B, 227-H
Breckenridge, William Clark, 860-D
Breckenridge, William K., 1222
Breda (musician), 548
Breedlove, Margaret G. Kilbourne, 544
Brees, Anton, 247, 752
Bremner, John, 1059
Bremond, Mary A., 490
Brenner, Walter, 847
Brescia, Domenico, 1333
Breslauer, Milton K., 949
Brethren church. See Church of the Brethren; Evangelical-United Brethren
Brewer, John Hyatt, 1061-A
Brewton, Sarah Jane Thorne, 270
Briard, George, 645
Bricher, Thomas, 701
Brick Presbyterian Church (New York), 825
Bricken, Carl Ernest, 227-F, 1580
Brico, Antonia, 227-F
Bridgeport (Conn.), 1030
Bridgeport (Conn.) Public Library, 173

Bridgewater (Va.) College, 1539
Bridgman, Frederick A., 317, 1053
Bridwell Theological Library, 1487
Briggs Family Collection, 698
Briggs, Mitchell P., 60
Brigham, Clarence S., 1031
Brigham, William, 302
Brigham Young College (Logan, Utah), 1519
Brigham Young University, 1520, 1521
Bright, Houston, 1481
Brighton Beach (N.Y.) Music Hall, 654
Brill, A. C., 843
Brillon de Jouy, Anne Louise Boyvin d'Hardancourt, 1327
Brimfield (Mass.), 707
Brinckle, Dr. John, 215
Briney, Mrs. Melville O., 531
Briscoe, Edward Eugene, 860-B
Brister, John, Library, 1452
Bristol Academy, 708
Bristol (Vt.) Band, 1529
Bristow, George F., 227-D, 227-F, 334, 1031, 1061-A, 1082, 1111
Britain, Radie, 84, 227-D, 227-F, 1473, 1477, 1507, 1580, 1646
British Broadcasting Corporation, 1670
British Columbia, 195
British Isles. See Anglo-American music; England; English music; Great Britain; Ireland; Irish music; Scotland; Scottish music; Welsh music
British Library, 1670
Britt, Horace, 227-F
Broadcast Music, Inc. (BMI), 227-G, 315, 949, 1040, 1061-D, 1108
Broadhead, Edward Hall, 1143
Broadhurst, Miss, 1031
Broadman Press, 1259
Broadside Television Incorporated, 1445
Broadsides, 106, 180, 227-M, 268, 302, 314, 315, 320, 340, 341, 391, 398, 544, 612, 614, 624, 701, 707, 721, 761, 814, 831, 939, 967, 977, 1059, 1077, 1143, 1174, 1193, 1299, 1333, 1338, 1340, 1375, 1396, 1402, 1405, 1463, 1496, 1520, 1528, 1530, 1556, 1560, 1591. See also Ballads
Broadus, Andrew, 1558
Broadway, 244, 256, 654, 828, 1055, 1208, 1350, 1477. See also Operetta and musical comedy; Tin Pan Alley; Theater music
Brock, Robert Alonzo, 127
Brockmann Music School & Orchestra, 1146
Brockway, Howard A., 227-D, 227-F, 317, 910, 1061-A, 1573, 1666

Broderick, Emma Maybelle Baker, 298
Brodhead (Wis.) Silver Cornet Band, 1612
Brody, Joseph, 1076
Broekhoven, John Andrew (Van), 1226
Bromo-Seltzer songs, 544, 618, 866
Bronck House Museum, 986
Bronson, C. P., 1611
Bronson, Charles, 1236
Bronson, Louis, 195-C
Bronson, Margaret, 1176
Brook Farm, 636
Brookline (Mass.), 227-B, 334
Brookline (Mass.) Public Library, 652
Brooklyn (N.Y.), 654, 1122
Brooklyn Academy of Music, 1083
Brooklyn Chamber Music Society, 349
Brooklyn College of the City University of New York, 1080
Brooklyn Music School and Playhouse, 1081
Brooklyn Public Library, 1082
Brooklyn Symphony, 55
Brooks, Anita (O'Hara) Comfort, 1172
Brooks, Elmer, 798
Brooks, Maud D., 646
Brooks, Phillips, 950
Brooks, Robert F., 1607
Brooks, Sydney, 180
Brooks, Tim, 1085
Broonzy, Big Bill, 610
Brosa, Antonio, 227-F
Bross, Gov. William, 314
Brower, Elizabeth Jordan, 3
Brown, Abbie F., 1541
Brown, Allen A., 636
Brown, Arthur King, 636
Brown, B. B., 1155
Brown, Campbell, 1463
Brown, Chamberlin & Lyman, 1061-L
Brown, David A., 1174
Brown, David McLaughlin, 707
Brown, Ed M., 874
Brown, Eddy, 421
Brown, Edwin R., 180
Brown, Francis H., 1404
Brown, Frank Clyde, 227-L, 1143
Brown, Gertrude, 1111
Brown, Henry, 1059
Brown, Hugo, 8
Brown, James M., 1274
Brown, John, 314, 1052, 1590
Brown, John Carter, Library, 1403
Brown, John M., 729-E
Brown, Lawrence, 1061-N
Brown, Lawrence W., 739
Brown, Les, 1143, 1646
Brown, Louisa, 635
Brown, Lyman (Chamberlin & Lyman Brown), 1061-L
Brown, Mayme, 396
Brown, Nancy, 1111

Brown, Ralph E., 1031
Brown, Sally, 1407
Brown, Seletha, 171
Brown, Sterling, 1451
Brown, Thomas S., 1591
Brown, Wade R., 1148
Brown, Wallee, 396
Brown, Warren, 349
Brown, William, 125
Brown, William A., 701
Brown, William M. S., 216
Brown County (Ind.), 227-K
Brown County (Ind.) Historical Museum, 434
Brown County (Minn.) Historical Society, 801
Brown University, 721, 1402, 1403
Brown-Clawson-Parvin family, 1274
Browne, A., 8
Browne, Benjamin K., 406
Browne, Benjamin P., Library, 351
Browne, J. F., & Co., 707
Browne, Scoville, 1031
Browne, William Hand, 1560
Browne (i.e., Van Volkenburg-Browne) Collection, 729-E
Browning, Elizabeth (Barrett), 1517
Browning, Mortimer, 1520, 1666
Browning, Robert, 1517
Browningsville (Md.) Coronet Band, 625
Brown's Opera House (Purcell, Okla.), 1258
Brubeck, Dave, 195-C
Bruce, George, 1639
Bruch, Fritz, 57
Bruch, Max, 1205
Bruckner, Anton, 1036
Brueggemann, John, 1643
Bruenner, Leopold, 810
Bruhl, Martin, 455
Bruner, David F., 489
Bruning, Harry F., 1520
Brunk, John David, 415
Brunnings, Florence E., 687
Brunnitt, Dan B., 398
Brunswick, Mark, 227-F, 1030, 1580
Brunswick records, 471, 1174, 1353, 1520
Brunswick and Topsham (Me.) Choral Society, 586
Brunswick (Me.) Juvenile Band, 586
Brunswick (Me.) Musical Education Society, 586
Brusiloff, Leon, 229
Bruyn, John W. de, 244
Bryan, Charles Faulkner, 227-D, 1441
Bryan, Charles Page, 314
Bryan, Gordon, 646
Bryant, Billy, 1176
Bryant, Laura, 1005
Bryden, John, 654
Brydges, Earl W., Public Library, 1091
Brymn, James T., 226
Bryn Mawr College, 1286

Bubalo, Rudolph, 1186
Buchanan, Annabel Morris, 1141
Buchanan County (Mo.) Historical Society, 853
Buchanan Glee Club, 1375
Buchannan, Jean Sinclair, 1333
Bucharoff, Simon, 311
Buchbaum, Charles, 1249
Buchhalter, Elisabeth H., 311
Buck, Carlton C., 1270
Buck, Dudley, 180, 182, 185, 208, 227-B, 227-E, 317, 606, 636, 951, 1018, 1053, 1061-A, 1083, 1111, 1222, 1534
Buck, Leonard W., 50
Buckingham County (Va.), 1560
Buckley, Martin E., 314
Buckley, Robert Jones, 1190
Bucknell University, 1313
Buckner, Teddy, 68
Bucks County (Pa.), 1333
Budapest (Hungary), 338
Buddhist music, 47
Buder, William E., 860-D
Buebendorf, Francis, 847
Buehler, A. C., Library, 352
Buehman, Henry and Albert, Collection, 30
Buell, Vai, 916
Bülow, Hans von, 642
Buena Vista (Mrs. Wallace Atkinson), 475
Buenger Memorial Library, 811
Buescher Saxophone Co., 433
Buesing, Charles, 195-C
Buffalo (N.Y.), 314, 334, 549, 977, 1130, 1174
Buffalo and Erie County (N.Y.) Public Library, 977
Buffalo (N.Y.) Symphony Orchestra, 549, 977
Buffalo Bill's Show, 167
Buffinton, Annie Burgess, 664
Bugatch, Samuel, 1076
"Bugler Bill" (Wilbur Wright Swihart), 443
Bugles, 230, 443, 815, 866, 1288, 1418. See also Drum and bugle corps
Buhlig, Richard, 68
Building of Arts Association, 579
Bukofzer, Manfred, 50, 1061-M
Bull, Alexander, 1611
Bull, George M., 150
Bull, Ole, 227-F, 314, 528, 707, 766, 802, 860-B, 1053, 1317, 1484, 1603, 1611
Bull, Olof, 1584
Bull, Storm, 1666
Bull, William, 662
Bullard, Ernest E., 203
Bullard, Frederick Field, 227-D
Bullard, Opal, 465
Bulliet, Clarence Joseph, 387
Bullock, A., 475
Bullock, Flora, 887
Bullock, Helen, 1567
Bunch, Pearl, 1477

Bunch, Sterling, 1477
Bunger, Richard, 68
Bunker Hill, Battle of, 663
Buonamici, Carlo, 1111
Burchenal, Elizabeth, 1372
Burchuk, David, 618
Burdett, John Lathrop, 1061-F
Burdick, D. C., 398
Burdick, Congressman Usher L., 227-A
Bureau of American Ethnology, 227-L
Bureau of Indian Affairs, 230
Bureau of Jewish Education, 117
Bureau of Music (Chicago), 314
Buren, Alicia van, 535
Buren, Lotta van, 1520
Burger, L., 868
Burgos, Francis de, 1477
Burgoyne, Gen. John, 1059
Burk, John N., 227-F
Burke, Harry R., 860-B
Burke (i.e., Triste-Burke) manuscripts, 1541
Burleigh, Cecil, 227-D, 1111, 1611, 1612
Burleigh, Harry Thacker, 195-B, 226, 268, 1053, 1148, 1187, 1294, 1298, 1573
Burlesque, 244, 476, 502, 815, 1064, 1364, 1611. See also Vaudeville
Burlesque Opera Troupe, 1364
Burlin, Natalie, 227-D, 227-F
Burling Library, 473
Burlington (Iowa), 475
Burlington (Iowa) Opera House, 475
Burlington (Iowa) Public Library, 454
Burlington Railroad, Lines West Band, 887
Burnet, Ulala Howard, 1477
Burns, Buddy, 68
Burns, Haydn, Library, 245
Burns, Joan Simpson, 1031
Burns, Robert, 1124
Burns Theater (Colorado Springs, Colo.), 153
Burnside, Robert H., 1061-A, 1061-L, 1061-M
Burrill collection, 907
Burriss, Helen, 1412
Burroughs, Bryson, 1053
Burrow Library, 1453
Burrows, Clyde, 738
Burton, Annie C. W., 348
Burton, DeWitt C., 1270
Burton, Frederick Russell, 227-D
Burton, Thomas G.,-Ambrose N. Manning Collection, 1445
Burton Historical Collection, 739
"Burying of the fiddle," 1188
Busby, Thomas, 406
Busch, Adolf, 227-D, 227-F, 1053
Busch, Carl, 227-F, 317, 398, 847, 931, 1668
Busch, Carl, Collection of Musical Instruments, 398

Busch, Fred, 410
Busch, Fritz, 406, 1053
Bush, Gladys Blakely, 847
Bush, Grace, 1127
Bush, John Wesley, 1524
Bush, Martin, 879
Bush, W. Foley, 227-F
Bush, William Herbert, 180
Bush Temple of Music and
    Conservatory, 314
Business organizations. See
    names of particular activi-
    ties; Corporate music
    ensembles
Busoni, Ferruccio, 639, 729-E,
    1448
Buszin, Walter E., 790, 856
Butler, Helen May, 234
Butler, Julia Colt, 939
Butler, Nicholas Murray, 1031
Butler, Pierce, 1352
Butler, Robert Cushman, Col-
    lection of Theatrical Illus-
    trations, 1573
Butler, Robert Ormond,
    Papers, 544
Butler, Thomas, and family,
    544
Butler, Walter, 510
Butler, Will George, 1298,
    1317
Butler County (Kan.) His-
    torical Society Museum, 497
Butler Library, 1031
Butler University, 421
Buttelman, Clifford V., 618
Buzzard, Joe, Jr., 150
Byers, A. L., 405
Byers, Mrs. M. Chapman,
    860-K
Byers, Roxanne, 68
Byers, S. H. M., 465
Bynum, Raymond T., 1501
Byrd, Frederick M., 1070
Byrne, Ellen Maria, 1402
Byrne, Thomas, Memorial
    Library, 10
Byron, Billy, 1480
Byzantine Catholic Seminary
    Library, 1357

C

Cabarrus County (N.C.), 1155
Cable, George Washington,
    568, 1457
Cabot, Jacob, 701
Cadek Choral Society, 15
Cadek Conservatory, 1439
Cadek Quartet, 15
Cadet Band (Salem, Mass.), 701
Cadet Choir (West Point), 1135
Cadet Glee Club (West Point),
    1135
Cadman, Charles Wakefield,
    115, 227-B, 317, 351, 398,
    590, 847, 887, 1018, 1052,
    1061-A, 1061-F, 1222, 1298,
    1359, 1385, 1666
Cadman Choral Club, 1622
Cadman Club (Houston Co.,
    Tex.), 1482
Cadman Club, Junior
    (Houston Co., Tex.), 1482

Cadmen, John Wakefield, 1487
Cady, Charles Earl, 1643, 1645
Cady, Henriette, 1061-F
Caesar, Irving, 227-F, 1611
Caffery, Sen. Donelson, 544
Cage, John, 68, 195-C, 227-D,
    227-F, 357, 1046, 1053, 1580
Cahn, Nellie, 153
Cain, Noble, 1573
Cairo (Ill.) Public Library, 303
Cajun music, 49, 73, 74, 271,
    542, 545, 563, 1477
Cakewalk, 543, 1061-N
Calbreath, Evelyn, 1270
Calbreath, Mary Evelene, 1274
Caldwell, Clarence, 1611
Cale, John G., 544
Cale, Rosalie Balmer Smith
    (Mrs. Charles Allan Cale),
    860-B
Calhoun, Benjamin C., 1338
Calhoun, James Edward, 1420
Calhoun, Rev. and Mrs., 195-C
Calhoun County (Iowa) His-
    torical Society, 486
Calhoun County (S.C.)
    Museum, 1424
Calhoun Opera Company, 103
California, 195-B, 227-H,
    227-K, 227-L, 354, 391, 398,
    433, 544, 549, 800, 815, 819,
    831, 888, 1061-F, 1061-M,
    1174, 1629
California Department of
    Parks and Recreation, 105
California Federation of Music
    Clubs, 227-H
California Historical Society
    Library, 118
California Music Teachers
    Association, 128
California State College, San
    Bernardino, 112
California State Library, 106
California State University,
    Fresno, 60
California State University,
    Long Beach, 68
California State University,
    Los Angeles, 72
California State University,
    Sacramento, 107
California, University of, at
    Berkeley, 50, 227-L
California, University of, at
    Davis, 59
California, University of, at
    Los Angeles, 74, 84
California, University of, at
    Riverside, 104
California, University of, at
    Santa Barbara, 131
Calker, Darrell W., 1646
Callahan, Charles S., 1064
Callanan College, Conserva-
    tory of Music, 465
Callender's Georgia Minstrels,
    544
Calliopes, 491, 523, 843, 1176
Callister, Francis, 612
Callister, Henry, 612
Calloway, Cab, 637
Calvary Episcopal Church
    (Pittsburgh), 1358

Calvé, Emma, 227-F
Camajani, G., 50
Cambria (Wyo.) Opera House,
    1647
Cambridge (Mass.), 701, 955
Cambridge (Mass.) Music
    Club, 701
Cambridge (Wis.), 802
Camden County (N.J.) His-
    torical Society, 920
Cameron, Giulia Valda
    ("Madame Valda"), 544
Cameron-Graham Memorial
    Band Library, 237
Camp, John Spencer, 182, 190
Camp Douglas, 314
Camp Haan (Cal.), 815
Camp meetings. See Revival
    meetings
Camp songs, 354, 679
Campaign songs, 36, 94, 128,
    227-A, 234, 314, 315, 320,
    398, 401, 424, 425, 490, 544,
    633, 636, 681, 742, 744, 761,
    977, 1003, 1193, 1207, 1218,
    1232, 1402, 1541, 1586, 1673.
    See also Political songs
Campanari, Giuseppe, 1053
Campbell, Alexander, 1589
Campbell, Charles Diven, 406
Campbell, Elsie Benjamin, 432
Campbell, Sir Francis Joseph,
    227-M, 1301
Campbell, James B., 314
Campbell, James Emmett, 432
Campbell, John C., Folk
    School, 1141
Campbell, John Charles, 1141
Campbell, Leroy B., 1387
Campbell, Nancy G., 1423
Campbell, Olive Arnold, 1141
Campbell, S. Verdi, 841
Campbell, Wallace, 187
Campbell, William Taylor, 636
Campbell and Colston Family
    Papers, 1141
Campbell House, 1578
Campos, Juan Morel, 1648,
    1651
Campton (N.H.) Sacred Music
    Society, 898
Canada, 144, 244, 456, 800,
    928, 1031, 1111, 1185, 1468,
    1612
Canaday, Dayton W., 860-G
Canadian County (Okla.) His-
    torical Society, 1249
Canady Library, 1286
Canal songs, 1193, 1197,
    1398. See also Boat songs
Cancion, 1651
Candler, Charles Howard, 269
Candlyn, T. Frederick H.,
    227-D
Caney Fork (Kenneport River,
    Cumberland Mountain,
    Tenn.), 1463
Canfield, Clara, 850
Cannon, Beekman, 195-C
Canon City (Colo.) Music
    Club, 151
Canonge, Louis Placide, 544
Canonza (club), 1518
Cantelo, Mr., 729-A

Canterbury Choral Series, 326
Canton (Ohio), 1296
Cantor, Eddie, 227-F
Cantorial music. See Jewish
    music
Cantors Institute Library, 1044
Cantrell, Barton, 398, 1029,
    1061
Cape Cod (Mass.), 673
Capen, Elizabeth (Mrs. George
    C.), 206
Capen, William, 706
Capes, S. J., 195-B
Capitol Record Co., 1353
Capitol Theater (Yakima,
    Wash.), 1587
Capitol Theatre (Newton,
    Iowa), 482
Caplan, Mike, 560
Caplet, André, 646
Capocci, Gaetano, 334
Capp, Oscar, Kid Band, 500
Cappelano's Band, 968
Carbondale (Ill.), 379
Carden, Allen, 860-A
Careless, George Edward
    Percy, 490, 1521
Carelli, Gabor, 1031
Carew, Eunice, 1402
Carey, Charles H., 606
Carey, Matthew, 1338
Carey, William, College, 825
Caribbean Sea, 1061-N
Carillon music, 247, 752, 1143.
    See also Bells and carillons
Carl, William Crane, 227-F,
    1359
Carle, Frankie, 1646
Carleton English Opera Com-
    pany, 314
Carley, Kenneth, 796
Carlisle, Kitty, 1611
Carlson, Charles Frederick,
    227-D
Carmalt, Ethel, 192
Carman, Bliss, 384
Carmer, Carl, 1095
Carmichael, Hoagy, 227-D,
    406, 1127, 1456
Carmina, 1616
Carncross & Dixie Minstrels,
    1333
Carnegie, Andrew, 1365
Carnegie Foundation, 1061-D
Carnegie Hall (New York),
    803, 1061, 1375
Carnegie Institute (Pittsburgh,
    Pa.), 1319, 1356, 1359, 1361
Carnegie Institute of Tech-
    nology, 1359
Carnegie Library (Pittsburgh,
    Pa.), 1354, 1359
Carnegie-Mellon University,
    1360
Carnegie Music Hall (Pitts-
    burgh, Pa.), 1354, 1356,
    1359, 1361, 1365, 1366, 1375
Carnegie Survey of the Archi-
    tecture of the South, 227-M
Carney Song Contest, 1165
Carols, 195-B. See also Sea-
    sonal and holiday songs
Carpathian music, 1357.
Carpenter, Mrs. Elbert L., 815

Carpenter, Elliot, 195-B
Carpenter, George Benedict, 314
Carpenter, Hoyle, 1111
Carpenter, Imogen, 36
Carpenter, James Madison, 227-K, 227-L
Carpenter, John Alden, 36, 227-B, 227-H, 317, 334, 549, 646, 729-E, 1011, 1018, 1053, 1080, 1111, 1580, 1666
Carpenter, Paul S., 1256
Carpenter, T. Leslie, 215
Carr, Benjamin, 227-D, 334, 544, 729-A, 1031, 1333, 1343
Carr, D., 860-D
Carr, Joseph, 612
Carre, John F., 1621
Carreño, Teresa, 195-A, 1107, 1111
Carriere, Joseph, 545
Carrillo, Julian, 227-F
Carrington, Otis M., 128
Carroll, Harry, 1270
Carroll, John, University, 1180
Carr's Music House, 612
Carruth, Margaret Scruggs, 1483
Carson, "Fiddlin'" John, 277
Carson, J. A., 307
Carson, William G. B., 860-C
Carson City (Nev.), 50
Carson County (Tex.) Square House Museum, 1507
Carter family, 1430
Carter, Alan, 1525
Carter, Elliott, 195-C, 227-B, 227-C, 227-F, 535, 1018, 1040, 1061-A, 1108, 1580
Carter, Gaylord, 68
Carter, John, 1111
Carter, Leslie, 1518
Carter, Mrs. Leslie, 1518
Carter, Robert, 1111
Carter-Owens Collection, 1141
Carton, J. Benoist, 860-D
Cartwright, Earl, 433
Caruso, Enrico, 83, 122, 227-F, 227-L, 313, 614, 820, 860-K, 907, 968, 1036, 1222, 1333, 1389, 1484, 1582
Caruso, Mrs. Enrico, 614
Carver, David L., 579
Carver, Walter Buckingham, 1005
Carver County (Minn.) Historical Society, 821
Carver (i.e., Dargan-Carver) Library, 1462
Carvers Quarter Ball, 176
Cary, Annie Louise, 598
Cary, Mary Flagler, Collection, 1053
Cary, Sylvester L., 544
Casa Blanca Compound, 1654
Casa Grande (Ariz.) Valley Historical Society, 20
Casaday, James Lewis, 448
Casadesus, Robert, 1177
Casals, Pablo, 227-B, 729-E, 1025, 1105, 1111
Case family, 860-D, 860-F
Case, George W., 255
Case, Henry Lincoln, 255

Case, Sallie, 860-D
Case Memorial Library, 183
Case-Western Reserve University, 1181
Cash, Owen C., 1607
Casino Theater (San Antonio, Tex.), 1205
Caspary, Vera, 1611
Cass, Alan, 150
Cass County (Neb.) Historical Society, 892
Cassel, Abraham, Collection, 1338
Cassell, Irwin, 1646
Cassell, Mana-Zucca, 248, 249, 1193
Cassell Collection, 380
Cassidy, Claudia, 315
Castelnuovo-Tedesco, Mario, 83, 227-C, 1580
Castine (Me.) Scientific Society, 587
Castle Garden, 1059
Caston, Saul, 157
Castrone, Mathilde (Graumann), Marchesi de (Mathilde Marchesi), 227-F
Catelinet, Philip, 1360
Cathedral of St. James (Chicago), 722
Cather, Willa, 893
Catherwood Library, 1005
Catholic University of America, 221
Cato, Minto, 227-F
Catskill, Mary Hills, 406
Catskill Mountain resorts, 986
Caughey, Annie M., 36
Cavalry Depot Band, 860-J
CBS (Columbia Broadcasting System), 227-H, 227-L, 349
CBS Records—Archives, 1028
Cecilia Society (Cincinnati), 1172
Cecilian Music Club, 469
Cedar Rapids Symphony Orchestra, 476
Cedarburg (Wis.) Public Library, 1598
Celestophone, 1249
Cello. See Violoncello
Centenary Institute (Summerfield, Ala.), 11
Centennial Exhibition (Philadelphia, 1876), 334, 1338
Center for Acadian and Creole Folklore, 545
Center for Creative Photography, 33
Center for Research Libraries, 312
Center for Southern Folklore, 1449
Center for Studies in American Culture, 979
Center for Studies in Ethnomusicology, 1031
Center for the Comparative Study of Folklore and Mythology, 74, 84
Center of Negro Art, 391
Central Arkansas, University of, 35
Central City (Colo.) Opera House, 155, 156, 860-B

Central College (Pella, Iowa), 475
Central Michigan University, 766
Central Minnesota Historical Center, 806
Central Music Hall (Chicago), 314
Central (S.C.) Wesleyan College, 1413
Central Vermont Music Association, 1530
Century Library, 1065
Century Music Publishing Company, 503
Century Theater (Jackson, Miss.?), 829
Century-Strand Theatre Lighting Archive, 1385
Le Cercle Gounod, 682
Cernkovic, Rudolph, 1372
Cervenka, George, 457
Chace, Frank W., 150
Chadwick, George Whitefield, 195-B, 227-B, 227-C, 317, 636, 646, 705, 863, 951, 1061-A, 1080, 1111, 1159, 1359, 1534, 1580
Chadwick, J. Raymond, Library, 479
Chajes, Julius, 739
Chaliapin, Feodor, 61, 227-B, 636, 860-D
Challis, John, 1069
Chamber ensembles, 15, 66, 68, 156, 157, 195-A, 227-E, 228, 349, 359, 535, 583, 618, 636, 646, 682, 719, 729-B, 815, 860-B, 916, 977, 1061-F, 1172, 1316, 1344, 1355, 1359, 1477
Chamber music collections, 7, 36, 50, 80, 84, 85, 89, 129, 142, 196, 206, 216, 227, 228, 244, 309, 323, 334, 349, 354, 398, 427, 455, 568-A, 583, 606, 636, 646, 667, 682, 706, 729-E, 860-F, 957, 977, 1046, 1050, 1071, 1082, 1105, 1107, 1111, 1161, 1176, 1183, 1184, 1192, 1200, 1222, 1267, 1270, 1289, 1312, 1333, 1336, 1359, 1375, 1477, 1517, 1520, 1540, 1541, 1543, 1567, 1593, 1621, 1676
Chamber Music Society (Ann Arbor, Mich.), 729-B
Chamber Music Society (Brooklyn, N.Y.), 349
Chamber Music Society (Buffalo), 977
Chamber Music Society (New Bedford, Mass.), 682
Chamber Music Society (Pittsburgh), 1355
Chamber Music Society (University of Louisville), 535
Chamber of Commerce (Tulsa, Okla.), 1256
Chamberlain, C. H., 302
Chamberlain, Millard, 1014
Chamberlin & Lyman Brown, 1061-L
Chaminade, Cecile, 631

Chaminade Club, 631
Chaminade Club (Jacksonville, Ill.?), 364
Chaminade Musical Club (Nashville, Tenn.), 1463
Champagne brothers, 676
Champion, Lucretia, 192
Chandler, Winthrop B., 68
Chanler, Theodore, 227-C, 227-H, 646, 1031, 1061-A
Chanteys, 62, 120, 227-K, 227-L, 683, 687, 1099, 1528. See also Naval songs
Chapek, Joseph H., 1622
Chapel Hill (N.C.), 1155
Chapelle, Kitty, 391
Chapin family, 1172, 1225
Chapin, Amzi, Sr., 1225
Chapin, Nathaniel Gates, 334
Chapin, Roy D., 729-B
Chapin Hall, 719
Chapin Library, 719
Chaplin, Charles, 227-F
Chaplin, Ralph, 1584
Chaplin, Saul, 1487, 1646
Chapman Family Papers, 1463
Chapman, J. Garfield, 1205
Chapman, Louise, 798
Chapman, Simon, 707
Chapman, William Rogers, 581
Chappell, Louis Watson, 1591
Charbonnel, Avis Vliben, 1397
Charette, E. H., 144
Charles City (Iowa), 465
Charleston (S.C.), 1143, 1420
Charleston Museum, 1415
Charleston County (S.C.) Library, 1414
Charleston (Mass.), 701
Charlotte (N.C.), 1141
Charlotte Court House (Va.), 1560
Charlton, Mary Ann, 1390
Charlton, Melville, 741, 1298
Charpentier-Morphy, Mrs. T. R., 334
Chart Music Publishing House, 357
Charters, John, 442
Chase family, 276
Chase, Caleb, 898
Chase, Edward, 860-D
Chase, Gilbert, 1061-B, 1580
Chase, Nelson A., 1530
Chase, Richard, 538
Chase, Theodore, 642
Chase Conservatory of Music, 276
Chasins, Abram, 68, 1031, 1292
Chassaignac, Eugene, 568
Chassaignac, S., 555
Chatfield, Mrs. A. H., 1172
Chatfield, A. W., 1172
Chatfield (Minn.) Brass Band Free Music Lending Library, 778
Chatham (Mass.?), 180
Chatham College, 1362
Chatham-Effingham Liberty Regional Library, 282
Chattahoochee (Ga.) Musical Convention, 270
Chattahoochee Valley Music Convention, 275

Chattanooga (Tenn.), 15
Chattanooga Music Club, 1439
Chattanooga Spring Festival, 1439
Chattanooga-Hamilton County (Tenn.) Bicentennial Library, 1439
Chatterton Opera House, 302
Chattle, Ann Agusta, 406
Chautauqua, 103, 163, 391, 398, 474, 475, 476, 511, 520, 982, 1272, 1317, 1428, 1429, 1432, 1515
Chavez, Carlos, 195-C
Chelsea (Vt.), 1530
Chemehuevi Indians, 31
Chenango County (N.Y.), 1005
Cheney, Alice, 1390
Cheney Singers, 1534
Cherokee Indians, 84, 939, 1255, 1264
Cherry, James O., 1487
Cherryfield (Me.) Marching Band, 577
Chesapeake and Ohio Historical Society, 1588
Chesapeake & Ohio Railway, 1588
Cheshire, John, 1061-A
Cheshire (Conn.), 180, 195-A
Cheslock, Louis, 614, 1061-A
Chester County (Pa.), 1333
Chester County Historical Society, 1390
Chestertown (Md.), 215
Chestnut Street Theatre, 1333
Chetek (Wis.), 611, 1614
Chevis-Samuel Collection, 841
Chiasera, Dorothy, 116
Chicago, 25, 36, 129, 227-L, 244, 315, 349, 351, 366, 375, 376, 391, 396, 398, 400, 476, 544, 598, 611, 613, 722, 729-B, 729-E, 734, 800, 802, 837, 860-K, 888, 1031, 1037, 1061-F, 1061-L, 1061-M, 1113, 1174, 1194, 1359, 1425, 1444, 1459, 1611, 1624, 1625, 1629, 1633, 1662, 1673
Chicago Architecture Foundation, 313
Chicago Auditorium Conservatory, 334
Chicago Band Association, 314
Chicago Business Men's Orchestra, 314
Chicago City Opera Company, 314
Chicago Civic Opera Company, 315
Chicago Classical Guitar Society, 391
Chicago Daily News, 387
Chicago Evening Post, 387, 1520
Chicago Grand Opera, 315
Chicago Grand Opera Company, 314
Chicago Historical Society, 314
Chicago Ideal Company, 314
Chicago In-and-about Music Educators Club, 618

Chicago Little Theatre, 729-E
Chicago Mendelssohn Club, 314, 398
Chicago Musical College, 338
Chicago Musicians' Union, 1609
Chicago Opera Company, 1031, 1037, 1061-F, 1061-L
Chicago Public Library, 315
Chicago Swedish Glee Club, 316
Chicago Symphony Orchestra, 314, 315, 317, 334, 357, 366, 433, 815, 1202, 1238, 1624
Chicago Tribune, 314
Chicago, University of, 340, 1005, 1481
Chicago World's Columbian Exposition (1893), 227-L, 314, 315, 334, 729-B, 1359
Chick, Annie Williams, 671
Chickering piano rolls, 916
Chickering-McKay pianos, 1017
Chiesa, Mary Tibaldi, 227-F
Child, Francis James, 654, 1541
Children's music, 54, 107, 113, 184, 195-A, 227-H, 336, 341, 344, 356, 376, 391, 406, 467, 531, 542, 544, 618, 636, 679, 687, 714, 729-E, 787, 798, 800, 822, 831, 854, 860-C, 866, 926, 948, 962, 1061-M, 1070, 1098, 1099, 1110, 1149, 1172, 1183, 1200, 1210, 1258, 1274, 1275, 1315, 1329, 1333, 1352, 1423, 1456, 1483, 1511, 1520, 1527, 1528, 1541, 1611, 1620, 1634, 1641, 1642, 1645, 1673, 1683. See also Lullabies
Childs, Barney, 101
Chinese music, 50, 61, 1665
Chippewa Falls (Wis.), 1601
Chippewa Indians, 355, 766
Chippewa Valley (Wis.) Historical Museum, 1600
Chippewa Valley (Wis.) Musicians Association, 1601
Chisholm Trail Museum, 518
Chittenden, Kate, 1107
Choctaw Indians, 355, 1255
Choirs. See Choral ensembles and singing societies
Chol, Emmanuel, 544
Chopin Singers (Chicago), 336
Choral Club (Concord, Mass.), 658
Choral Club (Hartford, Conn.), 181
Choral Club (Ithaca, N.Y.), 1005, 1006
Choral Club (St. Paul), 815
Choral ensembles and singing societies, 13, 15, 50, 78, 98, 103, 144, 180, 181, 187, 190, 192, 195-A, 195-B, 198, 216, 223, 227-B, 227-H, 230, 234, 242, 270, 275, 282, 310, 316, 320, 324, 325, 336, 348, 353, 356, 379, 388, 398, 401, 409, 419, 432, 437, 461, 462, 477, 488, 505, 509, 511, 514, 520,

529, 544, 579, 581, 586, 596, 609, 612, 613, 619, 633, 636, 642, 654, 659, 688, 693, 701, 705, 707, 716, 721, 729-B, 730, 739, 741, 757, 761, 794, 795, 800, 802, 803, 815, 818, 824, 837, 860-A, 860-B, 860-C, 860-E, 860-J, 866, 875, 879, 885, 892, 916, 917, 926, 940, 951, 977, 980, 991, 996, 1005, 1006, 1007, 1010, 1031, 1061-B, 1061-F, 1105, 1130, 1133, 1135, 1141, 1165, 1172, 1176, 1179, 1190, 1193, 1205, 1207, 1216, 1222, 1224, 1227, 1235, 1274, 1280, 1285, 1302, 1319, 1320, 1334, 1343, 1354, 1359, 1363, 1367, 1375, 1385, 1389, 1407, 1418, 1425, 1429, 1443, 1447, 1457, 1459, 1463, 1476, 1505, 1506, 1509, 1511, 1514, 1515, 1518, 1519, 1520, 1521, 1523, 1529, 1530, 1533, 1534, 1546, 1560, 1577, 1578, 1584, 1585, 1596, 1599, 1601, 1607, 1611, 1613, 1616, 1622, 1624, 1647, 1673, 1675, 1680, 1681
Choral music collections, 3, 50, 58, 80, 99, 115, 116, 117, 126, 129, 132, 140, 185, 192, 195-A, 216, 227, 324, 325, 326, 330, 334, 338, 345, 348, 350, 364, 368, 385, 398, 402, 432, 439, 452, 455, 462, 465, 469, 477, 481, 486, 489, 497, 501, 503, 509, 511, 522, 533, 534, 559, 566, 567, 569, 636, 644, 646, 667, 701, 705, 706, 711, 712, 723, 729-E, 794, 798, 800, 802, 803, 810, 819, 821, 835, 854, 856, 860-F, 866, 875, 896, 912, 926, 941, 944, 951, 952, 957, 977, 1061-N, 1111, 1124, 1161, 1165, 1167, 1174, 1176, 1180, 1183, 1194, 1200, 1201, 1202, 1207, 1211, 1216, 1220, 1235, 1245, 1252, 1259, 1274, 1277, 1285, 1302, 1315, 1320, 1333, 1340, 1343, 1359, 1363, 1457, 1459, 1481, 1487, 1493, 1509, 1514, 1520, 1521, 1522, 1523, 1534, 1541, 1543, 1593, 1604, 1607, 1615, 1617, 1619, 1621, 1632, 1636, 1649, 1653, 1665, 1673. See also Vocal music collections
Choral Society (Brunswick and Topsham, Me.), 586
Choral Society (Middlebury, Vt.), 1529
Choral Society (Rutland, Vt.), 1533
Choral Society (St. Louis), 860-C, 860-E
Choral Society (Salem, Mass.), 701
Choral Society (San Antonio, Tex.), 1511
Choral Society of Washington (D.C.), 223
Choral Society (Weymouth, Mass.), 916

Choral Society (Wilmington, Del.), 216
Choral Union (Kalamazoo, Mich.), 761
Choral Union (Marysville, Ohio), 1216
Choral Union (Milton, Wis.), 1616
Choral Union (Northborough, Mass.), 693
Choral Union (Worcester, Mass.), 721
Chotzinoff, Samuel, 637
Chou Wen-Chung, 535
Chowning, J. A. C., 1560
Christ Church (Mobile, Ala.), 8
Christ Church Cathedral (New Orleans), 552
Christadelphian church, 1471
Christensen, Harold, 122
Christensen, Lew, 122
Christensen, William, 122
Christian, D. Palmer, 729-B, 729-C
Christian and Missionary Alliance, 1094
Christian Church. See Disciples of Christ
Christian Church Band (Columbus, Ind.), 434
Christian Crusaders of Wisconsin, 729-B
Christian Science hymnals, 344
Christian Theological Seminary, 423
Christiansen, F. Melius, 802, 803, 808
Christiansen, Olaf, 803
Christmas music. See Seasonal and holiday songs
Christy, Edwin P., 127
Christy, G. P., 1329
Christy, Margaret, 15
Christy's Minstrels, 320, 544, 1395, 1484
Chromatic Club (Boston), 646
Church, John, Co., 227-G
Church Choral Association, 195-A
Church music, 265, 621, 636, 654, 663, 685, 689, 707, 815, 879, 914, 922, 940, 943, 944, 1006, 1083, 1125, 1141, 1161, 1202, 1207, 1228, 1274, 1281, 1285, 1312, 1325, 1358, 1418, 1420, 1462, 1477, 1521, 1611, 1649, 1653, 1658. See also specific denominations; Hymnals and tunebooks; Sunday-school songbooks; Jewish music
Church of England. See Episcopalian music
Church of God music, 405
Church of God Publishing House, 1440
Church of Jesus Christ of Latter-Day Saints. See Mormon music
Church of the Brethren, 350, 439, 506, 1302. See also Evangelical-United Brethren
Church of the Brethren General Board, 350

Church of the Messiah (Baltimore), 612
Church of the Nazarene. *See* Nazarene music
Churchill, Sarah J., 940
Cigarette cards with musical subjects, 234. *See also* Post cards
Cinatl, Ludwig, 1611
Cincinnati, 220, 314, 398, 523, 529, 531, 544, 568, 1113, 1193, 1222, 1245
Cincinnati College of Music, 1176
Cincinnati Conservatory of Music, 1112, 1174, 1177
Cincinnati Grand Opera, 1172
Cincinnati Haydn Society, 1176
Cincinnati Historical Society, 1172
Cincinnati Industrial Expositions, 1172
Cincinnati Literary and Musical Society, 1172
Cincinnati Männerchor, 398, 1172
Cincinnati May Festival, 1176
Cincinnati Music Hall Association, 1172
Cincinnati Music Hall Organ Association, 1172
Cincinnati Musical Club, 1172
Cincinnati Musical Festival Association, 1172
Cincinnati Orpheus, 398
Cincinnati Public Library, 1176
Cincinnati String Quartette, 1172
Cincinnati Summer Opera, 1176
Cincinnati Symphony Orchestra, 57, 549, 1172, 1173, 1176
Cincinnati, University of, College-Conservatory of Music, 1177
Cior, Charles, 544
Circus, 195-B, 234, 244, 379, 442, 544, 1172, 1333, 1396, 1477, 1511, 1594, 1595, 1662
Circus and Related Arts Collection, 379
Circus World Museum, 1594
Cisler, S. A., 530
Cities Service Concerts, 227-L
City Amateurs (New Brunswick, N.J.), 939
City Auditorium (Colorado Springs, Colo.), 153
City Auditorium (Lincoln, Neb.), 887
City College Archives, 1030
City College of the City University of New York, 1030
City College of New York, 1070
City Drummers' Association (St. Louis), 860-C
City of Detroit Arts Commission, 738
City Symphony (New York?), 1061-F

City University of New York, Brooklyn College, 1080
City University of New York, City College, 1030
Civic Arts Association (Louisville), 535
Civic Auditorium (Seattle), 1576
Civic Ballet (Pittsburgh), 1375
Civic Chorus (Holland, Mich.), 757
Civic Concert Series (Long Beach, Cal.), 70
Civic Light Opera (Long Beach, Cal.), 70
Civic Light Opera (Pittsburgh), 1375
Civic Light Opera Association (Los Angeles), 78
Civic Music Association (Battle Creek, Mich.), 730
Civic Music Association (Dallas?), 1483
Civic Music League (St. Louis), 860-D, 860-G
Civic Opera (Peoria, Ill.), 381
Civic Opera Building (Chicago), 391
Civic Opera Group (Ithaca, N.Y.), 1005
Civil rights songs, 742. *See also* Protest songs
Civil war music, 9, 43, 77, 127, 128, 214, 221, 227-A, 227-J, 227-M, 244, 280, 302, 314, 315, 319, 320, 340, 382, 390, 391, 413, 425, 465, 491, 523, 543, 544, 565, 568, 612, 623, 624, 636, 689, 691, 729-A, 729-B, 744, 761, 815, 833, 860-F, 860-G, 866, 887, 898, 909, 947, 955, 980, 985, 1008, 1059, 1061-M, 1095, 1111, 1143, 1155, 1161, 1174, 1189, 1190, 1193, 1208, 1232, 1295, 1333, 1389, 1402, 1405, 1432, 1444, 1463, 1467, 1471, 1477, 1497, 1541, 1590, 1591, 1595, 1596, 1611, 1612, 1618, 1639, 1673. *See also* Confederate music
Claggett, Rev. Thomas John, 612
Clapp, Margaret, Library, 716
Clapp, Philip Greeley, 227-D, 227-F, 476, 636
Claremont Colleges, 55
Claremont Graduate School, 55
Clarinets, 409, 425, 618, 663, 686, 701, 989, 1141, 1178, 1222, 1318, 1639
Clark, Charles, 195-C
Clark, Mrs. Charles, 195-C
Clark, Charles Badger, 1430
Clark, Mrs. Davis, 1172
Clark, Edgar Rogie, 741
Clark, Edward, 1670
Clark, Ella Anderson, 269
Clark, Frances Elliott, 618
Clark, Frank Albert, 226
Clark, George H., 234
Clark, Herald R., 1520
Clark, Herma Naomi, 314

Clark, Horace, 1477
Clark, James Osgood Andrew, 269
Clark, Kate Freeman, Manuscript Collection, 826
Clark, Keith C., 1002
Clark, Lucy A. Rice, 1524
Clark, Mary Vinson, 1591
Clark, Melville, 1127
Clark, Wallace R., 1480
Clark, Walter W., 1061-F
Clark, William Andrews, 84
Clark County (Kan.) Historical Society, 493
Clark County (Ohio) Historical Society, 1232
Clark County (Wis.) Historical Society, 1609
Clark Music Co., 1127
Clarke family, 1560
Clarke, Arthur Corning, 1668
Clarke, E. E., 227-H
Clarke, Harriet Orne, 701
Clarke, Helen Rand, 334
Clarke, Henry Leland, 398, 618, 661, 907, 1580
Clarke, Hugh A., 1352
Clarke, Rebecca, 227-F
Clarke, Robert Coningsby, 110
Clarke, S. A., 1274
Clarke, Samuel, 209
Clarke Historical Library, 766
Clarksburg (Md.) Band, 625
Classical Guitar Society (Chicago), 391
Clausen, Bernard, 1363
Clauson, Marge, 68
Clavichords, 1069
Clawson family, 1274
Clay, Frederic, 227-D
Clay (music publisher), 124
Clay Center (Kan.) Band, 514
Clay County (Mo.) Museum Association, 848
Clay Seminary, 848
Claypoole, Edward B., 227-D, 227-F
Clayton, Rev. J. B., 235
Cleary, Janice, 889
Clef Club (Northampton, Mass.), 688, 689
Clemenceau, Mrs. Pierre, 553
Clemens, Clara. *See* Gabrilowitsch, Clara (Clemens)
Clemens, Cyril, 860-D
Clemens, Samuel Langhorne ("Mark Twain"), 186, 839, 860-C, 871
Clement (Adams Clement) Collection, 234
Clements, William L., Library, 729-A
Cleveland, Grovenor, 1111
Cleveland, Grover, 681
Cleveland, William, 701
Cleveland (Ohio), 227-B, 800, 1172, 1611
Cleveland Conference for Educational Cooperation, 1190
Cleveland Federation of Musicians, 1182, 1190

Cleveland Institute of Music, 1183, 1190
Cleveland Music School Settlement, 800, 1058
Cleveland Musician, 1182
Cleveland News, 1190
Cleveland Orchestra, 1184, 1190, 1231
Cleveland Philharmonic Orchestra, 1181, 1190
Cleveland Plain Dealer, 1190
Cleveland Public Library, 1185
Cleveland State University, 1186
Cleveland Symphony Orchestra, 1238
Cleveland Vocal Society, 1205
Clifford, Charles V., 227-F
Clifton, Chalmers, 227-F, 1177
Clifton Music Club, 1172
Clinch Valley College, 1568
Cline, J. DeForest, 168, 1573
Clinton, Larry, 1646
Clinton (N.J.) Historical Museum Village, 921
Clippinger, David A., Collection, 1481
Clitherall, James, 1463
Clive, William C., 1521
Clokey, Joseph W., 55, 1573
Clopper family, 625
Cloppers (Md.), 625
Clough-Leighter, Grace Cotton Marshall, 227-D
Clough-Leighter, Henry, 227-B, 227-D
Club Montparnasse, 815
Clyde (N.Y.) Opera House, 1127
"CM" collection, 1185
Coast Artillery, 216th Regiment, Band, 815
Coates, Albert, 1053
Coates, Mary Weld, 1168
Coates, Thomas, 1291
Cobb, Charles M., 1530
Cobb, E. L., 209
Cobos, Ruben, 152
Cochran, Bywaters, 1483
Cochran, William C., 1222
Coci, Claire, 1295
Cocke County (Tenn.), 1459
Cockrell, W. Dale, 1527
Codman, Charles R., 1611
Cody, William S. ("Buffalo Bill"), 167
Coe, Charles W., Memorial Library, 80
Coe, George Albert, 354
Coe, Sadie Knowland, Collection, 354
Coe College, 457
Coerne, Louis Adolphe, 196, 227-D, 636, 654, 1580
Coffee, John, 1463
Coffey, "Happy" John, 1463
Coffey, Sam, 1463
Coffey, Walter Castella, 800
Coffman, Nano H., 410
Coffman, S. F., 415
Cogswell Music Library, 1304
Cohan, George M., 227-F, 624, 1057

Cohen, Cecil, 195-B
Cohen, Ethel S. (Mrs. Frank), 1061-B
Cohen, G. M., 1174
Cohen, Henry, 1477
Cohen, Israel L., 227-G
Cohen, Mendez, 227-A
Cohen, Norm, 73
Cohen, Ruth Steinkraus, 207
Cokato (Minn.) Historical Society, 779
Coke Collection, 523
Cole, John, 612
Cole, Robert, 226
Cole, Rossetter Gleason, 227-D, 227-F, 317, 326, 334, 646, 739
Cole, Russell D., Library, 481
Cole, Thomas, 227-M, 986
Cole, Ulric, 227-D
Colebrook (Pa.), 1315
Coleman family, 860-K
Coleman, Anne Eliza, 11
Coleman, George, 1005
Coleman, John, 612
Coleman, Robert H., 852, 1462
Coleman, Satis N., 1031
Coleman Memorial Library, 259
Coleridge-Taylor, Jessie F., 1031
Coleridge-Taylor, Samuel, 110, 142, 195-A, 195-B, 226, 636, 739, 1031, 1187, 1666
Colgate, Samuel, Library, 1109
Colgate Rochester/Bexley Hall/Crozer Theological Seminaries, 1110
Coliseum (Bloomington, Ill.), 302
Colket, Gordon Wright, 349
Collection of Business Americana, 234
Collections of music, biblio-philic, 183, 227-A, 227-K, 227-L, 227-M, 234, 334, 349, 391, 398, 406, 439, 440, 465, 484, 534, 646, 860-A, 860-B, 866, 1031, 1036, 1061-C, 1061-D, 1061-J, 1166, 1168, 1170, 1234, 1336, 1359, 1433, 1463, 1528, 1673, 1686. See also Autograph collections
College Band Director's National Association, 618
College Conservatory of Music (Cincinnati), 1172
College of Charleston (S.C.), 1416
College of Emporia, 498
College of Music Expression (Amarillo, Tex.), 1473
College of Music of Cincinnati, 1177
College of Saint Elizabeth, 923
College of William and Mary, 1560, 1566
College of William and Mary, Norfolk Division, 1554
College songs. See School songs
Collegium Musicum (Bethle-hem, Pa.), 1285

Collegium Musicum (Lititz, Pa.), 1285
Collegium Musicum (Salem, N.C.), 1161
Colles papers, 1061-M
Collier, Nina P., 234
Collingswood (N.J.) Free Pub-lic Library, 922
Collingwood Opera House, 1105
Collins, Carrie B. H., 1457
Collins, Cleota, 1555
Collins, Daniel, 195-B
Collins, Edward, 309
Collins, Ludie, 1457
Collins, Robert Hall, 1061-F
Collins, Thomas, 1333
Collins Collection of the Dance, 2
Colman, Howard, Library, 387
Colman, John, 195-C
Colón, Braulio Dueño, 1651
Colonial music, 219, 227-G, 227-M, 741, 1396, 1403, 1407, 1567. See also Revolu-tionary War
Colonial Williamsburg Foundation, 1567
Color music, 227-M, 636, 1338
Colorado, 142, 155, 156, 235, 334, 800
Colorado College, 152
Colorado Federation of Music Clubs, 157
Colorado Folklore Society, 150
Colorado Heritage Center, 156
Colorado Historical Society, 156, 169
Colorado Midland Band, 398
Colorado Normal School, 167
Colorado Springs (Colo.), 157
Colorado Springs Opera House, 153
Colorado, University of, 150
Colston family, papers, 1141
Colston, Frederick Mason, 1141
Columbia (Mo.), 860-B
Columbia (Pa.) Public Library, 1289
Columbia (Tenn.), 314, 1463
Columbia records, 104, 322, 471, 1061-J, 1272, 1353, 1520, 1640, 1665
Columbia Artists Manage-ment, Inc., 1031
Columbia Broadcasting Sys-tem, 227-H, 227-L, 349
Columbia Broadcasting Sys-tem Records—Archives, 1028
"Columbia, Columbia, to Glory Arise," 1059
Columbia Concerto Corpora-tion, 887
Columbia County (N.Y.) His-torical Society, 1008
Columbia Hall (Hopewell, N.J.), 929
Columbia Historical Society, 222
Columbia University, 1031, 1152
Columbian Exposition (1893). See World's Columbian Ex-position (1893)

Columbiana Collection, 1031
Columbus (Ga.), 1141
Columbus (Ga.) College, 276
Columbus (Ind.), 434
Columbus (Ohio), 1172
Columbus Beethoven Associa-tion, 1193
Columbus Maennerchor, 1193
Colville, Ruth Marie, 157
Comal County (Tex.), 1505
Comal Singers League, 1477
Combs, Josiah H., 84
Comden, Betty, 1057
Comfort, James H., 860-B
Comic opera. See Operetta and musical comedy
Command (Troop Carrier), 99
Commercial Club (Grand Forks, N.D.), 1165
Commercials and advertising songs, 135, 234, 543, 618, 824, 848, 860-E, 866, 1059, 1077, 1266, 1560, 1611
Commission on Worship, Liturgies, and Hymnology, 856
Committee on Social Thought, 340
Commonplace books, 127, 227-M, 398, 502, 611, 701, 1161, 1402, 1407. See also Daybooks; Lyrics of songs
Community and Settlement Music Schools, New York Association of, 1058
Community music schools. See Settlement music
Composer Facsimile Editions, 1019, 1111
Composers Forum, 1061-B
Composer's Forum-Laboratory, 636
Comstock Building, 1582
Concert halls. See Music halls; Opera houses; Theaters and auditoriums
Concert singers, 30, 129, 179, 266, 285, 314, 315, 334, 335, 433, 475, 544, 568-A, 598, 636, 646, 671, 677, 678, 709, 710, 741, 815, 860-B, 860-D, 896, 916, 939, 940, 975, 987, 1005, 1037, 1039, 1061-B, 1143, 1155, 1193, 1222, 1268, 1270, 1327, 1338, 1418, 1420, 1468, 1520, 1574, 1578, 1609, 1611
Concert-Program Exchange, 234
Concord (Mass.) Academy, 659
Concord Antiquarian Society, 658
Concord Choral Club, 659
Concord Free Public Library, 659
Concord (N.H.), 227-M
Concord Musical Society, 898
Concord (N.C.), 1155
Concord Series, 659
Concordia (Kan.) Band, 514
Concordia (Wis.), 1611
Concordia College (Moor-head, Minn.), 815

Concordia College (St. Paul), 811
Concordia Hall, 1631
Concordia Historical Institute, 856
Concordia Male Choir, 746
Concordia Seminary Library, 857
Concordia Teachers College, 385
Cone, Edward T., 1148
Confederate Army of Northern Virginia, 1141
Confederate music, 127, 195-A, 269, 314, 398, 544, 555, 568-C, 614, 624, 635, 744, 829, 848, 860-F, 967, 977, 1036, 1040, 1059, 1141, 1143, 1146, 1155, 1299, 1338, 1340, 1402, 1405, 1420, 1444, 1463, 1483, 1496, 1497, 1541, 1556, 1557, 1560, 1561. See also Civil War music
Conference for Educational Cooperation (Cleveland), 1190
Confrey, Zez (Edward Elezear), 227-D
Congregation B'nai David (Southfield, Mich.), 769
Congregation Rodfei Zedek (Chicago), 318
Congregational Library, 634
Congregationalist music, 180, 184, 598, 634, 656, 665, 786, 914, 1224
Congress Park (Saratoga Springs, N.Y.), 1117
Conn, C. G., Instrument Manufacturing Co., 433
Connecticut, 269, 696, 707, 721, 729-A, 815, 888, 905, 1030, 1061-M, 1402
Connecticut College, 196
Connecticut Historical Society, 180
Connecticut Second Regiment Band, 194
Connecticut State Archive, 181
Connecticut State Library, 181
Connecticut, University of, 203
Connecticut Valley (Mass.) Historical Museum, 704
Connell, Horatio, 1352
Connelly, John, 371
Conner, John E., Museum, 1500
Conner, Lemuel Parker, Family Papers, 544
Connick, Harris D. H., 50
Connor, William, 180
Conole, Frances R., Archive, 973
Conole, Philip, 973
Conrath, Louis, 860-F
Conrath's Conservatory of Music, 860-E
Conried, Heinrich, 1025
Conservatory of Music (Battle Creek, Mich.), 730
Conservatory of Music (Cin-cinnati), 1174
Conservatory of Music (Grand Rapids, Mich.), 748

Conservatory of Music
(Ithaca, N.Y.), 1005, 1006
Conservatory of Music
(Kansas City, Mo.), 847
Conservatory of Music
(Miami), 248
Conservatory of Music (Phila-
delphia), 1345
Conservatory of Music (St.
Louis), 860-B
Conservatory of Music
(Warren, Pa.), 1387
Constantinides, Dinos, 1580
Constitution Hall (Washing-
ton, D.C.), 226
Conterno, Giovanni E., 1030
Contests and awards, 121,
195-A, 227-B, 227-M, 379,
391, 398, 869, 958, 1061-B,
1133, 1148, 1165, 1233, 1234,
1343, 1359, 1374, 1448, 1477,
1494, 1579, 1646
Contin, Giovanni Batista, 314
Continental Vocalists, 190
Contrabass. See Bass viol
Convent of the Sacred Heart
(St. James Parish, La.), 544
Converse, C. C., 227-F, 317
Converse, Frederick S., 227-D,
227-F, 636, 642, 646, 654,
863, 1018, 1031, 1053, 1338
Converse College, 1425
Converse Hymnal Collection,
534
Conway, Patrick, 618
Conway, Patrick, Band, 618,
976
Conway, Patrick, Military
Band School, 1007
Conway, Patsy, 1006
Conway, Peter, 1395
Cook, B. Consuelo, 268
Cook, Harold, 697
Cook, Josephine P., 82
Cook, Russell Ames, 227-F,
1666
Cook, Will Marion, 226, 268
Cooke, James Francis, 227-F
Cooke, Judd, 195-A
Cooke, Nym, 775
Cooley, Carlton, 227-D
Coolidge, Arlan R., 1404
Coolidge, B. F., 1643
Coolidge, Elizabeth Sprague,
142, 227-B
Coolidge, Elizabeth Sprague,
Foundation, 227-B
Coon, Leland, 227-L
Coon songs, 198, 227-A, 244,
766, 866, 907, 1061-N, 1463
Cooper family papers, 1463
Cooper, E. Marie, 866
Cooper, George, 729, 1040
Cooper, Kate Holmes, 465
Cooper, Maude S., 815
Cooper, William F., 1463
Cooper Library, 1420
Cooper Union for the Ad-
vancement of Science and
Art, 1032
Coopersmith, Jacob Maurice,
729-C
Coosa County (Ala.), 1
Coots, J. Fred, 1611

Copeland, Carroll H., 430
Copland, Aaron, 195-C, 227-B,
227-C, 227-H, 227-M, 535,
800, 907, 1019, 1023, 1030,
1031, 1061-A, 1111, 1222,
1425, 1580
Copley, Richard, 227-F
Copp, Jonathan Shipley, 707
Coppet, Edward J. de, 1053
Copyright, 180, 227-A, 227-J,
227-M, 1270, 1464
Coral Gables (Fla.), 195-C
Corbett, Henry Clay, 514
Cordero, Roqué, 1580
Corgan, D. Leonard, Library,
1392
Corinth (Vt.), 707
Cornelissen, Arnold, 979
Cornelius, Rev. Edward, 432
Cornell College, 481
Cornell University, 227-H,
234, 1005, 1006
Cornet music, 192, 214,
227-J, 625, 665, 914, 942,
1098, 1100, 1236, 1267, 1272,
1291, 1530, 1612
Cornets, 209, 398, 470, 665,
681, 761, 906, 914, 1005. See
also Trumpets
Corning, Bly, 398, 729-A, 744
Corning-Painted Post (N.Y.)
Historical Society, 984
Cornish, John Hamilton, 1141
Cornish, Nellie C., 1577
Cornish music, 1612
Cornish School of Allied Arts,
1577
Cornplanter, Jesse, 1327
Coronation Hymnal, 717
Corporate music ensembles,
163, 305, 618, 730, 737, 815,
887, 1001, 1283, 1284, 1385,
1463
Corpus Christi, 334
Corridos, 33, 227-L, 1500
Cortissoz, Royal, 1053
Cortland County (N.Y.) His-
torical Society, 985
Cory, Eleanor, 195-C
Cory, Sarah F., 364, 940
Coryell, Marian, 739
Cosandy, Evelyn Graber, 815
Cosby, William, 1061-M
Coscia, Silvio, 646
Cossack, Don, Chorus, 1061-F
Cost, Herbert W., 860-D,
860-H
Costa, Wilhelm da, 896
Cothren, William, 181
Cotillions, 582
Cotlow, Marilyn, 1061-F
Cotner College of Religion, 888
Cotten, Elizabeth, 1445
Cotter, Joseph S., Sr., 268
Cotton, John, 636, 1541
Country and western music,
42, 49, 73, 74, 320, 406, 411,
495, 523, 557, 592, 747, 831,
927, 1170, 1174, 1234, 1430,
1438, 1442, 1454, 1455, 1469,
1472, 1477, 1480, 1525. See
also Hillbilly music
Country Dance & Song
Society of America, 1033

Country Music Foundation,
1455
Country Music Hall of Fame,
1455
Couper, Mildred, 227-F
Couret, William, 555
Course, Ray la, 1656
Covell, William King, 700
Covenanters, 1560
Coventry (Conn.), 192
Covert, Bernard, 1527
Covington (Ill.), 612
Cowboy songs, 32, 33, 107,
162, 687, 860-F, 1261, 1430,
1437, 1477
Cowell, Henry, 36, 76, 83, 87,
142, 227-C, 357, 398, 1031,
1040, 1061-A, 1061-B,
1061-D, 1061-J, 1080, 1108,
1111, 1301, 1420, 1580, 1666
Cowell, Henry, Music Center,
87
Cowell, Sidney Robertson
(Mrs. Henry), 50, 227-L
Cowley County (Kan.) His-
torical Society, 520
Cox, Ellen, M., 544
Cox, Henry Givin, 475
Cox, John Harrington, 1591
Coxe, Esther Maria, 314
Crabtree, Abram, Jr., 1141
Crabtree, Lotta, 36
Craft, George A., 486, 487
Cragin, G. Marshall, 866
Craig, Helen M., 227-A
Crain, W. H., Collection, 1477
Cramer, G. H. D., 1418
Cranch family, 643
Crandall, Frank M., 1611
Crandall Collection, 1143
Crandell, Alberta, 1616
Crane, Frederick, 474
Crane, Helen C., 227-D,
1061-A
Crane, Julia, 1104
Crane School of Music, 1104
Cranmer, Jean Chappell, 156
Cravath, Paul D., 1052
Cravens, Jane, 1463
Cravens, Lydia, 1463
Cravens (i.e., Helms-Cravens)
Library, 523
Cravner, William Charles, 15
Crawford, D., & Company,
860-K
Crawford, J. R., Theatre
Collection, 195-B
Crawford, J. W. ("Captain
Jack"), 398
Crawford, John Wallace, 157
Crawford, Rebekah, 227-H,
636
Crawford, Richard, 726
Crawford, Ruth Porter (Mrs.
Charles Seeger), 227-C,
227-F, 1481, 1580
Crawford, William Robert,
940
Crawford County (Ill.), 391
Crawfordsville (Ind.), 425
Creamer Hymnology Collec-
tion, 933
Creatore, Giuseppe, 195-C,
860-B

Creatore's Band, 618
Creek Indians, 1255
Creighton, John O., 831
Creighton Theater, 887
Cremona violins, 730
Creole music, 253, 545, 563,
860-C, 1118
Creston, Paul, 227-F, 1053,
1580
Cretan music, 1188
Crist, Bainbridge, 142, 227-F
Critchlow family, 102
Critchlow, Barbara N., 102
Critics, 50, 64, 115, 116, 122,
157, 192, 195-A, 227-H, 260,
265, 387, 398, 443, 444, 535,
611, 612, 636, 637, 691,
729-B, 739, 800, 847, 860-D,
876, 907, 916, 1031, 1061-B,
1061-F, 1061-J, 1061-L,
1061-M, 1067, 1093, 1111,
1137, 1143, 1177, 1190, 1270,
1327, 1333, 1355, 1366, 1381,
1416, 1457, 1484, 1520, 1577,
1592, 1611
Croatian-American Singers,
800
Croatian music, 800, 1188
Crockett, Albert Stevens, 1611
Croft, William, 1532
Crofts, Mrs. F. S., 227-F
Cromaine Library, 754
Cromwell, John, 1611
Crone, A. J., 776
Cronmiller, Thomas, 612
Crook, General, House, 879
Crook, John, 1521
Crook County (Ore.) Histori-
cal Society, 1275
Crosby, Bing, 465, 610, 1450,
1579, 1583
Crosby, Bob, 406, 1646
Crosby, Fanny, 306, 404, 1465
Crosby, George, 815
Crosby, John, 195-C
Crosby, Mary Inglehart, 1477
Crosby Brown Collection of
Musicians' Portraits, 1051
Crosby Library, 1579
Crosby's Opera House, 314,
315, 1061-M
Cross, Burnett, 195-C
Cross, Michael Hurley, 1333
Crouch, Frederick Nichols,
227-G, 1111, 1301
Crouch, Kenneth Elwood, 896,
1541
Crouch Music Library, 1517
Crouse, John Robert, 729-B
Crouse, Russel, 1611
Crow Wing County (Minn.)
Historical Society, 776
Crowell, Rhoda, 654
Crowninshield, Ethel, 110
Crozer Theological Seminary,
1110
Cruikshank, Martha, 800
Cruser, Sarah, 940
Crystal Gardens (Victoria,
British Columbia), 1665
Cue sheets. See Silent-film
music
Cueny, Alma, 860-D
Cueny, Elizabeth, 860-D

Cuesta, Arroyo de la, 71
Culbert, Ruth, 907
Cullen, Countee, 268, 1457
Cullinane collection, 1490
Culmell, Joaquin Nin, 1580
Culver Military Academy
    (Plymouth, Ind.), 443
Cumberland (Md.?), 654
Cumberland Methodist
    Church (Charleston, S.C.),
    1418
Cumberland Mountains, 1463
Cummin, John W., 686
Cumming, John, 766
Cummings, Michael, 680
Cummins, Lucile, 1270
Cumpson, Harry, 977
Cunningham, Arthur, 729-C,
    1457
Cunningham, Keith, 21
Curley Theatre, 302
Currier, Donald, 195-C
Currier & Ives, 624
Curry, Arthur Mansfield, 265
Curry, Beth, 1591
Curtis, Carlos, 1193
Curtis, Charles William, 1005
Curtis, Ford E., 1375
Curtis, Harriet R., 1375
Curtis, Herbert, 319
Curtis, John, 1338
Curtis, Marie, 766
Curtis, Moses Ashley, 1141
Curtis, Natalie, 1666
Curtis, Samuel R., 860-C
Curtis, Vera, 654
Curtis Institute of Music,
    179, 671, 1331
Curtis String Quartet, 1344
Curtiss, John F., 195-A
Curtiss, Minna, 1053
Cushing, Stella Marek, 1061-F
Cushman, Charlotte, 860-D
Cushman, Charlotte, Club,
    1332
Custer, Gen. George, 1435,
    1436, 1437
Custis family, 314
Custis, George Washington
    Parke, 1560
Cutler, Henry Stephen, 195-A
Cutter, Abram Edmands, 636
Cykler, Edmund A., 1270
Cylinders, 9, 17, 26, 37, 41, 50,
    61, 77, 82, 84, 105, 123, 126,
    133, 141, 142, 144, 156, 163,
    164, 167, 170, 171, 203, 210,
    227-L, 234, 237, 251, 277,
    285, 290, 299, 320, 344, 353,
    379, 395, 401, 406, 409, 471,
    472, 491, 493, 498, 502, 520,
    530, 545, 556, 568-B, 600,
    608, 618, 619, 620, 693, 730,
    733, 735, 736, 743, 744, 749,
    750, 764, 773, 774, 788, 792,
    801, 815, 820, 821, 823, 824,
    853, 893, 900, 921, 924, 932,
    934, 942, 945, 954, 964, 968,
    976, 987, 988, 991, 992, 1006,
    1017, 1041, 1061-J, 1079,
    1085, 1093, 1103, 1120, 1127,
    1129, 1132, 1143, 1146, 1155,
    1170, 1193, 1204, 1206, 1217,
    1221, 1223, 1246, 1248, 1253,

1268, 1272, 1275, 1292, 1353,
    1385, 1395, 1424, 1428, 1429,
    1431, 1433, 1442, 1483, 1488,
    1502, 1507, 1519, 1528, 1530,
    1531, 1534, 1546, 1571, 1578,
    1611, 1622, 1624, 1631, 1633,
    1640, 1642, 1645, 1655, 1659.
    See also Mechanical and
    electrical music-instrument
    discs, cylinders, and other
    media
Cyphers, Marie, 1364
Czech music, 398, 817, 895,
    1176, 1352, 1433, 1512, 1608
Czechoslovakia, 1176
Czopiwsky, Peter, 800

D

Dabney, Wendell Phillips,
    1172
Dacosta, Charles, 1551
Da Costa, Wilhelm, 896
Dacotah Prairie Museum, 1428
Dacus Library, 1423
Dahl, Ingolf, 76, 85, 227-D,
    227-F, 1580
Dahle, John, 802, 803, 808
Dahms, Walter, 227-F
Daib, Walter, 856
Dailey, Dan, 1487
Dailey, J. G., 356
Dakota Indians, 815
Dakota State College, 1429
Dakotah Prairie Museum, 1428
Daland, Mary Elizabeth, 1615
Daland, William C., 1615
d'Albert, Eugène, 195-A
Dalhart, Vernon, 495
Dalkullan Shop (Chicago), 339
Dalkullans Sångbök, 339
Dallas, 36, 1174, 1462, 1488,
    1501
Dallas Historical Society, 1483
Dallas Theatre History, collec-
    tion, 1484
Dallas Theological Seminary,
    1485
Daly, Augustin, 915, 1031
Daly's Theatre (New York),
    1031
Damenchor. See Women's
    choruses
Damenchor (Mayville, Wis.),
    1613
Dameron (i.e., Williams-
    Dameron) family, 1155
Dameron, Josie, 1155
D'Amico, Hank, 989
D'Amico, Marty, 989
Dammert, Mrs., 862
Damon, S. Foster, 1402
Damrich, Mrs. John J., 10
Damrosch family, 227-B, 349
Damrosch, Frank, 227-B,
    1061-A, 1061-F, 1580
Damrosch, Leopold, 227-B,
    1046, 1053, 1061-A, 1061-B,
    1083, 1174, 1338, 1580
Damrosch, Margaret Blaine
    (Mrs. Walter), 227-M
Damrosch, Walter, 84, 142,
    227-B, 227-L, 349, 729-E,
    907, 995, 1018, 1031, 1053,

1061-A, 1061-B, 1061-F,
    1063, 1111, 1177, 1301, 1359
Damrosch Music Club
    (El Reno, Okla.?), 1250
Dana, H. Douglass, 721
Danbury (Conn.) Scott-Fanton
    Museum and Historical
    Society, 174
Dance, 2, 16, 17, 26, 34, 50, 52,
    60, 75, 92, 115, 122, 156, 162,
    176, 184, 185, 195-A, 209,
    220, 223, 227-D, 227-G, 230,
    244, 265, 274, 285, 290, 305,
    334, 336, 341, 351, 398, 406,
    411, 438, 443, 478, 577, 582,
    586, 587, 624, 631, 654, 659,
    681, 699, 701, 704, 707,
    729-A, 729-D, 735, 736, 739,
    750, 761, 794, 795, 800, 815,
    846, 884, 907, 918, 939, 940,
    943, 976, 980, 1022, 1033,
    1034, 1059, 1061-K, 1077,
    1094, 1101, 1111, 1123, 1146,
    1161, 1234, 1252, 1267, 1295,
    1327, 1328, 1338, 1340, 1372,
    1375, 1402, 1418, 1435, 1461,
    1511, 1520, 1530, 1534, 1541,
    1550, 1558, 1560, 1576, 1577,
    1620, 1646, 1651, 1652, 1665.
    See also Ballet; and specific
    dance forms
Dance band music, 1, 17, 28,
    150, 151, 227-J, 228, 229,
    265, 349, 398, 406, 433, 441,
    457, 511, 568-B, 719, 729-D,
    736, 778, 793, 994, 1087,
    1111, 1166, 1194, 1206, 1270,
    1350, 1359, 1395, 1433, 1480,
    1488, 1519, 1543, 1576, 1577,
    1611, 1646. See also Band
    music
Dance bands (materials about),
    1, 406, 719, 730, 737, 747,
    798, 807, 989, 1059, 1124,
    1143, 1178, 1188, 1198, 1208,
    1487, 1501. See also Bands
Dance Films Association, Inc.,
    1034
Dancing Assembly (Philadel-
    phia), 1338
Daniel, Cyrus, 1459
Daniel, Harlan, 320
Daniel, Margaret Truman, 843
Daniel, Mrs. Mell (Minna
    Lederman), 195-C, 227-F,
    227-H, 1061-B
Daniel, Oliver, 1108
Daniels, Charles N., 739
Daniels, Mabel Wheeler, 227-F,
    398, 636, 646, 654, 1573
Danielson, Betsy, 1111
Danish Dramatic Club
    (Seattle), 1577
Danish Lutheran Church, 330
Danish music, 50, 316, 330,
    396, 464, 748, 791, 801, 845,
    878, 894, 1235, 1577
Danks, Hart P., 1040
Dann, Hollis, 227-F
Dannreuther, Gustav, 1107
Dansereau, H., 544
Danvers (Mass.), 701
Danville (Va.) Historical
    Society, 1542

Da Ponte, Lorenzo, 729-E,
    1111
Darby, Mrs. John F., 860-D
Darden Family Papers, 1463
Darensbourg, Joe, 68
Dargan-Carver Library, 1462
Darien (Ga.), 227-K
Darke County (Ohio) His-
    torical Society, 1208
Darley, Francis T. S., 1301,
    1343
Darling, David, 50
"Darling Nellie Gray," 1242
Darlington, William, 1059
Darlington County (S.C.) His-
    torical Commission, 1421
Darlington District (S.C.), 1420
Darmstadt (Germany), 195-A
Darst, W. Glen, 1477
Dartmouth College, 907
Daughters of the American
    Revolution, 226, 860-K
Daughters of the Republic of
    Texas, 1510
Davenny, Ward, 195-C
Davenport, Marcia, 227-M
David, Hans T., 1168
David, Mack, 85
David, Russ, 349
Davidoff, Ch., 281
Davids, R. B., 227-K
Davidson, James F., 837
Davidson, Levette, 161
Davidson, William Fuson, 815
Davidson Collection, 256
Davidson Theatre, 1624
Davies, W. P., 1165
Dávila, Rafael Balseiro, 1652
Davis, Albert, 1477
Davis, Arthur Kyle, Jr., 227-L
Davis, Auguste, 555, 568
Davis, Charlotte Jones, 636
Davis, Eleanor, 838
Davis, Evelyn, 1261
Davis, Gussie Lord, 226, 268
Davis, Harwell Goodwin,
    Library, 3
Davis, Jessie Bartlett, 314
Davis, John W., 1591
Davis, Katherine Kennicott,
    716, 847
Davis, Katherine Wallace, 854
Davis, Kay, 659
Davis, Lionel B., 795
Davis, Richard Bingham, 940
Davis, Ruby Shepperd, 1061-N
Davis, William Butler, 190
Davis, William James, 314
Davis, William Thomas, 698
Davis Entertainers of the
    Demoss Family Band of
    Oregon, 1268
Davise, Hugo, 68, 84
Davison, Archibald T., 227-F,
    636, 654
Davison, Martha Taylor, 1148
Davison-Belknap collection, 535
Dawes, Charles G., 317, 357
Dawes, Elizabeth F., 1327
Dawson, Carley, 1270
Dawson, Jane, 860-F
Dawson, Lois (Mrs. Neil), 487
Dawson, Mary Cardwell,
    227-F, 1061-N

Dawson, Thomas F., 156
Dawson, William Levi, 14, 195-B, 226, 729-C
Day, Ella Hudson, 1502
Day, Henry, Collection of Hymnology, Linguistics, and Ecclesiastical Law, 1070
Day, John Calvin, 184
Day, Katherine Seymour, 184
Day, Thomas D., 860-H
Day, Willard G., 612
Daybooks, 572, 707, 860-K, 985, 1052. *See also* Commonplace books; Lyrics of songs
Daynes, Joseph John, 1521
Dayton (Ohio), 432, 951
Dayton and Montgomery County Public Library, 1199
Dayton, University of, 1202
Deagan, J. C., Co., 321
Deakins, Duane D., 1127
Deal, Bruce E., 97
Dealers. *See* Merchants
Dean, Flora Ann, 815
Dean, Harry Arnold, 1521
Dean, Joseph H., 1521
Dean, Julia, 860-K
Deane, Julia Freeman, 356
De Angelis, Jefferson, 1061-L
Dearborn (Mich.) Historical Museum, 735
DeBaillou, Katherine Cowen, 265
DeBar, Ben, 860-K
DeBar's Opera House, 860-D
De Begnis, Giuseppe, 636
deBellis, Frank V., Collection, 123
DeBruyn, John W., 244
De Burgos, Francis, 1477
Debussy, Claude, 646
Decatur (N.D.), 761
Decca records, 104, 227-L
De Coppet, Edward J., 1054
De Cordova, LaUna Skinner, 1477
Dedham (Mass.) Historical Society, 660
De Donath, Jenö, 1338
Dee, Sylvia, 637
"Deep River," 1053, 1298
Deerfield (Mass.), 695
Defauw, Désiré, 227-F, 1580
Deger, Urban, Collection, 1202
De Gogorza, Emilio, 1054
DeGolyer Institute for American Studies, 1487
DeGraff, Grace Clark, 465
Deis, Carl, 227-D, 227-F
deJahn, Agnes G., 60
DeJong, Gerritt, Jr., 1520
DeKalb County (Ill.), 357
Dekalb County (Mo.) Historical Society, 850
De Koven, Reginald, 142, 227-D, 227-F, 712, 729, 1031, 1054, 1061-A, 1338, 1573, 1577, 1580, 1612
De Lacey, Zdenka Cerny, 314
De Laguna, Frederica, 1327
De Lamarter, Eric, 227-D, 227-F, 317, 334, 1046, 1111
Delaney, Robert, 1031, 1111

Delaney, William, 977
Delany, John O'Fallon, 860-D
De Lapouyade, Robert, Collection, 544
Delaware Division of Historical and Cultural Affairs, 210
Delaware Harmony, 216
Delaware Historical Society, 215
Delaware Regimental Band, Ninth, 214
Delaware, University of, 213
Delaware (River) Valley, 1333
Delaware (Ohio), 1244
Delay, Mike, 68
Delius, Frederick, 245, 246, 1580, 1671
Delius, Jelka Rosen, 214
Delius Trust, 1671
Deliz, Monserrate, 1650
Deller, Walter, 349
Dello Joio, Norman, 195-C, 227-D, 227-F, 1580
Delmark Records, 322
Del Marmol, Mrs. Alfonso, 549
DeLong, Richard P., 1486
Delord, Frances, 1101
Delord (i.e., Kent-Delord) House Museum, 1101, 1102
Del Puente, Giuseppe, 1053
Delta Omicron, 1176
Delta Queen (riverboat), 523
Demarest, Mary Lee, 1465
De Maria, Rosolino, 206
De Marsan, H., 1402
Deming, Adelaide, Collection, 188
Deming, O. V., 1518
DeMoss, James, 1268
DeMoss Concert Entertainers, 1270
DeMoss Family Bards, 1268
DeMoss Springs (Ore.), 1270
Dempster, William R., 1111
Den Akker, Nancy C. van, 570
Dencke, Jeremias, 1161, 1285
Denis, Ruth St., 84
Denison, Ella Strong, Library, 57
Denkmann Memorial Library, 386
Dennée, Charles Frederick, 227-B, 646
Dennof, Ben, 1111
Denny, William D., 227-D
Densmore, Benjamin, 815
Densmore, Frances, 82, 227-F, 227-L, 234, 804, 805, 815
Densmore, John Hopkins, 317
Denson-Parris Sacred Harp Singers, 1459
Dent County (Mo.) Historical Society, 867
Denton, Carl, 1274
Denver, 150, 164, 165, 168, 171, 235, 334
Denver Männerchor, 157
Denver Post Summer Operas, 156
Denver Public Library, 157
Denver Symphony Orchestra, 157

Denver, University of, 161
De Pachman, Vladimir, 227-F, 636, 1193
De Pasquale, Joseph, 227-F
De Pasquali, Bernice, 672
De Pasquali, Salvatore, 672
De Paul University, 323
De Paur, Leonard, 227-F
De Pauw University, 418
Derby (Conn.), 201
Derby (Conn.) Public Library, 175
Derlip, John R. van, 815
De Rubertis, Nazarene, 504
DeRyke, DeLores ("Fiddling De"), 884
De Saisset Art Gallery and Museum, 133
Des Moines (Iowa), 1031
Des Moines (Iowa) Public Library, 463
Des Moines County (Iowa) Historical Society, 455
De Sola, Abraham, 1174
Dessenbach Orchestra, 1111
Dessoff, Margarethe, 227-F
Destinn, Emmy, 61, 1111
Déthier, Édouard, 1053
Déthier, Gaston, 1053
de Treville, Yvonne, 860-D, 1061-F
Detroit (Mich.), 544, 729-B, 800, 1024, 1069, 1174
Detroit Conservatory of Music, 739
Detroit Federation of Musicians, 737
Detroit Institute of Arts, 738
Detroit News, 739
Detroit Opera Company, 739
Detroit Public Library, 739
Detroit Symphony Orchestra, 737, 739, 740
Detroit Symphony Society, 729-B, 739
Dett, R. Nathaniel, 226, 227-F, 268, 743, 1061-A, 1091, 1111, 1187, 1222, 1546, 1666
Detterer, Pauline, 1285
Detwiler, Lotte Lenya Weill, 1073
Deutsch, Adolf, 1646
Deutsch, Babette, 866
Deutsches Mandolin Club, 1172
DeVany, Aline Sue, 314
Deville, Edward, 171
Devincent, Sam, 411
Devol, Frank, 1646
Devon, Lewis, 1333
De Voto, Alfred, 1080
Devries, Rosa, 544
DeWeese, Alice Christine (Towne), 887
De Windt, Clara, 654
Dewing, Florence T., 761
De Witt, Isabel, 195-C
DeWitt, Mary Mildred Zick, 841
Dewitt Historical Society of Tompkins County (N.Y.), 1006
Dexter, Eleazer, 1530
Dexter, Julius, 1172

Dexter Cabin, 169
d'Hardelot, Guy, 1053
Diaghilev, Sergei, 122
Diamond, David, 221, 227-D, 227-F, 646, 977, 1031, 1111, 1148
Diapason, 105, 346
diBonaventura, Sam, 195-C
"Di Capi de Confucius," 1596
Dichter, Harry, 398, 889, 1333, 1339
Dick, Marcel, 227-D
Dicke, Lawrence, Collection, 315
Dickens, Hazel, 1445
Dickinson family, 1338
Dickinson, Clarence, 227-F
Dickinson, Clarence, Collection, 825
Dickinson, Edward, 1031, 1222, 1359
Dickinson, Emily, 195-B, 1425
Dickinson, George Sherman, 1107
Dickinson, Helen, 825
Dickinson, June M., 1011
Dickinson, Peter, 68
Dickinson College, 1287
Dickinson County (Kan.) Historical Society, 491
Dickore, Marie Paula, 1172
Dickson, William B., 940
Dido and Aeneas, 227-M
Diegueno music, 116
Diehl, Katherine S., 1477
Diehn, Friedrich Ludwig, 1553
Dieter, Wilhelm F., 850
Dieterick, Milton, 1270
Dietz, Howard, 227-D, 227-F, 1024, 1055, 1061-B
Dignam, Walter, 914
Digriam, Mary Alice, 1061-F
Diller, Angela, 227-F
Diller's Cornet Septet, 1005
Dillon family, 84
Dillon, Fannie Charles, 84, 227-D, 227-F, 1666
Dillon, William Austin, 985
Dillon, William A., Collection, 1006
Dilsner, Laurence, 227-D
Dimitroff, Celesta V., 984
Dimitroff, Lucienne Bloch, 63
d'Indy, Vincent, 639
Dingwall, Iva Andrus, 815
Di Pirani, Eugenio, 1053
Dippel, Andreas, 1053
The Disappointment, 1544
Disciples of Christ, 368, 422, 423, 434, 1456, 1589
Disciples of Christ, National Headquarters, 422
Disney, Walt, Archives, 54
Disney, Walt, Music Company, 54
Disney, Walt, Studios, 1177
District of Columbia, 612, 721, 815, 1111, 1426, 1477
District of Columbia Public Library, 223
Diton, Carl R., 226, 268, 741
Ditson, Oliver, 227-F, 227-G, 721, 916, 1298, 1333
Dix, John Adams, 1059

"Dixie," 11, 531, 558, 571, 1036, 1040
Dixon, John, Library, 930
Dixon, Roland, 227-L
Doak, Henry Melvil, 1463
Doan Memorial, 333
Doane, George Washington, 967
Doane, William H., 227-D, 1109, 1176
Dobbs, Mary B. Griffith, 266
Dobie, Charles Caldwell, 50
Dobie, James Frank, 1477
Dobson, Tom, 646
Dockstader minstrel troupe, 1333
"The Doctor and the Squire," 707
Dodge, John Wilson, 265
Dodge, Mabel Bourne Thompson, 1274
Dodge, Mary Mapes, 314
Dodge, May Hewes, 265
Dodge, Ossian E., 1527
Dodge, Robert G., Library, 647
Dodge Autograph Collection, 798
Dodge County (Neb.) Historical Society, 880
Dodridge, Philip, 1465
Dodson, Marion, 612
Dodson, Owen Vincent, 226
Doerner, Julius, 398
Dohnányi, Ernö, 729-E, 1580, 1670
Dohnányi, Mrs. Ernö, 227-F
Dolan, Robert Emmett, 1646
Dolan, W. O., 227-D
Dolmetsch, Arnold, 1333
Dolson, Carl ("Pappy"), 1487
Dominican College, 129
Don, Max, 95
Donahey, William, 1611
Donaldson, L. S., Co., 815
Donath, Jenö de, 1338
Donato, Anthony, 357, 1111
"The Done-Over Tailor," 612
Donelson, Bettie Mizell, 1463
Donnelley Library, 366
Donnelly, Joseph, 1172
Donner (i.e., Moses-Donner) Collection, 29
Donovan, Richard F., 195-A, 227-F, 1580
Doob, Leonard, 195-C
Doran Collection, 1338
D'Oranano, Mrs. A. Colonna, 1560
Dorati, Antal, 195-C, 227-F
Dorchester (Mass.), 707
Dorr, William Ripley, 132
Dorris, Jonathan Truman, Museum, 540
Dorset (Vt.), 1095
Dorsey, Tommy, 227-F, 610, 1124, 1270
Dorson, Richard, Collection, 406
Dossenbach Orchestra, 1111
Dossert, Frank C., 1061-F
Doster, Irma, 498
Douai, Adolf, 1477
Double bass music, 636
Dougherty, Celius, 227-F

Douglas, Bessie P., 815
Douglas, Charles Winfred, 157, 235
Douglas, George Perkins, 815
Douglas Collection, 235
Douglas County (Kan.) Historical Society, 503
Douglas County (Neb.) Historical Society, 879
Douglas County (Wis.) Historical Museum, 1633
Douglass College, 939
Dover (Ohio), 1161, 1285
Dover Historical Society, 1204
Dover-Foxcroft (Me.), 577
Doveren, Jo van, 379
Døving, Carl, 813
Dowagiac (Mich.), 761
Dowling, Benjamin, 701
Downes, Olin, 195-A, 227-F, 260, 265, 1053, 1359
Downing, L. J., 354
Downs, Alice E., 406
Downs, Joseph, Manuscript Collection, 217
D'Oyly Carte Opera Company, 1053
Dragon, Carmen, 1646
Dramatic music. See Opera; Operetta and musical comedy; Theater music
Draper, Ruth, 1053
Draper, Walter A., 1176
Draughon, Ralph P., Library, 1
Dreer, Ferdinand Julius, Collection, 1338
Dreger, Alvin, 7
Dreger, Oscar, 7
Dreiser family, 406
Dreiser, Theodore, 1352
Dresel, Otto, 398, 636, 1338
Dresser, Louise, 406
Dresser, Marcia von, 646, 1061-M
Dresser, Paul, 227-F, 406, 450, 1352
Dressler, John, 227-D
Dressler, William, 1477
Drew County (Ark.) Historical Society, 41
Drew University Library, 933
Drexel, Joseph, 1061-D
Dreyfus, Emma, 860-J
Driggs, Frank, 195-C
Driggs, William King, 1520
Drinker family, 1338
Drinker, Henry S., 227-F, 1333
Drinker, Sophie, 692
Drinker Library of Choral Music, 1333
Drinking songs, 65, 406
Driscoll, J. Francis, 227-A, 334
Driver, 701
Droescher, Georg, 227-B
Dromgoole, Edward, 1141
Droop, Edward H., 227-G
Druckman, Jacob, 195-C
Drugs, 119
Drum and bugle corps, 1598
Drum and fife corps. See Fife and drum corps
Drum corps, 577
Drum manufacturers, 321, 1395

Drummond, Alexander M., Papers, 1005
Drums, 191, 321, 653, 671, 814, 1639. See also Percussion
Drury, Elizabeth, 391
Drysdale, Anna Ludwig, 568
Dubensky, Arcady, 227-F
Dublin (Ireland), 244
Dubuque County (Iowa) Historical Society, 467
Duchin, Eddy, 1646
Duckwitz, Dorothy, 819
Ducommun, Helen, 478
Dudley, Bayard Turner Gross, Collection, 1498
Dueño, Colón, Braulio, 1651
Düring, Charles A. A., 1193
Düring, Heinrich J. G., 1193
Duffield, Ernest F., 1206
Duffield, George, 1465
Duffield, June, 1206
Duffy, J. J., 195-A
Duke, James B., 1422
Duke, John Woods, 691
Duke, Vernon, 207, 227-F, 1053
Duke University, 1143
Dukelsky, Vladimir (Vernon Duke), 207, 227-F, 1053
Dukes County (Mass.) Historical Society, 663
Dulcimers, 271, 980, 988, 1234
Duluth (Minn.), 800, 815, 1633
The Dumbells (Toronto), 1662
Dumler, Martin D., 1176
Dumont, Frank, 977
Dumont's Minstrels, 1333
Dunavan, Joseph M., 314
Dunbar Brothers, 917
Dunbar, Elijah, 544
Dunbar, Henry Ware, 917
Dunbar, James Munroe, 917
Dunbar, Paul Lawrence, 227-F, 1193
Dunbar, Quincy Adams, 917
Duncan, Isadora, 122
Duncan, James, 157
Duncan, Joseph Charles, 122
Duncan (Okla.) Public Library, 1247
Dunham, Katherine, 227-F, 305
Dunkley, Ferdinand, 552, 1061-M, 1137
Dunlap, William, 654, 1059
Dunn, James Philip, 227-D
Dunn, Julia Elizabeth, 1061-M
Dunn, Mary, 1477, 1501
Dunn, Rebecca Welty, 498
Dunn (N.C.), 1155
Duns Scotus College, 770
Dunton, Dr. W. R., Jr., 612
Dunwell family, 1059
Duo-Art piano rolls, 1333, 1436
DuPaur, Leonard, 1544
DuPont Library, 1467
Duport, Pierre Landrin, 227-D, 636
Duquesne University, 1058, 1372
Durand, Henry Strong, 195-B
Durand, Sara M., 180
Durang, John, 1352, 1396
Durgin, Dorothy, 897

Durham (N.C.), 1155
Durham (N.H.), 707
Durrell, Josephine, String Quartet, 916
Durrett, Reuben T., Collection, 340
Du Simitière, Pierre Eugène, 1340
Duss, John F., 1298
Dutch music, 227-L, 748, 757, 758, 759, 938, 979, 1008, 1083
Dux, Claire, 1061-F
Dvoracek Memorial Library, 895
Dvořák, Antonín, 815
Dwight, Catherine McFarland (Mrs. George M.), 465
Dwight, John S., 227-F, 636, 642, 1111
Dwight's Journal of Music, 636, 642
Dyas Collection, 1463
Dyche, Mamie Frances (Moser), 1463
Dye, Nathan, 1611
Dye, William Seddinger, 1385
Dye, William S., III, 1385
Dyen, Doris J., 308
Dyer, Charles J., 227-A
Dyer, Samuel, 612
Dyer & Hughes Co., 577
Dyke, Gerald M. van, 1256
Dykema, Peter, 227-F, 1573

E

E-Flat Cornet Windsor (Conn.) Band, 209
Eames, Emma, 227-B, 227-F, 654, 1053, 1222
Earhart, Will, 618, 1359
Earle, Mrs. Samuel L., 11
Earlham College, 444
Early School of Music, 1421
East, Ernest, 1445
East and West Association, 831
East Carolina University, 1149
East End Neighborhood House (Cleveland), 1190
East Frisian music, 398
East Greenwich (R.I.), 1407
East Haddam (Conn.), 192
East Haddam (Conn.) Historical Society, 176
East Jaffrey (N.H.), 1095
East Orange (N.J.), 1190
East Tennessee Historical Society, 1447
East Tennessee State University, 1445
East Windsor (Conn.?), 707
Eastchester (N.Y.), 406
Eastern Kentucky University, 540
Eastern Mennonite College, 1547
Eastern Music Camp (Sidney, Me.), 576
Eastern Orthodox church, 195-B, 760. See also Greek Orthodox church
Eastern Trails Museum, 1264
Eastern U.S., 1662

Eastern Washington State Historical Society, 1578
Eastham, Clark, 739
Eastman, Nikki, 1061-L
Eastman School of Music, 364, 1031, 1111, 1666
Eastman Theater (Rochester, N.Y.), 1005, 1111
Eastmond, Elbert H., 1520
Easton, Florence, 1053
Easton Area (Pa.) Public Library, 1290
The Easy Instructor, 729-A, 970, 1017
Eaton, Edward O., 544
Eaton, Quaintance, 636
Ebenezer (N.Y.), 453
Eberhart, Constance, 1487
Eberhart, Nelle Richmond, 887
Eberle, George, 719
Eccles, John, 741
Eckert, Louis, 553
Eckford Cornet Band, 761
Eckhard, Jacob, 1418, 1420
Eckhardt, Carl Conrad, 150
Eckstein, Louis, 815
Eckstorm, Fannie (Hardy), 592
Economy Village, 1281
Eddy, Clarence, 227-F, 1111
Eddy, Mary Olive, 1185
Eddy, Nelson, 227-E
Eden Publishing House, 1161
Edgar, Marjorie, 815
Edgar, William Crowell, 815
Edgecombe, David, 180
Edinburgh (Scotland), 334
Edison, Thomas A., 234, 395, 744, 766, 954, 1031, 1061-J, 1246, 1360
Edison, Thomas A., Foundation Re-recording, Laboratory, 1127
Edison Co., 133, 163, 164, 203, 290, 300, 370, 398, 409, 471, 476, 491, 493, 520, 608, 619, 693, 730, 736, 744, 800, 820, 821, 921, 932, 934, 945, 954, 968, 1006, 1103, 1120, 1127, 1129, 1132, 1146, 1223, 1246, 1268, 1272, 1275, 1278, 1410, 1424, 1429, 1431, 1471, 1502, 1519, 1522, 1530, 1531, 1571, 1611, 1631, 1633, 1640, 1642
Edison Fund, 37
Edison Institute, 736
Edison National Historic Site, 954
Edmonds, Shepard N., 227-F
Edmundson, Garth, 227-D, 1356
Edson, William, 1006
Edwards, Alice M., Collection, 477
Edwards, Gus, 747
Edwards, John, Memorial Foundation, 74
Edwards, Julian, 227-C, 317, 1061-D
Edwards, Mae, Collection, 1662
Edwards, Michael, 1124
Edwards Collection, 1046
Eells, Cushing, 180
Effinger, Cecil, 227-D, 227-F

Egan, Robert, 800, 1058
Eggelston-Roach papers, 544
Ehlen, Henry C., 1267
Ehlers, Alice, 84
Ehrlich slotted discs, 493
Eichar, Eugene, 349
Eichberg, Julius, 636
Eichheim, Henry, 227-D, 227-F, 317, 334, 1046
Eichhorn, Hermene Warlick, 1148
Einstein, Alfred, 50, 227-F, 265, 691, 1061-M, 1174, 1580
Eisenhower, Milton S., Library, 610
Eisenhower Library, 624
Eisteddfod festivals, 1132
El Paso (Tex.), 962, 1477
El Paso (Tex.) Public Library, 1489
El Reno (Okla.) Carnegie Library, 1250
Elder, Jacob D., 1352
Eldredge family, 707
Eldridge, Dr. E. F., 166
Eldridge, John, 59
Electric Theater (Saint Joseph, Mo.), 855
Electrical musical instruments. *See* Mechanical musical instruments
Eleutherian Mills-Hagley Foundation, 212
Elie, A. 555
Elie, Justin, 268
Elizabeth, Empress of Austria, 1111
Elk County (Pa.) Historical Society, 1379
Elkader Band, 472
Elkhart (Ind.), 433
Elkins, Kate Felton, 142
Elks Pepaz Band, 1395
Elkus, Albert I., 50
Ellerton, John Lodge, 646
Ellicock, J., 860-E
Elliker, Calvin, 1192
Ellington, Edward Kennedy ("Duke"), 195-C, 226, 406, 1061-A, 1127, 1488
Ellington, Mercer, 195-C
Ellington, Ruth, 195-C
Ellington (Conn.), 180
Ellinwood, Leonard W., 227-F
Elliot, Lewis, and Associates, 1469
Elliot's Academy of Music, 1393
Elliott, Alonzo ("Zo"), 195-A, 913
Ellis, Bruce T., 957
Ellis, Charles, 391
Ellis, Courtney M., 523
Ellis, Capt. Richard, 215
Ellis concerts (Pittsburgh), 1359
Ellis Opera Company, 860-D
Elliston, George, 1172
Ellstein, Abraham, 711
Ellsworth, Col., 315
Ellwood family, 344
Ellwood House Museum, 344
Elman, Mischa, 61, 227-F, 568, 637, 1061-F, 1105

Elmer, Nancy, 215
Elmhurst (Ill.) College, 352
Elmhurst (Ill.) Historical Museum, 353
Elmira (N.Y.) College, 990
Elmore, David, 110
Elmwood Opera House, 669
Elon College, 1144
Elred (Pa.), 618
Elrod, Mark, 623
Elsass, J. Frank, 618
Elson, Arthur, 227-F, 646
Elson, Louis Charles, 227-F, 646, 977, 1111
Elston, Arnold, 1580
Elsworth, John Van Varick, 700
Elwell, Herbert, 227-F, 1181, 1186
Elwes, Gervase, 1053
Ely, Richard T., Memorial Collection, 544
Emergency Committee in Aid of Displaced Foreign Scholars, 1061-M
Emerick, Albert, 1340
Emerson, Alice Edwards, 1005
Emerson, Edith, 1005
Emerson, Ellen, 659
Emerson, Irving, 180
Emerson, Luther O., 701
Emerson, Ralph Waldo, 659
Emerson, Ralph Waldo, Collection, 698
Emerson records, 471
Emerson Gounod Club, 314
Emilio, Manuel, 701
Emmett, Daniel Decatur, 11, 195-B, 227-F, 314, 729-A, 1193, 1195, 1541, 1639
Emmitsburgh (Md.), 729-A
Emory, Kenneth Pike, 285
Emory, Millie, 398
Emory University, 183, 269
Emporia State University, 498
Empress Hotel (Victoria, British Columbia), 1665
Emrick, Paul Spotts, 446
Enders, Harvey, 1666
Endicott, F. Monroe, 1402
Endo, Akira, 68
Endress, John P., 334
Enesco, Georges, 227-D
Enfield (Conn.), 195-A
Engel, Carl, 227-D, 227-E, 265, 646, 1031, 1659, 1666
Engel, Daniel, 1177
Engel, Lehman, 195-C, 227-F, 1040, 1544
Engel, Lehman, Collection, 828
Engelbrecht, Jacob, 621
Engelman, John B., 721
Engels, Harry, 1533
England, 268, 642, 849, 1190, 1683
Engle, W. H., 314
Engles, Hugo F., 1229
English, Granville, 1573
English music, 125, 129, 224, 227-G, 227-M, 245, 284, 406, 425, 729-E, 810, 938, 1005, 1070, 1528, 1612. *See also* Anglo-American music; England

English Theatre and Opera House, 427
Engraved plates for music, 60, 348, 794, 862, 868, 970, 1242
Engravers and printers of music, 76, 217, 638, 721, 866, 1112. *See also* Publishers
Enid (Okla.), 398
Enos, Sargeant Joseph, 214
Enright, William W., 1565
Ensemble of the Red Army, 1611
Ephemera. *See* particular forms, i.e., Postcards, Posters, Programs
Ephrata (Pa.), 227-G, 350, 380, 946, 948, 1031, 1061-M, 1116, 1299, 1302, 1319, 1333, 1334, 1338
Episcopal Church, Historical Society, 1474
Episcopal Diocese of Chicago, 324
Episcopal Divinity School, 653
Episcopalian music, 235, 324, 358, 440, 552, 567, 612, 653, 709, 1111, 1141, 1171, 1228, 1352, 1358, 1406, 1467, 1474, 1482, 1529, 1541, 1560
Eppert, Carl, 227-D, 227-F, 1624
Epstein, Ephraim M., 1174
Epstein, M. I., 860-F
Erb, John Lawrence, 227-F
Erbe, Ernst Immanuel, 1161
Erbe Collection, 1161
Erck, C. A., 227-D
Erhart, Victor J., 1483
Erie (Pa.), 36
Erie County (Pa.) Historical Society, 1294
Erlanger, A. L., 1061-L
Erlanger Amusement Enterprises, 1061-L
Ernestinoff, Alexander, 427
Ernst, Heinrich Wilhelm, 227-F
Ernst, Runyon G., 1300
Erskine, John, 227-F, 1031, 1183, 1580
Eskimo music, 16, 50, 195, 227-L, 760, 1581
Esperance (N.Y.) Historical Society, 991
Espinosa, Felipe Gutiérrez, 1643
Essex County (Mass.), 701
Essex County (Va.), 1560
Essex Institute, 349, 701
Estes, Carolyn Campbell, 432
Estes, Virgean England, 1477
Estey, J., & Co., 1329
Estonian music, 800
Estrellita (Stella Davenport Jones), 92
Estudios de Música Gustavo Batista, 1653
Ethiopian music. *See* Minstrelsy
Ethnic music. *See* specific ethnic groups; Folk music collections
Etler, Alvin, 227-C, 227-F, 398
Ettel, Mrs. Michael F., 812
Euclid Avenue Opera House, 1190

Eufaula (Ala.) Heritage Association, 5
The Eureka Messenger, 113
Eureka Publishing Co., 113
Eury, Jessie C., Library, 368
Eury, W. L., Appalachian Collection, 711
Euterpe Concerts (Boston), 636
Euterpiad, 1352
Euterpian Society (Allentown, Pa.?), 1280
Evangelical and Reformed Historical Society, 1306
Evangelical Church music, 591, 1059, 1201
Evangelical Covenant Church of America, 325
Evangelical (German) Church, 1306
Evangelical Lutheran Theological Seminary, 1196
Evangelical-United Brethren Church, Central Pennsylvania Conference, Archives, 1287
Evangelical-United Brethren music, 300, 355, 1201, 1287
Evans, Cheryl T., 1449
Evans, David H., 1449
Evans, George, 391
Evans, George T., 36
Evans, John Stark, 1274
Evans, May Garrettson, 606
Evans, Merle, 1594
Evans, Nathaniel, Family Papers, 544
Evanston Public Library, 354
Evanti, Lillian, 227-F, 739
Evelyn, Judith, 1662
Evening Ledger (Philadelphia), 1333
Evens, William, 1359
Everett, Edward, 544
Everett, Eleazar, 729-A
Evergreen House, 606
Ewell, D. Jesse, 227-G
Ewell, Elizabeth S., 1463
Ewell, Richard Stoddert, 1463
Ewen, David, 227-F
Examiner (San Francisco), 122
Excelsior (Mo.), 848
Exeter (N.H.) Brass Band, 901
Exeter (N.H.) Historical Society, 902
Exhibitions. *See* Fairs and expositions
Exposition & Music Hall (St. Louis), 860-E
Eyre, Alice, 1061-M
Eyre, Gardner (Agnes G. de Jahn), 60
Eyre, Lawrence, 1061-M
Ezekiel, Wellington, 1061-F
Ezpinal, Luisa, 30

F

F., W. S., 1232
Fabbri-Mueller, Inez, 50
Fackenthal Library, 1307
Faelten Pianoforte School, 636
Fahnestock, William F., 1116
Fairbank, Janet Ayer, 334
Fairbank, Margaret, 195-C, 1061-J

Fairchild, Blair, 227-D, 227-F, 1053
Fairclough, George Herbert, 815
Fairfax County (Va.) Public Library, 1543
Fairfield Academy, 1001
Fairlamb, James Remington, 646
Fairmont (W.Va.), 1591
Fairs and expositions, 122, 227-L, 234, 314, 315, 334, 460, 646, 681, 701, 729-B, 777, 860-C, 860-J, 1338, 1359, 1534, 1575. *See also* Festivals and pageants
Faith, Percy, 1520
Fake books. *See* Dance band music
Fales Library, 1062
Fall River (Mass.) Historical Society, 664
Fanciulli, Francesco, 1061-A
Fanfares, 228, 230
Fanning, Thomas, 721
Farber, Norma, 646
Farcloh, Anna, 815
Fargo, Milford H., 992
Farly, Job, 379
Farmers' Union (Mont.), 1466
Farmington (Conn.), 184
Farmington (Me.), 660
Farnam, Lynnwood, 227-F, 636, 1331, 1659
Farnam Street Theater, 887
Farnham, Joseph, 628
Farnsworth, Charles H., 1534
Farr, Charles, 195-C
Farr's Band, 947
Farrar, Augusta H., 406
Farrar, Geraldine, 83, 123, 227-B, 227-F, 227-L, 269, 692, 853, 1053, 1061-L, 1061-M, 1139, 1573, 1577
Farwell, Arthur, 227-D, 227-F, 646, 739, 974, 1031, 1061-A, 1061-B, 1061-F, 1080, 1111, 1261
Farwell, Brice, 974
Fashion-show music, 315
Fassett, Stephen, 1061-J
Father Kemp's Old Folks, 612, 699, 708
Father of the Blues, 6, 268
Faulds, David P., 535
Faulk, John H., 1477
Faulkner, Henry, 157
Fauré, Gabriel, 639
Faurot Opera House, 1215
Faust, Tony, & Sons, 860-K
Fay, Charles Norman, 227-F
Fay, Rodman, 227-F
Fearis, John S., 465
Febiger (i.e., Lea and Febiger) Collection, 1338
Federal Music Project. *See* WPA Federal Music Project
Federal Negro Theater Project, 244
Federal Street Theatre (Boston), 636
Federal Theater Project. *See* WPA Federal Theater Project

Federal Writers Project. *See* WPA Federal Writers Project
Federlein, Gottfried H., 84, 227-D
Feehan Memorial Library, 375
Feil, Hans C., 847
Feinberg, Benjamin F., Library, 1102
Feininger, Karl, 1061-M
Feist, Leonard, 195-C
Fekete, Zoltan, 227-F
Feldman, Mary Ann, 815
Feldman, Morton, 68
Felten, Geo. W. B., 406
Felton Institute and Classical Seminary, 215
Fenner, Miss A., 406
Fenwick Library, 1544
Ferber, Edna, 1611
Ferguson, Clarence, 395
Ferguson, Donald N., 800
Ferguson, Kate Lee, 544
Ferguson, Percy, 544
Fergusson family, papers, 1463
Fergusson, William Wallace, 1463
Fermin, Adelin, 1111
Ferrata, Ernest, 546
Ferrata, Giuseppe, 227-D, 546, 568
Ferrer, Thomas, 1546
Ferrer (Otero), Monsita, 1651, 1652
Ferrum Blues Festival, 1445
Ferrum (Va.) College, 1545
Festival Chorus (Charleston, S.C.), 1418
Festivals and pageants, 122, 150, 156, 157, 195-A, 213, 227-L, 230, 234, 241, 244, 263, 290, 305, 310, 314, 315, 334, 337, 354, 362, 363, 391, 398, 406, 460, 481, 488, 490, 505, 509, 522, 523 529, 576, 580, 618, 636, 646, 654, 681, 701, 703, 705, 707, 721, 729-A, 729-B, 748, 769, 770, 777, 782, 800, 854, 860-C, 860-E, 860-J, 860-K, 872, 907, 917, 939, 979, 980, 986, 1005, 1070, 1104, 1111, 1132, 1141, 1148, 1152, 1165, 1168, 1172, 1176, 1188, 1205, 1234, 1251, 1256, 1261, 1266, 1269, 1274, 1338, 1341, 1353, 1359, 1363, 1377, 1418, 1420, 1423, 1439, 1463, 1473, 1477, 1483, 1502, 1510, 1520, 1533, 1534, 1575, 1577, 1591, 1598, 1603, 1613, 1634. *See also* Fairs and expositions
Festivals of American Folklife, 234
Festivals of American Music, 1111
Few, William Preston, 1143
Fewkes, Jesse Walter, 227-L
Feyer, George, 1031
Il Fianciullo del oest, 1061-F
Fickensher, Arthur, 227-F, 1541, 1666
Fiddlers Carnival (Gallatin, Tenn.), 1463

Fiddles, 33, 34, 75, 213, 227-L, 271, 277, 278, 291, 398, 462, 523, 545, 582, 630, 636, 663, 727, 736, 768, 800, 884, 894, 898, 958, 980, 1141, 1188, 1234, 1270, 1364, 1389, 1445, 1463, 1528, 1534, 1600. *See also* Violin
Fiddlin' Powers family, 1444
Fiddling Archive, 884
Fiedler, Arthur, 142, 227-F, 1487
Field, Al G., & Co., Operatic Ministrels, 529
Field, Eugene, 314
Field, Harold, 816
Field, John, 1061-A
Field, Mary Slaughter, 334
Field recordings, 15, 23, 24, 27, 28, 29, 32, 33, 34, 36, 42, 50, 73, 75, 82, 84, 107, 116, 150, 152, 161, 162, 190, 213, 227-K, 227-L, 230, 234, 239, 260, 263, 265, 271, 278, 285, 291, 305, 308, 362, 398, 406, 499, 519, 522, 523, 537, 539, 542, 545, 563, 573, 592, 618, 630, 654, 673, 727, 760, 766, 768, 781, 782, 800, 832, 870, 907, 939, 957, 962, 964, 979, 983, 1005, 1021, 1031, 1061-J, 1061-N, 1076, 1095, 1140, 1141, 1149, 1170, 1185, 1188, 1212, 1255, 1270, 1297, 1327, 1352, 1389, 1392, 1430, 1433, 1445, 1477, 1488, 1518, 1520, 1523, 1525, 1528, 1541, 1545, 1577, 1591, 1596, 1611, 1612. *See also* Folk music collections; Non-commercial recordings
Fields, Lew, 1061-L
Fife, Austin E., and Alta, Collections, 1519, 1523
Fife and drum corps, 176, 178, 191, 1407, 1639. *See also* Drum corps
Fife music, 180, 191, 195-B, 319, 662, 701, 707, 1059, 1352, 1364, 1528, 1639. *See also* Flute music
Fillenger, Madeline James, 820
Fillmore, Henry, 239, 1191
Fillmore Museum, 239
Film music, 51, 54, 68, 83, 84, 85, 89, 90, 111, 116, 133, 227-H, 227-J, 227-L, 244, 269, 371, 394, 398, 433, 476, 624, 691, 796, 847, 1041, 1061-C, 1141, 1177, 1270, 1333, 1350, 1477, 1520, 1611, 1620, 1629, 1646, 1662, 1688. *See also* Silent-film music
Films and video tapes on music subjects, 29, 50, 75, 81, 84, 122, 195-B, 213, 227-B, 227-L, 230, 244, 271, 274, 360, 398, 440, 522, 535, 568-B, 646, 719, 729-C, 777, 803, 957, 983, 1031, 1034, 1041, 1054, 1055, 1056, 1140, 1141, 1152, 1188, 1333, 1372, 1375, 1385, 1430, 1445, 1452, 1455, 1466, 1577, 1594, 1611

Filson Club, 531
Fina, Don, 1606, 1611
Finck, Henry C., 1267
Finck, Henry T., 227-F
Finckel, John Alden, 227-D
Fine, Irving, 227-C, 227-D, 227-F
Fine Art Club (Chicago), 314
Fine Arts Society (Pittsburgh), 1355
Fink Collection, 1176
Finkelstein & Ruben Co., 815
"Finlandia," 458
Finney, Ross Lee, 227-C, 227-F, 691, 739, 1018, 1148, 1580
Finney, Theodore M., 1369
Finney, Theodore M., Music Library, 1375
Finnish-American Historical Archives, 753
Finnish music, 227-L, 636, 753, 777, 779, 781, 782, 795, 800, 815, 821, 1235
Finzel, William, 737
Fiot imprints, 556
Fire, songs about, 544, 624
Firelands Historical Society Museum, 1221
Firemen, 1001
Firestone, Idabelle, Audio Library, 646
Firestone, Marcella Schiller (Mrs. Morris), 1174
Firestone Tire & Rubber Company, 646
Firmin, Edmund, 707
First Baptist Church (Pittsburgh), 1363
First Presbyterian Church (Wilmington, N.C.), 1156
Fischer, Carl, & Co., 682, 1035
Fischer, J., & Bro., 227-G
Fischer, Louise D., 1477
Fischer Collection of Early Vocal Recordings, 561
Fish, Shepard, 643
Fish, Thaddeus, 707
Fishburn Library, 1550
Fisher, John M., 425
Fisher, Norman Z., 574
Fisher, William Arms, 227-F
Fisk, George, 167
Fisk Jubilee Singers, 739, 1179
Fisk University, 1457
Fiske, Dwight, 110
Fiske, Jim, 916
Fiske, John, 718
Fiske, May, 916
Fiske, Minnie Maddern, 227-F
Fitch, Dudley Warner, 465
Fitch, Finley, 1111
Fitch, Lorraine Noel Finley, 1111
Fitch, Theodore, 1111
Fitchburg (Mass.) Historical Society, 665
Fitchburg Public Library, 666, 667
Fitchburg State College, 666, 667
Fitelberg, Jerzy, 227-F
Fitelson, H. William, 195-B
Fithian, Philip Vickers, 1567
Fitzgerald, Bernard, 1477

Fitzgerald, Ella, 637, 1611
FitzSimons, H. T., Company, 326
Fitzwilliam, Sarah Raymond, 302
Five Civilized Tribes Museum, 1255
Flag, songs about, 744. *See also* "The Star-spangled Banner"
Flagg, Marion, 1484
Flagler, Harry Harkness, 227-F, 1053
Flagstad, Kirsten, 118, 1061-F
Flagstad, Kirsten, Memorial Collection, 118
Flaherty, Robert J., 1031
Flammer, Harold, 227-F
Flanagan family, 406
Flanagan, William, 227-F, 1061-A
Flanders, Helen Hartness, 227-F, 1528
Flanders, Helen Hartness, Ballad Collection, 1528
Flannery, Agnes V., 465
Fleischmann, Bianca, 1174
Fleisher, Edwin A., Collection, 272, 1333
Flemina, Mary Lou Robson, 253
Fleming, Robert M., 1172
Flesch, Carl, 227-F, 1177
Fletcher, Alice Cunningham, 227-F, 234, 654
Flexner, James, 195-C
Flinn, J. Hopkins, 103
Flint, Anne T., 1031
Flint (Mich.), 729-A
Flint Public Library, 745
Flonzaley Quartet, 636, 719, 1005, 1477
Florence (Colo.) Pioneer Museum and Historical Society, 163
Florida, 195, 227-L, 1059
Florida Agricultural and Mechanical University, 259
Florida Bandmasters' Association, 244
Florida Composers' League, 260
Florida Federation of Music Clubs, 263
Florida Folk Festival, 263
Florida Folklife Archive, 263
Florida State University, 260, 1670
Florida, University of, 244
Florio, Caryl, 227-D, 1061-A
Flotow, Friedrich von, 1113
Flowers, Robert Lee, 1143
Floyd, H. Alan, 1363
Flute music, 33, 180, 192, 227-A, 227-B, 227-G, 349, 548, 643, 645, 657, 701, 707, 838, 940, 1059, 1146, 1161, 1255, 1266, 1282, 1540. *See also* Fife music
Flutes, 33, 188, 227-B, 707, 986, 1190, 1274, 1375
Fluteville (Conn.), 188
Flying Dutchman Record Company, 936
Fobes, Azariah, 216

Fobes, Philena, 391
Foden, William, 860-B
Foerster, Adolph M., 227-D, 317, 1111, 1359, 1375
Foerster, Elsa, 1061-F
Fogler, Raymond H., Library, 592
Foley, Charles, 227-F
Foley, Eileen, 302
Foley, George H., 664
Folger Shakespeare Library, 224
Folk Arts Foundation of America, 815
Folk Music Archive of Tennessee Folksongs, 832
Folk music collections, 15, 16, 21, 23, 24, 27, 28, 29, 31, 32, 33, 34, 35, 36, 42, 49, 50, 73, 74, 75, 82, 84, 102, 107, 150, 152, 156, 157, 161, 162, 190, 196, 211, 213, 227-A, 227-K, 227-L, 230, 234, 239, 260, 263, 265, 271, 278, 285, 291, 293, 305, 308, 362, 391, 398, 406, 407, 456, 476, 499, 519, 522, 523, 531, 535, 537, 538, 542, 545, 563, 573, 592, 618, 626, 630, 654, 679, 687, 727, 729-B, 733, 741, 742, 769, 781, 789, 800, 815, 825, 829, 831, 832, 833, 836, 860-K, 870, 887, 888, 939, 957, 962, 963, 964, 979, 983, 1005, 1031, 1061-J, 1061-N, 1095, 1102, 1111, 1137, 1140, 1141, 1143, 1145, 1149, 1152, 1155, 1166, 1168, 1170, 1172, 1185, 1188, 1193, 1194, 1223, 1235, 1256, 1264, 1270, 1327, 1352, 1372, 1389, 1392, 1402, 1418, 1420, 1430, 1433, 1438, 1441, 1442, 1445, 1449, 1455, 1457, 1459, 1463, 1471, 1472, 1477, 1488, 1492, 1517, 1519, 1520, 1523, 1525, 1528, 1541, 1545, 1546, 1568, 1577, 1588, 1591, 1596, 1600, 1611, 1612, 1638, 1666. *See also* specific folk groups; Field recordings
Folke Bernadotte Memorial Library, 819
Folklore and Ethnic Art Center, 213
Folklore Archives (Brigham Young University), 1520
Folklore Archives (Indiana University), 406
FolKonvention (Greenville, Ill.), 362
Folksong. *See* Folk music collections
Folsom, Mrs. Willard M., 888
Folson, Honorable Mrs., 1111
Fondren Library, 1497
Fondren Library West, 1487
Foote, Arthur, 227-B, 227-C, 227-F, 317, 636, 642, 646, 701, 863, 951, 1061-A, 1080, 1111, 1338, 1359
Foote, Mrs. Arthur, 646
Foote, George Luther, 646
Foote, Rev. H. L., 50
Foote, Henry Wilder, 654, 1659

Forbes Library, 688
Forbes-Robinson, Sir Johnston, 1053
Force, Albert, Collection, 1006
Force, Peter, 227-M
Forchheimer, Dr. Frederick, 1176
Ford, Henry, 735, 736, 766
Ford, Jane Plonski, 588
Ford, Nita, 307
Ford Archive, 736
Ford Auditorium (Detroit), 740
Ford Model-T, 736
Ford Motor Company Band, 737
Ford Museum, 736
"Ford Sunday Evening Hour," 736
Ford's Theatre (Washington, D.C.), 612
Forest Glen (Md.), 625
Forest History Society, 135
Forestier, Auber (Mrs. Aubertine Woodward Moore), 1611
Forestry songs. *See* Loggers' songs
Forrest, Hamilton, 334
Forrest, Lillian, 514
Forst, Rudolf, 1061-A, 1061-B
Forsters, F. J. A., 1605
Forsyth, Cecil, 227-D
Fort Atkinson (Wis.), 1611
Fort Atkinson Historical Society, 1603
Fort Collins (Colo.) Museum, 164
Fort Davis (Tex.) National Historic Site, 1491
Fort Davis (Tex.) String Band, 1471
Fort Dayton (N.Y.?) Fireman's Band, 1001
Fort Delaware, 215
Fort Delaware Cornet Band, 214
Fort Delaware Society, 214
Fort Hays (Kan.) State College, 499
Fort Lauderdale (Fla.) Historical Society, 242
Fort Mason, 120
Fort McHenry National Monument and Historic Shrine, 607
Fort Morgan (Colo.) Heritage Foundation, 165
Fort Museum, 470
Fort Sheridan (Ill.) Museum, 1228
Fort Snelling (Minn.), 815
Fort Whipple, 26
Fort Worden, 1572
Fort Worth (Tex.), 1488
Fort Worth (Tex.) Public Library, 1492
Fortnightly Music Club (Cleveland), 1190
Fortnightly Music Club (St. Joseph, Mo.), 855
Forton Prison (Eng.), 227-M
Fortress Press, 1341
Foshay Tower (Minneapolis), 815

Foss, George, 1477
Foss, Lukas, 68, 195-C, 227-F, 977
Foster family, 1375
Foster, Ephraim, 701
Foster, Fay, 227-D
Foster, George, 227-H
Foster, Morrison, 127
Foster, Stephen Collins, 77, 116, 127, 185, 227-A, 227-D, 227-F, 240, 334, 521, 528, 531, 544, 618, 624, 729-A, 736, 744, 918, 1031, 1036, 1040, 1080, 1142, 1271, 1282, 1329, 1338, 1375, 1383, 1395, 1444, 1618
Foster, Stephen, Center and Florida Folklife Archive, 263
Foster, Stephen, Memorial Park, 263
Foster Hall, 334, 1031, 1374, 1375, 1383
Fouder, Sister M. Teresine, 1270
Foulke, William, 815
Foundation School (Berea, Ky.), 522
Fountainville (Pa.), 1299
Four Piano Ensemble, 1061-F
Four Saints in Three Acts, 206, 511
Four Season Players, 1012
Fourrier, Henri, 544
Fourrier, Joseph Amedee, 544
Fourrier Concert Band, 544
Fouser, Charles Elliott, 317, 345
Fowle, John, 654
Fowler, Frederick Acley, 195-B
Fox, Hannah, 227-A
Fox, Isaac, 1338
Fox, Mark, 875
Fox folios, 151
Fox Theatre (St. Louis), 398
Fox-trots. 846, 1061-N. *See also* Dance band music
Foxborough (Mass.), 707
Foxborough (Mass.) Historical Commission, 668
Fraenkel, Wolfgang, 1580
Fraker, Robert, 847
Framingham (Mass.) Historical Society, 669
Frampton, John Ross, 227-L
France, 939, 1155, 1611, 1683
France, Lela, 128
Franchetti, Arnold, 206, 227-D
Francis, D. R., 860-C
Francis, W. J., 555
Franciscan music, 133
Franciscan Sisters (Little Falls, Minn.), 787
Franco, Johan, 227-D, 227-F, 1553, 1580
Franco, José M., 1650
Franco, Sam, 1061-A
Frank, Leo, 1061-F
Frank, Marcel Gustave, 227-D
Frank, Paul, 1243
Frankel, Harry A. ("Singin' Sam"), 445
Frankel, Hiram Davis, 815
Frankenberg, Theodore Thomas, Theater Collection, 36

Frankenmuth (Mich.) Historical Museum, 746
Frankenstein, Alfred, 227-F
Franklin, Benjamin, 227-F, 1327, 1676
Franklin, Eduardo, 1651
Franklin, Malvin, 303
Franklin, William D., 190
Franklin and Marshall College, 1307
Franklin County (Ohio), 1193
Franklin County (Pa.), 1293, 1333
Franklin Institute, 1327
Franklin Music Warehouse, 1352, 1402
Franklin School Song, 1172
Franko, Nahan, 1061-B, 1061-F
Franko, Sam, 227-F, 1061-B
Franz, Chester, 860-E
Fras, Jim, 885
Fraser, Peter, 195-C
Fraternities and sororities, 190, 398, 511, 725, 866, 1005, 1176, 1260, 1274, 1377
Frazier, Janet White, 631
Frederick (Md.), 150
Frederick County (Md.) Historical Society, 620
Frederick County (Md.) Public Library, 621
Fredericksburg (Va.), 1560
Frederiksen, Sigurd, 227-D
Fredin, Aline, 1172
Fredonia (N.Y.) Normal School, 993, 994
Free and Accepted Masons of New York, 1038
Free Library of Philadelphia, 272, 1311, 1333
Free Will Baptist Historical Collection, 1154
Freed, Isadore, 195-A, 227-F, 1061-A
Freedmen's Aid Society (Cincinnati), 398
Freedman's Bureau School, 1141
Freeman, Harry Lawrence, 195-C, 226, 227-F
Freeman, Samuel T. (auction co.), 1352
Freeman, Valdo, 195-C
Freemasonry. *See* Masonic music
Freer, Eleanor (Everest), 227-C, 227-F
Freja Singing Society, 316
Fremont Club (Springfield, Ohio), 1232
Fremont County (Wyo.), 1643
Fremstad, Olive, 227-B, 227-F, 1053
French, 303
French, Christopher, 227-M
French, Edna, 154
French, Jonathan, 628
French, Katharine Jackson, 522
French, Myrta, 1111
French, Richard, 195-C
French horn. *See* Horn music
French music, 1, 50, 83, 115, 404, 542, 544, 545, 555, 560, 563, 568-A, 568-C, 620, 782,

791, 860-C, 860-F, 860-K, 1101, 1110, 1118, 1251, 1612
French Opera Company (New Orleans), 544, 560, 568
French Opera House (New Orleans), 555, 568, 569
French-Canadian music, 227-L, 676, 815, 1612. *See also* Cajun music
French's *New Sensation* (river showboat), 303
Fresno (Cal.), 50
Fresno (Cal.) City and County Historical Society, 61
Freund, John C., 1061-F
Friday Musicale (Jacksonville, Fla.), 245
Fried, Alexander, 122
Friedman, Arthur L., 949
Friedman, Mrs. Henry V., 334
Friedman, Ruth Klauber, 314
Friedman, Theodore Leopold (Ted Lewis), 1178
Friedrich Brothers Musical Journal, 748
Friedsam Memorial Library, 1116
Friend, Mr., 707
Friendly, Leonard, 1270
Friends of Art, Archaeology, and Music (Harvard University), 654
Friends of Chamber Music (Denver), 156
Friends of Chamber Music (Nashville), 1463
Friends of Music (Redlands, Cal.), 103
Friends of Music of San Mateo County (Cal.), 128
Friends, Society of. *See* Quaker music
Fries, Wulf, 642
Frieze, Henry Simmons, 729-B
Frieze Memorial Organ, 729-B
Friml, Rudolf, 84, 225, 1127
Frind-Sperling, Anni, 568
Friskin, James, 227-D, 227-F
Frissell, Hollis B., Library, 14
Fritch, Letitia, 860-H
Fritter, Genevieve Davisson, 227-D
Fritz, Chester, Library, 1165
Froehlich, Carl, 860-D
Froehlich, Egmont, 860-D
Frohman, Charles E., 1207
Frohman, Daniel, 1053, 1207
Frohsinn (Lindenhurst, N.Y.), 1010
Frohsinn Club (Mobile, Ala.), 9
Fromm, Herbert, 195-C
Fromm, Rudolph, 135
Frost, Thomas, 195-C
Frothingham, Robert, 227-K
Fruitlands Museums, 670
Fry, Edmund, & Co., 721
Fry, Jab, Library, 143
Fry, Noland, 171
Fry, William Henry, 1061-A, 1338, 1340
Fryberger, Agnes Moore, 815
Frykman, Nils, 325
Frysinger, J. Frank, 227-D

Fuchs, Dr. Julius, 334
Fuentes, Eduardo Sanchez de, 227-F
Fuerbringer, L. E., Hall, 856
Fuerstman, Joseph A., 940
Fulcher, Louise, Collection of Sacred Choral and Organ Music, 1604
Fuld, James J., 712, 1036
Fuleihan, Anis, 227-F
Fulkerson, Virginia (Vasey), 364
Fuller Public Library, 908
Fulton, Dorothy, 1172
Fulton County (Ill.) Historical Society, 304
Fulton County (Ind.) Historical Society, 446
Fulton Opera House, 1308
Funchess, Lloyd V. 544
Funderburg Library, 439
Funeral music, 219, 1327, 1560
Funk, Joseph, family, 721
Funk, Joseph, 568, 721, 1539, 1547, 1548
Funkes Opera House, 887
Furay, W. S., 1232
Furman University, 1422
Furst, William Wallace, 614
Furtwängler, Wilhelm, 729-E, 1025

G

G., H. L., 196
Gaal, Francis, 866
Gabriel, Charles Hutchinson, 465, 1465
Gabrielli, Edward, 544
Gabrilowitsch, Clara (Clemens), 227-E, 227-F, 636, 729-E, 839, 871, 1061-M
Gabrilowitsch, Ossip, 227-E, 227-F, 314, 636, 739, 839, 1061-B, 1111, 1177, 1580
Gachles, Philip Hante, 1560
Gachles pianos, 1560
Gadbold, Millie Moore, 1477
Gadeo Picó, Carlos R., 1651
Gadski, Johanna, 1053
Gaelic music, 227-L
Gaff family, 1112
Gaffney, Mamie, 1477
Gagaku, 47
Gage, Mrs. Lyman J., 227-D
Gale, Isabel, 800
Gale, Walter C., 1061-F
Gale, William T., 1061-F
Galesburg (Ill.), 391
Galesburg (Mich.) Musical Society, 761
Galesburg (Mich.) Musical Union, 761
Gallagher, William, 1193
Gallatin (Tenn.), 1463
Gallery Association (New York), 1053
Galli-Curci, Amelita, 227-B, 636
Gallison, Marie Reuter, 654
Gallo, Fortune, 227-F, 800
Galston, Gottfried, 1053, 1448
Galston-Busoni Archive, 1448
Galuska, J. F., 465

Galvin, William Richardson, 860-K
Gamble, Hamilton R., 860-D
Games. *See* Children's music
Gamut, 180, 204, 707, 977, 1530
Gamut Club (Los Angeles), 82
Gandy, Darius, 1420
Gange, Fraser, 1053
Gannett, Kent, 1111
Ganser Library, 1319
Gansevoort, Anna Maria, 227-A
Gansevoorts, Colonel, 1061-M
Ganz, Rudolph, 227-D, 227-F, 317, 334, 336, 338, 1061-A, 1111, 1580
Garbage collectors' songs, 742
Garcia, Eva R., 1477
Garcia, James, 1401
Garden, Mary, 227-F, 334, 636, 729-E, 907, 1053, 1061-L
Gardiner, Edward Carey, Collection, 1338
Gardiner (Me.) Drum Corps, 577
Gardini, Etelka Gerster, 1053
Gardner, Benjamin, 701
Gardner, Grace G., 1172
Gardner, Henry, 1521
Gardner, Isabella Stewart, 227-B, 639
Gardner, Isabella Stewart, Museum, 639
Gardner, Samuel, 1031
Garesche family, 860-C
Garesche, Lt. Col. Julius P., 860-C
Garesche, Marie R., 860-C
Garfield, James A., 1218
Garig, William W., 544
Garland, Hamlin, 1642
Garland, Judy, 783
Garlichs, Frank, 1052
Garnavillo (Iowa) Historical Society, 472
Garner, Claud, 43
Garner, Tom, 15
Garnett, Louise Ayers, 354
Garrett, Elizabeth, 960
Garrett, John Work, Library, 606
Garrett-Evangelical Theological Seminary Library, 355
Garriott, Jean E., 617
Garrison family, 654, 690, 692
Garrison, Ellen Wright (Mrs. William Lloyd Garrison II), 692
Garrison, Fielding H., 227-A
Garrison, Lucy McKim, 692, 1005, 1061-M, 1095
Garst, John, 264
Garst Museum, 1208
Gary, Mrs. James A., 227-A
Gary, Suson A., 1155
Gary (Ind.), 800
Gary Public Library, 414
Gassett, Henry, Jr., 642
Gaston, Marjorie, 418
Gaston, William, 1155
"Gastonia (N.C.) Strike Song," 1155
Gately automatic organs, 1631

Gates, Lucy, Opera Company, 1520
Gates, Susa Young, 1520
Gatti-Casazza, Giulio, 227-B, 227-F, 1052
Gattwood, Eldon J., 1459
Gatty, Alfred Scott, 1688
Gaucher, Valmore X., 721
Gaul, Alfred Robert, 1053, 1222
Gaul, Harvey Bartlett, 227-F, 1358, 1359
Gault, Pierce, 1426
Gauper, M. A., 462
Gauthier, Eva, 227-F, 1053, 1061-A, 1061-B, 1061-D
Gay, George, 1554
Gaylord, John, 209
Gaylord Music Library, 866
Gazzoli, Father G., 50
Gearhart, Livingston, 977
Gebhard, Heinrich, 639, 646
Gecks family, 860-B
Gecks, Francis, 860-K
Gecks, Frank, 860-B, 860-K
Gecks, John, 860-B
Gecks, Mathilde C., 860-K
Geer, Charles, 180
Geer, Ebenezer, 180
Geer, Moses F., 707
Gehring, Carl E., 729-B
Gehrkens, Karl Wilson, 1222
Gehrkens, Karl W., Music Education Library, 1222
Geidlinger Music Room, 1210
Geiger, Loren, 618
Geiger-Kullmann, Rosy, 1659
Geiringer, Karl, 227-F, 1061-M
Gelbart, Mikhl, 1076
Gelman, Harold, 68
Gemünder, August, 1051
Genêt, Edmond Charles, 227-A
Geneva (N.Y.), 1567
Geneva Historical Society, 996
Geneva (Switzerland), 1689
Gennett records, 471
George, James H., 128
George, Zelma Watson, 1187
George Mason University, 227-H, 1544
Georgetown (D.C.), 612
Georgetown (Mass.) Musical Union, 701
Georgetown (Tex.), 1493
Georgetown University, 225
Georgia, 195-A, 227-K, 260, 391, 544, 1141, 1143
Georgia Department of Archives and History, 270
Georgia Federation of Music Clubs, 267
Georgia Folklore Archives, 271
Georgia Folklore Society, 265
Georgia Historical Society, 280
Georgia State University, 271
Georgia, University of, 265
Gerard, W. C., 157
Gerhardt, Edwin L., 608
Gerhardt Marimba and Xylophone Collection, 608
Gericke, Wilhelm, 639
German, George B., 1430, 1437
German, George B., Music Archives, 1430

German Conservatory of Music (New York?), 1060
German music, 50, 56, 88, 89, 104, 115, 143, 157, 158, 160, 165, 167, 171, 217, 227-G, 227-H, 227-L, 230, 260, 284, 308, 314, 316, 329, 352, 359, 374, 380, 396, 398, 404, 406, 409, 415, 439, 443, 446, 453, 455, 465, 466, 468, 475, 478, 485, 503, 507, 509, 514, 518, 574, 611, 612, 613, 620, 693, 729-A, 729-B, 729-F, 730, 746, 764, 787, 791, 794, 801, 815, 821, 823, 824, 835, 836, 837, 853, 854, 856, 858, 860-A, 860-D, 860-E, 860-I, 862, 875, 878, 880, 888, 892, 948, 986, 1008, 1010, 1025, 1030, 1047, 1059, 1061-B, 1061-F, 1061-M, 1070, 1071, 1072, 1073, 1074, 1105, 1110, 1113, 1133, 1161, 1162, 1168, 1169, 1172, 1190, 1196, 1205, 1222, 1235, 1249, 1251, 1253, 1267, 1274, 1285, 1291, 1297, 1299, 1306, 1307, 1309, 1316, 1319, 1320, 1333, 1334, 1335, 1338, 1340, 1364, 1375, 1376, 1419, 1428, 1469, 1474, 1476, 1477, 1487, 1505, 1506, 1509, 1512, 1560, 1576, 1577, 1582, 1584, 1595, 1596, 1598, 1599, 1603, 1608, 1611, 1612, 1613, 1619, 1621, 1622, 1623, 1624, 1631, 1634, 1638, 1641, 1659, 1678, 1679, 1680, 1681. *See also* German-American musical organizations
German Society of Pennsylvania, 1334
German-American Bund, 230
German-American musical organizations, 156, 230, 314, 357, 398, 814, 837, 854, 860-D, 1010, 1061-F, 1061-M, 1172, 1190, 1193, 1291, 1334, 1375, 1476, 1506, 1509, 1559, 1599, 1608, 1611, 1621, 1624, 1680, 1682. *See also* German music
Germania (singing society; New Braunfels, Tex.), 1506
Germania Band (Battle Creek, Mich.), 730
Germania Club (Chicago), 314
Germania Männerchor, 613
Germania Musical Society of Worcester (Mass.), 721
Germania Orchestra of Philadelphia, 1287
Germania Singing Society, 1105
Germantown (Pa.), 217, 380, 1292, 1302, 1342
Germantown Historical Society, 1335
Germany, 729-B, 1061-M, 1113, 1222, 1338, 1468, 1611
Gerschefski, Edwin, 1425
Gershwin, George, 142, 177, 185, 195-A, 227-B, 227-F, 227-H, 227-L, 502, 527, 624, 636, 654, 800, 1031, 1036,

1057, 1089, 1111, 1416, 1457, 1477, 1580, 1611, 1666, 1689
Gershwin, George, Memorial Collection, 1457
Gershwin, George and Ira, Collection, 227-B
Gershwin, Ira, 227-B, 227-F, 1055, 1477, 1611
Gerstenberg, Julia, 314
Gert zur Heide, Karl, 253
Gesang-Verein (Port Washington, Wis.), 1599
Gesang-Verein (Zoar, Ohio), 1190
Gesangverein Germania, 1476
Gesang-Verein "Orpheus" (Boston), 1681
Gesang Verein Virginia (Richmond, Va.), 1560
Gesensway, Louis, 227-D
Gettysburg College, 1295
Geva, Tamara, 637
Giannini, Dusolina, 860-D
Giannini, Vittorio, 1160
Gibb, Robert Wilson, 227-D
Gibbons, James Sloan, 1040
Gibbs, Giles, 180
Gibson County (Tenn.) Public Library, 1470
Gibson Society, 640
Gideon, Miriam, 227-F
Gigante, Charles, 957, 1624
Gigli, Beniamino, 1031
Gilbert, B. F., 195-A
Gilbert, Henry F. B., 195-A, 195-C, 227-D, 227-F, 636, 1080
Gilbert, Henry S., 1031
Gilbert, James L., 195-A
Gilbert, L. Wolfe, 1646
Gilbert, Mabelle, 729-B
Gilbert, Richard B., 1171
Gilbert, T., 707
Gilbert, W. S., 1054
Gilbert & Sullivan, 234, 251, 406, 1005, 1053, 1061-M, 1143, 1349, 1358, 1544, 1572
Gilchrist, William Wallace, 227-D, 1333
Gilder, Richard Watson, 1031
Giles, Thomas E., 1524
Gill, Harold B., 1567
Gilles, Henri-Noel, 1343
Gillette, Elisabeth Hooker, 184
Gillette, James Robert, 227-D
Gilligan, Michael, 327
Gillis, Don, 227-C, 1488, 1494
Gillmour, Camille, 1477
Gilman, Benjamin Ives, 227-L
Gilman, Lawrence, 227-B, 227-F, 1061-B
Gilman, Maria Lawrence, 1053
Gilmer (Tex.), 1477
Gilmore, Joseph H., 1465
Gilmore, Patrick S., 195-A, 227-F, 618, 680, 701, 729-A, 860-J, 1522
Gilmore, W. E., 1618
Gilmore Band, 860-D, 1061-M
Ginn & Co., 618
Ginsburg, Henry, 168
Giorni, Aurelio, 227-D
Giraud, Ernest, 1040
Girault, August, 544
Girling, Robert, tune, 707

Glade, Coe, 1037
Glantz, Harry, 227-F
Glanville-Hicks, Peggy, 1040
Glarum, L. Stanley, 1270
Glasaw, Glenn L., 810
Glascow family papers, 1477
Glase, Paul E., 1333
Glasgow, Vaughn L., 554
Glasgow (Scotland) Orpheus
    Choir, 1675
Glass, Philip, 68
Glass Museum, 703
Glassell, John, 612
Glasser, Howard T., 630
Glaze, Tillman, 1276
Glaze, Warren, 1275, 1276
Glazer, David, 227-F
Glazer, Joe, 742
Gleason, Edward, 1520
Gleason, Frederic Grant, 334,
    1111
Gleason, Harold, 1111
Glee, Banjo, and Mandolin
    Club (Cornell University),
    1005
Glee Club (Salem, Mass.), 701
Glee clubs, 15, 190, 195-A,
    195-B, 244, 316, 402, 465,
    587, 642, 654, 701, 921, 939,
    1005, 1135, 1180, 1375, 1541,
    1577, 1581, 1591, 1616, 1621,
    1622, 1632. See also Male
    choruses; Women's choruses
Gleeson, Willard, 1520
Glen Plantation Collection,
    1161
Glendale Military Band, 1172
Glenn, Emma McHenry, 465
Glenn, John Carter, 195-A
Glessner, John Jacob, family,
    313
Glessner, Frances Macbeth
    (Mrs. John Jacob), 313, 314
Glessner House, 313
Globe Village, 707
Gloetzner, Anton, 225, 227-C,
    227-F
Glos Mansion, 353
Gloucester County (N.J.) His-
    torical Society, 955
Glover, Archibald, family, 218
Glover, Stephen, 356
Gluck, Alma, 123, 1054, 1111
Glynn, William C., 1477
Gobel, Mrs. Bailey, 779
Goddard, Heber Sutton, 1521
Goddard, Hez, 707
Godey's Lady Book, 862
Godowsky, Leopold, 227-B,
    227-F, 568, 907, 1111, 1580
Godowsky, Leopold, II, 195-C
Godrich, Israel, 905
Godwin, Harry, 1450
Goetschius, Percy, 1541
Goetz, Ruth Goodman, 1611
Goffstown (N.H.) Historical
    Society, 906
Gorgorza, Emilio de, 1053
Goins, Gregoria Fraser, 226
Golconda (Ill.) Public Library,
    361
Gold, Ernest, 1611
Gold, Julius, 334
Goldbeck, Robert, 860-C

Goldberg, Isaac, 654
Goldberg, Israel, 711
Golden, John, 1061-L
Golden (Colo.), 150
Golden Age Club (Gering,
    Neb.?), 881
"Golden Age of Bands" Collec-
    tion, 1433
Golden Gate National Recrea-
    tion Area, 121
Golden West Music Press, 76
Goldfaden, Abraham, 1076
Goldfarb Library, 712
Goldkette, Jean, 443, 737
Goldman, Edwin Franko,
    227-D, 227-F, 618, 1659
Goldman, Marcus Selden, 398
Goldman, Richard Franko,
    227-E, 618, 1124, 1666
Goldman Band, 398, 476, 618,
    1666
Goldmark, Carl, 227-F, 913,
    1025
Goldmark, Carl, Family Col-
    lection, 1025
Goldmark, Leo, 1025
Goldmark, Rubin, 227-F,
    729-E, 1025, 1030, 1666
Goldovsky, Boris, 227-F
Gold-rush songs, 195-B. See
    also Miners' songs
Goldsboro (N.C.), 1155
Goldschmidt, Otto, 142, 335,
    1328
Goldstein, Kenneth S., 1352
Goldstein, Kenneth S., Folk-
    lore Collection, 833
Golschmann, Vladimir, 227-F,
    860-C, 860-D, 1111, 1580
Goltra, Edward F., 860-D
Gombosi, Otto, 227-F, 340
Gomes, Antonio Carlos, 226
Gonzaga University, 1579, 1581
Gonzaga University Glee
    Clubs, 1581
Good, Harold & Wilma,
    Library, 416
Goode, K. M., 190
Goodhue County (Minn.)
    Historical Society, 804
Goodman, Alvin Harold, 1521
Goodman, Benny, 1031
Goodman, Ida Long, Memorial
    Library, 513
Goodman, Philip, 1611
Goodman, Saul, 1031
Goodrich, Frances, 1611
Goodrich, Frederick W., 1274
Goodrich, Wallace, 227-D, 646
Goodrich, Mrs. Wallace, 646
Goodrich Library, Inc., 1531
Goodrich Social Settlement,
    1190
Goodspeed Opera House, 177
Goodwin, George, 1061-C
Goodwin, Mary R. M., 1567
Goodwin, Parmelia Elizabeth
    (Cox), 391
Goodwin Library, 904
Goossens, Eugene, 227-D,
    227-F, 317, 1111, 1172, 1177,
    1580, 1666
Gordani, Nina, 1061-F
Gordon, A. J., 717

Gordon, Anna Adams, 356
Gordon, Asa. H., Library, 283
Gordon, Edgar B., 1611
Gordon, Eleanor Kinzie, 281
Gordon, Hally Wood, 1477
Gordon, Hugh, 1477
Gordon, Jacques, 227-F, 1111
Gordon, Jesse B., 1193
Gordon, Robert Winslow,
    227-K, 227-L, 227-M, 1270
Gordon, Taylor, 268
Gordon College, 717
Gorgas, Amelia Gayle,
    Library, 15
Gorin, Igor, 33
Goring-Thomas, A., 866
Gorno, Albino, 1176, 1177
Gorno Memorial Music
    Library, 1177
Gorton, Josephine, 977
Gorton, Thomas, Music
    Library 503
Goshen (N.Y.), 1017
Goshen College, 415, 416, 417
Gospel music, 36, 49, 74, 113,
    235, 271, 315, 320, 325, 333,
    404, 557, 559, 570, 948, 1031,
    1170, 1194, 1379, 1384, 1394,
    1413, 1442, 1443, 1459, 1462,
    1469, 1657, 1674, 1688. See
    also Gospel songbooks
Gospel songbooks, 3, 36, 109,
    113, 227-A, 235, 259, 284,
    308, 320, 333, 356, 398, 404,
    416, 432, 442, 452, 534, 559,
    570, 617, 775, 852, 866, 886,
    948, 1002, 1006, 1070, 1141,
    1166, 1194, 1200, 1263, 1376,
    1394, 1426, 1455, 1465, 1469,
    1493. See also Gospel music
Gospel Songwriters Museum,
    Inc., 1394
Gottlieb Musical Collection,
    606
Gottschalk, Louis A., 64
Gottschalk, Louis G., 555
Gottschalk, Louis Moreau,
    129, 227-D, 544, 555, 568,
    729-A, 744, 860-F, 863, 866,
    1005, 1036, 1040, 1061-A,
    1111, 1222
Gottschalk, Louis Moreau,
    Collection, 555
Gottschalk, Max W., 64
Goudy, Caspar J., 314
Gould, Archibald, 847
Gould, Hanna Flagg, 701
Gould, J. E., 721
Gould, Morton, 227-D, 227-F,
    1031, 1580, 1666
Gould, Olive, 730
Gould, Raymond, 730
Gould, William, 477
Gounod (i.e., Emerson
    Gounod) Club, 314
Gounod Club of Pittsburgh,
    1359
Gounod Society (New Haven,
    Conn.?), 195-A
Gouverneur (N.Y.) Historical
    Society, 998
Government Street Temple
    (Mobile, Ala.), 8
Governor's Foot Guard Band,

Second, New Haven
    (Conn.), 194
Graas, John J., 433
Graber, Albert, 815
Grabill, S. Becker von, 1308
Grace College, 452
Grace Episcopal Church
    (Sandusky, Ohio), 1228
Grace Hall, 719
Graceham (Md.), 1285
Graceland College, 477
Graceland Singers, 477
Graduate Theological Union
    Library, 46
Graffam, Clinton, 594
Grafulla, Claudio, 1618
Gragg family (N.C.), 1463
Graham, Alberta Powell Heald
    (Mrs. H. Austin), 465
Graham, Billy, Center, 404
Graham, Billy, School of
    Evangelism, 306
Graham, Frank M., 1413
Graham, Frank P., 1141
Graham, Gayle, 512
Graham, Lucia, 810
Graham, Mabelle, 465
Graham, Martha, 122, 227-F,
    1611
Graham, Otto, 401
Graham, Robert, 497
Graham, Stephen, 1155
Graichen, Jacob, 453
Graichen, William, 453
Grainger, Ella, 195-C, 1666
Grainger, Percy A., 99, 195-C,
    227-C, 227-F, 227-L, 314,
    317, 398, 729-E, 815, 925,
    1053, 1061-A, 1111, 1136,
    1177, 1580, 1666, 1669, 1670,
    1687
Grainger, Percy A., Band
    Library, 195
Grainger, Percy, Library
    Society, 1136
Grainger, Rose, 1666
Grainger Museum, 1666
Gram, Edmund, 1611
Gram, Hans, 227-D
Grambs, Fred L., 2
Gramley Library, 1163
Gramophone & Typewriter
    Co., Ltd., 227-L
Granby (Conn.), 180
Grand Army Hall and
    Memorial Association Col-
    lection, 315
Grand Exposition (St. Louis,
    1884), 860-J
Grand Festival (St. Louis,
    1900), 860-J
Grand Juvenile Orchestra,
    Victor J. Erhart's (Dallas),
    1483
Grand Lodge Library (New
    York), 1038
Grand Lodge of Iowa, Ancient
    Free and Accepted Masons, 458
Grand Lodge of Masons in
    Massachusetts, 641
Grand Lodge of the State of
    Washington, Sons of
    Herman (Tacoma, Wash.),
    1584

Grand Ole Opry papers, 1459
Grand Opera Association (Jackson, Miss.), 829
Grand Opera Association (St. Louis), 860-D
Grand Opera Committee (Baton Rouge, La.), 544
Grand Opera Company (New Orleans), 544
Grand Opera House (Bloomington, Ill.), 302
Grand Opera House (Burlington, Iowa), 454
Grand Opera House (Chicago), 315
Grand Opera House (Eau Claire, Wis.), 1600
Grand Opera House (Greensboro, N.C.), 1146
Grand Opera House (Minneapolis), 815
Grand Opera House (New Orleans), 544, 555
Grand Opera House (Omaha), 887
Grand Opera House (St. Louis), 860-A
Grand Opera House (St. Paul), 815
Grand Opera House (Springfield, Ohio), 1232
Grand Opera House (Toronto), 1662
Grand Rapids (Mich.), 729-B
Grand Rapids Public Library, 748
Grand Rapids Public Museum, 749
Grand View College, 464
Grandjany, Marcel, 227-D, 227-F
Grange songs, 761, 762
Grant, Anna, 707
Grant, Claude, 1445
Grant, Ken, 1607
Grant, Parks, 833, 1111
Grant, Ulysses S., 860-K
Grant, William Parker, 1477, 1520, 1521
Grant Park Symphony Orchestra, 315, 328
Grant-Schaefer, G. A., 354
Grasse, Edwin, 606
Grasselli Library, 1180
Gratz, Simon, Collection, 1338
Gratz College, 1336
Grau, Maurice, 1573
Grauman, Sid, 122
Graupner imprints, 334
Graupner, Johann Christian Gottlieb, 1402
Graves, Abraham D., 357
Graves, Juliette (Mrs. Crosby Adams), 227-F, 1148, 1153, 1222
Graves, Willis Frederick, 970
Gray family, 1560
Gray, C. O., Jr., 195-B
Gray, Jerry, 1487
Gray, Len, 682
Gray, Lillie Trust, papers, 544
Gray, Maxine Cushing, 1577
Graystone Ballroom (Detroit), 737

Gready, John, 398
Greason, Guy, 465
Great Britain, 1080, 1141
Great Falls (Mont.) Public Library, 873
Great Lakes Dredge and Philharmonic Society, 314
Great Lakes Historical Society, 1241
Great Lakes, songs about, 1241
Greater Cleveland Ethnographic Museum, 1188
Greek music, 729-F, 1352, 1377
Greek Orthodox church, 1188. See also Eastern Orthodox church
Greeley, William Roger, 718
Greeley (Colo.) Municipal Museum, 167
Green, Adolph, 1057
Green, Blaine, 1445
Green, Cordilia, 860-D
Green, Francis Harvey, Library, 1391
Green, Frank Searcy, 1463
Green, John, 860-D
Green, Joseph F., 1458
Green, Lenamay, 1463
Green, Martyn, 637
Green, Morris, 1061-L
Green, Paul Eliot, 1141
Green, Ray, 76
Green, Samuel, 180
Green, Zoe L., 50
Green Collection, 860-D
Green Collection of American Sheet Music, 244
Green Library, 142
Greene, Clay Meredith, 133
Greene, Howard F., Transportation Historical Collection, 1646
Greene, Thomas E., 1401
Greene County (N.Y.) Historical Society, 986
Greene's Opera House (Cedar Rapids, Iowa), 458, 465
Greenewalt, Mary Elizabeth (Hallock), 227-M, 636, 1338
Greenfield, Elizabeth T., 741
Greenfield (Mass.), 695
Greenfield Village and Henry Ford Museum, 736
Greenough, H. Rose, Jr., 227-L
Greensboro (N.C.) Historical Museum, 1146
Greenway, G. Lauder, 1061-J
Greenwich House, 800
Greenwood, John, 1059
Greenwood, Robert, 568
Greenwood (Va.), 227-K
Greer, I. G., 1140
Greer Music Library, 196
Gregorian chant, 133, 434. See also Roman Catholic church music
Gregorian Studio of Music, 226
Gregory family, 887
Gregory, L., 391
Gregory, Mahala Champman Mace, 1591
Gregway, William, 1099
Greiner, Seth, 866

Greissle, Felix, 68, 227-F
Grendysa, Peter A., 1597
Grey, William, 195-C
Grider, Rufus A., 1285, 1338
Gridley, Charles E., 298
Grieb, Herbert, 2
Grierson, Benjamin Henry, 391, 398, 1491
Griffes, Charles Tomlinson, 227-D, 227-F, 317, 990, 1061-A, 1061-B, 1080, 1580, 1666
Griffis, Elliot, 195-A, 227-D, 227-F, 465, 866, 1580
Griffith, Charles L., 484
Griffith, D. W., 1477
Griffith, James, 32
Griffith School of Music, 266
Griggs, G. W., 654
Griggs, Thomas Cott, 1521
Grignon, Charles, 1611
Griller, Sidney, 227-F
Grimm, Carl Hugo, 227-D, 1176
Grimm, J. D., 1161
Grinnell College, 473, 739
Griswold, Alexander H., 180
Griswold (Conn.), 707
Grobe, Charles A., 215
Grobe, D. M., 215
Grobe, J. A., 215
Grofé, Ferde, 142, 227-D, 227-F, 1580, 1648
Grofé, Ferde, collection, 1487
Grolier Club, 1053
Grolle, Johan, 800
Grombie, Ida Mae, 913
Gross, Carl R., 226
Gross, Walter, 1646
Gross, William, 1299
Grossman, Captain F. E., 50
Grossman, F. Karl, 1181, 1185
Grosvenor Library, 334, 377
Groton (Conn.), 180
Grout, Donald Jay, 1005
Grove, Dorothy Haverty (Mrs. Lon), 266
Groveland (Mass.) Organ Association, 701
Grove's Dictionary of Music and Musicians, American Supplement, 1359
Grubb, J. Allen, 157
Grubb, Margaret, 195-C
Grube, Bernhard, 1285
Gruen, Rudolph, 227-D
Gruenberg, Louis, 227-D, 227-F 1046, 1127, 1580
Grumman, Mr. and Mrs., 195-C
Grundtvig, F. L., 748
Gruner, N. G., 1161
Grunewald, Benedict, 553
Grunewald, Louis, 553, 555
Grunewald's Music Store, 553, 556, 568
Gruskin, Isadore, Library, 769
Gudbrandsdalen (Norway), 462
Gudehus, Heinrich, 1053
Guenther, Ralph, 1494
Guerber, Mary Edna, 156
Guest, Edgar A., 729-B
Guilbert, Yvette, 907

Guild, Courtney, 642
Guild of Carillonneurs in North America, 752
Guild of Harkness Bellringers (Yale University), 195-B
Guilford College, 1147
Guion, David, 227-D, 1477, 1501, 1502, 1517, 1541, 1666
Guitar and Mandolin Club (Harvard University), 654
Guitar Foundation of America, 1192
Guitar music, 7, 190, 227-L, 271, 412, 425, 465, 478, 654, 860-B, 987, 1015, 1155, 1192, 1299, 1327, 1401, 1407, 1420, 1424, 1448, 1487, 1540, 1599, 1660
Guitars, 7, 391, 654, 679, 761, 830, 860-B, 1192, 1322, 1401, 1560
Gullah music, 1352
Gulley, P. G., 1005
Gundlach, John H., 860-B, 860-C
Gundrum, Jacob, 1295
Gunn, Glenn Dillard, 227-E, 227-F
Gunning, Sarah Ogan, 1445
Gunnison (Colo.), 157
Gunther, Charles F., 314
Gurnee, Dwane, 68
Gustavus Adolphus College, 819
Guthrie, Mary, 860-B
Guthrie, Woodrow Wilson ("Woody"), 227-K, 227-L
Gutiérrez y Espinosa, Felipe, 1653
Gutman, Monroe C., Library, 654
Guy, Jack, Collection, 1140
Gwathmey Library, 1425
Gwin (i.e., Vardaman-Gwin) Collection, 1

H

H., T. W., 1560
Haas, Henry, 1059
Haas, Oscar, 1476, 1477, 1505
Haasis family, 1423
Haberl, Fred, 157
Hache, Theodore von la, 555, 561, 1477
Hackett, Albert, 1611
Hackett, Charles, 123
Hackett, James K., 1053
Hackett, Karleton, 1520
Hackett, Mrs. Karleton, 334
Hackley, E. Azalia, 268
Hackley, E. Azalia, Memorial Collection, 739
Hackman, Sterling, 398
Haden, Walter Darrell, 1469
Hadley, Henry K., 110, 227-B, 227-D, 227-F, 317, 398, 646, 951, 1018, 1040, 1053, 1061-A, 1061-B, 1111
Hadley, Mrs. Henry K., 1061-A
Haefer, Richard, 28
Haenschen, Gustave, 1007
Haesche, William E., 1549

Haeussler, Armin, 352
Hafley, W. C., 1463
Hageman, Richard, 646
Hagen, Francis Florentine, 1161, 1285, 1323
Hagen, Peter von, Jr., 701
Hagen Collection, 1161
Hager, Mina, 195-C
Hagerman, Benjamin F., 837
Hagerman-Hayden family, 837
Hagerty, Bernard, 1433
Haggin, B. H., 227-F
Haggin Galleries, 144
Hague, Mrs. Arthur, 195-C
Hague, Eleanor, 82
Hahr, Frederick C., 1559
Hahr Musical Society, 1560
Haieff, Alexei, 227-F, 977
Haifa Music Museum & Library, 1685
Haight, Fred Alton, 1272
"Hail Columbia!," 314, 465, 612, 1036
Haile, Eugen, 1061-A
Haimson, Naomi Carroll, 1451
Haines, Edmund, 227-D, 975, 1111
Haiti, 226, 739
Haldeman, Mrs. E. E. (Eliza Ewing Jacobs), 1315
Hale, Jonathan, 1190
Hale, Lucie, 815
Hale, Philip, 227-A, 227-B, 227-F, 555, 636, 691, 1177
Hale, William Dinsmore, 815
Halifax County (N.C.), 1141
Hall, Arthur Edwin, 195-C, 1497
Hall, Corinne Steele, 860-C
Hall, Elise Coolidge (Mrs. Richard J.), 646
Hall, James H., 1222
Hall, Jon F., 582
Hall, Joseph S., 75, 227-L
Hall, Robert Browne, 576, 599, 618
Hall, Sharlot, 26
Hall, Sharlot, Historical Society, 26
Hall, Wendell, 1611
Hall imprints, 1440
Hall-Stakely family, 1447
Hallam, Oscar, 815
Halpert, Herbert, 227-L, 523
Halstead, F. M., 1429
Hamberlin, L. R., 1477
Hamburg (Germany), 1113
Hamerik, Agsel, 614
Hamilton, Clara May Russell, 1477
Hamilton, Emory L., 1352
Hamilton, George E., 465
Hamilton, Thomas Hale, Library, 289
Hamilton (Mass.), 701
Hamlin, Anna, 1039
Hamlin, George, 1039
Hamma School of Theology, 1196
Hammer, Eleanor, 341
Hammer, William Joseph, 234
Hammered dulcimers, 988, 1234
Hammerstein, Louis, 860-H

Hammerstein, Oscar, 83, 225, 227-F
Hammerstein, Oscar, Jr., 227-E
Hammerstein, Oscar, II, 142, 1031, 1061-J, 1611
Hammond, John, 195-C, 1031
Hammond, John Hays, Jr., 227-M
Hammond (i.e., Weatherford-Hammond) Appalachian Collection, 522
Hammond Organ Co., 227-M
Hammond Organ "Stylings," 1270
Hampden, Walter-Edwin Booth Theatre Collection and Library, 1064
Hampden County (Mass.) Musical Association, 705
Hampton, Lionel, 321
Hampton Institute, 1546
Hampton Institute Choir (Va.), 1031
Hampton Singers, 1546
Hamstead (N.Y.), 502
Hanby, Benjamin R., 1189, 1242, 1243
Hanby House, 1242
Hancock, Frances A. J., 911
Hancock (Mass.), 697
Handbills. See Broadsides; Programs
Handel, George Frederick, 729-D, 1061-H, 1532
Handel and Haydn Society (Boston), 636, 916, 1061-B, 1061-M
Handel and Haydn Society (Lawrence, Kan.), 514
Handel and Haydn Society (New Albany, Ind.), 437
Handel and Haydn Society (Newark, N.J.), 940
Handel Choir of Baltimore, 609
Handel Society (Dartmouth College), 907
Handel Sodality (Harvard University), 654
Handleman Institute, 239
Handy, W. C., 6, 142, 185, 195-B, 226, 227-D, 227-F, 268, 564, 739, 860-D, 1061-N, 1450, 1451, 1452, 1457, 1463
Handy, W. C., Foundation for the Blind, 268
Handy, W. C., Home and Museum, 6
Handy Brothers Music Co., 268
Hanford, Charles B., 229
Hanford, James Holly, 227-K
Hanford, Rodney W., Collection, 1006
Hanks, H. L., 1483
Hanna, Benjamin, 227-D
Hannah family, 1560
Hannah, George, 1083
Hannas, Ruth, 2
Hanneman, Jacob, 262
Hannibal (Mo.), 270, 837
Hansen, Harold I., 1520
Hansen, Irene H., 1521

Hansen, John, 370
Hanson, Carl (Charles) F., 724
Hanson, Ethwell (Eddy), 1611
Hanson, Gladys, 269
Hanson, Howard, 84, 227-D, 227-F, 317, 1018, 1023, 1111, 1573, 1580, 1666
Hanson, Peter, 50
Hanson, William F., 1520
Harbach, Otto, 227-F, 360, 1031
Harburg, Edgar Y., 227-F, 1024
Harburg, E. Y., Archive, 195-B
Harby, Lee C., 1477
Hardanger fiddlers, 462, 800
Hardege, Richard, 1634
Hardelot, Guy d', 1053
Hardeman, Ella (Goode), 1141
Harden, Edward, 1143
Harder, Erwin E., 227-D
Harding, Albert Austin, 398
Harding, Walter N. H., 1673
Hardy, C. W., 913
Hardy, Ephraim B., 707
Hardy, Will, 663, 710
Hare, Maud Cuney, 268
Harker, F. Flaxington, 1558
Harkins, James E., 729-B
Harkness, 15
Harlan, Edgar R., 465
Harlem Damenchor, 359
Harlem Evening School, 226
Harlem Männerchor, 359
Harlem Renaissance, 12
Harline, Leigh, 1177
Harling, W. Franke, 111
Harmati, Sandor, 1053
Harmon, William Elmer, 227-M
Harmon Foundation, 227-M
Harmonia Club (Ithaca, N.Y.), 1005, 1006
Harmonic Orchestra (Manchester, N.H.?), 914
Harmonic Society (Baltimore), 612
Harmonic Society of Cincinnati, 1172
Harmonic Society (Woodbury, Conn.), 181
Harmonica music, 213, 227-L
Harmonie club (Appleton, Wis.), 1592
Harmonie Gesangverein (Philadelphia), 1334
Harmonie Society of Detroit, 739
Harmonien (Seattle), 1577
Harmony Associates, 1281
Harmony Hall, 1607
Harmony Old Singers Association, 1141
Harmony Society (Pa.), 1281, 1364
Harney County (Ore.?) Sagebrush Orchestra, 1274
Harnick, Sheldon, 1611
Harper, James C., 1151
Harper, Lila Edwards, 11
Harps, 334, 460, 707, 838, 1050, 1061-A, 1127, 1249, 1331
Harpsichords, 84, 713, 1069
Harpursville (N.Y.) Band, 1100

Harp-zither, 986
Harr, Haskell, 1595
Harrell, Mack, 1053
Harrigan, Edward ("Ned"), 83, 544, 624, 1061-L
Harrigan and Hart, 83, 624
Harrington, Calvin Sears 190
Harrington, John, 234
Harrington, Karl Pomeroy, 190
Harris family, 1338
Harris, C. Fiske, 1402
Harris, C. Fiske, Collection, 1402, 1405
Harris, Charles K., 1622
Harris, Daniel, 1222
Harris, Ethel Ramos, 227-F
Harris, George, Jr., 1541
Harris, Joel Chandler, 269, 1541
Harris, Lynn, 1487
Harris, Roy, 68, 227-C, 227-F, 317, 532, 1040, 1111, 1148, 1261, 1580
Harris, Victor, 1053
Harris Hymnal Collection, 1005
Harrison family, 424, 1560
Harrison, Abraham, 939
Harrison, President Benjamin, Foundation, 424
Harrison, Mrs. Benjamin, 424
Harrison, Birge, 698
Harrison, Dennis, 1190
Harrison, Edith Ogden (Mrs. Carter Harrison II), 314
Harrison, Frank, 12
Harrison, Guy Fraser, 1256
Harrison, Judith Williantina (Temple), 1560
Harrison, Lou, 68, 195-C, 227-D, 535, 1040
Harrison, Oswald Payne, 1477
Harrison, Peleg, 914
Harrison, William Henry, 425, 1193, 1232
Harrison (Me.), 707
Harrison Collection, 914
Harrison County (Tex.) Historical Society, 1502
Harrison (i.e., Pyne and Harrison) Opera Company, 544
Harriss, Robert Preston, 1143
"Harrying Chorus," 36
Harsh, Vivian G., Collection, 315
Hart, Annie J., 1420
Hart, Miss J. L., 227-A
Hart, Julia Duggan, 1501
Hart, Junius, 544, 555
Hart, Lela M., 730
Hart, Lorenz, 1031
Hart, Judge Louis Bret, 977
Hart, Margaret Grady, 195-C
Hart, Moss, 1611
Hart, Tony, 83, 624
Hart, Violet, 568
Hart, Weldon, 1111
Hartel, Master Freddy, 568
Harter, J., 1296
Hartford (Conn.), 269, 815
Hartford Public Library, 182
Hartford Seminary Foundation, 183

Hartford Theological Seminary, 269, 1369
Hartford, University of, 206
Hartland (Mich.) Music Hall, 729-B, 754, 755
Hartland (Vt.), 1530
Hartman, Frederick B., 1285
Hartman-Sutton Collection, 1141
Hartmann, Arthur, 465, 1111, 1333
Hartsville (Ind.) Serenaders, 409
Hartt, Charles Frederic, 1143
Hartt, Julius, 206
Hartt, Julius, School of Music, 181
Hartt College of Music, 181, 206
Hartwell, Thomas, 1017
Hartzler, Rev. J. D., 416
Hartzler Collection, 416
Harvard Musical Association, 642, 860-E
Harvard University, 227-L, 531, 625, 636, 654, 721, 1270
Harwell, Richard B., 398
Harwood-Arrowood, Bertha, 266
Hasidic music, 769. See also Jewish music
Haskins, Orren N., 1111
Hasselmans, Joseph, 544
Hasselmans, Louis, Collection, 544
Hast, Lisette, 531
Hast, Louis H., 531
Hastings, Alice O., 1622
Hastings, Benjamin, 180
Hastings, E. P., 739
Hastings, Frank Seymour, 1031
Hastings, George, 136, 138
Hastings, Martha Harris, 643
Hastings, Thomas, 739, 1338
Hastings Band (Santa Cruz, Cal.), 136, 138
Hastings (N.Y.) Historical Society, 1000
Hasty, Frank, 815
Haswell, Anthony, 721
Haswell, Nathan Baldwin, 721
Hatch, Harold A., 195-C
Hatch, Newton S., 707
Hatcher, Harlan, Research Library, 729-E
Hatfield, Edwin F., 1059
Hatzi, James, Collection of Violin Music, 1628
Haubiel, Charles, 227-D, 227-F, 1580, 1646
Hauerbach (Harbach), Otto A., 227-F, 360, 1031
Hauk, Minnie, 1053
Haun, Mildred, 1459
Hauser, Arthur, 227-H
Hauser, Carl, 227-D
Haverford College, 1301
Haverhill (Mass.), 906
Haverhill (Mass.) Public Library, 671
"Haverhill Commandry March," 901
Haverlin, Carl, Collection, 1040

Havlena, Charles, 457
Hawaii, 147, 195-B, 227-L, 1670
Hawaii State Archives, 286
Hawaii, University of, 289
Hawaiian Historical Society, 287
Hawaiian Mission Childrens' Society Library, 288
Hawaiian music, 74, 195-B, 227-L, 356, 1520, 1521, 1656, 1670
Hawes, William L., 555
Hawkins, Micah, 185, 227-A, 1058, 1123
Hawley, E. H., 234
Hawthorne-Longfellow Library, 585
Haxall, Octavia (Robinson), 1560
Hay, Rev. Horace, 143
Hay, John, Collection, 1402
Hay, John, Library, 1402
Hayde, Ron E., 1131
Hayden, A. S., 400
Hayden, Estelle, 544
Hayden, Isaac, 707
Hayden, Philip Cady, 465, 837
Hayden, William, 544
Haydn, Joseph, 212
Haydn Club (Portland, Me.), 596
Haydn Male Chorus (New Albany, Ind.), 437
Haydn Society (Brunswick, Me.), 586
Haydn Society (Cincinnati), 1176
Hayes (collector for Thomas A. Edison), 744
Hayes, Christie, 1129
Hayes, Fanny, 1207
Hayes, Mr. & Mrs. Patrick J., 227-H
Hayes, Roland, 36, 227-D, 227-F, 268, 1105, 1580
Hayes, President Rutherford B., 20, 1207, 1232
Hayes, Rutherford B., Library, 1207
Hayes, Mrs. Rutherford B., 1207
Hayes, Samuel P., Research Library and Music Library, 714
Hays, Dr., 1031
Hays, Theodore L., 815
Hays, Will S., 523
Hayward, Florence, 860-F, 860-H
Haywood, Beatrice Hereford, 715
Hazelman, Herbert, 1148
Hazelton, Mrs. John Morton (Maude V. Pepper), 931
Headley, Herbert Klyne, 1580
Heald, John Oxenbridge, 195-B
Healy, Rev. Sherwood, 334
Healy & Bishop organs, 1017
Healy House and Dexter Cabin, 169
Heard Museum, 24
Hearn, Lafcadio, 568, 1541
Hearst, Phoebe A., 50

Heart songs, 102
Heath, Fenno, 195-C
Heath, Robert C., 932
Heath, Susanna ("Sukey"), 651
Hebrew music. See Jewish music
Hebrew National and University Library, 1686
Hebrew Union College, 1172, 1174
Hecht, Elias, 1174
Heck, Thomas F., 1192
Hedden, Earl G., 435, 436
Hedden, Jennie Gebhart, Music Study Club, 435, 437
Hedden, W. R., Jr., 195-A
Hedden, Will J., 435
Hegner, Otto, 1222
Hehl, Matthäus, 1285
Heidelberg University (Germany), 465
Heiden, Bernhard, 227-D, 1580
Heifetz, Jascha, 227-F, 800, 1105, 1580
Heilbron, Julius, 815
Hein, Johann A., 810
Heine, Caroli Anthoni, 1299
Heineman, Dannie and Hettie, Collection, 1053
Heinrich, Anthony Philip, 227-C, 1031, 1111, 1338
Heinrich, Karl Gottlieb, 1375
Heinsheimer, Hans, 227-F
Heinz Hall for the Performing Arts, 1368
Heinz Memorial Chapel, 1375
Heisler, Tibor, Collection, 338
Heitz, Norman, 797
Helburn, Theresa, 1286
Helfer, Walter, 1148
Heller, Mrs. Albert, 334
Heller, Hans Ewald, 1270
Heller, James G., 227-D, 1174, 1176
Helmick, S. M., 465
Helms-Cravens Library, 523
Helsinki University (Finland) Chorus, 636
Helwig, Carl, 260
Hemans, Felicia, 698
Hemberger, Theodore, 614
Hemingway, Louis, 195-C
Hempel, Frieda, 1052, 1053, 1580
Hempstead (New York), 1270
Henckels, Theodore, 227-D
Hendershott, Chauncey Marion, 1477
Henderson, Edwin, 1172
Henderson, Knud, 802
Henderson, Skitch, 1611
Henderson, W. J., 142, 227-F, 1053
Henderson Settlement School, 524
Henderson-Wertmüller Papers, 1338
Hendricks, Francis, 227-D
Hendricks, George D., 1488
Hendrix, Glenn, 727
Henning, Ervin, 637
Henry, Betsy, 1338
Henry, Eliza, 1338
Henry, George E., 1148

Henry, Mellinger Edward, 227-K, 1402
Henry, S. R. (Henry R. Stern), 1270
Henry Street Settlement (New York), 800
Henschel, George, 639
Henschel, Gustav, 1338
Henschel, Isidor, 682
Henshaw, Dana, 689
Henshaw, Nevil Gratiot, 1541
Hentoff, Nat, 195-C
Hentz, Charles A., 1141
Hepburn, Katharine, 226, 959
Herbert, Victor, 79, 142, 227-C, 227-F, 317, 334, 398, 606, 624, 729-E, 747, 860-B, 862, 907, 1031, 1053, 1222, 1338, 1359, 1477, 1612
Herbst, Johannes, 1161, 1285
Heritage Military Music Foundation, 1618
Herkimer County (N.Y.) Historical Society, 1001
Herman, Rheinhold Ludwig, 646
Herman, Sons of, 1584
Hernández Bosch, José, 1651
Herold, Donald G., 1417
Herreshoff, Constance Mills, 115
Herreshoff, Sarah Brown, 1407
Herreshoff Music Collection, 1407
Herrick, Margaret, Library, 51
Herrmann, Bernard, 195-C, 227-D, 227-F
Herron, John W., 1141
Herron, William Edgar, 1439
Herschmann, I. A., 1058
Hershey School of Musical Art, 334
Herskovitz, Melville, 357
Hertz, Alfred, 50, 122, 1053
Hertz, Lily (Dorn), 50
Hertzberg, Harry, Circus Collection, 1511
Herwegh Sängerbund, 860-E
Herz, Gerhard, 1061-M
Herz, Otto, 1031
Herzberger, F. W., 856
Hesbacher, Peter, 1337
Hess, Dame Myra, 195-A, 1053
Hesser, Clifford, 476
Hessisches Hauptstaatsarchiv, 1683
Heth, Charlotte, 84
Heusen, Jimmy Van, 1579
Heussenstamm, George, 357
Hewitt family, 349
Hewitt, Eliza Edmunds, 465
Hewitt, Helen, 1488
Hewitt, Horatio D., 612
Hewitt, James, 729-A
Hewitt, John Hill, 127, 195-A, 227-D, 269, 612, 729-A, 1040
Hewitt, Peter, 68
Heye Foundation, 1059
Heyman, Edward, 1646
Heyn recitals (Pittsburgh), 1359
Heyward, DuBose, 227-F, 1477
Heywood, Donald, 226
Heywood, John H., 531

Hibberd, Lloyd, 1488, 1503
Hibbing (Minn.), 1633
Hibbing (Minn.) Historical Society, 784
Hicklin, Ralph, 1662
Hickman, Rev. Percival H., 235
Hickok, Charles, 1105
Hickok, Robert, 195-C
Hicks, Nathan, 1095
Hier, Ethel Glenn, 227-F, 1176, 1177
Higgins, May, 1487
Higgins imprints, 1123
Higginson, Henry Lee, 227-F, 636, 639, 654, 1111
Higginson, Thomas W., 268
High, Nellie E., 851
Highfill, Carroll, 1644
Highland County (Ohio) Historical Society, 1209
Highland Park (Ill.) Historical Society, 363
Highlander Folk School, 1463
Highlander Research and Education Center, 1466, 1611
Highlands University, 961
Hildegarde, Loretta, 1646
Hildreth Opera House (Charles City, Iowa), 465
Hill, Mrs. D., 1313
Hill, David J., 1313
Hill, Edward Burlingame, 227-B, 227-D, 227-F, 317, 636, 646, 654, 1018, 1111, 1177, 1580, 1648
Hill, Esther Clark, 498
Hill, Mrs. F. H., 1507
Hill, Grant L., Collection, 33
Hill, Inga, 800
Hill, Mabel Wood, 227-D, 227-F
Hill, Mildred J., 227-F, 531, 535, 1270
Hill, Ora, 862
Hill, Richard S., 227-E, 227-H
Hill, Samuel, 815
Hill, William E., Theater Collection, 1484
Hill Cumorah Pageant (Palmyra, N.Y.), 1520
Hill Ferguson collection, 15
Hill (i.e., Allston-Pringle-Hill) Papers, 1418
Hillbilly music, 49, 73, 74, 150, 163, 264, 277, 733, 924, 997, 1477. See also Country and western music
Hillegas, Michael, 1338
Hillman, Jessie, 994
Hillman Library, 1375
Hillman Memorial Music Association, 994
Himel family, 544
Hindemith, Paul, 195-A, 227-D, 227-F, 637, 949, 1580, 1670, 1679
Hindemith, Paul, Institut (Frankfurt, Germany), 1679
Hindemith project, 195-C
Hinderer, John C., 798
Hindsley, Mark, 398
Hiner, Dr. E. M., 846
Hiner Band Collection, 846

Hines, Earl ("Fatha"), 1031
Hines, James, 1551
Hinkle, Walter C., Memorial Library, 970
Hinkley and Singley sheet music collection, 606
Hinrichs, Gustav, 936
Hinton, Milton, 1031
Hippodrome (New York), 1061
Hiram College, 1210
Hirsch, Herbert Sachs, 968
Hirsch, Paul, collection (London), 1670
Hirschfeld, Max, 1544
Hirschfield caricatures, 729-C
Hisel, Mrs. O. R., 1256
Hispanic music. See Latin-American music; Mexican music; Spanish music
Histed, William, 683
Historic Buildings Survey, 227-M
Historic Deerfield (Mass.), Inc., 662
Historic New Orleans Collection, 555
Historic Popular Song Collection, 1624
Historical American Collection, 33
Historical and Genealogical Society of Indiana County (Pa.), 1303
Historical Association of Central Louisiana, 573
Historical Association of Southern Florida, 248
Historical Museum of the Darwin R. Barker Library, 993
Historical Society of Berks County (Pa.), 1378
Historical Society of Delaware, 215
Historical Society of East and West Baton Rouge, 544
Historical Society of Forest Park (Ill.), 359
Historical Society of Long Beach (Cal.), 69
Historical Society of Middleton (N.Y.) and the Wallkill Precinct, Inc., 1016
Historical Society of Pennsylvania, 1338, 1340
Historical Society of Princeton (N.J.), 947
Historical Society of Quincy and Adams County (Ill.), 382
Historical Society of St. James, 856
Historical Society of Saratoga Springs, 1117
Historical Society of the Tonawandas (N.Y.), 1129
Historical Society of Western Pennsylvania, 1364
Historical Society of York County (Pa.), 1396
Hitchcock, Champion Ingraham, 531
Hitchcock, H. P., 529
Hitchcock, Justin, 662

Hitchcock, Ripley, 1053
Hiwill, John, 314
Hjertaas-Roe, Ella, 803
Hjorth, Eric, 341
Hoard, Halbert L., 1603, 1611
Hoard, William Dempster, 1603
Hoard Historical Museum-Fort Atkinson (Wis.) Historical Society, 1603
Hoaré, Henry Royal, 334
Hobart, Henrietta, 1059
Hobart, Henry L., 1172
Hobart, William N., 1172
Hobart (Ind.) Historical Society, 419
Hobart College, 1005
Hoblitzelle Theatre Arts Library, 1477
Hoch, Oscar, family papers, 1270
Hoch, Theodor, 227-F
"Hoch, Amerika," 1036
Hodge Opera House, 1012
Hodges, George S., 227-A
Hodges, Joanna, 68
Hodges, Rev. John Sebastian Bach, 235
Hodges, Joy, 465
Hodgson, Richard, 215
Hoe, Robert, 1106
Hoff, W. C., 465
Hoffer, Mark, 434
Hoffman, Balzer, 1299
Hoffman, Christopher, 1325
Hoffman, Edwin M., 1222
Hoffman, J. S., Memorial Library, 318
Hoffman, Maurice, 913
Hoffman, Willi, 847
Hoffman, William, 1059
Hofmann, George, 195-C
Hofmann, Josef, 4, 227-F, 568, 729, 1053, 1061-F, 1177, 1470, 1484, 1573, 1580
Hogan, A. F., Collection, 1298
Hogan, Jasper S., 939
Hogan, William Ransom, 568
Hogan, William Ransom, Jazz Archive, 564, 568
Hogg, Ima, 1498
Hogg, William H., 939
Hohbargar, Roy A., 128
Hohengarten, Carl, 349
Hohf, Alice Pihl, 1436
Hohmann, Walter H., 509
Holabird, Mrs. John A., 334
Holberg, Anna, 8
Holchak, Bess, 1499
Holcman, Jan, 1061-J
Holcomb, Henry, 1190
Holden, Capt. John, 939
Holden, Oliver, 629, 636, 638, 643, 658, 935
Holiday songs. See Seasonal and holiday songs
Holiness Church (Chicago), 391
Holladay, Joseph, 1560
Holland, Justin, 268
Holland Library (Pullman, Wash.), 1573
Holley, Mary Austin, 528, 1477

Hollins College, 1549
Hollis Street Church (Boston), 654
Holloway, Mrs. Reuben Ross, 607
Hollowell, Miss Frank, 1463
Hollywood (Cal.), 433
Hollywood Bowl, 50, 78, 1261
Holman, Louise Stuart, 1516
Holman Library, 367
Holman, Louise Stuart, 1516
Holmberg, Fredrik, 1256
Holmen, Olga, 787
Holmes, Guy, 1595
Holmes, John S., 8
Holmes, Nathaniel, Fund, 1358
Holmes, Ralph F., 739
Holsinger, Clyde, 439
Holst, Gustav, 195-A, 729-E
Holstrom, Henning, 1577
Holt, Benjamin, 701
Holt, Frank, 1562
Holt, Frank G., 671
Holt, Nora Douglas, 268
Holt, Roland, Collection, 1141
Holt-Atherton Pacific Center for Western Studies, 145
Holvik, Johan A., 815
Holy Trinity Church (New York), 1083
Holyoke, Samuel, 195-A, 334, 502, 701
Homassell, Caroline, 841
Home Moravian Church, 1161
Homer, Mrs. Charles, 1061-F
Homer, George, 643
Homer, Louise, 123, 1061-D, 1573
Homer, Winslow, 624
Hommann, Charles, 1333, 1343
Honey Boy Minstrels, 391
Honnold Library, 55
Honolulu, 147
Honolulu Symphony Society, 287
Hood, Evelyn, 68
Hood, George, 636
Hood Collection, 1347
Hoogstraten, Willem Van, 84
Hooke, George Philip, 729-A
Hoover, Judge Earl R., 1172, 1174, 1189
Hoover, Herbert, Presidential Library, 490
Hoover Institution, 142
Hope, Constance, 1031
Hope, Laurence, 268
Hope (Kan.) Band, 514
Hope (N.J.), 1161
Hope College, 757
Hope Lutheran Church (Milwaukee, Wis.), 1619
Hope Publishing Company, 306
Hopekirk, Helen, 227-D, 227-F, 646
Hopewell, Bessie Richardson, 926
Hopewell (N.J.) Museum, 929
Hopkins, Charles Jerome, 227-D, 654, 1061-B
Hopkins Factory, 188
Hopkins, Johns, University, 606, 610, 612, 613, 624

Hopkinson family, 1338
Hopkinson, B. M., 606
Hopkinson, Cecil, 1031
Hopkinson, Francis, 127, 219, 227-D, 227-F, 227-M, 612, 1238, 1333, 1338, 1347, 1352
Hopkinson, Joseph, 314, 1338
Hopkinson Collection, 1333
Hopkinsville (Ky.) Community College, 527
Hopkinton (N.H.), 195-B, 227
Hopkinton (R.I.) Singing School, 1408
Horn, Charles Edward, 195-A, 224, 642, 847, 1059, 1338
Horn, LeRoy Van, 315
Horn music, 433, 646, 898
Horner, Joseph P., Collection, 544
Horner, Joseph, Memorial Library, 1334
Horner Institute 847
Horner Museum, 1268
Hornpipes, 582
Horowitz, Vladimir, 227-F, 1580
Horsman, Edward, 227-D
Horst, Charles, 555
Horst, Louis, 1061-A
Horszowski, Mieczyslaw, 1053, 1580
Horton, Mrs. Philip Gilbert, 195-C
Horton, Zilphia, 1466
Horton, Zilphia, Folk Music Collection, 1463
Hosen, Freda, 1431
Hoskins, Arthur C., Collection, 866
Hoskins, James D., Library, 1448
Hosmer, Helen, 1104
Hosmer, James Bidwell, 180
Hosmer Hall Choral Union, 180
Hospitals, music in, 1061-M
Houdini, Harry, 1477
Houghton, W. A., 50
Houghton Library, 654
Houghton, Mifflin, & Co., 654
"Hour of Charm," 1516
House of Patterson and Hopkins (music publishers), 1225
Houseley, Henry, 833
Housman, Rosalie, 227-F
Houston, 1477, 1478
Houston Public Library, 1496
Houston Symphony Orchestra, 1496, 1498
Houston, University of, 1498
Houston County (Tex.) Historical Commission, 1482
Hovdesen, Elmer Arne, 227-D
Hovhaness, Alan, 36, 227-C, 227-F, 535, 1040, 1108, 1580
How, Abiel, 654
How, Gordon, 815
Howard, Col. George S., 618
Howard, John Tasker, 227-F, 941, 1031, 1061-A, 1356
Howard-Tilton Memorial Library, 568
Howard University, 226
Howe, Elias, 1146

Howe, John, 1111
Howe, Julia Ward, 227-D, 227-F, 379
Howe, Mark Antony DeWolfe, 654
Howe, Mary, 227-D, 227-F, 1061-A, 1061-B
Howe, Stewart S., 398
Howe, Walter, 1111
Howell family, collection, 1156, 1157
Howell, Edward Vernon, 1141
Howell, Isabell, Collection, 1459
Howell, Jane Allette, 1031
Howell, Margaret Ann, 163
Howerton, George, 439
Howerton-Holsinger Collection, 439
Howland, R. S., 398
Howland Memorial Prize, 195-A
Hubard family, 1141
Hubard, E. W., 1141
Hubbard, Elbert, 1317
Hubbard, James Maurice, 195-B, 701
Hubbard, John Maynard, 314
Hubbard, Lester, Collection, 1523
Hubbard, Minnie Shoyen, 792
Hubbard, W. L., 611
Hubbell, Elizabeth, 443
Hubbell, Raymond B., 1024
Hubermann, Bronislaw, 1053
Hubley, Jacob, 1338
Hudgins, Mary Dengler, Collection, 36
Hudson, Arthur Palmer, Folklore Collection, 833
Hudson, E., 334
Hudson, J. L., Company Band and Orchestra, 737
Hudson (Wis.), 815
Hudson Collection, 841
Hudson River School of Art, 986
Hudson River Valley, 1008
Hudson-Fulton Celebration (1909), 1061-M
Huehn, Julius, 982
Huerter, Charles, 1127
Huger, Daniel, 1418
Huger (i.e., Bacot-Huger) Collection, 1418
Hughes, Adella Prentiss, 1190
Hughes, Charles W., 1137
Hughes, Edwin, 1420
Hughes, Gerald, 1170
Hughes, Langston, 268, 739, 1314
Hughes, Langston, Memorial Library, 1314
Hugo, John Adam, 173
Hulas, 285
Hull, Alexander, 1270
Hull, Anne A., 227-E, 227-F
Hull, Jesse B., 1541
Hull, Josephine Sherwood, 654
Hull House, 341, 800
Hullah, John, 606
Hulse, Camil van, 227-D
Human, Alfred, 227-F

Humboldt (Kan.), 398
Humiston, William Henry, 227-D, 227-F, 847
Humor, 116, 227-L, 244, 341, 391, 398, 624, 687, 1061-M, 1166, 1463, 1594, 1599, 1620
Humperdinck, Engelbert, 84
Humphrey, William T., 315
Humphrey family (Detroit), 739, 742
Humphrey, Martha, 739
Humphrey, Mary, 739
Hundling family, 482
Hundling, D. D., 482
Huneker, James Gibbons, 227-F, 907, 1061-D, 1061-L, 1611
Hungarian music, 260, 654, 1025, 1031, 1061-M, 1187
Hunkins, Eusebia, 1167
Hunleth Music Store (St. Louis), 398, 544
Hunt, Arthur Billings, 814, 1031
Hunt, Arthur Billings, Hymnology Collection, 814
Hunt, Franklin, 636
Hunt-Berol Collection, 1031
Hunt Library, 1360
Hunter, Max, 870
Hunter, Max, Folk Song Collection, 870
Hunterdon County (N.J.) Historical Society, 926
Huntington, Daniel Henry, 192
Huntington, Henry E., Library, 127
Huntington, John, 1524
Huntington, Joseph, 192
Huntington (N.Y.) Free Library and Reading Room, 1056
Huntington Hartford Foundation, 84
Hunton, John L., 1645
Huppert, Roy, 1376
Huré, Jean, 646
Hurlbutt, J. L., 1550
Hurlbutt, Minnie Mosely, 1550
Hurley, J. C., 664
Hurok, Sol, 227-F, 1061-L
Hurston, Zora Neale, 227-F, 244, 1022
Huss, Henry Holden, 227-D, 227-F, 398, 951, 1026, 1061-A, 1061-B
Hussey, Tacitus, 465
Husted, Benjamin, 1317
Husten, Harvey, 1333
Huston, Frank C., 1456
Hutcheson, Ernest, 227-D, 227-F, 1046, 1058, 1666
Hutchings-Koehlar papers, 425
Hutchins, Rev. Charles L., 653
Hutchins Library, 522
Hutchinson Family, 677, 701, 708, 785, 815, 898, 907, 915, 1527, 1673, 1675
Hutchinson, Asa B., 785
Hutchinson, Ernest, 227-F, 1031
Hutchinson, John W., 677
Hutchinson, Karl, 1270
Hutterites. See Anabaptist hymnals

Hutton family, 302
Huuse, Olaf Theodore Nielsen, 518
Hyde, Matilde, 662
Hyland, Robert O., 1234
Hymn Society of America, 1070, 1233, 1487
Hymn Society of America, Committee on Hymn Origins, 105
Hymnals and tunebooks—major collections (over 1000 items), 3, 56, 84, 158, 159, 185, 190, 227-A, 227-J, 228, 235, 269, 273, 306, 320, 330, 333, 334, 339, 368, 393, 398, 404, 405, 416, 534, 536, 559, 615, 634, 636, 637, 641, 643, 653, 654, 721, 798, 831, 847, 860-A, 862, 865, 885, 913, 933, 948, 988, 1002, 1045, 1049, 1061-D, 1070, 1110, 1143, 1161, 1169, 1207, 1222, 1233, 1235, 1259, 1263, 1309, 1311, 1347, 1350, 1369, 1375, 1376, 1402, 1433, 1440, 1455, 1464, 1465, 1474, 1477, 1487, 1493, 1521, 1522, 1529, 1530, 1565, 1636, 1664
Hymnology, 55, 58, 84, 129, 159, 183, 185, 190, 227-A, 227-M, 235, 238, 265, 269, 273, 306, 325, 330, 333, 352, 393, 415, 416, 440, 466, 496, 509, 534, 557, 622, 636, 637, 653, 654, 656, 721, 798, 813, 814, 825, 841, 844, 856, 858, 933, 948, 1002, 1031, 1070, 1092, 1115, 1137, 1161, 1201, 1233, 1259, 1285, 1296, 1300, 1321, 1338, 1347, 1352, 1369, 1376, 1380, 1422, 1426, 1456, 1458, 1459, 1474, 1487, 1521, 1525, 1565, 1658

I

Iadone, Joseph, 195-C
Iberville Parish (La.), 544
Iconography. See Pictures
Ida, Miss, 860-D
Idaho, College of, 291
Idaho Oral History Center, 290
Idaho State Historical Society, 290
Idaho State University, 294, 295
Idaho, University, of, 293
Ide, Chester, 1061-A, 1333
Idelsohn, Abraham Z., 1174
Ierardi, Joseph, Collection, 618
Ikelheimer, Desire, 1418
Iliff School of Theology, 158
Illini Theatre, 302
Illinois, 26, 36, 130, 227-L, 244, 476, 544, 598, 611, 612, 613, 722, 729-E, 734, 800, 837, 860-K, 866, 888, 1031, 1061-L, 1061-M, 1113, 1174, 1193, 1194, 1288, 1425, 1444, 1459, 1520, 1611, 1629, 1633
Illinois Federation of Music Clubs, 392

Illinois Historical Survey, 398

Illinois Infantry, 32nd Regiment, 391

Illinois National Guard, 2nd Regiment, Field Music Association, 314

Illinois Rural Music and Drama Festivals, 398

Illinois State Archives, 390

Illinois State Historical Library, 391

Illinois State University, 379

Illinois, University of, at Chicago Circle, 341

Illinois, University of, at Urbana-Champaign, 398

Illinois Valley Historical Society, 373

Illinois Wesleyan University, 301

Illinois Writers Project, 391

Imbrie, Andrew, 1108

Imhof, Roger, 503

Immigrant History Research Center, 800

Immigrant music, 227-A, 391, 800, 1021, 1076, 1179, 1330, 1336, 1611. *See also* specific national and linguistic groups; Folk music collections

Impresarios, 50, 79, 127, 195-A, 234, 314, 334, 340, 443, 531, 672, 800, 815, 854, 860-D, 940, 977, 1025, 1031, 1052, 1059, 1061-A, 1061-L, 1061-M, 1065, 1105, 1127, 1174, 1190, 1270, 1273, 1274, 1286, 1333, 1359, 1387, 1480, 1523, 1611, 1662, 1663

Inch, Herbert, 1111, 1148

Incidental music. *See* Silent-film music; Theater music

Independence Square Courthouse, 841

Indexes to music, 227-H, 227-J, 315, 398, 406, 437, 450, 561, 636, 687, 721, 726, 739, 740, 747, 816, 860-A, 862, 866, 977, 1033, 1061-C, 1061-E, 1061-H, 1061-N, 1141, 1151, 1161, 1194, 1244, 1285, 1333, 1338, 1359, 1369, 1455, 1459, 1463, 1488, 1519, 1541, 1544, 1576, 1594, 1612, 1633

Indian Exposition (Tulsa, Okla.), 125

Indian Fair (Heard Museum Guild), 43

Indian music. *See* American Indians

Indian River Community College, 243

Indiana, 398, 529, 800, 1172, 1193

Indiana Historical Society, 425

Indiana Society of Chicago, 341, 443

Indiana State Library, 426

Indiana University, 406, 409

Indiana University at South Bend, 448

Indiana University Southeast, 436

Indiana (Pa.) University, 1304

Indiana Volunteers, 1611

Indianapolis (Ind.), 409, 418, 1172

Indianapolis (Ind.) Männerchor, 406, 427

Indianapolis Matinee Musicale, 426, 427

Indianapolis Star, 387

Indianapolis Symphony Orchestra, 406, 421, 427

Indianapolis-Marion County (Ind.) Public Library, 427

Indochinese music, 305

Industrial Expositions (Cincinnati), 1172

Industrial music ensembles. *See* Corporate music ensembles

Industrial Workers of the World, 742, 743, 1445

Indy, Vincent d', 639

Infantry Band, 5th, 815

Infantry Band, 21st, 815

Infantry Division, 45th, Museum, 1257

Ingersoll, Janet T., Gospel Music Collection, 534

Ingram, Thomas, 1470

Inland Rivers Library, 1176

Inniskilling Dragoons, Sixth, 125

Instantaneous acetate discs. *See* Transcription discs and tapes

Institute for Music in Georgia, 278

Institute for Sex Research, Inc., 407

Institute for Studies in American Music (Kansas City), 847

Institute for Studies in American Music (New York), 1080

Institute of Arts and Science (Manchester, N.H.), 912

Institute of Arts and Sciences (Staten Island, N.Y.), 1090

Institute of Buddhist Studies, 47

Institute of History and Art (Albany, N.Y.), 966

Institute of Jazz Studies, 942, 1626

Institute of Music (St. Louis), 1448

Institute of Musical Art (New York), 227-B, 1046

Institute of Musical Pedagogy, 181

Institute of Texan Cultures, 1512

Institute of the American Musical, 1041

Instructional materials, 19, 20, 36, 50, 81, 84, 114, 145, 150, 157, 180, 181, 185, 192, 195-A, 195-B, 197, 218, 227-H, 227-J, 229, 270, 284, 301, 302, 312, 323, 341, 357, 361, 364, 379, 396, 398, 400, 406, 408, 416, 438, 455, 460, 465, 467, 475, 502, 529, 544, 608, 636, 654, 658, 662, 674,

694, 701, 707, 720, 721, 729-A, 787, 798, 800, 803, 847, 856, 907, 912, 955, 961, 977, 986, 995, 1017, 1030, 1031, 1080, 1096, 1101, 1111, 1120, 1135, 1141, 1155, 1161, 1177, 1193, 1210, 1213, 1222, 1235, 1249, 1270, 1285, 1315, 1323, 1327, 1333, 1338, 1340, 1375, 1401, 1447, 1459, 1463, 1520, 1525, 1530, 1534, 1541, 1546, 1591, 1596, 1599, 1621, 1639, 1673. *See also* particular instruments; Music education; Singing instruction materials

Instrument makers and repairers, 53, 124, 129, 164, 167, 188, 212, 227-B, 234, 321, 354, 391, 433, 491, 523, 539, 544, 577, 608, 612, 665, 671, 693, 697, 729-B, 736, 766, 837, 847, 860-J, 860-K, 894, 898, 1051, 1069, 1075, 1140, 1322, 1395, 1441, 1455, 1512, 1520, 1530, 1541, 1567, 1629. *See also* particular instruments

Inten, Ferdinand von, 1053

Interaliierten Musik-Leihbibliothek, 1684

Interlochen (Mich.), 398, 518, 729-B, 748

International Association of Music Libraries, 397

International Bach Society, 637

International Clarinet Society Research Center, 618

International Ladies Garment Workers Union, 1042

International Music Society, 729-C

International Percussion Reference Library, 28

International Piano Library, 1043

International Society for Contemporary Music, 1061-B, 1061-F

International Toy Festival, 800

Internationale Musikbibliothek (Berlin), 1684

Interviews. *See* Oral history

Iowa, 227-K, 416, 800, 1031, 1433, 1436

Iowa Band Law, 475

Iowa Department of History, Montauk, Division of Historic Preservation, 460

Iowa Federation of Music Clubs, 465

Iowa Masonic Library, 458

Iowa Society of Music Teachers, 465

Iowa, State Department of History and Archives, 465

Iowa State Historical Department, 465

Iowa Theater (Cedar Rapids, Iowa), 457

Iowa, University of, 475, 476

Iowa Wesleyan College, 479

Ipswich (Mass.), 701, 947

Ireland, George Thomas ("Tom"), 868

Ireland, 1080

Irish music, 181, 626, 657, 787, 907, 1005, 1122, 1146, 1188, 1352, 1471, 1528, 1669, 1673

Iron County (Mich.) Historical and Museum Society, 734

Iron Range (Minn.) Historical Society, 782

Iroquois County (Ill.) Historical Society, 399

Irving, Catherine, 1128

Irving, Charlotte (Van Wart), 1128

Irving, Sarah, 1128

Irving, Washington, 1128

Irving, Washington, House, 1128

Irwin, George M., 383

Irwin, May, 127

Isaacs, Edith J. R., 1611

Israel, Fanny, 1111

Israel, Julius, 1111

Israeli music, 23, 117, 769. *See also* Jewish music

Italian music, 50, 123, 133, 316, 391, 618, 781, 782, 800, 819, 860-D, 1059, 1188

Italian Opera Association (New York), 1059

Itasca County (Minn.) Historical Society, 783

Ithaca (N.Y.), 968, 976

Ithaca College, 1006, 1007

Ithaca Conservatory of Music, 1005, 1006, 1007

Iturbi, José, 1502

Itzel, John, 606, 614

Iucho, William (Wilhelm), 528, 1477

Ives, Bigelow, 195-C

Ives, Brewster, 195-C

Ives, Burl, 1061-B, 1061-L

Ives, Charles, 68, 76, 83, 99, 174, 195-A, 195-C, 227-B, 227-D, 227-F, 833, 1031, 1036, 1061-B, 1108, 1359, 1425, 1580

Ives, Mrs. Charles, 227-F

Ives, Chester, 195-C

Ives, John, 180

Ives, Richard, 195-C

Ivey, Jean Eichelberger, 195-C

IWW (Industrial Workers of the World), 742, 743, 1445

Ixion, 1208

J

Jablonski, Edward, 1477

Jackman, Harold, 268

Jackson, Arthur ("Peg Leg Sam"), 1141

Jackson, Caleb, Jr., 701

Jackson, Ernest H., 646

Jackson, George K., 379, 642, 648

Jackson, George Pullen, 84, 227-F, 1447, 1459, 1463

Jackson, Col. Henry, 1040

Jackson, John Herrick, Music Library, 195-A

Jackson, Leonora (Mrs. W. Duncan McKim), 227-B, 612
Jackson, Mahalia, 1450
Jackson, Ruth, 483
Jackson, Samuel C., 905
Jackson, Stonewall, House, 1550
Jackson, Walter Clinton, Library, 1148
Jackson (Miss.) Opera Guild, 829
Jackson (Miss.) State University, 827
Jackson County (Mo.) Historical Society, 841
Jackson County (Wis.) Historical Society, 1596
Jackson Piano Company, 1611
Jacksonville (Fla.) Public Library, 245
Jacksonville (Fla.) University, 246
Jacksonville (Ill.), 334, 391
Jacksonville (Ore.) Museum, 1272
Jacobi, Frederick, 227-D, 227-F, 227-H, 646, 1030, 1580
Jacobs, Carl, 960
Jacobs, David, 866
Jacobs, Eliza Ewing, 1315
Jacobs, Henry, 566
Jacobs, Melville, 1577
Jacobson, George, 195-C
Jaeger, John A., 1620
Jaffe, Alan, 195-C
Jalowitz, Heinrich, 729-E
Jamaica, 227-L, 1352
Jamaica Plain (Mass.), 656
James, Allen (Ellen Jane Lorenz), 3, 1200, 1201
James, Floyd Duke, 1477
James, George Watson, 1560
James, Harry, 1646
James, Herman G., 398
James, Philip, 227-C, 227-F, 1018, 1061-A, 1573
James, William L., 1141
"The James Boys in Missouri," 544
Jameson, Gladys, 522
Janesville (Wis.) Public Library, 1604
Janney, James C., 1420
Jannotta (Janotta?), Alfredo, 391, 398
Janssen, Werner, 227-D, 227-F, 317, 907
Japan, 618
Japanese Cultural Broadcasting Co., 1577
Japanese music, 574, 1251, 1469, 1541, 1577
Jardon, Dorothy, 1061-F
Jarnagin, Emily L., 939
Jarrell, Tommy, 1141, 1445
Jarvis, Anna, 1591
Jarvis, Charles H., 1331
Jasen, David A., 1086
Jasper County (Miss.), 829
Jaw harp. See Mouth harp
Jazz, 12, 33, 35, 38, 39, 40, 50, 122, 137, 142, 195, 226,

227-G, 227-L, 239, 258, 260, 264, 265, 315, 321, 322, 345, 349, 378, 398, 406, 433, 456, 466, 544, 550, 556, 561, 564, 568-B, 610, 631, 632, 636, 719, 747, 771, 779, 800, 845, 865, 888, 924, 930, 942, 969, 997, 1021, 1031, 1034, 1060, 1061-B, 1061-N, 1086, 1111, 1166, 1170, 1223, 1317, 1333, 1389, 1406, 1430, 1442, 1443, 1450, 1457, 1487, 1488, 1554, 1577, 1592, 1625, 1626, 1655, 1659, 1667
"The Jazz Singer," 398
Jefferson, Joseph, 1053
Jefferson, Martha (Randolph), 1541
Jefferson, Martha Wayles Skelton, 1541
Jefferson, Thomas, family, 1141, 1540, 1541
Jefferson, Thomas, 643, 1541
Jefferson County (Wash.) Historical Society, 1572
Jefferson Memorial Building, 860
Jencks, Chauncey C., 762
Jenkins, Iredell, 1541
Jenkins', J. W., Sons, 847
Jenkins, James Howard, 1053
Jenkins, Dr. Newell S., 642
Jenkins, Walter S., 547
Jenks, E. M., 1061-F
Jenks, Francis H., Collection, 666, 667
Jenks, Stephen, 334
Jennings, Alice C., 227-F
Jennings, Francis, 1338
Jensen, E., 802
Jepson, Henry Benjamin, 192, 195-A
Jericho Historical Society, 965
Jerome, Jerome, 1646
Jerseyville (Ill.), 364
Jessye, Eva, 511, 729-C
Jessye, Eva, Afro-American Music Collection, 729-C
Jesters of Jonathan Edwards College, 195-B
Jetter Collection, 1461
Jewell, William, College, 848, 849
Jewett, David, 701
Jewish Choral Society (Buffalo), 1130
Jewish Club of Milwaukee, 117
Jewish Community Centers of Chicago, 314
Jewish Community Library, 117
Jewish Institute of Religion, 1174
Jewish music, 23, 48, 50, 117, 189, 227-L, 254, 314, 318, 391, 549, 566, 711, 769, 815, 1021, 1025, 1030, 1044, 1061-B, 1061-J, 1076, 1172, 1174, 1336, 1371, 1477, 1686. See also Yiddish music
Jewish People's Institute, 391
Jewish Theological Seminary of America, 1044
Jews harp. See Mouth harp

Jig-saw puzzles, 922
Jigs, 907. See also Dance
Jirák, Karel, 338, 357, 1580
Jobes, Bob, 1208
Johansen, Gunnar, 227-F
Johanson, Rev. John H., 1161
Johanson Collection, 1161
John, Robert W., 284
"John Brown's Body," 1053
John Carroll University, 1189
John Edwards Memorial Foundation, 74
John Street Methodist Church (New York), 1045
Johns, Altona Trent, 1555
Johns, Clayton, 227-D, 639, 1061-A
Johns, Emile, 555
Johns Hopkins University, 606, 610, 612, 613, 624
Johnson, 1640
Johnson, Agnes Harris, 841
Johnson, Albert, 1611
Johnson, Edna (Evans), 1524
Johnson, Edward, 227-F, 1052, 1053, 1580, 1663
Johnson, Edward, Music Library, 1663
Johnson, Eldridge, 210, 1640
Johnson, Fannie C., 406
Johnson, Frances Hall, Program Collection, 183
Johnson, Francis, 227-D, 741, 1333, 1340
Johnson, Francis Marion, 391
Johnson, Frederick Ayres, 101, 227-D, 227-F, 1223
Johnson, Guy B., 227-K
Johnson, H. Earle, 192, 636, 951
Johnson, Hall, 195-B, 226, 1187
Johnson, Henry M., 349
Johnson, Horace, 1061-A
Johnson, Hunter, 1148
Johnson, J. Fred, Memorial, 1446
Johnson, J. H., 1402
Johnson, James, 1193
Johnson, James B., 226
Johnson, James P., 227-F
Johnson, James Weldon, 195-B, 226, 227-F, 245, 268, 1457
Johnson, Jennie, 776
Johnson, Joel Hills, 1520
Johnson, John Rosamond, 142, 195-A, 195-B, 226, 227-D, 1061-A
Johnson, Lockrem, 1576
Johnson, M., Jr., 654
Johnson, Malcolm, 1445
Johnson, Mary Ann, 612
Johnson, Merritt, 1428
Johnson, Orville S., 1643
Johnson, Robert, 90
Johnson, Robert Underwood, 104, 1053
Johnson, Thor, 99, 227-F, 1580
Johnson, William Spencer, 384
Johnson, William T., and Family Memorial Collection, 544
Johnson County (Wyo.), 1643
Johnson Organ Co., 700
Johnssohn, Esther, 1473

Johnston, Harrie W., 682
Johnston, John Sturge, 314
Johnston Collection, 817
Johnston Historical Museum, 937
Joint University Libraries (Nashville), 84, 1459
Jokl, Otto, 1580
Jolas, Jacques, 481
Jolson, Al, 1606
Jonas, Oswald, 104
Jones family (Long Island, N.Y.), 588
Jones, A. J., 1061-L
Jones, A. S., 1378
Jones, Ada Joyce, 227-H
Jones, Ada, Memorial Collection, 992
Jones, Allan, 1061-F
Jones, Archie H., 314
Jones, Carol, 1155
Jones, David E., 1381
Jones, Dyna, 1477
Jones, Edwin Arthur, 706
Jones, Fern Patterson, Memorial Music Library, 1168
Jones, Grandpa, 1445
Jones, Hattie, 860-D
Jones, Helen, 741
Jones, Hilton, 8
Jones, Col. John, 1338
Jones, Louis Vaughn, 226
Jones, Opal, 1591
Jones, Perrie, Rare Book Room, 817
Jones, Robert Edmond, 1061-L
Jones, Sissieretta, 226
Jones, Stella Davenport ("Estrellita"), 92
Jones, Susie, Collection, 1006
Jones, William Henry, 1155
Jones Beach (N.Y.), 588
Jones Liturgical Library, 1467
Jones Musical Collection, 1381
Joplin, Scott, 36, 741, 827, 836, 868, 1036, 1457, 1516
Jordan, Alice, 463
Jordan, Mrs. Jack, 1155
Jordan, Walter, 227-K
Jordan College of Music, Library, 421
Jores, Ernest, 1525
Jory, Margaret (Fairbank), 195-C, 1061-J
José, Richard J. ("Dickie"), 92, 896
Joseffy, Rafael, 195-A, 398, 1061-F, 1111
Josenhans, Alma, 739
Joslen, Abel, 707
Josten, Werner, 227-F, 691, 1061-A, 1580
Josten, Werner, Library, 691
Journal of Music and Dramatics, 815
Journals. See Periodicals
Joyce, James, 398, 502
Joyner, J. Y., Library, 1149
Jubilee Singers (Fisk University), 739, 1175
Jubilee Singers Collection, 1457
Judson, Arthur, 227-F, 1031, 1035, 1172, 1580

Judson College, 351
Judson Hall, 1035
Judson Press Collection, 1386
Jug bands, 997
Julliard Foundation, 1061-D
Julliard School of Music, 179,
227-B, 535, 1009, 1031, 1046,
1061-F
Juke boxes, 968
Jullien, Louis, 314
Juniata College, 1302
Juniata County (Pa.) Historical
Society, 1318
Junior Cadman Club (Houston
Co., Tex.), 1482
Junior League Concert Series
(Springfield, Mass.), 705
Junior MacDowell Club, 1265
Juniper, Walter, 1480
Juris, Frances, 1276
Jurren, James, 1433
Just, Robert H., 334
"Just Break the News to
Mother," 167
Juvenile Band (Brunswick,
Me.), 586
Juvenile Music Club (Rock
Hill, S.C.), 1423

K

Kahn, Erich Itor, 1047, 1061-A,
1580
Kahn, Frida, 1047
Kahn, Otto Hermann, 227-F
Kahn, Sammy, 1487
Kains, Sherwood, 1172
Kaiser, Kay, 1606
Kalkaska County (Mich). His-
torical Society, 762
Kalkman, Adelaide, 860-B
Kalsow, Fritz, 739
Kalsow, Hugo, 737
Kaminsky, Jack, 1557
Kamloops (British Columbia),
195
Kane, Elisha Kent, 1327
Kanetzke, Howard, 1611
Kanitz, Ernest, 85, 1061-M,
1580
Kansas, 144, 341, 847
Kansas City (Kan.), 847
Kansas City (Mo.), 476, 504,
841, 888, 1031
Kansas City Conservatory of
Music, 847
Kansas City Philharmonic, 847
Kansas City Public Library,
846
"Kansas Prize Song," 694
Kansas State Historical
Society, 514
Kansas State University, 507,
508
Kansas, University of, 502
Kansas War, 860-G
Kean Archives, 1339
Kearny, Gen. Stephen Watts,
860-D
Keating, Mr. & Mrs. George,
142
Kaper, Bronislaw, 1646
Kapp, Jack, 227-L
Kappa Kappa Psi, 1260

Karapetoff, Vladimir, 1005
Karnes County (Tex.) Library
System, 1499
Karolik, Maxim, 636
Karst, Emile, 860-H
Karsten, Helene P., 757
Katims, Milton, 227-F
Katterhorn, George H., 1172
Katwijk, Paul van, 1487
Katz, Hedi, 800
Katzman, Henry M., 502
Kauffman, Charles H., 195-C
Kauffman, George S., 1611
Kaufman, Harry, 84
Kaufman, Hattie F., 398
Kaufman, Louis, 1580
Kaufmann, Henry, W., 195-A,
195-C
Kaufmann, Irene, Settlement
Music School, 1355
Kaufmann, Walter, 1580
Kaun, Bernhard, 1111
Kaun, Hugo, 317, 1621, 1624
Kawecki, Joseph F., 756
Kay, Hershy, 1061-A
Kay, Ulysses, 195-C, 1040,
1580
Kaye, Nora, 637
Kaylor, J. Hurley, 851
Kaysville (Utah), 1521
Kazee, Buell, 522
KCRA (radio station, Sacra-
mento, Cal.), 108
KDKA (radio station, Pitts-
burgh), 1358
Kean Archives, 1339
Kearny, Gen. Stephen Watts,
860-D
Keating, Mr. & Mrs. George,
142
Kebo Valley (Me.) Golf Club,
579
Keck, E. D., 475
Keefe, Verna, 1596
Keeney, Russell, 195-A
Keepers, William Lloyd, 1048
Keffer, Edward I., 1333
Kehr, C. J. H., 1560
Keil, Frederick, 1267, 1274
Keil, Dr. William, 1267
Keim, George May, 1338
Keith, Alice, 1611
Keith, Edmond D., 273
Keith, Edmond D., Collection,
559
Keith/Albee Vaudeville Cir-
cuit, 476
Kelfer, General J. Warren,
1232
Kelle A. R., 1510
Keller, Homer, 1111, 1270,
1580
Kellerman, Sol, 258
Kelley family, 1223
Kelley, Edgar Stillman, 36,
227-B, 227-F, 317, 817, 1018,
1040, 1080, 1223
Kellogg, Clara Louise, 1052,
1338
Kelly, Dr. & Mrs. Emerson
Crosby, 1005
Kelly, Gene, 1487
Kelpius, Johannes, 948, 1338

Kelsey, Francis W., 729-B
Kelsey, Louis J., 465
Kelsey, Verne, 1580
Kemble, Fanny, 1352
Kemp, David, 1430, 1433
Kemp, Edward G., 729-B
Kemp, Hal, 1646
Kemp, Rev. James ("Father
Kemp"), 612, 699, 708
Kemper Family Papers, 1172
Kemper, Ruth, 1058
Kendal, Joseph, 185
Kendall, Messmore, 1477
Kendall, Raymond, 227-H
Kendel, John C., 150
Kendrick, Ben, 846
Kenin, Herman, 1274
Kennan, Kent, 1580
Kennedy, A., 349
Kennedy, Harriet (Tibbetts),
1274
Kennedy, John F., Memorial
Library, 72
Kennedy, Robert Emmet, 1118
Kenneport River, 1463
Kenney, Eudorus Catlin, 1005
Kenosha (Wis.), 1611
Kenosha County (Wis.) His-
torical Society, 1606
Kenreigh, James A., 1264
Kent, Richard, 898
Kent, Rockwell, 234
Kent Bugle, 1418
Kent Memorial Library, 205
Kent State University, 1211
Kent-Delord House Museum,
1101, 1102
Kentish Guards, 1407
Kenton, Stan, 1488
Kentucky, 84, 196, 227-K, 305,
314, 425, 435, 832, 1113,
1172, 1193, 1225, 1270, 1477,
1541
Kentucky Composers collec-
tion, 535
Kentucky Federation of Music
Clubs, 531
Kentucky Historical Society,
525
Kentucky Library, 523
Kentucky Music Educators'
Association Collection, 529
Kentucky School for the Blind,
531
Kentucky, University of, 529
Kerhin, Zlatko I., 800
Kern, Carl August, 866
Kern, Carl Wilhelm, 860-B,
860-F
Kern, Jerome, 227-D, 227-L,
527, 611, 624, 747, 1036,
1611
Kerr, Mrs. Arthur J., Jr., 1368
Kerr, Harrison, 227-D
Kerr, Jean, 1611
Kerr, John, 1190
Kerr, Walter, 1611
Kerr Opera House, 882
Keshena (Wis.), 1627
Kettering, Eunice Lea, 847, 957
Kewaunee (Wis.) Public
Library, 1608
Kewaunee County (Wis.) His-
torical Society, 1608

Key, Francis Scott, 227-F, 612,
1040, 1287, 1338, 1484
Key, Ollie Kidd, 1513
Key, Pierre van Rensselaer,
227-F
Key City Music Publishing
Co., 1606
Keyboard instruments and
music, 9, 68, 164, 195-A,
204, 207, 234, 391, 860-F,
860-K, 1061-A, 1061-C,
1161, 1222, 1312, 1323, 1364,
1407, 1448. See also Harpsi-
chords; Organs; Pianos
Keystone Broadcasting Sus-
taining Program Service,
1469
KGW (radio station, Portland,
Ore.), 1274
Kiallmark, George, 227-D
Kiburz, John, Jr., 349
Kidd Key College and Con-
servatory of Music, 1513
Kidder, Myron, 689
Kiepura, Jan, 1061-F
Kierney, Paul, 924
Kies, Paul P., 1573
Kilbourne, J. G., 544
Kilbourne, Margaret G.
(Breedlove), 544
Kilbreth, George Henry, 589
Kilgen Organ Co., 860-B
Killey, Richardetta (Beverley),
1560
Killingly (Conn.?), 180
Kilmer, Richard Longley, 314
Kilpatrick, Jack Frederick,
1483
Kilpatrick Society, 1483
Kiltz, John, 227-F
Kimball, J. J., 406
Kimball, Jacob, 701
Kimball House Historical
Society, 730
Kimberley, Edwin O., 1611
Kimberly, Dr., 314
Kimble, Stella, 1445
Kimble, Taylor, 1445
Kimmerle, Marjorie, 150
Kincaid, Bradley, 522
Kinder, Ralph, 227-D
Kinder, William, 396
Kindergarten songs. See Chil-
dren's music
Kinderhook (N.Y.), 707
Kindler, Hans, 223, 227-F, 1177
Kindler, Hans, Collection, 223
King, Charles, 286
King, E., 8
King, Frederick, 1477
King, Grace, 544
King, Julie Rivé, 227-F
King, Karl, 463, 470, 475, 618
King, LeEtta Sanders, 1577
King, M. I., Library, 529
King, Martin Luther, Memorial
Library, 223
King, Omega, 227-F
King, Stoddard, 1270
King, Sue, 860-D
King, Wayne, Collection, 28
King, Mrs. William Bruce,
227-H
King, William W., 544

King Sisters, 1520
Kingman (Kan.) Historical Museum, 500
King's College (Wilkes-Barre, Pa.), 1392
Kingsbury, Lilburn A., 860-D
Kinsey, Ruth, 1172
Kingsley, Elbridge, 688
Kingsley, George, 689
Kingsley, Luther, 202
Kingsport (Tenn.) Public Library, 1446
Kingston (Mass.), 707
Kingsville (Tex.), 227
Kinkeldey, Otto, 227-F, 1005, 1061-B, 1580
Kinscella, Hazel Gertrude, 227-F, 887, 1577
Kinsley (Kan.) Library, 501
Kipnis, Alexander, 195-C, 1061-F
Kirchner, Leon, 68
Kirkham, George, 1521
Kirkpatrick, John, 195-C, 227-F
Kirkpatrick, Ralph, 195, 227-F
Kirlin, June Caldwell, 1270
Kirshenblatt-Gimblett, Barbara, 1076
Kirstein, Lincoln, 227-F, 227-H
Kisinger, Everett D., 398
Kissel, Leo, Collection of Theater Orchestrations, 1612
Kistler, Marian, 171
Kitchens, Freeman, 523
Kittredge, George Lyman, 654
Kittredge, Walter, 314
KKK (Ku Klux Klan), 743, 1601
Klapper, Paul, Library, 1089
Klass, George, 815
Klatzko, Bernard, 997
Klau Library, 1174
Klaw, Marc, 227-F
Kleberg, Rudolph, 1477
Klein, Bruno Oscar, 227-D
Klemm, Gustav, 227-D
Klemperer, Otto, 72, 1025
Klinck Memorial Library, 385
Kline, John, 721
Kling's orchestral music library, 739
Klinke, Esther, 1480
Klio Association, 314
Klohr, John N., 1176
Kmen, Henry, 557
KMOX (radio station, St. Louis), 349
Knaebel, S., 707
Knapp, E. C., 356
Kneass, Nelson, 142, 866
Kneisel, Franz, 227-F, 583, 1053, 1111
Kneisel Hall, 583
Kneisel Quartet, 195-A, 227-E, 583, 682
Knell, John, 1611
Knickerbocker Little Symphony, 55
Knight, Abel Farnsworth, 699
Knight, Frederick, 463
Knight-Shaker Collection, 643
Knights of Pythias Band (Nashville, Ind.), 434

Knitzer, Joseph, 729-C
Knobloch, Davis, 1541
Knobloch, Fred F., 1541
Knoll, A. H., 398
Knott, James Proctor, 523
Knowland, Hannah B., 354
Knowles, Frederick L., 190
Knowleton, Eugene Bruce, 1277
Knox College, 360
KOA (radio station, Denver), 157
Kober, Arthur, 1611
Kobzev, Nicolai, 68
Koch, Caspar P., 1359, 1365
Koch, Paul, 1365
Kochanski, Paul, 1053
Kodály, Zoltán, 1031
Koehlar (i.e., Hutchings-Koehlar) papers, 425
Koenig, Clarence, 868
Koenig, Mrs. N., 150
Kohlenberg, Lee, Jr., 1382
Kohm, Joseph Anthony, 1005
Kohn, Miss, 860-D
Kohn, Solomon H., 1107
KOIN (radio station, Portland, Ore.), 1274
Koivisto, Edith, 800
Kolar, Victor, 1053
Koldofsky, Mrs. Adolf, 81
Kolisch, Rudolf, 195-C, 227-D, 1580
KOMO (Seattle) Radio Music Library, 1576
Det Kongelige Bibliotek, 1668
Konschine, Emma Mershon, 465
Kooper, Kees, 1026
Korda, Robert, 1061-A
Koreshan Unity, 241
Korn, Bertram W., 1174
Korngold, Erich Wolfgang, 84, 88, 89, 104, 227-F, 1025, 1580
Korngold, Ernst Werner, 88
Korngold, George, 89
Korngold, Julius, 88, 89
Korson, George, 227-L
Korson, George, Folklore Archive, 1392
Kortschak, Hugo, 227-F
Koshets, Nina, 227-B, 1053
Koshland Photograph Collection, 50
Kostelanetz, André, 227-C, 618
Kotzschmar Club (Portland, Me.), 576, 596
Koudelka, Josef, 636
Koussevitsky, Olga, 195-C, 227-B
Koussevitzky, Serge, 227-B, 227-F, 636, 654, 1031, 1580, 1670
Koussevitzky Foundation (Brookline, Mass.), 227-B
Koussevitzky Foundation (Washington, D.C.), 227-B
Koussevitzky Music Collection, 227-B
Koussevitzky Room, 636
Koutzen, Boris, 227-D, 1107
Koven, Reginald de, 142, 227-D, 227-F, 712, 729, 1031,

1053, 1061-A, 1338, 1573, 1577, 1580, 1612
Kowalski, Max, 1025
Kozinski, David, 216
Kozma, Tibor, 406
Kraehenbuehl, David, 195-C
Kraft, Edwin Arthur, 1190
Kraft, William, 68
Kraft Music Hall, 1579
Kramer, A. Walter, 227-D, 227-F, 1646
Kramer, Mrs. E. Burke, 1176
Kramer, Tosca Berger, 36
Krasner, Louis, 227-F, 654, 1127
Krauss, John, 1325
Krauth Memorial Library, 1342
Krehbiel, Henry Edward, 227-F, 227-H, 568, 1053, 1061-B, 1061-D, 1061-L, 1111, 1177
Kreider, Noble, 1061-A
Kreisarchiv Land Handeln, 1681
Kreisler, Fritz, 227-C, 227-F, 761, 860-C, 1053, 1111, 1148, 1359
Krenek, Ernst, 2, 68, 83, 96, 195-C, 227-C, 340, 535, 1061-M, 1111, 1155, 1292, 1359, 1580, 1670
Krepps, James, 1364
Krepps, William Taylor, 1364
Kress, Idabelle Haughey, 940
Kreutz, Arthur, 833
Kriebel, Christopher, 1325
KRKD (radio station, Los Angeles), 1577
KRLD (radio station, Dallas), 1501
Krodel, Sarah, 429
Kroeger family, 860-B
Kroeger, Adolph Ernst, 860-B
Kroeger, Alfred, 1111
Kroeger, Ernest R., 227-D, 860, 866
Krohn, Ernst, Sr., 866
Krohn, Ernst C., 860, 866
Krone, Max T., 1573
Kroyt, Boris, 227-F
Krueger, Karl, 227-H
Krummel, D. W., 397
KSCJ (radio station, Sioux City, Iowa), 1436
Ku Klux Klan, 743, 1601
Ku Klux Klan, Women's Auxiliary, 1601
Kubik, Gail, 227-F, 1061-A, 1580, 1646
Kuehn, Howard, 1378
Kuhn family (Brooklyn, N.Y.), 1122
Kuhn, Settie S., 1174
Kuhn, Walt, 234
Kuhnle, Wesley, 68
Kulp, Isaac Clarence, 1297
Kumlein, Thure L., 1611
Kunits String Quartet, 1359
Kunits, Luigi von, 1659
Kunkel imprints, 866
Kunkel, Charles, 860-B
Kunkel, Christian Charles, 860-B

Kunkel, Lloyd, 894
Kunkel, Mary Guthrie, 860-B
Kunkel Brothers, 860-E
Kunkel Collection, 860-B
Kunkel's Music Review, 860-E
Kunofsky, Edward, 1080
Kuntz, Emile, 568
Kuntz, Rosamonde E., 568
Kurath, Gertrude, 1327
Kurnik, Stanley, 68
Kuropas, Stephen, 800
Kursh, Maurice, 122
Kurth, Charles F., Jr., 1161
Kurth Collection, 1161
Kurtz, Edward, 1061-A
Kurtz, Samuel, 618
Kyle, Alexander, 227-D

L

Labadie collection, 729-E
Labor Management Documentation Center, 1005
Labor songs, 227-A, 227-L, 245, 391, 742, 1005, 1042, 1061-M, 1062, 1463, 1584, 1611. See also Occupational songs; Work songs
Labor Union Constitutions and By-Laws collection, 50
Labor unions. See Unions
Labrador, 1352
LaBrew, Arthur R., 741
Labunski, Wiktor, 847
Lachmund, Carl V., 1061-B
Lackawanna Historical Society, 1381
La Course, Ray, 1656
LaCrosse (Wis.), 1611, 1642
Lacy, Drucy, 1141
Laderman, Ezra, 227-C
Ladies' Concert Band (Kalkaska Co., Mich.), 762
Ladies' Hussar Band, 146
Ladies' Musical (St. Paul), 815
Ladies Musical Club (Cincinnati), 1172
Ladino music, 1021
LaDue, Mrs. Floyd, 838
LaFayette, Marie Joseph, Marquis de, 127, 729-A
Lafayette Square, 977
LaFlesche family, 887
LaFlesche, Francis, 887
Lagerstroms, Reinhold, 819
LaGuardia, Achille, 26
LaGuardia, Fiorello, 1031
Laguna, Frederica de, 1327
La Hache, Theodore von, 555, 561, 1477
Lahr, Bert, 1061-L
Laine, Frankie, 1487
Lajeunesse, Emma (Mme. Albani), 1054, 1061-B, 1659
La Jolla (Cal.) Playhouse, 115
Lajtha, Abel, 1031
Lake, M. S., 618
Lake County (Ill.) Museum, 400
Lake County (Minn.) Historical Society, 820
Lake County (Ohio) Historical Society, 1218

Lake Forest College, 366
Lake George (N.Y.), 179
Lakewood (Ohio) Historical Society, 1213
Lamarter, Eric De, 227-D, 227-F, 317, 334, 1046, 1111
Lamb, Annie, 1477
Lamb, John, 59
Lambert, Alexander, 1053
Lambert, Euphemie Aimée, 555
Lambert Castle, 944
Laments, 1155
Lamon, Bessie, 544
Lamoni (Iowa), 478
Lamont, Cedric, 866
Lampell, Millard, 1611
Lanaux, George, 544
Lancaster (Mass.) Town Library, 674
Lancaster (Ohio), 1193
Lancaster (Pa.), 1161, 1285
Lancaster Mennonite Conference, 1309
Lancaster Theological Seminary, 1306
Lancaster County (Pa.), 939
Lancaster County Historical Society, 1308
Landauer, Bella C., 185, 234, 1059
Lander, Edward J., 1165
Landers, Major George W., 465, 475
Landmichl, Ludwig Stanley, 1643
Landowska, Wanda, 1177
Landsberg, Sigmund, 357
Lane, Burton, 227-D, 1024
Lane, Margaret, 896
Lane County (Ore.) Museum, 1269
Lang, B. J., 636
Lang, Francis (Mrs. B. J.), 636
Lang, Henry Albert, 227-D
Lang, Malcolm, 636
Lang, Margaret Ruthven, 227-B, 227-D, 227-F, 636, 1573
Lang, Paul Henry, 227-F
Lang, Rosalie, 315
Lange, Hans, 1053
Lange, Juliette, 242
Langenus, Gustave, 1222
Langer, Pauline, 307
Langey, Otto, 1148
Langinger, Herman, 76, 195-C
Langlie, Dorothy Hatch, 815
Langlois (i.e, Amoureux-Langlois) family, 860-C
Langstroth, Ivan, 50
Lanier, Sidney, 606, 1560
Lanin, Jimmy, 1087
Lankford, Grace Ward, Collection, 1494
Lansing (Mich.) Opera House, 743
Lansingburgh (N.Y.), 1102
La Pine, A. J., 195-C
Lapouyade, Robert de, Collection, 544
Laramie (Wyo.), 1643
Laramie Plains Museum Association, 1645
Larcom, Lucy, 694, 701

Lardner, Ring, 729-B
Large, Laura Antoinette, 391
LaRocca, Dominic James ("Nick"), 227-F, 568
LaRoche, J. D., 1061-D
Larrabee, Mrs., 460
Larrabee, William, 460
Larson, Arne B., 1433
Larson, Earl Roland, 227-D
Larson, Louis E., 815
Larson's Theater, 1587
Lashanska, Hulda, 975
Laskiainen, 782
Laszlo, Alexander, 1646
Latella, Ann M. Pfeiffer, 1112
Lathrop, Orrin, Collection, 761
Latin-American music, 24, 29, 31, 49, 142, 213, 227-L, 291, 406, 800. See also Mexican music; Spanish music
Latin (language) music, 115, 316, 375, 791, 1059, 1571, 1579
Latrobe, Benjamin Henry, 612
Latter-Day Saints. See Mormon music
Latter Day Saints Tabernacle Choir, 1519, 1520, 1521, 1523
Lauder, Harry, 853, 1596
Lauff, Charles, 129
Laughlin, Estelle, 881
Laughry, Augusta, 1477
Laughton, Robert, 1674
Lauinger Memorial Library, 225
Laurance, Charles, 458
Laurence, Dan, Musical Comedy Collection, 1477
Lava, William, 1646
Laval, Université, 1670
La Violette, Wesley, 227-D, 227-F, 323
Law, Andrew, 180, 636, 729-A, 775, 955, 1292, 1333, 1338, 1402
Lawrence, A. F. R., 227-L, 1061-J
Lawrence, Gertrude, 1031, 1061-L
Lawrence, Jerome, 1061-J
Lawrence, John Porter, 1193
Lawrence, Lawrence Shubert, 1333
Lawrence, Lucile, 227-F
Lawrence, Marjorie, 305
Lawrence, Sarah, College, 975
Lawrence (Kan.), 514
Lawrence Musical Association, 514
Lawrenceville (N.J.) School, 930
Laws, Miss, 1172
Lawson, Warner, 227-F
Laycock, Harold, 1520
Layton, John Turner, 226
Lazar, Filip, 227-F
Lea and Febiger Collection, 1338
Leach, MacEdward, 1352
League of Composers, 1031, 1061-B, 1061-E
League of Composers, Review, 227-H

Learned Opera House, 1572
Leavitt, Burton E., 202
Leavitt, Theodore, Theatrical Print Collection, 398
Lebanese and Syrian music, 1188
Leblond, Caralie, 544
Lebow, Howard M., 627
Lechnyr, Joseph, 1525
Ledbetter, Lena Dancy, 1477
Lederman, Minna, 195-C, 227-F, 227-H, 1061-B
Leduc, Monique Schmitz, 195-C
Ledyard, Erwin, 1174
Lee family, 1560
Lee, Albert, 398
Lee, Angelica B., 713
Lee, Ann R. (McCarty), 1560
Lee, Carlton, 779
Lee, Mrs. Frances G., 642
Lee, Francis Wilson, 654
Lee, Harold B., Library, 1520
Lee, Henry, 1560
Lee, Mildred Childe, 1560
Lee, Nathaniel, 701
Lee, Noël, 195
Lee, Olav, 802
Lee, Philip Ludwell, 1560
Lee, Robert E., 1061-J, 1560
Lee, William, 1560
Lee (Me.), 729-B
Lee & Walker imprints, 467
Leeds, Philo, 1036
Lees, Benjamin, 83, 227-D, 535
Leese, Jacob, family, 65
Leeson, Cecil, 433
Leetonia (Ohio), 1309
Lefevere, Kamiel, 752
Leftwich, George E. ("Jelly"), 1143
Leginska, Ethel, 227-F
Lehigh County (Pa.), 1333
Lehigh County Historical Society, 1280
Lehigh University, 1284
"Lehigh Valley Waltz," 1291
Lehman, Mrs. A. H., 514
Lehman, E. Linwood, 1541
Lehman, F. M., 356
Lehman, Gottfried, 439
Lehman, William, 465
Lehmann, Liesel, 84
Lehmann, Lilli, 227-B, 227-F, 1111
Lehmann, Lotte, 131, 227-B, 1031, 1053
Lehmann collection, 1061-F
Leibowitz, René, 729-E
Leich, Roland, 1360
Leichtentritt, Hugo, 227-C, 227-F, 1523
Leide, Enrico, 266
Leigh, Mitch, 195-C
Leigh, Sam, 1477
Leighter, Grace Clough, 227-D
Leighter, Henry Clough, 227-B, 227-D
Leighton, George A., 1176
Leinsdorf, Erich, 227-F, 1031
Leipzig, 1222
Lejeal, Alois F., 227-D
Lekberg, Sven, 463
Leland, J. M., 815

Lenoir (N.C.) High School Band, 1143, 1151
Lenox, William J., 1139
Lenox Hill Neighborhood Association (New York), 800
Lenya, Lotte (Weill-Detweiler), 1073
Leo, Ernest, 465
Leonard, Clair, 1107
Leonard, Herman Burr, 30
Leonard, Jacob, 707
Leopold, Ralph, 1061-F
Lert, Richard, 68
Leschetizky, Theodor, 639
Leslie, Edgar, 1646
Lester, Thomas William, 317
Letter notation, 526, 670, 697, 1096, 1230. See also Shape notes
Leudeke, William, 977
Levant, Oscar, 227-F
Levassor family, 531
Levenson, Boris, 1111
Lever, Charles, 544
Levin, Sylvan, 1331
Levine, Marks, 637
Levine, Maurice, 195-C
Levine, Russ, Collection of Sheet Music, 465
Levitzki, Mischa, 1580
Levy, Ed, 712
Levy, Grace, 391
Levy, Hal, Collection, 84
Levy, Heniot, 334
Levy, Jules, 157
Levy, Lester S., 398, 610, 624
Levy, Will, 1174
Lewandowski, Manfred, 1025
Lewin, Frank, 195-C
Lewis, Eleanor Parke (Custis), 227-G
Lewis, Frank J., Center Library, 323
Lewis, Freeman, 1383
Lewis, Furry, 1451
Lewis, Hannah, 707
Lewis, Isabella W., 1611
Lewis, James, 1059
Lewis, James A., 238
Lewis, John Frederick, 1327
Lewis, John Leo, 324
Lewis, Joseph, 935, 1061-A
Lewis, Katherine Handy (Mrs. Homer), 1031
Lewis, Leo Rich, 227-D, 679
Lewis, Mrs. Leslie, 1643
Lewis, Mabel Claire, 913
Lewis, Nell Battle, 1155
Lewis, Ted, 1178
Lewis, Thomas W., 1193
Lewis, Walter H., 913
Lewis and Clark College, 1274
Lewis County (W.Va.), 1591
Lewis-Clark State College, 292
Lewisohn Stadium, 1030
Lewisson, Walter Updike, 127
Lewyn, Helena, 68
Lexington (Ky.), 425
Lexington (Mass.), 662
Lexington (Va.), 1560
Lhévinne, Josef, 227-F
Lhévinne, Rosina, 227-F
Liberal Arts Association of America, 55

Liberty (Mo.), 848
Liberty Hall (New Bedford, Mass.), 683
Librarianship, 227-H, 636, 979, 1111, 1326, 1352
Library Association of La Jolla (Cal.), 66
Library Association of Portland (Ore.), 1273
Library Association of Sandusky (Ohio), 1229
Library Company of Philadelphia, 1338, 1340
Library Hall (Warren, Pa.), 1387
Library of Congress, 101, 227, 272, 508, 722, 898, 909, 1152, 1270, 1546, 1685
Library of Congress classification scheme, 1111
Library of Congress, Archive of Folk Song, 27, 227, 1095, 1568
Library of Congress, Copyright Office, 227-J, 1106
Library Theater (Warren, Pa.), 1387
Libretti, 55, 81, 84, 100, 125, 127, 129, 195-A, 227-A, 227-J, 227-M, 265, 268, 269, 305, 314, 315, 334, 340, 354, 360, 366, 398, 476, 561, 576, 588, 612, 654, 712, 825, 977, 982, 995, 1005, 1037, 1041, 1042, 1046, 1061-D, 1061-L, 1065, 1141, 1174, 1210, 1226, 1277, 1285, 1338, 1340, 1402, 1459, 1461, 1518, 1520, 1594, 1612. See also Operas
Libretti, French texts from Louisiana, 1, 544, 555, 568-A, 568-C. See also French music
Lichtenwalter, Geneve, 847
Lichtenwanger, William, 227-F
Lieberson, Goddard, 195-C, 227-F, 1031
Liebesmahl, 1161, 1285, 1316
Liebling, Emil, 314, 1113
Liederkranz (Plattsmouth, Neb.), 892
Liedertafel (Cincinnati), 398
Liedertafel (New Braunfels, Tex.), 1506
Liepmann, Klaus, 195-C, 1155
Lieurance, Thurlowe, 465
Liggett, Carr, 1167
Light, David H., 1359
Light Guard Band (Marshall, Tex.), 1502
Light Infantry Company (Otisfield, Harrison, and Raymond, Me.), 707
Light Opera. See Operetta and musical comedy
Lili'uokalani, Queen of Hawaii, 285, 286, 1670
Lillenas Publishing Co., 113
Lilly, Josiah Kirby, 1375
Lilly Library, 406
Lilly Library Archives, 444
Lincoln, Abraham, 227-M, 314, 315, 340, 391, 398, 413, 885, 1402, 1444, 1590

Lincoln, Abraham, Library and Museum, 1444
Lincoln Grace Garrison, 1611
Lincoln, Jairus, 658
Lincoln, Jennette, E. C., 398
Lincoln, Mary Todd, 230
Lincoln (Ill.) Christian College, 368
Lincoln (Neb.) City Libraries, 885
Lincoln (Neb.) Symphony Orchestra, 887
Lincoln Center for the Performing Arts, 1031, 1053
Lincoln Library (Springfield, Ill.), 392
Lincoln Memorial University, 1444
Lincoln National Life Foundation, 413
Lincoln University, 1314
Lind, Jenny, 36, 142, 227-F, 305, 314, 335, 391, 544, 636, 654, 688, 689, 766, 815, 860-C, 860-D, 1054, 1059, 1111, 1222, 1305, 1328, 1461, 1463, 1484, 1502, 1511, 1603
Lindau, Harold, 1061-F
Lindbergh, Charles A., 195-B
Linden Hall, 1315
Lindenhurst (N.Y.) Historical Society, 1010
Lindenwood College, 306
Linder, Oliver A., 386
Lindgren, Dr. Ethel J., 334
Lindi, Aroldo, 1061-F
Lindsay, Anna L., 1555
Lindsay, Rev. E. H., 729-B
Lindsay, Howard, 1611
Lindsay, Jane Delany, 860-D
Lindsay, Vachel, 227-D, 227-F, 1270
Lineberger Memorial Library, 1419
Lines, A. E., 192
Lines West Band (Burlington Railroad), 887
Lions' Club (Hibbing, Minn.), 784
Lipscomb, Mance, 1487
Lissfelt, J. Fred, 1366
Lissfelt, Mrs. J. Fred, 1366
Listemann family, 1609
"Listen to the Mocking Bird," 1040, 1338
Liszniewski, Karol, 1172, 1177
Liszniewski, Marguerite Melville, 1172
Liszt, Franz, 708, 860-F
Litchfield (Conn.), 905
Litchfield (Conn.) Historical Society, 188
Litchfield County (Conn.) Choral Union, 187, 198
Literary and Musical Society (Cincinnati), 1172
Lithuanian music, 227-L, 391
Lititz (Pa.), 1161, 1285, 1320, 1402
Lititz Collegium Musicum, 1285
Lititz Moravian Church, 1316
Litta, Marie, 379
Litta Conservatory of Music, 398

Litten, William, 663
Little, Mr., 1463
Little, Amelia Timm (Mrs. F. H.), 465
Little, Dorothy, 587
Little, Phebe W., 587
Little, William, 729-A, 970, 1017
Little Rock (Ark.), 36
Little Rock Public Library, 40
Little Theatre (Chicago), 729-E
Littlefield, Warren ("Skip"), 138
Littleton (Colo.) Historical Museum, 170
Littleton Area (N.H.) Historical Society, 911
Liturgical Arts Society (University of Notre Dame), 440
Liturgical Commission, Episcopal Diocese of Chicago, 324
Liturgical music. See specific denominations; Church music
Liudkevych, 800
Liventhan, Sara Ida, 1061-A
Livingston, Brockholst, 1406
Livingston, Fud, 1420
Lloyd, Alice, College, 539
Lloyd, Norman, 195-C, 637
Lloyd, William Bross, 314
Lloyd Library, 1436
Loach, Don, 195-C
Locke, Mabel, 391
Locke, Ralph P., 1113
Locke, Robinson, 1207
Locke, Robinson, Collection of Dramatic Scrapbooks, 1061-L
Lockhart Society, 685
Lockwood, Albert, 729-E
Lockwood Normand, 227-D, 646, 1111, 1580
Lodge, William C., 215
Loeb, Eda Kuhn, Music Library, 654
Loeb, Harry Brunswick, 568
Loeb-Goehr, Susi, 84
Loeffler, Charles Martin, 195-C, 227-B, 227-F, 639, 646, 729-E, 1053, 1117, 1580, 1666
Loesser, Arthur, 227-F
Loesser, Frank, 1061-A
Löwenbach, Jan, 116
Logan, Frederic Knight, 465, 843
Logan, Joshua, 443, 1061-L, 1611
Logan, Sinclair, 646
Logan (Utah) Tabernacle Choir, 1521
Loggers' songs, 135, 592, 687, 766, 815, 1005, 1185, 1627
Lohn, Hermann, 142
Lohr, Lenox Riley, 341
Lolliman, Edgar, 1596
Lolliman, Pauline, 1596
Lomax, Alan, 227-L
Lomax, John A., 227-F, 1477
Lombard, Warren, 729-B
Lombard (i.e., Meadville/ Lombard) Theological School, 331

Lombardo, Guy, 1606
London, Charmian (Mrs. Jack), 62
London, George, 195-C
London, Jack, State Historic Park, 62
London (England), 244, 379, 568, 636, 707, 935, 1060, 1061-M, 1161, 1540, 1541
London records, 371
London University, 1672
Londonderry Cornet Band, 1530
Long, C. W., 398
Long, Earl K., Library, 569
Long, Harriet C. Bond, 636
Long, Huey P., 544
Long, Mrs. John Henry, 636
Long, Johnny, 1143
Long Beach (Cal.), 398
Long Beach Band, 1106
Long Beach Municipal Band, 398
Long Beach Public Library, 70
Long Beach Symphony Orchestra, 70
Long Island (N.Y.), 588
Long Island Historical Society, 1083
Longacre, Lindsay B., 158
Longfellow, Henry Wadsworth, 585, 654
Longley, E., 1172
Longmont (Colo.) Pioneer Museum, 171
Longstreet, Stephen, 1450
Longworth, Alice Roosevelt, 1172
Longy, Georges, 1053
Longy Club (Boston), 636
Loomis, Clarence, 961
Loomis, Harvey Worthington, 227-D, 1061-A
Loomis Temple of Music (New Haven, Conn.), 195-A
Loos, Armin, 195-A
Looscan, Adele, 1496
Lopatnikoff, Nikolai, 84, 227-D, 227-F, 1031, 1360, 1580
Lopez, Vincent, 1502
Lorch, Emil, 729-B
Lord, Bert, 1005
Lord, Mary, 227-D
Lord, Thomas, 947
Lorenz, Edmund S., 3, 1200, 1201, 1243
Lorenz, Ellen Jane, 3, 1200, 1201
Lorenz Publishing Co., 819
Loretto Heights College, 157
Loring, William C., 272
Los Angeles, 129, 195, 227-L, 391, 544, 888, 1061-M, 1174, 1662
Los Angeles Civic Light Opera Association, 78
Los Angeles Examiner, 1061-M
Los Angeles Master Chorale, 78
Los Angeles Music Center, Archives, 78
Los Angeles Philharmonic Orchestra, 72, 78, 84

Los Angeles Public Library, 79
Los Angeles Symphony Orchestra, 50, 127
Los Angeles Times, 1061-M
Los Angeles County (Cal.) Museum of Natural History, 77
Losey, F. H., 618
Losey, Joseph, 227-F
Lossing, Benson John, 1560
Loth, Louis Leslie, 227-D
Lothian, Napier, Theater Orchestra Collection, 646
Loud, Thomas, 935
Loudin Jubilee Singers, 1227
Loughridge, Rev. R. M., 1255
Lousiana, 1, 15, 38, 227-K, 268, 334, 406, 528, 654, 860-H, 980, 997, 1059, 1061-M, 1418, 1450, 1463, 1477, 1660
Louisiana College, 573
Louisiana Historical Association, 568
Louisiana News Index, 561
Louisiana Purchase Exposition (St. Louis, 1904), 460, 860-C
Louisiana State Library, 543
Louisiana State Museum, 556
Louisiana State University, 544
La Louisianaise, 555
Louisville, 227-K, 314, 398, 435, 529, 1172, 1270
Louisville Academy of Music, 532
Louisville Civic Arts Association, 535
Louisville Conservatory of Music, 535
Louisville Courier-Journal, 535
Louisville Free Public Library, 533
Louisville Herald, 387
Louisville Orchestra, 535
Louisville Philharmonic Society, 535
Louisville, University of, 535, 815
Louisville, University of, Chamber Music Society, 535
Lourié, Arthur, 227-F
Love family, 195-A
Love, Don L., Memorial Library, 888
Love, John W., Jr., 1659
Love, Lucy Cleveland Prindle (Mrs. Edward Gurley), 195-A
"Lovefeast Odes," 1161, 1285, 1316
Lovejoy Library, 349
Lovelace, Austin C., 159
Lovell, Malcolm, 239
Low, Juliette Gordon, Birthplace, 281
Low, Leo, 1076
Lowe, Mrs. John, 195-C
Lowell, Amy, 227-B, 227-F, 654
Lowell, Augusta, 227-D
Lowell, Isabel Pelham Shaw (Mrs. Frederick), 1031
Lowell Institute, 636

Lowell Offering, 676
Lowell (Mass.) Historical Society, 676
Lowell, University of, 676
Löwenbach, Jan, 116
Lowenhaupt, Warren, 195-B
Lowens, Irving, 611, 1061-H, 1161
Lowens, Margery, 611
Lowens Collection, 1161
Lowinsky, Edward, 329, 1061-M, 1155
Lowry, Earl, collection, 84
Lowry, Robert, 227-D, 259, 950, 1040
Lowville (N.Y.) Village Band, 1014
Lubbock (Tex.), 1477
Lucas Building, 886
Luce's Hall (Grand Rapids, Mich.?), 748
Lucke, Katherine, 614
Lucy Gates Opera Company, 1520
Ludden & Bates, 270
Ludlow, Dr. Clara S., 227-A
Ludlow, Fitz Hugh, Memorial Library, 119
Ludlow, Noah, 860-K
Ludlow & Smith's St. Louis Theatre, 860-C, 860-E
Luening, Otto, 227-F, 661, 1018, 1023, 1031, 1111, 1580
Lullabies, 107, 334. *See also* Children's music
Lumbard, Jules, 314
Lumbermen. *See* Loggers' songs
Lummis, Charles Fletcher, 82, 227-L
Lumpkin, Ben Gray, Colorado Folklore Collection, 150
Lunceford, Jimmy, 1143
Lund, John, 977, 1112
Lunenburg (Mass.) Academy, 707
Lunsford, Bascom Lamar, 227-F, 227-L, 522, 1152
Luoma, Agnes Helenius, 815
Lupton (Mich.), 729-B
Lurwick, Galen, 68
Luskin, Samuel S., Memorial Collection, 1130
Luther, Frank, 495
Luther College, 461, 1166
Luther Theological Seminary, 813
Lutheran Chaplains' Association, 856
Lutheran Church, Commission on Worship, Liturgics, and Hymnology, 855
Lutheran Church in America, 330, 1341
Lutheran Church-Missouri Synod, 811, 856, 858
Lutheran church music, 330, 353, 385, 386, 461, 466, 468, 622, 729-B, 777, 790, 791, 797, 802, 803, 808, 811, 813, 819, 835, 856, 858, 1196, 1235, 1296, 1320, 1341, 1342, 1419, 1428, 1619, 1633
Lutheran Liturgical Research Society, 856

Lutheran Publishing Co., 461
Lutheran School of Theology (Chicago), 330
Lutheran Studies Center, 1235
Lutheran Theological Seminary (Gettysburg, Pa.), 1296
Lutheran Theological Seminary (Philadelphia-Mount Airy, Penn.), 1342
Lutheran Theological Southern Seminary, 1419
Lutkin, Peter Christian, 354, 357
Lutz, Albert, 860-D
Lyceum Association (Tallmadge, Ohio), 1236
Lyceum Theatre (Ithaca, N.Y.), 1005, 1006
Lyceum Theatre (New York), 1065
Lyceum Theatre (Rochester, N.Y.), 1005
Lyceum Theater (Saint Joseph, Mo.), 855
Lyceum Theater (St. Louis), 860-C
Lyceum Theatre (Superior, Wis.), 1633
Lycoming Opera House, 1393
Lycoming County (Pa.) Historical Society, 1395
Lydon Library, 676
Lyman, Elizabeth, 1005
Lyman, Dr. John, 120
Lyme (Vt.), 1524
Lynchburg (Va.), 1541, 1560
Lynett, William, 1591
Lynn (Mass.), 815
Lynn (Mass.) Historical Society, Inc., 677
Lyon, Mrs. R., 829
Lyon, Susan Williams, 1080
Lyon & Healy, 244, 887, 1061-M
Lyon County (Kan.) Historical Society, 498
Lyons, James, 1517
Lyons, Lorenzo, 288
Lyre, Philip P., 215
Lyric Club (Poughkeepsie, N.Y.), 1105
Lyric Glee Club of Milwaukee, 1622
Lyric Male Chorus (Milwaukee), 1622
Lyric Opera (Ravinia, Ill.), 366
Lyric Theater (Fort Atkinson, Wis.), 1603
Lyric Theatre (Baltimore), 605
Lyrics of songs, 1, 11, 34, 45, 47, 50, 84, 85, 102, 116, 128, 142, 150, 181, 185, 192, 219, 227-B, 227-K, 227-M, 244, 269, 285, 293, 306, 376, 391, 404, 407, 425, 491, 502, 522, 523, 544, 568-C, 601, 606, 612, 694, 702, 707, 711, 721, 729-B, 742, 789, 815, 825, 829, 831, 833, 837, 860-C, 860-F, 860-K, 887, 907, 917, 940, 943, 967, 1040, 1052, 1059, 1061-M, 1061-N, 1066, 1070, 1077, 1091, 1119, 1127, 1143, 1149, 1161, 1174, 1232,

1233, 1264, 1267, 1270, 1274, 1299, 1338, 1340, 1490, 1511, 1541, 1556, 1568, 1577, 1591, 1611, 1614, 1647, 1673. *See also* Commonplace books; Daybooks

M

M. B. Music Club, 1439
Macalester College, 814
McAdams, Nettis F., 227-K
McAlexander, Eunice, 1445
McAllister, John A., 1340
McAllister, William, 914
McAneny, Herbert, 947
McBain, Lenora M., 730
McBride, Robert G., 227-F
McCaffrey imprints, 612
McCall, Daniel B. ("Banjo Dan"), 1049
Maccaroni, Angeline, 344
McCarthy, Harry, 555, 833, 1477
McCartie, D., 860-K
McCaskey, John P., 1308
McCaull Opera Comique Company, 860-J
McClain County (Okla.) Historical Society, 1258
McClane, Sykes S., 1499
McClellan, J. J., 1520
McClellan Opera House Collection, 156
McClintock, Walter, 227-L
McClung, Frank H., Museum, 1448
McClure, J. Clarendon, 8
MacColl, Hugh Frederick, 1402
McCollin, Frances, 227-D, 1333
McCollin Memorial Fund, 1342
McConathy, Osbourne, collection, 227-H
McCook, Martha M., 1364
McCord, Zeta, Theatre Collection, 1487
McCormack, John, 227-E, 227-F, 227-L, 1303
McCormick, Cyrus H., Jr., 1611
McCormick, Harold Fowler, 1611
McCormick, Mack, 1477
McCormick, Maria, 1401
McCosh, D. S., 164
McCoy, William J., 398
McCulloch family, 1207
McCulloch, Josephine, 1207
McCurtain, Green, 1255
McCutchan, Helen, 55
McCutchan, Robert G., Collection of Hymns and Hymnology, 55
McDaniel, David, Collection, 126
McDaniel, R. H., 950
McDaniel, William J., 36
McDermott, Mrs. D. R. P., 1483
McDermott, William Fee, 341
McDevitt, Josephine A., 1333
McDonald, Dan, 443

McDonald, Harl, 227-F
MacDonald, Jeanette, 84, 1031, 1061-F
McDonald, Paul, 798
MacDonald, Scott Richard and Kevin, Music Room, 684
Macdougall, Hamilton C., 716, 1402
McDowall, Mary Ann N., 1478
McDowell family (Mecklenburg Co., N.C.), 1141
MacDowell, Edward A., 195-A, 227-A, 227-B, 227-F, 227-M, 269, 317, 334, 590, 606, 611, 636, 639, 646, 900, 918, 936, 1031, 1053, 1061-A, 1061-B, 1080, 1111, 1222, 1338, 1375, 1502, 1549, 1577, 1580, 1659, 1666, 1670, 1689
MacDowell, Edward, Association, Inc., 227-M
McDowell, Fred, 1451
MacDowell, Marian, 227-B, 227-M, 636, 639, 646, 654, 815, 1031, 1549, 1577, 1580
MacDowell, Marian and Edward, Collection, 227-B
MacDowell Association, 1031
MacDowell Club (Boston?), 636
MacDowell Club (Flint, Mich.), 745
MacDowell Club (Nashville, Tenn.), 1463
MacDowell Club (New York), 1059
MacDowell Colony (Peterborough, N.H.), 84, 227-B, 227-M, 358, 654, 847, 1031, 1577
MacDowell Colony League of Southern California, 84
MacDowell Music Club, 1611
Macedonian music, 1188
McElhiney, G. W., 860-E
MacFadyen, Alexander, 227-D, 1621, 1622
McFarland, Frances, 800
McFarland, Robert E., 296
Macfarlane, Will C., 227-D
McFerrin, Robert, 227-F
MacGilder, Fluke, 157
McGill, Alma, 1230
McGill, Josephine, 535
MacGimsey, Robert Hunter, 227-F, 573
McGinnis, Joseph F., 227-K
McGoodwin, Henry Kerr, 523
McGranahan, James, 306, 333
McGrath, Edward J., 1172
McGregor, C. P., Co., 227-L
McGregor, Robert B., 465
MacGregor, Tracey, 1541
Machi, Sugi, 1577
McIlhenny, E. A., 227-K
MacIntosh, David, 305
McIntyre, Thomas, 1521
Mack, Alexander, Memorial Library, 153
Mack, Ted, 1520
Mackay, Aneas, 1059
Mackay, Clarence Hungerford, 127

McKay, Francis Howard, 227-D
McKay, George Frederick, 227-D, 227-F, 1111, 1148, 1576, 1577, 1580
MacKay-Smith, Alexander, 1541
McKaye, Percy, 1061
McKean, Thomas, 1338
McKeldin Library, 618
McKendree College, 367
Mackenzie, Findlay, 195-C
McKenzie, Kenneth G., 1665
Mackey Auditorium, 150
McKim, Leonora Jackson (Mrs. W. Duncan), 227-B, 612
McKim family, 654, 1005, 1061-M
McKim, Lucy (Garrison), 690, 692, 1005, 1061-M
McKim Fund, 227-B
McKinley, William, 1232
McKinney, Baylus Benjamin, 1259, 1462
McKinnon, Ruby, 1477
McKittrick, Mary, 860-C
Macklin, Hall, 398
McLaughlin & Reilly, 357, 854
McLean County (Ill.) Historical Society, 302
McLellan, Charles W., 1402
McLellan Lincoln Collection, 1402
McLeod County (Minn.) Historical Society, 785
MacMartin, Archibald, 1059
McMaster, Gilbert, 1370
McMillan, Malcolm Dana, 800
MacMurray College, 364
MacNaught, Mary Hoffman, 636, 916
McNeal, James, 806
McNeil, W. K., 42
McNeill, Normal L., 227-L, 1477, 1500
Macomb, "Czarina," 502
Macon (Ga.), 266
McPhee, Colin, 84, 227-D, 227-F, 1061-A
McPherson, Amie Semple, 404
McPherson, Mrs. Clifton, Jr., 1460
McPherson College, 506
McRay, Walter, 511
McTavish, Myron, 477
McWade, John E., 314
Maddox, Emily Harris, 1477
Maddox, Johnny ("Crazy Otto"), 1166
Maddox Performing Arts Collection, 1520
Maddy, Joseph E., 227-F, 518, 729-B
Madeira, Jean (Browning), 1407
Mader, Clarence, 84
Madison, Dolley, 1147
Madison (S.D.), 1432
Madison (Wis.), 1211
Madison Männerchor, 1611
Madison County (Ill.) Historical Society, 348
Madison County (N.Y.) Historical Society, 1097

Madison Township (N.J.) Historical Society, 934
Madrigal Club of Detroit, 739
Madrigal Club (Morningside College), 488
Madrigal Club (Salem, Mass.), 701
Madrigal Club (University of Chicago), 1481
Madrigals, 1481, 1544
Madsen, Florence J., 1520
Madsen, H. Franklin, 1520
Männerchor, 156, 314, 359, 398, 406, 427, 821, 1133, 1172, 1193, 1291, 1375, 1476, 1509, 1611, 1613, 1622. See also Male choruses
Männergesang-Verein (San Antonio, Tex.), 1509
Magazines. See Periodicals
Magennis Academy of Music, 199
Magill, Ellen, 860-D
Maginnis and Morgan (piano teachers), 180
Magnes, Judah L., Memorial Museum, 48
"Magnificat" collection, 1203
Magnus, Charles, 1402
Magnuson, Fred'rica, 315
Magnusson, A. A., 815
Mahler, Alma (Schindler), 88, 227-F, 654
Mahler, Gustav, 227-F, 1689
Mahoning Valley (Ohio) Historical Society, 1246
Mailamm, 1061-B
Main, Hubert P., 227-D, 227-G, 334
Maine, 227-L, 660, 707, 729-B
Maine Historical Society, 595
Maine Music Festival, 576, 577, 580
Maine State Library, 576
Maine State Museum, 577
Maine, University of, 592
Mainer, J. E., 884
Mainous, Jean, 195-C
Maisel, Edward M., 227-F
Majestic Theater (San Antonio, Tex.), 1511
Majestic Theater (Williamsport, Pa.), 1393
Major Figures in American Music project, 195-C
Makovsky, Boh, 1260
Malcolm, Alexander, 606
Male choruses, 61, 215, 314, 325, 401, 437, 453, 654, 746, 794, 803, 815, 824, 835, 879, 1200, 1274, 1446, 1447, 1575, 1596, 1607, 1622, 1632. See also Glee Clubs; Männerchor
Malibran, Maria (Garcia), 636, 1053
Malin, Don, 1573
Malin, William H., 489
Malkin, Joseph, 227-F, 1148
Malko, Nicolai, 227-F, 1053
Mallet instrument manufacturers, 321. See also Percussion
Maloche, Leslie, 68

Malone, Bill C., 557
Malotte, Albert Hay, 227-D, 614
Maltz, Bob, 1061-B
Man, William, 1338
Mana-Zucca, 248, 249, 1193
Managers. See names of specific musical organizations; Impresarios
Manchester (Ind.) Civic Symphony, 439
Manchester College, 439
Manchester (N.H.) City Library, 913
Manchester Historic Association, 914
Manchuria, 1222
Mandell, Eric, Collection of Jewish Music, 1336
Mandeville, Emma (Underhill), 1005
Mandeville, Dr. Frederick Austin, 1005
Mandeville, Henry D., Family Papers, 544
Mandolin Club (Fresno, Cal.), 61
Mandolin Club (Harvard University), 654
Mandolin/Guitar Co., 761
Mandolin, 61, 180, 195-A, 234, 271, 478, 510, 654, 761, 980, 1005, 1015, 1051, 1155, 1172, 1249, 1516, 1599
Manello, Angelo, 1051
Manhattan Opera Co., 636, 1061-F
Manhattan Opera House, 614
Manion, Dessa, 476
Manistee County (Mich.) Historical Museum, 764
Mank, Chaw, 394
Mankato (Minn.) Musical Association, 792
Mankato State University, 792
Manley, Basil, Jr., 1422
Manley, Mrs. N., 636
Mann, E. Richmond, 972
Mann, Elias, 127, 636
Mann, Klaus, 729-E
Mann, Monika, 729-E
Mann, Thomas, 227-F
Mannello, Angelo, 1052
Mannes, Clara Damrosch, 227-F
Mannes, David, 227-F, 1053
Mannes, Leopold, 227-F, 1050, 1111
Mannes College of Music, 1050
Mannheim, Ernest, 847
Manning, Ambrose N., Collection, 1445
Manning, William Hart, 1521
Manschinger, Kurt, 1580
Mansfeldt, Hugo, 50
Mansfield, Samuel, 215
McIntyre, Thomas, 1521
Mansfield (Conn.), 180
Mansfield Historical Society, 202
Mansfield (Pa.) State College, 1317
Mantel, George H., 1172
Manton, Robert W., 227-F, 900

Manuscript Society (Chicago), 334

Manuscript Society (New York), 1061-B

Maple Leaf Club, 868

Mapleson, Alfred, 544

"Mapleson cylinders," 1061-J

Maplewood Music Seminary, 176

Marathon County (Wis.) Public Library, 1638

Marcelli, Nino, 114

March, Flora, 1193

March, Susan L., 860-G

Marchant, Luther, 227-F

Marchant, Marian, 227-F

Marches, 9, 15, 142, 188, 195-A, 227-G, 228, 232, 285, 319, 334, 336, 338, 379, 398, 401, 490, 500, 502, 523, 544, 601, 628, 643, 654, 701, 707, 721, 744, 777, 815, 846, 860-K, 883, 894, 901, 939, 940, 947, 980, 986, 1014, 1016, 1061-C, 1061-M, 1061-N, 1106, 1122, 1135, 1151, 1162, 1190, 1207, 1267, 1268, 1288, 1327, 1421, 1429, 1435, 1550, 1572, 1611, 1631, 1665, 1673

Marchesi, Mathilde (Graumann), 227-F

Marchman, Virginia, 1207

Marcus, Antoinette Brody (Mrs. Jacob R.), 1174

Marcus, Merle Judith, 1174

Mardi Gras, 561

Mardi-Carnival Association, 302

Mare, Frank, 927

Marek, George, 637

Margetson, Edward, 226

Maria, Rosolino de, 206

Marian Library, 1202

Mariarden, 636

Mariarden School of Drama, 916

Marimba music, 608

Marine Bands. See United States Marine Bands

Maring, Joel, 1327

Marion (Md.?) Rifle Corps, 612

Maritime music. See Naval songs

Markham, George D., 860-C, 860-D

Markham, Mary McKittrick, 860-C

Marks, E. B., Printed Concert Music Collection, 1487

Marks, Fannie Blythe, Collection, 1264

Marks Brothers (Canadian touring company), 1662

Marlowe (i.e., Sothern and Marlowe) Shakespearean Company, 1459

Marmol, Mrs. Alfonso del, 549

Marquardt, P. A., 84

Marquardt, William, 1643

Marquette (Wis.), 235

Marquette College of Music, 1621

Marquette University, 1621

Mars Hill (N.C.) College, 1152

Marsan, H. de, 1402

Marsh, Charles, 642

Marsh, Julia, 642

Marsh, Simeon Buckley, 227-D

Marsh, William J., 1483

Marsh & Chase, 1530

Marshall, Arthur, 868

Marshall, Clarence A., 847

Marshall, Harriet Gibbs, 226, 227-F

Marshall, Napoleon Bonaparte, 226

Marshall County (Ind.) Historical Society, 443

Marshall County (Miss.) Historical Society, 826

Marshall-Wood Studios, 1516

Marshfield (Mass.) Historical Society, 678

Marsten, Mrs. Thomas, 334

Martens, Mason, 195-C

Martens Concerts, 427

Martin, Asa, 522

Martin, Bennett, Public Library, 885

Martin, C. F., guitars, 1322

Martin, Charles, 787

Martin, Clara Tull, 860-G

Martin, Deac, 1607

Martin, Ebenezar, 721

Martin, Emmy, 1168

Martin, H. B., 1473

Martin, Hugh, 227-D

Martin, Irving, Library, 145

Martin, J. Hill, 1338

Martin, John B., 730

Martin, John B., and Sherwood School of Music, 730

Martin, Mary, 1057

Martin, Mildred, 1333

Martin, Riccardo, 611, 1053

Martin (Tenn.), 1469

Martin Music Library, 559

Martin-Mitchell, Caroline, Museum, 376

Martinů, Bohuslav, 142, 227-F, 265, 1580

Marvel, Robert Wiley, 994

Marx, Josef, 195-C

Marxophones, 1249

Maryland, 129, 150, 213, 215, 227-H, 235, 654, 729-A, 1060, 1143, 1161, 1285, 1292, 1432, 1560, 1591

Maryland Diocesan Archives, 612

Maryland Folklore Archive, 618

Maryland Historical Society, 612

"Maryland, My Maryland," 314, 612, 1141

Maryland, University of, 618

Maryon, Edward, 636

Marysville (Ohio), 1193

Marysville Choral Union, 1216

Marzo, Eduardo, 227-D, 1061-A, 1061-F

Mascagni, Pietro, 227-F, 672

Maschinot, L. F., 1176

Masi, Francesco, 334

Mason, Daniel Gregory, 227-C, 227-F, 317, 636, 1031,

1053, 1061-A, 1061-B, 1148, 1573, 1666

Mason, George, University, 227-H, 1544

Mason, Henry Lowell, 195-A, 227-F, 618

Mason, Lowell, 195-A, 227-A, 227-D, 227-F, 227-H, 306, 379, 502, 618, 634, 636, 701, 729-A, 916, 994, 1031, 1036, 1040, 1088, 1099, 1111, 1245, 1338

Mason, Lowell, collection, 195-C

Mason, Luther Whiting, 618

Mason, Margaret, 1397

Mason, Morton F., 398

Mason, Redfern, 636

Mason, Stuart, 646

Mason, William, 227-D, 227-F, 636, 1031, 1040, 1061-B, 1061-F

Masonic Hall (Wilmington, Del.), 215

Masonic music, 233, 458, 641, 1005, 1038, 1537, 1584, 1673

Masons, Grand Lodge in Massachusetts, 641

Mason's Opera House, 1587

Mass, 962, 1653. See also Roman Catholic church music

Massachusetts, 83, 84, 130, 180, 181, 186, 217, 227-B, 227-H, 234, 252, 270, 334, 349, 379, 523, 544, 577, 618, 800, 815, 876, 906, 916, 923, 947, 977, 1031, 1052, 1061-B, 1061-J, 1142, 1143, 1174, 1177, 1207, 1352, 1359, 1402, 1522

Massachusetts Federation of Music Clubs, 636, 916

Massachusetts Historical Society, 643, 721

Massachusetts Institute of Technology, 655, 1261

Massachusetts, University of, at Amherst, 627

Massachusetts, University of, at Boston, 650

Massachusetts Volunteer Infantry, 25th Regiment, 721

Massett, Stephen, 65

Massillon (Ohio) Museum, 1217

Massud, Jean M., 701

Master Chorale (Los Angeles), 78

Master Melodiers (Morningside College), 488

Mather, Henry, 268

Mather, Richard, 636

Mather Collection, 1541

Mathieu, William, 314

Mathis, Rev. Michael, 440

Matinee Musical Club, 1207

Matinee Musical Club (Casa Grande, Ariz.), 20

Matinee Musical Club (York, Pa.), 1396

Matinee Musicale (Ann Arbor, Mich.), 729

Matinee Musicale (Indianapolis), 426, 427

Matinee Musicale, 780

Matlack, Hanna, 1315

Matlack, T. Chalkley, 1338

Matter, G., 133

Mattern, David E., 729-B, 729-C

Matteson, Maurice Jefferson, 1420

Mattfeld, Julius, 1025

Matthew, Paul, 1155

Matthews, Albert, 531

Matthews, Alexander, 227-D

Matthews, Brander, 1061-L

Matthews, Brander, Dramatic Museum Collection, 1031

Matthews, W. S. B., 334

Matthews, Washington, 227-L, 964

Matthews County (Va.), 1560

Mattick, Irvin, 866

Mattioli, Lino, 1176

Maude, Aylmer, 1053

Maude, Jenny, 1059

Maurer, Jacob, 1193

Maverick Concerts, 1138

Maxim, John, 643

Maxwell, Clara, 1172

Maxwell, Henry D., 227-G

Maxwell, Lawrence, 1172

Maxwell, Leon R., 568

Maxwell, Ruth Nottage, 568

Maxwell Music Library, 568

May, Joseph, 657

May Festival (Cincinnati), 1172, 1176

May Musical Festivals (Pittsburgh), 1359

May-Beegle concerts (Pittsburgh), 1359, 1375

Mayagüez (Puerto Rico), 1650

Mayer, Daniel (Co.), 860-D

Mayer, Elizabeth, 227-F

Mayer, Eugene, 574

Mayer Brass Band, 544

Mayfield, Alice, 1477

Mayfield, Doris, 362

Mayfield, Lyle, 362

Mayflower, Ballad of the, 698

Mayhew, Charles, 866

Maynard, Paul, 195-C

Maynor, Dorothy, 1031, 1546

Mayo, William T., 555

Mayo imprints, 556

Mayville (Wis.) Historical Society, 1613

Mazet, M., 568

Mazowsze Troupe, 336

Mazzeo, Mildred, 227-F

Mazzeo, Rosario, 227-F

MCA (Music Corporation of America), 1520

Mead, Edward Gould, 227-D, 227-F

Mead, Stith, 1538

Meadville/Lombard Theological School, 331

The Means Library, 672

Mears, Mary, 391

Mechanical and electrical music instrument discs, cylinders, and other media, 19, 26, 53, 153, 186, 210, 314, 344, 371, 406, 424, 493, 600, 821, 839, 959, 1204, 1245, 1278, 1471, 1578, 1611, 1623. See also Cylinders

Mechanical musical instruments, 395, 600, 636, 689, 750, 839, 968, 1245, 1578, 1629
Mechanics' Hall (Worcester, Mass.?), 724
Mecklenburg County (N.C.), 1141
Meder, John P., 896
Medford (Ore.), 1272
Meeker, Debby, 195-C
Meeker, Ezra, Historical Society, 1574
Mees, Arthur, 1061-D
Megee, Captain, 1403
Meier, Louis, 1633
Meignen, Leopold, 1343
Meine, Franklin J., 341
Meine, Franklin, Collection of American Humor, 398
Meisle, Kathryn, 860-D
Meister, Leila von, 646
Melba, Nellie, 83, 227-F, 639, 1177, 1222, 1484
Melbourne (Australia), University of, 925, 1111, 1666
Melchior, Lauritz, 860-J
Mele, 285, 286
Mellon, Arthur, 798
Mellon Library, 1362
Mellor, Charles C., 1359
Mellum, Horace Jay, 314
Melodant piano rolls, 1333
Melodeons, 65, 390, 665, 898, 1375, 1602
Melodrama. *See* Theater music
Melrose (La.), 544
Melton, James, 1061-F
Meltzer, Charles Henry, 1416
Melville, John, 1172
Memorial Hall (Springfield, Ohio), 1232
Memorial Library Archives, 1621
Memphis Commercial Appeal, 1452
Memphis State University, 1452
Memphis-Shelby County (Tenn.) Public Library, 1451
Mendel, Arthur, 195-C, 227-F
Mendelssohn, Eleanora, 712
Mendelssohn Choir (Pittsburgh), 1359, 1367
Mendelssohn Choral Society (Salem, Mass.), 701
Mendelssohn Club (Chicago), 398
Mendelssohn Club (Orlando, Fla.?), 251
Mendelssohn Quintet Club (Boston), 636, 646, 682
Mendelssohn Society (New Haven, Conn.?), 195-A
Mendocino County (Cal.) Museum, 147
Meneely Bell Co., 202
Meneger, Rev. Frank, 1581
Menges, Edward, 862
Menlo Park (Cal.) Public Library, 87
Mennonite Church, Archives of, 415
Mennonite Church, Historical Committee, 415

Mennonite Church Music Committee, 415
Mennonite Conference (Lancaster, Pa.), 1309
Mennonite Historians of Eastern Pennsylvania, 1297
Mennonite Historical and Research Committee, 415
Mennonite Historical Library, 417, 1169, 1547
Mennonite music, 415, 417, 509, 721, 1168, 1169, 1249, 1297, 1309, 1325, 1333, 1376, 1547
Mennonite Library and Archives, 509
Mennonite Song Festival Society, 509
Menominee (Mich.) Opera House, 765
Menominee County (Mich.) Historical Society, 765
Menominee Indian Historical Foundation, Inc., 1627
Menominee Logging Camp Museum, 1627
Menotti, Gian Carlo, 142, 227-D, 247, 1053, 1331
Menuhin family, 549
Mercantile Hall (Philadelphia), 564
Mercantile Library, 859
Mercantile Library Hall, 859
Merchants, 53, 84, 122, 180, 212, 213, 227-K, 227-L, 234, 270, 276, 282, 285, 321, 336, 339, 379, 391, 395, 398, 475, 515, 529, 544, 553, 554, 568-C, 577, 580, 654, 721, 743, 744, 748, 766, 815, 847, 860-E, 860-K, 887, 907, 977, 1015, 1061-H, 1061-M, 1075, 1105, 1127, 1141, 1159, 1161, 1193, 1207, 1211, 1267, 1272, 1285, 1322, 1333, 1338, 1359, 1402, 1418, 1433, 1443, 1529, 1530, 1560, 1611, 1635. *See also* Instrument makers and repairers; Recording companies
La Meri, 1511
Merman, Ethel, 1057
Mérou, Henri, 406
Mérou-Grevemeyer, Antoinie, 406
Merovich, Alexander, 1270
Merrick, Charles H., 1190
Merrill, A. M., 502
Merrill, Harrison R., 1520
Merrill, Joseph, 586
Merrill, William Stetson, 334
Merrill Library, 1519
Merriman, Oliver Paxton, 1375
Merritt, A. Tillman, 227-F
Merz, Karl, 1359
Mesang, Theodore Lawrence, 1268
Mesier, E. S., 721
Mesker Collection, 860-D
Messiah Festival, 505
Messiter, Arthur H., 1061-B
Mestrezat, Walter A., 1591
Metcalf, Clarence, 1185

Metcalf, Clarence S., Research Library, 1241
Metcalf, Frank E., 637
Metcalf, Frank J., 636, 721
Metcalf, Irving W., 1222
Method books. *See* Instructional materials
Methodist Book Concern, 1464
Methodist Historical Collection, 1168
Methodist Historical Society, 143
Methodist Hymnology Collection, 933
The Methodist Museum, 279
Methodist music, 97, 140, 190, 269, 279, 300, 301, 306, 355, 373, 393, 398, 418, 442, 451, 479, 496, 523, 637, 664, 725, 762, 786, 799, 834, 860-J, 886, 891, 922, 933, 1045, 1127, 1141, 1143, 1150, 1168, 1201, 1203, 1272, 1413, 1418, 1459, 1464, 1482, 1487, 1538, 1609, 1619, 1664
Methodist Theological School in Ohio, 1203
Methuen (Mass.), 654
Metro-Goldwyn-Mayer Library, 68
Metropolitan Museum of Art, 1051
Metropolitan Opera, 3, 83, 179, 227-B, 227-L, 244, 269, 314, 406, 544, 614, 654, 672, 710, 712, 807, 819, 1007, 1031, 1052, 1061-D, 1061-F, 1061-J, 1061-L, 1202, 1663
Metropolitan Opera Archives, 1052
Metropolitan Opera, Contest (1910), 1061-B
Metropolitan Opera Guild, 1031, 1052, 1061-F
Metropolitan Opera House (Grand Forks, N.D.), 1165
Metropolitan Opera House (Philadelphia), 1333
Metropolitan Opera House (St. Paul), 800
Metropolitan School of Music, 338
Metropolitan Theater (Seattle), 1575, 1576
Metropolitan Theatre (Minneapolis), 815
Metropolitan Toronto Library, 1662
Metsker, Mrs. John L., 1573
Mettetal, Jerome, 819
Mettke, Hans, 465
Metuchen (N.J.), 939
Metz (Mich.), 729-B
Metzger, Simon, 195-B
Metzger, Zerlina (Muhlmann), 314
Mexican music, 32, 33, 49, 130, 227-L, 291, 544, 957, 1475, 1477, 1500. *See also* Latin-American music; Spanish music
Mexican War, 195-B, 860-K
Mexico, 456, 1031
Meyer, Henry, 1493

Meyer, Julius Edward, 1060
Meyer, Max, 866
Meyerowitz, Jan, 227-D, 268, 1061-A, 1580
Meyrick, Edwin, 1477
Miami Beach (Fla.), 239
Miami Conservatory of Music, 248
Miami County (Ind.) Historical Museum and Puterbaugh Museum, 442
Miami-Dade County (Fla.) Public Library, 249
Miami University (Ohio), 1223
Miami, University of (Fla.), 239
Miami, University of, Band, 195-C
Michael, David Moritz, 1285
Michael, Jakob, 1686
Michael, Marion, 1477
Michaux, Lightfoot Solomon, 226
Michie, Mrs. Robert Lanlands, 860-K
Michigan, 398, 518, 544, 800, 1024, 1069, 1174, 1455, 1611
Michigan City (Ind.) Historical Society, 431
Michigan Federation of Music Clubs, 763
Michigan Historical Collections, 729-B
Michigan History Division, Department of State, 763
Michigan Music Club, 763
Michigan Music Teachers' Association, 766
Michigan State University, 406, 743
Michigan, University of, 393, 727, 729, 748
Michigan Youth Symphony, 98
Middelschuelte, William, 1359
Middle Eastern music, 626
Middlebury College, 1525, 1528
Middlebury Musical Institute, 1529
Middlesex County (Conn.) Historical Society, 190
Middlesex Musical Society, 657
Middletown (Conn.), 180
Middletown (N.Y.), 406
Middletown (Ohio), 1141
Midland (Tex.), 41
Midland Band, 153
Midland County (Tex.) Public Library, 1503
Mid-West Old Settlers, 480
Midwestern U.S., 98, 144, 227-H, 314, 349, 423, 480, 519, 847, 860-A, 1190, 1433
Mielke, Antonia, 1053
Miersch, Paul Th., 227-D
The Miessner Piano, 1611
Mietzke, George A., 1533
Migliaccio, Eduardo, 800
Milady, Samuel Lucas, 226
Mildenberg, Albert, 1061-A
Miles, C. Austin, 922
Miles, Grace Greenwood, 1061-M

Miles, Russell H., 398
Milhaud, Darius, 83, 91, 195-C, 227-D, 227-F, 654, 951, 977, 1053, 1061-B, 1425, 1670
Military Academy, 1135
Military balls, 26. *See also* Dance
Military bands (materials about), 19, 26, 194, 214, 227-E, 227-G, 228, 229, 230, 231, 232, 234, 314, 589, 602, 618, 623, 707, 730, 761, 815, 846, 847, 860-B, 860-J, 898, 909, 940, 1061-M, 1106, 1127, 1135, 1143, 1155, 1161, 1172, 1190, 1193, 1198, 1232, 1257, 1288, 1353, 1429, 1432, 1435, 1437, 1444, 1477, 1562, 1563, 1572, 1611, 1612, 1618, 1642. *See also* Bands
Military Historical Society of Massachusetts, 637
Military music, 214, 227-E, 227-G, 228, 229, 232, 336, 349, 353, 406, 465, 602, 624, 637, 669, 707, 721, 778, 800, 860-D, 874, 907, 909, 940, 941, 980, 1007, 1059, 1122, 1135, 1155, 1161, 1174, 1193, 1288, 1338, 1353, 1435, 1444, 1463, 1490, 1491, 1590, 1591, 1595, 1611, 1612, 1618, 1639
Military orchestras, 98, 228, 229, 232, 1471. *See also* Symphony orchestras
Military songs, 142, 176, 443, 544, 907, 1490, 1590, 1643. *See also* War songs
Militia of Massachusetts, 2nd Brigade, 7th Division, 707
Millard, Harrison, 729-A, 1404
Millard Club, 215
Miller, Alma Grayce, 1543
Miller, Anna, Museum, 1647
Miller, Annie Louise, 887
Miller, Carl, 195-C
Miller, Dayton C., 227-B, 227-F, 1181, 1190
Miller, Dayton C., Flute Collection, 227-B
Miller, Edward, 800
Miller, Elaine, 891
Miller, Elmer Joseph, 476
Miller, Eugene, 1655
Miller, Fred, 866
Miller, Frederick F., 544
Miller, Glenn, 150, 1143, 1198
Miller, Henry H., 314
Miller, Horace Alden, 465, 481
Miller, J. Roscoe, 357
Miller, Jacob, 1601
Miller, Laura, 465
Miller, Lois, 1298
Miller, Marilyn, 1061-L
Miller, Mitch, 1031
Miller, Philip L., 227-H
Miller, Russell King, 227-D
Miller, Susan, 1402
Miller, Terry E., 1212
Miller, Winfield, 514
Miller & Beacham imprints, 612

Miller Index of Songs, 816
Miller Library, 506
Millerite movement hymnals, 297
Millersville (Pa.) State College, 1319
Mills, Irving, 80
Mills, Randall V., Memorial Archive of Northwest Folklore, 1270
Mills College, 91
Mills Music Co., Inc., 80
Mills Music Library, 1612
Millsaps College, 828
Millsaps-Wilson Library, 828
Milltown (Me.?), 707
Milner, Arthur, 1333
Milner Library, 379
Milns, Rodney, 227-D
Milstead, Alma, 1502
Milstein, Nathan, 654
Milton (Wis.) College, 1615, 1616, 1617
Milton College Civic Orchestra, 1616
Milton (Wis.) Historical Society, 1616
Milwaukee, 375, 1174, 1611, 1612, 1629
Milwaukee Journal, 1611
Milwaukee Liedertafel, 1622
Milwaukee Auditorium, 1624
Milwaukee Grand Opera House, 1624
Milwaukee Music Center, 1623
Milwaukee Musical Society, 1622
Milwaukee Musikverein, 1624
Milwaukee People's Theatre, 1624
Milwaukee Public Library, 1624
Milwaukee State Teachers College, 1611
Milwaukee Symphony Orchestra, 1202, 1622, 1624
Milwaukee County Historical Society, 1622
Mims, Evelyn, 1477
Miner, Laura Shepherd, 1521
Miners' songs, 163, 227-L, 742, 1392, 1430, 1445, 1466
Ming, John H., 874
Minneapolis, 803, 815, 1436, 1629
Minneapolis History Collection, 798
Minneapolis Public Library, 798
Minneapolis Star, Star-Journal, 800
Minneapolis Symphony Orchestra, 798, 800, 815, 1238
Minnesingers, 860-B
Minnesota, 227-K, 396, 1433, 1436, 1611, 1629, 1633
Minnesota Amusements Co., 815
Minnesota Folklife Center, 815
Minnesota Historical Society, 815
Minnesota Music Teachers' Association, 815
Minnesota Orchestra, 798, 800, 814, 1238

Minnesota, University of, 800, 815, 1058
Minnesota, University of, (Duluth), 780
Minnesota, University of, Marching Band, 778
Minor family, 1560
Minsky, Harold, 1487
Minstrelsy (blackface and whiteface), 9, 116, 122, 127, 145, 185, 213, 227-M, 268, 298, 320, 334, 391, 398, 529, 544, 624, 628, 654, 721, 729-A, 729-B, 741, 815, 845, 906, 921, 945, 977, 1006, 1031, 1049, 1061-N, 1062, 1193, 1195, 1299, 1333, 1364, 1385, 1395, 1420, 1448, 1463, 1477, 1484, 1517, 1520, 1541, 1596, 1611, 1624, 1673, 1688
Miquelle, Renee Longy, 227-F
Miranda, Luis R., 1651
Misch, Ludwig, 1025
Misiewicz, Roger, 1657
Miss Montana Centennial, 872
Missia, Francis, 881
Mission music, 71, 77, 115, 129, 130, 133, 145. *See also* specific missions; Spanish music
Mission San Miguel (Cal.), 71
Missionaries, 1070, 1264, 1581, 1611, 1636
Missionary Research Library, 1070
Mississippi, 544, 860-D, 1449
Mississippi Collection, 833
Mississippi Department of Archives and History, 829
Mississippi Federation of Music Clubs, 829
Mississippi River, 865, 1600
Mississippi State University, 831
Mississippi, University of, 833
Missouri, 36, 130, 144, 227-K, 270, 305, 349, 379, 396, 398, 503, 544, 800, 831, 888, 1161, 1448, 1633
Missouri Baptist Convention, 849
Missouri Federation of Music Clubs, 836
Missouri Harmony, 315, 465, 836, 860-A
Missouri Historical Society, 860
Missouri Music Educators' Association, 869
Missouri Musical Fund Society, 860-D
Missouri State Music Teachers Association, 860-E
Missouri Theater, 853
Missouri 3rd Regiment Band, 847
Missouri Third Regiment National Guard, Band, 846
Missouri, University of, at Columbia, 837
Missouri, University of, at Kansas City, 847
Missouri, University of, at Saint Louis, 865

"The Missouri Waltz," 843
Missud, Jean, 701
Mitchell, Abbie, 741
Mitchell, Caroline Martin, 376
Mitchell, Charles S., 1459
Mitchell, Howard, 227-F
Mitchell, Margaret, 269
Mitchell, William E., 1487
Mitchell Memorial Library, 831
Mitropoulos, Dimitri, 227-F, 1031, 1580
Mitton, Samuel Bailey, 1521, 1524
Mobile (Ala.), 568, 1174
Mobile (Ala.) Historic Preservation Society, 8
Mobile Theatre (St. Louis), 860-C
Model-T Ford, 736
Modern Music, 227-H
Modlin Fine Arts Center, 1558
Moehlmann, R. L., 457
Mönkemöller collection, 142
Moffat County (Colo.) Museum, 154
Moffatt, Elizabeth Blackman, 332
Mohaupt, Richard, 227-F
Mohawk music, 355
Mohler, David, 349
Mokrejs, John, 227-F, 457, 465
Moldenhauer, Hans, 227-F, 1580
Moldenhaur Archives, 357, 1580
Moleux, Georges, 227-F
Moll, Ottmar, 860-B, 860-F, 866
"Molly Picon," 1336
Molnar, Ferenc, 227-F, 1061-L
Molnar, John, 1567
Monday Musical Club (Tillamook, Ore.), 1278
Monday Music Club (Youngstown, Ohio?), 1246
Monday Musicale (Michigan City, Ind.), 431
Monk, S. J., 1241
Monkton (Vt.), 379
Monogram Films, 1611
Monologues, 654, 715, 1352
Monongahela Musical Association, 1364
Monroe, Vaughan, 243, 637
Monson (Mass.), 707
Montana, 144, 291, 1466
Montana Historical Society, 874
Montana State University, 872
Montauk (Iowa), 460
Montclair (N.J.), 940, 1061-F
Montelius (Colo.?), 164
Montell, L., 523
Monteux, Pierre, 227-B, 227-F, 729-E, 1580
Montgomery, Mrs. Frank C., 514
Montgomery, James, 1465
Montgomery, Michael, 771
Montgomery County (Md.) Historical Society, 625
Montgomery County (Pa.), 1333

Monticello (Ill.), 391
Monticello College, 391
Monticello Female Seminary, 391
Monticello (Minn.), 777
Monticello (Va.), 1540, 1541
Montpelier (Vt.), 906, 1525
Montrose (Minn.), 777
Moodus Drum and Fife Corps, 176, 178, 191
Moody, Dwight L., 235, 306, 333, 1241
Moody Bible Institute, 333
Moor, Emil, 317
Moore family, 266
Moore, Mrs. Aubertine Woodward, 1611
Moore, Carol Jane, 1015
Moore, Clement C., 259, 1031
Moore, Cornelia Jackson, 266
Moore, Douglas Stuart, 195-B, 227-D, 227-F, 1018, 1031, 1111, 1292, 1580
Moore, Earl V., 227-F, 729
Moore, Eddie, 544
Moore, Francis, 1489
Moore, Grace, 1031, 1052, 1448
Moore, Homer, 1037
Moore, Isabelle Tompson, 646
Moore, Iva D., 1176
Moore, Mrs. John Trowtood, 1463
Moore, Mary Carr, 84, 227-D
Moore, S. T., 1477
Moore, Stuart, 1018
Moore, Thomas, 181, 1146
Moore, Undine S., 1553, 1555
Moore Theater (Seattle), 1575, 1576
Moorhead (Minn.), 815
Moorland, Jesse E., Collection of Negro Life and History, 226
Moorland-Spingarn Research Center, 226
Moran, John P., 1222
Moran, W. R., 142
Moravian Archives, 1285
Moravian Female Seminary (Bethlehem, Pa.), 1285
Moravian Historical Society, Inc., 1323
Moravian music, 1161, 1168, 1220, 1285, 1316, 1323, 1338, 1393
Moravian Music Foundation, 611, 1161
Moravian Symphony Orchestra, 1395
Moravian trombone choir (Lititz, Pa.), 1316
Moreau, Charles C., 636
Morehead, Ann, 1146
Morel Campos, Juan, 1648, 1651
Morena, Berta, 1052
Morey, Edna, 398
Morey, Lloyd, 398
Morgan (piano teacher), 180
Morgan, Bert, 304
Morgan, Charles, 302

Morgan, Eneas, 180
Morgan, Geoffrey Francis, 139
Morgan, Geraldine, 227-F
Morgan, Haydn M., 227-D
Morgan, Hannah R., 1105
Morgan, Hazel, 618
Morgan, Helen, 1333
Morgan, J. P., 227-F
Morgan, Mrs. John P., 227-F
Morgan, John Paul, 227-E
Morgan, Justin, 1530
Morgan, Pierpont, Library, 1053
Morgan, Russell, 618
Morgan, Shubael, 180
Morini, Albert, 227-F
Morlá Trenchs, Ramón, 1649
Morley, Thomas, 544
Mormon music, 50, 195-B, 477, 840, 949, 1518-24
Mormon Tabernacle Choir, 1519, 1520, 1521, 1523
Mormon Tabernacle Organ, 1520
Morning Choral Club (St. Louis), 860-C, 860-J
Morning Music Club (Cleveland), 1190
Morning Musical Club (Battle Creek, Mich.), 730
Morning Musicales (Watertown, N.Y.), 1134
Morningside College, 488
Moross, Jerome, 195-C, 227-F
Morrey, Grace Hamilton, 1193
Morrey School of Music, 1193
Morris brothers, 1445
Morris, Alton C., 245
Morris, Frank, 789
Morris, George S., 729-B
Morris, Harold, 227-D, 1111, 1477
Morris, Hugh M., Library, 213
Morris, James, 1378
Morris, John, 733
Morris, Miss L. W., 1399
Morris Library, 305
Morrison, Charles, 134
Morrison, Louisa, 142
Morrison County (Minn.) Historical Society, 787
Morrisson-Reeves Library, 445
Morristown National Historical Park Museum, 935
Morrow, Irving F., 50
Morrow, Stanley, Collection, 1432
Morse, Edward, 701
Morse, Samuel, 227-G
Morton, David, 523
Morton, Ferdinand ("Jelly Roll"), 227-L, 1433
Morton, J. Sterling, High School, 343
Morton, Lawrence, 81, 84, 195-C, 227-F
Morton, Zylpha S., 815
Mosenthal, Joseph, 227-D
Moses, Montrose Jonas, 1143
Moses-Donner Collection, 29
Mosher Library, 1485
Moten, Etta, 268
Mother's Club (Arlington Hills, Minn.), 815

The Mothersingers (Cincinnati), 1172
Motherwell, Hiram, 636
Motion pictures. See Film music; Films and video tapes on music subjects; Silent-film music
Moultonborough (N.H.), 701
Mount, Henry, 185
Mount, William Sidney, 1123
Mount Airy (Pa.) Seminary, 1342
Mount Marty College, 1434
Mount Olive College, 1154
Mount Prospect (Ill.) Historical Society, 374
Mount Saint Mary's College, 80
Mount Vernon (N.H.), 633
Mount Vernon (N.Y.), 1659
Mount Vernon (Va.), 1537
Mount Zion (Baptist) Church (Buckingham County, Va.), 1560
Mount Zion Hebrew Congregation (St. Paul), 815
Mountain and Plain Festival (Denver), 156
Mountain Lake, 1591
Mountain songs, 1185
Mountain Valley (Va.), 1539
Mourant, Walter, 1111
Mouth bow, 271
Mouth harp, 271
Movies. See Film music; Films and video tapes on music subjects; Silent-film music
Mowrer, Samuel, 654
Moyer, Karl, 1320
Moyle, James, Oral History Collection, 1521
Mozart, Wolfgang Amadeus, 708
Mozart Association (Richmond, Va.), 128, 1560
Mozart Association (Salem, Mass.), 701
Mozart Club (Ithaca, N.Y.), 1005, 1006
Mozart Club (Pittsburgh), 1359
Mozart Male Quartet, 879
Mozart Society (Fisk University), 1457
Mozart Society (Worcester, Mass.), 721
Muck, Karl, 227-F, 639, 1177, 1580
Mudd, Seeley G., Library, 1222
Mühlmann, Adolf, 314
Mueller, F. F., 1061-B
Mueller, Flora 1172
Mueller, Inez Fabbri, 50
Mueller, Robert Herman, 860-C
Mueller, Susanna, 1402
Muenscher, John, 1061-A
Muenzinger, Rudolf, 729-B
Mugar Memorial Library, 637
Mugler, Henri Jean, 1591
Muhlenberg, Rev. William A., 612
Muhlmann, Adolf, 1174

Muir, John, 227-F
Mulberry Hill (Tenn.), 1463
Muller, Joseph, 227-H, 1061-C
Muller, Joseph, collection, 1061-G
Mullet, Alfred Edgar, 636
Mullins, David W., Library, 36
Multnomah School of Music (Portland, Ore.), 1270
Munch, I. I., 1584
Mundwyler, Fred, 50
Mundwyler, J. Louis, 50
Munich (Germany), 1031
Municipal Auditorium (New Orleans), 561
Municipal Band (Grand Forks, N.D.), 1165
Municipal Chorus (St. Paul), 815
Municipal Opera (St. Louis), 860-A
Municipal Theatre Association (St. Louis), 860-C
Munn, John, 314
Munroe, Alexander Cole, 721
Munson, Esther, 514
Murat Theatre (Indianapolis), 427
Murdock, Henry T., 1333
Murphy, Edward, 227-G
Murphy, Lambert, 860-D
Murphy, Thomas P., 227-D
Murphy, Turk, 1450
Murray, Bain, 1186
Murray, Elsie, 1005
Murray, Lyn, 1646
Murray, Thomas, 644
Muscogee Indians, 274
Muse, Clarence, 795-B
Museo de la Música Puertorriqueña, 1654
Museum Contents, Inc., 548
Museum of Broadcasting, 1054
Museum of Fine Arts (Boston), 645
Museum of History and Industry (Seattle), 1575
Museum of Independent Telephony, 492
Museum of International Folk Art, 962
Museum of Modern Art, 1055
Museum of New Mexico, 962
Museum of Repertoire Americana, 480
Museum of Texas Tech University, 1501
Museum of the American Indian—Heye Foundation, 1056
Museum of the City of New York, 1057
Museum of the Confederacy Literary Society, 1556
Museum of the Society of the Cincinnati—Anderson House, 220
Museum of Western Colorado, 166
Museum Village in Orange County (N.Y.), 1017
Museums at Stony Brook (N.Y.), 1123
Museums of the City of Mobile (Ala.), 9

Music and Applied Arts Bureau (Minneapolis), 815

Music and Art Foundation (Seattle), 1577

Music Appreciation Hour, 227-B, 227-L

Music Arts Association (Cedar City, Utah), 1518

Music boxes. *See* Mechanical musical instruments

Music camps, 576, 729-B, 748

Music Center of the North Shore, 1058

Music Center Opera Association (Los Angeles), 78

Music Club (New Haven, Conn.), 195-A

Music Club (Temple, Tex.), 1515

Music clubs, 2, 5, 9, 11, 15, 20, 25, 30, 40, 50, 60, 61, 66, 69, 82, 84, 98, 103, 114, 128, 151, 157, 163, 165, 170, 173, 181, 188, 190, 192, 195-A, 195-B, 211, 212, 215, 226, 227-A, 227-G, 227-H, 245, 251, 253, 263, 266, 267, 282, 298, 302, 310, 314, 315, 334, 341, 354, 360, 364, 381, 391, 392, 398, 426, 429, 431, 435, 437, 442, 443, 459, 465, 469, 476, 479, 488, 501, 514, 515, 520, 523, 531, 576, 586, 595, 596, 597, 604, 606, 612, 631, 636, 646, 654, 657, 669, 682, 689, 699, 701, 705, 706, 719, 721, 723, 729-B, 730, 739, 745, 748, 751, 758, 763, 764, 772, 776, 780, 786, 787, 792, 798, 800, 815, 822, 829, 836, 855, 860-H, 860-J, 866, 873, 879, 881, 896, 898, 908, 911, 916, 918, 920, 939, 980, 1005, 1027, 1059, 1061-B, 1061-F, 1105, 1111, 1134, 1141, 1143, 1155, 1167, 1172, 1176, 1190, 1193, 1207, 1246, 1250, 1256, 1265, 1268, 1274, 1278, 1310, 1338, 1355, 1359, 1364, 1374, 1383, 1384, 1387, 1396, 1409, 1418, 1420, 1421, 1439, 1446, 1460, 1463, 1476, 1477, 1481, 1482, 1483, 1500, 1515, 1532, 1533, 1534, 1542, 1560, 1563, 1569, 1570, 1572, 1573, 1577, 1578, 1592, 1603, 1611, 1614, 1622, 1624, 1637, 1643, 1647

Music Commission, Episcopal Diocese of Chicago, 324

Music Corporation of America, 1520

Music Critics Association, 227-H

Music education, 10, 19, 30, 36, 50, 55, 60, 68, 81, 84, 85, 98, 114, 121, 122, 128, 129, 144, 150, 157, 167, 176, 179, 180, 181, 192, 195-A, 195-B, 199, 200, 206, 215, 227-A, 227-B, 227-H, 245, 248, 260, 266, 270, 276, 284, 293, 295, 299, 301, 302, 307, 309, 312, 314, 323, 329, 332, 334, 338, 340, 341, 357, 364, 365, 368,

370, 376, 381, 391, 398, 406, 409, 418, 430, 431, 437, 440, 443, 451, 457, 465, 472, 473, 475, 476, 479, 488, 494, 502, 509, 515, 523, 528, 529, 535, 539, 541, 544, 568-C, 576, 586, 612, 614, 618, 625, 636, 646, 654, 659, 671, 679, 707, 708, 716, 719, 721, 725, 729-B, 729-C, 730, 739, 743, 757, 766, 800, 803, 815, 822, 825, 827, 831, 837, 847, 860-B, 860-C, 860-D, 860-E, 866, 869, 879, 887, 888, 900, 912, 914, 926, 939, 940, 947, 982, 986, 993, 994, 1005, 1006, 1007, 1030, 1031, 1046, 1058, 1061-J, 1061-M, 1062, 1068, 1070, 1081, 1104, 1107, 1111, 1126, 1141, 1143, 1146, 1148, 1153, 1155, 1161, 1163, 1164, 1167, 1172, 1175, 1176, 1177, 1190, 1193, 1207, 1210, 1213, 1222, 1235, 1243, 1260, 1261, 1268, 1270, 1274, 1285, 1287, 1315, 1331, 1333, 1338, 1345, 1351, 1356, 1359, 1360, 1362, 1376, 1377, 1387, 1401, 1402, 1418, 1420, 1421, 1423, 1433, 1439, 1441, 1447, 1456, 1457, 1459, 1462, 1463, 1473, 1477, 1478, 1480, 1481, 1483, 1484, 1487, 1488, 1493, 1501, 1513, 1516, 1519, 1520, 1521, 1534, 1541, 1546, 1549, 1551, 1559, 1560, 1573, 1577, 1578, 1591, 1595, 1603, 1611, 1614, 1616, 1620, 1628, 1643. *See also* Instructional materials; Singing schools

Music Educators National Conference, 227-H, 618

Music Education National Conference Historical Center, 618

Music Festival (Columbia, S.C.), 1420

Music Festival (Evanston, Ill.), 354

Music Festival (Norfolk, Conn.), 195

Music Festival (Rutland, Vt.), 1533

Music Festival Association (Springfield, Mass.), 705

Music Hall Association (Cincinnati), 1172

Music Hall Organ Association (Cincinnati), 1172

Music halls, 195-B, 227-M, 290, 314, 654, 754, 755, 860-C, 860-D, 860-E, 868, 977, 1031, 1061-B, 1080, 1172, 1356, 1359, 1361, 1365, 1395, 1662. *See also* Opera houses; Theaters and auditoriums

Music Industries Council, 618

Music Library Association, 227-H, 979

Music Lovers' Club (Littleton, N.H.), 911

Music Lovers' Club (Cincinnati), 1172

Music Mart collection, 84

Music Memory Contest, 618

Music Research Club (Bridgeport, Conn.), 173

Music School Settlement (Cleveland), 1056

Music School Settlements, New York Association of, 1058

Music Study Club (Danville, Va.), 1542

Music Study Club (Duke University), 1143

Music Study Club (Evanston, Ill.), 354

Music Study Club (Fort Atkinson, Wis.), 1603

Music Study Club (Iowa City, Iowa), 475

Music Study Club (New Albany, Ind.), 435, 437

Music Study Club (Pensacola, Fla.), 253

Music Supervisors National Conference, 618, 860-J

Music Teachers Association, Arkansas, 36

Music Teachers Association, California, 128

Music Teachers Association (Jacksonville, Fla.), 245

Music Teachers Association, Michigan, 766

Music Teachers Association, Minnesota, 815

Music Teachers Association, North Texas, 1477

Music Teachers Association, Oregon, 1274

Music Teachers Association (Panhandle, Tex.), 1477

Music Teachers Association, South Plains, 1477, 1501

Music Teachers Association, Texas, 1477

Music Teachers Association (Washington, D.C.), 226

Music Teachers National Association, 227-H, 568, 1175

Music theory, 50, 68, 81, 302, 323, 379, 465, 476, 544, 613, 654, 1031, 1181, 1222, 1262, 1336, 1340, 1360, 1452, 1535, 1541. *See also* Acoustics

Music therapy, 1071

Music Vale Academy, 391

Music Vale Farm, 199

Music Vale Seminary, 180, 199, 200

Music Week in Pittsburgh (1924), 1359

Musical Academy (Philadelphia), 1345

Musical America, 1355

"Musical America" prize (1930), 121

Musical Art Association (Philadelphia), 1338

Musical Art Association (St. Louis), 860-E

Musical Art Society (Springfield, Mass.), 705

Musical Arts Club (Charleston, S.C.?), 1418

Musical Arts Club (Little Falls, Minn.), 787

Musical Arts Club (Long Beach, Cal.), 69

Musical Arts Conservatory (Amarillo, Tex.), 1473

Musical Arts Society (La Jolla, Cal.), 66

Musical Arts Society (Muskogee, Okla.), 1256

Musical Association (Baltimore), 612

Musical Association (Charleston, S.C.), 1418

Musical Association (Framingham, Mass.), 669

Musical Association (Hampden County, Mass.), 705

Musical Association (New Haven, Conn.), 195

Musical Association (Seville, Ohio), 1190

Musical Association, Western Vermont, 1529

Musical Association (Windsor County, Vt.), 1530

Musical Club (Fresno, Cal.), 60, 61

Musical comedy. *See* Operetta and musical comedy

Musical Education Society (Boston?), 636

Musical Education Society (Brunswick, Me.), 586

Musical Entertainments of the Young Ladies Seminary, 1285

Musical Evening (Wilmington, Del.?), 215

Musical Festival Association (Cincinnati), 1172

Musical Fund Society (Philadelphia), 212, 1333, 1338, 1340, 1343

Musical Heritage Studies, 295

Musical Institute (Middlebury, Vt.), 1529

Musical Institute (Pittsburgh), 1359

Musical Museum (Deansboro, N.Y.), 987

Musical plays. *See* Operetta and musical comedy

Musical Polyhymnia (St. Louis), 860-E

Musical saw, 779

Musical Society (Boulder, Colo.), 150

Musical Society (Charleston, S.C.), 1418

Musical Society (Concord, N.H.), 898

Musical Society (Galesburg, Mich.), 761

Musical Society (Jamaica, N.Y.), 1088

Musical Society (Kalamazoo, Mich.), 761

Musical Society (Milwaukee), 1611

Musical Society (New Albany, Inc.), 437

Musical Society (New Brunswick, N.J.), 939

Musical Society (Newark, N.J.), 815
Musical Society (Putney, Vt.), 1532
Musical Society (St. Louis), 860-E
Musical Society (St. Paul), 815
Musical Society in Stoughton (Mass.), 706
Musical Society of the City of New York, Inc., 1063
Musical theater. *See* Operetta and musical comedy; Theater music
Musical Theatre Collection, 177
Musical Union (Canton, N.Y.), 980
Musical Union (Galesburg, Mich.), 761
Musical Union (Georgetown, Mass.), 701
Musical Wonder House and Music Museum, 600
Musicians Association of Vermont, 1530
Musicians Club (Galesburg, Ill.), 360
Musicians' Club of Phoenix, 25
Musicians Club (Pittsburgh), 1355
Musicians Club of Women, 314
Musicians Emergency Fund, 1061-B
Musicians Foundation, Inc. (New York), 1027
Musicians Mutual Protective Union, Local 174-496, 558
Musicians Mutual Protective Union of San Francisco, 50
Musicians Mutual Protective Union of the Ohio Valley, Wheeling Local 142 (AFM), 1591
Musicians Protective Union (Santa Cruz, Calif.), 136
Musicians Protective Union (Ithaca, N.Y.), 1006
Musicians' Union (Chicago), 1609
Musicologists, 50, 68, 142, 195-A, 234, 265, 285, 329, 340, 406, 408, 538, 661, 679, 691, 692, 697, 790, 866, 941, 1005, 1025, 1031, 1061-B, 1061-L, 1061-M, 1074, 1107, 1111, 1155, 1168, 1459, 1477, 1488, 1503, 1520, 1521, 1523, 1541, 1577, 1659. *See also* names of specific musicologists
"Der Musikverein" (Milwaukee), 1622
Musin, Ovide, 862
Muskogee Indians, 274
Muskogee (Okla.) Musical Arts Society, 1256
Mussulman, Joseph, 876
Mutual Improvement Club of Galesburg (Mich.), 761
Muus, Bernt, 802
Muzio, Claudio, 1487
"My Country, 'Tis of Thee," 142, 950, 1040

My Old Kentucky Home, 521
Myer, Jean, 195-C
Myerberg, Michael, 1611
Myers, Alexander, 1575
Myers, Moses, House, 1552
Myrick, Julian S., 195-C
Myrow, Frederick E., 977

N

N., E., 314
NAACP (National Association for the Advancement of Colored People), 729-B
Naaltsoos Ba'Hooghan Library, 29
Nabakov, Nicolas, 227-D, 227-F
Nachod, Hans, 1488
NACWAPI Research Center, 618
Naff Collection, 1461
Nagy, Charles J., 1352
Nancrede, H. W., 1061-F
"Nancy Till," 157
Nanticoke Indians, 213
NAOB (National Academy of Broadcasting), 1611
Naperville (Ill.) Municipal Band, 377
Napier Lothian Theater Orchestra Collection, 646
Napoleon, Phil, 1450
Napoléonville (La.), 544, 555, 568
Napton, William B., 860-C
Nash, Bert, 907
Nash, Richard Nathan, 1611
Nash, William H., 50
Nashville, 84, 1040
Nashville Female Academy, 1463
Nashville Symphony Orchestra, 1463
Nason, Edward Shepard, 721
Nason, Elias, 721
Natal, University of, 1688
Natchez (Miss.), 544
Natchitoches Parish (La.), 544
National Academy of Broadcasting, 1611
National Air and Space Museum, 234
National anthem. *See* "The Star-spangled Banner"
National Anthropology Archives, 234
National Archives, 230
National Association for American Composers and Conductors, 1061-A
National Association for Music in Hospitals, 1061-M
National Association for the Advancement of Colored People, Battle Creek (Mich.) chapter, 729-B
National Association of American Composers and Conductors, 1061-D
National Association of College Wind and Percussion Instructors Research Center, 618

National Association of Negro Musicians, 226, 741
National Association of Negro Musicians, Detroit chapter, 739
National Association of Organists, Delaware Chapter, 215
National Automotive History Collection, 739
National Barn Dance, 1234
National Broadcasting Company, 227-B, 227-H, 227-L, 341, 1488, 1611
National Bureau for Advancement of Music, 618
National Collection of Fine Arts, 234
National Conservatory of Music, 612
National Convention of Women's Amateur Music Clubs, 314
National Council of the Southern Negro Youth Congress, 831
National Executive Committee of American Turners, 837
National Federation of Music Clubs, 227-G, 227-H, 263, 266, 618, 748, 800, 918, 1061-B, 1141
National Federation of Musicians, Cleveland, 1181
National Federation of Settlements, 1058
National Federation of Settlements and Neighborhood Centers, 800
National Flute Association, 33
National Folk Festivals (Chicago), 391
National Guard, Forty-fifth Infantry Division, 1257
National Guild of Community Music Schools, 800
National Guild of Community Schools of the Arts, Inc., 1058
National Institute of Arts and Letters, 195-A
National League of American Pen Women, 1061-B
National Library of Canada, 1659
National Library of Ireland, 1669
National Library of Scotland, 1687
National Maritime Museum, 120
National Museum of Natural History, 234
National Museum of Transport, 861
National Music Association, 887
National Music Camp, 398, 518, 729-B, 748
National Music Council, 227-H
National Music Week, 490, 618, 636, 1359
National Negro Opera Association, 227-H

National Negro Opera Company, 1061-N
National Opera Association, 33
National Oratorio Society, 99
National Orchestral Association, 1061-J
National Park Seminary, 625
National Peace Jubilee (Boston, 1869), 646, 701, 1534
National Portrait Gallery, 234
National Recreation and Park Association, 800
National School Band, Orchestra, and Vocal Association, 618
National songs, 228, 245, 455, 612, 616, 1061-D, 1111, 1453, 1611. *See also* "The Star-spangled Banner" and other specific song titles
National Summer School of Music, 618
National Symphony Orchestra, 223, 234
National Temperance Society, 577
National Theatre of Washington (D.C.), 223
National Trombone Association, 33
National War Labor Board (NWLB), 742
National Welsh Choir, 163
National Women's Christian Temperance Union, 356
National Youth Administration Music Program, 831
Native American music. *See* American Indians; also names of specific tribes
Natrona County, 1643
Naumburg, Elkan, 1174
Navajo Community College, 29
Navajo Indians, 31, 162, 190, 964
Naval Historical Center, 231
Naval songs, 120, 602, 624, 702, 1005, 1241. *See also* Boat songs; Chanteys; Steamships
Navarre-Bethlehem (Ohio) Historical Society, 1219
Navarro, Rafael, 1082
Navy. *See* United States Navy
"Navy Hour," 1106
Nazarene music, 113
Nazarene Publishing Co., 113
Nazareth (Pa.), 1161, 1285
Naze, W., 406
NBC, 227-B, 227-H, 227-L, 341, 1488, 1611
NBC Symphony, 227-L
Neal, Mabel Evangeline, 227-K
Neale, Maurice H., 730
Neale, William F., 730
Neave, William H., 1141
Neblett, Lizzie Scott, 1477
Nebraska, 144, 475, 1433
Nebraska Conference United Methodist Historical Center, 886

Nebraska State Historical Society, 887, 893
Nebraska Theater Programs Collection, 887
Nebraska, University of, at Lincoln, 888
Needham (Mass.) Historical Society, 681
Needmore Band, 434
Nef, Elinor Castle, 340
Nef, John U., 340
Negro Collection, 1457
Negro Light Opera Company (Chicago), 391
Negro music. See Afro-American music
Negro Theater Project, 244
Neibarger, Clyde, 847
Neidlinger, William H., 227-D, 951
Neisser, Georg, 1285
Nelson, Albert, 777
Nelson, Eitel Allen, 1477
Nelson, Robert E., 1181
Nelson, William Warville, 1436
Nelson County (Ky.) Public Library, 521
Netherlands Museum, 758
Netsorg, Bendetson, 730
Nettl, Bruno, 398
Nettl, Paul, 406, 1061-M
Nettleton, Asahel, 192
Neuhoff, Dorothy A., 860-C
Nevada, Emma (Emma Wixom), 227-F, 896
Nevada, 50
Nevada Historical Society, 896
Nevada Musical Club, 896
Nevin, Anne Paul, 646
Nevin, Arthur, 465, 1111
Nevin, Ethelbert, 227-D, 227-F, 639, 646, 951, 1040, 1053, 1222, 1298, 1375, 1666
Nevin, George Balch, 227-D, 317, 1298
Nevin, Gordon Balch, 442
New Academy of Music (Chicago), 315
New Albany-Floyd County (Ind.) Public Library, 437
New Bedford (Mass.) Free Public Library, 683
New Braunsfelser Männerchor, 1476
New Brunswick (Canada), 592
New Brunswick (N.J.) Theological Seminary, 938
New Castle County (Del.) Free Library, 216
New England, 219, 398, 476, 581, 700, 706, 707, 1031, 1402, 1525, 1528, 1541
New England Antiquities, Society for the Preservation of, 649
New England Conservatory of Music, 272, 646
New England Music Camp, 576
New Hampshire, 84, 195-B, 227-B, 227-L, 227-M, 593, 631, 633, 636, 645, 701
New Hampshire Antiquarian Society (Concord), 227-G

New Hampshire Antiquarian Society (Hopkinton), 227-G, 898, 909
New Hampshire Historical Society, 898, 909
New Hampshire Philharmonic Society, 907
New Hampshire State Library, 899
New Hampshire, University of, 900
New Hampshire Volunteer Infantry, 3rd, 227-G, 898, 909
New Harmony (Ind.), 425
New Harmony Workingmen's Institute Library, 438
New Haven (Conn.) Colony Historical Society, 192
New Haven Free Public Library, 193
New Jersey, 214, 395, 544, 815, 1052, 1061-F, 1161, 1190
New Jersey Historical Society, 940
New Jersey Music Collection, 940
New Jersey Regiment, 3rd, 195-B
New Lebanon (N.Y.), 697
New Lebanon (Ohio), 227-G
New London (Conn.), 180, 199
New London County (Conn.) Historical Society, 197
New Market (Tenn.), 1611
New Market (Va.), 1560
New Mexico, 142, 152, 1477, 1483
New Mexico Highlands University, 969
New Mexico State Records Center and Archives, 963
New Mexico State University, 960
New Mexico Symphony Orchestra, 957
New Mexico, University of, 152, 957, 962
New Moon records, 471
New Music, 68, 76, 1046, 1062, 1080
New Music Society, 1061-B
New Orleans (La.), 1, 15, 38, 268, 334, 406, 528, 544, 654, 860-H, 980, 997, 1061-M, 1418, 1450, 1463
New Orleans Baptist Theological Seminary, 273, 559
New Orleans Conservatory of Music, 544
New Orleans Grand Opera Company, 544
New Orleans Grand Opera House, 544
New Orleans Jazz Club Collection, 556
New Orleans Municipal Auditorium, 561
New Orleans Opera Association, 551
New Orleans Opera Company, 544
New Orleans Philharmonic Symphony Orchestra, 560
New Orleans Public Library, 561

New Orleans Sheet Music Collection, 568
New Orleans, University of, 569
New School of Music, Inc., 1344
New Sensation (showboat), 303, 1176
New Stuart Theater, 887
New Tribes Mission Bible Institute, 1636
New York (City), 36, 55, 84, 129, 133, 185, 188, 195-A, 212, 226, 227-H, 227-L, 242, 252, 266, 268, 270, 315, 349, 406, 503, 544, 577, 581, 654, 672, 682, 741, 800, 803, 807, 814, 819, 825, 831, 860-H, 860-J, 862, 864, 888, 921, 923, 930, 951, 968, 977, 987, 1000, 1017, 1095, 1111, 1122, 1142, 1174, 1190, 1207, 1243, 1270, 1285, 1322, 1336, 1350, 1375, 1395, 1402, 1416, 1423, 1425, 1444, 1459, 1463, 1483, 1611, 1629, 1678, 1686
New York (State), 36, 55, 84, 130, 133, 179, 185, 188, 195, 212, 226, 227-H, 227-L, 242, 252, 266, 268, 270, 314, 334, 349, 356, 395, 406, 453, 503, 544, 549, 577, 581, 588, 646, 654, 672, 682, 697, 707, 721, 729-A, 741, 800, 803, 807, 815, 819, 825, 831, 860-H, 860-K, 862, 864, 888, 921, 923, 930, 951, 1142, 1174, 1190, 1207, 1244, 1270, 1285, 1322, 1336, 1350, 1375, 1395, 1402, 1423, 1425, 1444, 1446, 1459, 1463, 1483, 1567, 1611, 1629, 1659, 1662
New York American, 195-A, 1061-B
New York Association of Community and Settlement Music Schools, 1058
New York Association of Music School Settlements, 1058
New York Association of Music Schools, 800
New York Bartók Archive, 981
New York Chamber Music Society, 1222
New York City Welfare Council, 800
New York Civic Orchestra, 55
New York Evening Mail, 1031
New York Evening Sun, 1031
New York Festival Orchestra, 55
New York Herald, 398
New York Hippodrome, 1061-A, 1061-M
New-York Historical Society, 721, 1059
New York Jazz Museum, 1060
New York Morning Telegraph, 1067
New York Philharmonic Orchestra, 195-A, 455, 1031, 1161, 1238, 1582
New York Philharmonic-Symphony Orchestra,

227-H, 654, 1031, 1053, 1061-F
New York Press, 195-A
New York Public Library, 721, 1026, 1061, 1666
New York Regiment, 2nd, 1060
New York State Historical Association, 983
New York State Library, 967
New York State Museum, 968
New York State School of Agriculture, 970
New York, State University of. See State University of New York
New York State Volunteers, 110th, Company "C", 1059
New York Symphony Orchestra, 1061-B
New York Times, 1031
New York Tribune, 227-H
New York University, 1062
New York World, 1061-B
Newark (N.J.), 939
Newark Public Library, 941
Newberry Library, 317, 334, 354, 1107
Newburgh (N.Y.), 1017
Newburyport (Mass.), 701
Newburyport Public Library, 684
Newcomb, Ethel, 1005
Newcomb, Mary, 227-K, 531
Newell, Laura E., 507
Newfoundland, 1352
Newland, William Augustine, 227-A
Newley, Anthony, 637
Newman, Alfred, 84, 85
Newman, Lionel, 133
Newman Collection, 1070
Newport (R.I.), 1268
Newport Folk Festivals, 979
Newport Historical Society, 1399
Newsboys' Band (Grand Rapids, Mich.), 748
Newsom, Hugh, 465, 613
Newton, John, 1465
Newton (Mass.), 654
Newtonville (Mass.), 1031
Nez Percé Indian music, 227-L
Niagara County (N.Y.) Historical Society, 1012
Niagara Falls, 1012
Nicholas, Joe, 1455
Nicholls State University, 575
Nichols, Arthur Howard, 635
Nichols, Ernest Loring ("Red"), 1270
Nichols, G. W., 1172
Nichols, John, 671
Nickerson, Camille, 226, 227-F
Nicolai, V., 587
Nicoll, Horace W., 1061-D
Nielsen, Alice, 123
Nies-Berger, Edouard, 227-F
"Night Hawks," 846
Nightclubs. See Theaters and auditoriums
Nijinsky, Kyra, 122
Nijinsky, Vaslav, 122
Nikisch, Arthur, 227-F
Nikoloric, Mrs. Artur, 195-C

Niles, Edward Abbe, 185
Niles, John Jacob, 227-D, 227-F
Nilsson, Christine, 227-F, 1111
Nimitz Library, 602
Nin-Culmell, Joaquin, 1580
Nisonen, Martti, 753
Nix, Mrs. Walter, 1477
No Man's Land Historical Museum, 1253
Noble, F. A., 707
Noble, T. Tertius, 227-D, 227-F
Nobles County (Minn.) Historical Society, 824
Noel, Amelia, 860-F
Noelte, Albert, 357
Noir, A., 1477
Nolan, Charles T., 1031
Nolen, W. W., 977
Non-commercial recordings, 1, 38, 68, 84, 111, 132, 167, 195-B, 227-L, 277, 398, 406, 427, 487, 819, 843, 884, 1061-J, 1061-N, 1139, 1141, 1244, 1438, 1450, 1488, 1657, 1663. See also 1667. See also Field recordings
Nono, Nuria Schoenberg, 195-C
Nordamerikanischer Sängerbund, 314
Nordeen, John, 1577
Nordic Choral Ensemble Association (Duluth, Minn.), 815
Nordica, Lillian, 50, 227-F, 590, 709, 710, 1052, 1338
Nordica Homestead Museum, 590
Nordoff, Paul, 227-F, 1580
Norfolk (Conn.), 195-A
Norfolk Historical Society, 198
Norfolk (Va.), 1551
Norfolk Public Library, 1552, 1553
Norfolk Green (N.Y.?), 1005
Norlin, Laura O., 1061-L
Normändenes Sangforening, 815
Normal Academy of Music (New London, Conn.), 180
Norman, Gertrude, 646, 1061-M
Normal (Ill.), 301
Norris, J. Parker, 1333
North, Alex, 84
North, Frank Mason, 933
North American Phonograph Company, 1640
North-American Sängerbund, 38th National Sängerfest (1934), 860-J
North American Singers' Union, 1375
North Andover (Mass.) Historical Society, 686
North Brevard (Fla.) Public Library, 262
North Carolina, 75, 227-K, 227-L, 906, 1225, 1445, 1463, 1477
North Carolina Department of Cultural Resources, 1155
North Carolina Federation of Music Clubs, 1155
North Carolina Infantry Band, 2nd, A.E.F., 1155

North Carolina Museum of History, 1155
North Carolina Regiment, 26th, 1161
North Carolina State Archives, 1155
North Carolina State Symphony, 1155
North Carolina Symphony Orchestra, 1155
North Carolina, University of, at Chapel Hill, 1141
North Carolina, University of, at Charlotte, 1142
North Carolina, University of, at Greensboro, 1148
North Carolina, University of, at Wilmington, 1158
North Central College, 378
North Dakota, 761, 800, 1611
North Dakota Institute for Regional Studies, 1164
North Dakota State University, 1164
North Dakota, University of, 1165
North Farnham (Richmond Co., Va.) Protestant Episcopal Church, 1560
North Lee County (Iowa) Historical Society, 471
North Park College, 325, 335
North Platte Valley (Neb.) Historical Association, 881
North Reading (Mass.), 1031
North Regional Library, 798
North Shore Music Festival, 354
North Texas Composers Archives, 1488
North Texas Female College, 1513
North Texas Music Teachers' Association, 1477
North Texas State University, 1488
Northampton (Mass.), 177, 181
Northampton Historical Society, 689
Northampton County (Pa.), 1333
Northampton County Historical Society, 1291
Northborough (Mass.) Historical Society, 693
Northcott, Henry Clay, 523
Northeast Archives of Folklore and Oral History, 592
Northeast Minnesota Historical Center, 780
Northeastern University, 647
Northern, George, 1560
Northern Arizona University, 21
Northern Book & Music Company, 802
Northern Colorado, University of, 167, 168
Northern Great Plains, 1433
Northern Illinois University, 345
Northern Indiana Historical Society, 449
Northern Iowa, University of, 456

Northern Ohio Opera Association, 1190
Northern Pacific Railway Records, 815
Northern Pacific Singers, 815
Northern State College, 1428
Northern Vermont Musical Association, 1530
Northfield (Mass.), 707
Northfield (Vt.) Singing Society, 1530
Northland College, 786
Northwestern U. S., 654, 1270, 1575, 1577. See also Pacific Northwest
Northwestern Singers' Association, 815
Northwestern University, 357, 1673
Norton, Amanda Allen, 590
Norton, Richard W., Memorial Library, 573
Norton, Spencer, 1256
Norton, William Frederick, 531
Norvo, Red, 321
Norwegian-American Historical Association, 802
Norwegian American Music Collection, 802
Norwegian music, 227-L, 316, 461, 462, 475, 777, 779, 782, 791, 794, 799, 800, 801, 802, 803, 813, 815, 819, 856, 1164, 1235, 1428, 1429, 1432, 1596, 1600
Norwich (Conn.), 180, 203, 1402
Noss, Luther, 195-C
Noss, Osea, 195-C
Notation. See Letter notation; Shape notes; Syllabic notation
Notations collection, 357
Notre Dame, University of, 440, 653
Nova Scotia, 1659
Novaes, Guiomar, 819
Novelty music, 239, 495
Novotna, Jarmilla, 1061-F
Noy, William Ray Van, 1521
Nuechterlein, Laura Bernthal, 746
Nunn, Rudolph, 1155
Nussbaum, Anna May Loewenstein, 866
Nutter, Charles Sumner, 190, 637, 1459
NWLB (National War Labor Board), 742
Nyack College, 1094
Nye, Captain Pearl R., 1193, 1197
Nyman, Uno A., 1624

O

Oakland, Ben, 1646
Oakland (Cal.) Museum, 92
Oakland (Cal.) Public Library, 93
Oakley, Annie, 1208
Oakley, Horace, 334
Oates, Henry F., 636
Oberhoffer, Emil, 798, 815

Oberlin (Ohio), 406, 837
Oberlin College, 1222
Oboe music, 729
O'Brien, George, Collection, 1614
O'Brien, J. Vick, 1359
Occupational songs, 227-A, 406, 1184, 1631. See also Labor songs; Work songs; and particular occupations (Cowboy songs, Loggers' songs, Miners' songs, Railroad songs, etc.)
Ocker, Olle Naomi, 1477
O'Connell, Charles, 227-F
Oconomowoc (Wis.), 1626
Oddfellows Band (Wayne, Mich.), 773
Odell, George C. D., 1031
Odell, L. Brevoort, 1127
Odeon Theatre (St. Louis), 860-C, 860-D
Odin Male Chorus, 794
Odnopossoff, Ricardo, 1061-F
O'Donnell, William, 1487
Odum, Howard W., 227-K
O'Hara, Geoffrey, 227-D, 227-F
Ohio, 36, 227-B, 227-G, 227-M, 314, 396, 398, 406, 432, 523, 529, 531, 544, 568, 729-B, 800, 815, 837, 860-B, 951, 1095, 1113, 1141, 1161, 1285, 1296, 1309, 1611
Ohio Historical Society, 1193
Ohio Infantry Regiment, 8th, 1190
Ohio Infantry, 122nd Regiment, 1193
Ohio Mechanics Institute, 1172
Ohio River Valley, 340, 1112
Ohio State University, 1194
Ohio University, 1167
Ohio Volunteer Infantry, 104th Regiment, 1190
Ohio Volunteer Infantry Band, 110th, 1232
Ohio Wesleyan University, 1244
Ojibway Indians, 815, 1611
Okies, 227-L
Oklahoma, 36, 113, 227-L, 398
Oklahoma Agricultural and Mechanical College, 1260
Oklahoma Baptist University, 1259
Oklahoma City (Okla.), 1260
Oklahoma City Symphony Orchestra, 1262
Oklahoma Federation of Music Clubs, 1256
Oklahoma State University, 1260
Oklahoma, University of, 1256
Olan, Levi A., 1174
Olathe (Kan.) Band, 514
Olcott, Chauncey, 1012
Old Colony Historical Society, 708
Old Dominion University, 1552
Old Dominion University, Library, 1554
Old Economy Village, 1281

Old Gaol Museum, 601
Old Globe Theatre (San Diego), 115
Old Harp Singers, 1358
Old Harp Singers of Nashville, 1459
Old Homestead recordings, 733
Old Kentucky Home, 521
"The Old North State," 1155
Old Ouaquaga (N.Y.) Historical Society, 1100
"The Old Rugged Cross," 729-B
Old Salem (N.C.), 1162
Old Slave Mart Museum and Library, 1427
Old Songs Library, 1607
Old South Church (Boston), 636, 707
Old Stoughton (Mass.) Musical Society, 706
Old Sturbridge Village, 707
Old Swedes Church, 215
Old Time Fiddlers Association, 884
Old-time music. See Country and western music; Folk music collections; Hillbilly music
Old Timer's Fiddle Contest, 1477
Old Village Hall Museum, 1010
Old Washington Historic State Park, 43
Oldberg, Arne, 227-C, 227-F, 317, 354, 357, 1026
Oldberg, Eric, 357
O'Leary, Mrs., 314
Oleson, O. M., 465
Olin Library, 190, 866, 1005
Olive, Jeanette Ramsey, 1501
Oliver, Benjamin Lynde, 701
Oliver, Henry K., 701
Oliver Theater, 887
Olivet (Mich.) College, 730, 767
Olivier, Louise, 563
Olmstead, Clarence, 1274
Olney, Marguerite, 1528
Olsen, Charles Ludwig, 1520
Olsen, Lars Jorgen Rudolf, 1051
Olson, Ben, 847
Olson, Evelyn N., 952
Olsson, Betty, 68
Olympia (Wash.) Band, 1571
Olympia Opera House, 1571
Omaha (Neb.), 475, 878, 887
Omaha Public Library, 890
Omaha Indians, 887
Omaha, University of, 879
O'Meara, Eva J., 195-C
Onans, Morris, 1061-M
Oncley, Alma Lissow, 1148
Ondricek, Franz, 1053
One-man bands, 777
Onegin, Sigrid, 1564
Oneida (N.Y.) Historical Society, 1132
O'Neill, Rose, 1127
Oneka, John, 742

Onnou, Alphonse, 227-F
Onondaga County (N.Y.) Public Library, 1125
Onondaga Historical Association, 1126
Ontario (Cal.) City Library, 95
Ontario (Canada), 1059
Opelousas (La.), 544
Opera (materials about), 3, 11, 15, 33, 36, 50, 55, 60, 70, 78, 83, 85, 104, 118, 122, 125, 127, 131, 142, 144, 155, 157, 163, 179, 182, 195-B, 206, 227-B, 227-H, 227-L, 227-M, 242, 244, 266, 270, 286, 298, 315, 319, 334, 337, 379, 391, 398, 442, 450, 511, 523, 544, 551, 568-C, 590, 598, 612, 613, 614, 636, 637, 638, 654, 712, 739, 742, 800, 815, 819, 837, 860-C, 860-D, 887, 916, 926, 973, 975, 982, 1005, 1007, 1031, 1037, 1052, 1059, 1061-F, 1061-K, 1061-L, 1064, 1137, 1141, 1155, 1165, 1172, 1202, 1222, 1229, 1326, 1333, 1338, 1340, 1359, 1396, 1407, 1416, 1452, 1459, 1461, 1463, 1507, 1511, 1524, 1577, 1596, 1603, 1611, 1626, 1643, 1646, 1663. See also Opera companies
Opera Association (Fresno, Cal.), 60
Opéra Comique (Paris), 544
Opera comique. See Operetta and musical comedy
Opera companies, 3, 15, 60, 70, 78, 83, 103, 115, 122, 124, 155, 156, 179, 195-B, 227-B, 227-H, 227-L, 230, 244, 269, 282, 314, 315, 337, 351, 381, 391, 406, 544, 551, 560, 568-C, 614, 636, 654, 672, 710, 712, 721, 739, 800, 807, 815, 819, 829, 860-A, 860-D, 860-J, 1005, 1007, 1031, 1037, 1052, 1053, 1059, 1061-B, 1061-D, 1061-F, 1061-J, 1061-L, 1061-N, 1065, 1172, 1176, 1190, 1199, 1202, 1272, 1333, 1349, 1368, 1375, 1420, 1483, 1520, 1576, 1578, 1663, 1678. See also Opera
Opera Festivals (Ravinia, Ill.), 337
Opera houses, 26, 37, 50, 59, 99, 129, 149, 153, 155, 156, 163, 167, 172, 177, 215, 224, 227-M, 251, 253, 276, 290, 302, 304, 314, 315, 382, 391, 400, 427, 438, 446, 450, 454, 458, 465, 476, 498, 528, 555, 568-A, 568-C, 569, 576, 647, 669, 743, 748, 761, 762, 765, 800, 815, 823, 860-A, 860-B, 860-E, 868, 872, 882, 887, 893, 911, 916, 944, 996, 1001, 1006, 1012, 1061-M, 1093, 1105, 1127, 1146, 1165, 1172, 1190, 1209, 1215, 1217, 1232, 1246, 1258, 1268, 1308, 1333,

1364, 1392, 1393, 1439, 1479, 1487, 1500, 1515, 1571, 1572, 1582, 1587, 1600, 1624, 1631, 1633, 1634, 1647. See also Theaters and auditoriums
Operas, 1, 3, 10, 15, 25, 33, 36, 50, 55, 84, 85, 89, 115, 118, 122, 130, 137, 142, 155, 173, 195-A, 196, 197, 227-J, 227-L, 227-M, 230, 242, 249, 255, 268, 286, 313, 315, 334, 340, 354, 398, 406, 502, 510, 523, 531, 544, 546, 555, 562, 569, 576, 590, 614, 618, 636, 637, 642, 646, 654, 711, 712, 729-B, 741, 793, 800, 810, 819, 827, 837, 855, 860-A, 860-F, 860-H, 866, 878, 896, 919, 936, 941, 949, 975, 977, 982, 984, 1007, 1031, 1039, 1052, 1061-D, 1061-F, 1061-J, 1061-N, 1067, 1070, 1082, 1088, 1121, 1183, 1194, 1267, 1298, 1352, 1359, 1375, 1402, 1435, 1477, 1515, 1518, 1520, 1528, 1534, 1541, 1543, 1564, 1576, 1596, 1611, 1612, 1646, 1663, 1673. See also Libretti
Operetta and musical comedy, 50, 51, 54, 66, 79, 83, 84, 115, 127, 128, 129, 130, 137, 139, 142, 146, 150, 177, 190, 195-B, 202, 207, 222, 224, 227-B, 227-H, 227-L, 230, 244, 251, 256, 265, 269, 285, 291, 313, 314, 315, 326, 340, 345, 347, 349, 354, 374, 381, 394, 396, 398, 401, 406, 443, 510, 527, 544, 612, 636, 654, 655, 691, 696, 698, 711, 712, 724, 729-B, 729-C, 739, 788, 796, 800, 828, 837, 854, 860-D, 860-F, 860-H, 860-J, 866, 878, 888, 923, 944, 949, 957, 977, 988, 1005, 1031, 1041, 1042, 1053, 1055, 1057, 1061-C, 1061-D, 1061-J, 1061-L, 1065, 1066, 1070, 1072, 1073, 1080, 1121, 1127, 1135, 1167, 1168, 1187, 1194, 1205, 1207, 1208, 1275, 1286, 1332, 1333, 1336, 1338, 1339, 1349, 1350, 1364, 1388, 1402, 1405, 1424, 1452, 1457, 1461, 1477, 1482, 1502, 1514, 1517, 1518, 1541, 1544, 1572, 1611, 1612, 1646, 1665, 1673, 1688
Ophicleide, 1267
Opper, Frederick H., 142
Opperman, Ella Scoble, 260
Oral history, 12, 38, 42, 44, 68, 84, 95, 102, 122, 141, 156, 167, 195-C, 248, 277, 278, 290, 308, 374, 406, 434, 443, 446, 475, 522, 523, 535, 539, 544, 545, 568-B, 592, 618, 654, 673, 736, 779, 798, 807, 815, 833, 865, 868, 872, 879, 888, 960, 992, 1024, 1031, 1061-J, 1061-N, 1099, 1119, 1144, 1174, 1187, 1234, 1297, 1423, 1430, 1433, 1450, 1451, 1452, 1454, 1462, 1463, 1466,

1472, 1487, 1501, 1516, 1517, 1521, 1525, 1528, 1541, 1544, 1577, 1597, 1611, 1643. See also Field recordings
Oral History of the Arts Archive, 68
Oranano, Mrs. A. Colonna d', 1560
Orange County (Fla.) Historical Commission, 251
Orange County (N.Y.), 406, 1017
Oratorical Association, 379
Oratorio societies. See Choral ensembles
Oratorio Society (Baltimore), 612
Oratorio Society (Grand Forks, N.D.), 1165
Oratorio Society (Hartford, Conn.), 181
Oratorio Society (New Haven, Conn.), 195-A
Oratorio Society (St. Louis), 860-B, 860-C, 860-E
Oratorio Society (Salem, Mass.), 701
Oratorio Society (Springfield, Mass.), 705
Orchesis (California State University, Fresno), 60
Orchestra Hall (Chicago), 314, 317, 391
Orchestral music libraries, 17, 28, 51, 54, 57, 68, 72, 79, 80, 83, 84, 85, 89, 98, 104, 111, 114, 115, 126, 129, 142, 151, 168, 173, 182, 195-A, 206, 223, 227-J, 227-L, 228, 229, 232, 304, 305, 307, 309, 315, 317, 326, 334, 339, 345, 354, 376, 383, 389, 391, 398, 427, 433, 441, 443, 477, 480, 481, 490, 497, 504, 517, 531, 532, 533, 535, 544, 605, 606, 618, 636, 654, 667, 682, 708, 723, 739, 749, 767, 778, 794, 798, 819, 821, 823, 846, 847, 860-F, 866, 885, 888, 896, 907, 951, 957, 977, 988, 1007, 1031, 1050, 1055, 1061-J, 1061-N, 1077, 1082, 1105, 1111, 1120, 1124, 1127, 1141, 1185, 1252, 1262, 1267, 1270, 1272, 1275, 1281, 1285, 1290, 1333, 1336, 1343, 1359, 1375, 1391, 1402, 1451, 1471, 1477, 1487, 1488, 1493, 1496, 1501, 1502, 1511, 1520, 1522, 1577, 1611, 1612, 1617, 1621, 1623, 1624, 1628, 1632, 1646, 1648, 1665, 1688. See also Theater music
Orchestral societies, 98, 103, 181, 195, 227-H, 266, 282, 287, 314, 357, 535, 544, 560, 605, 636, 729-B, 860-D, 739, 826, 860-E, 860-K, 887, 907, 1059, 1061-J, 1063, 1165, 1183, 1239, 1246, 1270, 1274, 1323, 1359, 1375, 1544, 1578, 1595. See also Symphony Orchestras

Orchestras (materials about). *See* Symphony Orchestras

Ordway, John P., 701

Oregon, 122, 291

Oregon Agricultural College, 1268

Oregon Historical Society, 1274

Oregon Music Teachers' Association, 1274

Oregon State Library, 1277

Oregon State University, 1268

Oregon Symphony Orchestra, 1273

Oregon Trail, 1266

Oregon Trail Pageants, 1269

Oregon, University of, 1269, 1270, 1274

Orendorff, George, 68

Orendorff (i.e., Parlin & Orendorff) Band, 305

Organ Association (Groveland, Mass.), 701

Organ Historical Society, 928, 1244

Organ instruction materials, 276, 308, 376, 510, 779, 868, 955, 1527, 1534, 1599

Organ manufacturing, 234, 391, 700, 729-B, 801, 860-B, 1244, 1325, 1329, 1356, 1611, 1629

Organ music, 58, 129, 185, 192, 195-A, 227-L, 271, 292, 294, 307, 324, 326, 334, 348, 351, 368, 375, 379, 390, 396, 398, 466, 478, 481, 486, 497, 552, 566, 569, 574, 638, 646, 700, 701, 719, 729-D, 786, 800, 819, 838, 885, 928, 934, 951, 977, 998, 1070, 1135, 1144, 1199, 1200, 1202, 1207, 1220, 1244, 1266, 1270, 1274, 1295, 1340, 1356, 1359, 1428, 1521, 1570, 1604, 1615, 1620, 1623

Organ rolls. *See* Piano and organ rolls

Organs (general collections devoted to), 8, 36, 55, 134, 150, 156, 157, 180, 188, 190, 215, 227-H, 227-M, 234, 235, 324, 356, 442, 460, 523, 544, 577, 580, 603, 636, 695, 701, 708, 719, 725, 729-B, 741, 825, 847, 866, 914, 920, 928, 939, 957, 977, 1005, 1017, 1030, 1059, 1070, 1117, 1125, 1143, 1144, 1159, 1172, 1193, 1222, 1244, 1270, 1274, 1325, 1338, 1356, 1358, 1361, 1363, 1365, 1373, 1375, 1382, 1385, 1396, 1406, 1418, 1459, 1463, 1495, 1520, 1521, 1525, 1529, 1533, 1577, 1611

Orient (N.Y.) Cornet Band, 1098

Oriental music, 68. *See also* Chinese music; Japanese music

Original Dixieland Jazz Band, 568

Orlando (Fla.) Opera House, 251

Orlando Public Library, 252

Ormandy, Eugene, 227-F, 314, 922, 1031, 1301, 1580

Ornstein, Leo, 195-A, 195-C, 227-D, 227-F, 1061-A, 1580, 1666

Oro Fino Hall, 1274

Orphéon Française de la Nouvelle Orleans Bibliothèque, 406

Orpheum Theater (Kalamazoo, Mich.), 761

Orpheum Theater (Omaha), 887

Orpheum Theater (Seattle), 1575

Orpheus (Cincinnati), 398

Orpheus (Newark, N.J.), 940

Orpheus Choir (Glasgow, Scotland), 1675

Orpheus Club (Cincinnati), 1172

Orpheus Club (Columbus, Ga.), 276

Orpheus Club (St. Paul), 800

Orpheus Club (Springfield, Mass.), 705

Orpheus Club (Wilmington, Del.?), 215

Orpheus Music Club (Brunswick, Me.), 586

Orpheus Music Club (Cincinnati), 1176

Orpheus Musical Society (Boston), 636

Orr, Mary Hamilton (Thompson), 1463

Orradre, Michel, Library, 133

Orrego-Salas, Juan, 1580

Orrell, E. M., 729-B

Orth, Jacob, 708

Orthodox church music, 195-B, 760, 1188

Ortmann, Otto, 613

Osborn, Fanny Scott (Beverley), 1560

Osborne, Stanley L., 1658

Oshkosh (Wis.), 1054, 1611

Oslin, S. J., 1255

Osser, Glenn, 729-D

Ossier, Julius, 847

Oster, Harry, 545, 1660

Oster, Phyllis, 1111

Osterman, Mark, 1395

Osterman, Susan, 1395

Otero, Antonio, 1651

Otero, Monsita Ferrer, 1651, 1652

Otis, Harrison Gray, House, 649

Otis, Philo A., 314, 334

Otisfield (Me.), 707

Otterbein College, 1243

Otterström, Thorvald, 317, 334, 800, 1061-A

Otto family (Ann Arbor, Mich.), 729-B

Otto, Herbert O., 568

Ouaquaga (N.Y.) Cornet Band, 1100

Oungst, Webb M., 465

Outagamie County (Wis.) Historical Society, 1592

Outer Banks (N.C.), 1095

Ovalle, Juan Rios, 1650, 1651

Over, W. H., Museum, 1432

Owen, Allison, 544

Owen, Barbara, 700

Owen, John Dale, 942

Owen, John Dale, Collection, 1626

Owen, Robert Dale, 425

Owen, William, 425

Owen, William Miller, Papers, 544

Owens, Tarry, 1477

Owens, William A., 1477

Owens (i.e., Carter-Owens) Collection, 1141

Owst, W. G., 606, 612

Oxbarn Museum, 1267

Oxford University, 1673

Oysterponds Historical Society, 1098

Ozark Folk Center, 42

Ozark Mountains, 35, 36, 42, 227-K, 227-L, 271, 836, 870, 979, 1452

Ozaukee County (Wis.) Historical Society, 1599

Ozawa, Seiji, 682

P

Pabst Auditorium, 1623

Pabst Theatre, 1623, 1624

Pachmann, Vladimir de, 227-F, 636, 1193

Pacific Islands, 285

Pacific Music Press, 76

Pacific Northwest, 1575, 1581. *See also* Northwestern U.S.

Pacific Ocean, 285

Pacific University, 1271

Paddon, John, 648

Paderewski, Ignace Jan, 61, 142, 195-A, 227-D, 313, 317, 336, 636, 639, 729, 1053, 1105, 1111, 1313, 1359, 1520

Page, Frank Crawford, Papers, 544

Page, Walter Hines, Library, 1538

Pageant and Drama Association (St. Louis), 860-E

Pageant and Masque (St. Louis), 860-E

Pageant Choral Society (St. Louis), 860-E

Pageants. *See* Festivals and pageants

Pagliughi, Lina, 1061-F

Paine family, 718

Paine, John Knowles, 227-B, 227-D, 227-F, 317, 636, 654, 718, 951, 1111, 1223, 1338, 1612

Paine, Robert Treat, 643

Paine, Silas K., 183

Paine Collection, 269

Painesville (Ohio), 1190

Paint and Powder Club, 612

Painted Post (N.Y.), 984

Paisley, William Merrell, 36

Pajaro Valley (Cal.) Historical Association, 146

Pakistani music, 398

Paldi, Mari, 227-D

Palestine, American, Musical Association ("Mailamm"), 1061-B

Palestine Orchestra Fund, 1174

Palestine Symphony Orchestra and Music Foundation, 1174

Palm, Augustus O., 1176

Palmer, Belle L., 1120

Palmer, Courtland, 1061-A

Palmer, Rev. David, 657

Palmer, George W., 636

Palmer, I. B., 860-K

Palmer, Ray, 950, 1465

Palmer, Robert, 227-D, 1111

Palmer, Saida Scott, 1591

Palmer (Mich.), 1455

"Palmolive Beauty Box Theatre," 227-L

Palmyra (N.Y.), 1520

Palo (Minn.), 782

Pampa Band, 1507

Panama-Pacific Exposition (1915), 122

Panchuk, John, 800

Panhandle Music Festival, 1473

Panhandle-Plains Historical Museum, 1480

Panhandle State University, 1253

Panhandle (Tex.) Music Teachers Association, 1477

Panizza, Ettore, 315

Panzeri, Louis, 562, 569

Papago Indians, 28, 31

Pape, Willie, 568

Paramount Records, 322, 1353, 1667

Paramount Pictures Corporation, 111

Paramount Studios (New York), 1270

Paramount Theatre (Toledo, Ohio), 1167

Paranov, Moshe, 206

Parcells, Walter H., 314

Paredes, Américo, 1477

Parelli, Attilio, 1053

Paris (France), 544, 555, 631, 1030, 1592

Parisot, Aldo, 195-C

Park County (Mont.) Museum Association, 875

Park County (Mont.) Pioneer Programs, 875

Parker, C. W., 491

Parker, Charles Astor, 815

Parker, Henry Taylor, 227-F, 636

Parker, Horatio, 195-A, 227-D, 227-F, 636, 646, 1018, 1031, 1053, 1061-A, 1080, 1107, 1111, 1177, 1338

Parker, J. C. D., 227-D, 227-G, 646

Parker, John Rowe, 721, 1352, 1359, 1402

Parker, Laura Bryan, 1477

Parker, Dr. Laurence, 787

Parker, Osborne, 142

Parker, Stephen, 698

Parker, Thurlow W., 227-A

Parker, Willetta, 314

Parker College of Music, 815

Parkersburg Musical Academy, 1591

Parkes, Olive Guild, 730

Parkes, Roger, 730
Parkman, Ebenezer, 643
Parler, Mary Celestia, 36
Parlin and Orendorff (farm implement manufacturer) Band, 304
Parlor music, 65, 379, 650, 998, 1536, 1541. *See also* Salon music
Parlow, Kathleen, 1520
Parrino, Ted, 1487
Parris, Hermann, 1333
Parris-Denson Co., 1440
Parry, David, 1390
Parry, Milman, Collection, 654
Parsifal, 860-B, 1515
Parsons, Elsie Clews, 1327
Parsons, Marion Randall, 50
Partch, Harry, 68, 195-C, 227-D, 227-F, 398, 1580
Partisan Prohibition Historical Society, 729-B
Party songs, 391, 407
Parvin (i.e., Brown-Clawson-Parvin) family, 1274
Pasadena (Cal.) College, 113
Pasadena (Cal.) Historical Society, 99
Pasadena (Cal.) Public Library, 100
Pascarella, Cesare, 68
Pashkoff, Christ, 349
Pasquale, Joseph de, 227-F
Pasquali, Bernice de, 672
Pasquali, Salvatore de, 672
Pasquet, Jean, 1553
Passaic County (N.J.) Historical Society, 944
Passamoquoddy Indians, 227-L
"Los Pastores," 1500
Patek, F. R., 1573
Patents, 234, 391, 612, 887, 1079
Paterson (N.J.), 939
Paterson Museum, 945
Paterson Opera House, 944
Paterson's Orchestral Concerts, 366
Patricks, Butterfield, 36
Patriotic songs, 92, 129, 185, 219, 227-A, 227-H, 314, 315, 406, 465, 544, 624, 625, 707, 721, 729-B, 744, 766, 800, 860-G, 887, 950, 1031, 1036, 1040, 1059, 1235, 1077, 1122, 1235, 1258, 1267, 1407, 1444, 1463, 1483, 1520, 1602, 1673. *See also* Political songs
Patrons, 129, 156, 160, 227-B, 227-M, 266, 268, 313, 334, 391, 568-A, 636, 729-B, 800, 814, 860, 1031, 1061-B, 1061-M, 1143, 1165, 1172, 1174, 1327, 1338, 1414, 1498, 1611
Pattee, Fred Lewis, Library, 1385
Patterson, Clara, 77
Patterson, Clinton H., 1031
Patterson, James, 1318
Patterson, John Brown, 1560
Patterson, Robert, 1225

Patterson, Robert Maskell, 1327
Patterson & Hopkins (music publishers), 1225
Patti, Adelina, 270, 544, 636, 815, 860-J, 1031, 1052, 1061-B, 1222, 1418
Pattison, Mrs. Everett W., 860-D
Pattison, Lee, 55, 646
Patton, Lowell, 1270
Patton, Willard, 798
Patz, Gustav, 665
Paul, H. M., 227-H
Paul, Robert L., 614
Paull, E. T., 544, 565, 1655
Paur, Emil, 1193, 1359
Paur, Leonard de, 227-F
Pavlova, Anna, 631, 1031, 1375
Payne, John Howard, 950, 1040, 1111, 1301
Payne, L. W., Jr., 1477
Paynter, William Garfield, 1113
Payson, Edward, 443
Paz, Pedro, Orchestra, 730
Pazmor, Radiana, 227-F, 1425
Peabody, Augustus, 654
Peabody, Charles, 642
Peabody, Elizabeth, House, 800
Peabody, George, Collection, 1546
Peabody, Margaret, 1107
Peabody Art Collection, 614
Peabody Conservatory of Music, 613, 614
Peabody Institute, 606, 613, 614
Peabody Museum of Archaeology and Ethnology, 227-L, 654
Peabody Museum of Salem (Mass.), 702
Peace Jubilee. *See* National Peace Jubilee (Boston, 1869); World's Peace Jubilee (Boston, 1872)
Peach, Bishop Robert W., 721
Peak Family Bell Ringers, 703
Peale, Charles Willson, 1327
Peale, Franklin, 1327
Peale's Museum, 1327
"Pealing Chord" collection, 943
Pearce, Thomas N., 957
Pearson, Norman, 195-C
Pearson, Samuel Arnold, 127
Pease, John, Jr., 663
Pedagogy. *See* Instructional materials; Music education
Pedersen, Elfrida J., 1577
Peel, Graham, 110
Peirce, Eli Harvey, Jr., 1521
Pejepscot Historical Society, 586
Peletier, Wilfred, 227-L
Pelissier, Victor, 1061-A
Pella (Iowa), 475
Peltz, Mary Ellis, 1031, 1052

Pember Library and Museum, 999
Pendleton, Edmund H., 1172
Penfield Library, 1099
Peninsula Philharmonic Orchestra, 128
Penn, William, College, 484
Penn, William, Memorial Museum Building, 1298
Penn School, 1141
Penn State Players, 1385
Pennsylvania, 36, 195, 212, 217, 220, 227-F, 227-G, 227-L, 334, 340, 350, 380, 391, 397, 400, 467, 556, 564, 606, 611, 618, 654, 679, 741, 800, 815, 860-B, 939, 944, 946, 1005, 1031, 1040, 1061-A, 1061-F, 1061-M, 1113, 1116, 1141, 1161, 1225, 1402, 1405, 1611, 1659
Pennsylvania Federation of Music Clubs, 1310
Pennsylvania German Collection, 1333
Pennsylvania Historical and Museum Commission, 1298
Pennsylvania History and German-American Collection, 1319
Pennsylvania militia, 1338
Pennsylvania State University, 1385
Pennsylvania, University of, 653, 833, 1327, 1352
Pennypacker, Samuel W., 1338
Penobscot (Me.), 587
Penrose Library, 161
Pensacola (Fla.) Historical Society, 253
Pentucket (Mass.) Orchestra, 671
People's Choral Union, 227-B, 636
Peoples Institute, 1032
People's Singing Classes (Pittsburgh, Pa.?), 1359
People's Song Library, 742
People's Theatre (Minneapolis), 815
Peoria (Ill.), 1520
Peoria Public Library, 381
Pepita, 576
Pepper, Buddy, 535
Pepper, Maude V., 931
Perabo, Johann Ernst, 636, 646, 1111, 1670
Percussion, 28, 245, 321, 618, 633, 643, 671, 815, 860-C, 1190, 1288, 1395, 1407, 1432. *See also* Drums
Performance rights, 391. *See also* American Society of Composers, Authors, and Publishers; Broadcast Music, Inc.
Performing Arts Research Center, 1061
Periman, Ken, 162
Periodicals, 68, 84, 122, 185, 192, 195-A, 227-A, 227-H, 227-K, 265, 320, 323, 325, 346, 349, 365, 398, 544, 611, 613, 636, 642, 674, 676, 721,

800, 860-E, 862, 939, 954, 977, 1005, 1059, 1061-N, 1077, 1352, 1359, 1402, 1403, 1530, 1594
Perkins, C. C., 636
Perkins, Elliam Oscar, 475
Perkins, Emily S., 190
Perkins, Frances, 1061-B
Perkins, Henry Southwick, 475
Perkins, Susannah, 721
Perkins, William R., Library, 1143
Perkins School for the Blind, 714, 1301
Perkins School of Theology, 1487
Perle, George, 227-C, 227-D, 1580
Perlet, Hermann, 50
Perlmutter, Sholem, Theatre Archives, 1076
Perry, Alfred, 183
Perry, Bliss, 1053
Perry, Josephine Hovey, 1533
Perry, Martha Scott, 1155
Perry County (Mo.) Lutheran Historical Society, 835
Perry Music Co., 868
Perschbacher, John H., 750
Persichetti, Vincent, 227-D, 1580
Persley, George W., 227-D
Persons, Mira H., 296
Pessl-Sobotka, Yella, 690
Pest, Annie Marie, 514
Peter, Johann Friedrich, 1161, 1285
Peter, Lily, 36
Peter codex, 1161
Peter Memorial Library, 1161
Peterborough (N.H.), 84, 227-B, 227-M, 636
Peterborough Historical Society, 917
Peterborough Town Library, 918
Peters family, 1338
Peters, Janet E., 854
Peters, Roberta, 1007
Peters, W. C., 535
Peters & Field, 314
Petersburg (Va.), 1061-A, 1560
Petersham (Mass.) Historical Society, 695
Peterson, Andrew, 815
Peterson, Clara Gottschalk, 555
Peterson, May, 1611
Peterson's 15th Massachusetts Regiment, 1059
Le Petite Théâtre du Vieux Carré, 555
Petrillo, James C., 227-L, 729-B
Pett, Ernest, 1611
Pettibone, W. H., 103
Pettigrew family, 1141
Pettigrew, Ebenezer, 1141
Pettis, Ashley, 227-F
Petzinger Library of Californiana, 144
Pevahouse, Jerry W., 1438
Peyre, Henri, 195-C
Peytavin, John L., 544
Pfatteicher, Carl, 227-F, 1352

Pfeiffer, Agatha, 854
Pfeiffer, Charles A., 854
Pfeiffer, Edward H., 1112
Pfeiffer, Henry, Library, 364
Pfeil, William R., 1622
Pfister, A. P., 15
Phelps, E., 1343
Phelps, S. Dryden, 950
Phelps County (Neb.) Histori-
    cal Society, 883
Phifer, Robert S., 1141
Philadelphia, 212, 334, 340,
    397, 467, 556, 564, 606, 741,
    815, 860-B, 1031, 1040,
    1061-A, 1061-F, 1113, 1161,
    1285, 1299, 1319, 1324, 1325,
    1338, 1385, 1402, 1403, 1611
Philadelphia American
    Musical Academy, 1340
Philadelphia Art Alliance,
    1352
Philadelphia Assembly, 1327
Philadelphia Centennial Exhi-
    bition (1876), 334, 1338
Philadelphia Civic Opera, 1333
Philadelphia College of Bible,
    1311
Philadelphia College of the
    Performing Arts, 1345
Philadelphia Conservatory of
    Music, 1345
Philadelphia Dancing Assem-
    bly, 1338
Philadelphia Divinity School,
    440, 653, 1352
Philadelphia Inquirer, 1333
Philadelpia Mayor's Commit-
    tee, 618
Philadelphia Musical
    Academy, 1333, 1345
Philadelphia Musical Saving
    and Loan Society, 212
Philadelphia Opera Co.,
    1061-F
Philadelphia Orchestra, 922,
    1346, 1498
Philadelphia Sunday Dispatch,
    1338
Philadelphia Theatre Index,
    1333
Philharmonia Club (Rutland,
    Vt.), 1533
Philharmonic Auditorium (Los
    Angeles), 78
Philharmonic Music Club
    (Jasper, Ind.), 429
Philharmonic Orchestra (St.
    Louis), 860-E
Philharmonic orchestras. See
    Symphony orchestras
Philharmonic Society (Bethle-
    hem, Pa.), 1285, 1323
Philharmonic Society (Chi-
    cago), 314
Philharmonic Society (Holly
    Springs, Miss.), 826
Philharmonic Society (Lititz,
    Pa.), 1285
Philharmonic Society (New
    Hampshire), 907
Philharmonic Society (New
    York), 1059, 1088
Philharmonic Society (Provi-
    dence, R.I.), 729-B

Philharmonic Society (St.
    Louis), 860-D, 860-E, 860-K
Philharmonic Society (Thibo-
    daux, La.), 544
Philharmonic Society (Vicks-
    burg, Miss.), 544
Philharmonic-Symphony So-
    ciety of New York Inc., 1063
Philip, L., 819
Philipp, Isidor, 227-F, 729-E,
    833
Philipp, Isidor, Archive and
    Memorial Library, 535
Philley, Grace C., 410
Phillipps, Adelaide, 678
Phillipps, Adelaide and
    Mathilde, Memorial Collec-
    tion, 646
Phillips, Burrill, 227-D, 227-F,
    1111, 1580
Phillips, Henry, Jr., 606
Phillips, L. A., 860-C
Phillips, R. W., 227-K
Phillips, Utah, 1445
Phillips Academy Archives,
    629
Phillips County (Ark.)
    Museum, 37
Phillips Exeter Academy, 903
Phillips Memorial Library,
    1589
Phillips University, 1251
Phillipson, Amanda, 866
Philomel Club (Warren, Pa.),
    1387
Phoenix Historical Society and
    Museum of History, 25
Phoenix Symphony Orchestra,
    30
Phonograph. See Recording
    companies; Recordings
Pianist's Club (Cincinnati),
    1172
Piano, H., 406
Piano (general collections de-
    voted to), 4, 68, 96, 195, 250,
    268, 390, 532, 580, 612, 627,
    636, 667, 691, 701, 712, 730,
    743, 847, 860-B, 885, 910,
    977, 1017, 1043, 1047,
    1061-F, 1061-M, 1080, 1093,
    1113, 1122, 1136, 1155, 1172,
    1177, 1193, 1222, 1269, 1289,
    1299, 1331, 1365, 1420, 1447,
    1448, 1470, 1520, 1529, 1577,
    1602, 1626, 1630
Piano and organ rolls, 26, 167,
    171, 195-B, 234, 349, 354,
    371, 398, 424, 446, 535, 556,
    568-B, 600, 689, 724, 735,
    743, 749, 750, 771, 774, 792,
    830, 853, 864, 868, 916, 942,
    949, 968, 978, 987, 1006,
    1017, 1065, 1066, 1086, 1111,
    1117, 1144, 1248, 1272, 1278,
    1292, 1333, 1433, 1436, 1520,
    1611, 1623, 1624, 1631, 1659,
    1666
Piano-harp music, 510
Piano instruction materials, 20,
    154, 169, 315, 326, 364, 376,
    398, 460, 497, 514, 535, 646,
    757, 773, 779, 794, 854,
    860-B, 866, 887, 891, 955,

1146, 1242, 1258, 1299, 1315,
    1403, 1428, 1472, 1502, 1510,
    1527
Piano makers and repairers,
    195-C, 200, 201, 227-M, 544,
    612, 707, 860-E, 935, 1013,
    1172, 1329, 1385, 1497, 1560,
    1611
Piano music collections, 17,
    50, 58, 62, 83, 92, 126, 129,
    154, 163, 169, 192, 195-A,
    196, 206, 216, 227-A, 227-B,
    227-J, 227-L, 228, 229, 236,
    249, 250, 260, 262, 307, 309,
    334, 336, 338, 348, 351, 354,
    369, 398, 412, 455, 457, 460,
    465, 477, 478, 496, 502, 517,
    533, 535, 544, 555, 569, 574,
    606, 642, 646, 667, 671, 701,
    712, 749, 767, 773, 776, 786,
    798, 819, 825, 838, 860-F,
    862, 863, 866, 880, 885, 889,
    895, 941, 977, 1016, 1046,
    1050, 1061-A, 1061-J, 1080,
    1082, 1107, 1111, 1138, 1143,
    1161, 1176, 1183, 1199, 1202,
    1207, 1243, 1269, 1272, 1280,
    1285, 1289, 1299, 1315, 1327,
    1338, 1340, 1359, 1375, 1378,
    1397, 1448, 1461, 1494, 1516,
    1528, 1540, 1543, 1557, 1615,
    1620, 1623, 1648, 1649, 1650,
    1665, 1673
Pianoforte Club (Fresno, Cal.),
    60
Pianolin music, 510, 750
Piastro, Michel, 227-F
Piatigorsky, Gregor, 227-F
Picard, Theodora, 391
Picerno, Leonard "Ned," 383
Pickaway County (Ohio), 1178
Pickett, Clarence E., 484
Pickhardt, Mary Howard,
    195-C
Pickman, Rebecca Taylor, 701
Pickman, Sally, 701
Picó, Carlos R. Gadea, 1651
Picó, Maria Teresa, 1651
Picon, Molly, 711
Pictorial Archives of Early
    American Architecture,
    227-M
Pictures (major collections), 6,
    30, 33, 50, 52, 54, 63, 65, 79,
    81, 83, 84, 105, 106, 120, 122,
    129, 156, 157, 160, 174, 193,
    195-B, 195-C, 200, 206, 226,
    227, 228, 229, 230, 231, 234,
    237, 244, 248, 265, 266, 285,
    290, 296, 313, 314, 333, 334,
    335, 349, 356, 364, 365, 379,
    387, 391, 394, 395, 398, 402,
    406, 408, 409, 418, 419, 420,
    421, 424, 426, 427, 430, 435,
    437, 438, 440, 442, 443, 446,
    447, 451, 454, 455, 457, 458,
    459, 460, 463, 464, 465, 469,
    472, 473, 475, 476, 480, 511,
    535, 554, 556, 561, 564, 565,
    568-B, 614, 624, 646, 654,
    676, 688, 721, 724, 729-A,
    729-C, 739, 766, 812, 815,
    866, 977, 1031, 1051, 1052,
    1056, 1059, 1061-G, 1061-L,

1064, 1077, 1079, 1084, 1111,
    1112, 1144, 1172, 1333, 1338,
    1339, 1352, 1359, 1402, 1405,
    1408, 1450, 1452, 1454, 1457,
    1477, 1484, 1502, 1512, 1518,
    1541, 1544, 1557, 1573, 1594,
    1609, 1611, 1646, 1655, 1666,
    1673
Pieran Sodality (Harvard Uni-
    versity), 642, 654
Pierce, Billie, 1450
Pierce, Brent, 68
Pierce, Dede, 1450
Pierpont, John, 1054
Pierpont Morgan Library, 1053
Pierre, Dorothi Bock, 52
Pierson College (Yale Univer-
    sity), 195-A
Pike, James, 1036
Pike, Lawrence, 1172
Pike's Opera House, 1172
Pikeville College, 537
Pilgrim Society, 698
Pilgrims, 698
Pillois, Jacques, 227-F
Pillsbury Foundation School,
    618
Pima Indians, 28
Pimsleur, Solomon, 1031, 1580
Pinart, Alphonse, 50
Pinder, Tom Wright, 1521
Pine, A. J. La, 195-C
Pine Barrens (N.J.), 939
Pine Mountain Settlement
    School, 538
Pine Ridge (S.D.), 27
Pine Ridge Agency, 156
Pine Street Synagogue (Buf-
    falo), 549
Pinkard, Maceo, 226
Pinkham, Daniel, 646, 1108
Pinson, Lois, 1477
Pioneer Collection, 30
Pioneer Mennenchor Associa-
    tion, 821
Pioneer Museum and Haggin
    Galleries, 144
Pioneer Museum of the Clark
    County (Kan.) Historical
    Society, 493
Pioneers' Museum, 153
Pipenhagen family, 1113
Piper, Edward, 50
Piper, Edwin Ford, 476
Piper, John, 50
Piper, Minnie Stevens, 1477
Piper Opera House, 50
Pirani, Eugenio di, 1053
Pisk, Paul Amadeus, 68, 81,
    83, 195-C, 227-E, 227-F, 866,
    1477, 1580
Piston, Walter, 227-C, 227-F,
    535, 636, 637, 654, 1040,
    1061-A, 1108, 1222, 1301,
    1580, 1648
Pitcher, Gladys, 580, 618
Pitchpipes, 188
Pitts family, 1560
Pitts, Lilla Belle, 618
Pitts Theology Library, 269
Pittsburg (Kan.) State Univer-
    sity, 511
Pittsburgh, 391, 400, 654, 800,
    1383, 1659

Pittsburgh Bach Choir, 1359
Pittsburgh Chamber Music Society, 1355
Pittsburgh Civic Ballet, 1375
Pittsburgh Dispatch, 1366
Pittsburgh May Musical Festivals, 1359
Pittsburgh Mendelssohn Choir, 1359
Pittsburgh Mozart Club, 1359
Pittsburgh Musical Institute, 1359
Pittsburgh (North Side) Organ recitals, 1375
Pittsburgh (Oakland) Organ recitals, 1375
Pittsburgh Opera, 1368, 1375
Pittsburgh Orchestra, 1359
Pittsburgh Orchestra Association, 1359
Pittsburgh Photographic Library, 1359
Pittsburgh Savoyards, 1358
Pittsburgh String Orchestra, 1359
Pittsburgh String Symphonic Ensemble Society, 1359
Pittsburgh Sun-Telegraph, 1366
Pittsburgh Symphony Orchestra, 1355, 1359, 1361, 1375
Pittsburgh Symphony Society, 1375
Pittsburgh Theological Seminary, 183, 1369
Pittsburgh, University of, 334, 1374, 1375
Pittsfield (Mass.), 217
Pitzinger, Gertrude, 1061-F
Placement Committee for German & Austrian Musicians, 1030
Plains Indians, 654
Plantation songs. *See* Minstrelsy
Plaquemine (La.), 544
Playbills. *See* Programs
Player pianos, 544. *See also* Mechanical musical instruments; Piano and organ rolls
The Players, 1064
Playground Association of America, 800
Plays with music. *See* Theater music
Plaza Music Company, 977
Pleasant Hill (Ky.), 529
Pleasanton, Gen. August, 1338
Pleasants, Henry, 637
Pleyel, 233, 555
Pleyela piano rolls, 949
Plimpton, Job, 1061-A
Plitt Theatre Collection, 315
Plogstedt, Lillian T., 1176
Pocahontas, U.S.S., 612
Pochon, Alfred, 1689
Podesta, Edward, Jazz Collection, 137
Poe, Edgar Allan, 606
Pohl, Otto, 880
Point Loma College, 113
Point Lookout (Md.), 1432
Point Pleasant (W. Va.), 227-K
Pointe Coupée Parish (La.), 544

Poister, Arthur, 1127
Polack, W. G., 856
Polah, André, 1127
Polish Museum of America, 336
Polish music, 336, 391, 756, 764, 787, 823, 1512, 1612
Political songs, 36, 94, 127, 219, 227-A, 228, 234, 314, 315, 320, 398, 442, 490, 610, 750, 986, 1172, 1217, 1232, 1329, 1430, 1463, 1560, 1577, 1586, 1606. *See also* Campaign songs; Patriotic songs
Polk, Eliza E., 1463
Polk, Leonidas, Library, 575
Polk (i.e., Yeatmann-Polk) Collection, 1463
Polkas, 398, 582, 701, 721, 807, 815, 895, 1135, 1187, 1188, 1194, 1298, 1550. *See also* Dance
Pollard, Edna, 850
Polley, Lillian Helms, 885
Polley Music Reference Library, 885
Pollock, Channing, Theatre Collection, 226
Polyhymnia Orchestra (St. Louis), 860-E
Polynesian and Hawaiian Club, 1520
Polynesian music, 285, 1520
Pomeroy, Rev. Howard E., 656
Pommer, Charles, 860-K
Pommer, William Henry, 860-B, 860-F, 860-K
Pomona (Cal.) College, 50, 55
Pompano Beach (Fla.) City Library, 256
Pomp's Cornet Band, 1291
Pond, William A., 555
Pons, Lily, 227-B, 227-F, 1031
Ponselle, Rosa, 123, 227-B, 227-L, 1111
Ponte, Lorenzo da, 729-E, 1111
Poole, Mrs. E. R., 227-A
Popper, Felix, 1031
Popper, Jan, 84
Popular Culture Collection, 743
Popular Culture Library, 1170
Popular Theater Collection, 743
Populist Party, 1430
Populist songs, 1430
Porcher Family Papers, 1418
Porgy and Bess, 142, 1286, 1416, 1477
Port Hope (N.C.), 906
Port Royal (S.C.), 227-G, 898, 909
Port Washington (Wis.) Gesang-Verein, 1599
Portage County (Ohio) Historical Society, 1227
Porter, Cole, 83, 195-B, 227-C, 227-F, 442, 527, 624, 719, 1031, 1036
Porter, Mrs. Cole, 195
Porter, John (Robert G. McCutchan), 55

Porter, Kaite A., 544
Porter, Marjorie Lansing, Collection, 1102
Porter, Quincy, 195-A, 195-C, 227-D, 227-F, 1018, 1023, 1111, 1580
Porter, Mrs. Quincy, 195-C
Porter, Solomon, 180
Porter, W. T., 1232
Porter Library, 511
Portland (Me.), 576
Portland Public Library, 596
Portland (Ore.), 122, 1270, 1272
Portnoff, Mischa, 1336
Portsmouth (England), 227-M
Portsmouth (N.H.), 645, 707
Portsmouth (Ohio), 406
Posner, Meyer, 1061-A
Post, Augustine, 1061-M
Post, Bill, 518
Post Theatre (Battle Creek, Mich.), 730
Postage stamps, 611, 1222
Postcards and similar ephemera, 53, 83, 227-H, 234, 237, 265, 357, 474, 556, 557, 580, 611, 636, 707, 721, 743, 866, 884, 1031, 1620, 1656, 1661
Posters (selected collections), 79, 81, 83, 124, 227-M, 234, 348, 398, 406, 568-B, 580, 637, 711, 807, 853, 1012, 1061-L, 1079, 1172, 1385, 1455, 1544, 1594, 1600, 1624
Poteat, Hubert McNeil, 1141, 1148
Potjes, Edouard, 1577
Potpeschnigg, Heinrich, 1039
Pottag, Max, 433
Potter, Barrett, G., 969
Potter, Edward C., 729-E
Potter, Martha Allen Woods, 523
Potter County (Pa.), 1005
Poughkeepsie (N.Y.), 1060
Poulton, J. P. C., 157
Pound, Ezra, 227-F
Pound, Louise, 887
Powell, Cuthbert, 157
Powell, Edward B., 84
Powell, Edward B., collection, 84
Powell, Eleanor, 1646
Powell, Ernest, 1502
Powell, Forest, 68
Powell, John, 227-F, 1053, 1177, 1541, 1559
Powell, John, Foundation, 1541
Powell, Laurence, 36
Powell, Maud, 227-F, 398, 739, 1061-F, 1111, 1177, 1502, 1573
Powell, Mel, 195-C
Powell, Reuben, 1234
Powell, Salley D., 1155
Powers ("Fiddlin' Powers") family, 1445
Powers, Fred Perry, Papers, 1338
Powers, James T., 227-H
Powers Opera House (Grand Rapids, Mich.?), 748

Powers Theater (Grand Rapids, Mich.), 749
Prairie Symphony, 317
Pratt, Enoch, Free Library, 614
Pratt, Frederick Alcott, 657
Pratt, Harry Rogers, 1541
Pratt, Selma Marian Urband, 1005
Pratt, Silas G., 1061-A
Pratt, Waldo Selden, 183, 206, 227-F, 1359
Pray, Mrs. James S., 636
Preble, Jack W., 1591
Prehn, Alyene Westall, 398
Prentiss, Francis, 1477
Presbyterian and Reformed Churches, Historical Foundation of the, 1153
Presbyterian Historical Society, 1347
Presbyterian music, 154, 315, 574, 819, 820, 825, 842, 860-J, 948, 1005, 1141, 1153, 1156, 1270, 1274, 1347, 1370, 1373, 1389, 1560, 1611, 1629
Presbyterian, Reformed, Theological Seminary, 1370
Prescott, Abraham, 898
Preservation Hall, 195-C
Presidential music, 94, 236, 424, 490, 544, 610, 624, 744, 843, 977, 1003, 1207, 1218, 1232, 1402, 1463, 1586, 1673. *See also* Political songs
Presser, Theodore, 227-F, 1333
Presser, Theodore, Music Building, 1549
Presser Foundation, 1061-B
Preston, John A., Collection, 646
Preus Library, 461
Prevost, Capt. A., 227-D
Preyer, Carl E., 502
Price, Carl Fowler, 190
Price, Clara, 95
Price, Florence B., 195-B
Price, Florence Beatrice Smith, 36
Price, Florence Bond, 226
Price, Percival, 247, 752
Price, Walter, 1256
Price (i.e., Teachout-Price) Memorial Library, 1210
Priebe, Mary Elizabeth Pfeiffer, 854
Priest, Edgar, 235
Primitive Baptist music, 522, 1141
Primrose, William, 227-F
Prince, Robert, 1061-A
Prince, Thomas, 636
Prince Edward Island, 592
Princeton Theological Seminary, 948
Princeton University, 939, 947, 949, 950, 1673
Pringle (i.e., Allston-Pringle-Hill) Papers, 1418
Printers. *See* Engravers and printers of music; Publishers
Prinz, LeRoy, 1487
Prison songs, 979, 1234
Pritkin, Joel, 78
Private recordings. *See* Non-commercial recordings

Prizes. *See* Contests and awards
Pro Musica Concert Series (Detroit), 738, 739
Procope, Russell, 195-C
Proetz, Arthur W., 866
Proffitt, Frank, 1095
Profitt, Josephine M. (Sylvia Dee), 637
Programs (selected collections), 2, 3, 7, 8, 9, 11, 12, 13, 15, 16, 19, 25, 26, 30, 36, 37, 41, 50, 55, 58, 59, 60, 61, 66, 68, 69, 77, 78, 79, 81, 83, 84, 85, 92, 93, 96, 98, 99, 100, 101, 103, 105, 106, 108, 113, 114, 115, 116, 118, 122, 124, 125, 128, 129, 132, 133, 134, 139, 140, 144, 145, 146, 147, 149, 150, 154, 155, 156, 163, 164, 165, 166, 167, 171, 172, 177, 179, 180, 181, 182, 183, 184, 185, 187, 188, 190, 192, 193, 195, 196, 197, 198, 200, 202, 206, 211, 212, 214, 216, 218, 222, 223, 224, 225, 226, 227, 228, 229, 232, 234, 239, 240, 242, 244, 245, 250, 251, 253, 254, 260, 265, 266, 267, 268, 269, 270, 276, 282, 285, 287, 288, 289, 295, 298, 299, 300, 301, 302, 304, 305, 306, 307, 310, 314, 315, 316, 317, 318, 319, 322, 328, 334, 336, 337, 338, 340, 341, 344, 348, 351, 353, 357, 359, 360, 364, 366, 369, 370, 376, 379, 381, 382, 384, 391, 394, 398, 400, 401, 402, 406, 408, 409, 418, 419, 420, 421, 424, 426, 427, 429, 430, 435, 437, 438, 439, 440, 442, 443, 446, 447, 451, 454, 455, 457, 458, 459, 460, 461, 463, 464, 465, 469, 471, 472, 473, 475, 476, 477, 478, 479, 480, 481, 486, 487, 488, 490, 496, 498, 500, 502, 503, 505, 507, 511, 514, 518, 520, 523, 528, 529, 531, 532, 535, 541, 544, 551, 555, 556, 560, 561, 568-C, 571, 576, 580, 585, 612, 613, 614, 636, 637, 639, 642, 646, 654, 679, 688, 701, 711, 721, 739, 743, 798, 815, 860-A, 860-J, 862, 866, 949, 977, 1005, 1031, 1036, 1041, 1052, 1059 1061, 1063, 1111, 1172, 1176, 1193, 1202, 1237, 1238, 1274, 1285, 1326, 1333, 1338, 1350, 1359, 1375, 1402, 1433, 1457, 1477, 1484, 1518, 1544, 1560, 1577, 1611, 1622, 1633, 1646, 1650, 1666
Prohibition and temperance songs, 43, 190, 227-A, 320, 356, 512, 577, 729-B, 802, 887, 986, 1070, 1098, 1193, 1614, 1673
Project in Ethnomusicology, 305
Prokofieff Society, 907
Prokofiev, Serge, 314, 729-E, 1053

Protest songs, 341, 391, 729-E, 742, 743, 815, 1008, 1061-M, 1155, 1223, 1463, 1466
Protestant Episcopal Church in Philadelphia Divinity School, 440
Protestant church music, 97, 163, 284, 288, 333, 416, 440, 637, 652, 662, 675, 685, 686, 695, 720, 1110, 1352, 1410, 1534, 1536, 1611. *See also* specific denominations
Providence (R.I.), 476, 729-B, 1061-A
Providence Public Library, 1405
Provincial Infantry, First Regiment (Charlotte, N.C.), 1463
Provo Marshal Band, 1521
Pruden, Albert Sears, 190
Pruett, Hubert S., 864
Pryor, Arthur, 239, 618
Psallonians, 1407
Psalmbooks, psalters. *See* specific denominations; Hymnals and tunebooks
Psalmody. *See* Hymnology
Public Library of Brookline (Mass.), 652
Public Library of Cincinnati and Hamilton County (Ohio), 1176
Public Library of Fort Wayne and Allen County (Ind.), 412
Public Library of Knoxville and Knox County (Tenn.), 1447
Public Library of Nashville and Davidson County (Tenn.), 1461
Publishers, 3, 38, 50, 54, 76, 80, 113, 124, 127, 164, 185, 195-A, 201, 227, 234, 268, 302, 306, 307, 315, 326, 334, 344, 357, 372, 384, 389, 391, 395, 396, 397, 398, 409, 433, 440, 452, 454, 455, 461, 503, 515, 535, 544, 553, 555, 556, 561, 568-A, 568-B, 568-C, 571, 606, 612, 618, 671, 676, 721, 724, 771, 802, 815, 819, 842, 847, 860, 864, 866, 868, 903, 907, 909, 916, 919, 977, 1019, 1024, 1031, 1035, 1046, 1061-B, 1061-H, 1066, 1111, 1123, 1124, 1141, 1142, 1161, 1200, 1207, 1225, 1243, 1249, 1259, 1261, 1266, 1270, 1298, 1299, 1333, 1334, 1338, 1341, 1386, 1402, 1418, 1420, 1440, 1444, 1462, 1463, 1464, 1473, 1539, 1541, 1547, 1548, 1560, 1576, 1605, 1606, 1611, 1673. *See also* Engravers and printers of music
Puccini, Giacomo, 1061-F
Puckett, Newbell Niles, 1185
Pueblo (Colo.), 800
Pueblo Indians, 31, 162, 962, 964
Puente, Giuseppe del, 1052
Puerto Rico, University of, 1650
Pugh, Ezra, 1421

Pukui, Mary K., 285
Pullen, William Russell, Library, 271
Pullman (Wash.) Music Club, 1573
Purcell, Margaret, 227-K
Purdue University Marching Band, 446
Purdy, Bertha, 896
Puring, John, 1061-M
Pusey Library, 654
Puterbaugh Museum, 442
Putney (Vt.) Historical Society, 1532
Pyle, Francis Johnson, 227-D
Pynchon, Bathshua, 704
Pyne and Harrison Opera Company, 544
Pyper, George D., 1523
Pythian Society (Corvallis, Ore.), 1268

Q

QRS Music Rolls, 853, 978
Quackenbush, Edward, 1274
Quadrangle Club (Washington University), 866
Quadrilles, 728. *See also* Dance
Quaker Collection, 505
Quaker music, 484, 1147
Quarles, James Thomas, 227-H, 837
Quaw, Gene, 872
Quebec (City), 549
Queens College, 1089
Queensborough Community College, 1087
Queens Borough (N.Y.) Public Library, 1088
Queyrouze, Leona, Papers, 544
Quick-step, 1135
Quilp, Daniel, 531
Quilter, Roger, 646
Quin, Mordecai, 1031
Quincy Public Library, 384
Quinn, J. Kerker, 398
Quintard, Charles Todd, 1467
Quintón, José I., 1650, 1651
Quitman, John A., and family, Papers, 544

R

Rabaud, Henri, 1053
Rabinoff, Max, 1031
Rabun, Margaret May Brewton, 270
Race records, 1443, 1449, 1667
Rachmaninoff, Sergei, 227-B, 227-L, 729-E, 1053, 1105, 1111, 1580
Rachmaninoff Archive, 227-B
Radcliff, Thomas, collection, 84
Radcliffe, Thomas A., 398
Radcliffe College, 654
Rader, Ben, 349
Rader, Henry H., 1611
Rader, Paul, 404
Radey, Hilda, 922
Radford, Annie, 1665
Radin, Paul, 1327

Radio Britain, 84
Radio City Music Hall, 1031
Radio Corporation of America, 234, 545, 1333. *See also* RCA-Victor catalogues
Radio-Keith-Orpheum (RKO) films, 1611
Radio-Keith-Orpheum (RKO) Vaudeville Collection, 1520
Radio music, 108, 195-B, 227-L, 237, 265, 278, 314, 349, 389, 398, 404, 427, 457, 502, 530, 533, 618, 632, 646, 719, 736, 800, 942, 973, 1007, 1031, 1052, 1054, 1061-J, 1065, 1106, 1141, 1170, 1177, 1194, 1234, 1270, 1333, 1336, 1430, 1436, 1437, 1443, 1450, 1451, 1452, 1459, 1469, 1488, 1501, 1520, 1544, 1576, 1579, 1611, 1646, 1662
Radio Pioneers, 1031
Radio stations and networks, 157, 195-C, 210, 213, 227, 234, 285, 322, 333, 338, 341, 349, 389, 398, 457, 533, 618, 1024, 1028, 1031, 1054, 1061-J, 1177, 1194, 1274, 1358, 1436, 1451, 1463, 1488, 1501, 1576, 1577, 1611, 1670
Rael, Juan B., Collection, 142
Rael, Juan D., 962
Raffaelli, Joseph, collection, 1061-F
Raffetto, Bertha Eaton, 896
Rafinesque, Constantine S., 528
Ragone, Vincent, 398
Ragtime, 35, 36, 226, 227-D, 268, 349, 406, 411, 516, 544, 564, 654, 741, 750, 771, 787, 847, 864, 866, 868, 997, 1059, 1086, 1061-B, 1061-N, 1086, 1166, 1339, 1457, 1497, 1577, 1625, 1655, 1659, 1673
Railroad and Historical Museum (Two Harbors, Minn.), 820
Railroad and Pioneer Museum, 1515
"Railroad Hour," 1061-J
Railroad songs, 624, 815, 820, 861, 887, 960, 1061-J, 1234, 1270, 1463, 1515, 1588, 1646
Raine, James Watt, 522
Rainer family, 863
Raksin, David, 227-C, 1487
Raleigh (N.C.), 1141
Ralston, Frances Marion, 84
Ramos, Heraclio, 1651
Ramos, Antonini, Ernesto, 1651
Ramsden, George, 682
Rand, Emily, 654
Randall, James Ryder, 314, 612, 1141
Randall, Kenn, Collection, 78
Randall, Lizzie, 544
Randall, Mary, 50
Randall, William H., Library, 1158
Randall, Willie, 1031
Randle, William, 1170

Randolph, George May, 1477
Randolph, Mrs. Harold, 227-A
Randolph, Martha Jefferson, 1541
Randolph, Vance, 36, 227-K, 227-L, 836
Randolph-Macon College, 1538
Random House, Inc., 1031
Range Symphony Orchestra, 815
Rankin, Jeremiah Eames, 950
Rannefeld, Herrmann, 1059
Ransom family, papers, 1463
Ransom, Ann P., 1463
Raphaelson, Samson, 398
Rapides Parish (La.), 544
Rapoport, Dr. Boris, 1031
Rapoport, Eda Rothstein, 1031
Rapp, George, 1281
Rappite and Harmony Society, 406
Rappite church, 425
Rappold, Edward, 1598
Rare Old Programs, Inc., 1031
Rascher, Sigurd, 227-F
Rasmuson, Elmer E., Library, 16
Ratcliffe, T. E., 398
Ratel, William, 1477
Rath, Erich, 1549
Rathaus, Karol, 1089
Rathburn Free Memorial Library, 178
Ratliff, B. E., 406
Ratterman, Heinrich A., 398
Rau, Robert, 1285
Rausch, Frederick, 1061-M
Rauth, Henry, 860-K
Ravenswaay, Charles Van, 860-B, 860-D
Ravinia (Ill.) Festival, 337, 363, 366
Rawdon, Lord Francis, 1059
Rawley family, 1005
Rawson, Edward, 1172
Rawson, Lucie Russell, 1172
Ray, Grant S., 442
Ray, Man, 949
Raymond, Annie Louise Cary, 598
Raymond (Me.), 707
Razaf, Andy (Paul Andrea-mentania Razafinlariefo), 226, 1061-N
RCA (Radio Corporation of America), 234, 545, 1333
RCA-Victor catalogues, 920, 922, 1333
Read, Daniel, 192, 636
Read, Gardner, 227-D, 227-F, 354, 636, 1111, 1580
Read, George F. H., 192
Reading, J. A. J., 314
Reading (Mass.) Antiquarian Society, 699
Reading (Pa.), 1333
Reading (Vt.), 1530
Ream, Vinnie, 1264
Reardon, James A., 860-C
Rebec, 860-D
Rebner, Edward, 68
Recording companies, 608, 618, 626, 733, 736, 744, 786,

853, 920, 934, 942, 945, 954, 968, 978, 1028, 1041, 1061-J, 1079, 1085, 1103, 1127, 1166, 1170, 1174, 1246, 1333, 1338, 1353, 1395, 1430, 1438, 1442, 1455, 1597, 1623, 1640, 1655, 1659, 1665, 1667. See also Publishers; and names of specific companies
Recordings—major collections (25,000 items or more), 73, 74, 84, 142, 195-B, 227-L, 237, 239, 357, 395, 398, 406, 533, 568-B, 736, 747, 888, 973, 1061-J, 1127, 1166, 1333, 1337, 1352, 1449, 1624, 1625
Recordings (subject), 234, 322, 1333, 1337, 1353, 1372, 1469, 1584, 1625
Red Cross, 876
Red Wing (Minn.) Public Library, 805
Reddington, Harriet, 599
Redman, May, 779
Redmond's Opera House, 748
Rednour, Samuel Allison, 434
Redpath Bureau, 476
Redway, Virginia Larkin, 1061-H
Redwood, Mrs. Francis Taze-well, 227-A
Redwood Library and Athenaeum, 1400
Reece, C. D., 1591
Reece, Florence, 1445
Reed family, 1560
Reed, Byron, 890
Reed, Ephraim, 1006
Reed, Janet, 122
Reed, Mary G., 636
Reed, Napoleon, 227-F
Reed, Neil, 1611
Reed, Robert B., 227-D
Reed Carol Collection, 195-B
Reed Library, 994
Reels, 815, 907. See also Dance
Reese, Gustave, 227-B, 227-F, 1061-B
Reese, Mrs. Gustave, 195-C
Reese, Leah H., 612
Reeves, David Wallace, 1405, 1407
Reeves (i.e., Morrisson-Reeves) Library, 445
Reform songs. See Protest songs
Reformed Church in America, 938
Reformed church music, 759, 938, 948, 1153, 1306, 1320, 1347
Reformed Presbyterian Theo-logical Seminary, 1370
Regenstein, Joseph, Library, 340
Regina music boxes, 1204, 1245, 1611
Reginaphone, 424
Reid, John D., Collection of Early American Jazz, 38
Reidenbach (Reidenbaugh), 1220
Reiff, Anton, 544

Reinagle, Alexander, 227-D, 866, 1338
Reinagle, George Anne, 227-D
Reinecke, George, 563
Reinecke, Zudie Harris, 535
Reiner, Carlotta, 357
Reiner, Fritz, 227-F, 357, 1031, 1580
Reinhardt, Jacob, 1558
Reis, Claire, 195-C, 227-G, 1061-B
Reiss, Gerald A., 349
Releider, Arnoldo (or Arnaldo), 133
Remenyi, Eduard, 104, 1053
Remington Band, 1001
Remington Co. (typewriter manufacturer), 1001
Renfro Valley (Ky.), 1234
Reorganized Church of Jesus Christ of Latter-Day Saints. See Mormon music
Repertorium (Milwaukee), 1624
Republic Pictures Music Col-lection, 1520
Republican Party, 398, 633, 1232, 1541
Resettlement Administration Collection, 227-L
Resettlement Administration Special Skills Division, 831
Resources of American Music History, 398
Ressler, Martin E., 1376
Resta, Colonel Francis E., 1135
Restoration History Manu-script Collection, 477
Retailers. See Merchants
Retana, R., 1651
Réti, Rudolf, 227-D, 227-E
Retter, Carl, 1359
Reuter, Rudolph E., 1573
Reuterdahl, Arvid, 815
Reuther, Walter P., Library, 742
Reutter, Hermann, 195-C
Revelli, William D., 729-B
Revival meetings, 45, 279, 284, 333, 391, 398, 452, 868, 933, 1141
Revolutionary War, 125, 127, 195-B, 227-M, 230, 314, 544, 721, 729-A, 935, 940, 1040, 1059, 1061-M, 1338, 1407, 1418, 1463. See also Colonial music
Revue. See Operetta and musi-cal comedy
Revueltas, Silvestre, 1475
Rexford, Eben E., 1040
Reyer, Henry, 1061-B
Reynolds, Horace M., 1402
Reynolds, Isham E., 1462
Reynolds, Jonathan, Jr., 707
Reynolds, Robert Burns, 1005
Reynolds, Roger, 68
Rhett (i.e., Bacot-Rhett) Papers, 1418
Rhoads, Harriet Thorne, 490
Rhode Island, 476, 707, 729-B, 1061-A
Rhode Island Black Heritage Society, 1406

Rhode Island Historical So-ciety, 1407
Rhodes, Willard, 27, 227-L
Rhythm and blues, 74, 1438, 1442, 1443, 1661
Rice family, 860-C
Rice, Cale Young, 523
Rice, John Blake, 314
Rice, M. E., 502
Rice, May, 860-C
Rice, T. D., 1484
Rice, Thomas D., 628
Rice, Thomas G., 1495
Rice University, 1497
Rice's Theatre, 314
Rich, Blanche Browning, Col-lection, 1519
Richard, James, 907
Richard, John, 907
Richards, Brinley, 555
Richards, J. J., 511
Richardson, Anna, 701
Richardson, Caroline Schetky, 227-A, 334
Richardson, Louise, 259
Richardson, Nathan, 227-F
Richardson, Nina Maud, 227-M
Richardson, Steven, 129
Richardson, Warren, 1643
Richardson, William (William R. Galvin), 860-K
Richardson, William H., 1190
Richardson (Tex.) Public Library, 1508
Richland Center (Wis.), 1611
Richman, Harry, 637
Richmond, Virginia (person), 646
Richmond (Ind.) Palladium and Sun-Telegram, 444
Richmond (Va.), 127, 1141, 1563
Richter, Eckhart, 195-C
Richter, Hugo, Jr., 763
Richter, M. A., 128
Richter, William Benson, 1351
Rickaby, Franz Lee, 1611
Rickard, Truman, 800
Rickel, Harry, 68
Rickett, Ezra E., 1193
Ricks College, 295
Ricksecker, Peter, 1161, 1285, 1323
Riddle, Nelson, 1611
Ridenour Collection, 1168
Rider, Claudius W., 1059
Rider, Sidney Smith, 1402
Riedel, Johannes, 815
Riegger, Wallingford, 227-D, 227-F, 535, 1040, 1061-A, 1108, 1111, 1580
Riemenschneider, Albert, 1168
Riemenschneider Bach Insti-tute, 1168
Riepel, Joseph, 1161
Riesenfeld, Hugo, 227-G
Riggs, George, 1155
Riggs, Lawrence, 1436
Riley, James Whitcomb, 531
Riley County (Kan.) Historical Museum, 507
Rinck, Johann Christian Heinrich, 195-A, 708

Rindge, Agnes, 1053
Rindlichbaker, Otto, 800
Ring, Emil, 1185
Ring, Stanley, 84
Ring shouts, 1141
Ringgold Brass Band, 1338
Ringling Circus Band, 1595
Ringling Museum Theatre Collection, 244
Ringwalt, Henry, 1359
Ringwalt Choral Union, 1359
Rinzler, Ralph, 545, 1352
Rios Ovalle, Juan, 1650, 1651
Rip Van Winkle Outdoor Commercial Production, 986
Ripon College, 739
Ritchie, Bell T., 61
Ritchie, Edna, 538
Ritchie, Jean, 538
Rittenhouse, George, 1031
Ritter, Frédéric Louis, 334, 636, 679, 1107
Ritter Library, 1168
Rivé-King, Julie, 227-F
Rivenburg, Leonard, 1226
River Falls (Wis.), 1611
Riverboats. See Steamships
Riverside (Cal.), 815
RKO films, 1611
RKO Vaudeville Collection, 1520
Roach family, 1471, 1472
Roach, Nessye Mae, 1471
Roach (i.e., Eggelston-Roach) papers, 544
Robb, John D., 152, 957, 962
Robbins, Charles Isaac, 1521
Robbins, Danny, 68
Robert, Kate Ayers, 8
"Robert Girling's tune," 707
Roberton, Sir Hugh, 1675
Roberton, Kenneth, 1675
Roberts, George, 195-C
Roberts, Mrs. George, 195-C
Roberts, Helen H., 82, 227-L, 285, 1327
Roberts, Henry C., 1560
Roberts, Kenneth, 718, 907
Roberts, Leonard, 537
Robertson, Hugh, 1388
Robertson, Leroy J., 227-D, 1523
Robertson, Sidney (Mrs. Henry Cowell), 50, 227-L
Robeson, Eslanda Goode, 268
Robeson, Helen Katz, 475
Robeson, Paul, 227-F, 268, 916, 1061-N
Robichaux, John, 568
Robinson family, 1560
Robinson, Albert F., 928
Robinson, Alexander C., Collection, 1383
Robinson, Avery, 1270
Robinson, Bill ("Bojangles"), 227-F, 268
Robinson, Carol, 265
Robinson, Earl, 227-F, 349, 1544
Robinson, Florence Price, 36
Robinson, Jim, 195-C
Robinson, John G., 215
Robinson, Sir Johnston Forbes, 1054

Robinson, Rowland E., Memorial Association, 1526
Robison, Carson J., 495
Robison, Robert A., 495
Robitschek, Robert, 817
Robjohn, William James (Caryl Florio), 227-D, 1061-A
Roble, August (August Wroblewski), 787
Robyn, Alfred, 860, 862
Robyn, Henry, 860-B
Robyn, Paul, 860-D
Robyn, William, 860-B
Rocca, Nick la, 227-F, 568
Rochberg, George, 1580
Rochester (Ind.) Band, 446
Rochester (N.Y.), 1005
Rochester Museum and Science Center Library, 1114
Rochester, University of, 1111, 1115
Rock County (Wis.) Historical Society, 1605
Rock Rapids (Iowa) Public Library, 485
Rock Springs (Wyo.), 1643
Rockefeller, John D., 163
Rockefeller, John Davison, 3rd, 1031
Rockefeller Chapel, 340
Rockford (Ill.) College, 387
Rockford (Ill.) Museum Center, 310, 388
Rockingham Public Library, 1548
Rockmont College, 160
Rockspring Sängerbund, 860-E
Rockwell, Julia Ludlow, 195-A
Rodda, Harriet Stryker, 1083
Rodef Shalom Temple (Pittsburgh), 1371
Rodeheaver, Homer Alvan, 36, 442
Rodeheaver Music Publishing Co., 452, 501
Rodgers, Goldie, 68
Rodgers, Jimmie, 831, 1455
Rodgers, Richard, 142, 227-C, 227-F, 624, 1031, 1036, 1611
Rodgers & Hammerstein Archives of Recorded Sound, 1061-J
Rodley Collection, 511
Rodrigues, José C., 1059
Rodzinski, Artur, 227-F, 1031
Roe, A. Stevens, 195-A
Röder, Martin, 227-D, 1053
Roedter, Emma L., 1172, 1176
Roemheld, Franz, 1646
Röntgen, Julius, 227-F
Roeschlaub, Alice, 157
Rogal, Stanley J., 834
Rogers, Bernard, 227-F, 1111, 1127
Rogers, Clara Kathleen, 227-D, 227-F, 636
Rogers, Mrs. E., 490
Rogers, Eddy, 36
Rogers, Francis, 1053
Rogers, Harold, 391
Rogers, Henry M., 227-G
Rogers, Irene, 1576
Rogers, James A., 393
Rogers, James G., 156

Rogers, James Hotchkiss, 1190
Rogers, Joseph, 1395
Rogers, Mary R., 227-F
Rogers, Robert Cameron, 1040
Rogers, Will, Library, 1254
Roggman, Lucille, 472
Rohland, Mrs. Q. B., 866
Rohm, William H., 957
Rokeby Museum, 1526
Rolling, Hubert, 544
Roman Catholic church music, 71, 77, 95, 115, 126, 130, 133, 145, 163, 327, 375, 428, 440, 523, 544, 549, 556, 570, 615, 644, 648, 756, 770, 810, 854, 1202, 1312, 1324, 1365, 1434, 1579, 1653. See also Mission music
Roman Polyphonic Singers, 636
Romberg, Sigmund, 50, 227-C, 227-L, 747, 1061-A
Rome, Harold, 227-D, 269
Romer collection, 249
Romeró Bravo, Alfredo, 1651
Rommel, Alexander, 479
Rommel Music Club, 479
Rondeau, Charles H., 1477
Rondeau, Gaston, 568
Ronnell, Ann, 227-F
Ronstadt, Frederic, 30
Rood, Katherine A., 1611
Roos, Charles, 815
Roosevelt, Eleanor, 226, 831
Roosevelt, Franklin D., Presidential Library, 1003
Roosevelt University, 338
Root, Anna, 707
Root, Deane L., 308
Root, Fred W., 315
Root, George F., 34, 227-D, 227-F, 314, 315, 334, 360, 729-A, 1111
Root, Juliett, 707
Root, Lora Ann, 707
Root, Minnie, 729-B
Root, Riley, 391
Root, Sarah A., 1031
Rorem, Ned, 535, 977
Roscoe Village Foundation, 1197
Rose, Al, 564, 568
Rosé, Alfred, 1176
Rose, Billy, 1031
Rose, Billy, Theatre Collection, 1061-L
Rose, Diana, 565
Rose, Harriet, 701
Rose, Jane L., 1567
Rose, Kenneth D., Sheet Music Collection, 1463
Rose, Kenneth Daniel, 1463
Rose, L. E., 860-D
Rose, Leonard, 1031
Rose, Mary S., 1567
Rosehill (N.Y.), 1567
Rosen, Jelka, 246
Rosenbach, Philip H. and A. S. W., Foundation, 1348
Rosenberg Library, 1495
Rosenfeld, Paul, 227-F, 1031
Rosenfield, John, 1484
Rosenthal, Moriz, 227-F, 1222
Roses, songs about, 565
"Rosita," 25

Ross, Alexander Coffman, 1193
Ross, Gilbert, 729-B
Ross, Hugh, 195-C, 227-F
Ross, Jerry, 1611
Ross, Orvis, 1666
Rossini, Gioacchino, 1418
Rossini Club (Portland, Me.), 595, 596, 597
Rothery, John H., 940
Rotschy, Edgar, 1577
Round, Bertha M., Collection, 1105
Rouse, I. E., Library, 825
Rouse's Hall (Peoria, Ill.), 1520
Roussain, Charles E., 815
Rowland, Orlando, 1031
Rowley, Daisy Woodruff, 15
Roy, James G., Jr., Collection, 315
Royal, George, 719
Royal Hawaiian Band, 286
Royal Music Library (London), 1670
Royal Philharmonic Society (London), 1270
Royce, Edward, 227-D, 1111
Roycroft, 1605
Rozsa, Miklos, 1127, 1580
Rubertis, Nazarene de, 504
Rubin, Ruth, 227-L, 1685
Rubinstein, Anton, 227-F, 860-B
Rubinstein, Beryl, 227-D, 227-F, 1183
Rubinstein Club (Cleveland), 1190
Rubinstein Club (New York), 581
Ruby, Harry, 85, 1611, 1646
Rudge, Olga, 227-F
Rudhyar, Dane, 68, 227-F
Rudie, Irene, 787
Rudolph, Bertha, 334
Ruebush & Kieffer, 1539, 1541, 1547, 1548
Ruff, Willie, 195-C
Rufser's Zither Club, 442
Rufty, Hilton, 1541, 1558
Ruger, Morris H., 68
Ruger, Robert, 68
Ruggles, Carl, 76, 195-A, 195-C, 227-D, 234, 239, 823, 1061-A, 1580
Rumsey, Nathan, 215
Rumshinsky, Joseph, 84, 1076, 1402
Runcie, Constance Faunt Le Roy, 855
Rund, Morris, 1174
Ruppel, Harry, Memorial Library, 342
Rusch, Robert, 1061-N
Rush, Benjamin, 1327
Rush, James, 1340
Rush, Samuel, 1327
Russak, Ben, 1544
Russell, G. D., & Co., 1142
Russell, George Alexander, 227-D
Russell, Henry, 729-A, 1174
Russell, Lillian, 1484
Russell, Olive Nelson, 847
Russell, William, 195-C, 568

Russia, 268, 1061-J, 1683
Russia, World War I, A.E.F. band in, 761
Russian Ballet, 631, 860-D
Russian music, 50, 195, 316, 636, 1061-E, 1122, 1222, 1357, 1541
Russian Symphonic Choir, 636
Rutgers, Catherine, 939
Rutgers, Gerard, 939
Rutgers University, 939, 942, 1626
Rutland Historical Society, 1533
Ryan, Hotel, 815
Ryan, Thomas, 636, 646
Ryan Library, 113
Rychlik, Charles, 1185
Ryder, Will, 195-C
Ryder, Mrs. Will, 195-C
Ryerson, Edward L., 314
Ryman Auditorium (Nashville), 1459

S

Saar, Louis Victor, 866
Saar, William, 1061-F
Sabata, Victor de, 1359
Sabbath-Day Lake, 1214
Sachse, Julius Friedrich, 946
Sacramento (Cal.), 50
Sacramento Junior College, 1518
Sacramento (Cal.) Museum and History Department, 108
Sacred and social harp, 263, 270, 271, 275, 398, 866, 1459
Sacred Harp Convention, 270
Sacred Music Association (Newark, N.J.), 940
Sacred Music Resource Center, 1434
Sacred Music Society (Baton Rouge, La.), 544
Sacred Music Society (Campton, N.H.), 898
Saenger Theater, 253
Sängerbund (St. Louis), 866
Sängerfest (Madison, Wis.), 1611
Sängerfest (St. Louis), 866
Sängerfest (Utica, N.Y.), 1133
Sängerfest Centennial Celebration, 1477
Sängerfest Zeitung, 1105
Saerchinger, César, 227-F
Sage Library, 938
Sagebrush Orchestra, 1274
Saginaw (Mich.) Academy of Music, 763
St. Albans (Vt.), 721
St. Albans Brigade Band, 1530
St. Bonaventure University, 1116
St. Catherine College, 810
St. Cecilia Hymnal, 1202
St. Cecilia Musical Club (Aurora, Ill.), 298
St. Cecilia Society (Flint, Mich.), 745
St. Cecilia Society (Grand Rapids, Mich.), 748

St. Cecelia Society (New York), 1061-M
St. Charles (Mo.), 306
St. Charles Borromeo Seminary, 1324
St. Clement's Church (Philadelphia), 1352
St. Cloud (Minn.) Musicians' Association, AFM Local 536, 806
St. Cloud State University, 806
St. Croix Valley Academy, 815
St. Cyr, Johnny, 1450
St. Denis, Ruth, 84
St. Edward's University, 1475
St. Helena Island (S.C.), 1141
St. James Cathedral (Chicago), 324, 722
St. James Parish (La.), 544
St. John's College, 520
St. Joseph (Mo.) Public Library, 855
St. Joseph Catholic Church (Baton Rouge, La.), 544
St. Joseph Catholic Church (Bowling Green, Ky.), 523
St. Lawrence County (N.Y.) Historical Association, 998
St. Lawrence County (N.Y.) History Center, 980
St. Louis, 129, 349, 379, 398, 460, 502, 544, 800, 831, 837, 847, 848, 864, 1161, 1633
St. Louis Academy of Music, 860-E
St. Louis Choral Society, 860-C, 860-E
St. Louis City Drummers' Association, 860-C
St. Louis Conservatory of Music, 860-B
St. Louis Exposition & Music Hall Association, 860-E
St. Louis Exposition Music Hall, 860-C
St. Louis Grand Exposition (1884), 860-J
St. Louis Grand Festival (1900), 860-J
St. Louis Historical Building, 860-K
St. Louis Institute of Music, 1448
St. Louis Musical Art Association, 860-E
St. Louis Musical Polyhymnia, 860-E
St. Louis Musical Society, 860-E
St. Louis Oratorio Society, 860-C
St. Louis Pageant and Drama Association, 860-E
St. Louis Pageant and Masque, 860-E
St. Louis Pageant Choral Society, 860-E
St. Louis Philharmonic Society, 544, 859, 860-B, 862
St. Louis Piano Manufacturing Company, 860-E
St. Louis Public Library, 862, 866
St. Louis School of Musical Art, 860-E

St. Louis Symphony Orchestra, 349, 860, 862, 866
St. Louis University, 863
St. Louis World's Fair (1904), 460, 860-C
St. Louis County (Minn.) Historical Society, 780
St. Luke's Choristers, 132
St. Luke's Library, 1467
St. Mary College, 504
St. Mary of the Lake Seminary, 375
St. Mary's Church (Charleston, S.C.), 1418
St. Mary's School (Raleigh, N.C.), 1141
St. Mary's Seminary and University, 615
St. Mathews (S.C.) Spirit Band, 1424
St. Maur Monastery, 428
St. Meinrad College & School of Theology, 447
St. Michael-Zion Church (Philadelphia), 1342
St. Michael's Church (Charleston, S.C.), 1420
St. Michael's College, 1535
St. Olaf College, 802, 803
St. Paul (Minn.), 800, 1633
St. Paul Opera Company, 800
St. Paul Public Library, 816
St. Paul Public Library, Highland Park Branch, 817
St. Paul Seminary, 818
St. Paul and Ramsey County (Minn.) War History Committee, 815
St. Paul's Cathedral (Boston), 648
St. Paul's Cathedral (Pittsburgh), 1365
St. Paul's Church (Baltimore), 235
St. Paul's Church (Paterson, N.J.), 944
St. Paul's Church (Philadelphia), 1338
St. Peters Church (Stevens Point, Wis.), 336
St. Peter's Presbyterian Church (Rochester, N.Y.), 1005
St. Petersburg (Fla.) Public Library, 257
St. Stephen's Church (Cohasset, Mass.), 636
St. Vincent College and Archabbey, 1312
Saint-Saens, Camille, 357
Ste. Genevieve (Mo.), 860-D
De Saisset Art Gallery and Museum, 133
Sajewski Music Store, 336
Salas, Juan Orrego, 1580
Salcedo, J., 398
Sale, B. H., 860-K
Salem (Conn. or Mass.?), 180
Salem (Conn.) Historical Society, 200
Salem (Conn.) Normal Academy of Music, 199, 200
Salem (Mass.), 349
Salem (N.J.), 214

Salem (N.C.), 1161, 1285
Salem College, 1161, 1163
Salem Collegium Musicum, 1161
Salem Female Academy, 1163
Salisbury, Captain B., 707
Salisbury, Mr. & Mrs. Frank C., 1149
Salloch, William, 84
Salmieri, Andrew, 610
Salmon, Alan Glover, 1122
Salmond, Felix, 1053
Salon music, 15, 794, 846, 1496, 1665. See also Parlor music
Saloon songs, 65. See also Drinking songs
Salt Lake City, 1270
Salt Lake City Bands, 1521
Salt Lake City Public Library, 1522
Salt Lake City Symphony Orchestra, 1523
Salt Lake City Theatre, 1523
Salt Lake Tabernacle Choir, 1519, 1520, 1521
Salt Lake Theatre, 1524
Salter, Hans J., 1646
Salter, Mary Turner (Mrs. Sumner Salter), 227-D
Salter, Sumner, 719
Saltiel, William David, 314
Saltzman-Stevens, Minnie, 302, 379
Salvation Army, 1070
Salz, Ansley K., 50
Salz, Henri E., 50
Salzburg (Austria), 131
Salzedo, Carlos, 227-D, 227-F, 1050, 1053, 1331
Samaroff, Olga, 227-F, 729-E, 1058, 1177, 1470, 1580
Samford University, 3
Samhold Sanger-Forbund, 802
Saminsky, Lazare, 195-A, 227-D, 227-F, 227-H, 1030
Samoa, 1521
Sampson, Henry T., Library, 827
Sams, William Raymond, 128
Samuels, William E., 1031
San Antonio (Tex.), 116, 1205
San Antonio Choral Society, 1511
San Antonio Public Library, 1511
San Antonio de Padua (Cal.) Mission, 129
San Carlo (Grand) Opera Company, 800, 860-D, 1037, 1061-F, 1578
San Diego Historical Society Library and Manuscripts Collection, 114
San Diego Public Library, 115
San Diego State University Library, 116
San Francisco, 50, 92, 127, 129, 133, 227-H, 227-L, 549, 800, 815, 819, 1061-F, 1174, 1272, 1629
San Francisco Ballet, 122
San Francisco Community Music School, 800

San Francisco Conservatory of Music, 121

San Francisco Examiner, 122

San Francisco Opera House, 819

San Francisco Public Library, 122

San Francisco State University, 123

San Francisco Symphony Orchestra, 50, 93, 122

San Jose (Cal.) Public Library, 126

San Juan County (N.M.) Museum Association, 959

San Luis Obispo (Cal.), 129

San Mateo County (Cal.) Historical Association, 128

San Miguel County (Colo.) Historical Society, 172

Sanborn, Elizabeth, 1534

Sanborn, Pitts, 227-F

Sanchez de Fuentes, Eduardo, 227-F

Sanctified church music, 997

Sandby, Herman, 1148

Sandburg, Carl, 185, 227-F, 360, 398, 1145, 1270

Sandburg, Carl, Home, National Historic Site, 1145

Sanders, Joe, 846

Sanders, Robert, 1111, 1148

Sanders, Robert L., 406

Sandler, Peretz, 1402

Sandor Teszler Library, 1426

Sandusky, Library Association of, 1229

Sandwich (Mass.) Historical Society, 703

Sanford, Charlotte Mead, 815

Sanford, Edward Rollin, family, 815

Sanford, Gertrude, 195-C

Sanford, W. D., 1631

Sanford Museum and Planetarium, 459

Sang, Philip D., Jazz Collection, 378

Sangamon Valley Collection, 392

Sangbog for det Danske folk in Amerika, 748

"Sangenfest" (Watertown, Wis.), 1634

Sanger, Eli, Collection, 1487

Sankey, Ira D., 227-D, 235, 306, 333, 1688

Sanromá, Jesús María, 227-F, 1648

Sans Souci, Gertrude, 815

Santa Barbara (Cal.) Mission Archive Library, 130

Santa Clara, University of, 133

Santa Cruz (Cal.) Public Library, 137

Santa Monica (Cal.) Municipal Band, 139

Santa Monica Public Library, 139

Sarah Lawrence College, 975

Saranec, Edmund, 195-C

Sarasate, Pablo, 860-B, 1111

Sargeant, Winthrop, 227-F, 637

Sargent, John Singer, 227-B, 639

Sarpy, J. B., 860-K

Saslavsky, Alexander, 1053

Satcher, H. B., 1061-F

Satin, Sophie, 227-B

Satterlee, Frances Mae Howe, 815

Saturday Club of Brunswick (Me.), 586

Saturday Club (Sacramento, Cal.), 50

Saturday Morning Junior Concerts (Boston?), 636

Saturday Morning Music Club (Tucson), 30

Saucier, Corinne, 545, 563

Saudek, Victor, 1359

Saudek Ensemble, 1359

Sauer (Saur), Christopher, Press, 380, 1292, 1334

Sauer, Robert, 1520

Sauk County (Wis.) Historical Society, 1595

Saul, George B., 1127

Saul, Jack, 1231

Saunders, Henry S., Collection of Whitmaniana, 1402

Saunders, Red, 1031

Sauter, Severin Robert, 860-K

Savage, Henry W., 1061-F

Savage, M. F., Collection, 1444

Savannah (Ga.), 142, 195-A, 266

Savannah Music Club, 282, 1143

Savannah Public and Chatham-Effingham Liberty Regional Library, 282

Savannah State College, 283

Savoca, Giuseppe, 1288

The Savoy Company, 1349

Savoyards (Durham, N.C.), 1143

Savoyards (Pittsburgh), 1358

Saw. *See* Musical saw

Sawyer, Antonia, 227-F

Sawyer, Milton, 761

Sawyer Library, 719

Saxe, Leonard, 227-B

Saxophones, 433, 646, 1053

Sayn, Elena de, 227-H

Sayre's Theater Collection, 1576

Scala, Francis, 227-E, 1618

Scalero, Rosario, 227-F, 1053

Scammill, Col. Alexander, 1040

Scandinavian music, 56, 681, 781, 815, 858, 1511, 1576, 1603, 1611, 1612. *See also* specific nationalities

Scandinavian Singers' Union of America, 815

Scarborough (Me.) Public Library, 598

Scarlatti, Domenico, 195-A

Scarmolin, A. Louis, 476, 923, 956

Schaack, P. Van, 707

Schaaf, Edward O., 941

Schaberg, Agnes M., 847, 860-F

Schad, Andrew, 612

Schaefer, Ferdinand, 406, 427

Schaefer, G. A. Grant, 354

Schaefer, Jacob, 227-D

Schaefer Library, 1118

Schaeffer, Paul, 50

Schaffenberg, Agnes, 296

Schaffter, Ferdinand, 567

Schaffter, Florian, 552

Schalow, Arthur, 142

Schang, Frederick, 1031

Scharf, Walter, 1646

Scharffenberg, Wilhelm, 636

Schauffler, Robert Haven, 1061-D

Schaum, J. O. H., 1323

Schaum, William, 1155

Schauwecker, Frederick, 819

Schehl, J. Alfred, 1176

Scheide, William H., 950

Scheide Library, 950

Schellenbaum instruments, 1267

Schelling, Ernest, 227-D, 227-F, 227-H, 317, 1031, 1053, 1063, 1580

Schemmer, O. H., 398

Schenck, Janet D., 800

Schenck, Ludwig, 1111

Schenck Orchestra, 1111

Schenectady (N.Y.), 654

Schenker, Heinrich, 104

Schetky, George J., 227-D

Schetky, J. G. C., 334

Scheuermann, John, 558

Schiff, Jacob H., 1174

Schifler, Rudolph, 913

Schiller, Rudolph, 914

Schillinger, Josef, 227-F, 1061, 1646

Schindler, Kurt, 227-D, 227-F, 1053, 1061-F

Schipa, Tito, 398

Schirmer family, 227-E

Schirmer, G., Inc., 227-B, 234, 854, 1061-B, 1420

Schirmer, Gustav, or Gustave, 227-F, 583, 636, 639

Schirmer, Rudolph, 227-F, 1053

Schirmann, Charles, 227-D

Schlappi, Elizabeth, 1455

Schlesinger, Arthur and Elizabeth, Library, 654

Schlesinger, Sigmund, 9, 10, 1174

Schley, Johannes, 620

Schlick, Lawrence A., 1640

Schlienman, Josephan, 1376

Schmeman, Hermann, 737

Schmidt, Arthur P., 227-B, 227-G, 357, 1031

Schmidt, Barbara, 1396

Schmidt, Harry, 1477

Schmidt, Wilmar R., 1549

Schmitt, Paul A., Music Co., 815

Schmitz, E. Robert, 227-F

Schmucker Memorial Library, 1295

Schnabel, Artur, 227-F, 340, 357, 729-E

Schnabel, John, 349

Schnabel, Karl Ulrich, 195-C

Schnabel, Therese, 357

Schneeloch family, 195-A, 195-B

Schnéevoigt, Georg Lennart, 227-F

Schneeweiss, Franz S. M., 939

Schneider, Alexander, 227-F, 1507

Schneider, Edward F., 1176

Schneider, F. J. C., 1059

Schneider, Karl, 1193

Schneider, Ludwig (Louis), 227-D

Schneider, Mischa, 227-F

Schnell, J. L., 860-D

Schnurr, Urban, Collection, 1202

Schock, Mabel, 8

Schoen, Isaac L., 860-H

Schoenberg, Arnold, 68, 81, 195-C, 227-F, 227-H, 227-L, 265, 340, 654, 729-E, 1025, 1031, 1053, 1061-B, 1174, 1488, 1580, 1670

Schoenberg, Arnold, Institute, 81

Schoenberg, Ronald, 195-C

Schoeneck (Pa.), 1285

Schoenefeld, Henry, 227-D

Schoenthaler, Mrs. J. G. W., 860-D

Schofield, Robert, 351

Scholer, Gustav, 1061-M

Scholes, Percy A., 618, 1659

Scholl, Walter, 379

Schomburg Center for Research in Black Culture, 1061-N

Schonberg, Harold, 637, 1580

School bands and orchestras, 1, 30, 114, 195, 398, 1005, 1040. *See also* Bands; Symphony orchestras

The School Musician, Director, and Teacher, 365

School of Fine Arts (Texarkana, Tex.), 1516

School of Music (Texarkana, Tex.), 1516

School of Musical Art (St. Louis), 860-E

School of Theology at Claremont (Cal.), 56

School songbooks. *See* School songs; Singing instruction materials

School songs, 11, 35, 68, 166, 190, 195-B, 227-A, 228, 284, 354, 366, 370, 373, 379, 391, 398, 401, 406, 440, 473, 481, 484, 523, 544, 618, 654, 694, 719, 725, 729-B, 761, 767, 800, 837, 878, 888, 896, 970, 995, 1005, 1006, 1036, 1077, 1143, 1172, 1210, 1217, 1223, 1268, 1287, 1362, 1423, 1459, 1463, 1616, 1641, 1645, 1673, 1688

Schoolcraft (Mich.) Musical Association, 761

Schools of music. *See* Music education; Singing schools; and names of specific institutions

The Schools of Theology in Dubuque (Iowa), 468

Schorr, Friedrich, 1053

Schorr, Laura Howell Norden (Mrs. Wallace), 1157
Schrade, Leo, 195-A
Schrader, D. G. von, 195-B
Schrag, Belle, 1477
Schreiber, Abner & Mary, Jewish Music Library, 1336
Schreiner, Alexander Ferdinand, 227-D, 1521
Schroeck, Albert F., 234
Schroeder, Henry, 612
Schryock, Buren Roscoe, 334
Schubert Club, 1596
Schubert Club (Grand Rapids, Mich.?), 748
Schubert Club (St. Paul), 815
Schubert Club (Salem, Mass.), 701
Schuhmann, George S., 398
Schuller, Gunther, 646
Schultz, Ferdinand Peter, 815
Schultz, Frances R., 541
Schultz, Herman, 977
Schuman, William, 195-C, 227-B, 227-C, 535, 907, 1018, 1040, 1580
Schumann, Clara, Club, 9
Schumann, Walter, 1646
Schumann-Heink, Ernestine, 55, 84, 227-F, 443, 636, 729-E, 853, 860, 1111, 1222, 1484, 1573
Schumer, Harry, 1061-D
Schurk, William L., 1170
Schuster, Gustav M., 1270
Schuyler, Philippa D., 268
Schuyler, William, 860-G
Schwab, Charles M., Memorial Library, 1283
Schwab, Joseph Maurice, 1312
Schwabisches Sängerbund of Brooklyn, 1680
Schwalbe, Ethel, 1472
Schwartz, Arthur, 227-D, 1024, 1611
Schwarzer, Franz, 698, 837, 847
Schwenckfelder Historical Library, 1325
Schwenckfelder music, 948, 1325
Schwerke, Irving, 227-F, 1592
Scofield-Hill Memorial Library, 1311
"The Scotch Nightingale" (May Fiske), 916
Scotia (N.Y.) History Center, 1119
Scotland, 140, 630
Scott family, 1560
Scott, Agnes, College, 278
Scott, Angelo Cyrus, 1260
Scott, Carlyle M., 800, 815
Scott, Ernest A., 398
Scott, Hollis, 1520
Scott, James, 868
Scott, L. E., 860-D
Scott, Louis N., 800
Scott, Raymond, 1646
Scott, Thomas, 1662
Scott, Verna Golden (Mrs. C. M.), 800, 815
Scott, Walter Dill, 357
Scott-Fanton Museum, 174

Scott-Palmer family, 1591
Scottish music, 140, 320, 334, 366, 404, 815, 1006, 1059, 1155, 1528
Scottish Rite Supreme Council, 233
Scouting, 353, 376, 937, 1061-M
Scraggs, T. W., 1176
Scranton, Helen Douglas (Love), 195-A
Scranton (Pa.) Tribune, 1381
Scripps College, 57
Scruggs, Earl, 1463
Scully, Emma Besser, 1176
Scully, George, 1364
Sea Islands (Ga.), 265
Seabury-Western Theological Seminary, 358
Sealevel (N.C.), 1149
Search, Frederick Preston, 1148, 1580
Sears School of Music, 299
Seashore, Carl E., 227-F, 476
Seashore tests, 1360
Seaside Company, 138
Seasonal and holiday songs, 117, 259, 334, 357, 636, 687, 802, 825, 935, 1082, 1096, 1161, 1165, 1188
Seat, John B., 860-A
Seaton, Horace, 823
Seattle, 1031
Seattle Historical Society, 1575
Seattle Public Library, 1576
Seaver, James E., 502
Seay, Albert, 195-C
Sebran, George W., 1440
Seckel, Ruth, 195-C
Secrist, John, 227-L
Secunda, Sholum, 1061-A
Sedalia (Mo.), 864
Sedgwick, Daniel, 1070
Seeboeck, William C. E., 317, 334
Seeger, Charles, 50, 84, 195-C, 227-F, 227-L
Seeger, Ruth Crawford, 227-C, 227-F, 1481, 1580
Seibert, George, 814
Seidel, Arthur, 398
Seidel, Emma, 779
Seidel, Lena, 779
Seidl, Anton, 84, 227-F, 1031, 1053
Seidl, Arthur, 1053
Seineke, Katherine Wagner, 314
Select School (Montgomery, Ala.), 11
Self-Improvement Club (Temple, Tex.), 1515
Sellers, Ernest O., 559
Sembrich, Marcella, 179, 227-F, 1009, 1053, 1117
Sembrich, Marcella, Memorial Association, Inc., 179
Sembrich, Marcella, Memorial Studio, 1009
Seminole Indians, 1265
Seminole Nation Historical Society, 1265
Semman, Lilorius, 1621
Semple, Amie, 404

Semsrott, William H., 860-D
Senate House (London), 1672
Seneca Falls (N.Y.) Historical Society, 1120
Sephardic music, 769, 1021
Serbian music, 227-L, 815, 1188
Seri Indians, 31
Serkin, Rudolf, 227-F
Serly, Tibor, 1580
Seroff, Doug, 1443
Seroff, Victor, 195-C
Servine, Marthe, 1061-A
Sessions, Roger, 83, 195-A, 195-C, 227-D, 227-F, 227-M, 535, 654, 691, 949, 1030, 1031, 1040, 1053, 1061-A
Settlement music, 341, 524, 538, 539, 800, 1058, 1068, 1190, 1351, 1355
Seuel, Edmund, 856
Seven Acres Museum, 395
Seventh-Day Adventist music, 298, 732, 761
Seventh Day Baptists, 946, 1615
Seventh Day Baptist Historical Society, 946
Severance Hall, 1183
Seville (Ohio) Musical Association, 1190
Sevitzky, Fabien, 227-E, 227-F
Seward, Philander, 398
Seward, William H., 398
Sewell, Arthur, 616
Sewell, W. Arthur, 30
Sewickley (Pa.) Music Club, 1383
Sewickley Public Library, 1383
Seymour, John Laurence, 55, 1518, 1520
Seymour Library, 360
Shaffer, Helen Louise, 84
Shaker Community, 697
Shaker Community (New Lebanon, N.Y.), 1091
Shaker (Ohio) Historical Society, 1230
Shaker Museum, 1096
Shaker music, 181, 195-A, 217, 227-G, 227-M, 523, 525, 526, 529, 593, 643, 670, 696, 697, 719, 729-E, 897, 967, 977, 1008, 1059, 1091, 1094, 1096, 1127, 1141, 1190, 1193, 1214, 1230, 1528
Shaker Village, Inc., 897
Shakertown at Pleasant Hill (Ky.), 526, 529
Shakersville (Ohio), 1190
Shakespeare, William, 224, 1459, 1612
Shan-Kar, Uday, 636
Shanklin family, 1005
Shannon, Marvin B., 1477
Shanties. See Chanteys
Shape notes, 67, 159, 260, 263, 265, 308, 320, 333, 510, 662, 729-A, 849, 888, 970, 993, 1095, 1137, 1141, 1161, 1172, 1176, 1190, 1212, 1220, 1297, 1299, 1389, 1440, 1448, 1454, 1527, 1534, 1548
Shapero, Harold, 195-C

Shapiro, Elliot, 1061-C
Shapleigh, Bertram, 833
Sharp, Cecil, 538
Shartkloff, Emilie, 606
Shattinger imprints, 866
Shattuck, Abel, 227-D, 227-G
Shattuck, Arthur, 1629, 1630
Shattuck, Mrs. S. F., 1630
Shaw, Artie, 637
Shaw, Clifford, 535
Shaw, Mrs. George, 1031
Shaw, Henry, 860-D
Shaw, Isabel Pelham (Mrs. Frederick Lowell), 1031
Shaw, J. Emory, 1477
Shaw, Levi, 729-E
Shaw, Mary McCulloch, 1111
Shaw, Robert, 195-C
Shawa, Nadonis, 1611
Shawe, Elsie M., 815
Shawnee County (Kan.) Historical Society, 515
Shea, John Gilmary, 225
Shearing, George, 714
Sheboygan (Wis.) Opera House, 1631
Sheboygan Theater, 1623
Sheboygan County (Wis.) Historical Society, 1631
Sheepskin Band, 434
Sheet music—very large collections (100,000 or more items), 33, 79, 84, 227, 334, 406, 411, 744, 977, 1048, 1061, 1270, 1333, 1339, 1402
Sheet music—large collections (20,000 to 100,000 items), 105, 122, 185, 195-B, 333, 349, 357, 398, 427, 568-A, 624, 654, 674, 721, 729-A, 739, 778, 796, 798, 847, 860-A, 866, 907, 949, 1007, 1031, 1049, 1077, 1111, 1166, 1176, 1350, 1372, 1375, 1433, 1477, 1492, 1517, 1520, 1576, 1607, 1624, 1636, 1646, 1673
Sheets, Jo, 434
Sheetz, William Leander, 454, 455, 475
Shelburne Falls (Mass.) Academy, 707
Shelby's Lost Cause, 1420
Sheldon, Edward Austin, 1099
Sheldon, Henry L., 1529
Sheldon, Mary, 188
Sheldon Art Museum, 1529
Sheldon Museum, 17
Shelley, Albertus, 1338
Shelley, Harry Rowe, 227-F, 1018, 1061-A
Shenandoah Valley (Va.), 1561
Shenk, Morris J., 94
Shepard, Thomas Griffin, 195-B
Shepherd, Anne Boyer, 1172
Shepherd, Arthur, 227-D, 227-F, 646, 1061-A, 1080, 1190, 1523, 1580
Shepherd, Richard, 111
Shepherd School of Music, 1497
Shepperd, Eli, 226
Sherburne (Mass.), 707

Sherman, John K., 800
Sherman, William T., 1611, 1612
Sherman and Clay imprints, 122, 124
Sherman and Hyde imprints, 124
Sherman Collection, 124
Sherrill family, 1225
Sherrill Memorial Library, 653
Sherrod Library, 1445
Sherwood, William H., 636
Sherwood School of Music, 730
Shettel, James Warren, 1396
Shields Library, 59
Shillito, John, 1172
Shillman, Alice Sheppard, 1502
Shipman, C. E., 465
Shipman, W. H., 465
Shippen family, 1338
Shipps, Barbara, 341
Shipps-Smith Collection, 341
Shirk, William Allen, 398
Shoemaker, Matthew H., Collection, 882
Shoen-René, Anna, 800
Shoninger Musical Monthly, 192
Shorney, George H., 306
Short, Jane, 425
Showalter, A. J., 1440
Showboats. *See* Steamships
Shrader, Pearl Hutton, 1578
Shrednick, Milton, 157
Shrine to Music Museum, 1433
Shubert Archive, 1065
Shubert Foundation (New York), 1065
Shubert Theatres (Philadelphia), 1333
Shuey, A. M., 798
Shull, Carl N., 1292
Shull, Sallie J., 398
Shurcliff, Margaret Homer Nichols, 635
Sibelius, Jean, 195-A, 260, 458
Sibley Music Library, 1111, 1666
Sidney (Me.), 576
Siegel, Charles L., 127
Siegel, Daniel, 712
Siegel, Ruth, 712
Siegling, John, 1418
Siegling Music House Collection, 1418
Siegmeister, Elie, 227-D, 227-F, 1031
Siemonn, George, 646
Sigma Alpha Iota, 511, 1061-B
Signora Ethiopian Minstrel Burlesque Troop, 815
Silent-film music, 51, 60, 84, 92, 154, 195-A, 292, 294, 349, 383, 398, 482, 565, 779, 847, 949, 1031, 1036, 1055, 1065, 1144, 1202, 1436, 1452, 1517, 1520, 1557, 1620, 1623, 1665. *See also* Film music
Siloti, Alexander, 1053, 1222
Silsbee, Mary, 701
Silva, Luigi, 1148
Silver, Mark, 1111

Silver Cornet Band (Brodhead, Wis.), 1612
Silver Cornet Band (Jacksonville, Ore.), 1272
Silver Lake Quartette, 356
Silverado Museum, 110
Silverman, Stanley, 1040
Silverton (Ore.) Marine Band, 1274
Silverton Trombone Band, 1274
Simi Valley (Cal.) Historical Society, 140
Simitière, Pierre Eugène du, 1340
Simms, Ernest W., 227-F
Simon, Alfred, 195-C
Simon, Charles Julius, 739
Simon, Dr. Frank, 228
Simonds, Bruce, 195-A, 195-C
Simonds, Robert A., 761
Simonds, Rosalind, 195-C
Simons, Elizabeth P., 1418
Simons, Menno, Historical Library and Archives, 1547
Simonson, Lee, 1061-L
Simplex piano rolls, 724
Simpson, A. Carson, 1352
Simpson, George Eliot, 847
Simpson, Samuel Robert, 1463
Sims, J. G., 1477
Simsbury (Conn.), 180
Sinatra, Frank, 1270, 1350
Sincese, Victor, 1605
Sinclair Library, 289
Sinding, Christian, 1111
Singenberger, Johann Baptist, 375
Singenberger, John, 375
Singer, Joshua Heschel, 549
Singer, Julius, 549, 1174
Singers, Loren, 461
"The Singers Assistant," 1399
Singers Club (Poughkeepsie, N.Y.), 1105
Singers Glen (Va.), 1539
Singers League in Texas, 1477
"Singin' Sam" (Harry A. Frankel), 445
Singing instruction material, 13, 17, 19, 22, 26, 128, 132, 133, 137, 146, 167, 169, 170, 171, 180, 184, 185, 188, 192, 195-A, 200, 205, 246, 262, 276, 284, 297, 298, 304, 344, 354, 364, 370, 373, 379, 385, 391, 401, 404, 416, 417, 419, 426, 437, 446, 453, 455, 460, 464, 475, 500, 503, 510, 514, 538, 544, 568-A, 577, 619, 625, 636, 646, 686, 707, 729-A, 746, 748, 749, 765, 773, 774, 777, 783, 798, 807, 823, 824, 829, 845, 850, 856, 867, 875, 878, 895, 896, 929, 939, 957, 976, 987, 993, 995, 1017, 1059, 1146, 1167, 1168, 1193, 1194, 1199, 1210, 1213, 1216, 1222, 1123, 1232, 1235, 1242, 1245, 1271, 1302, 1315, 1319, 1333, 1359, 1362, 1375, 1389, 1391, 1397, 1405, 1425, 1428, 1502, 1520, 1522, 1571, 1596, 1611, 1621, 1631, 1642, 1647

Singing School (Hopkinton, R.I.), 1408
Singing schools, 180, 297, 308, 357, 385, 417, 514, 589, 611, 636, 643, 654, 662, 701, 707, 729-A, 993, 1061-M, 1193, 1222, 1225, 1236, 1333, 1359, 1378, 1390, 1396, 1408, 1603
Singing societies. *See* Choral ensembles and singing societies
Singing Society (Hartland, Vt.), 1530
Singing Society (Hobart, Ind?), 419
"Single Sisters," 1161
Singley (i.e., Hinkley and Singley) Sheet Music Collection, 606
Sink, Charles A., 729-B
Sioux City (Iowa), 1436
Sioux Indians, 27, 815
Siouxland Heritage Museum, 1430
Sisler, Joseph, 1573
Sissle, Noble, 195-C, 226, 227-F, 268
Sisson, C. T., 1477
Sitherwood, G. H., 302
Sitka (Alaska), 19
Sizemore, Margaret, 4
Skelton, John, 391
Skidmore Guard, 544
Skiles, Marlin H., 1646
Skilton, Charles Sanford, 227-D, 227-F, 317, 502, 847, 862, 1061-A
Skinner, Constance, 1061-M
Skinner, Frank, 398
Skinner, LaUna De Cordova, 1477
Skinner, Ruth Hargrave (Mrs. Charles Wickham), 1172
Skinner School, 302
Skitswich Indians, 50
Skoog, A. L., 325
Skougaard, Lorentz S., 802
Skrainka, Philip, 860-H
Slade, Mrs. William Adams, 227-A
Slater, John R., 1111
Slater, Kenneth, 618
Slaughter, Henry P., Collection, 268
Slave songs, 282, 314, 315, 1054, 1095, 1142, 1223, 1299, 1400, 1427, 1688. *See also* Abolitionist songs
Slavic music, 349, 626, 781, 782. *See also* specific nationalities
Slavit, Lewis, 227-F, 862, 1666
Sleepy Hollow Restorations, 1128
Slezak, Leo, 395
Slick, Luke, 391
Slingerland Drum Company, 321
Slip ballads. *See* Broadsides
Slobin, Mark, 189
Slocum, Mrs. Don, 1270
Slonimsky, Nicolas, 68, 84, 195-C, 227-E, 227-F, 532, 636, 1111, 1580

Sloop, Jean, 508
Slovakian music, 825
Slovenian music, 391, 800, 1187
Slyck, Nicholas van, 398
Smedley, Peter, 1390
Smelzer, Hazel Dell Neff, 443
Smiley, A. K., Public Library, 103
Smit, Johannes, 1452
Smit, Leo, 977
Smith, Albert, 1511
Smith, Alexander MacKay, 1541
Smith, Mrs. Alfred F., 860-K
Smith, Bessie 610
Smith, Caroline Estes, 84
Smith, Carleton, 227-F
Smith, Carleton Sprague, 195-C, 227-F, 1580
Smith, Christopher, 226
Smith, Cora, 741
Smith, David Stanley, 195-A, 227-D, 227-F
Smith, E. J., 1510
Smith, Eleanor, 341
Smith, Elizabeth, 502
Smith, Frank Thornton, 144
Smith, Franklin G., 1490
Smith, Frederick Madison, 477
Smith, Frederick Madison, Library, 477
Smith, George Leslie, 84
Smith, Gerrit, 1125
Smith, H. D., 195-B
Smith, Harry B., Operetta Collection, 1477
Smith, Joel Sumner, 195-A, 195-B
Smith, John F., 522
Smith, Joseph Brown, 531
Smith, Julia, 1494
Smith, Kate Duncan, 11
Smith, Leland, 1274
Smith, Leonard B., 1124
Smith, Ligon, 1487
Smith, Lucia W., 103
Smith, Luther E., 860-C
Smith, Madeline P., 1031
Smith, May, 606
Smith, Melville M., 227-F
Smith, Moses, 227-F
Smith, N. Clark, 847
Smith, S. E. Boyd, 45
Smith, Samuel Francis, 142, 227-F, 314, 685, 798, 950, 1040, 1059
Smith, Sophia, Collection, 692
Smith, Stuart C., Collection, 940
Smith, Thomas Max, 195-A
Smith, Virgil, Collection, 1430
Smith, Warren Storey, 636
Smith, William, 729-A, 970
Smith, William Clifford, 1172
Smith, Wilson G., 1213
Smith College, 689, 691, 692
Smith Memorial Library, 982
Smith Opera House (Geneva, N.Y.), 996
Smith-Zimmerman Historical Museum, 1429
Smithdeal, J. D., 1421
Smith's Theatre, 860-G

Smithsonian Institution, 227-L, 234, 805
Smoak, Merril, 67
Smoky Mountains, 75, 227-L
Smolian, Steven, 1061-J
Smyth, Dame Ethel, 639
Smythe, Nellie Hobbs, 1626
Snaer, Samuel, 568
Snake River Basin (Idaho), 291
Snake River Valley (Idaho), 295
Snakenberg, James H., 406
Sneden, R. K., 1061-M
Snelgrove, Glen, 8
Snell, David L., 1646
Snell, Irene E., 190
Snell, Lila, 1603
Snell, Maddie, 1603
Snelling, Joseph, 1207
Snively, Joseph, 406
Snodgrass, Louis, 1176
Snooper's City Club, 866
Snoqualmie Valley (Wash.) Historical Society, 1570
Snow, Peter, 15
Snow, Willard C., 757
Snow Hill Cloister (Pa.), 350, 1293, 1299, 1333
Snyder, Franklyn Bliss, 357
Snyder, Richard N. M., 1290
Sobel, Bernard, 1611
Sobeski, Carl, 433
Sobolewski, Edward, 1624
Sobotka, Yella Pessl, 704
Social and sacred harp, 263, 270, 271, 275, 398, 866, 1459
Social Singing Society (Salem, Mass.), 701
Social Welfare History Archives Center, 800
Society for Ethnomusicology, 27
Society for the Foundation of a National Conservatory of Music, 227-H, 612
Society for the Preservation and Encouragement of Barber Shop Quartet Singing in America, 1607
Society for the Preservation of New England Antiquities, 649
Society for the Preservation of Spirituals, 1418
Society for the Preservation of the American Musical Heritage, 227-H
Society for the Publication of American Music, 195-A, 227-H, 1046
Society of American Symphony Conductors, 1061-B
Society of California Pioneers, 124
Society of Jesus, Oregon Province, Archives, 1581
Society of Oregon Composers, 1274
Society of the Cincinnati, 220
Society of the Friends of Music (New York), 1061-D
Society of Visual Education, 376
Soderlund, Gustave, 1111

Soderman, A., 724
Sofier, Joseph H., 181
Sokoloff, Nikolai, 227-F
Sola, Abraham de, 1174
Solar Festivals, 241
Solesmes, 1434
Sollers, Waldemar, 1647
Solm-Braunfels archives, 1477
Solomon, Izler, 227-F
Solomon, W. A., 1364
Solomons, Isaac, 215
Somers, Robert, 761
Sommers, Alfred, 471
Song Writers Hall of Fame, 1066
Songbooks. See Hymnals and tunebooks; Singing instruction materials; Songsters
Songsters, 45, 56, 65, 67, 109, 115, 127, 158, 171, 190, 195-B, 197, 213, 227-A, 227-M, 234, 269, 320, 333, 334, 340, 356, 379, 391, 398, 424, 611, 624, 633, 635, 636, 654, 681, 707, 721, 729-A, 729-B, 761, 837, 909, 966, 977, 1036, 1040, 1061-D, 1077, 1193, 1223, 1333, 1340, 1402, 1448, 1477, 1517, 1527, 1528, 1541, 1556, 1594, 1611, 1673
Sonkin, Robert, 227-L
Sonneck, Oscar, 227-D, 227-E, 227-F, 227-H, 265, 729-C, 1080, 1111, 1359
Sons of Herman, 1584
Sontag, Henriette, 1222
Sooladey, Edwin W., 1510
Sophienburg Memorial Museum, 1506
Sopkin, Stefan, 1061-A
Sororities. See Fraternities and sororities
Sosnik, Harry, 1611
Sothern and Marlowe Shakespearean Company, 1459
Souchon, Edmond, 1450
Souers, Mildred, 463, 465
Soule, Edmund F., 1270
Sound recordings. See Recordings—major collections
Sour, Robert B., Collection of Music of the Theatre, 949
Sousa, John Philip, 79, 142, 222, 227-C, 227-F, 229, 234, 317, 341, 343, 398, 442, 544, 618, 624, 729-A, 744, 815, 860-B, 1053, 1061-A, 1061-F, 1106, 1190, 1191, 1222, 1292, 1298, 1580, 1612
Sousa, John Philip, Museum and Collection, 398
Sousa Band, 229, 370, 398, 503, 671, 761, 1061-M, 1272, 1477, 1593, 1611
Sousa Band Library, 398
South, Mary Ellis, 406
South America, 1031. See also Latin-American music
South Bend (Ind.) Symphony Orchestra, 443
South Carolina, 227-G, 898, 909, 1053, 1141, 1143, 1463, 1477

South Carolina Historical Society, 1418
South Carolina Opera Workshop Guild, 1420
South Carolina, University of, 1420
South Caroliniana Library, 1420
South Dakota, 27, 475, 800
South Dakota, University of, 1432, 1433
South Florida, University of, 261
South Kingston (R.I.), 707
South Plains (Tex.) Music Association, 1477
South Plains Music Teachers Association, 1477, 1501
South Reading (Mass.), 699
South Royalton (Vt.), 1534
South Union (Ky.), 523, 525
Southard, Lucien H., 636
Southbridge (Mass.), 707
Southeast Minnesota Historical Center, 822
Southern, Eileen, 1457
Southern Appalachian region, 227-K, 1445
Southern Appalachian Video Ethnography Series, 1445
Southern Baptist Convention Historical Commission, 1462
Southern Baptist Theological Seminary, 534
Southern California, University of, 81, 85
Southern Conference for Human Welfare Collection, 268
Southern Folklore Collection, 1141
Southern Historical Collection, 1141
Southern Illinois University (Carbondale), 305
Southern Illinois University (Edwardsville), 349, 701
Southern Methodist University, 1483, 1487
Southern Music Archive (Memphis State University), 1452
Southern Musical Journal, 265
Southern Oregon Historical Society, 1272
Southern U.S., 227-M, 265, 271, 276, 530, 830, 979, 1095, 1141, 1143, 1185, 1200, 1452, 1454, 1611
Southern Utah State College, 1518
Southington (Conn.), 180
Southold (N.Y.) Historical Society and Museum, 1122
Southwest Arkansas Regional Archives, 43
Southwest Collection, 33, 1489, 1501
Southwest Folklore Collection, 152
Southwest Georgia Regional Library, 274
Southwest Louisiana, University of, 545

Southwest Missouri State University, 869
Southwest Museum, 82
Southwest State University, 793
Southwest Studies Program, 152
Southwest Tape Archive, 28
Southwestern at Memphis, 1453
Southwestern Baptist Theological Seminary, 1462, 1493
Southwestern College, 520
Southwestern Lore Center, 33
Southwestern U.S., 21, 28, 31, 33, 82, 145, 152, 227-L, 836, 957, 962, 965, 971, 1256, 1488, 1489
Southwestern University, 1493
Sowerby, Leo, 227-C, 227-F, 324, 334, 398, 722, 739, 1018, 1111, 1127, 1292, 1580, 1666
Spaeth (i.e., Vogelpohl & Spaeth), organs, 801
Spaeth, Sigmund, 227-F, 1031
Spain, Helen Knox, 266
Spair, Murphy, 853
Spalding, Albert, 123, 227-F, 637, 1053, 1222, 1580
Spalding, E. W., 707
Spalding, Ezekiel, 180
Spalding, Walter Raymond, 227-F
Spamer, Richard, 860-B
Spanier, Muggsy, 942, 1450
Spanish music, 28, 50, 65, 71, 82, 128, 129, 130, 137, 142, 145, 152, 162, 404, 475, 957, 962, 963, 1261, 1469, 1477, 1500. See also Latin American music; Mexican music
Spanish-American War, 227-A, 349, 475, 500, 1059, 1232
Sparks, Ned, 1662
Sparnon, Ken, 234
Spaulding, Harriet M., Library, 646
Spaulding, Walter R., 654
SPEBSQSA (Society for the Preservation and Encouragement of Barber Shop Quartet Singing in America), 1607
Speck, Frank Gouldsmith, 1327
Speed, Hattie Bishop, 532, 535
Speed Music Room, 535
Speer, Robert E., Library, 948
Speirachordeon Band, 183
Spell, Lota Mae (Mrs. Jefferson Rea), 1477
Spelman, Timothy Mather, 227-F, 1111
Spencer family, 180
Spencer, Alrick G., 896
Spencer, Francis G., Collection of American Printed Music, 1517
Spencer, Henry, 1593
Spencer, Kenneth, Research Library, 502
Spencer, Marion (Mrs. Henry), 1593

Spencer, Thomas J., & Co., 1560
Spengler, Jacob, 514
Spengler, William F., 1607
Sperati, Carlo A., 465
Spicer, Ishmael, 180, 729-A
Spiering, Lenore, 1172
Spiering, Theodore, 860-D
Spiering Collection, 860-D
Spiess, Lincoln B., 866
Spiller, I. J., 195-A
Spiller, Isabelle Taliaferro, 226
Spiller, William N., 226
Spiller School of Music, 226
Spilman, Jonathan E., 1189
Spinden, Herbert J., 227-L
Spingarn, Arthur B., 268
Spingarn, Arthur B., Collection of Negro Authors, 226
Spirituals, 142, 227-K, 267, 269, 271, 315, 340, 355, 573, 860-K, 1022, 1053, 1061-M, 1061-N, 1118, 1141, 1187, 1223, 1298, 1358, 1418, 1459, 1477
Spitalny, Phil, 1516
Spivacke, Harold, 227-F, 654
Spivakovsky-Kurtz Trio, 1061-F
Spofford, Grace, 671, 800
Spokane (Wash.) Public Library, 1582
Spooner, Alden, 1530
Sports, songs about, 624, 744, 796, 977, 1463
Spotsylvania County (Va.), 1560
Spottswood, Richard K., 626
Sprague, Albert A., 195-A
Spring Festival (Chattanooga, Tenn.), 1439
Spring Festival of the Arts (Potsdam, N.Y.), 1104
Spring Hill College, 910
Springer, Reuben R., 1172
Springer Opera House, 276
Springer Theatre Company, 276
Springfield (Mass.), 1051
Springfield (Mass.) City Library, 705
Springfield-Greene County (Mo.) Library, 870
Springfield (Ohio), 860-B, 1196
Springfield (Vt.), 1530
Springfield (Vt.) Military Band of Music, 707
Sproesser collection, 1635
Spross, Charles Gilbert, 227-D, 1105, 1573
Spross, William, 1477
Spry, Walter, 1425
Spurgeon, Charles Haddon, 849
Spurlock, Clifford, Collection, 1430
Square dance, 34, 75, 1034, 1061-K, 1402. See also Dance
Squier, Victor C., 729-B
Squier's Opera House, 748
Staatsarchiv und Personenstandsarchiv, (Detmold, W. Germany), 1678

Stack, A. Parker, 50
Stack, Richard, 962
Stadium Concerts (New York), 1063
Stadtarchiv Salzgitter, 1682
Stafford, Harry F., 1533
Stafford's, Mrs., Finishing School for Young Ladies, 11
Stage works. See Theater music
Stair, Patty, 227-D
Stakely (i.e., Hall-Stakely) family, 1447
Stakely, Carrie, 1447
Stalford, Ronald, 722
Stalker, Hugh, 654
Stambler, Benedict, 227-L, 1061-J
Stamford (Conn.), 888, 1061-M
Stamford (Conn.) Academy, 180
Stanbrough pianos, 1017
Stanchfield, Bessie Mae, 815
Standard Program Service, 1469
Stanford University, 142, 896
Stangl, Vera Stetkevicz, 800
Stanley, Albert A., 729-B, 729-C, 729-E
Stanton, Royal, 227-D
Stanton, Royal B., collection, 84
Staples, Samuel Elias, 721
Star Music Company, 618
"The Star-spangled Banner," 227-F, 227-H, 607, 612, 614, 616, 744, 914, 977, 1036, 1338, 1463, 1517
Star-spangled Banner Flag House, 616
Starbuck, Walter F., 646
"Stardust," 1274
Stark, John, 864, 868
Stark, Samuel, 142
Stark's Cornet Band, 906
Starr, Egbert, Library, 1528
Starr, Saul, Sheet Music Collection, 406
"The Stars and Stripes," 914
Starshak, Lieut. Joseph Benedict, 340
State and city songs, 227-A, 285, 303, 314, 315, 334, 426, 455, 465, 514, 516, 612, 694, 761, 815, 843, 850, 860-C, 872, 874, 879, 885, 896, 963, 1059, 1141, 1155, 1172, 1269, 1402, 1407, 1420, 1463, 1483, 1502, 1541, 1553, 1577, 1591, 1611, 1616, 1643
State Capitol (Wash.) Historical Association, 1571
State Fair Community College, 868
State Historical Society of Iowa, 475
State Historical Society of Missouri, 836, 837
State Historical Society of Wisconsin, 1611
State Library of Ohio, 1195
State Library of Pennsylvania, 1299
State Militia of Vermont, 2nd Regiment, 2nd Brigade, 1st Division, 707

State University of New York at Alfred, 970
State University of New York at Buffalo, 979
State University of New York at Stony Brook, 1124
State University of New York, College at Fredonia, 994
State University of New York, College at Oswego, 1099
State University of New York, College at Plattsburgh, 1102
State University of New York, College at Potsdam, 1104
State University of New York, College at Purchase, 1108
Stateburg (S.C.?) Literary and Musical Society, 1420
Staten Island, 1090
Staten Island Institute of Arts and Sciences, 1090
Staub, Augustus J., 9, 18
Stauffer, David McNeely, Collection, 1338
Staunton (Va.), 612
Stead, M., 314
Steamships, 30, 303, 523, 556, 865, 1176, 1403, 1463. See also Boat songs; Naval songs
Stearn, Noel Hudson, 360
Stearns, Frederick H., Collection of Musical Instruments, 729-B
Stearns, Peter Pindar, 1067
Stearns, Stanley W., 719
Stearns, Theodore, 1067
Stearns County (Minn.) Historical Society, 807
Stebbins, George C., 235, 333, 1031
Stebbins, George C., Memorial Collection, 235
Steckelberg, Carl-Frederic, 885, 887
Steckelberg, Ouida, 885
Stedman, Clarence, 84
Steel, David Warren, 728
Steel, Suzanne Flandreau, 728
Steel-workers' songs, 742
Steen, Ralph W., Library, 1504
Steers, Lois, 1274
Steers & Coman, 1274
Stein, Jules, 1520
Stein, Leon, 323
Stein, Leonard, 68, 81, 195-C
Steinberg, William, 227-F, 1375
Steiner, George, 1270
Steiner, John, 1625
Steiner, William K., 1359
Steinert, Alexander Lang, 227-F
Steinfeldt, John M., 1477
Steinmetz, Theodore A., 1611
Steinway, William, 1013
Steinway pianos, 129, 195-C, 1013
Steinway & Sons Project, 195-C
Steinway Hall, 1040
Stekert, Ellen, 1005
Stella music boxes, 1471
Steller, Mary B., 1403
Stephen F. Austin State University, 1504

Stephens, Edwin L., 544
Stephens, Evan, 1519, 1521
Stephens, Laura, 125
Stephens, Lincoln, 125
Stephens, R. Duane, 842
Stephens, Sister Rosetta, 1091
Stephens County (Okla.) Historical Museum, 1248
Sterling, Henry, 1375
Sterling, W. S., 1177
Sterling Memorial Library, 195-B
Sterling Piano Company, 201
Stern, Henry R., 1270
Stern, Jack, 1646
Stern, Joseph W., & Co., 1270
Sternberg, Constantin, 227-D, 227-F
Stetson, Augusta C., 227-D
Stetson, Mrs. E. G., 398
Stetson University, 229, 240
Steuben, Baron Friedrich, 1061-M
Steuermann, Eduard, 81, 227-C, 1580, 1670
Steuermann Collection, 81
Stevens, Halsey, 227-D, 227-F, 535, 1580
Stevens, Harry Robert, 1172
Stevens, Henry, 227-M
Stevens, Leith, 847
Stevens, Minnie Saltzman, 303, 379
Stevens, Risë, 637
Stevens, Sara, 180
Stevens, Solon, 676
Stevens, William Bacon, 440, 653, 1352
Stevens Point (Wis.), 336, 1611
Stevenson, Alice, 114
Stevenson, Henry J., 628
Stevenson, Robert Louis, 110, 129
Stewart, James M., 226
Stewart, Rose, 636
Stewart, Sir William Drummond, 860-D
Stiedry, Fritz, 81, 227-F
Stiedry-Wagner, Erika, 81
Stieff, Charles M., pianos, 612
Stigler, Eric, 391
Stigler (Okla.), 113
Stiles, John W., 601
Still, Vera Arvey (Mrs. William Grant), 68
Still, William Grant, 36, 142, 195-B, 226, 227-C, 227-F, 729-C, 827, 1111, 1127, 1212, 1425, 1580, 1646
Stillman, Edgar, 1018
Stillman, Jairus M., 1616
Stillman, Mitya, 398
Stillman, S., 398
Stimpson, Robert, 699
Stinchfield, Ben, 590
Stites, Edgar Page, 950
Stiven, Frederick B., 398
Stock, Frederick A., 227-D, 227-F, 314, 317, 334, 611, 729-E, 815, 1573, 1580
Stockton, Samuel William, 1560
Stockton (Cal.), 50
Stoddard, Mrs. Lynn, 761

Stoddard, Priscilla, 181
Stockton, Samuel William, 1560
Stoeckel, Carl, 195-A, 227-F, 1053
Stoeckel, Gustave, 195-A, 198
Stoehr, Richard, 1535
Stoepel, Robert, 636
Stoessel, Albert, 227-D, 227-F, 1053, 1666
Stoeving, Paul, 888
Stojowski, Sigismond, 227-F, 1053
Stokes, Anson Phelps, 227-F
Stokowski, Leopold, 195-C, 226, 227-B, 227-F, 406, 654, 729-E, 831, 951, 1031, 1040, 1061-B, 1061-M, 1301, 1359, 1580
Stokowski, Olga Samaroff, 227-F, 729-E, 1058, 1177, 1470, 1580
Stoller, Ben, 1430
Stolze, Robert H., 1270
Stone, Elijah, 707
Stone, Henry, 502
Stone, Joseph C., 84
Stone, Kurt, 195-C
Stone, Roberta Summers, 195-B
Stonehill, Ben, 1076
Stoner, George W., 1611
Stoner, Sara Augusta, 180
Stonewall Brigade Band, 1562, 1563
Stoney, Robert, 1521
Stopher, Henry Wallace, 544
Stor, Jean, 195-B
Stordahl, Axel, 1270
Storie, Austin, 1477
Storm, Charles W., 398
Storrs, A., 180
Story, William Cumming, 1061-M
Stoudemire, Mrs. Sterling, 1155
Stoughton (Mass.) Historical Society, 706
Stout, Mr. & Mrs. Owen, 441
Stout, Zacharias, 929
Stout Institute Band, 1614
Stout Institute Orchestra, 1614
Stowe, Harriet Beecher, 184
Stowe-Day Memorial Library and Historical Foundation, 184
Strachan, Pearl, 636
Strachwitz, Chris, 49
Strahm, Franz Joseph, 523
Strakosch, Maurice, 1040, 1052
Strakosch, Max, 1052
Strang, Gerald, 68, 81, 195-C, 227-F, 1580
Stransky, Josef, 227-F, 1193
Strassberger Conservatories of Music, 860-E
Strasser, William, 1331
Stratford (Conn.), 905
Stratford (Conn.) Historical Society, 204
Strathclyde Collaborative, 1084
Strathearn, Robert Perkins, family, 140

Stratton, George William, 919
Stratton Library, 919
Straus, Oscar, 1127
Strauss, Edouard, 646, 1061-M
Strauss, Johann, Jr., 639, 646
Strauss, John, 195-C
Strauss, Josef, 646
Strauss, Noel, 1061-F
Strauss, Richard, 636, 1061-F
Strauss, Therese Abraham, 1174
Stravinsky, Igor, 85, 142, 227-C, 227-F, 637, 949, 1061-B, 1111, 1222, 1580, 1670, 1689
Stravinsky, Soulima, 398
Strawbridge, Charles Heber, 314
Streed Family Orchestra, 475
Street music, 1090, 1118, 1418, 1528
Streeter, Amanda L. Dunwell (Mrs. Benjamin H.), 1059
Strickland, Lily, 227-D, 1411, 1412, 1420, 1425
Strickland, William, 227-D, 227-F
Strimer, Joseph, 1061-A
String Band (Ft. Davis, Tex.), 1471
String instrument music, 7, 34, 36, 278, 309, 338, 568-A, 630, 642, 646, 860-F, 888, 957, 1075, 1111, 1270, 1518, 1551, 1609. See also specific instruments
Stringfield, Lamar, 1141, 1148, 1155, 1666
Stringham, Edwin John, 227-D, 1111
Strohl, Joseph, 195-B
Strong, Anna Louise, 1577
Strong, Bill, 729-C
Strong, George Templeton (I), 1059, 1061-A, 1689
Strong, George Templeton (II), 227-B, 227-C, 227-F, 272, 1688
Strong, J., 192
Strong, Julia P., 1245
Strong, William Dietrich, 642
Stroud, Carolyn Stearns, 1148
Strozier, Robert Manning, Library, 260
Strube, Gustav, 227-D, 227-F, 605, 614
Strunk, W. Oliver, 195-C, 227-D, 227-F, 949
Struthers, William Wood, Collection of Historical Recordings, 1139
Stryker-Rodda, Harriet, 1083
Stubblebine, Donald J., 1350
Stucken, Frank van der, 729-E, 1111, 1176
Stuckenschmidt, H. H., 81
Stuntz, Mabel Hope, 1190
Sturgill, Virgil L., 1140
Sturgis, Sam, 729-B
Sturgis (Mich.) Public Library, 772
Stutler (i.e., Boyd Stutler) collection, 1590
Stuttgart (Germany), 544

Suburban Library System, 347
Such, Percy, 1148
Sudds, W. F., 980, 998
Sudler, Louis, 195-C
Suffield (Conn.), 180
Suffrage songs, 150
Suk, Josef, 227-D
Sul Ross State University, 1472
Sullivan, Arthur, 1054. See also Gilbert & Sullivan
Sullivan, Janet, 59
Sullivan, John T. S., 860-D
Sullivan, Maxine, 195-B
Sullivan's Island (S.C.), 1141
Sully, Robert Matthew, 1560
Summer Conference on Music Education, 729-B
Summer music, 1333. See also Seasonal and holiday songs
Summerfield (Ala.), 11
Summerhays, Margaret, 1520
Summers, George, 1662
Summy, Clayton F., Co., 227-H, 357
Summy-Birchard Co., 227-H, 357
Sumner, Arthur J., 1174
Sumner, Jezaniah, 406, 708
Sun Dance (Wyo.), 156
Sun Valley (Idaho) Folk Festival, 290
Sunday, Billy, 404, 452
Sunday-school songbooks, 376, 404, 465, 531, 591, 622, 664, 689, 802, 815, 1040, 1070, 1200, 1233, 1376, 1558, 1565, 1603
Sundborg, Vilma, 1577
Sunnyside (Washington Irving House), 1128
Suomi College, 753
Superstition Mountains, 25
Surdam, Henderson E. Van, 190
Surette, Thomas Whitney, 227-F, 659, 716
Surette School of Music, 659
Surinach, Carlos, 1108
Sutherland, Philip, 195-C
Sutro, Ottilie, 227-F, 612
Sutro, Otto, Wednesday Club (Baltimore), 612
Sutro, Rose Laura, 227-F, 612
Sutro Library, 125
Sutton, Maude (Minish), 1141
Sutton (i.e., Hartman-Sutton) Collection, 1141
Suzzallo Library, 1577
Sved, Alexander, 1061-F
Sverdrup, George, Library, 795
Svoboda Singing Society (Detroit), 800
Swall, Corinne, 36, 65
Swan, Alfred, 227-F, 1541
Swan, Howard, 68
Swan, Phebe, 977
Swan, Timothy, 180, 205, 636, 721
Swann, William F. G., 1327
Swanson, Howard, 195-B
Swarthmore (Pa.) Symphony Orchestra, 1327

Swarthout, Donald M., 227-F
Swartwout, Bernardus, 1059
Swasey, Ambrose, Library, 1110
Swayne, Noah Haynes, 1193
Swedish-American Lutheran Church, 330, 386
Swedish Club Foundation, 316
Swedish Festival Chorus, 815
Swedish Glee Club (Chicago), 316
Swedish Glee Club (Waukegan, Ill.), 402
Swedish Historical Society of America, 815
Swedish Lutheran Church, 330
Swedish music, 167, 171, 227-L, 310, 316, 325, 330, 339, 386, 388, 402, 419, 420, 478, 507, 776, 777, 779, 782, 791, 794, 809, 815, 819, 821, 856, 1235, 1251, 1328, 1428, 1469, 1577, 1645
Swedish Pioneer Historical Society, 339
Sweet, Albert Burbank, papers, 815
Sweet, Harry, 815
Sweet Briar (Va.) College, Library, 1564
Sweet Pea Carnival, 872
Swem, Earl Gregg, Library, 1560
Sweterlitsch, Richard, 1525
Swift, Cadet James Foster, 1135
Swift, John, 1327
Swift, Kay, 195-C, 227-F
Swihart, Wilbur Wright ("Bugler Bill"), 443
Swindell, Erwin, 465
Swing, Raymond Gram, 227-F
Swisher Library, 246
Swislowski, Jeno, 977
Swiss Bell Ringers, 1155
Swiss music, 234, 1155, 1267
Swiss Singing Society (Boston), 234
Switzerland, 33, 63
Switzer's Opera House, 1587
Swope, Wilmer D., 1309
Syllabic notation, 129
Sylvester, Stephen A., 1497
Symington, Edith, 1161
Symington Collection, 1161
Symphony orchestras (materials about), 2, 8, 30, 50, 55, 57, 61, 70, 78, 84, 93, 98, 103, 114, 115, 122, 127, 128, 129, 150, 154, 156, 157, 192, 195, 223, 226, 227-H, 227-L, 228, 230, 234, 244, 245, 253, 260, 266, 282, 287, 314, 315, 317, 328, 334, 366, 381, 406, 421, 427, 431, 433, 437, 439, 442, 443, 455, 463, 465, 476, 480, 529, 535, 544, 549, 560, 594, 605, 612, 613, 619, 636, 637, 642, 654, 671, 682, 705, 729-B, 730, 737, 739, 740, 748, 761, 763, 798, 800, 815, 823, 831, 845, 847, 859, 860-B, 860-C, 860-D, 860-E, 860-J, 862, 866, 882, 885,

887, 890, 894, 914, 921, 922, 953, 957, 977, 1005, 1031, 1053, 1061-B, 1061-F, 1061-M, 1063, 1105, 1111, 1115, 1143, 1146, 1155, 1161, 1165, 1172, 1173, 1174, 1176, 1181, 1184, 1190, 1199, 1202, 1207, 1231, 1237, 1238, 1239, 1246, 1262, 1273, 1274, 1285, 1287, 1316, 1327, 1333, 1343, 1346, 1355, 1359, 1361, 1375, 1393, 1414, 1418, 1425, 1459, 1463, 1473, 1483, 1489, 1496, 1498, 1511, 1516, 1521, 1523, 1525, 1533, 1544, 1560, 1576, 1578, 1582, 1600, 1603, 1608, 1611, 1614, 1616, 1622, 1624, 1633, 1642. *See also* Military orchestras; Orchestral societies
Symphony Society of New York, 1063
Synagogue music. *See* Jewish music
Syracuse (N.Y.), 987, 1065
Syracuse University, 1127
Syrian and Lebanese music, 1188
Szell, George, 227-F, 357
Szell, George, Memorial Library, 1184
Szell, Helene, 357
Szigeti, Joseph, 227-F, 398, 637, 1053, 1689

T

Tabor, Horace A. W., 156
Tabor Grand Opera House, 156
Tabor Opera Theatre, 156
Tacoma (Wash.) Public Library, 1583
Taft, William Howard, 1177
Taggard, Genevieve, 907
Tagliapietra, Giovanni, 1061-F
Taheitian music, 50
Tainter, Charles Sumner, 234
Tainter, Mabel, Literary, Library & Educational Society (Menomonie, Wis.), 1614
Talbott, Clarence Elzy, 293
Talbott, Ona B., Concert Series, 427
Talbott Library, 951
Talcott, Asa, 184
Tales of Cape Cod, Inc., 673
Talking Machine World, 744
Tall, Broughton, 227-H
Talladega College, 12
Tallmadge (Ohio) Historical Society, 1236
Tama County (Iowa) Historical Society, 489
Tamburitzan Institute of Folk Arts, 1372
Tamburitzans of Duquesne University, 1372
Tamiment Library, 1062
Tamiris, Helen, Collection, 1061-A
Tamkin, David, 1580
Tams, Arthur W., 234
Tams-Witmark Collection, 227-H, 949, 951, 1611, 1612

Tamworth (N.H.), 707
Tanglewood Festivals, 227-L
Tanguay, Eva, 36
Tannahill, Robert H., Research Library, 736
Tannenberg, David, 1161
Tansman, Alexandre, 91, 227-D, 227-F
Taos Indians, 1477
Tapley, Byron, 398
Tarahumara Indians, 31
Tarleton State University, 1514
Tatton, J. Meredith, 1477
Taube, Henry, 142
Tavárez, Elisa, 1651
Tavárez, Manuel Gregorio, 1652
Taverner, Albert, 1662
Taverner, Ida Van Cortland, 1662
Taverner Company, 1662
Taylor, Albert Alfred, 227-D
Taylor, Allen, 1149
Taylor, Archer, 265, 1352
Taylor, Bayard, 1060
Taylor, Bayard, Memorial Library, 1305
Taylor, Dana Boone, 1502
Taylor, Davidson, 227-F
Taylor, Deems, 142, 227-C, 227-F, 227-L, 1053, 1061-A, 1061-B, 1646, 1666
Taylor, Ira J., Educational Resources Library, 158
Taylor, John, 294
Taylor, John Lark, 1459
Taylor, John Wright, 654
Taylor, Phoebe Bloom, 1572
Taylor, Raynor, 227-D, 701, 1333, 1338
Taylor, Jessie Coleridge, 1031
Taylor, Samuel Coleridge, 110, 142, 195-A, 195-B, 226, 636, 739, 1031, 1666
Taylor, Virgil Corydon, 406, 465
Taylor, Warren, 1459
Taylor University, 451
Tchaikovsky, Peter Ilich, 1061-J
Tcherepnin, Alexander, 227-F, 323, 334, 1580
Tcherepnin, Nicolas, 227-F
Teaching materials. *See* Instructional materials; Music education
Teachout-Price Memorial Library, 1210
Tech Show, 655
Technicord records, 227-L
Tedesco, Mario Castelnuovo, 83, 227-C, 1580
Telephone, songs about, 142, 492, 796, 1040
Television music, 28, 84, 646, 719, 1007, 1054, 1177, 1234, 1333, 1445, 1450, 1520, 1611
Telford, Mrs. W. S., 227-A
Temianka, Henry, 84, 227-F
Temperance. *See* Prohibition and temperance songs
Tempest, Marie, 1662
Temple family, 1560
Temple, Clara Wright, 787

Temple Beth El (Tonawanda, N.Y.), 1130
Temple Beth Israel (Phoenix), 23
"The Temple of Minerva," 219, 227-M
Temple of Music and Art (Tucson), 30
Temple Sinai (New Orleans), 566
Temple Theater (Colorado Springs, Colo.), 153
Temple University, 1351
Templeton, Alec, 714, 1573
Templeton (Miss.), 860-D
Ten Hage, Jean, 1176
Tennant, John, 1142
Tennessee, 15, 75, 227-K, 314, 391, 832, 1040, 1140, 1174, 1611
Tennessee Electric Power Company, Historical Source Materials, 1463
Tennessee Federation of Music Clubs, 1460
Tennessee Historical Society, 1463
Tennessee Music and Printing Company, 1440
Tennessee State Library and Archives, 1463
Tennessee Technological University, 1441
Tennessee, University of, 1448
Tenney, Joseph, 1530
Tennyson, Jean, 1061-F
Tenor horn, 1267
Tenzler, Julius, 860-K
Ternini, Milka, 1053
Terteling Library, 291
Teszler, Sandor, Library, 1426
Tetlow, Helen Ingersoll, 646
Tetrazzini Concert Company, 860-D
Teutonia Männerchor, 314, 1375
Texarkana (Tex.) Historical Society and Museum, 1516
Texas, 36, 41, 43, 49, 104, 116, 528, 971, 1076, 1174, 1264, 1462
Texas A & I University, 227, 1500
Texas Christian University, 1494
Texas Department of Music Education, Applied Music Division, 1477
Texas Federation of Music Clubs, 1477
Texas Folklore Society, 1477
Texas Music Educators' Association, 1477, 1481, 1501
Texas Music Teachers' Association, 1477
Texas State Centennial, 1502
Texas State Library, 1476
Texas State Music Festivals, 1477
Texas State Music Teachers Association, 1477
Texas Tech University, 1501
Texas, University of, 1477
Texas, University of, at San Antonio, 1512

Textile workers' songs, 742
Texts. *See* Lyrics of songs
Thacher, Jane Scotford, 1269
Thacher, W. F. Goodwin, 1269
Thacher, Howland Guild, 398
Thatcher, G. W., Jr., 1519
Thatcher, Howard, 614
Thaxter, Joseph, 663
Thayer, Alexander Wheelock, 227-E, 636, 646, 729-B
Thayer, Arthur Wilder, 227-D
Thayer, Mary A., 227-G
Theater music, 23, 59, 60, 65, 83, 84, 129, 133, 142, 168, 184, 195-B, 203, 224, 226, 227-B, 227-J, 227-L, 227-M, 236, 244, 261, 268, 315, 334, 339, 340, 349, 364, 383, 398, 441, 448, 457, 465, 480, 482, 515, 595, 636, 646, 654, 655, 691, 696, 711, 729-E, 743, 810, 823, 828, 860-G, 894, 949, 992, 1005, 1021, 1031, 1041, 1053, 1057, 1061-A, 1061-J, 1061-L, 1064, 1065, 1076, 1077, 1080, 1111, 1135, 1144, 1174, 1208, 1286, 1333, 1336, 1402, 1452, 1459, 1477, 1487, 1500, 1512, 1518, 1519, 1520, 1521, 1541, 1544, 1573, 1576, 1577, 1594, 1611, 1612, 1620, 1623, 1624, 1641, 1646, 1662, 1667
Theater music, materials concerning, 16, 36, 50, 59, 60, 65, 77, 78, 79, 83, 84, 92, 93, 100, 105, 115, 116, 122, 124, 125, 127, 129, 133, 142, 144, 145, 150, 153, 156, 167, 172, 177, 180, 182, 190, 195-B, 222, 226, 227-H, 227-L, 227-M, 234, 244, 253, 260, 265, 266, 268, 269, 298, 308, 314, 315, 334, 336, 340, 341, 345, 369, 376, 386, 387, 391, 394, 398, 400, 406, 434, 438, 450, 457, 475, 476, 498, 502, 531, 533, 624, 636, 637, 638, 654, 655, 691, 711, 712, 715, 730, 737, 738, 739, 761, 792, 800, 810, 815, 828, 831, 837, 853, 854, 855, 860-A, 860-E, 874, 887, 888, 890, 921, 949, 966, 968, 985, 1005, 1021, 1031, 1041, 1053, 1057, 1059, 1061-L, 1061-M, 1064, 1065, 1076, 1114, 1127, 1135, 1141, 1143, 1144, 1146, 1165, 1172, 1174, 1199, 1207, 1256, 1261, 1274, 1286, 1329, 1332, 1333, 1338, 1351, 1352, 1364, 1375, 1378, 1385, 1387, 1396, 1399, 1402, 1403, 1407, 1428, 1439, 1447, 1452, 1459, 1461, 1477, 1484, 1487, 1511, 1520, 1521, 1523, 1524, 1536, 1541, 1544, 1559, 1560, 1564, 1567, 1571, 1573, 1575, 1576, 1577, 1584, 1587, 1591, 1594, 1603, 1611, 1613, 1621, 1629, 1631, 1633, 1646, 1662. *See also* specific theatrical forms; Broadway; Operetta and musical comedy

Theater, Music, Dance, and Art Miscellany, 50
Theaters and auditoriums, 25, 30, 77, 78, 92, 103, 115, 122, 153, 156, 195-A, 195-B, 222, 223, 227-M, 234, 244, 253, 276, 302, 314, 315, 317, 334, 340, 341, 382, 391, 398, 400, 427, 457, 476, 482, 502, 531, 535, 544, 555, 561, 612, 636, 654, 676, 683, 688, 689, 719, 724, 729-E, 730, 738, 748, 749, 761, 763, 801, 815, 829, 853, 855, 859, 860-A, 860-C, 860-D, 860-E, 860-J, 874, 887, 902, 929, 996, 1001, 1005, 1006, 1030, 1031, 1032, 1035, 1040, 1041, 1059, 1061-A, 1061-B, 1061-L, 1061-M, 1063, 1065, 1083, 1111, 1117, 1165, 1167, 1231, 1237, 1238, 1633. *See also* Music halls; Opera houses
Theatre and Film Arts, 83
Theatre Guild, 195-B, 1057, 1286
Theatre League (Fresno, Cal.), 60
Theatre Royal (New York), 502, 1059
Theil, K., 1571
Theory of music. *See* Music theory
Theremin, 234
Theremin, Leon, 227-F
Thetford (Vt.) Historical Society, 1534
Thibodaux (La.), 544
Thiele, Robert, 930
Thielepape, W. C. A., 1205, 1509
Third Presbyterian Church (Pittsburgh), 1373
Third Regiment Band, 442
Third Street Music School (New York), 1068
Thomas, A. Goring, 866
Thomas, Augustus, 127
Thomas, Charles John, 1521
Thomas, Christopher Joseph, 1148
Thomas, David C., 1225
Thomas, Helen S., 1596
Thomas, Isaiah, 721, 907, 1333
Thomas, Ivor, 1428
Thomas, Jean, 27, 535
Thomas, Jeannette Bell, 1193
Thomas, Jessie Beattie, 860-C, 1477
Thomas, John Charles, 614
Thomas, John D., 401
Thomas, Phyllis, 1410
Thomas, Rose Fay (Mrs. Theodore), 334, 729-E
Thomas, Theodore, 195-A, 227-E, 227-F, 313, 314, 317, 334, 639, 682, 1013, 1111, 1222
Thomas, Theodore, Orchestra, 613, 1061-M
Thomas Brothers Musical Journal, 986
Thomas Library, 1235
Thompson, Mrs. (May Peterson), 1611

Thompson, Aaron, 195-B
Thompson, Edgar, 68
Thompson, Eleanor P., 568
Thompson, Frederick Ferris, Memorial Library, 1107
Thompson, Gertrude, 292
Thompson, Henry S., 701
Thompson, J. H., 860-G
Thompson, J. Jørgen, 802
Thompson, John S., 195-C
Thompson, Oscar, 227-F
Thompson, Ralph, 181
Thompson, Randall, 227-D, 227-F, 637, 654, 1053, 1111, 1292, 1301, 1541, 1580
Thompson, T. P., 15
Thompson, William Hale, 314
Thompson (Conn.), 707
"Thompson ms. songster," 707
Thompson Memorial Chapel, 719
Thomson, Virgil, 91, 142, 195-A, 195-C, 206, 227-F, 268, 340, 477, 504, 511, 847, 1018, 1031, 1053, 1061-A, 1111, 1544, 1580
Thorburn, Grant, 1059
Thoreau family, 659
Thoreau, Sophia, 659
Thoreau Collection, 658
Thorn, Edgar (Edward A. MacDowell), 918
Thorne, Frank H., 1607
Thrasher, Herbert Chandler, 1405
Three Oaks (Mich.), 743
Thuer, John, 544
Thuman, J. Herman, 1172
Thumb, General Tom, 1511
Thumb, Mrs. Tom, 1511
Thurber, Mrs. Frances B., 1061-F
Thurber Community Building, 778
Thursby, Emma, 1053, 1059
Thursday Musical Clarion (Minneapolis), 798
Thursday Musical Club (Minneapolis), 798
Thurston, Samuel, 576
Thurston School of Music, 815
Tibaldi-Chiesa, Mary, 227-F
Tibbett, Lawrence, 227-F, 1061-D
Tibbs, LeRoy, Collection, 226
Tibbs, Marie Young, 226
Tichenor, Trebor Jay, 864
Tichenor, W. C., 1172
Tickle, William Fletcher, 1665
Tidewater (Va.), 1095
Tierney, Harry, 227-D
Tietjens, Paul, 862, 866
Tietjens, Terese, 1052
Tietze family, 1285
Tilden, Louis E., Collection, 949
Tiley, Herbert, 1333
Till, Jacob, 1285
Tillamook County (Ore.) Pioneer Museum, 1278
Tillett, W. F., 1459
Tilson, Ida, 1642
Tilzer, Harry von, 739
Timm, Henry C., 1061-F

Tin Pan Alley, 654, 1031, 1066. *See also* Broadway
Tindall, Glenn, 227-F
Tinney, Charles H., Collection of Circus Band Scores, 379
Tioga County (N.Y.), 1005
Tioga Point Museum, 1282
Tiomkin, Dimitri, 85
Tippecanoe (Ind.), 1193
Tirindelli, Pietro Adolfo, 639
Tischler, Hans, 408
Titon, Jeff, 654
Titus, Dr. Edward, 1059
Tobias, Henry, 1646
Toch, Ernst, 68, 83, 84, 227-D, 227-F, 535, 1111, 1292, 1580, 1670
Toch, Lilly, 84
Todd, Charles, 227-L
Todd, Mabel Loomis, 195-B
Todd, Maria C. (Mrs. William W.), 1059
Todd, T. M., 214, 215
Toledo (Ohio), 729-B, 1167, 1200
Toledo Museum of Art, 1238
Toledo Symphony Orchestra, 1207, 1239
Toledo-Lucas County (Ohio) Public Library, 1237
Tolland (Conn.), 707
Tollefsen, Carl, 349
Tollestrup, C. F., 1521
Tolstoy, Leo, 1061-J
Tone Circle (Cherokee, Iowa), 459
Toner, Joseph Meredith, 227-M
Tonning, Gerard, 1577
Toomer, Jean, Collection, 1457
Toomey, Mrs. William C. (Gertrude Sans Souci), 815
Toothaker, Esther, 507
Tootle Lyric Theater (Saint Joseph, Mo.), 855
Topeka (Kan.) Public Library, 516
Topsham (Me.) Choral Society, 586
Torello, Anton, 1331
Toronto, 398
Toronto, University of, 1663
Torrey, Col. Jay L., 1643
Torreyson Library, 35
Toscanini, Arturo, 122, 131, 195-A, 227-A, 234, 712, 729, 819, 968, 1031, 1036, 1053, 1061-F, 1061-H, 1078, 1488
Toscanini Memorial Archive, 1061-H, 1078
Tosti, Francesco Paolo, 639
Toubman, Ray, 1155
Touring musicians, 65, 83, 103, 118, 144, 157, 163, 179, 190, 195-A, 228, 269, 276, 298, 480, 535, 544, 618, 636, 654, 683, 719, 739, 801, 802, 803, 807, 815, 829, 843, 860-B, 878, 885, 896, 951, 991, 1000, 1031, 1052, 1053, 1065, 1111, 1191, 1208, 1273, 1396, 1428, 1457, 1479, 1487, 1526, 1546, 1549, 1576, 1594, 1595, 1603, 1609, 1634, 1642, 1662, 1675

Tourjeé, Eben, 646, 664
Tourjee Club, 699
Tours, Frederick, 986
Tovian Trio, 432
Towanda (Pa.) Museum, 1384
Tower, Luther Field, 544
Town Hall (New York), 234, 1061-B
Towne, John D., 729-B
Towner, Daniel B., 333, 1394
Townes, L. A., 1061-A
Towns, George Alexander, Collection, 268
Townsend, Charles, 1480
Towson State University, 608
The Tracker, 928
Traditional music. *See* Folk music collections
"Traipsin' Woman" collection, 535
Trajetta, Filippo, 1338
Trannum, Frances (Hannah), 1463
Transcription discs and tapes, 75, 195-A, 227-L, 237, 371, 427, 646, 733, 736, 742, 942, 1049, 1061-J, 1065, 1106, 1139, 1155, 1167, 1170, 1177, 1231, 1234, 1443, 1455, 1469, 1519, 1579. *See also* Folk music collections; Radio music
Transylvania University, 528
Transportation songs, 744, 796, 861, 977. *See also* specific modes of transportation
Traubel, Helen, 227-E, 860-J
Trebel Clef Club (Milton, Wis.), 1616
Treble Clef Club (New Albany, Ind.), 437
Treble Clef Club (Washington, D.C.), 226
Treble Clef Musical Club (Battle Creek, Mich.?), 730
Treble Clefs (Newcastle, Wyo.?), 1647
Tree, Beerbohm, Collection, 636
Tree Farm Archives, 201
Tregina, Arthur, 227-D
Tremaine, Charles M., 618, 729-B
Tremblay, George, 68, 1580
Tremont Beef Steak Club, 642
Tremont Theatre, 636
Trenchs, Ramón Morlá, 1649
Trenton (N.J.), 544
Trenton Free Public Library, 953
Treville, Yvonne de, 860-D, 1061-F
Tri-State and Texas Music Festivals, 1477
Tri-State Musical Festival (Enid, Okla.), 398, 1251
Triangle Club (Princeton University), 949
Tribal music. *See* Folk music collections
Tricentennial Ball (Sandwich, Mass.), 703

Trimble, William B., 11
Trinidad (West Indies), 1352
Trinity and Cumberland Methodist Church (Charleston, S.C.), 1418
Trinity College (Hartford, Conn.), 185
Trinity College (Durham, N.C.), 1143
Trinity Episcopal Church (New Orleans), 567
Trinity Lutheran Church (Altenburg, Mo.), 835
Trinity Lutheran Seminary, 1196
Trinity Methodist Church (Urbana, Ill.), 398
Trinta, Balbino, 1650
Il Trio Florentino, 1061-F
Tripp, Ruth, 1397
Trisobio, Filippo, 1324
Trist, Nicholas Philip, 1141
Triste-Burke manuscripts, 1541
Trombone Choir of Bethlehem (Pa.), 1285
Trombones, 33, 475, 1161, 1220, 1274, 1285, 1316
Trotter, John Scott, 84, 1646
Trotter, Robert, 84
Trousdale, Annie Lauri, 1477
Troy (Ala.) State University, Library, 13
Troy (N.Y.), 1105
Trued, S. Clarence, 1270
Truesdell, Ephraim, 1069
Truette, Everett E., 636, 1244
Truman, Harry S., 843, 1025
Truman, Harry S., Library, 843
Truman, Margaret, 843
Trumbull, Benjamin, 127
Trumpets, 486, 560, 707, 874, 1270. See also Cornets
Tuba music, 215, 1267
Tucker, George, 1445
Tucker, Henry, 1040
Tucker, Richard, 1025
Tucker, Sophie, 1061-L, 1208
Tuckerman, Samuel Parkman, 648
Tuesday Club of Annapolis (Md.), 606
Tuesday Music Club (Great Falls, Mont.), 873
Tuesday Music Club (Manistee, Mich.), 764
Tuesday Musical Club (Pittsburgh), 1359, 1374
Tuesday Musical Club (Port Townsend, Wash.), 1572
Tuesday Musicale (Detroit), 739
Tuesday Musicale (International Falls, Minn.), 786
Tuesday Musicale (Fort Omaha, Neb.), 879
Tuesday Musicale (Rochester, N.Y.), 1111
Tufts, Asa Alford, 679
Tufts College, 1107
Tufts University, 679
Tuit, Mr. & Mrs. Frank E., II, 177
Tulane University, 564, 568

Tully, Alice, Library, 1344
Tulsa (Okla.), 36
Tulsa Chamber of Commerce, 1256
Tulsa (Okla.) Indian Exposition, 1256
Tulsa County (Okla.) Historical Society, 1262
Tunbridge (Mass.), 977
Tunebooks. See Hymnals and tunebooks
Tuolumne County (Cal.) Museum, 141
Tureaud, Benjamin, Papers, 544
Tureck, Rosalyn, 637, 1061-F
Turkin, Marshall, 410
Turn und Gesang Verein (Boonville, Mo.), 837
Turnblad Society, 794
Turnbull, Edwin Litchfield, 606
Turnbull, Grace, 606
Turner, Alfred Dudley, 227-D
Turner, Althea Snider, 465
Turner, George E., 157
Turner, Godfrey, 227-D, 1580
Turner, William G. A., 227-H
Turner Hall (New Ulm, Minn.), 801
Turner Society, 837
Turner Society Pamphlets, 837
Turnham, Floyd, 68
Turnverein (Seattle), 1577
Turnvereine, 1577, 1681
Turrentine, Walter W., Sr., 1143
Turtle Bay Music School, 1058
Tuscaloosa (Ala.), 11, 15
Tuscarawas County (Ohio) Historical Society, 1220
Tuskegee Institute, 14
Tuthill, Burnet C., 227-C, 227-F, 1453, 1580
Tuthill, Burnet C., Library, 618
Tutors. See Instructional materials
Tuttle, Ada Alice, 1611
Twain, Mark, 839, 860-C
Twain, Mark, Birthplace, 871
Twain, Mark, Home & Museum, 839
Twain, Mark, Memorial, 186
Tweedy, Donald, 1111
Twichell, Mrs Burton, 195-C
Two-step, 544, 1061-N
Twyman, Mrs. W. G., 1502
Tydings, Senator Millard, 616
Tyler, Charles Ives, 195-C
Tyler, George, 195-C
Tyler, Gerald, 226
Tyler, Harry Linwood, 984
Typewriter manufacturer, 1001
Tyrolese singers, 863

U

UAW (United Auto Workers), 742
UCLA, 74, 84
Ufford, Edward S., 950
Uhler, John E., Sr., 544
Ukelin music, 510
Ukrainian music, 800, 1352

Ukulele music, 92, 1016, 1611
Ullman, Bernard, 1174
Ulman Opera House, 1395
Ulrich, Eugene J., 1232
Umlauf, C. J. F., 398
Uncle Tom's Cabin, 184
Unger, Claude W., Collection, 1338
Unger, Lillie Balmer (Mrs. Charles), 860-B, 860-D
Unger, Max, 1025
Union Brass Band (Marysville, Ohio), 1193
Union Chorus (Hartford, Conn.), 180
Union City (Tenn.), 1174
Union College, 654, 1118
Union County (Ohio) Historical Society, 1216
Union Evangelical Church (Greenville, Me.), 591
Union of American Hebrew Congregations, Committee on Synagogue Music, 1174
Union Theological Seminary, 825, 1070
Union Village (Ohio), 227-M, 1214
Unions, 50, 136, 227-A, 227-H, 227-L, 529, 558, 568-B, 729-B, 737, 742, 806, 843, 845, 985, 1006, 1020, 1042, 1182, 1190, 1274, 1375, 1463, 1466, 1480, 1591, 1601, 1611
Unitarian music, 331, 1115
Unite Club (Cincinnati?), 1172
United Artists Corp., 1611
United Auto Workers, 742
United Brethren Band (Columbus, Ind.), 434
United Brethren music. See Evangelical-United Brethren music
United Lutheran Church in America, 330
United Methodist music. See Methodist music
United Methodist Publishing House Library, 1464
United Neighborhood Houses, 800
United Society of Shakers, 593
United Service Organization, 227-H
United States Air Force Museum, 1198
United States Army, 874, 1135
United States Army Bands, 465, 761, 1127, 1288
United States Army Corps, 23rd, 2nd Brigade, 3rd Division, 1190
United States Army Military History Institute, 1288
United States Army-Air Force Band, 618
United States Army-Air Force Symphony, Troop Carrier Command, 99
United States Constitutional Centennial Commission, 1338
United States Department of Commerce, 490

United States Forest Service, 135
United States Infantry Band, 5th Regiment, 815
United States Infantry, 21st, 815
United States Infantry, 45th, 1257
United States Information Service, 1672
United States Marine Bands, 227-E, 228, 229, 234, 389, 1061-M, 1274
United States Marine Corps Museum, 229
United States Marine Orchestra, 228
United States Military Academy, 1135
United States National Archive, 230
United States Naval Academy, Museum, 602
United States Navy, 602
United States Navy Bands, 231, 232, 1106
United States Navy Orchestra, 232
United States Volunteer Cavalry, 2nd Regiment, 1643
United States Works Progress Administration. See WPA
United Swedish Singers of the Pacific Coast, 1577
United Theological Seminary (Dayton, Ohio), 1201
Unity Church (Chicago), 598
Universal Exposition (St. Louis, 1904), 460, 860-C
Universal piano rolls, 1333
Universalist Historical Society, 654
Universalist music, 331
Universalist Sacred Music Society (Cincinnati), 1112
Université Laval, 1660
University Artist Course (Minneapolis), 798
University of the Pacific, 145
University of the South, 1467
University Opera Company, 1520
University Settlement (New York), 800
University Settlement Records, 1190
Unnewehr, Jean, 1168
Untermeyer, Louis, 195-C
Upper Alton (Ill.), 334
Upper Room Devotional Library and Museum, 1465
Upsala College, 925, 1666
Upton, George P., 314, 334
Upton, James, 701
Upton, William Treat, 227-E, 227-F
Urban, Joseph, 1031
Urchs, Ernest, 227-G
Ursuline Convent (New Orleans), 549, 556
Urteaga, Juan, 1650
Usingen (Germany), 1683
Ussachevsky, Vladimir, 195-C, 1031, 1111

Ussher, Bruno David, 227-F
U.S.S. *Pocahontas*, 612
Utah, 291, 1270
Utah State Historical Society, 1524
Utah State University, 1519
Utah, University of, 1190, 1523
Utah, University of, Collection of Folk Songs ,1523
Ute Indians, 162, 1520
Utica (N.Y.), 987
Utica Männerchor, 1133
Utter, Ann H., 1006

V

"V-discs," 942
Vacher, Sgt. Eugene D., 1572
Vactor, David Van, 227-F, 443, 1111, 1666
Vagabondia (Ky.), 1270
Vail, George M., 1098
Vail, James, 195-A
Valda, Giulia Cameron, 544
Valdez (Alaska) Historical Society, 19
Valentine, Edward, 1559
Valentine, Mae, 334
Valentine, Mrs. Rodman S., 195-C
Valentine Museum, 1559
Valiant, Margaret, 227-L, 831
Vallamont Park Pavilion, 1393
Vallee, Rudy, 1487
Vallier, Jacque D., 1627
Valssi, 795
Valva, Fred D., Collection, 949
Valve Herald instruments, 487
Van, Guillaume de, 1676
Van Alstyne, John, 1061-L
Van Black, Amy, 1162
Van Broekhoven, John Andrew, 1226
Van Buren, Alicia, 535
Van Buren, Lotta, 1520
Van Cleave, Nathan, 1646
Van Cliburn International Piano Competition, 1494
Van Den Akker, Nancy C., 570
Van der Stucken, Frank, 729-E, 1111, 1176
Van Derlip, John R., 815
Van Doveren, Jo, 379
Van Dresser, Marcia, 646, 1061-M
Van Dyke, Gerald M. 1256
Van Dyke Bingham, Walter, 1360
Van Etten, I., 356
Van Heusen, Jimmy, 1579
Van Hoogstraten, Willem, 84
Van Horn, LeRoy, 315
Van Hulse, Camil, 227-D
Van Katwijk, Paul, 1487
Van Noy, William Ray, 1521
Van Pelt Library, 1352
Van Ravenswaay, Charles, 860-B, 860-D
Van Schaack, P., Jr., 707
Van Slyck, Nicholas, 398
Van Surdam, Henderson E., 190
Van Vactor, David, 227-F, 443, 1111, 1666

Van Vechten, Carl, 227-F, 739, 1061-L, 1457
Van Vleck, C. A., 1285
Van Wart, Charlotte Irving, 1128
Van Westerhout, N., 398
Van Vleck, C. A., 1285
Van Wart, Charlotte Irving, 1128
Van Westerhout, N., 398
Van Wyck, Amelia, 195-C
Van Wye, Ralph A., 1172
Vanderbilt University, 1459
Vandercook College of Music, 342
Vandergriff, Raleigh, 434
VanderKiste, Anna Edna, 406
Vann, R. D., 815
VanVolkenburg-Browne Collection, 729-E
Vardaman, John Forsythe, 1
Vardaman Gwin Collection, 1
Vartanian, Leon, 636
Vasa Glee Club (Seattle), 1577
Vashti Rogers Griffin Collection, 115
Vassar College, 679, 1107
Vassariana Collection, 1107
Vaudeville, 144, 234, 298, 383, 391, 457, 475, 476, 502, 655, 730, 750, 985, 1006, 1031, 1049, 1080, 1127, 1167, 1172, 1407, 1477, 1484, 1511, 1520, 1611, 1655, 1662, 1667. See also Burlesque; Theater music
Vaudeville Club (Cincinnati), 1172
Vaughan, John B., 265
Vaughan Williams, Ralph, 951
Vaughn, James D., 1440
Vavpetich, Rudolph, 860-D
Vawter (i.e., Redpath-Vawter) Bureau, 476
Vaxer, Menache, 1402
"V-discs," 942
Veasy, C. A., Jr., 1573
Veazy (Vesey), Maria R., 1031
Vechten, Carl van, 227-F, 739, 1061-L, 1457
Vechten, Carl van, 227-F, 739, 1061-L, 1457
Vengerova, Isabelle, 227-F
Venth, Carl, 227-D, 1477
Verdi, Giuseppe, 1061-F
Verein zum Schutze deutscher Einwanderer (Texas), 1477
Vereinigung fur Volkstum und Heimat, 1677
Vergennes (Vt.) Band, 1526, 1529
Vermont, 270, 379, 707, 721, 906, 1329
Vermont Historical Society, 1530
Vermont House of Representatives, 721
Vermont Music Journal, 1530
Vermont Musical Bulletin, 1530
Vermont Symphony Orchestra, 1525
Vermont, University of, 1525

Vernon County (Mo.) Historical Society, 851
Vernor, F. Dudleigh, 725
Verplanck, Mrs. William, 195-C
Verplanck, William, Jr., 195-C
Verrall, John, 227-F, 1576
Very, L. L. A., 701
Vesey (Veazy), Maria R., 1031
Vessella's Italian Band, 618
Vesterheim Norwegian-American Museum, 462
Veteran Association of the First Corps of Cadets, 637
Vezin family, 270
Vial, Mary M., Library, 1222
Vianesi, Auguste, 1053
Vick, Robert E., 227-D
Victor, Harry, 1166
Victor Corp., 104, 170, 443, 654, 786, 1129, 1353, 1520, 1531, 1640, 1665
Victor Talking Machine Co., 195-B, 210, 398, 618, 1061-J
Victor v. George (law suit), 1270
Victoria, Queen, 1670
Victoria, University of, 1665
Victoria University, Library, 1664
Victrola records, 460, 471, 853
Victrola (Camden) Co., 1395
Video tapes. See Films and video tapes on music subjects
Vienna (Austria), 131
Viereck, J. C., 555, 1061-A
Vietnamese music, 305
Vignaud, Henry, Papers, 544
Vigo County (Ind.) Public Library, 450
Vikoren, Ole, 883
Villa Pauline (N.Y.), 1078
Villard, Oswald Garrison, 654
Vinatieri, Felix, 1435, 1436, 1437
Vinatieri, Villiet, 1435
Vincent, John, 84, 227-F
Vincent, Matthew, 701
Vincentown (N.J.) Band, 939
Vineyard (Mass.) Public Library, 710
Viola music, 36, 379, 1111
Violano piano rolls, 750
Violette, Wesley La, 227-D, 227-F, 323
Violin (general materials), 50, 167, 226, 268, 349, 398, 421, 475, 487, 549, 583, 612, 689, 729-B, 730, 792, 815, 847, 860-D, 860-H, 885, 887, 898, 917, 1031, 1059, 1127, 1338, 1418, 1463, 1475, 1477, 1572, 1574, 1584, 1596, 1609, 1611, 1634. See also Fiddles
Violin instruction books, 204, 390, 460, 787, 887, 987, 1558, 1609
Violin makers and repairers, 167, 244, 671, 729-B, 847, 887, 894, 1051, 1075, 1253, 1323
Violin music, 7, 17, 36, 195-A, 209, 227-B, 227-G, 227-J,

345, 349, 369, 398, 460, 630, 728, 729-D, 838, 885, 888, 1046, 1061-A, 1082, 1111, 1127, 1141, 1185, 1275, 1276, 1359, 1516, 1540, 1628, 1634, 1660, 1665
Violoncello, 57, 443, 471, 860-D, 1148, 1327, 1609
Violoncello music, 7, 195-A, 203, 206, 642, 941, 1148
Virginia, 127, 213, 227-K, 227-L, 398, 544, 612, 721, 1061-A, 1111, 1141, 1225, 1352, 1477
Virginia (Minn.), 1633
Virginia Baptist Historical Society, 1558
Virginia City-Madison County (Mont.) Historical Museum, 877
Virginia City (Nev.), 50
Virginia Folklore Society, 227-L
Virginia Historical Society, 1560
Virginia Infantry, Fifth Regiment, 1563
Virginia Infantry, 13th, 1591
Virginia Military Institute, 1443
Virginia Minstrels, 1541
Virginia Normal Music School, 1560
Virginia Players, 1541
Virginia Polytechnic Institute and State University, 1554
Virginia State Committee for Rural School Music, 1560
Virginia State Library, 1561, 1563
Virginia State University, 1555
Virginia, University of, 1541, 1560
Virginia, University of, Clinch Valley College, 1568
Virginia, University of, Glee Club, 1541
Visiting cards. See Postcards
Vista recordings, 54
Vista, Buena (Mrs. Wallace Atkinson), 475
Vitaphone recordings, 371
Vivaldi Orchestra (Dallas), 148
Vleck, C. A. van, 1285
Vocal Club (Northampton, Mass.), 688
Vocal instruction. See Singing instruction materials
Vocal music collections, 33, 55, 126, 129, 137, 142, 168, 173, 195-A, 207, 216, 227-A, 227-G, 227-J, 227-L, 228, 256, 260, 305, 326, 334, 340, 354, 364, 369, 391, 398, 409, 412, 433, 455, 460, 487, 496, 497, 502, 507, 508, 517, 533, 535, 540, 569, 606, 636, 646, 654, 667, 689, 729-E, 749, 767, 773, 786, 798, 802, 819, 838, 860-F, 862, 866, 885, 889, 891, 896, 953, 957, 973, 1046, 1061-A, 1061-C, 1061-D, 1061-J, 1070, 1077, 1080, 1082, 1111, 1138, 1143,

1161, 1194, 1199, 1200, 1252, 1270, 1285, 1289, 1315, 1323, 1327, 1333, 1338, 1352, 1359, 1364, 1375, 1402, 1407, 1411, 1428, 1446, 1493, 1518, 1522, 1541, 1557, 1604, 1611, 1615, 1623, 1632, 1649, 1650, 1673. *See also* Choral music collections

Vocal Society (Cleveland), 1076

Vocal technique, 646, 1340

Vodery, William H., 195-B

Voegeli, Henry E., 314

Vogan, Charles E., 1553

Vogel, Guido B., 860-B

Vogelpohl & Sons organs, 801

Vogelpohl & Spaeth organs, 801

Vogrich, Max Wilhelm Karl, 227-D

Vogt, Augustus, 1053

"Voice of Firestone," 646

Voitier, Regina Morphy, 544

Volkoff, Boris, 1662

Vollintine, Edward, 398

Volpe, Arnold, 227-F, 1666

Von Meister, Leila, 646

Von Tilzer, Harry, 739

Voorsanger, Elkan, 1174

Vorhees, Donald, 1007

Vose, Edwin, 654

Voskuyl Library, 132

Vosseller, Elizabeth Van Fleet, 926

Voto, Alfred de, 1080

Vox Populi, 676

Vreede, Max E., 1667

Vrooman, Mrs. V., 896

Vulliet, A., 406

W

Wa Wan Society of America, 1261

Wabnitz, William S., 1172

Waco (Tex.), 104

Wade, Walter, 1607

Wadleigh High School, 226

Wadleigh Memorial Library, 915

Wadsworth, Joseph B., 707

Wagenaar, Bernard, 227-D, 227-F, 317, 1111

Wagmaster, Joseph W., 1172

Wagner, Abraham, 1325

Wagner, Charles Ludwig, 227-F

Wagner, Jacob, 406

Wagner, Joseph Frederick, 227-F

Wagner, Richard, 334, 642

Wagness, Olive, 786

Wahlert, Jennie, 860-K

Wainwright, John ("Jack"), 618

Waite, Clifford L. 190

Waite, Eliza Jane, 195-A

Waite, Isaac, 195-A

Waite, William, 195-C

Waitsburg (Wash.) Historical Society, 1585

Waldauer, August, 860-C, 860-D

Walden, Sylvia, 860-E

Waldman, Frederic, 1031

Waldron, Laura, 1143

Walker family, 1193

Walker, Barclay, 406

Walker, George Wesley, 625

Walker, Dr. James, 156

Walker, John D., 50

Walker, Joseph B., 227-M

Walker, Mae Ross, 1274

Walker, Pearl White, 306

Walker, William, 1422, 1425

Wallace, Lila Acheson, Library, 1046

Wallace, Oliver G., 1646

Wallace, Virginia Buckley, 314

Wallace, William Ross, 314

Wallace, William Vincent, 1477, 1520

Wallach, Sid, 866

Wallenstein, Alfred, 68, 227-F, 729-E

Wallenstein, Alfred, Collection, 618

Waller, Henry, 531

Waller, Thomas ("Fats"), 226

Wallerstedt Learning Center, 505

Wallerstein, Anton, 406

Wallgren Library, 335

Wallis, Hal, 88

Wallkill Precinct (N.Y.), 1016

Wallop, Lucille Fletcher, 195-C

Walls, Callie King, 1172

Walmsley, J. E., 1423

Walnut Grove (farm), 391

Walter, Bruno, 131, 227-F, 227-H, 340, 357, 1025, 1031, 1053, 1061-B, 1061-F, 1580

Walter, Bruno, Memorial Foundation, 1061-B

Walter, Bruno, Microfilm Collection, 227-H

Walter, Julius, 1274

Walter, Lotte, 357

Walter, Thomas, 195-A, 601, 628

Walter, William E., 636

Walters, Gibson, 309

Walters, Harold L., 36

Walters, Joseph Josiah, 226

Walthers, Ferdinand H., 860-C

Walton, Clarence, 1554

Walton, Ivan, 729-B

Walton, Ivan, Collection, 727

Walton, Julia A., 730

Walton, Mary Elizabeth, 636

Waltz, 195-A, 374, 379, 582, 636, 721, 789, 836, 843, 850, 860-F, 895, 947, 986, 1031, 1135, 1207, 1249, 1282, 1291, 1550, 1651, 1673. *See also* Dance

"Waltz, Spring in Norfolk," 195-A

Walworth County (Wis.) Historical Society, 1602

Wanamaker's store (Philadelphia), 1385

Wannamaker, William Hane, 1143

Wansborough, Harold, 406

War Department Collection of Revolutionary War Records, 230

War of 1812, 721

War songs, 68, 142, 195, 227-A, 227-M, 296, 354, 386, 406, 442, 461, 467, 475, 531, 544, 624, 636, 652, 721, 744, 800, 815, 850, 860-G, 920, 973, 977, 1006, 1008, 1059, 1141, 1146, 1155, 1208, 1232, 1463, 1673. *See also* specific wars; Military music; Military songs

Warburg, Felix, 1174

Ward, Anna Hazard Barker, 654

Ward, Charlotte B., 398

Ward, Edward, 84

Ward, Harriet Lucia, 1270

Ward, Joe E., Collection, 1477

Ward, Joseph, 544

Ward & Gow, 654

Ward-Belmont Conservatory of Music, 1459

Wardlow, Gayle Dean, 830

Wardwell, Hosea, 587

Ware, Catherine Ann, 544

Ware, C. P., 1095

Ware, Eleanor Percy, 544

Ware, Harriet, 1061-A, 1621

Ware, W. Porter, 1468

Warhurst, James Clayton, 920

Warner, A. J., 1111

Warner, Anne, 1095

Warner, Frank M., 1095

Warner, Jack, 88

Warner, Lydia C., 1338

Warner, Massah, 1285

Warner Brothers Films, 1611

Warner Brothers Orchestral Library, 847

Warren, Barney, 405

Warren, Harry, 1024, 1487

Warren, Harry, collection, 84

Warren, Henry, 314

Warren, Louis A., Lincoln Library and Museum, 413

Warren, Samuel Prowse, 227-E, 227-F, 227-H, 1244

Warren, William, II, 226

Warren, William L., 905

Warren (Pa.) Public Library, 1388

Warren County (Ohio) Historical Society Museum, 1214

Warren County (Pa.) Historical Society, 1387

Warrington, James, 183

Warrington Collection, 183, 269, 1369

Warroad (Minn.), 787

Warshaw, Isadore, 234

Wart, Charlotte Irving van, 1128

Wartburg Theological Seminary, 466

Washburn, Joseph, 195-B

Washburn, Watson, 195-C

Washburn University, 517

Washington family, collection, 227-G

Washington, Anne, 1537

Washington, George, 127, 314, 935

Washington, George, Masonic Museum, 1537

Washington, Leon, 1031

Washington (D.C.), 721, 815, 1111, 1426

Washington Cathedral Library, 235

Washington Choral Society, 227-H

Washington Conservatory of Music, 226

Washington Music Teachers Association, 226

Washington (Mo.), 398, 837, 847

Washington (State), 144, 1031

Washington State Capitol Historical Association, 1571

Washington State Historical Society, 1584

Washington State University, 1573

Washington, University of, 1577

Washington Benevolent Society of Massachusetts, 707

Washington County (Ky.) Historical Society, 541

Washington County (Neb.) Historical Association, 878

Washington County (Wis.) Historical Association, 1641

Washington Park (Ill.), 315

Washington University (St. Louis), 866

Washingtoniana Division, D.C. Public Library, 223

Wasner, Franz, 227-D

Wasson, D. DeWitt, 1092

Watauga County (N.C.), 1095, 1140

Watergate Concerts, 223

Waterhouse, Dorothy, 651

Waters, Edward N., 227-F

Waters, Ethel, 227-E

Watertown (Wis.), 1161, 1285

Watertown Historical Society, 1634

Watertown Musical Society, 1611

Watertown Public Library, 1635

Waterville (Me.) Historical Society, 599

Watkins, Carrie M., 314

Watkins, Doris John, 163

Watkins, Elizabeth M., Community Museum, 503

Watkins, R. B., 1367

Watkinson Library, 185

Watonwan County (Minn.) Historical Society, 789

Watson, Doc, 1445

Watson, Joseph, 227-D, 1420

Watsonville (Cal.) Band, 146

Watt, W. E., 398

Watts, H. Wintter, 227-F

Watts, Isaac, 67, 622, 658, 834, 1347, 1402, 1465, 1536

Watts, Llewellyn 936

Waukegan (Ill.), 400

Waukegan Historical Society, 401

Waukesha County (Wis.) Historical Museum, 1637

Waxman, Franz, 227-D, 1127

Wayland, John W., 1539
Wayland (Mass.) Free Public Library, 715
Wayles, John, 1541
Wayne (Mich.) Historical Commission, 773
Wayne State University, 742
Waynesburg College, 1389
WBAP (radio station, Fort Worth, Tex.), 1488
WCTU (Women's Christian Temperance Union), 356, 729-B, 1614
Weatherford-Hammond Appalachian Collection, 522
Weaver, Mary, 847
Weaver, Powell, 847
Weaver, Thomas, 847
Webb, Alice, 544
Webb, Emma, 1031
Webb, Frank Rush, 612
Webb, George James, 195-A, 636
Webber, Amherst, 639
Webber, Asa, 633
Webber, Buhamah, 633
Webber, F. R., 856
Webber, Harold A., 1274
Webber Academy of Music, 1274
Webber's Juvenile Orchestra, 1274
Webber's Juvenile Wranglers, 1274
Webber's Melodyphiends, 1274
Weber family (Nashville), 1463
Weber, Alice Lytle, 157
Weber, Carl Maria von, 1113
Weber, Eunice D., 976
Weber, Hannah, 1285
Weber, Henry, 1463
Weber, Johann, 860-K
Weber, Joseph M., 1061-L
Weber, Lisa, 1364
Weber, T. R., 1323
Webern, Anton, 654
Webern Archive, 1580
Webster, Bert, 1221
Webster, Beveridge, 1359
Webster, Mrs. Beveridge, 1359
Webster, Frederick, 1602
Webster, Joseph Philbrick, 314, 1602, 1611, 1612
Webster, Margret, 227-M
Webster, Paul F., 1127
Webster County (Iowa), 465
Wedding music, 860-G
Wednesday Afternoon Musical Club (Bridgeport, Conn.?), 173
Wednesday Morning Music Club (Austin, Tex.), 1476
Wesnesday Morning Musicale (Nashville), 1463
Wednesday Musical Club (Ann Arbor, Mich.), 729
Weeks, David, and family, papers, 544
Weeks, Eliakim, 1529
Weeping Water (Neb.) Little Symphony Orchestra, 894
Weeping Water (Neb.) Municipal Band, 894

Wegatchie Band, 980
Wegener, William, 1611, 1626
Wehrman, H. J., 1614
Wehrmann imprints, 556
Wehrmann, Henri, 544, 555, 568
Wehrmann, Henry, 568
Weidig, Adolf, 227-D, 317, 334
Weigand, Emil, 1176
Weigel, Eugene, 1580
Weigl, Karl, 1061-A, 1061-M, 1071, 1580
Weigl, Vally, 195-C, 1071, 1580
Weil, Oscar, 50
Weil's Band, 860-C
Weill, Kurt, 195-B, 227-B, 227-F, 1072, 1073
Weill, Kurt, Foundation, 1073
Weill-Detwiler, Lotte Lenya, 1072
Weinberger, Jaromir, 317, 1580
Weiner, Hal, 79
Weiner, Lazar, Archive, 1076
Weingartner, W., 406
Weinzweig, John, 1111
Weisgall, Hugo, 227-D, 606, 1018, 1580
Weisgarber, Elliot, 1148
Weiss, Adolph, 227-F, 1111, 1580
Weiss, Caspar, 948
Weiss, Georg, 948, 1325
Weissheimer, Marie, 1190
Welch (collector for Thos. A. Edison), 744
Welch, Roy Dickinson, 227-F
Welch, Walter L., 1127
Weld, Arthur, 1031, 1611
Welhafin, Fridrika, 406
Welles, Orson, 1544
Wellesley College, 716, 1005
Wellford, Ida Dulaney (Beverley), 1560
Wellman (Iowa), 416
Wells, Evelyn, 538
Wells, Gilbert, 465
Wells, W. G., 860-D
Welsh music, 163, 498, 574, 980, 1132, 1612
Welte-Mignon piano rolls, 1333
Wendall, 701
Wendell, Evert J., 654
Wendover, Jessie May, 939
Wennerburg Choral Society, 794
WENR (radio station, Chicago), 1194
Wenrich, Percy, 843, 868
Wentz, Abdel Ross, Library, 1296
Werfel, Alma Mahler, 1352
Werlein, Philip, Co., 544, 555, 558, 568
Werlein's for Music, 571
Werner, Eric, 1074, 1174
Werner, James Ritter, 1172
Werner, Leon L., 614
Werrenrath, Reinald, 123, 1573
Werthner, Mrs. Dell Kendall, 1172
Wertmüller (i.e., Henderson-Wertmüller) Papers, 1338

Wescott, D., 227-D
Wesley family, 834, 844
Wesley, Charles, 227-D
Wesley, John, 269
Wesley, Samuel, 1465
Wesleyan Methodist Church of America, 1413
Wesleyan University, 190
Wesleyana Collection, 269, 1413
Wessell, Nils Yngve, Library, 679
Wesson, Isabel, 636
West, Hedy, 1445
West, James, 671
West, John, 403
West, Julia Houston, 671
West Bay City (Mich.), 729-B
West Chester State College, 1391
West Chicago Historical Museum, 403
West Georgia College, 275
West Indies, 1323, 1352
West Liberty (Iowa) Band, 465
West Orange (N.J.), 395
West Point (N.Y.), 314, 729-A
West Point Bands, 1135
West Point Museum, 1135
West Salem (Wis.), 1611
West Salem (Wis.) Historical Society, 1642
West Texas Gebirgs-Sängerbund, 1505
West Texas Hill Singing Society, 1477
West Texas State University, 1480, 1481
West Virginia, 227-K, 630, 1095, 1352
West Virginia and Regional History Collection, 1591
West Virginia Department of Culture and History, 1590
West Virginia Folklore Society, 1591
West Virginia Music Educators Association, 1591
West Virginia State Fair, 1591
West Virginia University, 1591
Westborough (Mass.), 643
Westbrooke, Virginia, 568
Westcott, Thompson, 1338
Westerhout, N. van, 398
Westerly (R.I.) Historical Society, 1408
Westerly Public Library, 1409
Western Americana Collection, 195-B, 949
Western and west-coast U.S., 84, 118, 122, 124, 145, 150, 156, 157, 161, 195-B, 234, 476, 836, 866, 874, 1260, 1501, 1520, 1643
Western College Archives, 1223
Western Hennepin County (Minn.) Pioneers Association, 788
Western Historical Manuscript Collection, 837, 865
Western History Department, 156
Western Illinois University, 369

Western Jewish History Center, 48
Western Kentucky Folklore Archive, 84
Western Kentucky University, 523
Western Michigan University, 761
Western Musical Convention (1852), 860-E
Western New York Historical Collection, 970
Western New York Musical Association, 977
Western Reserve Historical Society, 1190
Western State College, 157
Western (i.e., Seabury-Western) Theological Seminary, 357
Western Theological Seminary of the Reformed Church of America, 759
Western Vermont Musical Association, 1529
Western Washington University, 1569
Westervelt, George C., 1222
Westervelt, Harman C., 1061-M
Westervelt, Leonidas, 1059
Westfield (Vt.), 721
Westlund, Bernhardt H., 1617
Westminster Choir, 1611
Westminster Choir (Dayton, Ohio), 432, 951
Westminster Choir College, 951
Westminster Choir School (Ithaca, N.Y.), 1006, 1007
Westmont College, 132
Weston (Vt.), 1530
Westphal, Gustavus A., 815
Westwood (N.J.) Musical Club, 939
Wethersfield (Conn.) Historical Society, 208
Wetmore, Dr., 970
Weyerhauser Library, 814
Weyman, Wesley, 1061-F
Weymouth (Mass.), 916
Weymouth Choral Society, 916
WFAA (radio station, Dallas), 1488
WFMT (radio station, Chicago), 338
WFPK-FM (radio station, Louisville), 533
WGN (radio station, Chicago), 398
Whaley, Carroll, 391
Wharton, Edward Clifton, Family Papers, 544
Wheat, John Thomas, 1141
Wheat, Leo P. (Leonidas Polk), 227-H, 1141
Wheatland, Stephen, 701
Wheaton (Ill.), 307
Wheaton (Ill.) College, 404
Wheaton (Mass.) College, 694
Wheaton (Mass.) Female Seminary, 694
Wheeler, Andrew C., 1059

Wheeler, Henry R., 695
Wheeler, J. W., 1533
Wheeler, Olin Dunbar, 815
Wheeler, Roger, 1031
Wheeling Sunday News (W.Va.), 1591
Wheelock, Mrs. Frank E., 1501
Wheelwright, Mary Cabot, 964
Wheelwright Museum of the American Indian, 973
Wheildon, Frederic Wilder, 636
Wheildon, William W., 646
Whiffenpoofs, 195-A, 195-B
Whipper, Leigh, 1061-N
Whistlers, 573
Whitaker, Lilla Seeligson, 1510
White, Mrs. Andrew Strong (Claire Alcée), 1005
White, Bukka, 1451
White, Clarence Cameron, 195-B, 226, 227-F, 268, 1061-N, 1546
White, Edward H., Collection, 949
White, Edward L., 701
White, Esther Griffin, 444
White, Garry, 68
White, Glenn, 1480
White, James, Library, 732
White, John G., Collection, 1185
White, Lew, 1061-F
White, Paul, 1111, 1148
White, Peter, 958
White, Mrs. R. Leon, 1477
White, Richard Grant, 1059
White, Richard Ross, 1560
White, Suza Doane, 636
White, Willy, 227-D
White House, 424, 490
White House, Office of Social Correspondence, 843
White Mountains Collection, 907
White Top Folk Festival, 1141
White-Sheetz Publishing Co., 454, 455
Whiteface. *See* Minstrelsy
Whitefield House, 1323
Whiteley, Bessie M., 227-D
Whiteman, James G., 1338
Whiteman, Paul, 227-F, 719, 1061-D
Whiteman Collection, 719
White's Scandals, 1061-L
Whithorne, Emerson, 227-D, 227-F, 1061-A, 1111
Whiting, Arthur, 227-D, 227-F, 1053, 1061-A, 1061-B, 1061-D, 1080
Whiting, George, 636
Whitley Opera House, 498
Whitman, Samuel, 180
Whitman, Walt, 1402
Whitmark Library, 195-A
Whitmer, Thomas Carl, 227-D, 646, 866, 1107, 1359
Whitmore, Alice Barber, 344
Whitney, Andrew, 665
Whitney, David, 943
Whitney, Jean, 1315
Whitney, Robert S., 535
Whittaker, Howard, 1058
Whittaker, James, 314

Whittall, Gertrude Clarke, 227-F
Whitten, Willie May (Mrs. James H.), 266
Whittier, John Greenleaf, 701, 1338
Whittingham, Rev. William R., 612
Whittingham (Vt.), 707
Whittle, Major D. W., 333
Whittlesey, Eliza, 199
Whittlesey, Henry, 200
Whittlesey, John, 200
Whittlesey, Karolyn Bradford, 180
Whittlesey, Orramel, 180, 199, 200
Whittlesey, Walter B., 1577
Whorf, Mike, 1024
Who's Who in America, 1061-B
Wichita (Kan.) Public Library, 519
Wichita State University, 519
Wichita Mountain (Okla.) Easter Pageant, 1256
Wichmann family (Berlin, Ger.), 1468
Wichmann, Theodore, 1414
Wick-Blachly-Colles papers, 1061-M
Wickham, Florence, 1052, 1061-A
Wickizer, Tom, 1262
Widener Library, 654
Widmeyer, Charles Brenton, 113
Wiegand, John, 227-D
Wiggin, Kate Douglas, 227-B
Wiggin, Lucy A., 860-D
Wiggins, Eugene, 277
Wiggins (Colo.) Beethoven Club, 165
Wiggs, Johnny, 1450
Wikoff, Dr. James, 947
Wilbur Collection of Vermontiana, 1525
Wilcox, Fannie M., 1476
Wilcox, Glenn, 536
Wilcox, John C., 157
Wilcox, Library, 484
Wilde, August E., 1172
Wilder, Alexander, 1111
Wildermuth, Judge Ora L., 406
Wiley, Annie L., 1338
Wiley, Dewey O., 1501
Wiley, Larry, 901
Wilgus, D. K., 84, 523, 1352
Wilgus Opera House, 1006
Wilke, Lucille, 68
Wilkin, Lucile K., 636, 721
Wilkins, Harold A., 1268
Wilkins, Raymond Sanger, 654
Wilkinson, Crowell, 940
Wilkinson, Winston, 1541
WILL (radio station, Urbana, Ill.), 398
Willard, Frances E., 356
Willard, Frances E., Memorial Library, 356
Willard, Joseph, Jr., 197
Willard, Rudolph, 1477
Willard, Samuel, 334, 695
Willes, William, 1521

William and Mary College, 1560
William Carey College, 825
William Jewell College, 848, 849
William Penn College, 484
Williams, Annie (Chick), 671
Williams, Arthur L., 1222
Williams, Bert, 739
Williams, Christopher à Beckett, 227-D
Williams, Clarence Agustus, 226, 1450
Williams, Egbert Austin, 226
Williams, Ernest, School of Music (Boston), 618
Williams, Florence Birdwell, 1477
Williams, Frances, 1061-L
Williams, Frederick P., 1353
Williams, George Frederick, 1143
Williams, Henry W., 860-D
Williams, Jean Elizabeth, 1270
Williams, John Davis, Library, 833
Williams, Rev. John Mott, 235
Williams, John Thomas, 1235
Williams, John W., 729-B
Williams, Joseph, 279
Williams, Nat, 1451
Williams, Rufus, 671
Williams, Samuel, Collection of Afro-Americana, 267
Williams, Spencer, 226
Williams, Sudie L., 1483
Williams, Vincent, 847
Williams, Walter, 868
Williams College, 719
Williams-Dameron family, 1155
Williamsburg District (S.C.), 1463
Williamsiana Collection, 719
Williamson, Eugenia, 860-C
Williamson, Evelyn Potter, 1420
Williamson, Hugh Philips, 1420
Williamson, John Finlay, 227-F
Williamstown (Mass.), 1031
Willig imprints, 556, 612
Willing, Mary, Collection, 1237
Willington (Conn.), 707
Willis, Eola, 1414
Willis, Mattie Azalia, 729-B
Willis, Richard, 1135
Willis, Richard Storrs, 1036
Willison, Nell Francis, 1572
Willman, Allan Arthur, 1643
Willman, Regina, 1643
Willow Grove (Pa.), 1333
Willows (Cal.) Public Library, 148
Wills, Bob, 1480, 1501
Wills, Bob, Memorial Archive of Popular Music, 1480
Wills, Johnnie Lee, 1480
Willson, Mrs. Charles C., 334
Willson, Meredith, 463, 465, 1031
Willson, Meredith, Library of Popular American Sheet Music, 84

Willson, Meredith/Stanley Ring Collection, 84
Wilmington (Del.), 213, 214, 215
Wilmington (Del.) Institute Free Library, 216
Wilmore, Carl, 636
Wilson, Carl, 1208
Wilson, Carol G., 142
Wilson, Carroll, 406
Wilson, Frank, 1208
Wilson, George H., 36, 1359
Wilson, George W., 1127
Wilson, Gilbert Livingstone, 815
Wilson, Hazel (Claus), 364
Wilson, Ira B., 465
Wilson, Keith, 195-C
Wilson, Louis R., Library, 1141
Wilson, Mark W., 1333
Wilson, Miriam B., Foundation, 1427
Wilson, Dr. Rex, 1472
Wilson, Robert, 1463
Wilson, Robert S., 1321
Wilson, Teddy, 12, 610
Wilson, Thomas E., 98
Wilson, Thomas J., 1141
Wilson, W. J., 1477
Wilson, Woodrow, 236, 1031
Wilson, Woodrow, House, 236
Wilson Collection of Folk Music and Folk Traditions, 1472
Wilson Museum, 587
Wiman, Dwight Deere, 1611
Wimmer Music Collection, 1312
Wimsatt, Margaret, 195-C
Winchell, Alexander, 729-B, 815
Winchell, Mrs. Horace V., 815
Winchell, Newton H., 815
Winchendon (Mass.) Historical Society, 720
Winchester (Va.), 1560
Winchester (Mass.) Orchestral Society, 636
Wind instruments, 898
Windsor (Conn.), 180
Windsor (Conn.) Historical Society, 209
Windsor County (Vt.) Musical Association, 1530
Windt, Clara de, 654
Windt, W. Bernard, 1266
Winfield (Kan.), 341
Winger, Betty Bush, 227-K
Winkler, Emil, 1463
Winn Library, 717
Winne, Jane Lathrop, 285
Winnebago (Minn.), 815
Winnebago County (Wis.), 1611
Winner, Septimus, 729-A, 1040, 1061-A, 1123, 1338
Winnetka (Ill.), 1056
Winnie family, 1483
Winona (Minn.), 815
Winona (Minn.) State University, 822
Winona County (Minn.) Historical Society, 823

Winslett, Rev. David, 1255
Winslow, Don Avery, 721
Winstein, Bernie, 558
Winston Family Papers, 1463
Winston, Nat, 1463
Winston, Nat, Jr., 1463
Winter, J. Angus, 636
Winter, Johann F. F., 835
Winterbotham, John M., 1611
Winterhalter, Hugo, 1646
Winterthur Museum, 217
Winterton, Henry J., 227-H
Winthrop, Robert Charles, 1541
Winthrop (Me.) Historical Society, 589
Winthrop (Minn.), 808
Winthrop College, 1423
Wintter-Watts, H., 227-F
Wisconsin, 227-L, 235, 336, 375, 396, 398, 729-B, 786, 800, 802, 815, 1054, 1161, 1174, 1285
Wisconsin Center for Film and Theater Research, 1611
Wisconsin College—Conservatory of Music, 1628
Wisconsin College of Music, 1628
Wisconsin Composers Concerts, 1617
Wisconsin Conservatory of Music, 1031, 1192, 1628
Wisconsin Federation of Music Clubs, 1611
Wisconsin State Historical Society, 1611, 1614
Wisconsin Infantry, 1611
Wisconsin State Musicians' Association, 1611
Wisconsin, University of, at Eau Claire, 1601
Wisconsin, University of, at Madison, 227-L, 739, 1611, 1612, 1673
Wisconsin, University of, at Milwaukee, 942, 1626, 1673
Wisconsin, University of, at Stevens Point, 1632
Wisconsin Volunteer Army, 1611
Wise County (Va.), 1352
Wisely, Edward B., 1080
Wismer collection, 50
Wissmiller, Emma, 302
Wistach, Carl, 227
Wister, Owen, 227-D, 227-M, 718, 1352, 1646
Witherell, W. Frank, 544
Witherspoon, Herbert, 1052, 1054, 1580
Witmark, Isidore, 1031, 1359
Witmark (i.e., Tams-Witmark) Collection, 949, 951, 1611, 1612
Witmer, Robert, 398
Witt, Isabel de, 195-C
Wittell, Chester, 1289, 1308, 1333
Witten, Laurence C., II, 195-B
Wittenberg Choir, 1235
Wittenberg College, 1232
Wittenberg University, 1196, 1233, 1235

Wittgenstein, Paul, 1061-D
Wixom, Emma (Emma Nevada), 227-F, 896
WJJD (radio station, Chicago), 389
WJJD Studio Orchestra, 389
WJR (radio station, Detroit), 1024, 1611
WKPFK (radio station, Los Angeles), 195-C
WLS (radio station, Chicago), 1234
WMBI (radio station, Chicago), 333
WMC (radio station, Memphis), 1451
WMT (radio station, Cedar Rapids, Iowa), 457
WNAX (radio station, Yankton, S.D.), 1436
WNEW (radio station, New York), 1061-J
Wobblies, 742, 743, 1445
Woelber, Henry, 636
Wofford College, 1426
Wohlberg, Max, 1044
Wohlgemuth, Paul W., 1263
Wold, Wayne, 622
Woldt, John, 195-C
Wolf, 406
Wolf, Albert, 195-B
Wolf, Hugo, 1039
Wolfe, Charles, 1454
Wolfe, Irving, 1456
Wolfes, Felix, 227-F
Wolhowe, Fred, 1166
Wolk, Abraham L., 1375
Wolle, Francis, 150
Wolle, Peter, 1285
Wolle, Theodore F., 1161
Wolpe, Stefan, 195-C, 227-D, 1580
Wolsey, Louis, 1174
Woltmann, Frederick, 1111
Woman's Club (Evanston, Ill.), 354
Woman's College of Duke University, 1143
Woman's Music Club (Cincinnati), 1172
Women in music, 146, 192, 226, 227-H, 314, 341, 354, 356, 359, 398, 469, 560, 596, 599, 636, 654, 676, 692, 694, 729-B, 739, 762, 776, 815, 866, 1061-B, 1061-M, 1107, 1161, 1163, 1167, 1172, 1285, 1315, 1375, 1385, 1463, 1483, 1510, 1516, 1518, 1520, 1560, 1569, 1591, 1601, 1613, 1614, 1616, 1632
Women's Amateur Musical Clubs, 314
Women's bands and orchestras, 146, 226, 341, 398, 654
Women's Choral Society (New Haven, Conn.), 192
Women's Chorus (Portland, Me.), 596
Women's choruses, 192, 359, 469, 596, 1161, 1518, 1613
Women's Christian Temperance Union, 356, 729-B, 1614

Women's Club (Littleton, Colo.), 170
Women's History Archive, 692
Women's Literary Society (Corvallis, Ore.), 1268
Women's Music Club (Bellingham, Wash.), 1569
Women's Symphony Orchestra (Long Beach, Cal.), 398
Women's Symphony Society of Boston, 636
Wonderland Music Company, 54
Wood, Benson, Library, 367
Wood, Carl Paige, 1577
Wood, Frank H., 860-K
Wood, Jule McIver, 36
Wood, Peggy, 1061-L
Wood, Ray, 1477
Wood, Simeon, 227-H
Wood, W., 701
Wood, William Halsey, 1059
Wood (i.e., Marshall-Wood) Studios, 1516
Wood-Hill, Mabel, 227-D, 227-F
Woodbury, Isaac Baker, 701, 847
Woodbury, William W., 815
Woodbury (Conn.) Harmonic Society, 181
Woodhouse, Harry, 84
Woodhouse, James, Co., 1141, 1560
Woodland, Harriet Vivian, 465
Woodland (Cal.), 59
Woodrow, J. W., 398
Woodruff, Mary B. (Marie), 406
Woodruff Library, 269
Wood's Opera House, 868
Woodside, Archible, 1141
Woodson Regional Library, 315
Woodson Research Center, 1497
Woodstock (N.Y.) Library, 1138
Woodstock (Vt.) Historical Society, 1536
Woodward, Blinn, 127
Woodward, Dorothy, 963
Woodward, Paul J., 1061-L
Woodward, Sidney C., 406
Woodwind music, 898, 1136. See also specific instruments
Woodworth, G. Wallace, 227-F, 654, 661
Woolf, Benjamin Edward, 1061-A
Woollcott, Alexander, 227-L
Woollett, Henry, 646
Woolson, Albert, 815
Woonsocket (R.I.) Historical Society, 1410
WOR (radio station, New York), 618
Worcester (Mass.), 270, 654, 707, 1174
Worcester (Ohio), University of, Conservatory of Music, 1359
Worch, Hugo, 234
Word, Charlotte Ingham, 1480

Work, Henry Clay, 227-E, 227-F, 314, 315, 369, 1618
Work, John Wesley, 226, 1457
Work songs, 245, 267, 679, 1061-N, 1546. See also specific occupations; Labor songs; Occupational songs
Workingmen's Institute (New Harmony, Ind.), 438
Workman, Donna, 360
Works Progress Administration. See WPA
World Music Archives, 190
World of Music, 899, 1530
World Peace Jubilee, 398
World Program Service, 1469
"The World Turned Upside Down," 1418
World War I, 5, 142, 227-A, 269, 296, 353, 386, 461, 475, 544, 624, 652, 761, 763, 800, 815, 850, 860-D, 860-G, 920, 977, 1008, 1031, 1107, 1127, 1141, 1146, 1155, 1208, 1232, 1256, 1389, 1402, 1519, 1570, 1629, 1662. See also War songs
World War II, 296, 406, 800, 1146, 1402. See also War songs
World's Columbian Exposition (Chicago, 1893), 227-L, 314, 315, 334, 729-B, 1359
World's Fair (Chicago, 1933), 777
World's Fair (1939), 234
World's fairs. See Fairs and expositions
World's Peace Jubilee (Boston, 1872), 646
Wornall, J. B., family, 841
Worrall, Harvey, 514
Worth, Amy, 1576
Worthington (Ohio), 1193
Worthington Historical Society, 1245
WPA (Works Progress Administration; Works Projects Administration), 79, 182, 315, 815, 1031, 1058, 1185, 1333, 1352, 1541, 1544, 1568, 1611, 1624, 1643
WPA—Louisiana, 561
WPA—Nevada, 896
WPA Federal Music Project, 55, 122, 226, 227-H, 227-K, 227-L, 230, 234, 636, 800, 1185, 1541, 1624
WPA Federal Music Project, Louisiana State-Wide Music Project, 544
WPA Federal Music Project, Music Education Division, 55
WPA Federal Music Project, Philadelphia Local Works Division, 1333
WPA Federal Music Project, Wisconsin, 1611
WPA Federal Theatre Project, 84, 154, 227-H, 227-K, 227-L, 739
WPA Federal Writers Project, 227-K, 227-L, 245, 963, 1541

WPA Folk Music Tour, 829
WPA Folklore Collection, 1541
WPA Illinois Music Project, 354, 391
WPA Illinois Writers Project, 391
WPA Joint Committee on Folk Arts, 227-L
WPA Music Periodicals Index, 323
WPA Orchestra, 1061-J
WPA Southern California Music Project, 104
WQXR (radio station, New York), 195-C
Wrangham, Francis, 1465
"Wreck of the Old '97," lawsuit, 1270
Wright, Edith A., 1333
Wright, Ellen (Mrs. William Lloyd Garrison II), 692
Wright, Ethel, 911
Wright, Helen Madeline, 195-A
Wright Isaac, 768
Wright, John, Jr., 1236
Wright, Kenneth, 230
Wright, Louise Drake, 227-D
Wright, Robert Craig, 227-D
Wright, Mrs. W. C., 334
Wright papers, 195-A
Wright County (Iowa) Historical Society Museum, 469
Wright County (Minn.) Historical Society, 777
Wright-Patterson Air Force Base, 1198
Wrightman, George A., 465
Wright's Book Shop, 1211
Wrigley, J., 1402
Wroblewski, August, 787
Wrongski, Thaddeus, 739
Wrubel, Allie, 190
WSM (radio station, Nashville), 1463
WTAM (radio station, Cleveland), 1611
Wulsin Family Papers, 1172
Wulsin, Lucien, 1172
Wulsin, Lucien, II, 1172
Wurlitzer, Marianne, 1075
Wurlitzer, Rembert, Co., 1075
Wurlitzer, Mrs. Rembert, 1075
Wurlitzer, Rudolph, Co., 1075
Wurlitzer piano rolls, 750
Wurtele, Mildred Orkney, 544
Wyandotte (Mich.) Historical Society, 774
Wyatt Theater, 103
WYBC (radio station, New Haven, Conn.), 195-C
Wyck, Amelia Van, 195-C
Wyckoff (N.J.) Public Library, 956
Wye, Ralph A. Van, 1172
Wyer family, 253
Wyer, Paul, 253
Wyeth, John, 1333
Wyld, Lionel D., 1398
Wyllie, John Cook, Library, 1568
Wyman, Loraine, 196
Wymon, Mabel, Collection, 147

Wyner, Yehudi, 195-C
Wynne, Michael D., Collection, 544
Wyoming, 291
Wyoming Federation of Music Clubs, 1643
Wyoming State Archives, 1643
Wyoming, University of, 1645, 1646

X

Xavier University of Louisiana, 572
Xylophone, 608

Y

Yaddo Colony, 1031
Yaddo Festival, 195-A
Yakima Valley (Wash.) Museum and Historical Association, 1587
Yale University, 195, 198, 1061-J
Yancy, Farrell, 982
"Yankee Doodle," 1036
Yankevich, Frankie, 1188
Yankton (S.D.), 475
Yankton College, 1436
Yankton County Historical Society, 1437
Yaqui Indians, 31
Yarnall Library of Theology, 1352
Yasser, Joseph, 227-F
Yates, Peter, 68, 84
Ybañez music manuscripts, 133
Yeamans, Laurel, 1222
Yeatmann-Polk Collection, 1463
Yiddish music, 32, 84, 117, 189, 227-L, 711, 1021, 1042, 1044, 1057, 1076, 1080, 1174, 1188, 1336, 1402, 1685. See also Jewish music
Yivo Institute for Jewish Research, 1076
Ylioppilaskunnan Laulajat, 636
YMCA, 860-J, 1611
Yoder, Paul V., 13
Yoder, Walter E., 415
Yolo County (Cal.) Historical Society, 149
Yon, Pietro Alessandro, 227-D, 854
Yonkers (N.Y.) Public Library, 1139
Yopp, Alfred Harding, 1159
Yopp, Mrs. Alfred Harding, 1159
Yorita, Mrs. Goro (Sugi Machi), 1577
York, Bill, 1256
York, James R., 1140
York, Rev. Terry W., 109
York County (Pa.) Historical Society, 1396
Yorkville Music School, 1058
Yost, Conrad, 1267
Yost, Gaylord, 1359
Youmans, Vincent, 227-D
Young, Lt., 860-D
Young, Barnard A., 1077

Young, Dorothy, 195-A
Young, Frank A., 1176
Young, Henry, 195-A
Young, Isaac N., 227-G, 697
Young, Morris N., 1077
Young, Victor, 636
Young, Virginia Bassett, 1477
Young America (Minn.), 821
Young Men's Christian Association, 860-J, 1611
Young Oregonians Accordion Club, 1274
Young People's Concerts (Cincinnati Symphony Orchestra), 1172
Ysaya, Theo, 111
Ysaÿe, Eugene, 227-D, 729-E
Yukon Territory, 18

Z

Zabriskie, John Goetchius, 944
Zachara, Francizek, 260
Zador, Eugene, 84, 86, 227-F, 1646
Zador, Leslie, 86
Zafren, Herbert C., 1172
Zanesville (Ohio), 1193
Zapf, Louise, 947
Zarzuelas, 957
Zeckwer, C. W., 1333
Zeigler, Julia, 195-C
Zeisl, Eric, 84
Zeisl, Gertrud, 84
Zeisler, Ernest B., 1174
Zeisler, Fannie (Bloomfield), 227-F, 334, 1053, 1174, 1222
Zeisler, Sigmund, 1174
Zelzer, Harry, Concert Management, 340
Zemachson, Arnold, 227-D
Zerrahn, Carl, 701
Zeuner, Charles, 1343
Ziegfeld, Florenz, 338, 1031, 1061-L, 1484
Ziegfeld Follies, 1031, 1477
Ziegler, Edward, 1053
Ziegler, Elmer, 239
Ziegler, Jacob H., 939
Zieglschmid, A. J. F., 415
Ziehn, Bernhard, 334, 729-E, 866
Zimbalist, Efrem, 227-F, 1331
Zimbalist, Mary Louise Curtis Bok, 227-B, 227-F, 1331
Zimmer, Edward, 1391
Zimmerman, Jacob, 425
Zimmerman, Max, 157
Zimmerman (i.e., Smith-Zimmerman) Historical Museum, 1429
Zimmermann, Charles A., 602
Zimmermann, Frederick, 1031
Zinsmeister, Alphonse, 1359
Zion Evangelical Church (New York), 1059
Zipper, Herbert, 84, 1058
Zirner, Ludwig, 398
Zithers, 398, 442, 510, 837, 847, 986
Zitterbart, Fidelis, Jr., 1375
Ziv, F. W., Radio Co., 1177
Ziv, Frederick W., Archive, 1177

Zoar (Ohio) Gesang-Verein, 1190
Zollars Memorial Library, 1251
Zonophone, 1640
Zoo Opera (Cincinnati), 1172
Zook, Florence, 68
Zucca, Mana (Augusta Zuckerman; Jesula Zuckerman), 248, 249, 1193
Zunser, Mirian Shomer (Mrs. Charles), 1061-B

Books in the series Music in American Life:

Only a Miner: Studies in Recorded Coal-Mining Songs
ARCHIE GREEN

Great Day Coming: Folk Music and the American Left
R. SERGE DENISOFF

John Philip Sousa: A Descriptive Catalog of His Works
PAUL E. BIERLEY

The Hell-Bound Train: A Cowboy Songbook
GLENN OHRLIN

Oh, Didn't He Ramble: The Life Story of Lee Collins as
Told to Mary Collins
FRANK J. GILLIS AND JOHN W. MINER, EDITORS

American Labor Songs of the Nineteenth Century
PHILIP S. FONER

Stars of Country Music: Uncle Dave Macon to Johnny Rodriguez
BILL C. MALONE AND JUDITH MC CULLOH, EDITORS

Git Along, Little Dogies: Songs and Songmakers of the American West
JOHN I. WHITE

A Texas-Mexican *Cancionero:* Folksongs of the Lower Border
AMÉRICO PAREDES

San Antonio Rose: The Life and Music of Bob Wills
CHARLES R. TOWNSEND

Early Downhome Blues: A Musical and Cultural Analysis
JEFF TODD TITON

An Ives Celebration: Papers and Panels of the Charles Ives
Centennial Festival-Conference
H. WILEY HITCHCOCK AND VIVIAN PERLIS, EDITORS

Sinful Tunes and Spirituals: Black Folk Music to the Civil War
DENA J. EPSTEIN

Joe Scott, the Woodsman-Songmaker
EDWARD D. IVES

Jimmie Rodgers: The Life and Times of America's Blue Yodeler
NOLAN PORTERFIELD

Early American Music Engraving and Printing: A History of Music Publishing in America
from 1787 to 1825 with Commentary on Earlier and Later Practices
RICHARD J. WOLFE

Sing a Sad Song: The Life of Hank Williams
ROGER M. WILLIAMS

Long Steel Rail: The Railroad in American Folksong
NORM COHEN

Resources of American Music History: A Directory of Source Materials
from Colonial Times to World War II
D. W. KRUMMEL, JEAN GEIL, DORIS J. DYEN, AND DEANE L. ROOT